THE ORIGINS OF THE WAR OF
1914

VOLUME II

Luigi Albertini

THE ORIGINS OF THE WAR OF 1914

Translated and edited
by
ISABELLA M. MASSEY
M.A.(Cantab.), Dr.phil. (Marburg).

VOLUME II

THE CRISIS OF JULY 1914.
FROM THE SARAJEVO OUTRAGE TO THE
AUSTRO-HUNGARIAN GENERAL MOBILIZATION

OXFORD UNIVERSITY PRESS

Oxford University Press, Amen House, London E.C.4

GLASGOW NEW YORK TORONTO MELBOURNE WELLINGTON
BOMBAY CALCUTTA MADRAS KARACHI LAHORE DACCA
CAPE TOWN SALISBURY NAIROBI IBADAN
KUALA LUMPUR HONG KONG

FIRST PUBLISHED 1953
REPRINTED LITHOGRAPHICALLY IN GREAT BRITAIN
AT THE UNIVERSITY PRESS, OXFORD
FROM SHEETS OF THE FIRST EDITION
1965

TABLE OF CONTENTS

XI. GERMAN POLICY AFTER THE AUSTRIAN DECLARATION OF WAR ON SERBIA; THE THREAT OF ENGLISH INTERVENTION. 466

XII. THE RUSSIAN GENERAL MOBILIZATION. 528

XIII. FRANCE AND RUSSIAN MOBILIZATION; LAST ENGLISH EFFORTS TO SAVE PEACE. 582

XIV. THE AUSTRIAN GENERAL MOBILIZATION.   651

APPENDIX: KING GEORGE'S WORDS TO PRINCE HENRY.
687

INDEX   689

ERRATA TO VOLUME I

PAGE

23 Superior [2] in line 13 should be at end of next paragraph.

24 Line 8.   For *hangman* read *henchman*.

59 Footnote 3.   For 1877 read 1887.

142 Line 24.   For *Prime* read *Foreign*.

142 Line 38.   For 1940 read 1904.

166 Line 35.   For *recognizes* read *recognized*.

169 Last line.   After *American* insert *Secretary of State*.

311 Line 14.   For *Signor* read M.

317 Line 32.   For 1916 read 1910.

340 Line 18.   For *England* read *Germany*.

358 Line 5.   For *Sergio* read *Serge*.

371 Line 26.   For *Prime Minister* read *Speaker*.

391 Line 17.   For *Department* read *Section*.

393 Line 41.   For *Semuprava* read *Samouprava*.

398 Line 30.   For 1812 read 1912.

415 Footnote 4.   For *Doumergues* read *Doumergue*.

430 Line 29.   For 1900 read 1910.

505 Line 2.   For *Beldimann* read *Beldiman*.

604 Column 1, line 26.   Read *Root, Elihu, United States Secretary of State*.

ABBREVIATIONS

Abbreviations are confined to works quoted more than three times. For the collections of diplomatic documents the number of the volume and the number of the document are given. The French diplomatic documents are divided into three series. For them and for the Russian documents (INT. BEZ.) the series number is given in the first place.

Authorized English translations are quoted, but not abridgements or selections.

A. F-R.: Ministère des Affaires Étrangères.—*L'alliance franco-russe. Origine de l'alliance* 1890–1893. *Convention militaire* 1892–1899, *et convention navale* 1912 (Paris, 1918).

ASQUITH: Asquith, Herbert Henry.—*The Genesis of the War* (London, 1923).

BACH: Bach, A.—Deutsche Gesandtschaftsberichte zum Kriegsausbruch 1914.—*Berichte und Telegramme der badischen, sächsischen und württembergischen Gesandtschaften in Berlin aus dem Juli und August* 1914. Im Auftrag des Auswärtigen Amtes herausgegeben von August Bach (Berlin 1937).

BAERNREITHER: Baernreither, Josef Maria.—*Fragmente eines politischen Tagebuches. Die südslavische Frage und Österreich-Ungarn vor dem Weltkrieg* (Berlin, 1928).
Fragments of a political diary (London, 1930).

BARNES: Barnes, Harry Elmer.—*The Genesis of the World War. An introduction to the problem of War Guilt* (New York and London, 1929).

BD.: *British Documents on the Origins of the War* 1898–1914. Ed. by G. P. Gooch and Harold Temperley. Vols. I–XI (London, 1926–38).

BENCKENDORFF: Benckendorff, Alexander Graf von.—*Diplomatischer Schriftwechsel hrsg. von Benno von Siebert* (Berlin and Leipzig, 1928).

BETHMANN: Bethmann Hollweg, Theobald von.—*Betrachtungen zum Weltkriege*. 2 vols. (Berlin, 1919–22).

BIBL: Bibl, Viktor.— *Die Tragödie Österreichs* (Leipzig, 1937).

BOGIČEVIĆ. *Aus. Pol. Serb.: Die Auswärtige Politik Serbiens*. 1903–14. ed. by M. Boghitschewitsch. 3 vols. (Berlin, 1928–31).

BOGIČEVIĆ, *Causes*: Boghitschewitsch, Miloš.—*Les causes de la guerre* (Paris, 1925); *Causes of the War* (Amsterdam, Rotterdam, 1919; London, 1920).

BOGIČEVIĆ, *Procès*: Boghitschewitsch, Miloš.—*Le procès de Salonique* (Paris, 1927).

BRANDENBURG: Brandenburg, Erich.—*From Bismarck to the World War* (London, 1933); *Von Bismarck zum Weltkrieg* (Leipzig, 1939).

BREDT: Bredt, Joh. Victor.—*Die belgische Neutralität und der Schlieffensche Feldzugplan* (Berlin, 1929).

BULG.: *Die bulgarischen Dokumente zum Kriegsausbruch* 1914, in *Kriegsschuldfrage*, March 1928 (Berlin).

BÜLOW: Bülow, Prince Bernard von.—*Memoirs* (1905–9) 4 vols. (London and New York, 1931).

CDD.: *Collected Diplomatic Documents relating to the Outbreak of the European War* (London, 1915).

CHLUMECKY: Chlumecky, Leopold Freiherr von.—*Erzherzog Franz Ferdinand. Wirken und Wollen* (Berlin, 1929).

CHURCHILL: Churchill, Winston Leonard Spencer.—*The World Crisis.* 6 vols. (London, 1923–31).

CONRAD: Conrad von Hötzendorf, Franz Graf.—*Aus meiner Dienstzeit 1906–1918.* 5 vols. (Vienna, 1921–5).

CRISPI, *Memoirs: Memoirs of Francesco Crispi.* 3 vols. (London, 1912–14).

CRISPI: Quest. Int.: Crispi, Francesco.—*Questioni Internazionali* (Milan, 1913).

CROKAERT: Crokaert, J. —*L'ultimatum allemand du 2 août*, in *Le Flambeau* of Brussels, 31 March 1922.

CZERNIN: Czernin, Ottokar Graf.—*In the World War* (London, New York, 1919).

DA.: Republik Österreich, Staatsamt für Äusseres.—*Diplomatische Aktenstücke zur Vorgeschichte des Krieges* 1914.—*Ergänzungen und Nachträge zum Österreichisch-Ungarischen Rotbuch.* 3 vols. (Vienna, 1919; *Deutsche Verlagsgesellschaft für Politik und Geschichte in Berlin*). Translated as: *Austrian Red Book. Official Files pertaining to Pre-War History.* 3 parts (London, 1920).

DD.: *Die Deutschen Dokumente zum Kriegsausbruch.*—*Vollständige Sammlung der von Karl Kautsky zusammengestellten amtlichen Aktenstücke mit einigen Ergänzungen. Neue durchgesehene und vermehrte Ausgabe.* 4 vols. (Berlin, 1927). *Outbreak of the World War.* Carnegie Endowment for International Peace. 1 vol. (O.U.P. 1924).

DENIS: Denis, Ernest.—*La grande Serbie* (Paris, 1919).

DIRR: Dirr, Pius.—*Bayerische Dokumente zum Kriegsausbruch und zum Versailler Schuldspruch* (Munich and Berlin, 1928).

DF.: Ministère des Affaires Étrangères. Commission de publication des documents relatifs aux origines de la guerre de 1914.—*Documents diplomatiques français* (1871–1914). III Série: 1911–14 (Paris, 1929–36). ·

DOBROROLSKI: Dobrorolski, Sergei Kostantinovich.—*La mobilisation de l'Armée russe en* 1914, in *Revue d'Histoire de la Guerre Mondiale* (Paris, April-July 1923).

FISCHER: Fischer, Eugen.—*Die Kritischen 39 Tage von Sarajevo bis zum Weltbrand* (Berlin, 1928).

FOERSTER: Foerster, Wolfgang.—*Graf Schlieffen und der Weltkrieg* (Berlin, 1925).

FRANGULIS: Frangulis, A. F.—*La Grèce et la crise mondiale*, 2 vols. (Paris, 1926–7).

FRIEDJUNG: Friedjung, Heinrich.—*Das Zeitalter des Imperialismus* 1884 *bis* 1914. 3 vols. (Berlin, 1919–22).

FRONT WIDER BÜLOW: Thimme, Friedrich.—*Front wider Bülow. Staatsmänner, Diplomaten und Forscher zu seinen Denkwürdigkeiten* (Munich, 1931).

GALET: Galet, Émile Joseph.—*Albert King of the Belgians in the Great War* (London, 1931); *S. M. le Roi Albert, Commandant en Chef devant l'invasion allemande. Préf. de S. M. le Roi Albert* (Paris, 1931).

GERIN: *Les responsabilités de la guerre. Quatorze questions par René Gerin; quatorze réponses par Raymond Poincaré* (Paris, 1930).

GIESL: Giesl, Wladimir Freiherr von.—*Zwei Jahrzehnte im Nahen Orient* (Berlin, 1927).

GIOLITTI: Giolitti, Giovanni.—*Memoirs of my life* (London and Sidney, 1923).

GOOCH, Before the War: Gooch, G. P.—*Before the War, Studies in Diplomacy.* 2 vols. (London, 1936–8).

GOOCH, Recent Revelations: Gooch, G. P. *Recent Revelations of European Diplomacy* (London, 1940).

GP.: *Die Grosse Politik der europäischen Kabinette* (1871–1914). *Sammlung der diplomatischen Akten des Auswärtigen Amtes.* 39 vols. and Index vol. (Berlin, 1922–7).

GR.: Ministère des Affaires Étrangères de Grèce.—*Documents diplomatiques 1913–1917* (Athens, 1917).

GREY: Grey, Sir Edward (Lord Grey of Fallodon).—*Twenty-five Years 1892–1916.* 2 vols. (London, 1925).

HAUSER: *Histoire diplomatique de l'Europe* (1871–1914) publiée sous la direction de Henri Hauser par J. Ancel, L. Cahen, R. Guyot, A. Lajusan, P. Renouvin et H. Salomon. 2 vols (Paris, 1929).

HERRE: Herre, Paul.—*Die kleinen Staaten und die Entstehung des Weltkriegs,* in *Berliner Monatshefte* (KSF.) of May and July 1933 and February and April 1934.

HOYOS: Hoyos, Alexander Graf.—*Der deutsch-englische Gegensatz und sein Einfluss auf die Balkanpolitik Österreich-Ungarns* (Berlin, 1922).

HUGUET: Huguet, Général V. J. M.—*L'intervention militaire britannique en 1914.* (Paris, 1928); *Britain and the War. A French indictment* (London, 1928).

INT. BEZ.: *Die internationalen Beziehungen im Zeitalter des Imperialismus. Dokumente aus den Archiven der Zarischen und der Provisorischen Regierung.* ed. O. Hoetsch. Reihe I, 5 vols. (Berlin, 1931–4).

ISAAC: Isaac, Jules.—*Un débat historique. 1914. Le problème des origines de la guerre* (Paris, 1933).

IZVOLSKY: *Der diplomatische Schriftwechsel Iswolskis,* 1911–14, ed. by Friedrich Stieve. 4 vols. (Berlin, 1924).

JOFFRE: *Memoirs of Marshal Joffre.* 2 vols. (London, 1932).

KANNER, *Katastrophenpolitik:* Kanner, Heinrich.—*Kaiserliche Katastrophenpolitik* (Vienna, 1922).

KANNER, *Schlüssel:* Kanner, Heinrich.—*Der Schlüssel zur Kriegsschuldfrage* (Munich, 1926).

KAUTSKY: Kautsky, Karl.—*The Guilt of William Hohenzollern* (London, 1920).

KRV SLOVENTSVA: 1914-1924 *Krv Sloventsva. Spomenica desetogodisnijce Svetskog Rata* (Belgrade, 1924).

KSF.: *Die Kriegsschuldfrage. Zeitschrift zur Vorgeschichte und Geschichte des Weltkrieges* (Berlin, 1923–8). Under the title *Berliner Monatshefte* edited by A. von Wegerer (Berlin, 1929–37).

LANGER, *Eur. All.:* Langer, William L.—*European Alliances and Alignments* 1871–1890 (New York, 1950).

LANGER, *Dipl. of Imp.:* Langer, William L.—*The Diplomacy of Imperialism* 1890–1902. 2 vols. (New York, 1951).

LAS.: *Correspondance diplomatique du gouvernement serbe.* 16–29 juin, 3–16 août 1914 (Paris, 1914; in CDD).

LEE: Lee, Sir Sidney.—*King Edward VII. A Biography.* 2 vols. (London, 1925–7).

LGB.: Royaume de Belgique: Ministère des Affaires Étrangères.—*Livre gris belge. Correspondance diplomatique relative à la guerre de 1914* (24 juillet–29 août 1914) (Paris, 1914; in CDD).

LICHNOWSKY: Prince Lichnowsky, *Heading for the Abyss* (London, 1928).

LJF.: Ministère des Affaires Étrangères. *Livre Jaune Français.*—*Documents diplomatiques 1914. La guerre européenne. Pièces relatives aux négotiations qui ont précédé les déclarations de guerre de l'Allemagne à la Russie* (1 août 1914) *et à la France* (3 août 1914). *Déclaration du 4 septembre 1914* (Paris, 1914; in CDD).

LLOYD GEORGE: Lloyd George, David.—*War Memoirs.* 6 vols. (London, 1933–6).

LN.: *Un Livre Noir.*—*Diplomatie d'avant-guerre d'après les documents des archives russes.* 1910–1917. 3 vols. in 6 parts (Paris, 1922–34).

LOUIS: Louis, Georges.—*Les Carnets.* 2 vols. (Paris, 1926).

LUTZ: Lutz, Hermann.—*Die europäische Politik in der Julikrise 1914. Gutachten* (Berlin, 1930).

MAGRINI: Magrini, Luciano.—*Il dramma di Sarajevo. Origini e responsabilità della guerra europea* (Milan, 1929).

MARGUTTI: Margutti, Albert von.—*La Tragédie des Habsbourg* (Paris and Vienna, 1919).

MICHON: Michon, Georges.—*La préparation à la guerre. La loi de trois ans.* 1910–1914 (Paris, 1935).

MOLTKE: Moltke, Helmuth von.—*Erinnerungen, Briefe, Dokumente 1877–1916.* Ed. by Eliza von Moltke (Stuttgart, 1922).

MONTGELAS: Montgelas, Max, Count.—*The Case for the Central Powers* (London, 1925).

MOUSSET: Mousset, Albert.—*Un drame historique: l'attentat de Sarajevo* (Paris, 1930).

MORLEY: Morley, John, Viscount, of Blackburn.—*Memorandum on Resignation, August* 1914 (London, 1928).

MUSULIN: Musulin, Alexander Freiherr von.—*Das Haus am Ballplatz* (Munich, 1924).

NICOLSON: Nicolson, Harold George.—*Sir Arthur Nicolson Bart., First Lord Carnock.*—*A Study in the Old Diplomacy* (London, 1930).

NINČIĆ: Ninčić, Momčilo.—*La Crise Bosniaque* (1908–1909) *et les Puissances Européennes.* 2 vols. (Paris, 1937).

OE-U.: Österreich-Ungarns Aussenpolitik von der Bosnischen Krise 1908 *bis zum Kriegsausbruch* 1914. 8 vols. and Index vol. (Vienna, 1930).

PALÉOLOGUE: Paléologue, Maurice.—*An Ambassador's Memoirs.* 3 vols. (London, 1923).

PFEFFER: Pfeffer, Leo.—*Istraga u Sarajevskom atentatu* (Zagreb, 1938).

POINCARÉ: Poincaré, Raymond.—*Au Service de la France. Neuf années de souvenirs.* 10 vols. (Paris, 1926–33).

POURTALÈS: Pourtalès, Friedrich Graf.—*Meine letzten Verhandlungen in St. Petersburg, Ende Juli* 1914 (Berlin, 1927).

PRIBRAM: Pribram, A. F.—*The Secret Treaties of Austria-Hungary.* Vol. I *Texts of the Treaties and Agreements.* Vol. II *Negotiations leading to the Treaties of the Triple Alliance* (Harvard University Press, 1920, 1921).

RECOULY: Recouly, Raymond.—*Les heures tragiques d'avant-guerre* (Paris, 1922).

RENOUVIN: Renouvin, Pierre.—*The Immediate Origins of the War.* (Yale U.P., 1928).
Les origines immédiates de la guerre (28 juin–4 août 1914) (Paris, 1927).

SALANDRA: Salandra, Antonio.—*La Neutralità italiana* (1914), (Milan, 1928). *Italy and the Great War* (London, 1923).

SALVATORELLI: Salvatorelli.—*La Triplice Alleanza* (Milan, 1939).

SANDONÀ: Sandonà, Augusto.—*L'Irredentismo nelle lotte politiche e nelle contese diplomatiche italo-austriache.* 3 vols. (Bologna, 1932).

SAZONOV: Sazonov, Serge.—*Fateful Years, 1909–1916* (London, 1928).

SCHÄFER: Schäfer, Theobald von.—*Generaloberst von Moltke in den Tagen vor der Mobilmachung und seine Einwirkung auf Österreich.* (*Kriegsschuldfrage,* Berlin, August 1926).

SCHILLING: *How the War began in 1914. Being the diary of the Russian F.O. from the 3rd to the 20th July 1914.* With a foreword by S. D. Sazonov and an introduction by Baron Schilling (London, 1925).

SCHMITT: Schmitt, Bernadotte E.—*The Coming of the War.* 2 vols. (New York, 1930).

SCHOEN: Schoen, Wilhelm Eduard, Freiherr von.—*Memoirs of an Ambassador* (London, 1922).

SELLIERS DE MORANVILLE: Selliers de Moranville, Liêutenant Général.— *Contribution à l'histoire de la Guerre Mondiale* 1914–1918 (Paris, 1933).

SENTENZA: *Il delitto di Sarajevo. Processo-Sentenza* (Bologna, 1930).

SETON-WATSON, *Roumanians:* Seton-Watson, R. W.—*A History of the Roumanians* (Cambridge, 1934).

SETON-WATSON, *Sarajevo:* Seton-Watson, R. W.—*Sarajevo* (London, 1926).

SHEBEKO: Schebeko, N.—*Souvenirs. Essai historique sur les origines de la guerre de* 1914 (Paris, 1936).

SIEBERT: Siebert, B. von.—*Entente Diplomacy and the World* (London, 1921).

SOSNOSKY: Sosnosky, Theodor. *Franz Ferdinand der Erzherzog-Thronfolger. Ein Lebensbild* (Munich, 1929).

SPENDER: Spender, John Alfred.—*Life of Herbert Henry Asquith, Lord Oxford and Asquith.* 2 vols. (London, 1932).

STANOJEVIĆ: Stanojević, Stanoje.—*Die Ermordung des Erzherzogs Franz Ferdinand* (Frankfort, 1923).

STEED: Steed, Henry Wickham.—*Through Thirty Years* 1892–1922. 2 vols. (London, 1924).

STIEVE, FRIEDRICH: *Izvolsky and World War* (London, 1926).

SZILASSY: Szilassy, Julius, Baron.—*Der Untergang der Donaumonarchie. Diplomatische Erinnerungen* (Berlin, 1921).

TAUBE: Taube, M.—*La politique russe d'avant-guerre* (Paris, 1928). Revised as *Der grossen Katastrophe entgegen* (Leipzig, 1937).

TIRPITZ, *Memoirs:* Tirpitz, Alfred von.—*My Memoirs,* 2 vols. (London, 1919); *Erinnerungen* (Berlin and Leipzig, 1927).

TIRPITZ, *Dokumente:* Tirpitz, Alfred von.—*Politische Dokumente.* 2 vols. Vol. I. *Der Aufbau der deutschen Wehrmacht* (Berlin, 1924). Vol. II. *Deutsche Ohnmachtspolitik im Weltkriege* (Berlin, 1926).

TITTONI, *Nuovi Scritti:* Tittoni, Tommaso.—*Nuovi Scritti di politica interna ed estera* (Milan, 1930).

TITTONI, *Sei anni:* Tittoni, Tommaso.—*Sei anni di politica estera* (1903–1909). *Discorsi pronunciati al Senato del Regno e alla Camera dei Deputati* (Turin, 1912); translated as: *Italy's Foreign and Colonial Policy* (London, 1914).

TOMMASINI: Tommasini, Francesco.—*L'Italia alla vigilia della guerra. La politica estera di Tommaso Tittoni.* 5 vols. (Bologna, 1934–41).

U.S.A.: State Department.—*European War.* No. 2, 3. *Diplomatic Correspondence with Belligerents* (Washington, 1915).

WEGERER, *Weltkrieg:* Wegerer, Alfred von.—*Der Ausbruch des Weltkrieges.* 2 vols. (Berlin, 1939).

WEGERER, *Widerlegung:* Wegerer, Alfred von.—*A Refutation of the Versailles War Guilt Thesis* (New York and London, 1930).

WERTHEIMER: Wertheimer, Eduard.—*Graf Julius Andrassy.* 3 vols (Stuttgart, 1910–13).

WOLFF: Wolff, Theodor.—*Das Vorspiel* (Munich, 1924).

WULLUS-RUDIGER: Wullus-Rudiger, J.—*La Belgique et l'équilibre européen* (Paris, 1935).

ZWEHL: Zwehl, Hans von.—*Erich von Falkenhayn, General der Infanterie. Eine biographische Studie* (Berlin, 1926).

CHAPTER I

ARCHDUKE FRANCIS FERDINAND AND THE SARAJEVO OUTRAGE

(1) *Archduke Francis Ferdinand, the Heir Apparent to the Austrian throne* (p. 1). (2) *The Archduke's attitude towards Serbia, Italy, Germany, and Russia* (p. 7). (3) *Francis Ferdinand's plans for the regeneration of the Monarchy* (p. 11). (4) *The Archduke's forebodings on the eve of the fatal journey; the state of revolution in which he found Bosnia* (p. 18). (5) *The Serbian Comitaji movement and* Mlada Bosna (p. 22). (6) *The* Narodna Obrana, *the* Black Hand, *and its leader, Colonel Dragutin Dimitrievič* (p. 25). (7) *The conflict between the* Black Hand *and the Prime Minister Pašić on the eve of the outrage* (p. 30). (8) *The Sarajevo outrage* (p. 35).

1. *Archduke Francis Ferdinand, the Heir Apparent to the Austrian throne.*

If the precariously poised political conditions within the Hapsburg Monarchy were a constant threat to the stability of Europe, a further imperfectly understood factor was the enigmatic figure of Archduke Francis Ferdinand, over whom there always hung the shadow of a tragic fate. He deserves our closer attention not only on account of the part he played in the life of the Monarchy, the plans he had for its regeneration and the influence he would have exercised, had he come to the throne, but also because the causes and circumstances which led to his assassination led also to the First World War.

A good deal is known to-day about this prince because many of those who knew him have felt moved to record their memories of him. Among them, besides Conrad von Hötzendorf, is Ottokar Czernin who, at the end of 1913, when Austro-Roumanian relations had shown themselves to be in a perilous state, was sent on the Archduke's initiative to be Austrian Minister at Bucharest. Had Francis Ferdinand succeeded to the throne, Czernin would have been his Foreign Minister and did in actual fact become Foreign Minister to the last Hapsburg ruler, Emperor Charles. Another of the Archduke's intimates and in full sympathy with his views was Leopold Chlumecky, editor of the *Österreichische Rundschau*. In his book on the Archduke, Chlumecky has published a correspondence of great interest between the Archduke, Conrad, and Colonel A. Brosch, who until 1912 was head of the Archduke's military chancery and his aide-de-camp. In 1913 the historian T. Sosnosky was selected by the Archduke to write the biographical introduction to a special issue of the *Österreichische Rundschau* in celebration of his fiftieth birthday.[1] In 1929 Sosnosky published a biography of Francis Ferdinand containing a valuable series of family letters.[2]

Francis Ferdinand was the son of Francis Joseph's brother, Archduke Charles Lewis. Born in 1863 he was little more than twenty-five when, as a result of the suicide of Archduke Rudolf, Francis Joseph's only son, he became heir to the thrones of Austria and Hungary. As he was consumptive, he was not expected to live long enough to reign, but after treatment at Brioni and Davos he recovered his health. He became a frequent visitor at the house of the Archduchess Isabella and it was expected that he would marry her daughter. But one day in a medallion belonging to Francis Ferdinand the Archduchess found the photograph of one of her ladies in waiting, Countess Sophie Chotek, whom she instantly dismissed. To the intense scandal of the Court the Archduke asked Francis Joseph for permission to marry the lady. It was flying in the face of all traditions and rules of etiquette to seek an alliance with the daughter of an ancient but impoverished Bohemian noble house and Francis Joseph would have liked to impose an outright veto on the marriage. But under the persuasion of his Empress, the Tsar, Kaiser Wilhelm, and Pope Leo XIII he gave consent to a morganatic union on condition that Francis Ferdinand, in the presence of the other archdukes and the Court dignitaries, should take an oath and sign a formal deed stating that his marriage was a morganatic union and would always remain so, and that consequently neither his wife nor his children could possess or claim the rights, titles or privileges normally appertaining to the wives and children of archdukes and that, above all, since the children and their descendants were not members of the Archducal house, they were excluded from the succession to the throne. This deed of renunciation was signed on 28 June 1900, the very day on which fourteen years later the Archduke was to meet his death at Sarajevo.

It was a document which Francis Ferdinand, deeply attached as he was to wife and children, was determined to submit to revision.[3] Although after her marriage the wife of the Archduke was created Duchess of Hohenberg, her order of precedence at Court was after the youngest of the Archduchesses and she was subjected to galling humiliations which caused her to refrain from taking part in official receptions. Kaiser Wilhelm, in marked contrast to Vienna and in order to gain influence over Francis Ferdinand, treated his consort with a deference which increased the Archduke's temptation to abjure the oath he had taken. It was widely believed that, on the death of Francis Joseph,

---

[1] Sosnosky, pp. iv–v.

[2] Nikitsch-Boulles, the Archduke's private secretary, and Dr. Eisenmenger, his personal physician, have also published their memories of him.

[3] Sosnosky, pp. 30–1.

Francis Ferdinand would ask for and without difficulty obtain an annulment of the oath from the Pope and it was known that Wilhelm would at once recognize Countess Chotek as Empress. King Edward VII, as he told Steed, would have followed suit.[1] All this intensified the rancour which Francis Joseph felt for the stubborn Heir Apparent who, moreover, sought to exercise an influence on the policy of the Monarchy which the Emperor could ill brook. Their frequent sharp discussions resulted in mutual feelings of fear and hatred.

Their relations had always been strained. From the time that Francis Ferdinand came to be Heir Apparent, he found himself held aloof by the Emperor. Despite his promotion to high military rank, he was entrusted only with purely decorative tasks and all military measures were taken without his knowledge.[2] In Court circles he was regarded as incurably ill and destined never to ascend the throne. Solicitude and adulation were concentrated on his younger brother Archduke Otto.[3] This led Francis Ferdinand to hate the Austrian Premier Goluchowski whom he had regarded as devoted to himself and who had then 'buried him alive' by saying to the Emperor that it was high time for Otto to take over the position of Heir Apparent which was due to him.[4]

This network of difficult and antagonistic relationships with his entourage had contributed to produce in Francis Ferdinand that harshness and violence of character which alienated popularity and good will. Colonel Brosch, who felt deep loyalty and admiration for him, describes him as endowed with energy which 'unfortunately acted rather explosively and impulsively' and with a tenacious will which his subordinates seldom managed to influence.[5] His character was complex and full of contradictions. He hated flattery and was wont to say of anyone who cringed to him: 'He is no good; he is a toady.'[6] But on the other hand—writes Brosch—'he could never bear direct contradiction', yet demanded the unvarnished truth and those around him had the difficult task of presenting the truth which he demanded in a tactful form acceptable to his pride.[7] Czernin, too, notes the profound lack of balance in this character whose every feeling ran to excess, even to mania. For instance, he had an inordinate love of the chase—in which his prowess was proverbial—of collecting antiques and of gardening, on which he spent enormous sums.[8] He could never strike the happy mean in his relations. He could only love or hate, and hatred was much more potent with him than love.

Those who were around him and loyal to him knew another side to

---

[1] Steed, I, p. 235. According to Czernin, the Archduke intended to confer on his consort not the title of Empress, but the highest rank in the Imperial family. But later he revealed a desire to introduce a change in the succession to the throne (Czernin, pp. 44–5).

[2] Chlumecky, pp. 359–60.   [3] Czernin, p. 36.   [4] Czernin, p. 36.

[5] Chlumecky, pp. 356–7.   [6] Czernin, p. 39.   [7] Chlumecky, p. 356.

[8] Czernin, Ch. II, *passim*.

his character. Conrad regarded him as 'a man of high intellectual abilities . . . who could be of winning affability with those whom he liked'.[1] And Brosch declares: 'no one can remain indifferent to the charm of Francis Ferdinand's conversation and all who have had the good fortune to be received by him have left the audience chamber radiant and absolutely enthusiastic about the personality of the Archduke.'[2]

Certainly he passed easily to the other extreme and beside the above, one must set the testimony of Czernin:

> Ministers and other officials rarely waited on the Archduke without beating hearts. He was capable of flying out at people and terrifying them to such a degree that they lost their heads completely.[3]

He made scenes with the Emperor, scenes with the other Archdukes, and with the Court dignitaries, scenes even with Conrad to whom he once said in 1909:

> When I am Commander-in-Chief I shall do as I will; if anyone does anything else, I shall have them all shot. [4]

Nevertheless beneath the asperities and inequalities of his character the heir to the Austrian throne possessed intellectual endowments of a high order.

> Whether Francis Ferdinand would have achieved the difficult task of constitutional reform, or merely precipitated disaster, will always remain an open question: but no one can deny that he was one of the strongest personalities whom the House of Hapsburg has produced—one of the great 'might have beens' of modern history.[5]

His acute comprehension and political intuition revealed to him with rare clarity the weak points and leaks in the structure of the Monarchy, while a shrewd sense of realities led him to ask the opinions of the men who worked with him, not only on their specific fields but in all fields whether military, political or economic, so that he heard other views beside the official opinion and was thus better informed than the Emperor as to what was really going on in the country.[6] A good judge of men, he rarely made a bad choice. In contrast to Francis Joseph, who favoured half measures and discouraged the emergence of masterful personalities, the Archduke surrounded himself with strong men, though this did not prevent him from being tormented by jealousy of the very personalities he had singled out for promotion. These feelings,

---

[1] Gina Conrad, *Mein Leben mit Conrad von Hötzendorf* (Leipzig, 1935), p. 67.
[2] Chlumecky, p. 358. See also Czernin, p. 39.   [3] Czernin, p. 39.
[4] Conrad, I, p. 158.   [5] Seton-Watson, *Roumanians,* p. 472.
[6] Chlumecky, p. 357.

however, he fought down when the interests at stake were those of his country which he loved with 'passionate' intensity.[1]

It is understandable that his outbursts of fury and his eccentricities sometimes raised doubts as to his mental condition. It was said that at shooting parties he would upon occasion blaze away at everything within range and was an object of general terror. Other anecdotes are recorded indicative of serious psychological disturbance and those around him feared that he would end in madness.[2] In 1913 there was a rumour that he had become mentally deranged and that measures were contemplated for excluding him from the throne, but no legal or constitutional means existed for preventing the Archduke's accession.[3]

These conflicting characteristics and the striking ways in which they manifested themselves exposed Francis Ferdinand to misapprehension and unpopularity. He was conscious of this and felt himself foredoomed to assassination. Czernin praises his great personal courage and contempt for danger, against which he took precautions purely in order to reassure his consort. At times it happened that news reached him of attempts organized against his person. He received such news with admirable coolness. He once told Czernin that a gipsy woman had foretold that 'he would one day let loose a world war' and this prophecy flattered his ambition.[4]

Latterly the Archduke had successfully broken down the isolation in which Court circles had sought to hold him and had gained considerable political influence. He had gathered around him generals and statesmen and some first-rate journalists whose loyalty he had won, and there was some truth in the talk of his forming a *Nebenregierung* (auxiliary Government). From his Vienna palace, the Belvedere, he exercised a powerful influence against Magyar encroachments at the Ballplatz, directing press campaigns against the 'pinchbeck' Magyars (*Talmimagyaren*), who hid their Jewish origins behind a mask of fanatical Magyar-Chauvinism, and making persistent efforts to get the leading political exponents of Magyarization replaced by men of his own way of thinking.[5] His letters[6] reveal the intensity and tenacity with which he pursued these aims, first skilfully testing the character and intelligence of the men of his choice and then using his characteristic violence and inflexibility to force his choice on the aged Emperor who ended by giving way for the sake of peace.[7] It is not surprising that relations were strained between the two, that they sought to keep out of each other's way and dreaded meeting alone. It made things particularly difficult for those in charge of the military and political affairs of the Monarchy; 'they had to execute a regular egg-dance between

---

[1] Sosnosky, p. 66.   [2] Seton-Watson, *Sarajevo*, p. 90; Steed, I, p. 367.
[3] Steed, I, p. 368.   [4] Czernin, pp. 44, 45–6.   [5] Sosnosky, pp. 54–5.
[6] Chlumecky, Ch. VI (*the Archduke's letters*), pp. 320 ff.   [7] Sosnosky, p. 117.

Schönbrunn and the Belvedere, always with the risk that an egg would get broken and that they would come a cropper'.[1] In the end the will of Schönbrunn prevailed. How long was this to be the case? This was the anxiety which haunted Francis Ferdinand.

Not only did he see the years slipping past and old age stealthily drawing nigh without his having the opportunity to employ his capacities as he would have wished: condemned to impotence he had to look on while the Emperor yielded more and more to a craving for quietness, a tendency to procrastination which fought shy of all decisions, a dangerous policy of drift which allowed internal conditions in the Monarchy to grow steadily more confused while the irredentist movements grew bolder and more hydra-headed, and the process of national disintegration gathered momentum and brought the danger of collapse ever nearer.[2]

The struggle between Schönbrunn and the Belvedere reached its maximum intensity in their respective military chanceries. The Archduke had accepted the supreme command of the army only on condition of receiving plenary powers.[3] On the one hand he had instituted a vigorous movement of technical reforms, especially in regard to the development of the navy, and on the other he strongly resisted Magyar tendencies to military separatism and the setting up of an independent Hungarian army. His ideal was a strong, unitary armed force which, together with the Hapsburg dynasty, should ensure the cohesion of any federal form that the Empire might assume. His 'little chancery', as it was called to distinguish it from Francis Joseph's 'great chancery', successfully checked the Magyar separatist tendency and Brosch writes:

If the Archduke had never accomplished anything else, he has earned an outstanding position in the military and political history of the Empire by his vigour and determination in maintaining the unity of the army and thereby the power of the Monarchy.[4]

His activity in the field of military reform produced good results from the moment he brought about the retirement of the elderly General Beck and the appointment of General Conrad von Hötzendorf as Commander-in-Chief. Conrad at that time was a simple commander of a division in the Tyrol and at first declined the onerous position, but ended by accepting it. He became one of the most valuable of the Archduke's collaborators, and when the pressure from the Belvedere for war against Italy roused Francis Joseph to remove Conrad from the Supreme Command, Francis Ferdinand persuaded him to accept the rank of Inspector General of the army as a 'post in the reserve', pending reinstatement in his previous office. Latterly friction developed between

---

[1] Sosnosky, p. 119.   [2] Sosnosky, p. 117.
[3] Chlumecky, p. 329.   [4] Chlumecky, p. 362; Czernin, p. 50.

the two men owing to temperamental incompatibility. Conrad could not endure the Archduke's habit of making scenes and went so far as to offer his resignation and—as his letters to his future wife reveal—to wish for the accession of Archduke Charles for whom he then felt warm admiration.[1] Despite all this the two men were united by a profound community of ideas, especially by their belief in the necessity for a war with Italy and their identity of views on the far-reaching reforms to be carried out in the army. At the same time Francis Ferdinand's more practical and realistic mind acted as a brake on the often unrealistic plans of the Commander-in-Chief.[2]

2. *The Archduke's attitude towards Serbia, Italy, Germany, and Russia.*

The only point on which the ideas of the Archduke and Conrad diverged was Balkan policy. The Archduke had a horror of war with Serbia, as sure to cause a breach with Russia with whom he was desirous of remaining on the best of terms. In 1908 he had not been in favour of annexing Bosnia-Herzegovina. On 20 October of that year he had written to Aehrenthal deprecating a war with Serbia and Montenegro and had instructed Brosch to restrain Conrad from a warlike policy. 'He really must give up this warmongering'.[3] It is true that the attitude of Serbia on that occasion and the pressure exercised by Conrad made him for a moment admit the possibility of a conflict, but he soon reverted to his earlier standpoint.[4] During the First Balkan war his attitude was no less firm. At the end of November 1912, when the Viennese Right-wing Clericals were making a *casus belli* of Serbian access to the Adriatic, and at the end of April 1913, when Montenegro occupied Scutari, the Archduke was obliged to swim with the current, which was clamouring that Austria could not submit to so great a humiliation. But these were impulses of brief duration, soon succeeded by a pacific frame of mind. Chlumecky narrates that Francis Ferdinand was in agreement with Berchtold over the sending to Belgrade in November 1913 of the deputy Redlich with proposals to Serbia for a customs union.[5]

Many historians, on the basis of a Belgian document, assert that, when the Archduke visited Wilhelm at Berlin and Springe on 22 and 23 November 1912 he voiced the views of the warmongers, asking for a free hand against Serbia, which the Kaiser refused.[6] But the first volume of the present work shows the absence of all foundation for this view.[7] Conrad, moreover, writes:

On the repeated opportunities I had of discussing with the Archduke the need for decisive action against Serbia, I could never be quite clear whether

---

[1] Gina Conrad, *Mein Leben mit Conrad*, p. 73.
[2] Chlumecky, p. 361.   [3] Chlumecky, p. 99.   [4] Conrad, I, pp. 153, 155.
[5] Chlumecky, p. 135.   [6] GP. XXXIII, note to 12405.   [7] See Vol. I, p. 401.

the Archduke in his inmost heart had decided on warlike action. He dealt with all matters bearing on it with an interest which suggested that he had its execution in view but yet seemed to me in his heart to have no real liking for it.[1]

And in February 1913 he reports Bardolff, the successor of Brosch, as saying:

The Archduke has sounded the retreat all along the line, he will on no account have war with Russia, he will not allow it. He wants not a plum tree, not a sheep from Serbia, nothing is further from his thoughts.[2]

And Berchtold said to Conrad:

The Emperor still has kingly feelings and would say: 'This is more than I can stand', but the Heir Apparent is all on the side of peace.[3]

Indeed at the beginning of 1913 when the Archduke entertained his brother-in-law Duke Albert of Würtemberg and Archduke Eugene to dinner, he expressed his agreement with the latter who said that 'a war and a conquest of Serbia was all nonsense', adding:

Even assuming the case that nobody else interferes: what should we gain from it? Only another pack of thieves and murderers and scoundrels and a few plum trees.

And next day at lunch he repeated:

A conquest of Serbia is a bit of nonsense; if on that account a general war were to threaten there would be no *casus foederis* for the allies.[4]

And to Conrad on 17 February he said:

It is a possibility that there will also be an attack on Serbia, but merely to chastise her and on no conditions to annex even a square yard from her.[5]

Thus in his endeavour for peace he was on the same side as Berchtold.

Berchtold alone understands me and is absolutely of my opinion and that is a lucky thing[6]

he told his brother-in-law, Duke Albert of Würtemberg. And on 15 March he again sent a message by Bardolff to Conrad not to urge the Foreign Minister to go to war.[7] Thus Berchtold had good grounds for saying to Tschirschky on 5 February 1913:

If it were known, how peaceably inclined the Archduke Francis Ferdinand is, the diplomats would be amazed at the wrongness of their ideas.[8]

So peaceably inclined was he that he wrote to the King of Roumania and Kaiser Wilhelm expressing his satisfaction over the Treaty of

---

[1] Conrad, II, p. 413. [2] Conrad, III, p. 127. [3] Conrad, III, p. 160.
[4] GP. XXXIV[1], 12788. [5] Conrad, III, p. 156. [6] GP. XXXIV[1], 12788.
[7] Conrad, III, p. 169. [8] GP. XXXIV[1], 12797.

Bucharest, which was generally regarded as a set-back for Austria.[1] And yet he was continually misunderstood. Public opinion dubbed him 'the leader of the war party' and the Tsar asked Prince Hohenlohe whether it were true that the Archduke's dream was to enter Moscow at the head of an Austro-Hungarian army,[2] which made Francis Ferdinand immediately send a telegram of denial. Eisenmenger well observes that the Archduke fell a martyr to a policy which he had opposed all his life.[3]

There was, however, as has already been stated, one Power which Francis Ferdinand, in full agreement with Conrad, heartily detested, namely Italy. Sosnosky writes:

In Italy he saw the hereditary arch-enemy of Austria and in the alliance with her a pointless farce, in which the Monarchy was condemned to a rôle unworthy of it. He thus regarded the alliance as a burden and a fetter which he would fain cast off at the first opportunity and which if he had come to the throne he would undoubtedly have brought to an end in order to win over Russia to be the third member of the alliance in Italy's stead.

His profound aversion for Italy arose from various good reasons. His origins were not such as to make him a friend of the House of Savoy and of a liberal Italy, for on his mother's side he was descended from the Bourbon Royal House which under Francis II, his uncle, had been deprived of its throne by Victor Emmanuel.[4] In addition to this emotional factor there existed a practical reason which carried much more weight: Francis Ferdinand knew that, in spite of the Triple Alliance, the Monarchy was hated in Italy, which harboured evil designs against Austria and was always on the alert to fall upon her, should a favourable chance offer itself. He knew that the alliance friendship was merely a mask to hide this hatred.[5]

Yet another biographer, the former director of the Vienna War Office Archives, Colonel Edmund Glaise-Horstenau writes:

More than any other country in the world the Archduke hated Italy whom he, like the Chief of Staff, regarded as the hereditary enemy. . . . He fiercely ridiculed the infrequent protestations of friendship from the Quirinale. The idea of having to meet Victor Emmanuel III at the impending German Imperial manoeuvres weighed like an incubus on the last weeks of his life. Italy was the one country in regard to which he from time to time thought of a war as even something attractive.[6]

---

[1] See Vol. I, p. 470.

[2] Sosnosky, p. 152.

[3] Victor Eisenmenger, *Archduke Francis Ferdinand* (London, 1931), p. 265.

[4] His mother was the daughter of Ferdinand II, the notorious King Bomba, the next-to-last king of the Two Sicilies. Bülow was struck by the forceful personality of the Archduke and writes that his eyes had something of the cruel expression of King Ferdinand (Bülow, I, p. 163).

[5] Sosnosky, pp. 133-4, 141.

[6] E. Glaise-Horstenau, *Franz Ferdinand*, in *Neue Österreichische Biographie*, Vol. III (Vienna, 1926), p. 26.

Sosnosky adds that if Austria had beaten Italy, Francis Ferdinand would have tried to revive the Papal States not merely for the benefit of the Pope, but in order to prevent a recovery of strength by Italy. He would, therefore, most likely not have confined himself to this one piece of political reconstruction, but have promoted the restoration of the 'Kingdom of the Two Sicilies', the dominions of his immediate ancestors on the maternal side. And presumably he would have demanded the return to Austria of Lombardy and Venetia.[1]

That he was thinking of Lombardy and Venetia we know from a remark he made to Conrad in the winter of 1913 at one of the most critical moments of the Balkan crisis to explain his opposition to a war against Serbia. He said:

Our chief enemy is Italy, against which war will some time have to be waged; we must regain Venetia and Lombardy.[2]

His very interest in naval matters was a reflexion of his animosity towards Italy. To him was due the increases in the navy to which Francis Joseph, who felt an instinctive repugnance towards naval questions and had never consented to wear admiral's uniform, had devoted scant attention. The reorganization of the navy was intended to assert the supremacy of Austria not only in the Adriatic but also in the Mediterranean.

In international politics the Archduke resented not only the ties with Italy but also the subordination of Vienna to Berlin. Relations between him and Wilhelm were at the beginning not cordial and Bülow takes credit for having brought about their friendship.[3] Francis Ferdinand was repelled by the Kaiser's histrionic posings. Furthermore his Austrian pride was deeply offended by German lack of esteem for his country's historic past and he was too steeped in the traditions of his royal house to attach himself unreservedly to a Hohenzollern. Wilhelm, realizing the influence that Francis Ferdinand would wield once he came to the throne, sought to put himself on good terms with him by showing great deference towards the Duchess of Hohenberg, as has been already mentioned. But General Joseph Stürgkh, son of the Austrian Prime Minister, writes:

I am sure that if Francis Ferdinand had succeeded to the throne and had come to the conclusion that another alliance would be more advantageous to the Monarchy, it would not have cost him any inward struggle to cast off Germany and her Kaiser.[4]

[1] Sosnosky, p. 142.   [2] Conrad, III, p. 156.
[3] Bülow, I, p. 397.
[4] Graf Joseph Stürgkh, General der Infanterie, *Politische und Militärische Erinnerungen* (Leipzig, 1922), p. 301.

What irked him most of all was the rôle of second fiddle assigned to the Monarchy in the alliance with Germany.[1]

He was opposed to any closer combine with Germany, not wishing to be bound to Germany more than to Russia, and the plan that was formulated later as 'Central Europe' (Mitteleuropa) was always far removed from his wishes and endeavours.[2]

With Russia he wished to be on the best of terms. He would have liked to see a revival of the *Dreikaiserbund* (if possible with the adhesion of England) as a political and social bulwark of Europe. Wilhelm in one of his marginal notes to a diplomatic document, justly remarks that Francis Ferdinand was Russia's 'best friend'.[3] Hence Austro-Russian friction in the Balkans greatly perturbed him, as threatening to involve Austria in a war with the Muscovite Empire, which he regarded as monstrous. With the death of the Archduke, writes Eisenmenger:

Friendship with Russia, which he had tried with all his might to maintain and strengthen, had lost its last support.[4]

3. *Francis Ferdinand's plans for the regeneration of the Monarchy.*

On home policy Francis Ferdinand had broad views. In a letter to Colonel Brosch he wrote:

I *must* have the nationalities with me, for this is the only salvation for the future.[5]

Hence he greatly disapproved of the repression of Czechs, Roumanians and Southern Slavs, which alienated them from Vienna. He laid the chief blame on the Dualistic system, so dear to Francis Joseph, and to that one of the two nations which most exploited it, i.e. the Magyars ('It was bad taste on their part ever to come to Europe')[6] who not only ruled the multi-lingual lands of the Crown of St. Stephen, but, as has been said, exercised a preponderant influence at Vienna and by their threats intimidated politicians and even the Emperor himself. Francis Joseph, for the sake of peace, yielded time after time to their growing demands while turning a deaf ear to requests from the other nationalities. The Heir Apparent on the contrary believed that unless the half-feudal domination of those sharp-tongued Magyar 'scarecrows with the big mustachios' was broken, the Monarchy must perish.[7]

The most important works which have been written on Francis Joseph, Francis Ferdinand, and the Emperor Charles reveal with considerable unanimity the parlous state to which the Compromise of 1867

[1] Sosnosky, p. 156.
[2] Czernin, p. 51.
[3] DD. I, 53.
[4] Eisenmenger, *op. cit.*, p. 266.
[5] Chlumecky, p. 323.
[6] Seton-Watson, *Sarajevo*, p. 84.
[7] Sosnosky, pp. 59–64.

and the policy of the aged Emperor had reduced the Monarchy. Redlich, Tchuppik, Bagger, Sosnosky, Chlumecky, Polzer-Hoditz, Bibl,
Friedjung, all tell the same story. Francis Joseph reigned too long and,
either did not perceive, or did not know how to remedy the malady
which was sapping the life of the Monarchy. As Polzer-Hoditz well
remarks,

> the Austrian problem was in large measure the problem of Hungary.

Only federalism could have regenerated the Hapsburg Empire, and the
Hungarians would not hear of federalism. Francis Joseph had hardly
breathed his last when Tisza appeared at Schönbrunn to ask the Emperor Charles to take the oath as King of Hungary, because once he had
done so, he could never have altered the foundations of the state.

Francis Ferdinand, as an assiduous reader of political publications,
was well informed on the various proposals for the salvation of the
Monarchy. He saw how Switzerland had achieved the conciliation of
its various peoples. Why could not Austria become a greater Switzerland? A Rumane political publicist of Hungary, bearing the Serbian
name of Aurel C. Popovici—as a student he had been sentenced in
Hungary to four years' imprisonment for a publication dealing with the
Magyar oppression of the Rumanes and had later taken refuge in Roumania—had devoted a book to the subject, formulating a plan which
won the warm approval of the Archduke.[1] The Monarchy was to be
divided up into fifteen national states, which were to be autonomous
and free to use their own language, but linked together, through the
intermediary of the German language, by a central government with the
Emperor at its head and a small parliament of not more than forty-two
deputies elected by the member states in proportion to their total of
inhabitants.

This plan, implying the dismemberment of the lands under the
Crown of St. Stephen and giving Hungary approximately the frontiers
she was to receive in the Peace Treaty of 1919, would in the opinion of
Vienna have led to a revolution in Budapest. But the prospect did not
dismay Francis Ferdinand who read and approved of Popovici's book.[2]
According to a statement of Baron Margutti, aide-de-camp in Francis
Joseph's Chancery, the Archduke, in considering the eventuality of a
Hungarian rebellion against the formation of a federal Austria, is re-
ported to have said:

> Very well, Hungary will have to be conquered once again at the point
> of the sword. I do not see how it would be possible to escape from this
> necessity.[3]

[1] Aurel C. Popovici, *Die Vereinigten Staaten von Gross-Österreich* (Leipzig, 1906).
[2] Sosnosky, pp. 71–4.   [3] Margutti, p. 68.

And to a Hungarian magnate who once sought an audience of him armed with a whole library of legal proofs of the rightness of the Magyar standpoint, he retorted: 'I snap my fingers at your laws.'[1] Nevertheless he was anxious to find a legal basis for his forceful method of procedure and took his stand on Article XLIV of the Hungarian Constitution of 1868 which in a restricted measure assured the rights of the nationalities to live according to their needs within the limits of loyalty and respect towards the Hungarian state. The Magyars had, of course, allowed this article to fall entirely into abeyance. In the Hungarian parliament the eight million non-Magyars (not counting the Croats) were represented by 21 deputies, and the eight and a half million Magyars by 392. Francis Ferdinand planned to restore the legal basis of national freedom by resorting to the simple device of universal suffrage, repugnant as it was to his aristocratic mentality.[2]

Meanwhile there had appeared a new device which promised to be easier of execution, namely trialism. This contemplated the formation within the frontiers of the Empire of a third state consisting of the territories inhabited by the Southern Slavs (Croats, Slovenes, Serbs). It would form a counterpoise to Magyar influence, transforming the centrifugal motion of the Slavs in the Monarchy into centripetal motion and, sooner or later, solving the problem of Jugoslav union by the forced or voluntary absorption of free Serbia into the new state. Except with the Magyars the trialistic solution would have found fewer opponents than that of absorbing the Slavs into a Greater Austria which would have violated historical tradition and offended the patriotism of the Crown Lands (*Kronlandsgefühl*)[3] although there were some fears that the new state might be capable of allying with Hungary against Austria and thus disappointing the hopes of those who sought in it a counterpoise to Magyar influence. Aehrenthal, himself, conceived the annexation of Bosnia-Herzegovina as a first step towards trialism, in that it would make possible a grant of autonomy to the Southern Slavs. Despite the deep antipathy existing between the Archduke and the Foreign Minister

their views coincided on one point: the juridical status of the Southern Slavs was to be restored as being the one effective weapon against the attraction of Pan-Serb propaganda.[4]

It may be objected that what has been said above of the Archduke's opinions, of his opposition to a war with Serbia, of his determination in the event of war not to annex 'even a square yard of her territory', would lead one to believe that he would be against the creation of Jugoslav unity by the absorption, voluntary or otherwise, of Serbia into the new state, and that as a fervent and uncompromising Catholic

---

[1] Czernin, p. 38.   [2] Giesl, p. 189.   [3] Sosnosky, pp. 73-6.   [4] Giesl, pp. 189-90.

he would not wish to incorporate millions of Orthodox Serbs in his state.[1] But there are testimonies to the contrary. For example Szilassy declares that in December 1912, when he was about to go to Athens as Austrian Minister, Francis Ferdinand summoned him for a talk on the international situation and showed no less desire for peace and for agreement with Russia than his uncle Francis Joseph:

> He regarded the realization of Southern Slav aspirations within the framework of the Monarchy as a possibility in the future and in sharp terms criticized Tisza's policy which made better relations with Serbia and Roumania impossible.[2]

Certainly a Jugoslav union achieved voluntarily would be a very different thing from union created by force.

By peaceful union, Serbia with its reigning house might one day have stood in the same relation to Austria as Bavaria and the Wittelsbach dynasty within the German Empire. The same holds good for Roumania, one of whose statesmen, Nicolai Filipescu, in March 1914, proposed to Czernin that Transylvania should be joined to Roumania and that Roumania in turn should unite with the Monarchy. Czernin welcomed the suggestion with enthusiasm and hoped for its realization on the accession of Francis Ferdinand, whose Foreign Minister he was to be and who approved of the project.[3]

Although trialism would in fact have been easier to put into operation, a federal Greater Austria still remained the Archduke's ideal.[4] Margutti states that in the summer of 1913 Francis Ferdinand said:

> I live and shall die for federalism; it is the sole salvation for the Monarchy, if anything can yet save it.[5]

Whether and how, on ascending the throne, he would have put the federal plan into execution is difficult to say. According to Czernin he had no concrete plans worked out.

> He was not clear himself into how many states the Hapsburg Monarchy should be converted.[6]

---

[1] On 30 June 1914, after the Archduke's death, Barrère wrote from Rome to the Quai d'Orsay: 'It is said that when Aehrenthal proposed to restore the Sanjak of Novibazar to Turkey, the Archduke on being consulted had simply asked how many Catholics there were in the Sanjak..On hearing there were none, he said that if this were so the abandonment of the Sanjak was of no importance.' DF. 3. X, 460.

[2] Szilassy, p. 259.

[3] See Vol. I, pp. 501–2. On 10 July 1909 on a visit to King Carol of Roumania at Sinaïa the Archduke had a confidential talk with Joan Bratianu, then Minister, inveighing against the Hungarians who could not be made to see reason except by force. One would have to wait for the end of the old gentleman (*alter Herr*) to restore order in the Monarchy which had come under the thumb of the 'wretches' in Pest. The Archduke added that in a federal Greater Austria, Roumania would have the position of Bavaria in the German Empire. (Diamandy, *La grande Guerre vue du versant oriental,* in the *Revue des Deux Mondes,* 15 December 1927, pp. 793–4.)

[4] Sosnosky, p. 75.   [5] Margutti, p. 69.   [6] Czernin, p. 50.

But there exists the minute of a proclamation which he was to make to his peoples on ascending the throne, stating that they were all to have equal rights and that each people was to be guaranteed freedom of national development within the framework of the common interests of the Monarchy. There also exists a programme of government which in the years 1910–11 he worked out with Colonel Brosch and with the advice of experts in constitutional law, among whom were Lammasch, Turba, Jäger, Czernin, Žolger, Steinacker and the Magyar Kristoffy.[1] This lengthy programme contained no mention either of federalism or of a trialistic solution, although there was a partial acceptance of the idea of trialism. But it was only a preliminary sketch for a more thorough-going transformation.

As Sovereign he intended to have taken the name of Francis II and, in order not to take an oath to observe the existing laws, would have had himself crowned as King of Hungary only after creating a stronger central authority under an Imperial Chancellor and enlarging the Delegations to constitute a genuine Imperial Parliament. The army was to be a single common unit. If, as seemed inevitable, the Magyars were to oppose these reforms, their resistance must be broken by imposing universal suffrage on them with the help of the many non-Magyar nationalities subject to the Crown of St. Stephen. Plans were in preparation for the creation of a Kingdom of Bosnia-Herzegovina, within the framework of the Empire. This would have been a kind of mitigated trialism which might have formed the starting point of a later union of Croatia and Dalmatia with Bosnia-Herzegovina. But, as laid down, it did not seem to promise advantages either in internal policy or in the Monarchy's relations with Serbia. The Archduke further proposed to introduce German as the official state language even in Hungary. He once said to the Breslau Bishop, Cardinal Kopp, that the Church, the Army, and Germanism (*Deutschtum*) would be the pillars of his rule.[2]

What prospects and what developments would such a programme have had? Conrad thinks that Austria might, perhaps in a new form, have flowered again under the leadership of Francis Ferdinand and summarizes the latter's guiding principles as follows:

National freedom as far as the interests of the collectivity permitted, the grouping together of the collectivity under a strong central power for the collective benefit, equality of rights for all, no privileged state within the Monarchy.[3]

Czernin, on the other hand says:

It is hardly conceivable that, once on the throne, the Archduke would have been able to carry out his plans. The structure of the Monarchy, which he

[1] Glaise-Horstenau, *Neue Österreichische Biographie*, Vol. III (Vienna, 1926), p. 22.
[2] Glaise-Horstenau, *Neue Österreichische Biographie*, III, p. 24.
[3] Conrad, IV, pp. 15, 16.

was so anxious to strengthen and support, was already so rotten that it could not have stood any great innovations, and if not war, then revolution, would have shattered it.[1]

Indeed one must ask oneself whether, in the precarious condition of the Hapsburg state, which seemed to exist only by the force of inertia, any vigorous attempt at a cure would not have brought down the whole structure in ruins. The Austrian ex-Minister Dzieduszycki once described Austria as

a broken pot held together with a piece of wire. It might do duty as long as it was treated with due precaution but woe if it were exposed to too hard knocks or got some kick or other. Then it would be liable to fall to pieces.[2]

Surely it would also have fallen to pieces in a war with Italy, hated at that time by all the nationalities of the Monarchy. To be fair it must be admitted that the dislike felt by the Heir Apparent, by Conrad and by diplomatic, military, and Catholic circles in Vienna was based on a pretty correct estimate of the obstacle that Italy represented to Austrian plans of expansion and of the line she would take in a European war. An insuperable conflict existed between Italian interests and those of her Austrian ally, and it must in fairness be recognized that the Italians had a right and a duty to settle the conflict, as they actually did, to their own advantage, bringing about the defeat and dissolution of a composite Empire which aimed at destroying their own national state. In any case the freedom movement of the oppressed nationalities had grown so irresistible that it could no longer be dammed back or diverted into other channels. To be successful, the consolidation of the Monarchy on the basis contemplated by Francis Ferdinand would have had to be carried out many years earlier. 'Seventy years' government of wasted opportunities!' exclaims Chlumecky who was as great an admirer of Francis Ferdinand as he was an unsparing critic of Francis Joseph.[3] The road of the peoples of Europe now led in another direction, and a stage on this road was the victory of the oppressed nationalities over Austria, not her victory over them.

It remains to be discussed whether it was not his very programme which cost the Archduke his life, before he ever came to the throne and whether Chlumecky is not mistaken in regarding it as 'particularly tragic that he should fall to the bullet of a Southern Slav'. Less strange it was, at any rate, than might seem at first glance. Chlumecky himself writes that

[1] Czernin, p. 48.
[2] Franco Caburi, *Francesco Giuseppe: La sua vita e i suoi tempi* (Bologna, 1920), II, p. 452.
[3] Chlumecky, p. 25.

to unite Dalmatia, Bosnia-Herzegovina, Croatia and Slavonia to form a unit of the Hapsburg state was the intention at which Francis Ferdinand arrived after long reflection and which at the end of 1913 he announced to me in the words: 'These lands all belong together'.[1]

But was it not perhaps the fear of his reforming the Monarchy, by making it tripartite which made those who planned the assassination want to do away with him, in order that Jugoslav unity should be brought about, not within the Monarchy but against it, by Serbia? We shall see about this further on.

One thing is certain, among the Serb nationalists and the Southern Slavs who drew their inspiration from Belgrade he was regarded as their worst enemy, and the rumours circulating about him depicted him as rabidly working for a war with Russia and Serbia. Thus after the Konopischt meeting, the Archduke's last political act before his tragic end, the legend won credence that Wilhelm and Francis Ferdinand had there together planned an attack on Serbia. At that meeting he was, as we have seen,[2] full of wrath against Italy which was still keeping Aliotti as Italian Minister in Albania and was making such a fuss over the Hohenlohe decrees. He further gave vent to his anger with Tisza and the Magyars. And before taking leave of his royal guest he had discussed the question of Austro-Serbian relations with him in terms of which Conrad records two conflicting versions. According to the one, at an audience of Francis Joseph on 5 July, after the assassination:

I expressed to His Majesty my view of the inevitability of a war with Serbia. . . . His Majesty looked at me questioningly and said: 'Are you sure of Germany?' He had, he said, enjoined on the Heir Apparent, Archduke Francis Ferdinand, to ask at Konopischt for a statement from the German Kaiser whether we could in future count unconditionally on Germany. The German Kaiser evaded the question and did not return an answer.[3]

But on returning to his office after the audience:

I outlined the main issues to Colonel Metzger, Chief of the Operational Section. When I spoke of doubts about German co-operation in the event of a war being forced on us and mentioned His Majesty's mistrust, Metzger interposed that on the last evening at Ilidže Archduke Francis Ferdinand had assured him Kaiser Wilhelm at Konopischt had said in reference to that very case: 'If we did not attack, the position would get worse.'[4]

Where does the truth lie? The Kaiser's behaviour in July 1914 makes it seem likely that Metzger's version is the right one. Possibly the Emperor may have thought it best not to give encouragement to his bellicose Chief of Staff, or it may even have been that Francis Ferdinand,

[1] Chlumecky, p. 194.
[2] See Vol. I, p. 533.
[3] Conrad, IV, p. 36.
[4] Conrad, IV, pp. 38-9.

who at the bottom of his heart did not believe in the desirability of an attack on Serbia, was not frank with the Emperor.[1]

Be that as it may, the fact that after the Konopischt meeting the Archduke went to Bosnia as Inspector General to direct manoeuvres which by some were regarded, wrongly, as a dress rehearsal for operations against Serbia, lent colour to the story that a decision for war was taken at that meeting. In reality the manoeuvres were to take place in a sector which was not at all the one from which an offensive against Serbia would have been begun. Moreover only two army corps took part in them whereas seven would have been necessary for an offensive against Serbia. And lastly the decision that the Archduke should attend them had been taken as far back as September 1913 and its intention had been to hearten the elements in Bosnia-Herzegovina which were loyal to the Monarchy and to demonstrate that there was no intention of yielding to the Pan-Serb movement.[2] In the event, with a manifest disregard of popular feeling, it was decided that the Archduke should visit Sarajevo on St. Vitus's day, the 525th anniversary of the Serbian defeat at Kosovo in 1389, which for the first time was to be solemnly celebrated now that in 1912 the defeat had been wiped out at Kumanovo.

4. The Archduke's forebodings on the eve of the fatal journey and the state of revolution in which he found Bosnia.

Conrad writes that on the eve of Francis Ferdinand's departure for Bosnia, he expressed doubts about his safety to the Emperor and asked whether it would not be better to give up his journey on account of the extreme summer heat. Conrad's informant was the Emperor himself, who, not wanting to cross his nephew, replied: 'Do as you think best.'[3] The Archduke's medical adviser, Dr. Eisenmenger, writes that Francis Ferdinand felt an unwillingness to undertake the mission laid upon him by the Sovereign and remarked that he would have much

---

[1] GP. XXXIX, 15720, 15732, 15734, 15735, 15736; Conrad, IV, pp. 36, 38-9; Magrini, p. 70. In this connexion it is worth recording that at the end of December 1915 Steed was told by a personage belonging to the Austro-Polish aristocracy intimate with the Archduke, the following story from a Vatican source. At the Konopischt meeting Wilhelm proposed, and the Archduke agreed, to make war on Russia and France (England was to remain neutral) in order to redraw the map of Europe: (1) Poland with Posen, Lithuania and the Ukraine were to form a kingdom from the Baltic to the Black Sea which would be given to Francis Ferdinand, who was to be succeeded by his eldest son Maximilian; (2) Bosnia, Hungary, the Jugoslav territories and Salonika were to form another kingdom destined for Ernest, the Archduke's second son; (3) German Austria with Trieste, with the Archduke Charles as its ruler would constitute a new federal state incorporated in the German Empire. Between these states and the German Empire there would be a permanent military and economic alliance. However Steed's story is not authenticated and finds no credence among historians. (H. Wickham Steed, 'The Pact of Konopischt', in the *Nineteenth Century* of February 1916, pp. 253-73).

[2] Conrad, III, pp. 445-6; Fay, II, pp. 43-8.   [3] Conrad, III, p. 700.

preferred if the Emperor had entrusted it to someone else.[1] Prince
Ludwig Windischgraetz relates in his memoirs having been told by
Countess Haugwitz, whose guest the Archduke was in the second half
of June, that Francis Ferdinand was extremely depressed and full of
forebodings.[2] His private secretary, Nikitsch-Boulles, narrates that,
when the Archduke arrived at the South Station in Vienna for his departure to Bosnia, he found that in the carriage reserved for his use the
electric light installation was out of order and could not be put right
in time, so that the carriage had to be lit with candles. 'Another pre-
monitory sign' remarked the Archduke to his suite, smiling. Nikitsch-
Boulles adds that, surrounded by burning candles, Francis Ferdinand
said to him:

What do you say to this lighting ? Like in a tomb, isn't it ?[3]

Nevertheless he started on the evening of 23 June in order to board
the *Viribus Unitis* at Trieste next morning, arriving on the 25th at Ilidže,
a little health resort near Sarajevo, where the Duchess awaited him and
where he had his headquarters.

The English Ambassador at Vienna reported to London on 29 June
that, as the Archduke's friendly feelings towards the Slavs were known
in Dalmatia, Herzegovina and Bosnia, he was given an enthusiastic
reception. Even the opposition press, with the exception of the irredentist *Narod*, accorded him a welcome.[4] On 26 and 27 June he attended
the manoeuvres and paid a private visit to Sarajevo amid acclamations.
But only superficial observers could be deceived by these appearances.
The events of the previous two years had widened the breach between
the Monarchy and the Southern Slavs and intensified their irredentism.
After the two Balkan wars Austria-Hungary came to have on her
frontiers a victorious 'Piedmont' of doubled size which, emboldened by
the success of its arms, openly directed its aspirations towards the territories of the Monarchy. The first victories over the Turks had sufficed
to create a state of mind in Serbia which the French Minister in Serbia,
Descos, on 26 November 1912 described as follows:

What King Peter at Uskub said to General de Sancy represents the
thoughts of the whole Serbian people: the Balkan war will necessarily bring
in its train an Austrian cataclysm and the only alternative is to know whether
it is advisable to let it loose at the present moment or hold it back for some
years more. In the camps and in the towns young and old know that the
Balkan question is in process of drawing to its close for good, while that of

---

[1] Eisenmenger, *Archduke Francis Ferdinand*, p. 264.

[2] Ludwig, Prinz Windischgraetz, *Vom Roten zum Schwarzen Prinzen* (Berlin, 1920),
pp. 49–50.

[3] Paul Nikitsch-Boulles, *Vor dem Sturm. Erinnerungen an Erzherzog-Thronfolger Franz
Ferdinand, Von seinem Privatsekretär* (Berlin, 1925), pp. 211–12.

[4] BD. XI, 21.

the Slavs in Austria is about to be opened and that the present military experiment is only the preparation for a more considerable and more decisive experiment, from which the whole Serbo-Croat people will come out liberated or introduced as a destructive element into the Austro-Hungarian organism. The Serbian officers . . . proclaim this to everybody they meet, the people shout it in the streets of Belgrade.[1]

If this was the state of mind in 1912 when the results of the first victories were still in doubt, it may be imagined to what diapason it swelled when the defeat of the Turks was succeeded in the following year by that of the Bulgarians. The resentment against Austria, who had barred the Serbs from access to the Adriatic for the benefit of the new state of Albania, knew no bounds and even broke out among the Slavs of the Monarchy, kindled by the newly won prestige of Serbia and the irredentist propaganda which fed on it.

The situation was extremely serious in Bosnia-Herzegovina where the agrarian question contributed not a little to exasperate popular feeling. Although as far back as 28 June 1878 Andrassy at the Congress of Berlin had declared that the Austro-Hungarian administration would regard it as their foremost duty to find a settlement of the agrarian question, practically nothing had been done. The Austro-Hungarian Joint Finance Minister, Kallay, who had administered the occupied region for twenty years, had come to an agreement with the 6,000 Musulman big landowners, placing at their mercy 100,000 *kmet* (peasants under a feudal regime).

Nothing has been done [wrote Baernreither from Sarajevo on 9 October 1913] for education, nothing to lighten the burden of mortgage, not a sod has been turned for railway building. I have travelled for hours through the countryside without coming across a school. Everywhere agriculture and rural conditions are trammelled by Turkish land law which prevails in Bosnia as in the time of the Turks.[2]

It is not pure chance that the perpetrators of the Sarajevo crime were sons of such *kmet*. Both Čabrinović and Princip, in the course of their trial, reproached Austria with not having solved the agrarian problem and with keeping the countryfolk in poverty and ignorance. Princip made the statement:

I have seen our people being steadily ruined. I am a peasant's son and know what goes on in the villages. That is why I meant to take my revenge and I regret nothing.[3]

During the First Balkan war the Bosnian Government, alarmed at the fervour of the population for the Serbian cause, closed the Diet granted in 1910 and declared a state of siege. Bilinski, who in 1911 became

---

[1] DF. 3. IV, 577.   [2] Baernreither, p. 277.   [3] Mousset, p. 130.

Finance Minister, tried to pursue a policy of conciliation by granting more freedom to the press, revoking the emergency laws and taking land reform in hand. But the reactionary Governor, General Potiorek, persisted in blindly repressive methods which only made the situation worse. If the middle classes and the older generation in general confined themselves to legal agitation, hoping that the accession of Francis Ferdinand would bring an improvement in conditions, the younger generation of the middle and lower classes, peasants, elementary school teachers, artisans and students, refused to accept the existing state of affairs, scorned legal propaganda, and circulated clandestine leaflets advocating 'Macedonian' methods. The young generation was the heart of this big political movement. In 1913 141 secondary school boys had appeared in the dock under accusation of belonging to secret societies of tendencies hostile to the state. The Mostar 'Gymnasium' had been closed. A year earlier all the secondary school boys of the Bosnian capital had demonstrated for several days in the Sarajevo streets, burning Hungarian flags. School strikes were an everyday occurrence and the pupils were filled with a spirit of revolt which refused to submit to the authority of masters friendly to Austria. Shouts of 'Long live King Peter' and 'Down with Francis Joseph' were increasingly frequent.

All those familiar with the country [writes Hoyos] had the impression that an explosion was imminent. Especially in the schools Pan-Serb propaganda had created such a state of chaos that the continuance of regular instruction seemed almost an impossibility.[1]

Gathered in secret societies, the students read and circulated books on economic, social and political conditions in Bosnia and Herzegovina and the works of Russian revolutionary authors, especially those of Kropotkin, Herzen, Bakunin, Stepniak, Gorki, Chernichevski and Plekanov. The members of the secret societies pledged themselves to awaken the peasantry to the miseries of their lot and incite them to rebellion. Each group had a leader who periodically reported to Gaćinović, the soul of the movement. Some Bosnians went abroad and made contacts with exiled Russian revolutionaries. In their exasperation with the brutality of the police and their eagerness to use terrorism as a means of rousing the masses against Hapsburg rule political assassination appealed to them.

The year 1913 in Bosnia [writes Jovan Jovanović, the former Serbian Minister at Vienna] was the year of revolutionary organization. . . . 'Action, action, enough of words' was the cry on all lips. The young dreamed of nothing but bombs, assassinations, explosives to blow up and destroy everything.[2]

[1] Hoyos, p. 74.   [2] Isaac, pp. 259–60.

5. *The Serbian Comitaji movement and* Mlada Bosna.

To understand the atmosphere in which this young generation lived one must bear in mind the Serbian Comitaji movement after the Second Balkan war. For ten years from 1902 to 1912 Comitajism was the leading element in all Balkan turbulence. The first Comitajism was of Bulgaro-Macedonian origins. In 1902 armed bands were formed in Macedonia, subsidized by the Bulgarian Government, for the purpose of causing disorders which would focus the attention of Europe on the Balkans and lead to European intervention such as would end Ottoman domination in Macedonia. This province was either to become autonomous or be annexed to Bulgaria. Alarmed by the claims which these bands were staking out for Bulgaria in Macedonia, Serb and Greek revolutionary circles, in touch with their respective governments, recruited armed bands in Serbia and Greece. In Serbia they arose as early as 1905. The Comitaji crossed into Macedonia provoking disorders, blowing up bridges, attacking small bodies of gendarmes, committing murders, acting not only against the Turkish authorities but also against the private property of Moslems. When Turkish troops intervened they disappeared over the frontiers into their respective states from whose governments they received arms and money. In the Balkan wars Greek, Bulgarian and Serbian Comitaji had moved in advance and in support of their respective armies, fighting without regard for the rules of warfare and often indulging in arson and massacre. One of these battalions of Comitaji fighters was commanded by Major Voja Tankosić, who in 1903 had taken part in the plot against the Obrenović royal pair and had ordered the shooting of Queen Draga's brothers. It mainly consisted of young Serbs who were Austro-Hungarian subjects. After the war the Serbian Government was unable to get rid of them. Crowded in Belgrade, they spent their time in cafés bragging of their exploits and dilating on plans for more wars and conspiracies. Their boastings, the atmosphere of excitement they maintained, their proposals for new ventures, the arms and bombs they still had hidden at their lodgings kept these Bosnian émigrés in a ferment. After the defeat of Turkey and then of Bulgaria their plots for wars and outrages took Austria-Hungary as their objective. One earlier act of terrorism found many would-be imitators, the attempted assassination of General Varešanin on 15 June 1910 at the opening of Parliament by the student Bogdan Žerajić, a Serb of Herzegovina. This youth had intended to assassinate the Emperor Francis Joseph, who was present in Sarajevo for the opening of the Diet, but remembering that the only result of this act would have been to bring Archduke Francis Ferdinand to the throne, he fired five shots at the Governor. The attempt failed and the would-be assassin committed suicide. His corpse was spurned by the General with his foot and buried among criminals and suicides. From that moment Žerajić was regarded as the first martyr of the Jugoslav cause. His memory was held sacred and his tomb covered with flowers by the adherents of *Mlada Bosna* (Young Bosnia).

Some historians have regarded *Mlada Bosna* as an actual political organization. Nothing is more erroneous. Investigations made in Sarajevo after the world war lead to the conclusion that no such organization existed. *Mlada Bosna* was nothing more than a collective term for a youth movement scattered in numerous societies and small revolutionary cells. Under the aegis at first of the *Narodna Obrana*, and later of the *Black Hand*—of which more will be said later—Pan-Serb propaganda was carried on all over Bosnia-Herzegovina in agricultural co-operatives, choral societies, the 'Pobratimstvo' (a Temperance 'Brotherhood') all of which cloaked political aims. There also existed student associations, above all the Sokols, which in Bosnia-Herzegovina numbered 40 groups totalling 3,000 members, and were affiliated to the Serbian Sokol association *Dušan Silni*.

The leading spirit in the *Mlada Bosna* was Vladimir Gaćinović, the son of a Herzegovinian priest. Having fled to Belgrade at the beginning of 1909, when the annexation crisis was at its height, intending to volunteer in a war against Austria-Hungary, if it were to arise, Gaćinović remained in Serbia for two years in close contact with the Comitaji and other violent nationalists who at that time still belonged to the *Narodna Obrana* which he also joined. Steeped in revolutionary ideas he went in 1912 to Vienna University and there wrote an anonymous pamphlet *The Death of a Hero* (*Smrt Jednog Heroja*) glorifying Žerajić.

The Serb revolutionary, if he wants to win [asserted the pamphlet] must be an artist and a conspirator, must have talent for strength and suffering, must be a martyr and a plotter, a man of Western manners and a *haiduk*, who will shout and wage war for the unfortunate and downtrodden.

The pamphlet quotes Žerajić's own phrase: 'I leave it to Serbdom to avenge me', and concludes with the appeal:

'Young Serbs, you who are rising from the ruins and foulness of to-day, will you produce such men?' It seems as though this sums up the whole Serbia problem, political, moral and cultural.[1]

The Sarajevo outrage and the mentality of those who took part in it can only be understood in the light of the influence exercised on the youth of Bosnia by this appeal which became rapidly known all over Bosnia. Gaćinović himself returned to Belgrade where in the meantime a more extremist revolutionary sect had been formed, the *Black Hand*,

---

[1] R. W. Seton-Watson, *Sarajevo*, pp. 69–71.

vowed to terroristic methods. This he joined, becoming one of its most active agitators. On the model of the *Black Hand* Gaćinović organized in Bosnia a network of revolutionary cells called *Kružok* whose members remained unknown to one another but were linked by intermediaries. There was a particularly active cell at Sarajevo. One of its members was a friend of Gaćinović, the young schoolmaster Danilo Ilić, who later became one of those involved in the assassination of Archduke Francis Ferdinand. The idea of the conspiracy originated partly with Gaćinović who, with the help of funds from Serbia, had gone to Lausanne to study sociology and learn how to carry out outrages and who there entered into relations with Leo Trotsky.

The ferment was not confined to Bosnia-Herzegovina, but spread to Croatia, Dalmatia and Slovenia. On 28 April 1912, 156 Croat, Serb, and Dalmatian students, accompanied by Professor Miller of Zagreb University, went in pilgrimage to Belgrade where they were officially welcomed by the authorities and the nationalists and expressed their enthusiasm for King Peter and Jugoslav unity. On 8 June 1912, in the streets of Zagreb a young Serbo-Croat, Luka Jukić, made an unsuccessful attempt on Baron Cuvaj, the Ban of Croatia. In August 1913 a young Croat student Ivan Dojčić, who had returned all the way from America on purpose, inflicted a severe wound on the new Ban, Baron Skerlecz; and in March 1914 another Croat, Jakob Šefer, was caught red-handed waiting to shoot Skerlecz at the Zagreb opera-house.

In vain the Budapest Government, unable to stem the Serbophil agitation by violence, at the end of 1912 suppressed the Constitution in Croatia where the Serbo-Croat coalition had a majority, and set up a dictatorship. Each repressive measure, each trial of conspirators gave fresh impetus to the liberation movement. One of the Ballplatz officials, Musulin, whose family belonged to Croatia, revisited his native district after a long absence in the summer of 1913 and noted a profound change there:

I found in Croatia that the differences between Serbs and Croats have largely disappeared among the educated classes and consequently there was a marked weakening of Croatian nationalist feeling. . . . Intellectual circles were, to an extent alarming to Austro-Hungarian patriots, impressed by the immense development of the Serb race on the other bank of the Drave. In many places I met with the conviction that national salvation will come only from there . . . . The political activity of Serbia makes itself felt everywhere.[1]

To such an extent did it make itself felt that, a few weeks before the Sarajevo outrage, the Serb and Croat student organizations at the universities of Vienna, Prague and Zagreb amalgamated into a single

---

[1] Musulin, p. 208.

society taking the name of 'Unified National Youth' with an un-equivocally anti-Austrian programme.[1]

6. *The* Narodna Obrana, *the* Black Hand, *and its leader Colonel Dragutin Dimitriević.*

It need hardly be said that the irredentist agitation among the Southern Slavs of Austrian nationality found whole-hearted support and encouragement from Serb nationalist societies, particularly the *Narodna Obrana* and the *Union or Death* (*Ujedinjenje ili Smrt*) more commonly known as the *Black Hand*. The former, founded in 1908 in connexion with the annexation crisis, has already been mentioned.[2] It has also been said that when the crisis of 1909 was over, the *Narodna Obrana*, though obliged to turn itself ostensibly into a cultural society, still carried on an active anti-Austrian campaign and showed approval of the Comitaji, though not of terrorism, to which its influential secretary, Milan Pribičević, was entirely opposed. In actual fact, however, the *Black Hand* placed beside him one of its own leading agents, Major Milan Vasić, who was general secretary of the two societies at the same time, and who fell in the Second Balkan war. And the *Black Hand* used the *Narodna Obrana* to provide 'tunnels' of communication between Serbia and Herzegovina operated by trusted agents. Thus the two societies had a certain common membership but it was the *Black Hand* which sought to influence the *Narodna Obrana*, not vice versa.

Before the World War and in the first three years after it was over very little was said or known of the *Black Hand*. Determined to place the guilt on Serbia for the Sarajevo outrage, Austria attributed it to the operations of the *Narodna Obrana*. It was the Serbs themselves who revealed the origins and crimes of the *Black Hand* when, after the end of the World War, discussions arose in Belgrade regarding the grounds of justification for the Salonika trial, which will be mentioned later. In that connexion a supporter of Pašić, Prof. Stanoje Stanojević of Belgrade University, published a pamphlet on the murder of Francis Ferdinand. In it he declared that the *Narodna Obrana* was not involved in the outrage, and that Colonel Dragutin Dimitriević, who had played a leading part in the Obrenović murders in 1903, was the moving spirit also in the conspiracy which led to the Sarajevo crime. The pamphlet threw light on the activities of the *Black Hand* of which the Colonel was the head.

Stanojević further revealed that the army officers implicated in the

[1] On the Jugoslav revolutionary question see: R. W. Seton-Watson, *Sarajevo*, Ch. III, pp. 63–79; Lončarević in *Jugoslaviens Entstehung* (Vienna, 1929), pp. 311–414; Fay, II, pp. 92–112; Schmitt, I, pp. 143–54; Bibl, pp. 438–68; Baernreither, pp. 274–7; B. Jevtić, *Sarajevski Atentat* (Sarajevo, 1923), pp. 3–21, Chs. I–VII translated in KSF, 1925, pp. 657–686; letter of Jovan Jovanović, quoted by Isaac, pp. 259–62.

[2] See Vol. I, pp. 297–8.

killings of 1903 had continued to remain in touch with one another and
exercised surveillance over the new dynasty and its Governments. In
1911 they had vainly asked for a renewal of propaganda and revolutionary agitation on Turkish territory which had been suspended after
the Turkish proclamation of a Constitution. It was as a result of this
refusal that on 22 May 1911 they had founded the *Union or Death*
society with Dimitrievié as its head and had at once begun to work
parallel with the *Narodna Obrana*.[1] But subsequent revelations by
Colonel Č. A. Popović, one of the founders, and in its latter years, secretary of the *Black Hand*, give a different account of the origins of the
association. According to him the idea originated with Radenković,
one of the leaders of the Serbian movement in Macedonia. The first to
join him was Tankosić and then Dimitrievié who at the beginning
promised only limited co-operation. Ten original members formed the
Central Committee.[2]

The character of this secret society, of which Dimitrievié became the
leading spirit and chief, is revealed in its statutes.[3] The purpose they set
forth is to realize the union of 'all the Serbs', giving preference to
'terrorist action over intellectual propaganda', bringing influence to
bear on Government circles and the various social classes of the Kingdom of Serbia which was 'regarded as the Serbian Piedmont', organizing revolutionary activity in all the territories inhabited by Serbs and
using every means available to fight opponents outside Serbia. A society
with such aims had necessarily to remain secret. Its members were
identified by numbers and remained personally unknown to one another.
Only the Central Committee knew their names. The *bona fides* of a new
member was guaranteed by the life of his sponsor. Every new member
pledged himself to convey to the Central Committee through channels
of the society hierarchy any information he might gain, whether as a
private citizen or in an official capacity, which was likely to prove of
use to the society. One of the conditions of membership was the 'for-
feiting of one's personality'. Once the Central Committee had pronounced a sentence of death 'all that mattered was that the execution
should take place without fail, no matter by what method'. The roman-
tic formula of the vow, the rites of the society were in keeping with its
spirit. In Serbia, members were recruited mainly from army officers,
but included also members of parliament, officials, members of the

[1] Stanojević, p. 48. It must be added that there were certain army officers implicated in
the killings of 1903 who refused to join the *Black Hand* and disapproved of its tendencies.
They were adherents of the Radical party and came to be known as the *White Hand*.

[2] Č. A. Popović, *Organizacija 'Ujedinjenje ili Smrt'* in *Nova Evropa*, 11 June 1927, p. 396.

[3] These statutes were the chief evidence for the prosecution against Dimitrievié in the
Salonika trial of 1917 (see pp. 30-1). But the judges in Salonika had before them only a
mutilated text. The full text was published in a Split newspaper by Oskar Tartaglia, reproduced in *Nova Evropa*, 21 October 1922 (pp. 182-90), translated into English in KSF of
September 1926 (pp. 681-9) and also given by Bogičević in *Le procès de Salonique* (pp. 41-53).

teaching profession, clergy, professional men. In the territories subject to the Monarchy, recruits came from the student youth and the working classes. It was even stated, according to Bogičević, that membership totalled 100,000 to 150,000,[1] but this was a gross exaggeration. Colonel Popović assured the present writer that it was not more than 2,500, but added:

Union or Death found wide approval, and membership would have been much higher if the doors had been open to all. Those who were admitted had to be of tested loyalty and capable of rendering practical service.

Did the *Black Hand* work only for the union of all Serbs, as its statutes state? Colonel Popović has assured the present writer that:

Union or Death had for its object the unification of all the Southern Slavs of the Austro-Hungarian Monarchy in a national unity. The Belgrade Central Committee comprised, in addition to the members from the Kingdom of Serbia, delegates representing all unredeemed Jugoslav territories: i.e. one for Bosnia-Herzegovina, who was Gaćinović, one for Old Serbia and Macedonia, one for Montenegro, one for Croatia, one for Slovenia and Syrmia, one for the Voivodina, one for Dalmatia, who was Oskar Tartaglia. It is affirmed that Dragutin Dimitriević, in 1917, died shouting: 'Long live Jugoslavia!'

But in the Slav territories of Austria-Hungary the number of members of the *Black Hand* cannot have been great. Oskar Tartaglia told the present writer that in Dalmatia there were two, in Croatia a dozen and in Bosnia-Herzegovina some thirty. Colonel Božin Šimić stated to the present writer that the *Black Hand* had as its object the union of all the Southern Slavs of the Monarchy and added:

We regarded the war against Turkey as a step in the war against Austro-Hungary which was our principal objective. Up to 1904 we were in favour of co-operation and union with Bulgaria. We aimed at the creation of a single Slav state in which the two parts would have equal rights, neither exercising political or military hegemony over the other. It was we who in 1912 urged Milovanović to sign the alliance with Bulgaria. In spite of this we raised the question of the Vardar valley in order to have our hands free in case of a war with Austria and in 1913 we resisted Russian pressure which supported Bulgarian territorial demands in Macedonia.

Shortly after the creation of the *Black Hand* the Serbian General Staff decided to set up six frontier posts, three on the frontiers of Bosnia-Herzegovina and three on the frontier between Macedonia and Turkey with instructions, not only to gather information on what went on on the other side, but also to make a study of the terrain in case of war. Popović told the present writer that Colonel Dimitriević managed to get six members of the *Black Hand* detailed to these posts and added:

[1] Bogičević, *Procès*, p. 3.

I was posted to the Bosnian frontier at Užice. To the tasks entrusted to me by the General Staff came a third on the part of the *Black Hand*, i.e. to organize revolutionary groups in Bosnia, discover trustworthy persons, foment revolutionary activity, form contacts with Bosniac agitators, in order both to enrol volunteers and to raise an insurrection in the event of war with Austria-Hungary. In Bosnia-Herzegovina the *Narodna Obrana* was known ever since the annexation and we thought that, if we said we were members of another organization, it might perhaps arouse distrust and hesitation. So we decided to give out that we belonged to the *Narodna Obrana* in order to benefit by the prestige this society enjoyed with the youth of Bosnia. Hence on this renewal of revolutionary activities, the Austrians thought they had the *Narodna Obrana* to deal with. Moreover, without the knowledge of its leaders, the *Narodna Obrana*, through the influence of Dimitriević, also came under the control of *Union or Death*, because besides its general secretary, Milan Vasić, several other influential members of the *Black Hand* were at the same time enrolled in the *Narodna Obrana*. The officer who during the First Balkan war recruited volunteers for the *Narodna Obrana* was also a member of the *Black Hand*.

In order to understand the influence exercised by the *Black Hand* on Serbian public life and the part it played in the Sarajevo conspiracy, it is necessary to examine more closely the figure of its leader Dimitriević. It is difficult to overrate the part which this Colonel—born in 1876, appointed head of the Intelligence Service of the Serbian General Staff in 1913, and known under the pseudonym of Apis—played in the history of his country, and the hold he still has over the minds of those who came close to him. Even his enemies pay tribute to his great gifts, his patriotism and his charm. Stanojević speaks thus of him:

Gifted and cultured, honourable, a convincing speaker, a sincere patriot, personally courageous, filled with ambition, energy and the capacity for work, Dragutin Dimitriević exercised exceptional influence on those around him, in particular on his associates and on junior officers who were all his inferiors in qualities of mind and character. He had the characteristics which cast a spell on men. His arguments were always striking and convincing. He could represent the most intractable matters as mere trifles, the most hazardous enterprises as innocent and harmless. Withal he was in every respect a remarkable organizer. He kept all the threads in his own hand and even his most intimate friends only knew what was their own immediate concern. But at the same time he was extraordinarily conceited and thoroughly affected. Ambitious as he was, he had a taste for working in secret, but he liked it to be known that he was doing secret work and that he kept all the threads in his own hand. He was incapable of distinguishing what was possible from what was not and perceiving the limits of responsibility and power. He had no clear conception of civil and political (*staatlichen*) life and its requirements. He saw only his own aims and pursued them ruthlessly and without scruple. He loved adventure and danger and secret meetings and mysterious activities. How far his private ambition reached it is hard to say.

His political ideas were dim and confused, but he was extraordinarily resolute in carrying out anything that he had set his mind on.

Dimitriević was convinced that his own ideas were the right ones on all
matters, events and circumstances. He believed that his opinions and activities enjoyed the monopoly of patriotism. Hence anyone who did not agree
with him could not in his eyes be either honourable or wise or a patriot. He,
without a doubt, was all this, but he found it hard to acknowledge it in
others, apart from those who obeyed his orders. It was for him to plan,
organize and command, for others to obey and carry out his orders without
questioning.[1]

A still more enthusiastic and quite uncritical appreciation of the personality of Dimitriević is to be found in the writings of the former
Serbian diplomat M. Bogičević, who describes him as a 'noble and
beautiful' soul and 'a terrorist despite his kindliness', 'the inspirer of all
the important deeds that were done in Serbia between 1903 and 1917'.
'A conspirator, a re-organizer, a leader of men and skilful politician,
all at the same time, he never sought satisfaction for his own ambitions
or glory. He was never seen about, but it was well known that he was
the mind directing everything.' In support of this eulogy Bogičević
published appreciations from several of Apis's comrades, one of
whom, for example, declares that 'he is something more than a man of
ability, he possesses a magnetic power which takes possession of all
who surround him'. Another says: 'For me he is something more than
an ordinary mortal, he is a hidden force to which I willingly submit
even if reason inclines me not to do so.'[2] For Tartaglia, Dimitriević
was a Mazzini and a Garibaldi rolled in one.[3] The surviving leaders of
the *Black Hand*, Colonel Velimir Vemić, Tucović, Čedomilj A. Popović,
Božin Šimić, when the present writer questioned them in November
1937, reaffirmed their devoted, unqualified admiration for Dimitriević.
The latter, a bachelor, lived in Belgrade at the house of his brother-in-
law, Professor Živanović, of Belgrade University. Dimitriević's nephew
and heir, Milan Živanović, in a statement made to the present writer says:

He was resolute and wise and had a shrewd political mind. He thought and
acted by himself without seeking the advice of others and, once a decision
was made, he went straight ahead with an iron will, without hesitation, without change of mind. He was a man of the utmost secrecy. He never spoke of
his intentions nor of his share in events even if these were long past. Many
times my father said to him that he had the temperament and the ability of a
politician rather than of a soldier and pressed him to write his memoirs or
describe the part he had played in the history of Serbia, my father being
deeply interested in history. He always answered that he had no time. In
reality he did not want to break silence. He was devoid of personal vanity.

[1] Stanojević, pp. 50-1.   [2] Bogičević, *Procès*, pp. 64-8.
[3] O. Tartaglia, *Dragutin Dimitrievič Apis* in *Nova Evropa*, 26 July 1927, pp. 67-74.

7. *The conflict between the* Black Hand *and the Prime Minister Pašić on the eve of the outrage.*

Here is the account given by Stanojević of what Dimitrievič was capable of doing and how his life ended:

A restless character full of the spirit of adventure Dimitrievič was continually planning conspiracies and outrages. In 1903 he was one of the chief organizers of the conspiracy against King Alexander, in 1911 he sent an emissary to assassinate either the Austrian Emperor or the Heir Apparent, In February 1914 he concerted with a Bulgarian secret revolutionary committee to assassinate the Bulgarian King Ferdinand. He took over and organized the outrage against the Austrian Heir Apparent in 1914. In 1916 from Corfu he sent an emissary to attempt the assassination of the Greek King Constantine and in the same year he seems to have sought contact with the enemy and organized an outrage against the Serbian Heir Apparent, Prince Alexander. It was for this reason that he was condemned to death and shot on the Salonika front in June 1917.[1]

As the source of his revelations Stanojević gives persons who took part in the events, including Dimitrievič himself, but produces no documents and his evidence therefore cannot be accepted unreservedly. There is no doubt but that Dimitrievič headed the conspiracy of 1903 and played the part in the Sarajevo crime which we shall soon consider. It also seems certain, as will be shown later, that he promoted the Jukić outrage, though of this Stanojević was not aware.[2] But while nothing is known of the other outrages attributed to him by the Belgrade professor—the surviving members of the *Black Hand* have no information about them—it is not true that Apis entered into relations with the enemy. And at the Salonika trial no evidence was produced that he was the organizer of the attempt on the life of the Regent for which he was arrested in December 1916, condemned to death on 5 June 1917 and shot on 26 June. On the contrary it is widely believed, even in Serbia that Pašić, who was bitterly hostile to Dimitrievič and above all feared his conspiracies, wanted him put out of the way when in the autumn of 1916 after the invasion of Roumania he, as Serbian Prime Minister, was considering the possibility of coming to terms with Austria. With this in view he instituted against Dimitrievič and his friends, who after the defeat and invasion of Serbia were no longer as dangerous as they had been, a trial based on a false accusation and ending with a sentence delivered on grounds which to a great extent corresponded with the facts as regards the *Black Hand*, but did not bring proof of the guilt of the accused men.[3] Hence the execution of the sentence on Dimitrievič and not on the other accused, especially as it was carried out in spite of intervention in high places on behalf of Apis,

---

[1] Stanojević, p. 51.   [2] See below, p. 75.
[3] See the findings in Bogičević, *Procès*, pp. 90–4.

rousing profound indignation and having repercussions which lasted long and left deep traces in Serbian life.[1]

We must cast a glance at the factors which gave rise to the conflict between Dimitrievć and the *Black Hand* on the one side and Pašić and his Cabinet of Old Radicals on the other, a conflict which was in full swing at the outbreak of the European war. When the *Black Hand* was founded, no difference of opinion existed between it and the Government, in fact Milovanović was in great sympathy with it. Popović made the statement to the present writer:

At the end of 1911 we decided to act in complete agreement with the Milovanović Government in all questions of foreign policy. Only three of us remained as officers on the Bosnian frontier, the rest were sent to the Turkish frontier. It was the *Black Hand* that insisted on the war with Turkey against the hesitations of Pašić, who, however, at this period was in full sympathy with us.

The Serbian Major Lazarević, who as early as 1917 revealed with many inaccuracies the importance of the *Black Hand* in a pamphlet entitled *La Main Noire* published at Lausanne, stated that its membership

---

[1] Those, besides Colonel Dimitrievć, condemned to death at the Salonika trial were Colonels Milan Miloranović, Radoje Lacić, Čedomilj A. Popović and Vladimir Tucović, Lieutenant-Colonel Velimir Vemić, Vice-consul Bogdan Radenković, Major Ljubomir Vulović and Rade Malobabić. But only Dimitrievć, Vulović and Malobabić were executed, the rest were reprieved and sentenced to life imprisonment, while General Damian Popović and Mohamed Mehmedbašić received a sentence of fifteen years' imprisonment. In 1919 all the accused who were still in prison were pardoned and restored to freedom. After the death of King Alexander they were reinstated in their rank, sent on leave 'and pensioned off. Oskar Tartaglia states that before the trial, i.e. just before the Serbian retreat across Albania, the dismissal took place of the Voivod Putnik, a good friend to the men of the *Black Hand*. As judges for the trial a choice was made of personal enemies of the accused. Admission was granted to the court-room only to holders of official passes. The accused deposed that they had never before heard of the attempt on the life of the Regent of which they were accused. Of the more than eighty witnesses for the prosecution none had been present at the outrage except a certain Velianović, who had been brought out of prison where he was serving a sentence for murder. Yet the accused had been under observation for a long time and all their movements shadowed (Oskar Tartaglia, *Veleizdajnik,* Zagreb, 1928, p. 29). Also R. W. Seton-Watson, who is certainly not suspect of animosity towards Pašić and defends him from the accusation of connivance in the conspiracy against the Archduke, expressed doubts as early as 22 August 1918 in *New Europe* as to the justice of the Salonika verdict, drawing attention to the following monstrous features of the trial: (1) while the attempt on the Regent was said to have taken place on 16 September 1916, the arrests were not made until 15 December and no investigation was made on the spot before 2 April 1917; (2) Apis and his friends were at first accused of high treason as having sought to make peace with the Central Powers, and only when this accusation could not be substantiated, were they accused of attempted assassination; (3) the only witness who claimed to have seen Malobabić (the alleged would-be assassin) discharge his weapon was a certain Velianović, who was in prison for a common murder; (4) none of those who had been in the Regent's carriage could bring concrete proofs; (5) the Minister of the Interior, Ljuba Jovanović, prevented the reading at the trial of a report by two French police who had followed the Regent's carriage. R. W. Seton-Watson also states that the Regent was reluctant to confirm the death sentences and only yielded to the pressure of Pašić, Protić and L. Jovanović (*Slavonic Review,* March 1928, pp. 704–6).

included the Serbian Crown Prince, the Prime Minister Pašić, the Minister of the Interior Protić, the Minister of Justice Stojanović and the Commander-in-Chief Putnik.[1] But the statement is devoid of support and the surviving members of the Central Committee of the *Black Hand* deny that these personages ever were members. Bogičević gives none of their names in the membership list, as he would undoubtedly have done if they had been members, because of the aversion he felt for them all.

However Bogičević declares, without bringing evidence, that the leaders of the *Black Hand* were on excellent terms with King Peter and Prince Alexander, and that the latter gave 26,000 dinars towards founding the journal *Piemont*, the organ of the society; also that in 1911 the Prince defrayed the expenses of a severe illness of Dimitrievič. He further says that the Prince expressed the wish to become head of the *Black Hand*, and felt resentment when the founder would not hear of it. Dimitrievič's disagreement with certain former associates who had gained an influence over the Prince aggravated this resentment.[2] Bogičević also writes that the officers sentenced at Salonika made a statement, which was brought up in the Skupština on 28 February 1924, to the effect that:

The *Union or Death* society was a patriotic society whose activities were always known to the relevant authorities and conformed to their intentions.[3]

Dimitrievič is further said to have stated at his trial that at the end of 1911 he informed Milovanović, then Foreign Minister, of the existence of the *Black Hand* and that Milovanović answered:

My young friend, put your *Black Hand* at my disposal and you will see what Milovanović will manage to do in a short time for the Serbian cause.

In this way, according to Popović, the society became in practice the executive organ of the Serbian Foreign Minister as regards Macedonian affairs.[4]

But this harmony was of short duration. In 1912 in the First Balkan war—says Stanojević—the *Black Hand* played a part of some importance. The success of Serbian arms increased the prestige of the army and of the military caste, and army officers exercised a considerable influence in affairs of state. Disagreements over policy led to the members of the *Black Hand* turning against the Government which was anxious to avoid a conflict with Bulgaria and ready to make concessions to her in Macedonia and submit the whole dispute to the arbitration of the Tsar. Pašić had to resign but the Russian Minister Hartwig contrived to have him reinstated. Only the sudden Bulgarian attack, by

---

[1] Dobrovoi Lazarewitsch, *La Main Noire* (Lausanne, 1917), p. 47.
[2] Bogičević, *Procès*, p. 10.   [3] Bogičević, *Procès*, p. 109.   [4] Schmitt, I, p. 197.

putting Bulgaria in the wrong, prevented a rupture between the *Black Hand* and the Serbian Government for the time being.[1]

But only for a short time, because after the Second Balkan war, when the problem of administration in the newly acquired territories arose, sharp conflicts flared up between the army and the police. The new officials sent to Macedonia by the Government were unequal to their admittedly difficult task, while at the same time a government decree, issued at the beginning of 1914, gave the civil authorities precedence over the military. This decree raised a veritable storm among the officers, who collectively petitioned that it should be rescinded. When at Uskub at the Easter Sunday ceremony the divisional commander, General Damian Popović, one of the regicides of 1903, tried to take the place on the bishop's right which belonged to the Prefect, the Government placed him on the retired list. In protest Popović was nominated chairman of the Officers' Club, whereupon the masterful Minister of the Interior, Stojan Protić, seized the club premises, ordered an inquiry into the deficit in its finances and is said to have concentrated 3,000 gendarmes at Belgrade as a safeguard against a military *coup d'état*, organized by Dimitrievic and the *Black Hand*.[2]

Colonel Čedomilj A. Popović told the present writer that

the crisis between the *Black Hand* and the Serbian Government, known under the name of the 'precedence of the military over the civil authorities' in the new provinces, was, in reality, a crisis caused by the misgovernment of the officials sent to Macedonia by Belgrade. The officers' protest caused acute tension. The Commander-in-Chief Putnik sent to Macedonia a trusted senior officer who on his return corroborated the accusations made by the *Black Hand*. Then Putnik went and protested to the King and Pašić had to resign.

In addition to 'precedence' there were other causes of friction between the Pašić Government and the *Black Hand*. Early in 1914 Pašić, alarmed at the activities of the 'frontier officers' at Šabac, Ložnica, and Užice, recalled them to the interior and gave them appointments as army instructors. In March 1914 the Government set up a commission of six to carry out an inquiry into the management of the officers' co-operative supply stores of which the *Black Hand* was in charge. The deficit was reported to amount to 300,000 dinars and this sum was said to have been used for the journal *Piemont*. The *Black Hand* rebutted this

---

[1] Stànojević, p. 53. According to Seton-Watson, however, the conflict between the Serbian Government and the *Black Hand* arose from the fact that Dimitrievic and his friends, being specially interested in Bosnia, favoured concessions to Bulgaria (*Sarajevo*, pp. 139–40). But Colonels Čedomilj A. Popović, Velimir Vemić, Vladimir Tucović and Božin Šimić have unanimously assured the present writer that Seton-Watson's statement is without foundation and that on the contrary Dimitrievic and the *Black Hand* were strongly opposed to concessions to the Bulgarians in Macedonia and the arbitration of the Tsar, fearing that the Tsar might pronounce in favour of Bulgaria.

[2] Seton-Watson, *Sarajevo*, p. 140.

accusation by declaring that the *Piemont* had 14,000 subscribers and was self supporting.[1]

In reporting to Paris on the dangerousness of the situation caused by the conflict between the *Black Hand* and Pašić, Descos, the French Minister at Belgrade, wrote on 7 May 1914:

The officers are in a ferment and hold meetings; the police keep them under observation and this irritates them. There are announcements of several resignations and placings on the retired list among the highest commands in the army. . . . The Minister of the Interior speaks of their 'Pretorian tendencies'. The army paper *Piemont* . . . recalls the memory of 29 May 1903, i.e. the assassination of King Alexander and Queen Draga, and forecasts fresh turmoil.[2]

On 26 May 1914, the *Piemont* wrote: 'Serbia is passing through anxious days. Never since 1903 has the political situation been so serious.' Matters were made worse by the parliamentary Opposition. In league with the *Black Hand* it first practised obstructionism and then left the Skupština. The royal family was without prestige, 'King Peter practically non-existent'.[3] Giesl, the Austrian Minister at Belgrade, reported to Vienna on 8 May:

The conflict between the Government and the conspirator party (*Crna Ruka*) . . . has become so aggravated in the last few weeks that a violent clash between the two rivals for power seems not impossible. . . . The King, who owes his throne to the conspirators, does not quite venture to side openly with them, but his sympathies belong to the *Crna Ruka*, as do those of the Crown Prince. . . . The *Crna Ruka* being probably none too fastidious in its choice of means to gain its ends, I regard the possibility of violent eruptions, even of an overthrow of the Government or a *coup d'état*, as not entirely inconceivable developments . . . unless the Government at the last moment capitulates to the military party, as it has done up to now.[4]

The King thus refused Pašić's request for a dissolution of the Government and Pašić resigned at the beginning of June. The King, it seems, promised General Putnik to entrust the formation of a new Government to the 'Young Radicals'. At this prospect Giesl warned Vienna that it would be a mistake for Austria to base any hopes on a change of Government:

The Old Radicals are certainly not pro-Austrian, but it would be a mistake to put any great hopes on the triumph of the Young Radicals, Progressives or Nationalists. . . . The determining factor in Serbia, the army, is filled with Jugoslav chauvinism and hate for Austria-Hungary and will force a nationalist-chauvinistic and anti-Austrian bias upon the policy of whatever Government there may be.[5]

[1] Oe-U. VII, 9485.   [2] DF. 3. X, 207.   [3] DF. 3. X, 285.
[4] Oe-U. VIII, 9649.   [5] Oe-U, VIII, 9819.

But the Russian Minister Hartwig, who carried great weight, and the Crown Prince Alexander persuaded King Peter to keep Pašić in power, though by so doing the King made his own position untenable. Pretexting health reasons, he left for the country, entrusting the regency to Prince Alexander. On 24 June the Skupština was dissolved and elections proclaimed for 14 August.

Such were the events which took place on the eve of the Sarajevo outrage. They throw light on the atmosphere in Belgrade after the annexation of Bosnia-Herzegovina and at the time when the assassination of the Archduke was planned. They help to explain the attitude both of the men of the *Black Hand*, who organized the crime, and of the Serbian Government which knew of the plot, could have frustrated it and did not do so.

8. *The Sarajevo outrage.*

On St. Vitus's day, 28 June, a radiant Sunday, the Archduke and his Duchess, after attending mass, left by train for Sarajevo to pay an official visit to the town. It was 10 a.m. when the procession of four cars entered the town proceeding in the direction of the Town Hall.

In the leading car was the mayor and the chief of police; in the second the Archduke in gala uniform, at his side his wife the Duchess of Hohenberg, facing them General Potiorek, the Governor of Bosnia, while beside the chauffeur was the owner of the car Count Harrach, the suite following in the other two cars. To reach the Town Hall the procession had to drive along the Appel Quay, bordered on one side by houses and on the other by a low embankment wall below which flowed the Miljačka river, generally almost dry in summer. Along the Appel Quay and near the bridges across the river joining the two parts of the town six conspirators had posted themselves. Near the Čumuria bridge on the riverside were Mohamed Mehmedbašić, Vaso Čubrilović and Nedeljko Čabrinović. On the landward side of the Appel Quay was stationed Cvijetko Popović and beside him was Danilo Ilić who, however, was regarded as an organizer, not as a perpetrator of the outrage. At the next bridge, the Latin bridge, on the riverside stood Gavrilo Princip by himself. Finally at the third bridge, the Imperial bridge, was Trifko Grabež. Such an array of conspirators drew the comment from the Archbishop of Sarajevo that for the Archduke to have left the town alive, he would have had to run the gauntlet of 'a regular avenue of assassins'. In reality the danger he ran was much less than it seemed and it was only by a singular chance that he was struck down.

The procession had drawn level with the Čumuria bridge when Čabrinović, after detonating the cap of a bomb by hitting it against a lamp-post, aimed the bomb at the Archduke seated in the open car.

The detonator, in flying off, inflicted a slight graze on the Duchess's neck. The bomb itself, according to the evidence of Count Harrach and of Colonel Bardolff, who followed in the fourth car, and to the deposition of Čabrinović,[1] fell on the folded-back hood of the Archduke's car and thence rolled off to explode with deafening noise against a back wheel of the car which followed, putting it out of use and wounding Colonel Merizzi, Potiorek's aide-de-camp. Perceiving that the car following his own was damaged, the Archduke ordered his own to stop and sent Harrach to inquire what had happened. After this, the procession, reduced to three cars, resumed its way, while Čabrinović who had jumped into the bed of the Miljačka river was pursued by police and taken to the police station.

On arriving at the Town Hall and learning of the graze inflicted on the Duchess, Francis Ferdinand said to Potiorek that he had prepared to ward off with his hand the infernal machine which the Duchess had seen thrown, but had said nothing to her for fear of alarming her. As the mayor was beginning to read his speech of welcome, the Archduke interrupted him sharply with the words: 'Mr. Mayor, I came here on a visit and I get bombs thrown at me. It is outrageous. Now you may speak.'[2] Harrach states: 'Their Highnesses displayed the greatest coolness and His Royal Highness only said to me: "To-day we shall get a few more bullets still." ' To Potiorek the Archduke confessed that he expected something of this kind and asked whether there were likely to be more bombs. The General, by his own account, replied that he did not think so, but that at all events it might be wise not to continue the programme as planned—which was to visit the museum returning along a part of the Appel Quay as far as the Latin bridge and then turning right along Francis Joseph Street—but to return straight to Ilidže driving at full speed along the Appel Quay, or else to go to the Konak, the Governor's official residence, and from thence to the station, since the population had merited this rebuke. The Archduke objected that he must first visit Colonel Merizzi at the garrison hospital, although his wound was known to be slight. Potiorek then suggested that they should go there avoiding the town and once more passing along the Appel Quay where—he said—no one expected the procession to pass. This was not true, because the press had published that on the return from the Town Hall the procession was to pass again along the Appel Quay as far as the Latin bridge. In any case this was the plan followed. The cars again took the route via the Appel Quay. The

[1] See the deposition of Harrach in Sosnosky, pp. 205–21; the report of Colonel Bardolff, the Archduke's private secretary in Conrad, IV, pp. 19–22; Potiorek's deposition in Mousset, pp. 440–3; Steed, I, pp. 400–1; Seton-Watson, pp. 102–3.

[2] Sosnosky, p. 206. Within the hearing of *The Times* correspondent the Archduke exclaimed: 'Now I understand why Count Tisza advised me to postpone my journey' (Steed, I, p. 400).

Duchess, who from the Town Hall was to have proceeded straight to the Konak, decided to accompany her husband and again took her seat beside him, while Harrach took up position on the running board on the left side of the car so as to cover the Archduke with his body.

But Potiorek and the chief of police, who did not expect a second attempt, not only failed to realize the danger of repassing along the first part of the Quay, but also omitted the essential precaution of giving clear instructions to the chauffeurs, particularly to the driver of the Archduke's car. What happened was that the front car containing the chief of police drove along the Appel Quay, but at the Latin bridge took a right-hand turn into the narrow Francis Joseph Street, the Archduke's car naturally following suit. Potiorek excitedly ordered the driver to continue along the Quay and the car was slowly backing out towards the embankment when Gavrilo Princip, the conspirator stationed at the Latin bridge, fired at close range.

At the trial he stated that when he heard the explosion of Čabrinović's bomb he moved with the crowd in that direction and saw that the procession had come to a standstill. Thinking that 'all was over', i.e. that the attempt was successful, and seeing Čabrinović taken away by the police, he thought of shooting him to prevent his talking and then committing suicide himself. But he gave up the idea when he perceived that the procession had moved off again. It moved past him at speed and he was not able to distinguish the Archduke. But having learnt from the press the route which the procession was to follow, he waited for its return from the Town Hall and took up a position on the other side of the Quay at the spot where the procession would have to turn to go to the Museum. The result of this change of position was that the assassin found himself on the right of the Archduke's car, the side opposite to where Harrach had placed himself as a shield. Just as the procession passed in front of him he fired two shots at Francis Ferdinand at a distance of four to five paces.[1] The first bullet wounded the Archduke in the jugular vein, the second inflicted an abdominal wound on the Duchess. A thin stream of blood spurted from the Archduke's mouth on to Harrach's right cheek. He himself relates:

While with one hand I drew out my handkerchief to wipe the blood from the Archduke's lips, Her Highness cried: 'For God's sake! What has happened to you?' Then she sank down from her seat with her face between the Archduke's knees. I had no idea that she had been hit and thought that she had fainted from shock. Then His Royal Highness said: 'Soferl, Soferl! Don't die. Live for my children!' Thereupon I seized the Archduke by the coat-collar to prevent his head from sinking forwards and asked him: 'Is Your Royal Highness in great pain?' To which he clearly replied: 'It is nothing.' Now his expression changed and he repeated six or seven times:

---

[1] Mousset, pp. 129-30.

'It is nothing', more and more losing consciousness and with a fading voice. Then came a brief pause followed by a convulsive rattle in the throat, caused by the loss of blood, which ceased on the arrival at the Konak. The two unconscious forms were carried into the Konak where death soon supervened.[1]

The Duchess was already dead and the Archduke expired ten minutes later. Meanwhile the assassin, who did not even know how many bullets he had fired, was raising his arm to turn his weapon against himself when the police were upon him, struck him and took him bleeding to the police station.[2]

If one considers that, apart from Čabrinović and Princip, none of the other conspirators dared use his arms (at the trial they confessed that their courage failed them) and that Princip was not able to fire the first time the procession went past him, one comes to the conclusion that, if he had not had the chance to fire at the Archduke at close range when the car was hardly in motion, if, in other words, the procession had passed at speed along the Appel Quay, as had been arranged, the second attempt either would not have taken place or most probably would have failed.

[1] Sosnosky, p. 220.·   [2] Mousset, p. 130.

CHAPTER II

THE THREADS OF THE CONSPIRACY

(1) *The identification of the perpetrators of the outrage and their personalities* (*p.* 39). (2) *The behaviour of the accused at the trial; their sentences* (*p.* 45). (3) *How and when the outrage was planned; the links between the conspirators and the* Black Hand (*p.* 51). (4) *The trial throws little light on the real instigator of the crime* (*p.* 58). (5) *Vienna's mistake in accusing the* Narodna Obrana *and not the* Black Hand (*p.* 64). (6) *The part played in the outrage by the head of the* Black Hand, *Colonel Dragutin Dimitrievié* (*p.* 68). (7) *The origins of the conspiracy* (*p.* 74). (8) *The Artamonov question* (*p.* 82). (9) *The real motive of the crime* (*p.* 86).

1. *The identification of the perpetrators of the outrage and their personalities.*

Much investigation has been carried out and many pages have been written on the conspiracy to end the life of the heir to the Austrian throne, but it will never be entirely cleared up because the few who knew the true facts either sought to tamper with and conceal them or kept silence and carried their secret with them to the grave. Thus the historian has to reconstruct the threads of the conspiracy from what emerged at the trial of the accused held at the Sarajevo Courts of Justice between 13 and 29 October 1914, from revelations emanating from Serbian sources, practically all of them inspired by political passion and therefore reliable only up to a certain point, and from personal inquiries of unequal value. The author of the present work entrusted his collaborator Luciano Magrini with the task of carrying out investigations in Serbia in the belief that after so considerable a lapse of time those best informed about the tragedy would speak more freely and frankly.

With this aim in view Magrini went to Serbia in October and November 1937 and was able to interrogate in detail two of those engaged to carry out the crime, Vaso Čubrilović and Mohamed Mehmedbašić; Colonels Čedomilj A. Popović and Velimir Vemić, founders of the Central Committee of the *Black Hand*, condemned to death at the Salonika trial and then reprieved; Colonels Vladimir Tucović and Božin Šimić, leading members of the *Black Hand* and personal friends of Colonel Dimitrievié; Oskar Tartaglia, a *Black Hand* member who represented Croatia in it and one of the organizers of Luka Jukić's attempt upon the life of the hated Dictator Cuvaj at Zagreb on 8 June 1912; Dr. Milan Živanović, secretary of the Belgrade Chamber of Commerce, nephew and heir of Colonel Dragutin Dimitrievié; Jovan Jovanović, former Foreign Minister, and Ambassador at Vienna at the moment of the crime; Slobodan Jovanović, Professor of Law and Rector of the University of Belgrade, who was in touch with Dimitriević and, during the hostilities between Austria and Serbia in 1914, was chief of the press section of the Serbian General Staff; Dr. Leo Pfeffer, the judge charged with the preliminary investigations into the outrage; the barrister Zistler, the boldest counsel for the defence at the Sarajevo trial; General Victor A. Artamonov, the Russian Military Attaché at Belgrade; and the mysterious Dr. Kazimirović whose name came up at the trial in curious circumstances.

Still to-day with such an abundance of witnesses and protagonists it is a difficult undertaking to reconstruct the exact lines of the tragedy, because most of them try to hide something or to elude some question or other. There are witnesses who attest something of which they have no knowledge, witnesses who remain dumb or give a false account of what they know, witnesses who add adornments to their statements or are mainly interested in self-justification. None the less by piecing together and sifting the information and impressions received, the present writer has come to an opinion on the origins of the conspiracy and the planning of the outrage which he believes to be substantially correct.[1]

Let us begin by ascertaining what happened after the outrage and the first results of the preliminary investigation. Together with bombs and revolvers the assassins had brought with them from Belgrade cyanide of potassium so that the one who carried out the deed should commit suicide and thus make sure of not betraying the names of the other accomplices and above all the origins and instigators of the conspiracy. Obeying their instructions Čabrinović and Princip swallowed their doses of poison, but it did not do more than cause slight injury to mouth and stomach. Čabrinović was dragged out of the waters of the Miljačka into which he had jumped after throwing the bomb and taken to the police first-aid post, where it was soon realized that he was an old acquaintance who had been banished from Sarajevo for five years for socialist opinions.

[1] This opinion practically coincides with that formed by Bruno Brehm, the author of *Apis und Este*, which is an account in the form of a novel of the historic events from the assassination of the Obrenović royal pair in 1903 to that of the Austrian Heir Apparent, ending with the Salonika trial and the death sentence on Dimitrievič, the hero of the tale. Brehm, who is the son of an Austrian officer, was badly wounded in the First World War. After the war he became an archaeologist, novelist and poet. The American historian Sidney B. Fay, in his preface to the English translation of *Apis und Este* entitled *They Call it Patriotism*, writes: 'While using the form of a novel, or rather of a series of vivid episodes in the lives of these two tragic figures, the author has at the same time shown extraordinary skill in interweaving a large amount of accurate historical material taken directly from the Sarajevo and Salonika official records.' This is so, and indeed Brehm has made judicious use of other material in addition to that of the two trials. But one cannot here quote a book of this kind, however excellent, as an authority, and must reconstruct the conspiracy from the documents and evidence available.

Unsuccessful in his studies Čabrinović, a Bosnian, had become a com-
positor and, after trying a variety of situations in his native place, had
moved from one town to another until in October 1913 he had settled
in Belgrade where he found employment in the Serbian state printing
office. As a habitué of the Žirovni Venac café, a meeting-place of
Serbian Comitaji and Bosnian refugees, he had absorbed their ideas.
Uneducated, irresponsible, vain, talkative, he was a revolutionary
whose muddle-headed ideas were sincerely held. His friends maintained
that he was anxious to clear his name of the disgrace of having a father
who was an Austrian police spy. Others give another picture of him.
These say that he had suspicious meetings at Fiume, Volosca, and Zagreb
(at the latter with the chief of police) and that, like his father, he had
become an Austrian secret agent, charged with organizing a fake conspiracy against Francis Ferdinand to provide Austria with a pretext for
attacking Serbia. Various circumstances are alleged in support of this
hypothesis and also of the theory that the Austrian Government had a
hand in organizing the conspiracy to get rid of the hated and feared
heir to the throne. It seems to be the case that at Volosca Čabrinović
had divulged to a fellow revolutionary his intention of killing the
Archduke; and after the murder, a Serbian paper asserted that the Belgrade police had wanted to expel him but that the Austrian consulate
vouched for him. Pašić repeated the same story in an interview with the
Budapest *Az Est* of 7 July and in the *British Documents* the item is
reproduced.[1] There followed denials in the Austrian semi-official *Frem-
denblatt* which, however, admitted that in December 1913 the Bosnian
police had given the Serbian police a good report on Čabrinović.
This they should not have done in view of the fact that Čabrinović was
banned from Sarajevo for five years. But it is not needful to go into
these accusations, since, whatever his past, he certainly took part in a
genuine and not a faked outrage against the Archduke. In other words
he acted not as an *agent provocateur* but as a fanatic bent on sacrificing
himself. Moreover Wiesner, the high official from the Ballplatz sent to
Sarajevo to investigate into possible Serbian complicity in the outrage,
maintains the baselessness of the allegations made against Čabrinović.[2]

Before knowing of the second attempt, the President of the Tribunal
at once instructed Judge Leo Pfeffer, who was with him at the police
station, to investigate the crime without delay. But the second attempt
quickly followed and the crowd fell upon Princip and began to lynch
him, so that the police rescued him and arrested him with difficulty.
He, too, was taken to the police first-aid post, hatless, with bleeding
head and vomiting.

[1] BD. XI, 80.
[2] Friedrich von Wiesner, *War Nedeljko Čabrinović ein österreichischer Konfident?* in KSF.,
September 1927, pp. 882–5.

Gavrilo Princip, the real leader, if not the instigator, of the conspiracy and the successful slayer of the Archduke and his consort, is without a doubt the outstanding figure in the group of assassins. Born in 1894 in a Bosnian village, he had an irregular schooling in various places. In May 1912 he went to Belgrade, prompted by political passion, and perhaps even at the suggestion of the agitator Gaćinović, mentioned above,[1] who had a considerable influence over him. At Belgrade during the First Balkan war Major Milan Vasić, the secretary of the *Narodna Obrana*, enlisted him in the Comitaji associated with this society and posted him to the group commanded by Major Tankosić, who, however, rejected him as physically unfit. Princip then returned to Bosnia, but in March 1913 again went to Belgrade to continue his studies. He was helped by the Education Minister Ljuba Jovanović who had him promoted through three secondary school classes in a few months. The winter of 1913–14 he spent in Bosnia maintaining close contact with Ilić and Gaćinović. He had conceived the idea of doing something big for the Pan-Serb cause, since he had not been able to serve as a Comitaji. In February 1914 he was again in Belgrade attending the top class of the secondary school which he only left at the end of May to carry out the assassination. As his school-mate Jevđević deposed, Princip had a great opinion of himself. He thought himself the cleverest of the class and the best in literature and boasted of being received in the best circles in Belgrade.[2] But Jevđević was trying to shield himself and his evidence is not trustworthy. Dr. Martin Pappenheim, who as prison medical officer took shorthand notes of repeated conversations with Princip, tells us that he was an 'emotional, solitary' youth who dreamed of the 'union of the Southern Slavs outside the framework of Austria', to be achieved by revolution for which the ground was to be prepared by the perpetration of assassinations. For all the young generation, assassins were heroes. Princip, however, 'did not aspire to becoming a hero, he only wanted to die for his idea' which he pursued with utter fixity of purpose and ruthless determination.[3] Colonel Čedomilj A. Popović who in 1914 was secretary to the Central Committee of the *Black Hand* and Oskar Tartaglia have assured the present writer that Princip, like Ilić, belonged to the *Black Hand*.

When the police doctor assured Judge Pfeffer that the injuries were not serious, though there might be complications, the Judge at once proceeded to the interrogation of Princip. He writes:

The young assassin, exhausted by his beating, was unable to utter a word. He was undersized, emaciated, sallow, sharp featured. It was difficult to imagine that so frail looking an individual could have committed so serious a

[1] See pp. 23–4.   [2] Mousset, p. 467.
[3] *Gavrilo Princips Bekenntnisse* (Vienna, 1926), pp. 11–14; *Princip o Sebi* (Zagreb, 1926), p. 28.

deed. Even his clear blue eyes, burning and piercing but serene, had nothing cruel or criminal in their expression. They spoke of innate intelligence, of steady and harmonious energy. When I told him I was the investigating judge and asked him if he had strength to speak he answered my questions with perfect clearness in a voice that grew steadily stronger and more assured. He confessed that already two years earlier he had vowed on the grave of Bogdan Žerajić to avenge the man who had sought the life of General Varešanin. When he learnt that the Archduke Francis Ferdinand was to visit Sarajevo, he decided to take his vengeance because he regarded the Heir Apparent as the embodiment of the supreme power which exercised its terrible pressure on the Jugoslavs. 'From the footboard'—he said—'I aimed at the Archduke, whose car had slowed down at the street corner. I do not remember what I thought at that moment. I only know that I fired twice or perhaps several times, without knowing whether I had hit or missed, because at that moment the crowd began to beat me.'[1]

At this first interrogation Princip mentioned no names; he said that he had no accomplices, that he had no knowledge of the other assassin, and had acted on his own initiative. The first to talk was Čabrinović, whose interrogation took place the following day, 29 June. He at once confessed, as Potiorek telegraphed to the Joint Finance Minister Bilinski, that he had concerted with Princip at Belgrade over the execution of the outrage. They had there been provided with bombs, revolvers, and money and also with Comitaji one of whom, Ciganović, he named.[2] For the first three days of the inquiry only two assassins' names were known. But from the first moment the police had made many arrests among Serbian elements. They arrested all the youths who had recently been in contact with Čabrinović and Princip, and the relations of both of them. Among the arrests was that of Danilo Ilić the ex-schoolmaster with whom Princip had lodged from his arrival in Sarajevo till the day of the murder.

According to the police report [writes Pfeffer] this Ilić was a highly untrustworthy person.[3]

Born in 1890 Ilić had early abandoned the career of an elementary schoolmaster and had gone to Sarajevo as a bank employee, then in 1913 to Belgrade where he and Princip, who had been friends since 1908, lodged together. He stayed there for two and a half months frequenting the cafés of the exiles and Comitaji. As a member of the *Black Hand*—the present writer was informed by Čedomilj Popović—he was in close personal contact with Colonel Dragutin Dimitriević and a long-standing friend of Gaćinović whose charm held him spellbound. He returned to Sarajevo, living on his mother, who let furnished rooms, and possibly on doles from the *Black Hand*. He devoted himself to revolutionary propaganda and was the leading spirit of the Sarajevo

[1] Pfeffer, pp. 27–8.   [2] Oe-U. VIII, 9947.   [3] Pfeffer, p. 48.

cell. Čedomilj Popović and Vaso Čubrilović have described him to the present writer as an energetic, secretive man, an able organizer and exercising a considerable influence on Bosnian youth. But from the moment of his arrest Ilić broke down and thought only of saving his own neck from the gallows.

At his interrogation on 1 July he said that he would confess everything if he were promised that he would not be sentenced to death chiefly because what had been done was done against his will. It was visible that Ilić was extremely depressed.[1]

The investigating judge answered that the law allowed extenuating circumstances to those making confessions in prison; he emphasized that Ilić's confession was necessary if only to save the many innocent people who had been arrested from suffering on his account, and that the men who had had the courage to carry out the outrage ought also to have the courage to shoulder the responsibility for it. Ilić then related that Princip, whose ideals he shared, had written him from Belgrade before Easter that he with two other men was soon to prepare an outrage against Archduke Francis Ferdinand on the occasion of the royal visit to Sarajevo, asking Ilić to find three more assassins in Sarajevo and saying that he would be given the necessary means of carrying out the deed. Ilić deposed that Princip's accomplices were Nedeljko Čabrinović and Trifko Grabež. The latter had lodged with Princip, and after the crime had gone first to the village of Pale, where his father was the Serbian pope, and then to Višegrad to escape into Serbia. Pfeffer stopped the interrogation and telephoned to the police at Sarajevo, Pale and Višegrad to arrest Grabež, and the arrest took place at Pale. Pfeffer relates that in the course of further interrogation Ilić named the three other assassins recruited by him at Sarajevo and those who had enabled the bombs to be taken into Bosnia.[2]

Thus the first threads of the conspiracy soon came to light. On 5 July Potiorek was able to telegraph to Bilinski that at the end of May Princip, after writing to Ilić that he had the 'things', i.e. the weapons for the outrage, ready, came to Sarajevo, saying that he had given the bombs and revolvers into the charge of Mihailo Jovanović, a Tuzla merchant, for safe custody. Ilić had gone on to state that at Mostar he met the Moslem joiner Mehmedbašić and persuaded him to take part in the crime and also recruited the students Vaso Čubrilović and Svijetko Popović. Čabrinović, Princip, and Grabež had made contact through Ciganović with the former Comitaji chief, Major Voja Tankosić, who had instructed them how to carry out the outrage and had enjoined on them not to let themselves be captured alive but to shoot themselves or take potassium cyanide so as to make no confessions. The day before

---

[1] Pfeffer, p. 48.   [2] Pfeffer, pp. 48–50.

the outrage Ilić had given the conspirators their bombs and revolvers, directing them what positions they were to take up along the Archduke's route in Sarajevo. The conspirators recruited in Sarajevo, he said, had no knowledge of the participation of the Belgrade group.[1]

It was as a result of Ilić's revelations that the other accomplices were arrested. Only Mehmedbašić succeeded in fleeing to Montenegro. The Austrian authorities asked Cetinje for his arrest and extradition but the Montenegrin authorities replied that he had been arrested but had escaped and his whereabouts were not known. He had gone to Serbia and enrolled in the Comitaji. Colonel Dimitrievič wanted to have him near and paid the expenses of his medical treatment when he fell ill. He was subsequently involved in the Salonika trial and sentenced to fifteen years' imprisonment.

2. *The behaviour of the accused at the trial; their sentences.*

Pfeffer writes that the perpetrators of the crime

were youths, almost boys still, callow, hesitant, not grasping the seriousness of the judicial inquiry, and that they involuntarily talked and disclosed things which were not asked of them.[2] It is really a miracle that with young men still so raw and irresponsible nothing leaked out beforehand of the preparations for the outrage. Each of them regarded himself as a hero, but not one of them had had the courage to fire.[3]

These remarks are applied by Pfeffer particularly to Vaso Čubrilović and Svijetko Popović, since Princip and Čabrinović actually carried out the deed. Except for Mehmedbašić, who was twenty-seven, and Ilić who was twenty-four, the others were minors. Princip was not quite twenty, Čabrinović and Grabež were nineteen, Popović eighteen and Čubrilović only seventeen.

How Grabež acted remains unexplained because at the preliminary investigation and the trial he gave divergent accounts of his intentions and of where he stood when the procession passed, but the fact is clear

[1] Oe-U. VIII, 10066.

[2] Their confessions were, however, not extracted under torture as has been represented by Borislav Jevtić in a play and by Dobroslav Jevdević in his book *Sarajevski Atentatori*. This book prints an alleged letter from Grabež to his father, describing horrible tortures (including being bitten by police dogs) by which his confessions were extorted (pp. 51–3). Nothing about such tortures came out in the trial where the accused would not have failed to reveal them if they had been subjected to them. The lawyer Zistler and the assassin Vaso Čubrilović have assured the present writer that torture was not used, and Princip never spoke of such a thing in his conversations with Dr. Pappenheim. One thing that is true is that Grabež was dipped in the river by the police to extract confessions and does not mention this in writing to his father. But Pfeffer—as he himself has told the present writer— firmly intervened so that the accused was no longer maltreated. Tartaglia, who after the Sarajevo crime was arrested and sentenced to five years' imprisonment, has assured the present writer that he never suffered the least violence. He and Colonel Popović regard the Grabež letter to his father as apocryphal.

[3] Pfeffer, pp. 64–5.

that he took no action. His friend Jevdević maintains that Grabež was pressed so tightly by the throng that he could not pull the bomb out of his pocket. By the time he had got out of the crush the Archduke was already at the Town Hall. Then he changed his place to wait for the Archduke near the Konak, beside the horse-chestnut tree near which Bogdan Žerajić had shot himself after his unsuccessful attempt on the Governor's life in 1910. But Grabež never saw the Archduke again. Princip had killed him.[1] Nothing of this appears in the letter to the father published by Jevdević. All it says is:

> From where I stood, I could not carry out the attempt because I should have killed many innocent victims.

Of the other two students recruited by Ilić at the last moment, Čubrilović deposed at the trial that he had not dared to pull out his revolver out of compassion for the Duchess, and at the preliminary interrogation he said that he felt pity for the Archduke while to his friends, immediately after the crime, he boasted that he had fired two shots at the same moment as Čabrinović threw the bomb.[2] But in his sentence it is stated that his revolver was found fully loaded and was thus never fired by him.[3] Questioned by the present writer twenty-three years later Čubrilović said that he did not fire and that Princip also did not fire the first time the Archduke passed by because the conspirators were ill placed in a long straight main road, whereas for the attempt a street with corners and curves would have been necessary. In reality he had not the courage, nor either had Popović, who honestly admitted that when he saw the Archduke his heart failed him and that after the explosion of the bomb he tried to run home.[4] Of him the Public Prosecutor Švara said at the trial in his speech for the prosecution:

> My lords, we should not believe, if we had not heard with our own ears, that this is how the thing happened: Vaso Čubrilović goes to Popović and bluntly says to him: 'Do you want to take part in the outrage?' Popović simply says 'Yes, willingly.' He consents to take part in it.[5]

But he did not fire.

Mehmedbašić, the only perpetrator who managed to flee, said when questioned by the present writer, that he did nothing because at the moment the procession was approaching a gendarme happened as if by chance to take his place behind him. He feared that if he brought out the bomb which he carried at his belt, the gendarme would seize him by the arm and this would have revealed the plot and prevented the other conspirators from doing anything. While he revolved these thoughts the Archduke's car went by and he had lost his oppor-

---

[1] Jevdević, *op. cit.*, p. 110.   [2] Mousset, pp. 213, 327.   [3] *Sentenza*, p. 96.
[4] Mousset, pp. 223–4.   [5] Mousset, p. 557.

tunity. In reality he, like the others, lacked courage and ran off as soon as he heard Čabrinović's bomb explode. Čabrinović was such a tyro that, as he was about to cross the frontier into Bosnia, he wrote post-cards which might have given the game away and this made Princip take his weapons from him and send him by a route different from his own. He had his photograph taken before starting out for the crime 'in order [he deposed at the trial] that there might remain some memento of me', and when the policeman who arrested him asked if he was a Serb, he answered: 'Yes, I am a Serb hero.'[1]

In passing verdict on this set of immature conspirators, only one of whom, Gavrilo Princip, fully understood what he was doing, the Tribunal could not impose the death sentence which in Austria could not apply to those who had not completed their twentieth year. There-fore Princip, Čabrinović and Grabež received sentences of twenty years' imprisonment, Vaso Čubrilović sixteen and Popović thirteen. The two latter were liberated after the Austrian collapse, but Princip and Čabrinović, who before the crime had suffered severe privations and were in bad health, probably tubercular, did not live to see the end of the war, nor did Grabež. Čabrinović died in January 1916, Princip in the spring of 1918,[2] and Grabež not long after. Čubrilović and Popo-vić lived on. In 1937 the former was professor of history at Belgrade University and Popović was director of the schools in Jagodina.

Of the adult assassins, Mehmedbašić, as already stated, managed to flee and at the end of 1937 lived in modest circumstances at Sarajevo working as a gardener and occasionally as a joiner. Ilić behaved at the trial just as at the preliminary investigation. He, who had been put in

---

[1] Mousset, pp. 94, 99, 485.

[2] Around Gavrilo Princip there concentrated all the admiration of the Serbs for political assassins. The remains of the three Belgrade conspirators who died in prison were trans-ferred in 1920 from the Bohemian fortress of Thereslenstadt to Jugoslavia accompanied by several Serbian members of parliament. The anniversary of the outrage was celebrated at Sarajevo by religious and patriotic speeches in honour of Princip. On 2 February 1930, on the house in front of which Francis Ferdinand and Duchess Sophia were assassinated a marble tablet was put up with the following inscription: 'On this historic spot, on 28 June 1914 on St. Vitus's day (*Vidovdan*) Gavrilo Princip proclaimed freedom.' The tablet was unveiled with a solemn religious ceremony over which the archbishop presided. It was attended by the relatives of Čubrilović, Grabež and Jovanović. Milan Božić, secretary of the *Narodna Obrana*, called to the crowd to sing hymns to the 'hero' Gavrilo Princip. In the winter of the same year at Theresienstadt in Czechoslovakia an avenue received the name of Principova Aley, in memory of Princip.

In connexion with him one of the survivors of the group of assassins, V. Čubrilović, said to the present writer: 'The Serbs carry on a hero-cult, and to-day with the name of Miloš Obilić they bracket that of Gavrilo Princip: the former stands for Serb heroism in the tragedy of the Kosovo Polye, the latter for Serb heroism in the final liberation.' The barris-ter Zistler, Čubrilović's defending counsel, in 1937 paid honour to the name of Princip at public gatherings and the funds raised by his lectures—more than 250,000 dinars—were to be used for erecting a memorial to Princip in his native place. Several volumes of epic verse, especially in Bosnia, celebrate the Sarajevo outrage and *guslars* chant their decasyllables about it at public gatherings, in squares and cafés.

charge of the whole conspiracy, maintained that he had tried to prevent the outrage and persuade Princip and Grabež not to act because of the terrible consequences for the whole Slav nation that would result. He even believed he had convinced Princip, but then Princip had firmly refused to give up his purpose and, when Ilić insisted, Princip said to Čabrinović that Ilić did not seem reliable and he did not feel full confidence in him.[1] The court gave no credence to the new story of this defendant, though the other accused tried to bear out his defence. He was reminded that far from being opposed to the outrage, he had recruited Mehmedbašić, Čubrilović and Popović to carry it out, pretending to them that he was also taking part in it, distributing revolvers and bombs to the conspirators and telling them where to stand. But in corroboration of his new line of defence Ilić deposed that he had written to Mehmedbašić not to come, explaining the contradiction by saying that, while he thought he had persuaded Princip and Grabež not to act, he felt sure that Čubrilović and Popović would in any case not do so. As regards Čabrinović, he knew from Princip and Grabež that he was very simple minded and incapable of perpetrating an outrage.[2] These shifts did not help him, nor did the plea of his defending counsel Malek who made the point at the trial that it was owing to Ilić's revelations that the number of accused had risen from four or five to a good twenty-five.

It is his revelations [said Malek] which have brought here all the accused except the principals. . . . I think there ought to be a penalty for those who have conceived the assassination, found the weapons and carried out the deed different from that of one who, after trying to dissuade his associates and refraining himself at the last moment from doing the deed, has made a clean breast.[3]

The court did not take this view. Ilić was sentenced to death and hanged.

It is contrary to all probability that as a member of the *Black Hand* and knowing its iron rules which threatened with death all who failed to carry out its orders, Ilić would have dared to oppose a conspiracy which he must have known through Princip to be engineered under the auspices of that terroristic secret society and its redoubted leader Colonel Dimitrievic, with whom Ilić was in direct contact. And in fact Čubrilović told the present writer that he was not aware of any change of mind on the part of Ilić on the eve of the outrage, or of any attempt at dissuasion. It was on the eve of the outrage that Ilić handed out the bombs and revolvers to himself and Popović explaining their use and firing a trial shot with Popović's revolver. Mehmedbašić on his part stated to the present writer:

[1] Mousset, pp. 128, 172–173, 189, 196–200.   [2] Mousset, p. 198.
[3] Mousset, pp. 235–6, 650, 657.

On the eve of the outrage Ilić introduced me to Princip in a Sarajevo café with the words: 'Mehmedbašić who to-morrow is to be with us.' We all three signed a postcard to Gaćinović at Lausanne. It is not true that at the last moment Ilić tried to persuade us not to carry out the deed; he simply expressed the fear that the police had got wind of something and might manage to hinder us. On the actual day of the outrage he was on the street where the assassins had gathered and went from one to the other. He came to me, too, and said, 'Be strong, be brave.'

In contrast with Ilić, the five youths behaved at the trial with great pluck. All, and especially those from Belgrade, acknowledged full responsibility for their acts, proclaiming their ideal of a liberated and united Jugoslav people, exonerating Serbia and the *Narodna Obrana* (all except Čabrinović who was less artful and more candid than the others and often let things slip out) whose responsibility for instigating the murder the prosecution tried to prove. They maintained that it was a purely cultural society and tried as far as they could to shield the other conspirators and their accomplices. For an understanding of their mentality and their disposition it will be useful to look at some of their depositions.

The most unshakable and resolute of the terrorists was their leader Gavrilo Princip who deposed in cross-examination: 'I am a Jugoslav nationalist and aim at the union of all Jugoslavs, whatever the political form, and their deliverance from Austria', to be achieved 'by terrorism', i.e 'by killing leading personages, eliminating those who stand in the way and harm or hinder the idea of union'. Serbia 'as the free section of the Jugoslav people' had 'a duty to devote herself to this union and to play the same part as Piedmont for Italy'. He had first fired at the Heir Apparent and had then aimed at Potiorek.

I have no regret because I am convinced that I have destroyed a scourge and done a good deed. Generally speaking he has done harm to everybody and is the originator of the exceptional laws and the treason trial (of Zagreb in 1909) . . . I have seen our people going steadily downhill. I am a peasant's son and know what is happening in the villages. . . . All this had its influence on me and also the fact of knowing that he [the Archduke] was a German, an enemy of the Slavs. . . . As future Sovereign he would have prevented our union and carried out certain reforms which would have been clearly against our interests.[1]

Was this an allusion to trialism? Very likely it was. When asked if he thought Jugoslav union could be carried out under Austria he answered: 'Heaven forfend!' Certainly he was ill-informed as to the political views and influence of Francis Ferdinand, which were very different from what he supposed. Indeed he confessed that the main motive of

---

[1] Mousset, pp. 115–31.

the outrage was vengeance which outweighed that of Jugoslav national unity. Žerajić—the medical student who committed suicide after failing in his attempt on the life of Varešanin[1]—

was my first model. When I was seventeen I passed whole nights at his grave, reflecting on our wretched condition and thinking of him. It is there that I made up my mind sooner or later to perpetrate an outrage.

Asked by the judge whether he did not realize that the assassination of the heir to the throne would have disastrous consequences, Princip replied:

Our enterprise was purely private and in no way official as the prosecution asserts. Serbia has no hand in it and cannot be held responsible for our deed. No one else knew of it beyond Ciganović and ourselves. How could Serbia be brought into the affair? [2]

Princip's main concern during the proceedings was to clear Serbia and the *Narodna Obrana*, not betray the men of the *Black Hand*, take full responsibility for the crime on himself and parry skilfully when the others committed dangerous indiscretions.

Čabrinović shared the cult of Žerajić's memory and regarded vengeance 'as a sacred duty of civilized men'. He wanted to avenge himself on Francis Ferdinand as being head of a clique which 'intended to conquer Serbia and the other Slav countries'. To the question what opinion his group had of the Archduke he replied that Francis Ferdinand was regarded as 'a man capable of action', 'one who thought of having a federal Austria and of bringing Serbia and Montenegro inside the Monarchy'.[3] Already at the preliminary investigation he had said that 'the Archduke purposed the creation of a federal monarchy which would have embraced Serbia as well' and this consideration, too, drove him to act 'because the Archduke was a danger to the Slavs and especially to Serbia.' These views on the Archduke were, according to him, those of the Serbian circles he frequented and he had also heard them in cafés from students and citizens.[4]

In the verdict it is stated:

It must be noted that at the trial all the arrested men modified their depositions made at the preliminary investigation. They now gave as their motive for the outrage their hatred of the Archduke because he was a representative of imperialism and Germanization and a persecutor of the Slavs, whereas before they had said that it was because he was in favour of the union of all Slav territories. The Tribunal is convinced, however, that the depositions made at the preliminary investigation correspond to their ideas and are sincere and that the later changes arise from and are due to the circumstance

---

[1] See p. 22.   [2] Mousset, pp. 151, 153–4.
[3] Mousset, pp. 82, 87–8.   [4] *Sentenza*, p. 77.

that they learnt from reading the statement for the prosecution that they were accused of high treason involving official circles in the Kingdom of Serbia. This made them endeavour to rebut the accusation under that heading.[1]

However at the end of his examination Čabrinović showed himself less consistent and more human than Princip. He said that he was glad it was not he who killed the Archduke because

if I had foreseen what was to happen I should myself have sat down on the bombs so as to blow myself to bits.[2]

Grabež also said that he would never have taken part in the assassination, had he known that it would lead to a European war.[3] In reality none of the conspirators, not even Princip, as we have seen, imagined for an instant that their deed would give rise to a European war. They were so raw that Grabež, despite his advanced studies, when asked to explain what he understood by political freedom, replied: 'I do not know very well either', and when asked if he were an advocate of terrorism, said: 'I do not quite know . . . Yes.'[4]

What a disparity between the level of intelligence and maturity of these young students and the appalling consequences of their deed! Seton-Watson who has studied the question and carried out investigations on the spot, expresses his agreement with the verdict of Jevtić that the crime was 'not the work of an isolated individual in national exaltation, but of the entire youth of Bosnia'. He goes on to say that 'the outrage of Sarajevo was the sixth in less than four years. All six were the work of Serbs or Croats from within the Monarchy.'[5] This is undoubtedly the case, but it is also undoubted that Serbian nationalists played a great part in creating the atmosphere in Bosnia and Croatia, and that the body of 'frontier officers' belonging to the *Black Hand*, called into existence, as has been already stated, by the Serbian General Staff in 1911, mainly busied themselves with fomenting revolutionary agitation and organizations in Bosnia and Herzegovina,[6] and that, in the Sarajevo conspiracy, the chief exponent of Serbian nationalism played a leading part, indeed was probably its actual instigator.

3. *How and when the outrage was planned; the links between the conspirators and the* Black Hand.

Let us first of all look at what the trial revealed. We must begin by recalling that, at his interrogation by the judge at the preliminary investigation on 28 June, Princip deposed that he had no accomplices,

---

[1] *Sentenza*, pp. 75–6.   [2] Mousset, p. 101.   [3] Mousset, p. 159.
[4] Mousset, pp. 160, 182.   [5] Seton-Watson, *Sarajevo*, pp. 144–5.
[6] Č. A. Popović, *Rad Organizacije Udjedinjenje ili Smrt*, in *Nova Evropa*, September 1927, pp. 139–52.

had been surprised to hear a bomb explode, and had acted without being instigated by anybody. Grabež, too, although arrested later, began by denials, but 'I changed my mind when I saw that the others did not preserve the same secrecy'.[1] Čabrinović, the most communicative of the accused, had stated at the preliminary investigation that he knew a lot more but did not mean to talk. At the trial, when interrogated on this point, he said he had been joking, but to the question whether he had been influenced by anyone he retorted 'That is my business. I am the one who is in the prisoners' dock and nobody must be held responsible for my doings. I shall carry my secret to the grave.'[2] In his last speech before being sentenced he said:

We did not seek to carry out this outrage against Francis Ferdinand and have deposed that the idea did not originate with us. In the company we frequented the conversations always turned on outrages. We read newspapers glorifying the deeds of Jukić and Žerajić. We thought that only noble characters are capable of committing assassinations. We had no idea of committing an outrage against Francis Ferdinand. . . . We believed that outrages against the mamelukes of the Diet, against Nastić [an *agent provocateur* in the pay of Austria] would be more necessary than the outrage against Francis Ferdinand. But the people among whom we lived spoke of Francis Ferdinand and saw him as an enemy of the Slavs. We have heard it said that he was an enemy of the Slavs. Nobody told us straight out: 'kill him', but in those circles we came round to the idea by ourselves.[3]

Princip must have thought that Čabrinović had gone too far in casting the responsibility for the instigation of the crime on others and jumping to his feet, made the following statement which closed the hearing:

It is a departure from the truth to insinuate that somebody else was the instigator of the outrage. The idea of it originated with us and it is we who carried it out. We have loved the people. I have nothing else to say in my defence.[4]

According to the findings of the Court, the idea originated in the following way. Čabrinović, who was the first to be interrogated, deposed that before Easter he happened on a newspaper cutting which stated that the Archduke was to come to Sarajevo and attend the manoeuvres.[5] After lunch he showed the cutting to Princip who read it

---

[1] Mousset, pp. 132, 234.   [2] Mousset, p. 229.
[3] Mousset, p. 670.   [4] Mousset, p. 671.
[5] This story of the newspaper cutting, which many have regarded as the germ of the outrage is related by Jevtić in *Sarajevski Atentat* as follows: When through the Zagreb newspaper *Srbobran* Sarajevo learnt of the manoeuvres in Bosnia and the visit of the Archduke, a few youths decided to pass on the news to the 'emigration', i.e. the Bosnians in Belgrade. 'The press cutting giving the item was pasted without comment on an ordinary sheet of paper and, on the envelope, Michael Pušara, who was then a municipal employee, wrote: Čabrinović, Belgrade, Café Zlatna Moruna. To lessen suspicion in case the letter was

without comment. But that evening after dinner Princip asked him to go out with him to talk over the news. ·

He suggested that we two should go together and perpetrate the outrage. It did not seem to me so impressive or so big an affair as it actually was. I thought that an outrage in the Diet would be more effective. . . . After a little opposition I agreed to the attempt on the life of the Heir Apparent. . . . We exchanged our word of honour and went our different ways.[1]

Princip in his turn maintained that, immediately on his arrival at Belgrade in March, he had read, probably in German newspapers, that the Heir Apparent was to visit Sarajevo. It was this news which suggested the idea of the outrage to him. A few days later he spoke of the matter with Čabrinović who showed him the press cutting. It was then that the 'definite decision' was actually taken. Before that 'I was the only one to think of the outrage'.[2]

It might have been worth while to go into the matter of the newspaper and find out where and when Princip read the news, about which he coolly asserted: 'I think they were German newspapers.' But it seems this is simply not true. If the Archduke's visit had been mentioned in the press 'at the time of my arrival at Belgrade', he would have decided on the outrage then, as he did when Čabrinović was said to have shown him the newspaper cutting and when, as we shall now see, Grabež spoke to him of the matter. In reality he behaved as one who, having heard from somewhere that the Archduke was to come to Bosnia and intending to make an attempt on his life, was only waiting for the news to be confirmed. This is clearly shown in the following deposition of Grabež who in the spring of 1914, having finished his year in the seventh class at school, left Belgrade, where he shared lodgings with Princip, and went to spend Easter at home in Bosnia.

At that time [i.e. before his return home] there had not been any question of an attempt on the life of the Heir Apparent; I only knew that I was capable of carrying out an assassination and would accomplish it, whatever it was. Princip said that Francis Ferdinand was to come and that the Bosnians must 'give him a reception'. Nothing else was settled. I was at home for a month and a half. Between times I went to Sarajevo and in the newspaper *Istina* I read that Francis Ferdinand was to come to Bosnia where the manoeuvres were to take place. The idea of those manoeuvres revolted me because they were to represent an attack on Serbia. It was then I became convinced of

opened Pušara took it next day to Senica and posted it there. . . . When Ilić heard of what the group had decided he approved. . . . He slipped away to Switzerland with a false passport to meet Gaćinović.' The 'emigration' was in sympathy with the idea that had prompted the sending of the cutting (*op. cit.*, pp. 24–25; KSF., 1925, p. 677). Actually there is nothing to show that Ilić ever went to Switzerland. What need had he to see Gaćinović when he was in direct contact with Dimitrievič?

[1] Mousset, pp. 75–8.   [2] Mousset, pp. 116–17, 150–1.

the necessity of doing away with him [the Archduke]. . . . On my return to
Belgrade I met Princip and told him about what I had read in the papers of
Francis Ferdinand's coming. He at once said he was ready to act. I answered:
'So am I.' He added: 'Čabrinović, too, is ready and steady.' [1]

Thus before Easter (which in 1914 fell on 12 April) Princip's purpose
of making an attempt on Francis Ferdinand's life was still vague and
had not taken shape. Only after the press, about Easter time, gave definite news of the visit did he make up his mind to carry out the deed and
persuade Čabrinović and Grabež to act with him. Princip must have
perceived how dangerous this admission of Grabež was, for, next day,
when the presiding judge drew his attention to the statement made by
Grabež that it was 'before his return to Serbia', i.e. before he left
Belgrade for his holiday in Bosnia, that Princip had discussed this plan
for an outrage with him [Grabež], Princip replied that they had only
spoken of an outrage in general, not of a specific one. Grabež corroborated this version by asserting that the attack on the Archduke had only
been spoken of after his return from Bosnia.[2] But his first deposition
was so precise and unhesitating that it deprives the denial of all value.

Having decided to perpetrate the outrage, Princip wrote to Ilić
about Easter time to initiate him into the plot, saying he had the necessary weapons and asking Ilić to find other accomplices. According to
Princip this letter was couched in an 'allegorical' form. But it seems unlikely that in such a form he could have made everything plain to his
Sarajevo friend if there had been no previous understanding between
them. That some such understanding had been arrived at can be deduced from the fact that at the preliminary investigation Ilić deposed
that he had had a meeting with Mehmedbašić, adding:

It was there that we agreed on the point that the outrage would be the
most useful deed for the realization of Jugoslavism and its practical aims.

Thus, as the presiding judge remarked, Ilić expressed himself in this
way before knowing that the Archduke was to visit Sarajevo. Consequently the first threads of the conspiracy had already been spun before

---

[1] Mousset, pp. 157–8, 161. Grabež's deposition finds confirmation in what Princip told
Dr. Pappenheim in prison. 'In March he had heard that the Heir Apparent was coming to
Sarajevo. He thought this would be the chance. Spoke of the matter to Čabrinović. He was
of the same opinion. . . . (Princip) had read a lot at Sarajevo. Every night he dreamt he
was an assassin and was struggling with gendarmes and police. He read a lot about the
Russian revolution. . . . In March Grabež passed the examination for the eighth class and
then returned to Sarajevo to work for the school leaving diploma. Princip told Grabež he
must let Ilić know about the idea and Ilić also agreed. . . . Ilić was under his [Princip's]
influence although five years his senior and already an elementary schoolmaster. . . . Ilić
wrote back that he was willing to take part. He sent word in code that Princip must get hold
of five or six revolvers. A fortnight later Grabež returned to Belgrade and decided to join
in. At first Princip had told him he must hold himself ready for another occasion, but when
he [Grabež] got back to Belgrade he said he wanted to join in' (*Gavrilo Princips Bekenntnisse*
(Vienna, 1926), pp. 15–16; *Princip o Sebi*, pp. 31–2).

[2] Mousset, pp. 184–5.

the press announcement of Francis Ferdinand's impending visit to Bosnia, but when, according to Grabež's deposition, Princip already knew of it and probably Ilić also. This is a point which it is of great importance to clear up, because as we shall see further on, it corroborates the most credible version of the origins of the plot.[1]

To carry out the crime Princip had to have arms, bombs, money and the means of making a clandestine entry into Bosnia. Did he apply to the *Narodna Obrana* and its secretary Pribičević? No! Princip did nothing of the kind. He applied to Milan Ciganović, a Bosnian settled since 1908 in Belgrade and holding a sinecure in the Serbian state railways. A rabid and prominent Comitaji, Ciganović had served as such in the Balkan wars under Major Tankosić, the right hand man of Colonel Dragutin Dimitriević, head of the *Black Hand*. With Dimitriević Tankosić had been deeply involved in the assassination of the Obrenović royal pair and the shooting of Queen Draga's two brothers. Later Tankosić became head of a Comitaji training school which was thronged with young Bosnians who came to Belgrade and on these he exercised a powerful influence. Tankosić was small and frail and in private life silent, quiet, and gentle. He seemed a timid character, but in reality was cruel and barbarous and, as a Comitaji leader, as ferociously severe as he was heroic and dashing. Honest and patriotic, he believed that his terrible deeds served his country.[2] Of course he was a member of the *Black Hand*. Another member of it was Ciganović, a dubious personage, who seems also to have spied on the society for Pašić.

Thus in applying to Ciganović, who was under the orders of Tankosić, who in his turn took his orders from Dimitriević, Princip was knocking at the door of the *Black Hand* of which, as already stated, he was a member. According to his deposition all he asked of Ciganović was bombs and 'after a moment's silence, Ciganović answered: "We shall see." In reality he at once agreed to let me have them.' But it was not until a little later that he formally promised the bombs and said he would do everything possible to find revolvers as well.[3] Čabrinović's

---

[1] See below, pp. 72–4.

[2] Stanojević, pp. 52–3. A similar description of Tankosić was given by Colonel Č. A. Popović and others who knew him intimately (cf. Magrini, pp. 92–3). In illustration of the influence and prestige Tankosić enjoyed Popović told the present writer the following : 'In private life Tankosić was unmethodical, and when he needed money he resorted to bills of exchange. Once an enemy of his protested one of his bills and brought the matter to the knowledge of Prince George. The Prince summoned Tankosić and rebuked him severely, saying that he had behaved dishonestly. Tankosić angrily replied that he tolerated no reproaches and remarks from the Prince on his private life. Prince George redoubled his reproaches. So Tankosić boxed his ears and cuffed him. Prince George himself related the scene to me. The fact was publicly known. Tankosić received no punishment.' Tankosić's mother was a peasant woman who told fortunes from cards. A good many officers of high rank resorted to her to have their futures told.

[3] Mousset, pp. 117–18.

story, however, is that it was he who first applied to Ciganović and was at once promised the necessary means. The explanation of this may be that Princip preferred not to let him know of his own contacts with the men of the *Black Hand*. Čabrinović certainly was in direct contact with Ciganović. He deposed that revolvers, ammunition and money were given by Ciganović to Princip and Grabež and that they were already practising firing with them in Topčider park before any were given to himself.

There was considerable delay in providing the arms.

For I should think a month [deposed Čabrinović] when we met, we used to say: 'Good morning. Any news?—No news.' That meant that the stuff had not come yet. . . . I thought that nothing would come of it.

But one day Ciganović greeted him at the café with *Sabaile* i.e. 'the day has dawned'.[1] The explanation of this delay is perhaps to be found in a telegram from Potiorek to Bilinski of 10 July stating that Grabež, on being interrogated, had stated that discussions about the projected outrage were on the point of coming to naught because of the Emperor's illness. Ciganović had then said to them:

Nothing doing, the old Emperor is ill and the Heir Apparent will not go to Bosnia. When the Emperor got better, Princip who acted as intermediary raised the matter again with Ciganović and brought it off.[2]

Did Princip raise the matter with Ciganović or with Tankosić himself? Princip and Grabež did everything not to compromise this officer, fearing perhaps that the investigation might reach higher still. Grabež went so far as to say that Tankosić was 'a secondary figure' and that in any case 'the main culprit' was Ciganović. This leads one to think that Grabež, too, was a member of the *Black Hand*. But Čabrinović had let out too much at the preliminary investigation for the three conspirators to make out that Major Tankosić had had no hand in the conspiracy. Judge Pfeffer told the present writer how he obtained confirmation of the name of Tankosić, which had first been mentioned by Ilić. Princip and Grabež in evidence had both described Čabrinović as not a trustworthy person and this had greatly annoyed him. Till that moment he had spoken vaguely of 'a gentleman'; but, taking advantage of his annoyance, Pfeffer managed to extract the confession that the 'gentleman' was Tankosić and that Grabež, too, had had dealings with him. Thereupon Grabež, also, owned up. Princip however, stuck to his statement that he knew nothing and kept great control of himself. When, however, Vienna insisted on Princip's being made to speak, Pfeffer, although averse to confronting one defendant with others, made Čabrinović and Grabež repeat their depositions in Princip's

---

[1] Mousset, p. 80.　　　　[2] Oe-U. VIII, 10184.

presence and then Princip confessed. At the trial Čabrinović, probably repeating what he had said at the preliminary investigation, also stated that Ciganović had received money from Tankosić 'who signed an order together with one of his colleagues'. (Does the double signature perhaps indicate that Tankosić acted not on his own account but on behalf of some association?) He added that of the three Grabež had been selected to go and deal with Tankosić.[1]

This visit to Tankosić is of considerable significance. Princip admitted that Tankosić himself desired it 'to see if we were any good'. Then, feeling he had said too much, he refused to say anything more on the matter.[2] Čabrinović, however, had already deposed that Tankosić had asked Grabež in the presence of Ciganović whether all was ready and 'whether he could count on us', receiving an affirmative reply. Grabež further reported the following dialogue with the Major:

Are you one of them and are you ready?—Yes—Are you quite sure of your own mind?—Yes—Do you know how to fire a revolver?—No—Then how do you expect to do the deed?—I think a revolver is the surest weapon.

After this Tankosić turned to Ciganović saying: 'Look, here is a revolver; practise firing at a target', and this Ciganović did in Topčider park.[3]

But it was improbable that Tankosić would have confined himself to seeing Grabež without getting in touch with the leader Princip. It was Ilić who threw light on this point when he confessed at the preliminary investigation:

Princip told me he went to see Tankosić who had given instructions for the outrage to be carried out and had added that those who carried it out were to take poison at once so that nothing should be found out from them.

At the trial Ilić denied that Princip had told him this,[4] but his denial found no credence. As has already been mentioned Ciganović actually

---

[1] Mousset, pp. 81, 82.

[2] Mousset, p. 118. Questioned by Luciano Magrini in October 1915 about the Sarajevo outrage, Tankosić made no secret of the part he had played: 'To hear himself held responsible for the Sarajevo outrage and the European war flattered his vanity; "Princip and Čabrinović—he exclaimed—what men they were! I knew they would not miss their aim! Reliable men who could keep their own counsel: they needed training and guidance." ... When asked whether the *Narodna Obrana* had taken part in the outrage, as the Austrians maintained, Tankosić replied: "The *Narodna Obrana* has nothing to do with it; the Government has nothing to do with it, but *other* resolute guardians of the destinies of Serbia knew and gave their sanction." And since it was openly said in Serbia that the plot was the work of the *Black Hand* and some officers had hinted at the name of Colonel Dragutin Dimitrievič as the probable arch-conspirator, Tankosić was asked whether by those "others" he meant the *Black Hand*. He only smiled and made no denial. ... Later Tankosić spoke of bombs and revolvers given by him to the conspirators and said it was his idea that the murderers should poison themselves with cyanide of potassium in order not to reveal the names of the other accomplices under police pressure' (Magrini, pp. 94–5).

[3] Mousset, pp. 162–3.   [4] Mousset, p. 192.

provided the assassins with potassium cyanide to be taken at the right moment. And Princip said that as soon as he had fired, he turned his weapon against himself, as he had promised Ciganović to do, but his arm was seized by the police; then he swallowed the poison but it did not act and he vomited it up.[1] Čabrinović also stated that Ciganović had advised them to commit suicide and that he took a double dose of poison which made him feel sick but did not act.

The complicity of Tankosić and Ciganović was not confined to providing the assassins with arms, bombs, money, and poison, but extended to enabling them to cross into Bosnia by means of one of the 'tunnels' consisting of trusted agents of the *Narodna Obrana*, who smuggled printed matter, arms, and conspirators into the Monarchy (here appears the link between *Narodna Obrana* and *Black Hand*). Provided with six bombs, four Brownings, 150 dinars, a map of Bosnia, cyanide of potassium, and a letter from Ciganović for Captain Popović (not to be confused with the often mentioned Colonel Popović) of the frontier guard, who the previous day had been in Belgrade and had there received the necessary instructions, the three conspirators entered upon what Princip called their 'mystic' journey to Šabac. From there Popović sent them to Ložnica with a letter for Captain Prvanović saying: 'Try to receive these people and see that they reach their destination as per instructions'.[2] Without asking the object of their journey Prvanović put himself at the conspirators' service so that they crossed the Drina at two different points and entered Bosnia. From that moment they were taken over by Bosnian trusted agents, who saw them as far as Tuzla whence they took the train for Sarajevo. At Tuzla, by way of precaution, they deposited arms and bombs which were collected by Ilić and given out by him at the last moment. Betrayed by Ilić, these other accomplices were arrested and tried with the chief conspirators. Some ten of them were acquitted, but four others—Veliko Čubrilović (brother of Vaso Čubrilović), Nedjo Kerović, Miško Jovanović and Jakov Milović—were, with Ilić, condemned to death and hanged. Mitar Kerović was sentenced to life imprisonment, five others to lesser penalties.[2] How much their participation was voluntary it is hard to say. At the trial they declared their lives, their families and their possessions to have been under threat from the assassins, who freely admitted that this was so, but at the preliminary investigation there was no word of any such thing.[3]

4. The trial throws little light on the real instigator of the crime.

The findings of the Court brought fully to light the part played by Ciganović and Tankosić in organizing the outrage. But they were not men who would undertake such an enterprise of their own initiative.

[1] Mousset, pp. 130, 138.   [2] Mousset, p. 141.   [3] Mousset, pp. 675–6.

In the course of the proceedings Čabrinović's counsel, Premužić, sought to impute the guilt to Freemasonry. According to what Vaso Čubrilović told the present writer, this accusation arose in the following way. After the first days of their arrest the defendants began to communicate among themselves by an alphabetical system made up of long and short knocks on the wall on a method they had all learnt from Stepniak's *Underground Russia,* thus keeping one another informed of the proceedings at the preliminary investigation. One day Čabrinović signalled:

Advocate Premužić [who was a Clerical under the influence of Archduke Francis Ferdinand's confessor, Father Puntigam] tells me that the Freemasons must have had a hand in the outrage and that it would be for the good of Serbia and myself if I made the confession that I am a Mason and that Freemasonry made me perpetrate the outrage. What shall I do?

The advice came back:

Let him believe it; it can't do us any harm and will draw off attention from Serbia.

This was the origin of the legend, which the accused, especially Čabrinović, in vain tried to substantiate in their evidence.

When asked by Advocate Premužić whether he was a Mason, Čabrinović answered that he did not want to admit it, that Ciganović and Tankosič were Masons and that Ciganović had told him it was the Masons who had doomed Francis Ferdinand to death. The presiding judge, himself a clerical who in later life lived in retirement in a Jesuit monastery at Sarajevo, described this assertion as fantastic. Premužić retorted that he would give proofs but did not venture to do so either in the course of the proceedings or in his final plea. In any case, under interrogation by the presiding judge Čabrinović ended by admitting that Masonry had no connexion with the outrage, which had been planned before it was known that Ciganović and Tankosić were Masons.[1] This was corroborated by Princip and Grabež who denied being Masons.[2] Towards the end of the trial Čabrinović made the statement that a friend and chief of Tankosić, a promoter of the outrage, was a Freemason. Of this personage we shall shortly speak. To finish with the episode let it suffice to add that no solid evidence ever came to light of any complicity of Freemasonry in the conspiracy. This is accepted by all leading historians and neither the Public Prosecutor in his indictment nor counsel for the defence in their pleas made any mention of an accusation against Freemasonry. In the summing up the statement occurs:

In regard to this particular the Court is of the opinion that the statements

---

[1] Mousset, pp. 85–7, 89–90.   [2] Mousset, pp. 134–5, 185.

on Freemasonry are part of the attempt to hide the activity of the *Narodna Obrana* and the complicity of Serbian official circles.[1]

This does not rule out the possibility that the friend and chief of Ciganović and Tankosić was a Freemason; very probably he was. But Apis took part in the plot not as a Mason, nor under orders from Freemasonry, but of his own free will. Here is how his name came up at the trial.

The proceedings were drawing to a close when Čabrinović who, as we have said, was the most garrulous and irresponsible of the assassins, came out with the statement: 'No one was able to know anything about the outrage except Ciganović, Tankosić and a friend of his.' The judge naturally asked who this friend was and Čabrinović answered: 'An ex-officer whose name I don't know.' Hearing this answer Princip broke in: 'Yes, an ex-officer. And a graduate in theology was also in the know.' Did he thus break in because he feared that Čabrinović had touched a dangerous theme? Was the graduate in theology brought in to divert the judge's attention from the ex-officer? The judge did, in fact, drop the ex-officer friend of Tankosić to ask who was the theology graduate. Čabrinović, who much earlier had mentioned the theology graduate Djuro Šarac and a certain Bukovac as having influenced the assassins after the decision to perpetrate the outrage[2] answered: 'We were told that it was Djuro Šarac.' He went on to say that nobody else knew of the conspiracy besides Ciganović, Tankosić, Bukovac, Djuro Šarac and the friend of Tankosič, who thus came up again and whom Čabrinović described as 'an altogether mystic personage'. His counsel asked if he knew the personage's name and Čabrinović replied that he did not; whereupon Princip at once burst in with the statement that it was Kazimirović, a man who had studied in Russia but had not wanted to become a priest. He had been told this by Ciganović who had said that he had talked of the outrage with Tankosić and a good, reliable friend Kazimirović.[3]

It must have appeared somewhat strange that two Comitaji and *Black Hand* members like Ciganović and Tankosić had to have discussions with a theologian Kazimirović, an unknown man of no importance in Serbian life. Anyway the subject was brought up again at the next

---

[1] *Sentenza*, p. 76. The foremost to believe in the complicity of Freemasonry in the conspiracy were Father Puntigam, Francis Ferdinand's confessor, who attended the trial and in 1918 under the pseudonym of Pharos published the depositions relating to the principal defendants, and Professor Kohler who wrote the preface to Pharos's book. Their opinion is also put forward in works by Karl Heise, Ernst Reventlow, H. Gruber and others. But the most notorious and noisy accuser of Freemasonry was General Ludendorff, who also attributed the outbreak of the World War to Freemasons, Jews, and Jesuits, and above all to the Vatican (General Ludendorff, *Wie der Weltkrieg in 1914 'gemacht' wurde* (Munich, 1934), pp. 28–34.

[2] Mousset, p. 107.   [3] Mousset, pp. 473–5.

hearing. Asked by the judge who was the friend of Tankosić mentioned by him, Čabrinović replied that he did not know whether Kazimirović was his name, but he had finished his studies in Russia and was a man of between thirty and forty well known in Belgrade. He further explained:

When I said to Ciganović that we must carry out the outrage and needed the wherewithal he told me that certain persons would provide it and that he would have a word with them. Later he told me he had spoken with Tankosić and that other man who is also a Mason and so to speak, one of their chiefs. Immediately after their conversation that other man went abroad, I was told, and made a tour of the whole Continent. He went to Budapest, France and Russia. Every time I asked Ciganović how things stood he answered 'Wait till that other man gets back.' One of those times Ciganović told me the Masons doomed the Austrian Heir Apparent to death two years ago, but did not have the men. When he gave me the Browning and the ammunition he said, 'That man got back last evening from Budapest.'[1]

The judge then asked Čabrinović whether he was not telling stories and the defendant sharply replied that it was

the pure truth, twenty times more true than all your documents on the *Narodna Obrana*

with which the conspirators had had nothing to do. He added that he had at first not said anything of that person because he did not know him and did not frequent his circles, adding:

I had no intention of saying anything about him. I did not mention his name and do not even know if that name [Kazimirović] is really his.[2]

Nor, indeed, was it, however much Princip insisted that Kazimirović was a friend of Tankosić. The judge remarked that a theologian could not be a Freemason if, as he actually did, he wrote religious articles for the *Christian Messenger*.[3] Traced down by Mousset who was formerly manager of the semi-official Serbian news-agency *Avala*, Kazimirović wrote him in 1929 to express amazement that his humble self had been mentioned at the trial and to give his word that he had never been a Freemason, that he had no knowledge of Tankosić, that he was a schoolmaster at Belgrade when Princip was preparing for his examinations and had thus known him but had never advised him to assassinate the Archduke.[4] Hence presumably Princip brought up the name of this extraneous schoolmaster to cover up that of the man to whom Čabrinović alluded. Kazimirović gave the present writer the same assurances in 1937, adding that Princip was 'a great patriot' who, on the two or three occasions when he saw him at the beginning of 1914, said that he

---

[1] Mousset, pp. 477–8.   [2] Mousset, pp. 478–80.
[3] Mousset, pp. 479–81.   [4] Mousset, pp. 26–7.

wanted to do something for the liberation of Bosnia and make an
attempt on the life of the Emperor of Austria. 'You will see'—he declared—'what we are capable of doing.' Kazimirović said to the present
writer, as he had written to Mousset—that in May 1913 he had made
a journey to Vienna, Prague and Teschen, and that on his return he
published an article against Austria in *Piemont*, the newspaper of the
Black Hand, on account of which after the Serbian retreat the Austrians
searched for him at Valjevo.

The present writer's impression is that this unassuming peaceable
schoolmaster with his limited views, who could not dissimulate his
admiration for Dimitrievic, in whose organ he had published that
article, was not telling the entire truth. He could not possibly have been
ignorant, as he claimed to be, of the existence of Tankosić, who was
well known in Belgrade. It was curious, too, that Princip should have
spoken to him of wanting to make an attempt on the life of the Austrian
Emperor at the beginning of 1914. At the beginning of 1914 Princip
was not at Belgrade and when he returned there at the end of February
it was Francis Ferdinand he planned to assassinate, not the Emperor.
Most likely Princip spoke the truth when he stated that Kazimirović
knew of the conspiracy; but this does not imply that he was the powerful friend of Tankosić to whom Čabrinović alluded. The probability is
that Princip brought up his name to distract attention from the personage whom Čabrinović, always kept much in the dark by Princip and
Ciganović, believed to be an ex-officer, a 'mystic personage' and 'so
to speak one of the chiefs' of Ciganović and Tankosić.

This personage could have been no other than the head of the *Black
Hand*, Dragutin Dimitriević. Apart from the story of the foreign
journey, no doubt invented by Ciganović to put Čabrinović off the
scent, all the indications given by the latter about this mysterious and
mystic personage whose name he did not know, reveal the lineaments
of Apis, not an ex-officer but an officer on the active list, who sought to
remain in the shade. Princip, however, in whom Tankosić had full
confidence and of whom, during the war, he said he had at once felt
he could be counted on to carry out the assassination,[1] was fully informed of everything and for that reason brought up the name of
Kazimirović at the trial to cover up Čabrinović's indiscretion. This
view is shared by the advocate Zistler, the most courageous of counsel
for the defence and by Kazimirović himself. In answer to a question by
Luciano Magrini as to how Princip came to bring in his name, he said:

Because besides Tankosić and Ciganović they were after a third man, and
Princip, perhaps to draw off the attention of the Austrian Court and keep
the name of Dragutin Dimitriević dark, mentioned my name, which might

---

[1] Magrini, p. 94.

easily occur to his mind because I was well known at the secondary school where I taught. Thus my name leapt into the limelight of the trial being brought into the Sarajevo outrage like the name of Pilate into the creed.

It is more probable that Princip brought up the name of Kazimirović because both the latter and the other theologian Djuro Šarac knew of his intentions. But this is of little importance. What matters is that the Court did not probe into the point. Both the presiding judge, the judges who assisted him, and the Public Prosecutor wanted to keep the trial within the lines laid down by the Vienna Government. On 1 October 1914 Berchtold had written to Bilinski, the head of the administration in Bosnia-Herzegovina, that:

the verdict by which the trial was to end should take full account of the for-midable international consequences of the crime. A verdict not correspond-ing to what is expected . . . would compromise the statements issued by the authorities of Bosnia-Herzegovina on the preliminary inquiry and thereby the first diplomatic move against Serbia; in general our right to enter Serbia in the conflict which has given birth to the World War would itself be called in doubt.[1]

In other words the Serbian Government was to be held responsible for the Sarajevo crime as protecting and promoting the activities of the semi-official, anti-Austrian *Narodna Obrana* which in the Austrian *dossier* to the Powers was accused outright of carrying on rabid Pan-Serb propaganda among the Serbs of the Monarchy and promoting con-spiracies and terrorism.[2] Now there is no doubt that the *Narodna Obrana* carried on anti-Austrian propaganda, especially in Bosnia, and aimed at the union of all the Serbs. But nothing at the trial showed it to have instigated or taken part in acts of terrorism, despite the fact that the conspirators were passed into Serbia by one of its 'tunnels'. Dimi-triević had attempted to gain control of it and its resources but had been prevented by its secretary Milan Pribičević. It has already been stated that the *Black Hand* had contrived to get one of its own men, Milan Vasić, appointed secretary of the *Narodna Obrana*. But after his death in the Balkan war the conflict between the two societies broke out afresh. Thus the defendants spoke the truth when they declared the *Narodna Obrana* innocent of the crime and said that Tankosić was in conflict with its members,[3] as he also was with the Prime Minister Pašić. Jovan Jovanović, the former Serbian Minister at Vienna, relates that after the outrage a rumour went round Belgrade that when Tankosić was asked why he gave the conspirators arms in May 1914 his reply was: 'To make trouble for Pašić and the Radicals.'[4]

---

[1] Mousset, pp. 16–17.
[2] Austro-Hungarian *Red Book*, 19; CDD., pp. 461–72.
[3] Mousset, pp. 21–2.   [4] Isaac, p. 256.

5. Vienna's mistake in accusing the Narodna Obrana *and not the* Black Hand.

Why, then, did the Vienna Government accuse the *Narodna Obrana* and not the *Black Hand*? Most historians have taken the view that the Austrian Government made a mistake and was in ignorance of the existence of the *Black Hand*, or at least had no suspicion of its complicity in the Sarajevo crime. But this is not the case. At Belgrade it had for a long time been well known to everybody that the regicides of 1903 had founded the *Black Hand*, that this organization was bitterly discontented with the Pašić Government and his party of Old Radicals, and that this feud overshadowed Serbian political life in the days preceding the outrage, forcing the resignation of Pašić, and, after his reinstatement in power, the dissolution of the Chamber and the calling of new elections. That Vienna knew of the *Black Hand* is shown by the reports of the Austro-Hungarian Minister to Belgrade one of which goes back as far as 12 November 1911,[1] and by polemics in the Serbian press which attracted the attention of the Austrian press.

In fact on 12 February 1912, Gellinck, the Austro-Hungarian Military Attaché at Belgrade sent information that the founders of the *Crna Ruka (Black Hand)* were 'Major Dragutin Dimitriević, called Apis, the leading spirit of the conspiracy of 1903, and Milan Milovanović, then his chief helper and intimate'. Gellinck added that

the founders of the new organization chose a current slogan 'Union or Death' which evidently means the union of all Serbs, the fulfilment of Pan-Serb aspirations.[2]

More precise information about the *Black Hand*, its organization, leaders, and bitter feud with the Pašić Government reached Vienna on 27 June 1912 in a detailed report from the chief of the Press Bureau of the Serbian Foreign Ministry, Stefanović-Vilovsky. The report stated that the activities of the *Black Hand* were increasing.

The *Black Hand* has become a factor in public life, though nothing positive is known about it. It is ubiquitous and has contacts with high and low, soldiers and civilians. Holding all the posts of command in the capital, the officers belonging to this organization have acquired a prestige which places them above the War Minister and even above the King himself.[3]

The reports of Giesl, the Austro-Hungarian Minister at Belgrade, of the first half of 1914, and particularly of May and June, are full of the struggle between the *Black Hand* and the Government. On 20 January 1914, in giving news of the appointment as Serbian War Minister of Colonel Stefanović-Vilovsky, who was one of the conspirators of 1903, Giesl stated:

[1] Oe-U. III, 2911.   [2] Oe-U. III, 3264.   [3] Oe-U. IV, 3590.

the *Crna Ruka* is again in full possession of its influence and all attempts of the Government and of the Radicals to rid themselves of it fail and lead again and again to their capitulation to the conspirators.[1]

On 18 March he reported that Pašić had ordered an inquiry into the running of the Officers' Co-operative Stores which was under *Black Hand* control and where embezzlements totalling 300,000 dinars were said to have taken place and to have been used for financing the *Black Hand* organ *Piemont*.[2] In another report of 8 May he wrote, as already mentioned, that the King's sympathies were all with the *Crna Ruka* and that there was a possibility of violent action unless at the last moment the Government yielded to the demands of the military party.[3] And similarly in succeeding reports.[4]

Besides this information from diplomatic sources the Ballplatz archives possessed a file headed *Secret society: The Black Hand in Serbia*, which, at any rate until the Anschluss, was still in the Vienna State Archives. It contained a collection of press cuttings from German, Viennese, Hungarian, Czech, Roumanian, Croat and French papers about the society. The cuttings were translated and classified as they came to the Ballplatz. This shows that the activities of the *Black Hand* were closely watched by the Austro-Hungarian Foreign Minister. Ludwig Bittner, the Director of the Vienna State Archives, has examined this file and states that it gives

a pretty faithful picture of the constitution, membership and aims of the secret society *Union or Death*, also known as the *Black Hand*.

Agreeing with the opinion expressed by Bogičević (who, however, claims that the Ballplatz knew nothing of the *Black Hand*) Bittner writes that it is

doubtful whether the Tsar and the English Government would have decided to support Serbia if the Austro-Hungarian Government in explaining its action against Serbia had produced its evidence about this association whose leaders were the regicides of 1903. It is tragic that the unsystematic methods in collecting the material implicating Serbia, and doubtless also the memory of the misdirection given in the Friedjung trial prevented this from being done.[5]

It might conceivably be thought that those who drafted and signed the ultimatum, and the enclosure containing the grounds on which it was based, refrained from accusing the *Black Hand* because, since it was

---

[1] Oe-U. VII, 9216.   [2] Oe-U. VII, 9485.   [3] Oe-U. VIII, 9649.
[4] Oe-U. VIII, 9734, 9809, 9819, 9844, 9908, 9919, 9922.
[5] Ludwig Bittner, *Die Schwarze Hand* in *Berliner Monatshefte*, January 1932, pp. 63–4; Bogičević, *Procès*, pp. 6, 170.

a secret society over which the Belgrade Government had no hold and with which it was at war, Pašić might have been enabled to elude the Austrian demands. But it is more likely that the Austro-Hungarian Government in the confusion of the moment never thought of the possible complicity of the *Black Hand* and concentrated all its suspicions on the *Narodna Obrana* whose activities for five years had been a constant source of worry to Vienna. Berchtold's ignorance of Balkan questions is well known. Jovan Jovanović, the former Serbian Minister at Vienna, told the present writer that it probably never entered Berchtold's head to connect the crime with the *Black Hand*, though he knew of its existence. None of Potiorek's telegrams from Sarajevo or those from Giesl, the Austrian Minister at Belgrade, mention the *Black Hand* as a possible instigator or accomplice in the outrage. The name never occurs in any Austrian document of July 1914, except in one from Nish of which we shall shortly speak. It is not to be found in the minutes preserved in the Vienna State Archives relating to the drafting of the ultimatum nor in those of the discussions in the Council of Joint Ministers. Giesl, whose reports of *Black Hand* activities we have already mentioned, stated to the present writer that neither before nor after his arrival in Belgrade did he have any grounds for suspecting the *Black Hand* of complicity. It was the *Narodna Obrana* which the Monarchy had found itself up against in 1908–9 and against which were concentrated the anger and suspicion of Forgach, the Counsellor on Serbian affairs at the Ballplatz. In any case, as the present writer was told by Musulin who actually drafted the ultimatum, it would not have been possible to ask for the dissolution of a secret society or measures against its members.

All this explains why Judge Pfeffer at the preliminary investigation, when told of the part played in the crime by Ciganović and the Serbian Major Tankosić, who belonged 'to the military party hostile to Pašić',[1] did not pursue the clue and was not urged by Vienna to do so. In the collection of Austrian diplomatic documents there occurs no telegram sent to Potiorek by Vienna, in reply to those he sent day by day on the proceedings of the preliminary investigation, asking for further inquiry into any aspect of it. If Vienna had known that the *Black Hand* was involved in the plot and had not been so slow to pursue the clue, it would have had an excellent opportunity to ask for the arrest not only of Ciganović and Tankosić but also of the members of the Central Committee of the *Black Hand*, in particular of Colonel Dimitriević, chief of Military Intelligence of the General Staff. And this would have been a request Pašić would have been forced to refuse, given the power of the *Black Hand* in Serbia. Moreover, it would have created a great sensation all over Europe if it had been made known that the outrage

[1] Oe-U. VIII, 10137.

was committed by the same regicides who in 1903 had perpetrated the massacre of the Obrenović royal pair.

Nevertheless immediately after the crime allegations arose in Belgrade circles that the *Black Hand* was behind it. This emerges in a report from the French Minister Descos of 1 July 1914, which stated that Serbism had

allowed itself to be dragged by the military party towards new methods and objectives, threatening to compromise the uninterrupted success of recent years. . . . The very circumstances of the crime betray the existence of a national organization the ends of which are easy to imagine.

Descos quoted the comment of the *Pester Lloyd* that

since the assassination of King Alexander and Queen Draga the methods of the conspiratorial officers had gained both in skill and in audacity.[1]

Not only this, but on 9 July there reached Vienna a report of 6 July from the Austro-Hungarian Vice-consul at Nish stating, among other things:

In the office of an engineer of Serbian nationality working in Serbian service but of Hungarian origin, Artillery Major Z. Andrejević exclaimed literally: 'There you see what the Serbian *Black Hand* can achieve, now you have the proof how it works and what it aims at. But that is only a beginning, a very lucky one, to be sure.'

The importance of this communication should not have escaped the attention of Vienna, containing, as it also did, the statement:

The bombs were personally distributed by Major Tanasić [a slip for Tankosić] corroborating what came out in the preliminary investigation at Sarajevo.[2]

But Vienna entirely overlooked this telegram and attached no importance to it, while no such voice as that òf Descos reached it from Belgrade. Thus it came about that only two fleeting allusions to the *Black Hand* occurred at the trial, where a witness described it as a subcommittee of the *Narodna Obrana*.[3] No one uttered the name of Dimitrievic and no one spoke of the activities of the *Black Hand*. The Public Prosecutor made a reference to Kazimirović's journey in proof that the outrage was not committed on the personal initiative of Ciganović and Tankosić and that

another influence intervened and willed that the Archduke should be slain.[4]

But he was not able to carry the matter further. The same is true of Princip's defending counsel Feldbauer who said:

Although Princip acted like a hero, I have the deep conviction that this youth has been influenced by a third party living outside the country,

[1] DF. 3. X, 469. [2] Oe-U. VIII, 10084.
[3] Mousset, pp. 90, 437. [4] Mousset, pp. 548–9.

and he recapitulated the names of Serbians which were brought up at the trial without making any reference to the chief criminal, the head of the *Black Hand*.[1] In spite of this absence of proof, the Sarajevo Court gained the impression that Serbian military circles were implicated in the outrage. Who they were it could or would not say. But the verdict runs:

The Court regards it as proved by the evidence that both the *Narodna Obrana* and military circles in the Kingdom of Serbia in charge of the espionage service, collaborated in the outrage. . . . There is no doubt that both the *Narodna Obrana* and military circles on the active list in the Kingdom of Serbia knew of the aims of the outrage and were prodigal of all possible assistance and all possible protection to the perpetrators for whom they actually procured the means of carrying out the assassination. The *Narodna Obrana* and military circles on the active list in the Kingdom of Serbia not only collaborated in the outrage in this way, but also found a means intended to prevent the discovery of their collaboration once the outrage was perpetrated (i.e. Ciganović had given poison to Princip and his associates, before they left Belgrade, advising them to poison themselves as soon as they had carried out the outrage, in order not to betray their accomplices).[2]

Thus, in spite of instructions to aim at the *Narodna Obrana*, the Sarajevo bench pronounced the guilt of Serbian 'military circles on the active list' for having known and approved of the aims of the crime, for having helped the conspirators by placing men of the espionage service at their disposal, and having taken the precaution, in order not to be discovered, of providing the conspirators with poison. But was not the expression 'military circles on the active list' synonymous with the *Black Hand* and its redoubtable chief Dragutin Dimitriević?

6. *The part played in the outrage by the head of the* Black Hand, *Colonel Dragutin Dimitriević.*

It was the Serbian Government which first accused Dimitriević whom it so feared and hated that, in 1917 after the Salonika trial, it replied to all who sought to intervene on behalf of the condemned man and even to the English Secretary of State for War that there was no doubt of the Colonel's complicity in the Sarajevo plot. A year later the Serbian Foreign Minister Stefan Protić in reply to an article of R. W. Seton-Watson deploring the recent execution of Apis, spoke of the existence of 'a written document which sufficiently proved the impossibility of reprieving Dimitriević'. In 1922 Protić wrote in his organ the Belgrade *Radical* that Dimitriević had signed an admission of his full responsibility for the outrage.

This document was never produced and it would be impossible to base any presumption of Dimitriević's guilt on assertions of the Pašić

---

[1] Mousset, pp. 567–9.　　　　[2] *Sentenza*, pp. 95–6.

Government, which trumped up the Salonika trial to rid itself of this enemy it feared. Nevertheless even Bogičević, the bitter enemy of Pašić and the eulogist, as we have seen,[1] of Dimitrievič, writes that after the end of the trial Dimitrievič is known to

have made a declaration that he alone was guilty of the Sarajevo outrage, but adding that the Court, the Russian Minister, and the Russian Military Attaché knew of the preparations for it.

Bogičević thinks that the document was probably in the possession of Ljuba Jovanović who was then Minister of the Interior and whose grave revelations, as we shall later see, produced a great sensation.[2] Bogičević has also published a testament of Apis which states:

I die innocent and in the belief that my death is necessary to Serbia for higher reasons.[3]

How are such words to be taken? And did Dimitrievič really avow his full responsibility for the Sarajevo crime in a signed document? The present writer has tried to probe into the matter and has found a general belief in Serbia that the confession does exist. Colonel Popović and the former Rector of Belgrade University, Slobodan Jovanović, though they say they know nothing precise about the part played by Apis in the outrage, agree that there certainly exists, or did exist, a statement by him on this matter which nobody has read but which was the decisive factor in the Salonika trial. Nothing is known of its whereabouts. All that is known is that certain important documents, instead of being deposited in the State Archives, went into the Royal Archives or were retained by the Prime Minister in office. If Dimitrievič's statement was retained by Pašić, it passed with other documents into the Royal Archives.

The reason why such a statement was demanded was given to the present writer by the former Serbian Minister at Vienna, Jovan Jovanović, who in 1914 was the *Black Hand's* and the military clique's choice for the office of Foreign Minister in the Government that was to succeed that of Pašić.[4] By his account the outrage was prepared at Sarajevo. The idea of it was in the air and found a favourable soil in Belgrade. Dimitrievič did undoubtedly draw up a written statement admitting that he was the organizer of the outrage, but it was probably extracted from him at the Salonika trial by promise of a free pardon in return. But the death sentence was pronounced and carried out all the same. One must not overlook the fact that between the Regent, Pašić, and Protić on the one hand and Dimitrievič on the other there was war to the knife. A fortnight before the outbreak of the war Dimitrievič was plotting to overthrow Pašić and sweep away the Government which

---

[1] See above, p. 29.   [2] Bogičević, *Procès*, pp. 39-40, 68; see pp. 92-8.
[3] Bogičević, *Procès*, pp. 68-9.   [4] DF. 3. X, 363.

met with much disapproval because of its oppressive and arbitrary policy and lack of political sense. In the crisis that followed it looked as if Pašić was done for, but through the intervention of the Regent and Hartwig he was again put in power and then called fresh elections. The King in displeasure withdrew into retirement, entrusting the Regency to the Crown Prince.

There thus was—according to Jovan Jovanović—a bitter feud between Dimitrievič and Pašić. It was Pašić's fear of the plots and conspiracies of Dimitrievič which was the chief motive for the Salonika trial. It came at one of the critical hours in the war when there seemed a likelihood of a stalemate. Prince Sixte of Bourbon had initiated conversations for a separate peace and Austria wanted assurances from Serbia that there would be no resumption of the political agitation which had led to the Sarajevo outrage, and that the secret societies working against Austria would be suppressed. Rumours of these conversations must have reached Serbia and it was said that Austria asked for the punishment of those who had perpetrated the outrage.[1] Hence it would be advisable to come to the peace negotiations already rid of that burden. This was the pretext for the Salonika vendetta. Dimitrievič's death was to enable Pašić to show that, before beginning peace conversations, Serbia had eliminated those responsible for the Sarajevo outrage.

This opinion is shared by Seton-Watson, who thinks it hard to doubt that the Pašić Government wanted not only to eliminate dangerous and hostile elements from the army but also to prepare the ground for the contingency of a separate peace with Austria, not as an act of treachery towards the Allies but as a necessity imposed by the way the war was going. Vienna would have to be convinced that the Pašić-Karageorgević regime was not implicated in the events which had brought on the war. And in fact the reason alleged for refusing a reprieve was the discovery of Dimitrievič's complicity in the Sarajevo outrage, something quite unconnected with the accusation on which he was being tried.[2]

As regards this complicity of his, it is worth mentioning that those whom the present writer questioned in Serbia, while not doubting the existence of the statement signed by Dimitrievič of his guilt, seem not to be equally certain of his entire guilt. In other words, Apis might have

---

[1] On this point Tartaglia writes that Pašić dispatched Protić to Switzerland where he made contact with the Austrian representatives (Adler and others) (Tartaglia, p. 30). In a letter to Prince Sixte of 24 March 1916, the Emperor Charles said that Serbia would be restored to full sovereignty and assured of an outlet to the Adriatic. But she must suppress 'all societies or groups, in particular the *Narodna Obrana*, the aim of which was the breaking up of the Monarchy' (Prince Sixte de Bourbon, *L'offre de paix séparée de l'Autriche* (Paris, 1920), pp. 41, 97.

[2] R. W. Seton-Watson, in *Slavonic Review*, March 1928, pp. 704-5.

got Tankosić and Ciganović to provide arms and means to carry out the outrage, without himself being the promoter of the conspiracy. In this case his guilt would be less great, because actually Princip could have procured a revolver without recourse to him. This more limited rôle played by Dimitriević in the plot seems to emerge from the revelations made in 1923 by Professor Stanoje Stanojević of Belgrade University, whom we have already met as an adherent of Pašić and of the *White Hand*, the society of officers opposed to the *Black Hand*.

According to Stanojević, though he never documents his statements, Dimitriević as early as 1911 sent an emissary to Vienna to make an attempt on the life of either the Emperor or Francis Ferdinand. But nothing more was ever heard of the emissary. Dimitriević became convinced of the necessity for the assassination when, after the Konopischt meeting of 2 June 1914, he was told by the Russian General Staff that Wilhelm had promised the Archduke German support in crushing Serbia. Dimitriević was in possession of the plan of the Austrian manoeuvres, and jumped to the conviction, as he himself related in 1915, that Serbia was about to be attacked and could only be saved by the assassination of Francis Ferdinand, who was regarded as her worst enemy. Hearing from Major Tankosić that there were two young Bosnians in Belgrade who wanted to carry out the crime, and had asked for advice and instructions, Dimitriević decided to make use of them and ordered Tankosić to instruct them in the use of firearms and bombs which he provided for them. On 15 June he communicated his intentions to the Central Committee of the *Black Hand*, who opposed the plan. Dimitriević thereupon promised to countermand it, but either came too late or was disobeyed by the perpetrators.[1]

From this account it would seem that the young conspirators had decided to make their attempt on the life of Francis Ferdinand quite apart from Dimitriević, who gave them aid only after learning of their intention. But Stanojević's version does not hold water, and his book itself bristles with inaccuracies and downright errors. Apart from the unlikelihood of that meeting of the Central Committee of the *Black Hand*[2] there is the fact that Princip, Čabrinović and Grabež went from Belgrade to Sarajevo to carry out the crime on 28 May, i.e. well before the Konopischt meeting. It is well, however, to bear in mind that on the tenth anniversary of the crime Colonel Č. A. Popović wrote that in 1915 he asked his friend, Dimitriević if it were true that he had taken

---

[1] Stanojević, pp. 52–6.

[2] Its unlikelihood is also to be inferred from the fact that Dimitriević was not wont to consult others, but acted on his own initiative. M. Ćurčin, editor of the Zagreb *Nova Evropa* who, though a Liberal, is also an admirer of Apis, told the present writer that Apis maintained the greatest secrecy about his plans and doings. The *Black Hand* was really Apis, himself; the others had only to obey. Even Tankosić was nothing more than his 'lackey'.

part in it and for what motive. On this occasion Dimitriević justified himself in the manner reported by Stanojević.[1]

Popović, when questioned by the present writer, said that when in 1915 he asked Dimitriević what part he had played in the outrage, he received the following reply:

I was convinced that the forthcoming manoeuvres in Bosnia were a pretext for an attack on Serbia, especially as they were to be under the command of the Austrian Commander-in-Chief, Archduke Francis Ferdinand. I intensely feared this development. You know that unfortunately at that moment the country was in a most critical state in its political relations and in its internal divisions. You are aware of what was our military position. Austria could have sent one or two cavalry divisions against us and nobody in Serbia could have stopped them. Our troops could not have got there in time from the south and all Serbia could have been overrun. Everybody, ourselves included, could have been faced with a *fait accompli*. Hence when Tankosić came one day into the office and told me: 'There are some young Bosnians asking to go to Bosnia. Am I to say yes?' I unreflectingly at once replied: 'Let them go.' Tankosić then added that these youths had come to an agreement with other Bosnian comrades that they were going to make some attempt on the Archduke Francis Ferdinand. I thought such an attempt would be impossible and that probably nothing would come of it. I imagined that the Archduke Francis Ferdinand would be well guarded and that nothing could happen to him. At best there might be an incident which would be a warning to him and those around him and would make them understand it was dangerous to attack Serbia. However after a certain time when I thought the matter over, I tried to call the youths back after they had crossed the frontier and at all events to prevent the outrage. My attempt was made through the Comitaji Djuro Šarac.[2] It was late. The perpetrators, both those from Serbia and those in Sarajevo, would not give up their purpose.

No faith can be put in this account, prompted no doubt by the wish to attenuate Dimitriević's guilt as much as possible. Above all, the descriptions given of him by all who knew him show that he was not the man to know hesitation, or to change his mind once he had made a decision. And then, if he had meant to prevent the outrage, a word from him would have been enough in view of the absolute obedience to superior orders binding all the members of the *Black Hand* to which the chief perpetrators belonged. The following circumstances make it highly probable that Dimitriević not only helped the conspirators but actually instigated the plot: (1) to get weapons and money, Princip applied straight to Ciganović, the agent of Tankosić and Dimitriević,

---

[1] Colonel Č. A. Popović, in the Zagreb *Novosti* of 28 June 1924.

[2] Djuro Šarac was a student of theology; but some members of the *Black Hand* think he was a spy of Pašić's. In fact at the Salonika trial he was one of the witnesses for the prosecution. Afterwards he was sent by Pašić to Switzerland to continue his studies at state expense and died there of tuberculosis before the end of the war.

as if he knew that they were the men to procure them for him; (2) Dimitrievič said to his friends that he thought the assassination of the Archduke necessary to the safety of Serbia. Now it seems unlikely that in an attempt on the life of no less a personage than the heir to the Austrian throne, the head of the *Black Hand* merely intervened by accident and that those raw youths acted on their own initiative and not on the suggestion of others.

Not only this. How could Princip, before the news appeared in the press, say to Grabež that the Archduke was to visit Sarajevo and that he must be 'given a reception', unless he had received the news from somewhere? There he was at Belgrade talking of the outrage without doing anything towards it, as if awaiting confirmation of the arrival of his victim and only making up his mind when the arrival and the visit to Sarajevo were announced in the press. Now who better than Dimitrievič, the head of Military Intelligence of the Serbian General Staff, was in a position to know beforehand that the Austrian manoeuvres were to be held in Bosnia and that the Archduke was to attend them? His Intelligence agent in Austria was none other than Rade Malobabič, one of the sixty-three Croatian Serbs sentenced in the notorious Zagreb (Agram) trial of 1909, the subject of a highly commendatory report by Dimitrievič of 1916 and sentenced and executed with him in 1917 as perpetrator of the attempt on the life of Prince Alexander. Always employed on difficult and dangerous missions Malobabič, according to Bogičevič, procured detailed information for his chief on the Austrian manoeuvres.[1] Did he not probably also provide information that the Archduke was to attend them, or even may the news not have come directly from the Serbian Military Attaché at Vienna, Colonel Lešanin? Be it noted, Francis Ferdinand announced the decision to Conrad as early as 16 September 1913 and Conrad discussed the subject with Potiorek on the 29th of the same month.[2] The then Serbian Minister at Vienna, Jovan Jovanovič has written to the present writer that

from the month of December onwards the manoeuvres in Bosnia were spoken of in Vienna. The Inspector General of the Austro-Hungarian army was to take part both as future Emperor and as Commander-in-Chief. It was to be, as was said towards the end of 1913, a lesson and a warning to the Serbs both of Bosnia and of Serbia.

If Dimitrievič knew of the Archduke's intention, he may well have thought that this would be the best opportunity for making an attempt on his life. It would then be understandable why, when questioned by Popovič, he alleged the manoeuvres as an explanation of the outrage. As a pretext this was worthless. Had Austria in the summer of 1914 been determined to attack Serbia, her determination could only have

---

[1] Bogičevič, *Procès*, pp. 78–80, 127.   [2] Conrad, III, p. 445.

been strengthened by her being put in a position to accuse the Serbian Government of being involved in the assassination of the Heir Apparent. Apis could not well avow his real motive for wanting to do away with Francis Ferdinand, but it is plain that the manoeuvres and the Sarajevo visit furnished him with the opportunity for carrying out the crime.

7. *The origins of the conspiracy.*

Among those who describe Dimitrievié as the instigator of the crime is Bogičević, the former Serbian diplomatist who from 1907 to 1914 was Serbian Chargé d'Affaires at Berlin. He had been sent there by Milovanović who wanted the post kept warm for himself but died before filling it. It must be borne in mind that Bogičević, who had been educated at the Vienna Theresianum, is one of those Germano-phils who prefer to cast the blame for the war on their own country rather than admit any responsibility on the part of the Central Powers. In May 1914 he was transferred from Berlin to Cairo as diplomatic agent. There in March 1915 he learnt from Constantinople that the Germans had decided to invade Serbia:

Without asking permission of his Government or even consulting it, he went to Paris and saw Jules Cambon, the former French Ambassador to Berlin. . . . At the end of August 1915 he was in Berlin

where he spoke with Zimmermann and sought to become an inter-mediary between France and Germany. The Serbian Government first thought of bringing him to trial but in the end he was only placed on the retired list.[1]

When the war was ended he poured forth a long indictment of the Serbian Royal House and of Pašić in *Die Kriegsursachen*, published in 1918. Later on, in the *Kriegsschuldfrage* and in *Évolution* he wrote a series of articles on the Salonika trial in which authentic documents and re-liable information are mingled with imputations inspired by blind resentment, so blind, indeed, that while accusing Pašić of foreknowledge of the plot and of failing to prevent it and showing his old friend Dimitrievié to have been its instigator, he lauds Dimitrievié to the skies as 'a noble and beautiful soul', as the man who "inspired all the outstanding deeds in Serbia from 1903 to 1917'.[2] The very violence of Bogičević's accusations against Pašić and the Royal Family made him the confidant of Dimitrievié's friends and of the surviving *Black Hand* members. With evidence provided by them he was enabled to recon-struct the threads of the Sarajevo plot.

The verdict at which he arrives is the opposite of that reached by

---

[1] This information is given in G. Demartial's preface to the French edition of Bogičević's *Les causes de la guerre*, pp. 3–5.

[2] Bogičević, *Procès*, p. 65.

R. W. Seton-Watson, who maintains that 'the initiative came from Bosnia not from Serbia'.[1] Bogičević's opinion is that a revolutionary movement certainly did exist in Bosnia but it was worked upon by the Serbian nationalists for their own ends. Thus Žerajić and Jukić, while preparing for their deeds, were trained in the use of firearms by the *Black Hand* members Božin Šimić and Tankosić. Moreover the perpetrators of the Sarajevo and other outrages received instruction in Belgrade from *Black Hand* elements such as the influential propagandist Gaćinović whose *Death of a Hero* was printed in Belgrade by the printers of the *Black Hand* paper *Piemont* for distribution in Bosnian schools. This makes it clear that 'the direction of the movement was located not in Bosnia-Herzegovina but in Belgrade'.[2]

Facts since brought to light strengthen this conclusion. Oskar Tartaglia, one of the organizers of a club of Serb, Croat and Slovene students of Zagreb University, describes the grand reception given by the leading members of the *Black Hand* to the club when it visited Belgrade in April 1912. Several students were invited to join the society, Tartaglia himself being received into it with impressive ceremonial on 27 April. He in his turn introduced Jukić, who was planning to make an attempt on the life of Cuvaj, the Ban of Croatia, to Dimitrievć

who at once agreed to the idea of the outrage and without ado put Jukić in the hands of the Comitaji leader Tankosić who trained Jukić in the use of the revolver and in bomb throwing. . . . The revolver was left in the hands' of Jukić and the bombs were conveyed to Zagreb.

Eventually they were thrown into the river Save. But with the revolver Jukić fired two shots at Cuvaj, killing first his secretary and then a policeman.[3]

These revelations show Dimitrievć acting already in 1912 as he was to do in 1914 but—if Bogičević's story is correct—with the important difference that in 1914, operating through the agency of Tankosić, he was the direct organizer of the Sarajevo crime. Bogičević bases his version on statements made to him by Mustafa Golubić and Paul Bastaić after his reading them the reconstruction of the plot made by Seton-Watson. These were two youths

one from Herzegovina and the other from Croatia, who took part in all the

---

[1] R. W. Seton-Watson, *Sarajevo*, p. 78.   [2] Bogičević, *Procès*, pp. 151–9.

[3] Oskar Tartaglia, *Veleizdajnik*, pp. 24–5, 55–6. At the present writer's inquiry in Serbia he checked up on the reliability of Tartaglia who at the beginning of the European war was arrested and sentenced by an Austrian court to five years' imprisonment for high treason. Professor Grka Novak of Zagreb University, who had known him for many years, and Dinko Sirovica, who was sentenced with Tartaglia to five years' imprisonment, assured the present writer that Tartaglia's book may be regarded as completely reliable. And this opinion was supported by Colonel Č. A. Popović of Belgrade.

acts of terrorism committed by the revolutionaries of Serbia and the Slav provinces then belonging to Austria.

In Seton-Watson's version the course of events was the following. In January 1913 Gaćinović

invited certain young Bosnians—among them two Moslems, Mehmedbašić and Mustafa Golubić—to meet him at Toulouse and here provided them with weapons and poison for the purpose of attempting the life of General Potiorek, the Governor of Bosnia, and forestalling their own capture by suicide. But the youthful conspirators' nerve failed them; fearing a Customs examination on their return across the Austrian frontier, they threw the weapons out of the carriage window, and nothing further came of this design. None the less, they, and others of their contemporaries, continued to dream of terrorist action and remained in continual correspondence with Gaćinović. . . . There was formed, mainly at his instance, a secret terrorist group or 'Kružok' in more than one of the Bosnian towns and notably in Sarajevo, where his friend Danilo Ilić, a young schoolmaster in Macedonia, was the link between those who were otherwise completely unknown to each other.

Ilić, as we have seen, was longing to organize some outrage but did not know where or against whom. It was at that moment (March 1914) that the news appeared in a Zagreb paper of forthcoming man-oeuvres in Bosnia to be attended by the Archduke. Pušara, one of Ilić's friends, sent the cutting to Čabrinović who showed it to Princip and Grabež, with the consequences we already know.[1] It is this which makes Seton-Watson say that

the initiative lay, not with those who so recklessly provided arms to three of them in Belgrade, but with Ilić and Pušara in Sarajevo and above all with Gaćinović in Lausanne.[2]

But when questioned by Bogičević, Golubić and Bastaić categorically denied several statements in Seton-Watson's account and made the following statements:

(1) The Toulouse meeting took place in the middle of January 1914, not 1913.
(2) It was attended only by Mustafa Golubić, Mohamed Mehmedbašić, and Vladimir Gaćinović.
(3) It took place at the Hôtel St. Gérôme, rue St. Gérôme.
(4) The idea of the meeting originated with Commander Voja Tankosić of Belgrade, no doubt with the consent of Colonel Dimitrievic. . . .
(7) Its purpose was in the first place to prepare an outrage against the Archduke Francis Ferdinand, then others against important civil and military personages in various parts of the Austro-Hungarian Monarchy, including

[1] See p. 52, *n.* 5. [2] Seton-Watson, *Sarajevo*, pp. 74–8.

Vienna. It was hoped by these means to incite the Slav element in Austria-Hungary to revolt and even to cause a general European war.

(8) The decision was taken to carry out this plan.

(9) As a result of the secret meeting Gaćinović wrote a letter to Gavrilo Princip, domiciled at Sarajevo, urging him to come to Lausanne with Danilo Ilić to settle the details of the outrages.

(10) At the end of January Mehmedbašić returned from Toulouse to Stolac in Herzegovina and a few days later went to Sarajevo and put himself at Ilić's disposition in order to assassinate General Potiorek, the Governor of Bosnia, immediately if necessary and, if not, to declare himself available for other outrages. Ilić told him that it was useless for the moment to assassinate Potiorek because it had been decided first to assassinate the Archduke, which was much more important.

(11) As soon as Ilić and Princip received Gaćinović's letter summoning them to Lausanne, Princip went to Belgrade to ask permission to make the journey; but Dimitrievič's right hand man Tankosić told him that it had become unnecessary because at Belgrade, too, it had been decided to assassinate the Archduke. On these grounds Princip was kept on in Belgrade until the end of May receiving instruction in the use of a Browning 9 mm. from Ciganović and Tankosić. All the Brownings for the outrage were bought by Dimitrievič himself.

(12) Ilić and Princip wrote to Gaćinović at Lausanne that they no longer needed to go there, because all preparations for the Archduke's assassination had already been made at Belgrade and Sarajevo.

(13) A few days before the outrage, Danilo Ilić went to Belgrade for last minute instructions and that time—an important detail—it was from Dimitrievič himself that he received them.[1]

Although coming from a suspect source, this reconstruction of the plot has found credence among historians by the fact that of the two youths questioned by Bogičević, one, Mustafa Golubić, actually attended the Toulouse meeting and the other, P. Bastaić was mixed up in acts of terrorism committed by young Bosnians. Tartaglia tells that with Bastaić was one of the three who had Jukić under their influence.

That part of what they said is true is corroborated by a French document. Mehmedbašić, another of the three who went to Toulouse, and one of the six perpetrators of the murder, when he made his escape to Montenegro and was arrested by the Montenegrin police, immediately confessed that he had taken part in the outrage and added that 'a meeting of the conspirators had taken place in France at Tours'. This was reported to Paris on 20 July 1914 by the French Minister at Cetinje who learnt it from the Foreign Minister Plamenac.[2] It is clear that the police understood Tours instead of Toulouse where the meeting really took place, not in January 1913, as Seton-Watson thinks, but in January 1914 as Bogičević's evidence states. The fact is that in January 1913

---

[1] Bogičević, *Procès*, pp. 160–3.   [2] DF. 3. X, 537.

—as the historian Fay remarks—Gaćinović was fighting before Scutari[1] and it is reasonable to suppose that a plot of such a kind would be hatched, not in the thick of a war with Turkey, but after the Serbian victories first against the Turks and then against the Bulgarians, when thoughts could turn to the fellow Slavs subject to the Dual Monarchy.

Hence it was the plot to kill Potiorek that was hatched at Toulouse, not, as Bogičević's account states, the plot to kill the Archduke. Therefore Gaćinović cannot have written summoning Princip and Ilić to Lausanne to prepare an outrage that had not yet been decided, nor can Ilić and Princip have needed to go to Belgrade to obtain permission for the journey. There is likewise no foundation for what is stated in §10 about Mehmedbašić's movements after the Toulouse meeting. In 1937, as already said, he was still alive in Sarajevo and in reply to questions from the present writer gave an exact account of the decisions taken at Toulouse and of what took place after the meeting, an account which differs from that of Bogičević.

His story is that his friend Golubić persuaded him to join the *Black Hand* and they were both eager to carry out an act of terrorism to revive the revolutionary spirit in Bosnia. He knew Gaćinović and Ilić, who had administered to him the oath required of all members of the *Black Hand*. At the end of December 1913 he received a letter from Golubić on behalf of Gaćinović asking him to go on an important matter to Toulouse. There, at the Hôtel St. Gérôme was Golubić who said that Gaćinović and Paul Bastaić were also expected. Actually only Gaćinović came and urged that Bosnia must be wakened up by acts of terrorism. Various possibilities were discussed, among them the idea of an attempt on the life of Francis Ferdinand.

But above all stress was laid on the importance of an attack on Potiorek for the effect that it would produce. Gaćinović thought it urgently necessary. So the others were dropped in favour of the attack on Potiorek. I was entrusted with the task of carrying it out. A dagger was chosen as the surest weapon, especially if poisoned beforehand. Gaćinović give me a little bottle of poison with which I was to moisten the blade of the dagger before doing the deed. From Toulouse I went to Marseilles and there embarked for Ragusa. At Ragusa I took the train but noticed that the gendarmes were searching the compartments for something. Fearing I was the man they wanted I threw away the dagger and poison in the lavatory. I afterwards found that it was a petty thief they were after. When I reached Stolac I wrote Gaćinović and, pending his reply, did nothing more about carrying out the outrage.

Some weeks later I received a letter from Ilić asking me to go to Mostar in an important matter. I went. Ilić told me that Francis Ferdinand was to visit Sarajevo, that the plot against Potiorek took a second place since the attack on the Heir Apparent was far more important, that Belgrade was of

[1] Fay, II, p. 106.

this opinion and would provide us with the necessary means: bombs and revolvers. He asked whether I would take part. I said I would, but reminded him that I had definitely promised Gaćinović to kill Potiorek.[1] I must therefore inform Gaćinović and get his consent to the change of plan. We both wrote the letter and a few days later came the reply: 'Forward Lions', giving his approval. I later again wrote Gaćinović who reiterated his full approval of the attempt on Francis Ferdinand's life. I settled with Ilić to go to Sarajevo on 25 July.

That the first idea of the assassins had been to murder Potiorek is also made clear by Princip's statements in May 1916 to his medical attendant Dr. Pappenheim, whose shorthand notes contain the following:

Čabrinović and Grabež were with him in Serbia. The three had made up their minds to perpetrate the outrage. The idea was his [Princip's]. Before that they had thought of an attempt on Potiorek. [Princip] had come from Belgrade to his brother's house in Sarajevo. He was always in company with Ilić who is now dead, and was his best friend. They made up their minds that one of them would make an attempt on Potiorek. It was October or November 1913.[2]

From Colonel Č. A. Popović also the present writer has the information that towards the end of October or in the first days of November 1913, Ilić came to his house at Užice to say that the youth of Bosnia was in a ferment and something had to be done. Popović replied that the thing to do was to strengthen the revolutionary organization and await the favourable moment. Ilić seemed not to be convinced, pressing his demand and asking what Popović would think of his going to Belgrade to talk things over with Apis whom he knew personally. Popović thought it an excellent idea and provided him with the necessary money and papers for crossing into Serbia, asking to be told by Ilić on his return what had been decided by Dimitrievič. He did not see Ilić again because Ilić returned by another route; but it is probable that, with Apis, Ilić talked over the question of an attempt on the life of Potiorek.

The present writer was able to consult the unpublished manuscript of a book by Oskar Tartaglia on the *Union or Death* society and the Sarajevo crime. In it he states that:

Princip, Čabrinović, Ilić, Grabež and Jovanović perpetrated the Sarajevo outrage solely and exclusively as members of the *Union or Death* organization

---

[1] This Mostar meeting figured largely in the trial. At the preliminary investigation Ilić admitted having arranged it, but at the trial said it was Mehmedbašić who asked him to come and suggested making an attempt on Francis Ferdinand's life. There is little doubt that the truthful account is that of Mehmedbašić, i.e. that where Ilić told the truth was at the preliminary investigation.

[2] *Gavrilo Princips Bekenntnisse* (Vienna, 1926), p. 15; *Princip o Sebi*, p. 31.

under orders from the head of that organization who held Princip and his
companions under his spell.

He declares that the Central Committee of the *Black Hand* was kept
completely in the dark about Apis's plans:

I have talked with all the surviving members of the Central Committee
and all have assured me that in the Central Committee there was never a word
spoken of the outrage and nobody dreamt of dissociating himself from Apis
after the crime was committed.

Apis—writes Tartaglia—was regarded as head of the *Black Hand*,
though he had never been elected to that office, and he acted not only
as a member of that organization but also independently of the Central
Committee as a Serb nationalist, army officer, and revolutionary, employing the services of the *Black Hand* members who were all devoted
to him.

Princip, Čabrinović and Grabež just before their departure for Bosnia
were continually in contact with the Comitaji leader, Major Voja Tankosić
and the Comitaji member Milan Ciganović. These two shared Apis's views
and did everything that he wanted. Dragutin Dimitrievič was the acknowledged head of *Union or Death*. He was the brain of the organization. Tankosić
was his right hand man and Ciganović was the right hand man of Tankosić.
Between them they carried out all Apis's orders and wishes.

Tartaglia asserts that the outrage was not organized by the Central
Committee of the *Black Hand* but, at the instigation of Dimitrievič, by
a certain number of the society's members, among them Tankosić,
Ciganović, Princip, Čabrinović, Grabež, Ilić, Gaćinović and the
Serbian frontier officers Major Rade Popović and Captain Jovan
Prvanović, who allowed the assassins and their arms to pass the
frontier. Tartaglia draws attention to the fact that four of those sentenced to death at the Salonika trial and then reprieved, Colonels Milovanović, Tucović, Čedomilj A. Popović, and Vemić, on 19 December
1923 published in the Belgrade newspaper *Glasnik* a statement that,
after the verdict of the lower military court, they were interrogated
about what they knew of the Sarajevo outrage. They answered that
they knew nothing.

We know [continued the statement] that the late Dimitrievič-Apis gave
the presiding judge Mišić a written document of a secret nature and we have
heard that this document was concerned with the Sarajevo outrage; we have
further learnt from those who had charge of him in prison that the interrogation which Apis underwent at the same time as ourselves was on the same
subject.

Tartaglia further adds that Captain Milan Stoikovič who drove

Apis, Vulović, and Malobabić to their place of execution, stated that in the motor lorry Apis said to him:

Now it is clear to me and clear to you, too, that I am to be killed to-day by Serbian rifles solely because I organized the Sarajevo outrage.

In the light of the data here accumulated there seems much verisimilitude in the following reconstruction of what happened, given to the present writer by Dimitrievíć's nephew and heir, Milan Živanović, whom the present writer interviewed in Belgrade.

My father questioned Dragutin Dimitrievíć various times on what he knew of the Sarajevo outrage and what part he played in it. Apis always made evasive replies saying that the main thing was that the outrage was perpetrated by young Bosniacs.

Though very young I spent a whole year with him at his office during the World War. I never heard him utter a word about the Sarajevo outrage. I have questioned some fifty people who were closest to him and they could none of them tell me anything definite that they had been told by him. Most of them had been told nothing, while to others vague and evasive statements had been made. I also questioned Colonel Milovanović, the intimate friend of Apis and, like him, sentenced to death at the Salonika trial, but then reprieved. He, too, knew little, having received only a vague and unconvincing answer.

Some of his comrades maintain that the motive of Dragutin Dimitrievíć's decision was the fear that the Austrian manoeuvres' in Bosnia might be a cover for making war on Serbia. But they forget that he was head of Military Intelligence of the General Staff and must have perfectly well known that Austria at that moment was not preparing for a war with Serbia. It is unthinkable that he could have been so irresponsible as to take up a suggestion emanating from Bosnian emigrés, still less take it up with the idea that it could not possibly be carried out. He was not a man to prearrange outrages with the thought that they would fail, nor to accept passively other people's suggestions and follow them out. It was always he who took the decisions after pondering on the means, the aims, the consequences, and the scope of his actions. He had a clear vision of things; he was the one to guide, not to be guided and dragged along in the wake. I am convinced that the initiative in the outrage against the Archduke was his.

The following reconstruction of events, though unsupported by evidence, is the one that in my opinion comes nearest to the truth. The young Bosnians were eager to do something to stir up revolutionary activity in Bosnia, but thought that this political aim would best be served by an attempt on General Potiorek, the Governor of Bosnia. They were attracted to it also by the memory of the unsuccessful attempt made by Žerajić and the spell which his name cast on the young revolutionaries of Bosnia. Probably in November or December 1913, not yet knowing of the Archduke's projected visit to Sarajevo, Apis gave consent to the attempt on Potiorek's life, and preparations for it were put in hand. But then he heard that the Archduke was coming to Sarajevo, realized that this was the great chance to eliminate the sponsor of trialism and that an attempt on Francis Ferdinand's life would have more far reaching effects than one on Potiorek. All that was necessary was to convince the young terrorists who were longing to perform some act of heroism.

Apis certainly never thought that the attempt would bring on a European war. Possibly he counted on the dislike felt for Francis Ferdinand by the Hungarians and even by the Viennese Court. In view of such an eventuality he probably thought it well to inform the Russian Military Attaché, Colonel Artamonov, in order to make sure of Russian aid in the event of an Austrian attack on Serbia. When questioned by his comrades on the part he had taken in the outrage, Dimitriević replied, it is true, that he had done nothing more than accede to a request from the young Bosnians transmitted by Tankosić. He could not do less than make this avowal since the names of Tankosić and Ciganović had come up in the Sarajevo preliminary investigation. But at the Salonika trial Apis drew up a statement, the text of which remains unknown, but in which, according to Protić, he admitted having organized the Sarajevo crime. And that he did so can be gathered also from the first lines of his will.

The reason of his extreme secrecy about his part in the outrage is to be sought not only in his taciturn nature and habit of keeping his own counsel, but also in his realization that after the war there would be a hunt for those responsible for the Archduke's death, which brought about the war. It was not yet clear how the war would end. Apis, I repeat, was head of Military Intelligence of the General Staff. If it became known that he was the instigator of the Sarajevo outrage, the impression would be created that the whole Serbian General Staff and probably the Belgrade Government itself was involved in the crime. This suspicion would have done untold harm to his country, which he loved beyond all else in life and for which he was ready to lay down his life.

8. *The Artamonov question.*

In Živanović's statement it will not have escaped the reader's attention that Dimitriević thought it necessary to make sure of Russian aid in case of an Austrian attack on Serbia, using as his channel the Russian Military Attaché at Belgrade, Colonel Artamonov. This is an obscure point in the question of responsibilities for the European war which needs to be cleared up. The first allegation that this colonel was party to the outrage which was being planned in Belgrade was made by the Austrian journalist Leopold Mandl in two articles published in the *Neues Wiener 6 Uhr Abendblatt* of 27 and 28 June 1924 in the following words:

The Russian Military Attaché at Belgrade, Colonel Artamonov, had long been working hand in hand with him [Dimitriević]. . . . When the Military Attaché heard from Dragutin Dimitriević of *Mlada Bosna's* plan, he asked for a short delay while he consulted St. Petersburg. A few days later he reappeared at the office of the Intelligence Section of the Serbian General Staff and declared that whatever happened Russia would back Serbia. While Artamonov was making this statement several members of the Central Committee of the *Black Hand* were present. 'We trembled—said my informant—to the depths of our being at the Russian Military Attaché's words, for we realized that now the axe was being laid to the foot of the tree of Austria.'[1]

Mandl does not divulge his source of information. There is some possibility that both he and Bogičević obtained their information from Colonel Božin Šimić. It is a fact that the latter was in close touch with Golubić and Bastaić, the two terrorists who were Bogičević's informants. These, after having belonged to the *Black Hand*, turned communist and in Vienna published a revolutionary weekly with the title *La Fédération Balkanique*.[2] After the war Šimić led a wandering life in Vienna, Paris, and Moscow. In an interview with Victor Serge, published in the Paris review *Clarté* of May 1925, Šimić made the following disclosures:

Apis worked daily in association with the Russian Military Attaché Artamonov. From Artamonov he learnt of the decisions taken at the Konopischt meeting. These decisions are perfectly comprehensible if one considers the discontent of the Slav element in the Austro-Hungarian provinces, which steadily assumed greater proportions as a result of the Serbian victories. From Artamonov he learnt that Archduke Francis Ferdinand was to attend the big manoeuvres in Bosnia, which were to take place in the summer of 1914. In Dimitrievié's eyes Francis Ferdinand was the man who had turned us out of Albania, Durazzo and Scutari, who wanted to tear up the Treaty of Bucharest. By his murder Dimitrievié hoped to sow confusion also in the Austro-German military camarilla and delay the latent world war for which we were unprepared. He saw the interruption of Austrian war preparations because of fresh hostilities arising from it [the murder]. This might rouse the Slavs in the Monarchy to revolt. When war had become practically unavoidable Apis thought it his duty, before taking decisive action, to come to an understanding with Artamonov. He informed him of the preparations for the Sarajevo outrage. A few days later Artamonov gave his reply which ran: 'Just go ahead! If you are attacked, you will not stand alone.' Artamonov had sought exact instructions from his superiors. Who were they? Very probably Hartwig. Hartwig knew everything, according to Apis's firm belief. Probably St. Petersburg, too, where Hartwig had personal friends. What about Sazonov? We cannot say with certainty, since the policy of ambassadors often differed in many details from that of ministers. Artamonov was well aware of the activities of the *Black Hand*. He personally paid Apis 8,000 French francs for propaganda in Austria.[3]

In December 1937 in the presence of Colonel Č. A. Popović the present writer submitted the text of this interview to Colonel Šimić and he confirmed that it was correct in all particulars except for certain

---

[1] The essential passage of this article was reproduced by Bogičević in KSF., June, 1925, pp. 388 ff.

[2] See Nos. 20–21, 31 May 1925, of *La Fédération Balkanique,* quoted in KSF., 1925, p. 441.

[3] Šimić's story is also published by Bogičević in KSF., July 1925, pp. 388–90.

formal details, but he assured the present writer that he had never stated that Hartwig knew everything, and that on this point his ideas had been wrongly reported. His opinion was that Hartwig was kept in the dark about the plot but that Artamonov—who sympathized with the *Black Hand*, to which he had contributed 8,000 francs, and above all with its chief Dimitriević, with whom he was in daily co-operation—was fully informed of everything. Šimić added that he had no idea whom Artamonov could have consulted in St. Petersburg before giving Dimitriević his reply, but it must have been somebody of more authority than himself, possibly the Russian General Staff, possibly the War Minister Sukhomlinov, possibly some Grand Duke, certainly not Hartwig, because in that case there would not have been a delay of several days before he could give his answer.

The present writer does not know for what reason Šimić altered his original version seeing that he had not troubled to rectify inaccuracies in his interview with Victor Serge as published in *Clarté*, if inaccuracies there were. It must, however, be added that Giesl, the Austrian Minister at Belgrade, when questioned by the present writer, also replied that he did not believe Hartwig was cognizant of the plot. Knowing the military weakness of Serbia he was opposed to war between Austria and Serbia and to anything that might cause it. Giesl thought, however, that Artamonov may well have been privy to the plot.

Artamonov himself, who meanwhile had risen to be a general and in 1937 was living in Belgrade, assured the present writer in answer to an inquiry that from 19 June to 28 July 1914 he was not in Serbia, being on two months' leave and his place being taken by Staff Captain Alexander Werchovski, an extremely able officer recently posted to Belgrade. Artamonov was at Zurich when on 29 June he learnt of the outrage. He did not return to his post, but went first to Milan and then to Lovrana. There on 24 July he heard the news of the Austrian ultimatum to Serbia. He rushed to Fiume to telephone to Werchovski who, regarding war as inevitable, had already left for St. Petersburg. Then Artamonov decided to return to Belgrade arriving on 28 July the day of Austria's declaration of war on Serbia. To Artamonov the present writer submitted Šimić's statements.

He declared them to be false and that Dimitriević never mentioned the outrage to him. Only after the war did he learn that Apis was implicated. They had been on the friendliest terms but had never discussed the impending Austro-Hungarian manoeuvres in Bosnia-Herzegovina or Francis Ferdinand's visit to Bosnia. They had never exchanged ideas on what might happen if the Heir Apparent were to die. On the present writer's remarking that it was strange he should absent himself from Belgrade at the very moment when the Austrian manoeuvres were on the point of beginning on the Bosnian frontier and the Archduke was expected at Sarajevo, Artamonov, after some embarrassed hesitation, said that he had not had any furlough for three years and permission had been given him in the first half of June when he had no idea of what was about to happen. He reiterated that he knew nothing of the outrage, and that in the little Belgrade of the time, where public life was confined to a very few cafés, the plot could not have been kept secret, and he added:

If Austria did not take adequate precautions for the protection of the Archduke's life, there must have been reasons for it. Perhaps the Sarajevo drama implies a mysterious Hapsburg drama. Probably this is the explanation why Jovan Jovanović's approach to Bilinski had no result.[1]

When the present writer asked Artamonov for his explanation of the statements made by Dimitriević to Colonel Šimić, his reply was:

Perhaps Dragutin Dimitriević gave this version to attenuate and cover up his own guilt or to boast of influences from high quarters. He was a strong, ambitious man who aimed at gaining complete and unconditional command of the State. His statements to Colonel Šimić as to my having agreed to the Sarajevo outrage on one hand whitewashed him for his part in the plot and on the other enhanced his prestige.

The present writer must honestly say he remained unconvinced by the behaviour of this officer, who struck him as being of limited intelligence with little strength of character, or by his explanations for his absence from Belgrade even after the outrage. He showed the present writer his note book of June–July 1914, a bald list of Swiss and Italian hotels, giving the room-numbers of the accommodation occupied by himself and his family in each hotel and the account of the day's expenses and nothing else. No mention of the Sarajevo outrage or Hartwig's death. Only the top of the page bearing the date 24 July 1914, under the name of his hotel at Lovrana are the words: *Austrian ultimatum to Serbia,* followed by the usual record of the day's expenditure beginning with: coffee—2 lire!

The present writer drew General Artamonov's attention to Bogičević's assertions in *Le Procès de Salonique* regarding the

close co-operation between the Russian and Serbian General Staffs and the intimate relation between Colonel Artamonov, Russian Military Attaché at Belgrade, and Colonel Dragutin Dimitriević, head of Military Intelligence, Serbian General Staff.[2]

Artamonov's reply was:

Of course I was in practically daily contact with Dimitriević. I was Military Attaché, Dimitriević was head of Military Intelligence of the Serbian

---

[1] An allusion to the attempt made by Jovanović to suggest to Bilinski that the Archduke's visit was inadvisable. More will be said of this in the next chapter (pp. 101–6).

[2] *Op. cit.,* p. 36.

General Staff. Serbia and Russia were on extremely friendly terms and had discussions on mutual co-operation in case of war. Moreover I had to follow Austrian military preparations in Bosnia, because, as an enemy frontier, it was of concern to the Russian General Staff in case of war. My relations with Dimitriević were entirely confined to intelligence on military matters.

Nevertheless, in view of the post he held, Artamonov did not succeed in giving the present writer a convincing explanation of his departure from Belgrade precisely on the eve of the Austrian grand manoeuvres in Bosnia. He simply repeated that he never had occasion to talk with Dimitriević either of the manoeuvres or of the possibility that Austria was planning a war on Serbia of which the manoeuvres were to be the prelude, nor of what might happen after the death of Francis Ferdinand, nor of the conspiracy against him.

Not until after the war did I learn that Dimitriević had instigated and organized the Sarajevo outrage.

After all, it is questionable whether Artamonov was in a position to guarantee Russian aid to Serbia in the event of an Austrian attack and whether Dimitriević would have been satisfied with such assurances. It does, however, seem certain—and this opinion is shared by Professor Slobodan Jovanović—that Artamonov was told of the plot, if not directly by Dimitriević, then by some other informant, and that he did nothing to thwart it.[1]

9. *The real motive of the crime.*

It still remains to say what reason can have induced Dimitriević to become the instigator of the outrage or at least to give it his help.

It is easy to suppose that he was well acquainted with the ideas and plans of the Archduke and, like everybody else, knew that, far from thinking of attacking Serbia and becoming involved in war with Russia, Francis Ferdinand was anxious to improve the conditions of the Slavs subject to Austria-Hungary and by introducing trialism prevent their uniting with the Kingdom of Serbia. Now trialism was what the Serb nationalists and militarists dreaded above all things. If it had no attraction for the youth of Bosnia, it found adherents among the Slavs of the

---

[1] In this connexion it must be added that in the *Deutsche Allgemeine Zeitung* of 13 April 1932, Wegerer, editor of the *Kriegsschuldfrage*, draws attention to the following: 'The Russian Polish archaeologist and member of the former Archaeological Institute of St. Petersburg, Louis de Trydar-Burzynski, states in his memoirs published in Florence in 1926 under the title *Le Crépuscule d'une Autocratie*: "The assassination was perpetrated with the support of the Russian Military Attaché at Belgrade. Captain Werchovski, who was assistant to the Military Attaché (Artamonov) and was later War Minister in the Kerensky Government, a young man whom I had known very well for years and all his family, told me quite frankly the truth about the origins, preparations and execution of the plot." Alexander Ivanovich Werchovski is still alive and holds a high command in the Red Army. His evidence, therefore, can still be obtained.' (KSF., 1932, pp. 490, 825.)

Monarchy. Had it been put into effect by Francis Ferdinand, it might have been fatal to the Pan-Serb movement.

If trialism had come about [writes B. Jevtić, the Bosniac revolutionary who boasts of having spent the night before the outrage with Princip] it would without doubt have meant the end of the ideals of *Omladina* [Serbo-Bosniac patriotic youth], their hopes for the liberation and union of all Jugoslavs and the destruction of Austria.[1]

Princip was alluding to trialism when he said at the trial that he thought Francis Ferdinand would do harm to the Serbs because

as future Sovereign he would have prevented our union by carrying through certain reforms which would have clearly gone against our interests.[2]

And Čabrinović went further in saying that the Archduke meant to create a federal Austria which would have included Serbia as well.[3]

Most likely the two assassins had learnt this lesson at the school of the men of the *Black Hand*. For them, however, the Archduke's plan must have been a secondary motive for the crime, while for Dimitrievič it may well have been the main motive. His nephew Živanović stated to the present writer:

The motive of the Sarajevo crime is to be sought in the Slavophil policy of Francis Ferdinand. The Archduke fell a victim of his political views favourable to trialism. If he had succeeded in carrying through this design, Serbia would have ended by gravitating towards Austria-Hungary. Apis, an acute political thinker, had grasped all the danger of the Archduke's plan. Austria meant to bring about Southern Slav union within the framework of the Danubian Monarchy. Dimitrievič, who had been for several months at the Serbian Legation in Berlin, must have been seriously perturbed by what he learnt of the political intentions of the Austrian Heir Apparent and the information, continually brought to him by Serbs and Croats from the Monarchy, of the growing sympathy which that programme roused among the Slav subjects of Austria. That is why he decided to seize the first occasion to eliminate Francis Ferdinand.

In his unpublished book on the *Black Hand* and the Sarajevo outrage Oskar Tartaglia writes:

Why did Apis have Francis Ferdinand murdered? The motive was the following: In Austria-Hungary the Slav element was the fifth wheel. The Heir Apparent was the representative of trialism. Trialism meant the death of the Jugoslav nationalist idea, the death of Jugoslav freedom and unity, the death of the idea embodied and proclaimed by *Union or Death* and by Apis. Apis knew all this and for that reason organized and prepared the Sarajevo outrage.

[1] Borivoje Jevtić, *Sarajevski Atentat* (Sarajevo, 1923), p. 16; KSF., 1925, pp. 669–70.
[2] Mousset, p. 131.　　　　　　　　　　[3] Mousset, p. 82.

Similarly the historian E. Anrich holds the view that the assassination of the heir to the Austrian throne was not purely an act of terrorism, but a political crime engendered by his ideas and that the Archduke died not because he aimed at creating a Jugoslavia within the Monarchy but because he was favourable to trialism. This is what he says:

Against whom was the outrage directed? Was it only to provoke Austria? It was directed against the one man in Austria who perhaps alone and by bloodless methods might have destroyed the Pan-Serb movement by a reorganization of Austria-Hungary in the sense that in place of its being constructed in two halves, Austria and Hungary (the so-called Austrian dualism), trialism would be introduced, the third group, liberated from Magyar national oppression, being Croatia with Bosnia, Herzegovina, Dalmatia and Slovenia. An idea which had powerful possibilities because at bottom between Croats and Serbs there existed profound religious, cultural and historical opposition. Only very late had Croatia become accessible to the Pan-Serb idea, only when the mistakes of the imperialistic Magyar-Hungarian rule had become unendurable. (Croatia had been assigned in 1868 to the Hungarian half of the Monarchy, although by historic territorial law it belonged directly to the House of Hapsburg.) Were a Croatian liberation to begin within the Austrian framework, then Croatia would be destined to evade capture by the Pan-Serbian idea. Whether Francis Ferdinand could successfully have carried through this transformation of Austria, it is not possible to say. The resistance of Hungary would certainly have gone to great lengths, moreover very deep shadows lie also on Francis Ferdinand's character. But one thing is certain, namely that this would have offered the only way of salvation. Thus the murder of just this very man is no mere demonstration, but an attempt to strike at Austria in her vital nerve.[1]

If this is so, it must be admitted that this assassination was not 'senseless', as the British Consul General at Budapest described it in a report of 14 July 1914.

It is surely the irony of fate—he went on—that the future ruler who was commonly regarded as a champion of Southern Slav rights should have fallen a victim to the criminal propaganda of Pan-Servian agitation.[2]

No! Francis Ferdinand was sentenced to death precisely because, by upholding the rights of the Slav subjects of the Monarchy, he was undermining the movement which aimed at detaching them from Austria and uniting them with Serbia. The outrage organized against him was not an irony of fate but inspired by nationalism, a political concept of great moment for the future of the Jugoslav people and the history of Europe. It gained its end by one of the greatest tragedies the human race has ever known.

[1] Ernst Anrich, *Europas Diplomatie am Vorabend des Weltkrieges* (Berlin, 1937), p. 35.
[2] BD. XI, 70.

CHAPTER III

THE SHARE OF RESPONSIBILITY BORNE BY BELGRADE AND VIENNA

(1) *Ljuba Jovanović's disclosure that the Serbian Government had foreknowledge of the plot; Pašić's tardy denials (p. 89). (2) Who was telling the truth, L. Jovanović or Pašić? (p. 94). (3) Evidence as to the information on the plot possessed by the Serbian Government and as to its having warned Vienna (p. 98). (4) The Serbian Minister to Vienna carries out badly the instructions given him by Pašić (p. 101). (5) Why Jovan Jovanović and Pašić took no effective action: the Oberdan precedent (p. 106). (6) The shadow of Dimitrievič; the Belgrade Government obstructs the search for the truth (p. 109). (7) The Austro-Hungarian authorities' neglect of all precautions at Sarajevo (p. 111). (8) The sense of relief in Austro-Hungarian political circles at the news of the Archduke's death; the disgraceful arrangements for the funeral of the Archduke and his consort (p. 115).*

1. *Ljuba Jovanović's disclosure that the Serbian Government had foreknowledge of the plot; Pašić's tardy denials.*

The fact that, in casting the blame for the Sarajevo crime on Serbia and sending a stern ultimatum, Austria did not mention the part played by the *Black Hand* was a piece of luck for the Serbian Government, in that the *Narodna Obrana*, which Vienna accused instead of accusing the *Black Hand*, could not be reproached with acts of terrorism. This does not mean that the Belgrade Government was free from all blame, nor is it correct to say, as does Seton-Watson, that Dimitrievič at all events acted as an individual. Princip at the trial made the same claim for Tankosić, in order to keep Serbia out of the question.[1] It may be objected that as Dimitrievič held a high post in the army, had taken a prominent part in the conspiracy of 1903, was a leading figure in the public life of his country, and represented a strong current of opinion in the army, the Serbian Government ought to have kept a watch on him and his society, knowing that they were dangerous. Now assuming Pašić and his colleagues to have been without complicity in the plot, as no serious historian seems to doubt, did they exercise the necessary vigilance? Or, on the contrary, assuming them to have had information of what the *Black Hand* and its chief were scheming, did they deliberately refrain from taking the necessary steps to frustrate it? Torrents of ink have flowed on this subject and the truth that has come to light is still denied by some. There was a moment after the war was over when, in the joy of victory and of Jugoslav union, Serbian politicians

[1] R. W. Seton-Watson, *Sarajevo*, p. 143.

and publicists indulged in disclosures and confidences in the fullness of their hearts. But the scandal thus caused was so great that silence fell once more on all that had happened, without entirely undoing the effect of the voices that had broken it.

As we have already seen,[1] Prof. Stanojević in 1923 began to lift the veil on the mystery surrounding the origins of the outrage and to accuse directly Apis and the *Black Hand*. His purpose in making these accusations was to demonstrate the complete innocence of the Serbian Government and the *Narodna Obrana* of whose activities the Government knew and approved. But in 1924 Ljuba Jovanović, who had been Minister of Education in 1914, having promised a contribution to a publication commemorating the tenth anniversary of the outbreak of the European war and not having anything prepared, sent in fragments of his memoirs. These figured as the first article in the publication which was entitled *Krv Sloventsva* (*The Blood of Slavism*). With complete uncon-cern Ljuba Jovanović relates:

I do not remember whether it was at the end of May or the beginning of June, when one day M. Pašić said to us (he conferred on these matters more particularly with Stojan Protić, who was then Minister of the Interior, but he said this much to the rest of us) that there were people who were preparing to go to Sarajevo to kill Francis Ferdinand, who was to go there to be solemnly received on *Vidov Dan*. As they afterwards told me, the plot was hatched by a group of secretly organized persons and in patriotic Bosno-Herzegovinian student circles in Belgrade. M. Pašić and the rest of us said, and Stojan agreed, that he should issue instructions to the frontier authorities on the Drina to deny a crossing to the youths who had already set out from Belgrade for that purpose. But the frontier 'authorities' themselves belonged to the organization, and did not carry out Stojan's instructions, but reported to him (and he afterwards reported to us), that the order had reached them too late, for the young men had already got across.

Thus the endeavour of the Government to prevent the execution of the plot failed, as did also the endeavour made on his own initiative by our Minister in Vienna, M. Joca Jovanović, in an interview with the Minister Bilinski, to dissuade the Archduke from the fatal journey which he con-templated. And so the attempt at Sarajevo was to be carried out, in more terrible measure than had been anticipated and with results which no one could then have pictured even in his wildest dreams.[2]

These few sentences give an accurate reconstruction of the plot, confirming that it was engineered by a secretly organized group of persons in collusion with Bosnian students and that the frontier auth-orities also belonged to this organization. Now the organization to

---

[1] See above, p. 71.

[2] *Krv Sloventsva*, p. 9; KSF., 1925, pp. 68–9; *Journal of British* [now *Royal*] *Institute of Inter-national Affairs* (March 1925), also issued as a separate off-print; *National Review* (April 1925).

which Ljuba Jovanović alluded was obviously the *Black Hand*, as he himself wrote in the Belgrade *Politika* of 22 March 1925, adding that this society was founded by elements dissatisfied with the Serbian Government. But though the society was secret, Pašić, according to L. Jovanović's account, was informed of what it was plotting and felt it necessary to raise the matter with his colleagues. They decided to prevent the plotters from entering Bosnia, and Protić, who was a man of decision and an enemy of Dimitrievic and the *Black Hand*, certainly cannot have failed to carry out the decision, but unfortunately came too late. The fact that the conspirators had crossed the frontier should have made Pašić try other means of preventing them from accomplishing their deed. What he actually did L. Jovanović does not explain. He goes on to relate:

I was personally acquainted with Gavril Princip, the chief conspirator. I saw him two or three times in my department, when he came to see me to ask me to allow him to sit privately for the examination at the 'Gymnasium', first for the fifth, and then for the sixth class.

Jovanović then describes his own feelings of shock and anxiety on hearing of the outrage. In making these disclosures, to which neither he nor anyone else in Serbia attached great importance, Ljuba Jovanović little dreamt of the indignation and amazement they were to cause, especially in certain circles abroad which were friendly to Serbia. The only new element contained in them was that they made clearer a fact which had already been stated indirectly immediately after the Sarajevo crime. Indeed, as we shall shortly see, as early as 30 June 1914 it had been authoritatively stated, and was repeated by Stanojević in 1923, that the Serbian Government had given timely warning to the Austrian Government of a plot that was being prepared at Sarajevo against the Archduke. If it could give this warning, this showed that the Serbian Government had information about the plot. Ljuba Jovanović now carried the matter further by disclosing that the plot was hatched at Belgrade and that the plotters were not stopped. After the war the tendency in Serbia was to boast of what had happened and to glorify the crime which had given rise to the liberation of the Southern Slavs and their union in an independent state. Italians can well understand this. They honour the memory of Guglielmo Oberdan, naming streets and squares after him and erecting monuments to his memory. Indeed no one in Belgrade dreamt of reproving L. Jovanović for what he had written, not even Pašić who was involved in the disclosures. In fact Jovanović was made Speaker of the Skupština, chairman of the elections committee, and other things which could only have happened by the will of Pašić.

But if the Serbia of that time and the Jugoslavia of later had influential and staunch friends and protectors, they also had bitter enemies. Among these was the Englishwoman Miss Durham, who at the end of 1924 began to make a stir in lectures and articles and also in the *Kriegsschuldfrage* about Ljuba Jovanović's disclosures[1] while on the other side of the Atlantic the well-known historian Fay on 24 December 1924 drew the attention of a gathering of American historians at Richmond (Va.) to the importance of these disclosures, to which he devoted certain of his writings. But the most intensive use of them was made, as might be expected, by the *Kriegsschuldfrage* which absorbed the facts brought to light by Ljuba Jovanović into its campaign for the revision of the Versailles verdict.[2]

This campaign forced that good friend of Serbia, R. W. Seton-Watson, who during the war had maintained the complete innocence of official Serbia and gave scant credence to the Jovanović revelations, to intervene in the hope of obtaining assurances and proofs from the Serbian Government which would demolish the accusations. In a letter to *The Times* of 16 February 1925 he publicly asked Pašić and Jovanović to clear themselves of the accusation of having had 'foreknowledge of and deliberate connivance at, the crime of Sarajevo'.

Pašić made no reply, but had an announcement published in the Belgrade press—but not, be it noted, by the official Press Bureau—that the Serbian Government had decided to publish another *Blue Book* on the origins of the war. This announcement caused Seton-Watson, a few weeks later, to write another letter to *The Times* saying that judgement should be suspended pending the publication of these documents. Meanwhile it happened that Ljuba Jovanović, who in 1924 had led the more moderate wing of the Radicals and had been asked by the King to form a Cabinet, seemed in a fair way towards superseding Pašić as leader of the party. But the sensation caused abroad by his notorious article provided the Belgrade press with a pretext for violent attacks which shook his political position. So in March and April 1925 in *Novi Zivot* and *Politika* he published a series of articles dealing with the part he had played for over thirty years in Serbian political life but evading the real issue, namely whether the Pašić Ministry had foreknowledge of the Sarajevo plot, and accusing Seton-Watson of having wrongly reported his statements. In an interview subsequently published in *Politika* of 17 April 1925 Jovanović stated: I made no revelations as people are being made to believe. I simply wrote what was known to everybody in Serbia in 1914.[3]

---

[1] Fay, II, p. 75.

[2] KSF., February 1925, pp. 68–72; April 1925, pp. 211–20; June 1925, pp. 393–8; April 1926, pp. 226–37; May 1926, pp. 318–21; June 1926, pp. 400–14; October 1926, pp. 767–785; August 1927, pp. 716–18; April 1929, pp. 361–4.

[3] Seton-Watson, *Sarajevo*, pp. 152–9; Belgrade *Politika*, 22 and 29 March, 6, 12, 17 April 1925; KSF., April 1925, pp. 211–20; *idem* May 1925, pp. 270–2; *idem* June 1925, pp. 393–402.

This line did not satisfy Seton-Watson who went to Jugoslavia to clear the matter up and published an open letter in the Zagreb *Nova Evropa* reproduced in *Obzor* of 13 May 1925.[1] The letter stated that more than two months had gone by since he had asked the Belgrade Government to make a pronouncement on the particulars given by L. Jovanović and that no reply had been yet forthcoming. He also took Jovanović apart and asked for a plain statement whether he confirmed what he had written as to Pašić's having informed his fellow ministers of the existence of the plot. If he did not deny it, then it was for Pašić to 'speak out plainly and place the facts in their true light'. But Pašić remained dumb and the *Blue Book* was never published. Therefore at the end of 1925 Seton-Watson published his book *Sarajevo*, in which he reproachfully drew attention to the fact that eight months had gone by and there was no sign of the *Blue Book*, so that it seemed probable that the announcement was merely tactical, to appease the critics until the whole agitation should die down.[2]

But in public opinion all over the world, especially in Germany, the sensation caused by the Jovanović disclosures lasted on and gave rise to polemics in Serbia. On 26 February 1926 at a meeting of the budget standing committee of the Skupština, the former Serbian Minister to Vienna, Jovan Jovanović (not to be confused with Ljuba Jovanović), begged Pašić to speak out frankly for the sake of Serbia's good name. Professor Jelenić, formerly Prince Alexander's private secretary and devoted to Pašić, addressed the Central Committee of the Radical party describing Ljuba Jovanović's story as 'a most perfidious levantine lie', and begging Pašić to contradict it. His own version was that the crime was engineered in Berlin, received the finishing touches at Konopischt and was 'perpetrated by means of the co-operation of the Vienna and Budapest camarilla with the Belgrade *Black Hand*'.[3] This assertion aroused the indignation of the two *Black Hand* survivors Colonels Popović and Milovanović who challenged Jelenić to prove his statements, in which case they would tell what they knew of the Sarajevo crime to clear the name of their dead comrades whose patriotism was beyond dispute.[4]

At this point Pašić felt obliged to break silence and throw to the wolves the Ljuba Jovanović who in 1917, as Minister of Home Affairs, had played a prominent part in the Salonika trial of Dimitriević and his associates. On 25 April 1926 at a meeting of the Radical Club Pašić declared that he had asked his former colleague to withdraw the allegation about his having had foreknowledge of the outrage on the Archduke, 'it being untrue that he had made any such statement to the

[1] Fay, II, p. 68.   [2] Seton-Watson, *Sarajevo*, p. 156.
[3] *Politika*, 26 March 1926; KSF., June 1926, pp. 400–3.
[4] *Politika*, 31 March 1926; KSF., June 1926, p. 406.

Cabinet'. The assertion had not been withdrawn. Pašić therefore re-iterated that he had never uttered the words attributed to him and that he had received corroboration of this from his colleagues of that time. He had no idea—he continued—why L. Jovanović had written what he did, but if that was the way he behaved, he had better leave the party because his conduct was unpardonable.

But this rebuttal by Pašić came too late—two years after the publica-tion of L. Jovanović's story—to receive credence. 'Nobody'—notes Jovan Jovanović, though he sides against his namesake—'took it seriously.' It 'politically buried' Ljuba Jovanović who was expelled from the Radical party, but refused to withdraw his story.[1] He wrote a reply saying he had stated that Pašić had spoken of the outrage in preparation against the Archduke not at a Cabinet meeting, but in the course of a private conversation. He offered to bring documentary proofs of the truth of this assertion if the then Prime Minister Uzunović and the then Foreign Minister Ninčić would take full responsibility for his doing so. This they both refused to do. So things remained as they were.[2] Pašić died in December 1926, Ljuba Jovanović in February 1928.

2. *Who was telling the truth, L. Jovanović or Pašić?*

Which of the two men was telling the truth? Seton-Watson thinks it was Pašić, though Pašić committed the mistake of showing amazing indifference to public opinion, particularly in foreign countries, made use of the incident not so much 'to defend the honour of his country' as to isolate a dangerous competitor for the party leadership, and failed to produce the proofs—which Seton-Watson believed him to possess —that

in 1914 he was ignorant, and even disapproved, of an underground move-ment which some admire as having led directly to national unity.

Seton-Watson regards L. Jovanović as

one of those politicians who like to exaggerate their own importance. . . . He was making a bid for the support of the Bosnian youth by showing that the Belgrade Government had sympathised with the revolutionary move-ment, though it is quite notorious that it did not do so.

Further, as one of the two statesmen mainly responsible for the execu-tion of Dimitrievič after the Salonika trial, he may have been seeking to remove the unfavourable impression caused by this action.[3]

The opinion of Seton-Watson is shared by the former Serbian Minister to Vienna Jovan Jovanović, as is shown in a letter written by

[1] Isaac, pp. 254–5.
[2] *Politika*, 26 April 1926; *Obzor*, 27 April 1926; KSF., June 1926, pp. 408–13.
[3] Seton-Watson, *Sarajevo*, pp. 157–9.

him to J. Isaac on 25 January 1933 in which he suggests that his name-sake had confused the Sarajevo outrage with another which he himself made public in 1926. According to this story, in April 1914 five young Bosnian Comitaji, one of whom was the Milan Ciganović whom we already know, asked Tankosić to give them arms and ammunition to go to Bosnia and assassinate the Governor, Potiorek. When Tankosić refused, they turned to Dimitrievic who agreed and sent the five to Šabac, where they were to cross the Drina into Bosnia. But one of the five got drunk and talked too much. All were arrested and sent back to Belgrade. The complicity of Dimitrievic having come to light, Pašić wrote to General Putnik complaining of the activities of his subordi-nate. This increased the tension between the Government and the *Black Hand* and did not prevent Dimitrievic shortly after from getting the Sarajevo assassins across into Bosnia. Thus probably L. Jovanović had confused the two incidents. The ex-Minister Jovanović added that Pašić did not at once contradict his former colleague because when the scandal broke out, this colleague in agreement with an exalted person-age (King Alexander?) was endeavouring to supplant him and Pašić allowed the doubt to remain as to the truth of his opponent's disclosures in order to entrap him and 'bury him' politically, as he then did at the Radical party meeting. Pašić did harm to Serbia by keeping silence for two years, but Ljuba Jovanović had acted out of personal vanity and in order to ascribe to his party the merit of having dealt the death-blow to the Hapsburg Monarchy.[1]

Few Serbian politicians seem so concerned to hide the truth in order to exonerate Serbia completely as was Jovan Jovanović, of whose line of action we shall shortly speak. Although he assured the American historian Bernadotte Schmitt that he had seen the official dossier of the earlier outrage which came to nothing, it is difficult to place faith in his disclosures[2] in the absence of more convincing evidence. Why did he suppress the names of all the conspirators except Ciganović, who in actual fact was never arrested at this time and retained his post in the State railways? And why did he state in *Politika* that the attempt was to be made against Francis Ferdinand while to Isaac he wrote that it was aimed at Potiorek?

When at the end of 1937 the present writer asked Jovan Jovanović for exact particulars in this matter, his explanations sounded em-barrassed and confused. It was clear that he was unwilling to enter into the question. He confined himself to repeating what he had already written without adding any new element to strengthen his statement. The present writer remarked to him that it was improbable that five

---

[1] Belgrade *Politika*, 4 December 1926; KSF., January 1927, p. 84; Isaac, pp. 254-5 (a variant account).

[2] B. Schmitt, I, p. 224.

young Comitaji would prepare an attempt on the life of Potiorek when preparations were going forward—as at least two of them knew—for the attempt against Francis Ferdinand. J. Jovanović agreed and replied that he had perhaps confused the dates and that the five youths, of whom he only knew the names of two, Ciganović and Djuro Šarac, had started off, not at the end of April, but at the end of January or in February, before there was any idea of the plot against the Archduke. A final question from the present writer elicited no better result. In 26 January 1938 J. Jovanović confined himself to writing in reply:

> The five young Comitaji who tried to cross the frontier near Šabac had no intention of committing an outrage against Archduke Francis Ferdinand. I suppose that their intention was more likely to put out of the way that arch enemy of the Serbs, Marshal Potiorek, the Governor of Bosnia. I cannot identify all five but only Ciganović and Dj. Šarac. It is owing to the indiscretion of a chambermaid at the hotel where one of the Comitaji spent the night previous to his departure from Šabac for the Drina that the police were informed and prevented all five from crossing. They would certainly have gone into Bosnia if this incident had not taken place.

However, L. Jovanović's story was so circumstantial and so exactly applicable to the Sarajevo crime as to rule out any possibility of confusion on his part. Nor is it true that Pašić maintained silence in order to trap his adversary. The friction between the two men arose much later than the disclosure, and after it Pašić still continued to entrust the highest posts to L. Jovanović. In short there are no grounds for the explanation suggested by Seton-Watson and repeated by J. Jovanović that it was vanity which caused L. Jovanović to write what he did and claim merit for a sympathetic attitude towards the plot in May–June 1914. He in fact confessed that with the other Ministers he had tried to foil the outrage and had felt the greatest horror on learning that it had taken place, in other words that he had opposed the act of terrorism. And if he had had the second aim attributed to him he would—as Schmitt well remarks—have made his disclosure in a more spectacular manner, instead of putting it into an article in an obscure publication.[1]

That in 1924 L. Jovanović candidly spoke the truth without considering what repercussions his memories would arouse and the trouble they would bring down on his own head is also manifest in two important pieces of evidence collected by Luciano Magrini. In October 1915 during the Serbian retreat—i.e. nine years before the appearance of the Jovanović article—Major Milan Georgević, formerly Chargé d'Affaires at Constantinople and son of a former Prime Minister Vladan Georgević, stated the same facts to Magrini in the presence of the *Daily Telegraph* correspondent George Stevens. Georgević's story was that several weeks before the crime, news leaked out in well-informed

[1] Schmitt, I, p. 235.

circles of the plot organized by the *Black Hand*. Pašić received information about it in the first fortnight of June. He remained in great uncertainty as to what steps to take in view of the strength of the *Black Hand* on one side and fear of complications with Austria on the other. After hesitating for several days he spoke to his colleagues who approved of his intention to frustrate the plans of the conspirators. But these had by then already crossed the frontier. Similarly in October 1915 the former Serbian Military Attaché in Austria, Colonel Lešanin, stated to Magrini that his Government had knowledge of the plot being hatched at Sarajevo and that, as we shall see, it passed on the information to the Serbian Minister in Vienna.[1]

Still further, there must also be taken into account a fact recorded by Ljuba Jovanović in proof of the veracity of his statements. He had written that the Ministers were in agreement that instructions should be sent by Pašić to the frontier authorities not to let the assassins get across, but that, as fate would have it, these authorities were also members of the organization (the *Black Hand*) and did not carry out the order. In *Politika*, 17 April 1925, L. Jovanović asserts that traces of these instructions were found by the Austrians when they captured Ložnica in 1914 and seized the papers of·the frontier official Kosta Todorović. Among them was a strict order from the Serbian War Minister to prevent the young men whose names were given from crossing the frontier.

Thus there seems no doubt that Pašić had knowledge of what was being hatched in Belgrade and nothing shows it more, as we shall see, than his behaviour after the crime.[2] He could not do otherwise than keep a watchful eye on the plottings of his enemies in the *Black Hand*. His informant on their activities seems to have been none other than the railway employee Ciganović who took so large a part in organizing the outrage. Of this there are no direct proofs but the indirect proofs carry considerable weight. When the Austrian Government in its ultimatum demanded the arrest of Tankosić and Ciganović, the Serbian Government replied that it had arrested Tankosić (who, as we know, was one of its opponents). As regards Ciganović, however, the Government replied that up to 28 June, the day of the outrage, he had been an employee of the State railways but that they had not been able to find him. It seems in reality that the Government itself caused his disappearance for fear he would tell tales. One sure fact is that at the Salonika trial Ciganović was one of the chief witnesses for the prosecution. Bogičević asserts that on 3 or 4 August 1914 the military commandant of an important railway station said to him in front of several witnesses that he had arranged for Ciganović's escape southwards. Bogičević also writes that before the Salonika trial Ciganović

---

[1] Magrini, pp. 106–8, 115.   [2] See pp. 98–101.

was known to be a spy and *agent provocateur* in the pay of Pašić. In March 1915 Pašić had his arrears of pay from June 1914 made up to him after the Salonika trial, and furnished him with a false passport and funds to go to America from whence he returned to Serbia in 1919 receiving a reward of agricultural land near Uskub from the Government.[1] Also Djuro Šarac, the graduate in theology, who knew everything about the planning of the Sarajevo outrage and whose name was mentioned at the Sarajevo trial by both Princip and Čabrinović, was subsequently one of the witnesses for the prosecution at the Salonika trial. After the trial he was sent to Switzerland at the expense of the Government to continue his studies.

One may well ask why, if Pašić had foreknowledge of a plot that might cause an international crisis in which Serbia would be caught unprepared and perhaps isolated, he did not do all in his power to bring about the arrest of the perpetrators, if not of the instigators, lest Serbia should be held guilty of the crime. Why did he not take vigorous measures? Most probably he was afraid of uncovering the activities of that powerful organization whose leaders would have had few scruples in having him assassinated. As Major Georgević told Magrini, Pašić hesitated at first and then took the steps which we have already noted. It is practically certain that in addition he took measures to warn Vienna of the dangers awaiting the Archduke in Sarajevo.

3. Evidence as to the information on the plot possessed by the Serbian Government and as to its having warned Vienna.

Such warning—which if proved would show foreknowledge of the outrage on the part of Pašić—was at once attested in an interview given by Spalaiković, the Serbian Minister to St. Petersburg, and published in a Russian journal two or three days after the crime.[2] On 30 June the acting French Consul at Budapest wrote to Paris:

To establish the responsibility of Serbia, who has not got his own little pointer? Everyone remembers the *démarche* said to have been undertaken a few days ago at the Ballplatz by the Serbian Minister, M. Jovanović, to draw attention to the dangers awaiting the Archduke in Bosnia.[3]

This *démarche*, therefore, was common knowledge and indeed on 30 June the Belgrade *Stampa* stated that shortly before Francis Ferdi-

---

[1] Bogičević, *Procès*, pp. 131–3, 143. J. Jovanović asserts that Ciganović entered the service of the Serbian Government only in 1916 after the Serbian withdrawal to Corfu and after the death of Tankosić (Isaac, p. 263). But the former Serbian Minister could not do otherwise than say this, because by admitting that in 1914 Ciganović was already a spy of Pašić's, he would have acknowledged that Pašić had received information about the outrage.

[2] According to Seton-Watson (*Sarajevo* p. 153, *n.* 2) the paper was the *Novoje Vremja* (30 June or 1 July). Fay on the other hand (II, p. 153), writes that it was the *Vecerne Vremja* of a day or two after the crime and that the interview was summarized in the *Neue Freie Presse* of 2 July.

[3] DF. 3. X, 463.

nand's departure for Bosnia Berchtold was warned by J. Jovanović against letting the Archduke go to Sarajevo

because the Serbian Government had come into possession of information which led it to believe that a plot had been engineered in Sarajevo to be carried out if the Heir Apparent were to go there.

Berchtold was stated to have thanked the Minister and informed the Emperor and the Archduke. But Berchtold at once issued a denial that he had received any such information[1] and three years later he repeated the denial when the French professor Denis in his book *La grande Serbie* (1915) made the same statement as emanating from authoritative Serbian sources.[2]

Pašić himself in the *Az Est* of 7 July 1914 denied foreknowledge of the outrage and having warned Vienna. Had he got wind of it—the Paris edition of the *New York Herald* of 20 July reports him to have said—he would certainly have informed the Austro-Hungarian Government. But an editorial in the *Temps* of 10 July 1914 attributes to him a statement to the opposite effect. Bogičević, on his part, asserts that, at a sitting of the Skupština of July 1914, Pašić in an answer to the deputy Petčić stated that he had sent a warning to Vienna.[3] This does not seem credible because the Skupština was dissolved on 24 June and the new one met only on 23 September. Similarly Stanojević, who is regarded as an apologist of Pašić, wrote in a publication of 1923 that, a few days before the outrage, the Serbian Minister to Vienna officially informed the Austro-Hungarian Government that the Serbian Government had reason to believe something was being engineered at Sarajevo against the Archduke. Asked by the *Kriegsschuldfrage* to authenticate this statement, Stanojević replied that he had the information from the Serbian Minister to Vienna, adding that the relevant document, of which he gave the number, existed in the Vienna archives. This, however, proved not to be true.[4]

This maze of statements and denials might tempt one to doubt whether Pašić really did instruct the Serbian Minister in Vienna to warn the Austrian Government of the danger which the Archduke would run if he went to Sarajevo. But to Pašić's denials little importance can be attached.[5] He was not accustomed to telling invariably the

---

[1] Oe-U. VIII, 9952.

[2] Denis, p. 277; Leopold Mandl, *Die Habsburger und die Serbische Frage* (Vienna, 1918) p. 152.

[3] Bogičević, *Procès*, p. 139.

[4] Stanojević, p. 61; KSF., October 1923, pp. 82-3.

[5] 'Those who knew Pašić intimately—writes L. Magrini—know how much weight can be attached to his statements and denials in the press. More than once the Serbian Premier's statements on one and the same theme were mutually contradictory, because in that way Pašić threw both friends and foes off the scent. He skilfully dispelled any uneasiness arising from these discrepancies by the convenient declaration that his ideas had been incorrectly

truth. Moreover if he had admitted giving that order to the Minister at Vienna it would have been the avowal that he had foreknowledge of the plot. It would have been awkward for Pašić to make such an admission and in any case, as L. Jovanović relates, he had decided not to do so. However the Serbian Government never officially denied what was stated by Spalaiković at St. Petersburg on 30 June, and it is unlikely that at that critical juncture he would have invented the story that the Austrian Government was forewarned of what was brewing at Sarajevo. That Spalaiković invented nothing is proved by a most important document brought to light by the publication in 1936 of Vol. X of the Third Series of the *Documents Diplomatiques Français* which reproduces the following note by Abel Ferry, the Under Secretary for Foreign Affairs, dated 1 July 1914:

I have received a call from Monsieur Vesnić, the Serbian Minister, with whom I keep up an old acquaintanceship and who as one friend to another (*en ami*) told me:

(1) That he regarded the outrage on the Archduke as a reply to the annexation of Bosnia. Prince (Alexander), moreover, was regarded as an *homme à poigne*. The Serbian Government had actually warned the Austrian Government that it had got wind of the plot.

(2) Discussing the disappearance of the aged Emperor from the scene, he said to me that the transfer of power would take place smoothly: the Jugoslav problem is evolving slowly and will not, in his opinion, be settled in less than some thirty years hence, unless some persecution and some policy à la Metternich came to hasten the evolution.[1]

An extraordinary document! The second part of it redounds to the credit of the Serbian authorities and corroborates that in 1914 when Serbia was finding it difficult to digest her enormous conquests made in the two Balkan wars, Pašić and the exponents of his views had no desire to bring about a hazardous settling of accounts with the Dual

---

reported. . . . His friends extolled his Byzantine quibbling, his craftiness, his coolness in moments of the greatest difficulty, his dissimulation which they interpreted as the supreme manifestation of his political wisdom. He was—they said—the most consummate Balkan political personality, an offshoot of the venerable Byzantine tree'. (Magrini, pp. 111–12.)

[1] DF. 3. X, 466. There is no reason to give credence to Henry Pozzi who in *Les Coupables* (Paris, 1935) asserts that on the morning of 9 July 1914, the French Government possessed definite evidence of Serbian guilt: 'The photograph of four telegrams in code addressed by Belgrade on 29 and 30 June and 1 and 2 July to Vesnić, the Serbian Minister in Paris; the photograph of a letter in which Colonel Dimitriević-Apis, Grand Master of the *Crna Ruka* (*Black Hand*) and organizer of the assassination, gave his Paris agent, the Military Attaché, details about the execution of the outrage; the original rough draft of Vesnić's reply; a copy of the Serbian Legation's secret code enabling the documents to be deciphered ' (p. 47). Not only does Pozzi give no proofs of his extraordinary statements, but it is improbable that Dimitriević, whose secretiveness is well known, would have hastened after the outrage to write a letter giving his friend details of its execution. This explains why Pozzi's book fell dead in France and England and practically so in Germany and why despite the serious nature of its alleged revelations it was never translated either into German or into English.

Monarchy. In the first paragraph there are phrases which are puzzling. Why, after linking the crime with the annexation of Bosnia-Herzegovina does Vesnić let fall the words: 'Prince (Alexander) moreover, was regarded as an *homme à poigne*?' Did the Serbian Minister peradventure suspect that the Prince had a hand in the plot? But that is by the way. What mainly concerns us is the statement in this first paragraph that the Serbian Government actually warned the Austrian Government that it had got wind of the plot. Now if on 1 July in. Paris Vesnić said the same thing as Spalaiković on the same or the previous day said in St. Petersburg, it is a sign that Pašić, possibly deeply concerned at the success of a plot which he had not seriously attempted to foil, telegraphed to both Ministers that Vienna had been put on its guard, regretting immediately afterwards that he had made the admission. That this is what he in fact did was told to Luciano Magrini as early as October 1915 by Major Milan Georgević and Colonel Lešanin who have already been mentioned. The Colonel, who was Serbian Military Attaché in Austria in 1914, and hence well informed, made his statement as follows:

The Serbian Government knew of the plot that was being hatched at Sarajevo; in fact a telegram from Pašić reached the Serbian Legation at Vienna in the first fortnight of June asking the Minister Jovan Jovanović to let the Austrian Government know that, owing to a leakage of information, the Serbian Government had grounds to suspect that a plot was being hatched against the life of the Archduke on the occasion of his journey to Bosnia. Since this visit might give rise to regrettable incidents on the part of some fanatic, it would be useful to suggest to the Austro-Hungarian Government the advisability of postponing the Archduke's visit.[1]

4. The Serbian Minister to Vienna carries out badly the instructions given him by Pašić.

All this shows that Ljuba Jovanović spoke the truth in disclosing that Pašić knew of the plot, and that the reports were true which stated that the Serbian Minister at Vienna received instructions to warn the Austrian Government. That, however, does not imply that the warning was actually given. It is a fact that J. Jovanović took no action in regard to Berchtold, whose statements to this effect are perfectly credible. J. Jovanović, previously consul at Uskub, was appointed Minister to Vienna at the end of 1912 in the middle of the First Balkan war. He was rumoured to have fomented disorders at the time of the annexation of Bosnia and even to have captained Comitaji bands. Thus he was not *persona grata* either at Court or at the Ballplatz. Dumaine, the French Ambassador to Vienna, in his book *La dernière ambassade de France en Autriche* writes of him as follows:

[1] Magrini, pp. 107, 115. See p. 97.

Feeling himself spied upon and traduced by the official world, slighted by his colleagues, who were disinclined to compromise themselves even for a just cause, he showed himself exceedingly grateful for the welcome I gave him. Count Berchtold was astonished that I should attach importance to anything he said and teased me for being so odd. 'Who ever believed the word of a Serb?' I heard the Archduchess Maria Josephine exclaim in all seriousness. . . . To be sure not all Serbs were of such candid innocence as the lamb in the fable; but the wolf in his ways of arguing did not show greater bias and effrontery than the Imperial Chancellery towards the Government of Belgrade.[1]

One thing is certain, that Jovan Jovanović had little contact with Berchtold, who preferred that he should deal with Bilinski, Joint Finance Minister and head of the administration of Bosnia-Herzegovina. Thus it was to Bilinski that J. Jovanović addressed himself in the matter of the Archduke's visit.[2] This is revealed by a letter signed H. Y. published in the *Wiener Sonn- und Montags-Zeitung* of 23 June 1924. It stated that on 18 June 1914 Pašić telegraphed to the Serbian Minister to Vienna requesting him

to dissuade the Archduke from going to Sarajevo or at least to warn him of the risk he would run.

The Minister reflected how to carry out so delicate a mission without damaging his own country and his first thought was to speak to Berchtold, but later he thought it would be better to bring up the matter with Bilinski which he did at noon on 21 June.

The authorship of this letter was attributed to G. Josimović who in June 1914 was Counsellor at the Serbian Legation to Vienna and who denied to Seton-Watson that he had written it. Seton-Watson thinks the writer was the anti-Serbian propagandist Leopold Mandl.[3] The disclosure in the letter of a *démarche* made by J. Jovanović with Bilinski led J. Jovanović to write to the *Neues Wiener Tagblatt* of 28 June 1924 that the warning had been given by him *of his own initiative*.

So far as I remember, my visit took place about 5 June. . . . I explained quite openly to the Minister what I had learned, namely that the manoeuvres were to be held in Bosnia on the Drin just opposite to Serbia, and that the Archduke himself would take command [in reality they took place elsewhere and the Archduke was not in command]. I said: . . . If this is true, I can assure your Excellency that it will arouse the greatest discontent among the Serbs who must regard this as an act of provocation. Manoeuvres in such circumstances are dangerous. Among the Serb youths there may be one who

[1] Dumaine, pp. 79–81.   [2] Fay, II, pp. 155–7.
[3] Seton-Watson, *Sarajevo*, p. 154.

will put a ball-cartridge in his rifle or revolver in place of a blank cartridge, and he may fire it, and the bullet might strike the man giving provocation. Therefore it would be good and reasonable that the Archduke should not go to Sarajevo; that the manoeuvres should not be held on *Vidov Dan*; and that they should not be held in Bosnia.

To these clear words Dr. von Bilinski replied that he . . . would inform me what result they had with the Archduke, although he himself could not believe in any such result of the manoeuvres as I foresaw; and that moreover he was in possession of information that Bosnia was completely quiet. A few days later I again called on Minister von Bilinski about this matter, but nevertheless had shortly to learn that the original programme would be followed and nothing changed in spite of my warning.[1]

Bilinski says nothing of all this in his *Memoirs*, merely deploring that he was not consulted on the measures to be taken for the protection of the Archduke—who, as we shall see, had desired that arrangements should be left in the hands of the local Governor, General Potiorek—and denying the rumour that he had made representations to the Emperor, a step which would have been quite out of place 'for I had no reason to interfere in this military journey'. And in fact at an audience granted two days after the crime the Emperor absolved Bilinski of all responsibility.[2]

Questioned during the war by an Austrian historian, Bilinski replied that he would like to spread the veil of oblivion over the whole subject.[3] But P. Flandrak, who in 1914 was chief of the Press department of the Austrian Finance Ministry, bore witness in the *Neues Wiener Journal* of 26 April 1925 to the *démarche* made by J. Jovanović, though without saying that the latter had mentioned the possibility of the Archduke's being hit by the bullet of a Serbian soldier and with the addition that, though Bilinski did not think it advisable for the Archduke to take the journey to Bosnia, he attached no importance to the Serbian Minister's words and did not report them to Berchtold, as was usual for him to do. Possibly the words were too general and there was too little mention of the reasons. One cannot, moreover, entirely overlook the fact that Bilinski felt a certain resentment against Francis Ferdinand for the latter's dislike of him. But in any case he would certainly not have remained indifferent and inactive if J. Jovanović had told him straight out that the Serbian Government had knowledge of a plot against the Heir Apparent. But this J. Jovanović did not do.

In a letter to J. Isaac of 31 December 1932, reaffirming that he had acted of his own initiative, Jovanović wrote:

Neither Pašić nor I knew that an outrage was being prepared at Sarajevo.

[1] *Neues Wiener Tagblatt*, No. 177, 28 June 1924; Fay, II, pp. 158–9.
[2] L. R. von Bilinski, *Wspomnjenja i Dokumenty* (Warsaw, 1924–5), I, pp. 273–7.
[3] L. Mandl, *Zur Warnung Serbiens an Österreich*, KSF., April 1924, pp. 108–9.

In a subsequent letter of 25 January 1933 he reiterated:

That the Serbian Government had any positive information, or that it planned or took part in the planning of the tragedy of St. Vitus's day, no, a thousand times no.[1]

All this emphasis, the unnecessary denial that Pašić had any hand in the plot—no one ever seriously suggested that he had—does not suffice to establish the view that Pašić remained without knowledge of the plot and was therefore in no position to telegraph instructing J. Jovanović to convey the information to Berchtold. Neither does it make one believe that the Serbian Minister to Vienna would have taken upon himself to advise the Austrian Government against proceeding with the plan of the Archduke's journey to Bosnia without instructions or permission from the Belgrade Government. It is true that at the beginning of the above-quoted letter to Isaac, J. Jovanović writes:

My warning was a suggestion to take certain measures in Bosnia and, as you know, Bilinski made attempts to tighten up the security service during the Archduke Francis Ferdinand's visit, running up against the opposition of the army authorities.

But to the *Neues Wiener Tagblatt* on the contrary J. Jovanović stated categorically that he ended his conversation with Bilinski not with a recommendation to take precautions but with the words:

Therefore it would be good and reasonable that the Archduke should not go to Sarajevo; that the manoeuvres should not be held on St. Vitus's day; that they should not be held in Bosnia.[2]

To form a clearer idea of what took place it is necessary to revert to the evidence collected in 1915 by Luciano Magrini from Colonel Lešanin, the former Serbian Military Attaché at Vienna, whom J. Jovanović at once informed of his talk with Bilinski. After giving details of the instructions telegraphed by Pašić to the Serbian Legation at Vienna,[3] Lešanin continues:

The Minister Jovan Jovanović felt extremely embarrassed; for two days he turned over in his mind the form that he would give to this delicate matter, which might be regarded as intimidation, to obtain the suspension of the journey. The telegram, moreover, was in general terms giving no particulars about the perpetrators. Personal relations between J. Jovanović and Berchtold were bad. What reception would Berchtold have given to a *démarche* of this kind and what interpretation would he have put upon it?

Jovan Jovanović decided to make his representations to the Finance Minister Bilinski, with whom he was on good terms and who had the adminis-

---

[1] Isaac, pp. 249–50, 255.
[2] *Neues Wiener Tagblatt*, 28 June 1924.   See above, p. 103.
[3] See above, p. 101.

tration of Bosnia-Herzegovina under his authority. J. Jovanović had no grounds for alleging the existence of a plot. Therefore he stressed in general terms the risks the Archduke might run from the inflamed state of public opinion in Bosnia and Serbia. Some serious personal misadventure might befall him. The journey might give rise to incidents and demonstrations which Serbia would deprecate but which would inevitably have repercussions on Austro-Serbian relations. It would be advisable to communicate these not entirely groundless fears of the Serbian Government to the Austrian Government before the journey was undertaken. He did not speak of the matter directly with Berchtold in order not to offend his feelings and because, in view of the relations between them, he feared to be misunderstood.

On his return to the Legation Jovan Jovanović said to Colonel Lešanin that he was concerned by the fact that, after a few minutes thoughtful silence, Bilinski showed no sign of attaching great importance to the communication and confined himself to remarking, when saying good-bye and thanking him: 'Let us hope nothing does happen.'[1]

It is of interest to note that J. Jovanović never denied the truth of what L. Magrini wrote and remained on the best terms with him. On the several occasions when Magrini questioned him, he displayed unwillingness to speak of the embarrassing question. It was evident that he was tied down by his earlier statements and was entirely engrossed in avoiding contradicting himself. This was also the impression gained by Slobodan Jovanović who had several conversations on the subject with his namesake and remained unconvinced of the truth of his account. On being reminded of Colonel Lešanin's statements, all that J. Jovanović answered was that he could not exactly remember what he had said, but that Lešanin had probably misunderstood his words and filled them out inaccurately. Asked later for a full and exact account of the terms he had used in his conversation with Bilinski, he replied on 11 January 1938 reverting to his first version.

It is understandable that Bilinski was not impressed by the vague expressions used. Certainly J. Jovanović could bring no proofs of the plot, nor was he in a position to name the perpetrators. But less than that would have sufficed to alert the Austrian authorities. He only needed to give the text of the telegram, i.e., in Lešanin's words, that

the Serbian Government had grounds to suspect that a plot was being hatched against the life of the Archduke on the occasion of his journey to Bosnia.

And to inform Berchtold, rather than Bilinski, of this news would not in the least have been an act of intimidation. It was far more serious and provocatory to warn against the Archduke's journey solely on grounds that the Austrian soldiers of Serbian race were in such a state of mind as to give rise to fears of an attempt on his life. This was indeed

[1] Magrini, pp. 115–16.

undue interference in the internal affairs of the Monarchy and Berchtold might have made a very different reply from that of the Slav Bilinski. Why, therefore, did Jovanović not take the straightforward course of calling on Berchtold and carrying out his instructions without delay and without taking any responsibility on his own shoulders?

5. Why J. Jovanović and Pašić took no effective action: the Oberdan precedent.

One cannot do otherwise than proceed by induction, noting that J. Jovanović was a frenzied Serb nationalist. On 23 May 1913 Descos, the French Minister to Serbia, notified Paris that J. Jovanović, then Serbian Minister in Vienna but home on leave in Belgrade, came to call on him full of the same fervour as at the time when the First Balkan war was in preparation. Descos's report continues:

> Now he is all against Austria: he says the time is drawing nigh; the Scutari question has deeply disturbed Austro-Italian relations; the Southern Slavs of the Austro-Hungarian Monarchy can no longer be held in; the effervescence among the Czechs is on the increase; before long the need will arise for an evolution towards federalism. Who is going to set in motion the downfall of Austria? It will be there and no longer in Montenegro that the next European crisis will originate.[1]

It is of interest to note this mention of the evolution toward federalism whose champion was Francis Ferdinand. In a letter to Isaac, J. Jovanović wrote that the Archduke

was immolated because at that moment he was the symbol of the tyranny, the yoke of the Jugoslavs in Austria-Hungary

and that

any other man in his place would have met with the same fate.[2]

We may be permitted to have doubts on this score and to think that the Archduke may have been immolated precisely because he had come round to the idea of federalism which seemed to perturb J. Jovanović. But to return to our story, in the very days when Pašić was sending instructions for giving Vienna warning of the plot, J. Jovanović was designated by the *Black Hand* to be Foreign Minister in the new Government which was to replace that of Pašić who had resigned. While the 'young Radicals' had expressed their readiness to adopt as their Foreign Minister Balugčić, the former secretary and friend of the King,

the *Black Hand* [reported Descos to Paris on 12 June 1914] which believed itself to be master of the situation, talked of putting into that office Jovan Jovanović, the Serbian Minister to Vienna, who is the diplomatist it trusts.[3]

---

[1] DF. 3. VI, 594.   [2] Isaac, p. 251.   [3] DF. 3. X, 363.

Pašić, however, was returned to power and J. Jovanović went back to Vienna. But was the embarrassment caused by Pašić's instructions (which were not in themselves embarrassing and did not require two days of meditation) partly due to fear of making a disclosure to the Austrian Government which would be extremely unwelcome to the *Black Hand* and its redoubtable chief? And was it consciousness of not having accomplished his duty which immediately made J. Jovanović anxious when Bilinski did not attach enough importance to his words, causing him to revert to the topic a few days later and, after the war, to deny the existence of the instructions telegraphed by Pašić and pretend that he had made those feeble representations on his own initiative, well knowing that Pašić could not contradict him, without admitting foreknowledge of the crime? We are—it is well to repeat—here in the realm of induction, not of proof, and it would be out of place to press the point. But it was needful to examine the question more closely because, if the Serbian Minister had informed Berchtold of what awaited the Archduke at Sarajevo, Francis Ferdinand in all probability would either not have gone there or would have been better guarded than he actually was, so that events would have taken another course. This hypothesis does not aim at attenuating the heavy responsibility that falls on Pašić. He knew that the conditions of his country and its army were extremely bad, and that Austria was watching her chance for a final round with Serbia. Consequently for all these reasons his craving was for peace. This is admitted even by one of Dimitrievič's brothers in arms when questioned by that bitter enemy of Pašić Bogičević. Here are his words:

Pašić seemed aghast that certain circles showed no sign of minding about peace. He feared that Tankosić's laboratory for making bombs and explosives would produce threats to peace. He feared that Austria would be provided with a pretext for an armed conflict with Serbia. For this reason in a confidential letter to Voivod Putnik, the Chief of Staff, Pašić drew attention to the fact that Colonel Dimitrievič was in touch with Bosnian student revolutionaries and that this might result in harmful consequences.[1]

It would be logical to suppose that on learning of the conspiracy against the life of Francis Ferdinand framed by Dimitrievič, a conspiracy which might well unleash the very conflict he feared, Pašić would resort to measures of the utmost vigour. His failure to do so can only be understood by taking account of his position between the *Black Hand* and Austria. On the one hand he dared not seize the conspirators and denounce their plot in Vienna. On the other hand he was afraid to allow a crime to be perpetrated which could be used by Austria as a pretext for attacking Serbia without intervention from her protectors. Yet another

---

[1] Bogičević, *Le Colonel Dragoutine Dimitrievič Apis* (Paris, 1928), p. 98.

factor to be taken into account is Pašić's own temperament. On 2 January 1938 the present writer wrote to Jovan Jovanović saying that in view of the fact that all the evidence which had come to light proved the Serbian Government's foreknowledge of the Sarajevo plot, he would beg Jovanović to tell him by whom and to what extent the Government was informed and what action it took. In his reply of 6 January Jovanović evaded the question with the following sibylline words which may be taken as an admission that Pašić had information of what was brewing but took refuge in a passive attitude:

The Serbian officers who participated in the plot of 29 May 1903, had taken the measure of enlisting in it also N. Pašić. When they divulged to him the preparations then being made against King Alexander Obrenović, Pašić replied that he would think the matter over and have a word with his friends. But when the day came for him to give his answer, he was absent from Belgrade: 'gone abroad'. Pašić never breathed a word to a single soul right until the end of the tragedy of 29 May 1903. In 1904 he was at daggers drawn with those very officers.

What else does this mean than that in 1914 Pašić was informed as he was in 1903? In 1914 he might mistakenly believe that by the orders sent to the frontier officials and by the warning given to the Austrian Government he could contrive to avert a catastrophe. He may even have reflected that conspirators and outrages rarely attain their object. In this case, however, none of his precautions took effect. Princip and his fellows slipped easily over into Bosnia, Bilinski kept Jovanović's words to himself, the outrage was attempted, and it succeeded.

Nevertheless Italians cannot judge the guilt of the Serbian Government by the same standards and with the same bitterness as the many whose main concern it is to lay the blame for the war everywhere except on Austria and Germany. Italians have every reason to know that those who govern a people struggling both to defend its own existence and to liberate its brothers from a foreign yoke have to reckon with emotions which sometimes burst forth in serious and dangerous manifestations. It is not always possible to oppose these with the necessary energy, more especially as the victories of the principle of nationality are won not only by the wisdom of the rulers but also by the co-operation of many diverse forces, some of which regrettably abandon legal methods and seek to cut the Gordian knot by rebellion, violence and terrorism. Were this not so, what right should Italians have to honour the memory of Guglielmo Oberdan?

In this connexion J. Jovanović in one of his conversations with the present writer made the following remark:

Even if the Serbian Government was aware of what was being prepared, it could not betray the perpetrators once they were across the frontier and send them to the gallows in Austria. Imagine the Rome Government having knowledge of the outrage planned by Guglielmo Oberdan. I believe that no Italian political figure could have betrayed him to the Austrian Government once he was across the frontier without causing an indignant and powerful revolt of public opinion.

The observation is to the point. It would be unfair, therefore, in judging the behaviour of the Serbian Government, to leave out of account the conditions prevailing at the moment in Serbia and in the Pan-Serb movement, just as it would be unfair to put the Serbian case and that of Austria on the same level. This, however, does not prevent our acknowledging that, by tolerating what he did, Pašić exposed his country to the danger of being attacked by Austria or of submitting to a drastic lowering of its political status without other countries coming to its aid.

6. The shadow of Dimitrievič; the Belgrade Government obstructs the search for the truth.

The *Entente*, after the Austrian ultimatum, took its stand with Serbia which thus escaped the danger of being left *tête à tête* with Austria-Hungary. Despite this support Serbia was invaded, and her Government, taking refuge in Corfu, in the darkest days of the war, had to face the problem whether to come to terms with the enemy. The allied victory saved her and enabled her to make the dream of Jugoslav unity come true.

It was, as has been said, the exultation engendered by the attainment of unity which gave the impetus to revelations as to the events leading up to it. Would it not surely have been more seemly, more worthy of all the sacrifices that had been made, the dangers run and the success that crowned them, would it not at the same time have been more intelligent not to suppress these revelations and leave history to tell the truth? Ljuba Jovanović, who more than all others was accused of indiscretions, remarked at the interview, already mentioned, which he gave *Politika* on 17 April 1925:

I have always held that in political life, whether in home or in international affairs, truth is the best ally and that a man does not err who takes his stand on the truth. In particular it is a sign of lack of good judgement to believe that the truth can be hidden about events which to-day interest the whole world and to the investigation of which the whole world devotes its attention. It cannot reasonably be imagined that in the face of such an impetus to investigate, any dissimulation, however skilful on our part, could successfully hide the truth.

So, indeed, it is! But the Serbian Government under Pašić let two years go by before contradicting L. Jovanović. Under Uzunović and

Ninčić the Government prevented Jovanović from producing proof of his assertions. It refrained from publishing the diplomatic documents relating to the whole tragedy. It stifled all disclosures, prohibited publications of which it did not approve, left points obscure which to-day still hinder a complete survey of events and a dispassionate assessment of responsibilities. To complete the picture it is here necessary to add that this behaviour of the Belgrade Government was motivated not only by fear of being saddled with the guilt for the war, but also by the repercussions of the Salonika trial.

If one talks with Serbs about the Sarajevo outrage and its origins, the conversation unfailingly comes round to the Salonika trial, whose chief victim dominates the background of the country's political life. Dimitrievič still enjoys widespread support and sympathy in Serbia. His case may be compared with that of Dreyfus and his death sentence is regarded even by independent minds as a vengeance on the part of the Regent, of Pašić, and of those working with him who feared Apis's powerful influence not only on the army but also in high spheres of public opinion and on the young generation. Those belonging to the Radical coalition, whose antagonist he was, would have had an interest in laying bare the part played by him in the assassination of the Austrian Heir Apparent. But, after the scandal aroused by the disclosures of Protić, Stanojević and L. Jovanović, they took refuge in silence for fear of the consequences to themselves. An example of this is the case of one of the perpetrators of the Sarajevo outrage, Vaso Čubrilović, professor of history at Belgrade University, who thus excuses himself for the evasive replies he gave the present writer:

It is still too early to speak of the Sarajevo outrage. It and the trial connected with it are still irons too hot to handle. Stanojević by attempting to write on the subject, rendered his last days wretched. L. Jovanović was attacked on all sides; a Serbian student, who was collecting material on the Sarajevo conspiracy and came also to me for information, had his house searched by the police and all the material which had cost him much time and money to collect was confiscated as soon as the police learnt what he was working on.

Years ago the Serbian Government published at its own expense an expurgated version of the proceedings of the Salonika trial. A few months later, concerned by the effects produced by this publication, they withdrew it from circulation and it is now impossible to procure a copy. The Marincović Cabinet contemplated the publication of the Serbian diplomatic documents and proposed to appoint a commission consisting of Professors Vlada Ćorović, Slobodan Jovanović and Jovan Jovanović which was to edit the material. But the Foreign Minister objected that this publication was a matter for his department. Slobodan Jovanović and Jovan Jovanović were left out, the documents were copied and Professor Ćorović—previously implicated in the Banjaluca trial and regarded as the obedient tool of the Foreign Ministry—was engaged to write a critical study of Austro-Serbian political relations in the last years before the outbreak of war on the basis of the diplomatic documents. Ćorović wrote his book which was weighed sentence by sentence at the Foreign Ministry before going to press. It was ready in 1935 but never appeared and it is impossible to procure a copy. Oskar Tartaglia's book *Veleizdajnik* dealing with the *Black Hand* and the Salonika trial was confiscated and the publication of another book by Tartaglia on the Salonika trial was prohibited.

A book on the Sarajevo plot written by Dragiza Stojadinović, the son-in-law of Ljuba Jovanović, was confiscated in 1936 when on the point of publication. An announcement had been made by the author that the book would reproduce important documents, and seems to have stated that the outrage was organized by Dimitrievic at the instigation of Berlin, which was seeking a pretext to start the World War —a grotesque supposition based perhaps on the partiality shown by the Germanophil Bogičević for Dimitrievic, on Dimitrievic's stay in Berlin in the summer of 1913 and probably on the desire of Dragiza Stojadinović to vindicate his father-in-law from the accusations and resentments aroused by the part he played in the Salonika trial. As if the confiscation were not enough, D. Stojadinović, who for years had carried on a violent campaign against the Prime Minister, his namesake but no relation, was arrested after there was an attempt on the Prime Minister's life in the Skupština, tried along with other political opponents and sentenced to three years' imprisonment. He was pardoned by the succeeding Government.

7. The Austro-Hungarian authorities' neglect of all precautions at Sarajevo.

If in Serbia the endeavour to suppress the truth has not prevented something of it from transpiring, in Austria no obstacle has been put in its path, not only because the downfall of the Monarchy threw open the doors of the archives, but also because the Austrians themselves contributed with scrupulous probity to the reconstruction of the facts. Thus it has become possible to refute the rumours of a complicity of Vienna and Budapest in the crime despite a series of circumstances such as might create the impression that the suppression of the Heir Apparent was desired in the two capitals, foremost among them being the failure of the authorities to take adequate measures for the Archduke's protection on his visit to Sarajevo.

No one in the Dual Monarchy could be ignorant of the state of mind prevailing in Bosnia or fail to foresee the dangers in store for Francis Ferdinand on a journey the announcement of which had brought threatening letters both to the Government and to the Archduke himself. In the Belgrade cafés, where Austrian agents abounded, it was openly said that he would never get back from Bosnia alive. Bosnian students who had come over into Serbia spoke in the same style. Pfeffer, an investigating judge at Sarajevo, writes that in his capacity as press monitor at the Governor's headquarters he had ample opportunities for following developments and observing the growth of fanaticism among both Serbs and Croats after the Serbian victories in the Balkan wars.

Having followed all this, I was amazed to read one day in the newspapers that Archduke Francis Ferdinand, actually on St. Vitus's day, was to visit Sarajevo officially and be welcomed by the mayor and municipality in the presence of all the citizens of Sarajevo.

He goes on to narrate that on the day before the outrage he met his brother-in-law, a judge in the penal division of the Provincial Governorship, with whom he discussed the Archduke's visit.

We both came to the conclusion that an outrage might very well happen because such a visit on that special day was a direct provocation to the Serbs.[1]

Bilinski was well aware of the state of things and warned the Sarajevo authorities.[2] It would have been incumbent on Bilinski to take measures, but he was on bad terms with the Governor, General Potiorek. The two men had conflicting views on the policy to be pursued in Bosnia. Bilinski on becoming, in 1911, Joint Finance Minister and thus also Minister for Bosnia-Herzegovina, sought with some success to attract the Bosnians into the orbit of the Monarchy. Potiorek on the other hand was an arrogant and violent reactionary and believed with Conrad that the Jugoslav question could only be solved by war. Hence he was by no means displeased with disturbances, demonstrations, and revolutionary deeds on the part of the youth of Bosnia as

---

[1] Pfeffer, pp. 22–3.

[2] Oe.-I'. VIII, 9663, 9693, 9882. During the World War a Croat, R. Bartulić, declared that, while in the service of the Austrian secret police, he learnt from a Zagreb municipal police official that the latter had anonymously received exact information about the plot with the names of the conspirators. This was transmitted to Budapest without effect, as was also a similar warning given to the police by Marco Gagliardi, a Zagreb lawyer, after a visit to Belgrade (G. Beck. *La Responsabilité de la Hongrie,* Paris, 1917, pp. 215–19). Later on Benno Klobučarić, in 1914 a Belgrade police commissioner, stated that he received information of the plot and was told not to attach any importance to the matter. Klobučarić also claims to have passed on Gagliardi's warning to Tisza, naming Princip and in vain asking for instructions (Milan *Secolo,* 28 July 1926). Raoul Chélard reports that Klobučarić was informed 'by anonymous letters first from Belgrade and then from America of all the names and particulars of the preparations for the outrage'. His superiors did not reply to his report and he received a discreet hint to take no action if one or other of the conspirators were to pass through his district. 'A few days later [continues Chélard] the Serbophil lawyer Marco Gagliardi, a Croat, arrived at Zagreb from Belgrade and also gave information of the plot that was being prepared' (Raoul Chélard, *La Responsabilité de la Hongrie,* Paris, 1930, pp. 162–3). These statements are undocumented and improbable. Historians attach no importance to them.

being conducive to war. While the Emperor approved of Bilinski and his policy, the Heir Apparent, by that very fact, suspected and opposed him and took sides with Potiorek.

It is a fact that Potiorek was informed by the Archduke of his forthcoming visit to Bosnia before Bilinski, who heard of it from Potiorek and was not consulted on the measures to be taken. He refrained from making objections on this score because, as he writes in his book, Francis Ferdinand had expressed the wish that the matter should be left in the hands of the Governor, as military chief. He did not warn the Emperor because he had no powers to act in the matter of a purely military journey, which became a political one without his being asked or informed.[1] Bilinski was so far ignored that, as a studied slight, the programme of the visit was circulated to all the other ministries except his and he received no invitation to the State ball at Ilidže.[2] This treatment was certainly no encouragement to him to report Jovan Jovanović's conversation to Berchtold, though Flandrak, one of his subordinates, contradicting statements of his own made in 1925, declared in 1928 that Berchtold was informed by Bilinski on the very day of the conversation.[3] Despite all this Bilinski, perturbed by the many letters he was receiving,

instructed Sarajevo to sound the local authorities as to their views on such a visit—with the result that practically all of them declined responsibility for the consequences. These reports were duly transmitted to Vienna and to the Court, but brought down upon Sarajevo a sharp reprimand: the responsibility of the civil authorities, they were told, was neither desired nor needed.[4]

The same reply was given by Potiorek to Zurunić, chief of the political department at Sarajevo, who twice called attention to the inadequacy of the police force in the town and to the difficulty of protecting the Archduke on the lengthy route he was to follow. 'The Archduke'—retorted Potiorek—'comes here as a general and you have nothing to do with the matter.' The Prefect of Sarajevo, too, was exceedingly perturbed, especially as the General's arrogance was not accompanied by any effective measures, although he perfectly well knew the state of mind prevailing among the young Bosnians and hence the danger of the Heir Apparent in making an official visit to Sarajevo on St. Vitus's day. But as J. Jovanović remarks in a letter to J. Isaac, all Potiorek's undertakings, whether military or civil, despite his reputation as one of the best generals of the Monarchy and the fact that he

[1] Bilinski, *Wspomnienia i Dokumenty* (*Reminiscences and Documents*) (Warsaw, 1924–5), I, p. 273.
[2] Seton-Watson, *Sarajevo*, p. 107.
[3] P. Flandrak, *Die falsche Deutung der Bilinskischen Warnung durch Senator de Jouvenel*, in KSF., December 1928, p. 1154.
[4] Seton-Watson, *Sarajevo*, p. 106.

was nearly made Chief of Staff instead of Conrad, were dogged by ill-luck, culminating in the Austrian defeat in Serbia at the end of 1914.[1] We learn from a telegram sent to Potiorek by Bilinski on 3 July that at Sarajevo there were only 120 police.

Moreover, though 70,000 troops were concentrated within no great distance for purposes of the manoeuvres, there was none the less no proper lining of the streets. In short, we can safely endorse the words of . . . Baron Margutti, who declares that the inadequacy of the precautions 'baffled every description'. The best proof of this is to compare them with those adopted on the very similar occasion of the Emperor's state visit to Sarajevo as recently as 1910. Every street along which he passed was lined with a double cordon of troops, the town swarmed with special police . . . and hundreds of individuals in Sarajevo were forbidden to leave their houses during the Emperor's stay.[2]

On 3 July, Bilinski wrote to Potiorek:

Had I been informed by reports from Your Excellency that the police administration was not equal to its task, it would have been our joint duty to prevent the journey at all costs. Already the fact, semi-officially published in the Sarajevo press, that the political authorities had only 120 police at their disposal, gave me a shock. Any request for a credit for an increase of the guard would of course have been granted immediately; moreover, I am sure that the gendarmerie would have acted as an excellent auxiliary to the police.[3]

Potiorek, at variance with the truth, defended himself by asserting that the precautions taken were the same as those for the Emperor's visit in 1910.

Against assassins who do not fear to die—he claimed—no lesser precaution would have sufficed than the total evacuation of the town.[4]

But the contrast was so great that at the Council of Joint Ministers held on 7 July the Hungarian Premier, Tisza, commented:

the most indescribable conditions must have reigned in the police force for six or seven individuals known to the police to be able on the day of the outrage to take up positions along the route of the murdered Heir Apparent armed with bombs and revolvers, without any of them being noticed and removed by the police.[5]

Seton-Watson writes:

Small wonder then if in the excited atmosphere of war many, both at home and abroad, should have rejected mere negligence as an adequate explanation of the crime, and if the theory of official complicity on the part of Vienna or Budapest gained considerable credence![6]

Even Judge Pfeffer does not hesitate to write:

[1] Isaac, pp. 256–8, 263–5.   [2] Seton-Watson, *Sarajevo*, pp. 108–9.
[3] Oe-U. VIII, 10029.   [4] Conrad, IV, pp. 65–6.
[5] Oe-U. VIII, 10118.   [6] Seton-Watson, *Sarajevo*, p. 111.

I had the impression that the Archduke Francis Ferdinand was sent on purpose to Sarajevo in the hope that this event would give rise to a demonstration which might provide a pretext for a conflict with Serbia. My brother-in-law (who is also a judge at Sarajevo) and I both, however, came to the conclusion that certainly the route would be lined by the troops present in Bosnia for the manoeuvres, exactly as it had been a few years before when the Emperor Francis Joseph came to Bosnia. In that case an outrage could hardly have been successful. But towards evening, as soon I as was alone, I came to the conclusion that there were two possibilities. Either ruling circles with their limited mental horizon had failed to foresee the danger to which they were exposing the Heir Apparent, or, if they did foresee it, they feigned to take so little account of it in order to provoke an incident.[1]

Things were in such a state that the inadequate precautions taken by the police were even revealed by an Austrian agent to the conspirator Čabrinović.[2] Another police agent, who recognized young Čabrinović on the street and knew that he had been expelled from Bosnia in 1912, warned the Chief of Police but received the reply: 'Leave him alone.' As the son of a notorious Austrian police *Konfident* the young man was assumed not to be dangerous.[3] Nevertheless there are not the slightest grounds for supposing that all this negligence was in accordance with Potiorek's wishes, even though to the general amazement he remained at his post unpunished after the crime. It is sufficient to bear in mind that, in not taking precautions against possible attack, he himself ran the risk of being assassinated, as he was to be seated in the Archduke's car. Čabrinović's bomb, for instance, might easily have hit him, and Princip at his trial deposed that, in firing his second shot which killed the Duchess, he was aiming at Potiorek.[4]

8. *The sense of relief in Austro-Hungarian political circles at the news of the Archduke's death ; the disgraceful arrangements for the funeral of the Archduke and his consort.*

Suspicions of Austrian complicity were certainly not dispelled by the behaviour of the Emperor and his Court on hearing the news of the outrage. It caused a real scandal to see how the antipathy felt for the Heir Apparent in the highest circles of the Monarchy stifled all sense of compassion in the presence of so great a tragedy, and gave rise to disgraceful funeral arrangements.

One of the leading Viennese journalists, Heinrich Kanner, editor of *Die Zeit* at the end of the war, writes that

the death of Archduke Francis Ferdinand, leaving aside the group of his special adherents, came as a relief in wide political circles even to the highest official circles.[5]

---

[1] Pfeffer, pp. 22-3.   [2] *Obzor*, 22 July 1926; KSF., September 1926, pp. 641, 722.
[3] Seton-Watson, *Sarajevo*, p. 113.   [4] Mousset, p. 130.
[5] Kanner, *Katastrophenpolitik*, p. 192.

Bülow, too, relates that the Austrian Ambassador to Berlin, the Hungarian Count Szögyény, said to him in conversation that the outrage was 'a dispensation of Providence' because the Archduke 'might have given rise to serious conflict, even perhaps to civil war. . . . '*Requiescat in pace*'—he ended.[1] This 'dispensation of Providence' brought the Monarchy to something worse than civil war, to its extinction. Francis Joseph's opinions on the crime seem not to have been very different from those of his Ambassador, to judge by what is narrated by Margutti, not, it is true, an altogether trustworthy witness:

On hearing the news—he relates—the Emperor collapsed into the armchair at his desk as if struck by a thunderbolt. He remained motionless for a long time. At the end he rose, paced the room a prey to the most violent agitation, his eyes rolling with terror. 'Horrible . . . Horrible! . . .' was the only word which escaped his lips. At last he seemed to have somewhat recovered his self control, for he exclaimed suddenly as if speaking to himself: 'The Almighty is not mocked! . . . Order, which I, alas, had not the strength to maintain, has been restored by a Higher Will.'[2]

The most widely believed version is that his words were: 'It is God's will.'

One thing certain is that he resigned himself so speedily and so easily to God's will that on 2 July, four days after the crime, granting an audience to the German Ambassador, he spoke of all kinds of things, shooting plans, the recent death of General Pollio, the Italian Chief of Staff, regarded as a faithful friend of the Triple Alliance, but not a word of the Archduke's murder.[3] When he saw Conrad on 5 July he never asked a question about the outrage nor an opinion on who were its instigators. Conrad remarked that he had been afraid of differences of opinion with the Archduke at the manoeuvres, but that they had remained on the best of terms. Francis Joseph replied that Francis Ferdinand had greatly improved of late and that he reproached himself for not having advised against the journey when the Archduke asked him whether it would not be advisable to drop it on account of the intense heat which was trying to one in his state of health.[4]

And that was all! But the true feelings of the Emperor and his Court were revealed at the funeral, the ceremonial of which was arranged by

---

[1] Bülow, III, pp. 135-6.

[2] Margutti, *La tragédie des Habsbourg* (Vienna, no year), pp. 81-2; *The Emperor Francis Joseph and his Times* (London, 1921), pp. 138-9. In an article published in the Vienna *Freiheit*, of October 1928, under the title *Franz Josef und Katharina Schratt*, the anonymous author, who derived his information from Frau Schratt herself, writes: It was known exactly what words were uttered by Francis Joseph on receiving the tragic news from Count Paar. The version which most deserves credence is that he exclaimed with a deep sigh: 'It is God's will!' It is certainly not true that he repeated the words he had uttered at the death of the Empress Elizabeth: '*Mir wird nichts erspart*' ('I am spared nothing') (Magrini, p. 143).

[3] DD. I, 11.   Conrad, IV, p. 37.

the Chief Controller of the Imperial Household, Prince Montenuovo. A grandson of Napoleon's second wife Marie Louise by her morganatic marriage with Neipperg, Montenuovo felt a special aversion for the Archduke and his consort. But in any case he could not do otherwise than carry out the orders from the Emperor who after the funeral thanked Montenuovo in an autograph letter for having carried out the ceremony 'in accordance with His Majesty's intentions'. The remains of the two deceased were conveyed from Sarajevo to the Dalmatian coast and thence by warship to Trieste, reaching Vienna at 10 p.m. on 2 July. Montenuovo had wished that nobody should be present at the station to receive them, so that the remains of the Duchess might be conveyed unobserved straight to Artstetten, the castle at which the Archduke had built a memorial chapel where he would be buried beside his wife. Thus the Duchess's funeral would not have taken place at the same time as that of the Archduke. But the new heir to the throne, Archduke Charles, attended at the station with the whole officer corps of the Vienna garrison and reverently escorted the cortège to the Hofburg Chapel where the coffins were placed side by side. Placed on different levels they were different in size and finish. That of the Archduke bore his full insignia, that of the Duchess only a pair of white gloves and a black fan, reminders of her former subordinate station as lady in waiting. Neither the Emperor nor the Archdukes sent wreaths. The only flowers were those sent by the diplomatic corps and the Hohenberg children, who, however, were not allowed to attend their parents' funeral service. It was also marked by the absence of all foreign royalties.[1]

As early as 28 June Tschirschky had telegraphed to Berlin that he had intimated to Avarna the advisability, in the interests of Austro-Italian relations, of Italy's being represented at the funeral with all possible solemnity and impressiveness.

The Duke of Avarna eagerly took up the idea and said it would be of great help to his endeavours in this matter in Rome, if he could officially hear from me as soon as possible that His Majesty, our Gracious Master, was going to attend the obsequies in person.[2]

On the same day Kaiser Wilhelm telegraphed to Tschirschky that he had decided to attend the Archduke's funeral at Vienna and that this information should be communicated to Avarna. The King of England was to be represented by Prince Arthur of Connaught.[3] But on the 29th, as is shown by a telegram from Bunsen, the English Ambassador to Vienna, Berchtold intimated to him and his colleagues that Francis Joseph, who had that morning arrived in the capital, had 'expressed the wish that the Archduke's funeral should not be attended

---

[1] Seton-Watson, *Sarajevo*, pp. 103-4.   [2] Bach, p. 11.   [3] BD. XI, 12, 26.

by any foreign royalties', because it was 'most important to spare the Emperor fatigue and keep the ceremony as short as possible'. Bunsen asked Berchtold whether Wilhelm would attend in any case and Berchtold answered that he did not yet know, but that in that case the Kaiser would do so as an intimate friend of the deceased.[1] But on 1 July Berlin received a telegram from the German Consul at Sarajevo advising against his Sovereign's visit to Vienna as being dangerous at the moment. Hence on the morning of the 2nd the Chancellor telegraphed to Tschirschky that he had persuaded the Kaiser not to go.[2]

'Thus unfortunately'—comments August Bach—'the chance was lost of personal conversations at Vienna.'[3] It has been said that Berchtold did not want foreign royalties to attend the funeral for fear their discussions with Francis Joseph might hinder his aggressive designs. Naumann, however, maintains on the contrary that Berchtold would have liked the Emperor to ask the royalties coming to Vienna for help in obtaining adequate compensation from Serbia, in the hope that from a sense of monarchical solidarity they would not refuse, and that he was sincerely distressed by Montenuovo's arrangements.[4]

The royalties did not come. The funeral, which should have been an impressive demonstration. of the unity and prestige of the Hapsburgs and their determination not to bend the knee to a fate that had doomed two Heirs Apparent to violent death, was a sorry and shabby affair. It only served to reveal the tottering condition of the Monarchy which even in the midst of such bereavement could not present a united front to the world. The funeral service on the afternoon of 3 July, conducted by the Cardinal-Archbishop in the tiny Hofburg chapel, was attended only by the Emperor and the Court. After the ceremony the chapel was closed, and not until after dark did the funeral procession leave the palace. Only at the last moment was permission given for troops to line the route, and this as the result of a protest from the aristocracy who had not been invited to the funeral. They were so indignant at the lack of respect shown to the two deceased that about 150 members of the highest Austrian and Hungarian families, headed by Count Chotek, the Duchess's brother, in gala uniform but on foot, forced their way into the procession and accompanied it as far as the station.

The train left at eleven o'clock reaching the little country station of Pöchlarn about one in the morning. . . . As though the very elements had conspired to mark the unusual tragedy of the occasion, one of the most terrific thunderstorms of recent years burst over the Danube at the very moment when the cortège was about to leave Pöchlarn. Torrential rain threw everything into confusion, the coffins were hastily carried into the tiny

[1] BD. XI, 18; DF. 3. X, 453; *Int. Bez.* i. IV, 17.
[2] DD. I, 6a and 6b; Bach, pp. 12–13.   [3] Bach, p. 13.
[4] Victor Naumann, *Profile* (Munich, 1925), p. 229.

waiting-room. . . . In the first summer dawn the victims of Sarajevo were borne across the Danube and up the hilly road to Artstetten where Francis Ferdinand had built his memorial chapel because the wife of his choice was too low-born to rest in the stifling Hapsburg vaults of the Capucine Church in Vienna.[1]

If this is what happened in Austria, still less was it likely that in Hungary adequate tribute would be paid to the memory of a prince who had planned to liberate the other nationalities from the yoke of the Magyar magnates. Max Müller, the English Consul-General at Budapest, sent a long report on this subject to Grey on 14 July, describing how the crime was followed by no sign of public mourning. However in the Chamber, Count Apponyi expressed regret that the funeral was not conducted with the ceremonial due to the Head of the Army and Navy and that the occasion had been lost for giving an impressive demonstration of national unity. Andrassy put his finger on the vital spot when he asked why the Archduke's visit to Sarajevo had been fixed for the day of the Serbian national holiday, why adequate precautions were not taken, and why the programme was proceeded with after the first attempt. Tisza extricated the Government by saying that the Archduke had made his journey as Commander-in-Chief of the Army without consultation with the two Governments.[2] But both Governments had known in advance of the journey and of the dangers it offered. Having made no attempt to prevent the outrage, they were then to exploit it by adopting that violent solution of the Serbian problem in regard to which the Archduke had opposed them since 1909.

Thus by the faults and negligence of both the Serbian and the Austro-Hungarian Governments, the tragedy was brought about which sent the Monarchy to its doom, caused the downfall of two other great empires, and had tragic consequences for European peace and civilization.

[1] Seton-Watson, *Sarajevo*, pp. 104–6; DF. 3. X, 494.　　　　[2] BD. XI, 70.

CHAPTER IV

AUSTRO-GERMAN INTENTIONS AFTER THE SARAJEVO DRAMA

1. *Reactions to the crime within the Dual Monarchy.*

The indignation aroused in the Dual Monarchy by the assassination played into the hands of those who, though they had hated the Archduke and feared his accession to the throne, now clamoured for vengeance against Serbia, on whose territory they assumed the outrage to have been planned. At Sarajevo, as in other Bosnian towns, anti-Serbian disturbances broke out which the authorities took no measures to prevent. The Hotel Europa and other premises belonging to rich Serbians, the Serbian school and the premises of two Serbian newspapers were wrecked and Potiorek proclaimed a state of siege. Disorders occurred in Dalmatia, and in Vienna there were demonstrations outside the Serbian Legation. All this, however, might be transient and without serious consequences. A greater danger was the immediate creation of a general opinion in responsible quarters that the moment had come for a final settlement of accounts with Serbia in order to prevent the Monarchy from disintegrating. All diplomatic reports to foreign governments agree on this, though some of the most authoritative Austro-Hungarian newspapers such as the *Neue Freie Presse* and the *Pester Lloyd*, as well as the official press, observed a moderation which may have been prompted by the necessity of concealing the true intentions of the Government but which did not counteract the impression produced by the violence of the rest of the press.

This violence was only to be expected. Ever since 1909 there had been the cry for war with Serbia. Several times it had been on the point of breaking out. But each time Russia had advised Belgrade to yield and Vienna had lacked the will to take the plunge, partly because of opposition from Francis Joseph and Francis Ferdinand, partly during the Balkan wars because of Berchtold's hesitation due to doubts of German support and the feeling that Italy could not be relied on. The Triple Alliance was in essence defensive, not offensive. Hence if Austria attacked Serbia and was then attacked by Russia, the *casus foederis* would not arise for the other allies. It is true that in January 1909 with the authorization of Bülow and the approval of the Kaiser a correspondence had taken place between Conrad and Moltke laying down that in case of war Germany would leave only thirteen divisions in East Prussia and would hurl the bulk of her forces against France while Austria would take the offensive against Russia in Galicia. To Conrad on 21 January 1909 Moltke had written:

It is to be foreseen that the time will come when the longanimity of the Monarchy in face of Serb provocation will come to an end. Then nothing will remain but for her to enter Serbia. I think that nothing else than the entering of Serbia by Austria would, in the event, lead to active intervention by Russia. This would provide the *casus foederis* for Germany. . . . The moment Russia mobilizes, Germany also will mobilize, and will unquestionably mobilize her whole army.

Moltke ended his letter with the assurance:

H.M. the Kaiser and His Grace the Prince Chancellor have taken cognizance of the content of the present letter.[1]

The 1909 arrangement did not give Austria a free hand to attack Serbia and start a European war without Germany's knowledge and consent. In other words, according to the letter, the Triplice remained unchanged. Nevertheless there was a change in the spirit of Austro-German relations. A momentous precedent had been set up, namely that in certain circumstances Germany might agree to let Austria-Hungary make an end of Serbia even if it meant Germany's supporting her in a clear act of aggression.

In the two years that had just passed the international situation had grown steadily worse because of the growing tension between Austria and Serbia. The General Staffs of the Triplice Powers had negotiated agreements in anticipation of a conflict which was regarded as imminent. The atmosphere was tense with expectancy of war, a spark would suffice to fire the powder barrel. What better card could Austria hold than the Sarajevo outrage? It was not then known that the crime was

[1] Conrad, I, pp. 379–84; see Vol. I, p. 270.

organized in Belgrade. Its perpetrators were actually Bosnians. But it was easy to believe—as was indeed the case—that it was the fruit of Serb irredentism and that this was a threat to the integrity of the Monarchy.

Indeed when Conrad learnt the news of the Sarajevo drama, he felt that for the Monarchy 'the hour had struck with shrill clangour'. He interrupted his tour of inspection and telegraphed the Emperor's military chancery then at Ischl, asking whether he should continue his tour or return to Vienna. The answer came back: 'Return to Vienna at His Majesty's command'.[1] Already in February he had written to Moltke: 'What are we waiting for?' On 16 March he had talked with the German Ambassador Tschirschky suggesting an early war with Russia. The Ambassador's reply had been: 'Two important people are against it, your Archduke Francis Ferdinand and my Kaiser' and he had added that only under the compulsion of a *fait accompli* would they resolve to go to war.[2] On 16 May he had at Carlsbad discussed the probabilities of war with Moltke who had said that the longer they waited the worse their chances would be.[3] After the Sarajevo crime Conrad said to Chlumecky:

In the years 1908–9 it would have been a game in which we could see all the cards ('*ein Spiel mit aufgelegten Karten*'), in 1912–13 it would have been a game with some chances of success ('*ein Spiel mit Chancen*'), now it is a sheer gamble ('*ein va banque-Spiel*').

But :

Now in 1914 we are under the compulsion of an unavoidable act of self-defence, which has been thrust upon us.[4]

On arriving at Vienna on 29 June Conrad said to his intimates who were waiting for him in his office

that the outrage was a Serbian machination, that it had created an extremely serious situation and would lead to war with Serbia; this brought with it the danger that Russia and Roumania would have to be counted as enemies.

It was not the professional soldier's hankering after a war that prompted him to speak thus. He was no less opposed than Francis Ferdinand to the dualism that was undermining the Monarchy and thought that Austria-Hungary should press forward into the Balkans and absorb Serbia and Montenegro. But as a preliminary he judged it necessary first to come to grips with Italy, and this had encountered opposition from Francis Joseph and Aehrenthal. Hence no time must now be lost in attacking Serbia after having missed the two opportunities

[1] Conrad, IV, p. 18. [2] Conrad, III, p. 597.
[3] Conrad, III, 670. [4] Conrad, IV, p. 72.

offered by the annexation of Bosnia and the Balkan wars. Conrad develops his views as follows:

Two principles stood in sharp conflict: the preservation of Austria-Hungary as a conglomerate of different nationalities, presenting a unity to the outer world under a single sovereign; the rise of separate independent national states which would attract their co-nationals in Austro-Hungarian territory and bring about the disintegration of the Monarchy.

The long smouldering conflict between these principles had, owing to the action of Serbia, assumed an acute form; a decision could no longer be postponed. That and not expiation of the murder was the reason why Austria-Hungary was forced to unsheath the sword against Serbia. That was what made the situation so serious. To take the side of Serbia was to will the downfall of the Austro-Hungarian Monarchy, or at least to work unwittingly for it.

Austria-Hungary cannot let the challenge pass with cool equanimity nor, after the blow on the one cheek, offer the other in Christian meekness, neither is it a case for a chivalrous encounter with 'poor little' Serbia, as she likes to call herself, nor for atonement for the murder—what is now at issue is the strictly practical importance of the prestige of a Great Power, of one which till now by continual acquiescence and long suffering (therein lay its mistake) had given an impression of impotence and allowed its enemies within and without to grow more and more arrogant, so that these enemies resorted to increasingly drastic methods to bring about the disintegration of the ancient empire.

Any further yielding now after Serbia's deed of violence would unleash those tendencies within the empire which in the form of Southern Slav, Czech, Moscowphil, Roumanian propaganda and Italian irredentism are already shaking at the foundations of the historic structure. Thus the Hapsburg Monarchy is left no other device than to cut the Gordian knot. . . . The favourable occasions for combating this inexorable menace were missed years ago. In vain did I at that time exhort to action. How easy would it be for me now to play the part of the unheeded warner, standing aside and saying 'You would not listen to me, now pull your own cart-wheels out of the quagmire'. But this is not the time for such reproaches. Duty now bids us place ourselves unreservedly at the service of those upon whose shoulders rests the burden of deciding this great question, strengthening them in their arduous task and concentrating all forces on the ordeal that lies ahead. The Sarajevo outrage has toppled over the house of cards built up with diplomatic documents, in which Austro-Hungarian policy thought it dwelt secure, the Monarchy has been seized by the throat and forced to choose between letting itself be strangled and making a last effort to defend itself against attack.[1]

From his own point of view Conrad may have been right. But even if he were not, the destinies of the Dual Monarchy at this critical turning point would have had to be in very different hands for the

[1] Conrad, IV, p. 30-1.

words of the Chief of Staff to encounter resistance. It is not impossible
to conceive that there might have been a statesman at the Ballplatz
strong enough after the Sarajevo tragedy to stand up against an environment which had long clamoured for war and now demanded it at all
cost. But certainly Berchtold was not the man from whom to ask such
a proof of strength. His prestige had been greatly shaken by his notable
failures in 1912–13. A great part of the attempts he had then made to
wrest from Serbia the fruits of her victories had failed. The Prince of
Wied, his choice for the throne of Albania, was about to lose his throne
ignominiously. Roumania had gone over to Russia and was lost to the
Triple Alliance. Between Serbia and Montenegro negotiations were in
train for a union which would but intensify the Serbian menace. With
Italy relations had grown steadily more strained in actual fact if not
officially. Something had to be done to remedy the situation. Should it
be a mobilization against Serbia, as Conrad proposed to Berchtold in a
conversation they had on 29 June? Berchtold objected that 'the outward occasion was lacking and that public opinion must first be prepared'. Did Conrad not think a revolution might break out in Bohemia?
Conrad answered: 'Do not let anyone persuade you of such a thing.'
But Berchtold still seemed disinclined to resort to force though agreeing
that the moment had come to settle the Serbian question and proposing
to raise the matter with the Emperor who had that day returned to
Vienna from Ischl. But how could the Serbian question be solved?

We send Serbia a demand to dissolve certain societies, relieve the Minister
of Police of his post etc.

Conrad replied:

The Serbs will calmly relieve the Minister of Police of his post; it will have
no effect; nothing will have effect but the use of force.

The discussion was renewed the following day, 1 July, Berchtold
saying that the Emperor was inclined to await the results of the inquiry
at Sarajevo while the Prime Ministers of Austria and Hungary were
advocating keeping a cool head.

Tisza is against war with Serbia, he fears Russia may strike at us and
Germany leave us in the lurch, Stürgkh on the other hand thinks that the
inquiry may furnish us with a reason for taking action.

Conrad however

took the point of view that only a display of force could avert the threat from
Serbia. The murder committed under Serbian patronage was the ground for
war. To the doubt, shared also by Berchtold, that Germany and Roumania
might leave us in the lurch, I answered that if that were the state of our
alliance with Germany, our hands were certainly tied. Berchtold told me

he had prepared a memorandum asking Germany to see that Roumania remained true to the Triple Alliance. I replied that Germany must first of all be asked whether she will cover our rear against Russia or not.[1]

These jottings of Conrad's would convey the impression that Berchtold had not yet made up his mind to drastic action against Serbia. In a note he sent to Conrad on 1 July there is no hint of any such move. He speaks of laying Austrian views on the Balkan situation before Berlin, stressing the need for a clarification of Austro-Roumanian relations both political and military.

I have had a memorandum drafted for His Majesty and Kaiser Wilhelm dealing with the whole complex of Balkan questions, in particular with the political relation of Roumania to the Monarchy and Triple Alliance. The military aspect is barely touched upon and the pamphlet would therefore need a short *aide mémoire* setting forth the effects which the neutrality and possible hostility of Roumania would have for the Monarchy and all the Triplice Powers in a European war. . . .[2]

But the fact remains that Tisza, who had gone to Vienna on 29 July to offer his condolences to the Emperor and had then called on Berchtold, learnt from the latter 'of his intention to make the Sarajevo outrage the occasion for a settlement of accounts with Serbia',[3] in other words for attacking her and putting her at the mercy of the Monarchy. So explicit was Berchtold on this point that Tisza, as we shall shortly see, was moved to send a protest to Francis Joseph. What is the explanation of the contradiction between Berchtold's language to Conrad and to Tisza? Obviously he could feign hesitancy with Conrad for fear the impetuous General might go prematurely into action, but not with the Hungarian Premier, the most forceful, dominating, and influential figure among the men who governed the Monarchy. Thus it would seem that what Berchtold said to Tisza was the expression of his real intentions. Hence those historians are right who, judging by appearances and by facts, conclude that Berchtold after the Sarajevo murder became the mouthpiece of the war party. It remains to be seen whether he did so from conviction or from inability to resist the pressure of those surrounding him. By temperament he was certainly not inclined to shoulder responsibilities and face storms of this kind. The German historian Hermann Lutz justly remarks:

He was by nature not of a martial turn of character but on the contrary soft, dependent, easily swayed, a man of exquisite manners and personal charm. His hesitating, irresolute behaviour in the Balkan wars had roused sharp criticism. Yet as early as the autumn of 1913 he had been won over to the idea of a war with Serbia. It seemed to him more and more necessary for the preservation of the Monarchy. After the assassination he seems to have

---

[1] Conrad, IV, pp. 33–5.   [2] Oe-U. VIII, 9976.   [3] Oe-U. VIII, 9978.

fallen deeply under the influence of the strong-willed Chief of Staff, Conrad.
Further as Chief of Section at the Ballplatz and regarded as its *spiritus rector*
there was Count Forgach, a bitter foe of the Serbs. And finally one must not
overlook the activities of Tschirschky, who at that moment did more to
stiffen Count Berchtold's backbone than was authorized by his instructions
from Berlin.[1]

That, once the decision was made, Berchtold appeared to hesitate,
and even ended by hoping Providence would work the miracle of
tiding him over this crisis, too, is highly probable, not to say certain,
as we shall later see.

2. *Tisza opposed to war. Francis Joseph's anger with Serbia. Victor Naumann
urges Vienna to go to war.*

This is the moment to give a rapid sketch of the man who opposed
Berchtold's intention and greatly outweighed him in authority, will
power, and strength of character, the commanding figure of Stefan
Tisza. The son of Koloman Tisza, leader of the Liberal party and Prime
Minister of Hungary from 1875 to 1890, he had been greatly helped in
his political career by his father's position. But he had also undergone
a sound training which included university studies at Berlin and Heidel-
berg. This was at the time when Bismarck was at the height of his glory
and the young Tisza learnt to admire the Iron Chancellor to whose
achievements he devoted the only book he ever wrote (*Von Sadowa bis
Sedan*).

There was a saying that all the Tiszas·had three ruling passions: the
Bible, politics and horses. Stefan Tisza was nicknamed the 'Bible man'.
His strict Calvinism revealed itself in his regard for principle, his sense
of duty and his complete straightforwardness. As a human being he
was devoid of charm but he had a compelling personality. 'After Bismarck'—writes one of his biographers—'no one ever produced a
deeper impression on those who surrounded him.' He was a harsh,
forceful character, as hard with himself as he was with others. One day
some members of his party complained of his neglecting them. His
answer was 'What would become of me if I had to be considerate even
to my friends?'[2] Adhering to his father's policy of loyalty to the Crown
and friendship with Austria, he was one of the foremost upholders of
the alliance with Germany, regarding it as the only possibility of salvation for his country in the event of a European war, the danger of
which he fully recognized. In his view the Dual Monarchy was a
necessity for Hungary and the King was the only link holding the other
nationalities of Hungary together under the Crown of St. Stephen. In
return Hungary was a necessity for the Monarchy, its healthiest and

---

[1] Lutz, p. 55.
[2] William Martin, *Les hommes d'état pendant la guerre* (Paris, 1929), pp. 80–3.

most vigorous element being the Magyars. Force was the only thing he understood and admired, and he thought that Hungary should be the dominant partner in the Monarchy as being the only strong element. He regarded the army as the foundation of the state and, while a large part of the Hungarian population demanded that Magyar should be the language used in the army, he accepted the King's point of view that there should be only one language of command and that the army should not be divided in two. A personality of this stamp could never be a popular figure. He was a King's man who would not hear of universal suffrage on the ground that the people were not sufficiently advanced. The nationalists of Kossuth's party demanded universal suffrage in order to impose the will of the nation on the King; Tisza on the contrary defended the Crown.

In political life he disdained cleverness, all the more because, not being gifted with eloquence, he could never hope to gain his way by the spoken appeal. He had a distaste for parliamentary tactics and preferred forceful means. Becoming Prime Minister in 1903 he tried in 1904 to break the obstructionism that was holding up parliamentary business by getting the Chamber to pass a new set of rules of procedure. The result was that the Opposition parties formed themselves into a *bloc* and came out victorious in the elections of 1905. After this defeat Tisza disappeared from the political scene for several years and devoted himself to managing his estate of Alsföld. But in 1912 he was chosen Speaker, and to break the resistance of the Opposition he called in the police and had the House cleared. A member then aimed three shots at him. Two men were wounded but Tisza remained uninjured and ruled that the debate should continue. But by violating the constitution and affronting his opponents he made all co-operation between the Hungarian parties impossible for the future. Thus, because Tisza had returned to power on 7 June 1913, Hungary was the only belligerent country during the war in which it was impossible to arrive at a party truce and create a national government.

War was abhorrent to Tisza both as a Magyar and as a Calvinist. The Magyar in him was opposed to the southward penetration of the Monarchy and the absorption of more Slavs as jeopardizing the dualist system and Hungarian predominance. The Calvinist in him revealed itself in a letter of 26 August 1914 to his young niece Margarete Zeik:

War, even if victorious, is terrible. For my soul every war means misery, anguish, devastation, the shedding of innocent blood, the suffering of innocent women and children.[1]

After the Peace of Bucharest he drew up a memorandum on 15 March 1914, defining his ideas on the policy to be pursued in order to maintain

[1] Graf Stefan Tisza, *Briefe* (Berlin, 1928), I, p. 62.

peace in the new conditions created by the Balkan wars.[1] It was adopted in its entirety by Berchtold and formed the basis of a document which was ready for dispatch to the Kaiser as early as 24 June. Tisza's opinion was that in the Balkans the Monarchy's main aim should be to preserve peace while losing no time in creating conditions in its own favour. The Archduke's death did not alter these views, and therefore, when Tisza learnt of Berchtold's intentions to go to war, he told him frankly that he would regard a war against Serbia as 'a fatal mistake'. He put his views to the Emperor in a memorandum of 1 July 1914:—

First of all we have so far no sufficient grounds for casting the responsibility on Serbia and provoking a war with her in spite of possible satisfactory explanations from the Serbian Government. We should find ourselves in an extremely weak position, appearing before the whole world as a disturber of the peace and kindling a major war in the most unfavourable conditions.

Secondly I regard the present moment as highly unfavourable, when we have practically lost Roumania, without any compensating gain, while Bulgaria, the only state on which we can count, is exhausted.

In the present Balkan situation my least concern would be that of finding a suitable *casus belli*. Once the moment to strike presents itself, a reason for war can always be found in the various questions. But before that a diplomatic constellation must be created which gives us a less unfavourable relative strength.

This involved winning over Bulgaria to the Triplice without alarming Roumania, in order to open the door to an agreement not only with Roumania but also with Greece. There was no time to be lost.

A last approach must be made to Germany to bring about the open accession of Roumania to the Triplice. If Germany cannot or will not carry out this mission, she must put up with our securing at least Bulgaria for the Triple Alliance.

Tisza begged the Emperor to bring up these points with Kaiser Wilhelm when the latter came to attend the Archduke's funeral and to make use of the recent monstrous events to combat the Kaiser's partiality for Serbia and win him over to wholehearted support of Austrian policy in the Balkans.[2]

What was the attitude of Francis Joseph? He was only just recovering from a serious illness which had befallen him in the winter. The longing to end his life in peace and the painful experiences of previous wars certainly did not induce him to seek adventure and stir up strife. Nevertheless, contrary to what certain historians would have us believe, it is certain that after the Sarajevo crime he came to the conclusion that things could not go on as they were with Serbia and that she would have to be taught a lesson. As supreme arbiter of the destinies of the

[1] Oe-U. VII, 9482.   [2] Oe-U. VIII, 9978.

Monarchy, he insisted on making his decisions on his own responsibility and it is a mistake to represent him as so weighed down with years that he agreed to whatever his ministers asked of him. All who knew him describe him as having the clear, firm mind of a fully responsible ruler. Conrad, whose sincerity is beyond question, protests against those who depict him as a shadowy figure, a weak-willed old man.[1]

Deeply embittered and indignant over the conduct of Austria-Hungary's enemies, perfectly aware of the aim of their machinations, well knowing what was at stake but convinced of the inevitability of the measure so ruthlessly provoked by Serbia, His Majesty during those days used the following words to me: 'If the Monarchy is doomed to perish, let it at least perish decorously!' It was the despairing resolve of an aged ruler driven to extremes by the enemies of his realm.[2]

Francis Joseph was so perturbed by the threat which Serbian agitation constituted for the Monarchy that, as we have already seen, he had commissioned Francis Ferdinand to inquire of Wilhelm at the Konopischt meeting whether Austria could in the future count unconditionally on Germany.[3] To Pallavicini, the Austrian Ambassador to Constantinople, the Emperor in June 1914 expressed the opinion that a war was the only way out of the existing situation.[4] The Sarajevo outrage could not but strengthen this conviction. Had he felt any doubts as to the course to pursue, Francis Joseph could easily have offset pressure from the war party by invoking Tisza's opposition to a war with Serbia. But he did not in fact summon Tisza to a discussion at all, though he feared him as he feared all Hungarians.

At this critical juncture Berchtold's *chef de cabinet*, Count Hoyos, on 1 July received a call from the influential German publicist Victor Naumann who was in close touch with the German Foreign Secretary Jagow, and with Stumm, the Political Director at the Wilhelmstrasse. The theme of his conversation was of such moment that it must here be quoted in full in the words of Hoyos:—

Dr. Naumann discussed the general political situation, dwelling on the great uneasiness felt in Berlin over Russian armaments and the test mobilization, recently fixed for the autumn, of considerable Russian forces. He himself

---

[1] To give an idea how Francis Joseph spoke and commanded his subordinates, it is worth while to reproduce a dialogue of 5 July between him and Conrad who was advocating the proclamation of martial law as a means of protecting the Monarchy against further Serbian outrages.

H.M.: 'All that is only when there is to be mobilization.'
Myself: 'Then it will be too late.'
H.M.: 'No—it cannot be done.'
Myself: 'There is no other way out.'
H.M.: 'I will not do it.'
Myself: 'As Your Majesty wills, but it was my duty to propose it.' (Conrad, IV, p. 37.)
[2] Conrad, IV, p. 162.   [3] Conrad, IV, p. 36; see p. 17.   [4] Conrad, IV, p. 107.

had observed that not only in army and navy circles but also in the Foreign Ministry the idea of a preventive war against Russia was regarded with less disfavour than a year ago. A settlement had been arrived at with England over Africa and the Portuguese colonies, and the visit of the English fleet to Kiel had been arranged to document the improvement in relations. For this reason there was believed to be the certainty that England would not intervene in a European war. The Foreign Ministry had been much impressed by the verbal account of the German consul until lately in Moscow who has now been appointed as *'vortragender Rat'* at the Foreign Ministry and has brought a great deal of information about Russian armaments. Herr von Stumm has spoken very seriously with Dr. Naumann of this danger and has described the war 'which Germany could have when she wants' as not impossible. I thanked Dr. Naumann for this interesting survey and let fall the remark that this state of affairs would be not unpleasing to us if we should ever find ourselves under the necessity of taking action against Serbia. Dr. Naumann eagerly seized on this remark and said that this was exactly what he had been going to suggest to me. In his opinion, after the Sarajevo murder, it was a question of life and death for the Monarchy not to leave this crime unpunished but to annihilate Serbia. For Germany such a course of action would be the touchstone whether Russia meant war or not. Berlin no longer counted on Roumania as an ally, but thought that the Roumanians would at first stay neutral. Opinion had come round to agreement to the accession of Bulgaria and Turkey to the Triplice and the Bulgarians would receive a subsidy. It was hoped that Greece could be forced to be neutral. France would probably be obliged by financial embarrassments to urge Russia not to go to war, but if a European war should come after all, the Triplice was now strong enough. Dr. Naumann thinks that if at the present moment, when Kaiser Wilhelm is horrified at the Sarajevo murder, he is spoken to in the right way, he will give us all assurances and this time go to the length of war, because he perceives the dangers for the monarchical principle. The Foreign Ministry will do nothing to oppose this state of mind because they regard this as the favourable moment for bringing about the great decision. Public opinion, says Naumann, would never have supported a war for Jakova but now he would guarantee that it would stand by the Austrian ally to a man and regard war as a liberating action. Austria-Hungary will be finished as a Monarchy and as a Great Power if she does not take advantage of this moment. I answered that I, too, regarded a solution of the Serbian question as urgently necessary and that it was of great value to us to reckon with the certainty that Germany will cover our rear. Dr. Naumann offered on his part, without mentioning me by name, to bring up the matter informally with Herr von Stumm and let me know his answer.[1]

Naumann's discourse perfectly summarizes the line of thought and action which in the days that followed was to be followed by those in charge of German policy. This in itself is confirmation that he spoke as their emissary.

On 2 July Francis Joseph received in audience the German

[1] Oe-U. VIII, 9966.

Ambassador Tschirschky who opened the conversation by conveying Wilhelm's regrets for not being present at the funeral of Francis Ferdinand. The Emperor replied that he would much have liked to see the Kaiser as there were so many political matters he would like to discuss with him.

For I see the future very black, said His Majesty, and conditions down there grow more disquieting every day. I do not know if we can continue any longer to look on passively and I hope that your Kaiser also measures the menace which the adjacency of Serbia signifies for the Monarchy. What particularly disquiets me is the Russian test mobilization which is planned for the autumn, just the time when we here have our change of recruits.[1]

Francis Joseph further added that he intended to send Prince Hohenlohe to Berlin for a frank discussion with Wilhelm. At the end of the audience, during which the Emperor had touched on all sorts of subjects, he reverted to the Serbian menace saying that they must take thought for the future and maintain the powerful position of the Triple Alliance.[2]

Of his own reply Tschirschky sent the following account to Berlin:

I took advantage of the Emperor's remark to point out once again—as I have already in these last few days emphatically pointed out to Count Berchtold—that His Majesty can surely rely on finding Germany solidly behind the Monarchy as soon as there is a question of defending one of its vital interests. The decision as to when and where any such vital interest is at stake must be left to Austria herself. Moods and wishes, however understandable they might be, could not be made the basis of a reliable policy. Before taking any decisive step it must be exactly estimated how far one meant to go and by

---

[1] DD. I, 9.

[2] To throw light on the situation, as seen at that moment from the Austrian point of view, it is perhaps worth while to give further particulars of what Francis Joseph said to Tschirschky at that audience. He lamented that in Albania everything was going wrong; nothing could be done with the people there; every Albanian was venal, not one was to be relied on. The Prince of Wied was not fit for his position. It was unsatisfactory that such a questionable type as Aliotti had been sent as Italian representative to Durazzo and only showed the weakness of the Rome Government. San Giuliano, however, was perfectly correct, and relations with Rome were decidedly better at the moment. Francis Joseph was glad that relations with Greece had improved. And although he had no great liking for King Ferdinand, Bulgaria seemed a country capable of great development and, except for Greece, perhaps the only Balkan state whose interests were not opposed to those of Austria. Hence he thought it a good policy to maintain and improve relations with Bulgaria. Roumania, on the other hand, was a sad chapter. 'I know that your Kaiser has full confidence in King Carol, but I have none.' King Carol had, moreover, frankly told Prince Fürstenberg that he did not feel in a position to fulfil his engagements towards the Triple Alliance.

The Emperor then went on to speak of the improvement in Anglo-German relations, saying that this would have favourable repercussions on those between London and Vienna. He was distressed at the unexpected death of General Pollio, the Italian Chief of Staff, which he regarded as a serious loss for Italy and also for Austria and Germany. 'Everybody is dying around me. It is too sad.' (DD. I, 11.)

what means the intended goal was to be attained. Before any important move the first point to be taken into consideration was the general political situation and the probable attitude of the other Powers and States, and the ground must be carefully prepared. I could only say once more that my Kaiser would back any firm resolve on the part of Austria-Hungary. His Majesty agreed heartily with these words of mine and said he thought I was undoubtedly right.[1]

This attitude on the Emperor's part, confirmed also by Conrad's account, warrants the query whether, instead of Berchtold's influencing his Sovereign, it was not rather Francis Joseph who overcame the doubts and hesitations of his Minister. Tschirschky had called on Berchtold before going to his audience of Francis Joseph and had said that in his opinion 'only vigorous measures against Serbia' would achieve Austria's object. Berchtold's report of the conversation continues:

As I well knew—said Tschirschky—Germany has several times during the crisis declared that in regard to Balkan policy she would always back us, if the need arose. On my remarking that this had repeatedly been promised but that in practice I had not always received the support of the Berlin Cabinet and was therefore not sure how far I could count on it, the Ambassador replied that, speaking quite privately, he attributed the attitude of his Government to the fact that we spoke a great deal about ideas without formulating a concrete plan of action, and Berlin would only intervene unreservedly on our behalf if such a plan were forthcoming.

Recently Prince Hohenlohe had spoken to him of the necessity for settling accounts with Serbia. He had answered that this was 'all very well', only one must be clear how far one meant to go and what were the plans in regard to Serbia. Moreover provision must be made for a favourable diplomatic situation and in particular the attitude of Italy and Roumania must be ascertained. To start a war with Serbia without being assured against attack from those countries would be a most risky undertaking. I answered that the question of how far one would go and what would in the end have to be done with Serbia would have to be decided by ourselves at the given moment in accordance with the circumstances. It could be decided at a later stage (*cura posterior*). In regard to Roumania, we could not raise the question there, because it would expose us to the demand for impossible compensations. . . . If we were to speak of the matter to the Rome Cabinet, Italy would presumably ask for Valona in compensation and to that we could not agree.[2]

Thus Tschirschky, while giving no absolute assurance on the attitude of Germany, urged Vienna to formulate a concrete plan of action, and Vienna received the impression that only by making a definite plan could Austria ensure that Berlin would intervene wholeheartedly in her support. Hence Berchtold's uncertainty in the past as to how far he could count on Germany had simply been due to the fact that Vienna had never yet formulated a definite plan.

[1] DD. I, 9 and 11.   [2] Oe-U. VIII, 10006.

Now if Germany thus urged extreme measures, Berchtold could expect no help from that quarter in resisting the demand for such measures from those around him and from his Sovereign. Yet on the other hand he could not but perceive that Tschirschky's incitements—partly spoken in strict confidence—left all doors of escape open to Germany. She could always declare that the diplomatic situation was unfavourable, that it was not certain whether Italy and Roumania would not range themselves against Austria, that the venture was too risky. The Austrian Ambassador Szögyény telegraphed on 4 July from Berlin that Zimmermann, the German Under Secretary for Foreign Affairs,

would regard as entirely understandable a strong line of action against Serbia on the part of the Monarchy which had on its side the universal sympathy of the whole civilized world, but he would recommend great prudence in this connexion and advise against making any humiliating demands on Serbia.[1]

On the other hand, Berchtold could take no action at all without the assent of the Prime Ministers of Austria and Hungary, and Tisza was firmly opposed to rash measures. What was Berchtold to do? To mobilize, as Conrad wanted, was impossible. Conrad himself had admitted that, before any action could be taken, the support of Germany must be definitely secured. Hence the only course was to inform Berlin of Vienna's readiness to go to war, asking whether Germany would give unqualified support if Russia were to take up arms in defence of Serbia. If Berlin wished Austria to seize this occasion to annihilate Serbia, Tisza would have to agree to the attack on Serbia.

3. *Vienna asks Berlin for its views and for support in an attack on Serbia: Francis Joseph's letter to Wilhelm and the Hoyos Mission.*

Certain historians, including Bernadôtte Schmitt, regard it as an adroit move on the part of Berchtold to refer the matter to Berlin.[2] Far from it! Berchtold was incapable of an adroit move. All he had done was to don his armour and leave it to his ally to decide whether he was to keep it on or doff it. Berlin was to say what course he should take. Outwardly Vienna was to choose its road; in reality Berlin was to say the decisive yea or nay. It is not impossible that at the bottom of his heart Berchtold would have liked Germany to prevent Austria from acting rashly and silence the Austrian war party.

It is significant that Vienna took the programme drawn up by Tisza[3] as the basis of a memorandum of 1 July and of an autograph letter of Francis Joseph to Kaiser Wilhelm dated 2 July which were to set forth Austrian views on the situation for the benefit of Berlin. Now Tisza's programme was one of peace, leaving no room for a war with Serbia.

[1] Oe-U. VIII, 10039.   [2] Schmitt, I, p. 347.   [3] See Vol. I, pp. 534-9.

So to adapt it to the project of perpetrating such an act of aggression, the memorandum received the following postscript:

The present memorandum was just ready when the terrible events of Sarajevo occurred.

The full consequences of the revolting murder can scarcely yet be assessed. But it has given undoubted proof, if such were necessary, of the unbridgeable antagonism between the Monarchy and Serbia and of the menace constituted by the Pan-Slav movement which stops at nothing.

Austria-Hungary has shown no lack of good will and readiness to meet Serbia half way, in order to create an endurable relationship with Serbia. But it has recently become evident that these endeavours were vain and that the Monarchy, in future, will still have to reckon with the stubborn, irreconcilable, and aggressive enmity of Serbia.

All the more imperative is the need for the Monarchy with a firm hand to sever the threads which its enemies seek to draw close into a net over its head.[1]

To give weight to these words Berchtold and his collaborators deemed it necessary to bring the memorandum to the notice of Kaiser Wilhelm by letting it be accompanied by a word from Francis Joseph. The Emperor accordingly signed a letter to Wilhelm placing the blame for the Sarajevo crime on Serbia and Pan-Serb propaganda and urging that an alliance should be concluded with Bulgaria in order to recall Roumania to a sense of her engagements towards the Central Powers, thus rendering it more possible for Greece to be reconciled with Bulgaria and Turkey. The real object of this unusual *démarche* was shown in the concluding sentences of the letter:

But this will only become possible if Serbia, which at present forms the pivot of Pan-Slav policy, is eliminated as a political power factor in the Balkans. You, too, since the recent terrible happenings in Bosnia, will feel convinced that a reconciliation of the differences which sunder us from Serbia is no longer to be thought of and that the stabilizing peace policy of all European monarchs will be menaced as long as this focus of criminal agitation in Belgrade lives on unpunished.

The postscript to the memorandum and Francis Joseph's letter leave no room for doubt as to the intentions of the Austrian Government towards Serbia. If the word war does not appear in either document, there are expressions which amount to the same thing. What is meant by 'with a firm hand sever the threads which its enemies sought to draw close into a net' over the head of the Monarchy, and by 'eliminate Serbia as a political power factor in the Balkans' unless it be that she was to be attacked and annihilated? If the official documents show a certain caution in their choice of terms, there is no doubt that this was prompted by the fear that Germany might oppose armed action such as

[1] Oe-U. VIII, 9984.

would endanger the peace of Europe. But to disclose unreservedly the Austrian Government's views, Berchtold decided not to send letter and memorandum to Berlin by diplomatic messenger but to entrust it to his *Chef de Cabinet* Hoyos, an ardent member of the war party, who was to convey by word of mouth his chief's intention of making war on Serbia and dividing her up among the adjacent states. With this the Emperor was substantially in agreement. When on 5 July Conrad had an audience of him and expressed his opinion of the inevitability of a war with Serbia, Francis Joseph replied: 'Yes that is quite true' but added: 'Are you sure of Germany?' He told Conrad that a note had gone off (by Hoyos) the previous evening asking for a definite answer. Hereupon Conrad asked:.

'If the answer runs that Germany will take her stand at our side, do we then make war on Serbia?' and the Emperor replied: 'In that case, yes.'[1]

These documents may suffice to show that after the Sarajevo outrage Vienna communicated to Berlin its intention to put an end to the Serb menace by war. Yet some of Berchtold's colleagues have not hesitated to ascribe to him and the Emperor the intention of eliminating the menace by peaceful means. Hoyos, for example, must have been perfectly aware of what was brewing. Yet at an interview which he gave to the present writer in November 1933 he began by saying that the Naumann visit had produced the impression on him that Berlin was urging the Monarchy to extreme measures. For reasons of home and foreign policy, Vienna had decided that Serbia must be put in her place, but neither Berchtold nor the Emperor intended to resort to force. Francis Joseph's autograph letter spoke merely of eliminating Serbia 'as a political power factor in the Balkans' and not leaving unpunished 'this focus of criminal agitation in Belgrade'. Berchtold, he added, differed from the prevailing opinion in Austria in wishing to confine himself to discussions with Serbia, if Berlin would agree to this. And, in fact, in the memorandum which he, Hoyos, laid before Berlin what stood in the foreground was the proposal to meet the Serb menace by an alliance with Bulgaria, to which Germany, distrusting the Bulgarians and fearing to alienate Roumania, had till then been opposed. In fact, said Hoyos to the present writer,

our attitude depended on Germany. We had taken no decision and pursued no policy of our own, however much we thought of the possibility of immediate action against Serbia and however much a war against her seemed sooner or later inevitable.

These reminiscences of Hoyos do not invalidate the evidence as to the warlike intentions of the Dual Monarchy provided by the postscript to the Tisza memorandum, Francis Joseph's letter to Wilhelm,

[1] Conrad, IV, p. 36.

Tisza's letter of 1 July to Francis Joseph, Tschirschky's dispatches, and Conrad's testimony.

The phrases from the Emperor's letter quoted by Hoyos form part of the documentation given above and prove the opposite of his thesis, while the political passages in which there is no mention of war were drafted before the Sarajevo outrage and thus do not support his thesis either. Nay more, Hoyos overlooks the fact that Tisza bears witness against him. At the meeting of Joint Ministers of the Dual Monarchy held on 7 July Tisza said that

he would never agree to a surprise attack on Serbia, 'sans crier gare' and without previous diplomatic action, as seemed to be the intention and as regrettably had been discussed in Berlin by Count Hoyos

and that even should war become unavoidable 'we must not aim at the complete annihilation of Serbia'.[1] There can be no doubt that in Berlin Hoyos spoke on instructions from Berchtold and, indeed, he complained to the present writer of Berchtold's subsequent disavowal.

That Berchtold at the bottom of his heart perhaps wished that Berlin would not support the war party is another matter belonging to the realm of theory and not of fact. In regard to the facts, no doubt is possible. It was Austria who asked Germany for support in the aggression planned against Serbia in full awareness of the repercussions that this might cause. At the same time the fact remains that, in deciding on aggression, Berchtold was influenced not only by the pressure of those around him but also by the fear lest a forbearing attitude might lower the prestige of Austria still more in German eyes, a fear more than justified by Naumann's move. And the further fact remains that the men who directed German policy, far from restraining Austria, urged her to resort to extreme measures, and renewed their pressure when she showed signs of perplexity and hesitation.

Having established these facts, let us beware of making them bear too wide a meaning. Let us make it quite clear that to attribute the responsibility for making war in July 1914 to the Central Powers is not to deliver judgement on the conditions which drove Austria to war with Serbia and led Germany to support Austria. To state that Austria and Germany acted as has already been shown and has yet to be shown is not to assert that from their own point of view they had not good reasons for seeking to change a state of affairs injurious directly to Austria and indirectly to Germany. The same holds good in respect of France and Russia. These two Powers manifested no great fear of the tempest that was being unloosed. Nay, they seemed almost ready to welcome it in certain conditions, hoping perhaps that its end might turn out to their advantage. The fact is that the question of the origins

[1] Oe-U. VIII, 10118; DD. I, 18.

of the war is an entirely different one from that of the rights and wrongs
of the war. This latter is an immense problem which we do not set
ourselves to solve. All that we can affirm, without entering into this
matter, is that even if one or both of the Central Powers had sufficient
reasons for starting a war, it would always have been a wrong decision
on their part to do so in conditions unfavourable to themselves, throwing the world into chaos only to bring about their own defeat and ruin.

4. *German pressure on Austria; the Kaiser in favour of a solution by force.*

On the day of the Sarajevo tragedy not one of the men in charge of
German policy was in Berlin. The Kaiser was attending the Kiel re-
gatta. The Chancellor was away at his country seat of Hohenfinow.
Jagow, the Secretary of State for Foreign Affairs, was on his honeymoon.
The Chief of Staff, Moltke, was taking the cure at Carlsbad, and the
influential Navy Minister, Tirpitz, was drinking the waters at Tarasp.
The Ministry of Foreign Affairs was thus in the hands of the Under
Secretary of State, Zimmermann. Having no authority to act on his own
judgement and mindful of the line taken by Germany in June 1913,
Zimmermann advised Belgrade not to be imprudent and Vienna to
show restraint. On 4 July as has already been noted, he said to Szögyény
that while vigorous measures against Serbia on the part of the Monarchy would be quite understandable

he would recommend great prudence in this connexion and advise against
making humiliating demands on Serbia.[1]

The German press, too, after using violent language in the first few
days, spoke with calmness and moderation. The Conservative *Deutsche
Tageszeitung* recommended that Austria should not make the crime the
starting point of a new Balkan policy. The Pan-German *Morgenpost*
expressed the hope that the Vienna Government would not lose its
head. The Liberal *Frankfurter Zeitung* advised against making reprisals.
The *Berliner Tageblatt* was alarmed by the Austrian demand for an
inquiry in Serbia.

But this was not at all the line taken by the Kaiser and army circles.
As early as 2 July Salza Lichtenau, the Saxon Minister in Berlin, telegraphed to Dresden:

From military quarters pressure is again being brought to bear to the effect
that we should let war come about now while Russia is not yet ready, but I
do not believe that H.M. the Kaiser will let himself be led astray into that.[2]

The following day the Saxon Military Plenipotentiary at Berlin
telegraphed to the Saxon War Minister an account of a conversation
he had had with Major-General Waldersee, the Quartermaster General

---

[1] Oe-U. VIII, 10039.   [2] Bach, p. 63.

at Supreme Command Headquarters, at the memorial service for Archduke Francis Ferdinand. What Waldersee said to him

seemed to be the view of the Chief of the Army General Staff. He gave it as his opinion that we might become involved in a war from one day to another. Everything, he thinks, depends on what attitude Russia takes in the Austro-Serbian business. In any case the course of events is being closely watched by Supreme Headquarters. I had the impression that they would regard it with favour there if war were to come about now. Conditions and prospects would never become better for us. But on the other hand H.M. the Kaiser is said to have pronounced in favour of maintaining peace.[1]

On this latter point the Saxon representative was mistaken. The Kaiser was overcome with consternation not only because of the outrage itself but also on account of his feelings of friendship for the victim. On his return to Potsdam his mood found utterance in marginal notes. No doubt crossed his mind as to where the guilt lay. 'Now or never' was his marginal note to Tschirschky's dispatch of 30 June reporting that responsible people in Vienna were saying 'there ought to be a thorough settlement of accounts with the Serbs'. And to Tschirschky's statement in the same dispatch:

I availed myself of all such openings, calmly but very emphatically and seriously, to utter a warning against hasty measures

the Kaiser's irate comment ran:

Who authorized him to do so? That is utterly stupid! It is not his business, since it is entirely Austria's own affair, what she intends to do. Later on, if things went wrong, it would be said: Germany was not willing! Will Tschirschky have the goodness to drop this nonsense! It is high time a clean sweep was made of the Serbs.[2]

On 5 July, on learning that Szögyény was to present to him the autograph letter from Francis Joseph brought by Hoyos, the Kaiser invited the Ambassador to lunch and after reading the letter and the memorandum expressed himself in terms which Szögyény in a telegram to Berchtold summarized as follows:

First His Majesty assured me that he had expected severe measures on our part in regard to Serbia, but he must confess that as a result of the analysis given by our august Sovereign he must not lose sight of possible serious European complications and thus would give no definite answer before consulting with the Imperial Chancellor. After luncheon when I laid great emphasis on the seriousness of the situation, His Majesty authorized me to convey to our august Sovereign that even in that case we may reckon on full support from Germany. As he had said, he must first hear the Chancellor's opinion but did not in the least doubt that Herr von Bethmann Hollweg

[1] Bach, p. 63.   [2] DD. I, 7.

would entirely agree with his own view. This was especially true in respect of any measure we might take against Serbia. In His Majesty's view there should be no delay in undertaking these measures. Russia's bearing would in any case be hostile, but for this he had been prepared for years. And even if matters went to the length of a war between Austria-Hungary and Russia, we could remain assured that Germany in her customary loyalty as an ally would stand at our side. Russia, by the way, was, as things stand to-day, not at all ready for war and would certainly think twice before resorting to arms. But she would certainly incite the other powers of the Triple *Entente* against us and fan the flames in the Balkans. He quite understood that His Imperial and Royal Apostolic Majesty with his well-known love of peace, would find it hard to march into Serbia, but if we have really recognized the necessity of military measures against Serbia he (Kaiser Wilhelm) would deplore our not taking advantage of the present moment which is so favourable to us.[1]

Wilhelm went on to say that an alliance with Bulgaria 'was not at all to his liking', as he had no confidence in King Ferdinand. But he would make no objection to a treaty between the Monarchy and Bulgaria, provided it did not in any way threaten Roumania and was made known to her. Wilhelm was to go next day (6 July) to Kiel to embark on his northern cruise, but on the evening of the 5th or the morning of the 6th he would have a talk with Bethmann Hollweg who had been specially summoned from Hohenfinow.

Let us make it quite plain that the only proviso made by Wilhelm in adopting this policy was that it should have the assent of the Chancellor and this, moreover, he regarded as certain. He never asked whether Vienna possessed proof of Serbian complicity in the crime. He set no limits to what Austria might do, nay took for granted that she would invade Serbia, a contingency not explicitly mentioned in the two Austrian communications, and he pressed for speedy action. It cannot be doubted that the Kaiser's attitude and the terms he used were influenced by what he learnt of the real intentions of the Monarchy by word of mouth from the Austrian Ambassador who on his part was speaking on the strength of what had been told him that morning by Hoyos.

Wilhelm was not in any way acting on the spur of the moment when he took the grave step of promising full support to Austria and urging her to take immediate action against Serbia. He believed that Russia was unprepared and could be dealt with by Germany. The problem of Austro-Serbian relations, raised afresh by the assassination of Francis Ferdinand, was very well known to him and if, as has already been narrated, he had in the 1912–13 crisis come down on the side of Serbia, from September 1913 onwards he had on several occasions, if not invariably, expressed himself in favour of a solution

<hr/>

[1] Oe-U. VIII, 10058.

by force. Such a solution could not but become an imperious demand after the outrage. Witness his marginal note to Tschirschky's telegram of 2 July in which he reprimanded the Ambassador for having enjoined moderation on Vienna adding: 'It is high time a clean sweep was made of the Serbs'. This note antedates the arrival of Hoyos in Berlin. The Kaiser doubtless received the Tschirschky telegram at once, annotating it probably on 3 July and returning it to the Wilhelmstrasse on the 4th. Lichnowsky, calling there on the 5th, prior to his return to London, was told by Zimmermann 'that Tschirschky had been reprimanded because he reported that he had counselled moderation in Vienna towards Serbia'.[1] It was that same morning of the 5th that Hoyos from Vienna had called on Zimmermann with the news of Austrian intentions towards Serbia. He was told that the Kaiser and the Chancellor 'regarded immediate intervention (*Einschreiten*) against Serbia as the most radical and best solution of our difficulties in the Balkans',[2] whereas the previous day Zimmermann had advised Szögyény that Vienna should show great restraint and not make humiliating demands on Serbia.[3] Thus it was clearly the Kaiser's marginal notes which made Zimmermann change his tune. Let it also not be forgotten that Victor Naumann made his appearance at the Ballplatz as early as 1 July, and that his mission was one which he had certainly not undertaken of his own initiative.

5. The Kaiser's discussions with his Chancellor and the military chiefs.

It may be presumed that the Chancellor was not altogether taken by surprise when he was summoned back from Hohenfinow and, together with Zimmermann, received in audience by the Kaiser at 6 p.m. on 5 July. Wilhelm gave them an account of what he had said to the Austrian Ambassador shortly before. Bethmann Hollweg's book, *Betrachtungen zum Weltkriege*, tells us that Wilhelm

declared he could be under no illusions as to the serious position in which the Danubian Monarchy had been placed by Pan-Serb propaganda. But it was not our business to advise our ally what to do as a result of the Sarajevo murder. On this Austria-Hungary must take her own decision. We must refrain from direct suggestions and advice all the more because we must use all means to prevent the Austro-Serbian conflict from widening into an international conflict. Emperor Francis Joseph must know that even in a critical hour we should not forsake Austria-Hungary. Our own vital interest requires the preservation of Austria intact. . . . These views of the Kaiser's coincided with my own opinions.[4]

But the Chancellor adapts his Sovereign's statements to fit the thesis that it was not Germany who kindled the flame of the European war.

[1] Prince Lichnowsky, *Heading for the Abyss*, p. 72.   [2] Oe-U. VIII, 10076.
[3] Oe-U. VIII, 10039.   [4] Bethmann, I, p. 135.

What the Kaiser actually did say emerges clearly from the actions and the subsequent statements of the two of them. After the war Zimmermann, appearing before the Commission of Inquiry to investigate the responsibility for the war appointed in 1919 by the German National Constituent Assembly, gave another account of the conversation:

After Mr. v. Bethmann Hollweg had briefly rehearsed to the Emperor the subject-matter of the Austro-Hungarian dispatches, already made known to the latter by Count Szögyény, His Majesty spoke without waiting to hear the Chancellor's propositions.[1]

This he no doubt did for fear that the propositions might conflict with the promise he had given Szögyény, although in point of fact this was not the case.

The German historian Lutz writes:

It has been said that Bethmann Hollweg regarded himself as bound by the consent which the Kaiser had given when speaking with the Austro-Hungarian Ambassador on 5 July 1914 and felt that he had been faced with a *fait accompli*. I cannot agree with this view. Wilhelm had told Syögyény that he could 'give no definite reply before consulting with the Chancellor', and later on in the conversation had again emphasized that he must 'first hear the Chancellor's opinion'. Hence Bethmann Hollweg was in a position to qualify the Kaiser's promises without in any way disavowing him. But even taking the standpoint that the Kaiser had made very definite promises and had never doubted that Bethmann Hollweg would be in full agreement with him, one must not overlook the fact that, on repeated occasions during his Chancellorship, Bethmann Hollweg took a stand against the Kaiser, as for instance over naval policy. It would have been his clear duty to do so again now if he regarded it as necessary. Since Jagow, the Secretary of State for Foreign Affairs, was away on leave, Bethmann Hollweg must bear the responsibility for what is called the 'blank cheque' of 5–6 July.[2]

Lutz writes in explanation that Bethmann

had pronounced inclinations towards philosophy, with a tendency to fatalism which at times made him regard war as inevitable. Thus it was after the Sarajevo murder.[3]

It cannot be doubted, however, that Bethmann Hollweg's attitude was influenced not only by that of the Kaiser but by that of military circles.

On the afternoon of 5 July the Kaiser summoned to the Neues Palais Colonel General von Plessen, his adjutant, General von Lyncker, the Chief of the Military Cabinet, and General von Falkenhayn,

[1] *Official German Documents relating to the World War* (Carnegie Endowment), (N.Y., 1923), I, p. 32.

[2] Lutz, p. 33.   [3] Lutz, p. 31.

the Minister for War, in order to bring the two documents received from Szögyény to their knowledge. General Plessen records in his diary:

His Majesty summoned me to the Neues Palais at 5 p.m. I there found Lyncker, Chief of the Military Cabinet and Falkenhayn the War Minister. His Majesty read us a letter from the Emperor of Austria and a memorandum from the Austrian Foreign Minister, Count Berchtold, according to which the Austrians are getting ready for a war on Serbia and want first to be sure of Germany. The Imperial Chancellor and the Secretary of State also attended. The opinion prevailed among us that the sooner the Austrians make their move against Serbia the better, and that the Russians—though friends of Serbia—will not join in. There is a threat of the withdrawal of Roumania from the Triple Alliance, and there appears on the horizon an alliance between Turkey and Bulgaria—His Majesty's departure on his northern cruise is to proceed without interruption.[1]

Next morning, 6 July, the Kaiser before his departure had talks with Admiral Capelle, the acting Navy Minister in Tirpitz's absence, and with General Bertrab of the General Staff, acting for Moltke while he was taking the cure at Carlsbad. To Admiral Capelle the Kaiser said:

He did not anticipate major military complications. In his opinion the Tsar in this case would not take the part of the regicides. Moreover Russia and France were not prepared for war—The Kaiser did not mention England. On the Chancellor's advice he was going on his northern cruise in order not to give room for disquietude.[2]

Bertrab after his audience at the Neues Palais on that morning of the 6th wrote to Moltke:

The Austro-Hungarian Ambassador submitted to His Majesty a *pro memoria* from his Government about the anti-Austrian machinations in the Balkans connected with the recent outrage and added that the Emperor of Austria-Hungary had resolved to march into Serbia. His Majesty in agreement with the Foreign Ministry and War Ministry approves this decision and has expressed his readiness to cover Austria in the event of Russia's intervening. It is true His Majesty does not think that Russia will intervene; particularly in view of the cause, the Tsar of Russia will hardly decide to do so. His Majesty therefore regards the affair as in the first instance a purely Balkan concern and signifies this conception by departing on his northern cruise according to plan.[3]

At 9.15 a.m. on 6 July the Kaiser left for his cruise.

It is certainly remarkable—writes Kautsky—that the Kaiser should have started on a cruise to the North in the midst of such a threatening situation. One thing, however, is clear: the most frivolous of Sovereigns would not

---

[1] Bach, p. 14.   [2] DD. I, p. XIX.   [3] Bach, p. 14.

have dared to do that without having first assured himself that the defences of the State were prepared for all possible emergencies.[1]

These talks gave rise to the rumour that a Crown Council was held at Potsdam on 5 July, at which the decision was taken to go to war. The publication of the German official documents by Kautsky and that of the proceedings of the Commission of Inquiry put an end to the legend of the Potsdam Council, which is the subject of an appendix to the present chapter. Evidence given before the Commission of Inquiry and documents which have subsequently come to light show that the Kaiser's intention was to inform the army and navy chiefs of what had taken place, so that they should be warned, and to make sure that the army was ready for anything that might happen. But his opinion was that Russia and France would not take the field on behalf of Serbia. There exists also a letter written to Moltke by Falkenhayn saying that the Kaiser had informed him of the intention of Austria to put Serbia in her place with or without the consent of Russia. Neither the Kaiser nor the Chancellor believed that Austria had come to an irrevocable decision to go to war, there being no mention of war in the Austrian memorandum. Thus, in view of the fact that the Kaiser had departed on a cruise, Moltke could proceed with his cure at Carlsbad.[2]

But if there is complete agreement among historians on this point, there are differences of opinion about the reactions of those in charge of German policy towards the Austrian intention to go to war with Serbia. What the Kaiser said to the Austrian Ambassador has been mentioned above. Here must be added that at that very same moment Hoyos was in conversation with the Under Secretary of State Zimmermann—in the absence of Bethmann and Jagow on holiday—and was telling him with complete frankness what he understood to be Berchtold's intentions. According to the minutes of the meeting of Austro-Hungarian Joint Ministers on 7 July it would seem that Hoyos had talked of 'a surprise attack without preliminary preparation' or, in the words used by Tisza at the meeting: '*sans crier gare*'. Hoyos further told Zimmermann that

---

[1] Kautsky, p. 79.

[2] Montgelas, pp. 119-20. Falkenhayn, according to Zwehl, urged the Kaiser to prepare for war. This the Kaiser refused to do for fear of interfering with the action of diplomacy (H. v. Zwehl, *Erich von Falkenhayn, eine biographische Studie*, Berlin, 1926, p. 55). On 5 July Falkenhayn then wrote to Moltke that, though not acting on official instructions, he thought it best to let the Chief of Staff know how tense the situation was, so that he should not be taken unawares by events (Montgelas, p. 119). The Chief of Naval Staff also took precautions tantamount to preparing for war. Despite all precautions, nervousness spread in Germany and Austria and led to a wave of selling and a fall of values on the Stock Exchange. If war preparations remained on a limited scale this was, as Waldersee wrote to Jagow, because on 17 July: 'We at Headquarters are ready for anything; for the time being we need take no further measures' (DD. I, 74). On 19 July, however, the Kaiser ordered Wedel to write to the Wilhelmstrasse that he thought it desirable to give timely warning to the Directors of the Hamburg-America and North German Lloyd steamship companies that an Austrian ultimatum to Serbia was to be expected on 23 July (DD. I, 80).

the plan was to partition Serbian territory between Austria, Bulgaria, and Albania. None of this aroused protest or objections on the part of Zimmermann, as he himself admitted before the Reichstag Commission of Inquiry.[1] When questioned by the present writer Hoyos stated that at his interview with Zimmermann on the afternoon of the 5th he delivered himself of the mission entrusted to him by Berchtold, handing over a copy of Francis Joseph's letter and of the Austrian memorandum. He explained to Zimmermann that the Sarajevo outrage touched vital Austrian interests in both home and foreign affairs, that Vienna found itself compelled to arrive at a definite settlement of accounts with Serbia, but that before taking a decisive step the Austrian Government needed to be certain that its intentions met with the full approval of Berlin. Hoyos assured the present writer that he had been surprised to find Zimmermann in wholehearted agreement that Austria-Hungary could no longer tolerate Serbian provocation. The decision of the Kaiser and Bethmann Hollweg was still awaited but there was little doubt that they would give Austria the assurance of unconditional support from Germany. Zimmermann inquired what steps Vienna proposed to take and Hoyos replied that so far no decision had been taken but that the idea was to impose severe conditions on Serbia and, if these were not accepted, go to war. Zimmermann replied that if Austria meant to act she must do so immediately without diplomatic delays which would waste precious time and give the alarm to *Entente* diplomacy.

We at Vienna—he said—have the defect of arguing too much and changing our minds. Once a decision was taken, there should be no time lost in going into action so as to take Serbia and the chancelleries of Europe by surprise. Austrian reprisals were amply justified by the Sarajevo crime.

Zimmermann felt sure that, if this course were pursued, the conflict would remain localized, but that, should France and Russia intervene, Germany alone with her increased military strength would be able to meet them. Hoyos told him that as soon as he was in possession of the German reply he would return to Vienna, and a Council of Joint Ministers would be summoned. Zimmermann replied that after the Council meeting it would be desirable that no further time should be lost.

Hoyos thus continues his narrative:

And as Tschirschky at Vienna had advised me to be very firm and detailed in my account of Austrian plans at Berlin, I carried out Berchtold's instructions by stating that, once we had beaten Serbia, we intended to partition her territory among Austria-Hungary, Bulgaria, and Albania. Zimmermann replied with a smile of satisfaction that this was a question concerning only

---

[1] *Official German Documents relating to the World War* (New York, 1923), I, p. 32.

ourselves and that he would raise no objections. Next day Bethmann officially informed Szögyény and myself in the presence of Zimmermann that
it was entirely for us to decide on the measures we were to take: in whatever
circumstances and whatever our decision we should find Germany unconditionally at our side in allied loyalty. Twice over he said to me, however,
that in his personal opinion, with things as they were, only 'immediate action
against Serbia' could solve our difficulties with her. 'The international
situation was entirely in our favour.' When I started out from Vienna,
despite all that had been said by Naumann and Ganz, I did not expect to find
in Berlin such instantaneous and complete understanding of our difficulties.
Our design of a decisive settlement of accounts with Serbia met with no
objection. On the contrary we were told that this was also the opinion of
Germany and we were advised to take 'immediate action'. This incitement,
expressed to me first by Zimmermann and then by Bethmann, made a great
impression on me and I did not fail to draw attention to it in the telegram[1]
which I sent to Vienna over Szögyény's signature after the conversation.

Zimmermann, in answer to an inquiry from the present writer, wrote
on 17 June 1938:

The Wilhelmstrasse, in coming to the conclusion that the war would
remain confined to Austria-Hungary and Serbia and that its spread to Europe
would be avoided, went on the assumption that the Dual Monarchy would
lose no time in proceeding against Serbia. To avoid the impression of exercising constraint, we unfortunately refrained from explicitly influencing our
ally in the sense of this assumption. Austria-Hungary failed to act without
delay and under the powerful impression of the Sarajevo murder. She allowed precious weeks to slip by in useless investigations; finally she sent an
ultimatum to Serbia without making the necessary military preparations to
invade Serbia immediately and occupy Belgrade in the event of a rejection,
which was surely to be expected. This mistake gave the *Entente* Powers the
welcome chance to exchange views and arrive at an understanding.

6. *A telegram from Szögyény falsely impugned; the evidence of Hoyos.*

On 6 June the Chancellor received Szögyény in the presence of
Hoyos and of the Under Secretary Zimmermann. Szögyény's report to
Vienna contains the following statements:

As to our relations with Serbia, the German Government takes the standpoint that it is for us to decide what has to be done in order to clear up these
relations, and that in so doing—whatever might be our decision—we could
reckon with the certainty that Germany would back the Monarchy as an ally
and friend. In the further course of the conversation I ascertained that the
Imperial Chancellor, no less than his Imperial Master, regards immediate
measures on our part against Serbia as the best and most thorough-going
solution of our difficulties in the Balkans. From the international standpoint
he regards the present moment as more favourable than a later one. He

---

[1] See below, p. 147.

entirely agrees to our not informing either Italy or Roumania in advance about any measures we might take against Serbia. But Italy is to be informed now by the German and our own Government of the intention of bringing about Bulgaria's accession to the Triple Alliance. . . . At the close of the conversation the Chancellor inquired about the present position in Albania and uttered an urgent warning against any projects such as might jeopardize our relations with Italy and the existence of the Triple Alliance.[1]

Evidently there were two parts to this conversation, an official part, summarized in the statements attributed by Bethmann Hollweg to his Sovereign, and a non-official part of far greater import in estimating how much responsibility Germany bears for what Austria decided to do. This second part tallies exactly with the line taken by Wilhelm. His marginal note 'Now or never', his strictures on Tschirschky and his remarks to Szögyény reveal similar opinions to those put in the mouth of Bethmann by the Austrian Ambassador. Bethmann, in telegraphing a summary of the conversation to Tschirschky, omitted this confidential part. After saying that Wilhelm fully understood Francis Joseph's wish for the accession of Bulgaria to the Triple Alliance and would use his influence with King Carol to hold Roumania to her duties as an ally, Bethmann ended his message:

Finally as regards Serbia, His Majesty, of course, cannot take any position in regard to the questions pending between that country and Austria-Hungary, as they are outside his authority. But Emperor Francis Joseph can rely on His Majesty's taking his stand loyally at the side of Austria-Hungary in accordance with his duties as an ally and his old friendship.[2]

No hint here of the desire that Austria should lose no time in attacking Serbia and should attack her without preliminary warning to Italy and Roumania. The silence of Bethmann's telegram on this point does not imply any contradiction between his version and that of Szögyény. But it has been used by German and non-German historians favourable to Germany to legitimate the assumption that Berlin never pressed Vienna to go to war and to accuse Szögyény of misunderstanding or gross exaggeration. They represent him as an old dotard on the point of being replaced by Hohenlohe, as under the thumb of military circles in Berlin and the like, the truth being that, like Pallavicini, he was regarded by the Ballplatz as one of its ablest diplomatists. His telegrams reveal him as an ambassador who knows his business. The telegram now under discussion, one of the most damning documents on German responsibility for the war, was published in 1919, a year before Bethmann Hollweg died and its authenticity was never called in question by him. How, indeed, could Szögyény have possibly invented a whole speech of this tenor if it had never been made? All that he would have achieved by so doing would have been a disavowal from Berlin and the

---

[1] Oe-U. VIII, 10076.   [2] DD. I, 15.

loss of his own credit. The speech, moreover, tallies exactly with the line taken by the Kaiser and is fully corroborated by Hoyos who was also present at the conversation. Hoyos has placed on record that both Szögyény and he carried away from Berlin

the impression that the German Government was in favour of an immediate offensive on our part against Serbia, although they clearly recognized that it might result in a world war.[1]

Questioned by the present writer at Vienna on 21 November 1933, Hoyos revealed that this telegram of Szögyény was drawn up entirely by Hoyos himself, who had been present at the conversation and that it accurately reflected the words uttered by the Chancellor. In proof of these statements Hoyos added that he had sent the very same account in a letter to Merey written on 20 July 1917 from Stockholm—where Hoyos was then Minister—and preserved in the Vienna State Archives. His account continues:

A few years ago in a series of articles published in the *Augsburger Allgemeine Zeitung*, which I believe to have been inspired by Zimmermann, I was represented as having said that Austria-Hungary was strong enough to oppose Russia and Serbia together while Germany was throwing all her strength against France. The very opposite of this is the truth. It was Zimmermann who said to me: 'We are strong enough to take on France and Russia at the same time, so you will be able to let all the weight of your army gravitate to the Balkans.' This too was an incitement. I never contradicted the German paper's statement because silence was enjoined on me and I was anxious to avoid all controversy.[2]

I had the clear impression that Germany was urging us to war because she felt that any further weakening of Austria would worsen the position of the Triple Alliance; and Germany needed a strong Austria-Hungary. When I got back to Vienna I made my report to Count Berchtold and was received by the Emperor. Francis Joseph was calm and understood the needs of the situation. After my report he said: 'Now we can no longer turn back. It will be a terrible war.'

Hoyos's letter to Merey has been found in the Vienna State Archives and is of much interest. It says that the Chancellor's last words confirmed his impression that the Germans meant in the future to place the responsibility for the outbreak of war entirely on Austria. For this reason he wondered whether it would not be useful if he drew up an account of his journey to Berlin for the Vienna Archives; but, as he was

---

[1] Hoyos, p. 80.

[2] In a letter to the present writer of 7 January 1935 Hoyos writes among other things: 'It is completely untrue that I told Zimmermann we had no need of German support even if Russia were to interfere in our conflict with Serbia. On the contrary he said to me in the course of the conversation that Germany was so strong since the increase in her military effectives that she could carry on a war against France and Russia on two fronts even without ourselves who would be sufficiently engaged in the Balkans. When on my return to Vienna I reported these statements to our Chief of Staff, Conrad, he only laughed.'

at Stockholm, he was without his pencilled notes, which were in the care of the *chef de cabinet*, and was without the Szögyény telegrams. Meantime he recounted what had taken place at Berlin as has been recorded here and then went on:

> The German Government was then perfectly free to say no to us and hold us back from taking measures against Serbia. Perhaps we should have taken it rather badly; but the German Government has certainly never let itself be influenced in its decisions by our good or ill humour.

The letter ended with a reminder to Merey of a message from Wilhelm in Berlin expressing the hope that Austria would not draw back and would carry out her measures boldly, and a reference to a telegram of Pallavicini's from Constantinople with an account of a conversation with his German colleague Wangenheim. Of this telegram mention will be made again later. Of Wilhelm's message no trace exists in the Vienna State Archives, and Hoyos after a three year interval was certainly making a confusion with a telegram to which we shall soon briefly refer, sent to Tschirschky, by him communicated to Berchtold and containing the message from Wilhelm just recorded.

Be it noted incidentally that when Hoyos writes that Germany was free to hold Austria back even if Austria took it badly, he unwittingly proves that those in charge of Austrian policy were then proposing to settle the conflict by force, not by diplomatic methods. Berlin could encourage and spur on to attack, but the initiative was taken by Austria.

Returning to our story, let us turn our attention to the fact that the original minute of the Bethmann-Szögyény talks, as drafted by Zimmermann, contains the statement of Germany's readiness to stand by Austria 'in whatever circumstances'.[1] The Chancellor suppressed these words in his telegram to Tschirschky, but if Zimmermann wrote them in his draft, it must have been because his chief had used them to Szögyény, i.e. gave Austria a free hand. It was this assurance which determined the subsequent action of Vienna. And in fact when on 7 July Tschirschky in Vienna listened to Szögyény's version of the talk read out to him by Hoyos, he wrote to Berlin that Szögyény's version 'entirely corresponded to the telegram sent me by Your Excellency on 6 July'.[2]

---

[1] DD. I, 15, *n.* 5.

[2] DD. I, 18. It may also be noted that on 9 July, four days after the Kaiser's promise to Szögyény, the Chancellor sent for the Minister of the Interior, Clemens Delbrück, and told him 'that an Austrian ultimatum to Serbia was to be expected'. Delbrück writes: 'My first thought was: "That means war." On my asking whether I ought not to take the necessary steps to make the requisite grain purchases in Holland, the Imperial Chancellor replied that . . . in his opinion things had not yet got to that point. We would have to avoid anything that might produce an impression that we were preparing for a war'. Clemens von Delbrück, *Die wirtschaftliche Mobilmachung in Deutschland 1914* (Munich, 1914), p. 96.

Wilhelm's ideas and intentions are also shown in a telegram addressed to Lichnowsky which the Wilhelmstrasse had drafted by Radowitz, the Counsellor at the Foreign Ministry, as early as 7 July. Its original text ran as follows:

The inquiry into the Sarajevo murder shows more and more clearly that its spiritual instigators are to be found in Belgrade political and military circles. *Austria seems decided not to allow this opportunity to slip of settling accounts with Serbia. We take a sympathetic attitude towards this idea, but are desirous that any resultant war should be localized.* To this end public opinion in Europe will have to render it possible for the Governments to look on at the fight between Austria and Serbia without taking sides. It is therefore already needful for a trend to be created in the English press representing this outrage and the earlier assassination of the Serbian King and Queen as manifestations of a criminal political mentality incompatible with the civilized conscience of Europe, thus creating an understanding for the action of the Monarchy in rising in self-defence against this long-standing menace from Serbia. Kindly use your influence with the English press in this sense but carefully avoid anything that might give the impression that we were hounding the Austrians into war.[1]

At that moment neither Berlin nor Vienna had information that the instigators of the outrage were to be found in Belgrade political and military circles. The signature appended to this telegram was that of Jagow and it was dispatched only on 12 July after Zimmermann had replaced the sentences in italics by the following:

In consequence of this the possibility exists that Austria might decide on more serious measures against Serbia and that this might lead to general complications. We are in all circumstances anxious for a localization of the conflict.

But the text, as drawn up immediately after the decisions taken on 5 and 6 July and more directly reflecting the ideas of the Wilhelmstrasse, states explicitly that Austria seemed decided on war with Serbia and that 'we take a sympathetic attitude towards this idea'.

The German historian Hermann Lutz comments:

In short-sighted misjudgement of the international situation the German Government thought that the moment had come for Vienna to take drastic action. Both Russia and France were thought to be unprepared and disinclined for war. England was drifting towards civil war and had made far-reaching colonial agreements with Germany opening prospects of lasting improvement in Anglo-German relations. It was thought that England and France would, if need be, restrain Russia and lastly great hopes were placed on the feeling of monarchical solidarity which, it was thought, would prevent the Tsar from drawing the sword on behalf of regicides. Thus on 5–6 July 1914 Austria received the intimation that it was for her to take the steps she

[1] DD. I, 36.

deemed necessary and that she could count on the loyal support of her ally Germany. As the German *White Book* of 1914 with rare candour expresses it: Austria was given '*a completely free hand in her action against Serbia*.'[1]

Lutz does not believe that Germany had no other choice open to her than to take her stand unreservedly on the side of the Danubian Monarchy and that any refusal would have destroyed the alliance.

Where would Austria-Hungary then have found a genuine ally? It was always much easier for Germany to come to an agreement, say, with Russia at the expense of Austria than the other way round. . . . And Vienna knew this.[2]

7. *Tschirschky's pressure on Vienna.*

But Berlin gave Austria-Hungary not only what Lutz describes as the 'curse' of a free hand.[3] It also gave her incitement and encouragement to take action against Serbia. We have already noted Naumann's call of 1 July on Hoyos. On 4 July Forgach drafted a note stating that he had seen Ganz, the Vienna correspondent of the *Frankfurter Zeitung*, who had that day been received by Tschirschky. Ganz had said that the German Ambassador had several times repeated to him with the obvious intention that the Ballplatz should be told of it

that Germany would support the Monarchy through thick and thin in whatever it might decide regarding Serbia. The Ambassador had added that the sooner Austria-Hungary went into action the better. Yesterday would have been better than to-day, and to-day would be better than to-morrow.[4]

To his English colleague Bunsen, as the latter on 5 July reported to the Foreign Office, Tschirschky said that relations between Austria and Serbia

must be bad, and that nothing could mend them. He added that he had tried in vain to convince Berlin of this fundamental truth. Some people in Germany still persisted in believing in the efficacy of a conciliatory policy on the part of Austria towards Serbia. He himself knew better.[5]

But after Sarajevo, even in Germany those in authority were converted to Tschirschky's thesis and he, in consequence, could speak a very different language to Berchtold than he had used on 2 July. This is shown by what Berchtold wrote to Tisza on 8 July:

Tschirschky has just left after having told me that he has received a telegram from Berlin containing instructions from his Imperial master to emphasize here that Berlin expects the Monarchy to take action against Serbia and that Germany would not understand our letting the opportunity slip without striking a blow. . . . From other utterances of the Ambassador I could see that Germany would interpret any compromise

[1] Lutz, pp. 31–2.   [2] Lutz, p. 34.   [3] Lutz, p. 60.
[4] Oe-U. VIII, 10038.   [5] BD. XI, 40.

on our part with Serbia as a confession of weakness, which would not remain without repercussions on our position in the Triple Alliance and the future policy of Germany.[1]

These documents, proving the pressure exercised by the German Ambassador on Austrian opinion, gave rise to a 'Tschirschky question' on which the German Commission of Inquiry sought to throw light by interrogating colleagues of the deceased diplomat. These latter denied that he had advised Austria to resort to violent measures. No telegram from Berlin was found ordering Tschirschky in the name of his 'Imperial master' to exercise the pressure attributed to him by Berchtold. Therefore Germans like Wegerer and pro-Germans asserted that Berchtold had invented this pressure to overcome the opposition of Tisza. But Berchtold reaffirmed it in the *Neue Freie Presse* (28 September 1919): 'Never should we have acted thus if Germany had not urged us to it', the pressure being applied first by the Kaiser and then by his Ambassador.

It seems difficult to believe that Berchtold, well knowing that Tisza frequented Tschirschky's society and could easily ascertain the truth, would in writing to Tisza dare to attribute such utterances to Tschirschky if the latter had never made them. Giesl, who was in Vienna during those days waiting to take up his post as Minister to Belgrade, has informed the present writer that he learnt from Berchtold of Tschirschky's having called at the Ballplatz with the Berlin telegram in question in his hands and having read it out to Berchtold. In answer to an inquiry from the present writer, Berchtold wrote on 3 December 1933:

I do not remember in what form Count Tschirschky made the communication which I reported in writing to Count Tisza on 8 July. But I can state with certainty that I was then entirely under the impression of this information and of its importance for our further procedure.

The point to be determined is, therefore, whether Tschirschky, who at first had preached prudence, did or did not receive instructions from Berlin to take the opposite line. Now, if it is undoubted that no telegram urging him to do so has come to light, it is no less undoubted that the Kaiser sharply disapproved of his first counsels of prudence. It cannot be ruled out, therefore, that, perhaps by letter from some high official at the Wilhelmstrasse, as Renouvin remarks,[2] or from some one at court, or by telephone, as Fischer writes,[3] Tschirschky may have

---

[1] Oe-U. VIII, 10145.   [2] Renouvin, pp. 67–71.

[3] In *Die kritischen 39 Tage* (pp. 63–4) Eugen Fischer, Secretary to the Reichstag Commission of Inquiry into the war guilt question, writes: 'Kaiser Wilhelm II wrote many a marginal note which he himself did not take seriously, many to which no attention was paid at the Foreign Ministry. But the one of 3 July 1914, to the report of the Ambassador to Vienna of 30 June, at once became a *mot d'ordre*. In Herr von Tschirschky at Vienna a transformation took place. On 30 June he had confidently reported home his serious attitude of

been told of the Imperial reprimand, especially as it seemed to be the Kaiser's wish that he should learn of it: 'Will Tschirschky have the goodness' etc.[1] However that may be, the news of the Imperial reprimand did not remain unknown to the Austrian Ambassador to Berlin, even if he did not know of the Kaiser's marginal note. On 8 July Szögyény telegraphed to Berchtold:

I was told at the Foreign Ministry that a report of his had shown him as having behaved with a certain half-heartedness towards Your Excellency. He is said to have received a reprimand from here on that account.[2]

It is of interest also to note that Lichnowsky, whose memoirs were written in 1916 before anything was known of the Kaiser's marginal notes, relates that, when at Berlin soon after the Sarajevo outrage, he learnt that:

Tschirschky had been reprimanded because he reported that he had counselled moderation in Vienna towards Serbia.[3]

After refusing to attach weight to Szögyény's telegrams, it is easy to say, as some German historians have done, that the references to pressure by Tschirschky are a sheer invention of the Ballplatz. But Lutz allows that Tschirschky 'did more to stiffen Berchtold's backbone than he was authorized to do by his instructions from Berlin' and comments that the chorus of accusations against Tschirschky in the publications of neutrals as well as of ex-enemies

cannot but impart the conviction that they are based on more than mere gossip. Prince Stolberg, the Counsellor at the German Embassy at Vienna under Tschirschky, has put forward as a possible explanation the theory that, in consequence of the reproaches levelled at German policy during the Balkan wars of not having sufficiently used its influence on behalf of Austrian interests, Tschirschky thought it incumbent on him for the sake of preserving the alliance to take a strong line in defence of the Austro-Hungarian point of view to the outer world.[4]

Too many sources bear witness to Tschirschky's pressure for the matter to be called in doubt. Giesl related to the present writer that

---

warning. On 2 July he still manifested to Emperor Francis Joseph and on the 3rd to Berchtold his aversion for a violently emotional policy in the Serbian question. On that same 3rd the Kaiser wrote his marginal note and on the 4th the daily report of the Viennese Foreign Ministry records that Tschirschky had said . . . with the obvious intention that it should be passed on: "Germany would support the Monarchy through thick and thin, no matter what it should decide to do against Serbia; the sooner Austria-Hungary started off the better" etc. . . . The transformation took place soon after the Kaiser had intimated his opinion. One must assume that the Kaiser's standpoint was at once telegraphed or telephoned on to Tschirschky. Any such telegram sent neither by nor on the instructions of the Chancellor or the Secretary of State need not have been preserved in such a way as to be available to us to-day.' (Cf. Oe-U. VIII, 10038.)

[1] See above, p. 138.   [2] Oe-U. VIII, 10127.]
[3] Lichnowsky, p. 72.   [4] Lutz, p. 50.

between 7 and 9 July he called on the German Ambassador, who asked him:

'What are you now going to do with Serbia?' I answered: 'That will probably mainly depend on the results of the investigation now in progress.' In the further course of the conversation Tschirschky observed: 'If you pocket that tamely as well, you are none of you worth . . ., and Germany would have to look round for another ally.'[1]

Later the present writer wrote asking Giesl whether he had told Berchtold of the tenor of this conversation at the time. Giesl replied that he did not remember so doing. Giesl raised the matter with Wegerer, the editor of the review *Kriegsschuldfrage*, who objected that his own investigations showed no trace of such expressions on Tschirschky's part. But to him Giesl emphatically reaffirmed his disclosure. Berchtold, in reply to a question from the present writer, also stated that Giesl had given him an account of the conversation and added that about the same time Tschirschky used the same expressions to Chlumecky as well. Czernin, too, lays stress on the pressure exercised by Tschirschky, saying that he was given to interfering in Austro-Hungarian affairs 'with a certain vehemence and not always in the most tactful way'. His speeches at the time were attuned to the tone of: 'Now or never.' He thought that the war had best break out in 1914 on the initiative of Austria. Czernin expresses the belief, however, that, in behaving as he did, Tschirschky was exceeding his instructions.[2] There is no room for doubt that, both by temperament and by the special position he enjoyed as having already directed his country's foreign policy, Tschirschky was perfectly capable of behaving as described above. He had his own ideas, predominant among them being that Austria was to pass across the prostrate body of Serbia. If he had at first given counsels of moderation, it was because he thought he was expressing the views of his Sovereign. But nothing was more welcome to him than to take the road in the opposite direction.

To form a correct picture of this diplomatist it is worth while to look at the profile of him drawn by Dumaine, the French Ambassador to Vienna:

Tschirschky was a colleague one did not care to meet save to the degree in which it was strictly necessary to converse with him. Under the exterior of a man of the best society, acquitting himself of the duties of courtesy with automatic exactitude and precision, it was impossible for him to hide for more than ten minutes the violence of his character, his arrogance, his will to dominate. . . . He constantly proclaimed himself an irreconcilable adversary of Serbia. . . . One day he said to me: 'I am so convinced of the necessity of crushing the Serbs that I should not fear to outstep my Government's instructions in order to make Austria decide to act. . . .' Until the

---

[1] Letter in the possession of the present writer.   [2] Czernin, pp. 10–11.

final break-up M. de Tschirschky's intransigence grew steadily more intolerable. A bad imitation of Bismarck, he reproduced only the defects. Strong in his authority as a former Secretary of State and boasting of the insight acquired in this high office, he laid down his opinions on every question in so peremptory a tone that it left no room for the expression of a contrary opinion. . . . Not content with making his weight felt heavily and ostentatiously on the decisions of the Austro-Hungarian Cabinet, he affected such airs of superiority towards his colleagues that most of them had given up frequenting his society.[1]

In this case, as it happened, Tschirschky in no way exceeded his instructions from Berlin. The telegrams reaching him were uncompromising in their demands that Vienna this time must take bold and thorough measures. The German historian Bach admits that after 5 July one guiding principle

dominated from now on the leading men at the Wilhelmstrasse: Austria-Hungary must herself decide the line she will follow. If she means to act she must do so quickly and decisively. Germany will take her stand at her side. But she will make every effort to localize any conflict between Vienna and Belgrade.[2]

And all the news reaching Berlin from Vienna from that day on was to the effect that Austria had decided on war with Serbia. On 7 July, Lieutenant-Colonel Kageneck, the German Military Attaché at Vienna, reported to Moltke that a well-informed officer at the War Ministry had intimated to him that

the Austro-Hungarian demands on Serbia are to be so harsh that evasion or submission seems impossible. That makes it look as if war with Serbia is a certainty.[3]

On 13 July Kageneck wrote to Moltke that he had been told by the War Minister's aide-de-camp that

the aged Emperor was still firmly resolved to undertake such an emphatic *démarche* at Belgrade as might well lead to the arbitrament of the sword. . . . People here seem to be quite uncertain as to what is to happen after the war with Serbia is over. Territorial acquisitions are not contemplated because that would mean giving compensation to Italy. Moreover in all the discussions taking place in the Delegations the point is stressed that the Monarchy is territorially saturated.[4]

General Moltke's marginal note to this letter was:

Austria must beat the Serbs and then make peace quickly, demanding an Austro-Serbian alliance as the sole condition. Like what Prussia did with Austria in 1866.

On 16 July Pallavicini, the Austrian Ambassador to Constantinople, telegraphed that he had talked with his German colleague Wangenheim

[1] Dumaine, p. 131.   [2] Bach, p. 15.   [3] Bach, p. 15.   [4] Bach, p. 16.

who had returned from Berlin that same day with the news that Berlin was

firmly resolved to go with us through thick and thin in Balkan affairs. But from his expressions I gathered that Berlin regards the present moment as decisive for the Triple Alliance. Everything, he said, would depend on our being able to achieve a complete success over Serbia. If we did so, the German statesmen saw the possibility of keeping Roumania in the Triple Alliance. A failure on our part, Baron Wangenheim gave me to understand, would imperil the existence of the Triple Alliance.[1]

8. *The views of the German supreme authorities on the Austrian situation.*

Wangenheim spoke the same language as Tschirschky, and Tschirschky as Bethmann Hollweg and as Wilhelm. The proofs are too numerous to be called seriously in question. All that has yet to be told will confirm that the Kaiser and his ministers asked Austria to hurl herself against Serbia as soon as possible. When they had not wanted her to do so, they had spoken in very different accents to hold her back. On 9 November 1912 Wilhelm, as has been shown in Vol. I of the present work, remarked to his Ministers that if a general war arose from Austria's refusal to have the Serbs in Albania and Durazzo, it would not be a *casus foederis* for Germany. And on 6 July 1913 the Chancellor warned Vienna not to take measures against Serbia for fear of causing a European war.

This would most seriously affect the vital interests of Germany and I must therefore expect that, before Count Berchtold makes any such resolve, he will inform us of it.[2]

It meant that Germany would not associate herself with Austria in a war provoked by Austrian aggression. Nothing of this kind was said in July 1914.

When on 20 July the Serbian Chargé d'Affaires called on Jagow to read him a *note verbale* in which Serbia, fearing an Austrian attack, expressed her readiness to offer Austria the satisfaction of all demands which were not incompatible with her own dignity and integrity, Jagow rebuffed him with the reply that he would communicate the message to Vienna.[3] Even going no further than the official German version, the statement was made that it was for Austria to decide what was to be done and that Germany would take her stand at her side.[4] Could Germany embark on a life and death gamble without even asking herself whether the gamble was actually necessary? The German statesmen would have been mad if they had never formed an opinion of their own as to what line their ally ought to take after the Sarajevo outrage.

[1] Oe-U. VIII, 10303.   [2] See Vol. I, pp. 455-6.   [3] DD. I, 91.   [4] DD. I, 15.

On one point they were clear from the beginning, even if at the eleventh hour doubts assailed them, namely that Austrian prestige was too much shaken, Austrian interests too much menaced for the Monarchy to do otherwise than seize the occasion to put Serbia in her place once and for all. If Austria failed to do so, if she contented herself with minor amends, she would prove herself to be an ally of no value and Germany would have to look around for other safeguards in Europe. This was the German thesis after Sarajevo, laid down by the Kaiser and countersigned by his Ministers.

Some historians make out that the Kaiser counted only up to a certain point. Let not too much weight be laid, they say, on his marginal notes which were often read at the Wilhelmstrasse only after decisions had been taken. Nothing is further from the truth! The Wilhelmstrasse could sometimes take action and make decisions without the Imperial consent, but only in matters of secondary importance and always in accordance with general instructions given by the Kaiser. In the absence of such instructions, when it was something more than a routine matter, anyone venturing to take a decision without consulting him would have incurred a disavowal and a reprimand. The fact is that instructions given in the marginal notes were scrupulously carried out and opinions expressed in them carefully conveyed to those concerned. The men in the Government were able to exercise some influence on Wilhelm's impulsive and changeable disposition and upon occasion make him change his mind, but they could never act contrary to his will. Bülow, for instance, in certain cases dragged him into courses which he was not inclined to pursue, but only by the exercise of consummate dexterity which ended badly for himself. At best, Bülow did not alter the basic lines of Wilhelm's policy, for which, as we shall soon explain, he bore the responsibility and which brought Germany to defeat. Bethmann, who was of far less account than Bülow, never dreamt in July 1914 of making a stand for his own pacific tendencies. He blindly followed instructions, whether he agreed with them or not.

These instructions are mirrored in a long telegram sent by Szögyény to Berchtold on 12 July:

Both H.M. Kaiser Wilhelm and all other responsible personages here not only stand firmly in allied loyalty behind the Monarchy but invite us most emphatically not to let the present moment pass but to take vigorous measures against Serbia and make a clean sweep of the revolutionary conspirators' nest once and for all, leaving it entirely to us what means we think right to select. . . . I think a certain explanation is necessary why authoritative German circles and not least H.M. Kaiser Wilhelm himself—one might almost say—press us to undertake possibly even military measures against Serbia. It is evident that after the deplorable events that have taken place the Monarchy must proceed with the utmost vigour against Serbia.

But that the German Government also from its own standpoint should regard the present moment as politically the most suitable needs further elucidation. The choice of the present moment is in the German view, which I altogether share, prompted by general political considerations and by special considerations arising out of the Sarajevo murder. Germany has recently been strengthened in her conviction that Russia is arming for war against her western neighbours. . . but is not at the present moment sufficiently forward with her preparations. Therefore it is by no means certain that, if Serbia becomes involved in a war with us, Russia would resort to arms in her support. And if she did so, she is far from being so militarily prepared and powerful as she will probably be some years hence. The German Government further believes it has sure indications that England would not join in a war over a Balkan country even should this lead to a passage of arms with Russia and eventually even with France. Not only that Anglo-German relations have so far improved that Germany no longer fears a directly hostile attitude on England's part, but above all England at the moment is anything but desirous of war and has no intention of pulling the chestnuts out of the fire for Serbia or ultimately for Russia. . . . Every nation condemns the bloody deed of Sarajevo and understands that we must call Serbia to account for it. . . . These no doubt are the political reasons why the German Empire frankly advocates our clearing up our relations with Serbia which it regards as intolerable.[1]

First-hand evidence of the mood at the Wilhelmstrasse is given in a letter from Jagow, the Under Secretary for Foreign Affairs, to Lichnowsky, the German Ambassador in London, who had reported Sir Edward Grey as having said on 9 July that much would depend on the measures Austria intended to take against Serbia and on 'whether they excited Slav feeling in such a way as to render it impossible for M. Sazonov to remain passive'.[2]

Jagow replied in a long private letter of 18 July:

But the fact remains that we have an alliance with Austria: *Hic Rhodus, hic salta*. Whether we have made a very good bargain in the alliance with that steadily disintegrating agglomeration of states on the Danube may be questioned. But I say with the poet—I think it was Busch—'If you're tired of the friends you've got, go, if you have them, with another lot.' Unfortunately we have not yet arrived at relations with England guaranteeing complete success, indeed we could not after all that has happened—if ever we shall be able to do so.

Austria, whose prestige has suffered more and more from her failure to take resolute action, now scarcely counts any longer as a full-sized Great Power. The Balkan crisis has further weakened her position. This recession in the Austrian power position has severely weakened our alliance group.

Austria is determined no longer to tolerate Serbian machinations and the consistently provocative behaviour of her diminutive neighbour in Belgrade —cf. the language of the Serbian press—and of Mr. Pašić. Austria recognizes

----

[1] Oe-U. VIII, 10215.   [2] DD. I, 30.

that she has let many chances slip, that she still has power to act but in a few years will no longer have it. She intends now to come to a settlement with Serbia and has conveyed this intention to us. During the whole Balkan crisis we have successfully used our good offices for peace. . . . We have not now driven Austria to her decision. We cannot and must not tie her hands now. If we did so, Austria (and we ourselves) could rightly reproach us with having deprived her of her last chance to rehabilitate herself politically. This would only hasten the process of gradual extinction and decay from within. Her position in the Balkans would be gone for ever. You will agree with me that a definite stabilization of Russian hegemony in the Balkans would indirectly be inadmissible for us. The preservation of Austria, and that Austria shall be as strong as possible, is essential to us on domestic and foreign grounds. . . .

We must see to localizing the conflict between Austria and Serbia. Whether this is possible will depend in the first place on Russia and in the second place on the moderating influence of the other members of the *Entente*. The more boldness Austria displays, the more strongly we support her, the more likely is Russia to keep quiet. There is certain to be some blustering in St. Petersburg, but at bottom Russia is not now ready to strike. France and England will not want war now. In a few years according to all expert opinion Russia will be ready to strike. Then she will crush us with the numbers of her soldiers, then she will have built her Baltic fleet and strategic railways. Our group meanwhile will be growing steadily weaker. Russia knows this well and therefore absolutely wants peace for several years more. . . . If localization is not attainable and if Russia attacks Austria, then the *casus foederis* will arise, then we cannot sacrifice Austria. We should then find ourselves in a not exactly proud isolation. I have no wish for a preventive war, but if the fight offers itself, we dare not flinch.

I still hope and believe that the conflict can be localized. England's attitude in this matter will be of great importance. I am quite convinced that public opinion there will not be enthusiastic about Austria's procedure. . . . But one must do what one can to prevent too great enthusiasm for Serbia. . . . Sir Grey always talks about the balance of power established by the two power groups. He must see that this balance would be totally upset if Austria were left in the lurch by us and shattered by Russia.[1]

---

[1] DD. I, 72.—Pierre Renouvin, whose work is basic for the French point of view, does not believe that in the days immediately preceding the sending of the ultimatum to Serbia Wilhelm still counted on the possibility of localizing the conflict and quotes the order given by Wilhelm to the fleet on 20 July to remain concentrated, despite advice to the contrary from his advisers. On 20 July he suggested to the Chancellor that the heads of the big steamship companies should receive warning (DD. I, 80). Moreover Tirpitz, who was informed on 13 July of the main points in the Austrian note, writes that he at once foresaw what would happen (Renouvin, pp. 77–9). Now it is possible that Tirpitz was pessimistic from the outset, but Wilhelm, while deeming it advisable to take precautions, nourished a series of graduated hopes, the main one of which was for English neutrality, and when it became apparent that this hope was fading, he in vain tried to avoid the conflict. Renouvin himself a few pages earlier writes (p. 51) of the German political leaders: 'A general war does not seem to have been a definite part of the programme adopted on 5 July, but it might easily follow as a consequence of such a programme. This risk the Central Powers clearly accepted.'

Let not this letter of Jagow's be regarded as a proof of German innocence. Nobody denies, and here it has been quite clearly demonstrated, that it was Austria who expressed to her ally the intention of settling accounts this time with Serbia. But this intention was a fulfilment of the ideas of Berlin, first made known to Vienna by Naumann and then expressed to Szögyény by the Kaiser and Bethmann. In other words Berlin held the opinion and communicated it to Vienna that Austria would no longer be worth anything and would fall to pieces if she did not, once and for all, eliminate the Serb menace. Now to express this opinion, as it was actually expressed, was to drive the Monarchy into making war on Serbia and thus plunging Europe into the most terrible war.

9. German hopes of a localization of the conflict; the precedent of 1909; *Bülow's share of responsibility.*

Not that the German leaders intended to let loose a general war on purpose. First of all they were not absolutely sure that the Monarchy this time really would go to extremes. Then they thought that if she did so, as was desirable, they would manage to localize the conflict because neither Russia nor France would act. We have seen Jagow writing this to Lichnowsky. And Biedermann, the Saxon Chargé d'Affaires at Berlin, reported the same thing on 17 July to the Minister for Foreign Affairs at Dresden:

If, contrary to expectations, Austria were obliged to take measures against Serbia, people here reckon on a localization of the conflict, because England is altogether peaceably minded and neither France nor Russia appears to feel any inclination for war.[1]

On 18 July Zimmermann, the Under Secretary for Foreign Affairs, told Dr. Schoen, the Bavarian representative at Berlin (who reported it to the Bavarian Prime Minister Hertling) that Russia would begin by bluffing but would be reined in by England and France.[2] On 20 July, Koester, the Baden Chargé d'Affaires at Berlin, wrote to Dusch, the Baden Minister for Foreign Affairs:

In circles here, even at the Foreign Ministry, the opinion prevails that Russia is bluffing and that, if only for reasons of domestic policy, she will think well before provoking a European war, the outcome of which is doubtful. Moreover it must not be overlooked that the personal sympathies of the Tsar for Serbia as the native country of the men who murdered the Austrian Heir Apparent and his wife, are extremely slight.[3]

[1] Bach, pp. 64–6.
[2] DD. IV, pp. 126–30; Dirr, pp. 6–9.
[3] Bach, pp. 66–7.

On 23 July Zimmermann said to Koester that he thought

it would be possible to induce Russia to remain neutral since she was beset with domestic difficulties of all kinds and since it might be assumed that there, as in the rest of Europe, a war on behalf of Serbia would not enlist many sympathies.[1]

Bach comments:

Parallel with optimistic estimates of the situation by Berlin went a profound underestimation of the extent to which the other side would be prepared to intervene. . . . This was a dangerous mistake, but up to 27 July it was so predominant that the Berlin statesmen during those days, even in the most serious communications from London and St. Petersburg, only looked for the few clues which seemed to point to a way of escape.[2]

The illusion as to the attitude of Russia lasted on at the Wilhelmstrasse far into the July crisis long after it ought to have faded. This is shown by a conversation which the English Ambassador in Vienna had with Tschirschky:

I have already reported the conviction expressed to me by the German Ambassador on 24 July that Russia would stand aside. This feeling, which was also held at the Ballplatz, influenced no doubt the course of events.[3]

And the English Ambassador to Berlin, on returning from leave on 27 July, wrote to Nicolson:

I found Jagow ill and tired but nevertheless optimistic—his optimism being based, as he told me, on the idea that Russia was not in a position to make war.[4]

As for the Chancellor, there is not the slightest doubt that he thought the same. In fact he believed that France was the chief one not to want war. On 16 July he telegraphed to Riedern, the Secretary of State for Alsace-Lorraine:

We have grounds to assume and cannot but wish, that France, at the moment burdened with all sorts of cares, will do everything to restrain Russia from intervention. . . . If we succeed in not only keeping France quiet herself but in getting her to enjoin peace on St. Petersburg, this will have a repercussion on the Franco-Russian alliance highly favourable to ourselves.[5]

In the correspondence of the representatives of the other German states at Berlin optimistic references to the situation are to be found even as late as 29 July. For instance the Baden Minister on that date, reporting his impressions of calls made by him on Delbrück, Lerchenfeld

[1] Bach, p. 71. [2] Bach, p. 20. [3] BD. XI, 676.
[4] BD. XI, 677. [5] DD. I, 58.

and Stumm, writes that the news of Russian and French preparations for mobilization seemed exaggerated, and that no conclusions
could be drawn from them.

The danger lies above all in the deplorable circumstance that the urgently
necessary decisive blow by Austria against Serbia is not to be expected in
less than ten to twelve days from now because deployment unfortunately
takes all that time. . . . Favourable to the prospects of peace is the fact that
the French now really do not desire war in any circumstances, in fact actually
fear it on account of their desperate financial position and perhaps also on
military grounds; that is why they are setting all levers in motion at St.
Petersburg to exercise a moderating influence there; but whether the peace-
loving ruler and his Foreign Minister will retain the upper hand against the
Pan-Slav currents is a thing no one can predict.[1]

And on that same 29 July the Saxon Chargé d'Affaires also wrote:

to-day the opinion in diplomatic and military circles is decidedly more optimistic, and satisfaction over this alleviation is already expressed in the *Norddeutsche Allgemeine Zeitung* of the 30th which has just appeared. It writes:
    'The peaceable tone of the official Russian communiqué of the 28th has
found a lively echo here. The Imperial Government shares the wish for the
preservation of peaceful relations. It hopes that the German people will
support its efforts by a temperate and quiet attitude.'[2]

Of course, once the war had broken out the German Government
had to put a good face on it. The preamble to the German *White Book*,
put together and published for the sitting of the German Reichstag of
3 August 1914, states:

From the bottom of our hearts we signified to our ally our agreement with
his estimate of the position. . . . In so doing we were fully aware that any
military measures against Serbia on the part of Austria-Hungary might bring
Russia on to the scene and involve us in a war in pursuance of our obligations
as an ally.[3]

'Fully aware' they were, but not fully convinced. However much the
German Government might affirm that if war had to come, it was
better for it to come at once rather than later, it may well be doubted
whether they would so lightheartedly have embarked on the adventure
if they had been convinced of immediate Russian intervention. They
took the plunge reckoning on the acquiescence of all the three *Entente*
Powers and at the worst on the neutrality of England.

An extraordinary illusion! It seems hard to believe that the rulers of
the German Empire can have been reckless and irresponsible to such
a degree. The World War sprang from this miscalculation of theirs,
not from the quite different mistake laid to their charge by S. Fay,

---

[1] Bach, pp. 90–1.   [2] Bach, p. 92.   [3] See CDD., p. 406.

a historian who has made a special study of the question of the origins of the war. He writes:

The Kaiser and his advisers on 5 and 6 July were not criminals plotting the World War; they were simpletons putting 'a noose about their necks' (the Kaiser himself noted frantically on 30 July. . . . 'the stupidity and clumsiness of our ally has been made a hangman's noose for us') and handing the other end of the rope to a stupid and clumsy adventurer who now felt free to go as far as he liked.[1]

To begin with, it is out of place to call Berchtold an adventurer and to overlook the fact that the Monarchy was in a position which, however much it may have been due to gross political blunders in the past, was now such as to convince the majority of Austrian political leaders, beginning with the aged Emperor himself, that there was no other way out than a war with Serbia. And in the second place it is not permissible for a historian like Fay to be oblivious of the admissions made immediately by the German Government in the *White Book*: 'We . . . permitted Austria a completely free hand in her action towards Serbia.'[2] The evidence here brought together demonstrates beyond a doubt: (1) that Germany in July 1914 wanted Austria to take advantage of the Sarajevo crime in order to finish with Serbia once and for all, and restore her own damaged prestige; (2) that, if Germany had not wanted this, neither Francis Joseph, nor Berchtold, nor even Conrad would have gone ahead with the venture.

Other documents show that Berlin did not change its mind in the days that followed and that the men at the Wilhelmstrasse never stopped prodding Austria to make haste, to take no half measures, to stick at nothing, right up to the moment when they realized that their reckoning on British neutrality was mistaken. On that day they sought to go into reverse, but too late. It may thus already be affirmed that, if for Austria the decision to go to war was an act of desperation, no such extenuating circumstances exist for Germany. To the German leaders, rather than to those of Austria, would apply the adjectives 'helpless and incompetent' used by Fay in describing the figure of Berchtold[3] who was certainly not a shining light either.

Bülow in his *Memoirs* relates that Pansa, a former Italian Ambassador to Berlin, said to him in May 1915: '*Vos gouvernants ont été au mois de Juillet dernier cent mille fois plus bêtes qu'aucune fantaisie ne peut se le figurer*'. He adds that German policy in the summer of 1914 illustrated the truth of Montaigne's saying '*que tous les maux de ce monde viennent de l'ânerie*'.[4]

Let him tell us wherein the *ânerie* of his successor consisted. His basic thesis is the following:

---

[1] Fay, II, p. 223.
[3] Fay, I, p. 469.
[2] *German White Book* in CDD., p. 406; see pp. 223–4.
[4] Bülow, III, pp. 148–9.

We have nothing at all to gain from war. An attempt to force the Danes, the Swiss, the Dutch or the Belgians on to our side is only conceivable to a madman. An extension of the Empire towards Eastern Europe would be a not less dubious undertaking.

As Jules Cambon said in Berlin to the Belgian Minister Beyens on 20 February 1914:

Germany need only be patient, she need only peacefully augment her economic and financial strength, and await the results of her growing birth-rate to dominate in Central Europe without a struggle, with no one to gain-say her.[1]

For this reason she ought to strive to maintain peace at all costs (i) by showing tact towards England and not forcing the pace of naval construction; rather than dreadnoughts it would be better to develop the U-boat, (ii) by not opposing Russian aspirations in the Dardanelles question, (iii) by holding the balance even between Russian and Austrian interests in the Balkans. For Bismarck the Dardanelles question had always formed a pretext for maintaining contact with Russia and Bülow claimed that for twelve years he had followed the same general policy. And then there had been the sending of Liman von Sanders to Constantinople with the result that Russia was annoyed beyond measure.[2]

All this is quite true. Only it must also not be forgotten: (i) that during Bülow's term of office German naval construction received its maximum impetus; offers of alliance made by the British Government were each time rejected, so that England found herself forced to compose her differences in 1904 with France and in 1907 with Russia, (ii) it was Bülow who in 1905 brought about the crisis over Morocco which nearly led to war and cemented the Franco-British *Entente Cordiale*, (iii) it was Bülow again who caused a gulf to open between Russia and Germany by supporting Austria to the utmost against Russia in the Bosnia-Herzegovina annexation crisis of 1908 and by the ultimatum of 1909 forcing Russia to recognize the annexation, and thereby to accept all the Austrian demands. And it was the success of this ultimatum which led his successor astray in encouraging the belief that by rattling the German sabre he could localize the Austro-Serbian conflict and thus avoid a European war. Bülow himself relates that on leaving office he warned Bethmann Hollweg not to try to repeat his own success of 1909: '*ne bis in idem*'. But Bethmann thought that, as Bülow had triumphed by daring, he, too, might have similar success. Bülow tried to warn him off with the tactless quotation: *Non cuivis homini contingit adire Corinthum* which Bethmann understandably resented. Jagow pertinently observes that the Bosnian crisis was but the prelude to the Serbian crisis of 1914:

[1] Bülow, III, p. 153.   [2] Bülow, III, pp. 12–18, 126.

Every policy has its consequences, even the policy of Bülow, although it had no steady line and scant farsightedness and consisted more of seesawing and juggling. We were thrown back on Austria not only by the treaty of alliance but also by the way the European Powers were grouped—to no small degree in consequence of Bülow's policy. In 1914 we had no intention of aping Bülow's performance in 1909. But how could we leave Austria in the lurch? When Bülow took his stand with Austria in the Bosnian crisis, it was not a matter of life and death for Austria but merely a kind of nominal alteration in the legal status of a province which she *de facto* governed. But in the Serbian crisis what was at stake was the existence of the Monarchy which was seriously threatened by Serbian agitation and machinations.[1]

But the fact is that except for the Ambassador to London, Lichnowsky, nobody in Germany from the Kaiser downwards saw the mistake that was being made in letting Austria declare war on Serbia. Not even Bülow shows any realization of it. If he had done so, it would have been his bounden duty to use all his influence to open the eyes of those in authority. But there is no evidence he can bring, no document he can quote, to show that he had understood what was at stake. A message of his to the *Hamburger Nachrichten* of 6 August was that of a thorough warmonger, and he made no attempt to warn the Kaiser when the latter summoned him to ask if he would go again to Rome as Ambassador. He only spoke out when defeat was already certain. And this was the case with all the Germans, beginning with the Socialists, who voted in favour of the war credits. The first to open his eyes to the mistakes he had made, was actually the Kaiser himself.

10. *The Austro-Hungarian Council of Joint Ministers of 7 July 1914; Tisza's opposition to a war with Serbia.*

The first telegram from Szögyény, summarizing his talk with the Kaiser, had already reached Vienna when on 6 July Berchtold received Conrad and said to him:

'You were yesterday with His Majesty. The Emperor says that you view the position very calmly.' Conrad: 'Yes—but I also told His Majesty that one can only expect a thorough solution from a war with Serbia. . . . Reverting to the possibility of war with Serbia, I emphasized that we must before anything know for certain whether Germany will take her stand at our side.' Berchtold: 'The answer will be here to-morrow. The German Kaiser says "Yes", but that he must first have a word with Bethmann Hollweg. How will His Majesty regard that?' Conrad: 'If Germany agrees, His Majesty will be for war with Serbia. . . .' Count Berchtold asked me what moment I thought the right one for the *casus belli*. He pointed out that it was now harvest time and the Monarchy would have to live for a year on the harvest. He suggested first proclaiming a test mobilization. To this I firmly objected saying that if there is to be mobilization, it must be total mobilization. Count

[1] *Front wider Bülow*, p. 217.

Berchtold went on: 'Tisza is against the war, he is afraid of a Russian invasion of Transylvania. What will happen about Galicia if we mobilize against Serbia? . . . The Germans will want to know from us what is to happen after the war.' Conrad: 'Tell them, we do not know that ourselves.'[1]

We reproduce this dialogue because it reveals Berchtold, in his uncertainty of mind, seeking through Conrad to probe into his Imperial master's real intentions, raising doubts and difficulties after having dispatched Hoyos to Berlin with instructions to take up a fighting attitude and to say that Serbian territory was to be partitioned between Austria, Bulgaria and Albania. Hoyos got back again to Vienna on the morning of 7 July and reported at once to Berchtold. Germany, he said, advised immediate action against Serbia even 'although our operations against Serbia should bring about the great war'.[2] Did he also report that he himself had drafted the second of Szögyény's telegrams? When the present writer put this question to Berchtold, he answered that he had no recollection of such a thing, but corroborated that Hoyos had given him the same account of the Hoyos-Zimmermann talk as was later given to the present writer by Hoyos himself. Zimmermann had assured Hoyos that Germany could perfectly well fight Russia and France, so that all Austria had to do was to concentrate her forces in the Balkans; Germany urged immediate action and had given the most solemn promises of unconditional support to the Monarchy. And in fact Berchtold, spurred on by this news, at once told Conrad:

Germany advises us to strike at once. . . . Germany will take her stand beside us unconditionally, even although our operations against Serbia should bring about the great war.

This caused Conrad to persuade Archduke Frederick, Francis Ferdinand's successor in the Supreme Command, to postpone his proposed journey to Hamburg. Conrad further held discussions with Colonel Metzger, the head of the operational branch, in regard to the necessary measures to be taken in view of possible mobilization.[3]

But would Tisza consent to a surprise attack on Serbia and her partition? Berchtold had been obliged to submit to him copies of the documents about to be sent to Berlin by the hand of Hoyos, and Tisza had telegraphed back the request that the most compromising phrases should be omitted from Francis Joseph's letter. But his request had not yet gone off when Szögyény was already presenting the letter to the Kaiser. Tisza also asked for a meeting of the Council of Joint Ministers of the Monarchy, and this was summoned for 7 July when the reply from Berlin could be laid before it. Previous to the meeting, Berchtold assembled the Prime Ministers Tisza and Stürgkh and the German

[1] Conrad, IV, pp. 39–40.   [2] Conrad, IV, 42.   [3] Conrad, IV, 42

Ambassador Tschirschky. Hoyos read the Szögyény telegrams out to them and gave an account of his interview with Zimmermann. Tisza was furious at the suggestion of a surprise attack on Serbia, let alone of partitioning her. He insisted that what Hoyos had said to Zimmermann, especially about the partitioning of Serbia, must be regarded by Germany as the expression of a purely personal opinion. To pacify him Berchtold had to disavow Hoyos.[1] But there is no room for doubt that at the beginning Berchtold did toy with projects for wiping Serbia off the map and partitioning her territory among her neighbours. The minutes of the meeting of the Council of Ministers for Joint Affairs of 7 July record that Berchtold opened the discussion by asking

whether the moment had not arrived to render Serbia innocuous once and for all by a display of force. Any such decisive blow could not be carried into execution without diplomatic preparation and he had accordingly got in touch with the German Government. The discussions in Berlin had had extremely satisfactory results, both Kaiser Wilhelm and Bethmann Hollweg having assured us of Germany's unconditional support in case of war complications with Serbia. Now we must reckon with Italy and Roumania and he shared the Berlin Cabinet's view that it would be better to act first and leave possible claims for compensation till later. He clearly saw that war with Russia would very likely be a consequence of our invading Serbia.[2] Russia was pursuing a policy which in the long run aimed at a league (*Zusammenschluss*) of the Balkan States, including Roumania, in order to play them off against the Monarchy when the moment seemed favourable. In his opinion we should realize that our position in the face of such a policy would grow steadily worse inasmuch as any passive letting things take their course on our part would necessarily be interpreted by our own Southern Slavs as a sign of weakness and would strengthen the gravitational pull of the two neighbour states. The logical consequence of what has been said surely is that we must forestall our adversaries and by a timely settlement of accounts with Serbia check the development which is already in full swing. Later on it will no longer be possible to do so.

The Hungarian Prime Minister agreed that in the last few days, because of facts revealed by the inquiry and the attitude of the Serbian press, the position had changed and that he, too, regarded the possibility of military measures against Serbia as less remote than he had believed immediately after the Sarajevo outrage. He would, however, never agree to a surprise attack on Serbia without preliminary diplomatic preparation, as seemed to be intended and as regrettably had been discussed in Berlin by Count Hoyos, because by so doing we should in his opinion thoroughly discredit ourselves in the

---

[1] DD., I, 18.

[2] Oe-U. VIII, 10118.—Later in revising the protocol, Berchtold attenuated the force of his statement by altering the wording to: 'an armed encounter with Serbia might have as its consequence a war with Russia'. Lutz, who gives the two versions, thinks that Berchtold may possibly have been prompted to use the stronger phrasing by the more confident views of Berlin on this point. (Lutz, p. 59.)

eyes of Europe and most probably have to reckon with the hostility of the whole of the Balkans—except for Bulgaria—without Bulgaria in her present state of weakness being able to give us corresponding help. We ought undoubtedly to formulate demands on Serbia and present an ultimatum if Serbia failed to meet them. The demands must be stiff but not impossible of fulfilment. If Serbia accepted them we should have scored a brilliant diplomatic success and our prestige in the Balkans would soar. Were our demands to meet with a rejection, then he, too, would be in favour of military operations, but he must from the outset emphatically state that any such operations, though they might result in a diminution of Serbia, must never aim at her destruction, because on the one hand this could never be conceded by Russia without a life and death struggle and because he himself as Hungarian Prime Minister could never agree to the annexation by the Monarchy of any part of Serbia.

It did not lie with Germany to judge whether or not we should now strike at Serbia. He personally took the view that there was no imperative reason to go to war for the time being. At the present moment it must be taken into account that the agitation against us in Roumania is very strong and that, in view of the inflamed state of public opinion, we should have to reckon with a Roumanian attack and in any case keep considerable forces in Transylvania, to overawe the Roumanians. Now, when Germany had gratifyingly thrown open the way to Bulgaria's accession to the Triple Alliance, a promising field of successful diplomatic activity opened up to us in the Balkans where, by an alliance (*Zusammenschluss*) between Bulgaria and Turkey and their accession to the Triple Alliance, a counterpoise could be created to Roumania and Serbia, thereby forcing Roumania to return to the Triple Alliance.

To this, Berchtold replied that

The history of recent years had shown that diplomatic successes against Serbia, while temporarily enhancing the prestige of the Monarchy, had only intensified the existing strain of our relations with Serbia. . . . A radical solution of the problem raised by the Pan-Serbian propaganda systematically carried out by Belgrade, the disintegrating effects of which is felt by us as far as Zagreb and Zara, is probably only possible by energetic intervention.[1]

Stürgkh, the Austrian Prime Minister, thought that

in the last few days the whole situation had taken on another aspect and a psychological situation had been created which in his opinion unquestionably called for a settlement with Serbia by war. He agreed with Tisza that we and not the German Government must judge whether a war was necessary or not; but he must say that it could not but exercise a great influence upon the decision we might take, if from the quarter which we must regard as the most

---

[1] It is interesting to note that in the minutes drawn up by Hoyos there stood: 'This was not possible save by war by which the Pan-Serb movement would be decapitated once and for all.' Berchtold suppressed this sentence with his pen, replacing the word 'war' by 'energetic intervention'. It looks as if at the sight of the word 'war' written in a historic document of this kind he took fright. This, too, is a pointer to his state of mind.

faithful supporter of our policy in the Triple Alliance, we were, as I have heard, assured of unconditional allied loyalty and in addition urged to act with speed, after our putting the question there. Count Tisza would do well to attach importance to this consideration and reflect that by a policy of hesitancy and weakness we run the risk at a later time of being no longer so sure of this unreserved support from the German Empire. . . . How the conflict should be begun, he regarded as a detail and if the Hungarian Government took the view that a surprise attack '*sans crier gare*', as Count Tisza put it, was not feasible, then another way must be found. . . . Therefore to-day the resolution should be passed in principle that action shall and must be taken. He shared Berchtold's opinion that the position could not be improved in any way by a diplomatic success. If on international grounds preliminary diplomatic action was the course taken, it must be taken with the firm resolve that it shall only end in war.

The Finance Minister Bilinski and the War Minister Krobatin associated themselves with this view. Thereupon the discussion turned upon the aims of military measures against Serbia, Tisza taking the standpoint that Serbia might be shorn of territory but, in deference to Russia, not entirely wiped off the map. At the end of the discussion the following resolutions were entered in the minutes:

1. All those present desire a speedy settlement of the conflict with Serbia by warlike or by peaceful means;

2. The Council of Ministers were willing to associate themselves with Tisza in the view that mobilization should only take place after concrete demands have been placed before and rejected by Serbia and an ultimatum has been presented.

On the other hand all those present, with the exception of Tisza, take the view that a purely diplomatic success, even were it to end with a resounding humiliation for Serbia, would be valueless and that, therefore, such far reaching demands must be made on Serbia as would render their rejection probable, in order to clear the road for a radical solution by way of military operations.

The latter part of this sentence is given as revised by Berchtold from the original draft by Hoyos which ran: 'present Serbia with unacceptable demands in order to make war certain'.

But this did not mean that unanimity had been reached. Tisza still refused to agree to the presenting of such stiff terms to Serbia that she would be unable to accept them and would thus put Austria in a position to declare war on her. He said

that he was anxious to meet the views of the other members and would therefore agree to stiff terms for Serbia but not terms that would clearly betray our intention to make impossible demands. Otherwise we should have an untenable juridical basis for a declaration of war. The text of the note must be very carefully thought out and he would attach importance to having it submitted to him before dispatch. He must make clear that if his point of view were not taken into consideration, he would be obliged to draw the necessary conclusions (*Konsequenzen*).

At the close of the afternoon session Tisza renewed his appeal to all present to weigh their decision carefully. The points under discussion at that session had been:

(i) Whether it would be possible to mobilize first only against Serbia and subsequently, if necessary, against Russia as well; (ii) whether large forces could be kept back in Transylvania to overawe Roumania; (iii) where the conflict with Russia was to start. In this connexion there followed a longish debate on the relative strength of the Powers involved and the possible course of a European war, a debate which on account of its confidential character is not of a nature to be included in the minutes.

Berchtold wound up the discussion by saying that though there was still a difference of opinion between Tisza and the rest of the Council, the gap had to a certain extent been narrowed by the fact that Tisza's proposals

would in all probability lead to the military solution of the conflict with Serbia which he and the other members of the conference regarded as necessary.

Berchtold then informed the Council that he intended to go to Ischl on 8 July to report to the Emperor.[1] Tisza asked him to submit at the same time a memorandum drawn up by himself giving his views on the situation.[2]

This memorandum dated 8 July begins:

The very satisfactory news from Berlin together with justified indignation over events in Serbia have caused all those present at yesterday's Joint Ministerial Conference to come to the resolve of provoking war with Serbia in order to settle accounts once and for all with this arch enemy of the Monarchy. I was not able fully to agree with this plan. Any such attack on Serbia would, as far as can humanly be foreseen, bring upon the scene the intervention of Russia and with it a world war, in which—despite all the optimism in Berlin—I cannot but regard the neutrality of Roumania as at least extremely doubtful. Public opinion there would passionately demand war against us. . . . Thus in this war of offence both the Russian and the Roumanian army would have to be counted among our enemies, which would make the chances of war highly unfavourable for us. . . . Hence in my opinion Serbia should be given the opportunity to avoid war by means of a severe diplomatic defeat, and if war were to result after all, it must be demonstrated before the eyes of all the world that we stand on a basis of legitimate self-defence. . . . But in order to obviate complications with

[1] Oe-U. VIII, 10118.   [2] Oe-U. VIII, 10116.

Italy, ensure the good will of England and render it possible for Russia to remain an onlooker in the war, we on our part would have to make a corresponding declaration at the suitable moment that we have no intention of annihilating, let alone of annexing, Serbia. After a successful war Serbia should, in my view, be reduced by the cession to Bulgaria, Greece and Albania of the territories she has conquered, we at the most only asking for certain strategically important frontier rectifications. We should, it is true, be entitled to indemnification of our war expenditure, which would give us a hold over Serbia for a long time to come. . . . Should Serbia meet our demands, we should, it is true, have to accept this solution in good faith and not bar her retreat. . . . For the moment I can only declare on my own behalf that in spite of my devotion to Your Majesty's service, or, better expressed, just because of it, I could not associate myself with responsibility for the sole solution by an aggressive war.[1]

· Both this memorandum and the minutes of the Council of Ministers show how large a part the decision of Berlin to support Austria played in determining the attitude of Vienna. The German historian Lutz writes:

In order to win Tisza over to the standpoint of the other ministers that the moment had come to 'render Serbia harmless for ever', Count Berchtold laid special emphasis on the unconditional support of the German Government which was pressing for a radical solution of the Serbian crisis. To Baron Conrad Berchtold went so far as to say on 10 July: 'On account of Germany if for no other reason, there could be no hanging back now'. Here is clearly to be seen the curse of the 'free hand' granted by Germany. Tisza's well-founded qualms would not have failed to impress Berlin, where it would have been highly desirable to summon a meeting of both the Crown Council and the Federal Council and this in its turn would have strengthened Tisza in his resistance to foolhardy moves.[2]

Tisza's memorandum also shows that he, the most influential statesman in the Monarchy, felt convinced of the inevitability of a world war in conditions unfavourable to Austria, if a 'war of aggression' were undertaken. In this he was entirely right. But he had already half capitulated to Berchtold's pressure and was soon to capitulate entirely.

11. *The laborious process of concocting the terms to be imposed on Serbia.*

Berchtold's remark at the Council of Ministers shows that he was now sure of war even if Tisza's suggestions as to procedure were adopted. To Tschirschky he said after the meeting that even if Francis Joseph were to take the standpoint of Tisza that in the first instance definite demands should be made on Serbia, he 'would advise his Sovereign so to formulate these demands that their acceptance appears

[1] Oe-U. VIII, 10146.   [2] Lutz, p. 60.

impossible'.[1] The Council of Ministers discussed the following demands to be presented to Serbia:

1. The punishment and expulsion from the Serbian Army of officers implicated in Pan-Serb propaganda;

2. an apology to be tendered by the Serbian Government for expressions used by Spalaiković, the Serbian Minister at St. Petersburg;

3. an investigation to be held into the circumstances in which the bombs were procured by the conspirators;

4. the dismissal of certain officials implicated in the earlier (Pokrayats) incident;

5. new legislation on the press and proceedings against the newspaper *Piemont*;

6. the revision of the Serbian law of associations;

7. the prohibition in officers' clubs and public places of journals hostile to Austria-Hungary.

These demands did not yet include those which were most burdensome and incompatible with Serbian sovereignty.[2]

Berchtold having put off his visit to the Emperor until the 9th, Conrad called on him on the 8th at 6 p.m. and was told of

the demands which were to be contained in an ultimatum to Serbia with a short time limit of twenty-four or forty-eight hours. It was to be presumed that Serbia would reject the demands so that on the expiry of the time limit mobilization and war would follow.

But Berchtold still had doubts about the whole business:

Berchtold: 'What happens if Serbia lets matters get to the point of mobilization and then capitulates all along the line?'

Conrad: 'Then we invade.'

Berchtold: 'Yes—but if Serbia simply does nothing?'

Conrad: 'Then Serbia remains occupied until the war expenditure is reimbursed.'

Berchtold: 'We shall not send the ultimatum till after harvest and after the close of the Sarajevo inquiry. . . .'

Conrad: 'When is the ultimatum to go off?'

Berchtold: 'In a fortnight's time. On 22 July. It would be a good thing if you and the War Minister would go away on leave for a while, so as to keep up an appearance that nothing is going on. . . .'

Berchtold: 'If we move into Serbia and occupy a sufficient area of territory, what then?'

Conrad: 'The occupation of territory does not settle anything, we should have to go on until we have beaten the Serbian Army.'

Berchtold: 'And if it gives us the slip?'

---

[1] DD. I, 19.

[2] Roderich Goos: *Das Wiener Kabinett und die Enstehung des Weltkrieges* (Vienna, 1919), p. 93–4.

Conrad: 'Then we insist on its being demobilized and disarmed. When we have reached that point, the rest will come of itself.'

Berchtold: 'On no account take any steps now which might betray us; nothing must be done that might attract attention.'[1]

In order to win Tisza over, Berchtold on the same day (8 July) wrote him a private letter:

Tschirschky has just left, after having told me that he has received a telegram from Berlin containing instructions from his Imperial master to emphasize here that Berlin expects the Monarchy to take action against Serbia and that Germany would not understand our letting the opportunity slip without striking a blow. . . . Tschirschky's declarations seem to me of such far reaching importance that they might well have some influence on your conclusions. That is why I hasten to communicate them to you and would beg you, if you think advisable, to telegraph (in code) to Bad Ischl where I am to spend to-morrow and could act as exponent of your views to His Majesty.[2]

As we have already seen, some historians deny that the Kaiser ever sent such orders to Tschirschky. But let it here be repeated that, given the intimacy of Tisza's relations with Tschirschky, Berchtold could never have made out to Tisza that Tschirschky told him something if Tschirschky had not done so. He and Tschirschky might, of course, have put their heads together to invent the story. If this were so, it had no effect on Tisza who did not send a telegram to Ischl, where Berchtold in consequence had on 9 July to tell Francis Joseph that there was a difference of opinion between himself and Tisza and explain the two points of view.

Information on what took place at Ischl is given by Conrad, and in a telegram sent by Tschirschky to Berlin on 10 July. Conrad relates:

On 10 July I called on Count Berchtold back from Ischl. He told me that he had found the Emperor very calm and resolute. His Majesty seemed to be in favour of action against Serbia and only had apprehensions about possible unrest in Hungary. Berchtold said that because of Germany, if for no other reason, we could not draw back now. Tisza, he says, is urging prudence, and opposes war; but Baron Burian is in Budapest for discussions with Tisza.[3]

Tschirschky's telegram informed Berlin that when Francis Joseph learnt of the difference of opinion between Berchtold and Tisza he

expressed the opinion that it might be possible to bridge it. But on the whole His Majesty rather leant to the view that concrete demands should be placed before Serbia.[4]

On 12 July Conrad had a talk with Berchtold:

He mentioned that Baron Burian is at Ischl. . . . The French President, Poincaré, he says, is on a visit to the Tsar, so he [Berchtold] wants to wait

---

[1] Conrad, IV, pp. 61–2.   [2] Oe-U. VIII, 10145; see pp. 150–1.
[3] Conrad, IV, p. 70.   [4] DD. I, 29; see p. 259.

until Poincaré's departure and postpone the ultimatum to Serbia until 23 July. It would expire on 25 July, and 28 July could therefore be the first day of mobilization.

I replied, that, if the military chancery agreed, I would go off on leave on 14 July and remain absent until 22 July, and so would the War Minister; but this programme would have to be changed if Serbia were to move troops northward. If that happened the ultimatum would have to be sent at once, because it would be a great advantage to us to cross the river barriers before the Serbs had taken adequate counter-measures. Count Berchtold said he needed this interval to await the end of the inquiry into the outrage and the getting in of the harvest and to carry out the diplomatic preliminaries.[1]

Before departing on 12 July Conrad wrote to Berchtold:

In my capacity as Chief of the General Staff I am only concerned with the exact terms of the decision, whether directly aiming at the outbreak of a war with Serbia or only reckoning with the possibility of a war. The diplomatic handling of either alternative lies, of course, outside my province; I must however again point out, as I explained verbally to Your Excellency with your complete approval, that in the diplomatic field everything must be avoided in the nature of protracted or piecemeal diplomatic action which would afford our adversary time for military measures and place us at a military disadvantage. . . . Hence it would be wise to avoid everything that might prematurely alarm our adversary and lead him to take counter-measures; in all respects a peaceable appearance should be displayed. But once the decision to act has been taken, military considerations demand that it must be carried out in a single move with a short-term ultimatum which, if rejected, should be followed immediately by the mobilization order.[2]

This letter gives the impression that, in spite of Berchtold's assurances, Conrad, because of Tisza's opposition, was not yet fully convinced that matters would come to a head. But Berchtold endeavoured to bring Tisza round by fixing a meeting with him for 14 July. By that day he would have received the full results of the inquiry into Serbian responsibility for the Sarajevo outrage which he needed for the drafting of the final form of the ultimatum. The drafting had been begun some time before. Tschirschky in his telegram of 10 July already, as we shall see, foreshadows some of the stiffest demands. But it was soon realized that more information must be obtained about the guilt of Belgrade. Therefore, on 10 July, Dr. Wiesner, the Legal Counsellor at the Ballplatz, an able and conscientious official, was sent to Sarajevo with instructions to report by telegram in forty-eight hours. On 13 July Wiesner telegraphed that the documents produced by the civil and military authorities gave no indication that the Belgrade Government had encouraged Pan-Serb propaganda but were enough to show that the movement had its origins in Serbia and was fostered by societies with the tolerance of the Belgrade Government.

---

[1] Conrad, IV, p. 72.   [2] Conrad, IV, p. 78.

There is nothing to show the complicity of the Serbian Government in the directing of the assassination or in its preparations or in the supplying of weapons. Nor is there anything to lead one even to conjecture such a thing. On the contrary there is evidence that would appear to show that such complicity is out of the question. . . .

. . . Depositions of accused place it practically beyond doubt that the outrage was decided in Belgrade and prepared with the help of the Serbian railway officials Ciganović and Major Tankosić, by both of whom bombs, Brownings, ammunition and cyanide of potassium were procured. . . . Bombs definitely proved to have come from Serbian army stores, but nothing to show that they had been taken out for this express purpose, since they might belong to the supplies of the Comitaji in the war. . . . Hardly room for doubt that Princip, Čabrinović and Grabež . . . secretly smuggled across the frontier by Serbian officials. . . . Other investigations after the outrage open a glimpse into propaganda organization *Narodna Obrana*. Received valuable utilizable material not yet examined, rapid inquiries in progress. If the intentions prevailing at my departure still exist, demands might be extended:

(A) Suppression of complicity of Serbian Government officials in smuggling persons and material across the frontier.

(B) Dismissal of Serbian frontier officers at Šabac and Ložnica and implicated customs official.

(C) Criminal proceedings against Ciganović and Tankosić.[1]

This report was not to the liking of the war party. Potiorek, writing to Conrad from Sarajevo on 14 July declared:

I regard it as utterly impossible but that at least one or other member of the democratic Government of so small a country as Serbia had knowledge of the preparations for the outrage. . . . It is moreover a fact that alongside of the official Government there is a military rival Government emanating from the army. That Serbian officers on the active list took part in the preparations for the outrage and took a leading part in the whole propaganda . . . is proved.[2]

But General Potiorek, who threatened to resign his command if military action were not taken, had no reason to be alarmed at the mildness of Wiesner's findings. He had both Berchtold and Conrad with him in his demand for stern measures. It seems, however, that right up to the previous day, 13 July, Berchtold continued to show hesitation. It was only on that 13 July that Tschirschky was able definitely to telegraph to Berlin.

Minister is *now himself convinced that speediest action is imperative* (the words 'now himself convinced' and 'speediest' are twice underlined by the Kaiser). He hopes to-morrow with Tisza to draw up an agreed text of the note to be sent to Serbia, would then submit it on Wednesday 15 July to the Emperor

---

[1] Oe-U. VIII, 10252-3; KSF., 1925, p. 653.   [2] Conrad, IV, 82-5.

at Ischl, after which without loss of time—perhaps even before Poincaré's departure—the handing over in Belgrade could take place.[1]

12. *Tisza comes round to the idea of war.*

On 14 July Berchtold finally succeeded in winning Tisza's consent to the dispatch of a short-term ultimatum to Serbia. Tisza surrendered on condition that before the sending of the ultimatum the Council of Ministers should pass a resolution that, in a war with Serbia, Austria aimed at no territorial acquisitions apart from slight frontier rectifications. He made this condition partly in the interests of Hungary which feared otherwise to lose its predominance within the Monarchy, partly to prevent Italy from claiming compensations, and partly to avoid giving the other Powers grounds for intervention. Chief among the reasons by which Berchtold persuaded Tisza to drop his opposition was, no doubt, the consideration that Germany regarded this demonstration of strength on the part of the Monarchy as necessary, failing which it would be regarded as unfit for alliance (*bündnisunfähig*). Berchtold cannot have failed to read Tisza the two telegrams from Szögyény at Berlin of 9 and 12 July. That of the 9th reported that Jagow

is in complete agreement with the line taken by the German Government as already indicated and assures me most emphatically that in his opinion, too, the projected operations against Serbia should be taken in hand without delay.[2]

That of the 12th said that

both H.M. Kaiser Wilhelm and all other responsible personages here not only stand firmly in allied loyalty behind the Monarchy, but invite us not to let the present moment pass but to take vigorous measures against Serbia and make a clean sweep of the revolutionary conspirators' nest there once and for all. . . . It is by no means certain that if Serbia becomes involved in a war with us, Russia would resort to arms in her support. . . . The German Government further believes it has sure indications that England at the present moment would not join in a war over a Balkan country, even should this lead to a passage of arms with Russia and eventually even with France.[3]

This telegram, as can be seen, meets the very objections which had caused Tisza to oppose a war which he regarded as holding out no hope of victory but which Berlin was prepared to face with the utmost optimism. This optimism must have turned the scales with Tisza, taken in conjunction with the arguments brought forward by Berchtold. These we shall shortly read in a report drawn up for Francis Joseph. Another factor which must have weighed with Tisza was that no reply

---

[1] DD. I, 40.   [2] Oe-U. VIII, 10154.   [3] Oe-U. VIII, 10215.

to his protests had come from the Emperor, showing that the decision had been taken to disregard them. What is certain is that, going to call on Tschirschky after this conversation, i.e. after his capitulation, Tisza told him that

the unconditional manner in which Germany has ranged herself at the side of the Monarchy had decidedly been of great influence on the firm attitude of the Emperor.[1]

Again some months later in a letter of 5 November 1914 to Tschirschky he was to reiterate:

We took counsel with Germany before entering upon our Serbian action and undertook the *démarche* at Belgrade with the direct encouragement of the German Government and the declaration that they regarded the situation as favourable for the more and more imminent settlement of accounts.[2]

In his talk with the German Ambassador on 14 July Tisza further said that

hitherto he had always been the one to recommend prudence but each day had strengthened him in the conviction that the Monarchy must come to a bold resolve to demonstrate its own vitality and put an end to the unendurable state of affairs in the south-east. The language of the Serbian press and of Serbian diplomatists was of unbearable presumptuousness. 'It has not been easy', said the Minister, 'to take the decision of advising war, but I am now convinced of its necessity and will use all my influence on behalf of the greatness of the Monarchy . . .' The note that was to be presented to Serbia has, he says, not yet received its final wording. That would not be done before Sunday (19 July). In regard to the date on which it would be handed to Serbia, the decision has been taken to-day rather to wait until after Poincaré's departure from St. Petersburg, i.e. until the 25th. Then if Serbia did not unconditionally agree to all the demands, mobilization would follow at once on the expiry of the appointed time limit. The note is to be so phrased that its acceptance will be practically impossible. . . . At the end Count Tisza warmly shook my hand, saying: 'We shall now united look the future calmly and firmly in the face.'

Wilhelm, always an admirer of Tisza, annotated these words with the remark: ' What a man he is !'[3]

Yes, but this man was now accepting full responsibility for the general war which at the beginning he had tried to prevent. And once he was converted, he did more than anyone to make matters worse for the Monarchy by vetoing the concessions to Italy which might have kept her neutral, if not actively friendly. The Hungarian press in those days, from the *Pester Lloyd* downwards, added fuel to the flames by baiting the Serbian press. Practically all those whose policy was leading the Monarchy into war were Magyars and it was Hungarian policy

---

[1] DD. I, 49.   [2] Stefan Tisza, *Briefe* (Berlin, 1927), p. 104.   [3] DD. I, 49.

that alienated Roumania from the Central Powers and blocked the trialistic solution of the Austro-Hungarian problem which might have saved the Danubian Monarchy.

But to return to our story. Berchtold had now been given the green light and he confided his relief to Tschirschky. It is symptomatic that no sooner had Tisza capitulated to Berchtold than he rushed to tell the German Ambassador all about it and that Berchtold in his turn hastened to summon the Ambassador to give him the joyful news. Hence Tschirschky was able to telegraph to Berlin on the 14th (the words in italics are those underlined by the Kaiser):

After Count Tisza had left me, Count Berchtold summoned me to let me know the results of to-day's discussion. To his great joy *agreement on all points* has been reached in regard to the *tenor of the note*, to be sent *to Serbia*. Count Tisza met the views·of the Minister in a gratifying manner and even stiffened up many points. Technical considerations, it is true, have rendered it impossible to hand the note to Belgrade as early as the 16th or 18th. Next Sunday at 9 a.m. the French text would receive its final revision at a meeting of the Ministers. He would submit the note to the Emperor at Ischl probably on Tuesday. He *guarantees* that His Majesty *will give it his assent*.

There was unanimity in to-day's discussion that it is advisable to wait until M. Poincaré's departure from St. Petersburg before carrying out the *démarche* at Belgrade (Kaiser's marginal comment: 'A pity!'). It will be better to avoid brotherhood being sworn at St. Petersburg over the champagne under the influence of Messrs. Poincaré, Izvolsky and the Grand Dukes, because that would affect and perhaps solidify the attitude of both Empires. It would also be a good thing if the toasts were all over before the note is delivered. Thus the delivery will be able to take place on 25 July (Kaiser's exclamation mark).[1]

Berchtold expressed himself in similar terms in a report drawn up immediately on the 14th for Francis Joseph:

All those present were of my opinion that the delivery of the ultimatum during the St. Petersburg meeting would be regarded as an affront and that a personal discussion between the ambitious President of the Republic and H.M. the Tsar of Russia on the international situation created by the dispatch of the ultimatum would heighten the probability of military intervention by Russia and France. Count Tisza has given up the objections which he raised against a short-term ultimatum, because I pointed out the military difficulties which would arise from a postponement. I put forward that even after mobilization a peaceable adjustment would be possible if Serbia would listen to reason in time. . . . The contents finally settled to-day of the note which is to be dispatched to Belgrade are such that the possibility of an armed conflict must be reckoned with. In the event of Serbia's yielding after all and accepting our demands, such a step on the part of the Kingdom would involve not only deep humiliation for itself and *pari passu* a loss of Russian

[1] DD. I, 50.

prestige in the Balkans but also certain guarantees for us in the sense of limiting Pan-Serb agitation on our soil.[1]

Let us linger a moment on this significant passage. It shows that on 14 July Berchtold had already taken another step backwards. At first he had pressed for a surprise attack against Serbia in order to destroy her and divide her territory among her neighbours. Then he fell in with Tisza's proposal to make stiff demands, stipulating, however, that they must be such that Serbia could not accept them and that war should be made on her. He also agreed to Tisza's wish that Serbia should not be destroyed and only territorially reduced for the benefit of her neighbours, but not of the Monarchy who was to be content with frontier adjustments and to declare to all the Powers that she did not aim at territorial acquisitions. Now in giving his views to Tisza and the Emperor, Berchtold envisaged the hypothesis that Serbia might yield 'even after [the Austrian] mobilization', in which case she would be made to bear the cost of that mobilization, but Austria would have to content herself with inflicting humiliation on Serbia and obtaining guarantees from her. Hence no longer the certainty, but only the extreme probability of war. This concession, too, must have been partly inspired by the need to overcome Tisza's opposition and Tisza did not remain insensible to the argument which offered him a gleam of hope that Serbia might end by giving way and that war might thus be averted. This is shown in a letter written by Tisza on 21 July to his daughter, telling that he had to go to Vienna because

owing to the insolence of the Serbs we must take a firm stand. The affair may pass off without war; God grant that it be so, but I cannot give you complete assurance that under no circumstances will there be war.[2]

However, it is clear that, little by little, Berchtold was coming round to toy with the possibility that an armed conflict might be avoided. We shall find more evidence of this when we examine the situation created by the breaking off of Austro-Serbian diplomatic relations.

APPENDIX TO CHAPTER IV

THE LEGEND OF THE POTSDAM CROWN COUNCIL

The report of a Crown Council held at Potsdam to decide on war, and giving Austria *carte blanche* against Serbia, was first published on 7 September 1914 by the Berlin correspondent of the *Nieuwe Rotterdamsche Courant*, then by the *Temps* of 21 January 1916. Later, on 4 May 1917, the Independent Socialist

Oe-U. VIII, 10272.   [2] KSF., March, 1932, pp. 284-7.

deputy Cohn affirmed it before a Reichstag Investigating Committee on the preliminaries of the war when accusing Falkenhayn. He alleged that it had been attended also by the Archduke Frederick and by Conrad. At the Socialist Peace Congress held at Stockholm in July 1917 Cohn made public the rumour, taken up by the (London) *Times* of 28 July 1917 'from a well-informed correspondent' that the Potsdam meeting had been attended also by Berchtold, Tisza and Conrad.

The German Government then decided on 31 July 1917 to publish an official denial. However the notice in the (London) *Times* gave occasion for the Italian deputy Barzilai to advert in the *Matin* to what purported to be revelations which he, as Minister, had made in a speech at Naples on 26 September 1915. These were particulars of a conversation alleged to have taken place at Constantinople on 15 July 1914 between the Italian Ambassador Garroni and the German Ambassador Wangenheim who had just returned from Berlin. Wangenheim had told the Italian Ambassador Garroni that war was imminent. It had been decided at a conference with the Kaiser at which he had been present. Serbia was to be presented with an ultimatum drawn up at Berlin and containing unacceptable terms. Garroni asked whether this would not lead to a European war and Wangenheim replied that this was so and that it was desired in Berlin. In the (London) *Times* of 4 August 1917 the American diplomat Lewis Einstein wrote that he, too, in June 1915 had heard this same story from Garroni and from 'another diplomatist' who later turned out to be the American Ambassador at Constantinople, Henry Morgenthau. The latter, first in the New York *World* of 14 October 1917 and then in his book *Ambassador Morgenthau's Story*, published in 1918, confirmed that the revelation was made also to him by Wangenheim giving details which are of no importance, as the whole story is devoid of foundation.[1]

Germanophil historians of course have made much ado about these allegations against Germany and her leaders, allegations which were used by the 'Commission on the Responsibilities of the Authors of the War and Sanctions' under the chairmanship of Lansing to justify Art. 231 of the Treaty of Versailles and adopted by French historians and by Poincaré himself.[2] But the German protests had no effect. The truth is:

(i) It is beyond doubt that the prime responsibility for the false statement lies with Wangenheim who told the story to Garroni and Morgenthau, perhaps, as Morgenthau suggests, to give himself importance as the possessor of private information. As ill-luck would have it, neither of the two Ambassadors telegraphed the conversation at once to his Government. But this does not mean that there are any grounds for believing it to be an invention of their own, and Bompard, the French Ambassador to Constantinople, testifies that Garroni spoke of it to him in August 1914.[3] Wangenheim himself is only partly to blame, because in Berlin diplomatic circles a rumour was certainly current that a Crown Council was held at Potsdam on 5 July 1914. The rumour was accepted even by the German Ambassador to London, Lichnowsky, for in his memorandum which was published in 1918 he speaks of the 'decisive conference' at Potsdam of 5 July.

[1] Schmitt, I, pp. 329–41; Fay, II, 167–82.   [2] Poincaré, IV, pp. 196–9.
[3] *Revue d'histoire de la guerre mondiale* (Paris, January 1930), pp. 45–50.

(ii) The legend of the Potsdam Council does not constitute a calumny of Germany. Even if it never took place, the fact remains that the Kaiser and Bethmann decided to give Austria a free hand though it might mean unleashing a European war. This was regarded as a possibility if not a probability and they preferred to have it then before Russian armaments were completed. In actual fact it was probably the separate conversations which during the few hours he was at Potsdam the Kaiser had with Szögyény, Bethmann Hollweg, Zimmermann, Falkenhayn and other military chiefs which gave rise to the rumour of an important council, a rumour collected on the very evening of 5 July at the Hotel Kaiserhof by Stein, the correspondent of the *Frankfurter Zeitung*.

Be it added that, if one omits the detail of the holding of a Crown Council, the original revelations of the Berlin correspondent of the *Nieuwe Rotterdamsche Courant* contain an account of what took place which is not at all exaggerated. The account states that Austria had made known her intention of sending a punitive expedition against Serbia. Though the Kaiser and his advisers were not in favour of war, their reply was that Vienna could count on Germany, whatever the consequences of the procedure against Serbia. The Kaiser and Chancellor did not regard the danger of war as great, while later it would become greater because of the greater preparedness of Russia and France. Not much that is wrong here any more than in what Lichnowsky wrote: 'At Potsdam on 5 July, the Vienna inquiry received the unqualified assent of all the leading people.'[1]

Then, of course, a more detailed legend grew up by degrees. German leaders who were absent from Berlin and Austrian leaders who never stirred from Vienna were said to have been at Potsdam. More or less dramatic particulars of the meeting were invented. All this is of no importance and the non-existence of the Council in no way lessens the responsibility of Germany.

[1] Lichnowsky, p. 72.

CHAPTER V

THE REACTIONS OF THE TRIPLE ENTENTE TO THE AUSTRO-SERBIAN TENSION

(1) *Alarming news reaches Russia of Austrian intentions; Sazonov's warnings* (p. 181). (2) *The visit of Poincaré and Viviani to St. Petersburg* (p. 188). (3) *The atmosphere of excitement at St. Petersburg and its effect on Sazonov* (p. 194). (4) *Sir Edward Grey's views on the Triple* Entente (p. 197). (5) *Lichnowsky's revelations and the optimism at the Foreign Office* (p. 203). (6) *Grey's proposal for direct conversations between Austria and Russia opposed by Poincaré* (p. 206). (7) *What Grey said to Lichnowsky and Mensdorff; the Kaiser's wrath; the English failure to understand the position* (p. 212).

1. *Alarming news reaches Russia of Austrian intentions; Sazonov's warnings.*

The man at the helm of Russian foreign policy and whose task it was to weather the storm about to be unloosed by the Austrian ultimatum to Serbia was no better fitted than were Bethmann Hollweg and Berchtold to meet the difficulties that lay ahead. In the crises of 1912 and 1913 the Tsar and the Prime Minister Kokovtzov were determined to keep the peace and Sazonov had no difficulty in resisting the pressure of the nationalists, of several ministers, and of Izvolsky who wanted Russia to remain inflexible. But the balance sheet of these crises seemed to show a deficit, in that the Balkan League had broken up and Bulgaria had slipped out of St. Petersburg's grasp. Dissatisfaction with the results of a policy whether of peace or of war has ever furnished matter for the verbiage of nationalism all the world over. Russian Pan-Slavs, officials and army officers who longed for adventure, grand dukes and diplomatists who looked to war for easily won laurels, complained that Russia had missed her chance to gain bigger and better rewards. Nationalists accused Sazonov of weakness, and since he was really weak and hesitating, the reproach stung him and goaded him to acts which were intended to prove that he was the contrary.

Then came the bombshell of the Liman von Sanders mission to reorganize and in reality to take command of the Turkish Army, which Sazonov regarded as a direct threat to Russian aspirations in the Straits. On no other sector of the map was Sazonov, the heir of Izvolsky's policy, so sensitive as on that of Constantinople and the Straits which the Pan-Slavs claimed for Russia. Hence he had begun to contemplate the possibility of war, and even to desire it in order to ward off the German menace and translate Russian dreams of the

Bosporus into reality. De Maistre has a saying: 'Bury a Slav desire beneath a fortress and it will blow it sky high.'

Withal, the flames of these passions were fanned by the French Ambassador recently arrived in St. Petersburg, Paléologue, a friend of Poincaré, one whose influence was to be similar to that exercised in Paris by Izvolsky.

In the period immediately preceding the outbreak of the World War, St. Petersburg felt a stronger hatred for Germany than for Austria. The aims of Russian statesmen were mainly directed towards Constantinople and the Straits. They had no desire to risk a war on behalf of the Balkan countries. But if Austria were to crush Serbia, the predominance of the Central Powers in the Near East would become a threat to Russian aims in the Straits. Sazonov writes:

> Germany decided to seize the opportunity thus offered of settling accounts with her Eastern and Western neighbours, and of crushing their power once for all. She could then proceed quietly to execute her plan of re-casting Central Europe on a new basis, transforming it, for her own purposes, into a corridor to the Near East. In order to realize this plan, it was necessary first to destroy Serbia, and then drive Russia out of the Balkan Peninsula, replacing her influence by that of Austria-Hungary.[1]

Behind Austrian moves, concealed and well thought out German plans were becoming visible. If in 1909 and in the First Balkan war the St. Petersburg Government had successfully resisted Slavophil pressure, it could now no longer do so. Not for nothing had Sazonov in the Duma on 23 May 1914 proclaimed the principle: 'The Balkans for the Balkan peoples', and had he, and indirectly the Tsar, given the Serbs the fullest assurances for the future.

This seems to have been very well understood by the German Ambassador to St. Petersburg, Pourtalès, who in the preface to his memoirs observed that the peace policy pursued by Sazonov in his first years of office was supported by his brother-in-law, the Prime Minister Stolypin, and, after the latter's assassination in the autumn of 1911, by his successor Kokovtzov, but that the nationalist and anti-German party won the victory when it got Kokovtzov replaced by the aged Goremykin, and the ambitious Maklakov appointed to the Ministry of the Interior. Thus Sazonov found himself powerless against the pressure of the Slavophils.

Already some months before the outbreak of war it became clear that he was not the man to take a strong stand alone against the growing nationalist onslaught. In these circumstances, it was to be foreseen that fresh differences with Austria-Hungary in the field of Near Eastern policy would lead to a more serious crisis than those that had gone before.[2]

---

[1] Sazonov, p. 164.
[2] Pourtalès, *Am Scheidewege zwischen Krieg und Frieden* (Charlottenburg, 1919), pp. 10–11.

But the truth is that Pourtalès took no steps to give timely notice of these impressions to Berlin. Among the German documents there is not a single telegram or report from him in this sense, while there exist telegrams to the opposite effect. For example on 23 July, speaking of the strikes which plagued the Russian capital during Poincaré's visit, he remarked:

In the event of foreign complications they might well create a difficult situation for the Government. ('Yes'—was the Kaiser's comment).[1]

In another telegram of the same date he gave it as his opinion that Sazonov 'was trying on a policy of bluff'.[2] But neither the environment nor the words of Sazonov were such as to produce the impression that the precedent of 1909 was likely to repeat itself. Let us look at them.

In a report of 13 July Pourtalès wrote:

Not only in the press, but also in society, one meets almost only with unfriendly judgements on the murdered Archduke and statements that Russia has lost a bitter enemy in him. (Kaiser's marginal note: 'Why! he always wanted to revive the old *Dreikaiserbund*! He was Russia's best friend!').[3]

This was true but the fact was that the Archduke was everywhere detested. Even the English Ambassador Sir George Buchanan had telegraphed to London on 9 July:

Now that the first feeling of horror evoked by the assassination of the Archduke Franz Ferdinand and His Consort has passed away, the general impression would seem to be one of relief that so dangerous a personality should have been removed from the succession to the throne.[4]

Sazonov [continues Pourtalès in his telegram of 13 July] when I first spoke to him after the outrage, dwelt only briefly on his condemnation of the crime while he could not find enough words of criticism for the behaviour of the Austro-Hungarian authorities who, he said, had permitted excesses against the Serbs . . . and had deliberately given rein to popular fury. . . . M. Sazonov denied the Austrian assertion that the outrage was to be attributed to a Pan-Serb plot. Of this he says there is till now not the slightest proof and it is utterly unjust to hold the Serbian Government, which is behaving with perfect correctness, responsible for the crime, as the Austrian press is doing. . . . It was the act of a few callow youths. . . . I pointed out that the outrage was a fresh, serious warning to the ancient Monarchies to be mindful of their common interests and the common dangers which threaten them. M. Sazonov could not but agree to this remark but with less warmth than I usually find when we are on the subject of monarchical interests. This reserve can only be explained by the Minister's irreconcilable hatred of Austria-Hungary, a hatred which here more and more clouds all clear, calm judgement. . . . All utterances about

[1] DD. I, 130.   [2] DD. I, 134.   [3] DD. I, 53.   [4] BD. XI, 49.

Austria-Hungary in official circles here testify to a boundless contempt for the conditions prevailing there.'[1]

Till now there was nothing in the way of a threat on the part of Russia, but only because after Austria's inaction in the recent crises, and given the estimate of her current in St. Petersburg, there was no suspicion of the moves she was preparing. Berchtold's precautions to keep them dark took in all the representatives of the Great Powers at Vienna. The English Ambassador, Sir Maurice de Bunsen, after warning his Government on 16 July:

that Austro-Hungarian Government are in no mood to parley with Servia, but will insist on immediate unconditional compliance, failing which force will be used. Germany is said to be in complete agreement with this procedure,[2]

neutralized the effect of his warning by telegraphing on 18 July:

Italian Ambassador does not believe that unreasonable demands will be made on Servia. . . . He does not think that either Minister for Foreign Affairs or Emperor would sanction such an unwise proceeding.[3]

After the memorial service for the Archduke, Sazonov on 14 July went to his country seat for five days' rest before the arrival at St. Petersburg of the President of the French Republic, Poincaré, and the French Foreign Minister Viviani on 20 July. During this interval two serious warnings reached Sazonov. At an evening party given by Countess Kleinmichel on 16 July, the Italian Ambassador Carlotti had a talk with Schilling, the respected and influential Head of Chancery who acted as a kind of Secretary General of the Russian Foreign Office. Carlotti inquired how Russia would behave if Austria decided on serious measures against Serbia. Schilling replied that Russia would not permit any weakening or humiliation of Serbia. Carlotti gave it as his impression

that Austria was capable of taking an irrevocable step with regard to Serbia based on the belief that, although Russia would make a verbal protest, she would not adopt forcible measures for the protection of Serbia against any Austrian attempts.[4]

On the same 16 July the Russian Ambassador to Vienna, Shebeko, sent the following telegram:

Information reaches me that the Austro-Hungarian Government at the conclusion of the inquiry intends to make certain demands on Belgrade, claiming that there is a connexion between the question of the Sarajevo outrage and the Pan-Serb agitation within the confines of the Monarchy. In so doing it reckons on the non-intervention of Russia and the sympathetic attitude of its own Southern Slav elements towards this measure. It would seem to me desirable that at the present moment, before a final decision on

---

[1] DD. I, 53.   [2] BD. XI, 50.   [3] BD. XI, 59.
[4] *Int. Bez.* i. IV, 245; Schilling, pp. 25–6. See pp. 225–6.

the matter, the Vienna Cabinet should be informed how Russia would react to the fact of Austria's presenting demands to Serbia such as would be unacceptable to the dignity of that state. The Austro-Hungarian Ambassador left for St. Petersburg yesterday evening.[1]

In his *Memoirs* Shebeko tells us that on 16 July he was told, evidently by the English Ambassador, that at a luncheon given by Lützow, a former Austrian Ambassador to Rome, who had that morning had a long conversation with Berchtold and Forgach,

there had been a discussion on the terms of the note which, when the inquiry would have terminated, the Austrian Government had decided to present to the Serbian Government. This note was drafted in extremely stiff terms and contained demands unacceptable to any independent State. The presentation of it was meant, therefore, to create a critical situation.[2]

Sazonov might have collated this piece of news with a telegram from Berchtold to the Austrian Chargé d'Affaires at St. Petersburg asking to be told the date on which Poincaré was due to leave St. Petersburg at the close of his state visit.[3] The telegram had been decoded by the Russian coding staff on the very day, 14 July, on which it reached the Russian capital and the staff had also decoded the Austrian Chargé d'Affaire's replies to Berchtold of 16 and 17 July saying that Poincaré was due to leave on the evening of the 23rd.[4]

Immediately on his return to his post on 17 July, Szápáry, the Austrian Ambassador to St. Petersburg, expressed the wish 'to see Sazonov as soon as possible'. Sazonov returned the following day and was met at the station by Schilling with news both of Shebeko's telegram from Vienna and of Schilling's talk with the Italian Ambassador on 3 July. Sazonov found the news disquieting, and when, immediately after his arrival at the Foreign Ministry, he received a call from Szápáry, he voiced his apprehensions about the latest news from Vienna and the nature of the terms to be presented to Serbia by Austria. Szápáry, following Berchtold's instructions not to let anything transpire of what was being engineered at Vienna, gave 'such positive' assurances—records Schilling in his diary—that they completely reassured Sazonov, who told Schilling after the conversation, that he had not needed to use threats since the Ambassador had given a guarantee of the pacific intentions of his Government: 'He has been as gentle as a lamb'.[5] But Sazonov cannot have been quite so reassured as all that, for on the same day he expressed to Buchanan

the great uneasiness which Austria's attitude towards Serbia was causing him. . . . Anything in the shape of an Austrian ultimatum at Belgrade

---

[1] *Int. Bez.* i. IV, 247.   [2] Shebeko, p. 213.
[3] *Int. Bez.* i. IV, 218.   [4] *Int. Bez.* i. IV, note to 218.
[5] Oe-U. VIII, 10365; *Int. Bez.* i. IV, 272; Schilling, pp. 26-7.

could not leave Russia indifferent, and she might be forced to take some pre-cautionary military measures.[1]

And on the day following his conversation with Szápáry he thought it wise to show the Tsar the text of Shebeko's telegram. The Tsar wrote the following comment as a footnote:

In my opinion a State should not present any sort of demands to another, unless, of course, it is bent on war.—Peterhof, 19/6 July, 1914.[2]

Other disquieting news had arrived and continued to arrive on the following days. On 16 July Shebeko sent a letter containing salient passages from the speech made by Tisza to the Hungarian Parliament on 15 July, the text of which had appeared in the press. Among other things he had said:

The Government does not think that the clarification [of relations with Serbia] must necessarily lead to warlike complications. In this connexion I will not be a prophet but only remark that war is a sad *ultima ratio* which should not be resorted to until all methods of peaceful solution are exhausted. But every state, every nation must be in the position to wage war and must desire war as *ultima ratio*, if state and nation are to continue to exist.

Shebeko, it is true, ended his letter with the words:

There is no doubt that by his speech of yesterday Count Tisza intended to make a certain impression in view of the impending negotiations which are to follow after the close of the secret inquiry which is being held at Sarajevo.[3]

But the Russian Chargé d'Affaires, Strandtmann, telegraphed·from Belgrade on 19 July:

Pašić is extremely anxious. Count Tisza's utterances at Budapest have made a profound impression on him. Moreover he has received information of Austrian troop movements towards Semlin and Mitrovitza and of the obviously irresponsible agitation of the Austrians all over Western Europe against Serbia.[4]

On 20 July Sazonov received from the Russian Chargé d'Affaires at Berlin, Bronewski, the text of the following note, published the previous evening by the semi-official *Norddeutsche Allgemeine Zeitung*:

In the utterances of the European press on the tension in relations between Austria-Hungary and Serbia, more and more voices are heard admitting that the desire of Austria-Hungary to bring about a clarification of her relations with Serbia is justified. In this connexion we associate ourselves with the hope,

---

[1] BD. XI, 60.
[2] *Int. Bez*. i. IV, 247.
[3] *Int. Bez*. i. IV, 249.
[4] *Int. Bez*. i. IV, 286.

expressed in more than one quarter, that a timely softening of attitude on the part of the Serbian Government will avoid the emergence of a serious crisis. In the common interest of Europe which has made itself felt in the preservation of peace among the Great Powers during the long Balkan crisis, it is desirable and imperative that the settlement of differences, which might in this connexion arise between Austria-Hungary and Serbia, should remain localized.[1]

By a telegram later on the same day, 20 July, Bronewski reported from Berlin that the correspondent of the Paris newspaper *Matin* had given him the following information, emanating, as it appeared, from the Austrian Embassy:

In the immediate future the Austro-Hungarian Government will communicate to the Governments of the Powers the results of the inquiry held in connexion with the Sarajevo crime and the name of all genuine Serbs from the Kingdom whose participation in it will have come to light. This information will then be given to the press, whereupon a *démarche* with the Serbian Government will follow.[2]

This was enough to alarm Sazonov, and on 21 July Pourtalès wrote to Bethmann Hollweg that

since Sazonov's return he has been very anxious about the relations between Austria-Hungary and Serbia. He told me that he had most alarming reports from London, Paris and Rome, where the attitude of Austria-Hungary was everywhere causing growing concern. . . . Sazonov seized the occasion to pour out once more in his usual manner his resentment against Austro-Hungarian policy. . . . There were, he said, powerful and dangerous forces at work . . . to plunge Austria into war . . . namely Count Forgach 'an intriguer of the worst sort' and Count Tisza, a half madman. . . . Their aim was the annihilation of Serbia (Kaiser's marginal note: 'would be the best thing, too!') . . . If Austria-Hungary was determined to break the peace, she would have to reckon with Europe (Kaiser's marginal note: 'No! but with Russia, yes!') . . . Russia would not be able to tolerate Austria-Hungary's using threatening language to Serbia or taking military measures (Kaiser: '*qui vivra verra*'). 'Russia's policy', said M. Sazonov, 'is pacific but not passive.'[3]

Sazonov's words cannot always be taken at their full value. As has been said, he was temperamental and changeable. In the succeeding days he can be seen making a series of suggestions for settling the conflict without sticking to any of them. But at this juncture it would have been difficult for him to show a spirit of accommodation and he was certainly not about to be urged to do so by the eminent personage who was soon to arrive at St. Petersburg, the President of the French Republic.

[1] *Int. Bez*. i. IV. 296.   [2] *Int. Bez*. i. IV, 297.   [3] DD. I, 120.

2. *The visit of Poincaré and Viviani to St. Petersburg.*

It fell to Viviani, as Foreign Minister, to accompany Poincaré to St. Petersburg on the President's state visit to the Tsar which had been arranged as early as January. On taking office Viviani had at once reaffirmed France's loyalty to the alliance with Russia and given assurances to Russia that the three year term of military service would be upheld. But he possessed neither the necessary experience nor the authority to direct French foreign policy. This consequently continued to be dominated by Poincaré whom the French pacifists saw with anxiety taking the road to the allied capital for the second time in two years. As early as May Georges Louis asked Caillaux to oppose this journey as likely to have serious consequences. After the Sarajevo tragedy the danger grew, and Jaurès vainly urged the Chamber to refuse the grant necessary for the visit.

On 15 July the President with Viviani embarked on the cruiser *France* to arrive at 2 p.m. on 20 July at St. Petersburg whither he had been preceded by Izvolsky and where his intimate friend Paléologue awaited him. The visit was to end at 11 p.m. on 23 July. Poincaré took with him an agenda which was very important for his future plans. He was anxious to compose certain differences between Russia and Sweden and still more to remedy the coolness between England and Russia arising from conflicting interests in India, Persia and the Persian Gulf. There was some danger that the Anglo-Russian Convention of 31 August 1907 might suffer the shipwreck so ardently desired by the pro-German party in Russia. This would have been a major disaster. It would have been the end of the Triple *Entente* and of all French hopes. What must be done was to consolidate it, strengthen the bonds between France and Russia, bring about the resumption of the suspended negotiations for an Anglo-Russian naval agreement and, above all, come to an understanding on the course to be followed in the Austro-Serbian conflict which was on the point of breaking out. On 4 July the President had given both the Serbian and the Austrian Ministers wise counsels of moderation.[1] But he could not but foresee that the matter would not settle itself so easily and there is no doubt that he wanted to ascertain the intentions of his ally and influence them in accordance with his views, the nature of which we have already seen. Several times in the two preceding years, as Izvolsky's dispatches show, the Russian attitude had been thought too submissive by France. Sazonov's defects were well known to Poincaré. In October 1912 he had described him to G. Louis as 'léger, mobile, et son esprit n'est pas très pénétrant'.[2] Later on, on 11 August 1914, shortly after war was declared, Poincaré was to describe him as 'ever disconcerting by the

[1] Oe-U. VIII, 10047; LAS. 13 ; in CDD., pp. 375-6.
[2] Louis, II, p. 35.

multiplicity of his improvisations'.[1] What was now necessary was to set him off on a steady course, but how far could this be done and what was to be the aim in view?

Very little is known of the talks which went on at St. Petersburg between 20 and 23 July. The preface to Vol. X of the Third Series of *French Diplomatic Documents* states that the Commission entrusted with the task of compiling the collection of documents made all possible investigations with the object of finding the minutes of the discussions.

These investigations have been almost entirely fruitless, as seem also to have been those made by the editors of the Russian documents. In the Foreign Ministry archives, where a file exists on preparations for the visit, there is only one single brief note, in M. Viviani's hand, which seems to refer to the talks. The telegrams exchanged between St. Petersburg and Paris during the visit are exclusively concerned with French home affairs. In the archives of the Presidency of the Republic no trace has been found. The archives of the French Embassy at St. Petersburg, which have been brought back to Paris, give no information. Efforts made to collect private papers have had the same negative result. M. Poincaré's papers, all deposited to-day in the archives of the Quai d'Orsay, contain no item for that period. It is in vain that the Commission has tried to find M. Viviani's papers, if such exist. M. de Margerie, then Director of Political Affairs and the Minister's *Chef de Cabinet*, who accompanied the President and Prime Minister on their journey, was good enough to inform the Commission that he did not possess any documents relating to the St. Petersburg conversations, that, moreover, he had not been present at the conversations of M. Poincaré and M. Viviani with the Russian statesmen and that he had never seen a report of them in the archives. Finally, M. Paléologue, the French Ambassador to St. Petersburg, who has already published his memoirs in the form of a *Diary*, has intimated that he had not preserved among his personal papers any document on this subject.[2]

Even Paléologue's dispatches on Russian reactions to the Sarajevo outrage are few and brief: just two laconic telegrams! A strange phenomenon in one who was hitherto so copious and detailed an informant. The telegram of 30 June begins:

The Russian press comments in decorous terms on the Sarajevo outrage, but is almost unanimous in implying that it is the expiation of the crime committed by Austria against Slavism in annexing Bosnia-Herzegovina.[3]

The one of 6 July runs:

M. Sazonov in a friendly tone pointed out to the Austrian Chargé d'Affaires the disquieting irritation that the Austrian press attacks on Serbia risk producing in Russia. Count Czernin having given to understand that the Austro-Hungarian Government would perhaps be obliged to seek the instigators of the Sarajevo outrage on Serbian territory, M. Sazonov cut him

---

[1] Poincaré, V, p. 71.   [2] DF. 3. X, pp. VI–VII.   [3] DF. 3. X, 459.

short: 'No country has had to suffer more than Russia from outrages prepared on foreign territory. Have we ever claimed to employ against any
country the procedure with which your newspapers threaten Serbia? Do
not engage yourselves on that road; it is dangerous.'[1]

Is it possible that Paléologue did not think necessary to send home
news of the Schilling-Carlotti conversation and the Shebeko telegram?[2]
In view of the journey that Viviani and the President were to make
to Russia, de Margerie had had a certain number of notes prepared
relating to the questions that Viviani was to discuss in his conversations with members of the Russian Government. The note entitled:
'Relations of Austria-Hungary and Russia' began with the statement:
'The point of departure of the Austro-Russian tension must be sought
in the Buchlau meeting of 15 September 1908.'

Further on in the note we read:

Can one glimpse an improvement in Austro-Russian relations in the
future? The reply will remain doubtful so long as the Vienna Cabinet, regarding the Bucharest Peace as a provisional peace, continues to encourage
Bulgarian claims to Ištip and Kočana and exercises a preponderating influence
at Sofia. Account must also be taken of Russian intrigues with the Southern
Slavs and Austrian intrigues with the Ruthenians. In regard to the Southern
Slavs, the Russian programme was defined in December last by the Tsar's
Minister to Belgrade, M. de Hartwig:—'After the question of Turkey, it is
now the turn of Austria. Serbia will be our best instrument. The day draws
near when you, Bulgarians, will have Macedonia and when Serbia will take
back *her* Bosnia and *her* Herzegovina.' Out of a total population of 1,800,000
inhabitants, this province numbers 800,000 Orthodox over whom the young
Serbian Kingdom hopes to be able to exercise a lasting ascendency with the
moral support of Russia. Did not M. Sazonov these last days in a talk with
the Austro-Hungarian Chargé d'Affaires at St. Petersburg rise in arms against
any attempt at a direct investigation at Belgrade in connexion with the
Sarajevo assassination?[3]

Among the meagre documents of the St. Petersburg visit is an
undated note in de Margerie's hand giving the headings of the subjects for discussion with Sazonov. The fourteenth on the list was:
'Austria-Hungary; assassination of the Archduke and Serbia'.[4]

Certainly by 20 and 21 July de Margerie regarded the international situation as extremely disquieting. Victor Margueritte, a life-
long intimate friend of Berthelot, de Margerie's Assistant Director for
European Affairs at the Quai d'Orsay, has assured the present writer
that when on the evening of 21 July, he questioned Berthelot on the
international situation, he received the answer: 'The situation is extremely serious, we are going towards war.' Nor was St. Petersburg
less aware of the seriousness of the situation. Poincaré and Viviani

[1] DF. 3. X, 477.   [2] See pp. 184–5.   [3] DF. 3. X, 500.   [4] DF. 3. X, 502.

there learnt news of the Schilling-Carlotti talk and of the Shebeko telegram which had so much alarmed Sazonov. Another to feel alarm was the wise French Ambassador to Berlin, Jules Cambon. On 21 July Paris received a dispatch from him dated the 20th with the warning:

Within a few weeks from now the Triplice will find itself to have assembled an exceptional armed mass. From this it may be inferred that towards that moment it expects to have to make an effort, or at least it wants to give everybody the impression that it has prepared everything to support its policy by force. It is probable that Austro-Serbian difficulties play a large part in this attitude. The *Norddeutsche Allgemeine Zeitung* of 19 July is at pains to express the hope that the Powers will show themselves united as they did during the Balkan crisis and that the difficulties which might break out between Austria and Serbia will remain *localized*; there will therefore be difficulties, although the Austrian Government is long in bringing to the light its grievances against Belgrade. . . .

The *Lokal-Anzeiger* charitably warns us that Germany will not let herself be perturbed.[1]

A further dispatch from Jules Cambon, received on the early afternoon of the 21st, ran:

The Berlin Bourse has been very weak to-day. This drop of several points on the most reliable securities is attributed to the disquiet which is beginning to arise on the subject of Serbia. The *Lokal-Anzeiger* of this evening publishes a note intended to inform opinion that there are no grounds for anxiety.

Confidential. I am however entitled to think from information reaching me from sources worthy of credence that when Austria makes the *démarche* at Belgrade, which she deems necessary in consequence of the Sarajevo outrage, Germany will support her with her authority and has not any intention to play the rôle of mediator.[2]

Both these documents were immediately communicated to Poincaré in Russia and to the French Embassy at St. Petersburg. On 22 July another dispatch from Jules Cambon was telegraphed on to St. Petersburg. It ran:

The Bourse continues to fall. The Chargé d'Affaires and I have each spoken to the Secretary of State about the article in the *Norddeutsche Allgemeine Zeitung* expressing the hope that the Austro-Serbian difficulties will be localized. I asked Herr von Jagow what the Austrian note would contain. He assured me that he does not know at all. I am surprised at this as Germany affects to range herself beside Austria with particular energy.

Highly Confidential. I am assured that, as during the periods of tension in 1911 and at the moment of the Serbian crisis in 1912, the first preliminary notices of mobilization have been issued in Germany. I acquaint the Department with this information with all reserve.[3]

[1] DF. 3. X, 538.   [2] DF. 3. X, 539.   [3] DF. 3. X, 551.

An alarming telegram from Barrère also reached the Quai d'Orsay on the evening of the 21st, a short summary of which was telegraphed on to St. Petersburg. Barrère wrote:

Marquis San Giuliano shows great anxiety on the subject of the Austro-Serbian conflict. Germany, he says, would make no effort to restrain Austria, and Vienna imagines that Russia will let Serbia be violated. The Foreign Minister assures that he is doing all he can to lead the Austrians to demand of the Serbs only things they can carry out; the dissolution of Bosnian political clubs would seem to him in that category and he seems to understand that the Belgrade Cabinet on the other hand could not accept a mixed commission of inquiry into the causes of the Sarajevo outrage. According to Marquis San Giuliano Roumania would be particularly well placed to exercise a pacifying influence on the Vienna Cabinet, but action should be taken as soon as possible, for, once the note has been delivered, the Minister is convinced that Austria will make it a duty to obtain what she has demanded. The German Ambassador likewise deems the present situation very disquieting. He says that his Government 'has had enough' of always restraining Austria-Hungary. I believe it to be the case that Marquis San Giuliano has endeavoured, without success, to gain cognizance of the Austrian note in order at once to induce the Serbs to make the necessary sacrifices, even before the note has been delivered.[1]

On the evening of 22 July, Bienvenu-Martin, the interim Foreign Minister, telegraphed to the French Ambassadors at St. Petersburg, London and Vienna:

M. Jules Cambon asked Herr von Jagow what the Austrian note to Belgrade would contain and the Chancellor [sic] answered that he had no idea. Our Ambassador showed surprise at this; he notes that the fall on the Berlin Bourse continues and that pessimistic news is circulating.

M. Barrère has spoken on the subject of Austro-Serbian tension with Marquis San Giuliano who shows anxiety about it and assures that he works on Austria in order that Serbia may be asked things that can be carried out, for example, the dissolution of the Bosnian club, and not an inquiry into the causes of the Sarajevo outrage.

Generally speaking it seems that the Austrian Government, feeling itself overborne by its press and the military party, seeks to obtain the maximum from Serbia by preliminary intimidation, direct and indirect, and to this end leans on Germany.[2]

No great effort is needed to imagine the impression produced on Poincaré not only by the news he learnt at St. Petersburg but also by the disquieting dispatches from Jules Cambon whom he knew to be a diplomatist of great judgement and moderation. The St. Petersburg conversations must have dealt above all with the Austro-Serbian tension and the eventualities that might result from it. Both Poincaré and

---

[1] DF. 3. X, 546.   [2] DF .3. X, 555

Paléologue in their memoirs describe the externals of the visit but are silent on its political fruits. Paléologue paints a picture of the meeting of the two heads of state:

The President of the Republic stepped on board the *Alexandria*. The Tsar received him at the gangway. As soon as the presentations were over the Imperial yacht steered for Peterhof. Seated in the stern the Tsar and the President immediately entered into conversation, I should perhaps say a discussion, for it was obvious that they were talking business, firing questions at each other and arguing. As was proper, it was Poincaré who had the initiative. Before long he was doing all the talking. The Tsar simply nodded acquiescence.[1]

Next day, the 21st, the two had a long talk 'on all the questions at the moment on the diplomatic chessboard', ending up with 'the problem of the Austro-Serbian dispute'. In connexion with the application of the Anglo-Russian agreements in Persia, Buchanan on 22 July telegraphed to Grey:

The President of the Republic told me yesterday that he had discussed Persian question with Emperor and Minister for Foreign Affairs, and that both had given him most satisfactory assurances. . . . Emperor had declared in the most positive terms that he would [not] allow Persia to cause division between England and Russia.[2]

Poincaré was also due to visit Stockholm and was charged with a message from the Tsar to the King of Sweden to say how much the Tsar desired the maintenance of friendly relations.

In the afternoon of 21 July Poincaré's reception of the members of the Diplomatic Corps at the Winter Palace gave rise to a significant incident between Poincaré and the Austrian Ambassador Szápáry. Poincaré asked the Ambassador: 'Have you any news of Serbia?' and received the evasive reply: 'The judicial inquiry is proceeding.' Paléologue narrates that Poincaré rejoined:

'Of course I am anxious about the results of this inquiry. . . . I can remember two previous inquiries which did not improve relations with Serbia. Don't you remember the Friedjung affair and the Prohaska affair?' . . . Szápáry replied in a dry tone: 'Monsieur le Président, we cannot suffer a foreign government to allow plots against our sovereignty to be hatched on its territory!' In a more than conciliatory tone Poincaré endeavoured to point out that in the present state of public feeling in Europe every Government should be twice as cautious as usual. 'With a little good will this Serbian business is easy to settle. But it can just as easily become acute. Serbia has some very warm friends in the Russian people. And Russia has an ally, France. There are plenty of complications to be feared!'[3] Then he thanked

---

[1] Paléologue, I, p. 13.　　　　　　　　　　[2] BD. XI, 75.

[3] A blunt warning that 'localization' of the war would not be attainable, had the Central Powers but had ears to hear. [Tr.]

the Ambassador for his call. Szápáry bowed and went out without a word.

When we three were alone again Poincaré said:

'I'm not satisfied with this conversation. The Ambassador had obviously been instructed to say nothing. . . . Austria has a *coup de théâtre* in store for us. Sazonov must be firm and we must back him up.'[1]

Paléologue's account finds corroboration in Szápáry's own report to Vienna in which he comments:

The threatening attitude of the President, so strikingly in contrast with the reserved, circumspect bearing of Sazonov, confirms the anticipation that M. Poincaré will exercise anything but a calming influence here.[2]

Sazonov, on his part, telegraphed on 22 July to Shebeko in Vienna:

From my discussions with the French Foreign Minister it clearly emerges that also France, who is greatly concerned about the turn which Austro-Serbian relations might take, is not inclined to tolerate a humiliation of Serbia unwarranted by the circumstances.[3]

And he writes in his *Fateful Years*:

The three days that the President of the French Republic spent at Peterhof were passed under the shadow of impending calamity.[4]

3. *The atmosphere of excitement at St. Petersburg and its effect on Sazonov.*

In truth the atmosphere created by the excitement of the visit with its toasts and champagne was beginning to infect Sazonov. Already a clamour for war was making itself heard.

Paléologue narrates how, arriving early for a banquet given on the evening of the 22nd by the Grand Duke Nicholas after a military review, he chatted with the Grand Duchess Anastasia and her sister Grand Duchess Militza, the two Montenegrin princesses. The Grand Duchess Anastasia told him:

'I've had a telegram (in prearranged code) from my father [the King of Montenegro] to-day. He tells me we shall have war before the end of the month. . . . Just look at this little box I always take about with me. It's got some Lorraine soil in it, real Lorraine soil I picked up over the frontier. . . . Look there, at the table of honour: it's covered with thistles. . . . They are Lorraine thistles, don't you see!' . . . At dinner . . . the rhapsody continued, interspersed with prophecies: 'There's going to be war. There'll be nothing left of Austria. You're going to get back Alsace and Lorraine. Our armies will meet in Berlin. Germany will be destroyed! Then suddenly: 'I must restrain myself. The Emperor has his eye on me.'[5]

---

[1] Paléologue, I, pp. 18–19.   [2] Oe-U. VIII, 10461.   [3] *Int. Bez.* i. IV, 322.
[4] Sazonov, p. 151.   [5] Paléologue, I, pp. 22–3.

This scene reveals the atmosphere at St. Petersburg under the influence of which Sazonov's attitude grew more decided. Following him about in those days was his predecessor and former chief Izvolsky who went around repeating that Russia could not evade the German challenge; that for over a year France had been surprised at the passivity shown by Russia in questions which touched her closely; and that the Dual Alliance would be in mortal danger if the Russian passivity continued. Responding to this impulsion Sazonov in the night of 22–23 July sent Austria a warning for which he had not till now gathered courage. At 4 a.m. on the 23rd he wired the Russian Chargé d'Affaires at Vienna asking him to call Berchtold's attention 'cordially but firmly' to the dangerous consequences to which 'such a step may lead if it is of a character unacceptable to the dignity of Serbia'.

He added that the French and English Ambassadors to Vienna had been instructed to enjoin moderation on the Government there.[1]

It was, as we shall see, not true that England intended to take such a step. But Poincaré agreed to do so, and Viviani, in leaving St. Petersburg, wired instructions to Paris for Dumaine. They went off at 2.5 a.m. on 24 July.[2]

Sazonov's note also arrived too late. The Russian Chargé d'Affaires received it at 3 p.m. on the 23rd and went at once to the Ballplatz. But Berchtold sent a message that he was busy and could only see him next morning. At 6 p.m. on the 23rd the ultimatum was in the hands of the Serbian Government. Its dispatch, as we know, had been intentionally timed so that it was received just before Poincaré left Russian waters. In his farewell toast on board the *France*, thanking the Tsar for his welcome, Poincaré amid the enthusiasm of those present said that their two countries cherished 'the same ideal of peace in strength, honour and self-respect'.

That is just what wanted saying—commented the Montenegrin princesses —just what we have been waiting for so long. Peace in strength, honour and

<hr/>

[1] *Int. Bez.* i, IV, 322.

[2] DF. 3. XI, 1; LJ. 22; CDD., pp. 154–5. The *Yellow Book* gives this telegram as having been dispatched from Reval at 1 a.m. on the 24th, but the *Documents Français* show that it in fact went off from St. Petersburg at 2.5 a.m. and a footnote comments: 'This telegram had evidently been drafted on the evening of the 23rd before the President of the Republic and the Prime Minister embarked.' However as early as at 1.46 p.m. on 22 July Buchanan had telegraphed information to Grey of the *démarche* desired by Sazonov, saying that 'to-day' Sazonov would bring the matter up with Poincaré (BD. XI, 76), and no doubt Sazonov did in fact receive Poincaré's assent before sending off, at 4 a.m. on the 23rd, his own message to Vienna. Viviani's instruction, therefore, was not drafted until nearly a day later, and was sent, not directly to Vienna, but to Paris for re-transmission. In truth, despite general apprehension and uneasiness, the Austrian ultimatum seems to have taken everybody by surprise. Even from Vienna, writing at 4.45 p.m. on the 24th, Dumaine remarks: 'The suddenness and the extreme nature of the demands formulated in the Austro-Hungarian note or ultimatum to Belgrade have surprised . . . the most rabid enemies of Serbia' (DF. 3. XI, 16). [Tr.]

self respect. Remember those words, Monsieur l'Ambassadeur, they will mark a date in the history of the world.[1]

Indeed they were spoken only a few moments before the curtain rose on the first act of the tragedy. A year later, in recalling this farewell, Nicholas II was to say to a former French Cabinet Minister, Cruppi:

I have always present in my memory the firm words spoken to me by the President of the Republic on 23 July 1914 when he was on the point of leaving Russia.[2]

What exactly was said during the three days that the visit lasted, is something that perhaps will never be known. Georges Louis in his *Carnets* records Millerand as having said: 'I asked Poincaré: "But what did you say to the Russians?" I never succeeded in making him tell.'[3] It should have been the duty of the Prime Minister Viviani to draft minutes of what was said in the talks, as Poincaré had done on the occasion of his visit of 1912. If it was not done, there must have been good reasons for this. Some light is thrown by a dispatch of 24 July from Buchanan to Grey:

Minister for Foreign Affairs and French Ambassador told me confidentially that result of the visit of the French Republic had been to establish the following points:

1. Perfect community of views on the various problems with which the Powers are confronted as regards the maintenance of general peace and balance of power in Europe, more especially in the East.

2. Decision to take action at Vienna with a view to the prevention of a demand for explanations or any summons equivalent to an intervention in the internal affairs of Servia which the latter would be justified in regarding as an attack on her sovereignty and independence.

3. Solemn affirmation of obligations imposed by the alliance of the two countries.[4]

The import of these vague and mysterious formulae was made clear by subsequent events. The third point seemed to the British Government of such a nature that it was omitted from the version of Buchanan's dispatch published in the English *Blue Book* of 1914. There can be no doubt that the stiffening of Russia's attitude was in some measure due to the heated atmosphere arising from Poincaré's visit and to his promptings. What went on in Poincaré's mind is hard to say. Did he merely desire that in this set of circumstances Russia and the Triple *Entente* should show themselves strong and not capitulate to an 'either —or' from the Central Powers? Or else did he deem that the hour had struck for the *revanche* and that it could not come in conditions more

[1] Paléologue, I, p. 28; *Int. Bez.* i. V, 1.   [2] Paris *Matin*, 26 August 1915.
[3] Louis, II, p. 180.   [4] BD. XI, 101.

favourable for France? On 25 December 1914 Ernest Judet, the editor of *L'Éclair*, related to G. Louis that when Poincaré held a press conference to urge the formation of a united front

he shook hands with all of us present. When my own turn came, I said to him: 'A year ago you predicted war for 1914. We have got it!' This reminder somewhat disconcerted him and he replied with a certain embarrassment: 'Yes, but it is Kaiser Wilhelm who predicted the war. We knew of it through the King of the Belgians.'[1]

Certainly there were respected politicians and diplomatists in France who accused Poincaré of having used influence on Russia in favour of war. Louis's *Carnets* bring direct and indirect evidence that this view was held by Pichon, Deschanel, the two Cambons and the War Minister, Messimy. On 26 June 1915 Deschanel said to Louis:

nobody speaks more severely than Messimy of the part played by Poincaré. . . . The majority of the men who were Ministers in July openly say that Poincaré is the cause of the war.[2]

However Louis is not an impartial witness and though his statements have not been denied by those concerned, not even by Poincaré, it is fantastic to put the blame for the European war on Poincaré. No! Those responsible for the war before and more than Poincaré are the rulers of the Central Powers, and, as we shall later see, even Sazonov, who at a certain point let the helm of the ship of state slip from his grasp. The French President's share was in availing himself of the mistakes committed by Austria and Germany to carry through the *revanche* and restore to France Alsace and above all his own Lorraine.

4. *Sir Edward Grey's views on the Triple* Entente.

So far we have shown that the respective attitudes of Germany and Austria on the one hand and France and Russia on the other were already clearly defined on the eve of the delivery of the Austrian ultimatum to Serbia. The aggressor states, having a definite objective, shaped the course of events, while the other group had no clear plan beyond not allowing Serbia to be overwhelmed. Both sides, therefore, were deeply concerned to know what would be the line taken by England and Italy. Whether one or both of them intervened or stood aside, the consequences would be incalculable. They were thus both in a position to exercise an enormous, if not decisive, influence in the diplomatic struggle which would in any case precede the armed conflict. England of course carried more weight than Italy because of her economic strength, her naval superiority, her position and prestige in the world and the effects which would result from her decisions. But Italy, too,

---

[1] Louis, II, p. 157.   [2] Louis, II, p. 193.

whose example would presumably be followed by Roumania, was in a position to speak a very effective word to her allies, and admonish them to ponder well, before they acted, on what would be the consequences of their actions.

The tension between England and Germany had been the most serious of those that tormented Europe before the war. Either Germany would have to recognize that for England it was a question of life and death to have a much more powerful fleet than Germany, or the matter would have to be fought out between the two countries. They could not stand the strain of an unending naval armaments race. However in 1914 nobody in England thought that the conflict was imminent, and few even regarded it as sooner or later inevitable. The Haldane mission in 1912 had failed to arrive at an agreement on the rate of naval construction and Germany had turned a deaf ear to the proposal of a naval holiday. But

The spring and summer of 1914 were marked in Europe by an exceptional tranquillity. Ever since Agadir the policy of Germany towards Great Britain had not only been correct, but considerate. All through the tangle of Balkan Conferences British and German diplomacy laboured in harmony. Some at least of those who were accustomed to utter warnings began to feel the need of revising their judgement. The personalities who expressed the foreign policy of Germany, seemed for the first time to be men to whom we could talk and with whom common action was possible. . . . Some there were who looked forward to a wider combination in which Great Britain and Germany, without prejudice to their respective friendships or alliances, might together bring the two opposing European systems into harmony and give to all the anxious nations solid assurances of safety and fair play. Naval rivalry had at the moment ceased to be a cause of friction. We were proceeding inflexibly for the third year in succession with our series of programmes. . . . Germany had made no further increases since the beginning of 1912.[1]

Grey in his *Twenty-five Years* says much the same thing. Recalling the successive European crises from 1906 on, he writes of 1914:

European peace had weathered worse storms than any that were now visible above the horizon. I had been more than eight years at the Foreign Office in the centre of all the troubles; it was natural to hope, even to expect, that the same methods which had preserved peace hitherto, when it had been threatened, would preserve it still. . . . The peril of German aggression was possible, but seemed less likely than in 1905 and 1911. Germany showed no signs of attempting again to break or test the strength of the Franco-British *Entente*. We had shown our readiness to meet her over the Bagdad railway, and (as far as we could honourably do so) in the matter of the Portuguese Colonies; and an agreement on these subjects had practically been

[1] Churchill, I, pp. 178–9.

completed in the early months of 1914. In spite of the rebuff about the naval holiday, relations with Germany seemed to be really improved.[1]

In proof of this Grey reproduces a conversation he had with the German Ambassador Lichnowsky as he had reported it in his own dispatch of 24 June to Sir Edward Goschen in Berlin:

Herr von Bethmann Hollweg had instructed Prince Lichnowsky to tell me that he hoped, if new developments or emergencies arose in the Balkans, that they would be discussed as frankly between Germany and ourselves as the difficulties that arose during the last Balkan crisis, and that we should be able to keep in as close touch. . . . I most cordially reciprocated what Herr von Bethmann Hollweg had said. . . . I was most anxious not to lose any of the ground that had been gained then for good relations between us. The British Government belonged to one group of Powers, but did not do so in order to make difficulties greater between the two European groups; on the contrary, we wished to prevent any questions that arose from throwing the groups, as such, into opposition. . . . Prince Lichnowsky cordially agreed. He said that our being in the group we were was a good thing, and he regarded our intimacy with France and Russia without any misgiving, because he was sure that it was used for peace. I said that he was quite justified in this view. We should never pursue an aggressive policy, and if ever there was a European war, and we took part in it, it would not be on the aggressive side, for public opinion was against that.[2]

Grey was speaking with the utmost sincerity. To be sure, pseudo-historians of the type of Mathias Morhardt and Alberto Lumbroso are not lacking, who deny this sincerity and assert that Grey and his officials wanted war and wittingly dragged Europe into it.[3] But their case is disproved by unassailable documents and is quite untenable. All sorts of criticisms can be made against Grey. It can fairly be said that he was deficient in political intuition and that his handling of the situation in 1914 was so inept and dilatory that it failed to avert the catastrophe. But there exists no shadow of a doubt that he was an upright and straightforward character, perhaps even too upright and straightforward.

Grey had entered parliament as a Liberal in November 1885 at the age of twenty-three. From 1885 to 1902 British foreign policy was that of the Conservative Prime Minister and Foreign Secretary Lord Salisbury, even during the two short terms of Liberal Government within that period. Gladstone kept foreign affairs out of party politics and indeed said in one election speech that he did not find fault with the foreign policy of Lord Salisbury from 1886 to 1902; this policy being 'that of direct friendship with the Triple Alliance'.[4]

[1] Grey, I, pp. 302-3.   [2] Grey, I, pp. 304-5.
[3] M. Morhardt, Les preuves (Paris, 1924); Alberto Lumbroso, Le origini della guerra mondiale (Milan, 1928).
[4] Grey, I, p. 4.

Grey was thirty when in August 1892 he first took office as Under Secretary for Foreign Affairs in Gladstone's Liberal Home Rule Cabinet which lasted until June 1895 and in which Lord Rosebery was Foreign Secretary. In taking office Lord Rosebery had informed the Ambassadors of the Triple Alliance that he intended to continue the policy of Lord Salisbury. And when in June 1895 Lord Salisbury again returned to power his Government even 'went further on the road of complaisance and advance to Germany than before'.[1] In practice, therefore, except for a brief interlude, the Conservative leader Lord Salisbury governed from 1885 to 1902 when he resigned, his place being taken by Arthur Balfour. The Balfour Government only lasted until December 1905 when it resigned owing to the opposition aroused by Joseph Chamberlain's proposals for tariff reform. The 1906 elections gave an overwhelming victory to the Liberals under Campbell-Bannerman, whose illness and death in 1908 was to lead to the appointment of Asquith as his successor. Grey had been out of office for over ten years (1895–1905) when in 1906 Campbell-Bannerman asked him to take the Foreign Office. He hesitated for a long time, either because he wished to remain free, or because he thought that the leadership of the House would be better in the hands of Asquith. Finally he accepted unwillingly, remaining in office for over ten years.

During the years when he had been out of office British foreign policy had slowly been taking a new direction. Joseph Chamberlain's offers of alliance to Germany had been made and rebuffed and Balfour's Foreign Secretary, Lord Lansdowne, was turning to a policy of friendship with France. The immense Liberal majority in the 1906 elections placed the new Government in a very strong position, but it was a Government divided within itself, a veiled coalition. On the one side there was a small right wing of Liberal Imperialists who had been supporters of the Boer war. They counted among their numbers Grey, Haldane, the Secretary of State for War, Asquith, the Chancellor of the Exchequer, and Churchill, President of the Board of Trade. On the other side was a large radical-pacifist left wing, constituting the bulk of the party and of the Cabinet and including Lloyd George, John Burns, and John Morley. Churchill writes that Campbell-Bannerman's

word was law to the extremists of his Party. They would accept almost anything from him. Thus he was able to authorize Grey to support France strongly at Algeciras. He also authorized . . . the beginning of military conversations between the British and French General Staffs with a view to concerted action in the event of war. . . . Mr. Asquith had been far from 'sound' about the Boer War. . . . He was therefore in a certain sense suspect, and every step he took in external affairs was watched with prim vigilance by the Elders. If the military conversations with France had not

[1] Grey, I, p. 34.

been authorized by Sir Henry Campbell-Bannerman, and if his political virtue could not be cited in their justification, I doubt whether they could have been begun and continued by Mr. Asquith. . . . Henceforward the relations of the two Staffs became increasingly intimate and confidential. Mutual trust grew continually in one set of military relationships, mutual precautions in the other. However explicitly the two Governments might agree and affirm to each other that no national or political engagement was involved in these technical discussions, the fact remained that they constituted an exceedingly potent tie.'[1]

The 'sound' radical pacifists who formed the bulk of the Government would not hear of an alliance with France, still less with Tsarist Russia. They wanted to work in agreement with Germany but to have no ties with any Power. Grey had therefore to walk warily for fear of incurring the displeasure of his radical-pacifist colleagues. But even apart from this necessity, he was not inclined either by temperament or by opinions to carry on a policy of hostility to Germany or to support France and Russia in any such policy. He had a deep abhorrence of war and welcomed the Anglo-French agreement of 1904, less as rendering England independent of Germany in Egypt, than as ending the exasperating friction with France. In his *Twenty-five Years* he asks the question:

Was it in the minds of those who made the simple, straightforward Agreement for the settling of present differences that it would develop into something more, into what was called the *Entente Cordiale*—a general *diplomatic* alliance with no new obligations, but with preparations for the contingency of a German attack on France? . . . I cannot say. There is in great affairs so much more, as a rule, in the minds of the events (if such an expression may be used) than in the minds of the chief actors. . . . It was obvious that Germany would not like the Agreement. She had profited by the constant dissensions between Britain and France. . . . But really good relations with Germany could not be founded on bad relations with France; I saw no reason why we should be hostile to German interests, where Germany was expanding, and, if we were not, why should the Agreement with France mean bad relations with Germany? In British minds, certainly in my own, the Anglo-French Agreement was not regarded as more than I have described it. It was the subsequent attempts of Germany to shake or break it that turned it into an *Entente*.[2]

There is much truth in this last statement, but it also cannot be doubted that Delcassé and Paul Cambon sought a reconciliation between France and England in view of its potential further development, and that Balfour, Chamberlain and Lord Lansdowne, after the failure of their efforts for an alliance with Germany, accepted the French offer as a means of ending Britain's isolation, i.e. in self-protection. Grey's

---

[1] Churchill, I, pp. 32–4.   [2] Grey, I, pp. 51–3.

slow mind probably, if not certainly, failed to perceive at first the full import of the 1904 Agreement, any more than did European public opinion or even the Chancelleries of Europe. And it is indisputable that it was the mistakes of Germany which strengthened the *Entente*, turned it into a potential weapon of war and rounded it off by the Anglo-Russian Agreement of 1907.

Be it remembered that on two occasions, at the time of Algeciras (1906) and that of Agadir (1911), England showed readiness to resort to war in support of France; that, as already said, from 1906 onwards the General Staffs of the two countries discussed plans of concerted action in the event of war, growing more and more convinced that war would come; and that in 1912 England recalled her battleships from the Mediterranean while France concentrated her fleet there, leaving her northern and western shores undefended under the implicit understanding that their defence would be undertaken by Britain. Grey never failed to warn France that this could not be regarded as pledging Britain to come in on the side of France in the event of war. Facts spoke louder than words and moral obligations were stronger than ones put down in writing. Churchill writes:

> It is true to say that our *Entente* with France and the military and naval conversations that had taken place since 1906, had led us into a position where we had the obligations of an alliance without its advantages. An open alliance, if it could have been peacefully brought about at an earlier date, would have exercised a deterring effect upon the German mind, or at the .east would have altered their military calculations. Whereas now we were morally bound to come to the aid of France and it was our interest to do so, and yet the fact that we should come in appeared so uncertain that it did not weigh as it should have done with the Germans. Moreover, as things were, if France had been in an aggressive mood, we should not have had the un-questioned right of an ally to influence her action in a pacific sense: and if as the result of her aggressive mood war had broken out and we had stood aside, we should have been accused of deserting her, and in any case would have been ourselves grievously endangered by her defeat.[1]

Grey must undoubtedly have been aware of the false situation which nad arisen in regard to Anglo-French and indirectly Anglo-Russian relations. He could not but feel the force of the appeals coming from St. Petersburg at the beginning of 1914 to transform the *Entente* into an alliance which would have been a safeguard of European peace.[2] But his own mentality and that of the nation was averse to forming ties of that sort. Even had he himself been convinced that an alliance would be better than the *Entente* both for Britain and for the peace of Europe, he would never have gained the assent either of his colleagues in the Cabinet, or of Parliament, or of public opinion, least of all of

[1] Churchill, I, p. 205.   [2] See Vol. I, pp. 571-4.

his colleagues for the reasons given above, which were specially strong in the period of calm in Anglo-German relations signalized by the visit of the British fleet to Kiel at the end of June 1914 amid demonstrations of extreme cordiality.

5. Lichnowsky's revelations and the optimism at the Foreign Office.

In the midst of the ceremonies at Kiel there arrived the news of the Sarajevo outrage. But nobody there at first thought that thirty days later the two navies would be at war with each other. Certainly no such idea crossed the minds of the English political leaders whose whole attention was focused on the serious situation created at home by the revolt of the Protestant counties of Ulster against the imminent passage into law of the Irish Home Rule bill. In this revolt they were supported and encouraged by the whole Conservative party. It was more than probable that the troops sent to keep order in Ulster would fraternize with the Orangemen. Churchill writes:

These shocking events caused an explosion of unparalleled fury in Parliament and shook the State to its foundations. . . . We cannot read the debates that continued at intervals through April, May and June without wondering that our Parliamentary institutions were strong enough to survive the passions by which they were convulsed. Was it astonishing that German agents reported and German statesmen believed, that England was paralysed by faction and drifting into civil war, and need not be taken into account as a factor in the European situation? . . . During the whole of May and June the party warfare proceeded, but underneath the surface negotiations for a settlement between the two great parties were steadily persisted in. These eventuated on 20 July in a summons by the King to the leaders of the Conservative, Liberal and Irish parties to meet in conference at Buckingham Palace.[1]

But no agreement was reached and the threat of civil war was not removed when the European war was about to break out.

These preoccupations at home prevented the Foreign Office from giving much heed to the alarming news coming in from Vienna and Belgrade until Lichnowsky called on 6 July on his return from his short visit to Berlin. Grey's report to Sir Horace Rumbold in Berlin runs:

The Ambassador then went on to speak to me privately, he said, but very seriously, as to the anxiety and pessimism that he had found at Berlin. He explained that the murder of the Archduke Franz Ferdinand had excited very strong anti-Servian feeling in Austria, and he knew for a fact, though he did not know details, that the Austrians intended to do something and that it was not impossible that they would take military action against Servia. I said that

[1] Churchill, I, pp. 181-6.

surely they did not think of taking any territory? The Ambassador replied that they did not wish to take territory, because they would not know what to do with it. He thought their idea was that they must have some compensation in the sense of some humiliation for Servia. The situation was very difficult for Germany; if she told the Austrians that nothing must be done, she would be accused of always holding them back and not supporting them; on the other hand if she let events take their course there was the possibility of very serious trouble. The Ambassador earnestly hoped that, if trouble came, we would use our influence to mitigate feeling in St. Petersburg.

A second thing which caused anxiety and pessimism in Berlin was the apprehension in Germany about the attitude of Russia, especially in connection with the recent increase of military strength. He was told that Russia now had a peace footing of one million men and the impression in Germany was that Russian feeling towards Germany was very unfavourable.

A third thing was the idea that there was some Naval Convention between Russia and England. He had reported to his Government all I had said to him recently. . . . They accepted the statement that there was nothing between the British and Russian Governments, but they felt that, nevertheless, there might be some understanding between the British and Russian naval authorities. If there was such an understanding for co-operation directed against Germany, it would strengthen the chauvinistic feeling in Russia, it would make Pan-German feeling quite irresistible, and lead to an increase in the German Naval Law, which otherwise was not intended.

The Ambassador went so far as to say that there was some feeling in Germany . . . that trouble was bound to come and therefore it would be better not to restrain Austria and let the trouble come now, rather than later. He impressed on me more than once that he was speaking quite privately and on very delicate matters, but he was anxious to keep in touch with me. . . . He quoted Herr von Bethmann Hollweg as being pessimistic. . . . I was disturbed by what the Ambassador had told me about the form that anti-Servian feeling might take in Austria. If trouble did come, I would use all the influence I could to mitigate difficulties and smooth them away, and if clouds arose, to prevent the storm from breaking. I was glad that he had spoken to me; I should like to talk the whole matter of his conversation over with him later on, when I had had time to consider it.[1]

Grey's apprehension was expressed on 8 July to the Russian Ambassador Benckendorff, to whom he repeated the substance of what Lichnowsky had told him on the 6th:

Benckendorff said that he would write to Sazonov. He expressed himself quite conscious of the apprehension felt in Berlin; of the danger that lay in it, especially at this moment when Austria was excited against Servia, and of the desirability of preventing the horrible situation of having the Servian question forced open.[2]

---

[1] BD. XI, 32. Lichnowsky's own dispatch to his Government (DD. I, 20) omits all mention of his warning to Grey about Austria's intentions towards Serbia. [Tr.]

[2] BD. XI, 39.

But the fears of the Foreign Office were allayed by a dispatch from Sir Maurice de Bunsen, the English Ambassador to Vienna:

I had some conversation to-day with M. Schebeko, Russian Ambassador, concerning the feeling of bitterness which exists here against Serbia and its possible consequences. M. Schebeko doubts if the animosity penetrates deep down among the Austrian people . . . He cannot believe that the country will allow itself to be rushed into war, for an isolated combat with Serbia would be impossible and Russia would be compelled to take up arms in defence of Serbia.[1]

Had Shebeko known what Lichnowsky had said to Grey, he would certainly have been alarmed. But at the Foreign Office the Permanent Under Secretary of State, Sir Arthur Nicolson, remained deaf to Lichnowsky's warning. His annotation to Bunsen's dispatch runs:

I have my doubts as to whether Austria will take any action of a serious character and I expect the storm will blow over. M. Schebeko is a shrewd man and I attach weight to any opinion he expresses.

Grey's account to Sir Horace Rumbold (acting during Goschen's absence on leave) in Berlin of his talk with Lichnowsky on 9 July shows that the first subject discussed between them was 'the apprehension in Germany of an Anglo-Russian Naval Convention directed against Germany' in regard to which Grey gave emphatic assurances that 'the hands of the Government were quite free'. Only then did they pass on to discuss the Serbian question:

I told the Ambassador that, since I saw him last Monday, I had expressed to Count Benckendorff the apprehension that the Austrian Government might be forced by public opinion to make some *démarche* with regard to Serbia . . . Prince Lichnowsky expressed himself as hopeful, though he had no information, that the German Government might have succeeded in smoothing the Austrian intentions with regard to Serbia. He hoped that in any circumstances, if England and Germany kept in touch, we might be able to keep things right. I said that, if Austrian action with regard to Servia kept within certain bounds, it would, of course, be comparatively easy to encourage patience at St. Petersburg; but there were some things that Austria might do that would make the Russian Government say that the Slav feeling in Russia was so strong that they must send an ultimatum or something of that sort. I assured Prince Lichnowsky that I would continue the same policy as I had pursued through the Balkan crisis, and do my utmost to prevent the outbreak of war between the Great Powers.[2]

Lichnowsky's dispatch to his Government reported fully the assurance given by Grey that no binding engagement existed between Great Britain on the one hand and France and Russia on the other, though they remained on terms of close intimacy. The dispatch continues:

[1] BD. XI, 40.   [2] BD. XI, 41.

Since our last conversation, added Sir Edward, he had made inquiries about the feeling towards us in Russia and had found no basis for anxiety; he seemed also to be ready, if we wished it, to exercise his influence with Russia. He had already made efforts to persuade the Russian Government to take a calm and conciliatory attitude in the event of the Vienna Cabinet finding itself obliged in consequence of the Sarajevo murder to adopt a stiffer attitude towards Serbia. Much would depend, said Sir Edward, on the nature of the measures contemplated and whether they did not excite Slav feeling in such a way as to render it impossible for M. Sazonov to remain passive. On the whole the Minister was in a confident mood and said cheerfully that he felt no reason to be pessimistic about the situation.[1]

After another talk on 15 July Lichnowsky telegraphed to Berlin:

Sir E. Grey said it would all depend on what form the intervention might take, in no case could there be a question of a reduction of Serbian territory. He has endeavoured to use his influence at St. Petersburg in support of Austrian claims. But if intense excitement were caused in Russia by Austrian military measures, he would not be in a position to keep Russian policy in hand and would, in view of the present unpopularity of England in Russia, . . . have to be careful of Russian feelings. He will, I am convinced, if a conflict were to break out between Austria and Serbia, do his utmost to restrain Russia. But I do not think that he is in a position to say the decisive word there as he is in Paris.[2]

6. *Grey's proposal for direct conversations between Austria and Russia opposed by Poincaré.*

The sense of grievance in Russia against England which Grey gave as a reason for not putting too much pressure on St. Petersburg was due to grave differences which had arisen in Asia. The Russians·were greatly dissatisfied with what seemed to them to be undue advantages which the British Government had gained in the oilfields of Mesopotamia by the Anglo-Persian Oil Agreement of 1913. This had given the British Admiralty, which had gone over to the use of oil fuel for its new capital ships, the monopoly of the oilfields of the 'neutral zone' of the Persian Gulf, the value of which was estimated at £200,000,000. On the English side there were also grievances. For long the action of Russian Consuls in Persia had given grounds for complaint and there were also apprehensions, felt largely by the Government of India, concerning the situation in Afghanistan. This mutual distrust might conceivably have had serious consequences. Sazonov's position was not secure and if he fell from power no one could foresee by whom he would be succeeded:

There was always at the Court, and to a large extent in the army, a strong German party; the growing danger of revolution would almost inevitably

[1] DD. I, 30.   DD. I, 52.

have had the effect of causing the Russian Government to turn for support to Germany and of reviving the old understanding between the two nations for the maintenance of monarchical institutions against the forces of disorder. Anything of this kind would have had the gravest effect; at once the whole settlement in Asia would have been in jeopardy.[1]

The two Governments were seeking ways of coming to agreement over their points of variance. Sazonov on 7 July suggested to Sir George Buchanan

that a formula might be found under which we might mutually guarantee the inviolability of each other's Asiatic possessions. On my replying that our Allies, the Japanese, might regard such a guarantee on our part as directed against themselves, Sazonov said that there was no reason why they should not be brought in also.

Again on 19 July Buchanan telegraphed to Grey that Sazonov

would accept almost any formula that would in our opinion achieve the result of allaying the suspicion. I thought it best not to pursue the conversation further, but I gathered that, should the idea of such a triple guarantee commend itself to His Majesty's Government, Minister for Foreign Affairs will leave it to them to suggest what form it should take.

To this, the next day, Sir Edward Grey answered:

I am personally attracted by idea of triple guarantee, and am very glad that Minister for Foreign Affairs has made it a serious proposal. I will consult Prime Minister and, if he approves, the Cabinet, as soon as the Parliamentary and Irish situation gives them time.[1]

This is where the matter stood when Grey alluded to English relations with Russia in his conversation with Lichnowsky, as a reason for not bringing pressure to bear on St. Petersburg. The truth was that it was on Berlin and Vienna, not on St. Petersburg, that he should have brought pressure to bear. But the Foreign Office was still blind to this and remained so even after receiving other alarm signals contained in two dispatches from Bunsen in Vienna. That of 16 July ran:

I gather that situation is regarded at the Ministry for Foreign Affairs in a serious light and that a kind of indictment is being prepared against the Servian Government for alleged complicity in the conspiracy which led to the assassination of the Archduke. . . . My informant states that the Servian Government will be required to adopt certain definite measures in restraint of nationalist and anarchist propaganda, and that Austro-Hungarian Government are in no mood to parley with Servia, but will insist on immediate compliance, failing which force will be used. Germany is said to be in complete agreement with this procedure, and it is thought that the rest of Europe will sympathize with Austria-Hungary in demanding that Servia shall adopt in future more submissive attitude.[2]

[1] BD. XI, pp. X–XI.   [2] BD. XI, 50.

That of 17 July ran:

From all I hear the Ballplatz is in an uncompromising mood. . . . The authority for the telegram I sent yesterday was Count Lützow, ex-Ambassador at Rome. . . . He had seen both Berchtold and Forgach at the Ballplatz the day before. . . . He put on a serious face and said he wondered if I realized how grave the situation was. This Government was not going to stand Servian insolence any longer. . . . A note was being drawn up . . . demanding categorically that Servia should take effective measures to prevent the manufacture and export of bombs. . . . No futile discussion would be tolerated. If Servia did not at once cave in, force would be used to compel her. Count Lützow added that Count Berchtold was sure of German support and did not believe any country would hesitate to approve—not even Russia. . . . It all agrees strangely with the language of most of the Press, and almost all the people one meets. . . . Count Lützow said Austria was determined to have her way this time and would refuse to be headed off by anybody. Count Tisza's speech does not seem to me to read very reassuringly. He said: 'We must have a settlement (*Klärung*) with Servia, and we may possibly achieve it without war.'[1]

A similar hint as to the true situation was given to Sir Eyre Crowe, Assistant Under Secretary of State, by the Counsellor of the Austrian Embassy, presumably in order to sound Foreign Office opinion.[2]

This opinion had been expressed by a *Times* leader of 16 July which, while couched in restrained language, was not at all favourable to the use of force by Austria. But on the following day J. A. Spender, who was on terms of intimacy with Grey, published a leading article in the *Westminster Gazette*, of which he was editor, containing the following statements:

We cannot deny that Austria-Hungary has a *prima-facie* case for desiring to clarify her relations with Servia. . . . It is suspected in Vienna and Buda-Pesth that a deliberate attempt is being made to work on the population of Servian nationality in the Empire, in order to prepare their separation from the Monarchy. . . . In such circumstances the Government cannot be expected to remain inactive, and Servia will be well advised if she realizes the reasonableness of her great neighbour's anxiety, and does whatever may be in her power to allay it, without waiting for a pressure which might involve what Count Tisza calls 'warlike complications'.[3]

The Viennese press was delighted with this article and it also raised the hopes of Lichnowsky who already in his dispatch of 6 July had reported that Grey

seemed to understand that for a leading Austro-Hungarian statesman it would be difficult to refrain altogether from more vigorous measures.[4]

---

[1] BD. XI, 56.
[2] BD. XI, 50, minute.
[3] BD. XI, 58.
[4] DD. I, 20.

On 17 July Lichnowsky telegraphed to Berlin in regard to the article:

In view of the friendly relations between the editor Mr. Spender and Sir Edward Grey it is natural to assume that the Minister's views have not been without influence and that my repeated conversations with him have contributed to his taking Austria's right to satisfaction into consideration.[1]

Three days later, 20 July, Lichnowsky had to report:

The Minister has sent a statement to Vienna that the recent *Westminster Gazette* article . . . was not inspired by him.[2]

Grey's own account of the interview states:

I asked the German Ambassador to-day if he had any news of what was going on in Vienna with regard to Serbia. He said he had not, but Austria was certainly going to take some step, and he regarded the situation as very uncomfortable. . . . I said that . . . the more Austria could keep her demands within reasonable limits, and the stronger the justification she could produce for making any demand, the more chance there would be of smoothing things over. I hated the idea of a war between any of the Great Powers, and that any of them should be dragged into a war by Serbia would be detestable.[3]

It was evident that there could be no question of merely 'any one' of the Great Powers being dragged into a war by Serbia, and the fear that they would all be dragged in might well have been awakened in Grey not only by Lichnowsky's repeated warnings but by the calculated indiscretions of Lützow and by Buchanan's message from St. Petersburg of 18 July

that anything in the shape of an Austrian ultimatum at Belgrade could not leave Russia indifferent, and she might be forced to take some precautionary military measures.[4]

But still on 20 July Grey's eyes were not opened to the seriousness of the crisis. Lichnowsky's dispatch to Berlin of that date says that Grey

still takes an optimistic view of the Austro-Serbian dissension and believes in a peaceful solution of the question.[5]

However, on the evening of the 20th, he did go so far as to send the following suggestion to Sir G. Buchanan at St. Petersburg:

It is possible that Servian Government have been negligent, and that proceedings at the trial at Sarajevo will show that the murder of the Archduke was planned on Servian territory. If Austrian demands in Servia are kept within reasonable limits and if Austria can produce justification for making them, I hope every attempt will be made to prevent any breach of

[1] DD. I, 76.   [2] DD. I, 92.   [3] BD. XI, 68.   [4] BD. XI, 60.   [5] DD. I, 92.

the peace. It would be very desirable that Austria and Russia should discuss things together if they become difficult. You can speak in this sense if occasion seems to require it.[1]

The idea of conversations between St. Petersburg and Vienna, thus thrown out casually, was developed on 22 July by Grey in conversation with the Russian Ambassador:

I said I had been thinking what might be done if I were in M. Sazonov's place. It might be possible for M. Sazonov to send for the Austrian Ambassador in St. Petersburg; to refer to the statements in the press that Austria was going to make some demand on Servia; to emphasize the strength of pro-Serb feeling in Russia . . . and then to ask the Austrian Government to take Russia into their confidence. . . . It might then be possible for the Russian Government to get the Austrian demand kept within reasonable limits. . . . Count Benckendorff spoke of the difficulty of Russia making a friendly communication in Vienna.[2]

Buchanan put the idea to Poincaré whom he met on 21 July:

His Excellency expressed opinion that a conversation à deux between Austria and Russia would be very dangerous at the present moment, and seemed favourable to moderating counsels by France and England at Vienna.[3]

Of this reply, Fay makes a capital charge against Poincaré:

'Very dangerous' to what? Certainly not to the peace of Europe. But perhaps to M. Poincaré's policy of having the Triple *Entente* stand as a solid block in opposition to Germany and Austria. . . . For more than two years he had sought to tighten the Triple *Entente* in every way possible, and to prevent separate understandings by any one of its members with Germany or Austria. He had repudiated M. René's efforts at conciliation by greater autonomy to Alsace-Lorraine. When M. Crozier, the French Ambassador at Vienna, sought to establish better relations between Austria and Russia and France, and the listing of Austrian securities on the Paris Bourse, M. Poincaré thwarted his efforts. . . . According to Izvolski, M. Poincaré claimed also to have prevented the success of the Haldane Mission and the Anglo-German negotiations for a naval understanding. . . . M. Poincaré's contemporary telegrams and his later memoirs continually reiterate the desire to have the Triple *Entente* always concert together their line of action before any one of them approached Germany or Austria. So now, in the more serious crisis of July 1914, quite in keeping with his whole policy since he became Minister of Foreign Affairs in January 1912, he thought 'a conversation à deux between Austria and Russia would be very dangerous'.[4]

When on 22 July Buchanan passed on to London a proposal from Sazonov for the three *Entente* Governments to counsel moderation at Vienna, Crowe at the Foreign Office minuted it on the 23rd:

[1] BD. XI, 67.   [2] BD. XI, 79.   [3] BD. XI, 76.
[4] Fay, II, pp. 366–7; LN. II, 275; Poincaré, I, pp. 125ff.

Any such communication at Vienna would be likely to produce intense irritation without any beneficial other effect.[1]

Fay is doubtless right in his interpretation of Poincaré's motive in disapproving of direct talks between St. Petersburg and Vienna. Besides disapproving of them on principle, the President must have been apprehensive lest Sazonov should be too weak in a *tête-à-tête* with Berchtold. But it is altogether out of place to attach importance to Grey's suggestion, which Buchanan was not instructed to lay before Sazonov —in fact he seems never to have done so—and to make out that if it had not been rejected by Poincaré it might have been of use. Any such move would have had to be made much earlier at the very first signs that a serious crisis was developing. Renewed warnings of danger reached London on 22 July. Writing to Grey from Rome on 20 July Sir Rennell Rodd reported in reference to

your conversation with the German Ambassador on the subject of the anxiety and pessimism prevailing in Germany with regard to the position between Austria and Servia. I find exactly the same feeling of uneasiness prevailing at the German Embassy here. . . . I asked what the attitude of Germany would be and my informant was convinced that if the issue remained between Austria and Servia, Germany would have nothing to say, but that if Russia intervened on behalf of Servia, Germany was bound to intervene on behalf of Austria.[2]

Again on 22 July Rodd wrote that San Giuliano,

who is in constant touch with Austrian Embassy, told me that he feared that communication to be made to Servia had been drafted in terms which must inevitably be inacceptable. . . . He is convinced that a party in Austria are determined to take the opportunity of crushing Servia, which would be quite against the interests of Italy.[3]

On the 22nd there also arrived a dispatch of 20 July from Sir H. Rumbold in Berlin quoting a passage from the *Norddeutsche Allgemeine Zeitung* of 19 July:

We share the hope expressed in more than one quarter that a serious crisis will be avoided by the Servian Government giving way in time. In any case the solidarity of Europe . . . demands and requires that the discussions ('*Auseinandersetzungen*') which may arise between Austria-Hungary and Servia should remain localized.[4]

A dispatch from Rumbold of 22 July brought the information that the German Secretary of State for Foreign Affairs, Jagow, 'admitted that he had practically drafted the statement' published in the *Norddeutsche Allgemeine Zeitung.*

[1] BD. XI, 76, 84.   [2] BD. XI, 74.
[3] BD. XI, 78.   [4] BD. XI, 73. See p. 191.

He insisted that question at issue between Austria and Servia was one for discussion and settlement by those two countries alone without interference from outside. That being his view, he had not considered it opportune to say anything to Austro-Hungarian Government.[1]

These last two documents began to throw light on the true state of affairs and the game played by the Central Powers. Their import did not escape the most astute of the Foreign Office officials, Sir Eyre Crowe, the immediate subordinate of Sir Arthur Nicolson, but his chief's superior in ability. Crowe, whose mother and wife were both German, was, though not hostile to Germany, clearsighted about her and understood the threat that her armaments represented to the existence of Britain. To Rumbold's dispatch he wrote the following penetrating comment:

It is difficult to understand the attitude of the German Government. On the face of it, it does not bear the stamp of straightforwardness. If they really are anxious to see Austria kept reasonably in check, they are in the best position to speak at Vienna. All they are doing is to inflame the passions at Belgrade and it looks very much like egging on the Austrians when they openly and persistently threaten the Servian Government through their official newspapers. . . . They appear to rely on the British Government to reinforce the German and Austrian threats at Belgrade; it is clear that if the British Government did intervene in this sense, or by addressing admonitions to St. Petersburg, the much desired breach between England and Russia would be brought one step nearer to realization. But I admit that all this is speculation. We do not know the facts. The German Government clearly do know. They know what the Austrian Government is going to demand, they are aware that those demands will raise a grave issue, and I think we may say with some assurance that they have expressed approval of those demands and promised support, should dangerous complications ensue. So much can, I think, be read in the present telegram.[2]

Nothing could be more true. Grey, of course, read both telegram and footnote and added his own: 'I will answer this telegram to-morrow after I have seen Count Mensdorff.' So here was 22 July and Grey had not yet seen fit to inquire of the Austrian Ambassador to London how matters stood, or to give him an idea of the English attitude! And the morrow was the very day on which the Austrian ultimatum was to be presented at Belgrade.

7. *What Grey said to Lichnowsky and Mensdorff; the Kaiser's wrath; the English failure to understand the position.*

However, on 22 July Grey saw Lichnowsky and for the first time showed an adequate appreciation of the situation. The 'British Documents' show no trace of the conversation, but it can only have been

[1] BD. XI, 77.   [2] BD. XI, 77.

from Grey himself that Lichnowsky learnt what was to be said to Mensdorff by Grey on the morrow. On 23 July Jagow sent Lichnowsky's dispatch on to the Kaiser:

Sir Edward Grey, as I am confidentially informed, will tell Count Mensdorff to-morrow that the British Government will use its influence in the sense that the Austro-Hungarian demands, *provided they are moderate and reconcilable with the independence of the Serbian State*, might be accepted by the Serbian Government. (Kaiser's marginal note: He has no right to lay down the law about that. It is the business of H.M. the Emperor Francis Joseph.) He thinks that Sazonov will use his influence at Belgrade in the same sense. But the presupposition for this attitude is that Vienna shall produce no accusations à la Friedjung, and that the Austro-Hungarian Government is in a position to prove beyond doubt the connexion between the Sarajevo murder and Belgrade political circles ('That is its own affair'). All depends on the way the note has been drawn up in Vienna and the results of the previous inquiry.[1]

Lichnowsky went on to speak of his endeavours to persuade London to urge unconditional acceptance of the Austrian demands by Belgrade 'even if they should not fully take account of the *national dignity of Serbia*' ('no such thing!'). The dispatch continues:

In this I run up against the expectation that our influence with Vienna has succeeded in getting all unrealizable demands dropped ('How could I do such a thing! None of my business! What does unrealizable mean? the fellows have carried on agitation with murder and have got to be taken down a peg.') There is a definite assumption that we should not identify ourselves with demands manifestly aiming at bringing about a war, and that we are not supporting any policy to use the Sarajevo murder as a pretext for Austrian desires in the Balkans and the tearing up of the Peace of Bucharest ('That is a monstrous piece of British impudence. I am not called upon to give H.M. the Emperor directions à la Grey as how to preserve his honour!')

In communicating Lichnowsky's dispatch to the Kaiser, Jagow added that the Ambassador was being sent instructions to say

that we had no knowledge of the Austrian demands and regarded them *as an internal question for Austria-Hungary* in which we had *no competence to intervene*.

(The passages in italics above are those underlined by the Kaiser.) This elicited the following outburst from the Kaiser:

Just so! That must be said to Grey with the utmost seriousness and clarity! To let him see that I am not to be joked with. Grey makes the mistake of putting Serbia on a level with Austria and the other Great Powers! That is unheard of! Serbia is a band of brigands who must be arrested for crime! I shall not interfere in anything that the Emperor is alone competent to judge! I have been expecting this dispatch and it does not surprise me! Just

[1] DD. I, 118, 121.

the British way of thinking and condescendingly ordering people about, which I am determined to see rebuffed! Wilhelm. I.R.[1]

The Kaiser's ludicrous rages and vainglory were to give way to terror when he at last understood better the effects of the Austrian action and of the support he had given the Vienna Government in their dangerous adventure. From this adventure Grey was too late to hold them back when on the 23rd he had his talk with Mensdorff. With Berchtold's permission[2] Mensdorff told Grey

that he would be able to-morrow morning to let me have officially the communication that he understood was being made to Servia to-day by Austria. . . . I said that it was not a matter on which I would make any comment until I received an official communication, and it seemed to me probably a matter on which I should not be able to make any comment at first sight. But when Count Mensdorff told me that he supposed there would be something in the nature of a time-limit, which was in effect akin to an ultimatum, I said that I regretted this very much. To begin with, a time-limit might inflame opinion in Russia, and it would make it difficult, if not impossible, to give more time, even if after a few days it appeared that by giving more time there would be a prospect of securing a peaceful settlement. . . . A time-limit was generally the thing to be used only in the last resort, after other means had been tried and failed. Count Mensdorff said that if Servia had voluntarily instituted an inquiry on her own territory, all this might have been avoided. . . . I said that I would not comment upon or criticize what Count Mensdorff had told me this afternoon, but I could not help dwelling upon the awful consequences involved in the situation. . . . If as many as four Great Powers of Europe— let us say Austria, France, Russia and Germany—were engaged in war, it seemed to me that it must involve the expenditure of so vast a sum of money and such an interference with trade, that a war would be accompanied or followed by a complete collapse of European credit and industry. In these days, in great industrial States, this would mean a state of things worse than that of 1848, and, irrespective of who were victors in the war, many things might be completely swept away. Count Mensdorff did not demur to this statement of the possible consequences of the present situation, but he said that all would depend upon Russia. . . . I hoped very much that if there were difficulties, Austria and Russia would be able in the first instance to discuss them directly with each other.[3]

This conversation took place on the very afternoon when the ultimatum was presented at Belgrade. Can it be said that Grey had done all in his power to prevent this fatal step from being taken? The answer must be: No. It is not possible to absolve Grey, as does, for example, Bernadotte Schmitt, who is indulgent towards him, by claiming that he could not have acted otherwise because the struggle over Irish Home Rule entirely absorbed the attention of the country which took no interest in Austro-Serbian squabbles, or that he had to be extremely

[1] DD. I, 121.   [2] Oe-U. VIII, 10535.   [3] BD. XI, 86.

careful of Russian feelings, or that Berlin and Vienna paid no heed to his advice, in short that: 'All Sir Edward Grey could do was to wait'.[1]

Wait for the catastrophe to happen? In his talk with Mensdorff he mentioned the danger that four of the Great Powers might become involved in war. This would mean leaving England and Italy out of the European war, and gives a glimpse of what his ideas were at that moment. His was a slow-thinking mind. At first he was incapable of realizing that the murder of the Archduke revived the whole problem of Austro-Serbian relations which in 1913 had overhung the labours of the Ambassadors' Conference, held under his own chairmanship, and had on so many occasions threatened the peace of Europe. His failure to understand the danger seems still more inexplicable when one remembers the warnings given him by Lichnowsky and confirmed by Lützow's 'indiscretions' to Bunsen. Not until he read Jagow's plain statements to Rumbold and Crowe's comments did Grey's eyes begin to be opened, but not so far as to see that the Four Power war he spoke of would inevitably pose the problem of English intervention. It never entered his head that, in speaking to the Austrian Ambassador of a Four Power war, without so much as hinting that England might become involved, he was encouraging Berlin and Vienna to intransigence and war. Yet he was well aware that in the preceding years the German rulers had made every effort to get a pledge of neutrality out of him, in the hope of being able to conquer France and Russia without Britain's command of the sea coming to their aid and tipping the scales in their favour.

Hence during this first phase of the July crisis at any rate, the hesitancy and ineptitude of British policy is not to be sought in Cabinet dissensions, the Irish question, fear of offending Russia and the like. A perusal of the documents shows that up to 23 July there is one explanation pure and simple; namely Grey's utter failure on the one hand to understand what was going on, what was told him and what was reported from the various Embassies, and on the other to grasp that Austrian aggression against Serbia would bring in first Russia and then Germany and France. He saw that these would be disastrous developments but thought that they would only indirectly affect England and that, as he was to say in the following days, she had no reason to let herself be drawn into purely Balkan troubles. As if any outbreak of war in the Balkans did not raise all the European problems, first and foremost that of Anglo-German relations! And as if England, who had composed her differences with France and Russia precisely to safeguard herself against Germany, could see her *de facto* if not *de jure* allies defeated without being defeated herself!

[1] Schmitt, I, pp. 431–2.

The most that can be said in Grey's defence is that his state of mind was that of the immense majority of English politicians and of his fellow-countrymen in general. A certain ingenuousness, more than anything else, prevents them from penetrating easily into the psychology and underlying tendencies of other peoples. Even after light had been thrown on the line pursued by Poincaré and Paléologue, Grey was capable of writing:

The statement about the pacific disposition of France was certainly right: her whole conduct in 1914, up to the very outbreak of war, proved her desire to avoid a conflict.[1]

And Churchill, though of greater discernment than Grey, writes:

Justice to France requires the explicit statement that the conduct of her Government at this awful juncture was faultless.[2]

The English are traditionally averse to dealing with problems before they have become urgent and to seeking solutions in advance which would necessarily restrict their freedom of action when the time came.

What still remains to be seen is whether, with a better understanding of the situation and the demands it made, Grey would have been in a position to take action and whether any action on his part could have changed the course of events. These queries will find their answer in the account of what came after and the reflexions suggested thereby. Now our attention must turn to the attitude of the other Great Power which was in a position to exercise a determining influence on the decisions of the Central Powers, i.e. Italy.

[1] Grey, I, p. 306.   [2] Churchill, I, p. 205.

CHAPTER VI

ITALY'S RELATIONS WITH HER ALLIES
BEFORE THE ULTIMATUM TO SERBIA

(1) *Francis Ferdinand and the real relations between Austria and Italy* (p. 216). (2) *Berchtold's reasons for keeping Italy in the dark about his plans; Flotow's indiscretions* (p. 220). (3) *A conversation between San Giuliano and Flotow; Italy's warning to Berlin; Jagow's request to Vienna* (p. 226). (4) *Berchtold's refusal to recognize Italy's right to compensation* (p. 231). (5) *Berchtold's instructions to the Austro-Hungarian Ambassador at Rome* (p. 235). (6) *The guiding lines of San Giuliano's policy; the Consulta's inaction; its silence on the precedent of 1913* (p. 241). (7) *San Giuliano's views and moves* (p. 245). (8) *The three courses open to San Giuliano; his mistaken choice* (p. 247).

1. *Francis Ferdinand and the real relations between Austria and Italy.*

On 30 June 1914 Krupensky, the Russian Ambassador to Rome, wrote privately to Sazonov that in Italy

indignation at the monstrous deed is mingled with a feeling of liberation from an undefinable danger. . . . San Giuliano said to me: 'The crime is horrible, but world peace will not mourn over it.' Worse and more heartless is a strange demonstration in a Rome cinema packed with a Sunday crowd where, on learning of the Sarajevo tragedy, the public demanded the Royal March and the orchestra played it amid applause.[1]

Rodd, too, wrote to Grey on 7 July:

While ostensibly the authorities and the press have been loud in their denunciations of the crime and full of sympathy with the Emperor, it is obvious that people generally have regarded the elimination of the late Archduke as almost providential.[2]

It was even the case that there were public demonstrations of this feeling. A Sicilian nationalist society went so far as to publish a manifesto expressing satisfaction over the crime and even the Foreign Minister San Giuliano's commemorative speech in the Senate spoke so unfeelingly of the victims as to rouse a protest from the Socialist *Avanti*. Still more callous was San Giuliano in telephoning the news of the outrage to the Prime Minister Salandra:

Is that you, Salandra? Do you know, we shall have no more bother about

---

[1] *Int. Bez.* i. IV, 29.   [2] BD. XI, 36.

the Villa d'Este affair.—How do you mean?—This morning they've mur-
ered the Archduke Francis Ferdinand at Sarajevo.[1]

In the eyes of the Italians the Archduke was the most influential exponent of the strong aversion, compounded of hate and contempt, felt
for Italy by military, diplomatic and Catholic circles in Austria and
which not only gave rise to odious measures against Italian subjects
of the Monarchy but were even a menace to the existence of Italy.
It must in fairness be said that this aversion was fully reciprocated by
the Italians and was partly justified by Italian irredentist manifestations.
Salandra truly states that 'even after 1866 and after 1870 Italy felt incomplete' and that 'each one of us had at the bottom of his heart a germ
of irredentism never to be stifled, though held in check by the more
pressing demands of home affairs, economic reconstruction and international politics which made the first decades of the new State difficult
and toilsome'.[2] The disharmony between the two states was not,
however, confined to the frontier question but was to no small extent
due to the feeling that the territorial integrity, prosperity, and expansion
of the one were threatened by the other. Francis Ferdinand, as already
noted, cherished the desire to regain Venetia and Lombardy, shattering
Italian unity by undoing the work of the Risorgimento. The Italians,
besides wanting to take away the Trentino, Trieste and Istria from the
Monarchy, sought to prevent its gaining the upper hand in Albania and
pressing on to Salonika whereby it would have become so powerful
as to threaten the existence of Italy. And if the Italians had no thoughts
of attacking Austria, knowing their own inferiority in resources,
Austria, or at any rate certain of its leading personalities, beginning
with Conrad, the Chief of Staff, meditated attacking Italy as the main
obstacle in the way of Austro-Hungarian expansion, hence of her
safety. A paradoxical situation! Austria and Italy were allies in order
not to be enemies and their hostility broke out at every moment despite

[1] Salandra, p. 16.—Negotiations were in process for the acquisition by the state of the
Villa d'Este at Tivoli which was the property of Francis Ferdinand, the negotiations being
conducted by the Austrian Ambassador Merey with his characteristic insolence. When
Salandra hesitated to bring the bill before the Chamber enabling the purchase to be carried
out Merey said to him: 'The fact is that yours is a weak Government. Your predecessors
would have brought it in.' To this Salandra replied: 'If that is so, you only have to wait a
few months until my predecessor has returned to this place' (p. 19). Salandra goes on to
note that on the day after the crime he received a dispatch from Avarna of whom he had
inquired what he was to make of a threat, uttered by Merey in connexion with the dispute
over Albania, 'of a bold step which would cause the most painful surprise in Italy'. Did this
mean the occupation of the Lovčen? inquired Salandra. Avarna replied that he did not
know, but supposed that the threat had been uttered 'under pressure from an exalted
personage who since the Emperor's recent illness, has been taking a still more active part
in the home and foreign policy of the Monarchy and not infrequently conveys instructions in an indirect way to ambassadors, as Merey told me confidentially some time ago'
(pp. 19–20).
[2] Salandra, pp. 28–9.

the alliance. The chief phases of Austro-Italian relations have been amply dealt with in Vol. I. It is enough here to recall that on the eve of the outbreak of the European war, the Governments of the Dual Monarchy and of Italy were at variance, not only over anti-Austrian demonstrations in Italy resulting from conflicts in Trieste between Italians and Slovenes—demonstrations which led to the Prefect of Naples being relieved of his office—but also on account of the activities of Aliotti, the Italian Minister in Albania, whose recall was asked for by Vienna. But while the disease of irredentism was chronic and did not occasion immediate anxiety, the struggle for influence in Albania had reached an intensity which threatened to wreck the peace between the two countries. It led Bollati, the Italian Ambassador to Berlin, to write the following dispatch on 8 July:

It is impossible to imagine a stranger or more dangerous situation and it is urgent to rush to the rescue. But how? If there were nothing more than the Albanian question dividing us! But there are so many other causes of dissension, so many other areas of friction: the Lovčen question, the possible conflict between Austria and Serbia, the awful problem of a possible union between Serbia and Montenegro, which is no doubt maturing towards a settlement in the near or distant future; not to speak of further long standing disputes, more serious and less easily resolved: the possession by Austria of provinces of Italian race and tongue which, in the consciousness of, to say the least, nine-tenths of the Italians of the Kingdom, belong *de jure* to Italy and must one day or another belong to her also *de facto*; the treatment by Austria of the populations of those provinces; the clerical question; the failure to return our Sovereign's visit. . . . I touch very briefly; but one knows that in such conditions the slightest incident is sufficient to cause complications and jeopardize the stability of the alliance.

In reality there is not one single question in which the interests of Italy are not, or are not thought to be, in conflict with those of Austria, in which the policy of each of the two Governments is not intent on jealously watching and often opposing that of the other, on setting up safeguards against it and is not inspired by the conviction that what helps the one must necessarily hinder the other.

Bollati went on to praise the efforts made by San Giuliano in four years of office 'to reconcile the supreme needs of our international position with the unconcealed repugnances of Italian popular feeling and consciousness'. He had 'accomplished a magnificent task, characterized by a series of partial successes' but 'alas it was a labour of Sisyphus'. And although the most formidable enemy of a policy favourable to Italy, i.e. Francis Ferdinand, was no more, there was no hope of an improvement in the position. One could not but ask oneself the question whether it would not be better to dissolve the alliance in order to create 'easier or at least more straightforward relations between the two

States'. But what a leap in the dark it would be to 'break with the system which has so long formed the basis of all our foreign policy!' Shrinking back 'in fear' from this prospect Bollati concluded that he could see no remedy for the inexpediencies and perils of the situation. The German Government—he added—attached 'the highest importance to maintaining Italian co-operation in the Triple Alliance'. But if faced with a conflict between Austria and Italy 'Germany, forced to choose between the two, would opt for Vienna and not for Rome'.[1]

This gives a very true picture of the Italian position within the Alliance on the eve of the European war, omitting just one particular. Bollati forgot to say that San Giuliano's predecessors, beginning with Visconti Venosta, because they perceived the unsatisfactoriness of the position, had formed bonds of friendship outside the Triplice for which they were reproached by their allies, but which, if kept within limits, gave Italy added strength and prestige, thus enabling her better to safeguard her interests. Now San Giuliano had repudiated these friendships in order to draw closer to the allies and earn their trust more fully. The result had been, to use Bollati's phrase, 'a labour of Sisyphus', and worse. Italy had lost her friends and was on strained terms with one of her allies into whose power she had put herself, by, among other things, a naval agreement that was the climax of self immolation, since it entrusted the command of the Italian Navy, which was superior to that of Austria, to an Austrian Admiral. As a result, Vienna and Berlin took so little account of Italy that, in open violation of the Triplice Treaty, they decided that Austria should set fire to the European powder magazine without so much as consulting or informing Italy.

2. Berchtold's reasons for keeping Italy in the dark about his plans; Flotow's indiscretions.

For so doing Vienna had a variety of reasons: fear that the Consulta would warn Belgrade and St. Petersburg; the conviction that in disapproval of Austria's action Italy would veto it, as she had done the previous year; the anticipation that Italy would at once demand compensation which could not be granted her. What form would the demand take? When Tschirschky on 2 July mentioned to Berchtold that 'in view of their alliance Italy should be consulted before the initiation of military action', Berchtold objected:

if we were to put this question to the Rome Cabinet, Italy would presumably demand Valona as compensation, which we could not concede.[2]

Hoyos, who was Berchtold's immediate colleague, writes:

It was only by creating a *fait accompli* that Italian neutrality might perhaps have been obtained for a certain period of time which would end with Italy's

---

[1] Salandra, pp. 50–6.   [2] Oe-U. VIII, 10006.

entering the war either with us or against us according to the fortunes of war. If he [Berchtold] had informed the Italian Government as fully of his plans as the German, Italy would probably at once have asked for the cession of the Trentino in compensation. In the circumstances of the time this demand would have been rejected as not within the field of discussion and the outcome would have been a clash which would have driven Italy much earlier to join our enemies.[1]

These words, together with the contemptuous assumption that Italy would join the winning side, tacitly imply that Austria counted on Italy's remaining neutral, though knowing that she would have a claim to compensations which were to be refused her. But is it so certain that Austria did not care whether Italy declared her neutrality or not? In answer to a question from the present writer, Berchtold replied by letter on 23 November 1933:

Conrad did not expect much from Italy, if she had gone with us, since, in consequence of the Libyan campaign, she was militarily disorganized, especially in respect of artillery, and a high value could not, as far as one could foresee, be placed upon her aid. But at that time nobody here thought of a long war.

But in this Berchtold's memory has misled him. It is quite true that Conrad had no high opinion of the immediate usefulness of Italian co-operation and in a note of 2 July 1914 he wrote:

The numerical comparison of combined military effectives is for the Triplice affected unfavourably by the fact that Italy for years to come will have considerable forces tied down in Libya and that the full and timely deployment of the military strength of the Kingdom for the early decisive engagements in the Triplice war will encounter great obstacles even when that military strength is placed unreservedly at the service of the common cause.

But in writing thus Conrad was not in the remotest degree suggesting that it was indifferent to him whether Italy joined the allies or not. The note shows him already considerably perturbed at the possibility that Roumania might remain neutral, since that would set free three Russian army corps for other uses while obliging the Monarchy to provide for the defence of its common frontier with Roumania.[2] If he was concerned over Roumanian neutrality, how much greater would have been his concern over Italian neutrality, the possibility of which had never entered his head! On the contrary he counted on Italy's contributing 34 divisions (ten of them second line troops) to the total effectives of the Triplice, which would then amount to 160 divisions against the 211 of Russia, France, Serbia, Montenegro and Roumania. If Italy

---

[1] Hoyos, pp. 65–6.   [2] Oe-U. VIII, 9995.

were to remain out of the war the 160 divisions would drop to 126. In this case Conrad would never have advised mobilization and war. This is shown by his saying to Berchtold on 23 July: 'If we have to fear Italy as well, then let us not mobilize'.[1]

This being Conrad's attitude, why did Berchtold, by keeping Italy in the dark about his intentions and refusing her compensations, make it seem that he attached no value to Italian co-operation, whereas to Roumania he paid great attention while taking active steps to hold Montenegro back from making common cause with Serbia? When the present writer put this question to Musulin, a very senior official at the Ballplatz, his reply was that, in the first place, Berchtold until 31 July did not think there would be war and that secondly he, in common with all those at the Ballplatz, was firmly persuaded that, if a European war broke out, Italy would range herself with the Triplice. Therefore he paid no heed to Italy but devoted his attention to Montenegro whose neutrality might carry weight with Russia, when in reality it was the Italian attitude which ought to have been regarded as the decisive factor. The truth is that, as Musulin wrote the present writer,

to turn the fortunes of war in our favour it would have sufficed for Italy, even without declaring war, to dispatch several army corps to the French frontier.

Of the above explanation the most convincing part is that Berchtold hoped that there would be no European war and that the quarrel with Serbia could be patched up after all. But at the back of his mind there was probably the further thought that it would be no great disaster if Italy did declare herself neutral, seeing that all Merey's reports went to show she would never throw her weight against the Monarchy. Confirmation of this is given in Berchtold's replies to Stolberg and Tschirschky of 17 and 20 July which we shall consider later.[2] It certainly was extraordinary levity on Berchtold's part to regard Italy in that light but it is so much in keeping with his character that it need not surprise us. The really amazing thing is that Berlin should have agreed to the proposal of keeping Italy in the dark when Germany counted on Italian support for the achievement of her lightning victory over France. So incredible is Szögyény's message of 6 July to Vienna:

The Chancellor is in full agreement with our not informing either Italy or Roumania in advance of any action we may take[3]

that Fay thinks it a fabrication:

This policy of deceiving Italy, or of delaying to inform her, was so completely contrary to the German attitude just before and after 5 July, that one is forced to doubt the accuracy of the Austrian Ambassador's assertion.[4]

[1] Conrad, IV, 108.   [2] See pp. 231–5.   [3] Oe-U. VIII, 10076.   [4] Fay, II, 217.

But Fay has a personal antipathy to Szögyény which makes him overlook the telegram sent on the evening of 11 July by Jagow to Flotow, the German Ambassador to Rome. This gave information of Francis Joseph's letter to Wilhelm expressing 'the need to take vigorous measures against the agitation carried on by Russian and Serb Pan-Slavs' and went on:

we have left it to the Austro-Hungarian Government to take the steps it deems suitable and have promised, if need be, our support in accordance with the alliance.

The message then went on:

The above is for Your Excellency's purely personal information. Communication of it to Marquis San Giuliano is at present scarcely to be recommended because of his leanings towards Serbia, but I beg you to draw his attention to the unmeasured language of the Serbian press and to remark that it would hardly be possible for Austria-Hungary to take such provocation quietly. Further it might be well to prepare Marquis San Giuliano carefully for the idea that we are contemplating a *rapprochement* with Bulgaria, avoiding however anything in the nature of opposition to Roumania.[1]

Luigi Aldovrandi Marescotti, who in July 1914 was First Secretary at the Italian Embassy in Vienna, narrates the following:

After a series of conversations on the general political situation with the German Foreign Minister Jagow, the Italian Ambassador to Berlin, Bollati, asked Jagow, whom he had known for many years and on whose friendship he believed he could rely, whether it would be wise for him to go on leave for three weeks to undergo a cure. Jagow replied in the affirmative and Bollati left Berlin on 20 July but he returned on the 23rd on instructions from San Giuliano.[2]

After Italy had declared her neutrality and immediately on the publication of the German *White Book*, Bollati telegraphed an account of it to Rome on 5 August:

In the *White Book* which has been laid before the Reichstag, after a brief account of the Sarajevo outrage and the circumstances preceding and following it, the German Government expresses itself in the following terms: 'Under those circumstances it was clear to Austria that it was not compatible with the dignity and the spirit of self-preservation of the Monarchy to view idly any longer this agitation across the border. The Imperial and Royal Government appraised Germany of this conception and asked for our opinion. With all our heart we were able to agree with our ally's estimate of the situation, and assure him that any action considered necessary to end the

[1] DD. I, 33.
[2] Luigi Aldovrandi Marescotti, *Guerra diplomatica: Ricordi e frammenti di diario* (Milan, 1938), p. 22.

movement in Serbia directed against the conservation of the Monarchy would meet with our approval. We were perfectly aware that a possible warlike attitude of Austria-Hungary against Serbia might bring Russia upon the field, and that it might therefore involve us in a war, in accordance with our duty as allies. We could not, however, in these vital interests of Austria-Hungary, which were at stake, advise our ally to take a yielding attitude not compatible with his dignity, nor deny him our assistance in these trying days. We could all the less do this as our own interests were menaced through the continued Serb agitation. . . . We, therefore, allowed Austria a completely free hand in her action towards Serbia, but have not participated in her preparations.'[1]

All this is so clear that no comment is necessary to show that Austria-Hungary's action has been previously concerted with Germany, also in anticipation of the war complications which might arise from it. The only limit to this preliminary agreement is contained in the phrase 'We . . . have not participated in her [Austria's] preparations.' I said this to Jagow this morning, adding that nothing of all this was made known to Italy, who was kept in the dark about everything up to the last moment and only on the very eve received information from Austria-Hungary of what steps were to be taken against Serbia. To all the questions with which I daily plied Jagow about the plans of Austria-Hungary, he had always answered that he had no information; that he knew Austria-Hungary meant to make stiff demands on Serbia for satisfaction and that he thought her intention reasonable, but that he knew nothing of the form her action would take and that in any case no serious complications were likely to ensue. To my repeated objections that measures against Serbia would inevitably entail Russian intervention, Jagow had always replied that Russia would confine herself to platonic protests and diplomatic notes but in the end, as on previous occasions, would not do more than bluff. Now by an official publication it is demonstrated beyond all possibility of doubt that, in giving previous consent to the Austro-Hungarian action, Germany clearly realized what might be its consequences in regard to France. This being so, it was the absolute duty of Austria-Hungary and Germany, not only in virtue of the treaty of the Triple Alliance, to inform the remaining ally in order that she might be in a position to express her views in a matter of such extreme importance and to make at least the necessary preparations. This Austria-Hungary and Germany did not do; they confronted Italy with a *fait accompli* previously concerted between themselves and they made it impossible for her to take measures; they failed to honour their pledges to us and hence there ceased to exist for us the undertakings laid down by the treaty. . . .[2]

Here we have the evidence that Berlin persisted in keeping Italy in the dark[3] and now moreover, barring fresh revelations, it becomes

---

[1] See CDD., p. 406.

[2] Aldovrandi Marescotti, *op. cit.,* pp. 23–4.

[3] It should be added that in Berchtold's talks with Stolberg, the Counsellor at the German Embassy, on 18 July and with Tschirschky on the 20th, he reminded Berlin that it was agreed between them not to keep Italy informed (DD. I, 84).

clear at what precise moment San Giuliano learnt of what was brewing. On 18 July Merey wrote from Rome to Berchtold complaining:

From utterances of Count Berchem, the Secretary at the German Embassy, to two gentlemen of my Embassy, the latter have gained the impression that the German Ambassador, who has been staying for the last fortnight at Fiuggi, has been making confidences to the Italian Foreign Minister about our intentions with regard to Serbia . . . Perhaps this is connected with the fact that Marquis San Giuliano . . . is coming on Tuesday for two days to Rome. . . . I must be prepared to be questioned by the Minister on Tuesday on the subject of our strained relations with Serbia.[1]

Thus we learn that Flotow had lost no time in carrying out Jagow's instructions of 11 July. Merey had reason to feel aggrieved. A letter written to Salandra on 16 November 1915 by the former Italian Ambassador to Constantinople, Garroni, and published in Salandra's *La Neutralità Italiana (1914)*[2] shows that on 16 July 1914 San Giuliano sent two telegrams, one to the Italian Ambassadors at Vienna and Berlin, and the other to those at St. Petersburg and Belgrade, in which he mentioned having during those days had several conversations with Flotow

from which he had drawn the conclusion that the Austro-Serbian conflict would be *inevitable* because of the excessive demands made by Vienna.[3]

It was certainly San Giuliano's telegram which alerted Carlotti, the Italian Ambassador at St. Petersburg, and led to the following conversation with Schilling:

The Italian Ambassador asked Baron Schilling what attitude Russia would adopt should Austria decide to take action of any kind against Serbia. Baron Schilling unhesitatingly replied that Russia would not endure any infringement by Austria of the integrity and independence of Serbia. Marquis Carlotti remarked that if this was Russia's firm determination it would be well that she should make a plain representation to Vienna to that effect, because it was his impression that Austria was capable of taking an irrevocable step with regard to Serbia, based on the belief that, although

---

[1] Oe-U. VIII, 10364.   [2] Salandra, pp. 119 ff.

[3] Garroni read these telegrams in the collection of diplomatic documents circulated to the Embassies. They did not surprise him, as his German colleague, Wangenheim, had already said to him on 15 July: 'Nous sommes à la guerre', and told him of the impending ultimatum couched in terms that Serbia could not accept. But Garroni seems not to have reported Wangenheim's words at once to the Consulta. He only revealed them to Sonnino and Salandra in September 1915 and the revelation was mentioned in a speech of Barzilai in the Chamber. As there were protests in Italy over Garroni's silence, he wrote the above quoted letter to Salandra, claiming to have telegraphed the whole story to San Giuliano on 16 July 1914. But the archives show only one report from him of 20 July 1914, received in Rome on the 25th, summarizing a trivial talk with Wangenheim which had nothing to do with that of 15 July. Be it added that Garroni, a former Prefect of Genoa, was an improvised ambassador, created by Giolitti and, like him, a neutralist.

Russia would make a verbal protest, she would not adopt forcible measures for the protection of Serbia against any Austrian attempts. If, however, Vienna had to reckon with the inevitability of a collision with Russia, in all probability the Government there would begin to consider the results of adopting a too energetic policy with regard to Serbia.

Baron Schilling said to the Ambassador that he was in a position to emphasize his declaration that Russia was firmly determined not to permit any weakening or humiliation of Serbia, and it was therefore the duty of Austria's allies to warn her of the dangers arising from her present policy, as Russia's determination to protect the independence of Serbia could no longer be doubted.

The Ambassador promised to telegraph to Rome to this effect and to request the Italian Government to draw the attention of the Vienna Cabinet to the foregoing, but remarked that in his opinion it would produce a greater impression in Vienna if a declaration of this sort were made there by Russia herself rather than by Italy who was an ally.

Baron Schilling said to the Ambassador that, on the contrary, if Russia made such a declaration in Vienna, it would perhaps be regarded as an ultimatum and so render the situation more acute whereas insistent advice proffered by Italy and Germany—that is by allies—would certainly be more acceptable to Austria-Hungary.[1]

This conversation is of great importance. It was Carlotti's revelations to Schilling which opened Sazonov's eyes to what was brewing in Vienna and the suggestion made to Schilling by Carlotti, no less than Schilling's reply, laid down lines of action which should have been followed respectively by Russia and by Italy to prevent the disaster happening. We have already seen what line Russia took. As for Italy, it is clear that Carlotti telegraphed Schilling's suggestions to the Consulta and that San Giuliano failed to speak to Vienna on the lines suggested. Not that he did not appreciate the perils of a general war or did not know what ought to be done. He was not so slow of the up-take as his English opposite number, moreover, a year earlier, on 12 July 1913, acting on Giolitti's instructions, he had flatly told Merey that if the aggression Vienna was then planning against Serbia were to lead to a European war, Italy would not recognize the *casus foederis*. This time he took a different line which will be considered later. Meanwhile we pursue the narrative of events.

3. *A conversation between San Giuliano and Flotow; Italy's warning to Berlin; Jagow's request to Vienna.*

On 12 July at Fiuggi San Giuliano said to Flotow that

immediately after the murder of the Archduke he instructed the Italian representative in Belgrade very strongly to urge the Serbian Government to

[1] *Int. Bez.* i. IV, 245; Schilling, pp. 25–6.

moderation. He believes this advice is being followed. Governments in democratic countries cannot, he said, be held responsible for the transgressions of the press and the Austrian Government ought not to put itself in the wrong in that matter.[1]

On 14 July San Giuliano told Flotow that, although

the reports of the Italian Ambassador at Vienna about Serbia were not pessimistic in tone, he has already taken the opinion of the International Law expert, Signor Fusinato, on the legal position and tells me that, according to Italian opinion, a Government can only claim in respect of crime against common law not in respect of political propaganda, unless this leads to action. He fears, therefore, that Italy would not be able to support Austrian claims without coming into conflict with the deeply rooted conviction of the Italian people and with liberal principles. I replied that one must first await the content of the Austrian claim but that, if a conflict should arise, political and not juridical questions would be at stake. San Giuliano insisted, however, that the Italian Government could never take up a position hostile to the principle of nationality. He apparently is preparing us for his not standing shoulder to shoulder with Austria in the event of further complications. The Austrian Government will have to reckon with this possibility.[2]

San Giuliano's fear was, as Flotow telegraphed on the 15th,

that Austria, in a conflict with Serbia, was planning territorial acquisition which Italy could not tolerate.[3]

On 16 July Flotow from Fiuggi sent three letters to Berlin, two to Bethmann Hollweg and one to Jagow. The first reached Berlin on the afternoon of the 18th and on the 19th was communicated to Tschirschky in Vienna for his personal information. It does not tell much more than the telegram but is worth considering as giving a picture of the situation at the moment.

To my previous communication on the expert opinion given by the Minister of State, Fusinato, respecting the Austro-Serbian conflict and Marquis San Giuliano's position, I should like to add that he strongly took the standpoint that Austria has no right to make claims on Belgrade on account of Pan-Serbian propaganda as long as the latter does not translate itself into action in Austria. The murder of the Archduke could not be so regarded as it was not committed by a Serbian subject. If Austria intended to suppress Serbian national aspirations, no Italian Government could follow her in this course; all traditions of the idea of nationality and the liberal principle would force Italy to hold aloof.

All who know the power of words over the Latin peoples will not fail to perceive that it is, indeed, not easy for an Italian Government to take any other attitude. Already voices are raised describing opposition to

[1] DD. I, 38.   [2] DD. I, 42.   [3] DD. I, 51.

Serbian national strivings as impossible in view of Italy's similar historic national struggle. For public opinion here the Austrian procedure has a thoroughly bad platform. If I expressed strong disagreement with the Minister, it was not so much because I did not understand the standpoint, as because I wanted to elicit a hint from him as to whether in the event of serious European complications he would refuse to help his ally. The Minister could not go to the length of a conclusive pronouncement because Austrian demands have not yet found a formulation. But I have the impression that it will be extraordinarily difficult, if not impossible, to bring Italy into line in this field. Factors to be taken into account are not only the present acute question, but still more the prevailing feeling against Austria and even Marquis San Giuliano's personal frame of mind. As late as a year ago things were quite different. But since Prince Hohenlohe's notorious Trieste decrees the traditional antipathy for Austria, only just subsiding, has gradually reawakened and it is, in fact, difficult at the present moment to conceive of extensive practical co-operation between Austria and Italy. Marquis San Giuliano, who has regarded the advancement of relations with Austria as a kind of political programme of his ministry, is disappointed and feels himself no longer supported by public sentiment. He was saying to me only yesterday that he saw so many black spots in the further shaping of Italo-Austrian relations that he almost despaired of further efforts.

I produced many reasons for saying that I was still convinced that the alliance with Austria was the best policy for Italy. Temporary disturbances, like the present, must be got over. The Minister said that, as long as he was there, he would of course carry on in that sense. But he was working without much hope.[1]

The second letter followed on the same 16 July. It said:

Marquis San Giuliano is sceptical of the diplomatic measures planned by Austria against Serbia. In his view they cannot lead to results. Even if Serbia yielded to Austrian demands, i.e. prohibited and dissolved Pan-Serb associations etc., the agitation would simply go underground. That would even be the case if Austria occupied Belgrade. National aspirations of such strength cannot nowadays be suppressed by force. It was the old Austrian mistake of believing in the omnipotence and effectiveness of the police in such national questions. Italian history of the last century was an example. The analogy of the situation was so striking that on those grounds alone Italians could not be expected to sympathize with the Austrian measures.[2]

More vivacious and interesting was the letter to Jagow with whom Flotow was on terms of friendship. Although it was of a private nature a copy of it was placed by Jagow in the archives.

I am glad you have no illusions about the difficulty of the position here; I regard it as hopeless if Austria, in view of the danger, does not pull herself together and realize that if she means to take any territory she must give Italy compensation. Otherwise Italy will attack her in the rear. That is such a

---

[1] DD. I, 64.   [2] DD. I, 73.

serious matter for us that we must consider whether we shall not have to come to definite terms with Vienna. S. G.'s state of mind you will see from my reports. More than ever all depends on him, for Salandra does not support him as did Giolitti. Salandra makes no secret of his anti-Austrian feelings and Merey has not handled him skilfully. S. G. is pessimistic, depressed, discouraged and very ill.[1]

Flotow's dispatch of 14 July and the letters of the 16th had not reached Berlin when Jagow on the 14th sent a telegram to Rome with instructions to Flotow to work for the 'localization' of the conflict:

Should the results of the inquiry into the Sarajevo murder cause Austria-Hungary to take more serious measures against Serbia, it would be to the greatest interest of ourselves and the rest of Europe to localize the conflict that might arise. This will depend on public opinion all over Europe making it possible for the Governments to be inactive onlookers at the settlement of differences between Austria and Serbia. For this the view must prevail in the press that the conflict is a matter which only concerns the two participants. . . . Please do what you can to influence the Italian press, though carefully avoiding everything that might make it seem that we were urging the Austrians to go to war.[2]

Jagow saw at once that it would not do to buy over some discredited newspaper. He had been Ambassador to Rome and understood what effect would be produced in Italy, despite the pro-Triplice sentiments of San Giuliano, by any step on the part of Austria in the Balkans such as the one Vienna was contemplating. Jagow's attitude, as reflected in the documents, throws a favourable light on the line taken by Italy in regard to the Austrian aggression and its consequences. The accusation that Italy failed in her duty as an ally is rebutted by German diplomacy which saw in advance what line she would adopt. This fact is illustrated by the telegram which Jagow sent to Tschirschky on 15 July to inform him of what Flotow had reported on 14 July, adding a comment of great interest and—one can say—of extreme clearsightedness.

Italian public opinion has till now in general been no less hostile to Austria than friendly to Serbia. There is no doubt in my mind that in an Austro-Serbian conflict, it would side with Serbia. A territorial extension of the Austro-Hungarian Monarchy, even a further spread of its influence in the Balkans, is viewed with horror in Italy and regarded as an injury to Italy's position there. By an optical illusion the imagined threat from her Austrian neighbour makes her overlook the in reality much greater Slav peril. Apart from the fact that Government policy in Italy to no small extent depends on the state of public opinion, the above idea still dominates the minds of the majority of Italian statesmen. Each time there was any threat to Serbia from Austria I saw that it gave rise to an extraordinary feeling of tension. If Italy took the side of Serbia that would unquestionably encourage Russia to act.

[1] DD. I, 75.   [2] DD. I, 44.

St. Petersburg would calculate that Italy would not only fail to fulfil her duties under the alliance, but might even intervene against Austria-Hungary. A collapse of the Monarchy would of course open to Italy the prospect of gaining long coveted territories.

It is therefore in my opinion of the highest importance that Vienna should discuss with the Rome Cabinet the aims it proposes to pursue in the conflict and should bring it over to its side or—as a conflict with Serbia does not in itself constitute a *casus foederis*—keep it strictly neutral. Under her agreements with Austria, Italy has a right to compensation for every change in the Balkans in favour of the Danube Monarchy. This, therefore, would be the object and the bait of the negotiations with Italy. According to our information the cession of Valona, for instance, would not be regarded in Rome as acceptable compensation. In fact Italy for the time being seems to have given up her wish for a foothold on the opposite shore of the Adriatic.

In strict confidence, the only compensation regarded as adequate in Italy would be the acquisition of the Trentino. This would be so rich a mouthful that it could stop the mouth of public opinion hostile to Austria. That the renunciation of an ancient portion of the territory of the Monarchy would be difficult to reconcile with the feelings of the Sovereign and of the people in Austria, cannot be overlooked. But on the other hand the question arises what is the value to Austrian policy of the attitude taken by Italy, what price is one willing to pay for it and whether the price would be in proportion to the gain elsewhere.

I would ask Your Excellency to make the Italian attitude the subject of a detailed confidential conversation with Count Berchtold and in so doing to touch on the question of compensations. Whether in this conversation the question of Trento can be mentioned, I must leave to your judgement and knowledge of the conditions in Vienna.

The line taken by Italy will certainly be of influence on Russia's behaviour in regard to the Serbian conflict; if this develops into a general war, Italy's attitude would be of the highest military importance to us.[1]

The statements contained in this document are made, not by an Italian, but by the German Secretary of State for Foreign Affairs. It is he who sees that: (1) 'a territorial extension of the Austro-Hungarian Monarchy, even a further spread of its influence in the Balkans, is viewed with horror in Italy'; (2) a conflict between Austria and Serbia did not constitute a *casus foederis* for Italy; (3) Italy had a right to compensation for any change in the Balkans in favour of Austria; (4) according to information in Berlin, Valona would not be regarded as adequate compensation, what Italy would want was the Trentino.

It is not fortuitous that Jagow named the Trentino. On 10 July Flotow had hinted to San Giuliano the possibility that Austria might agree to a union between Montenegro and Serbia on condition that she herself received Mount Lovčen. San Giuliano at once indignantly reacted by threatening

[1] DD. I, 46.

that we must not for a minute be in doubt that such a step on the part of Austria would mean not only the end of the Triple Alliance but an Italian war against Austria. This war would be fought with all weapons, with the revolutionizing of Austria and with the aid of the Serbs and Russians.

In reply to further insistence on the part of Flotow, San Giuliano

hesitatingly came out with the idea that the only possible way to render this eventuality acceptable to Italian public opinion would be a cession of territory in the Trentino to Italy.[1]

On 15 July Flotow again telegraphed from Fiuggi:

Marquis San Giuliano fears that Austria in her conflict with Serbia is planning territorial acquisitions which Italy could not tolerate. I replied that I thought Austria simply wanted to stop continual threat from Pan-Serb propaganda. Minister said it would be impossible to stop it by force. Propaganda would simply go underground. It was urgently to be desired that Austria should be moderate.[2]

This was telegraphed on immediately by Jagow to Tschirschky in Vienna. Flotow's informative reports to Berlin were in great contrast to those sent to Vienna by Merey whose only idea was to get Berchtold's consent to communicating the Austrian ultimatum to San Giuliano one day earlier than it was presented at Belgrade. Again on 17 July Flotow telegraphed from Fiuggi:

In a purely theoretical discussion of the potential Austro-Serbian conflict —for he is not yet in the secret—Marquis San Giuliano said that an overthrow of Serbia or an Austrian annexation could be tolerated neither by Italy nor by Roumania.[3]

This also was telegraphed on to Tschirschky by Jagow on 18 July. A letter written on the same day by Jagow to Tschirschky, after expressing disbelief in the rumour that Italy planned to occupy Valona, warned Vienna

not to have any illusions but that an Austrian attack on Serbia would not only meet with a most unfavourable reception in Italy but would probably encounter direct opposition. . . . I therefore regard a speedy discussion between the Vienna and the Rome Cabinet as an urgent necessity and think that this could be greatly facilitated if Italy, with Austrian consent, were involved in Albania. Will Your Exeellency be so good as to urge this on Count Berchtold.[4]

4. *Berchtold's refusal to recognize Italy's right to compensation.*

What was Vienna's reaction to the pressure from Berlin? Tschirschky seems to have preferred not to broach the theme of compensation himself, but in consequence of the telegram of 15 July he sent the

[1] GP. XXXVIII, 15555.   [2] DD. I, 51.   [3] DD. I, 60.   [4] DD. I, 68.

Embassy Counsellor, Stolberg, on the 17th to see Berchtold and ask whether before taking action it would not perhaps be advisable to get into touch with Italy. Berchtold replied—runs Stolberg's report—

that up to now he had not let a word transpire and in fact was intending to confront the Italian Government with a *fait accompli*, as he could not be quite sure of their discretion and they might with their pro-Serb attitude easily let something percolate through to Belgrade. On this point Berlin had agreed with Hoyos, with whom the matter had been discussed. From Hoyos himself also I obtained confirmation of this. Thereat I . . . earnestly explained to the Minister how enormously important it seems to us that people here should have a discussion with Rome over the aims to be pursued in the dispute and try to keep it on their side. Berchtold evinced great optimism and said Italy could surely never be so mean as to turn against the Monarchy. I replied that in a preliminary conflict with Serbia alone the alliance would not come into question and that Italy might well, even if only morally, take the side of Serbia and that this might be disastrous to the solidity of the Triplice and would undoubtedly strengthen the readiness of Russia to take action. The Minister saw that, but did not of his own accord bring up the subject of possible compensations. Even when Hoyos, who had been called in, made the remark that the Italians would in any case have to be given something, he let the matter drop. . . . But I had a long conversation immediately after with Hoyos in which he brought up the subject of Trento, asking me if this was the compensation we had in mind, which I agreed it was. He by no means rejected this and was not insensible to the argument that it would put an end to irredentism. I said to him that in this case it need only be a matter of the relatively small area of the diocese of Trento. He took all this in a very friendly spirit but went on to mention as a possible compensation for Italy that she might be given the Dodecanese.[1]

But Hoyos was not Berchtold, and when it became clear that Stolberg's *démarche* had produced no effect Tschirschky himself had to take up the matter with Berchtold on 20 July. We have seen how Jagow on the 17th had telegraphed instructions that Tschirschky should inquire what Austria meant to do with Serbia, as this might affect the attitude of Italy and England. Tschirschky was, however, to be careful

not to give the impression that we meant in any way to put obstacles in the way or lay down limits of objectives for her.[2]

The German query was not out of place. Its purport was explained four days later in a telegram which Szögyény sent summarizing a conversation with Jagow of 21 July:

Herr von Jagow, without wishing to give us direct advice, expressed the idea that it would be expedient, in order to make sure of Italy, for us in view of the possibility of our becoming involved in hostilities with Serbia to have a confidential discussion with Italy about our aims. Were we to declare in

---

[1] DD. I, 87.   [2] DD. I, 61.

advance that we envisaged only a provisional occupation of certain parts of Serbian territory, a declaration which Herr von Jagow, however, did not regard as particularly desirable, Italy would probably be satisfied with this, but if such were not the case, she would certainly make the usual demands for compensation, in which case an understanding ought to be arrived at right from the beginning.[1]

In other words Berlin would prefer that Austria should cede the Trentino to Italy and recoup herself by annexing the whole or a part of Serbia, but if Vienna did not intend to proceed to a permanent occupation of Serbian territory, let it quieten Italy by saying so and thus justifying the refusal of compensations.

The momentous conversation between Tschirschky and Berchtold of 20 July is preserved in two not greatly differing versions. Tschirschky's account runs:

I went on to explain that it will be of decisive importance for the future attitude of Italy and for public opinion in that country as well as for the attitude of England what the Austro-Hungarian statesmen's ideas are about the future of Serbia. Count Berchtold replied . . . that at yesterday's discussion, particularly as a result of representations made by Count Tisza, who insisted that neither he nor any other member of the Hungarian Government could be counted on to agree to a strengthening of the Slav element in the Monarchy, it was decided to refrain from any permanent acquisition of foreign territory. Thus no valid reason would be given for Italy to make claims for compensation. On my observing that Italy might regard the expansion of Austrian influence in the Balkans as prejudicial to her own position and possibly as a basis for putting in claims, Berchtold replied that such a standpoint would be inconsistent with the repeated assurances of Marquis San Giuliano that Italy needed a strong Austria, if only as a bulwark against the Slav flood. . . . That, moreover, Italy herself does not respect the principle of nationality and only demands its observance from others is made clear by the occupation of Libya which is in direct conflict with this principle. . . . If Rome at present regards large-scale Austro-Italian co-operation as impracticable, there is actually no need for any such co-operation, Austria asks neither for co-operation nor for support but merely for Italy's abstention from hostile acts against her ally [another confirmation of Berchtold's attitude towards Italy]. He will certainly do everything possible, he says, to spare Italian feelings and has already considered granting the Italians within the Monarchy some satisfaction. This idea I welcomed most warmly and recommended Berchtold to develop further. Count Berchtold also told me that Herr von Merey, who had strictly avoided the Serbian affair in talking with San Giuliano, because he was sure that the slightest hint to Italy would at once be passed on to Russia and used for counter-moves and claims to compensation, cherished no illusions as to the anti-Austrian and pro-Serb tendencies of San Giuliano and the Italians, but was firmly convinced that military and domestic considerations would render it hardly feasible for Italy

[1] Oe-U. VIII, 10448.

to contemplate active intervention. Herr von Merey believes, and in this
Berchtold agrees with him, that San Giuliano's main purpose is to bluff
Austria, taking cover behind Italian public opinion. He has indications that
San Giuliano is trying to use his Russian connexions for this end. Herr von
Merey suggests that as a sop to Italy, so that the note does not first become
known there through the press, it should be communicated by himself to
Marquis San Giuliano on the actual day it is presented at Belgrade. Berchtold
is to follow this suggestion. Because it is important to make it possible for
Italy to range herself on the side of Austria and to obviate all misunderstanding, he will in handing the note to Rome accompany it with a statement that,
in taking measures against Serbia, Austria does not contemplate making any
additions to her territory.[1]

Berchtold's own version brings out some other items of the con-
versation. He felt rather upset at finding that Italy had somehow got
wind of what Vienna was planning against Serbia and suspected the
German Ambassador Flotow of having committed some indiscretion.
There were already indications that Italy was making efforts to thwart
Austrian plans.

I could thus not yet contemplate an exchange of views with the Italian
Government about our action, this in fact having been agreed at the time in
the Berlin discussions between the Under Secretary of State and Count Hoyos.
Our intention was to inform the Rome Cabinet one day in advance of the
delivery of the note to Serbia, which seems to me perfectly adequate as an
act of courtesy towards an unreliable ally. . . . As regards Valona there
exists here such a stormy current of public opinion against allowing Italy to
establish herself on the opposite shore of the Adriatic that I could not enter
into a deal on this point. . . . I urged Herr von Tschirschky to have San
Giuliano's attention called by Berlin to the contradiction between his repeated protestations that Italy needs a strong Austria-Hungary as a bulwark
against the Slav flood and his policy at critical moments of working with
Russia, the predominant Power of the Slavic world, along lines which would
deprive the Monarchy of the possibility of preserving her existing territorial
integrity. Finally I emphasized that it would not do for us to let ourselves
be frightened or diverted from our appointed path, all the more as I gather
from the report of our Ambassador to the Quirinal that Italy as a result of
the Libyan campaign is in no fighting mood and will vent her discontent
with us in words but hardly in deeds.[2]

Here, therefore, was a categoric refusal to acknowledge the right of
Italy to compensation, the reason being that Berchtold did not regard
Italian co-operation as necessary or think he need be afraid of her be-
cause she would not go beyond words. But if such blindness seems
almost incredible, it must be added that Berlin was not much less blind.
It was when Austria asked leave to attack Serbia with the promise of
German support that the Wilhelmstrasse ought to have made this

[1] DD. I, 94.   [2] Oe-U. VIII, 10398.

support conditional on Vienna's coming to an agreement with Rome. For Italy this would have been a misfortune, because if Austria had promised the Trentino, the Rome Government might have succumbed to the temptation and given Austria a free hand with what disastrous results Heaven only knows. But from the Austro-German standpoint the step was imperative and Berlin would have been in a position to insist on its being carried out by Vienna as a condition of her own promise of support. This had been Tschirschky's first idea when on 30 June he pointed out to Berchtold that:

the pros and cons of any action must be carefully weighed and the fact not lost sight of that Austria-Hungary does not stand alone in the world, that it was her duty . . . to take into account the reactions of Italy and Roumania in all matters affecting Serbia.[1]

and on 2 July he had repeated the warning to Francis Joseph.[2] Instead of which Bethmann Hollweg agreed to the Austrian request that Italy should be kept in the dark and it was only when Flotow's first dispatches arrived with news of San Giuliano's reservations that the Wilhelmstrasse saw the danger of going to war without coming to a previous agreement with Italy. And even when they did see it they did not draw the necessary consequences and tell Berchtold to stay his hand. They let things take their course with the consequences we know.

5. Berchtold's instructions to the Austro-Hungarian Ambassador at Rome.

Immediately after his talk with Tschirschky on 20 July Berchtold sent Merey a series of telegrams revealing his lack of all sense of reality. The first told Merey that San Giuliano had learnt, probably through Flotow, 'of our intention of taking vigorous measures concerted with Germany' against Serbia, and had

at once sent instructions to Italian representatives at St. Petersburg and Bucharest to induce the Governments there to take up a threatening attitude at Berlin and Vienna to stop our taking action. Of course any such attempts at intimidation would have no effect on us.[3]

There was some truth in his assertion, a proof that Italian dispatches were being intercepted and decoded. The second telegram suggested that Merey should say that Vienna had evidence which would justify the use of stern language at Belgrade, but assuring San Giuliano

that we in our *démarches* at Belgrade regarded their peaceful success as quite within the bounds of possibility and that in any case we were convinced of being able to count on Italy's loyalty as an ally in the clarification of our relations with Serbia. Both to you and to me at Abbazia, Marquis San Giuliano, with a just appreciation of the international situation, has often said

[1] DD. I, 7.   [2] DD. I, 9.   [3] Oe-U. VIII, 10418, 10419, 10420.

that Italy needs a strong Austria-Hungary. The clarification of our so un-satisfactory relations with Serbia seemed an absolute necessity for the pre-servation of the present position of the Monarchy and the solidity of the Triple Alliance. . . . At the present juncture it was to Italy's interest to come out publicly on our side. . . . In the further course of the conversa-tion Your Excellency might, as a personal opinion, express the conviction that, even if peaceful methods were to fail, the Vienna Cabinet does not con-template a campaign of conquest or any acquisition of Serbian territory. Your Excellency might seize the occasion to give a categoric denial of the tendentious invention of the *Temps* that we were planning an attack on the Lovčen. On the contrary we should be greatly obliged to the Italian Govern-ment if it would use its influence at Cetinje to tranquillize Montenegro—whose attitude is widely different from that of the Belgrade Government and which has had bad experiences with bombs imported from Serbia—on the subject of our conversation with Belgrade.[1]

Be it remembered that at the Council of Joint Ministers on 19 July Berchtold, on the insistence of Tisza, had undertaken to notify the Powers of the Monarchy's territorial *désintéressement* in the event of war with Serbia. Next day he had promised Tschirschky to communicate this declaration without delay to Italy. Here is the way he carried out that promise. Merey was to express, merely as a personal opinion, the conviction that Austria was not contemplating a campaign of conquest, evidently because Berchtold saw that what lay ahead was a war of con-quest even if he had agreed with Tisza to the contrary. We shall see in a moment how Merey carried out his instructions. But first we must look at the third of the telegrams which Berchtold sent to both Rome and to Berlin. It warned the two Austrian Ambassadors:

The possibility cannot be discounted that the Royal Italian Government in the event of our becoming involved in war with Serbia will seek to inter-pret Article VII of the Triplice Treaty in a sense acceptable to itself and raise the question of compensations. Enclosed Your Excellency will receive a confidential note whose content is to serve Your Excellency as guidance in conversation with Marquis San Giuliano in taking a stand against the Italian interpretation of the above Article.[2]

This note began by stating:

In the event of it becoming necessary to declare war on Serbia, Austria-Hungary does not pursue the purpose of making territorial gains. . . . But the nature of the war necessitates the transfer of the operational bases to Serbian soil and it . . . is to be foreseen that a provisional occupation of Serbian territory will be maintained until the required guarantees have been fulfilled and Serbia has paid back the expenditure on mobilization or war, as the case may be, in which Serbia's original refusal has involved the Mon-archy. It would be a thorough misinterpretation of the Triplice Treaty for Article VII to be so interpreted that the temporary occupation of an adjacent

---

[1] Oe-U. VIII, 10419. [2] Oe-U. VIII, 10420.

Balkan state with which the Monarchy was at war was to be dependent on a previous agreement with Italy reached on a basis of compensation.

The note went on to explain that when Article VII speaks of the *status quo* 'in the regions of the Balkans or of the Ottoman coasts and islands in the Adriatic and in the Aegean Sea' the wording shows that only Turkish territory was meant, not that of other Balkan states.[1]

By a further telegram on 21 July Merey was instructed that if San Giuliano remained unyielding in his interpretation of Article VII, Merey was

to avoid further discussion of this topic on the plea that neither side will be likely to convince the other and that Your Excellency thought it expedient . . . to review the situation from the standpoint of the many joint interests of Austria-Hungary and Italy as friends and allies. . . . It would seem to me anything but expedient if discussion of Article VII should arouse feelings of irritation and in the last resort perhaps culminate in jeopardizing the whole treaty.[2]

By these three telegrams dispatched between 5.30 and 10 p.m. on 20 July, Berchtold imagined he had settled the matter of Italy! Among his arguments the only one that held water was that San Giuliano had repeatedly emphasized Italy's need for a strong Austria. That being so 'it was to Italy's interest to come out publicly on our side'. But the real truth was that it was not at all necessary to Italy to have a strong Austria, the Slav menace being far less serious for Italy than it was for the Dual Monarchy. San Giuliano's phrase was one of those remarks which represent the opposite of the truth and met with not the slightest credence from the men who governed Austria.

Berchtold's failure to grasp the importance of Italy and her claims can in part be explained by the information and advice he received from the arrogant, superficial and ill-informed Merey whose one idea was that the way to deal with Rome was to adopt a bullying tone and refuse to budge an inch. He started from the assumption, expressed by Aehrenthal in February 1911 to dispel his own alarm at the development of Italian armaments, that 'in Italy the Government, army, navy, parliament, press and a large part of the population are dominated by the most Italian of all emotions, fear'.[3]

Merey was convinced, as he wrote to his friend Berchtold on 25 July in congratulating him on the ultimatum, that all offers of mediation should be rejected and a final settling of accounts with Serbia carried through, there being no possible worse misfortune for the Monarchy than for Serbia to yield to the demands made by Vienna. This diplomat, who as a Hungarian may be counted as a member of the

---

[1] Oe-U. VIII, 10392; Pribram, I, p. 155.   [2] Oe-U. VIII, 10458.
[3] Conrad, II, p. 225.

Hungarian camarilla, was like the rest of the Hungarians a disastrous counsellor for Berchtold. On 18 July, before knowing the nature of the demands to be contained in the ultimatum, he sent a report of the state of mind in Italy:

In the press here the general assumption is that moderate demands on our side and a conciliatory reception of them by Serbia will bring about a peaceful settlement. . . . But if we push matters as far as an armed conflict . . . the traditional friendliness to Serbia, Italian aspirations in the Balkan Peninsula, the danger of a European outbreak for Italy with her now disorganized army and bad financial position, and the abhorrent prospect that after over-throwing Serbia we might restore our diminished prestige in the Balkans and even acquire territorial advantages, all this will automatically draw Italian sympathies to the other side. Article VII of the Triplice Treaty will be invoked against us. . . . In this situation the Italian Government, partly as a speculation, partly under the impetus of public opinion, might feel tempted to break the agreement with us over Albania and make a separate move in South Albania. Italy would then have a gage in her pocket in the shape of Valona and could view with more calmness what went on in the north of the Balkan Peninsula. These are all merely suppositions . . . only one thing seems to me certain, namely that in the event of our settling accounts with Serbia by military action our relations with Italy for years to come . . . will be extremely bad. Not that I want to argue against war with Serbia. Nothing is further from my thoughts, but one does not make an omelette without breaking eggs. . . . I do not in any sense plead for previous consultations and negotiations with the Italian Cabinet. . . . But there seems to me to be an indispensable minimum of courtesy due to Marquis San Giuliano, so that he should learn of the outbreak of hostilities not from the press but a day in advance from me.[1]

Such were Merey's ideas when Berchtold's three telegrams of the 20th reached him, and certainly met with his full approval. On 21 July he saw San Giuliano whose expressions of anxiety over the forthcoming Austrian *démarche* at Belgrade gave Merey an opening to guide the conversation along the lines laid down in his instructions.

On the subject of the clarification of our relations with Serbia, the Minister again dwelt at great length on the possibility of our healing the breach not by humiliation and force but by conciliation. . . . Italy, he continued, wants a strong Austria-Hungary, but as it is now, without territorial enlargement. Anything of that sort—he must frankly say—would be regarded by Italy, who pursues a policy of conciliation and equilibrium, as injurious to her interests. My explanation that we did not aim at annexation of territory was received with satisfaction by the Minister, in regard to the Lovčen with ill-concealed jubilation. I answered in the negative his question whether he could use this in the press and I stressed the fact that this confidential com-munication was in the nature of a sincere intention to abstain from territorial

[1] Oe-U. VIII, 10308.

gains but not of a pledge. (In view of the possibility of war and of the further eventuality that Montenegro will perhaps make common cause with Serbia, I thought it would be dangerous to embark on more far-reaching promises.) Marquis San Giuliano declared in conclusion that it was his firm intention to support us if our demands on Serbia were such that their fulfilment seemed equitable. Were the opposite the case, he would have the whole of public feeling in the land against him, as it was unalterably liberal, mindful of its own revolutionary origins and in sympathy with irredentist manifestations everywhere. He emphasized that his position would be rendered easier if our *démarche* at Belgrade were based—if not entirely at least mainly—on the Sarajevo catastrophe and less on other agitation. I argued against all these limitations which I described as theoretically unsound (as placing Serbia on the level of a modern civilized state) and practically deficient in friendship and solidarity. . . . He promised to send instructions to-day to Montenegro in the sense desired by us. In Belgrade, too, he had already given advice to be conciliatory and to add to its weight had ordered the Minister to return to his post.[1]

A strange dialogue! The Ambassador announcing, in so serious a matter as the annexation planned against Serbia, first that there was to be no annexation, then, mindful of Berchtold's instructions that he was only to give a personal opinion, adding that this was an intention but not a pledge. If that was not playing a double game! And there was San Giuliano taking it all in, never asking, as was laid down in the treaty of alliance (Articles I and VII), to be informed in advance of the demands that were to be made on Serbia, even promising in certain conditions to support Austria and only on the 23rd getting Fasciotti, the Italian Minister to Bucharest, to make a *démarche* which tells its own tale. On that date Fasciotti, in an audience of King Carol of Roumania, said it was the opinion in Rome

that Austria was going to make excessive demands on Serbia in order, on her refusal, to declare war on her. The Italian Government desires that Roumania should intervene at Vienna to bring it about that the Austrian terms should be such that Serbia could accept them.[2]

This was asking Roumania at the eleventh hour to do what Italy, though warned of Austrian intentions already ten days previously, had failed to do, San Giuliano having avoided the subject with both Ambassadors. On 19 July Flotow telegraphed to Berlin from Fiuggi that Avarna was sending home pessimistic reports about Serbia and that San Giuliano regarded the situation as serious, but avoided all discussion with him on the subject.[3] Another dispatch from Flotow sent early on the 23rd informed Berlin:

From a remark of San Giuliano the Austrian Minister has in general informed him of the Austrian intention to proceed against Serbia. The note is

---

[1] Oe-U. VIII, 10460.   [2] KSF., 1929, p. 276.   [3] DD. I, 78.

to be communicated here as soon as its final form is settled. Austria claims
not to intend at present to acquire territory or to occupy the Lovčen. Minister does not regard this declaration as a permanent undertaking and is
therefore not entirely reassured on this point. He avoided further discussion
with the remark that the Prime Minister Salandra desired on Friday 24 July
(i.e. after the ultimatum) to discuss the position with me in San Giuliano's
presence. . . . San Giuliano could not conceal his fears of excessive terms
which would rouse all Europe and Italian public opinion against Austria.[1]

Doubtless he felt anxious, but he remained inactive, nor were the
Italian Ambassadors less inactive than he. The Austrian documents
show no trace of conversations between Avarna and Berchtold in the
period from 18 July to 24 July. What was the reason? Probably a
political calculation on which we shall now try to throw light.

But before so doing and after extracting what information we can
from German and Austrian documents, we must not omit to take into
account what Salandra writes in *La Neutralità Italiana*. Speaking of the
policy of the Government under his Premiership he claims:

We formulated it with clarity and firmness even when the conflict outlined itself as a mere possibility. . . . On 18 July Bollati had reported a talk
with Jagow, who while the Austrian demands on Serbia were still pending,
had expressed the hope that they were moderate (he then knew perfectly well
that they would intentionally be excessive). Nevertheless Jagow could not
rule out the possibility of a conflict. But he relied on Russia's not being ready
to take the field. To restrain her it seemed to him expedient that the Triplice
should show itself united. And on the 20th San Giuliano hastened to reply
that we could not support the Austrian demands on Serbia if they ran
counter to the principles of our liberal code of public law and might create a
precedent also in regard to ourselves. Further: it was to our interest that
Serbia should not be crushed and that Austria-Hungary should not be territorially enlarged; nor could we second a policy contrary to our interests; that
this was also to the interests of Russia who would probably be forced to take
action. In conclusion, in reference to Jagow's opinion that Russia might be
restrained from acting by the conviction that she would find herself confronted by a compact Triple Alliance, the comment was that 'Italy is not
bound to take part in an eventual war provoked by an aggressive action of
Austria against Serbia which the entire political world will condemn; nor
can we take any step favourable to Austria-Hungary without first being sure
of the interpretation of Article VII of the treaty and until the question of
compensations has been settled.'

This clear telegram—the only one to which for the sake of brevity I refer,
but not the only one sent in this sense—was communicated to Avarna to
whom similar instructions were given.[2]

Now, after having taken cognizance of what the published documents tell of the Italian Government's attitude during the period lead-

[1] DD. I, 119.   [2] Salandra, pp. 71–2.

ing up to the presentation to Serbia of the Austrian ultimatum, we can pass judgement.

6. The guiding lines of San Giuliano's policy ; the Consulta's inaction ; its silence on the precedent of 1913.

The Sarajevo crime should hardly have failed to make it a foregone conclusion in the chancelleries of Europe that Austria was going to take some kind of action against Serbia. It was therefore incumbent on them, if they meant to avert a European war, to keep a close watch from the beginning on all that the Monarchy set about doing. But nothing of the kind did any of them do, while Germany on the contrary urged her ally to extreme measures. Towards the middle of July the intentions of Vienna leaked out, and from that moment duty should have called the Powers no longer merely to keep a watchful eye, but to do all they could to prevent the sending of an ultimatum which Serbia would be forced to reject and which would thus lead to an Austro-Serbian war, with all the likelihood that it would involve the whole of Europe. The sending of the ultimatum would set forces in motion which shortness of time, reasons of prestige on both sides, and mobilization measures would make it difficult, if not impossible, to arrest before all Europe was drawn into war. This was a prospect which Germany was prepared to face, though wrongly regarding it as unlikely. France in the view of some of her most influential public men was also prepared. In Russia opinions were divided, but the war party, held in check in 1908–9 and 1912–13, showed signs of coming to the fore. England and Italy on the other hand were bent on peace.

Of England we have already said that a complete unawareness reigned there of what was brewing. Now we must turn our attention to Italy who did not feel militarily prepared or economically strong enough to be attracted by the gamble of a war. The whole idea was abhorrent to both the governing classes—save for a handful of nationalists—and the masses. What reason had Italy to fight a war at the side of the Monarchy to consolidate its structure and assure its future in return for some paltry territorial reward? Italy had entered the Triple Alliance to secure herself against both Austria and France, not to make war on anyone. If she was to be called upon to make war on any Power in support of her allies, that Power could only be France. But in 1902 Italy had made an agreement with her French neighbour to observe neutrality towards France in any conflict not provoked by France herself. Nay more! To go to war with France was almost certainly to go to war with England. That was something which all Italian statesmen had utterly refused to contemplate, friendship with Britain being the basis of Italian foreign policy. Italy, therefore, had a supreme interest in intervening in time to avert a disaster which would place her in the painful dilemma of not being able to fulfil her engagements as they appeared to be laid down in the alliance. How could this be averted? There existed a precedent which should have shown her how to act, that of July 1913. Then also Berchtold had threatened intervention in Serbia.[1] San Giuliano had consulted Giolitti and had been told to tell Vienna 'in the most formal manner':

If Austria intervenes against Serbia it is clear that a *casus foederis* cannot be established.[2]

Unlike Grey, San Giuliano perfectly understood what was in the wind and in July 1914 he ought to have repeated to Merey what he had said to him in July 1913, without changing a single comma. It might be objected that in 1913 Italy had Germany with her in holding Austria back from attacking Serbia and that her success was due to this fact, while in 1914, when Austria had the assurance of German support, the word of Italy would have counted for nothing. But this is a vast mistake. Berchtold might well in the days before sending the ultimatum say that Italian co-operation did not matter much and that she was too exhausted by the Libyan war to do anything. But at the moment of dealing the blow on 23 July he seems to have been assailed by anxieties about Italy which he unburdened to Conrad. Conrad's reply was: 'If we have to fear Italy as well, then let us not mobilize'[3] and Conrad goes on to say: 'This reply corresponded to my opinion that we were not equal to a war on three fronts (Balkans, Russia and Italy).' Still more, as we have already seen, did Berlin feel confident that Italy could be counted on to attack France and send troops to the Rhine. On 26 July 1914 Bethmann Hollweg telegraphed to Tschirschky in Vienna:

Also the Chief of the General Staff regards it as urgently necessary that Italy be kept firmly with the Triplice. An understanding between Vienna and Rome is therefore necessary. Vienna must not equivocate with questionable interpretations of the treaty and must take resolutions commensurable with the seriousness of the situation.[4]

Berlin had no doubt that if Vienna would only make up its mind to offer compensations, Italy would march with the allies. Hence an unequivocal statement from Rome that a war caused by Austrian designs on Serbia would not be regarded as a *casus foederis* would undoubtedly have had a powerful if not decisive influence on the line taken by the Central Powers, especially by Germany, who was ready to carry on a war with France and Russia but only when sure that Italy was on her side and England neutral. As things turned out, as soon as English neutrality seemed to be in doubt, Berlin, too late, tried to

---

[1] See Vol. I, pp. 457-9.   [2] CDD., p. 401; Giolitti, II, p. 503.
[3] Conrad, IV, p. 108.   [4] DD. I, 202.

scurry to shelter. The same effect, but with better success, would probably have been produced if Italy straightforwardly and in good time had announced the line she was going to take.

That she did so is asserted by Salandra in passages of his book which have been quoted. But the present writer maintains that this is not true. The German and Austrian diplomatic documents which were never destined for publication and were made public only after the Central Powers had collapsed, are so unanimous in their portrayal of the undecided, vacillating, ambiguous attitude of San Giuliano as to leave no room for doubt. Kept in the dark, only half informed at the last moment, he put up no fight against the threat to Italian interests in the Near East and the violation of the Triplice Treaty, nor did he remind Berchtold of the veto that he and Aehrenthal had placed on Italian operations against Turkey. And when on 21 July Merey told him that Austria had no annexionist aims, but objected to this being published in the press as being only an intention not a pledge on the part of the Austrian Government, San Giuliano not only refrained from protesting at such duplicity of language but went to the length of saying that Italy would support Austrian demands if they were reasonable. As if it were possible that in the life and death struggle between Austria and Serbia Vienna would make 'reasonable' demands! Not a single diplomatic document of the Central Powers shows San Giuliano speaking before the ultimatum as he had spoken in 1913. When in 1913 he spoke those words, his warning was scrupulously reported to Vienna by Merey. This time he should have spoken them not only to Merey but to Flotow and have had the same words said at Berlin by Bollati and at Vienna by Avarna, if need be in a note. Now Merey reports nothing and Flotow only half words which merely gave Jagow the impression that Italy needed only to be compensated by the Trentino in order to march at the side of the Central Powers. But to mutter grumbles, express doubts, ask for compensation is something very different from announcing Italian neutrality clearly in advance, as would have been the straightforward, honest, and only rightful course to take.

So elastic and vague were the instructions emanating from the Consulta that a scrupulous diplomat like Avarna made statements to his German colleague which were the opposite of what he ought to have been saying, if what Salandra says is true. An Austrian dispatch of 21 July records:

Tschirschky recently had a talk with Duke Avarna who expressed the conviction that the Italian Government in the Austro-Hungarian-Serbian dispute will faithfully fulfil its duty as an ally and—even though voices should be heard to the contrary in Italy—would take its stand by Austria-Hungary.[1]

[1] Oe-U. VIII, 10439.

A clear sign that the Italian diplomats had not received adequate instructions and were acting on their own initiative. But there is still worse. When, as we shall see, after the delivery of the ultimatum the rumour went round that Fasciotti, the Italian Minister at Bucharest, had said that if war broke out 'Italy could not take part in it', San Giuliano on 27 July told Flotow that Fasciotti had exceeded his instructions and would be called to order.[1] On 29 July Szögyény in Berlin asked his Italian colleague Bollati whether Fasciotti's reported words represented the views of the Rome Cabinet. He received the answer that Fasciotti had been rebuked and that such was 'quite categorically not the view of the Rome Cabinet'.[2] What further proof is needed that San Giuliano did not either before or after the ultimatum make any such statement to Berlin or Vienna as that of 1913, and that in consequence the allies were left in doubt about his intentions? The further course of the narrative will bring convincing confirmation of this impression and will show that even if war could not have been averted, Italy could have arrived at her declaration of neutrality by a different and more honourable road.

But then what of the telegrams mentioned by Salandra? It can be shown and proved that various documents used by him in his Campidoglio speech and in his books are not to be relied on. All the Governments, at the time of the European war, were guilty of manipulating the diplomatic documents that preceded it. Not that Salandra was a man capable of such conduct. What he did was to use material provided by the Consulta. The present writer does not, however, cast doubt on the telegram sent to Bollati by San Giuliano on 20 July the contents of which we will now examine. It stated that 'we could not support the Austrian demands on Serbia if they ran contrary to the principles of our liberal code of public law'; that it was 'to our interest that Serbia should not be crushed and that Austria-Hungary should not territorially be enlarged'; that 'Italy is *not bound* to take part in an eventual war provoked by aggressive action by Austria against Serbia which the entire political world will condemn'.[3] But to declare that Italy was not bound to take part in such a war is not at all the same as a flat declaration that Italy *would refuse* to take part in such a war. And in fact the telegram went on to state: 'nor can we take any step favourable to Austria-Hungary without first being sure of the interpretation of Article VII of the treaty and until the question of compensations has been settled'.

Therefore if Article VII were interpreted as Italy desired and Vienna came to terms with her over the compensations to be given her in return for Austrian gains from Serbia, all Italian moral considerations would fall to the ground and Italy would take 'steps favourable to Austria-Hungary'. Among these steps there might of course be—why not,

[1] DD. I, 261.   [2] Oe-U. VIII, 10943.   [3] Salandra, pp. 71-2.

if it were made worth her while?[1]—even intervention on the side of Austria. It would not be easy for public opinion to come round to it. But the eventuality was taken under consideration.

7. San Giuliano's views and moves.

To understand the course pursued by San Giuliano we must know something of the man himself. Of quick intelligence, well travelled and thoroughly trained—he had an excellent knowledge of languages, especially German—he had made a special study of foreign affairs on which he wrote articles and made speeches in the Chamber. He had great powers of application, plenty of wit and guile and the manners of a lord and he was sceptical to the point of cynicism. He was Under Secretary for Agriculture in the Giolitti ministry in 1892 and then Postmaster General in the Pelloux ministry in 1898–1900. In the second Fortis ministry at the end of 1905 he received the portfolio of Foreign Affairs which he had coveted from his youth. But Fortis fell after two months and his successor Giolitti appointed San Giuliano as Ambassador to London, where he remained for three years, then to Paris whence he was called to Rome as Foreign Minister by Luzzatti in March 1910, retaining this office under Giolitti and Salandra until his death on 16 October 1914. Thus it was San Giuliano who took Italy into Libya, directed foreign policy during the Libyan war and the·Balkan wars and renewed the Triple Alliance in 1912.

His policy was one of utter, unreserved surrender to the Central Powers, inspired by sympathy and admiration for them, especially for Germany, by fear of their strength and by the opposite feelings towards the *Entente* Powers whom he had not learnt either in London or Paris to know, to like and to judge at their true value. At bottom, also, San Giuliano had no belief in the strength and hence in the destiny of his own country and that is another reason why he was such a devotee of the Triple Alliance and hostile to the policy of holding the balance between the alliance with the Central Powers and the friendship with England, France and Russia—the first of these an old friendship, the other two formed later. This course of policy had been set in 1896 by Visconti Venosta, and to it all his successors had remained faithful. San Giuliano however, drew closer to the Central Powers, tagging along behind Austria in the Balkan wars whose significance and fatal consequences for Austria he never perceived, and going to the length of authorizing the enormity of the Austro-Italian Naval Convention of 1914 which, in case of war, placed the Italian Navy, which was superior in strength and number to the Austrian, under the command of an Austrian admiral.[2]

---

[1] Salandra, p. 90. See Vol. I, p. 422, *n.* 2.
[2] See Vol. I, pp. 555–9.

Giolitti, who understood little of foreign affairs and only paid attention to them when there was a hint of trouble, gave San Giuliano a free hand, merely intervening with firm orders when there was a danger that San Giuliano's devotion to the Triplice and to Austria might threaten to drag Italy into hazardous adventures. This had been the case during the Balkan wars when San Giuliano would have let Italy take part with Austria in an expedition against Montenegro when the latter refused to evacuate Scutari which had been awarded to Albania. Giolitti again intervened in 1913, as has been narrated, and San Giuliano had then made no objection to telling Austria that Italy would not recognize the *casus foederis* in the case of a war caused by an Austrian attack on Serbia, because he knew then that he had Germany on his side. But in July 1914 Germany had changed her attitude, Giolitti was no longer in power and in his place since March 1914 was Salandra who had none of Giolitti's personal authority and with whom San Giuliano felt he had more freedom to follow his own bent.

This is proved beyond all shadow of a doubt by a very damaging piece of evidence. The reader will have already realized the importance of the caution given by San Giuliano to Austria in July 1913. When a year later precisely the same situation recurred it should have been San Giuliano's imperative duty to inform the new Head of the Government of the precedent of 1913. This he failed to do. And when on 5 December 1914 Giolitti rose in the Chamber and made known the warning he had conveyed to Austria by San Giuliano in 1913, both Salandra and Sonnino were thunderstruck. Salandra writes:

It was a revelation to me also. San Giuliano had not informed me of the important precedent. Sonnino was ignorant of it too.[1]

So amazed was Salandra that at first he was inclined to disbelieve Giolitti's statement and expressed his suspicions to the present writer that it might be an attempt on Giolitti's part to claim credit for having discovered and vindicated Italy's right to remain neutral before Salandra did so and to win the applause which in fact followed the announcement. As San Giuliano had died shortly before, the chief witness was lacking. But search was made in the records and revealed the following:

It brought to light that Giolitti had made a mistake of no importance in the date: the incident took place in July not in August 1913. More important was the discovery that at that time we had Germany in full agreement with our point of view. Merey had spoken confidentially to the Secretary General De Martino (San Giuliano being at the moment away from Rome) of the aggressive designs of Austria on Serbia in order at all costs to prevent the latter from making excessive territorial gains in the event of a Serbian victory

[1] Salandra, p. 450.

over Bulgaria in the last Balkan crisis then in progress. The conversation had taken the form of a confidential communication to our Government of a telegram addressed by Berchtold to the Austrian Ambassador to Berlin. It was, thus, at Berlin that the question had its focal point. San Giuliano had given immediate instructions to Bollati to speak to Berlin in the sense desired by himself and Giolitti. On 11 July, Bollati telegraphed from Berlin that he had seen Jagow who gave him an account of a conversation which had taken place between the Austrian Ambassador and the German Chancellor during Jagow's absence. On many different grounds into which it is not now necessary to enter, Bethmann had ended by advising Berchtold emphatically to maintain an attitude of prudent reserve. 'Any intervention by Austria-Hungary on behalf of Bulgaria, if confined to a diplomatic form, would be destined to certain failure; if, on the other hand, it manifested itself in military action, it would undoubtedly lead to a general war which was contrary to the interests of Germany.'

Therefore the Chancellor 'explicitly urged upon Berchtold that if such were his designs he should do nothing to transform them into actions without first informing Germany who did not desire to find herself faced with a *fait accompli*'. Jagow added on his own account that he did not see what could be meant by the allegedly defensive character of an eventual Austro-Hungarian action, save in the inconceivable case of Serbia's invading Hungarian territory. Jagow ended by concurring in our own interpretation of the treaty and gave the assurance that Germany, too, would refuse to follow Austria-Hungary in that course.[1]

Thus, as we see, the Italian *démarche* was confined to Berlin and was not a caution given by Italy directly to Vienna. This fact gave Salandra the mistaken impression, not mentioned in his book but voiced to the present writer, that what had taken place was merely a clarification of the Italian interpretation of the Triple Alliance and was, therefore, less important than Giolitti had let it be believed. The reason for this impression of his was that at the Consulta no trace was found of a report by San Giuliano on what he had said to Merey. By all the rules of good diplomacy he should not only have at once drafted a report of their conversation but had it at once communicated to Avarna at Vienna. Had there been such a document Salandra would have realized that the episode of 1913 was vitally important, that Germany cautioned Austria before telling Italy she had done so and that the Italian warning ranked as a definitive interpretation of the Triplice Treaty. Had there been a report on the matter, Salandra would have attached more weight to it than he did. He merely described it as 'important', whereas it was, in fact, decisive.

8. *The three courses open to San Giuliano; his mistaken choice.*

What now remains to be seen is why San Giuliano left no proper account of the conversation. The reason was that his words to Merey

[1] Salandra, pp. 450-2.

were merely the echo of Berlin's ideas at the moment, not an expression of his own convictions. It was simply an embarrassing incident not to be writ large in the Consulta records or in the history of the Triplice. His lapse from the rules of good diplomacy was less serious than was his keeping the incident from Salandra's knowledge. The present writer abstains from expressing condemnation of this silence. It was, in his opinion, rooted in the fear that if Salandra were to learn of the precedent he would undoubtedly follow it, both as approximating most closely to the course to which he inclined and in fact, finally took, and as having been laid down by Giolitti whose parliamentary strength he well knew. San Giuliano, on the contrary, did not think that Italy should take the same line as in 1913 because Germany's line was now different and he feared to offend her, and also because, in the diplomatic gamble now beginning, he thought he held good cards which would win him a big prize for small stakes. Let us examine his chances.

The Austrian move opened up several courses from which he could choose. He could regard the Austrian ultimatum to Serbia as the necessary response to Serbian provocation and therefore take the line laid down in Article III of the treaty which runs:

Article III: If one, or two, of the High Contracting Parties, without direct provocation on their part, should chance to be attacked and to be engaged in war with two or more Great Powers non-signatory to the present Treaty, the *casus foederis* will arise simultaneously for all the High Contracting Parties.[1]

This article implies that if France followed the lead of Russia in going to war with the Central Powers, Italy, recognizing that the provocation had been given by Serbia and Russia, was bound to take her stand at the side of her allies. But San Giuliano did not go to the length of regarding Austria as the one who had received provocation, not given it. There were some in Italy who went even as far as that, but he was not of their number, and, even if he had been, he would not have been followed by Salandra and the rest of the Cabinet.

The second possible course was the opposite of the one just outlined and would have been based on the spirit and the letter of Articles I and VII of the treaty which ran as follows:

Article I. The High Contracting Parties . . . engage to proceed to an exchange of ideas on political and economic questions of a general nature which may arise, and they further promise one another mutual support within the limits of their own interests.

Article VII. Austria-Hungary and Italy, having in mind only the maintenance, so far as possible, of the territorial *status quo* in the Orient, engage to use their influence to forestall any territorial modification which might be

---

[1] Pribram, I, p. 153.

injurious to one or the other of the Powers signatory to the present Treaty. To this end, they shall communicate to one another all information of a nature to enlighten each other mutually concerning their own dispositions, as well as those of other Powers.

However, if, in the course of events, the maintenance of the *status quo* in the regions of the Balkans or of the Ottoman coasts and islands in the Adriatic and in the Aegean Sea should become impossible, and if, whether in consequence of the action of a third Power or otherwise, Austria-Hungary or Italy should find ·hemselves under the necessity of modifying it by a temporary or permanent occupation on their part, this occupation shall take place only after a previous agreement between the two Powers, based upon the principle of a reciprocal compensation for every advantage, territorial or other, which each of them might obtain beyond the present *status quo*, and giving satisfaction to the interests and well founded claims of the two Parties.[1]

It was plain that before sending Serbia an ultimatum which might bring about the intervention of Russia and hence create the *casus foederis* first for Germany and then (after the intervention of France) for Italy, Austria should, under Article I, have consulted not only Germany, which she actually did, but also Italy, which with German concurrence, she abstained from doing. What alliance could ever permit one partner to commit acts such as might create an obligation for the other partners to come to the rescue without their having previously been consulted and having expressed their approval? To quote some precedents: When Poincaré on 1 April 1912 received from Izvolsky the first intimation that the Balkan states had formed a league and perceived the danger of a war which did not suit his purpose, he bluntly cautioned Sazonov that Russia must not act without the agreement of her ally France; if there were agreement, the alliance would hold good; if not, the one who acted would bear the risk alone. Similar words were said to Austria by Wilhelm after the outbreak of the First Balkan war, and repeated by Bethmann Hollweg to Szögyény on 6 July 1913 during the Second Balkan war. Italy had the manifest right, therefore, to be fully informed of the ultimatum to Serbia and to express agreement with it before its consequences could constitute a *casus foederis* on her part on behalf of Austria. And Austria's failure to consult her was an open violation of the provisions of Article I of the treaty.

But it was a no less flagrant violation of the provisions of Article VII which bound the high contracting parties 'to use their influence to forestall any territorial modification' in the Balkans and to 'communicate to one another all information of a nature to enlighten each other mutually concerning their own dispositions'. Now Austria had not officially communicated her intentions to Rome, had in fact deliberately

[1] Pribram, I, pp. 155-7.

withheld knowledge of them. Not only that, Article VII laid it down that

if Austria-Hungary or Italy should find themselves under the necessity of modifying it by a temporary or permanent occupation on their part, this occupation shall take place only after a previous agreement between the two Powers, based upon the principle of a reciprocal compensation.

But what Austria was now about to do was to go to war with Serbia without having come to any such previous agreement.

Berchtold objected that when Article VII spoke of 'regions of the Balkans or of the Ottoman coasts and islands in the Adriatic and in the Aegean Sea', it only referred to Turkish possessions.[1] Not so! It referred to a region which when Article VII was drawn up was in Turkish possession, but which Italy could not regard as having ceased to be of interest to her, at least in respect of Austria, even after it had ceased to be Turkish. This was so much the case that, even though the region had already been conquered by the Balkan League at the time when the last renewal of the Triple Alliance was signed on 5 December 1912, Austria made no request for the suppression of this article. Another childish remark made by Berchtold was that it would radically change the scope of Article VII if it were to be interpreted in the sense that the temporary occupation of territories belonging to a Balkan state at war with the Monarchy could not take place except after an understanding with Italy on a basis of compensations. Quite the contrary, Article VII expressly makes this very declaration and the reason is plain. There was little likelihood that Austria would attack Serbia unless she had in view some direct or indirect advantage to herself. Any such advantage gained by Austria was to be counterbalanced by an advantage for Italy. Once the deed was done, it would be too late for Italy to take measures for safeguarding her interests.

Berchtold went on to say:

During the Libyan campaign Italian troops occupied a number of Ottoman islands in the Aegean, which would have been a ground for a demand on our part for compensation. . . . I did not then raise a claim.

This is true but only up to a certain point. The right of Italy to occupy Tripoli was recognized by Austria in the second renewal of the Triple Alliance. Article III of the treaty of 1887 laid down that:

If it were to happen that France should make a move to extend her occupation . . . under any form whatsoever, in the North African territories, whether of the Vilayet of Tripoli or of the Moroccan Empire, and that in consequence thereof Italy, in order to safeguard her position in the Mediterranean, should feel that she must herself undertake action in the said

[1] Oe-U. VIII, 10715.

North African territories, or even have recourse to extreme measures in French territory in Europe, the state of war which would thereby ensue between Italy and France would constitute *ipso facto*, on the demand of Italy and at the common charge of the two allies, the *casus foederis*.[1]

It was, therefore, the bounden duty of Vienna not to deny Italy the means of availing herself of this article against Turkey. But instead of this, when she sought to carry the war against Turkey into the European continent (because without this she could not force Turkey to accept peace) Italy met with an absolute veto from Aehrenthal, a veto subsequently confirmed by Berchtold. She had to remain at war for over a year longer without winning a victory over her enemy who only capitulated on being attacked by the Balkan states. Berchtold, it is true, agreed to the Italian occupation of certain islands, but not of others, a sign that those occupied did not constitute a threat to Austrian interests. An Austrian aggression against Serbia was a quite different question. By entirely changing the balance of power in the Balkans it would so seriously affect Italian interests that it was regarded by many as an injury for which no compensations could be regarded as an adequate indemnity.

In short: an Austrian aggression against Serbia would be such a serious violation of Articles I and VII that Italy would be compelled in advance to deny the existence of the *casus foederis* and to take still more drastic action if, in spite of this warning, the Dual Monarchy persisted in its aggression.

Lastly, the third course open under the treaty was that suggested by Article IV:

Article IV: In case a Great Power non-signatory to the present Treaty should threaten the security of the states of one of the High Contracting Parties and the threatened Party should find itself forced on that account to make war against it, the two others bind themselves to observe towards their Ally a benevolent neutrality. Each of them reserves to itself, in this case, the right to take part in the war, if it should see fit, to make common cause with its Ally.[2]

Actually the state which threatened the security of Austria was not a Great Power, but in consideration of the probability of Russian intervention, this article might suggest a line of action, i.e. not recognize the *casus foederis* as of right, therefore not promise Italian intervention on the side of the Central Powers, but on the other hand not rule it out as a possibility, nay regard it even as possible; in either case insist on Italy's right to compensation under Article VII and remain within the Triple Alliance.

This third alternative was the one chosen by San Giuliano. It had

[1] Pribram, I, pp. 112–13.　　　　　　[2] Pribram, I, pp. 152–3.

certain advantages. It avoided a rupture with Vienna and above all with Berlin, the object of his reverential awe. It would open the way for negotiation over compensations on a scale which would be greater or smaller according as Italy joined in with the Central Powers or merely undertook to observe neutrality. We shall shortly see San Giuliano confessing in a letter to the King that this was, indeed, his plan. And to win over Salandra to this plan San Giuliano found it necessary to keep him in the dark about the precedent of 1913. It was this plan which prevented San Giuliano from taking a firm line to avert the outbreak of an Austro-Serbian war and made him say under his breath that though by rights the *casus foederis* did not arise, since it was a question of Austrian aggression repugnant to the liberal Italian spirit, Italy might perhaps carry out 'acts favourable' to Austria-Hungary (later he even did not rule out the possibility of Italy's marching side by side with her) if she could be perfectly sure about the interpretation of Article VII of the treaty and if 'the question of compensations were satisfactorily settled'. Here we also have the explanation why San Giuliano made no protest when Merey told him that Austria did not intend to occupy Serbian territory but did not engage not to do so. He did not want to imperil his bargaining for compensations by employing pressure and threats which might only annoy Vienna and antagonize Berlin, with both of whom he desired to remain on good terms. Be it noted that as late as the days when war was regarded as imminent, San Giuliano was still thinking of a possible expedition against Albania in agreement with Austria. On 20 July Flotow sent Berlin the following account of a conversation with him:

Marquis San Giuliano does not on his information regard an attack by Epirotes on Valona as probable. If contrary to expectation an Italian expedition were to become necessary, it would only take place in agreement with Austria. He hopes to maintain this agreement as long as possible, but is doubtful of its being possible on account of Serbia. He intends to have a meeting with Prime Minister Salandra to-morrow to discuss their future attitude. Two Italian warships are lying off Valona. In Brindisi two transport vessels lie ready.[1]

Apparently this enterprise was to fall within the framework of compensations which Austria would be expected to give to Italy. What an ignominious standpoint to take at so grave and critical a moment! It is impossible to condemn too strongly this whole policy of San Giuliano's. It revealed a total absence of all sense of horror at the tragedy that was about to be enacted and did not raise a finger to avert it. Despite protestations to the contrary it showed not the slightest regard for the feelings of the Italian people, friendly to Serbia and hostile to

---

[1] GP. XXXVI², 14540.

Austria, and for Italian liberal traditions. It tried to drive a bargain by which Italy would round off her own territory by conniving at the sacrifice of Serbia which was the incarnation of the principle of nationality. It allowed Italy's hereditary enemy to extend and strengthen her domination with evil consequences for Italy which would in no way be offset by the vaguely outlined compensations which Sonnino was later to ask for in more precise terms and which fortunately were refused by Berchtold and his successor.

Inspired partly by obsequiousness and fear of the Central Powers, partly by misapprehended Machiavellism, aimed at holding all roads open and at driving a bargain no matter what turn was taken by events, this line of conduct was blind to all moral considerations and ruinous to Italian interests and good name. For Italy there was but one suitable and honourable course and that was to refuse all complicity in aggression and warn the aggressor. Had this truth been recognized from the beginning no accusation would have been raised against Italy of betraying her alliance, or if raised, it could have been conclusively rebutted. The possibility of such an accusation being made should have been foreseen. And the only way to prevent this happening was for Italy before the war broke out to tell her allies that the treaty did not bind her to involve herself in an adventure which conflicted with her interests, her feelings and her love of peace.

CHAPTER VII

THE PRESENTATION OF THE AUSTRIAN
ULTIMATUM AT BELGRADE

*(1) The Council of Joint Ministers on 19 July approves the text of the ulti-
matum on conditions laid down by Tisza (p. 254). (2) The Kaiser in favour of
the reoccupation of the Sanjak of Novibazar; German impatience and dissatisfaction with Austrian delays (p. 258). (3) The belated communication of the
ultimatum to the Wilhelmstrasse; the implausible statements of Jagow
and Bethmann Hollweg (p. 264). (4) The efforts of those directing German policy
to wear a face of innocence (p. 268). (5) The Serbian Government's inaction
after the Sarajevo outrage (p. 270). (6) Pasić's memorandum to the Great
Powers (p. 274). (7) Hartwig's sudden death at the Austrian Legation in
Belgrade (p. 276). (8) The first news in Belgrade of what Austria was planning;
Pašić goes off on an electioneering campaign (p. 280). (9) The delivery of
the ultimatum at Belgrade; the text of the Austrian note to Serbia (p. 284).*

1. *The Council of Joint Ministers on 19 July approves the text of the ultimatum on
conditions laid down by Tisza.*

We have seen that at the first moment on 29 June when Conrad advocated mobilization and immediate hostilities against Serbia, Berchtold
objected that there was no outward occasion for such measures and
public opinion would first have to be prepared.[1] As an outward occasion he envisaged the presenting of definite demands to Serbia for the
dissolution of certain societies and the dismissal of the Minister of
Police. The idea of an ultimatum to Serbia occurred to Berchtold right
from the beginning but it is not unlikely that, not feeling sure how to
set about it, he had second thoughts of taking immediate action and
confronting Europe with a *fait accompli* and that it was Tisza's opposition and the time and means needed to overcome this, which made him
revert to his original idea of an ultimatum. In the discussion which
took place at the Council of Joint Ministers on 7 July seven points were
drawn up of which only three were to figure in the ultimatum. As yet
there was no word of the dissolution of the *Narodna Obrana*, but there
was mention of a lawsuit against the Belgrade journal *Piemont*. And
there was no hint of the stiffest demands which form points 5 and 6 of
the ultimatum. The idea of asking Serbia to receive an Austrian Government representative at Belgrade must have arisen in the minds
of Berchtold and his advisers when they were thinking up a way of

[1] Conrad, IV, pp. 33-4.

rendering the ultimatum impossible for Serbia to accept. It was on 10 July in conversation with Tschirschky that Berchtold for the first time mentioned that among the demands to be made on Serbia there might be one for the acceptance of an Austrian Government authority in Belgrade to keep watch on Pan-Serb machinations, perhaps also one for the dissolution of certain societies and the dismissal of some of the army officers implicated.[1] A letter from Tschirschky informed Jagow on 11 July that Belgrade was to be asked for a public and official declaration by the King of Serbia and the setting up of an Austrian Government authority to supervise the fulfilment of this undertaking.[2] On 13 July Bethmann was informed that a demand would be made for the participation of a senior Austrian official in the inquiry into the outrage. To collect evidence in support of the Austrian demands showing the complicity of the Serbian Government Dr. Wiesner had been sent to Sarajevo and had returned with empty hands. After Tisza's conversion the task of drafting the ultimatum was entrusted to Musulin, the senior official and Balkan expert at the Ballplatz and it was revised by Berchtold and Forgach. The section most difficult to draft was Point 6. Already Point 5 had demanded that Belgrade should accept the collaboration in Serbia of organs of the Austro-Hungarian Government in the repression of the subversive movement directed against the integrity of the Monarchy. The present writer was allowed to examine at the Vienna State Archives the minutes which served for the final draft of the ultimatum. They show that, in Musulin's draft, Article 6 ran:

To open a judicial inquiry against those implicated in the plot of 28 June who are at present on Serbian territory and to take summary proceedings by indictment against Major Voja Tankosić of the Serbian Army and the Serbian railway employee Ciganović, incriminated in the concordant depositions of the conspirators arrested at Sarajevo.

In this formulation the point might have been acceptable to Serbia. The task of modifying it was performed by Berchtold who of his own initiative rephrased Musulin's text to run:

To allow the agents of the Imperial and Royal police to proceed, together with the Serbian authorities, to search for the accomplices of the plot of 28 June who are on Serbian territory, to open a judicial inquiry against those incriminated who shall be indicated by the Imperial and Royal Government in consequence of this search, and to take summary proceedings against them.

Musulin accepted Berchtold's suggestion and gave the point the following form:

To open a judicial inquiry against those implicated in the plot of 28 June who are on Serbian territory and to permit agents of the police of the

---

[1] DD. I, 29.   [2] See p. 260.

Monarchy to participate with the Serbian authorities in the investigation relating thereto; to proceed summarily to the opening of criminal proceedings against Major Voja Tankosić and the individual named Ciganović, a Serbian State employee incriminated by the results of the preliminary investigation at Sarajevo.

The final revision was carried out by Forgach. Point 6 was divided into two parts and was given a more peremptory tone, as is shown in the final text.

To open a judicial inquiry against the accomplices of the plot of 28 June who are on Serbian territory; organs delegated by the Imperial and Royal Government will take part in the investigations relating thereto.

Another of Berchtold's preoccupations was that of disguising Austrian intentions so that nothing would transpire such as might awaken suspicion and that the utmost secrecy should be observed. Conrad and the War Minister Krobatin were away on leave and this, as Szögyény telegraphed from Vienna on 16 July, was regarded as a reassuring sign by the Italian Ambassador Bollati who had been 'extremely disquieted over the situation'.[1] On returning to his post at St. Petersburg on 18 July, the Austrian Ambassador Szápáry gave the most pacific assurances to Sazonov. Notwithstanding all Berchtold's precautions for keeping the secret, news of Austrian designs leaked out after 16 July to the chancelleries of the Great Powers, despite the fact that the meeting of Joint Ministers of 19 July, to discuss and pass the text of the ultimatum, was held at Berchtold's private residence, the ministers arriving singly and not in official cars.

Berchtold told the ministers that the note would be handed to the Serbian Government on 23 July at 5 p.m., in order that the forty-eight hour time limit might expire on Saturday 25th at 5 p.m. and the order for mobilization be given in the night of Saturday to Sunday.

For diplomatic reasons he was obliged to pronounce definitely against a further postponement as Berlin was already beginning to feel edgy and news of our intentions has trickled through to Rome.

Tisza reiterated that the assent of the Royal Hungarian Government must be conditional on the unanimous acceptance by the Council of Ministers of the resolution

that no plans of conquest by the Monarchy are linked with the action against Serbia and that except for frontier rectifications for military reasons not an inch of Serbian territory will be annexed by us.

Berchtold replied that he could only accept Tisza's standpoint with certain reservations. If Austria did win the war against Serbia she

---

[1] Oe-U. VIII, 10296.

would not herself make annexations but would seek to reduce Serbia o a size small enough to be no longer a menace by forcing her to make the largest possible cessions of territory to Bulgaria, Greece and Albania, eventually even to Roumania.[1] But the situation in the Balkans might change. It was not impossible that Russia might bring about the fall of the existing Sofia Cabinet and bring a regime to power hostile to the Monarchy. Albania, too, was a far from dependable factor.

He, as responsible for foreign policy, must reckon with the possibility that conditions at the end of the war might make it no longer possible for us not to make annexations if we meant to create better conditions on our frontiers than exist at present.

Tisza remained obdurate, saying:

He did not make this demand only on grounds of domestic policy but because he was personally convinced that Russia would be forced to offer resistance à outrance if we were to insist on the complete annihilation of Serbia.

The Austrian Premier, Stürgkh, pointed out

that even if acquisition of Serbian territory by the Monarchy were ruled out, it should still be possible, by the deposition of the dynasty, a military convention, and other appropriate measures, to place Serbia in a relationship of dependence on the Monarchy. Moreover the resolution passed by the Council of Ministers must not be such as would render impossible any strategic frontier rectifications that might prove necessary.

The War Minister Krobatin

said that he would support this resolution on condition that, in addition to frontier rectification, the permanent occupation of a bridgehead on the further bank of the Save such as the Šabac district were not ruled out.

Thereupon the following resolution was unanimously passed:

The Joint Council of Ministers agrees to the proposal of the Royal Hungarian Prime Minister that immediately on the outbreak of war the foreign Powers shall receive a statement that the Monarchy is not waging a war of

---

[1] Oe-U. VIII, 10393. The first trace of the idea of ceding Serbian territory to Bulgaria, Greece and Albania appears in one of Czernin's reports from Bucharest of 11 March 1914 (Oe-U. VIII, 9463) reproduced by Conrad (III, p. 781–2). In this report Czernin states that it would certainly be desirable to draw Roumania, Bulgaria and Greece together and attach them to the Triplice. 'But I do not believe that this alliance would be permanently possible, without satisfying Bulgarian claims in some way, which in this case would presumably have to be done at the expense of Serbia, hence could not take place peacefully. . . . After a successful campaign one could satisfy Bulgaria and Greece—and thereby indirectly Roumania—with Serbian territory, one could round off Albania and make it a frontier state of the Monarchy and reduce Serbia to a minimum.'

conquest and does not purpose to annex the Kingdom. Strategically necessary frontier rectifications and such temporary occupation of Serbian territory as may eventually become necessary are not ruled out by this resolution.

Nothing throws more light on the bearing of this vote of territorial
désintéressement than Conrad's words to Krobatin at the end of the
meeting:

Well, we shall see; before the Balkan war the Powers talked about the
status quo—after the war nobody bothered about it any more.[1]

Except for Tisza all the other ministers felt sure, like Conrad, that
when it came to the point the pledge of territorial *désintéressement* would
remain a dead letter, and it could not be otherwise. Would it in fact
have been worth while to plunge into so terrible an adventure—an
adventure which was to cost Austria her existence—in order, if successful, to emerge from it with empty hands, without having solved the
Southern Slav problem once and for all by annexing the Slavs to the
Monarchy? But this would have meant the end of dualism to which
Hungary owed her predominance, and therefore Tisza would not hear
of it. Thus it came about that Europe was thrown into chaos by
schemers who were devoid of any plans for a sound and reasonable
new order. Berchtold in those days thought he could somehow get
round Tisza's veto and, as we shall see, took care not to promise
Austrian territorial *désintéressement* to Italy. And not until 28 July did
he make that promise to Russia.

2. *The Kaiser in favour of the reoccupation of the Sanjak of Novibazar; German
impatience and dissatisfaction with Austrian delays.*

On 20 July the note to Serbia was sent to the Austrian Minister at
Belgrade, to the Ambassadors to the Great Powers, and to the Ministers
to the minor nations. The Austrian Minister at Belgrade was to present
it to the Serbian Government at 5 p.m. on 23 July, the others were to
present it on the morning of the 24th. The note was dispatched before
being read by Francis Joseph. Only on the morning of the 21st did
Berchtold lay it before him at Ischl. But the Emperor was already in
agreement and gave it his authorization. On receiving this, Berchtold
from Ischl telegraphed to Macchio to tell Tschirschky that the document would be submitted to him the next day because there were a few
modifications to it still to be made. This was not true, seeing that the
note had gone off to all the various capitals on the 20th.

Why this falsehood? Did Germany not yet know the text of the note,
though called upon to bear its consequences? Let us examine how the
Kaiser and his subordinates followed the course of events. Wilhelm
had gone off on a cruise on 6 July but had telegrams daily sent on to

[1] Conrad, IV, p. 92.

him and was impatient with the slowness of Vienna. On 10 July
Tschirschky reported having heard from Berchtold that at the audience
of the previous day Francis Joseph had expressed his gratitude to
Wilhelm and had said

that he was *now* entirely of our opinion that a *decision* must be made to put an
end to the intolerable situation in regard to Serbia.

The two words *now* and *decision* were underlined by the Kaiser and his
marginal comment was: 'It is taking a very long time.' Neither he nor
Tschirschky made any protest against Francis Joseph's ascribing to
Germany the decision he was taking. Nor did they take exception to
the general character of the note, as indicated in Tschirschky's telegram
of 10 July (the Kaiser's comments are inset in italics):

The Minister hereupon acquainted the Emperor with the two modalities
which were under consideration in respect of the first measures to be taken
against Serbia. His Majesty expressed the view that this difference [between
Berchtold and Tisza] could perhaps be bridged over. On the whole His
Majesty inclined to the idea that concrete demands must be made on Serbia
(*Very much so! And in plain terms*). He, the Minister, does not underrate the
advantages of such a procedure. It would mean that the odium of attacking
Serbia unawares, which would fall on the Monarchy, will be avoided and
Serbia put in the wrong. Moreover this procedure would considerably
facilitate an, at least, neutral attitude on the part both of Roumania and of
England. The formulation of appropriate demands on Serbia forms at
present the main concern here (*They have had time enough for it*), and Count
Berchtold says he would be glad to know what Berlin thinks about it. He
thinks one demand might be that an organ of the Austro-Hungarian Government should be set up at Belgrade to keep an eye on the Pan-Serb agitation
there, perhaps also the dissolution of associations and the dismissal of some
incriminated army officers. The time limit for the reply must be made as
short as possible, presumably 48 hours. It is true that even this short limit
would be enough for Belgrade to get directions from St. Petersburg. Were
the Serbs to accept all the demands, this will be a solution that would not
be to his liking and he is turning over in his mind what demands could be
made that would render acceptance by Serbia absolutely impossible.[1]

The Kaiser was ready with a suggestion. His marginal comment
runs:

*Tell them to clear out of the Sanjak! Then the row will be on at once! Austria must
unquestionably have it back again, so as to prevent the union of Serbia and Montenegro
and the access of Serbia to the sea.*

Only four months earlier this union had been regarded by the Kaiser
as inevitable! Now his impatience was such that, when on 14 July
Vienna telegraphed that the ultimatum could not be presented earlier

[1] DD. I, 29.

than the 23rd because it must wait until Poincaré had left St. Petersburg, he wrote in the margin: 'What a pity.'[1]

The Kaiser's state of mind was shared by his ministers. As we have already noted, Szögyény telegraphed Vienna on 9 July that he had been most emphatically assured by Jagow that 'in his opinion, too, the projected action against Serbia should be taken in hand without delay'.[2] But what was this action to be? Did Berlin expect Austria to attack Serbia without ado and partition her on the lines of Berchtold's original plan explained verbally by Hoyos, or did it prefer the procedure of a previous ultimatum?

We have just seen that on 10 July Tschirschky telegraphed that Berchtold would be glad to know what were Berlin's ideas about the demands to be made on Serbia. On 11 July Jagow replied:

> As to the formulation of the demands on Serbia we can take no position, as this is a matter for Austria. To us it only seems desirable that Vienna should collect enough material to prove that in Serbia a Pan-Serb agitation exists which endangers the Monarchy. . . . This material would best be published —not singly but as a whole—shortly before the presenting of the demands, or ultimatum to Serbia.[3]

This was an indirect hint that what Austria was advised to present was an ultimatum. Tschirschky reverted to the question of the demands to be included in the Austrian note in a letter which he wrote to Jagow on 11 July saying that, according to what he had heard, Belgrade would be asked for:

(1) a public and official statement by the King of Serbia that he renounced the policy of a Greater Serbia; (2) the creation of an Austro-Hungarian organ to supervise the carrying out of this pledge. A time limit of only forty-eight hours would be allowed for the reply. If it were not satisfactory, mobilization would follow.[4]

Not a word of response came from Berlin. On 5 July, when Berchtold had intimated his intention of withholding his 'projected strong démarche at Belgrade' until after Poincaré's departure from Russia, Berlin had registered emphatic displeasure. Jagow had then said to

---

[1] DD. I, 50.   [2] Oe-U. VIII, 10154. See p. 175.   [3] DD. I, 31.

[4] *Beilagen zu den stenographischen Berichten über die öffentlichen Verhandlungen des Untersuchungs-ausschusses*, No. 1, *Zur Vorgeschichte des Weltkrieges* (Berlin, 1920), I, 119-20. Tirpitz narrates that on 13 July Bethmann Hollweg 'had been informed on the essential points of the intended ultimatum on which I received a communication from my deputy while in Tarasp. The portion of the letter sent to me ran as follows: "Our Ambassador in Vienna, Herr v. Tschirschky, has learnt privately, and also from Count Berchtold, that the note to be sent by Austria to Serbia will put the following demands: i. A proclamation from King Peter to his people, calling upon them to dissociate themselves from the Greater-Serbian agitation. ii. The participation of a high Austrian official in the inquiry into the assassination. iii. The dismissal and punishment of all officers and officials who are shown to have had a share in it." ' (Tirpitz, *Memoirs*, pp. 244-5.)

Szögyény that while understanding the necessity for the postponement 'he quite extraordinarily regrets this delay'.[1] The displeasure was certainly partly due to the impression that Vienna was not showing the requisite spirit of resolution. Tirpitz narrates:

From reports of 11 July I find that it was conjectured in the [German] Foreign Office at the time, that the Austrians would have preferred us to refuse them our help as an ally against Serbia. Our ally knew so little what she wanted, it was said, that she now asked us what she was actually to demand of the Serbs. This impression was scarcely correct. It showed how little Berlin ought to reckon on Austria remaining firm in the course which she had taken to save her honour.[2]

On 17 July Biedermann, the Saxon Chargé d'Affaires at Berlin, wrote to Vitztum von Eckstädt, the Saxon Foreign Minister:

The Vienna Government seems to have difficulty in mustering the energy necessary for a *démarche* and has now definitely postponed until the 25th the handing in of the note which was planned for 15 July. What the nature of the demands will be still remains to be seen but it is not to be ruled out that they will be 'hard for Serbia to swallow'. If care is being taken here not to spur on our ally, equal care is being taken not to weaken her resolve in any way, on the contrary a vigorous *démarche* would be welcomed, because it is the opinion here that it would re-establish Austro-Hungarian prestige in foreign eyes, especially those of the Balkan peoples and that resolute action would be likely to halt the inner disintegration of the Monarchy at least for some time. It is thought that Germany can only look for support to a strong, united ally. . . .[3]

On 18 July Zimmermann told the Bavarian representative: 'it is still extremely doubtful whether Vienna will gather itself together for this effort'. And he went on to say: 'Vienna seems not to have expected Germany to give such whole-hearted support to the Danubian Monarchy' and that his impression was 'that the ever timid and irresolute authorities in Vienna felt it almost unpleasant not to be admonished by Germany to act with prudence and restraint'.[4] However there is room for doubts whether this string of misgivings and grumblings was not prompted also by a general low opinion of Austria and her tardy ways and by regret that the measures she now proposed to take were not those foreshadowed by Hoyos on 5 July which comprised not only an immediate attack but also the partitioning of Serbia. It is true that on 15 July Jagow motivated his regrets over the postponement of the ultimatum by alleging 'that the sympathetic concurrence and interest in this *démarche* would be cooled even in Germany by this delay'.[5] But the following day on receiving the above quoted comments by the

---

[1] Oe-U. VIII, 10296.   [2] Tirpitz, *Memoirs*, p. 260.   [3] Bach, pp. 64-6.
[4] Dirr, pp. 6-7.   [5] Oe-U. VIII, 10296.

Kaiser to the Tschirschky dispatch of 10 July in which Wilhelm advised Austria to reoccupy the Sanjak, Jagow with his own hand wrote Tschirschky a letter which is a most revealing document:

As is known to Your Excellency from a perusal of Count Hoyos's notes of his conversation with the Under Secretary of State, Count Hoyos there states that Austria must partition Serbia. Count Berchtold and Count Tisza commented on this statement by saying it was the expression of Count Hoyos's personal views and explicitly dissociated themselves from it; they did not, however, enter further into their territorial plans.

For the diplomatic handling of this conflict with Serbia it would not be unimportant to know from the first what views the Austro-Hungarian statesmen have about the future shape of Serbia, since this question will have a decisive influence on the attitude of Italy and on the public opinion and attitude of England.

That the plans of the statesmen of the Danubian Monarchy may be influenced and modified by the course of events is doubtless to be regarded as inevitable, but it should be possible to assume that the Vienna Cabinet has already formed a general picture of the aims it intends to pursue also in the territorial question. Will Your Excellency be so good as to attempt to elicit an explanation on this point in conversation with Count Berchtold, while avoiding giving the impression that we had any wish to stand as a hindrance in the way of Austrian action or to prescribe definite limits or aims for it. It would merely be useful to us to gain some idea of what direction it is to take.[1]

Here it is necessary to read between the lines. The first sentences sound as if the German leaders were concerned about the impression that might be created in Italy and England by Austria's plan of annexing Serbian territory and that they were anxious to restrain her on this point. But it soon becomes apparent that Tschirschky is being advised not to give Vienna the impression that Germany meant *'to stand as a hindrance in the way of Austrian action or to prescribe definite limits or aims for it'*. To give such advice to an Ambassador of Tschirschky's temperament was to tempt him to invite Berchtold to cut off a fat slice of Serbia for himself. And in any case Jagow's instructions indirectly but clearly laid down the principle that Austria might do as she pleased, even to the point of carrying out the plan announced by Hoyos on 5 July, without meeting any objections from Germany. And if Germany raised no objections, why then—Jagow seemed to ask—was Austria so loth to destroy and partition Serbia? So much concern did he feel that on 21 July he reverted to the question in conversation with Szögyény. The latter's account, written on the same day, ends:

In conclusion I think I must again emphasize that the Secretary of State gave me clearly to understand that Germany will unquestionably back us un-

[1] DD. I, 61.

conditionally and with her whole strength but that for this very reason it is a vital interest of the German Government to be informed in good time 'whither our way leads us', especially whether we contemplate merely a provisional occupation of Serbian territory, or whether, as Count Hoyos foreshadowed in his last conversation with the Imperial Chancellor, we purpose a partition of Serbia as *ultima ratio*.[1]

What else was this harping on Hoyos's plan than a way of telling Vienna to adopt it?

It is in the light of such documents that Berchtold's line of conduct must be viewed. There can be no doubt that his fear was of being regarded by Berlin as too weak and yielding. Thus when on 14 July he and Tisza agreed to postpone the sending of the ultimatum from the 16th or 18th July to the 25th when Poincaré would have left St. Petersburg, his great concern was with the impression that the postponement would produce at Berlin. He summoned Tschirschky, whose account of the interview, telegraphed that same evening, ends:

Count Berchtold, explicitly and repeatedly begged me, as did Count Tisza also, not to let my Government be in any doubt that no other reason than the presence of Poincaré in St. Petersburg causes the postponement of the handing of the note to Belgrade and that Berlin may be quite sure that *there is no question of hesitancy or indecision*.

The Minister said in conclusion that after the final drafting of the text on Sunday he will without delay communicate it confidentially to the Imperial German Government before submitting the note to his Emperor.[2]

The words in italics are those underlined by the Kaiser who was annoyed by the postponement and took note of these assurances that Vienna really meant business, assurances given because Vienna felt watched over and under suspicion. It was to placate this German distrust that Berchtold promised Tschirschky to send the text of the ultimatum to Berlin before submitting it to Francis Joseph. On learning from Szögyény on 15 July of Jagow's disapproval of the postponement, he let him know on the 17th that the delay would be shortened by two days so that the note would go off in the afternoon of the 23rd, i.e. before Poincaré's departure, on the calculation 'that the President would already have gone on board ship by the time the Belgrade *démarche* became known in St. Petersburg'.[3] And at the Council of Ministers of 19 July he explained, as has been noted above, that it could not be postponed, because Berlin 'was beginning to feel edgy.' And this was so much the case that on the 19th Jagow was anxiously telegraphing Tschirschky asking for a copy of the promised document and on the 20th repeated the request.[4] Tschirschky replied that he would receive and transmit it on the evening of the 21st. How was it

---

[1] Oe-U. VIII, 10448.   [2] DD. I, 50.   [3] DD. I, 65.   [4] DD. I, 77, 83.

then that Berchtold failed to keep his promise of sending it on the 19th, and why did he from Ischl telegraph to Macchio to transmit it only on the 22nd under the pretext that changes had still to be made in the text?

3. The belated communication of the ultimatum to the Wilhelmstrasse; the implausible statements of Jagow and Bethmann Hollweg.

The general tendency is to believe that Berchtold acted thus for fear that Germany might ask for a softening of the wording and substance of the note. How could he fear such a thing, when all that reached him from Berlin was pressure not to lose time in taking stern measures and when the German Ambassador, following out the instructions so concordant with his own views,

avoided giving the impression that we had any wish to stand as a hindrance in the way of Austrian action or to prescribe definite limits or aims for it?

Logic compels one to come to the opposite conclusion, namely that Berchtold feared pressure might come from Berlin to make stiffer demands, to go to still greater lengths and that he therefore sought to confront the German ally with a *fait accompli*.[1] This conclusion finds support in the behaviour of the Wilhelmstrasse in the days that followed up to the moment when fear of English intervention and of Italian neutrality caused her to go into reverse.

The line taken by the German Government is shown beyond all possibility of doubt by the circular instructions sent to the German Ambassadors in St. Petersburg, Paris and London on 21 July, before the contents were known of the Austrian ultimatum which was to go off to Belgrade only on the afternoon of the 23rd. The Ambassadors were told in advance: 'The action and the demands of the Austro-Hungarian Government can only be regarded as fair and moderate.'[2] And they were instructed

to give emphatic expression to the view that the present question is purely a matter for settlement between Austria-Hungary and Serbia and that the earnest endeavour of the Powers must be to limit it to those directly concerned. We anxiously desire the localization of the conflict because any

---

[1] Among those who hold the general opinion is Fay who asserts that 'Berchtold, after 14 July, having been promised German support and having converted Tisza, no longer showed the same consideration for Germany, and gave little heed to her advice and requests' (II, p. 255). But after the understanding with Tisza on 14 July, Berchtold was as open as usual with Tschirschky, promising to give him the text of the ultimatum before submitting it to Frances Joseph. The change in him came later. Was it not perhaps brought about by what Tschirschky said to him on the 17th on Jagow's instructions? The question is legitimate. In any case it is well to note that, in order not to raise it, Fay entirely omits the relevant passage from Jagow's instructions to Tschirschky of 17 July.

[2] DD. I, 100.

intervention by another Power might in consequence of the various alliances bring incalculable consequences in its train.

The 21st was the very day of the reception at St. Petersburg at which Poincaré warned the Austrian Ambassador:

Serbia has some very warm friends in the Russian people. And Russia has an ally, France. There are plenty of complications to be feared![1]

And the Wilhelmstrasse had still not seen the text of the Austrian note! So imprudent was this circular letter that, when it was published in the German *White Book* in 1914, the Chancellor dated it 23 July,[2] while in reality it was sent on the 21st to St. Petersburg, Paris and London.

Only on the evening of 22 July did the Wilhelmstrasse at last receive a copy of the ultimatum. It came about in the following way. We know that Szögyény received a copy of it on 20 July,[3] and on the 21st begged Berchtold for permission to communicate it at once to the Berlin Government before it went to the other Powers.[4] Berchtold answered on the 22nd that formally Berlin should be given communication of the ultimatum on the same footing as the other Powers but that Tschirschky had confidentially been given a copy on the 21st so that it was doubtless by the 22nd in the hands of the German Government.[5] In fact Forgach, not knowing of Berchtold's order to Macchio of the 21st not to let Tschirschky have the note before the 22nd, had given it to him on the 21st. But Tschirschky (possibly in order not to betray the German code to Austria) instead of telegraphing it, sent it by post to Berlin where it was received on the 22nd at 8 p.m. But before that hour Szögyény, knowing that Tschirschky was already in possession of it, thought himself authorized to communicate it and Jagow was in the act of perusing it when Tschirschky's copy arrived. What Jagow's impressions were we learn from his book *Ursachen und Ausbruch des Weltkrieges*:

After reading through the lengthy text I at once gave my opinion to the Ambassador that its content seemed to me to be pretty stiff and going beyond its purpose. Count Szögyény replied that it was too late to do anything about it, for the ultimatum had already gone off to Belgrade and was to be handed over next morning and published at the same time in the official Viennese *Telegraph*. I expressed my pained surprise to the Ambassador that the decisions of his Government had been communicated to us so tardily that we were deprived of the possibility of giving our views on it. The Chancellor, too, to whom I at once submitted the text of the ultimatum, was of the opinion that it was too harsh.[6]

---

[1] Paléologue, I, p. 19. See p. 193.   [2] CDD., p. 424.   [3] Oe-U. VIII, 10445.
[4] Oe-U. VIII, 10448.   [5] Oe-U. VIII, 10478.
[6] Gottlieb von Jagow, *Ursachen und Ausbruch des Weltkrieges* (Berlin, 1919), p. 110.

Although Bethmann Hollweg[1] also states that Jagow reported to him the protest made to Szögyény and the latter's reply, it is not easy to believe that Jagow actually made it. He was not good at telling the truth when he thought his country's interests demanded its suppression. He claims to have complained to Szögyény of having been deprived of the possibility of passing an opinion on the Austrian Government's decisions. He can hardly have done so in view of the fact that, when asked by Berchtold for advice on the 10th, he had on the 11th replied: 'As to the formulation of the demands on Serbia we can take no position, as this is a matter for Austria.'[2] Even when pressing for a copy of the ultimatum, Jagow had not motivated this by the need for discussions on the text between Berlin and Vienna. All he had said was that it would guide him in his dealings with the other Powers and in giving directions to the press. We have also seen that he had no intention of standing as an obstacle in the way of Austrian action. In short: a free hand, no discussions about what was to be done.

But even assuming, purely for the sake of argument, that when the ultimatum was read at the Wilhelmstrasse, the opinion was that it went beyond the limits, would there have been no time left for discussions on it? Jagow says there would not, because Szögyény told him the ultimatum was to be presented the following day. But how could Szögyény have told such a lie to Jagow who perfectly well knew that the handing over was not to take place till the 23rd at 5 p.m.? So well did he know this that on the morning of the 22nd, i.e. some hours before receiving the copy of the ultimatum, he had telegraphed to Vienna that if the Austrian *démarche* at Belgrade were made at 5 p.m. on the 23rd, it might become known at St. Petersburg before Poincaré left there[3] because of the difference of Central European time. Berchtold had replied, thanking and saying that the handing over would be put off until 6 p.m.[4] Not that a single day would have sufficed for discussions on such a question between the two allies. But if Germany had really thought that to leave the ultimatum as it was would be to risk bringing on a European war, which she did not desire, she had the perfect right and duty to demand, and Vienna would have had the time to agree, that the Austrian Minister to Belgrade should be instructed by telegram to postpone the delivery of the note in order that changes should be made in it. But the fact is that the Wilhelmstrasse made no request for changes, it sent no telegram to Tschirschky saying that a bad impression had been produced in Berlin by the reading of the Austrian demands, and the terms used to Szögyény were such that he telegraphed to Vienna:

Herr von Jagow sends thanks for the communication and assures me that

[1] Bethmann, p. 139.   [2] DD. I, 31. See p. 260.   [3] DD. I, 112.   [4] DD. I, 127.

the German Government is entirely in agreement with the contents of the note.[1]

It would have been difficult for the Austrian Ambassador to express himself thus if Jagow had said the very opposite. And had Jagow done so, would he not surely have telegraphed to Tschirschky the objections he was making? Let him believe that who can! Here again, in the opinion of the present writer, the one who tells the truth is Szögyény and his truthfulness is demonstrated not only by the considerations just mentioned but by a scrutiny of Jagow's own statements. Did he or did he not know of the substance, if not the actual text, of the stiffest of the demands which Austria intended to make on Belgrade? Without the slightest doubt he did know. It was he who on 11 July had given Vienna the excellent advice to preface the note by documents on the Pan-Serb movement in justification of Austrian action before world opinion[2] (instead of which, Berchtold circulated the documents to the Powers some days later, when they had other things to think of). It was he who had bestirred himself to have the handing of the ultimatum delayed by one hour. He had been informed of its three stiffest demands already by Tschirschky's telegram of the 10th and letter of the 11th. Of all this no shadow of a doubt can exist. The German historian Lutz pertinently remarks that if after the war Bethmann, Jagow and Zimmermann all declared that they regarded the note as 'altogether too stiff', they ought to have let the Austrian Government know this and made an effort to have the handing of the note suspended, modifying instruction No. 100, i.e. the circular telegram sent by the Chancellor on 21 July to the Ambassadors at St. Petersburg, Paris and London. This instructed them to say to the Foreign Ministers of the Triple *Entente* that if the Austro-Hungarian Government

does not mean definitely to renounce its position as a Great Power, it cannot do otherwise than press its demands with the Serbian Government and if need be enforce the same by appeal to military measures, in regard to which the choice of means must be left with it,[3]

and going on to state that Germany hoped for a localization of the conflict

because any intervention by another Power might in consequence of the various alliances bring incalculable consequences in its train.

Lutz points out: 'Nothing is known of any German criticism of Vienna' and that

Vienna it is true, would by that time hardly have consented to any change; the 'free hand' so lightheartedly granted, gave it the right to refuse. But

---

[1] Oe-U. VIII, 10582.   [2] DD. I, 31.   [3] DD. I, 100; CDD., p. 424.

representations against the note which was seen to be too stiff would have had a moderating effect on Vienna later on. Worse than this omission was the fact that Berlin made no change in the Instruction No. 100. . . . Taking all this with what has preceded, the claim of the three German statesmen to have criticized the note *at once* as too stiff does not seem altogether convincing so far as concerns the period before 24 July.[1]

4. The efforts of those directing German policy to wear a face of innocence.

What still has to be seen is why Jagow and Bethmann Hollweg wanted to make believe the contrary. There can be only one reason and it is revealed not by a chain of reasoning but by the documents. It had been agreed beforehand that, when the ultimatum was presented, Germany was to pretend not to have had previous knowledge of what it contained. This was in order that she might proclaim her innocence and disclaim all responsibility for causing a European war. On 22 July, in the expectation that Serbia would not agree to all the demands and that, therefore, following orders, the Austrian Minister at Belgrade would hastily take his departure, Macchio was concerned about how to deliver the declaration of war on Serbia which was to follow. He asked Tschirschky whether the German Minister at Belgrade could not undertake to do this.[2] Jagow answered in the negative alleging that if the German Legation were to do so, the public, not familiar with diplomatic usage, would gain the impression that 'we had hounded Austria-Hungary into the war'.[3]

Here we have the consideration which was uppermost in the minds of the German rulers and caused them to feign ignorance of the Austrian note and to pretend afterwards, when the war had broken out, that they thought it too stiff but had not the time to get it modified. And it is solely in order to keep up this fiction that they declined to participate in drafting the note, as if it were no concern of theirs.

In short all the acts and all the rôles in the tragedy were settled in advance in Berlin. This is clearly shown in a document which has attracted much attention on account of the light it throws on German war guilt. On 18 July, Schoen, the Counsellor at the Bavarian Legation in Berlin, sent to Munich a detailed telegram reporting what he had been

[1] Lutz, pp. 75-6.
[2] DD. I, 138.
[3] DD. I, 142.—On 5 February 1915 in a conversation with Theodor Wolff, the editor of the *Berliner Tageblatt*, Bethmann Hollweg said: 'We were unacquainted with the terms of the Note. I deliberately avoided acquaintance with its contents. I did not want to make any amendments in it—if one makes amendments it always proves afterwards that the mistake that was made was one's own, and I had no desire for that. We simply felt that Austria's hand must be strengthened, that at the moment when at last she was determined to act with firmness she must not be left in the lurch' (Theodor Wolff, *The Eve of 1914*, London, 1935, p. 620).

told by Zimmermann, Jagow's Under Secretary of State. It is worth quoting the relevant passage almost in full:

As Zimmermann told me, the note, as far as at present known, contains the following demands:

i. The issue by the King of Serbia of a proclamation to the effect that the Serbian Government is in no way associated with the Pan-Serb movement and disapproves of it.

ii. The opening of judicial proceedings against the accomplices of the Sarajevo murder and participation of an Austrian official in these proceedings.

iii. Measures against all involved in the Pan-Serb movement.

For the acceptance of these demands a time limit of 48 hours is said to have been given. That Serbia čannot comply with demands incompatible with her dignity as an independent state is self evident. The consequence therefore is no doubt war.

Here with us it is absolutely agreed that Austria is to use the favourable moment even at the risk of further complications. Whether Vienna will really pull herself together and act still seems rather doubtful to Herr von Jagow and Herr von Zimmermann. The Under Secretary of State expressed the view that owing to her indecision and vacillation, Austria-Hungary has now succeeded Turkey as the sick man of Europe, with Russians, Italians, Roumanians, Serbs and Montenegrins waiting for her to be carved up among them. A strong and successful intervention against Serbia would lead Austrians and Hungarians to feel themselves once more a powerful state. It would revive the flagging economic life and repress the aspirations of the foreign elements for years to come. The indignation felt to-day in the whole Monarchy over the outrage will no doubt make it possible for even the Slav troops to be depended on. In a few years, as General Conrad von Hötzendorf himself admits, the further activity of Slav propaganda will make this no longer the case. . . . How the other Powers will take up position to an armed conflict between Austria and Serbia will, it is thought here, mainly depend on whether Austria contents herself with a chastisement of Serbia or demands territorial compensation for herself. In the former case it may be possible to localize the war, in the latter major complications would probably be inevitable.

In the interests of a localization of the war, the heads of the Imperial Government will, immediately after the delivery of the Austrian note at Belgrade, take diplomatic steps with the Great Powers. They will point to the fact that the Kaiser is away on his northern cruise and the Chief of the General Staff and the Prussian War Minister are absent on leave as proof that Germany has been no less taken by surprise by the Austrian action than the other Powers. . . . They will represent that it will be in the common interest of all monarchical states if the 'Belgrade nest of anarchists' is cleared out and will try to bring the Powers round to the view that the settlement between Austria and Serbia concerns these two states. There will be no mobilization of German troops and our military authorities will persuade Austria not to mobilize her whole army, in particular not the troops in Galicia, in order not to produce a Russian counter-mobilization which would force us and France to take corresponding measures and thus bring about a European war.[1]

Indeed, this is precisely what happened. Schoen's telegram fully and accurately defines the rôle played by Germany up to the sending of the ultimatum to Serbia and immediately after as far as the moment when it dawned on the Wilhelmstrasse that it had made a mistake in its basic calculation that, if the worst came to the worst and France and Russia came into the war, England could be counted on to remain neutral and Italy to enter the war with her allies.

It was an ill-contrived rôle. How could the other chancelleries be expected to believe that Austria was venturing on this enterprise without a full understanding with Germany? The English Government and the interim French Government were, it is true, slow in finding their bearings as was also a considerable section of the European press. But when the Austro-German manoeuvre became apparent and it transpired that Berlin was anything but ignorant of Austrian designs and, indeed, held all the threads, then such an avalanche of general indignation and mistrust descended on the German rulers that they were totally discredited and all attempts to save the peace were vain.

5. The Serbian Government's inaction after the Sarajevo outrage.

If the disappearance of the Archduke produced a feeling of relief in Italy and other countries, it certainly did not give rise to demonstrations of grief in Serbia. The Austrian Chargé d'Affaires at Belgrade telegraphed on 29 June: 'The people are said (by eyewitnesses) to have hugged one another for joy'.[2] The non-Government press mirrored the same feeling and employed violent and provocative language about Austria which played into Berchtold's hands. In the *dossier* circulated to the Powers after the ultimatum he collected a good number of specimens of this language. *Piemont*, for example, the organ of the *Black Hand*, described Princip as a 'young martyr'. The *Odjek* remarked that Francis Ferdinand's visit 'could not but arouse brutal feelings of resistance, hatred and revenge'. The *Balkan* demanded that Austria 'should be put under international control'.[3] Such utterances, fully reproduced in the Viennese press, not only inflamed Austro-Hungarian public opinion and enraged Tisza, but aroused censure in the diplomatic documents of the time and inspired severe comment in the English and Italian press.

The German Minister to Belgrade wrote to the Chancellor on 30 June:

It was at once instinctively felt here that the responsibility for the bloody

---

[1] DD. IV, pp. 126–8.   [2] Oe-U. VIII, 9943.
[3] Austro-Hungarian *Red Book*, 19; Mach, pp. 135–6; CDD., pp. 494–5.

deed committed by Serbs falls not only on the brethren in Bosnia but on the whole Slav world.

If the Serbian Government dissociated itself from the perpetrators by issuing a communiqué severely condemning the crime and if the *Samouprava* published a semi-official article showing that it came as a blow to Serbia at the very moment when highly important negotiations with the Monarchy were approaching a settlement and when Serbia, exhausted by ceaseless agitation, needed above all a period of peace and quiet, the general feeling was very different.

To say nothing of the tactless comparisons, such as with William Tell's heroic deed and that of the Serb Miloš Obilić who assassinated Sultan Bajasid on the Kosovo Polye and is still celebrated as a national hero, it is pointed out how thoughtless it was to hold manoeuvres in fanaticized Bosnia at the very moment when the St. Vitus day festival filled impressionable minds anew with patriotic fervour. A considerable section of the Serbian press re-echoes this mood and speaks of the provocation to Serbian patriotism by the holding of the manoeuvres. These tactics have of course no other aim than to parry accusations which might be raised by Austro-Hungarian public opinion against the Pan-Serb agitation methodically carried on in Serbia.[1]

Descos, the French Minister at Belgrade wrote on 1 July to Viviani:

The Serbian crowd is quiet and intent; it does not let itself be surprised by events and accepts them, whatever they are, with apparent indifference. . . . The press shows no regret for what has happened; only the *Samouprava* slightly hints at a feeling of humiliation, with the regret that the crime should have been committed at the moment when so many political and economic questions raised by the Balkan wars seemed to be on the way to settlement between Austria and Serbia. The delegates of the Austrian and Hungarian Governments who had come to negotiate the railway agreement in fact left Belgrade on the morrow of the outrage. . . . For the first time for six years Serbism finds itself in the wrong: escaping from the wise direction of M. Pašić, it has let itself be dragged by the military party towards new methods and aims, threatening to compromise the uninterrupted success of recent years. The *Politika* insists that the outrage can only be the deed of isolated elements; the *Pravda* imagines a plot set afoot as the vengeance of another Archduke on Francis Ferdinand. But the actual circumstances of the crime betray the existence of a nationalist organization of which it is easy to suppose the aims. The *Pester Lloyd* notes that since the assassination of King Alexander and Queen Draga the method of the conspiring officers has gained in technique and daring. The interests of the present situation prevent the Russian Minister from relaxing his guidance of the Crown Prince and the press draws attention to the frequency of their interviews. The heedless hand of the Sarajevo schoolboy doubtless closes a period in the history of Jugoslavism. English arbitration, pontifical mediation, all the artifices

[1] DD. I, 10.

accumulated by the Konopischt and Constantza meetings have at one blow become a dead letter. The actual facts of the outrage and the hunting down of Serbs in the streets of Sarajevo and Agram betray the strength of extremist ideas and the difficulties of compromise.[1]

It is understandable that the Serbs did not view with favour the presence in Belgrade of a French Minister who was so outspoken, knew and disapproved of the activities of the. *Black Hand,* and had a clear perception of the difficulties and .weaknesses of the Serbian Government. As early as 1 July 1914 Vesnić the Serbian Minister at Paris, said to Abel Ferry, the Under Secretary of State for Foreign Affairs, that the Serbian Government would like Descos to be replaced by Boppe.[2] A footnote to this document runs:

This indication gives rise to the thought that from that moment M. Descos's state of health caused it to be expected that he would soon resign.

But the *French Diplomatic Documents* of 1 July to 14 July bring five other long reports from this diligent and clear-sighted representative of France, which reveal no trace of impaired health nor the slightest hint of his resignation. The last of these reports bears the date 14 July and it is not known what reports, if any, he may after then have sent from Belgrade. Nor is it known whether and how the French Government was informed from Belgrade of the delivery of the Austrian ultimatum to Serbia. In any case Paris acceded to the Serbian request and replaced Descos by Boppe who arrived in Belgrade on the morning of 25 July.[3]

On 6 July the German Minister at Belgrade sent Berlin a long report on the Pan-Serb revolutionary agitation of the *Narodna Obrana* ending as follows:

However much the Serbian Government may show horror and indignation at the Sarajevo murder, however it may protest innocence and point out how senseless and pointless the crime is and how it has damaged the Serb cause more than it has furthered it, one thing it cannot deny. It, itself, has created the atmosphere in which alone such explosions of blind fanaticism are possible. In its land and under the eyes of its authorities the elements have been reared who have disgraced Serbia before the whole civilized world and reduced it again to the level of the atrocious regicide of 1903.[4]

The Kaiser underlined various phrases of this report annotating them as 'Very good'.

It is highly probable that the Serbian Prime Minister Pašić, who had weathered the storms of 1912–13 and well understood Austrian ways of thinking, cherished no illusions about the probable consequences of the Sarajevo crime. It is told of him that after he had heard the news he remarked to his first visitor: 'It is very bad. It will mean war' and retired

---

[1] DF. 3. X, 469.   [2] DF. 3. X, 466.   [3] DF. 3. XI, note to 62.   [4] DD. I, 19a.

to bed to give undisturbed thought to the problem.[1] He issued an order closing all places of entertainment, including cafés, and stopped all ceremonies in honour of the Vidovdan. He caused the *Samouprava* to publish a leading article expressing deep regret for this sad event detrimental to the interests of Serbia who is now convinced that it is to her interest to be on friendly terms with Austria-Hungary.[2] He sent to Vienna the condolences of the Serbian Government which

on their part will certainly most loyally do everything to prove that they will not tolerate within their territory the fostering of any agitation or illegal proceedings calculated to disturb our already delicate relations with Austria-Hungary.[3]

Wise moves all of them but not enough. What Serbia ought to have done to prove her innocence and render it more difficult for Austria to hold her responsible for the crime was to open a judicial inquiry into the possible complicity of Serbian subjects and take the necessary measures in that event. This was the advice given the Serbian Government by Zimmermann, the German Under Secretary for Foreign Affairs on 30 June, before Germany decided to back Austrian action and while she still wished for a peaceful settlement.

At the Foreign Ministry here—wrote Lerchenfeld, the Bavarian Minister in Berlin, to his Government at Munich—it is hoped that Serbia will make every effort to bring to account those guilty of the conspiracy. Zimmermann has in the first instance seriously drawn the attention of the Serbian Chargé d'Affaires to the consequences which might follow a failure of Serbia in this respect and has urged the Russian Ambassador to induce his Government to speak in a similar way at Belgrade.[4]

But Pašić turned a deaf ear. And when on 30 June the Austrian Chargé d'Affaires at Belgrade called·at the Foreign Ministry and asked unofficially whether the Government did not consider it advisable to hold an investigation, Gruić replied that 'nothing had been done so far and the matter did not concern the Serbian Government'. High words were spoken on both sides.[5] Gruić's answer shows that the Government had no intention of taking the initiative in investigating what complicity existed on Serbian territory. They would leave it to Austria to bring forward proofs and would then consider what steps to take. In regard to the deplorable behaviour of the Serbian press, Pašić stated in a circular of 14 July to all Serbian Legations that as it was 'absolutely free' the Government possessed no 'means, constitutional or legal', for controlling it.[6]

---

[1] H. F. Armstrong, *Three days in Belgrade* in *Foreign Affairs* (N.Y. January 1927), V, p. 267.
[2] BD. XI, 27, 35.   [3] LAS. 5 ; CDD., p. 371.   [4] Dirr, p. 118.
[5] BD. XI, 27; DD. I, 12; Oe-U. VIII, 9950.
[6] LAS. 20 ; CDD., p. 379.

6. *Pašić's memorandum to the Great Powers.*

This was hardly the way to avert or parry a dangerous move on the part of Austria, nor does it seem to have been the result of promptings from Russia or from Hartwig, the Russian Minister at Belgrade. The latter was a fanatical Pan-Slav who in the past, by no means always following instructions, had continually egged Serbia on to resist Austria and fanned the flames of Slav irredentism. However, on hearing of the Sarajevo crime, he is reported to have been horrified and to have exclaimed: 'For Heaven's sake! Let us hope that it is not a Serb.'[1] This is easily explained. Hartwig knew very well the condition of Serbia and that, exhausted by the wars of 1912–13, she was in no condition to withstand an armed attack which it also suited Russia to defer. On 7 July Sazonov had telegraphed Hartwig to enjoin on the Serbian Government extreme caution in all questions liable to intensify the anti-Serb feeling in Austria and create a dangerous situation.

On this account we think it would be desirable to let the negotiations wait relating to a *rapprochement* between Serbia and Montenegro, they having attracted the attention of the Austro-Hungarian and even of the German Government.[2]

Hartwig replied on the 9th that Pašić had broken off conversations with Cetinje and had told him that the Serbian Government

was fully conscious of the need to display caution at the present disturbed juncture and to show no reaction to the disgraceful provocation from Austria. He himself had severely condemned the foul deed of Sarajevo and had at once answered the request of the Austro-Hungarian Legation here to set a watch on the behaviour of suspicious elements previously banished from Bosnia and Croatia.[3]

If Pašić had indeed acted thus, he would not have done so except with the consent of Hartwig. But there is no evidence either that Austria at that time had formulated the demand or that the Serbian Government had agreed to it. All the evidence points in fact to the contrary.

On 8 July, when the new German Military Attaché presented his credentials, Pašić expressed to the German Minister Griesinger his horror and indignation at the crime and

affirmed that a civilized Government could not possibly be held responsible for the excesses of callow and overwrought lads. . . . The surveillance of nationalistic associations and their contacts at home and in foreign countries was a most difficult task for the Serbian Government; the liberal, democratic constitution of the country, particularly in the field of association and press, afforded the Government practically no hold, and all attempts to widen the powers of the Government and enable it to take vigorous measures had

---

[1] DD. I, 10; Gooss, p. 72.   *Int. Bez.* i. IV, 112.   [3] *Int. Bez.* i. IV, 148.

foundered on the resistance of the Skupština. As far as was in his power within existing legislation he would exercise strict control over the nationalistic organizations and expel all elements seeking a hiding place here.

To two of these statements the Kaiser's marginal comment was: 'Bunkum' and his footnote was: 'Blah'.[1] On 9 July the French Minister Descos reported to Paris:

Serbian opinion has furiously broken loose against the demonstrations to which in all the Southern Slav lands of Austria-Hungary the Sarajevo outrage has given rise: it no doubt rightly sees in them the hand of the Imperial and Royal authorities, desirous of checking the Serb elements. If the demonstrations have been brief and few in Croatia and Dalmatia where the position of Serbism is weak, they have been violent and widespread in Bosnia-Herzegovina which is its main stronghold. The Sarajevo outrage seems to have given rise there, if not to a racial war, since the three elements of the population are equally Jugoslav, at least to a war of religion, setting the musulman and catholic majority against the orthodox . . . The Serbian press follows with anxiety the Sarajevo preliminary inquiry. . . . The crimes organized by secret societies show a finesse beyond the mediocre powers of the literary bureau of the Ballplatz and, to put a finger on the activities of the *Black Hand* and the *Narodna Obrana* in the Sarajevo outrage, more wide-awake methods would be needful. . . . In the necessary investigations Austro-Hungarian policy will find its best helpers in the neighbouring nationalities, who are *ipso facto* enemies of Serbism, i.e. the Croats, Hungarians and Bulgars, the latter especially having a most exact knowledge of Serbian organizations. The announcement that Austro-Hungarian diplomacy is planning a *démarche* with the Royal Government following the close of the Sarajevo preliminary inquiry in order to secure the pursuit of the criminals shown to be on Serbian territory greatly disquiets the Government and public opinion.[2]

But despite this anxiety Pašić did little or nothing to avert the Austrian *démarche*, merely instructing all Serbian representatives to proclaim the Belgrade Government's innocence and good intentions. On 17 July the *Leipziger Neueste Nachrichten* published statements by Pašić made to its Belgrade correspondent on 12 July:

In answer to a question on the Sarajevo outrage, the Prime Minister expressed himself in severe terms about it but did not allow it to be laid at the door of the Serbian Government and people. 'We do not interfere in the internal affairs of Austria-Hungary, but we ought after all to be left in peace. We have enough to do with our own internal problems without occupying ourselves with those who call themselves Serbs outside the Kingdom. We are so accustomed to see our fellow countrymen oppressed and hated in Hungary that we are no longer perturbed by it. We take no part in plots but we know that time works in our favour.'[3]

---

[1] DD. I, 32.   [2] DF. 3. X, 488.   [3] DF. 3. X, 548.

The interview was disavowed by Pašić, but few attached any importance to the Serbian Premier's disavowals. On 19 July he telegraphed to the diplomatic representatives of Serbia to say that

during the whole of this period, from the date of the perpetration of the outrage until to-day, not once did the Austro-Hungarian Government apply to the Serbian Government for their assistance in this matter.[1]

And on 20 July, before going on an electioneering tour, he instructed the Serbian Ministers to the Great Powers to present a *note verbale* stating that immediately after the Sarajevo outrage the Austro-Hungarian press had started putting the blame on Serbia and the Pan-Serb idea.

The Royal Government immediately declared its readiness to take judicial proceedings against any Serbian subject against whom there were proofs of complicity in the Sarajevo crime.

The Austro-Hungarian Government up to the present has made no requests to the Royal Government for investigation and judicial proceedings in respect of any persons. Only details of the whereabouts of certain students expelled from the priests' seminary at Paverac were asked for and immediately furnished.

Public opinion in Austria-Hungary and Europe is still being excited against Serbia by the press campaign, and how intense the excitement is appears from the questions of some Hungarian party leaders in the Hungarian parliament and the replies of the Hungarian Premier. The debates show that the Monarchy intends to undertake *démarches* with the Royal Government—in what sense and in what form is not indicated. . . . The Royal Government fears lest the excited public opinion in Austria-Hungary might offer an occasion for the Austro-Hungarian Government to take a step for the purpose of inflicting a humiliation on Serbia, which Serbia could not accept.

After expressing readiness to meet any Austro-Hungarian requests in regard to judicial proceedings against accomplices 'if there should be any', the note went on to state:

The Royal Government would be unable to fulfil only such demands as any other state mindful of its dignity and independence could not fulfil

and ended by asking the German Government, 'if occasion offered', to use its influence towards conciliation.[2]

7. *Hartwig's sudden death at the Austrian Legation in Belgrade.*

A week earlier the powerful influence of the Russian Minister at Belgrade had come to an end and the Serbian Government appeared to have lost all sense of direction.

On 10 July, hearing that the Austrian Minister Giesl had that day returned to his post at Belgrade, Hartwig went to call on him the same

---

[1] LAS. 30, in CDD., p. 385.   [2] DD. I, 86.

evening at 9 p.m. After expressing 'his personal and sincere condolences for the atrocious outrage', he cleared up false rumours that he had had a bridge party on the evening of the outrage and had failed to fly the Legation flag at half-mast during the memorial service for the Archduke. He then went on to speak of his heart trouble which made it urgent for him to go to Bad Nauheim. He had only put off his journey until after the King of Serbia's birthday on 12 July. He next asked what would be the attitude of the Austrian Government towards Serbia in the matter of the assassination and was visibly reassured by Giesl's soothing reply. Suddenly at about 9.20 p.m. without a sound he collapsed and slid unconscious from the divan to the carpet. A doctor was on the scene in a few minutes but Hartwig was already dead, death being due to angina pectoris from which he had suffered for years.[1] Giesl had at once sent Hartwig's waiting carriage to fetch his daughter Ludmilla, and Baroness Giesl tried to proffer words of sympathy, but the girl brusquely replied that 'Austrian' words did not interest her. Her manner was cold and hostile and she made a quick inspection of the room, sniffing at the Eau de Cologne bottle standing on a piece of furniture, rummaging about in some large Japanese vases and asking whether her father had partaken of anything at the Austrian Legation. Fortunately he had not and had only smoked some Russian cigarettes which he had brought with him. Giesl gave Ludmilla the ends of two cigarettes which she carefully put in her purse. Rumours at once arose that Hartwig had not died a natural death and that he had been poisoned by Giesl. A Serbian journal called Baron and Baroness Giesl 'modern Borgias'. Giesl himself narrates that a few days later when at the barber's he heard one customer say to another:

Austria sends us strange ambassadors. First we had an imbecile [Forgach] and now we have an assassin. Giesl has brought an electric chair from Vienna which causes the immediate death of anyone who sits down on it and leaves not the slightest trace.[2]

A friend of Hartwig's, General Artamonov, informed the present writer that Hartwig's death did not come as a surprise to him.

His heart was in a very bad state, he was terribly stout and suffered from asthma. Every year after the King's birthday, which fell on St. Peter's day, he used to go to Bad Nauheim and leave it with his weight reduced by ten kilograms.

Hartwig's last letter reached Artamonov after the news of his death, and spoke of the general excitement in Belgrade, Pašić's absence on an electioneering tour and his own impending journey to Nauheim on

---

[1] Oe-U. VIII, 10170, 10193.

[2] DF. 3. X, 499; Giesl, pp. 259–61; certain details were given orally to Dr. Magrini by Giesl. [Tr.]

16 or 17 July. Less than an hour after his death a Serbian police official appeared at the Austrian Legation to make investigations, but Giesl claimed his right of extra-territoriality and refused him entry. The Belgrade *Politika* commented that Hartwig very rarely paid calls and preferred to receive visitors at his own house. What could have taken him to the Austrian Legation at 9 p.m.? The *Politika* put it down to his wish to clear up the various hostile rumours as soon as possible. The *Pravda* was sure he was acting on orders from St. Petersburg. Descos who quotes these theories thinks that Hartwig may have been anxious not to lose touch with the Austrian Legation as that would have been playing into the hands of Pašić, or that he may have felt the urgency of scotching rumours so damaging to the representative of the Tsar.[1] The Hungarian *Pester Lloyd* pointed out that Hartwig died on Austrian soil

at the moment when the representative of our Monarchy was telling him about the attitude that Austria-Hungary proposes to take towards Pan-Serb propaganda. Perhaps in dying he asked himself the anguishing question: would the Pan-Serb idea, of which he was the champion, triumph in the crisis or would it suffer lamentable collapse?

Descos gave it as his own opinion that:

The consequences of M. de Hartwig's death seem infinitely more serious for Serbism than the disappearance of the Archduke can be for the Dual Monarchy.

His death meant that

the force is spent which for more than two years dragged Serbia into unknown paths. Prince Alexander is only a passive tool in the hands of a reckless military party. Deprived of the needed fulcrum, M. Pašić was losing the balance he was trying to maintain, finding himself hemmed in between the demands of the Austrian Legation and the injunctions of the *Black Hand*. . . . Hartwig has died at the very moment when his indomitable will had just won for him the realization of his ambitions by imposing on Serbism his absolute authority and on Europe the Serbian question in the violent form dear to his heart.[2]

Belgrade gave Hartwig a magnificent funeral. The Municipal Council named a street after him and a committee was formed to set up a statue to him. In reporting these facts to Paris on 14 July Descos gives his own estimate of his late colleague:

M. de Hartwig's death is an irreparable loss for Serbia. From his long service in the Asiatic Department, he had derived an incomparable knowledge of Balkan affairs, the way they worked and the Russian traditions. He

---

[1] DF. 3. X, 449.   [2] DF. 3. X, 499.

was able, energetic and implacable. Led by temperament and circumstances into the ways of revolt, he had a success in Belgrade which general conditions in Teheran had not allowed him to achieve and he used the Serb cause as a weapon in his struggle against his own Government. With the support of conservative and orthodox circles at St. Petersburg he withstood M. Sazonov, about whom he openly expressed himself in the most contemptuous terms and he dragged Russian diplomacy towards the Balkan evolution of the last two years which he had the merit of conceiving and carrying out. During the five years that he lived at Belgrade he never went to St. Petersburg except on the occasion of King Peter's brief visit there and when, last winter, he asked permission to go there during the visit of M. Pašić and Prince Alexander, it was relentlessly refused. M. Sazonov lost no time in replying affirmatively to the request of the Belgrade municipality that M. de Hartwig should be buried in Serbia, and on his tomb Serbian tributes took the place of the scanty tributes from Russia. Disregarded by his own people and without great means, he was a valuable and reliable weapon for the Serb cause: the arbitrator between the parties, the support of the Royal family, the protector of Serbia and Serbism as representative of Russia and champion of the Slav race. To this task which was in keeping with his Slavophil sentiments and flattering to his taste for power he brought knowledge and experience of outstanding maturity. He has died at the very moment when his developing personality became most necessary to Serbia if she was to hold her own against Austria in the Bosnian business and against Europe in the matter of Macedonia. . . . It is by no means sure that he would have been successful and it is highly probable that he had just raised problems too vast and too multiple for the weakness of Serbia.[1]

Even Giesl expresses the view that Hartwig's death at that moment was a misfortune. He says that in their talk that last evening Hartwig showed himself convinced that the Serbian Army was too severely weakened and that Russia was too unprepared for war. For these reasons he would have used his influence with St. Petersburg and Belgrade and

would certainly have managed to persuade the Serbian Government to agree to unconditional acceptance of all our demands. Of course he would have held out prospects of a full and successful settlement of accounts at a later date, the time for which would come when—round about 1916—the Tsarist army would have returned to full strength. Serbia must husband her forces till then. Had Hartwig been alive on the critical 25 July, the World War would not have broken out.[2]

Giesl may be exaggerating, but it is legitimate to believe that Hartwig would never have let Pašić sit with folded hands when the Austrian threat began visibly to outline itself, as it did during the week preceding the ultimatum.

[1] DF. 3. X, 511. [2] Giesl, p. 260.

8. *The first news in Belgrade of what Austria was planning; Pašić goes off on an electioneering campaign.*

The silence maintained by Austria was in itself an evil omen. On 15 July Dumaine, the French Ambassador to Vienna, discussed with the Serbian Minister Jovanović the possibility that Austria would ask the Belgrade Government to give guarantees against Pan-Serb agitation not only by a strict policing of the frontier but also by dissolving various nationalist associations scheduled as suspect.

In that case—replied Jovan Jovanović at once—it is the whole of Serbia that will have to be dissolved. Not one of us but cherishes the hope of a union of all Serbs! To the extent that, to get it, Milovanović formerly even resigned himself to the idea of bringing about the union under the Hapsburg sceptre! To it he would even have sacrificed the independence of our small kingdom. Austria-Hungary failed to understand; she heaped mistake upon mistake. The evil is now beyond remedy. However if, treating us with the respect due from one independent state to another, she asks us politely to assist her investigations and second her in her safety measures, we shall not refuse. But let her be regardful of our national dignity or she will find us ready to take up the fight.[1]

On 15 July the Serbian Minister at Vienna telegraphed Belgrade that he thought the Monarchy was about to take some action[2] and the Serbian Minister in London on the 17th advised his Government not to place any reliance on the ostensibly pacific statements of Austria-Hungary

as the way is being prepared for diplomatic pressure upon Serbia which may develop into an armed attack.[3]

Probably the Serbian Minister in London had been told by the Foreign Office of Bunsen's dispatch of 16 July from Vienna reporting Lützow's 'indiscretion' that

a kind of indictment is being prepared against the Servian Government for alleged complicity in the conspiracy which led to the assassination of the Archduke.[4]

This dispatch was communicated also to Crackanthorpe at Belgrade, who reported home on 17 July:

Servian Prime Minister has declared to Austrian Minister in unofficial conversation that Servian Government are prepared to comply at once with any request for police investigation and to take any other measure compatible with dignity and independence of State.[5]

---

[1] DF. 3. X, 516.   [2] LAS, 25, CDD., p. 382.   [3] LAS. 27, CDD., p. 386.
[4] BD. XI, 50.   [5] BD. XI, 53.

This shows that Pašić was anxious about Vienna's intentions. 'But'—continued Crackanthorpe:

general feeling is that a demand on the part of Austro-Hungarian Government for appointment of a mixed commission of inquiry, for suppression of nationalist societies and for censorship of press, could not be acceded to, since it would imply foreign intervention in domestic affairs and legislation.[1]

This dispatch gives the gist of the stiffest demands which Austria was to make on Belgrade and shows that towards the middle of July Belgrade got wind of what was preparing. But Pašić made not the slightest move to forestall Austrian designs. On 18 July, possibly as a result of Bunsen's telegram, Crackanthorpe called on Gruić, the Secretary General of the Serbian Foreign Ministry, and

alluded to the suggestion made in the *Times* of the 16th instant to the effect that the wisest course for Serbia would be to undertake herself of her own motion an inquiry into the alleged South Slav conspiracy on Servian soil. M. Gruić pointed out the impossibility of adopting any definite measures before learning the findings of the Sarajevo Court which had hitherto been kept secret. . . . On the publication of the result of the inquiry, the Servian Government would be fully prepared to comply with whatever request for further investigation the circumstances might call for and which would be compatible with international usage.

With regard to Čabrinović, who had made the first attempt on the Archduke's life, it was already public knowledge that on his arrival in Belgrade recently the Servian Government had, as is usual with Austrian subjects coming to reside in Belgrade, made the customary inquiry of the Austrian consulate as to his antecedents and had received satisfactory information on this point. Of Princip the Servian Government knew nothing.

The Secretary General said he was aware that there was an influential party in Austria who wished to take advantage of the present conjuncture to press Servia to extremes. But the Servian Government had certain knowledge that restraint would be exercised on Austria from Berlin. Should, however, the worst come to the worst and Austria declare war, Servia would not stand alone. Russia would not remain quiet were Servia wantonly attacked, and Bulgaria would be immobilized by Roumania. Under present conditions a war between a Great Power and a Balkan State must inevitably, in the opinion of the Secretary General, lead to a European conflagration.[2]

In this Gruić was right and was more clear-sighted than Grey to whom the dispatch was addressed. But he was wrong about the line Germany would take and soon saw his mistake, when the Serbian Chargé d'Affaires in Berlin telegraphed Belgrade the reply he had received on 20 July from Jagow to his assurances that

it was Serbia's intention to maintain the best and most correct relations with the Monarchy and she was prepared to fulfil all Austro-Hungarian demands

[1] BD. XI, 53.   [2] BD. XI, 80.

for a strict investigation into the Sarajevo outrage in as far as these were compatible with the honour and sovereignty of the Kingdom. The Serbian Chargé d'Affaires at the same time requested the German Government to exercise a conciliatory influence on the Vienna Cabinet.

Herr von Jagow's reply had been—added Herr von Tschirschky—that, in the view of the German Government, Serbia in these last years had been so wanting in correct neighbourly behaviour towards Austria-Hungary that it was only too understandable if, in making its demands known, the Vienna Cabinet were to make use of very vigorous language.[1]

Jagow's words foreshadowed a very strong note from Austria. From Vienna on the same 20 July came a still more disturbing warning from Jovan Jovanović that in all probability Austria was making ready to go to war with Serbia. But by the time these two messages reached Belgrade Pašić had departed on an electioneering tour through Southern Serbia. Was this from lack of awareness on his part or was he unable to act otherwise? There is no doubt that he was to some extent hampered by the general elections in which the country was called upon to choose between his own party and the military party, ruled by the *Black Hand*. This is even admitted by the German Minister in Belgrade who on 21 July wrote to his Government that

any conciliatoriness on his part towards the Monarchy is interpreted by the united Opposition as weakness.[2]

But election meetings were not the crafty statesman's sole preoccupation. He was very well aware of the seriousness of the situation. On 19 July, the day he left Belgrade, he had a talk with Strandtmann, the Russian Chargé d'Affaires, who described him as 'extremely anxious'.

Count Tisza's utterances at Budapest have made a profound impression on him. He has also received information of Austrian troop movements.[3]

The truth is that there were strong reasons why Pašić took no effective steps to ward off the threat from Austria by himself instituting preliminary investigations into the ramifications of the plot in Serbia. In other words he knew that it had been hatched in Belgrade and that it was Serbian officers, leaders of the *Black Hand*, who held all the threads of it, provided the perpetrators with weapons, bombs and funds and helped them to cross the frontier into Bosnia. The go-between who had kept these officers in touch with the three young conspirators was, as we have seen, that railway employee Ciganović, who, while a member of the *Black Hand*, was probably also Pašić's informer about what went on in that society, on which the Serbian Government had every reason to keep a watchful eye. Hence the opening of proceedings against the accomplices in the outrage would have caused a most

[1] Oe-U. VIII, 10440.   [2] DD. I, 137.   [3] *Int. Bez.* i. IV, 286.

terrific scandal, which would have done immense harm to Serbia and served as a justification for extreme demands on the part of Austria. And where would the scandal have stopped seeing that the *Black Hand* had contacts with the highest in the land? And what would be the consequences if it were discovered that Pašić had been notified of the plot?

That this danger did exist was shown on 6 July when Jovan Jovanović reported from Vienna that the inquiry held by the Austrian authorities at Sarajevo had shown that the plot had been hatched at Belgrade and that in it was implicated a Serbian employee of the Ministry of Public Works, a certain Ciganović. It is maintained by Ljuba Jovanović, then Minister of Education,[1] that Pašić pressed for the identification of Ciganović and that he would in the end have been discovered in the railway administrative service. But on 8 July the Austrian Legation at Belgrade telegraphed Vienna that Ciganović had left Belgrade on a month's leave three days before the crime. The prefect of police said he knew nothing about the man, but it transpires that it was he who brought about the man's departure.[2] Thus it came about that when the Austrian ultimatum asked for the arrest of both Tankosić and Ciganović, the Serbian Government arrested the former (and let him go immediately) while in regard to the latter it replied that as a

subject of the Monarchy who until 28 June had been an employee in the railway administration, he had not yet been found and a warrant of arrest had been issued against him.

It was later shown that immediately after the outrage Ciganović's name was removed from the list of railway employees. When mobilization was ordered, Ciganović rejoined Tankosić's company.

Bogičević states that the Salonika trial of Colonel Dragutin Dimitrievič proves beyond doubt what was known beforehand, namely that

before the war Ciganović had been a spy and *agent provocateur* for Pašić and that, as a member of the *Black Hand*, he kept the Government faithfully informed of what went on in it.[3]

These are circumstances which support the supposition that there was contact between Pašić and Ciganović and help to explain Pašić's fear of bringing the threads of the conspiracy to the light of day. He was afraid politically, and no doubt also physically. The men of the *Black Hand*—the Serbian Chargé d'Affaires in Paris used often to say to an intimate friend—

were so powerful and had succeeded so well in concealing their actions and in placing accomplished facts before those who, like Pašić, condemned their

---

[1] *Krv Slovenstva*, p. 14.
[2] Friedrich von Wiesner, *Ciganović* in KSF., November 1927, pp. 1041-8.
[3] Bogičević, *Procès*, pp. 131-3.

revolutionary methods of direct action, . . . that it was impossible to stop them. Pašić knew! We all knew! But nothing could be done. If Russia had not supported us, if we had had to submit to the inquest which the Austrian ultimatum exacted in July 1914, we should have been caught with our hand in the sack.[1]

And these were men whose threats were to be feared. On the evening of 29 June three Comitaji sought out the owner of the journal *Balkan* and told him on behalf of Tankosić that he had better not publish anything about any contacts the murderer Čabrinović may have had with people in Belgrade or write anything that might implicate Serbs, if he did so, it would be the worse for him.[2] It is not out of place to suppose that it would also have been the worse for Pašić if he had opened judicial proceedings which brought to light the criminal activities of Tankosić and his powerful and unscrupulous chief Dimitrievič, even apart from the political consequences of such a step and the risks of bringing Ciganović into the matter as well.

It is legitimate to ask oneself the question whether events would have taken a different turn if Pašić had behaved differently. Austria had made up her mind this time to make an end of Serbia but would undoubtedly have found it difficult if Belgrade had shown willingness to meet her demands for the exposure of any on Serbian territory who might be involved in the crime. But on the other hand, as has been indicated, the investigation would have reached up into such exalted circles and would have uncovered such widespread anti-Austrian activities in Serbia that it would only have armed Austria with stronger arguments in support of her demands. Such must have been Pašić's calculation in acting as he did.

9. The delivery of the ultimatum at Belgrade; the text of the Austrian note to Serbia.

Pašić was absent from Belgrade when on the morning of 23 July, Giesl telephoned to the Foreign Ministry that at 4.30 p.m. he would have an 'important communication' for the Serbian Premier.[3] On 21 July Giesl had received instructions from Berchtold to make this communication between 4 and 5 p.m. This preliminary message was to be regarded as a simple act of courtesy to enable Pašić to hasten back, but if he had still not returned, the delivery of the note was to take place 'in any case' to the minister taking Pašić's place or to the senior official present at the Foreign Ministry.[4] And as Vienna had considered the

---

[1] Henri Pozzi, *Black Hand over Europe* (London, 1935), p. 82.

[2] Belgrade police report to the Minister of the Interior, Protić, reproduced by Pharos in his book: *Der Prozess gegen die Attentäter von Sarajevo* (Berlin, 1918), p. 81, *n.* 45.

[3] KSF. (1935), p. 579, *n.* 2.

[4] Oe-U. VIII, 10435.

possibility that, at the moment of the delivery of the ultimatum, Pašić might have resigned, Berchtold instructed Giesl on 23 July that

the resignation of the Government could not of course have any influence either on the presentation of our demands or on the forty-eight hour time limit, since it is well known that a Government after resigning still has entire responsibility for the conduct of affairs until the formation of a new ministry.[1]

Earlier the same day Berchtold had telegraphed Giesl to postpone the presentation of the note until a few minutes before 5 p.m. at the earliest and if possible until 6 p.m.[2] The ministers present in Belgrade were Paču, Stojan Protić, Djuričić, Ljuba Jovanović and Colonel Stefanović. All the others were away electioneering, and the Regent on the 22nd had signed a *ukaze* nominating the Finance Minister Paču to replace Pašić during the latter's absence. The Minister of the Interior, Stojan Protić, was tied to his house with a bad foot.[3] On receiving the message in the forenoon Paču managed to get on the telephone to Pašić who was at Nish. Pašić's answer was: 'Receive him in my place' and, despite all appeals to return to Belgrade at once, he continued his tour. At 6 p.m. Giesl appeared at the Foreign Ministry and was received by Paču in the presence of Gruić, the Secretary General. Giesl handed him the ultimatum, a two-page annex, and a brief accompanying letter addressed to Dr. Paču as representative of the Prime Minister. He added that the time limit fixed for the reply would expire on Saturday at 6 p.m. and, if by then no reply were received or the reply were unsatis-factory, he would leave Belgrade with the whole Legation staff. He also asked to be given, at the same time as the Serbian reply, the Serbian text of the two official enunciations, in order to check them. Paču, without reading the note, replied that because of elections many of the ministers were away and that he feared it would be impossible to call a full Cabinet meeting in the time. Giesl replied

that the return of the ministers in the age of railways, telegraph and telephone in a land of that size could only be a matter of a few hours and that he had already that morning suggested Pašić's being informed. In any case this was a private matter for the Serbian Government in which he had nothing to say.[4]

Giesl told the present writer that Paču still seemed to hesitate and repeated that he could not receive the note. Giesl told him that if he would not take it from his hands he would leave it on the table. Then Paču could do what he liked with it. After saying this Giesl took his leave. Paču and Gruić read the note and showed it to Ljuba Jovanović and Diuričić who were waiting in an adjoining room.

[1] Oe-U. VIII, 10519.　　[2] Oe-U. VIII, 10518.
[3] *Krv Sloventsva*, p. 20.　　[4] Oe-U. VIII, 10526.

The text was as follows:

On 31 March 1909 the Serbian Minister at Vienna on the instructions of his Government made the following declaration to the Imperial and Royal Government:

'Serbia recognizes that her rights have not been affected by the *fait accompli* created in Bosnia-Herzegovina and that consequently she will conform to such decisions as the Powers may take in conformity with Article XXV of the Treaty of Berlin. In deference to the advice of the Great Powers, Serbia undertakes henceforward to renounce the attitude of protest and opposition which she has adopted with regard to the annexation since last autumn and she further engages to modify the direction of her present policy with regard to Austria-Hungary and to live henceforward with the latter on a footing of good neighbourliness.'

The history of recent years and in particular the painful events of 28 June have demonstrated the existence in Serbia of a subversive movement the aim of which is to detach from the Austro-Hungarian Monarchy certain parts of its territories. This movement which had its birth under the eye of the Serbian Government has gone so far as to manifest itself beyond the territory of the Kingdom by acts of terrorism, by a series of outrages and by murders.

The Royal Serbian Government, far from fulfilling the formal pledges contained in the declaration of 31 March 1909, has done nothing to repress these movements; it has tolerated the criminal machinations of various societies and associations directed against the Monarchy, unrestrained language on the part of the press, glorification of the perpetrators of outrages, participation of officers and officials in subversive agitation, unwholesome propaganda in public education, in short tolerated all the manifestations of a nature to inculcate in the Serbian population hatred of the Monarchy and contempt for its institutions.

This culpable tolerance on the part of the Royal Government of Serbia had not ceased at the moment when the events of 28 June last revealed its disastrous consequences to the whole world.

It is shown by the depositions and confessions of the criminal authors of the outrage of 28 June that the Sarajevo murders were planned in Belgrade, that the arms and explosives with which the murderers were found to be provided had been given them by Serbian officers and officials belonging to the *Narodna Obrana* and finally that the passage into Bosnia of the criminals and their arms was organized and effectuated by chiefs of the Serbian frontier service.

The results here mentioned of the preliminary investigation do not permit the Imperial and Royal Government to pursue any longer the attitude of expectant forbearance which they have for years observed towards the machinations concentrated in Belgrade and thence propagated in the territories of the Monarchy; the results on the contrary impose on them the duty of putting an end to the intrigues which constitute a permanent threat to the tranquillity of the Monarchy.

It is to achieve this end that the Imperial and Royal Government sees itself obliged to demand from the Serbian Government the formal assurance that it condemns the propaganda directed against the Austro-Hungarian Monarchy, that is to say the aggregate of tendencies, the ultimate aim of which is to detach from the Monarchy territories belonging thereto, and that it undertakes to suppress by every means this criminal and terrorist propaganda.

In order to give a formal character to this undertaking the Royal Government of Serbia shall cause to be published on the front page of the *Official Journal* of the 26/13 July the following declaration:

'The Royal Government of Serbia condemns the propaganda directed against Austria-Hungary, i.e. the aggregate of tendencies, the ultimate aim of which is to detach from the Austro-Hungarian Monarchy territories which form part thereof, and it sincerely deplores the fatal consequences of these criminal proceedings.

'The Royal Government regrets that Serbian officers and officials have participated in the above-mentioned propaganda and thereby compromised the good neighbourly relations to which the Royal Government had solemnly pledged itself by its declaration of 31 March 1909.

'The Royal Government, which disapproves and repudiates all idea or attempt of interference with the destinies of the inhabitants of any part whatsoever of Austria-Hungary, considers it its duty formally to warn the officers, officials and all the population of the Kingdom that henceforward it will proceed with the utmost rigour against all persons who may render themselves guilty of such machinations which it will use all its efforts to forestall and repress.'

This declaration shall simultaneously be communicated to the Royal Army as an order of the day by His Majesty the King and shall be published in the 'Official Bulletin of the Army'.

The Royal Serbian Government further undertakes:

1. To suppress any publication which incites to hatred and contempt of the Monarchy and the general tendency of which is directed against its territorial integrity;

2. To dissolve immediately the society styled *Narodna Obrana*, to confiscate all its means of propaganda, and to proceed in the same manner against the other societies and their branches in Serbia which engage in propaganda against the Austro-Hungarian Monarchy; the Royal Government will take the necessary measures to prevent the dissolved societies from continuing their activities under another name and form;

3. To eliminate without delay from public instruction in Serbia, both as regards the teaching body and the methods of instruction, all that serves or might serve to foment the propaganda against Austria-Hungary:

4. To remove from the military service and the administration in general all officers and officials guilty of propaganda against the Austro-Hungarian Monarchy and of whom the Imperial and Royal Government reserves to itself the right to communicate the names and deeds to the Royal Government;

5. To accept the collaboration in Serbia of organs of the Imperial and Royal Government in the suppression of the subversive movement directed against the territorial integrity of the Monarchy;

6. To take judicial proceedings against the accessories to the plot of 28 June who are on Serbian territory;

Organs delegated by the Imperial and Royal Government will take part in the investigations relating thereto;

7. To proceed without delay to the arrest of Major Voija Tankosić and of a certain Milan Ciganović, a Serbian State employee implicated by the findings of the preliminary investigation at Sarajevo;

8. To prevent by effective measures the co-operation of the Serbian Authorities in the illicit traffic in arms and explosives across the frontier; to dismiss and severely punish the officials of the Šabac and Ložnica frontier service guilty of having assisted the authors of the Sarajevo crime by facilitating their crossing of the frontier;

9. To furnish the Imperial and Royal Government with explanations regarding the unjustifiable utterances of high Serbian officials both in Serbia and abroad, who, notwithstanding their official position, have not hesitated since the outrage of 28 June to express themselves in interviews in terms of hostility towards the Austro-Hungarian Monarchy, finally;

10. To notify the Imperial and Royal Government without delay of the execution of the measures comprised under the preceding heads.

The Imperial and Royal Government expects the reply of the Royal Government at the latest by Saturday 25 of this month at 5 p.m.[1]

A memorandum dealing with the results of the preliminary investigation at Sarajevo with regard to the officials mentioned in Points 7 and 8 is annexed to this Note.

Annex.

The criminal investigation opened by the Sarajevo Court against Gavrilo Princip and associates on the count of assassination and complicity therein, in respect of the crime committed by them on 28 June last, has up to the present led to the following conclusions:

1. The plot having as its object the assassination of the Archduke Francis Ferdinand on the occasion of his visit to Sarajevo was formed at Belgrade by Gavrilo Princip, Nedeljko Čabrinović and one Milan Ciganović and Trifko Grabež with the help of Commander Voija Tankosić.

2. The 6 bombs and 4 Browning pistols with ammunition with which the malefactors committed the outrage were delivered to Princip, Čabrinović and Grabež at Belgrade by a certain Milan Ciganović and Commander Voija Tankosić.

3. The bombs are hand grenades from the munitions depot of the Serbian Army at Kragujevać.

4. To assure the success of the outrage, Ciganović instructed Princip, Čabrinović and Grabež in the use of grenades, and, in a forest near the rifle-range at Topčider (Park), gave Princip and Grabež shooting practice with Browning pistols.

5. To enable Princip, Čabrinović and Grabež to cross the frontier of Bosnia-Herzegovina and to smuggle in clandestinely their contraband arms, a secret system of transport was organized by Ciganović.

---

[1] The figure 5 is struck out and replaced by 6.

As a result of this organization the introduction into Bosnia-Herzegovina of the criminals and their arms was effected by the frontier captains of Šabac (Rade Popović) and Ložnica, and the customs official Rudivoj Grbić of Ložnica with the aid of various individuals.[1]

There is no need to dwell on the serious and far-reaching character of this note, which is only too apparent. It was at once termed an ultimatum, and Grey described it as 'the most formidable document he had ever seen addressed by one State to another that was independent'.[2] On all sides it was seen as the clarion call to war which it was intended to be. There seemed no possibility that Serbia could unconditionally accept many of its points. Particularly Points 5 and 6 infringed her sovereignty by demanding acceptance of the collaboration of Austrian representatives in the suppression of the Pan-Slav movement and in the hunt for those who took part in the plot. Were these points thus framed in order that Serbia should reject them and the Monarchy could attack her, or did Vienna cherish the illusion that she would submit in the end? This question will be answered in Chapter IX, but first we must see what attitude the Triple *Entente* Powers and Italy took in regard to the Austrian *démarche* and how Serbia replied to it.

[1] Oe-U. VIII, 10395.   [2] BD. XI, 91.

CHAPTER VIII

RUSSIAN REACTIONS, ITALIAN RESERVATIONS, THE ABSENCE OF THE FRENCH LEADERS, ENGLISH INACTION

(1) Sazonov foresees a European war and proposes partial mobilization (p. 290). (2) France offers support; England is asked to give hers (p. 294). (3) The German demand for 'localization of the conflict' (p. 297). (4) On 25 July St. Petersburg decides on partial mobilization in principle; the 'period preparatory to war' (p. 304). (5) War is in the air; Sazonov appeals to London and Rome (p. 308). (6) The text of the Austrian ultimatum is communicated to the Consulta on the morning of 24 July; the discussion between Salandra, San Giuliano and Flotow (p. 311). (7) The Italian Government's views set forth by San Giuliano in a letter to the King of Italy (p. 318). (8) Perplexity and confusion at the Quai d'Orsay; Bienvenu-Martin at first favourable to Austria; the belated arrival of instructions from Viviani. (p. 322). (9) English désintéressement in the Austro-Serbian conflict; the mistake made by Grey (p. 329). (10) Grey shrinks from the only effective measure and urges mobilization and mediation (p. 334). (11) Germany's bogus acceptance of Four Power mediation (p. 340).

1. Sazonov foresees a European war and proposes partial mobilization.

At 9 p.m. on 23 July after the farewell banquet to Poincaré, Count Montereale, Counsellor at the Italian Embassy in St. Petersburg, told Butzov, an official of the Russian Foreign Office, that the Italian Ambassador had just received news from Italy that Austria that very day had presented an unacceptable ultimatum to Belgrade. This shows that the Consulta had immediately communicated to Carlotti the substance of a *démarche* carried out that day at Rome by Ambrozy acting on instructions from Berchtold which we shall examine further on.[1] That same evening the Austrian Ambassador Szápáry asked for an interview with Sazonov for the following day. But until late at night St. Petersburg knew nothing more than this. Then at 7 a.m. on the 24th there came a telegram from Belgrade which confirmed what Montereale had said. Schilling thereupon ordered Izvolsky and Shebeko back to their respective posts at Paris and Vienna and when at 10 a.m. on Friday Sazonov returned from Tsarkoe Selo to the Russian Foreign Ministry he was informed of the news. 'C'est la guerre européenne!' was his

[1] See pp. 312–13.

shocked reply. He instantly sent for Szápáry and telephoned the news to the Tsar who exclaimed, 'This is disturbing!'[1]

C'est la guerre européenne! The words cast a searchlight into Sazonov's mind and explain much of what was later to happen. No doubt it is true that he was suffering nervous strain from the late nights, the banquets and speeches, the round of ceremonies, the general enthusiasm and excitement of the previous days, not to speak of the talks with Poincaré who had only departed a few hours earlier. But it is also true that the nature of the demands made on Serbia, the short time limit granted for unconditional acceptance, the presentation of the note at the very moment when Poincaré was on the point of leaving Russian waters, all indicated that this time Austria, in collusion with Germany, had made up her mind to go to extremes and carry out the destruction, material or moral, of her small Slav neighbour without regard for the prestige, feelings and interests of its protectress Russia. In Russia herself nationalistic tendencies had gained the upper hand and could no longer be quietened down as they had been in 1909 nor persuaded to pursue a policy of peace as in 1912–13. Austria and Germany on their side could hardly be expected to make a right-about turn. In all probability therefore Europe was on the brink of war. Such was Sazonov's summing up of the situation and he acted accordingly but with characteristic haste and impulsiveness and with effects that were fatal.

His first action was to receive Szápáry who officially acquainted him of the Austrian note, justifying it with the arguments laid down by Berchtold in two telegrams circulated to the Austrian representatives at St. Petersburg, Paris, London, Rome and Constantinople[2] and saying that he would soon be bringing a *dossier* of documents proving Serbian guilt. (The *dossier* was not yet ready and by the time it was circulated to the various Governments some days later, it was too late to be of any interest.) In his reports of the interview Szápáry said that Sazonov listened to him 'relatively calmly' and gave an impression 'more of disheartenment than of excitement', but his quotations of what Sazonov actually said produce the opposite effect. The stiffest demands of the ultimatum had roused him to protest:

I know what it is. You mean to make war on Serbia. . . . You are setting fire to Europe. It is a great responsibility that you are assuming, you will see the impression that it will make here and in London and Paris and perhaps elsewhere. It will be regarded as an unjustifiable aggression. . . . Why was Serbia given no chance to speak and why the form of an ultimatum? . . . The monarchic idea has got nothing to do with it. . . . The fact is you mean war and you have burnt your bridges. . . . One sees how peace loving you are, seeing that you set fire to Europe.

[1] *Int. Bez.* i. V, 25; Schilling's *Diary*, pp. 28–9.
[2] Oe-U. VIII, 10399, 10340.

It is not surprising that Szápáry's fourth telegram concludes:

In spite of the Minister's relative calmness, his position, as was scarcely to be expected otherwise, was definitely adverse and hostile.[1]

Still more hostile even than Szápáry imagined! Sazonov had a fixed idea which had germinated in the preceding days. Already on 18 July, as has been noted, he had said to the English Ambassador Buchanan that anything in the nature of an Austrian ultimatum at Belgrade could not leave Russia indifferent, and that she might be forced to take some precautionary military measure.[2]

After the delivery of the ultimatum he decided to ask the consent of the ministers and of the Tsar to a partial mobilization against Austria which could be put into operation at the necessary moment and need never take place if Austria drew back at the mere announcement of the measure and if Germany, against whom the mobilization was not directed, restrained her ally and opened up the possibility of successful diplomatic action. To this end as soon as Szápáry had taken his leave, Sazonov received the Russian Chief of Staff General Janushkevich with whom he discussed this partial mobilization against Austria. The substance of the discussion is given by General Dobrorolski, then Chief of the Mobilization Section. He was summoned between 11 a.m. and noon on 24 July by General Janushkevich who told him 'The situation is very serious', and went on to ask:

Have you everything in readiness for the proclamation of the mobilization of our army? . . . In an hour you will bring me all arrangements for putting the army on a war footing, the intention being, if need arises, to proclaim only partial mobilization against Austria-Hungary. Hence as regards this mobilization nothing must give Germany occasion to perceive in it any hostile intentions against herself.[3]

The arrangements were to be submitted to a Council of Ministers called for 3 p.m.

Let us pause a moment to consider this bright idea of Sazonov's of a mobilization against Austria alone, which at the given moment, as we shall later see, was to have fatal consequences. Mobilization against Austria alone had no sense, since if Russia attacked Austria, Germany would go to the help of her ally, and Russia would have to mobilize against Germany as well, in other words, to carry out general mobilization. It may be objected that mobilization against Austria, both as a means of intimidating Austria and putting pressure on Germany, without directly

---

[1] Oe-U. VIII, 10616–9.   [2] BD. XI, 60.

[3] General Dobrorolski's account appeared first in the Belgrade Army Bulletin, *Vojni Zbornik*, I, pp. 91–116 (August–September 1921); it was then translated into German: *Die Mobilmachung der russischen Armee, 1914* (Berlin, 1922), and into French: *La Mobilisation de l'Armée Russe en 1914* in *Revue d'Histoire de la Guerre Mondiale*, I, April–July 1923. Here the quotation follows the German version (pp. 17–18).

bringing her into the conflict, would not prevent a subsequent mobilization against Germany as well, if it were to prove necessary. For this to be feasible the Russian General Staff would have had to include among its preparations a plan for mobilization against Austria alone, to be followed, if need be, by the mobilization of the remainder of her forces against Germany. But the General Staff had planned on the understanding that, if war came, Germany and Austria would make common cause and had worked out a scheme for general mobilization against both Empires. It therefore had no plan ready for mobilization against Austria alone and could not in the space of a few hours carry out the detailed work necessitated by such a proposal. This meant that no partial mobilization was feasible. Either Russia must not mobilize at all or she must mobilize against both Austria and Germany.

By ill-luck Janushkevich had become Chief of Staff only five months previously, and was not familiar with the details of the mobilization plan. Whether for this reason or because he did not venture to oppose Sazonov, the fact is that he did not on the spot say that the plan was unworkable. Dobrorolski did not fail to point out to his Chief that this was the case, not only because no plans had been made but also because, as early as 1892 during the negotiations for a Franco-Russian alliance, the Russian General Staff had firmly laid down that in the event of war strategic requirements would make it necessary to fight against both the Central Powers. In 1914 the situation was still the same. Sazonov's idea was to mobilize only the four Military Districts of Kiev, Odessa, Moscow and Kazan. This would give thirteen army corps (1,100,000 men) while the plan of operations against Austria involved the use of fifteen army corps. Moreover, to operate against Austria, a part of these army corps would have to march through the Warsaw district and this could not be done for fear of alarming Germany. Further, if the Warsaw district were not to be included in the mobilization, not only would there be a shortage of three army corps but the Austrian frontier facing Poland would remain uncovered. And when later, in consequence of Germany's coming into the war, general mobilization became necessary the result would be utter confusion, since, among other things, the Warsaw district would be deprived of its reserves which under the mobilization plan were to be drawn partly from the Moscow and Kazan districts.

These arguments were so obvious that they might have appeared convincing even to one who had no inside knowledge. But the Chief of Staff must have had some reason for not wanting to offend Sazonov and refused to admit their force.

General Janushkevich [writes Dobrorolski] again commanded me to report within an hour in the sense that he had already ordered.[1]

---

[1] Dobrorolski, p. 18.

This was a real disaster. Had Janushkevich from the beginning warned Sazonov of the mistake he would be making in proclaiming partial mobilization, Sazonov would never have got the Council of Ministers on 24 July and the Tsar on 25 July to approve it in principle, nor would he have proclaimed it on the evening of 28 July with incalculable consequences. If he had been asked to choose between no mobilization and general mobilization against the Central Powers, Sazonov would have hesitated to plunge headlong into the venture, whereas, believing he could threaten Austria without provoking Germany, he found out too late that this could not be done. Thus Janushkevich's acceptance of his idea had fatal consequences.

2. *France offers support; England is asked to give hers.*

In the hope of preventing war Sazonov as early as 24 July sought to persuade England to make a clear statement which would convince Germany that it was an illusion to think she could have a war with Russia and France alone. He writes in *Fateful Years*:

I had a vivid recollection of the impression produced everywhere, and especially in Germany, by Mr. Lloyd George's speech in 1911, when, owing to the Agadir incident, Europe was on the brink of war. A decisive statement on the part of the British Government of its solidarity with France had then been sufficient to dispel the gathering storm clouds. I was profoundly convinced at the time and am still convinced now that, had the British Government sided with Russia and France on the Serbian question from the first, Berlin would not have encouraged Austria in its policy of aggression, but would on the contrary have advised caution and moderation, and the hour of reckoning between the two hostile camps into which Europe was divided would have been postponed for years if not for ever.[1]

This was a perfectly correct view which Sazonov had for some time been putting forward. On 19 February 1914 he had written to Benckendorff, the Russian Ambassador in London:

It must be said that the peace of the world will only be secure on the day when the Triple *Entente*, whose real existence is not better authenticated than the existence of the sea serpent, shall transform itself into a defensive alliance without secret clauses and publicly announced in all the world press.[2]

He now reverted to the subject on 24 July in a conversation with the English and French Ambassadors at a lunch given by Paléologue.[3] Paléologue records in his *Memoirs* the ideas that he put forward:

[1] Sazonov, p. 180.   [2] *Int. Bez.* i. I, 289. See Vol. I, p. 571.
[3] According to Schilling's *Diary* it was Paléologue who called a meeting of Sazonov, Buchanan and Diamandy, the Roumanian Minister. 'It was of the greatest advantage for us that Roumania should be drawn in on our side, while for Roumania it was manifestly flattering to participate as an equal in the diplomatic steps taken by the Great Powers.' (Ibid., p. 30). But Buchanan writes that Diamandy arrived towards the close of his own talk with Sazonov and that Sazonov in a private conversation 'invited also Roumanian Government to make representations at Vienna' (BD. XI, 101).

Taking my stand on the toasts exchanged between the Tsar and the President, the declarations of the two Foreign Ministers and the communiqué to the Havas Agency yesterday, I had no hesitation in advocating a policy of firmness.

'But suppose that policy is bound to lead to war?' said Sazonov.

'It will only lead to war if the Germanic powers have already made up their minds to resort to force to secure the hegemony of the East. Firmness does not exclude conciliation. But it is essential for the other side to be prepared to negotiate and compromise. You know my own views as to Germany's designs. The Austrian ultimatum seems to me to provoke the dangerous crisis I have anticipated for a long time. Henceforth we must recognize that war may break out at any moment. That prospect must govern all our diplomatic action.'[1]

To talk like that was to add fuel to the flames. But the English Ambassador, who had no motive for attributing to his French colleague anything that he did not say, telegraphed an account of the conversation to London which shows Paléologue going very much farther:

The French Ambassador gave me to understand that France would not only give Russia strong diplomatic support but would, if necessary, fulfil all the obligations imposed on her by the alliance.[2]

The seriousness and effect of such an affirmation, made when Poincaré and Viviani had scarcely left Russian waters, must be obvious to everyone. Repeated with increasing warmth during the days that followed and not counteracted by telegrams from Paris in the opposite sense, they must have exercised a powerful influence on Sazonov, who, feeling fully assured of French support, felt less concern about gaining the support of England. To Buchanan he

expressed the hope that His Majesty's Government would proclaim their solidarity with France and Russia. He characterized Austria's conduct as immoral and provocative. Some of the demands which she had presented were absolutely inacceptable and she would never have acted as she had done without having first consulted Germany. . . . I said that I could not speak in the name of His Majesty's Government, but that I would telegraph all that they had said. I could personally hold out no hope that His Majesty's Government would make any declaration of solidarity that would entail engagement to support France and Russia by force of arms. We had no direct interests in Servia, and public opinion in England would never sanction a war on her behalf. Minister for Foreign Affairs replied that the Servian question was but part of general European question and that we could not efface ourselves.

I said that I gathered that His Excellency wished us to join in telling Austria that we could not tolerate her active intervention in Servian internal affairs. If she paid no attention to our representations and took military action

[1] Paléologue, I, pp. 31–2.　　　　[2] BD. XI, 101.

against Servia, did Russia propose to declare war upon her? Minister for Foreign Affairs said that the whole question would be considered by a Council of Ministers to be held this afternoon, but that no decision would be taken till a further Council of Ministers had been held under the presidency of the Emperor, probably to-morrow. He personally thought that Russia would at any rate have to mobilize.

I suggested that the first thing to be done was to try to gain time by bringing our influence to bear to induce Austria to extend term of delay accorded to Servia. The French Ambassador replied that time did not permit of this, either Austria was bluffing or had made up her mind to act at once. In either case a firm and united attitude was our only chance of averting war. I then asked whether it would not be advisable to urge Servian Government to state precisely how far they were prepared to go to meet Austria's wishes. Minister for Foreign Affairs said that some of the demands contained in ultimatum might no doubt be accepted, but that he must first consult his colleagues.

As they both continued to press me to declare our complete solidarity with them, I said that I thought you might be prepared to represent strongly at Vienna and Berlin danger to European peace of an Austrian attack on Serbia. You might perhaps point out that it would in all probability force Russia to intervene, that this would bring Germany and (? France) into the field, and that if war became general, it would be difficult for England to remain neutral. Minister for Foreign Affairs said that he hoped that we would in any case express strong reprobation of Austria's action. If war did break out, we would sooner or later be dragged into it, but if we did not make common cause with France and Russia from the outset we should have rendered war more likely, and should not have played a 'beau rôle'.

From French Ambassador's language it almost looked as if France and Russia were determined to make a strong stand even if we declined to join them. Language of Minister of Foreign Affairs, however, was not so (? decided) on this subject.[1]

Buchanan's language was as temperate and conciliatory, as that of Paléologue was the contrary. Without pledging his Government to unconditional solidarity, he showed that he realized the European character of the conflict, and while rightly thinking that Austria should be requested to extend the time limit she had imposed on Serbia, he thought that without going too far Grey could give Vienna and Berlin a warning of the consequences which a war with Serbia might and in fact did bring in its train. These were the very things that Grey did say in the end, but, alas, too late.

[1] BD. XI, 101.—In Paléologue's *Diary* as published in the *Revue des Deux Mondes* of 15 January 1921, p. 248, it is stated that to his appeal Buchanan replied: 'You do not know our present rulers. Oh! if the Conservative party were in power, I am certain that they would understand that the national interest commands us with so much evidence'. In his book *An Ambassador's Memoirs*, which he published subsequently, this was toned down to: 'I'm afraid public opinion with us is still far from realizing what our national interests so imperiously require' (I, p. 32).

3. The German demand for 'localization of the conflict'.

At 3 p.m. on 24 July a meeting of the Russian Council of Ministers was held at which Sazonov gave a survey of the diplomatic situation, asking for authorization to proclaim partial mobilization and take other measures. There was a lengthy discussion which ended with the adoption of the following decisions:

(i) Jointly with the other Powers to address a request to Austria for a prolongation of the time limit for the Serbian reply, in order to give the Powers time to acquaint themselves with the findings of the Judicial Inquiry into the Sarajevo murder as suggested by Austria herself;

(ii) to advise Serbia not to engage in hostilities with the Austro-Hungarian troops, but to withdraw her forces declaring that she entrusts her fate to the judgement of the Great Powers;

(iii) to ask the Tsar to authorize in principle the mobilization of the four military districts of Kiev, Odessa, Moscow and Kazan, and of the Baltic and Black Sea fleets;

(iv) to urge the War Minister without delay to speed up the completion of supplies of army equipment;

(v) to authorize the Minister of Finance to take measures immediately to reduce the amount of funds belonging to the Finance Department at present deposited in Germany and Austria-Hungary.[1]

The first decision, which had been suggested by Buchanan, was put into operation on the 24th. A telegram was sent to the Russian Chargé d'Affaires at Vienna and to the Russian representatives at Berlin, Paris, London, Rome and Bucharest to say:

As Austria-Hungary has only addressed herself to the Powers twelve hours after the delivery of her ultimatum to Belgrade, it is impossible for the Powers in the short time remaining to undertake anything useful towards the settlement of the complications that have arisen. . . . Since Austria has declared her readiness to acquaint the Powers with the results of the inquiry on which the accusations are based, the Powers should be given the opportunity to form an opinion on the matter. . . . The rejection by Austria of our proposal for dealing with the matter would rob the declaration made by her to-day of all meaning and be openly at variance with international 'ethics'.[2]

Also on the 24th the second resolution voted by the Council of Ministers was carried out, and Serbia was advised not to oppose an eventual Austrian invasion which it was feared might take place on the expiry of the forty-eight hour time limit. Sazonov's telegram conveying these instructions to Belgrade will be dealt with more fully in Chapter IX, which is devoted to the reply returned by Serbia.

[1] *Int. Bez.* i. V, 19; *Current History*, January 1926, p. 533.
[2] *Int. Bez.* i. V, 23.

After Spalaiković's departure, Sazonov at 7 p.m. at length received Pourtalès who was to make a very serious communication symptomatic of the attitude Germany proposed to take to the conflict. Already on 21–22 July the Chancellor had sent a circular of instructions to St. Petersburg, London and Paris (not to Rome) expatiating on the wrongs done to Austria by Serbia, culminating in the Sarajevo crime which had been hatched in Belgrade:

It has become clearly evident that it would not be consistent either with the dignity or with the self-preservation of the Austro-Hungarian Monarchy still longer to remain inactive in face of this movement on the other side of the frontier. . . . But the apprehension cannot be excluded that the Serbian Government might refuse to comply with those demands. . . . For the Austro-Hungarian Government there would be no choice, if it does not wish definitely to abandon Austria's position as a Great Power, but to obtain the fulfilment of its demands from the Serbian Government by strong pressure and, if necessary, by using military measures, the choice of the means having to be left to them.

I beg to ask Your Excellency to express yourself to M. Sazonov in the above sense and in so doing to give emphatic expression to the view that the present question is purely a matter for settlement between Austria-Hungary and Serbia, and that to confine it to the parties directly concerned must be the earnest endeavour of the Powers. We urgently desire the localization of the conflict because any intervention by another Power might in consequence of the various alliances bring incalculable consequences in its train.

For the especial benefit of Sazonov Pourtalès was instructed to dwell on the serious consequences for the monarchical principle if the monarchic Powers failed to make common cause against a 'political radicalism in Serbia that does not shrink from crimes against members of its own royal family'. The telegram ended: 'I cherish the hope that M. Sazonov will not be insensible to this fact.'[1]

Let us not dwell on this puerile appeal to monarchical solidarity which could have no effect when the action against Serbia was such that Russian prestige and Russian interests were seriously involved. Let us rather turn our attention to the fact that Germany demanded a free hand for Austria against her small Slav neighbour under threat otherwise of going to the help of her ally. This thesis was summarized in the expression 'localization of the conflict' which has remained notorious and which will be regularly used in that sense in the present work. Let us pause a moment to analyse this thesis, bearing in mind that it formed the basis of German diplomatic action from 24 July onward and that the European conflagration broke out precisely because at the opportune moment the German Government refused to renounce it,

---

[1] DD. I, 100; BD. XI, 100.

and in order to ensure its success, urged the Austrian Government to make haste and declare war on Serbia.

'Localization of the conflict' meant that: 1. no one else was to have a say in the Austrian ultimatum to Serbia (not that this would have been possible in the brief time limit set for the reply); 2. unless Belgrade played the dirty trick on Austria of submitting for the time being to all her demands, the invasion of Serbia would take place, and if it took place, no one was to interfere on pain of war. It is sufficient to define the terms of this injunction to measure the immensity of the miscalculation it contained. It was universally admitted that Russia, for reasons of kinship and because of her own designs on Constantinople and the Straits, had a special interest in the autonomy and evolution of the small Balkan States. The history of Europe in the previous half-century was shot through and through with disputes between Russia and Austria over their rival claims for hegemony in the Balkans. War had been just round the corner in 1908–9 and 1912–13 over the struggle between Austria and Serbia in which Russia had always taken her stand with Serbia. And now the rulers in Berlin thrust themselves forward and thought they could solve the knotty problem once and for all by confronting Russia, her ally France, her all-but-ally England, and indirectly Italy as well, with a blustering *aut-aut* in the misguided notion that they would all bow to the German fiat. But this was tantamount to willing war, the war of which, when it did break out, they declared that their hands were clean. We have in fact already seen that they were prepared to have a war, while at the same time thinking it on the whole improbable and counting above all on England's standing aside and letting them have an easy victory. The reasoning was absurd, almost unbelievable, all the more as the German rulers were on the point of violating Belgian neutrality in order to make a speedy end of France.

Discussing this point in his *Memoirs* Prince Bülow writes:

The gravest fault of these blind leaders was their refusal to seek or take advice, share their intentions with anyone, or confess the clumsy moves already made. . . . Had my advice been asked, I should have tried to find out first if Berlin was aiming at preventive warfare.

If they had said yes, Bülow would have quoted the authority of Bismarck against the idea. But:

Let us suppose that Bethmann and his colleagues had answered me that 'prophylactic warfare' was an idea that had never crossed their minds—that they merely believed it might be possible to 'localize' this Austro-Serbian conflict. Then I should naturally have warned them that theirs was a most dangerous illusion; that it could only have arisen from their ignorance of the whole situation in Russia, in England, France—all over the world! Never would the Russians allow the Austrians to organize punitive measures against the Serbs. Unless the most cautious diplomacy were employed, the antagonism created by such a measure between Russia on the one hand, and with her Serbia, and the Dual Monarchy on the other, would have as its result a dangerous crisis. This, in its turn, would mean further armaments, that is to say, the menace of imminent World War. France would at once champion Russia. For twenty-five years it had been an axiom that though, in any Franco-German conflict, Russia for a time might hesitate to take up arms against our Empire, the moment we were at war with Russia, French rifles would go off automatically. And I should have added 'once we are at war with Russia and France, it is more than likely that Great Britain will seize on such a favourable chance to strangle, without undue risks, her rival in commerce, navigation, and industry—the most powerful Continental State, and so, by British tradition, her enemy'. I should have asked if we were really so certain that Italy and Roumania were our friends. I repeat that such reasoning as this would have been no proof of unusual diplomatic experience, or exceptional political acumen. I am convinced that any normal German diplomat—Metternich, Bernstorff, Mumm or Rosen, Mühlberg or Brock-dorff-Rantzau, would have said the same in July 1914.[1]

Bülow's opinion finds confirmation from another German of unimpeachable credentials, Grand Admiral Tirpitz, who relates that when, while taking the waters at Tarasp, he learnt of the ultimatum his 'first impression was that this ultimatum was unacceptable to the Serbians and might easily lead to a world war'. He continues:

I never believed in the possibility of 'localizing' the Austro-Serbian passage of arms, just as little as I had any faith in England's neutrality in a continental war. I wrote to my deputy in this sense and recommended an agreement with the Tsar. This suggestion had no effect.[2]

This digression, the purpose of which is to clear up the fundamental point in the controversy which developed in the days that followed, enables us to form some idea of the violent reaction produced in the mind of the impulsive Sazonov by the German proposal of a 'localization of the conflict'. The account sent to Berlin by Pourtalès on 25 July tells us:

The Minister, who was extremely agitated and vented his feelings in boundless accusations against Austria-Hungary, declared with the utmost decision that Russia could not possibly admit that the Austro-Serbian difference should be settled between the two parties alone. The engagements into which Serbia entered after the Bosnian crisis and to which the Austrian note alludes, were made to Europe, consequently the matter was a European concern and it was for Europe to investigate whether Serbia had fulfilled her undertaking. He, therefore, demanded that the dossier of the investigation should be laid before the Cabinets of the six Powers. Austria could not be

[1] Bülow, III, 156, 157-8.   [2] Tirpitz, Memoirs, I, p. 245.

prosecutor and judge in her own cause. Sazonov declared he could in no way regard the facts alleged by Austria-Hungary in the note as proved, the inquiry filled him with the greatest (mistrust). He went on to say that in the purely legal question Serbia could, if the alleged facts were proved, give Austria satisfaction, but not in the demands of a political nature.[1]

Pourtalès replied that Austria would never consent, any more than would any Great Power, to submit the matter to European arbitration, and, according to his instructions, brought forward the plea: 'Russia cannot possibly defend the cause of regicide'. Sazonov referred to earlier crimes of this nature, saying that 'never have Governments and peoples been held responsible for the acts of individuals'.

M. Sazonov gave me to understand that the 'proofs' brought forward by Austria-Hungary in no way convinced him and indulged in the most unmeasured accusations and imputations against the Austro-Hungarian Government. . . . I could not do otherwise than express the fear that he was under the sway of his blind, relentless hatred against Austria. . . . 'Hatred is not in my character' replied the Minister, 'I therefore feel not hatred for Austria but contempt'. M. Sazonov added that in his belief Austria-Hungary was seeking a pretext to 'swallow' Serbia. 'In that case however', he said, 'Russia will go to war with Austria' ('*All right! Let her*' runs the Kaiser's marginal note on the first of the two dispatches). . . . I expressed my conviction that in the most extreme case it would only be a matter of an Austrian punitive expedition against Serbia and that Austria was far from contemplating territorial acquisitions. At this M. Sazonov shook his head incredulously and spoke of far-reaching plans of Austria's. First Serbia was to be devoured, then it would be Bulgaria's turn and then 'we shall have them at the Black Sea'. I answered that such fantastic exaggerations did not seem to me worthy of serious discussion.[2]

Schilling writes that those who after an hour saw Pourtalès emerge from Sazonov's cabinet noticed that he was extremely agitated and taken aback by the determination Sazonov had shown to resist the Austrian demands.[3] And Pourtalès himself confided to his diary his impression that the Council of Ministers had 'seriously considered the eventuality of a breach with Austria-Hungary and Germany' and 'resolved not to hang back from an armed (*scharfen*) conflict'.[4]

But in his dispatch to Berlin, on the contrary, he expressed the supposition

that Russia will not take up arms except in the case that Austria were to want to make territorial acquisitions at Serbia's expense. Even the wish for a Europeanization of the question seems to indicate that an immediate Russian intervention is not to be anticipated.[5]

---

[1] DD. I, 160.   [2] DD. I, 160, 204.   [3] *Int. Bez.* i. V, 25.
[4] Pourtalès, p. 19.   [5] DD. I, 160.

In the letter that followed he gave as his general impression
that in spite of M. Sazonov's extremely agitated state of mind he seems most
of all to want to temporize, and that this wish above all is the reason for his
proposal to bring the matter before the tribunal of Europe. It is true that a
dangerous factor in the present situation is Sazonov's passionate nationalism,
particularly also his religious hatred of Austria-Hungary. Public opinion has
till now shown remarkable indifference towards the Austro-Serbian conflict.
This may, it is true, change in the next few days as to-day's papers already
foreshadow.[1]

This was an understatement if not a falsification of the truth. But—
as Sazonov in his book rightly observes—the German diplomatic
representatives in the European capitals were careful not to oppose the
prevailing mood in Berlin for fear of falling into disfavour, well knowing that the only one among them who boldly spoke the truth and
opposed the plans of the Wilhelmstrasse was derided there as 'good old
Lichnowsky'.[2]

The anxiety to send pleasant reports to the Wilhelmstrasse and the
Kaiser, to suppress as long as possible anything that might offend them
and hence not to give an unvarnished account of what he saw and heard
is evident in all Pourtalès's dispatches. When the war was over he declared, as has been indicated, that it was obvious that Russia would not
this time yield to the wishes of Vienna and Berlin. Thus in writing
on 24 July that, apart from official honours 'it could not be said that
the reception of the French visitor here was particularly warm',[3] and on
the 25th that 'public opinion here has till now shown remarkable indifference towards the Austro-Serbian conflict'[4] neither he, nor Szápáry
in his messages to Vienna, made any mention of the angry comments
of the Russian press, or spoke of the distant rumble of disaster which
grew louder in the following days when an official communiqué, not reported by Pourtalès to Berlin, announced that the Russian Government
'is closely following the course of the Austro-Serbian dispute to which
Russia cannot remain indifferent'.[5]

Sazonov ended the day of the 24th by receiving Paléologue who
narrates in his *Memoirs* that he saw Pourtalès emerge from Sazonov's
cabinet 'his face purple and his eyes flashing'. Sazonov 'still agitated

---

[1] DD. I, 204.   [2] Sazonov, pp. 165–6.
[3] DD. I, 203.—The German military plenipotentiary, General Chelius, went to the
length of writing to the Kaiser on the 26th that the 'Tsar, as often as I was able to observe,
treated Poincaré very coldly and condescendingly, as was remarked by the whole entourage.
Army Headquarters pay altogether scant regard to the *entente* with France and incline much
more to the imperial alliance with Germany. The Tsar himself, as Baron Grünwald said to
me, has no liking for the whole friendship with France, and is said to have many times said
so.' (DD. II, 291.) This is the way the Kaiser was served by his loyal henchmen!
[4] DD. I, 204.
[5] Russian *Orange Book*, 10; CDD., p. 269.

over the dispute in which he had just been engaged' told him what had happened. Paléologue commented:

'If conversations between St. Petersburg and Berlin are to continue in this strain they won't last long. Very soon we shall see the Emperor William rise in his "shining armour". Please be calm. Exhaust every possibility of compromise! Don't forget that my Government is a government based on public opinion and can only support you effectively if it has public opinion behind it. . . . Can I give my Government an assurance that you have not yet ordered any military preparations?' 'None whatever.'[1]

If this is the truth, Paléologue was speaking that evening very much more restrainedly than he had done with Buchanan a few hours earlier. But his account needs checking, even down to details, with the very much more trustworthy day's report of the Russian Foreign Ministry which records that Paléologue arrived while Sazonov was in conversation with Pourtalès, but did not see Pourtalès leave, because in order to avoid meeting the latter, he had gone to wait in Schilling's room 'which Pourtalès could not pass through'. Far from predicting that Wilhelm would soon be standing 'in shining armour', Paléologue told Schilling he

considered the situation as by no means hopeless. He founded his optimism on the supposition that Germany would scarcely decide to support Austria since she knew to what serious consequences this would inevitably lead at the present moment. 'We have never been in a better position—he said —for our views are in perfect agreement, . . . we have four fresh documents of great importance confirming this.' Baron Schilling asked him what the nature of these documents was. . . . It appeared that M. Paléologue regarded as such documents the speeches recently exchanged by the Tsar and the President of the French Republic at Peterhof and on board the battleship *France*. As soon as Pourtalès had left, the French Ambassador was received by the Minister who promptly informed him of the Cabinet's decisions and of his conversations with the Serbian Minister and the German Ambassador.[2]

In other words, far from assuring Paléologue that no military measures were to be taken, Sazonov told him of the decision in principle to call a partial mobilization. But none of this did Paléologue telegraph to Paris.

With the talk with Paléologue Sazonov ended this fateful 24 July, during which the first outlines had taken shape of firm resistance, even to the length of using military measures, against the intention imputed to the Central Powers of crushing Serbia in order to gain a free hand in the Balkans and strike at Russan interests in the Near East. On the following day the seriousness of the situation was revealed to the public by the above mentioned proclamation and became fully apparent to the foreign diplomats gathered at Krasnoe Selo,

---

[1] Paléologue, I, p. 33.   [2] Schilling, *Diary*, pp. 31–2; *Int. Bez.* i. V, 25.

where the Tsar, amid omens of war and revolution, was to hold the
summer review of Russian troops. St. Petersburg was in the grip of a
huge strike which made many think of war as a desperate way of escape
from domestic difficulties. It is even not impossible that this consideration carried some weight with the Council of Ministers presided over
by the Tsar and attended by Grand Duke Nicholas, the Commander-in-
Chief to be, and General Janushkevich, which met before the military
review in order to submit for the Sovereign's approval the measures
decided on the previous day and any others that were judged necessary.

*4. On 25 July St. Petersburg decides on partial mobilization in principle; the 'period
preparatory to war'.*

What the discussions were that went on at this Council is not known.
Sazonov who had first dropped in at the Foreign Ministry to read the
telegrams which had come in during the night[1] must have pressed for
authorization to proclaim partial mobilization, though he had learnt
that on the 24th Berchtold had summoned Kudashev, the Russian
Chargé d'Affaires in Vienna, and had made important statements to
him. Berchtold's minute records:

> I said that nothing was further from our thoughts than the wish to humili-
> ate Serbia. . . . Our aim was purely to clear up the untenable relations of
> Serbia with the Monarchy and to this end induce her Government on the
> one hand publicly to disavow the tendencies directed against the existence of
> the Monarchy and suppress them by administrative measures and on the
> other hand to afford us the possibility of convincing ourselves of the con-
> scientious execution of these measures. . . . Finally I pointed out that
> we aimed at no acquisition of territory, but only at the preservation of the
> existing order, a standpoint which should be appreciated by the Russian
> Government.

To Kudashev's question: 'What will happen if the time limit expires
without Serbia's having given a satisfactory answer?' Berchtold replied
that Giesl and the Legation staff would leave Belgrade. To that Kudashev's remark was: 'Then it is war!'[2]

Now if Austria were to go to war with Serbia what value would
there be in Berchtold's assurances of territorial *désintéressement* and
respect of Serbian independence? Such promises were therefore not
likely to induce Sazonov to turn back and refrain from asking the
Tsar's approval of the military measures. The proposal for partial
mobilization was not called in question either by the War Minister or
by the Chief of Staff. The *Journal of the Russian General Staff Committee*
records for 25 June:

> The Chief of the General Staff informed the members of the General Staff
> Committee that H.M. the Tsar had been graciously pleased to declare that it

---

[1] *Int. Bez.* i. V, 51.   [2] Oe-U. VIII, 10615.

was necessary to support Serbia even if it were necessary to proclaim mobilization and begin military operations, but not earlier than after Austrian troops had crossed the Serbian frontier. According to information received, certain preparatory measures for mobilization were being taken in Austria-Hungary and Italy. Therefore H.M. the Tsar had been graciously pleased to confirm the order of the Council of Ministers that in the night of 25/26 July the pre-mobilization period shall begin. Should it prove necessary to proclaim mobilization, in view of the fact that operations are to be confined solely to action against Austria, His Majesty has commanded that mobilization shall take place in the military districts of Kiev, Odessa, Kazan and Moscow. The remaining military districts shall only be mobilized in the case that Germany joins Austria, not earlier, in order to avoid major diplomatic complications.[1]

At the same time the Tsar ordered a series of other measures, including the return to winter quarters of the troops who were on manoeuvres, the proclamation of the state of war in the fortified cities and frontier forts, the recall of officers on leave, the promotion of cadets to be officers.

The most serious of these measures, be it noted, was not the partial mobilization, since it was not to be carried out for the moment, but another which came into force in the night of 25/26 July. This was the proclamation of what the General Staff Gazette called 'the pre-mobilization period', but which was officially termed the 'period preparatory to war'.[2] Did the General Staff possibly prefer to use the former term in order not to alarm the Tsar and Sazonov? It is a curious fact that Dobrorolski, Sukhomlinov and other high-ranking officers always say 'pre-mobilization period'. In either case one and the same thing is meant, and it is certain that however much the General Staff regarded partial mobilization as a mistaken, dangerous and impracticable measure, they were only too ready to carry out the provisions of the 'Regulation concerning the period preparatory to war', which had been approved by the Tsar on 2 March 1913 and partly made up for the slowness of Russian mobilization operations.

According to this regulation:

'Period preparatory to war' means the period of diplomatic complications which precedes the opening of hostilities in the course of which all Government departments must take the necessary measures for the preparation and smooth execution of the mobilization of the Army, the Navy and the Fortresses, as well as for the deployment of the army at the threatened frontier.[3]

One of these measures was the recall of reservists to bring the frontier troop divisions up to strength, and this in the districts near to the

---

[1] *Int. Beʐ.* i. V, 79.   [2] Fay, II, p. 316, *n.* 90.
[3] Gunther Frantz, *Russlands Eintritt in den Weltkrieg* (Berlin, 1924), 30, p. 189.

frontiers operated almost as a general mobilization.[1] As a result of the measures which began to be carried out on 26 July, the Russian armies when war broke out were able to take the field sooner than was expected. But the measures had been designed for the whole of Russian territory, without distinguishing between the Austrian and the German frontiers, hence they also operated against Germany and this explains the alarm of the German military authorities who in the following days learnt from many quarters of Russian military preparations and got Bethmann to make protests to Sazonov.

The latter on the afternoon of that same 25 July had a talk with Buchanan and Paléologue and informed them of the measures approved that morning by the Tsar, including the mobilization, when the Foreign Minister should judge necessary, of 1,100,000 men. This important conversation, also, has left no trace in the *French Diplomatic Documents*, despite the importance of the statements made at it by Paléologue. However, having kept from his Government's knowledge the decisions taken at the meeting of the Council of Ministers the preceding day, he could not go on hiding news that Paris might perfectly well learn from London. Hence at 6.22 p.m. on the 25th he telegraphed to Paris that at the Council of Ministers held at Krasnoe Selo that morning under the presidence of the Tsar, it had been decided in principle to mobilize the thirteen army corps which were destined if necessary to operate against Austria. '. . . Secret preparations will commence from to-day'.[2]

The 'secret preparations' were those resulting from the proclamation of the 'pre-mobilization period'. When Buchanan heard of the mobilization of 1,100,000 men he expressed the earnest hope that Russia would not precipitate war by mobilizing until Grey had had time to use his influence in favour of peace.

His Excellency assured me that Russia had no aggressive intentions and that she would take no action until it was forced on her. French Ambassador then said he had received a number of telegrams from Minister in charge of Ministry for Foreign Affairs, that no one of them displayed slightest sign of hesitation, and that he was in position to give His Excellency formal assurance that France placed herself unreservedly on Russia's side. After thanking him, Minister for Foreign Affairs turned to me with question 'And your Government?' I repeated what I had said to Emperor in audience that England could play rôle of mediator at Berlin and Vienna to better purpose as friend who, if her counsels of moderation were disregarded, might be one day converted into an ally, than if she were to declare herself Russia's ally at once.

[1] Fay (II, pp. 303–21) gives a full account of these military measures.
[2] DF. XI, 50.

Sazonov pertinently observed to Buchanan that

unfortunately Germany was convinced that she could count upon our neutrality. With the exception of *The Times*, nearly the whole of English press was on the side of Austria. . . . He did not believe that Germany really wanted war, but her attitude was decided by ours. If we took our stand firmly with France and Russia there would be no war. If we failed them now, rivers of blood would flow and we would in the end be dragged into war.

The French Ambassador remarked that French Government would want to know at once whether our fleet was prepared to play part assigned to it by Anglo-French Naval Convention. He could not believe that England would not stand by her two friends, who were acting as one in this matter.[1]

Buchanan's report ends as follows:

I said all I could to impress prudence on Minister for Foreign Affairs, and warned him, if Russia mobilized, Germany would not be content with mere mobilization or give Russia time to carry out hers, but would probably declare war at once. His Excellency assured me once more that he did not wish to precipitate a conflict, but unless Germany can restrain Austria I can regard situation as desperate. Russia cannot allow Germany to crush Serbia and become predominant Power in Balkans, and, secure of support of France, she will face all the risks of war. For ourselves position is a most perilous one, and we shall have to choose between giving Russia our active support or renouncing her friendship. If we fail her now we cannot hope to maintain that friendly co-operation with her in Asia that is of such vital importance to us.[2]

Buchanan had every reason to utter the warning that 'if Russia mobilized, Germany would not be content with mere mobilization or give Russia time to carry out hers, but would probably declare war at once', for this was exactly what came to pass. And he was wise to impress prudence on Sazonov, while Paléologue worked in the opposite direction. In truth, the news soon leaked out that serious decisions had been taken that morning. On seeing that the Council of Ministers was holding such a long meeting, all who were gathered at Krasnoe Selo were seized with a feeling of anxiety, especially as the review had been rushed through in a hurry and it was announced that the manoeuvres had been suspended and troops were returning to their standing quarters. That evening, too, came the ceremony at which the military cadets received promotion as officers, and at the banquet that followed the newly promoted officers voiced their joy at marching against Austria. The banquet was followed by a dramatic show at which

---

[1] At this point the *British Documents* (XI, 125) in a footnote refer to a sentence from the Introduction (page xii): 'In raising this question the French Ambassador was acting without instructions from his Government. He was only with characteristic impulsiveness giving expression to his own personal view.'

[2] BD. XI, 125.

occurred a great demonstration in favour of war organized by Grand Duke Nicholas. All these signs did not escape General Chelius, the German Military Plenipotentiary at the Russian Court. On the 25th he telegraphed and on the 26th he sent a written report on them to Berlin: 'I have the impression that all preparations are being made for mobilization against Austria' and on the 26th he wrote that the Master of the Horse, the Germanophil Baron Grünwald had said to him at dinner:

the situation is very serious; what was decided on this morning I cannot tell you, you will no doubt soon learn it yourself; but you may take it that matters look very serious.[1]

5. *War is in the air; Sazonov appeals to London and Rome.*

It is true to say that by the threat of mobilizing Sazonov simply meant to put pressure on Austria and Germany and make them draw back from the dangerous course on which they had embarked. But those around him who were most in a position to know, regarded the taking of this decision as a sure step towards war. In the late afternoon of the 25th Paléologue, who seems to have lost all control of his language, confided to the Italian Ambassador Carlotti:

that the Council of Ministers this forenoon has taken decisions on the necessary directives and measures to be put into force in the war against Austria and Germany, now regarded as imminent. He added that France was ready to fulfil her duty as an ally to the full. To my query whether he thought the situation hopeless he answered that in his opinion the dispute presented itself no longer exclusively as between Austria and Serbia but between Germany and Russia and that the attitude of the Vienna Cabinet, impervious to all idea of conciliation, indicated its firm decision to provoke war. To my extremely emphatic objections he answered that the facts would confirm his statements, but that the Triple *Entente*, although convinced of the uselessness of its endeavours will do everything possible to avert a European catastrophe, or at least to make it clear on whom the terrible responsibility rests. Paléologue ended with the remark that the only gleam of hope left comes from London and Rome where perhaps an effort is being made to use their great influence in Berlin in order to make an attempt at mediation for the preservation of peace.[2]

Paléologue himself narrates:

At 7 o'clock this evening [the 25th] I went to the Warsaw station to say good-bye to Izvolsky who is returning to his post [in Paris] in haste. There was a great bustle on the platforms. The trains were packed with officers and men. This looked like mobilization. We rapidly exchanged impressions and came to the same conclusion: 'It is war this time.'[3]

[1] DD. I, 194, 291.

[2] Carlotti towards midnight telegraphed Paléologue's impressions to San Giuliano and his telegram is reproduced in KSF., May 1924, p. 164.

[3] Paléologue, I, p. 35.

The Russian generals all took the same view. Dobrorolski writes that after 24–25 July

war was a foregone conclusion and the whole deluge of telegrams between the Governments of Russia and Germany was only the *mise en scène* of a historical drama.[1]

It may be said that Paléologue, Izvolsky and the generals were taking their fancies for facts. War had not been decided, the Russian partial mobilization had been sanctioned but was not yet to be promulgated. However the proclamation of the 'pre-mobilization period' set in motion one cogwheel of the sinister war machine and brought on to the scene the army chiefs who with their technical demands were to frustrate all attempts at a peaceful settlement. The first critical date in the progress of the Great Powers towards the catastrophe of the war had been 5 July, when Germany agreed, and indeed urged, that Austria should take action against Serbia. The second critical date is 25 July when the first Russian military measures were decided on. But however serious the error of judgement made by Sazonov, and attributable as it in some measure was to the influence of Paléologue, and however much Sazonov in his heart of hearts doubted that war could be averted, he does not seem to have had any conception of what would be the consequences of the actual measures he proposed. He was under the illusion that he could at will regulate their application and scope and that they could be set in motion without any danger to the peace which he was so genuinely seeking to safeguard. This sincere desire he showed by refraining from mobilizing against Germany, sending agitated appeals to England and Serbia and not overlooking the potentialities of Italy.

On 25 July besides talking to Buchanan, as we have seen above, he telegraphed to Benckendorff, the Russian Ambassador to London, asking him to say to Grey:

So long as it is possible to avert a European war, it is easier for England than for any other Power to exert a moderating influence upon Austria. . . . Unfortunately, according to our information, Austria on the day prior to that on which she took action in Belgrade thought she was justified in hoping that she would meet with no opposition from England. . . . It was therefore very desirable that England should firmly and clearly make it understood that she considers Austria's action unjustified by the circumstances and extremely dangerous to European peace. . . . In the event of the situation becoming more acute . . . we rely upon England's not delaying to range herself definitely on the side of Russia and France in order to maintain that European balance for which she has always stood in the past, and which in the event of Austria's victory will undoubtedly be broken.[2]

---

[1] Dobrorolski, pp. 21–2.
[2] Schilling, p. 86–7.

Besides appealing directly to London, Sazonov also advised Serbia to do the same on her own account, telegraphing instructions to the Russian Chargé d'Affaires at Belgrade to suggest to Pašić that:

In view of the special position of England . . . war between Austria and Serbia might perhaps yet be averted if the Serbian Government addressed a request for mediation to the English Government.

And to Benckendorff he telegraphed the text of this telegram adding: 'Should the Serbs take a step of this kind, please support them energetically'.[1]

But this the Serbian Government declined to do. On 27 July Strandtmann telegraphed from Nish that Pašić had that morning promised him to submit Sazonov's suggestion to a Cabinet meeting. But an hour later he had said

that the insufficiently clarified position taken up by England towards the events that are developing and her tendency, shown in the news that is coming in, not to let herself become involved in any conflict which may arise, causes the Serbian Government to be apprehensive about the success of a *démarche* which might give England a pretext for not adopting a definite attitude towards Austria and Germany.

Strandtmann's dispatch continues:

I have the impression that the Serbian Government [i.e. Pašić] now after the delivery of its reply to Austria, in which the most far-reaching concessions have been made, fears by any request for mediation to rouse the suspicion that it could go any further to meet the demands addressed to it. I further believe that under the influence of telegrams coming in from Spalaiković depicting the enthusiasm with which Russia has been seized, Pašić thinks it would be disadvantageous to Serbia to displace the centre of gravity of the question from St. Petersburg to another European capital.[2]

In truth the Serbs had every reason to be mistrustful of Grey, since he had shown not the slightest regard for their interests. As for Sazonov, the same thing was probably happening with him as had happened in 1912 when he first egged on Serbia and Bulgaria to attack Turkey and then in vain sought to hold them back. Hence it came about that neither London nor Belgrade paid any heed to Sazonov's appeals.

And Rome was equally deaf to them. When Pašić got back to Belgrade on the morning of the 24th, he fell in at once with Strandtmann's suggestion that it would be a good idea if Serbia were to ask for mediation by the King of Italy, uncle of the Prince Regent.[3] Strandtmann's next dispatch accordingly reports that the Cabinet meeting which had just been held had resolved that the Regent should send a telegram to

---

[1] Schilling, pp. 87–8.   [2] *Int. Bez.* i. V, 149.   [3] *Int. Bez.* i. V, 35.

the Italian King asking for his good offices to obtain an extension of
the time limit and a softening of the demands conflicting with Serbian
law.[1] We have already seen that on the evening of the 24th Sazonov had
adopted the suggestion of asking for an extension of the time limit.
Now on the 26th he took the further step of sending to Krupensky,
the Russian Ambassador to Rome, the following telegram, which was
communicated also to London and Paris:

> We are of the opinion that Italy might play a prominent part in safe-
> guarding peace if she would adequately use her good offices with Austria and
> take up a definitely adverse attitude towards the conflict, as the latter cannot
> remain localized. It would be desirable if you would give it as your personal
> conviction, that it would be impossible for Russia to refrain from going to
> the help of Serbia.[2]

Sazonov was perfectly right in thinking that both Italy and England
had a duty to perform in so grave a crisis. But neither country showed
itself capable of fulfilling this duty, as we shall now proceed to see.

6. *The text of the Austrian ultimatum is communicated to the Consulta on the morning
of 24 July;.the discussion between Salandra, San Giuliano, and Flotow.*

We have already seen that the Austrian ultimatum was presented at
Belgrade on 23 July at 6 p.m. The Italian Government, which under the
terms of the Triple Alliance should have had advance knowledge of it,
only received communication of it on the following day.

Berchtold, it is true, had inquired of Merey

whether it would not be useful to advise Marquis San Giuliano one day or
several hours beforehand in order to avoid offending him and to enable him
to exercise influence on the Italian press and public in favour of loyalty to the
alliance.[3]

Merey on the 14th had replied advising that San Giuliano be appraised one day in advance. On 15 July Berchtold had agreed and on
20 July had said to Tschirschky that 'in order to show the utmost consideration towards Italy' a general communication to her might now
be made.[4] But the same day he telegraphed to Merey to let San Giuliano
know the actual text of the note only on the morning of 24 July, i.e.
after it had been delivered to Serbia.[5] These conflicting instructions led
Merey to telegraph on 22 July: 'I think I must assume that Your
Excellency—unfortunately without informing me—has changed your
mind'.[6]

This was exactly what had happened, probably under the influence
of Forgach and Musulin. They on the evening of 22 July obtained

---

[1] *Int. Bez.* i. V, 36.   [2] *Int Bez.* i. V, 84.   [3] Oe-U. VIII, 10221.
[4] Oe-U. VIII, 10264, 10289; DD. I, 104.   [5] Oe-U. VIII, 10400.
[6] Oe-U. VIII, 10496.

Berchtold's signature to a telegram instructing Merey to appraise San Giuliano in the afternoon of 23 July in the strictest confidence that the *démarche* at Belgrade would be carried out that very Thursday 23 July 'in the afternoon', giving him a general notion of the note in terms to which we shall revert later, and letting him see the text only on 24 July, the day after its delivery at Belgrade. The object of these precautions is obvious: 'We wish at all costs to prevent the news from reaching St. Petersburg from Rome on the actual day'.[1] The exasperated Merey replied on 23 July that on the 14th and 15th Berchtold had sent him other instructions, that there could be no more question of an act of courtesy towards Italy, as had been agreed with Tschirschky, since Rome would be acquainted with the text of the note only on the same afternoon as it was delivered (in fact it was not until the following day). As ill-luck would have it, he himself had fallen ill, so that the task of making the communication would fall to Count Ambrozy, who would drive over to Fiuggi for the purpose.[2] Ambrozy saw San Giuliano at 4 p.m. on 23 July and handed him a note reproducing the content of Berchtold's telegram:

The Minister of Austria-Hungary to Belgrade has been instructed to make the *démarche* on Thursday 23 July in the afternoon. He will hand to the Serbian Government a note containing a certain number of requests which Austria-Hungary finds herself obliged to present in consequence of the findings resulting from the Sarajevo inquiry and after having recognized that we must put an end to the seditious agitation fomented from Belgrade in our southern frontier provinces. We have given the Serbian Government a time limit of 48 hours for the acceptance of our demands, since we cannot tolerate the habitual delays of the Belgrade Cabinet.

The signatory powers will officially be appraised of the contents ·of our note on Friday the 24th. A similar communication is being made only to Rome, Berlin and Bucharest as an act of special courtesy towards the allied Powers.[3]

San Giuliano's reply can be learnt from Merey's telegram of 1 a.m. on the 24th to Berchtold giving the substance of the San Giuliano-Ambrozy interview.

He could not—he said—express any view without knowing what demands the Imperial and Royal Government had made on the Belgrade Cabinet and discussing them with the Prime Minister. The latter was due next day at Fiuggi where a discussion would take place between him and San Giuliano and the German Ambassador who was also there. Privately and unofficially San Giuliano expressed concern about the effect on public opinion. He gave

---

[1] Oe-U. VIII, 10494.   [2] Oe-U. VIII, 10542.

[3] Salandra, p. 74. Salandra gives this communication as having been made to De Martino not to San Giuliano, but the following lines show that it was San Giuliano who sent Ambrozy on to De Martino.

Count Ambrozy a letter for the Secretary General De Martino said to contain instructions to calm the press down as soon as the news of our delivery of the ultimatum reaches Rome. Herr von Flotow, on whom Ambrozy also called, told him that San Giuliano was not only concerned about the attitude of Italian public opinion in the event of our demands being very humiliating for Serbia, but also anxious to know whether we would carry out our intention of refraining from territorial acquisition. To Count Ambrozy's remark that we had given no engagement on this head the Ambassador replied that he could understand that we would not be willing to give a binding undertaking. But he thought that if we could decide to do so it would be easier to keep Italy in step with us.[1]

From Fiuggi Flotow telegraphed to Berlin on the morning of 24 July mentioning Ambrozy's calls on himself and San Giuliano of the previous day and adding that San Giuliano had said to him that he

feared the bad impression that the time limit would produce and had in the night sent directions through the Prime Minister to all prefects to suppress anti-Austrian demonstrations and prevent any recruiting of volunteers for Serbia. He thinks it contrary to spirit of the Triple Alliance to have undertaken such action without first taking counsel with allies.

This dispatch was sent on to Tschirschky in Vienna with the comment in Jagow's hand: 'The Vienna Cabinet, according to this, has not after all kept the promise made to Your Excellency'.[2] Tschirschky answered on 25 July:

I to-day took Baron Macchio to task, asking why the promise made to me to communicate the note to Marquis San Giuliano through Herr von Merey before its delivery at Belgrade . . . had not been kept. Macchio's explanation was that the unfortunate conduct of the matter had been the consequence of a misunderstanding of Merey's. He had been informed that Marquis San Giuliano was to come to Rome from Fiuggi and had therefore intended to make communication of the note in Rome. San Giuliano had in fact gone to Rome but had again left when the Ambassador asked to speak to him. Merey then suddenly fell ill and had to send the Embassy Counsellor to Fiuggi on the following day.[3]

A tissue of falsehoods on the part of Macchio which completes the documentation on the shameless way in which Vienna violated both letter and spirit of the engagements entered into under the Triple Alliance.

The actual text of the ultimatum was made known to the Consulta on 24 July when before noon Ambrozy handed it to De Martino. The impression it produced could not be other than painful. It was patent that many of the demands were so injurious to the honour and independence of Serbia that they could not be accepted by Belgrade, while

[1] Oe-U. VIII, 10544.   [2] DD. I, 136.   [3] DD. I, 187.

acceptance of part of them would enable the Monarchy to invade at once and smash its diminutive enemy. It might have occurred to the Consulta that European public opinion would rise against such a clear case of aggression which showed that Austria-Hungary had no other means of prolonging her existence than by the increasing oppression of her non-German and non-Magyar populations. The Italian nation had gained its unity by suffering the same calvary and would, better than any other, share the feelings of the Serbs and espouse their cause, all the more because Serbia's interest in saving her present and future existence coincided with the interest of Italy not to strengthen the Dual Monarchy or let it extend further into the Near East. But the Consulta lived in a world of its own with its windows closed to the realities outside. De Martino read the note without finding anything objectionable in it. He only said at the end: 'We seem to have come to a turning point in history'. When Ambrozy enlarged on the purely defensive character of the Austrian action, he replied:

Certainly I should never have believed it possible to uncover and prove the complicity of Serbian officers and officials in the Sarajevo drama.[1]

This stupidity on the part of the senior permanent official at the Consulta reflects the attitude of San Giuliano who despite what he had gleaned of the nature of the note had issued no instructions to his staff as to what line to take.

Suffering from painful and crippling gout which was soon to bring him to his grave, San Giuliano was, as we know, at Fiuggi where Flotow was also staying and where Salandra joined him on the morning of the 24th. The three men were in conversation awaiting the text of the note when towards noon it was telephoned on to them from the Consulta.

When we read the note [writes Salandra] all the colour left our faces. We had the vision of impending catastrophe. Even Flotow paled visibly and said that until that moment he had not known the text of the note.[2]

This was, indeed, true, whereas it is not correct that the Italian Government—as Salandra maintains, blaming Garroni the Italian Ambassdor to the Porte, for not having informed him—was completely in the dark about the Austrian Government's designs.[3] The documents quoted above prove the opposite to be true. Salandra and San Giuliano were prepared for a blow of that sort, for they at once took measures which had clearly been concerted in advance, it being inconceivable that they could have made their decisions as to what was to be done in the very presence of the German Ambassador. Their plans were formulated in a telegram to the Italian Ambassadors to Vienna and Berlin,

[1] Oe-U. VIII, 10611.   [2] Salandra, p. 75.   [3] Salandra, p. 69.

drafted by San Giuliano and summarizing the Fiuggi conversation. In Salandra's famous Campidoglio speech he read the first part of this telegram which runs as follows:

To-day we have had a long conversation between the Prime Minister, Flotow and myself, which I summarize for the personal information of Your Excellency and for your guidance in further conversations.

We, Salandra and I, first of all drew the Ambassador's attention to the fact that Austria has no right, according to the spirit of the treaty of the Triple Alliance, to undertake a *démarche* such as she has made at Belgrade without previous agreement with her allies.

By the style in which the note is couched and the demands it contains, which, while ineffective against the Pan-Serb danger are deeply offensive to Serbia and indirectly to Russia, Austria has plainly shown that she means to provoke a war. We therefore told Flotow that, in view of this behaviour on the part of Austria and of the defensive and conservative character of the treaty of the Triple Alliance, Italy is under no obligation to go to the help of Austria in case that, as a result of this *démarche* of hers, she finds herself at war with Russia, since any European war in this case is the consequence of an act of provocation and aggression by Austria.

No obligation, therefore, for Italy to intervene! But would she intervene or not? The reply to this question is contained in the further part of the telegram which Salandra in his Campidoglio speech thought fit to suppress, feeling that at the moment it would produce an unfavourable impression. He only published it thirteen years later in his *La Neutralità Italiana*. Here it is:—

However the fact that we are under no obligation [to take part in a European war provoked by Austrian aggression against Serbia] does not exclude the possibility that it may suit us to take part in the eventual war, if this were to correspond with our vital interests.

In view of the political regime in our country any such participation by us would in no case be possible if the Government could not give the country beforehand the certitude of an advantage commensurate with the risks and of a nature to surmount the opposition of public opinion to a war fought in the interest of Austria. The latter of late has committed a good many mistakes which have brought about a recession by not a few steps in the work of progressive mutual *rapprochement* which was being carried out, thanks in part to Your Excellency's intelligent co-operation.

We also brought it to Flotow's notice that it is not possible for the Royal Government to lay down its line of conduct in the present question without first knowing whether our allies concur in our interpretation of Article VII. I have the impression that Flotow regards it as correct. If we are not sure that it is accepted by our allies, we shall be compelled to follow a policy contrary to that of Austria in all Balkan questions except Albania, on which special agreements exist between Italy and Austria.

Flotow several times in the course of the conversation hinted at the necessity for territorial compensations for us in case of territorial acquisitions by Austria.

Salandra and I further pointed out to Flotow, who signified his assent, that the Austrian communication does not for the time being require a reply and consequently we for the moment have no motive for pronouncing an opinion.[1]

This is as much as to say that in a European war developing out of Austria's action there would be no *casus foederis* for Italy, but she might come into the war if assured beforehand, or rather if able to persuade the nation beforehand, that there was the certainty of her obtaining 'an advantage commensurate with the risk and of a nature to overcome the opposition of public opinion to a war fought in the interests of Austria'. Let her allies, therefore, set about recognizing Italy's right to compensation under Article VII. Only on such terms would Italy pursue a Balkan policy favourable to Austria.

Here we have had San Giuliano's version of the conversation of 24 July. We must now look at Flotow's account given in a telegram of 25 July, following after another much shorter one of 24 July, and copiously underlined and annotated by the Kaiser as is here partly shown:

In a rather excited conversation of several hours with Prime Minister Salandra and Marquis San Giuliano, the latter said that in the case of an aggressive action by Austria and one bringing so many consequences in its train, the spirit of the Triplice Treaty would have demanded that she come to a previous understanding with her allies. As in respect of Italy this has not taken place, Italy cannot regard herself as bound by the further consequences of this *démarche*.

Moreover Article VII of the Triplice Treaty lays down that in case of changes in the Balkans, the contracting parties are to consult together beforehand and that if one were to acquire an addition of territory there, the other would receive compensation.

Upon my observing that, as far as I knew, Austria had declared she did not purpose to make territorial acquisitions, the Minister said that such a declaration had been only very provisional. It had been rather that Austria had declared she did not now propose to make territorial acquisitions, leaving the way open for later different decisions, should they become necessary. The Minister did not think it could be taken ill if he took precautionary measures in good time.

The text of the Austrian note was so aggressively and clumsily worded that the public opinion of Europe and also of Italy would be against Austria and no Italian Government could make headway against that.

After Marquis San Giuliano forcibly represented, on the basis of the Triplice treaty, that the Treaty is binding for a war of defence but that Austria is now proceeding aggressively and that therefore, even in the case of Russian intervention, Italy would not be bound, I vigorously combated this stand-

---

[1] Salandra, pp. 76–8.

point and after long discussion elicited the statement that in this and the above quoted utterances of Marquis San Giuliano it was only a question of taking up a *position in principle* (*'vanity therefore'*) which would not exclude other decisions on the part of the Italian Government. I explained at length that at this stage what was of importance was not *what might have to happen* later, but at the present moment to display *to the world the compactness and unity of the Triple Alliance* (*'Just so'*) and to avoid everything that might lead Russia and France to an assumption of inner disunity among the allies. I therefore was obliged to insist on influence being brought to bear on the press in this sense. Austria did not demand an answer, there was thus for the present no embarrassing necessity to make one. In the end I secured assent on this point.

My impression is that the only way of holding Italy is *to promise her compensations in good time*, if Austria takes territorial possession of the Lovčen or occupies it (*'the little thief must always get his bit to gobble up as well'*).

I found Salandra fairly easy to convince. He grasped that Austrian vital interests are involved.[1]

We need not linger to comment on the Kaiser's vulgar taunts at Italian wavering, nor single out discrepancies, which are more of form than of substance, between the two versions. If anything, Flotow's telegram gives the impression that San Giuliano was being wary about defining what line Italy would take if war broke out, when he said that the refusal to recognize the *casus foederis* was only a 'position in principle', whereas Salandra was 'fairly easy to convince'. On the whole Flotow remained puzzled, and on the following day, the 25th, sent the Chancellor a letter which reached Berlin on the 27th and gave less hope of Italy's making common cause with Austria but thought the possibility remote that she might, if denied satisfaction, range herself against Austria. This third dispatch runs:

From yesterday's discussion with Salandra and Marquis San Giuliano which at several points gave rise to sharp clashes between Marquis San Giuliano and myself, three points seemed on the Italian side to take definite shape. Firstly, fear of Italian public opinion, secondly the consciousness of military weakness, and thirdly the desire to turn the occasion to good account and win something for Italy, if possible the Trentino.

The possibility that Italy might eventually even turn against Austria was not directly expressed by Marquis San Giuliano, it only sounded faintly in slight hints. I did not seize upon these hints, as I thought it better not to admit any such possibility. I have the impression that even the occupation of purely Serbian territory would not necessarily lead to such a step on the part of Italy. It would only render Italy's already by no means unimpeachable relations with Russia still more close knit. On the other hand I should regard it as extremely desirable if Austria, especially at the beginning, could avoid the occupation of the Lovčen. If that is not possible then Austria must first make offers of compensation here. For the occupation of the Lovčen would

[1] DD. I, 156, 168.

in fact alarm all Italy and force the Government further than it would wish. In all these things one must bear in mind that this Cabinet is far less strong and therefore less capable of resistance than the Giolitti Ministry.

His Majesty the King in the parliamentary and democratic conditions here will not be in the position to exercise a decisive influence.

As already reported, Marquis San Giuliano, on grounds of the wording of the Austrian note, emphatically maintains that Austria's procedure against Serbia is an aggressive one and that therefore any intervention of Russia and France that might result would not turn the war into a defensive one and produce the *casus foederis*. I vigorously attacked this standpoint for tactical reasons. But it is to be foreseen that Italy will keep tight hold of this possibility of slipping out.

Net result therefore: Active help from Italy in any European conflict that may arise is scarcely to be counted on. A directly hostile attitude to Austria on the part of Italy could, as far as can to-day be seen, be averted by a wise policy on Austria's part.[1]

These varying shades of emphasis in the different accounts of the Fiuggi conversation of 23 July give the impression that feeling ran high and that San Giuliano passed through several states of mind without leaving the German Ambassador with any clear impression of what line he intended to take.

7. *The Italian Government's views set forth by San Giuliano in a letter to the King of Italy.*

There is another document which reveals the true views of the Italian Government at this first moment when the European war began to loom up. It is a letter revealed by Salandra which San Giuliano wrote to the King:

Fiuggi, 24 July 1914.

Sire,

As Your Majesty will have seen from the telegrams going off, both I in my instructions to Your Majesty's representatives and in conversations with foreign representatives, and Salandra and I in our to-day's conversation with Flotow, have up to the present said and done nothing that might limit Italy's freedom of action in the events which may derive from the Austrian *démarche* at Belgrade.

It was, indeed, our duty to await and we do await Your Majesty's orders; and to Your Majesty's high wisdom I submit the line of conduct proposed by me to the President of the Council and approved by him, subject to Your Majesty's approval.

We are both convinced that it is most difficult, perhaps impossible, and certainly extremely dangerous to drag Italy into taking part in an eventual war provoked by Austria and waged in the interest of Austria.

It is also necessary before committing ourselves to a definite line of conduct

[1] DD. I, 244.

to assure ourselves that it will be the one most corresponding to our interests. It seems to me, then, that what is expedient for us is:

1. to maintain to our allies that for reasons adduced in the telegrams now being dispatched we are under no obligation to take part in the eventual war.

2. to assure ourselves, before supporting our allies even diplomatically, that they accept our interpretation of Article VII of the treaty of the Triple Alliance;

3. to assure ourselves of eventual compensations for any increase of territory whatsoever on the part of Austria;

4. to assure ourselves of eventual compensations for our eventual, but not probable participation in the war, a participation to be decided *pro* or *contra* freely when the time comes;

5. possibly also to secure for ourselves doubtless very minor compensations, or at least guarantees that our interests shall not be damaged, in return for any diplomatic support given to our allies.

This attitude on our part is for the moment facilitated by the fact that Austria-Hungary has not up to the present asked us for any support or even for any opinion whatever regarding her note to Serbia.[1]

The present writer has often wondered why Salandra thought fit to publish this document. If he did so in the interests of pure historic truth, there can be nothing but praise for his act of self-abnegation. If San Giuliano's letter proves anything, it proves that the Italian Government at that juncture was miles away from perceiving the sole road that, both for her honour and for her interest, Italy ought to have chosen. It did, indeed, lay down that Austria's action was aggressive and that therefore Italy was absolved from the obligation of going to her support if a general war were to result. It put forward various suggestions as to the line Italy was to take in such a war, a line that was to be subject to the treatment Italy would receive from Austria. But having formulated these reservations, it expressed the view that the Austrian communication did not require an answer and that consequently for the time being Italy had no reason to voice an opinion. In fact the last thing that San Giuliano thought of was to avail himself of Italian rights and Austrian obligations for the one purpose of blocking Austria's way, as should have been his sole aim if he did not mean to have war. He had received from Russia the advice, backed by solid arguments, to warn Vienna in time, and yet he took no account of this appeal.

It goes without saying that to block Austria's way, San Giuliano would have to be determined not to join the fight at her side and to say so right from the beginning both at Berlin and Vienna, without renouncing, nay, demanding recognition of Italy's rights under Article VII. Instead of this what San Giuliano did was to admit that it would be 'most difficult, perhaps impossible and certainly extremely

[1] Salandra, pp. 78–80.

dangerous to drag Italy into taking part in an eventual war provoked by Austria and waged in the interest of Austria', but he did not rule out the possibility entirely. What concerned him was 'to assure ourselves of eventual compensations for our eventual, but not probable, participation in the war, *a participation to be decided pro or contra freely when the time comes*'. It never occurred to him that there could be no such freedom for Italy, since in 1902 she had concluded an agreement with France pledging her to remain neutral in a war of aggression provoked by the Central Powers. Either it was not now a question of an aggressive war and then Italy was bound to recognize the *casus foederis*, or Italy refused to recognize the *casus foederis* and then she must herself recognize that France had the right to Italy's neutrality. There was no escaping the horns of this dilemma. For Italy in 1914 only two courses were open: either to march forthwith at the side of her allies, or to declare her neutrality. To march with her allies later when suitable compensation had been guaranteed was not possible without a breach of contract. And if the first alternative was 'most difficult, perhaps impossible and certainly dangerous' then the second alternative must be chosen at once.

The great mistake committed by Salandra and San Giuliano was not to be certain from the first that it was disastrous and impossible for Italy to intervene with her allies in a war of this kind and that she must shape her course accordingly. This mistake—and let this be admitted by the present writer who in almost all things has been Giolitti's political adversary—would never have been made by Giolitti, as is proved by his firm attitude in July 1913. And it is the present writer's conviction that it would never have been made by Salandra, either, if this precedent had been brought to his knowledge. Knowing nothing of it, he let himself be carried along in the wake of San Giuliano. Both men flattered themselves that they were being super diplomats. They had no realization of the fact that by posing the question in such terms, by letting Austria have her will without putting in their veto, by confining themselves for the moment to declaring that for the time being there was no obligation for Italy to intervene, by making their subsequent action depend on an agreement on compensations, and by regarding Italian participation in the war on the side of the Central Powers as even remotely possible, they were losing sight of the nature and aims of the Austrian aggression against Serbia and bartering away the supreme interests, both material and moral, of Europe and Italy in return for a strip of national territory which Italy ought to gain by more honourable means.

Years later Salandra was to write a magnificent page in his book summarizing the motives which, when the time came, were to induce the two Ministers to decide on neutrality. There he says that the attack

on Serbia, whether or not ending in her loss of territory, would imply
'the definitive hegemony of Austria and thereby the triumphant invasion of the Balkan peninsula by *Deutschtum*, the end of all possibility
of Italian expansion, the commercial and military loss of the Adriatic'.
And then he continues:

from the wedge of the Trentino pointing at the heart of the Peninsula, from
Garda rapidly becoming Germanized, from Trieste the German emporium
for the Near East, we should have been more and more irrevocably surrounded, penetrated, strangled by *Deutschtum*. . . . The kingdom of Italy,
even if sharing in their victory, would have been at best the first vassal state
of the Reich.[1]

These are indisputable facts, yet they played no part in, and indeed
stand in direct contradiction to, both the diplomatic action deployed
by Italy before and after the ultimatum to Serbia, and Sonnino's later
negotiations with Vienna. The conception by which the Prime Minister
Salandra was guided was none other than that, if Italy could not join
with Austria in making war, she could 'secure doubtless very minor
compensations . . . in return for any diplomatic support given to our
allies', support, that is, for a venture so counter to Italian feelings,
interests and future prospects. The following coherent principles, were,
alas, recognized by Salandra only much later: 1. it should have been
realized already on 15 July that public feeling in Italy no less than the
true interests of the country would make it impossible for her to join
in the Austrian venture; 2. Italy's allies should have immediately been
notified that they could not undertake anything without Italian consent
except in violation of the letter and spirit of the alliance and on pain
of obliging Italy to deny the existence of the *casus foederis*, if not to take
still more drastic action; 3. efforts should have been made, by seeking
especially the co-operation of England, to prevent war from breaking
out; 4. Austria's attention should have been drawn to the violation of
Article VII, but without any reference to compensations due to Italy,
since these could only have been obtained to the detriment of Italy's
good name and of the European balance of power, which were interests infinitely transcending the satisfactions provided by any obtainable
concessions. This would have been a farsighted policy, rich in moral
prestige, capable of being developed, as it actually was later, and, above
all, such as to spare Italy the accusations of treachery subsequently
levelled against her. If, when the war was on, Italy had been able to
bring forward proofs of having made efforts to avert it, efforts based on
her rights under the alliance and on the duties which the alliance imposed upon the Central Powers, her decision in May 1915 to enter the
war against the Central Powers would have gone down to history as a

[1] Salandra, pp. 87–8.

great deed. This decision she could have reached in her own good time by the open high road, not down back streets where she forfeited every shred of dignity by seeking rewards without fighting for them and running the risk of being defrauded of them after all.

Let it for the moment suffice to make clear that, after remaining passive in the days preceding the delivery to Serbia of the Austrian ultimatum while being well aware of its nature and its dangers, San Giuliano now, once the ultimatum had been presented, denied that a *casus foederis* existed, but not that it could not be allowed to exist if suitable compensations were forthcoming. He made not the slightest effort to put up opposition such as might cause the Central Powers to think twice about the possible effects of the aggression into which Austria was now about to plunge. He opined that 'for the time being no motive for pronouncing an opinion' existed, and in the succeeding days, as we shall see, he did still worse. By acting thus, he gave the green light to the general war that was on the point of breaking out. All he attempted was to make a proposal to London for the settlement of the conflict which will be discussed at a later moment and which was still-born, both as coming too late and as being too favourable to the Austrian thesis and contrary to that of Russia.

8. *Perplexity and confusion at the Quai d'Orsay; Bienvenu-Martin at first favourable to Austria; the belated arrival of instructions from Viviani.*

The Austrian ultimatum and the German circular note supporting it were of course made known to Paris and London also on 24 July. As we know, both the French President and Viviani, the Prime Minister and Foreign Minister, were absent from Paris. The Quai d'Orsay was left in the charge of Bienvenu-Martin, the Minister of Justice. His report made to Viviani on the communications made to him on the 24th by the Austrian Ambassador Szécsen and the German Ambassador Schoen and on his replies—published as Nos. 25 and 28 in the French *Yellow Book*—differs considerably from the telegrams sent home by the Austrian and German Ambassadors. But the suppressions, alterations, and falsifications that characterize this collection leave little room for doubt where the truth lies. The Ambassadors of the Central Powers had no reason to hide what they learnt from their Governments. The Quai d'Orsay, however, was for the moment totally unequal to dealing with the situation and in addition, as in the crisis of 1908–9, animated by such strongly Austrophil sentiments as could not be avowed when the *Yellow Book* came to be published. Hence the documents had to be falsified to make them fall into line with the instructions arriving from Poincaré and Viviani in St. Petersburg and above all with the events leading up to the war. This can easily be understood.

Bienvenu-Martin's first telegram, giving a summary of the ultimatum from the copy handed him by Szécsen, gives no hint of any exchange of ideas between himself and the Ambassador, but says that after their meeting Szécsen saw Berthelot who, on Bienvenu-Martin's instructions, pointed out to the Ambassador

the feeling of anxiety caused by the information available this morning about the contents of the Austrian note and the painful impression which could not fail to be produced on French public opinion by the time chosen for so categorical a *démarche* with so short a time limit; that is to say, a time when the President of the Republic and the President of the Council and Minister for Foreign Affairs of the Republic had left St. Petersburg and were at sea, and consequently were not able to exert, in agreement with those Powers which were not directly interested, that soothing influence on Serbia and Austria which was so desirable in the interest of general peace.[1]

In vain in Vol. XI of the French Diplomatic Documents would one seek a trace of this Szécsen-Berthelot conversation, which must thus be regarded as an interpolation in the *Yellow Book*. The telegram of 24 July sent to Viviani via the French Minister at Stockholm only gives a summary of the Austrian ultimatum, making no mention of any conversation with Szécsen.[2] According to the account given by Szécsen, which also says nothing of a conversation with Berthelot,

Bienvenu-Martin . . . seemed considerably perturbed by my communication . . . but readily admitted that the events of recent date and the bearing of the Serbian Government render a forceful *démarche* on our part quite understandable. Point V of the note seemed particularly to strike the Minister, for he had it read over to him twice. The Minister thanked me for my communication which, he said, would be carefully examined . . . . He agreed that it was the duty of Serbia to take strong measures against any accomplices in the Sarajevo murder. . . . Laying great emphasis on French good will towards Austria-Hungary . . . he expressed the hope that the dispute will be peacefully settled in a manner agreeable to our wishes. The Minister avoided any attempt to defend or extenuate in any way the attitude of Serbia.

The dispatch ends with the words of warning: 'On the conduct of foreign policy M. Martin has of course no influence.'[3] They show that Szécsen himself did not think any weight could be attached to the faint reactions of the Minister of Justice.

In the second telegram informing Viviani of Schoen's call with the circular note from the German Government asking for the 'localization of the conflict', Bienvenu-Martin states that he pointed out to the German Ambassador that:

Much as it might appear legitimate to demand the punishment of all those who were implicated in the Sarajevo outrage and *although it could be admitted*

[1] LJF. 25; CDD., pp. 156-7.   [2] DF. 3. XI, 13.   [3] Oe-U. VIII, 10606.

that Austria might desire to obtain guarantees of the ending and the repression of anti-Austrian propaganda, no less did it seem difficult on the contrary to demand measures incompatible with the dignity and sovereignty of Serbia; the Serbian Government, even were it willing to submit to them, would risk being swept away by a revolution. . . . I added that if the aim pursued by Austria was legitimate, the means of obtaining it (les modalités) might lend themselves to discussion and that if Serbia gave obvious proofs of good intentions, Austria ought to lend herself to discussions. It should perhaps not be made too difficult for third Powers, who neither morally nor in sentiment could do otherwise than take an interest in Serbia, to take an attitude in conformity with the desire expressed by Germany to localize the conflict.[1]

Here, too, there are marked differences from Schoen's version which says that Bienvenu-Martin

was visibly relieved at our view that the Austro-Serbian conflict should be settled between the two parties concerned. . . . He says the French Government will make efforts in this sense in the interests of the preservation of European peace. It can, however, not conceal that a power such as Russia, which has Pan-Slav currents to reckon with, will not find it so easy to disinterest itself completely, especially if Austria-Hungary were to insist on immediate fulfilment of all demands, even of those which are hard to reconcile with Serbian sovereignty or are materially not immediately executable. French Government thinks there is no question but that Serbia should make reparation in convincing manner and assure Austria-Hungary of the punishment of delinquents and the prevention of conspiracies against her. From here advice has been sent to the Serbs to yield all they possibly can.[2]

Nay more, Szécsen sent Berchtold another telegram on the same day saying that Berthelot had also been present at the Bienvenu-Martin interview with Schoen and had expressed the opinion that

the Serbian Government ought at once to declare its acceptance of the note in principle, but ask for explanations and further details on certain points.[3]

And these impressions of the two Ambassadors find confirmation in a telegram from Sevastopulo, the Russian Chargé d'Affaires at Paris, telling St. Petersburg that Schoen's tone left the impression 'that hope had not been given up of settling the incident by Austro-Serbian negotiations'.[4]

What a contrast to the line taken by Poincaré and Paléologue! But it was above all Bienvenu-Martin's lack of comprehension that led the Ambassadors to take such an optimistic view of the Paris situation. Victor Margueritte has informed the present writer that Berthelot on 24 July actually said to him that a European war was now inevitable

---

[1] LJF. 28; DF. 3. XI, 20.—The sentence in italics is omitted in the *Yellow Book* which contains other variants; CDD., pp. 159-60.
[2] DD. I, 154.   [3] Oe-U. VIII, 10608.   [4] *Int. Bez.* i. V. 26.

and that it would break out in the course of a few days. And the *Temps*, in its leading article, inspired by Berthelot and appearing on the evening of 24 July, said that the Austrian note

is an unprecedented document as regards the arrogance of its tone and the outrageousness of its demands. . . . What is asked of Serbia is not only the acknowledgment of vassalage implicit in paragraphs V and VI of the note; but also a public general confession by which Serbia is to recognize herself responsible for all the difficulties which the Austro-Hungarian authorities will encounter in their relations with their Slav subjects. . . . The blow threatening the Balkans and Slavism also threatens the European balance of power. . . . To-day's discussion ranges beyond Austria and Serbia; it concerns all Europe.

The dispatches reaching the Quai d'Orsay from London and Vienna that day were alarming. Paul Cambon telegraphed:

If Russia takes the part of the Serbs, she will have the initiative in an aggression against Austria, and Germany will be obliged to support the latter Power. It will be a general war.[1]

A few hours later he telegraphed: 'The situation is most serious and we see no means of arresting the march of events.'[2] Dumaine telegraphed from Vienna that it seemed 'almost impossible that the Austro-Hungarian Government whose military preparations are, it seems, complete, should not this time proceed to putting its threats into execution'.[3] From Berlin Jules Cambon telegraphed: 'Most of the Chargés d'Affaires at present in Berlin came to see me this morning. They show little hope of a peaceful issue.'[4] From Cetinje the French Minister reported that the Montenegrin Foreign Minister, in acquainting him with the news from Belgrade that Giesl was to leave his post on Saturday (25th) if the Serbian answer were not satisfactory and that the Serbian Government was taking steps to remove its archives and funds to the interior, added: 'I think that Austro-Hungarian troops will be entering Serbian territory without delay.'[5]

Bienvenu-Martin immediately passed on all the most important dispatches to Stockholm but took no steps on his own account and on the contrary gave the Austro-Hungarian and German Ambassadors the impression that France would place no impediment in the way of Austrian measures to exact satisfaction from Serbia. It is true that he was without news from St. Petersburg. He had on receiving a copy of the Austrian ultimatum, at once asked Paléologue to let him know 'the views and intentions of the Russian Government'.[6] But Paléologue was uninformative and kept Paris in ignorance of what was going on in St. Petersburg. His first telegram of the 24th gave no hint of the conversation which had taken place between himself, Sazonov

---

[1] DF. 3. XI, 12. [2] DF. 3. XI, 23. [3] DF. 3. XI, 28.
[4] DF. 3. XI, 11. [5] DF. 3. XI, 24. [6] DF. 3. XI, 8.

and Buchanan, the content of which we know from Buchanan's own dispatch.[1] It simply said that he and Sazonov had acquainted Buchanan with the general conclusions of the conversations which had taken place during Poincaré's visit.[2] It was not until the evening of the 25th that Bienvenu-Martin learnt of the contents of Buchanan's telegram from de Fleuriau, the French Chargé d'Affaires at London to whom it had been read by Nicolson. Through this channel he further learnt that Sazonov had told Buchanan that

agreements had been reached during M. Poincaré's stay providing for an action at Vienna with a view to preventing the Austro-Hungarian Government from adopting a threatening attitude towards Serbia. . . .

and that if the Austrian ultimatum were put into execution

measures would be taken to-day (Friday) at a Council presided over by the Tsar and that the execution of the Austrian ultimatum would probably be followed by the mobilization of the Russian Army. M. Paléologue added that France would conform to the conditions of her treaty of alliance.[3]

In a second telegram sent off on 24 July at 9.12 p.m., Paléologue gave no hint of the decision taken at the Council of Ministers to ask the Tsar on the following day to order partial mobilization. All that he says is:

As the President of the Republic and the Prime Minister have been able to see for themselves, the disposition of the Emperor of Russia and his Ministers is entirely pacific. But the ultimatum which the Austro-Hungarian Government has just handed to the Belgrade Cabinet brings a new and disquieting element into the situation. Russian [public] opinion would never tolerate Austria's doing violence to Serbia. The shortness of the time limit granted by the ultimatum renders still more difficult the moderating action which the Powers of the Triple *Entente* might develop in Vienna. On the other hand M. Sazonov presumes that Germany will wish to support her ally and I fear that this impression is correct. The solidarity of the Triple *Entente* must therefore be resolutely displayed. Any wavering would encourage the Teutonic Powers to accentuate their provocative attitude and would hasten events. Speaking to me of bellicose German *arrière-pensées*, the Russian Emperor said to me some months ago: 'If France and Russia really mean peace, they must put themselves in a state to uphold it, if need be, by force.' The Triple *Entente* disposes of sufficient strength to safeguard peace. It must not hesitate to show that strength.[4]

In a third telegram dispatched soon after midnight, Paléologue still maintained silence on the Council of Ministers which had been held at St. Petersburg and of whose decisions he had been acquainted by Sazonov. Nor did he breathe a word of the communiqué which the Russian Government had published in its official journal. All that he divulged was that 'a Council of Ministers will be held to-morrow [25th]

---

[1] BD. XI, 101.   [2] DF. 3. XI, 21.   [3] DF. 3. XI, 51.   [4] DF. 3. XI, 21.

presided over by the Emperor. M. Sazonov will endeavour to win the day for ideas of moderation'.[1] The truth being that Sazonov was going to obtain the Tsar's approval for the Council of Ministers' decisions involving partial mobilization!

Kept thus in the dark and, one may really say, deceived by Paléologue about what was going on at St. Petersburg, imperfectly evaluating the telegrams passing through his inexperienced hands and probably not enlightened by Berthelot on the seriousness of the situation, Bienvenu-Martin had no idea of the import of the advice given by Berthelot to the Serbian Minister at Paris. He telegraphed to Stockholm, to reach the Prime Minister Viviani, that Vesnić had asked advice and had been told, as a personal opinion,

that Serbia should try to gain time . . . there might be grounds, for example, for offering immediate satisfaction on all points that were not incompatible with the dignity and sovereignty of Serbia; for drawing attention to the fact that the findings of the investigation at Sarajevo were unilateral and that, while ready to take severe measures against all the accomplices of a crime she abhorred, Serbia asked to be furnished with the proofs in order to verify them rapidly; for seeking above all to escape the direct grasp of Austria by declaring herself ready to submit to the arbitrage of Europe.[2]

The man who from the first clearly saw what was happening was Jules Cambon, the French Ambassador to Berlin, the gist of whose conversation with Jagow is given in a dispatch from Sir Horace Rumbold of 24 July:

Ambassador said that German Government could not maintain fiction that question at issue between Austria-Hungary and Servia was an internal one and could be localized. . . . On Secretary of State saying that Servian Government would doubtless give way, French Ambassador asked whether Secretary of State seriously thought that Servian Government could accept certain demands in note. . . . Secretary of State suggested that it was for the *Entente* Powers to advise moderation and compliance at Belgrade. Ambassador inquired whether German Government would not also enjoin moderation on their ally. Secretary of State, after some reflexion, said that 'that would depend on circumstances. . . .' French Ambassador is inclined to think that Austro-Hungarian and German Governments are playing a dangerous game of bluff, and that they think they can carry matters through with a high hand.[3]

---

[1] DF. 3. XI, 34.   [2] DF. 3. XI, 15.

[3] BD. XI, 103. Very different was the estimate formed by Dumaine, the French Ambassador to Vienna, who on 22 July, the eve of the delivery of the ultimatum, called at the Ballplatz and 'painted a very black picture of the dangers of an Austro-Serbian war'. Yet he ended by saying 'that he had come to the conviction, that Russia had no intention of making a strong stand on behalf of Serbia . . . but would rather make efforts that the war should remain localized' (Oe-U. VIII, 10491). Macchio of course assured him that the tone of the Austrian note was such as to 'allow us to count on a peaceful result' (LJF. 20; CDD., p. 152). How Dumaine, given his relations with Shebeko, could think such a thing, is inconceivable

It was no question of bluff this time. Berlin was in deadly earnest. On 25 July Paris was given the alarm by the *Écho de Paris* which published details of Schoen's visit to the Quai d'Orsay and explained that the meaning of the demand for 'localization of the conflict', was: 'Leave Austria to crush Serbia or you will have to reckon with Germany'. The Triple *Entente* was to submit to a collective humiliation; if not, there was to be war. They were faced with a fresh 'Agadir coup' engineered when England was all taken up with the Irish problem and Russia with the St. Petersburg strike and when Poincaré and Viviani were on the high seas. This article led the German Ambassador to call on Berthelot that same day and protest against its indiscretion and its misinterpretation in attributing a threatening tone to his warning against the intervention of other Powers. The Quai d'Orsay assured him that it had no hand in the article and he took the matter up with the Havas agency.[1] The indiscretion probably originated with the Russian Embassy with which, as Sir Francis Bertie telegraphed that same day to Grey, 'the *Écho de Paris* is known to be in close relation'.[2]

It shows that Bienvenu-Martin had still not tumbled to what it all meant, and Sevastopulo telegraphed on the 25th to St. Petersburg:

> The fact that Baron von Schoen has thought it necessary to make this new *démarche* has had a somewhat reassuring effect at the Foreign Ministry as a sign that Germany does not want war no matter at what price.[3]

No doubt Germany did not actually want war, but she wanted complete submission from Serbia and Russia. Failing that, war. Thus it was not in Schoen's power to give the German note a different interpretation from the threatening one ascribed to it not only by the *Écho de Paris*[4] but by other journals such as Clemenceau's *L'Homme Libre* and the *Temps* and by public opinion generally.

> Public opinion and the press—wrote Sevastopulo in the telegram just quoted—without distinction of tendency, are exceedingly indignant about it, and even M. Jaurès sharply condemns the Austrian *démarche* as likely to provoke a general war.

There was not the slightest doubt that the ultimatum had a bad reception in Paris and gave rise to demonstrations outside the Austrian

---

though it is true that Shebeko himself was untroubled enough to go away on holiday. On 29 July at the height of the crisis Bunsen telegraphed to Grey that Dumaine was now convinced 'that growing condition of unrest in Southern Slav provinces of Dual Monarchy was such that Austro-Hungarian Government were compelled either to acquiesce in separation of these provinces or make a desperate effort to retain them by reducing Serbia to impotency. . . . French Ambassador thinks this shows that conflict is not due to German instigation and that it does not necessarily show that Germany desires European war, as is thought by many in France' (BD. XI, 265). The *Yellow Book* shows no trace of either of these judgements of Dumaine. They are in keeping with the Austrophil tradition at the Quai d'Orsay.

[1] DD. I, 170.   [2] BD. X, 123.   [3] *Int. Bez.* i. V, 59.   [4] BD. XI, 123.

Embassy.[1] The hours were passing and the time limit would soon be up. Swift action would have been necessary which the Quai d Orsay, with its leaders absent, was too much thrown out of its bearings to undertake.

9. *English* désintéressement *in the Austro-Serbian conflict; the mistake made by Grey.*

What was the effect in London? Grey, as has been said, had known since the previous day the substance of the Austrian note. When on the morning of the 24th Mensdorff communicated the text to him, Grey, as his telegram informed Bunsen on the same day, said

that the murder of the Archduke and some of the circumstances stated in the Austro-Hungarian note with regard to Servia naturally aroused sympathy with Austria, but I thought it a great pity that a time limit, and such a short time limit, had been introduced at this stage, and the note seemed to me the most formidable document I had ever seen addressed by one State to another that was independent. Demand No. 5 might mean that the Austro-Hungarian Government were to be entitled to appoint officials who should have authority in Servian territory, and this would hardly be consistent with maintenance of the independent sovereignty of Servia.

I was not, however, making these comments in order to discuss the merits of the dispute between Austria-Hungary and Servia; that was not our concern. It was solely from the point of view of the peace of Europe that I should concern myself with the matter, and I felt great apprehension. I must wait to hear the views of other Powers and no doubt we should consult with them to see what could be done to mitigate difficulties.

The Austro-Hungarian Ambassador observed that there had been so much procrastination on the part of Servia that a time limit was essential. Some weeks had elapsed since the murder of the Archduke and Servia had made no sign of sympathy or help; if she had held out a hand after the murder the present situation might have been avoided.

I observed that a time limit could have been introduced at any later stage if Servia had procrastinated about a reply; as it was, the Austro-Hungarian Government not only demanded a reply within forty-eight hours, but dictated the terms of the reply.[2]

Thus Grey had fully understood the seriousness of the Austrian note. We must now see how he prepared to ward off its consequences when in the afternoon of the 24th he received the French Ambassador Paul Cambon. The account he sent off that same day to Sir Francis Bertie runs:

I told M. Cambon that this afternoon I was to see the German Ambassador, who some days ago had asked me privately to exercise moderating influence in St. Petersburg. I would say to the Ambassador that, of course, if the presentation of this ultimatum to Servia did not lead to trouble between

---

[1] BD. XI, 192.   [2] BD. XI, 91.

Austria and Russia, we need not concern ourselves about it; but, if Russia took the view of the Austrian ultimatum which it seemed to me that any Power interested in Servia would take, I should be quite powerless, in face of the terms of the ultimatum, to exercise any moderating influence. I would say that I thought the only chance of any mediating or moderating influence being exercised was that Germany, France, Italy and ourselves, who had not direct interests in Servia, should act together for the sake of peace, simultaneously in Vienna and St. Petersburg.[1]

Obviously Grey was leaving the time factor entirely out of account. But the wise and experienced Cambon had taken counsel with his Russian colleague immediately on learning the contents of the ultimatum and had come with the purpose of suggesting:

The important thing was to gain time by mediation in Vienna. The best chance of this being accepted would be that Germany should propose it to the other Powers.

So he pointed out to Grey

that we could not say anything in St. Petersburg till Russia had expressed some opinion or taken some action. But, when two days were over, Austria would march into Servia, for the Servians could not possibly accept the Austrian demand. Russia would be compelled by her public opinion to take action as soon as Austria attacked Servia, and therefore, once the Austrians had attacked Servia, it would be too late for any mediation.

I said that I had not contemplated anything being said in St. Petersburg until after it was clear that there must be trouble between Austria and Russia. I had thought that if Austria did move into Servia, and Russia mobilized, it would be possible for the four Powers to urge Austria to stop her advance, and Russia also to stop hers, pending mediation. But it would be essential for any chance of success for such a step that Germany should participate in it.

M. Cambon said that it would be too late after Austria had once moved against Serbia. The important thing was to gain time by mediation in Vienna. The best chance of this being accepted would be that Germany should propose it to the other Powers.

I said that by this he meant mediation between Austria and Servia.

He replied that this was so.

I said that I would talk to the German Ambassador this afternoon on the subject.[2]

In these conversations with Mensdorff and especially with Paul Cambon, Grey took up a position which he was to define and develop

[1] BD. XI, 98.
[2] BD. XI, 98; DF. 3. XI, 12.—In the text of Cambon's dispatch as published in the LJF. 33 (CDD., p. 164), the following passage is omitted from the latter part of it. 'If Russia takes the part of the Serbs she will have the initiative in an aggression against Austria, and Germany will be obliged to support the latter Power. It will be a general war. It would be advisable to obtain from Berlin a proposal for a conference which would suspend the effect of the ultimatum. I will let you know the feelings of Sir Ed. Grey on this delaying device which seems very belated but which must be tried.' The telegram went off on the evening of the 24th to Viviani at Stockholm. But nothing came of it.

in his subsequent diplomatic activity and the underlying principles of which it is necessary to examine. Grey started out from the assumption that the Austro-Serbian conflict was of no immediate concern to England and that the two countries should be left to settle it between themselves. But an Austro-Russian conflict would be another matter, since it would be a threat to the peace of Europe. And since there was a prospect of an Austro-Russian conflict, the four Powers not involved should at once devise means of intervening between the two contending parties. Grey thought it difficult if not impossible to stop Austria from invading Serbia, and Russia from mobilizing in aid of Serbia. But Austria might be appealed to not to advance too far and both might be appealed to not to cross their respective frontiers but to give time for the mediation of Germany, France, Italy and England, which would be easy to arrange if Germany were willing. It was a policy which showed Grey's complete lack of understanding of the situation created and revealed by the ultimatum.

In the first place it was foolish and dangerous, if not also politically immoral, to regard the Austro-Serbian dispute of no concern of Britain and to think it could be kept separate from an Austro-Russian dispute. All that had happened from 1908 onwards served to prove that Austro-Serbian relations were one of the fundamental European problems, as involving the future of Austria-Hungary and indirectly that of German expansion in the Balkans and Near East from Constantinople to the Persian Gulf. For this reason, as well as for reasons of kinship, the conflict was a concern of Russia, who connected the crushing of Serbia with German policy in Turkey and had a few months previously contemplated going to war over the appointment of the German General Liman von Sanders to reorganize and command the Turkish Army. England had no less grounds for not remaining indifferent to questions raised by the ultimatum, in view of the repercussions that a triumph of *Deutschtum* in the Balkans would produce in Europe and beyond. Even apart from that, the relations between Russia and Serbia were such that the one conflict could not be kept separate from the other. The only way of preventing a war between Austria and Russia was to intervene at once between Austria and Serbia. This is what Grey abstained from doing. He held no communication at all with Vienna, nor did he, as he should have done, begin in the early hours of 24 July pressing with the requisite forcefulness and perseverance for a prolongation of the time limit in order to give time for the Powers to take measures to affect a conciliation. By keeping the two questions separate Grey was supporting the German thesis of the localization of the conflict, which Russia would never have accepted, and was thus fanning the flames instead of putting them out.

Another move which fanned the flames was the attempt to restrain

Austria and Russia, not from mobilizing, but from fighting once they had mobilized. As is already known and as the present account will show, the European war resulted directly from the Russian mobilization which led to that of Germany. And this in its turn, since it involved an immediate opening of hostilities, brought about the outbreak of the war. If it is understandable that Grey, like many others, was ignorant of the fact that for Germany mobilization and the beginning of hostilities were simultaneous acts, it is incredible that he failed to perceive how extremely dangerous were the Russian and Austrian mobilizations, not only intrinsically but also in their repercussions on the systems of alliance. This danger, as we have seen, was fully appreciated by the English Ambassador at St. Petersburg and also, at bottom, by Sazonov himself. True, Sazonov only intended partial mobilization as a threat to call Vienna and Berlin to order, to be left unused as long as possible. But he, too, made a terrible mistake in setting in motion the military machine which swept himself and the cause of peace to destruction. But Grey's blindness altogether surpassed that of Sazonov and was only equalled by that of the English press, the comments of which, especially of the Liberal organs, were as favourable to Austria as they were hostile to Serbia and Russia.

Another serious mistake made by Grey was not to perceive or even suspect, that before sending an ultimatum of such a kind Vienna must necessarily have secured the approval of Germany and that it was therefore a foolish waste of time to call for the help of Berlin by means other than those which would put the fear of God into Germany and make her give up her idea of localizing the conflict. One would imagine that the naked threat of calling the alliances into operation might well have opened Grey's eyes and made him talk to Lichnowsky on lines different from those he had indicated to Cambon. But not at all! To Sir Horace Rumbold he telegraphed a summary of what he said on 24 July to Lichnowsky:

I said that if the Austrian ultimatum to Servia did not lead to trouble between Austria and Russia I had no concern with it; I had heard nothing yet from St. Petersburg, but I was very apprehensive of the view Russia would take of the situation. I reminded the German Ambassador that some days ago he had expressed a personal hope that if need arose I would endeavour to exercise moderating influence at St. Petersburg, but now I said that, in view of the extraordinarily stiff character of the Austrian note, the shortness of the time allowed, and the wide scope of the demands upon Servia, I felt quite helpless as far as Russia was concerned, and I did not believe any Power could exercise influence alone.

The only chance I could see of mediating or moderating influence being effective, was that the four Powers, Germany, Italy, France and ourselves, should work together simultaneously at Vienna and St. Petersburg in favour of moderation in the event of the relations between Austria and Russia becoming threatening.

The immediate danger was that in a few hours Austria might march into Servia and Russian Slav opinion demand that Russia should march to help Servia; it would be very desirable to get Austria not to precipitate military action and so to gain more time. But none of us could influence Austria in this direction unless Germany would propose and participate in such action at Vienna.[1]

From this summary, dictated by Grey himself, it would seem that he thought mobilization inevitable and never even asked for the prolongation of the forty-eight hour time limit, but only that Austria should not go to war immediately, to which, as we shall now see, Berchtold was ready to agree. However Lichnowsky's dispatch of the 24th to Berlin reported Grey as having said

he would be prepared together with us to make representations to Vienna in favour of a prolongation of the time limit, since a way out might then be found. He made the further suggestion that in the event of a dangerous tension between Russia and Austria, the four not directly interested Powers, England, Germany, France and Italy, should undertake mediation.[2]

But the time limit was to expire at 6 p.m. the following day. Was there any likelihood that a request for prolongation sent via Berlin would arrive in time? And would Berlin be in any haste to ask for it in time when at the same time it was circulating the statement:

The Imperial Government want to emphasize their opinion that in the present case there is only question of a matter to be settled exclusively between Austria-Hungary and Servia, and that the Great Powers ought seriously to endeavour to reserve it to those two immediately concerned

and adding:

The Imperial Government desire urgently the localization of the conflict because every interference of another Power would, owing to the different treaty obligations, be followed by incalculable consequences.[3]

The Assistant Under Secretary, Sir Eyre Crowe's minute to this document begins:

The answer is that owing to the extreme nature of the Austrian demands and the time limit imposed, the localization of the conflict has been made exceedingly difficult. Because the Austrian terms bear on their face the character of a design to provoke a war.

But the Under Secretary, Sir Arthur Nicolson, optimistically added:

Telegrams are posted at the Clubs that the Conservative Press at Berlin have veered round, and are protesting against Germany being implicated in a conflict which Austria-Hungary has conjured, and because Germany was

[1] BD. XI, 99.   [2] DD. I, 157.   [3] BD. XI, 100.

not consulted beforehand in regard to the ultimatum. I do not know if this change of front has any significance.

Grey in his turn commented:

If true, it is a very surprising change of front. I have assumed in my conversations with Prince Lichnowsky that a war between Austria and Servia cannot be localized.

It was in fact true that German nationalist papers like the *Post* and the *Rheinisch-Westfälische Zeitung*, not to speak of the Liberal *Frankfurter Zeitung* and the Socialist *Vorwärts* had made this change. But it was by no means general and the semi-official *Lokal-Anzeiger* took a very different line. But even had the opposition been general, to hope for a change of front in the face of an *aut-aut* of that character was beside the point. It was, indeed, true that Grey had assumed in his conversations with the German Ambassador that a war between Austria and Serbia could not be localized, but he had done so in terms that were reported by Lichnowsky to Berlin as follows:

The danger of a European war will, if Austria enters Serbian territory, be brought into immediate proximity. The consequences of such a Four Power war, he expressly emphasized the figure four, and meant thereby Russia, Austria-Hungary, Germany and France, would be entirely unpredictable.[1]

Wilhelm's marginal note was: 'He forgets Italy' (which shows that Wilhelm was counting on Italy as an ally). But it was far worse that Grey 'forgot' England and so led Berlin to believe that it could remain unyielding because, if war were to come, England would look on from the side-lines.

10. *Grey shrinks from the only effective measure and urges mobilization and mediation.*

We now resume the narrative of events. After his talk with Lichnowsky Grey telegraphed to Crackanthorpe at Belgrade:

I have urged upon German Ambassador that Austria should not precipitate military action. It seems to me that Servia ought certainly to express concern and regret that any officials, however subordinate, should have been accomplices in the murder of the Archduke, and promise, if this is proved, to give fullest satisfaction. . . . I cannot tell whether anything short of unconditional acceptance will avert military action by Austria on expiry of time limit, but the only chance would be to give a favourable reply on as many points as possible. Servian Minister here implores us to give some indication of our views, but I cannot undertake responsibility of giving more advice than above.[2]

Hardly had Grey left his office on the afternoon of the 24th than Mensdorff rang asking to see him that same evening. The Chief Clerk,

[1] DD. I, 157.   [2] BD. XI, 102.

Mr. Montgomery, who answered the telephone, called in at the Austrian Embassy on his way home and was told that Mensdorff

had just received a telegram from his Government authorizing him to explain to you that the step taken at Belgrade was not an ultimatum but a '*démarche* with a time limit', and that if the Austrian demands were not complied with within this time limit his Government would break off diplomatic relations amd commence military preparations (not operations).[1]

In another chapter we shall examine the motives which led Berchtold to make this move. Grey received it as good news, telegraphing to Sir George Buchanan and Sir Francis Bertie: 'it makes the immediate situation seem less acute',[2] and, after it was far too late to do any good, he sent instructions to Bunsen in Vienna 'to support in general terms the step taken by your Russian colleague' who had said to Berchtold: 'The Russian Government trust that the Austro-Hungarian Government will prolong the time limit.' Grey added that:

If the Austro-Hungarian Government consider it too late to vary the time limit already stated, I trust that they will at any rate give time in the sense and for the reasons desired by Russia before taking any irretrievable steps.[3]

At 8 p.m. on the 24th Grey had received from St. Petersburg the important telegram[4] fully summarizing Buchanan's first conversation with Sazonov and Paléologue earlier in the day. The reply which this communication received from Grey on 25 July runs as follows:

You spoke quite rightly in very difficult circumstances as to the attitude of His Majesty's Government. I entirely approve, and I cannot promise more on behalf of His Majesty's Government.

I do not consider that public opinion here would or ought to sanction our going to war in the Servian quarrel.

But if war does take place we may be drawn into it by development of other issues, and I am therefore anxious to prevent war.

The brusque, sudden and peremptory character of the Austrian *démarche* makes it almost inevitable that in very short time Austria and Russia will both have mobilized against each other. In this event, it seems to me that the only chance of peace is for the other four Powers to join in asking Austria and Russia not to cross the frontier, and to give time for the four Powers acting at Vienna and St. Petersburg to endeavour to arrange matters.

If Germany will adopt this view, I am strongly of opinion that France and ourselves should act upon it. Italy no doubt would gladly co-operate.

But the co-operation of Germany would be essential.[5]

Let us look more closely at this document. Here was Grey telling Buchanan that Russian mobilization was 'almost inevitable' and that Buchanan was to take this for granted in talking with Sazonov. This,

[1] BD. XI, 104.   [2] BD. XI, 105.   [3] BD. XI, 118.
[4] BD. XI, 101.   [5] BD. XI, 112.

given Sazonov's state of mind, was a most dangerous thing to say. Instead of restraining St. Petersburg, this was the very thing to drive it forward. As regards Grey's opening words of approval for the line taken by Buchanan in his talk with Sazonov and Paléologue, it must be noted that Buchanan had been intentionally reticent. He had said that he 'could hold out no hope that His Majesty's Government would make any declaration of solidarity that would entail engagement to support France and Russia by force of arms' but added 'that I thought you might be prepared to represent strongly at Vienna and Berlin the danger to European peace of an Austrian attack on Servia' and

that it would in all probability force Russia to intervene, that this would bring Germany and (? France) into the field, and that if war became general, it would be difficult for England to remain neutral.[1]

Did Grey approve of this way of talking? It certainly showed to him a landscape he had not discovered for himself, and revealed the one path he should have chosen, which would almost certainly have led to a splendid success. The man who tried to guide him on this path was Sir Eyre Crowe, the ablest mind at the Foreign Office, who minuted the Buchanan dispatch as follows:

The moment has passed when it might have been possible to enlist French support in an effort to hold back Russia.

It is clear that France and Russia are decided to accept the challenge thrown out to them. Whatever we may think of the merits of the Austrian charges against Servia, France and Russia consider that these are the pretexts, and that the bigger cause of the Triple Alliance versus Triple *Entente* is definitely engaged.

I think it would be impolitic, not to say dangerous, for England to attempt to controvert this opinion, or to endeavour to obscure the plain issue, by any representation at St. Petersburg and Paris.

The point that now matters is whether Germany is or is not absolutely determined to have this war now.

There is still the chance that she can be made to hesitate, if she can be induced to apprehend that the war will find England by the side of France and Russia.

I can suggest only one effective way of bringing this home to the German Government without absolutely committing us definitely at this stage. If, the moment either Austria or Russia begin to mobilize, His Majesty's Government gave orders to put our whole fleet on an immediate war footing. this may make Germany realize the seriousness of the danger to which she would be exposed if England took part in the war.

It would be right, supposing this decision could be taken now, to inform the French and Russian Governments of it, and this again would be the best thing we could do to prevent a very grave situation arising as between England and Russia.

[1] BD. XI, 101.

It is difficult not to agree with M. Sazonov that sooner or later England will be dragged into the war if it does come. We shall gain nothing by not making up our minds what we can do in circumstances that may arise to-morrow.

Should the war come, and England stand aside, one of two things must happen:—

(*a*) Either Germany and Austria win, crush France and humiliate Russia. With the French fleet gone, Germany in occupation of the Channel, with the willing or unwilling co-operation of Holland and Belgium, what will be the position of a friendless England?

(*b*) Or France and Russia win. What would then be their attitude towards England? What about India and the Mediterranean?

Our interests are tied up with those of France and Russia in this struggle, which is not for the possession of Servia, but one between Germany aiming at a political dictatorship in Europe and the Powers who desire to retain individual freedom.

Under this Nicolson in his turn wrote:

The points raised by Sir Eyre Crowe merit serious consideration, and doubtless the Cabinet will review the situation. Our attitude during the crisis will be regarded by Russia as a test and we must be most careful not to alienate her.[1]

But Grey evaded the issue raised by Crowe as is shown in his footnote:

Mr. Churchill told me to-day that the fleet can be mobilized in twenty-four hours, but I think it is premature to make any statement to France and Russia yet.

In this he was by no means ill advised. While Crowe's analysis of the situation was singularly correct and penetrating, reminding his Chief of the logical necessities of the policy of *entente* with France and Russia, the remedy suggested by him was hardly powerful enough, while to give France and Russia an assurance of unconditional solidarity at that moment would have encouraged them to be aggressive. The best advice was that given by Buchanan to tell Germany 'that if war became general, it would be difficult for England to remain neutral'.

But both in his comment to Crowe's minute and in his reply to Buchanan Grey evaded the fundamental issue which it was his duty to face, and his behaviour confirmed Berlin in the belief that there would be no general war because England did not oppose the localization of the conflict, and that even if it were to come it would only involve the Continental Powers, and then Germany would be the victor. Let Vienna, therefore, not give way, but forge ahead at full speed.

In a later chapter we shall discuss the question whether, considering

[1] BD. XI, 101.

the ultrapacifist pro-German and anti-Russian feelings of many of his colleagues, Grey would or would not have been able without Cabinet consent to make the statement to Germany suggested explicitly by Buchanan, implicitly by Crowe, and soon after, as we shall see, by the Russian Ambassador Benckendorff. We shall then show that he could have easily done so, in fact did so, but not until it was too late. But for the moment he clung tenaciously to his idea of mediation by the four Powers after Russia and Austria had mobilized, reverting to it in a talk with Lichnowsky on the morning of 25 July.

I have told the German Ambassador that Austrian Ambassador has been authorized to inform me that rupture of diplomatic relations and military preparations but not operations on part of Austria would be the method of procedure on expiry of time limit. I said that this interposed a stage of mobilization before actual crossing of frontier, which I had urged yesterday should be delayed.

We should now apparently be soon confronted by a moment at which both Austria and Russia would have mobilized. The only chance of peace would be for the four Powers . . . to join in asking Austria and Russia not to cross the frontier till there had been time for us to endeavour to arrange matters between them.

German Ambassador read me a telegram from German Foreign Office.[1]

Zimmermann's telegram begins:

In diplomatic circles here, the opinion is current that we instigated Austria-Hungary to the stiff note to Serbia and took part in drafting it. Rumour seems to have originated with Cambon. Please contradict where possible. We have exercised no influence on content of note and have, like other Powers, had no opportunity to take up a position with regard to it before publication. That we cannot suggest to Vienna to withdraw, now that Austria-Hungary of her own initiative has decided on sharp language, goes without saying. Austria-Hungary's prestige at home and abroad would in the event of retreat be finally ruined.[2]

Lichnowsky after reading out this dispatch went on to say to Grey that

what I contemplated was mediation between Russia and Austria; this was a different question, and he thought Austria might with dignity accept it. . . . I endorsed his observation, saying that between Servia and Austria I felt no title to intervene, but as soon as the question became one between Austria and Russia it was a question of the peace of Europe, in which we must all take a hand.

I impressed upon him that if Austria and Russia mobilized the participation of Germany would be essential to any diplomatic action for peace. We could do nothing alone. I had had no time to consult the French

[1] BD. XI, 116. [2] DD. I, 153.

Government, who were travelling at the moment, and I could not be sure of their views, but if German Government were prepared to agree with my suggestion, I was prepared to say to the French Government that I thought it the right thing to do.[1]

Thus Paul Cambon's wise suggestion of mediation between Austria and Serbia to which Grey had at the time agreed, was dropped because Germany would never have accepted it. One reason why Grey let it drop was that Paul Cambon was for the moment absent, having gone to Paris after his interview on the 24th, to ask for or give guidance to the leaderless Quai d'Orsay, only returning late on the 27th. Had this experienced and respected diplomatist remained at his post, there is a possibility that Grey might have behaved more wisely. All he could think of doing for the moment was to seek German support for his idea, which had by now become an obsession, of preventing a mobilized Austria and Russia from going to war. He did not desist even in the afternoon when the Russian Ambassador Benckendorff, on learning of Grey's suggestion to Lichnowsky that morning of Four Power mediation, showed only apprehension

that what I said would give Germany the impression that France and England were detached from Russia. . . . Count Benckendorff urged that I should give some indication to Germany to make her think that we would not stand aside if there was a war.

I said that I had given no indication that we would stand aside; on the contrary, I had said to the German Ambassador that, as long as there was only a dispute between Austria and Servia alone, I did not feel entitled to intervene; but that, directly it was a matter between Austria and Russia, it became a question of the peace of Europe, which concerned us all. . . .

In effect I was asking that if Russia mobilized against Austria, the German Government, who had been supporting the Austrian demand on Servia, should ask Austria to consider some modification of her demands, under the threat of Russian mobilization. This was not an easy thing for Germany to do, even though we would join in at the same time in asking Russia to suspend action. I was afraid, too, that Germany would reply that mobilization with her was a question of hours, whereas with Russia it was a question of days; and that, as a matter of fact, I had asked that if Russia mobilized against Austria, Germany, instead of mobilizing against Russia, should suspend mobilization and join with us in intervention with Russia, thereby throwing away the advantage of time, for, if the diplomatic intervention failed, Russia would meanwhile have gained time for her mobilization. It was true that I had not said anything directly as to whether we would take any part or not if there was a European conflict, and I could not say so; but there was absolutely nothing for Russia to complain of in the suggestion that I had made to the German Government, and I was only afraid that there might be difficulty in its acceptance by the German Government. I had made

[1] BD. XI, 116.

it on my own responsibility, and I had no doubt it was the best proposal to make in the interests of peace.[1]

Thus Grey imagined himself to be rendering Russia a service by letting her gain time if she began at once to mobilize. It was a ridiculous idea to think that, if Russia mobilized, the German Government would wait with folded arms and act the peacemaker. The one mobilization brought on the other and together they led to war. The only way to have stopped it was that advised by Benckendorff, Buchanan and Crowe, namely to make Germany understand the risks she ran if she did not rein in her ally: risks of Italian neutrality and English intervention.

How far Grey was from this realization he showed on the afternoon of the 25th when he sent a brief message to Lichnowsky not with a threat to Germany but with an appeal to her good nature! That afternoon a telegram had come in from Crackanthorpe in Belgrade saying that the Serbian reply to the Austrian note was being·

drawn up in the most conciliatory terms and will meet Austrian demands in as large measure as possible. . . . Opinion of Servian Government is that, unless Austrian Government desire war at any cost, they will accept full satisfaction offered in Servian reply.[2]

Pleased with this news, Grey sent Crackanthorpe's forecast on to Lichnowsky with the

hope that if the Serbian reply when received at Vienna corresponds to this forecast, the German Government may feel able to influence the Austrian Government to take a favourable view of it.[3]

Having so done Grey, with his conscience at rest, departed for his customary week-end in the country. True at 6 p.m. that Saturday the forty-eight hour time limit given to Serbia was due to expire. Grey however, was not concerned with the Austro-Serbian conflict, but only with the Austro-Russian conflict which had not yet broken out. So the matter was not pressing!

Nothing more reveals Grey's incomprehension of what was threatening than that he should have left the Foreign Office to look after itself at this juncture and gone off for his usual week-end. It would have shaken him up if he could have had a glimpse of how his suggestion was being received at the Wilhelmstrasse and what was going on there.

11. *Germany's bogus acceptance of Four Power mediation.*

Let us now consider the reactions of the Wilhelmstrasse to the first suggestions from London. At 1.16 a.m. on the morning of the 25th

[1] BD. XI, 132.   [2] BD. XI, 114.   [3] BD. XI, 115.

Lichnowsky's telegram reached Berlin giving an account of his conversation with Grey of 24 July at which Grey suggested that Germany should join with England in asking for the extension of the time limit and that 'in the event of a dangerous tension between Russia and Austria, the four not directly interested Powers, England, Germany, France and Italy, should undertake mediation' between Russia and Austria.

It is futile [wrote Wilhelm in the margin]. I will not join in; only if Austria expressly asks me to do so, which is not likely. In points of honour and vital questions one does not ask others for advice.[1]

The Wilhelmstrasse thought likewise and put Lichnowsky's telegram aside for the time being. When at the end of the morning Sir Horace Rumbold called in, Jagow told him that the telegram had come in only at 10 a.m. and that he had at once instructed Tschirschky to pass on to Berchtold the proposal 'for an extension of the time limit', and to 'speak to' his Excellency about it.

Unfortunately it appeared from the press that Count Berchtold is at Ischl and Secretary of State thought that in these circumstances there would be delay and difficulty in getting time limit extended. . . . He admitted quite freely that Austro-Hungarian Government wished to give the Servians a lesson, and that they meant to take military action. He also admitted that Servian Government could not swallow certain of the Austro-Hungarian demands.
Secretary of State said that a reassuring feature of the situation was that Count Berchtold had sent for the Russian representative at Vienna and had told him that Austria-Hungary had no intention of seizing Serbian territory. This step should in his opinion exercise a calming influence at St. Petersburg. I asked whether it was not to be feared that, in taking military action against Servia, Austria would dangerously excite public opinion in Russia. He said he thought not. He remained of opinion that crisis could be localized. . . . If the relations between Austria and Russia became threatening, he was quite ready to fall in with your suggestion as to the four Powers working in favour of moderation at Vienna and St. Petersburg. . . . Secretary of State again repeated very earnestly that he had had no previous knowledge of contents of Austro-Hungarian note. . . . He confessed privately that, as a diplomatic document, note left much to be desired.[2]

A tissue of lies from first to last. Lichnowsky's telegram had arrived nine hours earlier. It was not communicated to Tschirschky either at 10 a.m. or at noon, but at 4 p.m., in order that it might reach Vienna after the time limit had expired. Neither was Tschirschky instructed to 'speak to' Berchtold about it. What was actually sent to Tschirschky was a copy of the dispatch with the comment:

[1] DD. I, 157.   [2] BD. XI, 122.

I have replied in London that I would communicate Sir E. Grey's suggestion to Vienna, but that as the ultimatum expires to-day and Count Berchtold
is at Ischl, I did not think that prolongation would be possible.[1]

This was tantamount to telling Vienna not to pay any attention to
the proposal and to go quietly ahead. The same treatment was meted
out to the Russian Chargé d'Affaires whom Jagow did not see until
5 p.m. and then only to tell him that it was too late to make representations at Vienna.[2] And it was no different with Grey's plea, on learning
the forecast of the Serbian reply, that 'the German Government may
feel able to influence the Austrian Government to take a favourable
view of it'. On the evening of the 26th Zimmermann telephoned Rumbold to say that the plea had been passed on to Vienna.

Under Secretary of State considers very fact of their making this communication to Austro-Hungarian Government implies that they associate
themselves to a certain extent with your hope.

The mockery in this statement did not escape the permanent officials
at the Foreign Office. Crowe minuted it: Very insidious on the
part of the German Government', and Nicolson added: 'This is the
second occasion on which Herr von Jagow has acted similarly'.[3]
But the proposal made by Grey to Lichnowsky on 25 July that if
Austria and Russia mobilized, the other four Powers should join in
asking them not to cross their respective frontiers until an effort had
been made at mediation, was hailed at the Wilhelmstrasse as a proof
that Grey was no longer talking of mediation between Austria and
Serbia, as, at Cambon's suggestion, he had done on the 24th, but of
mediation between Austria and Russia. Now this would have tied
Russia's hands while Austria was getting away with the attack on
Serbia and so would have brought about the desired 'localization of the
conflict'. Thus Germany could safely give London the little satisfaction
of accepting it in principle. On 25 July Lichnowsky sent no less than
three telegrams to Berlin urging acceptance. In the first of them he
wrote: 'I see in this the only possibility of avoiding a world war in
which we should risk everything and gain nothing', and he added that
he 'did not believe that, if France were to become involved, England
could remain indifferent'.[4] The second telegram ended with the
warning:

The rejection of the proposal to mediate between Austria and Russia, or
an unaccommodating attitude that might lead to the assumption that we
want a war with Russia would probably have the result of driving England
unconditionally to the side of France and Russia.[5]

[1] DD. I, 171.   [2] Int. Bez. i. V, 63.   [3] BD. XI, 149.
[4] DD. I, 179.   [5] DD. I, 180.

It was not politic to neglect Lichnowsky's advice and offend London on the very evening when the rupture of diplomatic relations between Vienna and Belgradé was taking place which was the prelude to the Austrian war on Serbia. Therefore at 11 p.m. on the 25th Jagow answered Lichnowsky:

Sir E. Grey's distinction between Austro-Serbian and Austro-Russian conflict is perfectly apposite. In the former we, no more than England, are willing to interfere, and take standpoint, as before, that question must remain localized by abstention of all Powers. We therefore urgently hope that Russia, conscious of the seriousness of the situation and her responsibilities, will abstain from any active intervention. Should an Austro-Russian conflict arise, we are prepared, subject to the reservation of our well-known alliance obligations, together with the other Great Powers, to cause mediation to take place between Austria and Russia.[1]

Did Germany by accepting mediation subject to localization of the conflict and 'subject to the reservation of our well-known allied obligations' mean to allow Russia, as Grey had contemplated, to mobilize? Was this, in other words, a sincere acceptance without equivocation? No! nothing of the kind! At 1.35 p.m. on 26 July Bethmann Hollweg telegraphed to Lichnowsky:

Austria has made an official declaration to Russia that she does not intend territorial gains in Serbia and on her part will not infringe integrity of the Kingdom but only restore order. According to so far unconfirmed news from reliable source the call-up of several classes of reservists is immediately about to take place in Russia, which would be the equivalent of mobilization also against ourselves. Should this news be confirmed we should against our wish be driven to counter measures. Our endeavour even now is to localize the war and preserve the European peace. We therefore ask Sir Edward Grey to use his influence in this sense at St. Petersburg.[2]

This telegram from Bethmann Hollweg and the one from Jagow of late on the night of the 25th reached Lichnowsky on Sunday the 26th when Grey was at Itchen Abbas. Lichnowsky therefore wrote:

Dear Sir Edward, I hear from Berlin that they hear from a good source that Russia intends to call out several classes of reserves. In this case we would have to follow as it would mean a mobilization also against us. As my Government still hopes to be able to localize the war and to keep up the peace of Europe, they instruct me to request you to use your influence in St. Petersburg in that sense.

PS.—My Government accepts your suggested mediation à quatre.[3]

By a strange irony the very document which announces the acceptance of Grey's proposals offers the proof that Berlin accepted it in bad faith. The truth was that Russia had not called any reservists to the

[1] DD. I, 192. [2] DD. I, 199. [3] BD. XI, 145.

colours, and Germany was already threatening to do so. But how could Russia, following Grey's suggestion, mobilize against Austria without calling up reserves? The fact is that Berlin did not, indeed could not, seriously mean to let Russia make preparations, even against Austria alone, because that would have gained her time for mobilization. Grey's proposal was impracticable not only for that reason but because, once Russia had mobilized against Austria the 'well-known alliance obligations' would come into play to which the Chancellor's reservations alluded.

It would not have been needful to linger on proving this point if the acceptance by Germany of mediation *à quatre* had not been used by various pro-German historians and the American Fay[1] as a proof of Germany's good will and of the lack of good will on the part of France and Russia, whose Ambassadors disapproved of Grey's proposal. It was these Ambassadors who were right. No mediation could take place between Austria and Russia that was not preceded by mediation between Austria and Serbia. And to mediate between Austria and Russia without intervening in the Austro-Serbian dispute was to play into the hands of the Central Powers. It meant giving Austria a free hand against Serbia. It was the fulfilment of Vienna's and Berlin's dreams of 'localization of the conflict'. Thus the proposal was still-born and was soon swept aside by events, not by the opposition of the French and Russian Ambassadors which was a purely personal expression of opinion on a suggestion put forward by Grey. Berlin accepted it *pro forma* without a shred of sincerity, merely to flatter the English hope. Indeed a few hours before sending the telegram of acceptance Jagow was saying to Szögyény, as the latter telegraphed to Vienna, and as we shall see in another chapter, that Berlin

takes for granted that upon eventual negative reply from Serbia, our declaration of war will follow, joined to military operations. Any delay in beginning warlike operations is regarded here as a great danger im respect of intervention of other Powers. We are urgently advised to go ahead at once and confront the world with a *fait accompli*.[2]

Hence we must conclude that now, as before the first Austrian *démarche* at Belgrade, English diplomatic activity in the two days following the ultimatum was characterized by a complete failure to understand what was at issue. It should have been the duty of the Foreign Secretary not to lose an instant in giving Germany and Austria a severe warning which would have made them retrace their steps. He should especially have urged Germany to restrain Austria and make her agree to a prolongation of the time limit in order to give the Powers opportunity to intervene between Vienna and Belgrade. At the same time he

[1] Fay, II, p. 377.   [2] Oe-U. VIII, 10656.

should have recommended to St. Petersburg to refrain from all measures of mobilization, promising to use his whole influence to bring about a peaceful settlement of the dispute. Grey did none of these things. Indeed, he did the very opposite. He made not the slightest inquiries at Vienna, he led Germany to believe that the conflict could be localized, he regarded Russian mobilization as something to be expected, when he ought to have known that it might be—as it actually became—the immediate cause of catastrophe.

At the point which matters had reached on the evening of the 25th only Serbia could have remedied the consequences of Italian and English inaction by accepting unconditionally the Austrian demands, leaving it to the Powers to vindicate her sovereign rights. But Serbia, as we shall see, took a middle course which failed to avert the tragedy.

CHAPTER IX

THE SERBIAN REPLY AND THE RUPTURE OF AUSTRO-SERBIAN RELATIONS

(1) *The Serbian Government appeals to the Great Powers* (p. 346). (2) *Serbia's serious plight in July* 1914 (p. 350). (3) *The lacunae in the Serbian diplomatic documents. Sazonov's advice to Serbia and its import* (p. 353). (4) *Pašić acquaints the friendly Powers of the Serbian acceptance of the ultimatum; a reservation on Point 6 later changed into a rejection* (p. 358). (5) *The drafting and delivery of the Serbian reply* (p. 361). (6) *The text of the Serbian reply; its true character* (p. 364). (7) *Giesl leaves Belgrade; he reports to Tisza and Francis Joseph* (p. 372). (8) *After the first heat of anger Vienna beats a series of retreats* (p. 376). (9) *The Austro-German thesis that the ultimatum was one which could be accepted by Serbia* (p. 380). (10) *Austria-Hungary mobilizes against Serbia; the Ballplatz still hopes to avoid war* (p. 385).

1. *The Serbian Government appeals to the Great Powers.*

As soon as Giesl had left the Serbian Foreign Ministry on Thursday 23 July after presenting the Austrian ultimatum at 6 p.m., the members of the Serbian Government still in Belgrade set to work in Pašić's absence on studying the document. Their emotion grew as they realized the nature of its contents. Ljuba Jovanović writes:

We . . . quickly saw that it was not an ordinary Note but an ultimatum. . . . Paču himself had not up till then been at all willing to admit the possibility of such a thing, because he had believed that Germany would never approve of a step on the part of Austria-Hungary which might drag her also into war and compromise her brilliant economic progress.[1]

Slavko Gruić, Secretary General of the Serbian Foreign Office, recording his memories in an article written for the Belgrade *Politika*, narrates:

We had no need to read the ultimatum from beginning to end to grasp the significance of the Austro-Hungarian note. For a while there was a deathly silence because no one ventured to be the first to express his thought. The first to break the silence was the Minister of the Interior, Ljuba Jovanović. After several times pacing the length of the spacious room, he stopped and said: 'We have no other choice than to fight it out.'[2]

[1] Article in *Krv Sloventsva* (Belgrade, 1924, p. 22), translated for the British (*now* Royal) Institute of International Affairs, London, 1925, p. 14. *See* Fay, II, p. 61, n. 12.
[2] *Politika* (Belgrade, 22–6 July 1934).

Ljuba Jovanović writes further:

As for myself I was immediately certain that, notwithstanding all the intentions of my colleagues to satisfy Austria-Hungary this time, matters would nevertheless turn out as we feared. Even if we, or some other Government, accepted to the letter everything that the ultimatum demanded, I was convinced that the dispute would not be settled, for the execution of the obligations which we should have undertaken on behalf of Serbia would have given innumerable occasions for new complications which would in the end have had to be settled by war. But, as I had long since been reconciled to the inevitability of what had begun to come to pass, I was now fairly cool. I saw clearly and I felt very deeply that there was nothing left for us all but bravely to meet our destiny.[1]

Gruić gives the following account of the initial difficulties of getting the news through to Pašić:

It was extremely difficult to communicate the text of the Note to the Prime Minister. First of all it was difficult to discover his whereabouts. That morning he had left for Radujevac and from thence was to go to Zaječar, Knjaževac and Nish. In all these places he had made speeches. According to the account of Šajinović [Chief of the political section of the Foreign Ministry, who accompanied Pašić] Pašić had said to him after his speech at Nish: 'It would be a good thing if we were to take a little rest. What do you think of going off to Salonika where we could stay two or three days incognito?' Šajinović had therefore ordered the Premier's coach to be coupled on to the Salonika train. While the two were waiting for the train, the Prime Minister was told that there was a telephone call for him from Belgrade. He went to the station-master's office. When he returned he told Dr. Šajinović that Lazar Paču had asked him to return to Belgrade because at 6 p.m. the Austro-Hungarian Minister was to deliver a note. 'I told Laza—said Pašić—that he was to receive the note; when I get back [to Belgrade] we shall give the answer. Laza told me that from what he had heard it was not to be an ordinary note. But I stood firmly by my reply.' After this conversation the train drew in and the Prime Minister started off for Salonika with Dr. Šajinović. When they arrived at Lescovac, the station-master informed Pašić that he was asked to return at once to Belgrade and also handed him a telegram from the Regent recalling him. Pašič then told Dr. Šajinović to get on to the Foreign Minister and find out about the note. I personally answered the call and gave briefly in French the substance of the ultimatum. Later I tried at two or three intermediate stations to communicate to Dr. Šajinović by telephone or code the most important points of the ultimatum, but could not make contact with him.[2]

This narrative gives a picture of the mentality of Pašić. In the most critical hour he sought to evade direct responsibility and, although warned in good time of the importance of the note, the arrival of which Giesl had announced in advance, he pursued his journey to Salonika

---

[1] *Art. cit.* p. 23 (English translation, p. 14).   [2] *Politika* (Belgrade), 23 July 1934.

for a few days' rest incognito. In fact even before starting for Salonika Pašić knew that from one moment to the next Vienna would be sending Belgrade a stiff note. Did he imagine he could gain time by his absence or did he not rather want to let others bear the burden of the decisions that would have to be taken in his absence?

Ljuba Jovanović writes that Paču, who was a man of energy, acted at once on the evening of the 23rd.

> That same evening he sent a circular telegram to all our Legations in which he told them about the Note and at the same time gave it as his opinion that the 'demands upon us were such that no Serbian Government could accept them in their entirety'. By those words he desired to emphasize that any Government which might be formed for that special purpose, and which should do so, would not be a *Serbian* Government.[1]

The telegram told of the arrival of the note and said that the reply had to be given within forty-eight hours, adding that in the absence of several members of the Cabinet no decision had yet been taken, but that it could be said already that the Austrian demands were 'such that no Serbian Government could accept them in their entirety'.[2] The same statement was made on the evening of the 23rd by Paču to the Russian Chargé d'Affaires Strandtmann in informing him of the text of the note.[3] Paču afterwards told Spalaiković that he had said to Strandtmann that

> the Serbian Government would appeal to the Governments of the friendly Powers to protect the independence of Serbia

but that 'if war was inevitable, Serbia would make war'.[4]

Late that same night the Regent, Prince Alexander, went to the Russian Legation

> to express his despair over the Austrian ultimatum, compliance with which he regards as an absolute impossibility for a state which has the slightest regard for its dignity. His Royal Highness said he placed all his hopes on H.M. the Tsar of Russia whose powerful word could alone save Serbia. He will take no decisions before Pašić's return at 5 a.m. to-morrow. As the most insulting points he regards Point 4 and those which press for the admission of Austrian agents to Serbia.

Strandtmann's dispatch ended with the suggestion that Sazonov might appeal to the King of Italy, the Prince Regent's uncle, to offer himself as mediator.[5]

Pašić was of the same opinion when he arrived back in Belgrade at 5 a.m. on the 24th and called in at the Russian Legation on his way to the Cabinet meeting.

[1] *Art. cit.* p. 14.   [2] LAS. 33; CDD., p. 388.   [3] *Int. Bez.* i. V, 10.
[4] LAS. 34; CDD., p. 388; Russian *Orange Book*, 9; CDD., p. 269.   [5] *Int. Bez.* i. V, 75.

His first impression is—telegraphed Strandtmann to St. Petersburg—that it is not possible either to accept or to reject the Austrian note; time must be gained at all costs. . . . He intends to give Austria his answer at the appointed time, i.e. to-morrow, Saturday at 6 p.m. But now at once an appeal will be made to the Powers to protect the independence of Serbia. 'But,' said Pašić, 'if war is unavoidable—we shall fight.' It is not intended to defend Belgrade, the foreign legations will be asked to follow the Government into the interior of the country. Pašić sees the future extremely dark.[1]

As ill luck would have it the friendly *Entente* Powers were at the moment not very effectively represented at Belgrade. Hartwig was dead and the Chargé d'Affaires Strandtmann had none of his authority. Des Graz, the English Minister, was on leave, his place being taken by Crackanthorpe; the newly appointed French Minister Boppe had not yet transferred from Constantinople and the French Legation was leaderless. Crackanthorpe's dispatch of the 24th runs:

Prime Minister who returned to Belgrade early this morning is very anxious and dejected. He begged me earnestly to convey to you his hope that His Majesty's Government will use their good offices in moderating Austrian demands which he says are impossible of acceptance.[2]

Pašić saw the Greek and Montenegrin Ministers and no doubt asked them for their countries' support. According to Giesl's dispatch of the same day the Greek Minister refused Pašić a new alliance or any change in the alliance of the last Balkan war and seemed to be uncertain what line his Government would take.[3] Pašić got the Cabinet to decide that the Regent should telegraph to the King of Italy asking him

to use his good offices at Vienna in favour of an extension of the time limit and a softening of those terms of the ultimatum which conflict with Serbian law[4]

and that he should also send an urgent appeal to the Tsar. Strandtmann's telegram to St. Petersburg on 25 July gave the text of the appeal to the Tsar as follows:

Yesterday evening the Austro-Hungarian Government handed the Serbian Government a note on the subject of the Sarajevo outrage. Conscious of her international obligations, Serbia from the first days after the terrible crime declared that she condemns violence and that she is ready to institute an inquiry on her territory, if the trial conducted by the Austro-Hungarian authorities were to prove the complicity of known Serbian subjects. But the demands contained in the Austro-Hungarian Government's note are incompatible with the dignity of Serbia as an independent state and are unnecessarily humiliating. For instance we are asked in a peremptory tone for a declaration by the Government in the Official *Gazette*, for a Royal order

---

[1] *Int. Bez.* i. V, 35.   [2] BD. XI, 92; LAS. 35; CDD. p. 389.
[3] Oe-U. VIII, 10578.   [4] *Int. Bez.* i. V, 36.

to the army condemning the spirit of hostility towards Austria-Hungary and
for us to level the reproach against ourselves of criminal negligence towards
subversive agitation. Further the demand is made that Austro-Hungarian
officials shall come to Serbia both to collaborate with our officials in these
measures and to supervise the execution of the other measures indicated in
the Note. We are given a time limit of 48 hours to accept integrally, failing
which the Austro-Hungarian Legation will withdraw from Belgrade. Of
the Austro-Hungarian terms we are disposed to accept those which are
compatible with the status of an independent state and those advised by
Your Majesty after taking cognizance of them. We shall severely punish all
persons whose participation in the outrage shall be proved. Among these
demands are some which require an alteration in our laws and this alteration
needs time. The time limit is too short, the Austro-Hungarian army is being
concentrated on our frontier and can attack on the expiry of the time limit.
We cannot defend ourselves. Therefore we pray Your Majesty to lend help
as soon as possible. Your Majesty has given us so many proofs of your
precious good will and we confidently hope that this appeal will find an echo
in your generous Slav heart. I am the interpreter of the feelings of the
Serbian nation which in this dark hour prays Your Majesty graciously to
intervene on behalf of the destinies of Serbia. Alexander.[1]

2. *Serbia's serious plight in July* 1914.

These documents give the impression that the Serbian Government
had at once decided not to accept the Austrian demands which infringed its sovereign rights, hence not to accept the ultimatum in its
entirety, accepting the risk of the serious and obvious consequences.
And indeed the great majority of historians take this view. But a
quantity of evidence exists which proves the contrary. First of all we
must make clear that not too much importance is to be attached to the
declarations of resistance in the telegrams and conversations of Paču
and Pašić. Balkan politicians were habitually free with their threats
and talk of war while perfectly prepared to pipe down when safety
demanded. In the present case it would never have done for the
Serbian Government to let the Powers, and especially Russia whose
support they were seeking, perceive any sign of willingness to yield.
But what they said was one thing and what they thought was another.
They could not but remember that in 1909 Russia had induced them
to consent to recognizing the annexation of Bosnia-Herzegovina, that
in 1913 they had had to give up the claim for an outlet to the Adriatic
because St. Petersburg had bowed to Vienna's insistence on this point,
that for the same reason Montenegro had had to withdraw from
Scutari. In short Russia had never been willing to risk a European
war for the sake of Serbia. Would she do so now? It was highly
unlikely, if not impossible. And unless Russia gave whole-hearted

[1] *Int Bez.* i. V, 37.

support, no alternative remained but unconditional submission to avert invasion and the wiping out of Serbia.

Moreover the country was in a disastrous state. It was passing through a serious political crisis. A bare four days before the Sarajevo outrage, i.e. on 24 June, King Peter had laid down his powers and Prince Alexander had taken over the Regency. General elections had been called to break the power of the Opposition to which belonged, as we have already seen, the powerful military party and the *Black Hand*. Already in the Albanian campaign of the autumn of 1913, as Seton-Watson remarks, the peasantry had shown a marked reluctance to return to the colours, and now it was harvest time. In conquered Macedonia things were not going well and were aggravated by friction between the civil and military authorities. Most serious of all, the army was in a bad state. It possessed only 120,000 small arms of various types, hardly any light and no heavy guns, there was a shortage of uniforms and supplies of all kinds. The result was that when, at the end of May 1914, Greece thought of sending an ultimatum to Constantinople over the persecution of the Greek population in Asia Minor, Prince Alexander told the Greek Military Attaché on 2 June, as the latter reported to Athens:

Serbia is entirely unable to aid us. The Serbs lack everything. They have no ammunition, no artillery, no rifles. They have nothing at all and even if they were to mobilize, there would be no response to the call-up.

The following day the Belgrade Government said the same thing in its reply to Athens, alleging also a complete lack of financial resources.[1] The problem to be solved was therefore how to gain time by an immediate acceptance of the Austrian demands which would save the existence of the Kingdom and give it the chance to elude the demands later by the arts in which Balkan statesmen are past masters.

That this was the state of mind prevailing in Belgrade between 23 and 25 July is shown by Luciano Magrini in an article published in the *Secolo XX* of 1 May 1916. He had been in Serbia in the autumn of 1915 when the Austrians and Germans, commanded by General Mackensen, were launching their offensive against Serbia. Moving with the Serbian Army and Government in the tragic retreat through the mountains of Albania he had been in constant contact with Serbian officers, politicians and higher officials. Dealing with the immediate origins of the war Magrini's article tells of the deep impression caused by the Austro-Hungarian ultimatum in a Serbia which had only just emerged exhausted from the Balkan wars. The Serbs would have had no chance alone against the Austrian Army and all their hopes turned on Russia without whose aid 'Serbia would have found herself forced to

[1] Frangulis, I., pp. 131–4.

swallow the Austrian ultimatum whole'.[1] Later Magrini published more material supporting this view in his book *Il dramma di Sarajevo*:

During the Serbian retreat in October 1915 Colonel Pavlović talked to me of his memories of those critical days. All the members of the Cabinet realized the aim and the seriousness of the note and well understood that if the ultimatum were not accepted outright, war would follow. All were exceedingly alarmed and saw no other way out of the difficult situation than that of acceptance. In answer to a question Colonel Pavlović assured me that Serbia was not in a condition to fight a war with Austria. The tension of the previous weeks made it certain that any attempt to gain time would lead to disaster. No great hopes were placed on support from Russia and the other *Entente* Powers. People had not forgotten that in the crises of 1908–9 and 1912–13 it was Russia who had advised Serbia to comply with the Austrian demands. Most disquieting of all was the military state of Serbia, which had been bled white by the two Balkan wars. Both the Cabinet and Colonel Popović regarded it as advisable to accept the ultimatum in its entirety to prevent worse from happening. None of them contemplated the eventuality of war. They believed that by yielding to force they could weather the threatening storm.[2]

On the evening of 23 July a Cabinet meeting was held, presided over by Prince Alexander, and attended by Colonel Pavlović as acting Chief of Staff. In the absence of Pašić, no decisions were taken, and as soon as he returned the Cabinet met again and the same views were expressed, the acting Chief of Staff again giving his opinion. Pašić, however, asked that no decision should be taken before Russia's opinion had been asked. Prince Alexander then telegraphed to the Tsar that Serbia was prepared to accept not only 'the terms compatible with the status of an independent state', but also those 'whose acceptance shall be advised by Your Majesty'. Now this—as Magrini observes—meant 'that if Russia were to advise unconditional acceptance of the Austrian ultimatum, Serbia would accept without raising objections'. Spalai-ković, the Serbian Minister at St. Petersburg, was asked to ascertain the views of the Russian Government, at the same time informing Sazonov on behalf of the Serbian General Staff that Serbia was in no state to resist an invasion by Austria.

Up to the late afternoon of 24 July Belgrade was optimistic about the situation. It was thought that in the condition she was known to be in, Serbia would not be expected to do otherwise than yield to so terrible a threat in order to avoid war. But in the afternoon a telegram from Spalaiković arrived to say that Sazonov had given the opinion that the Austrian ultimatum was unacceptable as a whole and that Serbia, as a proof of good will, should accept those parts which she thought compatible with her independence,

---

[1] Luciano Magrini, *La tragedia della Serbia*, in *Secolo XX* (Milan, May 1916), p. 390; *La Serbia invasa* (Milan, 1922), p. 43.

[2] Magrini, *Il dramma di Sarajevo*, pp. 203–4.

but that if she meant to save her honour she must reject such demands as Points V and VI which infringed Serbian sovereign rights. Russia could not remain indifferent to an Austrian outrage against Slav interests, and, making the Serbian cause her own, would vigorously support and defend legitimate Serbian interests.[1]

The existence of this telegram from Spalaiković, vouched for by Colonel Pavlović, is not proved by the Serbian documents which have been made public, but that does not mean anything, because the Serbian diplomatic documents of the period have never been published in full. This may well be due to the unwillingness of the Serbian Government to confess that Serbia would have accepted the ultimatum unconditionally if Russia had not advised her otherwise. The following facts, however, do emerge. Schilling's diary contains an entry stating that after the meeting of the Russian Cabinet he saw Spalaiković and enjoined on the Serbian Government 'extreme moderation' in its reply to the Austrian note.[2] Sazonov in his *Fateful Years* writes that he advised Spalaiković that the Serbian Government should accept all the points of the ultimatum not incompatible with Serbian sovereign rights. He also adds that he telegraphed Belgrade in the same sense.[3] But his telegram has not turned up among the Russian documents, while of the documents published in the Serbian *Blue Book* for 24 July the only telegram from Spalaiković is No. 36 which merely states that on leaving Sazonov's cabinet at 7 p.m. on the 24th he ran into the German Ambassador Pourtalès who was just about to be admitted and that when Pourtalès put forward to him the thesis of the localization of the conflict, Spalaiković answered that he was under a misapprehension and would see before long 'that this was not a question between Serbia and Austria but a European question'.[4]

3. *The lacunae in the Serbian diplomatic documents. Sazonov's advice and its import.*

This telegram proves that the Serbian Government has suppressed certain communications from its St. Petersburg representative. Spalaiković had a talk with Sazonov after the Russian Cabinet meeting at which important decisions were taken such as were certainly not withheld from his knowledge. Yet in telegraphing to Belgrade what he reports are words exchanged with Pourtalès as he was leaving Sazonov's cabinet, not the things Sazonov had said to him ! How can one believe him and how can one further believe that Sazonov only got into touch with him on the evening of the 24th and gave him no more definite advice than the vague words recorded by Schilling? The seriousness of the omissions from the Serbian documents was denied by Jovan

---

[1] Magrini, pp. 205–6.   [2] Schilling, p. 31; *Int Bez.* i. V, 25.
[3] Sazonov, p. 177.   [4] LAS. 36; CDD., p. 389.

Jovanović, the former Serbian Minister in Vienna, in a letter to Jules Isaac of 31 December 1932 in which he claims to have read the Spalaiković dispatches and found nothing in them that had to be kept from public knowledge. But Jovanović was a disciple and admirer of Pašić and may well have wished not to rob his chief of the glory of having rejected the most offensive points of the Austrian note. In any case Jovanović admitted the existence of four other Spalaiković dispatches which were never published, one of which, received at Belgrade on the 24th, stated:

> that Sazonov condemns the Austro-Hungarian ultimatum, that Serbia may count on Russian aid, but that Sazonov does not say what form this aid will take because it is for the Tsar and France to decide and that, in view of Serbia's lack of resources to carry on a war, she was to make a declaration and allow the Austrians to enter Serbia without putting up any resistance.

Another telegram which reached Belgrade at midnight on the 24th brought news that 'a bold decision is expected from one moment to another'.[1] The awaited decision or rather decisions were obviously those about to be taken at the Russian Cabinet meeting, including that of an eventual partial mobilization. Thus the telegrams whose existence is admitted by Jovanović show that Spalaiković saw Sazonov or his representative twice before the Cabinet meeting. Acting on instructions, as Pavlović indicates,[2] he must have told Sazonov that Serbia was in no state to resist the threatening Austrian attack and asked what she ought to do. Sazonov can certainly not have regarded it as possible for Serbia to accept all the Austrian demands, seeing that he condemned them, promising Russian aid in a form still to be determined and above all advising the Serbian Government to submit to invasion. Having brought up the question at the Cabinet meeting, and before sending the request to Vienna for a prolongation of the time limit, he telegraphed to Strandtmann at Belgrade:

> If Serbia's helpless position really is such as to leave no doubt of the outcome of her armed struggle with Austria, it would perhaps be better that in the event of invasion by Austria the Serbs for the time being should make no attempt at resistance, but withdraw, leaving the enemy to occupy the land without fighting and making a solemn appeal to the Powers. In this appeal the Serbs might draw attention to their difficult situation after the recent war, during which they had earned the gratitude of Europe by their moderation and they might base their appeal on the grounds that it was impossible for them to maintain the unequal struggle, asking the Powers for aid which would be founded on a sense of justice.[3]

---

[1] Isaac, p. 249.   [2] See p. 252.

[3] *Int Bez*. i. V, 22. This telegram of Sazonov's might be thought to be an indirect reply to the Regent's telegram to the Tsar. But the Regent's message, decided on in the forenoon of the 24th and transmitted by Strandtmann in the afternoon, could hardly have reached

This, like the advice which Sazonov relates that he gave to Serbia to accept the points of the ultimatum not incompatible with her sovereign rights, implied that she should not yield unconditionally. If she was to yield unconditionally there would have been no need to consider the possibility of war and invasion. The assumption was, on the contrary, that upon accepting only a part of the demands, she would in all probability be attacked. If that took place Russia would intervene,[1] and then either Austria would desist from her plan or there would be a European war. In this case the affair would not be decided in Serbia, and Serbia would have to resign herself for the time being to invasion. To give such advice was to say in advance that Russia would intervene so that Pašić was relieved of all doubt as to how to act. And if any doubt lingered after Spalaiković's first telegram, which left unspecified the form to be taken by Russian aid (on grounds that the decision rested with the Tsar and France, i.e. that without the certainty of French support Russia could not take the field), that doubt vanished when it was known that St. Petersburg was about to take a bold decision and when the further news came that the decision had been made, i.e. that, if need be, Russian mobilization would take place against Austria.

News of the partial mobilization and of the other decisions taken at the St. Petersburg Cabinet meeting of 24 July must—it is reasonable to suppose—have been given in Spalaiković's telegram No. 36 which has certainly been cut, or else in his previous one summarizing his conversation with Sazonov at 7 p.m. This must have been a very fateful conversation since after it Spalaiković was able to tell the German Ambassador that the conflict could not remain localized because it was a 'European question'. This was, in all probability, the telegram to which Colonel Pavlović alluded in his talk with Magrini and which

Sazonov before the morning of the 25th. Certainly the Tsar did not receive it until the 26th, since under the date: 'Peterhof, 26 July,' he wrote as a footnote: 'Very modest and dignified telegram. How is it to be answered?' (*Int. Bez*. i. V, 37). The reply sent to Belgrade on 27 July runs:

'In appealing to me at a moment of peculiar difficulty Your Royal Highness has made no mistake about my feelings for you and my heart-felt good will towards the Serbian people. The present situation occupies my most serious attention, and My Government is using every effort to compose the existing difficulties. I do not doubt that Your Highness and the Royal Government are eager to facilitate this task by leaving no avenue unexplored which might lead to a solution such as would avert the horrors of a fresh war while upholding the dignity of Serbia. As long as the slightest hope exists of avoiding bloodshed, all our efforts must be directed to this aim. Should we be unsuccessful in this, in spite of our most sincere desire, Your Highness may rest assured that Russia will in no case remain indifferent to the fate of Serbia' (*Int. Bez*. i. V, 120). Strandtmann received this dispatch at Nish on the 28th and travelled overnight to Belgrade to show it, in the Prince Regent's absence, to Pašić, who crossed himself, exclaiming 'O God! The Tsar is great and merciful!' and was overcome with emotion (Russian *Orange Book*, 57; CDD., p. 287; Mach, p. 316).

[1] The *Novoje Vremia* of 23 October 1914 states that Sazonov assured Spalaiković that 'in no case would Russia tolerate Austria's attacking Serbia'.

finally dissuaded the Serbian Government from the idea of escaping catastrophe by unconditional acceptance of the ultimatum. Indeed if Russia were willing to mobilize against Austria, it was a sign that she did not intend this time to let Serbia be attacked and mutilated and hence that Serbia could not and should not do otherwise than follow the guidance of St. Petersburg. Pavlović's statement that the telegram which changed the whole situation arrived on the afternoon of the 24th is evidently due to a slip of memory which has led him to confuse the 24th with the 25th. In the afternoon of the 24th Belgrade could not have known anything of Sazonov's intentions, seeing that they were not formulated until that very afternoon. And from Jovanović we know that Spalaikovic's telegram foretelling that a bold decision would be taken from one minute to the next, only reached Belgrade at midnight of the 24th.[1] Therefore the one summarizing his conversation with Sazonov of 7 p.m., written between 8 and 9 p.m. and then encoded, cannot have left St. Petersburg earlier than the last hours of 24 July and been decoded and given to Pašić earlier than the morning of the 25th.

Various other factors confirm this hypothesis. Wegerer maintains that up to midday on the 25th the Serbian Government still intended to accept the Austrian ultimatum. He recalls that the Sofia journal *Utro* of 27 July contained a telegram from Belgrade of the 25th stating that the decision to reject certain demands was taken in consequence of a promise telegraphed by Sazonov that Russia would support Serbia even by war.[2] Wegerer also tells that the proprietor of the Belgrade *Politika* said on the 25th to Dušan A. Lončarević that a sensational change had come about at the beginning of that same afternoon as a result of a telegram from St. Petersburg calling on Serbia to mobilize.[3] The present writer does not know whether it will ever be

---

[1] Slavko Gruić, the Secretary General of the Serbian Foreign Office, writes: 'On returning home in the night of the 24th to 25th at 2 a.m. I packed the bare necessities of clothes and linen in two small suit cases which I hid under the bed so that the servants and neighbours, who kept on asking questions, should not know that I was preparing to leave Belgrade. For the same reason I left everything in the house just as it was. I was just about getting to bed when a dull roar made me look from the window at the street. I lived in the last house at the end of the street now known as the "Boulevard of the Liberation", opposite the Observatory. The noise was coming from the Slavija [cross roads] and I at once recognized horses' hoof-beats and the rumble of the wheels of field-artillery and ammunition wagons on the paved street. The Belgrade artillery regiment was leaving Belgrade! And because I knew that there existed a definite decision not to defend Belgrade in the event of war with Austria-Hungary, it was depressing to me to see and hear our army abandoning the capital even before the clash' (*Politika*, Belgrade, 22–5 July 1934; translated into German in KSF. (1935), p. 589).

[2] KSF. (1931), pp. 635–6.

[3] Wegerer, *Refutation*, pp. 80–1.—Schmitt states (I, p. 532) that Lončarević, the Belgrade representative of the Vienna *Telegraph Bureau* who received his information from the head of the press bureau of the Serbian Foreign Office, made somewhat different statements. He said that at first the Belgrade Government was prepared to accept the ultimatum if at the

possible to establish that it was St. Petersburg which advised Serbia to mobilize as she did on the 25th. But it is likely that the news of Russian mobilization in certain districts, which was decided in principle on the 24th, led Serbia to mobilize and to conclude that St. Petersburg did not want Serbia to submit unconditionally to the Austrian demands.

Giesl, too, bears testimony that, but for advice from Russia, Serbia would have submitted:

A number of foreign journalists had chosen my legation as the best observation post. From them I learned at noon that they had talked with Pašić and that he had confidently held out prospects of a peaceful solution of the crisis by the acceptance of our demands. . . . But in the early hours of the afternoon, the situation took a thorough turn for the worse. I ascertained that a lengthy telegram had reached King Peter from the Tsar. It was being stated that Serbia had been strengthened in her resistance by the assurance that she had the backing of the entire strength of Russia. It was further said that Crown Prince Alexander had gone with the telegram to the officers' club where it was read aloud and gave rise to tumultuous demonstrations in favour of war.[1]

The Tsar's telegram did not exist, but there did exist telegrams from Spalaiković giving news of unmistakable significance about Russia's intentions, and on top of them, there came about noon communication by the Russian Chargé d'Affaires of Sazonov's message of the evening of the 24th advising Serbia to allow herself to be invaded.[2] Let it be said once again that to make such a suggestion was tantamount to advising Serbia to resist. And the same advice was contained in another document which became known at Belgrade probably on the morning of the 25th. It was the Russian official communiqué which said that the Russian Government is 'closely following the course of the

expiration of the time limit no favourable reply had been received to the Prince Regent's telegram to the Tsar and that the reply to Austria was so drafted as to permit of last-minute changes according to the nature of the Russian reply. He also stated on the authority of a former Serbian minister that half-way through the afternoon (of the 25th) an answer came from Russia 'which ran favourably' and led the Serbian Government to order mobilization and prepare for war.

[1] Giesl, pp. 267–8.

[2] It is true that telegrams from St. Petersburg took a long time to reach Serbia. Seton-Watson declares (*Sarajevo*, p. 257), that he was told on first hand authority at Belgrade that this telegram from Sazonov to Strandtmann, which has never been published, reached the Serbian Government after the latter had sent its reply to the Austrian note. But so great a delay seems hardly believable even though the English Chargé d'Affaires telegraphed at 12.30 p.m. on the 25th that his Russian colleague was still without instructions from his Government (BD. XI, 111). Counting the time needed for drafting and encoding the telegram, one must assume that it transmits information received first thing on the morning of the 25th. All other evidence, including that of J. Jovanović, makes it certain that the news and advice from Russia arrived in time. Indeed J. Jovanović reveals that the advice to Serbia to allow herself to be invaded was given to Belgrade in the first telegram of which Spalaiković tells us and which arrived in the course of the 24th.

dispute between the two countries to which Russia cannot remain indifferent'.[1]

Jules Isaac, whose book *Un débat historique, le problème des origines de la guerre* devotes special attention to this point, also comes to the conclusion that 'between the morning and afternoon of 25 July the Serbian Government changed its mind'. Asking himself the question why, after contemplating acceptance *in toto* (with reservations), it ended by accepting only nine, returning a refusal on Point 6 and only on that point, and after mustering the statements and evidence collected by Wegerer, Isaac comes to the conclusion:

> One may believe, without claiming as certain, that the information awaited and received from St. Petersburg—in one form or another—made the Serbian Government revoke its earlier decision and bravely accept the break; whether because of a telegram from the Tsar or not is of little importance, a simple telegram from M. Spalaiković announcing the decisions taken at Krasnoe-Selo would be enough.[2]

It must be made plain in the first instance that the decisions taken at Krasnoe Selo on the morning of the 25th could not be known at Belgrade by the time the Serbian reply was handed to Giesl. But those of the 24th were already enough to enlighten Pašić and his colleagues as to Russian intentions. Let us further dwell a moment on the 'acceptance *in toto* (with reservations)' mentioned by Isaac. Was, in fact, the acceptance which the Serbian Government intended to give to the Austrian demands unconditional or accompanied by some reservation? At this point it becomes necessary to consider three documents which, if read in the light of all that has just been said, prove beyond all possibility of doubt that as late as the morning of the 25th the Serbian Government had the intention of sending a reply of a very different character to the one actually delivered to Giesl, a reply which might have caused events to take quite another turn.

4. *Pašić acquaints the friendly Powers of the Serbian acceptance of the ultimatum; a reservation on Point 6 later changed into a rejection.*

On 25 July Pašić sent a telegram to all the Serbian Legations:

A brief summary of the reply of the Royal Government was communicated to the representatives of the allied Governments at the Ministry for Foreign Affairs to-day. They were informed that the reply would be quite conciliatory on all points and that the Serbian Government would accept the Austro-Hungarian demands as far as possible. The Serbian Government trust that the Austro-Hungarian Government, unless they are determined to make war at all costs, will see their way to accept the full satisfaction offered in the Serbian reply.[3]

[1] Russian *Orange Book*, 10, in CDD., p. 269.   [2] Isaac, pp. 118–23.
[3] LAS. 38, in CDD., pp. 389–90.

It is difficult to understand why so few historians have paid attention to this telegram in which Pašić announces the acceptance in principle of all the Austrian demands. They thus have failed to ask themselves how it came about that he later in the final reply made reservations on many points and rejected one outright. We must examine whether the reservations embodied in the final reply were already contained in this statement of the 25th to the friendly Powers. Crackanthorpe telegraphed to Grey at 12.30 p.m. on the 25th:

The Servian Government consent to publication of declaration in *Official Gazette*. The ten points are accepted with reserves. The Servian Government declare themselves ready to agree to mixed commission of inquiry, provided that appointment of such commission can be proved to be in accordance with international usage. They consent to dismiss and prosecute those officers whose guilt can be clearly proved and they have already arrested officer (Tankosić) mentioned in Austrian note. They agree to suppress *Narodna Obrana*.[1]

This telegram indicates only vaguely some of the reservations to be included in Pašić's reply. Further light is thrown by the more detailed account sent to Paris on the 25th by the newly arrived French Minister Boppe:

M. Pašić has just acquainted me of the note which will be handed this evening to the Austrian Minister. The Serbian Government agrees to publish to-morrow in the *Official Gazette* the declaration which has been required, they will also communicate it to the army by an order of the day; they will dissolve the societies of national defence and all other associations which might agitate against Austria-Hungary; they undertake to modify the press law, to dismiss from the army, public instruction and other administrations all officials whose participation in the propaganda shall be proved; they request that the names of these officials may be communicated to them.

As to the participation of Austrian officials in the inquiry, they ask for explanations; they will only agree to that which is consonant with international law or to relations of good neighbourliness; they accept all the other demands of the ultimatum and declare that if the Austro-Hungarian Government is not satisfied with this, they are ready to defer the matter to the decision of the Hague Tribunal or to that of the Great Powers who took part in drawing up the Declaration of 31 March 1909.[2]

This document shows that the reservations were of small account. In fact there was substantially only one, which did not invalidate the acceptance in principle and which it will be well to regard more closely. It related to Point 6 of the Austrian note requesting the Serbian Government

---

[1] BD. XI, 114.   [2] LJF. 46; in CDD., p. 172; DF. 3, XI, 63.

to take judicial proceedings against the accessories to the plot of 28 June who are on Serbian territory; Organs delegated by the Imperial and Royal Government will take part in the investigations relating thereto.

Why was Vienna to be asked for explanations on that precise point and on that point alone and why was it stated that the participation of Austrian officials in the inquiry would be agreed to only if consonant with international law and relations of good neighbourliness? Opinions as to the severity and unacceptability of the various Austrian demands varied greatly in the course of the crisis. The Prince Regent Alexander on the evening of the 23rd thought the most serious demands were Point 4 asking for the dismissal of all officers and officials guilty of propaganda against the Monarchy and the points connected with the intervention of Austrian representatives in Serbia.[1] Sazonov regarded as one of the harshest Point 2 which demanded the dissolution of the *Narodna Obrana*, and also Point 5, which dealt with the participation of officials of the Monarchy in the suppression of the anti-Austrian movement.[2] Grey took special exception to Point 5 giving the short time limit and dictating the terms of the reply,[3] while the French press, according to Szécsen's dispatch, considered Points 1, 3, 5, and 9 to be impossible of application.[4] The Belgrade Government, however, concentrated its opposition on Point 6, first inclining to accept it with the above-mentioned reservations and then, in the final text of the reply, rejecting it outright. It, moreover, was the only point rejected.

This line of conduct can only be explained in the light of what has been said above[5] of Pašić's fears that Austria might gain an insight into the ramifications of the conspiracy and discover guilt in high places. This in fact was the astute Pašić's main concern and, when seeming ready to bow to all Vienna's demands, he appended to Point 6 an apparently mild and purely formal reservation which in reality would have enabled him subsequently to reject it, as for the moment he deemed it too dangerous to do. But once he felt himself sure of Russian support he took courage and returned an outright refusal to Point 6, transferring the reservation originally formulated against it to Point 5 and regarding this reservation as an excellent expedient by which to elude the fulfilment of his undertakings.

The above is the present writer's reconstruction of what happened, based on the documents and on verified evidence. The conclusion drawn from this reconstruction is that, if assurances of full support had not come from St. Petersburg, the Serbian reply would have followed the lines indicated in Boppe's dispatch, i.e. full formal acceptance of the ultimatum with a reservation on Point 6 so skilfully worded as

---

[1] *Int. Bez.* i. V, 75.   [2] Oe–U. VIII, 10616, 10617.   [3] Oe–U. VIII, 10600.
[4] Oe–U. VIII, 10679.   [5] See above, pp. 282–4.

to make it very difficult for Austria to construe it into a rejection. What would have happened was the eventuality most dreaded by Austria and which for a moment alarmed Griesinger, the German Minister in Belgrade. Magrini in his article in *Secolo XX*, relates that Vilovsky, the chief, and Sinobad, an official of the Belgrade press bureau, which was an important department of the Serbian Foreign Office, ran into Griesinger in front of the Royal Palace on 24 July and the following conversation took place:

'What news?' asked the German Minister with a smile.

'What you know: the Austrian ultimatum. We have hope of avoiding war, indeed we believe that war will be avoided. You know that we cannot measure up to Austria. . . .'

At these words the German Minister uttered an exclamation of annoyed amazement.

'But surely, do you not feel that this ultimatum means war? It is utterly impossible for you to accept the Austrian demands; no people in the world could accept that ultimatum without committing suicide.'

'It is war'—repeated the Minister with an angry air; and after a short silence, as it were to strengthen his conviction, he added:—'You ought to know that Baron Giesl is already all packed up and ready to leave! . . .'[1]

Things turned out as Griesinger wished; but they could have gone differently if it had depended only on Belgrade. This fact is of no little importance in the inquiry into the responsibility for the acts which led to the European war. This does not mean that Russia should have tolerated the humiliation and violation of Serbia which might have had incalculable repercussions in the Balkans and on the future position of the Dual Monarchy, nor that Serbia should or could have accepted the Austrian demands. If the Serbian Government contemplated yielding, it was not because this was regarded as a feasible and honourable way out, but because it was rendered inevitable by the serious state of the Serbian nation and army. San Giuliano later on, as we shall see, thought to gain acceptance for a proposal of his for composing the Austro-Serbian difference on a basis of full acceptance by Serbia of the ultimatum. But he, too, in this belated move, was guided solely by the desire to avoid the catastrophe at any price, making the Great Powers shoulder the responsibility of suggesting it to Belgrade.

5. The drafting and delivery of the Serbian reply.

The general impression at the time was that certain points in the note were such that they must necessarily be rejected, and, as we have seen, they were planned in order to produce this effect. Even Grey, who felt no concern for Serbian independence and prestige and would

---

[1] Magrini, *art. cit.* in *Secolo XX*, p. 390; *La Serbia invasa*, p. 44.

have left Austria to do what she liked with Serbia, if it did not lead to war, did not venture to advise unconditional acceptance of the Austrian note. We have already seen that Pašić at once appealed to him via Crackanthorpe. On the evening of the 24th Grey replied:

It seems to me that Servia ought certainly to express concern and regret that any officials, however subordinate, should have been accomplices in murder of the Archduke, and promise, if this is proved, to give fullest satisfaction. For the rest, I can only say that Servian Government must reply as they consider the interests of Servia require. I cannot tell whether anything short of unconditional acceptance will avert military action by Austria on expiration of time limit, but the only chance would be to give a favourable reply on as many points as possible within the limit of time, and not to meet Austrian demand with a blank negative.[1]

It is not very clear whether similar advice came from Paris. In the circular telegram of 24 July Bienvenu-Martin stated that Berthelot had personally advised Serbia to 'play for time', it might be well,

for example, to offer immediate satisfaction on all points not inconsistent with the dignity and sovereignty of Serbia and to point out that the findings of the Sarajevo inquiry were unilateral and that Serbia . . . asked to be shown the proofs in order rapidly to verify them; above all to try to escape the direct grip of Austria by declaring her willingness to submit to the arbitrage of Europe.[2]

Szécsen telegraphed from Paris on 24 July that the German Ambassador Schoen had been told by Berthelot that 'the Serbian Government should declare acceptance in principle but ask for explanations and further details on certain points'.[3] Schoen's own dispatch said that 'Serbia has been advised from here to yield as far as possible'.[4] But to his intimate friend, Victor Margueritte—as the latter informed the present writer—Berthelot said that the Serbian reply was in its essentials inspired by the advice given by him to Vesnić, the Serbian Minister in Paris.

However, with Poincaré and Viviani absent, the advice from Paris could not carry the same weight with Pašić as that from London and from St. Petersburg which were identical in substance. By not yielding everything and accepting the Austrian challenge Pašić gained the approval of Serbian military and nationalist circles, who might have revolted—as Griesinger telegraphed to Berlin on the 24th—if the order of the day had been issued to the Serbian Army, as demanded by the Austrian note.[5] Thus, the course to be followed became plain and it was pursued by Pašić and his colleagues with consummate diplomatic skill and to the immediate great advantage of Serbia.

---

[1] BD. XI, 102.   [2] LJF. 26; in CDD., pp. 157-8; DF. 3. XI, 15.
[3] Oe-U. VIII, 10608.   [4] DD. I, 154.   [5] DD. I, 159.

Before Giesl received his answer, military preparations were begun and arrangements made for the removal from Belgrade to the interior of Government offices, archives, and the Treasury and for the evacuation of the capital by the army.[1] Mobilization was proclaimed.[2] It seems pretty clear that, by ordering mobilization before handing the reply, Pašić intended to assure the military party of his intention to resist and thus gain their acceptance of an apparently extremely mild reply. In fact, being convinced that Austria would take nothing less than unconditional acceptance of her note, Pašić saw to it that the Serbian reply agreed to the greatest possible number of Austrian demands and was couched in calm and conciliatory terms. By this he would win the sympathy and approval of the Chancelleries and public opinion of Europe and would put the Monarchy in the wrong, if it seized upon partial acceptance as a pretext for war. The Serbian Ministers weighed every word of the first draft, making an infinite number of changes, so that the text given to Gruić for translation and recopying was so full of crossings out and additions as to be almost incomprehensible.

Slavko Gruić, then Secretary General of the Serbian Foreign Office, and later Jugoslav Minister in London, has narrated to the present writer that the first text of the Serbian reply came into his hands for translation at 11 a.m. The drawing up of the reply had been carried out mainly by Protić, Pašić and Janković, then Minister of Public Education, but the Ministers Ljuba Jovanović and Djuričić had also contributed to it. At many points the text was almost illegible, there were many sentences crossed out and many added. While the work of translation was proceeding, between noon and 5 p.m., the text was several times taken away again and the Ministers, in continuous session in an adjoining large room, made many changes, additions and completions. At last after 4 p.m. the text seemed finally settled and an attempt was made to type it out. But the typist was inexperienced and very nervous and after a few lines the typewriter refused to work, with the result that the reply had to be written out by hand in hectographic ink, copies being jellied off. Towards 5 p.m. when the copying out of the translation was not yet quite finished, Gruić was summoned into the Cabinet room and asked for the first part of the Serbian text for the introduction of one more change. Gruić declared that it was not possible to make any fresh corrections or the text would never be ready in time. The last half-hour was one of feverish work. The reply was corrected by pen here and there. One whole phrase placed in

---

[1] Oe-U. VIII, 10645.

[2] Griesinger had already telegraphed on the 24th at 11.50 p.m.: 'Mobilization is already in full swing.' (DD. I, 158.) It was understandable, if not inevitable, that military preparations began at once in view of possible developments. But the order for mobilization was not given until 3 p.m. on the 25th.

parenthesis was crossed out in ink and made illegible. At 5.45 p.m. Gruić handed the text to Pašić in an envelope.

Pašić [continues Gruić] looked around, then turned his gaze meaningly on me and asked: 'Well, who will take it?' I felt not the slightest desire to be the messenger. I had barely time to get to the station and if I had first to take the note to the Austrian Minister, I might lose my train, which would have waited for the Prime Minister or a Cabinet Minister but not for me. So I felt relieved when, amid general silence, Pašić said: 'Very well, then I will take it myself.' He put the envelope with our reply under his arm and descended the stair with measured tread followed in silence by Ministers and officials who hastened off to the station to catch the train which soon after 6 p.m. was due to leave for Nish.

6. *The text of the Serbian reply; its true character.*

There now follows a translation of the Serbian reply with the comments made by the Austro-Hungarian Government beside each point of the note in a document which was circularized to all Austrian representatives abroad on 28 July after the declaration of war and was meant to serve as a justification for the war. As this document was not transmitted by telegraph, it arrived at the various capitals so late that it could not be communicated to all the Powers, not to England certainly,[1] and thus failed to produce much effect.

Text of Serbian Reply[2]	*Remarks of Austrian Government*
The Royal Serbian Government have received the communication of the Imperial and Royal Government of the 10th inst. [old style], and are convinced that their reply will remove any misunderstanding which may threaten to impair the good neighbourly relations between the Austro-Hungarian Monarchy and the Kingdom of Serbia.	The Royal Serbian Government confine themselves to asserting that, since the declarations on 18 March 1909 no attempt has been made by the Serbian Government and their agents to change the position of Bosnia and Herzegovina.
Conscious of the fact that the protests which were made both from the tribune of the national Skupština and in the declarations and actions of the responsible representatives of the State—protests which were cut short by the declarations made by the Serbian Government on the 18th March, 1909 [old style]—have not been renewed on any occasion as regards the great neighbouring Monarchy, and that no attempt has been made since that time, either by	Thereby they deliberately and arbitrarily shift the ground on which our *démarche* was based, as we did not maintain that they and their agents have taken any official action in this direction.
	Our charge, on the contrary, is to the effect that the Serbian Government, notwithstanding the obligations undertaken in the above-quoted note, have neglected to suppress the movement directed against the territorial integrity of the Monarchy.
	Their obligation, that is to say, was that they should change the

---

[1] Schmitt, I, p. 536.   [2] DA. II, 96, Annex; CDD., pp. 507–14.

successive Royal Governments or by their agents, to change the political and legal state of affairs created in Bosnia and Herzegovina, the Royal Government draw attention to the fact that in this connexion the Imperial and Royal Government have made no representation except one concerning a school book, and that on that occasion the Imperial and Royal Government received an entirely satisfactory explanation. Serbia has several times given proofs of her pacific and moderate policy during the Balkan crisis, and it is thanks to Serbia and to the sacrifice that she has made in the exclusive interest of European peace that that peace has been preserved.

The Royal Government cannot be held responsible for manifestations of a private character, such as articles in the press and the peaceable work of societies—manifestations which take place in nearly all countries in the ordinary course of events, and which, as a general rule, escape official control. The Royal Government are all the less responsible, in view of the fact that at the time of the solution of a series of questions which arose between Serbia and Austria-Hungary they gave proof of a great readiness to oblige, and thus succeeded in settling the majority of these questions to the advantage of the two neighbouring countries.

For these reasons the Royal Government have been pained and surprised at the statements, according to which members of the Kingdom of Serbia are supposed to have participated in the preparations for the crime committed at Sarajevo; the Royal Government expected to be invited to collaborate in an investigation of all that concerns this crime, and they were ready, in order to prove the entire correctness of their attitude, to take measures against any persons concerning

whole direction of their policy and adopt a friendly and neighbourly attitude towards the Austro-Hungarian Monarchy, and not merely that they should refrain from officially attacking the incorporation of Bosnia in the Monarchy.

The proposition of the Royal Serbian Government that utterances in the press and the activities of societies are of a private character and are not subject to official control is absolutely antagonistic to the institutions of modern States, even those which have the most liberal law with regard to press and associations; this law has a public character and subjects the press, as well as associations, to State control. Moreover, Serbian institutions themselves contemplate some such control. The complaint against the Serbian Government is in fact that they have entirely omitted to control their press and their associations, of whose activities in a sense hostile to the Monarchy they were well aware.

This proposition is incorrect; the Serbian Government were accurately informed of the suspicions which were entertained against quite definite persons and were not only in a position but also bound by their internal laws to initiate spontaneous inquiries. They have done nothing in this direction.

whom representations were made to them. Falling in, therefore, with the desire of the Imperial and Royal Government, they are prepared to hand over for trial any Serbian subject, without regard to his position or rank, of whose complicity in the crime of Sarajevo proofs are forthcoming, and more especially they undertake to cause to be published on the first page of the *Journal Official*, on the date of the 13th (26th) July, the following declaration:—

'The Royal Government of Serbia condemn all propaganda which may be directed against Austria-Hungary —i.e., the general tendency, the final aim of which is to detach from the Austro-Hungarian Monarchy territories belonging to it, and they sincerely deplore the fatal consequences of these criminal proceedings.

Our demand ran:—

'The Royal Government of Servia condemn the propaganda directed against Austria-Hungary . . .'

The alteration made by the Royal Serbian Government in the declaration demanded by us implies that no such propaganda directed against Austria-Hungary exists, or that they are cognizant of no such propaganda. This formula is insincere and disingenuous, as by it the Serbian Government reserve for themselves for later use the evasion that they had not by this declaration disavowed the then existing propaganda, and had not admitted that it was hostile to the Monarchy, from which they could further deduce that they had not bound themselves to suppress propaganda similar to that now being carried on.

The wording demanded by us ran:—

'The Royal Government regret that Serbian officers and functionaries . . . participated. . . .'

By the adoption of this wording with the addition 'according to the communication from the Imperial and Royal Government' the Serbian Government are pursuing the object that has already been referred to above, namely that of preserving a free hand for the future.

'The Royal Government regret that, according to the communication from the Imperial and Royal Government, certain Serbian officers and functionaries participated in the above mentioned propaganda, and thus compromised the good neighbourly relations to which the Royal Serbian Government was solemnly pledged by the declaration of 31 March 1909 [new style].

'The Government, etc. . . .' (identical with the text as demanded).

The Royal Government further undertake:—

1. To introduce at the first regular convocation of the Skupština a provision into the press law providing for the most severe punishment of

We had demanded of them:—

1. 'To suppress any publication which incites to hatred and contempt of the Austro-Hungarian Monarchy and the general tendency

incitement to hatred and contempt of the Austro-Hungarian Monarchy, and for taking action against any publication the general tendency of which is directed against the territorial integrity of Austria-Hungary. The Government engage at the approaching revision of the Constitution to cause an amendment to be introduced into Article 22 of the Constitution of such a nature that such publication may be confiscated, a proceeding at present impossible under the categorical terms of Article 22 of the Constitution.

of which is directed against the territorial integrity of the Monarchy.'

We wished therefore to ensure that Serbia should be obliged to see to it that press attacks of that nature shall be discontinued in future; we wished therefore to know that a definite result in this connexion was assured.

Instead of this Serbia offers us the enactment of certain laws which would be calculated to serve as a means towards this result, viz:—

(a) A law under which the press publications in question which are hostile to the Monarchy are to be punished on their merits (subjectiv) a matter which is of complete indifference to us, all the more as it is well known that the prosecution of press offences on their merits (subjectiv) is only very rarely possible, and, if any law of the sort is laxly administered, even in the few cases of this nature a conviction would not be obtained; this therefore, is a proposal which is no way meets our demand as it does not offer us the slightest guarantee of the result which we wish to obtain.

(b) A law supplementary to Art. 22 of the Constitution which would permit confiscation—a proposal which is equally unsatisfactory to us, as the existence of such a law in Serbia is of no use to us, but only the obligation of the Government to apply it; this, however, is not promised us.

These proposals are therefore entirely unsatisfactory—all the more so as they are evasive in that we are not told within what period of time these laws would be enacted, and that in the event of the rejection of the Bills by the Skupština—apart from the possible resignation of the Government—everything would be as it was before.

2. The Government possess no proof, nor does the note of the Imperial and Royal Government furnish them with any, that the *Narodna*

The whole of the public life of Serbia teems with the propaganda against the Monarchy, of the *Narodna Obrana* and of societies affiliated to

Obrana and other similar societies have committed up to the present any criminal act of this nature through the proceedings of any of their members. Nevertheless, the Royal Government will accept the demand of the Imperial and Royal Government, and will dissolve the *Narodna Obrana* Society and every other society which may be directing its efforts against Austria-Hungary.

it; it is therefore quite impossible to admit the reservation made by the Serbian Government when they say that they know nothing about them.

Quite apart from this the demand we have made is not entirely complied with, as we further required:—

That the means of propaganda possessed by these associations should be confiscated.

That the re-establishment of the dissolved associations under another name and in another form should be prevented.

The Belgrade Cabinet maintains complete silence in both these directions, so that the half consent which has been given offers us no guarantee that it is contemplated to put a definite end to the activities of the associations hostile to the Monarchy, especially of the *Narodna Obrana*, by their dissolution.

3. The Royal Serbian Government undertake to eliminate without delay from public instruction in Serbia[1] everything that serves or might serve to foment the propaganda against Austria - Hungary, whenever the Imperial and Royal Government furnish them with facts and proofs of this propaganda.

In this case also the Serbian Government first ask for proofs that propaganda against the Monarchy is fomented in public educational establishments in Serbia, when they must know that the school books which have been introduced into Serbian schools contain matter of an objectionable nature in this respect, and that a large proportion of the Serbian teachers are enrolled in the ranks of the *Narodna Obrana* and the societies affiliated with it.

Moreover, here, too, the Serbian Government have not complied with a portion of our demand as fully as we required, inasmuch as in their text they have omitted the addition which we desired 'both as regards the teaching body and also as regards the methods of instruction'—an addition which quite clearly shows in what directions the propaganda against the Monarchy in the Serbian schools is to be looked for.

4. The Royal Government also agree to remove from the military

Inasmuch as the Royal Serbian Government attach to their consent

[1] Here thirteen words were crossed out and rendered illegible before the handing of the note to Giesl.

service all such persons as the judicial inquiry may have proved to be guilty of acts directed against the integrity of the territory of the Austro-Hungarian Monarchy, and they expect the Imperial and Royal Government to communicate to them at a later date the names and the acts of these officers and functionaries for the purpose of the proceedings which are to be taken against them.

5. The Royal Government must confess that they do not clearly grasp the meaning or the scope of the demand made by the Imperial and Royal Government that Serbia shall undertake to accept the collaboration of the representatives of the Imperial and Royal Government upon their territory, but they declare that they will admit such collaboration as agrees with the principle of international law, with criminal procedure, and with good neighbourly relations.

6. It goes without saying[1] that the Royal Government consider it their duty to open an inquiry against all such persons as are, or eventually may be, implicated in the plot of 15 June [old style], and who happen to be within the territory of the kingdom. As regards the participation in this inquiry of Austro-Hungarian agents or authorities appointed for this purpose by the Imperial and Royal Government, the Royal Government cannot accept such an arrangement, as it would be a violation of the Constitution and of the law of criminal procedure; nevertheless in concrete cases communications as to the results of the investigation in question might be given to the Austro-Hungarian agents.

to the removal of the officers and functionaries in question from military and civil service the condition that these persons should have been convicted by judicial inquiry, their consent is confined to those cases in which these persons are charged with a crime punishable by law. As we, however, demand the removal of those officers and functionaries who foment propaganda against the Monarchy, a proceeding which is not generally punishable by law in Serbia, it appears that our demand under this head also is not complied with.

International Law has just as little to do with this question as has criminal procedure. This is purely a matter of State police, which must be settled by way of a separate agreement. Serbia's reservation is therefore unintelligible, and would be calculated, owing to the vague and general form in which it is couched, to lead to unsurmountable difficulties when the time comes for concluding the prospective agreement.

Our demand was quite clear and did not admit of misinterpretation. We desired:—

(1) The opening of a judicial inquiry (*enquête judiciaire*) against accessories to the plot.

(2) The collaboration of representatives of the Imperial and Royal Government in the investigations relating thereto ('*recherches*' as opposed to '*enquête judiciaire*').

It never occurred to us that representatives of the Imperial and Royal Government should take part in the Serbian judicial proceedings; it was intended that they should collaborate only in the preliminary police investigations, directed to the collection and verification of the material for the inquiry.

If the Serbian Government misunderstand us on this point they

---

[1] Here a word is crossed out.

must do so deliberately, for the distinction between '*enquête judiciaire*' and simple '*recherches*' must be familiar to them.

In desiring to be exempted from all control in the proceedings which are to be initiated, which if properly carried through would have results of a very undesirable kind for themselves, and in view of the fact that they have no handle for a plausible refusal of the collaboration of our representatives in the preliminary police investigations (numberless precedents exist for such police intervention) they have adopted a standpoint which is intended to invest their refusal with an appearance of justification and to impress on our demand the stamp of impracticability.

This answer is disingenuous.

The inquiries set on foot by us show that three days after the crime, when it became known that Ciganović was implicated in the plot, he went on leave and travelled to Ribari on a commission from the Prefecture of Police at Belgrade. It is, therefore, in the first place incorrect to say that Ciganović had left Serbian State Service on 25–8 June [old style]. To this must be added the fact that the Prefect of Police at Belgrade, who had himself contrived the departure of Ciganović and who knew where he was stopping, declared in an interview that no man of the name of Milan Ciganović existed in Belgrade.

7. The Royal Government proceeded, on the very evening of the delivery of the note, to arrest Commandant Voja Tankosić. As regards Milan Ciganović, who is a subject of the Austro-Hungarian Monarchy and who up to 15 June [old style] was employed (on probation) by the directorate of railways, it has not yet been possible to arrest him.

The Austro-Hungarian Government are requested to be so good as to supply as soon as possible, in the customary form, the presumptive evidence of guilt, as well as the proofs of guilt, if there are any (*eventuelles*), which have been collected up to the present, at the inquiry[1] at Sarajevo for the purposes of the later inquiry.

8. The Serbian Government will reinforce and extend the measures which have been taken for preventing the illicit traffic in arms and explosives across the frontier. It goes without saying that they will immediately order an inquiry and will severely punish the frontier officials on the Šabac-Ložnica line who have failed in their duty and allowed the authors of the crime of Sarajevo to pass.

---

[1] The original word '*instruction*' was replaced by '*enquête*'.

9. The Royal Government will gladly give explanations of the remarks made by their officials whether in Serbia or abroad, in interviews after the crime which, according to the statement of the Imperial and Royal Government, were hostile towards the Monarchy, as soon as the Imperial and Royal Government have communicated to them the passages in question in these remarks, and as soon as they have shown that the remarks were actually made by the said officials, although the Royal Government will themselves take steps to collect evidence and proofs.

10. The Royal Government will inform the Imperial and Royal Government of the execution of the measures comprised under the above heads, in so far as this has not already been done by the present note,[1] as soon as each measure has been ordered and carried out.

If the Imperial and Royal Government are not satisfied with this reply, the Serbian Government, considering that it is not to the common interest to precipitate the solution of this question, are ready, as always, to accept a pacific understanding, either by referring this question to the decision of the International Tribunal of the Hague, or to the Great Powers which took part in the drawing up of the declaration made by the Serbian Government on the 18th (31st) March 1909.[2]

The interviews in question must be quite well known to the Royal Serbian Government. By requesting the Imperial and Royal Government to communicate to them all kinds of details about these interviews, and keeping in reserve the holding of a formal inquiry into them, they show that they are not willing to comply seriously with this demand either.

The Austrian comments give a good idea of the extent to which Belgrade had acceded to the demands of the ultimatum: no reservations made on Points 8 and 10; Points 1, 2, 3 partially accepted. But the replies to Points 4, 5, 9 were couched in such a way as to evade their demands. To Point 8 the reply was untruthful, since Ciganović, as the Austrian comment stated, had been got away by the Serbian authorities. Finally a negative reply was given to the paramount demand in Point 6 for the participation of organs of the Austro-Hungarian Government in the investigations into the plot of 28 June.

[1] Here a word is crossed out and made illegible.

[2] Oe-U. VIII, 10648, 10860. The mistakes in spelling and grammar can be seen in the original of the Serbian reply preserved in the Vienna State Archives.

While undoubtedly incompatible with Serbian sovereign rights, it would also have been dangerous in bringing to light the activities of the *Black Hand* and its redoubted chief.

There is no need to linger over a discussion of the Austrian reasons for making such demands and the Serbian right to reject not only the one she did but several others as well. Pašić told the Bulgarian Minister on 27 July that 'if Serbia had been sure of being supported to such an extent by Russia she would never have conceded so much'.[1] From his own point of view he may have been right, but it was none the less true that Serbian officials were implicated in the Sarajevo crime and that it was directly connected with Pan-Serb activity and propaganda. A further question is whether politically and morally Austria had the better right to defend her existence or Serbia to liberate her brethren. Italians who have suffered the same calvary (Schmitt recalls that Cavour was asked by Buol to suppress Piedmontese journals and gave much the same reply as Pašić gave to Berchtold),[2] and who, in the final phases of the war, aimed at the dissolution of Austria-Hungary and achieved it, will be the last to uphold the cause of Austria against that of Serbia.

But leaving aside all discussion of the merits of the question, one may draw attention to the cleverness displayed in drafting the reply, which was described by the man who framed the Viennese note as 'the most brilliant specimen of diplomatic skill that I know'.[3] Indeed unless one collates the two texts, one gets the impression that Serbia was agreeing to practically all the Austrian demands. If, as might well be expected, she did not agree to the participation of Austrian officials in a judicial inquiry or Serbian territory (Point 6), she yielded on Point 5, which was not less injurious to her sovereignty and independence, in that she accepted 'such (Austrian) collaboration as would correspond with the principles of international law and penal procedure and also to good neighbourly relations'. This sounded a lot and meant nothing at all. But it turned out that not only European public opinion and the *Entente* Chancelleries, but also Kaiser Wilhelm[4] and his Chancellor, carried away the impression of a full capitulation on the part of Serbia such as ought to render a peaceful solution of the dispute possible.

Vienna thought otherwise and Berlin was unable to exercise restraint.

7. *Giesl leaves Belgrade; he reports to Tisza and Francis Joseph.*

The instructions telegraphed by Berchtold to Giesl on 20 July as to how he was to behave in connexion with the Serbian reply were extremely precise. No prolongation of the time limit could be granted on any pretext of the Serbian Government's wanting further informa-

---

[1] *Die Bulgarischen Dokumente zum Kriegsausbruch*, KSF., March 1928, p. 245.
[2] Schmitt, I, 537.   [3] Musulin, p. 241.   [4] DD. I, 271.

tion on particular points, nor could there be any negotiations on the demands. Only their unconditional acceptance within the time limit would be regarded as satisfactory and 'prevent the Austrian Government from drawing the further consequences'. Giesl was not to discuss the contents of the note or the meaning of particular demands. On the expiry of the forty-eight hour time limit, if the note had not been unconditionally accepted, Giesl was to send a note to the Serbian Government informing it that he was leaving Belgrade with the Legation staff.[1] On 24 July Berchtold repeated the order that 'any conditional acceptance, or one accompanied by reservations is to be regarded as a refusal'.[2]

By 3 p.m. on the 25th Giesl knew that acceptance would not be unconditional. The Minister of Commerce, Janković, had come asking a small personal favour and as a return service had let out what was happening. At 5.55 p.m. Pašić arrived at the Austrian Legation and handed over the Serbian note, saying in broken German:

Part of your demands we have accepted . . . for the rest we place our hopes on your loyalty and chivalry as an Austrian general.[3]

Giesl actually was a general, and, as a good general, he carried out his instructions to the letter. He quickly glanced through the document and, seeing that it did not fulfil the conditions laid down by Berchtold, signed the already prepared note and sent it by an official to Pašić. The note said that as the time limit of the note delivered to the Minister Paču had expired and he had not received a satisfactory reply, he was leaving Belgrade that same evening with the Legation staff. The protection of the Legation premises and of Austro-Hungarian subjects and interests was entrusted to the German Legation. From the moment Pašić was in receipt of this letter, Austro-Serbian diplomatic relations were to be regarded as broken off.[4] Having burnt the code books, the luggage being ready packed and cars at the door, Giesl, with his wife and Legation staff reached the Belgrade station in time for the 6.30 p.m. train, and ten minutes later crossed the Austrian frontier at Semlin.[5]

---

[1] Oe-U. VIII, 10396.   [2] Oe-U. VIII, 10571.
[3] Giesl, pp. 268-9.   [4] LAS. 40, in CDD., p. 390.
[5] In a letter written to the present writer on 18 December 1932 Giesl writes that even before receiving the Serbian reply he was convinced that the Austro-Hungarian ultimatum would not be accepted integrally by the Belgrade Government. 'The events of the afternoon of 25 July: the Minister Janković's call, mobilization, departure of the garrison, convinced me that in no case would Serbia accept the note without reservations (communication from the Minister Janković). Independently of Pašić's decisive reply, this conviction was strengthened when at 6.15 p.m. I found the streets leading to the station and the station itself occupied by the military. Moreover part of the diplomatic corps was at the station, whereas on my part only the German Minister had been informed of my departure. I certainly attribute to the Russian telegram the origin of the change in the situation which took place immediately after noon.'

This haste was also in response to Berchtold's orders. On 24 July he had telegraphed that, in the event of a rupture, Giesl was to leave Belgrade by the 6.30 p.m. train and to telegraph immediately on reaching Semlin *en clair* and in a minimum of words to the Imperial Chancellery, to the Foreign Minister and to Tisza, and this he did. He further was to get on at once by telephone to the railway head offices at Budapest and through them communicate with Tisza, who had been asked to hold the Semlin–Budapest telephone line after 6 p.m. for Giesl's use and to relay the message he received at once to the Ballplatz. By these means Berchtold calculated that he could have information of Giesl's departure as early as 7 p.m.[1] Thus the first to get news of the break was Tisza. Recognizing Giesl's voice, and without giving him time to speak Tisza asked: 'Did it have to be?' (*Musste es denn sein?*) to which Giesl replied with the single word: 'Yes.'[2] Giesl's telephone message to Budapest was relayed to Vienna where at 7.45 p.m. it became known that, as the Serbian note was not satisfactory on several points, Giesl had broken off diplomatic relations and left and that the Serbian Government at 3 p.m. had ordered general mobilization and had withdrawn with the diplomatic corps to Kragujevac.[3] Giesl's telegram to Berchtold only arrived at 9 p.m.[4] Next morning, the 26th, Giesl arrived in Budapest where Tisza was at the station to meet him, read the Serbian reply and approved of the rupture. Giesl then continued his journey to Vienna which he reached in the early hours of the afternoon.[5]

Margutti narrates that Francis Joseph at Ischl awaited the result of the Austrian *démarche* at Belgrade in great anxiety. At 2.45 p.m. he entertained the Duke and Duchess of Cumberland to lunch with their daughters and the Duke and Duchess of Brunswick.

It was the most mournful meal at which I have ever been present in my life. The Emperor was unrecognizable. He hardly opened his lips and his preoccupied, absent-minded glance showed that his thoughts were far away. As soon as he could do so without discourtesy he rose from table and withdrew after abruptly taking leave of his guests. . . . At 5.30 p.m. Berchtold arrived [at Margutti's office]. He knew that I was directly connected by telephone with the War Ministry at Vienna and had come to my office to wait for the telephone call. He was as pale as death. After greeting me he sank into an armchair and relapsed into complete silence. On the stroke of

---

[1] Oe-U. VIII, 10571.

[2] Giesl, p. 271. In an interesting letter containing his diary for 25, 26 and 27 July, sent to Luciano Magrini on 11 January 1935, Giesl writes: 'Count Tisza first of all had the Serbian note read to him, then read it attentively through and had it copied. Then a discussion arose between us during which, after I had recounted the last events in Belgrade, he absolved me with the words: "You could not have done differently".'

[3] Oe-U. VIII, 10646.   [4] Oe-U. VIII, 10647.

[5] Giesl, pp. 271–2.

6 p.m. he rose as if on springs. 'It is hardly likely that anything will come now,' he said. 'I am going out for a breath of air. If I am needed I am at my *pied-à-terre* at the Hotel Elisabeth.' And he took his leave. He had hardly been gone for five minutes when the telephone bell rang. The aide-de-camp at the War Ministry was telephoning me that a few seconds before 6 p.m. the Serbian Government's reply had been handed to Baron Giesl and that he, regarding it as unacceptable, had at once left Belgrade for Semlin with all his staff. . . . Without losing a minute I rang up the Hotel Elisabeth and asked for Count Berchtold. . . . He was not back yet. . . . I wrote the text of the message on a loose leaf and flew rather than ran to the Imperial villa. . . . The Monarch rose from his desk without a word. . . . With wide eyes he listened and, when I had finished, said: '*Also doch!*' ('So after alll') in a voice hoarse with emotion.

The exclamation reveals that a dreaded possibility had become a certainty. Then after a long silence he exclaimed: 'After all, the rupture of diplomatic relations is not necessarily a *casus belli*!'[1]

These words have never received much attention from historians, partly because they are reported by the not always reliable Margutti, partly because they were not sufficiently authenticated and might be the expression of a fleeting mood. But this is not the case. The same idea was expressed by Berchtold when talking to Giesl immediately on the latter's arrival at the Ballplatz. In Giesl's above quoted letter to the present writer, he says in his diary extract for 26 July:

Vienna. Afternoon at the Foreign Ministry where Count Berchtold . . . awaited me. . . . Count Berchtold approved my conduct, was interested especially in the Tsar's intervention by the telegram of the 25th which brought about the change of attitude. He emphasized in the conversation that: 'The breaking off of relations is not by any means war.'

And in the diary entry for the 27th contained in the same letter, Giesl records:

In the course of the audience lasting one hour, the Emperor also repeated the view of Count Berchtold: 'The breaking off of relations is still not necessarily war.'

In his earlier letter to the present writer of 18 December 1932 Giesl had given a fuller account of this audience:

When I entered Francis Joseph rose and said: 'You will give me a report on what took place. But first of all I say to you that you could not have acted otherwise, and I must bear this too. However this still does not mean war!' Then he bade me be seated and make my report. I spoke little and at the end he repeated: 'You could not have acted otherwise. We must bear this too.

---

[1] Margutti, pp. 116–18; the news cannot have reached Ischl much before 7 p.m.

Conrad is a noble spirit and can guide the Archduke;[1] but we are not at war yet, and if I can, I shall prevent it.'[2]

What is the explanation of this change from Francis Joseph's attitude in the early days of July?[3] Then he spoke of resorting to extreme measures against Serbia, as is also visible in his autograph letter to Wilhelm of 2 July and in his words to Conrad, when Conrad asked: 'If the answer runs that Germany will take her stand at our side, do we then make war on Serbia?' and Francis Joseph replied: 'In that case, yes.'[4]

Why twenty days later did he seem to have changed his mind and to be hoping to go into reverse? Historians, in the opinion of the present writer, have not paid sufficient attention to the series of retreats from earlier decisions shown in the Austrian documents of those days and of which several phases have been illustrated above.[5] First a surprise attack on Serbia was contemplated, to be followed by her partition between Austria, Bulgaria and Roumania; next, at the insistence of Tisza, Serbia was to be presented with demands so harsh that she would be bound to reject them and war would follow, but on the understanding that the territory taken from her was to be assigned to her Balkan neighbours, not to the Monarchy, which was to confine itself to frontier rectifications and notify the Powers that it did not aim at territorial conquests. Next, after Tisza's surrender, Berchtold, as he himself wrote in his report to the Emperor of 14 July,

put forward that even after mobilization a peaceable adjustment would be possible if Serbia would listen to reason in time. . . . The contents . . . of the note . . . are such that the possibility of an armed conflict must be reckoned with.

But a loophole still was left for 'Serbia's yielding after all and accepting our demands'.[6]

8. *After the first heat of anger Vienna beats a series of retreats.*

These retreats denote a sharp drop in the temperature from that of the first heat of anger at Vienna. They are explained both by the temperament of the man who directed Austrian foreign policy and by the opposition he encountered from the Hungarian Prime Minister as

[1] Archduke Frederick had been nominated by the Emperor Commander-in-Chief. He was the grandson of Archduke Albert, the victor of Custoza. But he was to be assisted by Conrad who was given the widest military powers and exercised in fact the supreme command of the army.

[2] In a letter of 18 January 1933, written by Giesl to the present writer, he adds: 'By the words "This does not yet mean war" the Emperor clearly referred solely to the war with Serbia. There was not yet the thought of a world war breaking out, seeing that not even mobilization against Serbia had as yet been ordered and nothing was yet known exactly of the Russian and French will to war.'

[3] See pp. 128-32.   [4] See p. 135.   [5] See pp. 170-5.

[6] Oe-U. VIII, 10272. See pp. 177-8.

well as by the Emperor's age and craving for peace. As the days passed, a faint hope seems to have dawned in the hearts of all these leaders that the crisis would pass without need for the use of force. On 25 July the English Ambassador to Vienna telegraphed to Grey: 'Language of press this morning leaves the impression that the surrender of Servia is neither expected nor really desired.'[1] But this did not entirely represent the state of mind either of Tisza, or of Berchtold or of Francis Joseph on whose shoulders rested the whole responsibility for an immense tragedy. The two latter in particular, Berchtold from weakness of character, Francis Joseph from the weight of years, seemed to shrink from facing it. And while of the Emperor's views no more is known than has been recorded above, Berchtold's are mirrored in documents almost wholly neglected in the works dealing with the subject.

When, in his telegram of 23 July, Giesl described the note he was to deliver that evening as an ultimatum, as it was also termed by Mensdorff and other Ambassadors, Berchtold corrected him by wiring:

The term ultimatum chosen by you for our to-day's step at Belgrade is incorrect inasmuch as fruitless expiry of time limit will be followed only by breaking off of diplomatic relations, not by immediate commencement of state of war. State of war will begin only with declaration of war or Serbian offensive.[2]

This intention not to resort immediately to war was, as we have seen, intimated to London on the evening of the 24th.[3] On the previous day Mensdorff had telegraphed expressing the fear that Grey would criticize the style of the note and the shortness of the time limit as that of an ultimatum and Berchtold had replied instructing Mensdorff to explain immediately to Grey that it was 'not a formal ultimatum but a démarche with a time limit'. The telegram, drafted by Musulin, one of the few men at the Ballplatz who did not belong to the war party, went on:

If the time limit expires without result, it will for the time being be followed only by the breaking off of diplomatic relations and the beginning of necessary military preparations, since we are quite determined to insist on our justifiable demands. Your Excellency is empowered to add that if Serbia were to yield after expiry of time limit only under the pressure of our military measures, we should have to hold her responsible for the reimbursement of our expenditure arising therefrom; we have, as is known, had in 1908 and 1912 twice to mobilize on account of Serbia.[4]

[1] BD. XI, 110.   [2] Oe-U. VIII, 10521.   [3] BD. XI, 104.
[4] Oe-U. VIII, 10599.—The idea that Serbia might save herself from war by paying the cost of mobilization was perhaps suggested to Berchtold by a conversation he had with Conrad on 23 July: 'I remarked [writes Conrad] that if there was mobilization, there would have to be war. The Minister interposed enquiringly: "But if Serbia yields on the second day of mobilization?" I answered: "Then Serbia must pay the costs" meaning the expenditure arising out of mobilization' (Conrad, IV, p. 108).

Mensdorff saw Nicolson at once and gave the message, which greatly relieved Grey.[1] Berchtold's purpose in sending it was the opposite of the one which had originally inspired his proposal to make a surprise attack on Serbia and confront the Powers with a *fait accompli* and was the purpose behind all the advice he received from Berlin. To tell London that for the moment there was no intention of going to war but only of making war preparations was to give Grey to understand that there was still time for him to make representations at St. Petersburg and Belgrade that Serbia should yield and an armed conflict be avoided.

On the same morning of the 24th Berchtold received the Russian Chargé d'Affaires Kudashev and tried to calm St. Petersburg's anxiety by assuring him that:

nothing was further from our thoughts than the wish to humiliate Serbia which was not in the least to our interest. My endeavour had been to eliminate everything from the note which could produce any such impression. Our aim is purely and simply to clarify the untenable relations of Serbia with the Monarchy. . . . Finally I pointed out that we did not aim at territorial gain but merely at the preservation of the *status quo*.

Kudashev asked what would happen if the time limit expired without Serbia's returning a satisfactory reply. 'On my replying that our Minister and the Legation staff were to depart, Prince Kudashev reflected and remarked: "Then it is war." '[2]

On that same day (24th), in anticipation of an unsatisfactory reply from Serbia, the Ballplatz drafted a coded message which was sent, not by wire but by courier, to St. Petersburg, arriving there only on the afternoon of the 27th. It gave Szápáry instructions on what he was to say in his conversations with Sazonov, particularly confirming Austrian territorial *désintéressement*:

The Monarchy is territorially saturated and does not covet Serbian possessions. If the conflict with Serbia is forced upon us it will on our part not be a war for territorial gain but purely a means of self-defence and self-preservation. . . . Also we do not meditate infringement of the sovereignty of the Kingdom, but will on the other hand go to extreme lengths to obtain the fulfilment of our demands and not recoil from the possibility of European complications.[3]

On the morning of 25 July Berchtold received Szápáry's five dispatches from St. Petersburg[4] and hastened to send a message to Szápáry telling him to assure Sazonov that the insertion into the note of Point 5 asking for the participation of Austrian officials in the suppression of the anti-Austrian movement

[1] BD. XI, 104, 105.   [2] Oe-U. VIII, 10615.
[3] Oe-U. VIII, 10685.   [4] Oe-U. VIII, 10616–20.

was due to purely practical considerations and not at all to an intention of infringing the sovereignty of Serbia. We contemplate in Point 5 collaboration in the setting up of a secret 'bureau de sûreté' in Belgrade which should function after the style of the analogous Russian institutions in Paris and Berlin and co-operate with the Serbian police and administrative authorities.[1]

Having written this message Berchtold took his departure for Ischl, whither he was pursued by a telegram from Macchio, saying that Kudashev had again called that morning after Berchtold had left and had been firmly told that no extension of the time limit could be granted and that 'we regard our action as a matter concerning only ourselves and Serbia'.[2] It must have been on receiving this blunt answer that Kudashev telegraphed direct to Berchtold en route: 'I am instructed as a matter of urgency to ask the I. and R. Government for an extension of the time limit laid down in the ultimatum to Serbia.'[3] On receiving Kudashev's telegram in the train Berchtold telegraphed to Macchio from Lambach that after refusing Kudashev an extension of the time limit he was to add

that even after the breaking off of diplomatic relations, Serbia can bring about a peaceful solution by unconditional acceptance of our demands, but we should in this case be obliged to request from Serbia the repayment of all our costs and damages caused by military measures.[4]

This message corresponds exactly to what Berchtold said in his instructions on the 24th to Mensdorff telling him to inform Grey that 'the note is not to be regarded as an ultimatum but as a *démarche* with a time limit', concluding:

Your Excellency is empowered to add that if Serbia after the expiry of the time limit were to yield only under the pressure of our military measures, we should certainly have to insist on the repayment of the expenses we had incurred.[5]

But when Macchio reported the blunt refusal he had returned to Kudashev before this instruction reached him, Berchtold replied approvingly all the same.[6]

All this took place before Serbia had given her reply. After receiving it, Berchtold on the afternoon of the 26th had a frank talk with Giesl on the question. According to information given by Giesl to the present writer, Berchtold told him that he did not expect Serbia would resist and thought that at the last moment she would accept the ultimatum unconditionally. He added: 'You did well to act as you did; but that still does not mean war'—the very words he had used on the 25th and which Francis Joseph was also to use to Giesl on the 27th.

[1] Oe-U. VIII, 10682. [2] Oe-U. VIII, 10703.
[3] Oe-U. VIII, 10686. [4] Oe-U. VIII, 10704.
[5] Oe-U. VIII, 10599. [6] Oe-U. VIII, 10705.

I got the impression—commented Giesl—that Berchtold was still optimistic and thought that Serbia would give in as soon as Austria began mobilization, in which case the solution would be that she would indemnify Austria for the cost of the mobilization.[1]

And in answer to an inquiry from the present writer, Berchtold himself corroborated that he had still gone on hoping to avoid war. In a letter of 3 January 1933 he writes:

As long as we remained in contact with Russia I believed in the possibility that a European war might be avoided. Possibly it is actually the case that on 26 July, when Giesl made his report on the breaking off of diplomatic relations, I was still 'optimistic'. In any case it is true, as far as my memory goes, that in the course of the talk I said: 'This is still not war.' Moreover it was then still possible for Serbia to choose more moderate counsels and avert the outbreak of hostilities. My efforts were directed to avoiding everything that might bring Russia into the conflict and that also explains my apprehensions about Conrad's pressing for mobilization.[2]

9. The Austro-German thesis that the ultimatum was one which could be accepted by Serbia.

This would make it appear as if Austria could not be said to have wanted war at all costs and to have sent an unacceptable ultimatum in order to get it. Some reference to this thesis has been made in earlier pages when the weakness was shown of the claims made by Hoyos and other colleagues of Berchtold's that Austria at the beginning meant to settle her dispute with Serbia by peaceful methods.[3] Now the story must be taken up again in the light of events and documents subsequent to the Hoyos mission to Berlin of 5 July and the question answered: Did the first warlike intentions calm down to the point of making way for the formulation of demands which the Serbian Government could with propriety accept?

Alfred Wegerer, the editor of the *Berliner Monatshefte* (earlier *Kriegsschuldfrage*), and leader of a campaign to absolve Germany from all guilt for the First World War, maintains the thesis that the note was drawn

---

[1] In the letter of 11 February 1933 to the present writer Giesl writes: 'When I spoke with Berchtold on 26 July, the only theme [of the conversation] was the study of the Serbian reply and of the decisions to be taken as a result of this study. In the conversation *there was no word* of an immediate declaration of war on Serbia and the firm hope was still maintained that Serbia would come to reason. In particular the diplomatic efforts of the *Entente* Powers and the influence of the German Kaiser on the Tsar might have effect.' In his later letter of 11 January 1935 to the present writer, Giesl writes that at his meeting with Berchtold, on his arrival from Belgrade on the 26th, when Berchtold had affirmed that the rupture of relations was not war by a long way, Giesl had noticed 'that hopes were being placed on the feeling of solidarity between the Monarchs and that the influence was underestimated of the Tsar's entourage which was pressing for war. . . .'

[2] In conversation and by letter Berchtold has repeatedly assured the present writer of his firm hope of avoiding a conflict with Russia.

[3] See pp. 135–6.

up in terms that Serbia might perfectly well have accepted.[1] Musulin, who drafted the ultimatum, has written:

Never in the confidential discussions between the Ministers was the thought expressed that the terms of the note must be so worded that they would be regarded by Serbia as unacceptable. . . . In formulating each individual point of the list of demands . . . the question was considered whether the demand in question would and could be accepted by Serbia and in each case the wording . . . was only regarded as final when this question had been answered in the affirmative. . . . Nobody even thought of a refusal by Serbia of her own free will.[2]

The exact opposite was the case.

The documents show that, contrary to what Musulin maintains, Berchtold, at least at the beginning, wanted the terms presented to Serbia to be such as she could not but reject. It will be remembered that, at the Council of 7 July, the Austro-Hungarian Ministers, with the exception of Tisza, took the view

that a purely diplomatic success, even if it were to end with a resounding humiliation of Serbia, would be valueless and that therefore such far reaching demands must be made on Serbia as would render their rejection probable in order to clear the road for a radical solution by way of military operations.[3]

On his return from Ischl on 10 July Berchtold, in telling Tschirschky of some of the demands to be included in the ultimatum, had said:

Were the Serbs to accept all the demands, this will be a solution that would not be to his liking and he is turning over in his mind what demands could be made that would render acceptance by Serbia absolutely impossible.[4]

It was after 10 July, when he was endeavouring to overcome Tisza's opposition, that Berchtold considered the possibility that Serbia might yield to the ultimatum which was in preparation, but this did not lead him to moderate its terms. Indeed in the already quoted text of his report to the Emperor of 14 July it is stated that

the content of the note to be presented to Belgrade, which had been agreed upon that same day, is such that the probability of settling the question by war must be reckoned with.

This meant that the note was to contain terms which Serbia could not accept or, to continue with the words of the report:

However, if, after all, Serbia were to yield and meet our demands, such a procedure on the part of the Kingdom would mean not only deep humiliation for it and *pari passu* a lowering of Russian prestige in the Balkans, but

---

[1] Wegerer, *A Refutation*, pp. 66–73. [2] Musulin, pp. 225–6.
[3] Oe-U. VIII, 10118. See p. 169. [4] DD. I, 29. See p. 259.

also involve certain guarantees for us in the sense of a limitation of Pan-Serbian agitation on our territory.[1]

Such a solution did not find favour with Berlin where there was a fear that Vienna would not make the terms stiff enough to ensure their rejection. On 18 July, Prince Stolberg, Counsellor at the German Embassy in Vienna, wrote privately to Jagow:

> Berchtold hopes that the Austrian demands, which he did not divulge in detail, will not be accepted by Serbia, but he is not absolutely sure.

Stolberg thought it would be incomprehensible 'why such demands should not have been framed as would make a breach inevitable'. But at the end of his letter he is able to reassure Jagow that he has just heard from Hoyos 'that the demands are such as any State possessed of a remnant of self respect and dignity could not possibly accept'.[2] And the general opinion among the public was that Serbia would return a refusal. This is shown in the report, drawn up for Sir Edward Grey on 1 September after the outbreak of war by Sir Maurice de Bunsen, describing the events of his last days in Vienna:

> On 24 July the note was published in the newspapers. By common consent it was at once styled an Ultimatum. Its integral acceptance was neither expected nor desired, and when on the following afternoon it was at first rumoured in Vienna that it had been unconditionally accepted, there was a moment of keen disappointment. The mistake was quickly corrected, and as soon as it was known later in the evening that the Servian reply had been rejected . . . Vienna burst into a frenzy of delight, vast crowds parading the streets and singing patriotic songs until the small hours of the morning.[3]

One who did not share in this joy was the man most responsible for what had happened, Berchtold. His state of mind on the eve of the presentation of the ultimatum is revealed in a private letter written by him on 21 July to his intimate friend Merey, the Austrian Ambassador in Rome, the obvious sincerity of which deserves attention. He begins by saying that motives of home and foreign policy have led to his decision that the dangerous subversive movement in Bosnia-Herzegovina with its ramifications in Dalmatia, Croatia, Slavonia and Hungary could only be halted

> by bold measures in Belgrade, where all the threads come together . . . In our exposed position, with the unreliability and jealousy of our Italian ally, the hostility of Roumanian public opinion, the pressure of Slavophil advisers at the Court of the Tsar, the responsibility, as I am well aware, is no light one. But the responsibility for doing nothing, for letting things take their course till the waves engulf us, seems to me still more grave— if momentarily less arduous—than to offer resistance and accept its consequences. In drawing up the note to Serbia we were guided by the intention

[1] Oe-U. VIII, 10272.   [2] DD. I, 87.   [3] BD. XI, 676.

of proving to the whole world our good right to make certain demands on Serbia for the maintenance of peace within our frontiers, and to formulate these demands in such a way that Serbia, whether for the past or for the future, would set her face against propaganda hostile to the Monarchy and the possibility should be given us of being consulted in this matter. It was not our concern to humiliate Serbia but to bring about a clear-cut situation in respect of her neighbourly relations with the Monarchy and as a practical result to achieve—in case of acceptance, a thoroughgoing purge in Serbia with our co-operation or—in case of rejection, a settlement by force of arms, followed by the greatest possible weakening of Serbia.

This meant that the 'practical' result could be reached, if Serbia were to accept all the Austrian demands. Yet a few lines further on Berchtold says:

Tisza thinks of even a merely diplomatic success as a means of strengthening our position in the Balkans, and wants if possible to avoid the breach, whereas I, on grounds of the diplomatic successes of 1909 and 1912 which had no effect in the long run and only made our relations with Serbia more difficult, am extremely sceptical of another peaceful triumph.[1]

There is an evident contradiction between this feeling of the uselessness of a peaceful triumph and the idea that if Serbia yielded on all points, the matter could be settled. Which was his real standpoint? Here let us look at Merey's reply, written on the 29th, after the rupture of Austro-Serbian relations. It throws light also on Merey's own views:

I shall regard it as a piece of real good fortune if war with Serbia does come about. Supposing a European conflagration does result, that will seem to me to prove that it was in the air and would have come sooner or later for one cause or another, and there is no doubt that for the Triple Alliance the present moment is more favourable than another later. So I sincerely congratulate you on your, as I well understand, difficult resolve, so full of responsibility. As is clear from what I have said above my approval is only of the eventuality of a real war with Serbia. In the opposite case, i.e. of Serbia's yielding at the eleventh hour, or worse, of our acceptance of mediation or similar negotiations, I am, as is logical, of the opposite opinion, and would regard this as nothing less than a catastrophe. On this point our views do not seem entirely to coincide. You seem to regard such an eventuality perhaps not as desirable, but as anyway a certain diplomatic success and to expect a 'thoroughgoing purge' in Serbia as the result of acceptance of our demands. My view is that Serbia's acceptance of our demands within the forty-eight hour time limit would have been a petty, purely diplomatic success for us, with all its exclusively harmful consequences and without the slightest real benefit. Serbia could have done us no worse service than to say: Yes to everything.[2]

[1] Oe-U. VIII, 10459.   [2] Oe-U. VIII, 10991.

This letter seems to give a very good interpretation of Berchtold's thought, making it clear that he did not want war for its own sake, but thought it preferable to a diplomatic success that would most probably be sterile. He thought it of prime importance that the Monarchy should be given a voice in the suppression of the Pan-Serb movement in Serbia. This condition could not be accepted by a country which meant to safeguard its sovereignty and independence. But had Serbia felt herself deserted by Russia and the Powers, she might well have felt obliged to accept it, to save herself from worse. This would have been a surrender such as nations usually only make after military defeat, i.e. Austria would have won the war (in appearance at least and save for possible later disappointments) without firing a shot. She had done all she could to come to blows and, if that did not happen, it was not because of the moderation of her demands, but because of the supine acquiescence of her adversary. This would have enabled Berchtold to hold up his head in his dealings with the war party in Austria and Germany, while avoiding the risks of a 'decisive' military encounter. No doubt he thought a war inadvisable for the country but it was not repugnant either to himself or his Emperor.

This, in the present writer's opinion, is the position Berchtold arrived at after his first bellicose fancies had evaporated: behave to Serbia in a way to make war all but unavoidable, but hold in reserve, though without enthusiasm, the possibility that she might escape war by submitting to Austrian supervision, thus enabling the Government of Vienna to achieve a diplomatic and practical success out of all comparison with those that had gone before. Therefore no softening of any of the terms, no extension of the time limit, in fact no concessions of any sort. Either diplomatic victory all along the line or the opening of hostilities. And if war were to come, some way must be found of getting round Tisza's stipulation that no territory was to be taken from Serbia. This pledge to the Hungarian Premier was a sore point with Berchtold who may have thought, with good reason, that it was hardly worth while going to war and risking setting Europe alight, if nothing was to be gained in the end. This conclusion may be drawn from the following circumstance. After sending to Szápáry by courier on the 25th the telegram, mentioned above, instructing him to give Sazonov an assurance of Austrian territorial *désintéressement*,[1] Berchtold read the summary of the Sazonov-Pourtalès interview of the 25th.[2] This caused him to change his instructions to Szápáry by a telegram sent off the same night which said: 'Request Your Excellency for the present not to touch on the topic of territorial *désintéressements* either with M. Sazonov or your Italian colleague',[3] Carlotti. It was only on 27 July and apparently at the express command of Francis Joseph that

[1] Oe-U. VIII, 10685 ; see p. 378.   [2] DD. I, 160.   [3] Oe-U. VIII, 10684.

he authorized Szápáry to say both to Sazonov and to Carlotti 'that as long as the war remains localized between Austria-Hungary and Serbia, the Monarchy has no designs of territorial conquest'.[1]

10. *Austria-Hungary mobilizes against Serbia; the Ballplatz still hopes to avoid war.*

Which of Berchtold's two alternatives—Serbian submission, or war —was to be fulfilled depended not on Serbia but on Russia. And there is no doubt that Berchtold at the beginning had a clear perception of what would be the Russian reaction. At the Council of Ministers of 7 July he said, 'he was clear in his own mind that a war with Russia would be the most probable consequence of our entering Serbia'. This is the original wording of the minutes as written by Hoyos and preserved in the Vienna State Archives. But Berchtold, taking fright at so forthright a statement, altered it to: 'that a passage of arms with Serbia might result in war with Russia',[2] which comes to much the same thing. And it may be said that at that moment, in contrast to the German Chancellor, Berchtold was not buoyed up by the hope that the conflict would remain localized. His views changed in the next few days when he began to toy with the hypothesis that Serbia might resign herself to integral acceptance of the Austrian demands. Was this escapism, or did he really believe that Russia would advise submission as in 1909 and 1912?

Probably it was both. One must not forget Szögyény's important telegram of 12 July reporting the belief in Berlin that Russia was not prepared or willing to go to war.[3] No doubt it was this message that gave rise to Berchtold's hope or dream that war might be averted by the unconditional submission of Serbia and that he began his endeavours to make this possible by (as he wrote to the present writer) 'trying to avoid everything that might draw Russia into the conflict', while making no concessions for the reasons we already know. One way of not drawing Russia in was not to rush matters, while going forward with the necessary preparations and giving an impression of war both at home and abroad. Hence Berchtold's telegram to Mensdorff of 24 July directing him to tell Grey that

if the Austrian demands were not complied with within the time limit, his Government would break off diplomatic relations and begin military preparations (not operations).[4]

so that Serbia would still have time to comply. Hence also on 25 July his instructions to Macchio to tell the Russian Chargé d'Affaires the same thing.[5] At the same time the order was given for mobilization

---

Oe-U. VIII, 10834. [2] Oe-U. VIII, 10118. [3] Oe-U. VIII, 10215. See pp. 156–7.
[4] BD. XI, 104. [5] Oe-U. VIII, 10704.

2 C

against Serbia. As early as the 24th Berchtold had received a telegram from Tisza asking him to impress on Francis Joseph in Tisza's name and his own that, if the Serbian answer were not satisfactory, the order for mobilization would be necessary without delay ; 'any hesitation in this respect would bring fatal consequences'.[1] Still more. On 25 July Tisza telegraphed direct to the Emperor

the urgent entreaty, in the event of an unsatisfactory answer from Serbia, to be graciously pleased to order mobilization at once. From the tenor of our note no other way seems to me to be possible. The slightest delay or hesitation would gravely injure the reputation of the Monarchy for boldness and initiative and would influence the attitude not only of our friends and foes but of the undecided elements and result in the most fatal consequences.[2]

By these means the Emperor was persuaded to sign the mobilization order on the evening of the 25th. Berchtold and the War Minister, Krobatin, were closeted in audience with him after the arrival of news of the rupture of relations. The order reached Conrad at 9.23 that same evening and he immediately directed that the 27th should be the first 'alarm day' and the 28th the first day of mobilization.[3]

It is also a fact that at 4.30 p.m. on 26 July four telegrams all ready in code went off to Berlin, Rome, London and Paris saying that war was imminent.

To our regret and much against our will we are placed under the necessity of enforcing on Serbia by the sharpest means a fundamental change in her hitherto hostile attitude.

The telegrams for London and Paris asked the respective Governments to 'understand that after exhausting peaceful means we now finally must regard the moment as arrived . . . to appeal to the arbitrage of war'. Those for Berlin and Rome said that it was 'an act of self defence if after long years of patience we resolve to oppose Pan-Serbian machinations by the sword'. The telegram for Berlin ended:

We confidently hope that our coming dispute with Serbia will not occasion further complications; but should this be the case, we acknowledge with gratitude that Germany in often-tested loyalty will be mindful of her duties as an ally and support us in any conflict with another opponent which may be forced upon us.

The telegram for Rome reminded the Consulta that Austria had 'as a loyal ally hailed with joy the success of Italian arms' in the war for Tripoli and had 'most readily welcomed the extension of the Italian sphere of influence resulting therefrom'.[4] But one must not overlook

---

[1] Oe-U. VIII, 10637.   [2] Oe-U. VIII, 10708.
[3] Conrad, IV, p. 122.   [4] Oe-U. VIII, 10714.

that the words said to Giesl on the afternoon of 26 July ('That still does not mean war') are later than the drafting of these telegrams which must have taken some time to encode. Berchtold may still have hoped that an announcement of imminent war would spur the Powers to prevent it by putting pressure on Serbia to accept all the Austrian demands. This indeed had been the Italian proposal as we shall see in the next chapter. The supposition finds support in another symptomatic document. After war had been declared on 28 July at 8.30 p.m., Berchtold telegraphed to Merey:

Declaration of war, as Your Excellency knows, issued to-day. Beginning of military operations must, however, await the completion of mobilization. . . . For this a certain time will be necessary, as we, warned by the experiences of recent years, did not want to begin large-scale military measures before it was certain that war will really come about.[1]

'While there's life, there's hope', must have been Berchtold's thought, although after the 26th he cannot have had many illusions left. On that afternoon he learnt from Giesl that the Serbian Government was inclining towards acceptance to avoid war when the whole situation was changed by the arrival of a telegram from the Tsar urging Serbia to resist and promising full support from Russia. If this were true (though Francis Joseph told Giesl he did not think it possible) there could be no idea that Serbia would beat a retreat. Russia might suggest her making limited concessions later but not accepting the note as it stood. In fact, as we shall soon see, this was the very course that Sazonov tried to take, but in which Berchtold, bent on carrying off an outright diplomatic victory even at the price of resorting to arms, refused to follow him. It was this that led to the catastrophe, because, though Berchtold feared war, he did not fear it to the point of averting it by making some concession.

The interpretation offered here of Berchtold's behaviour finds support in the account given to the present writer by Musulin, the man who drafted the ultimatum, in a conversation which took place at Vienna on 30 November 1933. Here is what Musulin said:

Berchtold, like the majority of the officials at the Ballplatz, although sceptical as to the outcome of a peaceful solution, nevertheless at the bottom of his heart hoped and wished for it. No preliminaries of mobilization were begun precisely because of the persuasion that Serbia would accept the note. The General Staff on their side were unwilling to mobilize if there was no certainty of war, because, as Conrad had said, 'a horse three times taken up to an obstacle and each time reined back will refuse to jump it'. In short the mood of the Ballplatz in July 1914 was like that of someone who is to undergo an operation and more or less confidently hopes to be able to escape it.

[1] Oe-U. VIII, 10910.

Undoubtedly the form of the ultimatum was categoric and gave Serbia no loophole for discussion, but that was from a desire to prevent tricky answers, in short to obtain some practical result. And in fact if Russia had not intervened and advised against acceptance, the Serbian Government would have given in. It did not do so and instead replied with so astute a note as to produce the impression, when read out to Berchtold by Giesl in the presence of various officials, of being a severe blow to the Monarchy, cheating it of diplomatic victory and placing it at a disadvantage in the eyes of public opinion all over the world. Nevertheless even after the rupture of diplomatic relations, itself intended as a form of pressure, Vienna cherished the hope that Serbia would give way under pressure from the Powers. This is shown in the telegram to Mensdorff saying that Serbia could avert war by integral acceptance and payment of the costs of Austrian mobilization necessitated by the unsatisfactory reply.

Even the declaration of war was regarded by Berchtold as not more than an extreme form of pressure to obtain a diplomatic surrender from Serbia who still had nearly twenty days for reflexion, seeing that operations did not commence until 15 August. It would not have been the first declaration of war not to be followed by military action. The same thing happened under Maria Theresa at the time of the so-called 'potato war', the memory of which was present in the discussions at the Ballplatz during the last week of July 1914. From the moment Austria undertook not to violate the territorial integrity and sovereignty of Serbia, it was taken for granted that Russia would not intervene and that war would be avoided. Tisza, moreover, thought that even if Russia did take the field, she would carry on a feint of war which would end in a settlement honourable to both sides; and if this was to be possible, it would be better for Germany to remain neutral and act as mediator between Austria and Russia at the suitable moment. Thus peace would be made after a short campaign. This way of thinking offered no inducement to accept a European conference or any other expedient that would place the Monarchy on a level with Serbia, a discussion of the various points of the ultimatum being neither possible nor desirable, since the diplomatic victory had to be complete.

Musulin's brief sketch of the psychology of Berchtold and his colleagues in the crisis of July 1914 harmonizes with what we know from the documents and in the opinion of the present writer gets very near to the truth, save in respect of the terms of the ultimatum. Contrary to what Musulin maintains, these were, according to the first documented decision, to be such that Serbia would be obliged to reject them and this would lead to war. It is possible, nay probable, that Berchtold, with his easy-going temperament, and the other Ministers, knowing the Emperor's wish for peace, subsequently changed their minds and for the sake of quietness gave Musulin instructions along other lines, but the documents show nothing of it. In any case the picture drawn by this high official reveals how low was the level of political intelligence at the Ballplatz and how short-sighted and unenlightened were the men in charge of the destinies of the Dual Monarchy, if they deluded themselves that they could act as they did without causing the most appalling conflagration and thought only of a 'potato war' or some kind of a muted war. They should have known that Russia could never allow Serbia to submit, because this would have been a far greater humiliation to herself than the one she suffered in 1909, which was still acutely resented by those in charge of Russian policy. Austria had to choose between two alternatives: either she made up her mind for a European war to make an end of Serbia and eliminate Russian influence for ever from the Balkans, and then the only thing was to go ahead as she actually did, or she tried to find a way out which would enable her in some way to control the Pan-Serb agitation, and then she could not afford to be stiff-necked and refuse all discussion. On the contrary she should have talked the matter over with St. Petersburg, taking account of Sazonov's promises and the assurances he declared himself ready to give Vienna, thus tying his hands and gaining his consent to the repression of the anti-Austrian movement and obtaining the support of the other Powers. The Powers had no wish to shed their blood to vindicate the claims of Serbia whom they were pretty generally prepared to throw to the wolves.

It is true to say that in this phase of the crisis Berlin refused to hear of compromise and pressed for war. But this does not do away with the fact that, if the rulers of Austria had meant not to have war, they should not have behaved as they did. One has the impression that at the last moment Berchtold, seized by belated misgivings, staked the fate of the Monarchy on a gambler's throw and thus sent it to its doom.

CHAPTER X

THE FAILURE OF MEDIATION PROPOSALS; AUSTRIA DECLARES WAR ON SERBIA

(1) *Berlin rejects the English proposal for a conference (p. 390). (2) Italian acceptance of the English proposal; confusion in Paris (p. 395). (3) Sazonov prefers direct conversations between St. Petersburg and Vienna (p. 403). (4) Grey's urgent appeal to Germany; Mensdorff informed of the concentration of the British fleet (p. 410). (5) A proposal put forward by San Giuliano is dropped by Grey and rejected by Vienna (p. 417). (6) Berlin presses for the 'localization of the conflict' (p. 424). (7) German intransigence and Lichnowsky's warnings (p. 429). (8) Kaiser Wilhelm's frame of mind; the Potsdam meeting of 27 July (p. 433). (9) The Grey-Lichnowsky conversation of 27 July; the German Government's duplicity; a telegram from Szögyény (p. 441). (10) Bethmann Hollweg's double game and the motive of his démarche at Vienna (p. 447). (11) German pressure for immediate war on Serbia and Conrad's objections (p. 453). (12) The Austrian declaration of war on Serbia (p. 460).*

1. *Berlin rejects the English proposal for a conference.*

The news that Serbia had ordered mobilization and that diplomatic relations between Austria and Serbia were broken off reached London from Belgrade at 11.30 p.m. on 25 July.[1] At 8 a.m. on the 26th came a telegram from Bunsen in Vienna confirming the news of Giesl's departure and saying: 'War is thought imminent. Wildest enthusiasm prevails in Vienna.'[2] From St. Petersburg at 10.30 p.m. on the 25th had arrived the telegram from Buchanan with Sazonov's statement: 'Russia cannot allow Austria to crush Serbia and become predominant Power in the Balkans', and warning that

this morning Emperor had sanctioned drafting of Imperial *Ukaze*, which is only to be published when Minister for Foreign Affairs considers moment come for giving effect to it, ordering mobilization of 1,100,000 men. Necessary preliminary preparations for mobilization would, however, be begun-at once.[3]

This was the alarming situation which awaited the Permanent Under Secretary at the Foreign Office, Sir Arthur Nicolson when he reached his office on the morning of Sunday 26 July. To Grey, absent on his usual week-end at Itchen Abbas, Nicolson at once telegraphed:

[1] BD. XI, 130, 131. [2] BD. XI, 135.
[3] BD. XI, 125 ; see above, pp. 306-7.

I think that the only hope of avoiding a general conflict would be for us to take advantage at once of suggestion thrown out by Sazonov[1] . . . that you should telegraph to Berlin, Paris, Rome, asking that they shall authorize their Ambassadors here to join you in a Conference to endeavour to find an issue to prevent complications and that abstention on all sides from active military operations shall be requested of Vienna, Servia and St. Petersburg pending results of conference.[2]

The idea was suggested to Nicolson by Sazonov's words to Buchanan:

Obligations taken by Servia in 1908 (*sic*) to which reference is made in Austrian ultimatum were given to Powers and not to Austria, and he would like to see question put on an international footing. Were Servia to appeal to Powers, Russia would be quite ready to stand aside and leave question in hands of England, France, Italy and Germany.[3]

This was Nicolson's way of adopting the suggestion, but it was a proposal made without much faith. During the course of that Sunday further disquieting news rolled in. From Christiania came two dispatches: 'Morning papers report that German fleet, numbering twenty-eight large ships, received orders to concentrate during the night at predetermined point off the Norwegian coast.' (They were in fact ordered back to Kiel.) And: 'It is reported that the Emperor William left Balestrand at 6 o'clock last night and is proceeding direct to Kiel.'[4] From Berlin Rumbold telegraphed: 'Last night large crowds paraded principal streets singing patriotic songs and Austrian national anthem. German public opinion continues to support Austria-Hungary strongly.'[5] Lichnowsky came to the Foreign Office with an urgent telegram from his Government

to say they had received information that Russia was calling in 'classes of reserves' which meant mobilization. If this mobilization took place on the German frontier, Germany would be compelled to mobilize.[6]

All this was such bad news that Nicolson wrote a letter to Grey later on that same day describing his suggestion of a conference as

I admit, a very poor chance—but in any case we shall have done our utmost. Berlin is playing with us. Jagow did not really adopt your proposal to intervene at Vienna, and to be backed up by us and France, but simply 'passed on' your suggestions and told his Ambassador to speak about it. This is not what was intended or desired.

Nicolson hit the nail on the head, as we already know, and indirectly administered a merited rebuke to his Chief by adding that 'Lichnowsky

---

[1] BD. XI, 125.   [2] BD. XI, 139.   [3] BD. XI, 125.   [4] BD. XI, 137, 138.
[5] BD. XI, 147.   [6] DD. I, 199; BD. XI, 146; see p. 343.

was convinced we could stand aside and remain neutral—an unfortunate conviction'.[1] But what he had not seen was that, if war was to be prevented, not only 'active military preparations' would have to stop but also all orders for mobilization, as Buchanan indeed had perceived. Nicolson had said that day to Lichnowsky: 'It would be difficult and delicate for us to ask Petersburg not to mobilize at all—when Austria was contemplating such a measure' and that 'the main thing was to prevent, if possible, active military operations'.[2] What Austria was actually doing was merely to mobilize a few army corps against Serbia. But the real fact of the matter was—as events soon showed—that any mobilization would mean war.

Grey had at once telegraphed back his approval of the idea of a conference and in his name, instructions were sent to the British representatives at Vienna, St. Petersburg and Belgrade to inform the respective Governments of the suggestion and 'to request that pending results of conference all active military operations should be suspended'.[3] Grey in his *Twenty-Five Years* writes:

In discussing the situation with Nicolson, it had been agreed between us that at an opportune moment, or as a last resort, we should propose a Conference. It would be on the lines of the Conference of Ambassadors in 1912–13. . . . The same personnel was still in London. . . . We were all loyal colleagues who not only knew but trusted each other. If our respective Governments would only use us and trust us and give us the chance, we could keep the peace of Europe in any crisis. And it would be an honourable peace. . . . After the submission of the Serbian reply to Austria, how easy it would be to arrange peace with honour, at any rate to Austria! On the other hand I felt some hesitation about again proposing a Conference. . . . Was I to be always putting myself forward as the composer of Balkan troubles? . . . I left Nicolson in charge that day, 26 July. He judged it desirable not to delay any longer the proposal for a Conference and sent it. . . . I entirely approved of what Nicolson had done, but I was not altogether hopeful about the answer we should get from Berlin. I believed German preparations for war to be much more advanced than those of France and Russia; the Conference would give time for the latter Powers to prepare and for the situation to be altered to the disadvantage of Germany, who had now a distinct advantage. I was prepared for some stipulations from Germany and apprehensive that she would not give an immediate acceptance. We must be ready . . . to give or get guarantees that there would be no mobilizations during the Conference.[4]

Grey's memory deceived him when he wrote these words. Nicolson's telegram and still more his letter, beginning: 'I telegraphed to you an idea which occurred to me after reading Buchanan's telegram' show that the idea of a conference emanated from Nicolson, not from Grey, and that he circulated the suggestion after receiving Grey's approval.

[1] BD. XI, 144.   [2] BD. XI, 146.   [3] BD. XI, 140.   [4] Grey, I, pp. 314–16.

Grey also overlooks the fact that he never made any attempt to prevent the various mobilizations, in fact regarded them as inevitable, when the Powers concerned were not yet thinking of, or at least still hesitating about, such measures. On the other hand he was quite right in thinking that a conference would be the best way of preserving peace and that it would be opposed by Berlin. But he does not see that he himself could have overcome that opposition if he had spoken plainly to Berlin.

There would have been several differences between the conference of 1912–13 and that proposed on 26 July 1914. First of all Germany in 1912–13 was working with the Triple *Entente* and Italy to safeguard peace against the wish of Austria who would have liked to dispute the fruits of Serbian victories, accepting the conference against the grain and retaining bad memories of it. The 1912–13 conference moreover was attended by the Austrian and Russian Ambassadors who would have been excluded from that of July 1914. Further still, the subject of the 1912–13 conference was the assigning to the Balkan States of Turkish territory which only indirectly touched Austrian interests. In 1914 Austria and Russia were to be regarded as parties in the dispute on a similar footing to Serbia. This was to adopt the thesis which Paul Cambon had put forward in his talk with Grey on 24 July that the Austro-Serbian and the Austro-Russian conflicts were inseparable, whereas Grey had regarded them as distinct, as Germany wanted when she agreed to mediation between Austria and Russia but not between Austria and Serbia. Bethmann Hollweg writes:

It would have been a serious offence against the interests of our ally if we had taken part in such a court of arbitration, as the Secretary of State Jagow has rightly called it, so long as Austria-Hungary herself did not desire the intervention of the Powers in her dispute with Serbia.

But what other means existed for preventing a conflict between Austria and Russia than to call in the non-interested Powers to compose the Austro-Serbian dispute? To rule this out was to maintain that the conflict must remain localized, in other words that Russia and Europe must capitulate to the German pronouncement of 24 July. And it was because he wanted to obtain this capitulation, as Bülow had done in 1909, that Bethmann rejected Grey's proposal. He writes:

No one could assume that the German member of the Conference could make headway against the representatives of England and France, who were swimming with the Russo-Serbian current, and also against the Italian representative.[1]

It was not this fear which brought about its rejection. There was no question of decisions being taken on a majority vote, and Germany

[1] Bethmann Hollweg, I, p. 145.

could have fought as hard as she liked in defence of the Austrian demands. But it would, of course, not have been possible for her to win over the Great Powers, Russia especially, to allowing Serbian independence and integrity to be destroyed by any 'localization of the conflict'. It was precisely because the conference proposed by Grey would mean the end of any 'localization' that Bethmann would have none of it, more especially as he thought it necessary for Austrian prestige that the ultimatum should be immediately followed by war. Had he been willing to preserve peace by insisting on the most stringent measures to safeguard Austria against Pan-Serb propaganda, he would have welcomed Grey's proposal with open arms and would have got the guarantees sanctioned by the conference of Great Powers, who to avert war would have had to consent to measures which would have dealt a severe blow to Jugoslav national aspirations.

Bethmann's rejection was dispatched to Lichnowsky at 1 p.m. on 27 July, the latter having telegraphed news of the proposal to Berlin at 8.25 p.m. on the 26th as soon as he had heard of it from Nicolson and before the official *démarche* was made.[1]

Bethmann's reply ran:

Nothing is yet known here of Sir Edward Grey's proposal to hold a Four Power Conference in London. We could not take part in such a conference as we cannot drag Austria in her conflict with Serbia before a European tribunal. Sir Edward Grey, as your message expressly states, draws a sharp distinction between Austro-Serbian and Austro-Russian conflict and is as little concerned with the former as we ourselves. Our efforts at mediation must confine themselves to an eventual Austro-Russian conflict. In the Serbo-Austrian conflict the possible course seems the one indicated by St. Petersburg, of direct discussions between St. Petersburg and Vienna. I therefore urge representations in London of the necessity and possibility of localization,[2]

i.e. of allowing Austria to do as she liked with Serbia. It was on the afternoon of the 27th that Goschen, who had just returned to his post, made the official *démarche* proposing the conference. His dispatch of 6.17 p.m. describes how it was received at the Wilhelmstrasse:

[Jagow] says that Conference you suggest would practically amount to a court of arbitration, and could not, in his opinion, be called together except at request of Austria and Russia. . . . I said I was sure that your idea had nothing to do with arbitration, but meant that representatives of the four nations not directly interested should discuss and suggest means for avoiding a dangerous situation. He maintained, however, that such a conference as you proposed was not practicable. He added that news he had just received from St. Petersburg showed that there was an intention on the part of M.

---

[1] DD. I, 236.   [2] DD. I, 248.

Sazonov to exchange views with Count Berchtold. He thought that . . . it would be best before doing anything else to await outcome of the exchange of views between the Austrian and Russian Governments.[1]

Once again Jagow was uttering an untruth. What he wanted was not successful discussions between St. Petersburg and Vienna but the immediate opening of hostilities against Serbia.

2. *Italian acceptance of the English proposal; confusion in Paris.*

Somewhat different from the German reaction was that of Italy. At 10 p.m. on the 26th Sir R. Rodd, the English Ambassador to Rome, was able to telegraph:

Minister for Foreign Affairs welcomes your proposal for a conference. . . . He thinks that it would be prudent that Italy in her position as an ally should refer to Berlin and Vienna before undertaking formally to request the latter to suspend all action.[2]

Strange that Italy should not venture to make the suggestion to an ally who was acting in violation of both the letter and the spirit of the treaty of alliance!

In Paris, pending the return of Poincaré, Viviani, and Izvolsky, confusion reigned supreme. Bernadotte Schmitt remarks:

It is striking to observe that whereas in the great majority of cases in which the documents of July 1914 record the version of both parties to a conversation, the accounts tally very well indeed, the reports of the acting French Foreign Minister and the German Ambassador in Paris of what they said to each other on 26 and 27 July create very different impressions.[3]

But the discrepancies in the documents of 26 and 27 July, as in those of 24 and 25 July, are explained by the notorious fact that the documents as published in the *Yellow Book* were manipulated.[4] At 5 p.m. on the afternoon of 26 July, Schoen, the German Ambassador to Paris, called and saw Bienvenu-Martin at the Quai d'Orsay to make the statement on behalf of his Government that

Austria has officially declared that she purposes no territorial gains from Serbia. . . . The decision whether a European war is to arise lies at present entirely with Russia. We rely on France . . . to make her influence felt in St. Petersburg to quieten matters down.[5]

Schoen was able to inform Berlin at 7.40 p.m. that Bienvenu-Martin had assured him 'that our appeal to the solidarity of the endeavours for preserving the peace was gratifying and greatly valued'. Bienvenu-Martin personally

was most willing to exercise a quietening influence in St. Petersburg now that, by the Austrian declaration that no annexation was intended, the

---

[1] BD. XI, 185.   [2] BD. XI, 154.   [3] Schmitt, II, p. 11.
[4] See pp. 322-4.   [5] DD. I, 200.

conditions for so doing had been created. He could not yet make a formal statement on behalf of the French Government as to the mode of influence as he
must first consult the absent Prime Minister. Speaking personally he asked
whether there could not also be a question of a quietening influence in
Vienna, seeing that Serbia had apparently yielded on most points and thus
made room for negotiations. I replied that joint representations in Vienna
on the part of the Powers seemed to me incompatible with our view that
Austria-Hungary and Serbia were to be left to themselves. The place to use
influence was St. Petersburg. M. Bienvenu-Martin agreed confidentially in
the course of the conversation that Sazonov's idea that only the Powers
acting jointly could pass a verdict on Serbia's attitude was juridically hardly
tenable. He also expressed regret that my earlier *démarche* was so misinter-
preted by the press here and assured me that the indiscretion did not emanate
from the Quai d'Orsay.[1]

More complaisant it would have been impossible for Bienvenu-
Martin to be. But in the *Yellow Book* he is made to cut a very different
figure:

*I replied to this suggestion that Russia was moderate, that she had not committed
any act which allowed any doubt as to her moderation, and that we were in agreement
with her in seeking a peaceful solution of the dispute. It therefore appeared to us that
Germany on her side ought to act at Vienna, where her action would certainly be
effective, with a view to avoiding military operations leading to the occupation of
Serbia.* The Ambassador having observed to me that this could not be
reconciled with the position taken up by Germany 'that the question concerned only Austria and Serbia', I told him that the mediation at Vienna
and St. Petersburg could be the act of the four other Powers less interested
in the question. Herr von Schoen then entrenched himself behind his
lack of instructions in this respect and I told him that in these conditions
I did not feel myself in a position to take any action at St. Petersburg
alone.[2]

Which of the two accounts is speaking the truth? In the present
writer's opinion there is no doubt that it was that of the German
Ambassador, who had no interest in telling his Government otherwise
than what happened, while it was to the French interest to make
Bienvenu-Martin cut a more intelligent figure than he actually did. In
actual fact the text of the corresponding document published in Vol. XI
of the Third Series of *French Diplomatic Documents* show not a trace of
the italicized first passage given above, which was obviously invented
by the compilers of the *Yellow Book*.[3] It is true that in this authentic text
there is also a suggestion of Four Power mediation. And there exists
a version of the same conversation telegraphed to St. Petersburg on
the 26th by the Russian Chargé d'Affaires, Sevastopulo, which confirms
that Bienvenu-Martin had dropped a hint of Four Power mediation

---

[1] DD. I, 235.   [2] LJF. 56; CDD., p. 179.   [3] DF. 3. XI, 98.

while declining to enjoin moderation on St. Petersburg, but had given as the reason for declining: 'because of the absence of Viviani'.[1] This last phrase meant that Bienvenu-Martin would have no objection in principle to urging moderation at St. Petersburg but only refrained in Viviani's absence, and, as we shall soon see, Sazonov resented this strongly. What still remains to be determined is whether Sevastopulo was told the truth and, if so, whether he had it from Bienvenu-Martin himself or from another official at the Quai d'Orsay, its acting Political Director, Philippe Berthelot. Now there is no doubt that the latter had perfectly understood the situation. He had, in fact, on the 26th expressed to Sevastopulo his personal impression

that the successive German *démarches* at Paris had the object of intimidating France and inducing her to exercise pressure at St. Petersburg. From the whole circumstances and the whole behaviour of Germany and Austria, he inclined to believe that those Powers aimed at a brilliant diplomatic victory but not at war at any price, although in the extreme case they would not recoil from it. He regarded an urgent and vigorous *démarche* on the part of England at Berlin as useful.[2]

This clearsighted estimate guided Berthelot in his talks with Schoen. There exists a memorandum on the call paid by Schoen on Berthelot at 7 p.m. after leaving Bienvenu-Martin. Schoen came to ask whether

in order to avoid the appearance in the newspapers of comments intended to influence public opinion . . . a brief statement should be communicated to the press . . . : 'During the afternoon the German Ambassador and the Minister for Foreign Affairs had a fresh interview, in the course of which, in the most amicable spirit, and acting in an identical feeling of peaceful co-operation (*sentiment de solidarité pacifique*), they examined the means which might be employed to maintain general peace.'

The Acting Political Director replied at once, 'Then, in your opinion everything is settled, and you bring us the assurance that Austria accepts the Serbian note or will enter into conversations with the Powers on this matter?' The Ambassador having appeared surprised and having vigorously denied the suggestion, it was explained to him that if there was no modification in Germany's negative attitude, the terms of the suggested 'note to the press' were exaggerated, and of a nature to give a false security to French opinion by creating illusion on the real situation, the dangers of which were only too evident. . . .

M. Berthelot then said that to any simple mind Germany's attitude was inexplicable if it did not aim at war. . . . Was it probable that Germany would have arrayed herself on the side of Austria in such an adventure with her eyes closed? . . . The breaking off of diplomatic relations by Austria, her threats of war, and the mobilization which she was undertaking make pacific action on the part of Germany peculiarly urgent, for from the day

---

[1] *Int. Bez.* i. V, 92.   [2] *Int. Bez.* i. V, 93.

when Austrian troops crossed the Serbian frontier, one would be faced by an act which without doubt would oblige the St. Petersburg Cabinet to intervene and would risk the unloosing of a war which Germany declares that she wishes to avoid. Herr von Schoen . . . added finally that he did not say that Germany on her side would not give some advice to Vienna. In these conditions the Political Director announced that he would ask the Minister if it appeared to him opportune to communicate to the press a short note in a moderate tone.[1]

The views of Berlin being what they were it was certainly not the moment to make joint communiqués of any sort. But this whole story receives no corroboration from Schoen whose brief dispatch of 7.50 p.m. runs:

From a confidential talk with acting Political Director I have the definite impression that Viviani's answer will be that he is ready to exercise calming influence in St. Petersburg if we are prepared to advise moderation in Vienna seeing that Serbia has fulfilled almost all demands.[2]

This shows that Paris had promised to restrain St. Petersburg if Viviani agreed. And one thing is certain, namely that the French press next morning published the following communiqué:

The German Ambassador and the Acting President of the Council have had a fresh conversation in the course of which they considered what measures could be taken by the Powers for the maintenance of peace.[3]

The communiqué was colourless enough, but in reporting it to Grey, Sir Francis Bertie's comment was:

This . . . has doubtless been issued to check a chauvinistic movement in the press. . . . The object of this movement was to make the public believe that the German Ambassador in Paris had, by orders of his Government, made a *démarche* at the Ministry for Foreign Affairs which amounted to giving France brutally to understand that, unless other Powers kept out of the quarrel, they would have Germany to deal with and the prospect of a general European conflagration.[4]

There is something here that is not quite clear. Such a *démarche* had actually been made by Schoen on the 24th by order of his Government. And possibly Bienvenu-Martin, who had no understanding of foreign affairs, was partly incapacitated by inexperience and unfamiliarity with his temporary duties, partly anxious to avert war if this could be done by not taking the Serbian business too much to heart and keeping Russia quiet. In this he may have been prompted by the interests of the Viviani Government and the majority in the Chamber supporting it

[1] LJF, 57; DF. 3. XI, 109; CDD., pp. 179–81.   [2] DD. I, 241.
[3] BD. XI, 184.   [4] BD. XI, 193.

which, as Szécsen remarked on 28 July, had many links with socialist circles.[1] But, on the other hand, as Szécsen went on to say, the Russian alliance was the lodestar of every French politician and the press spoke its mind freely. Schoen telegraphed to Berlin on 27 July (and this is a proof that he made no attempt to mislead his Government or let them think Bienvenu-Martin had said pleasant things he did not say) that there was a general feeling in Paris that the 'decision on war or peace now lies essentially with Berlin'.[2] Even the Socialist *Humanité* inquired why, if Germany wanted France to restrain Russia, she did not herself restrain Austria. And the interim Premier should have had better inside information than the daily press. He had Berthelot to advise him, and on the evening of the 24th there arrived from London the wise and experienced Paul Cambon who did not return to his post until 27 July. In telling his memories of those last days before the outbreak of war to R. Recouly, Paul Cambon begins his story only on the 31st, saying nothing of the visit he had just paid to Paris.[3] But if he left London at that tragic moment, it was certainly not on a light errand. He may well have thought that with Poincaré and Viviani absent from the capital it would be well for him to be there to offer advice. It have may been he who opened the eyes of the Quai d'Orsay as to what was really going on. However the later behaviour of Bienvenu-Martin shows no signs of having been influenced by Paul Cambon, while, in the opinion of the present writer, he was considerably influenced by the lately appointed British Ambassador to Paris, Sir Francis Bertie.

Bertie has left a diary which opens on 26 July with a statement frankly antagonistic to support of the pro-Serbian policy of Russia.[4] And on 25 July he had sent a dispatch to Grey saying that he had said to Bienvenu-Martin

that in democratic countries such as England and France war could not be made without the support of public opinion, and I felt sure that public opinion in England would not sanction a war in support of Russia if she, as protector of the Slavs, picked a quarrel with Austria over the Austro-Servian difficulty. He admitted, but not as Minister, that it would be difficult to bring French public opinion to fighting point in such a case as present one.[5]

And Bertie drew the conclusion that 'the French Government will probably advise the Russian Government to moderate any excessive zeal they may be inclined to display to protect the Servian client'.[6] This was advice to Grey to do the same. On 27 July Bertie reported:

German Ambassador is much dissatisfied and has expressed his desire for stronger wording (of the communiqué to the press) and for phrase indicating

[1] Oe-U. VIII, 10907.   [2] DD. I, 252.   [3] Recouly, Chap. II.
[4] Bertie, I, p. 1.   [5] BD. XI, 129.   [6] BD. XI, 134.

'solidarity' between the Powers and for description of conversation as 'very friendly'. . . . I think we ought to urge French Government to issue notice suggested by German Ambassador.[1]

On the same day in a letter to Grey he wrote:

I am sure that the French Government do not want to fight and they should be encouraged to put pressure on the Russian Government not to assume the absurd and obsolete attitude of Russia being the protectress of all Slav States, whatever their conduct, for this will lead to war. I do not believe that the German Emperor and Government were accessories before the fact to the terms of the Austrian note. If they had been the Emperor would not have been away yachting. . . . Izvolsky is expected back here to-day or to-morrow and he is not an element of peace. If you get together meetings between yourself and the French, German and Italian Ambassadors, call them consultations, for the Austrians would resent a sort of repetition of the London reunions which ended in being dubbed the London Conference. They would consider that they were being treated as a Balkan Minor State. The Quai d'Orsay represented by M. Berthelot is not sufficiently *coulant* with the German Ambassador. . . . Some mention should be made of *solidarité*.[2]

It seems hardly credible that a diplomatist occupying so important a post could have had so little understanding. Grey briefly replied on the 28th: 'I suppose French reluctance is due to desire to avoid appearance of being detached from Russia, and I cannot urge them to risk that.'[3] It was a needful lesson but it arrived too late when the inexperienced Bienvenu-Martin had already come under Bertie's influence. There is little doubt that, if he had been differently advised, Bienvenu-Martin would have sounded a note which would have shattered the German illusion that they could save the peace while sacrificing Serbia and humiliating the other Great Powers. This does not mean that it would not have been wise to calm down St. Petersburg. The Power that was giving its support to its ally had every right at the same time to impart advice and urge circumspection. But in so doing it would have been needful before all else to identify the aggressor. This would have put an end to any idea of the 'localization of the conflict', uncovering Germany's double game and letting her know that, as it was she who held all the threads of the Austrian action in her hands, it was for her to make a move for peace, failing which there would be war, for which the responsibility would be hers. The misfortune was that from neither London nor Paris nor Rome did any such warning come to the Wilhelmstrasse, nay more, that from London and Paris the statements that came were such as to give Berlin hope that its schemes would work out successfully.

[1] BD. XI, 184.   [2] BD. XI, 192.   [3] BD. XI, 204.

The attitude of Paris had in itself little positive effect, but we have followed it through the records in order to point out the shortcomings of other Powers besides Austria and Germany. After the 27th the French attitude became less confused and more decided. On that day Izvolsky resumed his post at the Russian Embassy and was able to send a reassuring telegram to St. Petersburg, saying that he had discussed the situation with Bienvenu-Martin in the presence of Berthelot and Abel Ferry (the Under Secretary at the Foreign Ministry) and was

surprised how justly Bienvenu-Martin and his colleagues size up the situation and how penetrated they are with firm and calm determination to give us full support and avoid the slightest hint of a difference of opinion with us.[1]

Sazonov, however, had been by no means pleased at Sevastopulo's account of the conversation between Bienvenu-Martin and Schoen of 26 July and it led him to send the following telegram:

I should like to clear up a misunderstanding in Bienvenu-Martin's answer to Schoen. If it is a question of any pressure for moderation at St. Petersburg, we reject this from the outset, as we have from the beginning adopted an attitude which we cannot modify, since we have already met all acceptable demands on the part of Austria.[2]

Izvolsky's reply of 28 July runs:

I regard it as my duty to state, as is evident from my yesterday's conversation at the Quai d'Orsay, that the Minister of Justice never for a moment contemplated the possibility of a moderating influence at St. Petersburg. He only answered the German Ambassador that not Russia but Austria was the threat to peace and that if there were to be any question of moderating influence it would have to be exercised not only at St. Petersburg but also and chiefly at Vienna. The upshot of the conversation with Baron Schoen was Bienvenu-Martin's reply that he declined the German proposal.[3]

It was not quite that, but matters were straightening themselves out to some degree. The German Ambassador, who was genuinely anxious not to have war, redoubled his efforts, knocking at every door, but making no headway against the irresistible course of events. On the morning of the 27th he sent a private letter to Berthelot urging again that France should calm her ally.[4] Then he called on Abel Ferry to propose 'an intervention on the part of France and Germany between Russia and Austria', receiving the reply that the intervention should be left in the hands of the (four) Powers.[5]

The *Yellow Book* quotes Bienvenu-Martin as expressing the opinion to Viviani that it 'is most probable' that Schoen's letter

'has as its object . . . an attempt to compromise France in the eyes of Russia and, in case of failure, to throw the responsibility for the eventual war on

[1] *Int. Bez.* i. V, 129.   [2] *Int. Bez.* i. V, 116.   [3] *Int. Bez.* i. V, 177.
[4] LJF. 62; DF. 3. XI, 133; CDD., p. 185.   [5] *Int. Bez.* i. V, 129.

Russia and on France . . . and to mask the military action by Austria in Serbia intended to complete the success of Austria'.

But in the authentic text of the *French Diplomatic Documents* the 'most probable' is replaced by the tentative phrase: 'M. de Schoen's letter tends perhaps to throw' . . . . Moreover the *Yellow Book* omits the suggested alternative explanation:

A simpler explanation would be to think that M. de Schoen may have feared that the note to the press might be interpreted by his Government as a sign that he had carried out his instructions badly, their main object being to ensure against an eventual Russian mobilization on German frontiers properly speaking, a mobilization destined to provoke similar measures in Germany and bring on war, as M. de Jagow has indicated.[1]

Schoen and Szécsen made efforts to avert the catastrophe and Szécsen did not fail to point out the true state of things to Vienna. He did not conceal from Berthelot his amazement that Giesl should have regarded the Serbian reply as unsatisfactory.[2] On 27 July on Berchtold's instructions Szécsen called on Bienvenu-Martin bringing the official Austrian intimation that

since the Serbian Government had not given a satisfactory reply to the requirements of the Imperial Government, the latter found themselves obliged to take strong measures to induce Serbia to give the satisfaction and guarantees that are required of her. . . . I asked the Ambassador to acquaint me with the measures contemplated by Austria, and Count Szécsen replied that they might be either an ultimatum, or a declaration of war, or the crossing of the frontier. . . . I then called the Ambassador's attention to the fact that . . . Austria . . . was assuming a grave responsibility in running the risk of precipitating a war the limits of which it was impossible to foresee.[3]

These remonstrances had the effect of making Szécsen telegraph to his Government at 8.5 p.m. on the same evening that Bienvenu-Martin had been 'painfully surprised' by his communication and had warned him of the possibilities of a general war.

The far-reaching compliance of Serbia, which was not regarded as possible here, has made a strong impression. Our attitude gives rise to the opinion that we want war at any price. . . . M. Poincaré returns on Wednesday, M. Izvolsky to-day or tomorrow. We shall now no doubt get spoken to in a sharper key.[4]

The return of the influential, indefatigable and interfering Izvolsky was certainly bound to harden the attitude of the Quai d'Orsay, which

[1] LJF. 62; CDD., pp. 184–5; DF. 3. XI, 133.   [2] *Int. Bez.* i. V, 94.
[3] LJF. 75; CDD., p. 193; DF. 3. XI, 147.   [4] Oe-U. VIII, 10822.

until the 27th had been so undecided as to leave unattended to for forty-eight hours Grey's first proposal, transmitted by Bertie in his note of 25 July, for mediation by the four disinterested Powers at Vienna and St. Petersburg. That the Foreign Office was much perturbed by this silence we learn from Mensdorff who telegraphed from London at 5.55 p.m. on the 26th:

I have communicated rupture of diplomatic relations with Serbia to Government. Sir A. Nicolson, whom I saw in Sir Edward Grey's absence, is extremely disquieted. . . . He has till now practically no news from Paris.[1]

Paul Cambon, as has been said, was absent from London during these days, his place being taken by de Fleuriau who, without instructions, advised Paris on the 27th to agree to Grey's proposal for a conference of the four Ambassadors which implicitly cancelled the earlier one for mediation at St. Petersburg and Vienna.[2] Thus it came about that on the 27th the Quai d'Orsay was faced with the task of replying to both of Grey's proposals and it did so by a note in which it accepted them both.[3] This note elicited an approving telegram on 28 July from Viviani on board the *France* in which he said he was glad that 'Sir E. Grey grasps the logic of the situation' in not excluding St. Petersburg from the discussions, offering the German Government a dignified method of withdrawing from the standpoint that the Austro-Serbian affair was not of general interest, and indicating that the mediation of the Four Powers was needed primarily at Vienna and Belgrade.[4]

3. *Sazonov prefers direct conversations between St. Petersburg and Vienna.*

If the Foreign Office found the silence of the Quai d'Orsay disconcerting, it was dismayed by the nature of the Russian reply. First, however, we must take account of what had taken place at St. Petersburg before the arrival of Grey's proposal. Russian public opinion had been incensed by the news of the rupture of Austro-Serbian relations. In St. Petersburg, Moscow, and other centres demonstrations had taken place against Austria and in support of Serbia, to whom, as the majority of the press in defiant articles asserted, Russia must lend her aid also on the grounds that the minor Slav states covered the Russian flank against the German 'Drang nach dem Osten' in the direction of the Dardanelles.[5] But Sazonov did not allow the outcry to throw him off his balance. Pourtalès writes:

I was confirmed in my opinion that Sazonov still firmly hoped to avoid war when I met him on the morning of the 26th in the train, as he and I in the summer months lived at Tsarkoe Selo.

[1] Oe-U. VIII, 10735.   [2] LJF. 69, CDD., p. 188; DF. 3. XI, 116.   [3] BD. XI, 194.
[4] LJF. 76, CDD. pp. 194–5; DF. 3. XI, 190.   [5] DD. II, 288.

The two had a long talk at the station when they got out of the train.

To my surprise I found the Minister much more conciliatory than two days earlier. M. Sazonov overflowed with professions of peaceful intentions and assured me that he was only seeking means of procuring legitimate satisfaction for Austria-Hungary without abandoning the standpoint, to which Russia must firmly adhere, that Serbia's sovereignty must not be infringed. He expressed his readiness to discuss any proposal which could lead to that end. I availed myself of the Minister's propitious mood to dissuade him from the idea of bringing the Austro-Serbian conflict before a European forum. I reminded him of the experiences during the Balkan wars with the unwieldy apparatus of the London Ambassadors' Conference and how slowly it worked. I urgently recommended a direct, frank discussion with the Vienna Cabinet or in the first place with my Austro-Hungarian colleague. . . . Austria-Hungary I declared does not think of swallowing Serbia, but only wants to give her a well-merited lesson. M. Sazonov promised to follow my advice and get at once into touch with Count Szápáry.[1]

In his dispatch to Berlin dealing with this meeting Pourtalès adds:

Some of the [Austrian] demands constituting direct attacks on Serbian sovereignty would—he [Sazonov] said—have to be moderated, and in the interests of peace he pleads insistently for the co-operation of all the Powers, including Germany, to persuade Vienna Cabinet to soften several points. It was wrong to think that Russian policy was being guided purely by 'sympathies'. For Russia the balance of power in the Balkans was a vital interest and she could therefore not on any account tolerate the reduction of Serbia to a vassal state of Austria.[2]

Acting on the suggestion of Pourtalès to use the favourable moment Szápáry called on Sazonov in the early afternoon of the 26th. He had no recent instructions from Berchtold because, as we have seen, those of the 24th telling him to assure Sazonov that Austria did not 'aim at territorial gain' or infringement of Serbian sovereignty, had not been sent by telegraph but by courier, only reaching St. Petersburg on the afternoon of the 27th.[3] But even had they arrived without delay, they would have been cancelled by the telegram sent off the same night instructing Szápáry 'not to touch on the topic of territorial désintéressements' with Sazonov.[4] However the conversation of the 27th was very friendly:

In contrast to his very snuffy attitude on Friday (24th) M. Sazonov greeted me very cordially . . . and said that if I had not called he would have asked me to come for a frank talk. On Friday he had been taken by surprise

---

[1] Pourtalès, pp. 22–3.   [2] DD. I, 217.
[3] Oe-U. VIII, 10615. See p. 378.   [4] Oe-U. VIII, 10684. See p. 384.

and had not displayed all the self command he could have wished. . . . I replied that I had the impression that Russia was under a misapprehension as to the character of our action. It was imputed to us that we meant to make a drive into the Balkans as the beginning of a march to Salonika or even to Constantinople. Others went so far as to call our action the opening bar of a preventive war against Russia planned by Germany. . . . The aim of our action was self-preservation and self-defence against hostile propaganda by the spoken and written word and by deeds threatening our integrity. No one in Austria-Hungary dreamt of threatening Russian interests or picking a quarrel with Russia. But we were absolutely determined to achieve the aim we had set ourselves, and the way we had chosen seemed to us the most suitable one. But as it was a question of self-defence I could not conceal from him that it would be carried through regardless of consequences. I could see that if the affair were to develop into a conflict between the Great Powers, this must necessarily have the most terrible consequences. . . . M. Sazonov fully agreed and expressed his pleasure at what I had said. He was profuse in his assurances that in Russia not only he but the whole Cabinet and, still more important, the Tsar were animated by similar sentiments towards Austria-Hungary. . . . He had no feelings for the Balkan Slavs. They were actually a heavy burden on Russia and we could hardly imagine how much trouble they had already given Russia. Our aims, as described by me, were perfectly legitimate but he thought the way we had chosen to attain them not the safest. The note presented by us was not in a happily chosen form. He had since studied it and if I had time he should like to go through it with me. . . . I remarked that I was not authorized to discuss the text of the note with him . . . though his comments would of course be of interest. The Minister then went through all the points of the note and to-day thought 7 of the 10 points acceptable without too great difficulty. Only the two points 5 and 6 regarding the co-operation of I. and R. officials in Serbia and the point 4 concerning the dismissal at our discretion of officers and officials seemed to him unacceptable as it stood. On Point 5 I was able to give him an authoritative interpretation on the basis of your telegram of 25 July.[1] M. Sazonov suggested that one might envisage the presence of a consul at the inquiry and would need to produce evidence against those whose dismissal was demanded. Otherwise there would be the risk that King Peter might be assassinated. . . . I answered . . . that this showed how necessary our measures against Serbia were. Summing up, Sazonov said he thought the difficulty regarding the note was one of wording and perhaps an acceptable way might be found of getting over this difficulty. Were we prepared to accept the mediation of our ally the King of Italy or of the King of England?—I replied that I was not in a position to express an opinion. . . . The Serbs had yesterday mobilized. . . . At the close of his talk M. Sazonov again warmly expressed his pleasure at the explanations I had given which had greatly reassured him. He would report them to Tsar Nicholas whom he is to see the day after to-morrow. Russian policy has gone a long way in two days from the first abrupt rejection of our

[1] Oe-U. VIII, 10682. See pp. 378-9.

action and sitting in judgement over our dossier to the transforming of the whole affair into a European concern and from there further to a recognition of the legitimate nature of our claims and a search for mediators. However it must not be overlooked that along with this regressive diplomatic movement there runs lively military activity by which Russia's military position, and with it our own diplomatic position, daily threatens to turn more and more in our disfavour.[1]

[After this conversation Pourtalès telegraphed to Berlin]: Both of those concerned, when I saw them later, had the same satisfactory impression of it. . . . Sazonov begged me to tell him whether I could not make some kind of proposal. I emphasized that I was not empowered to make proposals and could only express my own thoughts, but the following seemed to me perhaps a practicable way. If, as from Count Szápáry's utterances did not seem quite impossible, the Vienna Cabinet were to agree to tone down the wording of its demands, the attempt might be made to contact Austria-Hungary at once for this purpose. If agreement were to follow, Serbia might receive advice from Russia to comply with the Austrian demands on a basis agreed between Austria and Russia and to intimate this to the Austrian Government by the intermediary of a third Power. Sazonov . . . said he would at once telegraph in the sense of my suggestion to the Austrian Ambassador in Vienna.[2]

And that same evening Sazonov did so in a telegram summarizing his talk with Pourtalès in which he said that

to end the present tense situation with all possible speed [he thought it desirable] that the Austro-Hungarian Ambassador should be empowered to have a private exchange of ideas with him for the purpose of a joint revision of some articles of the Austrian note of 23 July. It might thus be possible to find a formula acceptable to Serbia and at the same time giving satisfaction in principle to Austria's demands.[3]

Pourtalès ended his account of the conversation with Sazonov quoted above with the words: 'I gained the impression that he had perhaps received news from Paris and London which did not encourage

[1] Oe-U. VIII, 10835. This dispatch is stated in the Austrian diplomatic documents to have been sent off from St. Petersburg at 2.15 p.m. on 27 July arriving at 4.30 p.m. in Vienna. Telegrams from Pourtalès and Sazonov, however, show that it belongs to the 26th. Pourtalès's telegram to Berlin of 10 p.m. on 26 July begins: 'Count Szápáry had a long talk with Sazonov this afternoon' (DD. I, 238). It should also be noted that Sazonov's summary of the talk sent to Shebeko on the 26th shows several differences in regard to the 10 points of the Austrian ultimatum. Szápáry says that Sazonov thought points 4, 5, 6 unacceptable. Sazonov telegraphed to Shebeko on 26 July: 'Points 1 and 2 could not be fulfilled without changing the Serbian law on the press and associations, to which the Skupština would hardly give consent. The fulfilment of Points 4 and 5 would inevitably lead to very dangerous consequences and threaten even the members of the Royal Family and Pašić with acts of terrorism, which would scarcely be to Austria's interest. On the other points, given certain modifications of detail, it should not in my opinion be too difficult to find a basis of understanding if the accusations contained in them are confirmed by sufficient proofs.' (Int. Bez. i. V, 86.)

[2] DD. I, 238.   [3] Int. Bez. i. V, 86.

him to a continuance of the aggressive tone in which he had spoken two days earlier' and this impression was confirmed by a telegram of the 25th from Jagow saying that Bienvenu-Martin had 'held language showing understanding and amounting to an admission that France, too, desired a localization of the conflict'.[1] But here Pourtalès was mistaken. It was he himself who had taken a long step forward in saying that Austria was ready to 'tone down her demands'. He attributed this admission to statements made by Szápáry, but no such statement was authorized by Berchtold or made by Szápáry to Sazonov. Sure of French support after the assurance given by Poincaré at St. Petersburg, Sazonov also felt relieved by these conversations with Szápáry and still more with Pourtalès. He spoke of this relief both to Paléologue[2] and to Buchanan:

> He would, he said, use all his influence at Belgrade to induce the Servian Government to go as far as possible in giving satisfaction to Austria. . . . He suggested that in order to safeguard Austria against any revolutionary Servian propaganda in future and to dispose her to renounce some of her extreme demands, Powers might come to a private understanding to instruct their Ministers at Belgrade to keep in constant touch with each other, and to interchange all the information which any one of them might receive with regard to any Servian machinations or plots directed against Austria. In the event of any such information reaching them, they should be empowered to exercise pressure on Servian Government with a view to preventing such plots maturing.[3]

Thus the attitude of the two Ambassadors, especially that of Pourtalès, had induced a mood of compliance and optimism in Sazonov, who readily passed from one mood to the opposite. The Austrian Government might, if it had chosen, have taken advantage of this mood to its own benefit and the hurt of Serbia. Instead of so doing, it rejected Sazonov's proposals and when in 1914 it published the Austrian *Red Book* it thought better to suppress several essential points of Szápáry's dispatch.

While he was hugging the hope of coming to a friendly understanding with Austria, Sazonov received Grey's proposal to submit the quarrel to a conference of the four Ambassadors. He, of course, did not reject it but thought it could wait for the moment, because as he told Buchanan:

> I have begun *pourparlers* with the Austro-Hungarian Ambassador in conditions which I trust are favourable. However I have not yet received a reply to the proposal I have made of a revision of the note by the two Cabinets. If direct explanations with the Vienna Cabinet prove unattainable, I am

---

[1] Pourtalès, p. 26. [2] LJF. 54, CDD., p. 177; DF. 3. XI, 103.
[3] BD. XI, 198.

ready to accept the English proposal, or any other of a nature to resolve the conflict favourably.[1]

This reply annoyed Nicolson who, as we have seen, had proposed the conference of the four Ambassadors to please Sazonov, and whose comment was:

In three consecutive days M. Sazonov has made one suggestion and two proposals all differing from each other. . . . One really does not know where one is with M. Sazonov and I told Count Benckendorff so this afternoon.[2]

It is no doubt true that Sazonov was impulsive, easily passing from angry words to conciliatory acts and expressions, in short not very well balanced. But the idea of direct conversations had first been mooted by Grey on 20 July, and Buchanan asked Sazonov on the 27th

whether he would prefer direct exchange of views, which he had proposed, to such a conference. German Ambassador, to whom I had just spoken, had expressed personal opinion that former would be more agreeable to Austria. His Excellency said he was perfectly ready to stand aside if conference was accepted by other Powers.[3]

And Grey himself on 28 July reverted to the idea of direct conversations and that, together with the German refusal, put an end to all talk of a conference of Ambassadors.

The German refusal was not yet known in London (the telegram conveying the news arrived at 9 p.m. on the 27th) when on that day a strong revulsion of feeling took place at the Foreign Office against the behaviour of the Central Powers in consequence of events which gradually opened Grey's eyes. His better grasp of the situation was partly due to the efforts of his subordinates, Nicolson, Crowe, Tyrrell and the Ambassador Buchanan, the only one of the British Ambassadors whose dispatches and whose actions reveal diplomatic ability. In a dispatch of the 27th reporting his conversation with Sazonov on the 26th Buchanan writes that he warned Sazonov that he

was wrong in believing that we should promote cause of peace by telling Germany if she supported Austria by force of arms she would have us to deal with as well as France and Russia. . . . His Excellency must do nothing to precipitate a conflict, and I therefore trusted that mobilization *ukaze* would be deferred as long as possible and that when it was issued troops would not be allowed to cross frontier.[4]

In speaking thus Buchanan, who as early as the 24th had urged Grey to talk plainly to Berlin,[5] was expressing Grey's views rather than his own. And Sazonov's reply was 'that he did not believe we should

[1] BD. XI, 206.　　　[2] BD. XI, 179 n.　　　[3] BD. XI, 198.
[4] BD. XI, 170.　　　[5] See above, pp. 295-6.

succeed in winning over Germany to cause of peace unless we publicly proclaimed our solidarity with France and Russia'. It would not have been needful to make any public statement, although in 1911 at the time of Agadir it had been Lloyd George's threatening speech which had caused Berlin to drop its unyielding attitude. On this point, therefore, Sazonov was right. On the question of mobilization, he told Buchanan:

> No effective steps could be taken until Imperial *ukaze* was issued, and if it was deferred too long Austria would profit by delay to make her military preparations complete, while Russia could do nothing. . . . He could not tell me when *ukaze* would be issued, but spoke of day on which Austrian Army entered Servia as a likely date.[1]

Crowe's minute to this dispatch runs:

> I am afraid that the real difficulty to be overcome will be found in the question of mobilization. Austria is already mobilizing. This, if the war does come, is a serious menace to Russia, who cannot be expected to delay her own mobilization which, as it is, can only become effective in something like double the time required by Austria and Germany. If Russia mobilizes, we have been warned that Germany will do the same, and as German mobilization is directed almost entirely against France, the latter cannot possibly delay her own mobilization even for the fraction of a day. . . . This however means that within 24 hours His Majesty's Government will be faced with the question whether, in a quarrel so imposed by Austria on an unwilling France, Great Britain will stand idly aside, or take sides. . . . It is difficult not to remember the position of Prussia in 1805 when she insisted on keeping out of the war which she could not prevent from breaking out between other Powers over questions not, on their face, of direct interest to Prussia. This war was waged without Prussia in 1805. But in 1806 she fell a victim to the Power that had won in 1805, and no one was ready to help her or to prevent her political ruin and partition.

Nicolson was of the same opinion. His views are revealed not only in his minutes drawing attention to Germany's double game in pretending to want peace while refusing to restrain Austria in any way, but also in a confidential letter to Buchanan of 28 July in which he writes:

> I can quite understand Russia not being able to permit Austria to crush Servia. I think the talk about localizing the war merely means that all the Powers are to hold the ring while Austria quietly strangles Servia. . . . I do not understand after the very satisfactory way in which Servia has met the Austrian requests, how Austria can with any justification proceed to hostile measures against her. If she deliberately provokes war with Servia with the intention of giving her what she calls a lesson, she is, I think, acting most wrongly, for she must know very well that such action on her part would in all probability lead to a general European conflagration.[2]

[1] BD. XI, 170.   [2] BD. XI, 239.

Grey's private secretary, Sir William Tyrrell, was of the same opinion as Crowe and Nicolson, as is shown in a telegram from Lichnowsky to Berlin of Sunday, 26 July, after Tyrrell had warned him that if the Serbian frontier were crossed, the war would become general. 'The localization of the war hoped for by Berlin was utterly impossible.'[1]

4. Grey's urgent appeal to Germany; Mensdorff informed of the concentration of the British fleet.

Under the influence of this environment Grey on his return to London on the evening of the 26th spoke in similar terms to Lichnowsky who earlier in the afternoon had sent him a letter saying in a postscript: 'My Government accepts your suggested mediation *à quatre*', and asking Grey to use his influence with St. Petersburg to localize the war.[2] Grey saw him late in the forenoon of the 27th and told him that the Serbian reply had given complete satisfaction to Austrian demands

in a measure which he would never have believed possible. . . . If Austria was not satisfied with this reply, or if this reply were not regarded in Vienna as a basis for peaceful negotiations, or if Austria proceeded to the occupation of Belgrade, which lies completely defenceless, then it would be absolutely clear that Austria was only looking for a pretext to crush Serbia. But through Serbia Russia would also be hit and Russian influence in the Balkans. It was clear that Russia could not look on unconcerned but must take it as a direct challenge. This would give rise to the most terrible war which Europe had ever seen and none knew whither such a war would lead. We, said Grey, had repeatedly and as late as yesterday addressed the request to him to exercise a moderating influence in St. Petersburg. He had always willingly responded to these appeals and drawn upon himself reproaches from Russia in the last crisis that he placed himself too much on our side and too little on theirs. Now he made an appeal to us to use our influence with Vienna to have the reply from Belgrade regarded either as satisfactory or as a basis for negotiations. He was persuaded that it lay with us to settle the matter by suitable representations and he would regard it as a good omen for the future if we two were once again successful in assuring the peace of Europe by our influence on our respective allies.[3]

---

[1] DD. I, 236.   [2] BD. XI, 145. See p. 343.

[3] DD. I, 258. Summarizing the conversation in a telegram to Goschen, Grey said he had told Lichnowsky 'that if Germany assisted Austria against Russia, it would be because . . . Germany could not afford to see Austria crushed. Just so other issues might be raised that would supersede the dispute between Austria and Servia and would bring other Powers in, and the war would be the biggest ever known.' (BD. XI, 176.) This is a veiled threat not included in Lichnowsky's dispatch. But in a later telegram of the same date Lichnowsky gave as his impression 'that the whole Serbian question is leading up to a trial of strength between Triple Alliance and Triple *Entente*. If Austria's intention to use the present occasion to crush Serbia should become more apparent, I am convinced that England will take her stand unconditionally by France and Russia, in order to show that she does not mean to tolerate a moral or military defeat of her group. If war comes in these conditions, we shall have England against us' (DD. I, 265).

This was a renewed and formal request for mediation at Vienna which Grey was addressing to Berlin, more explicit but not essentially different from those that had gone before. But its greater solemnity and warmth made a deep impression on Lichnowsky as we shall see when we come to examine its results.

In the afternoon of the 27th Grey saw Mensdorff. He told him the substance of his conversation with Lichnowsky in the morning, and went on to use a most unfortunate expression:

I said that it seemed to me as if the Austrian Government believed that, even after the Servian reply, they could make war on Servia anyhow, without risk of bringing Russia into the dispute. If they could make war on Servia and at the same time satisfy Russia, well and good; but, if not, the consequences would be incalculable.

This is hardly the way an English statesman ought to regard the problem of the sovereignty and independence of a free European nation. Grey ended by telling Mensdorff:

Our fleet was to have dispersed to-day, but we had felt unable to let it disperse. We should not think of calling up reserves at this moment, and there was no menace in what we had done about our fleet; but, owing to the possibility of a European conflagration, it was impossible for us to disperse our forces at this moment. I gave this as an illustration of the anxiety that was felt. It seemed to me that the Servian reply already involved the greatest humiliation to Servia that I had ever seen a country undergo, and it was very disappointing to me that the reply was treated by the Austrian Government as if it were as unsatisfactory as a blank negative.[1]

This was no news to Mensdorff. The press of Monday morning (27th) had published a communiqué saying that the First Fleet, concentrated at Portland, had received orders not to disperse and the Second Fleet to remain at their home ports in proximity to their balance crews. We have the account of this written by Winston Churchill, then First Lord of the Admiralty. In his narrative he records an episode which deserves attention. At the end of an inconclusive Cabinet discussion on 24 July on the boundaries of Fermanagh and Tyrone

the quiet grave tones of Sir Edward Grey's voice were heard reading a document which had just been brought to him from the Foreign Office. It was the Austrian note to Serbia. . . . This note was clearly an ultimatum; but it was an ultimatum such as had never been penned in modern times. . . . I went back to the Admiralty at about 6 o'clock. I said to my friends . . . that there was real danger and that it might be war.

That same Friday night (the 24th) at dinner Churchill and the Secretary of State for War, Haldane, met one of the foremost German-

[1] BD. XI, 188.

Jewish business magnates, Albert Ballin, head of the Hamburg-America Steamship Line, who had on previous occasions been used by the German Government for negotiations of a delicate nature. He had just arrived from Germany.

With the first few words he spoke—narrates Churchill—it became clear that he had not come here on any mission of pleasure. He said the situation was grave. 'I remember,' he said, 'old Bismarck telling me the year before he died that one day the great European war would come out of some damned foolish thing in the Balkans.' These words, he said, might come true. It all depended on the Tsar. What would he do if Austria chastised Serbia? . . . 'If Russia marches against Austria, we must march; and if we march, France must march, and what would England do?' I was not in a position to say more than that it would be a great mistake to assume that England would necessarily do nothing, and I added that she would judge events as they arose. He replied speaking with very great earnestness, 'Suppose we had to go to war with Russia and France, and suppose we defeated France and yet took nothing from her in Europe, not an inch of her territory, only some colonies to indemnify us. Would that make a difference to England's attitude? Suppose we gave a guarantee beforehand!

This veiled proposal was one to give rise to the most serious suspicions. How did Churchill receive it? He himself tells us: 'I stuck to my formula that England would judge events as they arose and that it would be a mistake to assume that we should stand out of it whatever happened.'[1] Ballin, however, went away with another impression. Haldane narrates that

after dinner he spoke to Grey and myself separately about the position of Great Britain and our relations with Germany. We both told him that so far these were quite good, but that their maintenance was dependent on Germany not attacking France. In such a case Germany could not reckon on our neutrality. Just before England declared war on Germany on 4 August, Ballin sent me by messenger a letter recalling the dinner . . . and expressing the hope, based on what he imagined we had said, that if Germany did not try to 'swallow up' France, England would be neutral. I did not answer this letter, which arrived only the day before war broke out. The only material point about it was that Ballin had represented Grey and myself as having used the words 'swallow up' whereas we had really said 'attack' when we defined the condition.[2]

Ballin, however, according to his biographer,

returned on 27 July to Berlin with the impression that a moderately skilled German diplomatist could very well have come to an understanding with England and France, which could have assured peace and prevented Russia from beginning war. England and the leading English political men were

[1] Churchill, I, pp. 195–6.
[2] R. B. Haldane. *An Autobiography* (London 1929), pp. 270, 271–3.

absolutely pacific and the French Government was so little inclined for war that its representation in London, to use his expression, was 'very slight' and would do everything to prevent war. England was, however, pledged to support France in an unprovoked attack, for instance, would certainly not allow us to march through Belgium using our old plan of war. . . . But how much the Cabinet desired the preservation of peace, is shown, surely, by the fact that Churchill at parting begged Ballin almost with tears: 'My dear friend, don't let us go to war.'[1]

The important thing about this episode is that it was after Ballin's return, i.e. on 29 July, that Bethmann Hollweg made the proposal that England should remain neutral on the very conditions outlined by Ballin. And as those conditions were indignantly rejected by Grey as dishonourable, it seems hardly possible that he and Haldane could have taken them into consideration a few days earlier. One can only conclude that Ballin had not made himself clear. But it must also be allowed that he was not spoken to plainly enough and that no advantage was taken of this good opportunity to give Germany a serious warning and dispel the illusions she was harbouring.

To come back to Churchill, the latter tells us:

I discussed the situation at length the next morning (Saturday) with the First Sea Lord. For the moment, however, there was nothing to do. At no time in all these last three years were we more completely ready. The test mobilization had been completed, and with the exception of the Immediate Reserve, all the reservists were already paid off and journeying to their homes. But the whole of the 1st and 2nd Fleets were complete in every way for battle and were concentrated at Portland, where they were to remain till Monday morning (27th) at 7 o'clock when the 1st Fleet would disperse by squadrons for various exercises and when the ships of the 2nd Fleet would proceed to their Home Ports to discharge their balance crews. Up till the Monday morning, therefore, a word instantaneously transmitted from the wireless mast of the Admiralty to the *Iron Duke* would suffice to keep our main force together.[2]

On Saturday afternoon Churchill followed Grey's example and departed to Cromer to spend the week-end with his family. No doubt he felt reassured by Crackanthorpe's optimistic telegram from Belgrade[3] saying that Serbia was accepting the ultimatum. But he called up the Admiralty several times and on the Sunday afternoon (26th) decided to return to London.

Prince Louis (of Battenberg) awaited me at the Admiralty. . . . The First Sea Lord told me that in accordance with our conversation he had told the Fleet not to disperse. . . . I then went round to Sir Edward Grey. . . . No one was with him except Sir William Tyrrell of the Foreign Office. . . .

---

[1] B. Huldermann, *Albert Ballin* (Berlin, 1922), pp. 301-2.
[2] Churchill, I, pp. 194-5.   BD. XI, 114; see p. 340.

I learnt from him that he viewed the situation very gravely. . . . I asked whether it would be helpful or the reverse if we stated in public that we were keeping the Fleet together. Both he and Tyrrell were insistent that we should proclaim it at the earliest possible moment: it might have the effect of sobering the Central Powers and steadying Europe.[1]

And in fact on Monday 27th, as we have seen, Grey used the news to caution Mensdorff and also to reassure the Russian Ambassador Benckendorff, who complained to him 'that impression prevails in German and Austrian circles that we shall stand aside in any event', which up to that moment was certainly true. Grey

pointed out that orders we have given to First Fleet, which happens to be concentrated at Portland, not to disperse for manoeuvre leave ought to dispel this impression, though Russian Ambassador must not take my reference to it as meaning that we promised anything more than diplomatic action.[2]

Grey's mind was slowly beginning to move. The movement can be traced in Benckendorff's dispatches. As late as the 26th Benckendorff was writing a despairing letter to Sazonov saying that Nicolson had just shown him Buchanan's dispatch of the 25th, telling of the conversation between himself, Sazonov and Paléologue, before Grey had yet read it,[3] that Grey was still entrenched behind the thesis that his language gave Berlin no grounds for counting on English neutrality, and that he still expressed confidence in the success of his proposal for mediation. Paul Cambon unfortunately had not yet come back to London, and Benckendorff thought that Grey was afraid to engage himself too far for fear of not being supported by the English press. But the Conservative papers were beginning to move and even the anti-Serb Radical press had no word of criticism against the Russian attitude or against the Triple *Entente* as such.

But that is a long way off from going to war. Hence, in my opinion, all the hesitation. England is only slowly awakening out of her entire absorption in Ulster. Since yesterday she has learnt that war is in prospect and begins to feel uneasy, but the slow English imagination has not yet taken in that England might herself be drawn into it. It is unfortunate but that is how it is. It is clear that the Foreign Office is opening its eyes more quickly than elsewhere. I still hope to get Grey to drop the mask in these days but I cannot promise this.[4]

After his seeing Grey on the Sunday evening, Benckendorff's dispatches of the 27th were more cheerful. One of them gives the substance of what Grey had said to Lichnowsky that same day[5] and Benckendorff expressed the hope to Grey that his words would open

---

[1] Churchill, I, pp. 196–8.   [2] BD. XI, 177.   [3] BD. XI, 125. See pp. 306 7.
[4] *Int. Bez.* i. V, 91.   [5] BD. XI, 176.

the eyes of the German Government which was still under the impression that England was going to remain neutral.

Grey answered that, without being in a position to give a definite undertaking, he thought he had made himself sufficiently plain to-day, to destroy that impression. He said that the orders just issued to the English fleet would serve to clarify matters without being a threat to anybody. He told me he was going to make a statement in the Commons, basing himself on the Serbian reply. He expects there will be many questions. If he is asked whether England will remain neutral whatever happens, he will answer: 'Certainly not.' If he is asked whether the orders to the fleet have any reference to events of the day he will answer: 'Yes, certainly.'[1]

A later dispatch from Benckendorff on the same day is more confident:

Since to-day Grey's language is more unambiguous, noticeably more decided than till now. He places much reliance on the impression which will be produced by the orders to the fleet which were published this morning and decided on on Saturday evening. A telegram from Buchanan which arrived yesterday evening has, I believe, made a very useful impression. In any case the confidence of Berlin and Vienna in the neutrality of England has no longer any foundation.[2]

This was saying too much. Up to the 29th Germany still went on being sure of English neutrality. Moreover Grey's statement in the Commons on the 27th was cold and colourless and gave rise to no questions such as might have led him to make some enlightening answers as Buchanan's dispatch of the 26th had asked of him:

I venture to hope that, in any statement you may make in Parliament, you may find it possible to show that if European peace is being endangered it is not Russia but Austria who is at fault. . . . It would, I think, be most inadvisable to allow belief to gain ground here that our sympathies are on the side of Austria. As it is our position is a very delicate one and Minister for Foreign Affairs told me yesterday that Emperor had expressed great disappointment on hearing from him what I had said with regard to probable attitude of His Majesty's Government.[3]

But Grey paid no heed to this plea. His speech gave a rapid summary of what had happened and of the two proposals he had made to deal with the crisis, to the second of which, the conference of ambassadors, he had not yet received answers from all the Powers. He said that if the dispute spread beyond Austria and Serbia and involved another Great Power, it would end in the greatest disaster that could befall the Continent of Europe—in short he reiterated in the Commons the well-worn distinction between an Austro-Serbian and an Austro-Russian

---

[1] *Int. Bez.* i. V, 122.   [2] *Int. Bez.* i. V, 124.   [3] BD. XI, 153.

conflict, so pleasing to the ear of the Central Powers: 'As long as the dispute remained only between Austria-Hungary and Serbia, I felt that we had not the right to intervene.' And as he puts it in his memoirs: 'it was better that Serbia should give way than that European peace should be broken'.[1] This theory, which would plead for the toleration of any violence a Great Power might inflict on a weaker state, is no more practicable than it is moral, and if Grey had not countenanced it, he might have followed another line of action which would have led to very different results.

No doubt the concentration of the British fleet, which had been made known by the press, added something that was lacking in Grey's speech. But in Russia, despite Benckendorff's report, the dissatisfaction was intense. Izvolsky told Lord Granville, whom he met at a dinner in Paris on the 27th that in his belief

war is inevitable and by the fault of England; that if England had at once declared her solidarity with Russia and France, and her intention to fight if necessary, Germany and Austria would have hesitated.[2]

No doubt it was in connexion with such news that Nicolson in his already mentioned private letter to Buchanan of 28 July writes:

What has preoccupied, and I confess has troubled me very much, is satisfying Russia's very natural request as to what we should do in certain eventualities. . . . We, of course, living under such conditions as we do here, when no Government practically can take any decided line without feeling that public opinion amply supports them, are unable to give any decided engagements; . . . but I think we have made it perfectly clear that in any case neither Germany nor Austria could possibly rely with any certainty upon our remaining neutral. . . . There is no doubt whatsoever that, were we drawn into this conflagration, we should be on the side of our friends. Although therefore we were unable to give Sazonov a definite undertaking as to what our attitude would be, I think you will see that there is very little doubt, supposing we were called upon to take a share, that we should not hesitate to do our duty.[3]

But the real problem was, would England feel called upon to 'take a share'. It was a problem which Grey's own conduct had helped to create. On the one hand he had made no attempt to restrain Russia from pressing forward with mobilization and had even regarded it as necessary and inevitable, with no perception of the danger it involved. On the other hand he left the German leaders with the conviction, on which they based all their plans, that England would remain neutral. By encouraging Berlin to be intransigent and St. Petersburg to order mobilization, he was unleashing war. If he had made up his mind in time he would have had the right and the means to restrain Russia and

[1] Grey, I, 310.   [2] BD. XI, 216.   [3] BD. XI, 239.

he would have given Germany a warning which would have made her retrace her steps, as the story of events will show. Was it true that the mood of Parliament and public opinion rendered it impossible to make a decision earlier and hence to give timely admonitions to both parties? This is maintained by Grey's fellow countrymen and by many historians who are well disposed towards him. But it will soon be proved by facts that the contrary is the case. John Morley, one of Grey's colleagues in the Government, who was himself opposed to entering the war, has placed it on record that it was at the Cabinet meeting of Monday 27 July that Grey made the straightforward and honourable statement (to which we shall come later) that the moment had come for England to decide whether or not to go to the aid of France and Russia. 'If the Cabinet was for neutrality, he did not think that he was the man to carry out such a policy.'[1]

It was a manly statement, but it could not take the place of the words and deeds which duty demanded of one who, as his country's Foreign Secretary, was in large measure arbiter of the situation and whose every word and deed should have been directed towards averting the catastrophe.

5. *A proposal put forward by San Giuliano is dropped by Grey and rejected by Vienna.*

The Italian Government also made an effort to stay the course of disaster. It took action on receiving the text of the ultimatum on 24 July. What this action was will be told in Vol. III of the present work,[2] but it is necessary for the understanding of events to speak now of one effort it made to settle the dispute. As early as 25 July, De Martino, the Secretary General of the Consulta, told the English Ambassador, Sir Rennell Rodd, that 'Austria-Hungary will only be restrained by unconditional acceptance of note by Servia'.[3] It was a true intuition. Indeed a perusal of the diplomatic documents giving the opinions of the Rome Government on the situation leaves the present writer with the impression that they grasped what were the intentions of the Central Powers more rapidly and more clearly than any other Government. If only they had acted accordingly! Returning to Rome on 27 July San Giuliano had a talk with Rodd:

He greatly doubts whether Germany will be willing to invite Austria to suspend military action pending conference (of ambassadors), but had hope that military action may be practically deferred by fact of conference meeting at once. He does not, as at present informed, see any possibility of Austria receding from any point laid down in note to Servia, but believes that if Servia will even now accept it Austria will be satisfied, and if she had

[1] John Viscount Morley, *Memorandum on Resignation* (London, 1928), p. 2.
[2] See Vol. III, Ch. VI.   [3] BD. XI, 113.

reason to think this will be advice of Powers, Austria may defer action. Servia may be induced to accept note in its integrity on advice of four Powers invited to conference. This would save her face in allowing her to think she had yielded to Europe and not to Austria alone. This is also the view of Servian agent here, provided some explanation could be given as to how points 5 and 6 of conditions would be applied.[1]

San Giuliano, also on the 27th, told Flotow that:

According to his information [he gives no particulars] Serbia would be prepared to comply with the Austrian demands if they were presented by Europe (Kaiser's marginal note: 'Rubbish!') On the other hand Russia would only intervene if Austria permanently occupied Serbian territory.[2]

This last idea was devoid of foundation. Thus far San Giuliano had only expressed an opinion; he had made no proposal. But on the morning of the 28th he had a talk with the Serbian Chargé d'Affaires, Ljuba Mihailović, who repeated (we say 'repeated' because Rodd's dispatch of the 27th shows that San Giuliano had already heard this opinion from Mihailović) that,

he thought Servia might still accept the whole Austrian note if some explanations were given regarding mode in which Austrian agents would require to intervene under Article 5 and Article 6.

San Giuliano therefore saw Rodd in the afternoon and asked him to propose to London that:

such explanations might be given to the Powers engaged in discussions, as it was not to be anticipated that Austria would give them to Servia. The Powers might then advise Servia to accept unconditionally.

Many points in the Austrian official explanation of the grounds on which the Servian reply was considered inadequate seemed to San Giuliano 'quite childish', but where this explanation stated that the co-operation of Austrian agents in Servia was not to be in judicial or administrative measures, but only in investigation,

he thought that ground might be cleared. . . . Above all, Minister impressed upon me his anxiety that discussion should begin at once. He had given Italian Ambassador a wide general latitude to accept at once every point or suggestion on which he could be in agreement with ourselves and Germany.[3]

He evidently did not yet know that the Conference had been rejected by Germany. But Grey knew this, as is shown in his telegram of 4 p.m. on 28 July to Goschen in Berlin whose dispatch of 27 July had conveyed the rejection of the idea of a conference on grounds that it 'would practically amount to a court of arbitration'. Grey tells Goschen

---

[1] BD. XI, 202.   [2] DD. I, 249.   [3] BD. XI, 231.

that he was right in replying: 'It would not be an arbitration but a private and informal discussion to ascertain what suggestion could be made for a settlement.' But he adds: 'I entirely agree that direct exchange of views between Austria and Russia is the most preferable method of all, and as long as there is a prospect of that taking place I would suspend every other suggestion.'[1] Accordingly when San Giuliano's proposal reached him on the evening of the 28th he at once replied:

I understand from Austrian Minister for Foreign Affairs that Austria will not accept any discussion on basis of Serbian note, and the inference of all I have heard from Vienna and Berlin is that any form of mediation by the Powers as between Austria and Servia will not be accepted by Austria. It is therefore impossible for me to initiate discussions with Ambassadors here, and Italian Minister for Foreign Affairs must speak at Berlin and Vienna. I shall be glad if any suggestions he can make there are favourably received.[2]

This telegram left London at 12.45 a.m. on 29 July and crossed with one from Rodd sent off that same night at 12.5 a.m. This began by drawing attention to the discrepancy between what Lichnowsky had said to Grey on the 27th i.e. 'that the German Government accept in principle mediation between Austria and Russia by the four Powers',[3] and what Jagow said on the same day to Goschen, i.e. 'that the conference you suggest would practically amount to a court of arbitration'. San Giuliano, however—writes Rodd—understands from Berlin

that it is rather the 'conference' than the principle which creates difficulty. He is telegraphing to Berlin to-night urging that the idea of an exchange of views in London should be adhered to and suggests that German Secretary of State for Foreign Affairs might propose formula which he could accept. Minister for Foreign Affairs thinks that this exchange of views might be concomitant with direct communication between St. Petersburg and Vienna and would keep door open if latter fail to have any result. He is also informing Berlin that public opinion here will not pardon the Government if every possible step has not been taken to avoid war and urging that in this Germany must co-operate. Even if it proved impossible to induce Germany to take part he would still advocate that Italy and England should still continue to exchange views, as each represented one group. He added that there seemed to be a difficulty in making Germany believe that Russia was in earnest and thought it would have a great effect if she believed that Great Britain would act with Russia and France, as Germany was really desirous of good relations with ourselves.[4]

This last sentence contained a remarkable and valuable piece of advice, coming from a member of the Triple Alliance. Again the able Sir Eyre Crowe was the only one to perceive its importance. His brief

[1] BD. XI, 218.　　[2] BD. XI, 246.　　[3] BD. XI, 176.　　[4] BD. XI, 252.

minute runs: 'The last paragraph is significant, coming from Italy', in other words: 'It is high time we told Berlin where we stood.' All that Nicolson could find to say (it was the 29th) was: 'I ask myself what is the use of exchanging views at this juncture. . . . I am of opinion that the resources of diplomacy are, for the present, exhausted.' And even San Giuliano at about the same moment told Rodd that he 'now thinks moment is past for any further discussions on basis of Servian note'.[1]

Grey, meanwhile, on the morning of the 29th received a dispatch of the evening of the 28th from Bunsen in Vienna saying:

> Russian Ambassador informs me that Austro-Hungarian Government have declined suggestion of Russian Government that the Austrian Ambassador at St. Petersburg should be authorized to discuss directly with Russian Minister for Foreign Affairs means of settling Austro-Servian conflict.[2]

Thoroughly perturbed by this news, Grey summoned Lichnowsky, whose report to Berlin of their important talk will engage our attention later. For the moment what concerns us is that, towards the end of it, Grey revived San Giuliano's proposal stating that he had referred him to Vienna and Berlin.[3] Berlin had already heard of it direct from Flotow on the 27th.[4] However, for reasons we shall soon consider, Bethmann at 12.30 a.m. on the 30th communicated Lichnowsky's telegram to Vienna adding: 'Please communicate enclosed at once to Count Berchtold and say that we regard this compliance on the part of Serbia as suitable basis for negotiations. . . .'[5] But in the afternoon of the 30th the answer came from Tschirschky:

> It is a mistake to assume that acceptance of Points 5 and 6 of the Austrian note means its integral acceptance, as Serbia has made reservations on several other points. As long as peaceful settlement of the conflict between Serbia and Monarchy was in question, the integral acceptance of the demands of the note were regarded here as sufficient. Now that the state of war has come into force, Austria's conditions would of course be formulated differently.[6]

Thus the failure of Grey's proposal was now followed by the failure of San Giuliano's. There are historians put the blame for this on Grey on grounds that he did not take the Italian proposal seriously enough. Mathias Morhardt, at one time General Secretary of the 'Ligue des Droits de l'Homme' goes so far as to describe Grey's attitude to the proposal as 'criminal'.[7] But he is one of those who, without basis of proof, ascribe the attitude of the Foreign Office in the July crisis to unscrupulous duplicity and whose opinion it is not possible to share. Let us, therefore, now try to form a more objective judgement.

[1] BD. XI, 268.   [2] BD. XI, 248.   [3] DD. II, 357.
[4] DD. I, 249.   [5] DD. II, 384.   [6] DD. II, 432.
[7] Morhardt, *Les Preuves*, pp. 255 ff., especially p. 273.

It cannot be doubted that San Giuliano's proposal was in theory the only one which might have averted the European war. But to be successful, it ought to have been made in good time, i.e. on 24 July before Serbia gave her reply to Austria, or at the latest on the morning of the 26th, before Grey took another line. Actually, however, it reached London on the morning of the 29th slipped inside the English proposal for an ambassadors' conference, which had already been rejected by Berlin, and when it seemed that St. Petersburg and Vienna were on the way to opening direct conversations on which Grey, by whom they were first suggested, Pourtalès, who had recommended them to Sazonov, and Sazonov, who had sought to initiate them, all placed their greatest hopes. London could thus not do otherwise than answer Rome as it did. San Giuliano's idea, in fact, came too late. Even had Grey seriously taken it up, it would have been swept away both by the Austrian declaration of war on Serbia and the Russian mobilization.

Nay more! To have been successful the proposal would have had to be launched by a strong *démarche* with Italy's partners in the Triple Alliance to make them understand that Italy was determined to avert war, and it would have had to be solidly based on the willingness both of Belgrade, and of St. Petersburg, to accept it. San Giuliano made no official communication of it either to Berlin or to Vienna and in suggesting it to London, he only had the more or less explicit consent of the Serbian Chargé d'Affaires in Rome. And even the Serbian Chargé d'Affaires, besides having no official authority, was only expressing a personal opinion of little value. What would have been the effect in Belgrade? We already know that Belgrade would not have refused more or less integral acceptance of the Austrian demands, if advised to do so by St. Petersburg at once, but not later. This is proved by the Serbian Government's rejection of Sazonov's advice transmitted by Strandtmann to ask for English mediation, of which we have already spoken.[1] St. Petersburg was in any case against full submission by Serbia and expressed its dislike of the Italian suggestion. On 29 July Buchanan brought to Sazonov's knowledge San Giuliano's first tentative proposal embodied in Rodd's dispatch of 27 July and sent on by Grey. Buchanan

asked whether he would raise objections if this suggestion were carried out. His Excellency said he could not be more Servian than the Servians and would agree to anything four Powers could arrange provided it was acceptable to Servia. Sharpness of ultimatum, however, would have to be toned down by some supplementary statement or explanations.[2]

This was tantamount to a rejection of the proposal, the basis of which was precisely the integral acceptance of the ultimatum, which alone, if made in time, could have halted Austria.

[1] See pp. 310-11.   [2] BD. XI, 276.

This chain of reasoning leads us to the conclusion that San Giuliano's suggestion, valuable in itself, suffered shipwreck because it was both belated and unsupported by the consent of the Serbian Government, by which Mihailović was not authorized to say what he did. In making his proposal, San Giuliano had another way out of the difficulty at the back of his mind. To Krupensky on the 27th he revealed this: 'Well, what does that matter? Let them [the Serbs] accept, even if they do not carry out what they agree to.'[1] However London was not alone in rejecting the proposal. It was not favourably received in either Berlin, or St. Petersburg or Vienna, while Paris, still off the map, expressed no opinion whatever. But granting all that, it remains to be said that Grey's manner of rejection showed less deference and consideration than characterized his relations with the other Great Powers. A laconic sentence suffices to convey it and the advice 'to speak at Berlin and Vienna' is coupled with the half ironical remark: 'I shall be glad if any suggestions he can make there are favourably received.'

The truth is that the Foreign Office at that time apparently regarded Italy as a negligible quantity. Among the 677 British Diplomatic Documents contained in Vol. XI of the collection dealing with *The Outbreak of the War*, those which in a few lines summarize dealings with the Italian Ambassador Imperiali can be counted on the fingers of one hand. Never a thorough talk between him and Grey, no inquiry on the part of Grey as to what was the Italian attitude. Vol. XI, however, contains an account of two curious conversations between San Giuliano and Rodd, one at a banquet at the Persian Legation on 21 July and the other at the Consulta on the morning of the 22nd. They are both contained in a letter of 22 July from Rodd to Grey:

As I was placed next to His Excellency we had an opportunity for some conversation and he at once began to speak of the grave situation existing between Austria-Hungary and Servia. He was afraid a dangerous spirit of excitement and self-confidence existed at Belgrade. He, however, still had hopes that the known pacific aims of the Emperor would prevent the precipitation of a crisis. Should Servia, as she anticipated, be supported by Russia, there was no doubt that Germany would join Austria. This did not merely depend on her obligations as an ally, but Germany believed that it was a vital question for Austria if she was to maintain her position and prestige, to achieve a success, and it was Germany's interest to promote it. What then, I asked, would Italy do and how far did her obligations bind her? He said the Triple Alliance was purely for defensive purposes. It remained to be seen in what direction events would move. Obviously nothing could be further from Italy's desire than to become a party in such a struggle. I saw His Excellency again this morning and he then told me that he had every reason to fear that the communication which the Austro-Hungarian Government were about to make to Servia had been drafted in

[1] *Int. Bez.* i. V, 131.

terms which Servia must regard as unacceptable. There was just a hope that,
as Count Berchtold had been to Ischl, the Emperor might cause its terms to
be somewhat modified. There was, however, a party in Austria—the strongest
party—which aimed at taking this opportunity for crushing Servia. It was
not of course Italy's interest that Servia should be crushed.

I said it was to be hoped that both our countries would be able to steer
clear of any conflict. It was hardly conceivable that we should be drawn into
a struggle where no direct interests of our own were involved, where, in fact,
in the case of Italy, she would probably be siding against her own interests.

The Marquis di San Giuliano said that as our two nations were associated
with groups which were by force of circumstances likely to be ranged in
antagonism, it seemed quite conceivable that in the special circumstances of
the case, we might arrange to 'pair', like members of the British Parliament.

We were of course only discussing hypotheses which it is earnestly to
be hoped may never be realized, but this new form of counter-insurance
seemed rather to commend itself to him.[1]

To this bright idea Grey vouchsafed no reply, and for this he cannot
be blamed since it was as preposterous from the English as it was from
the Italian point of view. Neither England nor Italy could ever have
undertaken to remain outside a conflict involving the whole balance
of power in Europe. To neither country could it be a matter of
indifference which side would win. Had Germany and Austria, for
example, been the victors, as well might have happened if Russia and
France had been denied English help, both Italians and English would
have paid their abstention dearly.

The above document furnishes another proof of San Giuliano's
inability to frame a policy to meet a situation which he himself clearly
foresaw and which imposed heavy responsibilities no less on Italy
than on England. He should have seized the occasion of the banquet
to impress the English Government with the imminence of the danger
and suggest that the two Governments should seek to act as mediators
between the two groups in order to impose peace on them both. That
idea seems to have dawned on San Giuliano on the evening of the 28th
when he said to Rodd that, 'even if it proved impossible to induce
Germany to take part, he would still advocate that Italy and England
should still continue to exchange views, each representing one group'.[2]
But the idea dawned too late and in too vague a form, since San
Giuliano thought of each country representing its own group. On the
contrary what each country ought to have done was to make the
weight of its own will to peace felt within its own group, London by
threatening Berlin that it would support St. Petersburg and Paris, while
reining St. Petersburg firmly back from precipitate moves, Rome by
bluntly telling Berlin and Vienna that it would not join them in a war

[1] BD. XI, 161.   [2] BD. XI, 252.

of aggression contrary to Italian interests. When, as we have just seen, San Giuliano said to Rodd on the 29th that he 'thought it would have a great effect if Germany believed that Great Britain would act with Russia and France',[1] he showed that his quick mind had grasped what influence Grey could exercise. It is all the more unpardonable that he should not have grasped that Italy could achieve a similar effect by destroying her allies' illusions about the certainty of her support. But certain calculations of his own prevented him from wanting or daring to take this step and so he deprived himself of all means of influencing the situation as did his British opposite number for other reasons.

Nothing shows better the lack of comprehension of Grey and the miscalculation of San Giuliano than the fact that they did not from the first act in close agreement, seeing that as early as 21 July *inter pocula* San Giuliano gave Rodd a sort of pre-announcement of Italian neutrality when he said that the crushing of Serbia 'would be quite against the interests of Italy',[2] a statement of which neither Rodd nor the Foreign Office perceived the importance. Again on the 26th Rodd reported:

I gather that Italian Government will endeavour to argue, even if Russia should intervene in support of Servia, that inasmuch as Austria did not consult Italy before delivering note, and inasmuch as by her mode of attack on Servia she would be constructively provoking Russia, the *casus foederis* contemplated by alliance would not arise.[3]

But the news went unheeded in London, where Grey had not even yet perceived that English intervention would be inevitable, far less grasped what the threat of English intervention and Italian neutrality could have done to stop the war from breaking out.

And so because no action was taken by either of the two men who had it in their power to extinguish the first flames, the fire went on spreading until it engulfed both their countries.

6. Berlin presses for the 'localization of the conflict'.

We have already examined the attitude of Berlin towards the English and Italian proposals for the settlement of the conflict. We must now view in greater detail the thoughts and actions of the German leaders in the period preceding the Austrian declaration of war on Serbia. It was the period in which these leaders were under the illusion that the Austro-Serbian conflict could remain 'localized', and convinced that they would get this proposal accepted by the other Powers. We have shown above the folly of this illusion.[4] But the news coming in on 24 and 25 July gave the impression that Paris and London were amenable, and that, if they both at that moment put pressure on St.

---

[1] BD. XI, 252.   [2] BD. XI, 78.   [3] BD. XI, 148.   [4] See pp. 298-9.

Petersburg, Russia would feel herself unsupported and would not go further in support of Serbia. Never can enough stress be laid on the disastrous consequences of the lack of policy and the unguarded language of both Grey and Bienvenu-Martin. Tirpitz writes of the harm done by Grey's reference to a Four Power war, i.e. one not involving England. It strengthened the Chancellor, Jagow, Stumm and others in their expectation of English neutrality, so that they went boldly ahead on the wrong road they had chosen.[1] Not less mischievous was Grey's repeated statement that he had no intention of interfering in the conflict between Austria and Serbia. It was tantamount to a declaration that he had nothing to say against the localization of the conflict.

But if the German thesis was to prevail, there was no time to lose, because prolonged diplomatic tension might throw it into jeopardy. Grey had already asked Germany to propose an extension of the time limit and Berlin had made a feint of compliance which did not hoodwink the clear-sighted Crowe and Nicolson.[2] Next Grey had proposed Four Power mediation at Vienna and St. Petersburg to which Germany, again in bad faith, expressed agreement on the evening of the 25th, regarding it as no hindrance to Austria's attacking Serbia, i.e. to the localization of the war.[3] But Berlin could not hope to carry on this double game indefinitely without being found out. Paris had only discovered it up to a certain point, and Schoen's dispatches were still reassuring. But Poincaré and Viviani would soon be back home again and then the tune would change. Added up, this meant that Austria must go ahead and invade Serbia without loss of time.

Austria, meanwhile, seemed about to go to sleep and unable to make up her mind. The Wilhelmstrasse, as we have seen, had been all along doubtful of the steadfastness of her intentions.[4] These doubts revived when on 24 July Berchtold telegraphed to Mensdorff that he was

to make clear to Sir Edward Grey that our yesterday's *démarche* at Belgrade is not to be regarded as a formal ultimatum; it is a *démarche* with a time limit which, as Your Excellency will confidentially convey to Sir E. Grey—if the time limit expires without result—will for the time being be followed only by the breaking off of diplomatic relations and the beginning of necessary military preparations [i.e. not by war]. . . . If Serbia were to yield after the expiry of the time limit only under the pressure of our military measures we should have to hold her responsible for the reimbursement of our expenditure arising therefrom.[5]

Berlin asked itself what could be the motive for this move. Did it mean that Vienna had changed its mind and was trying to avoid war? After what had happened Berlin did not think this likely. German prestige was now bound up with that of Austria. Szögyény was

---

[1] Tirpitz, *Memoirs*, p. 252.   [2] See pp. 340-2.   [3] See p. 342.
[4] See p. 261.   [5] Oe-U. VIII, 10599. See p. 377.

therefore summoned on the 25th and given a suitable talking to, which his dispatch summarized as follows:

Regarding concluding paragraph of Your Excellency's telegram of yesterday [Count Mensdorff's answer to Sir E. Grey] I should like to say that here it is universally taken for granted that an eventual negative reply by Serbia will be followed immediately by a declaration of war from us and military operations. Any delay in commencing military operations is regarded here as a great danger because of the interference of other Powers. They urgently advise us to go ahead and confront the world with a *fait accompli*. I completely share this opinion of the Foreign Ministry.[1]

This telegram by itself sufficiently reveals the part played by Germany in driving Austria into making war on Serbia. The pro-German historians, faced with similar documents, take refuge in accusing Szögyény of having misunderstood and misreported, but this time they are silenced. Their usual excuses fail them because Berchtold at once read the dispatch out to Tschirschky and he repeated the substance of it back to Berlin,[2] where, as we shall see, far from being disavowed, it was confirmed by a message from Jagow on the 27th deploring that the commencement of Austrian military operations was, for practical reasons, having to be deferred until 12 August.[3] Thus while the men at the Ballplatz hesitated and, after the rupture of diplomatic relations, consoled themselves with the thought that war was not yet upon them, the Wilhelmstrasse clamoured for 'a declaration of war and military operations'. Nothing is more revealing of the intentions of Berlin than its behaviour over the Serbian reply, its taking for granted that this justified an immediate break of diplomatic relations followed by the opening of hostilities, its tacit assumption that Belgrade would not submit entirely to the ultimatum. Had the men of Berlin not intended that there should be war between Austria and Serbia they would at once have asked to see a copy of the Serbian note and studied its implications and possible repercussions. Only after that would they have decided what action was to be taken. Nothing of this did they do, and the note came into their hands in circumstances which will be described later. Their procedure shows that the last thing they cared about was whether the break of diplomatic relations followed by war was really justified by the attitude of Serbia. All they cared to know was that the ultimatum had not been accepted integrally, that Giesl had in consequence taken his departure and that therefore it was now the guns which could, indeed should, speak in such a way as to confront Europe with a *fait accompli*.

And yet the news arriving in Berlin on the 25th and the morning of the 26th was not wholly satisfactory. Not counting the appeals and laments from that Cassandra, Lichnowsky, there was the attitude of

---

[1] Oe-U. VIII, 10656.   [2] DD. I, 213.   [3] Oe-U. VIII, 10792.

Italy which was anything but certain, and Italian support was something that Moltke regarded as absolutely essential. On learning this, Bethmann Hollweg, who had fallen in with Berchtold's proposal to keep Italy in the dark about the whole affair, thought he could make up for this mistake by telegraphing to Tschirschky on the 26th:

An understanding between Vienna and Rome is necessary. Vienna must not evade this with questionable interpretations of the treaty, but take decisions in keeping with the seriousness of the situation.[1]

From St. Petersburg, too, came the disquieting news that Sazonov had on the 24th been highly indignant about the ultimatum and had given Pourtalès a hostile reception, and then on the 26th a telegram from the German General Chelius to say that on the 25th the manoeuvres at Krasnoe Selo had been suddenly called off, that the regiments were returning to garrison, that great excitement reigned at Headquarters over the Austrian *démarche* and that, in his opinion, all preparations were being made for mobilization against Austria.[2] This sent the Chancellor off in quest of a life-belt and he thought he had found one in a dispatch from Tschirschky of 24 July reporting from Vienna that Berchtold had asked the Russian Chargé d'Affaires to call on him and had given him assurances that Austria had no intention of taking territory from Serbia.[3] This was in flat contradiction to the ideas and expectations of Berlin in the preceding days[4] and indeed, as we shall see, earned for Berchtold the epithet 'donkey' from Wilhelm. But Pourtalès's dispatch reporting his conversation with Sazonov on the 24th had quoted textually Sazonov's words: 'If Austria-Hungary swallows Serbia, we shall make war on her'[5] and had concluded from them that what Sazonov perhaps meant was 'that Russia would only take up arms if Austria sought to make territorial gains at the expense of Serbia'. This gave Bethmann the idea that he could reach the safe harbour of 'localization' by jettisoning something of the German expectations and so he seized upon Berchtold's declaration of territorial *désintéressement* and telegraphed in the afternoon of 26 July to Pourtalès:

Now that Count Berchtold has declared to Russia that Austria plans no territorial gains in Serbia but only means to restore peace and quiet, the preservation of European peace depends entirely on Russia. We rely on Russia's love of peace and our long-standing good relations for her taking no steps which could seriously imperil European peace.[6]

At the same time, as we have seen, the Chancellor asked London and Paris to restrain St. Petersburg on grounds of Austrian territorial *désintéressement*, threatening that otherwise Germany would take countermeasures.[7] Then, fearing he had been too mild and not sufficiently

[1] DD. I, 202.   [2] DD. I, 194.   [3] DD. I, 155.   [4] See pp. 261-5.
     [5] DD. I, 160.   [6] DD. I, 198.   [7] See p. 343.

explicit in his previous telegram to Pourtalès he now (at 7.15 p.m. on the 26th) sent him another marked 'urgent' saying:

Preparatory military measures on the part of Russia directed in any way against ourselves would force us to take counter measures which would have to consist in mobilizing the army. Mobilization, however, means war, and would moreover have to be directed simultaneously against Russia and France, since France's engagements with Russia are well known. We cannot believe that Russia means to unloose a European war of this kind. In view of Austria's territorial *désintéressement* we rather take the view that Russia can adopt a waiting attitude towards the issue (*Auseinandersetzung*) between Austria-Hungary and Serbia. Russia's desire not to have the integrity of the Serbian Kingdom called in question can receive our support, the more as Austria-Hungary has stated that she does not intend to call this integrity in question. This might provide a common basis of agreement also in the further course of the affair.[1]

The objects of this dispatch are patent: to scare St. Petersburg and Paris; to offer St. Petersburg a way of escape by guaranteeing the Austrian territorial *désintéressement* which Berchtold had been simple-minded enough to promise, and from which, in consequence, it was better to draw such advantage as was possible; but to insist on the settlement of the 'issue' [euphemism for war] taking place without outside intervention, thus procuring for the Central Powers and for himself, the successor of Bülow, a triumph still more brilliant than that won by the Prince in 1909. All this shows that in spite of Italian reserve, Sazonov's protests, and the threat of Russian mobilization, the Chancellor regarded the attitude of Paris and London as the decisive factor and therefore on 26 July still nursed the illusion of being able to 'localize' the war. He who had telegraphed to the Kaiser on the 25th: 'Paris and London are actively working for localization of the conflict,'[2] further informed him on the 26th:

Should Russia make ready for a conflict with Austria, England intends to attempt mediation and hopes in this for French support. So long as Russia takes no hostile action, I am of the opinion that our attitude in view of localization must be one of calmness.[3]

---

[1] DD. I, 219. [2] DD. I, 191.

[3] DD. I, 197.—On board the *Hohenzollern* on 25 July there was none of Bethmann Hollweg's optimism. Colonel-general Lyncker, the Chief of the Military Cabinet, who attended the Kaiser on his cruise, wrote on that day to his wife: 'To-day's news is pretty serious. Russia, as is to be expected, sides with Serbia, and the Austrian Minister in Belgrade takes his departure to-night, if the reply to the ultimatum is not satisfactory. That pretty certainly means war. We are prepared to return home at once and indeed ought to do so. Why we do not, I cannot imagine.' At 5 p.m. that same day Lyncker further told his wife: 'The Kaiser on the basis of a dispatch from Belgrade has decided to leave here for Cuxhaven [changed to Kiel] in an hour. Apparently the Serbian Government has refused to comply with the Austrian demands and intends to transfer itself to Nish. That looks pretty bad and we are all glad to be on the homeward course. Possibly this homeward journey is the first step to war for ourselves as well' (Bach, pp. 19–20).

It was rather an overstatement to say that Paris and London were actively working for localization, but Bethmann had his reasons for seeking to inspire his Sovereign with an optimism greater than his own, especially as this optimism found corroboration on the afternoon of the 26th in an excellent piece of news from the Naval Attaché in London. Prince Henry of Prussia had that morning breakfasted with King George V and the latter had said to him: 'We shall try all we can to keep out of this and shall remain neutral.' This actual quotation comes from Prince Henry's own letter to the Kaiser of 28 July,[1] but the Naval Attaché had also reported:

King of Great Britain told Prince Henry of Prussia England would remain neutral in the event of war breaking out between Continental Powers. Fleet has dismissed reservists and sent crews on leave according to programme.[2]

This last item of news was true on the morning of 26 July, but was no longer so in the afternoon when the First Sea Lord issued the order to the fleet not to disperse.[3] But Berlin did not know this and felt a sense of relief. It was no doubt in virtue of this telegram from the German Naval Attaché that to Jules Cambon, who expressed his conviction that England would stand by France and Russia, Jagow replied:

You have your information. We have ours which is quite to the contrary. We are sure of English neutrality.[4]

7. *German intransigence and Lichnowsky's warnings.*

Further support for this optimism was furnished by the later and better news coming in from St. Petersburg on the 26th. Pourtalès, having called that morning on Sazonov, telegraphed that he found him 'much calmer and more conciliatory', and that

he begs us to help find a bridge in order to procure satisfaction of Austrian demands which he recognizes as justifiable in as far as they relate directly to the prosecution of the originators of the outrage. Some demands, however, which constituted a direct attack on Serbian sovereignty would have to be toned down. . . . There was no more word of a revision of the Austrian inquiry by the Powers. Instead there seems to be some idea in his mind of mediation in which Germany and Italy might play a part.[5]

This idea, of course, found no favour with Berlin. What the Wilhelmstrasse wanted was that there should be no discussion of the Austrian ultimatum, and that St. Petersburg should put up no opposition to the war which Austria was on the point of starting, contenting herself with Vienna's assurances of territorial *désintéressement*. Meanwhile it was

---

[1] DD. II, 374. See appendix on p. 687.   [2] DD. I, 207.   [3] Churchill, I, p. 198.
[4] Recouly, p. 23.   [5] DD. I, 217.

satisfactory to note Sazonov's change of tone which might be the precursor of other steps along the road of compliance. In forwarding this dispatch to Tschirschky at Vienna, Bethmann suppressed its final sentences which run:

I drew Sazonov's attention particularly to the fact that if, as he thought, Austria really sought a pretext to attack Serbia, there would already be news of the beginning of the Austrian action. This indication seemed to contribute to reassuring the Minister.[1]

The reason of this suppression is that Pourtalès's words were not to be taken by Austria as a loophole to evade going to war, as was expected of her.

Pourtalès, himself, wrote them because he had not divined the hidden intentions of his superiors and, indeed, by his sincere efforts for peace was at cross purposes with them. In a telegram of the evening of the 26th, arriving on the morning of the 27th, he reported that Sazonov and Szápáry had had a friendly talk about the ultimatum and that he, himself, in his private capacity had advised Sazonov to get into direct touch with Vienna to obtain a softening of some of the demands.[2] This was the last thing the Wilhelmstrasse wanted! The only thing that would satisfy Berlin was war. But what Pourtalès regarded as a piece of good news could be put to a useful purpose as a blind. Jagow used it in this way on 27 July when, in rejecting Grey's proposal for a Four Power Conference, he told Goschen that 'news he had just received from St. Petersburg showed that there was an intention on the part of M. Sazonov to exchange views with Count Berchtold'.[3] And to Jules Cambon on the same day he told the same half-truth.[4] To make London think that Germany was making efforts for conciliation, Jagow also communicated Pourtalès's telegram to Lichnowsky with suitable omissions and modifications.[5] What he carefully refrained from doing was to advise the Austrian ally to follow up Pourtalès's suggestion and open direct conversations with St. Petersburg. When on 27 July the Russian Chargé d'Affaires, Bronevski, approached him with the plea that he would advise Vienna to adopt Sazonov's proposal for direct conversations, Jagow replied that he agreed with Pourtalès in thinking that Szápáry might continue his talks with Sazonov:

To my request—reported Bronevski—that he would on his own behalf urge Vienna to adopt this conciliatory course, he answered, he could not advise Austria to yield, but the mere communication of the Pourtalès telegram to Vienna meant that he rather recommended this way out of the situation.[6]

[1] DD. I, 217.   [2] DD. I, 238. See p. 406.   [3] BD. XI, 185.
[4] LJF. 74; CDD., pp. 191–2; DF. 3. XI, 167.   [5] DD. I, 238, n.
[6] Int Bez. i. V, 134.

This hypocritical answer had already done duty the previous day when Rumbold telegraphed to Grey that Zimmermann

has just telephoned me to say that German Ambassador at Vienna has been instructed to pass on to Austro-Hungarian Government your hopes that they may take a favourable view of a Servian reply if it corresponds to the forecast contained in Belgrade telegram No. 52. Under Secretary of State considers very fact of their making this communication to Austro-Hungarian Government implies that they associate themselves to a certain extent with your hope.[1]

In fact the exact opposite was the case. The passing on of Sazonov's suggestion for direct conversations to Vienna without comment was tantamount to advising its rejection.

How, indeed, could Germany do otherwise when she had asked her ally to attack at once and face the world with a *fait accompli*? This is the sole key which enables the historian to decode the Berlin diplomatic documents of 25 to 28 July. The same key explains the rejection of Grey's proposal for a Four Power Conference, the preliminary announcement of which was made to Berlin in a telegram from Lichnowsky at 8.25 p.m. on the 26th. He had called at the Foreign Office that Sunday to speak of the question of Russian mobilization with Nicolson and Tyrrell, Grey being away for the week-end.

The two gentlemen regard Sir E. Grey's proposal . . . as the only possibility of avoiding a general war and hope it will succeed in providing Austria with full satisfaction, since Serbia would be more likely to yield to pressure from the Powers . . . than to threats from Austria. . . . Once the Serbian frontier was crossed, all would be lost since no Russian Government could tolerate this. . . . Berlin's hopes for a localization of the war were completely impossible and must be left out of practical politics. If we, i.e. H.M. the Kaiser and his Government and representatives, in co-operation with Sir E. Grey were successful in saving the peace of Europe, Anglo-German relations would be placed on a firm foundation for all eternity.

Lichnowsky's dispatch ended with the solemn words:

I would like to give you the urgent warning no longer to believe in the possibility of localization and I would voice the very humble plea that our attitude should be entirely dictated by the need to spare the German people a struggle in which they have nothing to win and everything to lose.[2]

Lichnowsky's moving plea was as courageous as it was proper. He was to suffer the execrations of his fellow countrymen for his revelations during the war, but he saw clearly from the first the dangers to which Austria, with Germany's support, exposed his native land. We have seen that he was in Berlin during the very days when the whole venture

---

[1] BD. XI, 149. See p. 342.   [2] DD. I, 236.

was being planned, and on returning to his post he never hid his apprehensions. When Jagow on 18 July wrote to persuade him that Austria must use drastic methods with Serbia[1] Lichnowsky replied with Bismarck's warning that Germany should never allow Austria to drag her into a Balkan quarrel which would bring her into conflict with Russia, and he went on to say:

> As to the localization of the conflict, you will agree that this will go the way of all pious wishes if it does come to a passage of arms with Serbia. Hence the chief thing seems to me that the Austrian demands should be worded in such a manner that with some pressure on Belgrade from St. Petersburg and London they will be acceptable, not in such a manner that they will necessarily lead to a war *ad majorem illustrissimi comitis de Berchtold gloriam*.[2]

What did then come instead was the Austrian ultimatum.

'The general impression produced by it in London'—reports Lichnowsky on the 25th—'is utterly devastating.'[3] And in a later dispatch of the same day he warned: 'I do not believe that if France becomes involved England could possibly remain indifferent.'[4]

On the 26th he again warned:

> I doubt that Sir E. Grey will be able to influence Russia in the proposed sense since after the publication of the Austrian demands no one here believes in the possibility of localizing the war. That Austria's procedure will lead to a world war, nobody here doubts.[5]

But his words fell on deaf ears. Berlin regarded the proposal for a Four Power Conference as—to quote Lerchenfeld's words to the Bavarian Prime Minister Hertling—'completely inopportune, since, because of its request that hostilities should be suspended for the time being, it is not acceptable to Austria-Hungary'.[6] It was rejected on the 27th before it had officially been made.[7] Neither Bethmann nor Jagow saw any reason for Lichnowsky to take such a pessimistic view. It did not seem to them that France and England were showing much concern and they knew what King George V had said to Prince Henry of Prussia. Moreover Pourtalès's telegram of the 26th telling of Sazonov's talk with Szápáry had ended with the words: 'I have the impression that Sazonov, perhaps because of news from Paris and London, has rather lost heart and now seeks ways of escape.'[8] In another telegram of somewhat earlier on the same day Pourtalès had said that Sazonov had guaranteed 'that no mobilization order had been issued, that the Cabinet had decided not to issue one until Austria-Hungary assumes a hostile attitude towards Russia'. 'Towards Russia', not 'towards

---

[1] DD. I, 72. See pp. 157-8.   [2] DD. I, 161.   [3] DD. I, 163.   [4] DD. I, 179.
[5] DD. I, 218.   [6] Dirr, p. 154.   [7] See p. 394.   [8] DD. I, 238.

Serbia'. All that Sazonov admitted was that 'certain military preparations were now being made to prevent surprise'.[1] Thus Berlin could not regard the prospect as too gloomy and Grey could be firmly told No! while Austria was given a free hand and Germany pressed for the 'localization of the conflict'.

So after neglecting to read the Serbian reply as being something devoid of importance, after refraining from making any recommendation that Vienna should fall in with Sazonov's suggestion of direct conversations, the Chancellor and Jagow refused to submit the question to a Four Power Conference. Bethmann having on the 26th wirelessed to Wilhelm on board the *Hohenzollern* that 'St. Petersburg is visibly hesitating',[2] described the situation on the 27th in a telegram as follows:

Austria seems not to be able to begin war operations until 12 August, Serbia seems to intend to stand entirely on the defensive. Serbia's reply to the ultimatum, the text of which has not yet been obtainable, is said to have accepted all points, including punishment of all officers excepting those in senior command; also collaboration but with certain reservations. The diplomatic situation not quite clear. England and France desirous of peace, Italy likewise, the issue being unpopular and allegedly against Italian interests. Russia on the latest reports seems not yet to be mobilizing and to be willing for negotiations with Vienna over slight modifications of the demands not yet met by Serbia. Vienna's attitude to this so far unknown. I have sent word to all Cabinets that we regard Austro-Serbian conflict as an affair concerning these two states alone and have drawn Russia's attention to the consequences of any military measure in any way directed against ourselves.[3]

8. *Kaiser Wilhelm's frame of mind; the Potsdam meeting of 27 July.*

The reader will have been struck by the negligent, pedestrian style of this report, hardly calculated to give the Kaiser much enlightenment. He will further note: i. that up to the time the telegram was dispatched, i.e. 11.20 a.m. on Monday the 27th, Berlin had not yet read the text of the Serbian reply which had been handed to Giesl at 6 p.m. on the 25th, and which Jagow did not ask Tschirschky to let him have by wire until ten minutes after this telegram had gone off to the Kaiser,[4] a point to which we shall return later; ii. that this telegram and the one preceding it are completely silent on the pressure put on Vienna to attack Serbia without delay; iii. that there is no hint of Grey's proposal for a Four Power Conference and of the refusal which Berlin was about to return and did in fact return by a telegram dispatched at 1 p.m.[5] These omissions were all as intentional as was the loose uninformative style. It was clearly meant to avoid upsetting the Kaiser and make him

[1] DD. I, 230. [2] DD. I, 221. [3] DD. I, 245.
[4] DD. I, 246. [5] DD. I, 248.

think all was well, for fear that otherwise he might, by one of his sudden changes of front, topple over the beautiful castle that Bethmann and Jagow were busy building for his and their own glorification. For this same reason the dispatches sent on to him were often expurgated. Thus from Lichnowsky's telegram of the 26th the passages were omitted in which he gives Nicolson's and Tyrrell's opinion that no Russian Government could allow the Serbian frontier to be crossed and that in such an event Russia would be forced to attack Austria, and also Lichnowsky's warning that the localization of the conflict was an illusion.[1]

However the Kaiser, finding himself in the dark and mistrustful of what the Wilhelmstrasse was doing, had suddenly given the order for the return and, much to his Ministers' dismay, (Jagow voiced his 'regret' to Rumbold on the 26th[2]) arrived towards 1 p.m. on the 27th at Wildpark station, where he was met by Bethmann bringing the morning's dispatches. In what mood was Wilhelm? We know a certain number of his marginal notes to documents reaching him on his cruise, all in his most blustering, swaggering style clamouring for Austria to go ahead full speed and without fear. A dispatch from Schoen of 24 July provokes the outburst: 'Ultimata are either accepted or they are not! There is no discussion! That is why they have that name!'[3] That is the way the Kaiser solved problems. A little more political common sense is contained in his marginal note to a dispatch of Tschirschky's of 10 July:

The Sanjak is what Austria must definitely have back, so as to prevent the union of Serbia and Montenegro and the Serbs from reaching the sea.[4]

And to the news that Berchtold had promised Austrian territorial désintéressement to Kudashev his comment was: 'Donkey! They *must* take back the Sanjak, otherwise the Serbs will get to the Adriatic.' Berchtold's disclaimer of any intention on the part of Austria to shift the balance of power in the Balkans elicited the dictum:

That will and *must* come automatically. Austria must become preponderant over the other minor ones in the Balkans at the expense of Russia; otherwise there will be no peace.[5]

As might be expected, Grey's proposal for Four Power mediation found no favour with Wilhelm: 'I won't join in, or only if Austria expressly asks me to, which is not likely. In questions of honour and existence one does not consult others' runs a marginal note to Lichnowsky's dispatch of 24 July.[6]

[1] DD. I, 236.   [2] BD. XI, 147.   [3] DD. I, 154.
[4] DD. I, 29. See pp. 259–60.   [5] DD. I, 155.   [6] DD. I, 157.

The mediation was accepted by the Wilhelmstrasse in spite of the Imperial marginal notes, but that may have been because telegrams reached the *Hohenzollern* with delay and the comment was wirelessed to Berlin only at 11 p.m. on the 26th while Jagow's acceptance of mediation was telegraphed to Lichnowsky on the evening of the 25th.[1] How much authority Wilhelm exercised is illustrated by the following episode. The Chancellor heard from the Naval Chief of Staff that 'in consequence of a Wolff telegram' the Kaiser had ordered the fleet to prepare at once to return to base. He therefore 'ventured respectfully to suggest that Your Majesty should not for the moment order a premature return of the fleet'. Wilhelm was furious and his marginal comment, of which as usual the Foreign Minister took cognizance when the relevant document was returned to him, runs:

Incredible presumption! Unheard of! Never thought of such a thing!!! It was because of my Ambassador's announcement of the mobilization in Belgrade!! This *may* involve the mobilization of Russia; *will* involve the mobilization of Austria! In this case I must have my forces on land and sea together. There is not a single ship in the Baltic!! I am, moreover, not accustomed to taking military measures on the basis of a Wolff telegram, but in consideration of the General Situation and that the civilian Chancellor has not yet understood.[2]

Bethmann reverted to the subject on the 26th when news came in from the Naval Attaché in London that the English fleet was dismissing its reservists:

In view of this I humbly venture to propose that Your Majesty order the High Sea Fleet to remain in Norway for the present as this would considerably lighten England's planned mediation at St. Petersburg which is visibly faltering.[3]

Wilhelm's note runs:

There exists a Russian fleet! In the Baltic now on exercises are 5 Russian torpedo boat flotillas, all or part of which in 16 hours could be in position before the Belts and cut communications through them. Port Arthur should be a lesson! My fleet has orders to proceed to Kiel and to Kiel it shall go! W.

The fact is that the temperamental monarch did not feel able to stay still in the midst of so many threatening complications. When Bethmann telegraphed him on the 26th that in view of Germany's aim to localize the conflict it was necessary to keep calm so that Russia should not resort to any act of hostility, Wilhelm placed an exclamation mark against the word 'localization' and the words 'keep calm' were annotated: 'Quietness is the prime civic duty! Just quietness, always just quietness!! A quiet mobilization is certainly something new.'[4] And he hastened back home to watch events from close at hand.

[1] DD. I, 192. See p. 343.   [2] DD. I, 182.   [3] DD. I, 221.   [4] DD. I, 197.

In this he was not altogether wrong, at least from his own point of view. Things were moving towards war. How could one not take precautions and continue to see everything through rose-coloured spectacles like the Chancellor? Not that Wilhelm had any wish for war, as will soon become apparent. Bülow writes of him:

William II did not want war. He feared it. His bellicose marginal notes prove nothing. His exaggerations were mainly meant to ring in the ears of Privy Councillors at the Foreign Office, just as his more menacing jingo speeches were intended to give the foreigner the impression that here was another Frederick the Great or Napoleon. . . . William II did not want war, if only because he did not trust his nerves not to give way under the strain of any really critical situation. The moment there was danger His Majesty would become uncomfortably conscious that he could never lead an army in the field. . . . He was well aware that he was neurasthenic, without real capacity as a general, and still less able, in spite of his naval hobby, to have led a squadron or even captained a ship.[1]

When the others showed they were not afraid and held their ground, above all when Perfidious Albion raised her voice, the Kaiser prudently drew in his horns. Thus it had happened at Algeciras in 1906 and after Agadir in 1911, thus it would have happened in July 1914 if Wilhelm had had at his side a less inept Chancellor than the untrained, incapable, dull-witted Bethmann Hollweg. Tirpitz comes to similar conclusions:

When the Emperor did not consider that peace was threatened, he liked to give free play to his reminiscences of famous ancestors. In moments which he realized to be critical, on the other hand, he proceeded with extraordinary caution. If the Emperor had remained in Berlin, and if the normal government machinery had been at work, then the Emperor in spite of his only intermittent attention to foreign policy would probably have found ways and means of evading the danger of war about the middle of the month [of July]. As, however, the Chief of the General Staff, the Minister for War, the Chief of the Naval Staff, and myself were kept away from Berlin during the succeeding days, the whole business was monopolized by the Chancellor, who, having no experience himself of the larger European world, was unable to estimate correctly the value of his colleagues at the Foreign Ministry.[2]

Bülow writes:

Bethmann, so as not to be disturbed in the achievement of his 'diplomatic masterpiece' had advised his Sovereign on no account to abandon the usual North Sea trip.[3]

---

[1] Bülow, III, p. 149.
[2] Tirpitz, *Memoirs*, pp. 242-3.
[3] Bülow, III, p. 160.

He adds:

> When at last on 27 July, the Kaiser reached Berlin . . . his Chancellor awaited him on the platform, very humble, and with a pale and wretched face. His Sovereign put . . . the question: . . . 'How did it all happen?' . . . Count August Eulenburg was present at this scene. . . . He told me later that Bethmann, utterly cowed, admitted that all along he had been deceived and offered the Kaiser his resignation. His Majesty answered: 'You've cooked this broth and now you're going to eat it.'[1]

Something similar may have taken place, not on the 27th (even though Wilhelm's greeting to Bethmann on the 27th may have been not very friendly) but on the 29th when he summoned the military chiefs to tell them, as Tirpitz says, of his exchange of views with the Chancellor 'who had collapsed completely'.[2] On the 27th Wilhelm did not yet view the situation as beyond remedy.

During the afternoon of the 26th the information sent by Bethmann resulted in an optimistic estimate of the situation by those on board the *Hohenzollern*. At 4 p.m. Lyncker wrote to his wife:

> the Chancellor announces to the Kaiser that he and England are employed in localizing the war, i.e. limit it to the two Powers, or in other words keep Russia out of it. For us everything depends on the success of this. According to Russian press opinions, it is doubtful.

At 6 p.m. Lyncker wrote again:

> It looks like beginning to disentangle itself. Count Platen has just told me the Kaiser has just wirelessed to the Kaiserin that as soon as he has got the hang of the situation in Berlin he intends to go to Wilhelmshöhe. That does not look as if a European war were on the point of breaking out. Probably the Kaiser, who thought this morning that there would be war, has meanwhile had more reassuring news.[3]

Meanwhile Pourtalès's telegram, reporting his first conversation with Sazonov after the delivery of the ultimatum,[4] had been forwarded to the *Hohenzollern* on the evening of the 26th and produced the impression that 'the Russian Government does not intend to go to war immediately',[5] thus feeding the hope that Berlin diplomacy would manage to avert a conflict between the Great Powers.

When he got to Potsdam on the 27th the Kaiser immediately summoned the Chancellor and the Army chiefs to meet him at 3.10 p.m.

Moltke, the Commander-in-Chief of the army, who had arrived at Potsdam on the previous evening, wrote on the 27th to his wife that 'the situation continues to be extremely obscure. . . . It will be about another fortnight before anything definite can be known or said.[6]

---

[1] Bülow, III, p. 161. [2] Tirpitz, *Memoirs*, p. 274. [3] Bach, p. 20.
[4] DD. I, 160. [5] Bach, pp. 20-1. [6] Moltke, p. 381.

From this it would seem that it was not yet known whether Austria had declared war against Serbia or not, and it was understood that the Monarchy would not be ready to begin operations before 12 August. Moltke's letter was written in the forenoon of the 27th before the Potsdam meeting.

What happened at this meeting and what decisions were taken is not definitely known since no records of its proceedings exist. General Plessen, who was present, notes in his diary:

> First a long private talk with the Reichskanzler, after that with us soldiers. The Austrians are not nearly ready! It will be.the beginning of August before operations can begin. It is hoped to localize the war! England declares she means to remain neutral. I have the impression that it will all blow over.[1]

Falkenhayn, who was then Minister for War, was not present at this conference (any more than was the Navy Minister Tirpitz who returned to Berlin on the 27th of his own initiative and against the wishes of Bethmann Hollweg). Falkenhayn—according to his biographer—learnt by a side wind (*unter der Hand*) that the decision had been taken to 'fight the business out (*die Sache durchzufechten*), cost what it may'.[2] From this Bernadotte Schmitt concludes that at the Potsdam conference on 27 July no decision was taken to change the attitude of Germany towards Austria, even though it might involve her in war.[3]

The present writer put the question by letter to the ex-Kaiser Wilhelm and on 11 March 1936 received the following reply from his aide-de-camp:

> General Falkenhayn's remark that on 27 July he learnt *unter der Hand* that a decision had been taken 'to fight the business out, cost what it may' finds no support in the documents. And in fact it is without consistency. The remark probably only meant that the intention was to carry on honestly the policy pursued since 5 July of unconditional support for Austria-Hungary even in face of the threat of intervention by the *Entente* Powers. Decisions in this sense were not taken on 27 July. The best proof of this is the Kaiser's marginal comment to the Serbian note of reply to the Austro-Hungarian note. This marginal note which was immediately followed by His Majesty's letter to the Secretary of State, Jagow, with the proposal for a *Halt in Belgrade* was the beginning of the change in German policy towards Austria. Nay more: apart from the fact that Falkenhayn's source for this remark is rightly open to doubt, and therefore quoted even by him simply as *unter der Hand*, the expression *durchzufechten* does not in current usage mean that the aim pursued is to be attained by armed force. The word means rather that the line of policy pursued up to a given moment is to be maintained even in spite of certain circumstances.

---

[1] Bach, p. 22.   [2] Zwehl, p. 56.   [3] Schmitt, II, pp. 62-8.

It must be said that Falkenhayn's diary contains many inaccuracies even when speaking of occasions when he was present and took an active part, hence his statement carries no authority.[1] Moreover he adds that it still remained open whether this decision was final. In actual fact, if the decision had actually been taken, Falkenhayn would have been officially informed of it and not have learnt of it *unter der Hand*. It must be remembered that on 27 July Berlin still regarded the position as satisfactory. August Bach explains:

The reason for this was the reassuring news from St. Petersburg. In particular Count Pourtalès's proposal, which Sazonov accepted, that Sazonov should negotiate directly with Vienna on the basis of a softening of the Austrian demands seemed to offer prospects of an easing of the tension and to promise more success than Sir Edward Grey's proposal for a conference which the Chancellor and Foreign Office declined that same day.[2]

Thus no doubt the Chancellor's report to the Kaiser was optimistic in tone and General Plessen's diary entry accurately reflects this optimism. Bach explains:

Since the beginning of Austrian operations against Serbia was not to be reckoned on for another couple of weeks, it is clear that on 27 July the political and military directors in Berlin thought that they had enough time ahead of them for diplomatic negotiations.[3]

One thing is certain, namely that Wilhelm on the afternoon of the 27th did not have the text of the Serbian reply laid before him. The question is whether it had yet been received by the Wilhelmstrasse. We have already seen that neither Bethmann nor Jagow had taken the trouble to ask Vienna for it at once. They only began to think of such a thing on the morning of the 27th. They knew that the Kaiser had been incensed at learning of the Austrian note not from his Government but from a press agency.[4] Now he was coming home again and nobody was able to tell him the exact terms of the Serbian reply! Therefore at 11.30 a.m. on the 27th Jagow had telegraphed to Tschirschky: 'Please wire text of Serbian reply by return.'[5] Lest this request might be regarded in Vienna as a symptom of a change of mind Jagow hastened to reassure Szögyény that it was needed

in order to demonstrate the wrongness of the statement made in England that the Serbian answer meets our wishes on the main points.[6]

But the text of the Serbian reply had been telegraphed on the evening of the 25th by the Serbian Government to the Serbian Chargé d'Affaires

---

[1] In this connexion the differences may be noted between Falkenhayn's diary and the more reliable diary of Moltke in their account of the events of 1 August. (Zwehl, p. 59; Moltke, pp. 19–23.)

[2] Bach, p. 22.   [3] Bach, p. 22.   [4] DD. I, 231.

[5] DD. I, 246.   [6] Oe-U. VIII, 10790.

at Berlin. He received it on the evening of the 26th and left it with Jagow on the 27th. At what hour? Szögyény, who learnt of the fact from Jagow, gives the hour as 'noon' in a dispatch sent off at 5.50 p.m.[1] Jules Cambon in a dispatch of the 27th to the Quai d'Orsay reports that he asked Jagow whether he had studied the Serbian reply 'which the Serbian Chargé d'Affaires had handed him this morning' and had received the reply: 'I have not yet had time.'[2] It seems possible, therefore, that the note may have been left with Jagow by the Serbian Chargé d'Affaires after Jagow had telegraphed Vienna for the text in order to study it. This would bring the time very close to 'noon'. One thing certain is that in the archives of the Wilhelmstrasse the document is entered as having arrived in the afternoon of the 27th.[3] But if Jagow had it by noon why did he not bring it to the Potsdam meeting?

A footnote to the *Deutsche Dokumente*[4] says that the 'somewhat illegible' telegram was handed over with a brief accompanying note during the day of the 27th and that the exact hour could not be determined. But it was not the note's illegibility which Jagow alleged as his reason for not having yet studied the note, nor does any such illegibility figure in the telegram to Szögyény asking for the text.[5] And how was it rendered legible for submission to the Kaiser? Was this achieved by the copy sent by return from Vienna? The answer to this question is no! because Vienna made no haste to send it. Tschirschky did not answer until 1.45 a.m. on the 28th, having been told by Macchio that

the office was too overburdened to prepare a copy of the lengthy note so quickly. But everything possible would be done to let me have the note this evening (i.e. the 27th).

---

[1] Oe-U. VIII, 10790.—Hein Sasse in a study 'Daten zum Kriegsausbruch' published in the *Berliner Monatshefte*, August 1934, p. 712, also gives 'noon' as the hour.

[2] LJF. 74; CDD., pp. 191–2; DF. 3. XI, 167.—J. Cambon replied: 'I regret this. You would see that except on some points of detail Serbia has yielded entirely. It appears then that, since Austria has obtained the satisfaction which your support has procured for her, you might to-day advise her to be content or to examine with Serbia the terms of the latter's reply.' Cambon pressed Jagow to agree to Grey's proposal for a conference and received the usual reply that Jagow ' did not refuse to act to settle the Austro-Russian conflict but could not intervene in the Austro-Serbian conflict'. J. Cambon asked him 'whether Germany wanted war' and said that, if not, Jagow must act accordingly. Jagow 'said he was ready to unite with England and France in a common effort but a form must be found for this intervention which he could accept'. Then with the usual hypocrisy he added: 'Moreover, direct conversations have been entered upon between Vienna and St. Petersburg and are in progress; I expect very good results from them and am hopeful.'

[3] DD. I, 270, 271.—Jules Cambon wrote to Luciano Magrini that Jagow received the Serbian reply at 11 a.m. on the 27th and that his own conversation with Jagow took place at 4–5 p.m. on the same day.

[4] DD. I, 270.

[5] Oe-U. VIII, 10790.

He got it at 11.30 p.m. on the 27th, but as it had been given to the press that same evening, he did not think it worth while to telegraph it.[1] The delay in Vienna was obviously intentional. But to the present writer it seems that Jagow's delay in laying the Serbian note before the Kaiser was no less intentional. Even supposing it to have been impossible for him to bring it personally at 3 p.m. why did he wait to send it to Potsdam by special messenger leaving Berlin only at 9.30 p.m.? It certainly looks as if he meant it to come so late that the Kaiser would not read it till the morning of the 28th, when Austria was to declare war on Serbia, as was made known to Berlin at 4.37 p.m. on the 27th as we shall see. The Chancellor was to use similar tactics next day to make an order from the Kaiser arrive too late. The Wilhelmstrasse must have acquired considerable skill in circumventing the unexpected moves of its impulsive Sovereign. In this case, it happened that he began to perceive the true situation sooner than did his advisers.

We have already seen that the telegram sent to catch the Kaiser en route in the royal train on the morning of the 27th said nothing of the proposal made by Grey on the 26th to submit the whole Austro-Russo-Serbian dispute to a conference of ambassadors.[2] But at Potsdam Bethmann can hardly have continued to hide the fact. What the Kaiser said, we do not know. But just before going to Wildpark station to meet him, Bethmann had telegraphed to Lichnowsky declining the proposal and must have told Wilhelm of this, if not of the official rejection conveyed by Jagow to Goschen. Thus Wilhelm was confronted with a *fait accompli* which he could not undo. Would he have done so, had he been able? We have the answer in a marginal note to Flotow's dispatch of the 27th from Rome which reached Berlin at 1.28 p.m. and outlined San Giuliano's proposal for getting the Great Powers to dictate terms which Serbia would then accept. That Serbia would do this was described by the Kaiser as 'rubbish'. And beside Flotow's news of Grey's proposal for an ambassadors' conference he wrote: 'I will not have anything to do with such a thing.'[3] However, a telegram sent to the Kaiser by the Chancellor to arrive first thing on the 28th[4] indirectly shows that at Potsdam it was decided to show more regard for the English proposal since Lichnowsky was reporting that Germany's refusal to restrain Vienna was arousing mistrust in London.[5]

9. *The Grey-Lichnowsky conversation of 27 July; the German Government's duplicity; a telegram from Szögyény.*

On the morning of Monday, the 27th, Lichnowsky had called on Grey who had returned from the country on the Sunday evening.

[1] DD. II, 280.   [2] DD. I, 245.   [3] DD. I, 249.

[4] DD. II, 283.   [5] DD. I, 258.

Grey had told him that the Serbian reply had complied with the Austrian demands

to a degree which he would never have thought possible. . . . Now he made an appeal to us to use our influence with Vienna to have the reply from Belgrade regarded either as satisfactory or as a basis for negotiations.

Lichnowsky in making this report had added that Grey had spoken very seriously and had for the first time seemed out of humour. His own conviction was

that if war now comes, we could no longer count on English sympathies and British support, since the Austrian action would be regarded as showing all signs of lack of good will. Everybody here is convinced, and I hear the same thing from my colleagues, that the key to the situation is Berlin and if Berlin seriously means peace, Austria can be restrained from pursuing a foolhardy policy, as Grey calls it.[1]

This telegram had been followed on the same day by two others, sent off at 5 p.m. and 6.27 p.m. respectively. The first of these said: 'our entire future relations with England', 'the most important point in our foreign policy', would now be decided. If Germany held Austria back from making war 'our relations to Great Britain would in all the foreseeable future have the confidential and intimate character which has signalized them for the last eighteen months'. If the opposite were to be the case 'I think that it will never again be possible to reconstitute the threads which have latterly bound us together'. The warning message continued:

Here the impression gains ground, and I noticed it clearly in my talk with Sir Edward Grey, that the whole Serbian question is working up to a trial. of strength between Triple Alliance and Triple *Entente*. Should Austria's intention to use the present occasion to crush Servia, as Sir E. Grey expressed it, become still more evident, England will, I am convinced, range herself on the side of France and Russia, in order to show that she does not mean to tolerate a moral or still more a military defeat of her group. If war comes in these conditions we shall have England against us. The feeling that, in view of the far-reaching compliance of the Serbian Government, the war might have been avoided will be of decisive importance for the attitude of the British Government.[2]

The second of these telegrams continued to warn that Grey

makes a sharp distinction between the Austro-Serbian and Austro-Russian conflict, i.e. he would not interfere in the Austro-Serbian, as long as it did not develop into an Austro-Russian conflict. But now he finds himself obliged to intervene, since it threatens to develop into an Austro-Russian and hence a European conflict. Thus the Austro-Russian conflict is inseparable

[1] DD. I, 258. See pp. 410-11.   [2] DD. I, 265.

from the Austro-Serbian . . . as Grey said to me. An understanding between Austria and Russia hangs on the settlement of the Austro-Serbian rift. Without this settlement, according to opinion here, all mediation is useless. How can I advocate localization of the conflict when nobody here doubts that Austria-Hungary's procedure jeopardizes serious Russian interests, and that, if we exercise no pressure on Austria, Russia will be forced to intervene against her will? I only make people shrug their shoulders in amusement.

If an agreement between Vienna and St. Petersburg on the basis of the Serbian note were attainable without the use of military measures against Serbia, Sir E. Grey would have achieved all that he desires. What he wants to avoid is an Austrian passage of arms with Serbia because he fears this will disturb the peace of Europe. He confirms, to-day, that no Russian call-up of reserves has taken place.[1]

If after reading these telegrams one looks again at Grey's own account of the conversation of the 27th written to Goschen at Berlin[2] one receives the impression that he was far from displaying the force, the warmth, the close-knit reasoning attributed to him by Lichnowsky and that he did not use all the arguments put in his mouth. This is not so much the case in the first telegram which is approximately identical with that of Grey, as in the second and third. *Facit indignatio versum*, and Lichnowsky's indignation, basing its language on words used by Grey which were beginning to be very downright, did not remain without influence on the German Government. Their effect was strengthened by the news, reaching Berlin on the 27th, that the English fleet, which was to disperse on that day, had received the order to remain together. Did this mean that the Chancellor's basic calculation was wrong and that England would not remain neutral in a possible Continental war? Bethmann did not yet think so. However on receiving Lichnowsky's first telegram at 4.37 p.m. and the two others at 8.40 p.m. he telegraphed to Tschirschky at 11.50 p.m. the text of the first one with the omission of its last paragraph which runs:

Everybody here is convinced, and I hear the same thing from my colleagues, that the key to the situation is Berlin and if Berlin seriously means peace, Austria can be restrained from pursuing a foolhardy policy, as Grey calls it.

In place of it, he wrote:

After our having declined an English proposal for a conference, it is impossible for us to reject this English suggestion *a limine*. By a rejection of all mediatory action we should be held responsible for the conflagration by the whole world and be represented as the real warmongers. This would make our own position in the country impossible where we should appear as having been forced into war. Our position is all the more difficult as

---

[1] DD. I, 266.   [2] BD. XI, 176.

Serbia has apparently yielded very much. We cannot therefore reject the rôle of mediator and must submit the English proposal to the Vienna Cabinet for consideration, as London and Paris are all the time using their influence with St. Petersburg. I want Count Berchtold's views on the English suggestion and on M. Sazonov's desire to negotiate directly with Vienna.[1]

Five hours later, i.e. at 5 a.m. on the 28th, the Chancellor was sending the following letter to the Kaiser:

I humbly submit to Your Majesty a telegram that has just arrived from Prince Lichnowsky. On Your Majesty's instructions I have submitted Sir Edward Grey's suggestion to Count Berchtold. It will be for Austria to decide what attitude she will take to it. Were we to reject the rôle of mediator *a limine*, since London and Paris are all the time using their influence with St. Petersburg, we should stand before all the world as responsible for the conflagration and as the real war makers. That would on the one hand make it impossible for us to maintain the present good mood in our own country and on the other cause England to give up her neutrality.[2]

Thus Grey's latest plea that Germany should use persuasion in order that Vienna might accept the Serbian reply or regard it as a basis for negotiation was submitted 'to Berchtold by Bethmann Hollweg *on Wilhelm's instructions*. And since Wilhelm had not yet seen it when he came to Potsdam to meet the Chancellor—the relevant telegram not having yet arrived in Berlin—and since Bethmann had no further communication with Wilhelm after that meeting, it follows that, even if at Potsdam Wilhelm did not favour the acceptance of Grey's proposal of the 26th to submit the Austro-Serbo-Russian dispute to a conference of the four ambassadors in London (a proposal already rejected by Bethmann), he at least must have thought that it would be wise to be more considerate in dealing with England. Otherwise the Chancellor's allusion to Wilhelm's 'instructions' would not make sense. It now remains to be seen whether, in passing on Grey's proposal, Bethmann was acting in good faith, i.e. whether Berlin did or did not want it to be accepted by Vienna.

The German historians all claim that he was acting in good faith, that his telegram to Tschirschky of 27 July is the first sign of a German change of attitude to one of sincere endeavour to bring about Austrian acceptance of compromise and conciliation. This is, however, far from being the case. Bethmann Hollweg did, indeed, change his attitude, but not until 48 hours later. On the evening of the 27th all the Chancellor sought to do was to throw dust in the eyes of Grey and lead him to believe that Berlin was seriously trying to avert a conflict, that if war broke out it would be Russia's fault and that England could

---

[1] DD. I, 277.   [2] DD. II, 283.

therefore remain neutral. To convince oneself of this one must carefully read the text of the telegram to Tschirschky. It did not withdraw the pressure on Austria to begin military operations against Serbia at once, nor did it make any suggestion that Vienna should defer the declaration of war, which Berlin expected to take place on the following day, the 28th, or at the latest on the 29th. On the contrary, the Chancellor coolly talks of a European conflagration, which he does nothing to prevent, his only concern being that he shall not appear to have provoked it. Hence no message was sent recommending that Vienna fall in with the English suggestion, which Berlin could not do otherwise than pass on there. What Bethmann asked to know was simply Berchtold's opinion on the matter. Nor is this all. The Chancellor could not but have an opinion of his own on a question involving German solidarity with Austria in a possible European war. That opinion was that Austria should remain intransigent and lose no time in attacking Serbia. All this is made unmistakably clear in the astounding and notorious dispatch sent to Berchtold by the Austrian Ambassador Szögyény at 9.15 on the 27th, more than two hours before Bethmann sent his telegram to Tschirschky, and here reproduced in full:

The Secretary of State told me very definitely in a strictly confidential form that in the immediate future mediation proposals from England will possibly (*eventuell*) be brought to Your Excellency's knowledge by the German Government. The German Government, he says, tenders the most binding assurances that it in no way associates itself with the proposals, is even decidedly against their being considered, and only passes them on in order to conform to the English request. In so doing the Government proceeds from the standpoint that it is of the greatest importance that England at the present moment should not make common cause with Russia and France. Consequently everything must be avoided that might disconnect the telegraph line between Germany and England which till now has been in good working order. Were Germany to say flatly to Sir E. Grey that she is not willing to pass on his wishes to Austria-Hungary, by whom England believes these wishes will sooner find consideration if Germany is the intermediary, then the situation would arise which, as has just been said, must at all costs be avoided. The German Government would, moreover, in respect of any other request of England to Vienna, assure the latter most emphatically that it in no way supports any such demands for intervention in regard to Austria-Hungary and only passes them on to comply with the wish of England. For instance only yesterday the English Government approached him, the Secretary of State, through the German Ambassador to London and directly through its own representative here, asking him to support the wish of England in regard to a toning down by us of the note to Serbia. He, Jagow, gave answer that he would certainly fulfil Sir E. Grey's wish and pass on England's desire to Your Excellency, but that he could not support it himself, since the Serbian conflict was a question of prestige for the Austro-Hungarian Monarchy in which Germany was also involved. He, the Secretary of State, had therefore passed on Sir E. Grey's note to Herr von Tschirschky, but without giving him instructions to submit it to Your Excellency; thereupon he had been able to inform the English Cabinet, that he did not directly decline the English wish, and had even forwarded it to Vienna. In conclusion the Secretary of State reiterated his standpoint to me and, in order to prevent any misunderstanding, asked me to assure your Excellency that, also in the case just adduced, he, in acting as intermediary, was not in the slightest degree in favour of consideration being given to the English wish.[1]

This amazing document proves: (i) that the telegram sent by Bethmann to Vienna at 11.50 p.m. communicating Lichnowsky's dispatch and submitting Grey's proposal for mediation to Berchtold had the sole aim of creating an alibi for Germany in the eyes of Grey; (ii) that Vienna was flatly to reject both this proposal and any other that Germany might be obliged to pass on to her in order not to 'disconnect the telegraph line between Germany and England which till now has been in good working order'. No stronger shaft of light could fall on the guilt and duplicity of the German Government, and the propagandists of German innocence ought to have been silenced by it. But they have recourse to their usual expedients, indeed display special zeal in view of the gravity of the speech attributed to Jagow. They maintain that Szögyény was an old dotard who misunderstood what was said to him and who was on the point of being replaced by Prince Hohenlohe. Questioned by the commission of four German experts at the Peace Conference, Bethmann Hollweg and Jagow denied ever having made the statements alleged by Szögyény in the first two sentences of the dispatch. Jagow stated that he found it difficult and often exasperating to talk with Szögyény. Another assertion made by German or pro-German historians is that the form of the dispatch is obscure at certain points and that it makes statements contradicted by the facts. For instance, there has been a lot of discussion to decide whether in the sentence beginning: 'The German Government would moreover (*Die deutsche Regierung würde übrigens*)' the word 'the latter' (German *demselben*) refers to England or Vienna. Both are neuter and hence in gender the word could agree with either. Renouvin accepts Montgelas's interpretation that England is meant.[2] Berchtold, in a letter of 29 January 1934 to the present writer, takes it as referring to Grey who is only mentioned in the preceding sentence!

[1] Oe-U. VIII, 10793.

[2] Renouvin, pp. 121–5. The German historian Hermann Lutz notes that Szögyény's account finds confirmation in the whole behaviour of Berlin up to that moment and in its pressure for a declaration of war, and that it completely coincides with the attitude of Berlin towards Tschirschky's telegram of the 27th reporting that the declaration of war would follow 'to-morrow, at the latest the day after to-morrow, in order to cut away the ground from any attempt at intervention' (DD. I, 257), i.e. that Berlin raised no objections to this decision and therefore approved of it (Lutz, pp. 141–2).

10. *Bethmann Hollweg's double game and the motive of his* démarche *at Vienna.*

There is no need to weary the reader with a detailed examination of every phrase in a dispatch which Szögyény probably dashed off in haste before going to dinner. It is of minor importance whether in this or that particular it is inaccurate or whether *demselben* refers to Vienna or London. Even if it does refer to London, this does not change the general import of the dispatch which is our concern here. Now is it conceivable that the experienced Ambassador Szögyény, whose dispatches were usually read by Tschirschky, could have invented all of a piece the speech which he puts into the mouth of Jagow packed with news and confidences which Jagow alone was in a position to give? And what, in such a case, would have been his aim? Moreover, how could he give advance information of Bethmann's next step, unless he had been told of it by the Secretary of State? But this is not all. There is a further and still more important consideration, namely that this dispatch of Szögyény's, like others of his that have or have not been called in question, forms so necessary a link in the chain of diplomatic documents, that without it the logical reconstruction of the actions of Berlin, and thus indirectly of Vienna in the days preceding the Austrian declaration of war on Serbia, would be rendered impossible. If in studying the documents of the various countries there is one fact which particularly strikes the student who approaches them with an open mind, it is that the documents fit together to perfection, for example Lichnowsky's version of a talk with Grey finds perfect corroboration in Grey's account of the same talk sent to Rumbold or Goschen. The same holds good of Berchtold's talks with Tschirschky and so forth. There is nothing strange in this, since normally neither ministers nor ambassadors have any motive for falsifying the character of the things they hear and say. But the concordance even exceeds all that the student might expect, and when, as sometimes in the French Diplomatic Documents, he finds versions which reveal discrepancies, he has little difficulty in distinguishing the false from the true. But in the present case of Szögyény's dispatch there is no need to make any such investigation. It tallies perfectly with all the other known documents and is indeed, an indispensable link in the series.

To convince ourselves still further of this, let us first investigate what were the English proposals for mediation which 'will possibly (*eventuell*) be brought to Your Excellency's (i.e. Berchtold's) knowledge'. Were they those for an ambassadors' conference put forward by England on the 26th, or those made by Grey to Lichnowsky on the morning of the 27th that Germany should resolve 'to use her influence with Vienna to have the reply from Belgrade regarded either as satisfactory or as a basis for negotiations'? German historians generally assume the latter. Indeed what motive could Jagow have for getting

Szögyény to report to Vienna, with such circumspection and apologies, that it was Grey's proposal for an ambassadors' conference which would 'possibly (*eventuell*) be brought' to Berchtold's knowledge? This proposal, made known to Vienna in the afternoon of the 27th by a telegram from Mensdorff in London, had already been flatly rejected by Bethmann and Jagow.

Had Jagow intended a reference to that, he would have accompanied the allusion with news of his having rejected it as a gesture of solidarity with Austria. He would never have assumed, as he does, the contrite air of one who on somebody else's behalf has to pass on a disagreeable message to a friend and begs him not to bear a grudge on that account and to take no notice of the message. Indeed the fact that the English proposal for an ambassadors' conference was never passed on by Berlin to Vienna is made perfectly plain in DD. I, 277 which states: 'After our having already declined an English proposal for a conference. . . .' What DD. I, 277 does pass on to Vienna is Lichnowsky's telegram of 27 July reporting his conversation with Grey in which the latter asked Berlin to use its good offices so that Vienna should consider the Serbian reply 'either as satisfactory or as a basis for negotiation'. Thus Jagow's apologetic message transmitted by Szögyény can only be the preliminary announcement of the instruction telegraphed by Bethmann to Tschirschky two and a half hours later. And the 'possibly' can only mean that when Jagow spoke to Szögyény Bethmann was still uncertain whether or not to pass on Grey's last suggestion to Vienna and in fact only made up his mind at 11.50 p.m.

While most historians take this view, the American professor Fay, one of the most able and temperate in the defence of Germany, endeavours to prove the other thesis. His motive is clear and is, indeed, stated by himself: 'If Szogyény's telegram is trustworthy, it would throw a sinister light upon the sincerity of Bethmann's action'.[1] And as there is no doubt that Jagow's allusion was to Grey's proposal of the 27th, and as there is no valid reason to impugn the trustworthiness of Szögyény's report to Berchtold of what he had been told by Jagow, it may in truth be said to 'throw a sinister light upon the sincerity' of the German *démarche* for mediation on the evening of the 27th.

Let us try to reconstruct how this *démarche* was carried out. Grey in his talk with Lichnowsky had reasoned approximately as follows: since Germany can do anything she likes with Vienna and since the Serbian reply complies practically entirely with the Austrian demands, it is for Germany to prove her love of peace by persuading Austria either to be satisfied with this reply or to regard it as a basis for negotiation. Lichnowsky made a moving appeal to Berlin to meet the English

[1] Fay, II, 414.

wish, pointing out the dangers of yet another refusal. But the Chancellor was on the one hand not yet convinced of the danger and still hoped to cover himself with glory by inducing Europe to accept the 'localization of the conflict', while on the other he was not in a position to beat a retreat easily because—and this is the key to the whole matter—it was Germany who had driven Austria on to act immediately against Serbia and had got her to the point of declaring war. By a most singular stroke of fate Lichnowsky's dispatch reporting his conversation of the morning with Grey arrived at 4.37 p.m. on the 27th, the exact moment of arrival of Tschirschky's telegram saying that the Austrian declaration of war on Serbia was to take place on the 28th or at the latest on the 29th.

What was Bethmann to do? Was he to perform an act of supreme courage, admit the mistakenness of the course he had taken and the impossibility of 'localizing the conflict', and appeal to Vienna to postpone the declaration of war and declare willingness to negotiate? This would have been the best moment to draw back. Later on, retreat would be more difficult if not impossible. But Bethmann either could or would not understand this. He obviously thought he could stand firm and that the best solution (in conformity with an order of which we do not know the nature, received from the Kaiser at Potsdam) would be to pass Grey's new suggestion on to Vienna with advice to reject it, and to tell London that German mediation, in accordance with Grey's suggestion, was being undertaken in order that Grey might believe in Germany's innocence and love of peace. Why, then, did he not give this advice openly to Vienna in the telegram sent to Tschirschky? This is a fair question which pro-German historians may ask their opponents. They can justifiably object that if Bethmann wanted to say something to Vienna it could be said directly without recourse to the subterfuge of making it known through Szögyény. But in fact the subterfuge is easily explained. The Chancellor's double game of feigning to satisfy Grey while advising Berchtold not to yield was not one of which Wilhelm would have approved. He had been kept in the dark about the pressure put on Vienna to attack Serbia at once and now he was not told of what Jagow said to Szögyény, who had come to be used as the go-between when messages had to be conveyed to the Ballplatz of which it was not desired to keep a documentary record at the Wilhelmstrasse. Bethmann probably feared that Wilhelm might not approve of his manoeuvre and might take some vigorous action of his own. Moreover at Potsdam he had given Bethmann orders which the latter says he was obeying in sending Lichnowsky's telegram on to Tschirschky. Did these orders perhaps conflict with what Jagow said to Szögyény?

This seems very likely. And it is certain that there was the intention to leave no trace of the double game in the records of the Wilhelm-strasse. This explains why Szögyény was summoned to listen to Jagow's message (which he telegraphed on at 9.15 p.m. on the 27th) that an English proposal for mediation would possibly (*eventuell*) be passed on, at the same time giving Vienna a formal assurance that the German Government did not associate itself with the proposal, in fact actually advised its rejection and only passed it on in deference to Grey's wish. All misgivings as to the wisdom of this manoeuvre must no doubt have vanished when at 8.40 p.m. on the 27th Lichnowsky's two later telegrams came in. Hence at 11.50 p.m. the telegram went off to Tschirschky with instructions to make the sham *démarche* at Vienna; at the same moment another, of course, was dispatched to Lichnowsky saying:

In the sense desired by Sir Edward Grey we have at once begun mediatory action at Vienna. In addition to the English suggestion we have also sub-mitted to Count Berchtold Sazonov's wish for direct discussions.[1]

Lichnowsky was completely taken in and on the 28th hastened to write the glad news to Grey adding in good faith: 'I begin to hope that it has once more been possible, owing to Anglo-German col-laboration, to save the peace of Europe.'[2] He must no doubt have per-ceived the baselessness of this hope very soon after, on learning of the Austrian declaration of war on Serbia. And here it is necessary to revert to an observation already made which supports the assumptions now being put forward. Since the Chancellor already knew that, far from accepting the Serbian note as satisfactory or as a basis for negotia-tion, Austria was to declare war on the 28th or at the latest on the 29th, would not Bethmann's first request, if his move for conciliation had been sincere, have been to ask for a postponement of the declara-tion of war? His complete silence on this point shows that he wished the declaration of war to be made, so that Europe should be faced with a *fait accompli*. His calculation was that Grey would be satisfied with Germany's show of good will and would resign himself to the *fait accompli*, concentrating his efforts on composing the Austro-Russian conflict, a matter which Berlin also had at heart and would gladly help to bring about, once the 'localization of the conflict' had been achieved.

That this was the train of reasoning may also be deduced from another singular telegram sent by Bethmann to Lichnowsky that same night. The night of 27/28 July was one of great activity for the Chan-cellor. At 11.50 p.m. on the 27th, as we have seen, he offered his mediation to Vienna, at 5 a.m. on the 28th he gave news of this to the Kaiser, and between these two messages, he sent off another to Lichnowsky which has received little attention from historians.

[1] DD. I, 278.   [2] BD. XI, 236.

Referring to Grey's wish that Austria should regard the Serbian reply as satisfactory or as a basis for negotiation Bethmann writes:

The former demand is impracticable. We cannot possibly advise Vienna subsequently to sanction the Serbian reply which, at the first moment and without our seeing it, they had rejected as unsatisfactory. We have gone very far towards meeting England by undertaking mediatory action in respect of the second request. I definitely rely on England's duly appreciating the step we have taken to meet her wishes. Whether the Serbian reply goes to the limits of what is possible I have not yet been able to examine, as it has only just come into my hands. It is a suspicious fact that Serbia has mobilized before giving her reply. That looks as if she had a bad conscience.

Sir Edward's assumption that Austria has designs to overthrow Serbia seems to me the more groundless as she has expressly declared to Russia that she has no territorial ambitions and does not intend to infringe the integrity of the Serbian Kingdom, a declaration which has not failed to produce its effect on Russia. Austria on the other hand wants, and has not only the right but the duty to want, security against having her existence further undermined by Pan-Serb agitation which has finally found its expression in the Sarajevo crime. That is absolutely nothing to do with a policy of prestige or with playing off the Triple Alliance against the Triple *Entente*.

Much as it is our endeavour to maintain European peace in full harmony with England and, it is to be hoped, in further co-operation with her, we cannot admit the right of Russia or even of the Triple *Entente* to take sides against Austria in favour of Serbian intrigues.

I request Your Excellency to frame your language in accordance with these views.[1]

Thus Grey's first proposal of an ambassadors' conference was impracticable. In regard to the second the German Government did not decline to offer mediation but did not say that Vienna ought to accept it and regard the Serbian note as a basis for discussion. On the contrary a series of arguments was brought forward to prove Austria's good right, as against the Triple *Entente*, which had no right to interfere. And not a word was mentioned of the imminent declaration of war, although Bethmann knew that Grey's proposal was aimed at preventing an armed clash between Austria and Serbia which would drag Russia into the conflict. Nor was it said that, once war was declared, all discussion on the Serbian reply would become impossible.

Tschirschky had no great difficulty in fathoming the wish of Berlin. Instead of losing no time on the morning of the 28th in acquainting Berchtold with the contents of Bethmann's telegram, he waited until after the Austrian declaration of war had gone off at 11 a.m.[2] and then saw Berchtold in the afternoon.[3] Whether he did this of his own initiative or acting on instructions remains to be seen. But in any case

[1] DD. II, 279. [2] DD. II, 311. [3] DD. II, 313.

Tschirschky perfectly acted up to the Chancellor's double game. It failed because it gambled on cards which did not and, indeed, could not turn up in the pack. But its failure does not entitle historians to assail the truth, established by a series of documents all proving that on the night of 27–28 July the 'localization' thesis still determined the actions of the German Government, so that it did nothing in good earnest or in good faith to brake the downward course to catastrophe and that its change of front does not date from that night in which, had it so willed, it would have been in time to hold Austria back from declaring war on Serbia with all the fatal consequences which this act brought in its train. Thus Montgelas has no grounds for his statement that Bethmann's telegram of the evening of the 27th was sent in good faith and to base on this the assertion: 'The fixed principle of non-interference in the Austro-Serbian conflict was thus abandoned by Germany.'[1]

On the contrary it is Kautsky who correctly summarizes the Chancellor's moves as follows:

Nor does he recommend the English proposal, he merely transmits it, and apologizes for the fact that circumstances oblige him to do so. To London, however, he telegraphs: 'We have at once undertaken mediation movement in Vienna in the sense desired by Sir Edward Grey.' The result of the 'mediation movement' was that Austria declared war on Serbia on 28 July.[2]

Poincaré, too, makes a very accurate and apt reconstruction of Bethmann's acts on the evening of the 27th:

In conclusion the Chancellor asks Count Berchtold for his opinion and with Lichnowsky takes credit to himself for having at once begun a mediatory action at Vienna in the direction desired by Sir Edward Grey. But, as M. Sazonov remarks, 'the principal occupation of M. Bethmann Hollweg then was, not to save the peace, but to present events in a light which would create the impression that Germany had been forced into war'. Thus the Imperial Chancellor only seeks to cover himself. At the hour in which he is writing he knows from Tschirschky's telegram, which had arrived in Berlin at 4.30 p.m., that Count Berchtold is about to send off the declaration of war to Serbia. He knows that the English proposal has by Sir E. Grey been made dependent on the essential condition that Austria shall abstain from all military operations. And yet he does not give up his obstinate idea of not intervening between Austria and Serbia. He makes no gesture, he utters no word to stop the firing of the first shell.[3]

Not even on the 28th did the Chancellor change his mind since, as Bernadotte Schmitt pertinently observes,[4] he sent a round telegram to

---

[1] Montgelas, *The Case for the Central Powers*, p. 135.   [2] Kautsky, pp. 183–4.
[3] Poincaré, IV, p. 353.   [4] Schmitt, II, p. 74.

the Prussian envoys to the Governments of the other member States of the Reich in which he said:

The Serbian Government's reply to the demands presented by the Austro-Hungarian Government on the 23rd of this month through its representative at Belgrade makes it clear that responsible quarters in Serbia do not intend to give up their previous policy and subversive activity. Consequently the Austro-Hungarian Government, if it does not mean definitely to renounce its position as a Great Power, has no other choice than to enforce its demands by strong pressure and, if need be, by resort to military measures.[1]

Further developments and further warnings were to be necessary before the Chancellor became convinced of his error and began to make desperate efforts to beat a retreat. By then, alas, it was too late.

11. *German pressure for immediate war on Serbia and Conrad's objections.*

That Berchtold did not mean to go to war with Serbia after the breaking off of diplomatic relations is beyond doubt. On 24 July he had sent word to Grey that if the '*démarche* with a time limit' at Belgrade expired without a result, it would be provisionally followed by the breaking off of diplomatic relations and the beginning of military preparations, i.e. not of operations. In the matter of the declaration of war he had not kept his word and, indeed, had instructed Mensdorff to say, as his own personal opinion, to Grey that Serbia would still have time to comply with the Austrian demands by accepting them integrally and reimbursing the expenditure incurred by the Monarchy for mobilization. Thus in the period between the rupture of diplomatic relations on 25 July and the beginning of operations, fixed by Conrad for 12 August, the Powers would have ample time to exert pressure on Belgrade to submit and thereby avoid all complications. And that Serbia should submit was perhaps the wish both of Berchtold and of Francis Joseph, who had repeatedly said that the break did not yet mean war, as Berchtold said to Giesl on 26 July.[2]

But while Berchtold was at Ischl the Ballplatz received Szögyény's telegram, which had left Berlin at 2.12 p.m. on the 25th reaching Vienna at 8 p.m. and which said:

Here it is universally taken for granted that an eventual negative reply by Serbia will be followed by a declaration of war from us and military operations. Any delay in commencing military operations is regarded here as a great danger because of the interference of other Powers. They urgently advise us to go ahead and confront the world with a *fait accompli*.[3]

Finding this telegram on returning to his office on the morning of the 26th Berchtold decided to summon the Chief of Staff, Conrad, and

[1] DD. II, 307.   [2] See pp. 374-7.   [3] Oe-U. VIII, 10656. See p. 426.

the German Ambassador Tschirschky, whose report of the conversation to Berlin at 4.10 p.m. runs:

Count Berchtold read out to me Count Szögyény's telegram saying that
to avoid the risk as far as possible of intervention by third parties, Berlin
regarded the greatest speed in military operations and the earliest declaration of war as advisable. The Minister had already summoned Baron von
Hötzendorf to discuss this point and he appeared while I was with the
Minister. To the Commander-in-Chief I warmly advocated our standpoint
which was fully shared by Count Berchtold. Baron von Hötzendorf alleged
that it was above all necessary to avoid opening the campaign with inadequate
forces. The Hungarian army corps on the Serbian northern frontier would of
course be ready to march in a very short time. But the Austrian deployment
on the Serbian western frontier would take some time because of lack of
communications and things must be held up till then. He calculated on
beginning the general advance about 12 August. However a formal declaration of war would doubtless be necessary since he assumed that in the next
few days armed Serbian incursions on the Bosnian frontier would take
place.[1]

We shall not dwell on the attitude of Berchtold who was clearly
unwilling to appear hesitant or changeable in the eyes of the domineering and interfering German diplomat and so expressed agreement with
the German standpoint. Let us rather examine the views of Conrad.
Ever since September 1913, when Serbian operations in Albania
seemed to offer Austria a pretext for war, he had said that sixteen days
were needed to carry out mobilization and that war could not be
declared and operations begun before mobilization was completed.
Foreseeing a period of extreme diplomatic tension and pressure from
the Powers, Berchtold had on 29 September 1913 proposed the immediate occupation of the Serbian town of Šabac with such troops as
were available. '*Ultimatum und Einmarschieren*' (ultimatum and invasion)
was his formula. He would have liked to say to the Serbs: 'Until you

---

[1] DD. I, 213. Conrad's book does not give us these particulars about the first part of the
talk on the 26th, i.e. of what was said while Tschirschky was present. But it gives other
valuable information: 'At 12.30 p.m. of the same day (26 July) I was with Count Berchtold.
I met Herr von Tschirschky there. Later Baron Macchio and Count Forgach also appeared.
Herr von Tschirschky read out several notes. . . . He said that Sweden had told M.
Poincaré that if war came with Russia, she would unreservedly stand on the side of the
Triple Alliance. I said I thought it would be advisable to bring this statement to the knowledge of Russia, it would make her more careful. In Italy, said the German Ambassador,
the behaviour of the press was good. But San Giuliano was very anxious and had stated
that if the great war were to break out because of Austria-Hungary's action, Italy was not
obliged to keep the engagement under the Triple Alliance, and I interposed: "I fear this is
Cadorna's influence, he was described to me as Francophil." Count Berchtold remarked
that Italy probably wanted to do a deal and gain some territory, if we were to gain any.
Herr von Tschirschky advised us not to act in a hurry and to tell Italy that compensations
would be discussed at the appropriate moment. He went on to speak of Germany's *démarche*
at Paris and Bratianu's excitement, adding, however, that King Carol of Roumania would
remain on the side of the Triple Alliance' (Conrad, IV, p. 131).

leave Albania we shall stay in Šabac.' Conrad had objected: 'Either the Serbs leave us sitting there and laugh at us or they attack us; the first is a fatal course, the second is war.' He explained that with a cadre army it was not possible to invade Serbia without preparation.[1] A few weeks later on 20 October Berchtold had returned to the idea of occupying Serbian territory with troops of the peace-time army and Conrad had replied that Potiorek had only 25,000 men in the whole of Bosnia-Herzegovina, whereas mobilization would bring them up to 80,000.[2] On 26 July Berchtold was greatly dismayed by the fact of the long wait between mobilization and attack, but Conrad bluntly told him that nothing could alter this and that he must stand firm against the intervention of the Powers during that period.[3]

The discussions of 1913 were thus resumed in July 1914. It will be remembered that Berchtold's original plan, which Hoyos took to Berlin, was to make a surprise attack on Serbia *sans crier gare*, without either ultimatum or mobilization. Therefore on 6 July he had proposed to the Chief of Staff that he should order a test mobilization (*Probemobilisierung*). But Conrad had replied that mobilization could only be undertaken in view of certain war.[4] Now Szögyény's telegram of 26 July had brought the matter up afresh. After Tschirschky's departure, leaving Berchtold alone with Conrad, Berchtold said:

'We should like to send the declaration of war to Serbia as soon as possible in order that various influences may cease. When do you want the declaration of war?' Conrad: 'Only when we are at the stage when operations can at once begin—say on 12 August.' Berchtold: 'The diplomatic situation will not hold so long. One cannot be sure that there will not be clashes at the frontier.'

Conrad thought one might wait a few days, it was not so urgent as all that. In the end they agreed to postpone the declaration of war, but if diplomatic reasons made haste necessary the matter would be discussed again.[5] This delay caused Berchtold uneasiness. Reverting to it on the morning of the 27th he sent Hoyos to get Conrad to agree to an immediate declaration of war which, even if not immediately followed by the opening of hostilities, would at least achieve the effect desired by Germany of 'confronting the world with a *fait accompli*'. Conrad

---

[1] Conrad, III, pp. 443-4.   [2] Conrad, III, p. 474.
[3] Conrad, III, p. 444.   [4] Conrad IV, p. 40.
[5] Conrad IV, pp. 131-2.—Conrad adds that he suggested that Montenegro should be kept out of it as long as possible and Bulgaria not incited against Roumania. 'But the most important thing is to find out what Russia's attitude will be, it would be desirable to know this by the 4th or at the latest by the 5th of August. Berchtold: " It cannot be done!" I summed up: it was like this, if by that date we were sure that Russia would go in against us, we should proceed straight against Russia, otherwise it would be against Serbia, but then, if Russia went in against us later, we should at first be the weaker in the northern war sector' (Conrad IV, 131).

gave his consent 'provided diplomatic considerations made it seem necessary'.[1] Thereupon Berchtold hastened to give the news to Tschirschky, who, as we have seen, telegraphed it on to Berlin where the telegram arrived at 4.37 p.m.:

It has been decided here to send official declaration of war to-morrow, at the latest the day after, in order to cut away the ground from any attempt at intervention.[2]

That Berchtold's action was dictated by the desire to please Berlin is obvious. In a letter written to Luciano Magrini on 20 January 1933 he states that 'the contents of the Szögyény telegram of 25 July had a certain influence on the Austro-Hungarian decisions and measures'. This is easy to believe in view of our knowledge of all that had gone before. If Vienna had retreated this time it would have been regarded by Berlin as unfit to be an ally (*bündnisunfähig*). If operations could not begin earlier than 12 August, it was necessary at least to declare war, especially as Berlin was not at all pleased at the delay. Indeed when Jagow read Tschirschky's dispatch of the 26th, mentioned already, which reported that Conrad could not take the field before 12 August, he poured out his displeasure to Szögyény, who telegraphed at 5.50 p.m. on the 27th:

The Secretary of State tells me Herr von Tschirschky has telegraphed that General Conrad von Hötzendorf had told him in confidence, that in order to proceed against Serbia with the necessary military strength, our mobilization could not be complete until 12 August. The Secretary of State tells me he regrets that the date for the beginning of our military action should have had to be delayed so long.[3]

Lerchenfeld, the Bavarian Minister at Berlin, in his turn wrote to Hertling:

Here very little edification is felt at Austria-Hungary's declaring herself not in a position to open the attack earlier than in a fortnight or ten days at the least.[4]

These two documents taken with Szögyény's dispatch throw a clear light on the true intentions and the responsibilities of the German Government. They are never quoted by the historians who impugn the validity of Szögyény's dispatch of the 27th, well knowing that dispatch and documents corroborate one another completely. One of these historians explains the declaration of war on Serbia by the fact that, when Vienna learned of the good impression produced by the Serbian reply and when on the 26th Berlin passed on Grey's wish that Vienna should favourably consider it,[5] Berchtold began to doubt the

---

[1] Conrad, IV, p. 132.   [2] DD. I, 257.   [3] Oe-U. VIII, 10792.
[4] Dirr, p. 154.   [5] See p. 342.

wisdom of remaining inactive and 'about noon on the 26th' put the question to Conrad.[1] Now it has been shown above that the question was put to Conrad on the morning of the 26th in Tschirschky's presence as the result of Szögyény's dispatch of the 25th in a conversation which these historians pass over in silence, while it is further obvious that the simple passing on by Berlin of a wish of Grey's without any expression of opinion was tantamount to advising Vienna to take no account of it. It is true that in reporting on the 27th Vienna's decision to declare war, Tschirschky's dispatch said it was inspired above all by the aim of 'cutting away ground from any attempt at intervention'. But Berchtold could hardly avow to Tschirschky that he had taken the decision because of pressure from Berlin. He alleged the reason which Jagow had given in asking for it and which in itself —that is to say apart from the risk it involved—was unexceptionable. But his real state of mind was very different. He had still not replied to Szögyeny's telegram of the 25th asking for an immediate declaration of war and the opening of hostilities. His reply was given at 11.10 p.m. on the 27th when he was in a position to announce the impending declaration of war, but he added:

Opening of military operations must be delayed until the end of deployment in order then to deal the decisive blow with full strength. For this a certain time will be necessary, as the experiences of the last years have warned us not to begin large-scale military measures before being sure that war is certain.[2]

Thus Berchtold justified the delay not only by the need not to begin operations before preparations were completed but also by the need to be sure that war was really going to result. This shows that he still did not regard the declaration of war as inevitably followed by the

---

[1] Fay, II, p. 417. The opinions furthest removed from documentary proof are those of Barnes. No German has ventured on statements so much at variance with the facts as he. He writes: 'Germany, impressed by the extensive submission of Serbia, alarmed at the prospect of Russian intervention, and urged on by Sir Edward Grey, began on 27 July to press Austria for suspension of military activities and the opening of negotiations with Russia on the Serbian issue. To forestall further progress in this policy Berchtold declared war on Serbia at noon on 28 July, and then contended that negotiations concerning the Austrian policy in Serbia were no longer possible on account of the outbreak of war' (Barnes, p. 211). Elsewhere he states: 'Germany . . . opposed the Austrian declaration of war on Serbia. When the prospect of Russian intervention threatened to precipitate a general European war, Germany severely pressed Austria to begin conversations with St. Petersburg in regard to the Austro-Serbian dispute, but Austria refused to yield at all for four days, and when she simulated consent on 31 July it was too late' (Barnes, p. 223). The documents, however, prove: (i) that Germany never asked Austria to suspend military action against Serbia; (ii) that Austria declared war on Serbia against the advice of the Austrian Chief of Staff and under German pressure; (iii) that Bethmann's telegram of the evening of the 27th, which contained no suggestions to Austria and was moreover neutralized by Jagow's statements to Szögyény, came into Berchtold's hands only on the afternoon of the 28th, after the declaration of war had gone off.

[2] Oe-U. VIII, 10783.

outbreak of hostilities and judging by 'the experiences of the last years' he thought that the fortnight intervening between the declaration of war and the opening of hostilities might give room for some kind of intervention or development such as might render war unnecessary. He repeated the same idea in a telegram to Merey also on 28 July, of which we have already spoken:

Warned by the experiences of recent years we did not want to begin large-scale military measures before it was certain that war will actually come about.[1]

The only way that war might be avoided after the declaration of war was by the unconditional submission of Serbia. In this Berchtold held fast to what he had written in his report to Francis Joseph of 14 July: 'even after mobilization has taken place a peaceful settlement might be possible if Serbia were to yield in time'.[2] The impression given by all this is that, in spite of everything, Berchtold still hoped for some miracle of Providence which would avert the tragedy by causing Serbia to yield on all points, for this complete submission he was determined to have, cost what it may. It is quite likely that he thought of the declaration of war as a way either of cutting short all offers of mediation or of spurring on the Powers to put pressure on Belgrade or of pacifying public opinion and the press which was clamouring for a settlement of accounts with Serbia.

The news reaching him on 26 and 27 July was such as to make him think that the Triple *Entente* had no desire to allow a general war to come about for the sake of Serbia, so that by standing firm he would be forcing Serbia to capitulate. On 25 July Szögyény reported Jagow's impression that the French Cabinet was anxious to avoid a major war and Pourtalès's news from St. Petersburg that for the moment Russia was not contemplating military measures.[3] From Paris on the 25th Szécsen telegraphed that a European war would be highly unpopular and that Bertie had given it as his opinion that Russia would not take up the challenge.[4] From St. Petersburg also, Szápáry telegraphed Carlotti's impression that both England and France were pressing for localization.[5] No less optimistic were the dispatches reaching Vienna on the 27th. Szécsen again wrote of the French wish for a settlement of the conflict.[6] Szögyény said that Berlin had no confirmation of the recall of four classes of Russian reservists and that Sazonov had told Pourtalès 'that Russia would only mobilize if and when Austria-Hungary were to assume a hostile attitude towards Russia'.[7] From St. Petersburg

[1] Oe-U. VIII, 10910. See p. 387.   [2] Oe-U. VIII, 10272.
[3] Oe-U. VIII, 10658, 10659.   [4] Oe-U. VIII, 10679.
[5] Oe-U. VIII, 10688.   [6] Oe-U. VIII, 10741.
[7] Oe-U. VIII, 10788.

Szápáry reported that he had found Sazonov calmer and more con-ciliatory and that Sazonov had thought the Austrian aim as expounded by Szápáry 'perfectly legitimate'. In two days the Russian attitude had changed from indignation to a 'diplomatic movement in the opposite direction'.[1]

It might be objected that such promising news ought to have spurred Berchtold on to go full speed ahead in the belief that the locali-zation of the conflict had been achieved. Tschirschky also can hardly have failed to express to him the opinion he gave on the 26th to the English Ambassador

that Russia, having received assurance that Austria-Hungary will annex no Serbian territory, will keep quiet during chastisement which Austria-Hungary is determined to inflict on Servia. . . . Nor was France at all in a condition to face war. . . . Italian Ambassador says that the German Ambassador has held exactly the same language to him and that it is founded on similar opinions of both German and Austrian Ambassadors at St. Petersburg.[2]

But it is likely that Berchtold had less belief than Bethmann in the possibility of localizing the war, moreover his temperament did not lead him to indulge in bold adventure. In any case he certainly showed no symptom of quickening the tempo except when urged by Berlin to do so. The 'certain influences' to which he alluded in his talk with Conrad were nothing else than those exercised by the German ally. And the nexus between them and the declaration of war is so evident that it is not possible to attribute the declaration to other reasons which at best could be but of secondary importance. Germany, therefore, bears the responsibility for this first declaration of war which started the race for mobilization, which in its turn led to the outbreak of the European war. It was Germany who: (i) made Szögyény write to Vienna that a Serbian rejection of the Austrian demands ought to be at once followed by the declaration of war and the opening of hostili-ties; (ii) 'vigorously supported' this same course through its representa-tive Tschirschky in his conversation with Berchtold and Conrad on 26 July; (iii) expressed regret on the 27th because the action against Serbia could not begin earlier than 12 August; (iv) raised no objection on learning at 4.37 p.m. on the 27th that Austria was to declare war on Serbia on the 28th, or at the latest on the 29th, i.e. that on one of those two days the critical step would be taken which was of the utmost gravity and peril for the peace of Europe. Germany made no request for postponement, no attempt to restrain her ally, because Austria, in acting as she did, was fulfilling Germany's desire, her only fault, if she

[1] Oe-U. VIII, 10835.   [2] BD. XI, 150.

had one, being that of not beginning military operations earlier than 12 August.

12. *The Austrian declaration of war on Serbia.*

Having made this clear, we now turn our attention to the moves made by Berchtold to bring about the declaration of war. It was necessary to obtain the assent of Francis Joseph and this was the object of a report to him drawn up by Berchtold on the 27th:

> With reference to the very skilfully phrased answering note of the Serbian Government handed by M. Pašić to Baron Giesl on 25 July which is quite valueless in content, but courteous in form, I regard it as not impossible that the Triple *Entente* might make another attempt to achieve a peaceful settlement of the conflict unless a clear situation is created by the declaration of war. According to a report from the Command of the 4th Corps, Serbian troops yesterday fired on our troops from Danube steamers near Temes-Kubin, and the return of their fire led to a considerable skirmish. Thus hostilities have in fact been begun and it seems all the more advisable to ensure the army's entire freedom of movement in respect of international law; and this can only be effected by the initiation of the state of war. . . . I beg to mention that His Royal and Imperial Highness Archduke Frederick, the Commander-in-Chief of the Balkan forces, and the Chief of Staff have. no objections to the dispatch of the declaration of war to-morrow morning.[1]

Appended was the draft of the telegram which was to be sent *en clair* to the Serbian Foreign Minister at Belgrade or Kragujevac.

> The Royal Government of Serbia not having replied in a satisfactory manner to the note which had been handed to it by the Minister of Austria-Hungary at Belgrade dated 23 July 1914, the Imperial and Royal. Government finds it necessary to see to the safeguarding of its rights and interests and with this object to have recourse to force of arms, all the more so since Serbian troops have already attacked a detachment of the I. and R. army near Temes-Kubin. Austria-Hungary accordingly regards herself from this moment as in a state of war with Serbia.
>
> The Minister for Foreign Affairs of Austria-Hungary
>
> Count Berchtold.

Francis Joseph on the 28th gave his assent in the following terms:

> I approve the enclosed draft of a telegram to the Serbian Minister for Foreign Affairs which contains the declaration of war on Serbia and grant you the required authority. Bad Ischl, on 28 July 1914. Francis Joseph.

Thus the die was cast.

Berchtold did not know how to serve the declaration of war on Serbia and as early as 22 July asked Berlin to perform the office through the German Legation. Jagow, however, refused this on grounds that

---

[1] Oe-U. VIII, 10855.

'it might awaken the impression in the public unfamiliar with diplomatic usage that we had hounded Austria-Hungary into war'. Thereupon Tschirschky reported on the 25th:

The declaration of war will in the event be served on the Serbian Government by telegraph or post, at the same time being communicated to all the Powers in order to deprive the Serbian Government of any pretext of not having been informed.[1]

Thus for the first time in history a declaration of war was made by telegram. But the method was not without its inconveniences. Pašić told Magrini in 1915 that when he received Berchtold's telegram at 1 p.m. on 28 July and learnt a little later that an identical telegram had also gone to army headquarters, doubts rose in his mind of their authenticity. It might be an Austrian trick to get Serbia to attack and take the responsibility for the war on her own shoulders. Pašić's suspicions were heightened when an hour later he asked the German Minister Griesinger for news and received the reply that the latter knew nothing and could say nothing. Pašić thereupon remarked that he was inclined to regard the telegram as a hoax, since direct telegraphic communication with Austria was cut off and he could not see how the telegram could have come via Bucharest while mediation was in progress. Since Griesinger continued to declare himself entirely in the dark and as much in doubt as Pašić, the latter telegraphed to St. Petersburg, London and Paris to tell them of the strange telegram he had received and to ask whether it was true that Austria had declared war on Serbia. In due time the replies came back in the affirmative.

There had, however, been no fighting at Temes-Kubin. And on the 29th Berchtold wrote this to Francis Joseph to explain the omission from the telegram, as sent, of the words 'all the more so' to the end of the sentence. This has led Tittoni to associate himself with the accusation raised in many quarters against Berchtold of having deceived the Emperor 'even as regards the immediate reasons for the declaration of war on Serbia', taking advantage of the enfeeblement which age had brought about in Francis Joseph's will power and mental faculties.[2] On the Austrian side, however, it is maintained that no political personage would ever have dared to play such a trick on the Emperor, that his mind was clear and his will strong and that Berchtold actually did receive news from the military authorities of fighting at Temes-Kubin, had used it without checking it and had issued a rectification on learning that it was without foundation. Giesl, who on 27 July was at the Ballplatz, has stated by letter to the present writer that it was only known in the evening of the 27th that the incident was devoid of significance. A steamer carrying Serbian reservists had been

---

[1] DD. I, 138, 142, 206.   [2] Tittoni, *Nuovi Scritti*, p. 61.

prevented by rifle shots from approaching the Hungarian bank. Thus
there was no question of Serbian aggression and Berchtold in the night
of 27/28 July deleted the accusation from the declaration of war. On
the Austrian side it is further maintained that no expedients of such a
kind were needed to obtain the assent of the aged Emperor to a war
of whose necessity he was now entirely convinced. And to the present
writer Berchtold himself wrote on 23 November 1932:

> The view that the Emperor 'was pushed into war' is totally false. His
> Majesty was in full possession of a clear mind and unimpaired judgement
> and convinced of his lofty mission. In his decisions on such serious questions
> he consulted only his own conscience and would never have allowed himself
> to be 'pushed'. Germany's advocacy of active measures, her assurance of
> help under the alliance and on the other hand the unsatisfactory attitude of
> official and unofficial Serbia were the deciding factors for the Emperor, who
> during the course of July became increasingly sceptical of the possibility of
> preserving the peace. The view that the arrival at a given moment of the later
> unconfirmed military report on a Serbian attack near Temes-Kubin was of
> decisive importance is a baseless legend. Political considerations—the
> unsatisfactory reply to the note containing the demands—were operative
> in the decision to draw the final consequences.

All this, no doubt, is very true, and it may be remembered that, as
early as 5 July, Francis Joseph had said to Conrad that if Germany were
with Austria, he would make war on Serbia.[1] But it is also true, as has
been said above, that, both on the 25th, when the news of the rupture
of diplomatic relations reached Ischl, and two days later in the audience
granted to Giesl, the aged Emperor distinctly said that the rupture did
not yet mean war and he spoke in the tone of one who hoped that war
might be avoided.[2] It is, therefore, comprehensible that Berchtold, to
overcome these last possible hesitations, may have, if not invented, at
least exploited the Temes-Kubin episode for his ends, even knowing
it to be a fabrication.[3] And that this is the case may be judged from
the fact that on 28 July when he already knew that there had been no
incident at Temes-Kubin, Berchtold declared that war was inevitable
because the Serbs had opened hostilities at Temes-Kubin.[4]

Already on 26 July he was not very straightforward in his telegram
to Mensdorff instructing the latter how to reply to the wish expressed
by Grey to Lichnowsky and passed on to Berchtold by Tschirschky,

---

[1] Conrad, IV, p. 36. See p. 135.   [2] See p. 375.

[3] According to a revelation attributed to Colonel Seeliger, head of the press bureau of
the Austrian War Ministry, Francis Joseph refused to sign the declaration of war until
Berchtold read out a telegram stating that 'Serbians' had raided Bosnian territory and in the
fighting there some 400 soldiers had been killed. This in reality was a falsification of a telegram to the effect that four gendarmes had been wounded in a border fray (Schmitt, II,
p. 83, on the authority of the *New York Times*, 20 August 1924). This story is devoid of all
proof, unsupported by other testimony and may be regarded as unfounded.

[4] OeU. VIII, 10915.

that the German Government might feel able to influence the Austrian Government to take a favourable view of the Serbian reply.[1] Berchtold's telegram to Mensdorff of 26 July runs:

I regard it as opportune that Your Excellency should take up the matter again with the Foreign Secretary and point out to him that almost at the very moment when he was writing to Prince Lichnowsky, i.e. yesterday at 3 p.m., Serbia had already ordered the general mobilization of her army, a proof that no inclination for a peaceful solution of the affair existed at Belgrade.[2]

And on the 28th he telegraphed again to Mensdorff in the same sense,[3] though well aware that the Serbian mobilization was a purely precautionary measure and that Serbia would never be able or willing to play the Austrian game by assuming the offensive. Thus he was distorting the truth in attributing an aggressive purpose to Serbian mobilization and his artifice entirely failed of its effect. Still less straightforward was he on the 28th with the Russian Ambassador Shebeko who, returning from a brief leave of absence in Russia, came to carry out the instructions given him by Sazonov after the latter's conversation with Szápáry at St. Petersburg of 26 July, i.e. to have the first and last of those 'direct conversations' which were to save the situation.

Let it here be said once again that these direct conversations were undertaken at the suggestion of the German Ambassador Pourtalès who, sincerely desirous of an agreement between Russia and Austria on the Serbian note—an agreement not at that time in the intentions of Berlin—had raised hopes in Sazonov that Vienna might soften some of its demands. Encouraged by the success of this talk with Szápáry, Sazonov had taken up Pourtalès's suggestion of asking Berchtold that Szápáry might be authorized to discuss with him at St. Petersburg the rephrasing of some points of the Austrian note to render them acceptable by Serbia and in this sense he had telegraphed to Shebeko. The latter had already called once at the Ballplatz and had a general talk on the situation with Macchio without touching on Sazonov's plea which had probably not yet reached him.[4] Berchtold, who was bent on declaring war on Serbia, had decided to be 'not at home' on the 27th,

---

[1] BD. XI, 115.   [2] Oe-U. VIII, 10733.   [3] Oe-U. VIII, 10891.

[4] *Int. Bez.* i. V, 139.—In Shebeko's report on this talk the following passage is noteworthy: 'Here, apparently under the influence of assurances from the German Ambassador in Vienna who during the whole course of the crisis has played the rôle of a warmonger, they reckon on the probability of the localization of the conflict with Serbia and the possibility of dealing her a severe blow with impunity.' In a later telegram, dated the 29th, Shebeko reports Tschirschky as saying to him 'that in his opinion any pressure on Austria would be doomed to failure. This statement does not surprise me since he himself is a zealous adherent, if not the instigator of the "active" procedure of Austria towards Serbia' (*Int. Bez.* i. V, 243). These impressions of Tschirschky's are to be noted because it is impossible to overestimate the pressure exercised at the Ballplatz by this overbearing diplomatist and the influence he had on Berchtold.

thus avoiding also the visit of Bunsen who was intending to ask him to put forward some suggestions for a way out of the crisis.[1] Berchtold did not see Shebeko till the 28th after war had been declared and then of course gave him an answer in the negative. His own account of the conversation, telegraphed to Szápáry at 11.40 p.m. on 28 July, runs:

In my reply I emphasized that I could not entertain any such proposal. Negotiations on the text of the note of reply which we had described as unsatisfactory would not meet with the understanding or approval of anyone here. It was all the more impossible in that, as the Ambassador knew, both here and in Hungary a profound general excitement had taken possession of public opinion and that, moreover, we have to-day declared war on Serbia. . . . The Serbian attitude on receipt of our note had, moreover, not been such as to render a peaceful settlement possible, inasmuch as Serbia, even before returning her unsatisfactory answer, ordered general mobilization and thereby in advance performed a hostile act against us. In spite of this we waited three more days. Now yesterday the Serbs had opened hostilities against us on the Hungarian frontier. This made it impossible for us to persevere in the longanimity hitherto displayed by us towards Serbia. The attainment of a thorough rehabilitation (*Sanierung*) of our relations with Serbia on peaceful lines had now been rendered impossible for us and we found ourselves obliged to reply to Serbian provocation in the only manner which in the actual circumstances befits the dignity of the Monarchy.[2]

Note that in this document Berchtold rejects the proposal to discuss not the Austrian note, but the text of the Serbian reply. Sazonov, at that moment, had not yet seen the text of the Serbian reply and in his talk with Szápáry had suggested discussions on ways of rewording some points of the Austrian note to make them acceptable to Serbia. And in fact it is on these lines that Shebeko spoke to Berchtold, telegraphing to St. Petersburg on the 28th that Berchtold had refused

to draw back and enter into a discussion of the text of the [Austrian] note . . . all the more as the Serbian reply gave the proof of the insincerity of their assurances for the future. From my conversation I have received the impression that the Austro-Hungarian Government at the present moment has decided to deal Serbia a blow to restore its own prestige in the Balkans and at home, and, for the localization of the conflict, counts on Germany's support and the other Powers' love of peace.[3]

In reporting to Berlin what Berchtold had said to Shebeko, Tschirschky telegraphed:

Count Berchtold told me that the Russian Ambassador was very conciliatory in form but inwardly, as it seemed, decidedly perturbed, for he was as white as chalk. . . . The Minister in friendly tones replied that he, the Ambassador, will have noticed the mood of the population in Vienna and

---

[1] BD. XI, 175.   [2] Oe-U. VIII, 10915.   [3] *Int. Bez.* i. V, 188.

the Monarchy these last days and realized that further discussion of Serbia had become quite impossible for any Austro-Hungarian Government; it would simply be swept away.[1]

Hence Tschirschky's dispatch reports that Berchtold was rejecting not conversations with St. Petersburg but conversations with Belgrade, whilst Sazonov, basing himself on Shebeko, told Pourtalès that Berchtold refused conversations between St. Petersburg and Vienna.[2] The discrepancy disconcerted Bethmann and gave rise on the evening of the 29th to one of his agitated telegrams.

Ostensibly war had been declared because the Serbs had begun hostilities at Temes-Kubin. The same reason was alleged by Tschirschky in a dispatch to Berlin as the reason for the rejection, in accordance with the desire of Berlin, of Grey's plea for mediation by Germany. Let it here in this connexion be repeated that Bethmann's telegram, dispatched at 11.50 p.m. on the 27th, arrived in Vienna at 5.30 a.m. on the 28th. On receiving it, Tschirschky, knowing that war was to be declared that same day, ought to have gone straightway to see Berchtold. What he did, or said he did, was to go only in the afternoon, after the declaration had been made. At 4.55 p.m. he was in a position to send two telegrams to Berlin, the first to say that the declaration of war had gone off at 11 a.m.[3] the other to report that Berchtold cordially thanked the Chancellor for passing on the English proposal for mediation to which he would reply later. For the moment he

observed that after the opening of hostilities on the part of Serbia and the declaration of war which has meanwhile taken place, he regarded the English démarche as coming too late.[4]

Bunsen at 4.10 p.m. on the 25th reported to Grey in much the same sense:

Minister for Foreign Affairs said quietly, but firmly, that no discussion could be accepted on basis of Servian note. . . . This was a matter that must be settled directly between the two parties immediately concerned.[5]

The two partners in Vienna and Berlin hoped with their prearranged artifices to throw dust in the eyes of the other Powers and obtain their assent to the punitive expedition against Serbia, which, whatever the promises to the contrary, could not but end with the crushing of Serbia or at least her reduction to the rank of a vassal state of the Dual Monarchy. But they were deceiving only themselves, Germany in demanding and Austria in agreeing to make a fatal move, which they were neither of them able to undo when there arose before their eyes the spectre, perceived first by Germany, of a conflagration destined to bring them to abysmal defeat.

[1] DD. II, 356.   [2] DD. II, 365.   [3] DD. II, 311.
          [4] DD. II, 313.   [5] BD. XI, 230.

CHAPTER XI

GERMAN POLICY AFTER THE AUSTRIAN
DECLARATION OF WAR ON SERBIA;
THE THREAT OF ENGLISH INTERVENTION

1. *The Kaiser finds a conciliatory formula.*

On the morning of 28 July Wilhelm was at last able to read the text of the reply given by Serbia at 6 p.m. on 25 July. As has been said, the German political chiefs could have obtained it in the course of the 26th, had they taken the trouble to do so. And about noon on the 27th it was communicated to them by the Serbian Chargé d'Affaires in Berlin. The Kaiser could thus have seen it by the afternoon of the 27th, but in fact it was sent to Potsdam by a special messenger who did not leave Berlin until 11.30 p.m. This seems to have been done in order that Wilhelm should not see it until the following day, when he would be too late to prevent Austria from sending off the declaration of war for which Bethmann and Jagow had asked and which Tschirschky had told them was to be expected on the 28th or at the latest on the 29th. It is quite clear that the Kaiser read the Serbian document on the 28th and not on the evening of the 27th because at the top of it is written: 'Read at the N(eues) Pal(ais). 28. VII, 1914. W.'

It must be admitted that from their own point of view the men at the Wilhelmstrasse had good reasons for withholding knowledge of the Serbian reply as long as possible from the Kaiser. Presumably at the meeting on the 27th he had shown himself rather favourable to a peaceful solution of the crisis. Undoubtedly it was 'in accordance with His Majesty's orders' that on the evening of the 27th Bethmann had forwarded Lichnowsky's telegram to Tschirschky, so that Berchtold should be informed of Grey's hope, expressed on the morning of the 27th, that Germany would use her influence at Vienna to get the Serbian reply regarded 'as satisfactory or as a basis for conversations'.[1] Together with the Serbian reply, Wilhelm had before him in the early morning of the 28th that grave dispatch from his Ambassador in London and also Bethmann's telegram stating that his orders had been carried out but maintaining silence about the tortuous and disingenuous comment which had accompanied his proposal to Vienna and about what Jagow had said to Szögyény on the evening of the 27th in order to induce Berchtold to refuse the English wish.[2] The reason for Bethmann's silence must have been his perception that the Kaiser was inclining towards a search for a way out of the crisis. And in this Bethmann was not mistaken. General Plessen notes in his diary for the 28th.

> I go riding with H.M. at 7.30 a.m. He tells me England thinks the Serbian answer to the Austrian ultimatum such that in essence all the demands are conceded and therewith all reason for war is gone. I said I thought Austria must at least lay hands on some gage which should serve as guarantee for the carrying out of the concessions.[3]

Wilhelm's astonishing footnote to the Serbian reply runs:

> A brilliant achievement in a time limit of only forty-eight hours!
> It is more than one could have expected!
> A great moral success for Vienna; but with it all reason for war is gone and Giesl ought to have quietly stayed on in Belgrade!
> After that I should never have ordered mobilization.[4]

What a contrast to the bellicose thought and language of earlier marginal notes urging Austria to go ahead against Serbia at full speed! It has already been noted that Wilhelm was full of bluster when danger was a long way off but piped down when he saw a real threat of war approaching. The neutral attitude of London had led him to hope that Austria would be allowed to bring Serbia to reason without causing a European war. But now the news from England was not at all reassuring and Lichnowsky's warnings sounded extremely serious. Lichnowsky had reported Grey as saying that Serbia had 'given satisfaction to Austrian demands in a measure which he would never have believed possible'[5] and had added that, if Austria was not satisfied with this reply the most terrible war might break out that Europe had ever

---

[1] DD. I, 258. See p. 444.   [2] See pp. 445–6.   [3] Bach, p. 23.
[4] DD. I, 271.   [5] See p. 442.

known. And if it did, Lichnowsky maintained that Germany would not receive support from England. Moreover there was Italy saying she was under no obligation to take part in a war of aggression and asking for compensations which Austria was not yet ready to grant. In fact the situation was beginning to look very black for the Central Powers. It was under these impressions that the Kaiser read the Serbian reply and realized that Grey was right in saying that it ought to be regarded as substantially satisfactory. But Germany had given Austria her promise of unconditional support, and Wilhelm, though not knowing that the very day before Austria had been urged to open hostilities without delay, was conscious that, after she had been given such assurances, she could not be asked to reverse her whole course. The only thing to do was to find some expedient which would enable her to take action, but action to which Russia could not raise objection. The Kaiser formulated his conclusions in the following letter, sent at once to Jagow, bearing the date 10 a.m., 28 July, and written with underlinings which are here reproduced in italics:.

On reading through the Serbian reply which I received this morning I am persuaded that on the whole the wishes of the Danubian Monarchy are met. The few reservations made by Serbia on single points can in my opinion well be cleared up by negotiation. But capitulation of the most humble type is there proclaimed *urbi et orbi* and thereby *all reason for war* falls to the ground.

Nevertheless this scrap of paper together with what it contains can only be regarded as of limited value as long as it is not translated into *deeds*. The Serbs are Orientals, therefore liars, deceitful, and master hands at temporizing. In order that these fine promises may become truth and fact, the exercise of *gentle (douce) violence* will be necessary. This will best be done by Austria's occupying Belgrade as *security* for the enforcement and execution of the promises and remaining there until the demands are *actually* carried out. This is also necessary in order to give an outward *satisfaction d'honneur* to the army which has for a third time been mobilized *to no purpose*, an appearance of success in the eyes of the rest of the world and enable it to have at least the consciousness of having stood on foreign soil. Without this the calling off of the campaign might give rise to an ill feeling towards the dynasty which might be extremely hazardous. Should Your Excellency share this opinion of mine, I should propose to say to Austria: the retreat of Serbia in a very humiliating form has been attained and we congratulate her on this. Thereby of course *a reason for war no longer exists*, but what is necessary is a *guarantee* that the promises would be put into execution. This would doubt-less be attainable by the *temporary* military occupation of a part of Serbia. Just as we in 1871 left troops posted in France until the milliards were paid up. On *this basis* I am ready to *mediate* for *peace* in Austria. Contrary proposals or protests from other states I would firmly reject, especially as they all more or less openly appeal to me to help to preserve the peace. This I will do in my own way and thus in a manner sparing of Austrian *national sentiment* and the *military honour* of her *army*. The latter has already been appealed to by the supreme war lord and is about to respond to the appeal. It must therefore unquestionably have a visible satisfaction d'honneur; that is a *prerequisite* of my mediation. Will Your Excellency therefore submit to me a proposal in the sense here outlined which shall be communicated to Vienna. I have ordered Plessen who entirely shares my views to write in the above sense to the Chief of the General Staff.[1]

The idea of a *Halt in Belgrade*, as this proposal is generally called by historians, was quite ingenious. Wilhelm was, after all, more quick-witted, intelligent, and perspicacious than his Ministers and put forward an expedient which held the balance well between the two sides. Something similar had already been thought of by Avarna, the Italian Ambassador to Vienna, as appears from a telegram sent by Bunsen to Grey on 27 July:

Italian Ambassador is greatly concerned and is casting about for a means of circumscribing conflict which he regards as inevitable. He asked me this morning if I thought following might be usefully proposed:—

Austria to repeat to Powers in form of positive engagement promise already made to Russia to the effect that she desires neither to annex any territory nor to crush Servia, nor to deprive her of her independence, but merely to obtain guarantees for future.

His Excellency thought that possibly Russia might consent to keep quiet. He would think it over and perhaps communicate with Italian Minister for Foreign Affairs as to terms of possible formula. He begged that his name might not be mentioned as having thrown out this suggestion, which is still in a very crude form.[2]

What Grey thought of Avarna's proposal is not known, but it is a fact that two days later (on 29 July) he took the same line, making a suggestion to Lichnowsky very like that of Avarna and almost identical with Wilhelm's *Halt in Belgrade*.

This formula was, indeed, not such as would find favour with Serbia and with those who had her freedom at heart, but from the point of view of European peace it was skilful in giving Austria satisfaction in both the political and military field while asking her not to embark on a real war and to confine herself to the occupation of Serbian territory as a guarantee and while not demanding from Serbia unconditional acceptance of the Austrian demands. She had made certain reservations which could be 'settled by negotiation'. Now this was exactly what Russia wanted. Even Sazonov in a talk with Pourtalès on the morning of the 30th in which he put forward a formula embodying his final demands—a formula to which we shall return later[3]—

---

[1] DD. II, 293.
[2] BD. XI, 175.—It is not known whether Avarna submitted the idea to San Giuliano. He very likely did so, but there is no indication that San Giuliano followed it up.
[3] See pp. 562-3.

did not demand the cessation of Austrian operations. But if the Kaiser's initiative was to have any influence on the course of events, it would have to be taken up at once and put into execution in its entirety with maximum energy. Without heavy pressure Vienna would not comply. During these tragic last eight days of July every hour was of decisive importance. The loss of a few hours meant that proposals and the response to them became outdated and useless. And this fact was realized by protagonists in the drama who in certain instances practised delay as a means of reciprocal deception.

2. *The Chancellor's delay; his aim is not 'to hold Austria back' and to cast the blame on Russia if a general war results.*

At what time did Jagow read the Kaiser's letter? The present writer put this question to Wegerer who replied that the exact hour cannot be ascertained, but that as the Kaiser wrote it at 10 a.m. and had it forwarded by special messenger 'it may be supposed that Herr von Jagow received it in the forenoon of 28 July'. Did the Kaiser realize that unless his proposal was at once sent on to Vienna it would arrive too late? The answer is that he did not. He actually wanted it taken to the Ballplatz by an official from the Wilhelmstrasse, and Bethmann at 10.15 p.m. explained to him that, as there was no more regular railway communication with Vienna that night, he had had to send it by telegraph.[1] But there was nó reason for Wilhelm to feel the need of haste since he had no idea that Austria was on the point of declaring war and that his proposal had been formulated barely an hour before the declaration of war was telegraphed to Belgrade. Bethmann, however, knew this, and the Kaiser's instructions must have upset his plans to a degree that is easily imaginable. After urging Austria on to speed up military action (and indeed by his insistence causing her to declare war), after telling her the previous evening not to pay any attention to the English proposals for mediation which were sent on merely for tactical reasons, how were the German leaders to avow to their Austrian colleagues that their calculations had been wrong and oblige them to take a more prudent line? This, nevertheless, not only lay within their power, but was their duty, since it had become clearly apparent that 'localization of the war' was not possible, that there was neither hope of English neutrality, on which the Wilhelmstrasse had reared its plans, nor likelihood of Italian co-operation. But neither Chancellor nor Secretary of State was a man of quick intuition or of rapid and courageous decisions. They still had no intention of drawing back from the adventure into which they had plunged and did not share the Kaiser's opinion of the Serbian reply.

[1] DD. II, 308.

In a circular of instructions to the Prussian envoys to the other Governments of the Reich Bethmann stated:

The Serbian Government's reply . . . makes it clear that authoritative quarters in Serbia do not intend to give up their previous policy and subversive activity. Consequently, if it does not mean definitely to renounce its position as a Great Power, the Austro-Hungarian Government has no other choice than to enforce its demands by strong pressure and, if need be, by recourse to military measures.[1]

Lutz remarks that this circular may have been drafted before the Serbian reply was exactly known; 'but in any case it was not changed even after, and the critical reader again carries away the impression that Berlin still, on 28 July, consented to the Austro-Hungarian war against Serbia'.[2] Thus while Wilhelm was coming round to a peaceful solution of the conflict, the Wilhelmstrasse was deceitfully evading the spirit of his instructions while feigning to obey them. The Kaiser was out at Potsdam and did not, like the Tsar, use the telephone to communicate with his Ministers. They on their side were apt to be late in forwarding to him the documents they received, and subjected them to a certain measure of censorship, while, in carrying out his orders, they did so with delays which neutralized their effect.

They could and should have telegraphed the Kaiser's proposal to Tschirschky as soon as it reached them. But they took no action until 10.15 p.m., obviously for two reasons: (i) because they were awaiting news of the declaration of war, which Vienna might have suspended if the Kaiser's *démarche* had been put into execution; (ii) because if Tschirschky had received the relevant telegram in the afternoon or early evening, he would have had time to carry out the *démarche* that same day; but this was not possible if it was telegraphed to him only at 10 p.m. Thus the matter would not receive attention till the 29th when it was too late. Hence on the 28th the Chancellor carried on a diplomatic activity at complete variance with the letter and spirit of his Sovereign's orders and inspired by the intention of offering St. Petersburg and London explanations, assurances, and soft words meant to neutralize the effects of the declaration of war and safeguard the underlying principle of the 'localization of the conflict'. This principle they meant to uphold even at the cost of a more or less probable European conflict, for the outbreak of which not Germany but Russia was to be made the guilty party. And this would absolve the German leaders in the eyes of their people and avert English intervention. Let us prove this.

From Vienna Tschirschky had telegraphed on the evening of the 27th that Conrad

takes the view that the moment has come, if there is confirmation in Berlin of Russian military measures, to state at St. Petersburg, in the interests of a

---

[1] DD. II, 307.   [2] Lutz, pp. 147–8.

desirable clarification of military situation, that this mobilization constitutes such a threat on the Russian southern and western frontier that corresponding measures would have to be taken.[1]

At 3.20 p.m. on the 28th Bethmann replied that the rumours of Russian military preparations were not confirmed and that he and Moltke thought it premature to make a categoric statement of that kind at St. Petersburg.[2] In fact relations with Russia were going quite well. On the morning of the 28th a telegram from Pourtalès of the previous evening had brought news of Sazonov's favourable reception of Pourtalès's representations based on two telegrams from the Wilhelm-strasse of 26 July[3] alleging the good relations between the two Empires and the Austrian assurances of territorial *désintéressement* towards Serbia as reasons why Russia 'might adopt a waiting attitude towards the issue between Austria-Hungary and Serbia'. Sazonov's reply to Pourtalès had been that

as Austria had declared her territorial *désintéressement* and had not yet undertaken hostile measures against Serbia, the moment, in his opinion, had come, by an exchange of views between the Powers, to seek means of 'building golden bridges' for Austria . . . . He urges us to reflect that if the Austrian demands which affect Serbian sovereign rights were fulfilled, a revolutionary régime would come to power that would be worse than the present one. . . . He urgently begged for our co-operation in this sense. It must be possible to find some way of giving Serbia a well merited lesson while respecting her sovereign rights.[4]

What a marvellous chance was thus offered by Sazonov for dealing a mortal blow to Pan-Serb propaganda! But all that Bethmann did was to send a telegram at 3.35 p.m. on the 28th thanking Sazonov and expressing the hope 'that Austria's declaration of *désintéressement* will satisfy Russia and serve as a basis for further understanding'.[5] When at last at 6.39 p.m. on the 28th Tschirschky's telegram reached the Wilhelmstrasse bringing news that war had been declared on Serbia at 11 a.m.,[6] Bethmann at 11 p.m. with the utmost coolness sent Pourtalès the following telegram in his own hand:

We are continuing our endeavours to persuade Vienna to have a frank discussion with St. Petersburg for the purpose of clarifying the aims and extent of the Austrian procedure in Serbia in an unexceptionable manner which it is hoped will be acceptable to Russia. The declaration of war issued in the meanwhile does not change this in any way.[7]

The declaration of war did not change this in any way! Well, if it made no change, why issue it? Because, as the words of the telegram

[1] DD. II, 281.   [2] DD. II, 299.   [3] DD. I, 198, 219. See pp. 427–8.
[4] DD. II, 282.   [5] DD. II, 300.   [6] DD. II, 311.   [7] DD. II, 315.

indicate, it would be followed by 'Austrian procedure against Serbia', of which only the 'aims and extent' were to be clarified between St. Petersburg and Vienna. In other words St. Petersburg was to acquiesce in the 'procedure' and only discuss its 'extent'. The conflict was to go its way, remaining 'localized'. This still continued to be the thesis the triumph which Bethmann was determined to bring about, even though he camouflaged it with non-committal phrases, like those used above which deceived no one, and like those he telegraphed at 8.40 p.m. on the 28th to Lichnowsky for use with Grey:

If the British Government sees its highest interest in the preservation of European peace on the basis of equilibrium between the groups, it will not expect us in our mediatory action to go to the length of trying to coerce Austria-Hungary into indulgence towards Serbia. We should thereby contribute to the undermining of Austria-Hungary's position as a Great Power and to a shift of the European balance of power to the disadvantage of the Triple Alliance. We are, however, far from regarding the Austro-Serbian conflict as a trial of strength between the two European groups. We regard the Austro-Hungarian procedure purely as a means of finally removing the Serbian provocation which had grown unbearable and now, for the third time in five years, seriously threatens the peace of Europe. . . . We still pursue our efforts for mediation at St. Petersburg and hope for success.[1]

And to the British Ambassador, whom he summoned on the evening of the 28th, Bethmann said not a word of the Kaiser's proposal which he was about to forward to Vienna, and merely talked in soothing generalities which Goschen at midnight telegraphed to Grey as follows:

He had not been able to accept your proposal for a conference of the representatives of the Great Powers, because he did not think it would be effective and because such a conference would in his opinion have had the appearance of an 'Areopagus' consisting of two Powers of each group sitting in judgement upon the two remaining Powers. . . . You could be assured that he was doing his very best both at Vienna and St. Petersburg to get the two Governments to discuss the situation directly with each other in a friendly way. He had great hopes that such discussions would take place and lead to a satisfactory result, but if the news were true which he had just read in the papers, namely that Russia had mobilized fourteen army corps in the south. . . . Austria . . . would have to take similar measures and if war were to result, Russia would be entirely responsible. . . . Austria's quarrel with Serbia was a purely Austrian concern with which Russia had nothing to do. His Excellency further said that he resented articles in the French press which stated that decision of peace or war rested with the German Emperor. This decision rested with Russia and Russia alone. In conclusion His Excellency reiterated his desire to co-operate with England and his intention

[1] DD. II, 314.

to do his utmost to maintain general peace. 'A war between the Great Powers must be avoided' were his last words.[1]

So if war broke out it was clearly to be recognized that the guilt lay with Russia 'and Russia alone'. This was also the main point of the long telegram[2] circulated to the Prussian envoys at the capitals of the other member states of the Reich, which from the number it bears, later than those of the telegrams sent off in the afternoon, must certainly have been issued after the Kaiser's letter had been received at the Wilhelmstrasse. But whereas Wilhelm declared that Serbia had humbled herself and conceded more than could be believed, Bethmann asserted that the Serbian reply

makes it clear that authoritative quarters in Serbia do not intend to give up their previous policy and subversive activity. Consequently, if it does not mean definitely to renounce its position as a Great Power, the Austro-Hungarian Government has no other choice than to enforce its demands by strong pressure and, if need be, by recourse to military measures. . . . If Russia thinks it necessary to intervene in this conflict with Serbia . . . she must be clear . . . that she alone bears the responsibility if the Austro-Serbian quarrel, which all the other Great Powers want to localize, gives rise to a European war. . . . Only under compulsion shall we draw the sword, but then in the calm consciousness that we bear no guilt for the calamity which a war must bring to the peoples of Europe.[3]

It had become Bethmann's obsession to put Russia in the wrong in the eyes of the world in the hope of clearing Germany of all responsibility for a European war and thus cutting out English intervention. Here even Fay admits:

He was too much concerned with preventing the odium of responsibility for a war from falling on Germany and Austria, rather than with preventing such a war altogether.[4]

All his actions were motivated by this concern. For instance, on the evening of the 28th he wrote to the Kaiser asking him to undertake a direct exchange of telegrams with the Tsar, which we shall examine later. 'A telegram of this kind would, if war were to come about, place the guilt of Russia in the strongest light.'[5] Even his fulfilment at 10.15 p.m. on the 28th of the Kaiser's order to send his proposal to Vienna was motivated by the same consideration:

It is an imperative necessity that the responsibility for a possible extension of the conflict to the Powers not immediately concerned should in all circumstances fall on Russia.[6]

And in order that the two Central Powers should be guiltless of any such responsibility it was necessary that Austria should not play a double game in regard to her true intentions towards Serbia.

[1] BD. XI, 249.   [2] See p. 471.   [3] DD. II, 307.
[4] Fay, II, p. 425.   [5] DD. II, 308.   [6] DD. II, 323.

3. Austrian evasiveness on the subject of territorial désintéressement.

Almost all the telegrams sent by Berlin to St. Petersburg, London and Paris from 25 July onwards show that Bethmann was basing his diplomatic action chiefly on Austria's declaration of territorial *désintéressement* reported to Berlin in a dispatch from Tschirschky on 24 July[1], his line being that as Austria had no territorial aims and only sought to obtain solid guarantees against Slav irredentism, she ought to be given a free hand. We have seen that it was only at the instances of Tisza that the Joint Ministers had agreed to say that the Dual Monarchy had no intention of increasing her territory at the expense of Serbia, hoping in their hearts not to keep the promise. We have also seen that if, after victorious war, the promise had to be kept, Serbia was in any case to be mutilated for the benefit of Bulgaria, Greece and Albania.[2] Bethmann might well have imagined all this and understood that Austria did not mean to run the mortal risk of a European war in order to re-emerge from Serbian territories empty handed. But either he did not or he pretended not to understand this, hoping to make port safely with his 'localization of the conflict'. In all the chancelleries of the Triple *Entente* he chanted his litany that Austria, in invading Serbia, only sought guarantees against a repetition of crimes such as that which had brought about the death of the Heir Apparent. He was, therefore, deeply disturbed when at 3.45 p.m. on the 28th there arrived a dispatch from Lichnowsky:

The staff of the Austrian Embassy here, including Count Mensdorff, in talking with Embassy staff and myself make not the slightest secret of the fact that Austria is only out for the overthrow of Serbia and that the note was intentionally so worded that it could not but be rejected. When the news was circulated here on Saturday evening by the *Central News* that Serbia had given way, the gentlemen in question were positively shattered. Count Mensdorff said again yesterday evening to me in confidence that Vienna absolutely wanted war, because Serbia was to be 'flattened out'. The same gentlemen also say that the intention is to present Bulgaria (and presumably also Albania) with portions of Serbia.[3]

Noting by the way that the confidences of Mensdorff and his staff at the Austrian Embassy in London confirm that the note of 23 July 'was intentionally so worded that it could not but be rejected', let us turn our attention to the marginal note written by Bethmann on the 28th against these utterances:

This ambiguity on the part of Austria is intolerable. To us they refuse information about their programme and expressly say that Count Hoyos's remarks about a partitioning of Serbia were purely personal; in St. Petersburg

[1] DD. I, 155. [2] See pp. 256–7. [3] DD. II, 301.

they are lambs without evil intentions and in London their Embassy talks of giving away Serbian territory to Bulgaria and Albania.[1]

This was a very different state of mind from that of Jagow on 17 July when he asked Tschirschky to make inquiries as to

what views the Austro-Hungarian statesmen have about the future shape of Serbia . . . while avoiding giving the impression that we had any wish to stand as a hindrance in the way of Austrian action or to prescribe definite limits or aims for it.[2]

Then Berlin had no misgivings, indeed wanted Austria to make an end of Serbia, annexing a large part of her territory and thus putting herself in a position to offer Italy handsome compensation, perhaps even the Trentino. But now the difficulties the Powers were creating over the 'localization of the conflict' lent special value to the declaration of territorial *désintéressement* which had earned for its author the epithet of 'donkey' from Wilhelm. Thus making up his mind after long delay to carry out the *démarche* at Vienna as commanded by his Imperial master, Bethmann at 10.15 p.m. on the 28th telegraphed to Tschirschky:

The Austro-Hungarian Government has definitely stated to Russia that it does not contemplate territorial acquisitions in Serbia. This tallies with Your Excellency's report that neither the Austrian nor the Hungarian statesmen regard an increase in the Slav elements of the Monarchy as desirable. Apart from this, the Austro-Hungarian Government in spite of repeated inquiries has left us in the dark about its intentions. The Serbian Government's reply to the Austrian ultimatum, now before us, makes it clear that Serbia has after all met the Austrian demands in so considerable a measure that a completely intransigent attitude on the part of the Austro-Hungarian Government would bring about a gradual revulsion of public opinion all over Europe.

According to information from the Austrian General Staff active military measures against Serbia will not be possible before 12 August. The Imperial Government in consequence is placed in the extraordinarily difficult position of finding itself exposed to proposals for mediation and conferences from the other Cabinets and, if it persists in its previous reserve towards such proposals, the odium of having caused a world war will fall on it even in the eyes of the German people. It is not possible on such a basis to begin and wage a successful war on three fronts. It is an imperious necessity that the responsibility for a possible spread of the conflict to the Powers not immediately involved should in all circumstances fall on Russia. In M. Sazonov's last talk with Count Pourtalès, the Minister already admitted that Serbia must be given the 'well merited lesson'. He no longer took up so adverse an attitude towards the Austrian standpoint as previously. From thence it is not far to the conclusion that the Russian Government will not refuse to

[1] DD. II, 301.   [2] DD. I, 61. See p. 362.

recognize that now the mobilization of the Austro-Hungarian army has begun its military honour requires its march into Serbia. The Russian Government will the more easily reconcile itself to this idea if the Vienna Cabinet reiterates at St. Petersburg the definite statement that territorial gains in Serbia are remote from its thoughts and that its military measures are aimed purely at a temporary occupation of Belgrade and other definite points on Serbian territory in order to force the Serbian Government to integral fulfilment of Austrian demands and to furnish guarantees for future good behaviour, to which, after her experiences with Serbia, Austria-Hungary has an unquestioned right. The occupation, like the German occupation in France after the Peace of Frankfort, would be intended as a guarantee for the demand for a war indemnity. As soon as the Austrian demands are met evacuation will follow. Should the Russian Government fail to recognize the justice of this standpoint, it will have against it the public opinion of all Europe which is on the point of turning against Austria.[1]

A cursory perusal of this document might leave the impression that the Chancellor had taken a big step along the road to reasonableness in admitting: (i) that Serbia had 'met the Austrian demands in so considerable a measure that a completely intransigent attitude on the part of the Austro-Hungarian Government would bring about a gradual revulsion of public opinion all over Europe'; (ii) that, since Austria could not begin operations before 12 August, Germany would find it difficult to reject proposals for mediation without incurring the odium of causing a European war; (iii) that Sazonov had drawn closer to the Austrian standpoint to the extent that he might be thought likely to agree to such a proposal as the temporary occupation of Belgrade. But what terms would he have demanded in return for his consent?

Here lies the crux of the question. The Kaiser proposed a conciliatory solution, Bethmann an attitude of complete intransigence. Being obliged to carry out his Imperial master's order, he did so along the lines of his own opinions, changing its spirit and refusing Sazonov's paramount wish. While the Kaiser thought it sufficient if Austria barely crossed the frontier, occupying Belgrade without further invasion of Serbia, Bethmann proposed the occupation of Belgrade and other specified points on Serbian territory. But this is a minor point. More serious is the fact that Bethmann wanted the occupation 'in order to force the Serbian Government to integral fulfilment of Austrian demands' whereas Wilhelm had said: 'The few reservations made by Serbia on single points can in my opinion well be cleared up by negotiation.' This was the kernel of the whole dispute. As has already been shown, up to the eleventh hour the Russian idea was

[1] DD. II, 323.

to negotiate with Austria or to submit to mediation those points of the Austrian note on which Serbia had made reservations as infringing her sovereign rights. Hence, by changing the Kaiser's proposal to one that Serbia must accept the ultimatum terms integrally, Bethmann condemned it to failure even in the event of its acceptance by Austria, because it would never have been accepted by Russia. He was aspiring to a showy success like that of Bülow in 1909 and this would be spoiled if the Austrian ultimatum were subjected to discussion or modification. It looks as though he perfectly realized the consequences of this line of his, if he did not perhaps even want Vienna to return a flat refusal to Wilhelm's proposal, for his telegram ends with the astonishing words:

Will Your Excellency be good enough to have a talk immediately in this sense with Count Berchtold and suggest a relevant *démarche* at St. Petersburg. You will in so doing have carefully to avoid giving the impression that we wish to restrain Austria. It is merely a question of finding an arrangement to render possible the achievement of the aim pursued by Austria-Hungary of severing the vital nerve of Pan-Serb propaganda without at the same time bringing on a world war, and if this latter is not avoidable, to improve for us as far as possible the conditions in which it will be waged.[1]

The German historian Hermann Lutz recognizes and deplores that Berlin did not act at Vienna in the sense of the Kaiser's proposal and with the speed demanded by the seriousness of the situation. He writes:

As I have already shown, Berlin was not at all totally in the dark about Vienna's intentions. The intention was after all to reduce Serbia in size, eliminate her as a power factor and 'sever the vital nerve of Pan-Serb propaganda'. Jagow at least was aware of the far-reaching intentions of the Monarchy when he made the suggestion about the Trentino. . . . The passages dealing with 'war on three fronts', and how to achieve the best conditions for this, show that Bethmann Hollweg still weighs the possibility of a world war with surprising fatalism. . . . The mood that echoes in his instructions seems to be: 'If Russia intervenes, there will simply be war.' The measures recommended by the Chancellor are totally inadequate. He still deludes himself that territorial *désintéressement* can satisfy Russia after not only St. Petersburg but even London, Paris, and Rome have repeatedly emphasized that it is Serbian sovereignty which is the issue. . . . Bethmann Hollweg knew as well as every other diplomat in Europe that besides territorial integrity there exists also sovereignty. . . . It is remarkable how deaf the diplomats of the Central Powers in 1914 almost always were as soon as anybody from the other camp touched on the question of Serbian sovereignty . . . It is true that the promise of Serbian sovereignty would have implied a certain renunciation by Austria-Hungary of the idea of 'dealing the death blow to Pan-Serbism'. At the same time as these instructions were dispatched

[1] DD. II, 323.

to Tschirschky, Bethmann Hollweg was solemnly assuring the British Ambassador that he was doing 'his utmost' for the preservation of the general peace and his last words to Sir Edward Goschen were: 'A war between the Great Powers must be avoided.' These doubtless sincere words, however, were in no way in accord with what Bethmann was doing at that very moment. For nobody will wish to maintain that the above quoted instructions to Vienna were the 'utmost' that could and should have been done in the existing situation. The cleavage between the instructions to Tschirschky and the contemporaneous words to Goschen finds its explanation in the fact that the Chancellor had his hands tied on the one hand by the *carte blanche* he had given to Vienna and on the other by his wish to see a general war averted. Moreover he was not to know that the German Ambassador to Vienna manifestly toned down the instructions given him very considerably.[1]

It is obvious that if Austria was not to be made to understand that Germany wanted to hold her back, and meant to hold her back at all costs, Berchtold would pay no attention to any admonitions and a general war would in all probability result. The Chancellor's words seem to say that this would not be desirable but that, if it were unavoidable, the endeavour must be to fight it in the best conditions for the Central Powers, in other words by keeping England neutral and throwing the odium for the war on Russia. It was the ever recurrent *Leitmotiv* of Bethmann's policy throughout the whole terrible crisis, the bankruptcy of which he was to perceive a few hours later. And when this happened and Bethmann changed over to the idea that Austria should agree to the *Halt in Belgrade*, Berchtold first did not reply and then answered in the negative.

4. *The implications of mobilization not grasped by the leaders of the Great Powers.*

One of the decisive factors in the crisis of July 1914 was the absence of all understanding of military matters on the part of the responsible statesmen who had to make the decisions on war or peace, decisions which were closely connected with military problems, in particular with those of mobilization. They had no knowledge of what mobilization actually was, what demands it made on the country, what consequences it brought with it, to what risks it exposed the peace of Europe. They looked on it as a measure costly, it is true, but to which recourse might be had without necessarily implying that war would follow. They thought that as long as armies remained within their own frontiers, diplomacy could still continue to work for peace not only while mobilization was in progress but even after it was completed.

To say nothing of Berchtold who at the beginning had wanted to attack Serbia *sans crier gare* even before mobilizing and was disconsolate that the attack would have to be postponed until mobilization was

---

[1] Lutz, pp. 150–2.

completed, there was also Grey, who when the dispute first broke out, thought it natural that Austria and Russia should mobilize forthwith, while he still hoped to avert war. Sazonov, likewise, thought at once of partial mobilization against Austria as a means of frightening her and Germany into willingness to negotiate. He induced the Tsar to give his assent in principle as early as 25 July, never reflecting on the effects the measure might produce in Austria and that Russian partial mobilization meant full mobilization against Austria-Hungary who would reply by her own general mobilization. Nor did he stop to consider that by repercussion German solidarity with Vienna would manifest itself also in military matters. When later the Tsar ordered general mobilization, he telegraphed on 31 July to Wilhelm that it was 'technically impossible to stop our military preparations' but that 'as long as negotiations with Austria on Servia's account are taking place my troops shall not make any provocative action. I give you my solemn word for this.' And on 1 August he again telegraphed to Wilhelm:

Wish to have the same guarantee from you as I gave you, that these measures *do not* mean war and that we shall continue negotiating for the benefit of our countries and universal peace dear to all our hearts.[1]

There is not the slightest doubt that Grey, Sazonov and the Tsar were acting in perfect good faith. Indeed from a theoretical point of view their idea was legitimate (assuming that two or more armies can be kept standing face to face for ten days or three weeks without a single incident occurring to upset the peace). But it would only be possible on condition that each of the possible belligerents had a strategic plan laying down that no crossing of the frontier should take place before mobilization was complete. If a single one of them had a plan in which the beginning of mobilization and the crossing of the frontier were virtually simultaneous or at least correlated, that Power was not in a position to stand at ease within its frontiers while mobilization proceeded; mobilization in that case was identical with going to war. Now this was precisely the case with Germany. Bethmann seemed to know this when on 26 July he instructed Pourtalès to say to Sazonov that

preparatory military measures on the part of Russia directed in any way against ourselves would force us to take counter measures which would have to consist in mobilizing the army. Mobilization, however, means war, and would moreover have to be directed simultaneously against Russia and France, since France's engagements with Russia are well known.[2]

In another telegram of the 29th, which will be considered later, we shall see that Bethmann informs Sazonov that if Germany were forced

[1] DD. III, 487, 546.   [2] DD. I, 219. See p. 428.

to mobilize, a European war would be 'scarcely to be prevented (*auf-zuhalten*)'.[1] The truth was that there would then be no means of preventing the war. But even if he knew this, Bethmann never went on to explain why for Germany mobilization meant war, nor did he make any effort to open Grey's eyes to the danger and mistakenness of thinking it natural that Russia and Austria should mobilize. Hence Sazonov failed to understand the full meaning of the warnings addressed to him, thinking them only vague threats, especially as Bethmann was talking of 'military measures in any way directed against us' while Sazonov had no other mobilization in mind than that against Austria, if it should prove needful. Had Sazonov known that for Germany any mobilization was equivalent to war there is no doubt that he would have shaped his course differently. It is the present writer's opinion that Sazonov regarded mobilization as quite distinct from war. This can be seen from the account Pourtalès gives of a talk he had with Sazonov on 26 July at which they spoke of the Russian military preparations:

I made detailed and urgent representations to the Minister about how dangerous it seemed to me to attempt to strengthen diplomatic action by military pressure. When the Minister objected that the taking of military measures in order not to be surprised by events was far from meaning that war was intended, I replied that the danger lay in the possibility that as soon as such measures were initiated, the General Staff and not the diplomatists would have charge of the situation. . . . Sazonov put the question: 'Surely mobilization is not equivalent to war with you, either. Is it?' I replied: 'Perhaps not in theory. But . . . once the button is pressed and the machinery of mobilization set in motion, there is no stopping it.'[2]

If not even the German Ambassador knew that the frontiers of his country would be crossed a few hours after the order for mobilization, it was not possible that Sazonov could know it, and his optimism was further supported by the fact that Germany raised no objection to a Russian mobilization against Austria alone. This is a most important point and deserves close attention. It finds further confirmation in Lichnowsky's words to Nicolson on 26 July (while Grey was away on his week-end) that 'the Germans would not mind a partial mobilization, say at Odessa or Kiev—but could not view indifferently a mobilization on the German frontier'.[3] That this was not a purely personal statement of Lichnowsky's is shown by Jagow's saying to Goschen on the following day

that if Russia mobilized against Germany, latter would have to follow suit. I asked him what he meant by 'mobilizing against Germany'. He said that if Russia only mobilized in south, Germany would not mobilize, but if she

---

[1] DD. II, 342. See p. 491.   [2] Pourtalès, p. 27.   [3] BD. XI, 146.

mobilized in north Germany would have to do so too, and Russian system of mobilization was so complicated that it might be difficult exactly to locate her mobilization. Germany would therefore have to be very careful not to be taken by surprise.[1]

And to J. Cambon also on the 27th Jagow said much the same thing:

He remarked to me that if Russia mobilized, Germany would be obliged to mobilize at once. . . . I asked him if Germany would regard herself as bound to mobilize whatever the military measures taken by Russia. He said no and that she would only mobilize if Russia mobilized on the German frontier. He authorized me formally to acquaint you with this limitation.[2]

Thus at the beginning the Wilhelmstrasse took up an attitude of tolerance towards a partial mobilization by Russia, without for the moment perceiving that this was a mistake. In other words, the German statesmen knew that, for Germany, mobilization was tantamount to war, but they did not realize that if Russia mobilized against Austria, Austria would have to order general mobilization and this in its turn, under the terms of the alliance and the interpretation given to them, and because of the assurances given to Austria in July, would call forth German mobilization and, consequently, war. There was still a further point. The Austrian General Staff needed to be quite certain of Russia's intentions before going ahead with mobilization against Serbia. If Russia were not to intervene, Conrad would take the offensive against Serbia with seven army corps, i.e. 412,000 men (Case B, i.e. war in the Balkans). But if Russia came in, he would remain on the defensive on the Serbian front with three army corps (190,000 men) and send the remaining four corps to Galicia together with nine others (Case R, i.e. war against Russia). All doubt on the point must be cleared up by the fifth day of mobilization (1 August) when he must decide whether the four army corps were to be sent against Serbia or against Russia.

This is an aspect of the 'localization of the conflict' which had never been considered by the statesmen of the Central Powers. For Austria to take the field against Serbia it was needful, not only that Russia should not come in, but that she should pledge herself *a priori* not to come in. Suppose that she had given no hint of any intention to mobilize and that Conrad after 1 August had sent towards the Save those four army corps that would have been needed in Galicia. Then if after 1 August Russia had gone over from words to deeds, Austria would not have had sufficient forces to meet her and the consequences might have been incalculable. Conrad, therefore, ought to have brought this matter to the attention of the statesmen in order that they should

---

[1] BD. XI, 185   [2] LJF. 67 ; CDD. p. 187 ; DF. 3. XI, 134.

include it in their calculations. But he only did so on 27 July after agreeing to the declaration of war against Serbia as if it was this declaration which created the danger of Russian mobilization. This turned out in fact to be the case, but the upshot would have been the same if no declaration of war had been made against Serbia or if one had been made only at the moment of opening hostilities.

When on 27 July rumours of Russian mobilization reached Vienna and Berchtold asked Conrad what ought to be done, Conrad's reply was:

Germany must be called upon to state that she stands on our side and that she is sending a note to St. Petersburg worded as follows: 'We hear that Russia is mobilizing the military districts of Kiev, Odessa and Moscow; we see in this such a threat to Austria-Hungary that, if this mobilization is confirmed, Germany will at once order mobilization against Russia.[1]

This note did not enter into explanations about the particular mobilization problem of which we have just spoken, since if Russia mobilized it was clear that the four army corps would be sent to Galicia and not against Serbia and it was urgent to make sure of German support. But Berchtold did not act on Conrad's suggestion, and late on the 27th went to discuss the matter with Tschirschky, speaking, however, in terms rather different from those of the note. Tschirschky's dispatch reported:

Chief of General Staff takes the view that moment has come, if there is confirmation of Russian military measures in Berlin, to state at St. Petersburg, in the interests of desirable clarification of military situation, that this mobilization constitutes such a threat on Russian southern and western frontier that corresponding measures would have to be taken.[2]

Bethmann, as we have seen, replied on the 28th that in his and Moltke's opinion 'a categorical statement of that kind at St. Petersburg would seem to be premature'.[3]

However in the afternoon of the 28th, after the declaration of war had gone off to Serbia, Conrad again took up the matter with Berchtold. Present at the discussion were the War Minister, Krobatin, Burian, Stürgkh, Forgach, Macchio; and Conrad gives us the following account of it:

I submitted to Count Berchtold the proposal for the mobilization of the whole fleet to be addressed to His Majesty—he signed it with some hesitation. . . . Count Berchtold pointed out that the big question was whether we could carry on a war with Russia when Serbia had to be fought with 400,000 men. Now that the action against Serbia was already proceeding this objection certainly seemed belated. I answered that I must know by

---

[1] Conrad, IV, p. 133.   [2] DD. II, 281.   [3] DD. II, 299. See p. 472.

1 August whether we should also be obliged to go to war with Russia, because if that were not certain all transports would move off against Serbia. If Russia mobilized, Germany must also intervene and nothing would be left us but also to mobilize against Russia. Count Berchtold interposed that the *démarche* we asked of Germany must not take the form of an ultimatum, as Germany wanted to avoid this. I replied that there was no need to choose the form of an ultimatum but of a polite letter. And the same also to Roumania. What I, for obvious military reasons, needed to know above all was whether a Russian war was to be reckoned with or a localized war against Serbia.[1]

This time Berchtold seems to have been convinced, for at 11 p.m. on the 20th he sent Szögyény a long telegram on the subject.

According to concordant reports from St. Petersburg, Kiev, Warsaw, Moscow, and Odessa, Russia is making extensive military preparations. M. Sazonov and the Russian Minister for War have assured on their honour that mobilization has not so far been ordered, but the latter told the German Military Attaché that the military districts of Kiev, Odessa, Moscow and Kazan, facing Austria, would be mobilized if our troops crossed the Serbian frontier. In these circumstances the Chief of General Staff regards it as absolutely necessary to ascertain without delay whether we can march with strong forces against Serbia or will have to employ our main strength against Russia. On the answer to this question depends the whole plan of campaign against Serbia. If Russia actually mobilizes these military districts it would be essential, in view of the great importance to Russia of gaining time, that not only Austria-Hungary, but, from the whole situation, also Germany should at once adopt the most extensive counter-measures. Conrad's opinion seems to me worthy of the closest attention and I should like to beg the Berlin Cabinet most urgently, to weigh the question whether Russia should not be given a friendly reminder that the mobilization of those districts is tantamount to a threat to Austria-Hungary and therefore, if put into execution, would have to be answered by the most extensive counter-measures on the part both of the Monarchy and of its ally the German Reich. . . . This clarification, to be of use, would have to be carried out at the latest by 1 August. . . . I assume that the German authorities will agree to my proposals in view of the threat to both our Empires from Russia's attitude.[2]

Szögyény lost no time in seeing Jagow on the morning of the 29th, and Jagow asked him to draw up a memorandum on the subject which the Wilhelmstrasse had under consideration in the afternoon. Jagow must have been perturbed by this demand, seeing that he had expressly consented to the Russian partial mobilization and he did not at first know how to reply. On the 30th St. Petersburg made the fatal mistake of ordering general mobilization, while on the 29th the order had been given for partial mobilization in circumstances which will be discussed later. But if this mistake had never been made, how could Germany

---

[1] Conrad, IV, p. 137.   [2] Oe-U. VIII, 10863.

request Russia not to pursue military preparations against Austria alone, in view of the fact that she had already given her consent to them? And if she did not make the request, how would she find herself placed with regard to Austria, whom she had urged to attack Serbia without delay and who now saw the menace of Russia peering over her shoulder? Nor can it be said that this German lack of foresight had no actual consequences because the Russian general mobilization led to that of Germany and thus to war. On the contrary, we shall see that on the 29th, in order to deter Sazonov from the partial mobilization to which Jagow had given his assent, Bethmann sent Pourtalès a telegram containing such threats that they powerfully contributed to persuading Sazonov that he must mobilize not only against Austria but also against Germany.

5. Moltke's views on preventive war, his memorandum of 28 July.

The chain of recklessness and error which brought Europe to catastrophe is made up of a series of links which cannot be taken apart and each one of which must be examined, if it is to be understood how the war came about. Berlin ought at once to have shattered Sazonov's illusion that he could mobilize against Austria without forthwith bringing Germany into the fray. The danger of the various mobilizations, the nexus existing between them, the effect that one might have by setting all the others in motion, one after the other, should have been calmly and thoroughly thought out. The sole excuse for neglecting this precaution possessed by the men in power in 1914 is that they were in fact ignorant of the problem in all its many aspects.[1]

But Moltke understood the problem and on 29 July began to take up position to the conflict. He had not been consulted on the 26th, the day of his return to Berlin; he was never asked whether, if the attempt to 'localize the conflict' were not successful, Germany would be capable of facing a European war with hope of success! But no doubt if he had been asked the question, he would have answered it with the forecast he made in a letter to Conrad of 21 January 1909 in which he said:

I think that only an Austrian invasion of Serbia could in the event lead to active intervention by Russia. This would provide the *casus foederis* for

[1] It is curious to see that Jagow in his *Ursachen und Ausbruch des Weltkrieges* (Berlin, 1919, p. 123), admits having said to Goschen that 'if Russia mobilized only in the south we should not mobilize'. He takes care not to confess that this was a tremendous blunder and glides over the consequences for which it was partly responsible. This he was able to do because Russia ordered general mobilization, i.e. mobilization also against Germany, before Germany took the same step. But it is quite clear that even if Russia had confined herself to ordering partial mobilization, the logic of the case as presented by Conrad and Moltke would have forced Germany to demand that it be cancelled, or, in case of a refusal, mobilize in her turn in order to go to the help of Austria. In short partial mobilization would have led to war no less surely than general mobilization.

Germany. . . . The moment Russia mobilizes, Germany also will mobilize and will unquestionably mobilize her whole army.[1]

And he would probably have chimed in with the views of the Wilhelmstrasse that if war was to come, it had better come now.

This must be stated because there are people in Germany, among them Theobald von Schäfer, the Director of the Potsdam Archives, who maintain that Moltke did not want a preventive war,[2] and others like Lutz who timidly maintain the contrary.[3] Let us briefly examine the documents. On 19 April 1909, when the Bosnian crisis had subsided, Moltke, replying to a letter from Conrad of 10 April, wrote that he did not feel he was authorized to give his views 'on the desirability or undesirability of war in this case'. But privately he 'ventured' to say that he felt

the deepest regret that an opportunity has been allowed to slip by unused which would probably not so soon recur in such favourable conditions. I am firmly convinced that the war between Austria-Hungary and Serbia could have been successfully localized and the Monarchy, internally consolidated and externally strengthened by its victorious prosecution, would have won a preponderance in the Balkans which could not very easily have been shaken. Even were Russia to have become belligerent and a European war to have developed, the preconditions for Austria and Germany would have been better now than, as far as can be foreseen, they will be a few years hence. . . . As long as Austria and Germany stand shoulder to shoulder, each ready to recognize in the actions of the other the *tua res agitur*, we shall be strong enough to break through all encirclement. Against this Central European block many a one may break his teeth.[4]

On 19 August 1911, during the Agadir crisis, Moltke wrote to his wife:

If we again slink out of this affair with our tail between our legs, if we cannot pull ourselves together to present demands which we are prepared to enforce by the sword, then I despair of the future of the German Reich. Then I shall get out. But first I shall put forward the proposal to abolish the army and put ourselves under the protectorate of Japan, then we can make money in peace and sink back into idiocy (*'versimpeln'*).[5]

He seems to have been less ebullient during the Balkan wars. On 16 February 1913, writing to Conrad, he said he thought the conflagration would break out sooner or later 'but the attack must be started by the Slavs'. It was perhaps the peaceable frame of mind of Wilhelm

[1] Conrad, I, pp. 380–1. See Vol. I, pp. 269–70.
[2] Theobald von Schäfer, *Wollte Generaloberst v. Moltke den Präventivkrieg?* KSF., June 1927, pp. 543–60.
[3] Hermann Lutz, *Moltke und der Präventivkrieg*, KSF., November 1927, pp. 1107–20.
[4] Conrad, I, p. 165.
[5] Moltke, p. 362.

during the years 1912–13 which prompted his Chief of Staff to abstain at that time from bellicose language. All the same, in the Vienna War Archives under the rubric *Akten aus dem Nachlass Schemuas* (folder 161) there is preserved a report of a conversation which took place between Marshal Schemua, then Austrian Chief of Staff, and Wilhelm and Moltke, which states that Moltke

repeatedly maintained his loyalty to the alliance and declared that we could place full reliance on German help if ever Russia threatened us, since it was also a paramount interest of Germany's that we should not be weakened.

True, these statements were not calls for a preventive war. But, on the eve of the Sarajevo crime, Moltke was more explicit. The witness is Conrad. Neither Schäfer nor Lutz mentions the incident. Conrad had a meeting with his German opposite number at Carlsbad on 12 May 1914 and they spoke of the probability of a war.

General Moltke said that delay meant a lessening of our chances; we could not compete with Russia in masses. And he continued: 'Here people go on expecting a statement from England that she will not join in. This statement England will never make.'[1]

That these views of Moltke's were known to Berlin is clear from a private letter written on 31 July 1914 by Lerchenfeld, the Bavarian envoy in Berlin, to the Bavarian Premier Hertling, which runs:

Months ago the Chief of the General Staff, Herr von Moltke, expressed the view that the moment is from the military point of view favourable to a degree which cannot occur again in a foreseeable future.[2]

The reasons he gave were the German superiority in artillery and small arms and the inferior training of the French troops.

These documents leave no doubt as to the views of the German Chief of Staff. Let us now see how he acted on his return to Berlin. A telegram sent on 26 July by Bethmann to Tschirschky reports Moltke as saying that he 'also regards it as urgently necessary to hold Italy fast to the Triple Alliance'.[3] Then he drafted and forwarded to Jagow the text of the ultimatum to be presented at Brussels at the moment of mobilization. His plan of campaign was based on the passage of the German right wing through Belgium. He thus needed to have the document ready requesting the Belgian Government to grant the army right of passage. On the morning of the 27th he was again in conference with the Chancellor and in the afternoon was summoned by the Kaiser to the Potsdam meeting. That same day he wrote to his wife: 'The situation continues to be extremely obscure. . . . It will be about another fortnight before anything definite can be known or

[1] Conrad. III, pp. 669–73.   [2] DD. IV, p. 151.   [3] DD. I, 202.

said,'[1] meaning probably that Austria would not begin operations until about 12 August. But what Moltke on the 27th did not know, as indeed the Kaiser also did not, was that Jagow had instructed Tschirschky to ask Vienna to declare war and that the declaration was to be made on 28 July. As soon as the declaration was made he must certainly have understood that this seriously aggravated the situation and he began to step into the foreground. May he not have been encouraged to do so by things Conrad had said to him? Surely it is likely that Conrad drew his attention to the problems which the threatened partial mobilization in Russia would raise for Austria. It would be strange, had Conrad not done so. But however that may be, on the 28th Moltke drew up an important memorandum which he sent on the 29th to the Chancellor and which discussed those very problems, arriving at the same solutions as had Conrad. The document begins by expatiating on the misdeeds of Serbia and the longanimity of Austria. The issue between them could have been settled locally to the general relief of Europe but for the fact that Russia now threatened to intervene.

What will and must be the further consequence? Austria, if she enters Serbia, will be faced not only with the Serbian Army but with strong Russian superiority; she will thus not be able to wage war with Serbia without making Russian intervention certain. That means she will be forced to mobilize the other half of her army, for she cannot possibly put herself at the mercy of a Russia ready for war. The instant Austria mobilizes her whole army, the clash between her and Russia will become inevitable. Now that is for Germany the *casus foederis*. Unless Germany means to break her word and allow her ally to succumb to Russian superior strength, she must also mobilize. That will lead to the mobilization of the remaining Russian military districts. Russia will then be able to say, 'I am being attacked by Germany' and that will make her sure of the support of France who is bound by treaty to go to war if her ally Russia is attacked. The Franco-Russian agreement, so often praised as a purely defensive alliance brought about only to meet German plans of aggression, comes thereby into operation and the civilized states of Europe will begin to tear one another to pieces.

This line of thought more or less coincided with that of Conrad. Moltke laid down it that: (1) Austria could not go to war against Serbia without mobilizing against Russia, since, if she ventured into Serbia without taking this precaution, she would find herself at the mercy of Russia, whose intentions were not reassuring; (2) Austrian mobilization would make an Austro-Russian clash inevitable; (3) this clash would call Germany to the scene and she would therefore have to mobilize. In making these points Moltke was demonstrating that to enter Serbia was to unleash a European war and to make oneself

---

[1] Moltke, p. 381. See p. 437.

responsible for causing it. Moltke realized this and, not knowing that Russian partial mobilization was on the point of being ordered, he ruefully remarked that if Austria were to mobilize first, as he himself wished, Russia could say to her: 'You, Austria, are mobilizing against us, that means you intend to make war on us.' Likewise, even when Germany was obliged to mobilize, Russia would say to the world: 'I never wanted war. It is Germany who brought it on.' But these consequences Moltke seemed prepared to accept, for he proceeds to arrive at the same conclusions as Conrad:

This is the way things will and must develop, unless, one might almost say, a miracle takes place to prevent at the eleventh hour a war which will annihilate the civilization of almost the whole of Europe for decades to come.

Germany does not want to bring about this terrible war. But the German Government knows that it would fatally wound the deeply rooted sentiment of allied loyalty, one of the finest traits of the German spirit, and place itself at variance with all the feelings of its people, if it were unwilling to go to the help of its ally at a moment which must decide that ally's fate. . . . Germany therefore, if the clash between Austria and Russia is inevitable, must mobilize and prepare to wage war on two fronts.

In connexion with the military measures which are to be taken by us if the case arises, it is of the greatest importance to ascertain, as soon as possible, whether Russia and France are disposed to go to the length of war with Germany. The greater the progress of our neighbours' preparations, the sooner they will be able to complete their mobilization. The military position will thus grow day by day more unfavourable for us and may, if our prospective opponents go on preparing at their leisure, lead to fatal consequences for us.[1]

Moltke's memorandum was entitled: *Towards an estimate of the political situation* and this is a correct description. It constitutes an invasion by the military authorities of the political field which lies outside their province. Kautsky is right in asserting that in this document

the central military organization raises the claim to take the decision of questions of foreign policy into its own hands, and to hasten on a warlike solution, even at the very moment when the civil authority is preparing to yield so far as to take a step, although a small one, towards peace.[2]

Lutz, too, describes the document as 'an inroad into the province of the Imperial Government likely, indeed no doubt calculated, to influence the political leadership'.[3]

He summarizes Moltke's memorandum as follows:

In this memorandum Moltke took the standpoint that Germany must mobilize if Russia mobilized against Austria, therefore that in this case the

---

[1] DD. II, 349.   [2] Kautsky, p. 198.   [3] Lutz, pp. 200–1.

casus foederis for Germany would arise, since Russian partial mobilization against Austria would force the latter into general mobilization, from which war would necessarily result. As we have already seen, however, the Reich Government had made a statement that the *casus foederis* would arise, not as a result of Russian partial mobilization against Austria, but only after a Russian attack on Austria, or as a result of Russian general mobilization. The difference is an essential one.[1]

All the same Moltke does use certain expressions which convey a sense of horror at the prospect that the civilized states of Europe will tear one another to pieces,

unless, one might almost say, a miracle happens to avert at the eleventh hour a war which will annihilate for decades to come the civilization of almost the whole of Europe. Germany has no desire to bring about this terrible war.[2]

Though resolved to go to the ally's help, he seems at the critical moment to have perceived the terribleness of the tragedy towards which events were moving and to have been somewhat more cautious than the War Minister Falkenhayn.

6. *Bethmann's threatening telegrams to Paris and St. Petersburg; his dissatisfaction with Vienna.*

Falkenhayn had kept the troops in garrison that were to have gone on manoeuvres, had ordered the guarding of the railways by railway authorities and the purchase of grain. On the 28th he ordered the troops already away on manoeuvres return to garrison. Bethmann objected to this but the Kaiser gave his authorization.[3] Thus far no harm was done. Wilhelm's consent meant nothing, since as Falkenhayn's biographer writes: 'the Kaiser was entirely averse to war and even disposed to take a different line from Austria'.[4] But on the 29th Falkenhayn put forward much more serious demands in a conversation which he and Moltke had with Bethmann at a time that is not exactly known but was probably during the morning. Writing on the 29th before knowing the results of the conversation, but on the authority of information obtained from Falkenhayn, General Wenninger, the Bavarian Military Attaché at Berlin, gave it as his impression that Moltke and Falkenhayn were in conflict with Bethmann and Jagow. They were only at one in their annoyance with Austria for not beginning military operations for another fortnight. The War Minister and Chief of Staff wanted military measures to be taken at once. Indeed

the Chief of Staff wants to go further. He is throwing his whole weight in favour of using the exceptionally favourable position to strike hard. He

---

[1] Lutz, p. 203.   [2] Lutz, p. 202.   [3] Zwehl, p. 56.   [4] Zwehl, p. 56.

points out that France is actually in military embarrassment, that Russia feels anything but secure from the military point of view, that the season is right, the harvest practically in, the year's training completed. Against this impetus the Chancellor is applying the brakes with all his might. He is anxious to avoid anything that might give rise to similar measures in France or England and start the stone rolling.[1]

This statement however is not entirely correct, since in the talk on the morning of the 29th Moltke did not at all support the extremist views of Falkenhayn. The latter's biographer, the sole source of information about this conversation, writes:

The news to hand on the 29th was that France and England, the latter only in respect of her navy, had started mobilizing. Falkenhayn feared lest Germany might 'sit quiet' while this was happening. He did not succeed in gaining the Chancellor's approval of his wish to proclaim the 'imminent danger of war' (*drohende Kriegsgefahr*) because Moltke would not go further than giving military protection to important railway key points.[2]

The proclamation of the *Kriegsgefahrzustand* (state of war danger) meant putting into operation the military measures preceding mobilization. It was, therefore, a big step towards general mobilization, i.e. in the case of Germany, towards war. It is understandable that the Chancellor was unwilling to authorize it and he had Moltke on his side. However Bethmann entirely agreed with Moltke in the opinion that the intentions of St. Petersburg and Paris must be ascertained without delay. At 12.50 p.m. on the 29th he telegraphed Schoen to warn the French Government:

We are having to proclaim '*Kriegsgefahr*' which, though not mobilization or recall to the colours, does mean a heightening of the tension.[3]

The telegram to Pourtalès was couched in more imperious terms:

Kindly impress on M. Sazonov very seriously that further progress of Russian mobilization measures would compel us to mobilize and that then European war would be scarcely to be prevented.[4]

This telegram communicated to Sazonov on the afternoon of the 29th and regarded by him as an ultimatum, produced, as we shall see, the opposite of the effect intended. It betrayed the state of nerves which gained hold of the Chancellor as a result of the situation that presented itself to him on 29 July. News of the measures taken by the British Admiralty had caused panic on the Stock Exchange. From St. Petersburg in the course of the night had come a telegram from Chelius, the German Military Plenipotentiary at the Russian Court,

---

[1] DD. IV, Annex IVa, No. 2; in 1927 edition, pp. 153-4.
[2] Zwehl, p 56.　　　[3] DD. II, 341.　　　[4] DD. II, 342.

reporting a conversation he had had with Prince Trubetzkoi, a member of the Tsar's entourage, who had said:

We have no love for the Serbs but they are our fellow Slavs and we cannot leave our brethren in the lurch when they are in a tight place. . . . The return of your Kaiser has greatly reassured us, for we trust His Majesty and do not want war. . . . It would be well if the two Monarchs would have a word with each other by telegraph.[1]

This had actually been done during the night. From various quarters news was coming in of mobilization measures in South Russian districts and of preparations in France. And during the morning Szögyény called to put forward Conrad's suggestion that St. Petersburg should be threatened with not only Austrian but also German counter-measures if the news of Russian partial mobilization were confirmed. A similar request was made in Moltke's memorandum and in the talk Bethmann had with Moltke and Falkenhayn. The threatening telegrams to St. Petersburg and Paris were Bethmann's way of carrying out the request.

Another cause of anxiety and annoyance to Bethmann was Austria's attitude towards Italy. Under pressure from Tschirschky Berchtold had gone to the length of telling Italy that Austria did not intend to make territorial acquisitions in Serbia and that, therefore, if she were obliged to proceed to an occupation of Serbian territory that was more than temporary, she was ready in such an event to enter upon an exchange of views with Italy.[2] But Bethmann did not think this statement satisfactory and wrote to Jagow on the 29th asking whether it would not be

necessary to send another telegram to Vienna, in which we sharply declare that we regard this way of handling the question of compensation with Rome as absolutely unsatisfactory and hold Vienna entirely responsible for any attitude Italy may take in a possible war. If on the eve of a possible European conflagration Vienna threatens in this way to shatter the Triple Alliance, the whole alliance system will be undermined. Vienna's statement that it will behave itself properly with Italy in the event of a permanent occupation of Serbian territory stands in contradiction with the assurances it gave St. Petersburg of territorial *désintéressement*. The statements made in Rome will certainly become known in St. Petersburg. We as allies cannot support a policy with a false bottom. . . . Otherwise we cannot continue to mediate at St. Petersburg and will find ourselves hitched to the towline of Vienna. This I will not do, even if I risk being accused of turning tail.[3]

It is obvious that the Chancellor wanted Italy to be kept within the Triple Alliance by the promise of compensations not conditional on territorial gains which Austria was prevented from making by her

---

[1] DD. II, 337.   [2] DD. II, 328.   [3] DD. II, 340.

pledge to Russia not to strip Serbia of any territory. After sending off this letter, Bethmann at 8 p.m. on the 29th, passed on to Tschirschky the telegram from Lichnowsky[1] which had caused him so much alarm the previous day and to which he appended the following comment:

These utterances of the Austrian diplomats would seem to be reflexions of fresh wishes and aspirations. I view the behaviour of the Vienna Government and its diverse procedures with the different Governments with growing disapproval. At St. Petersburg it declares its territorial *désintéressement*, us it leaves completely in the dark about its plans, Rome it fobs off with meaningless phrases about the question of compensations; in London Mensdorff gives away parts of Serbia to Bulgaria and Albania and comes into conflict with the solemn declarations of Vienna at St. Petersburg. From these contradictions I can only draw the conclusion that its disavowal of Count Hoyos contained in telegram No. 83 was only meant for the gallery, and that the Vienna Government cherishes plans which it thinks had better be concealed from us, in order to make sure of German support in any event and not to expose itself to a possible refusal by making them known.[2]

Let it be said that there undoubtedly was an incompatibility between mentioning to Rome the possibility of a not merely temporary occupation of Serbian territory and giving St. Petersburg promises of Austrian territorial *désintéressement*. But there was no incompatibility between the promise of *désintéressement* and that of giving away parts of Serbia to her neighbours. In fact to guarantee that Austria would not enlarge herself at the cost of Serbia was not the same as to guarantee the integrity of Serbian territory. And if Bethmann and Sazonov did not perceive the deception lurking in the Austrian formula, the fault was theirs for not having made sure of its full meaning. However the strong disapproval voiced in the first part of the above telegram was followed by instructions which should have made Tschirschky act with the greatest prudence:

The above observations are in the first instance for Your Excellency's personal enlightenment. I only ask you to indicate to Count Berchtold that it would be advisable to take precautions to avert mistrust of his declarations to the Powers on the subject of Serbian integrity.[3]

But that amount of pressure was not enough to make Austria do all she could to keep Italy inside the Triple Alliance, had that ever been possible. Nor could diplomatic jugglery ensure the neutrality of England for which Bethmann still continued to hope on 29 July, though realizing that it was growing increasingly difficult to propitiate Grey.

Indeed, on the evening of the 28th, a telegram from Tschirschky had, as Bethmann had asked, brought Berchtold's rejection of Grey's

[1] DD. II, 301.   [2] DD. II, 361.   [3] DD. II, 361.

suggestion that Austria should regard the Serbian reply either as satisfactory or as a basis for negotiation.[1] This rejection had to be communicated to Goschen. How could it be made palatable to Grey after the refusal of a conference? From Goschen at 4.27 p.m. came the account of how Bethmann set about it.

Imperial Chancellor sent for me to-day. He informed me that he had at once communicated to Vienna your opinion that Servian reply might form basis of discussion. He regretted to state that Austro-Hungarian Government had answered that it was too late to act upon your suggestion, as events had marched too rapidly. Upon receiving their answer his Excellency had sent a message to Vienna stating that while he was of opinion that Servian reply had shown a certain desire to meet Austrian demands, he quite understood that in view of past experiences Austro-Hungarian Government could not rest satisfied without some sure guarantees that demands they had made upon Servia would be scrupulously carried out in their entirety. He had added that he presumed that hostilities about to be undertaken against Servia had exclusive object of securing such guarantees, particularly as Austro-Hungarian Government had already given assurances at St. Petersburg that she had no territorial designs. If this view was correct he advised Austro-Hungarian Government to speak openly in that sense, for he hoped that by holding such language all possible misunderstanding might be set aside.

This was a distant allusion to the *Halt in Belgrade* proposal of the previous evening. And Grey was to be placated and reassured by being made partner in a secret:

His Excellency begged me most urgently to request you to regard this communication of language he had held at Vienna as most secret and confidential and not to mention it to representatives of any other Power. He had not even mentioned it to Prince Lichnowsky. That he now communicated it to me was a proof of confidence he felt in you and of his desire that you should know how sincerely he appreciated your efforts in the cause of general peace and that he was doing his best to support them.[2]

7. The Potsdam meeting of 29 July; the Russian announcement of partial mobilization.

Bethmann's technique of diplomacy was as perfidious as it was clumsy and puerile. At Vienna he spoke in one voice, at St. Petersburg and London in another. He asked Vienna to begin hostilities against Serbia to enforce the complete fulfilment of its demands. To Grey and Sazonov he put on a face of innocence and expected to be regarded by them as a mediator and peace maker. He carried out the Kaiser's order while radically altering it and holding it back to make sure it would have no effect. Tirpitz, who must have known Bethmann pretty well, had noticed that he 'avoided straight and open discussions'.

[1] DD. II, 313. See p. 465.   [2] BD. XI, 264.

His aim was

to avoid the world war. But the means used to this end . . . helped considerably to promote the world war. Bethmann did not see that ambiguity did not bring us any respect in such a matter, and was extraordinarily dangerous.[1]

Moreover

the Chancellor had not known how to keep the Kaiser really in touch with events. The Kaiser found it difficult to find a clear starting point for effective diplomatic action. He said he did not know what the Austrians wanted. The Serbs had conceded everything but a few bagatelles. Since 5 July the Austrians had said nothing about their intentions.[2]

This is anything but the truth. The statesmen at Vienna were but puppets whose movements were controlled by wires held by Bethmann and Jagow, though the Kaiser did not realize this.

Tirpitz goes on to say:

This statement was made in the evening of 29 July in the Neues Palais at Potsdam, whither the Kaiser had summoned the military chiefs in order to inform them of his negotiations with the Chancellor who had collapsed completely. We had no idea at the time of the doubts which Bethmann must have had about his policy during the first weeks in July. We only saw with consternation what was taking place before our eyes, including the Kaiser's, who expressed himself without reserve regarding Bethmann's incompetence, as he had done many times before. He gave the opinion, however, that he could not separate himself from this man now, as he enjoyed the confidence of Europe.[3]

The meeting of the 29th has been sometimes called the Potsdam Crown Council. And in fact it was a council or series of ordinary councils in which the Kaiser consulted his chief subordinates. According to the day's record made by the aide-de-camp on duty, the Kaiser at 4.40 p.m. received the Chancellor, Falkenhayn, Moltke, and Lyncker, the Chief of his Military Cabinet. At 6.10 p.m. he saw his brother, Prince Henry of Prussia, at 7.15 p.m. Tirpitz, Pohl, the Naval Chief of General Staff and Müller, Chief of the Navy Cabinet.[4]

Goschen, however, wrote to Nicolson:

His Excellency sent for me about 10.30 p.m.; told me that he had just come from a Council at Potsdam, at which the Emperor, Admiral v. Tirpitz and the Minister of War had been present.[5]

If this were so, it looks as if Bethmann had been present at a series of audiences given that evening by the Kaiser and had stayed on even

---

[1] Tirpitz, *Memoirs*, I, pp. 259–60.   [2] Tirpitz, *Memoirs*, I, p. 272
[3] Tirpitz, *Memoirs*, I, pp. 273–4.
[4] A. von Wegerer, in KSF., July 1923, pp. 8–12.   [5] BD. XI, 677

after they were over. But Tirpitz and the aide-de-camp both record that the Chancellor left Potsdam before Wilhelm saw his brother Prince Henry. If this point is not at all certain, still less is known of what was said and decided at the meetings. The *Yellow Book* represents Jules Cambon as telegraphing from Berlin to Paris on 30 July:

> It seems certain that the Extraordinary Council held yesterday evening at Potsdam with the military authorities under the presidency of the Kaiser decided on mobilization . . . but that from various causes . . . the serious measures which had been decided upon were suspended.

This is one of the usual falsifications of the *Yellow Book*. The great collection of *French Diplomatic Documents* gives nothing of this kind in the two dispatches telegraphed on 30 July to Paris by Jules Cambon, from which Document No. 105 of the *Yellow Book* is derived with considerable alterations and additions.[1] Some light on what went on at Potsdam on the 29th is thrown by the minutes of a Prussian Council of Ministers held on the 30th, at which the Chancellor acquainted the Prussian Cabinet of the position. With reference to his own *démarche* at Vienna on the evening of the 28th in connexion with the proposal for a *Halt in Belgrade*, he made the statement:

> H.M. is agreed that, before further decisions, the above-outlined action at Vienna should first be brought to a conclusion: a declaration of threatening danger of war means mobilization and this in our circumstances, mobilization, on two fronts, means war. It is not practically possible to carry on at the same time political and military action. . . . On the part of the military the desire had been expressed to proclaim the 'threatening danger of war' but he had successfully carried his different standpoint with His Majesty and the limit was drawn at military protection for the railways.[2]

These statements clearly refer to a meeting at which the Kaiser, the Chancellor and the military chiefs were present. Such a meeting cannot have been other than the Potsdam Council. However it appears that Moltke was not one of those who asked for the proclamation of 'the threatening danger of war'. On the contrary Falkenhayn's biographer Zwehl writes that Falkenhayn was concerned about the beginnings of mobilization of the French Army and British Navy but

> did not manage to gain the Chancellor's approval of his wish to proclaim the 'threatening danger of war' because Moltke would not go further than giving military protection to railway key points. Nor was more obtained in a joint verbal report to the Kaiser, although in those days he [the Kaiser] inclined to the view that the ball had started rolling and it was too late to stop it. Falkenhayn's comment was that he would have understood the Kaiser's hesitating attitude in the interests of preserving peace, if he had still believed in, or at least wished for, peace. . . . Though Falkenhayn rightly

---

[1] LJF. 105; CDD. p. 214; DF. 3. XI, 330 and 339.   [2] DD. II, 456.

emphasizes that the delay was to our military disadvantage, the War Ministry had no right to oppose it, if Moltke felt able to take the responsibility for it.[1]

The truth probably is that it was the Kaiser's pacific attitude which calmed down both Moltke and Falkenhayn.

But such scraps of information certainly do not complete the chronicle of the decisions and discussions which took place at Potsdam. The problem most discussed must have been that of English neutrality which mattered to the Chancellor above all else and which he sought much more than he sought to avoid war, his great fear being that the many refusals returned by Germany and Austria to the proposals put forward both by Grey and the Kaiser might end in the loss of English neutrality and in England's taking the side of France and Russia. Prince Henry had only just returned from London when the Kaiser received him at 6.10 p.m. He, as we know, had seen King George V on the 26th, coming away with the impression that England would remain neutral.[2] Tirpitz says Prince Henry reaffirmed this impression on the 29th and adds that, when he himself expressed some doubts, the Kaiser silenced him by saying: 'I have the word of a King: that is sufficient for me.'[3] But this assurance must have related only to the immediate attitude of England, since on 28 July Prince Henry wrote to the Kaiser from Kiel:

Before my departure from London on Sunday morning I had, at my own request, a short talk with Georgie who was perfectly clear about the seriousness of the present situation and assured me that he and his Government would no leave stone unturned to localize the war between Austria and Serbia; that is why his Government made the proposal, as you already know, that Germany, England, France and Italy should intervene to try to hold Russia in check, and that he hoped Germany would be able in spite of her alliance with Austria to associate herself with this proposal in order to avert European war, to which, he said, we were nearer than ever before; he further said literally 'we shall try all we can to keep out of this—and shall remain neutral'. That the words were sincerely meant, I am convinced; as also of England's remaining at the beginning neutral, whether she will be able to do so in the long run, I cannot judge, but have my doubts on account of her relations with France.[4]

Now Prince Henry cannot have spoken otherwise than he wrote. This impression of his, combined with that produced by the British Admiralty's orders to the fleet and Lichnowsky's warnings, must have persuaded Bethmann to suggest to his Imperial master a move of extreme daring and singular clumsiness, namely openly to ask the English Government to remain neutral, offering guarantees and making promises such as seemed adequate to the occasion. The details of this

---

[1] Zwehl, p. 56.
[3] Tirpitz, *Memoirs*, I, p. 275.
[2] See pp. 429 and 687.
[4] DD. II, 374.

proposal were put into writing by the Chancellor. He knew that besides being concerned for the fate of France, Great Britain strongly desired an agreement with Germany on naval limitation. This agreement she had several times sought to obtain, the last attempt being the Haldane mission of 1912, and had never succeeded owing to the intransigence of Tirpitz with the Kaiser's backing. Bethmann, therefore, thought it would be a bright idea to tempt Grey with the bait of a naval agreement by which Germany would have to make certain concessions. Tirpitz tells us:

The Kaiser informed the company [on the 29th] that the Chancellor had proposed that, in order to keep England neutral, we should sacrifice the German fleet for an agreement with England, which he, the Kaiser, had refused to do. Consequently, after his return from Potsdam on the evening of the 29th, the Chancellor had to put some restraint upon himself with regard to the fleet, when he summoned the British Ambassador to him and made high bids for English neutrality in the event of a Franco-German war.[1]

What these bids were will be seen later.[2] Now our attention must be turned to serious news which reached the Wilhelmstrasse on the afternoon of the 29th. On learning of the Austrian declaration of war on Serbia of 28 July, Sazonov had immediately telegraphed to Bronevski, the Russian Chargé d'Affaires at Berlin, that as a result of it the Russian Government had ordered for the next day, the 29th, mobilization in the districts of Odessa, Kiev, Moscow and Kazan, i.e. against Austria. 'Bring this to the knowledge of the German Government [added Sazonov] emphasizing that no aggressive intention exists on the part of Russia towards Germany.'[3] The instruction was carried out not by the Chargé d'Affaires but by the Ambassador Sverbeev, who had returned to Berlin on the 29th. Calling on Jagow at 5 p.m. for the first conversation after his return, Sverbeev entered into a lengthy discussion of the events following the Sarajevo crime on which it is not necessary to dwell here. The discussion had not ended when a paper was brought to Jagow which he read with 'consternation' and passed to the Ambassador, asking him if what it said were true. It was a dispatch from Pourtalès, which had reached the Wilhelmstrasse at 2.52 p.m. and summarized a conversation Pourtalès had had that morning with Sazonov. We shall return to this conversation later. Sazonov had told Pourtalès that since Austria had mobilized eight corps

this measure must be regarded as directed partly against Russia. Therefore Russia likewise saw herself obliged to mobilize the military districts on the Austrian frontier. The relevant order will be given to-day.[4]

[1] Tirpitz, *Memoirs*, I, p. 274. [2] See pp. 505–7.
[3] *Int. Bez.* i. V, 168. [4] DD. II, 343.

Here follows an account of the further conversation with Jagow according to the version given by Sverbeev in a later report, substantially identical with that telegraphed by him to St. Petersburg on the evening of the 29th[1]:

It was the news of our mobilization against Austria-Hungary with which I had orders to acquaint him. In confirming this news I emphasized—as I had orders to do—that this measure had no point of hostility directed against Germany and I added that the mobilization on the Austrian frontier had all the more foundation as the Hapsburg Monarchy, according to trustworthy information reaching me, was itself making extensive military preparations in Galicia.

Herr von Jagow denied the alleged preparations and declared that since we had mobilized against Austria-Hungary, Germany was likewise obliged to mobilize; there was therefore nothing else left to be done and the diplomatists must now leave the talking to the cannon.

I could not conceal from my interlocutor the amazement which this statement evoked in me. For still on the previous evening he had been saying to Cambon that our mobilization against Austria would not bring German mobilization in its train. Herr von Jagow answered with great embarrassment: 'Yes, but as Germany has learnt that Russia is placing her troops ready on the German frontier, she was of course obliged to mobilize on her part.'

I declared, that, as far as we were concerned, I knew nothing of this, and doubted that this news was correct. Of Germany, on the other hand, I knew definitely from trustworthy information that she was assembling her military strength only against us.

Herr von Jagow vigorously called in question these alleged preparations and, naturally without success, attempted to persuade me that all that had been done was to recall officers on leave and troops which had taken part in manoeuvres.[2]

The conversation ended with Jagow's saying that he had been expressing a purely personal point of view and adding that he would give a definite reply after consulting with the Chancellor and that a Cabinet meeting was to be held that evening.[3]

It seems clear that Bethmann did not know of the Russian partial mobilization when he went to Potsdam, since the Kaiser received him at 4.30 p.m., whereas the telegram from Pourtalès only came into Jagow's hands, after decoding, at 5 p.m. Certainly the telegram was not discussed at Potsdam, for the Chancellor sent it to the Kaiser on the morning of the 30th. Had the conference known of it, the Russian partial mobilization would have been the main topic of dis-

---

[1] *Int. Bez.* i. V, 241.
[2] Schilling, pp. 102–10; *Int. Bez.* i. V, p. 336. The English edition of Schilling's diary gives the French original of this text.
[3] *Int. Bez.* i. V, 241.

cussion and would have affected the decisions taken. When the Kaiser
did read it at 7 a.m. on the 30th he annotated it with angry marginal
notes: 'That means I've got to mobilize as well!'[1] Thus the Chancellor
must have found the bad news awaiting him on returning to his office
after the conference at which he had looked 'completely collapsed' and
at which the Kaiser had certainly not given him a flattering reception
and had rejected his proposal to offer England a naval agreement.
The news of Russian mobilization must have increased his dismay.
Germany had consented to this Russian partial mobilization, but that
very morning Berchtold's telegram and Moltke's memorandum were
showing that the two Chiefs of Staff regarded the Russian measure as
one which made it necessary for Austria and Germany to mobilize and
that meant war. What was he to do?

The situation was growing more and more disquieting. At 3.15 p.m.
Berlin received yet another telegram dispatched from St. Petersburg
at 2.30 in which Chelius reported:

> In the Tsar's entourage yesterday there were still high hopes of a peaceful
> solution; to-day, since the declaration of war [on Serbia], a general war is re-
> garded as almost inevitable. . . . Since the rejection of the Serbian reply,
> which is here regarded as extremely compliant, the conviction prevails that
> Austria has acted in bad faith and means war. . . . They do not want war
> and deplore that no Power has been able to hold Austria back from this
> dangerous step.[2]

At 4 p.m. on the 29th the General Staff had learnt that Belgium was
raising her effectives from 55,000 to 100,000 men by calling up three
class of reservists, was equipping fortifications and reinforcing frontier
defences, with the intention of resisting invasion, whether coming
from France or from Germany. The news, which was at once passed on
to the Wilhelmstrasse,[3] was very disturbing from the point of view
of the German war plan. Next the Naval Attaché in London sent word
on the 30th that, if Germany made war on France, the British Navy
would immediately attack Germany[4] (actually on the 29th the British
First Squadron had moved to concentrate at Scapa Flow and the
Second and Third were being kept together at their bases).[5] The news
from Roumania was bad, from Italy none too reassuring, from England
doubtful. On the 28th Lichnowsky had not seen Grey. But on the 29th,
in a telegram reaching Berlin at 4.40 p.m., he reported Tyrrell as saying
that the Triple Alliance would never stand the strain of a world war
and that Italy would not take part in a war which broke out over
Serbia.[6] In a later telegram, arriving at 5.7 p.m., Lichnowsky summarized a conversation which he had with Grey on the morning of

[1] DD. II, 399.   [2] DD. II, 344.   [3] DD. II, 372.
[4] DD. II, 402.   [5] Churchill, pp. 210-13.   [6] DD. II, 355.

the 29th. Grey had learnt from a dispatch of Bunsen's of the 28th that Berchtold had rejected the proposal for direct Austro-Russian conversations. Grey

still thought a direct exchange of views between Vienna and St. Petersburg the best method and asked me what is to happen if, as the telegram from Vienna foreshadowed, the discussions were to break down. Were we in that case in a position to make some proposal? He had suggested the conference of ambassadors here, which did not seem to us practicable, but we had accepted Four Power mediation and he would be glad if we were in a position to make a proposal of some kind. . . . He hoped that some means would be found of enabling Austria to receive full satisfaction without expecting Russia to look on quietly until Austria had carried her military enterprise to its extreme end. . . . I replied that Serbia was not really a direct concern of Russia, and Russia had all the less cause to interfere in this fight between neighbours as Austria had no intention of annexing Serbia. He replied that even without annexation there was a way of transforming Serbia into a vassal state of Austria's. This Russia never could or would let happen. . . . He at this point let fall the idea whether it might not be possible to bring about an understanding as to the extent of Austrian military operations and demands. From the Minister's words to-day I again gathered the impression that there is a firm conviction here, as I have repeatedly reported to Your Excellency, that, failing readiness on the part of Austria to enter into a discussion of the Serbian question, world war will be unavoidable.

Sir E. Grey remarked half jokingly that there was no knowing what houses would be spared in such a conflagration, now that even little Holland was arming. He was visibly cheered by my news that Your Excellency, so far with good success, was endeavouring to mediate between Vienna and St. Petersburg and declared his readiness to join in anything that offered a prospect of success. . . .

In conclusion the Minister told me that the Serbian Chargé d'Affaires at Rome had told Marquis San Giuliano that under the presupposition of certain elucidations as to the manner of participation of Austrian agents, Serbia would be inclined to swallow even Articles 5 and 6 of the Austrian note, thus her entire demands. As it was not to be assumed that Austria would enter into direct negotiations with Serbia, the matter might reach Serbia as advice through the channel of the Great Powers. Marquis San Giuliano thinks that on this basis agreement might be reached. Above all he desires the immediate opening of the discussion. Sir E. Grey has referred Marquis San Giuliano to the Vienna and Berlin Cabinets, he, without their agreement, not being in a position to open discussions.

In conclusion the Minister read me a telegram from Sir G. Buchanan, saying that the Russian Ministry for Foreign Affairs had informed the representatives of the foreign press that, since negotiations between Vienna and St. Petersburg had been without result, Russia saw herself obliged to regard an entry of Austrian troops into Serbian territory as a *casus belli*.[1]

[1] DD. II, 357.

Such was the pile of documents accumulated on the Chancellor's desk in the afternoon of the 29th. They showed that the Austrian declaration of war on Serbia, which he had desired and which, he had sent word to Sazonov, 'does not change anything'[1] had in fact changed everything for the worse. Bethmann must have been aghast. Europe was being set ablaze and the means of extinguishing the flames were few. They must all be tried without being too finicky, without bothering too much about what advice had been given to Vienna. If not, not only would there be war, but it might even bring in England. These are the considerations underlying the agitated diplomatic steps taken or countersigned by Bethmann during that anguishing night, steps which now show an unmistakable imprint of sincerity, born of sheer panic.

The news of Russian partial mobilization necessitated in the first place fresh consultations with the military authorities. It was to be feared that they would ask for mobilization at any cost or at least the proclamation of the 'state of imminent danger of war'. But the discussion, which was attended by Bethmann, Jagow, Moltke and Falkenhayn, went off more quietly as a result of the attitude taken by both generals. The problem under discussion was—as we read in Falkenhayn's biography—whether Russian partial mobilization rendered German mobilization inevitable:

This was negatived [runs a note by Falkenhayn] by the Chancellor against slight, very, very slight opposition from Moltke, because Bethmann took the view that, as, according to a statement by Sazonov to Pourtalès, Russian mobilization did not mean war, the *casus foederis* did not arise. We were bound to await until this arose, because otherwise we should not have public opinion with us either at home or in England. It is desirable to have it because, in the Chancellor's opinion, England would not be able to side with Russia if Russia unleashed a general war by an attack on Austria and thus took on her own shoulders the guilt for the whole *Kladderadatsch* (smash-up).

. . . I [Falkenhayn] personally regard Sazonov's statement as a direct lie, as is also the communication of the Russian War Minister and Chief of Staff, Sukhomlinov, to our Military Attaché Eggeling at St. Petersburg. But I did not make this reply to the Chancellor, since it is not my business to direct policy and there can be no interference from military advisers, except where an essential military interest is at stake. This was, however, not the case here, for it was to be assumed that our mobilization, even if two or three days later than that of Russia and Austria, would be more rapid than theirs. If we had acted resolutely we should, by my proposal, have proclaimed the 'threatening danger of war' this morning. Now a few hours sooner or later are of no importance.[2]

[1] DD. II, 315.   [2] Zwehl, p. 57.

Thus not even now did the generals become very insistent, probably because, as must once more be repeated, they realized that their Imperial master was bent on pursuing his peace move. The discussion resulted in a decision to send a special messenger to Brussels that very evening taking with him in a sealed envelope for delivery to the German Minister there the text of the ultimatum to Belgium drawn up by Moltke on the 26th. The envelope was to remain unopened except on orders from Berlin.

8. The Chancellor's agitated telegrams; his request for English neutrality.

We now turn attention to the diplomatic action taken by the Chancellor after his return from Potsdam. There it had been decided to take no further steps until the result would be known of the Kaiser's proposal for a *Halt in Belgrade* sent to Vienna on the evening of the 28th. Bethmann had carried out the command against his will and with intentional delay, altering its character in important respects, and again giving Vienna to understand that Germany expected her ally to take speedy action against Serbia. He ought, therefore, not to have had very high expectations of the success of the *démarche*. But by the evening of the 29th he was in a very changed state of mind and was desperately clutching at the hope of its acceptance by Vienna, especially after hearing from Lichnowsky of Grey's idea that it might 'be possible to bring about an understanding as to the extent of Austrian military operations and demands'. This idea which Grey adumbrated in a later conversation with Lichnowsky was not far removed from that of the *Halt in Belgrade*, put forward by the Kaiser on the evening of the 28th. The coincidence seemed to be of happy augury. But how was it that no reply came from Vienna? If only there were a favourable reply, the matter might be taken seriously in hand.

But how, alas, could the Chancellor cherish the illusion that Vienna would take a suggestion seriously that was put forward in such a manner? Had he not instructed Tschirschky:

> You will have carefully to avoid giving the impression that we wish to restrain Austria. . . . It is merely a question . . . of severing the vital nerve of Pan-Serb propaganda without at the same time bringing on a world war, or if this latter is not avoidable, of improving for us as far as possible the conditions in which it will be waged,[1]

i.e. by persuading England to remain neutral? Bethmann's dispatch was studied by both Tschirschky and Berchtold in the light of Szögyény's report of the evening of the 27th which explained that Berlin had passed on Grey's proposal in order to avoid everything 'that might disconnect the telegraph line between Germany and England

[1] DD. II, 323.

which till now has been in good working order'.[1] To obtain a reversal of Viennese policy, which had been thus pursued at the wish of Berlin, Bethmann would have had to make a new approach with a new sense of urgency. But this he did not realize because his nerve was failing him, and at 10.18 p.m. on the 29th he sent an open telegram (so great was his haste) asking if his instructions relating to the *Halt in Belgrade* had been received in Vienna.[2] At 10.30 he again wired: 'Expect by return discharge of instruction No. 174.'[3] This telegram went off only at 12.30 a.m. on the 30th because of the time needed for encoding. Immediately afterwards he forwarded on to Tschirschky Lichnowsky's long dispatch in full including also San Giuliano's proposal based, as we know, on integral acceptance by Serbia of the Austrian ultimatum. He ended the telegram with the following words:

> Please communicate the enclosed to Count Berchtold at once, adding that we regard such compliance on the part of Serbia as suitable basis for negotiations on condition of an occupation of Serbian territory as a guarantee.[4]

The Chancellor was going too far in assuming that Serbia had yielded and accepted the ultimatum integrally. He cannot but have known that he was exaggerating. But this time he was in earnest in wanting Vienna to accept the *Halt in Belgrade* and did not care whether he was misleading if he could gain his point. And in a telegram, which also went off at 12.30 a.m. on the 30th, he went to the length of begging Vienna not to break off the direct conversations with St. Petersburg which on the 27th Jagow had refused to recommend to Vienna when they were suggested by the Russian Chargé d'Affaires[5] and which Berchtold on the 28th had rejected.[6] This telegram told Tschirschky he was to say that St. Petersburg declared:

> Russian mobilization by no means implies war as in Western Europe [meaning Germany], the Russian Army can stand at ease for a long while without crossing the frontier; relations with Vienna are not broken off and Russia is anxious to avoid war if at all possible. . . . Russia complains that conversations have been continued neither through M. Shebeko nor through Count Szápáry. Therefore, in order to prevent general catastrophe, or at any rate put Russia in the wrong, we must urgently desire that Vienna should begin and pursue conversations as indicated in Telegram No. 174,[7]

i.e. for the *Halt in Belgrade*. Conversations were thus to be resumed on a basis of the occupation of Belgrade and some other places as guarantees of Serbian acceptance and execution of Austrian demands. This took for granted the carrying out by Serbia of all the Austrian demands without discussion. Rather than allow the Serbian reservations

---

[1] Oe-U. VIII, 10793. See pp. 445-6.   [2] DD. II, 377, n.   [3] DD. II, 377.
[4] DD. II, 384.   [5] See p. 430.   [6] See p. 463.   [7] DD. II, 385.

to be settled by negotiation, as suggested by the Kaiser, the mulish
Chancellor was prepared to go to war.

Meanwhile he anticipated the effect of a Viennese acceptance of the
Halt in Belgrade proposal by sending to Pourtalès at 11.5 p.m. on the
29th a dispatch calmer than the menacing one of 12.50 p.m.:

> Russian mobilization on the Austrian frontier will, I assume, lead to
> corresponding Austrian measures. How far it will still be possible to stop
> the avalanche then it is hard to say and I fear that the pacific intentions of
> M. Sazonov will not be fulfilled. In order to avert, if possible, the threatening
> catastrophe, we are acting at Vienna to persuade the Austro-Hungarian
> Government, in confirmation of its previous assurance, once more formally
> to declare to Russia that it does not contemplate territorial acquisitions in
> Serbia and that its military measures aim purely at temporary occupation in
> order to force Serbia to give guarantees for future good behaviour. If
> Austria-Hungary makes this declaration, Russia will then have attained all
> she wanted. For that the Serbs must receive a 'well merited lesson' has
> already been admitted to you by M. Sazonov. We therefore expect that if our
> step at Vienna is successful Russia will not provoke a military conflict with
> Austria.[1]

This dispatch was drafted by Rosenberg, amended by Jagow, and
signed by Bethmann. Rosenberg's draft began: 'In order if possible
still at the eleventh hour to avert probably inevitable catastrophe. . . .'
It was Jagow who amended 'inevitable' to 'threatening', but the correc-
tion is no less indicative of the state of mind prevailing at the Wilhelmstrasse.[2] The most revealing demonstration of it is the proposal, made
with the authorization of the Kaiser still in the night of the 29th, to
the English Ambassador Goschen. After war had broken out Goschen
wrote to Nicolson, as has already been said, that Bethmann sent for
him towards 10.30 p.m. and told him that he had just come from a
Council at Potsdam,[3] that he had dined in ten minutes and that, tired

---

[1] DD. II, 380.

[2] Another sign of this state of mind is the telegram which Jagow at 9.15 p.m. on the
29th sent to the German Minister at Copenhagen and which ended: 'In a European conflagration we have no intentions of endangering the integrity of the Danish state. But
military events, without our wish or design, might entail the spread of operations into
Danish waters. Denmark must then be alive to the seriousness of the situation and make
up her mind what attitude she would take in the event' (DD. II, 371).

[3] Let it here be repeated that there is no evidence of the Chancellor's having stayed so
late at Potsdam, in view of the telegrams signed by him between 10.18 p.m. on the 29th
and 12.30 a.m. on the 30th. Counting the time needed for encoding them, it is not possible
that he could have studied the dispatches awaiting him, decided what action was to be
taken and signed those telegrams after Goschen had left him towards 11 p.m. Thus, either
his talk with Goschen took place much earlier than 10.30 p.m., or, if it took place then, as
it probably did, the Chancellor had already previously done all those things and had his
consultation with Moltke and Falkenhayn as to how to act in consequence of Russian
partial mobilization. He must have got back from Potsdam somewhere about 7 p.m. and
in fact signed telegram No. 361 which went off at 8 p.m. (see p. 493). Why then tell Goschen
that he had just returned from a Council attended by the Kaiser? It looks as if he did it
to heighten the impressiveness of the extraordinary proposal he was about to make.

as he was, he had to have a long talk with Jagow after he had finished with Goschen[1]:

He spoke to me from typewritten notes, which, however, he would not show me. I asked him as it was a matter of such importance whether I might draft my telegram there and then read him what I had written. So I made a draft and read it to him. He suggested one or two slight alterations and then told me that it was exactly what he meant to say.

There is, therefore, practically complete identity between Goschen's account and the text of the verbal statement made by the Chancellor preserved among the German documents:

Our efforts continue to be aimed at preserving peace. If, through a Russian attack on Austria and the resultant duties incumbent on us as allies, a European conflagration were after all, to our great regret, to become unavoidable, we hope that England will remain a spectator. As far as we can judge English policy, she would, on considerations of the European balance of power, not be willing to allow the crushing of France. This is also not at all within our intentions. We can assure the English Cabinet—on the assumption of its remaining neutral—that, even in the event of a victorious war, we aim at no territorial gains at the expense of France. We can further assure them that we shall respect the neutrality and integrity of Holland as long as it is respected by our opponents. As regards Belgium we do not know to what counter-operations French action in a possible war might oblige us. But, assuming that Belgium does not take sides against us we would also in her case be ready to give an assurance that there must be no infringement of Belgian integrity after the end of the war. These eventual assurances appear to us to be a suitable basis for a further settlement with England for which our policy hitherto has steadily worked. The assurance of a neutral attitude on the part of England in the present conflict *would enable me to a general neutrality agreement in the future, of which it would be premature to discuss the details at the present moment.*[2]

The words in italics are in English in the original. In Jagow's first draft as submitted to the Kaiser there stood instead of them 'and the prospect of a general neutrality treaty for the future we should be able to respond to with a naval agreement'. But, as already stated, the Kaiser would not agree to the proposal of a naval agreement, therefore the Chancellor struck out the words and substituted

would open up to us the possibility of contemplating a general neutrality treaty in the future. I cannot of course today speak more fully on the details and basis of such a treaty as England would of course express her opinion on the whole question.

But this did not quite satisfy Bethmann either and he replaced it by the words in English italicized above.

[1] BD. XI. p. 362.   [2] DD. II, 373.

The German offer contained an omission which was at once perceived by Goschen whose dispatch reports:

In answer to a question from me, his Excellency said that it would not be possible for him to give such an assurance as regards [the French] colonies. . . . His Excellency asked me how I thought you would view his request. I replied that I thought that you would like to retain full liberty of action.[1]

The Ambassador might have found stronger terms in which to reply, even if he could not describe the whole offer, as Grey himself described it, as 'infamous'. It was not only infamous, it was unintelligent, a revelation of utter political incompetence. Even at this critical juncture the men to whom English neutrality was of supreme importance could not make up their minds either to accept an agreement regulating the pace of naval construction or to keep their hands off French colonies. In this way they showed their hand. Their game was, to demand a free hand in Europe in order to enforce their will on the Continental Powers at Serbia's expense, retaining a free hand for themselves at sea, so that, once they had gained military supremacy in Europe, they could overcome English supremacy at sea. And they expected the statesmen on the other side of the Channel to be blind enough to fall into so clumsy a trap, despite the fact that when in previous years a neutrality agreement had been made a condition of a naval accord, the whole matter had been dropped by Downing Street.

Jagow writes that the Chancellor put forward his proposal in the belief that, if England had remained neutral, neither France nor Russia would have dared to go to war. 'The neutrality of England would thus have signified the preservation of peace.'[2] The German Secretary of State for Foreign Affairs did not excel at telling the truth, and in this, as in other instances, it is easy to perceive how he has falsified it. The offer made to Goschen was openly and exclusively concerned with the case of war, and neither its aim nor its character was pacific. Determined up to the last to obtain the triumph of his demand for the 'localization of the conflict'—the fighting might be on a limited scale but its purpose was to wring from Serbia integral acceptance of the ultimatum and thus to achieve for Bethmann a diplomatic triumph more brilliant than that of Bülow in 1909—the Chancellor, rather than retreat a single step, was prepared to face a European conflagration and not regard himself its originator simply because Russia was in appearance to have begun it. In appearance, but not in reality. The fact is, if Bethmann had punctually and faithfully carried out his Sovereign's instructions as they were intended on the 28th, acting on the principle laid down by Wilhelm that the Serbian reservations on certain points

[1] BD. XI, 293.
[2] G. von Jagow, *England und der Kriegsausbruch* (Berlin, 1925), pp. 33–4.

of the ultimatum should be 'settled by negotiation', war would not have broken out. But Bethmann flattered himself that England would be hoodwinked by the show he had staged to put Russia in the wrong and Germany in the right, with the corollary of a neutral England and a German victory on the Continent. Not only, however, was nobody deceived by his contrivances, but even if it had been true that Russia was in the wrong, never could Germany have been able to count on the neutrality of the Power whose maritime supremacy she was challenging, whose existence she was threatening and to whom, by the invasion of Belgium, she was about to offer fresh justification for intervention in the conflict.

It is astounding that this was not perceived and foreseen by the men in charge of the fate of Germany in those days when it was grasped by everybody in Europe who had the slightest notion of international affairs. The only extenuating factor that can be put forward in their defence is that, having once made their colossal miscalculation, they were confirmed in it by the behaviour of Sir Edward Grey. We shall shortly see that, as soon as Grey made up his mind to speak as he ought to have done from the beginning, Bethmann made desperate efforts to stop war, but his efforts came, alas, too late.

9. *Germany threatened with English intervention.*

When Grey spoke in the House on 27 July, he was not in a position to announce that Germany had rejected his proposal for an ambassadors' conference. This news came in a dispatch from Goschen reaching London at 9 p.m. on the 27th and was probably made known to Grey the following day together with a minute from Crowe: 'So far as we know, the German Government has up to now said not a single word at Vienna in the direction of restraint or moderation.'[1] The officials at the Foreign Office lost no opportunity of opening Grey's eyes. On the same day (27th) the French Ambassador gave Nicolson information on conversations between Bienvenu-Martin and Schoen, and Nicolson minuted this report:

The German attitude is, to my mind, an untenable one if Germany really, as she so profusely professes, desires peace. . . . A long telegram from Vienna by Dr. Dillon in to-day's *D.T.*[2] is worth reading. Dr. Dillon is an intimate friend of Count Berchtold and he is evidently stating Austrian case with a naked simplicity which is notable. He avows that the Servian 'question' is merely a pretext for an endeavour, in conjunction with Germany, to re-establish Austria's position in the Balkans and to displace Russia and it is stated that no intervention or mediation will be allowed. We are witnessing a most cynical and desperate measure and Germany should, for her own

---

[1] BD. XI, 185. [2] *Daily Telegraph.*

reputation, show facts that she is not willing to associate herself with it or in any case assist in mitigating its effects and limit its scope.[1]

Grey relates:

I remember well the impulse to say that, as Germany forbade a Conference, I could do no more, and that it was on Germany that the responsibility must rest if war came. But this impulse was put aside, to have acted on it would have been . . . to make it the object of diplomatic action to throw the blame for war on Germany in advance. . . . With good-will, direct negotiations between Austria and Russia might succeed; von Bethmann Hollweg might have in mind some other means by which his influence could be used for peace. . . . Let it not be supposed [Grey continues with his usual ingenuousness and lack of penetration] that I thought von Bethmann Hollweg or von Jagow insincere. . . . I was sure they did not want war. I was, therefore, still ready to co-operate in any other way for peace that von Bethmann Hollweg could devise and preferred. In that sense I replied.[2]

This is anything but accurate, and Grey's memory has betrayed him. What roused him to anger was the Austrian declaration of war on Serbia, not the rejection of the conference, which he did not take in bad part, as is shown by his message to Goschen of 28 July:

I entirely agree that direct exchange of views between Austria and Russia is the most preferable method of all, and as long as there is a prospect of that taking place I would suspend every other suggestion.[3]

Indeed it was he who at the beginning had suggested direct conversations between St. Petersburg and Vienna. This message crossed with one from Goschen of the 28th reporting that both Goschen and J. Cambon and the Italian Ambassador Bollati had gathered from Jagow that it was the word 'conference' which gave offence to Germany.

We were wondering whether it might be possible for you to put proposal in another form omitting the word 'conference', or perhaps even to propose to him that he himself should suggest lines on which he would find it possible to work with us.[4]

This was also suggested by San Giuliano, probably on advice from Bollati, in a talk he had with Rodd on the evening of the 28th.[5] The idea was sound 'if, as Germany says, she is so anxious to work for peace', wrote Crowe in his minute to Goschen's telegram, commending the suggestion to his Chief. But Grey was still hoping for direct conversations and therefore replied to Goschen, still on the 28th:

I am ready to propose that German Minister for Foreign Affairs should suggest lines on which this principle may be applied, but I will keep the idea

---

[1] BD. XI, 174.   [2] Grey, I, pp. 321–2.   [3] BD. XI, 218.
[4] BD. XI, 215.   [5] See p. 419.

in reserve till we see how the conversations between Austria and Russia progress.[1]

It was, indeed, a misfortune that Grey did not, before it was too late, adopt the suggestion made by the three Ambassadors and call Germany's bluff by a plain demand that she herself should now put forward a proposal by which the peace could be preserved. It happened by a strange fate during the course of this crisis that the good proposals, such as San Giuliano's for a *Halt in Belgrade*, came to naught because they were made too late and were overtaken by events, while the diplomats wasted time over methods of conciliation which had no chance of success, such as direct conversations, not wanted by either Berlin or Vienna, though put forward in good faith by Pourtalès at St. Petersburg.

Grey's telegram to Goschen had only just gone off when, at 6.45 p.m. on the 28th, there came one from Crackanthorpe at Nish, with news that Austria had declared war on Serbia,[2] and at 7.45 p.m. one from Bunsen in Vienna summarizing in a few words a talk with Berchtold:

The upshot of our conversation is that Austria-Hungary cannot delay warlike proceedings against Servia and would have to decline any suggestion of negotiations on basis of Servian reply.[3]

Direct conversations had thus come to naught, as was confirmed at 1.30 a.m. on the 29th by another dispatch from Bunsen,[4] and the frail bark of European peace was flung on the rocks by the tempest roused by this declaration of war. Even before learning that war was declared, Sazonov had said to Buchanan

that no engagement that Austria might take on Servia's independence and integrity would satisfy Russia, and that, on day that Austria crossed Servian frontier, order for mobilization against Austria would be issued.[5]

In the face of such facts and prospects what value could be attached to Bethmann's statement to Goschen on the 28th

that he was doing his very best both at Vienna and at St. Petersburg to get the two Governments to discuss the situation with each other in a friendly way. He had great hopes that such discussions would take place and lead to satisfactory results.[6]

Crowe minuted this: 'It is difficult to believe that the German Government have done anything at all' and Nicolson added: 'I suppose Germany wishes Russia to join with the other Powers in keeping the ring while Austria strangles Servia'.

This time Grey really did lose patience. Sending for Lichnowsky he

[1] BD. XI, 223.   [2] BD. XI, 225.   [3] BD. XI, 227; also BD. XI, 230. See p. 465.
[4] BD. XI, 248.   [5] BD. XI, 247.   [6] BD. XI, 249.

talked to him in a way which has been fully discussed in the preceding chapter in connexion with the summary of the conversation telegraphed by Lichnowsky to Berlin.[1] But in putting forward the idea suggested by Goschen, Cambon and Bollati, Grey did so with a warmth to which Lichnowsky's dispatch probably hardly does justice. Grey himself wrote to Goschen on 29 July:

I urged that the German Government should suggest any method by which the influence of the four Powers could be used together to prevent war between Austria and Russia. France agreed, Italy agreed. . . . In fact, mediation was ready to come into operation by any method that Germany thought possible if only Germany would 'press the button' in the interests of peace.[2]

Mensdorff telegraphed to Vienna that Grey was 'extremely anxious' about the approaching danger of European complications:

He said repeatedly that we should, as far as could be seen, have the support and sympathy of all the Powers, if we would be satisfied with the acceptance by Serbia of all our demands and in addition a guarantee from the Powers that these promises should be kept. I remarked that after the declaration of war and opening of hostilities it was probably too late. 'Then it is perhaps too late also to avert a general war,' he exclaimed. I continually returned to the point that the question of the Austro-Serbian conflict must be kept apart from that of a general war and that Russia must be persuaded not to bring on the latter by her intervention. To this Grey observed: 'If the Powers are to advise only Russia to remain passive, that would be tantamount to giving you a free hand, and this Russia will not accept. You would have to give us at least something that we could make use of at St. Petersburg.' He did not want to discuss the pros and cons of our standpoint, what concerned him were facts, the most important being how can a European war still be averted. Even without territorial gains, we might reduce Serbia to the rank of vassal to us and thereby eliminate Russia from the Balkans.[3]

But the proposal that Berlin should suggest her own solution and the warnings to Vienna came too late. On the morning of the 29th the Russian Ambassador Benckendorff forwarded to the Foreign Office two telegrams from Sazonov. One to the Russian Ambassador at Berlin stated that:

In consequence of the declaration of war addressed by Austria-Hungary to Serbia, the Imperial Government will to-morrow declare mobilization in the military districts of Odessa, Kiev, Moscow and Kazan.

The other, addressed to Benckendorff, ran:

Urgent. The Austrian declaration of war manifestly renders vain my *pourparlers* with the Austro-Hungarian Ambassador at St. Petersburg. The

---

[1] DD. II, 357. See p. 501.   [2] BD. XI, 263.   [3] Oe-U. VIII, 10973.

action of the London Cabinet in favour of mediation and also to suspend Austrian military operations against Serbia seems to me altogether urgent. Without the suspension of military operations, mediation would only serve to drag matters on and would enable Austria meanwhile to crush Servia.[1]

Grey also received a telegram from Rodd at Rome containing a suggestion from San Giuliano

that there seemed to be a difficulty in making Germany believe that Russia was in earnest and he thought it would have a great effect if she believed that Great Britain would act with Russia and France, as Germany was really desirous of good relations with ourselves.[2]

We have already noted that this suggestion was minuted by Crowe: 'The last paragraph is significant, coming from Italy', while Nicolson merely thought:

The resources of diplomacy are, for the present, exhausted. We have two undoubted facts before us—1. Austria will invade and endeavour to crush Servia. 2. If Austria invades Servia, Russia will act in support of Servia. Appeals either to Austria or Russia to alter their course would be futile and would lead to misunderstandings.[3]

But would it, in fact, have been useless to make such an appeal, or rather to give Germany a warning which would cure her of her illusions, as had been advised explicitly by San Giuliano and implicitly by Crowe, and had been asked for by Sazonov and proposed by Buchanan?

Grey had refused to pay any attention to the idea. Now he perceived the bankruptcy of all his moves and the inexorable approach of the spectre of war. Mensdorff's impression of Grey's attitude, confirmed by words from Tyrrell, is summed up in Mensdorff's dispatch of the 29th as:

to stay outside any European complication if at all possible; Russian interests leave England cold but if French vital interests or the power position of France is at stake, no English Government will be in a position to hold England back from taking part on the side of France.[4]

And this was, indeed, the case. Grey felt it, but up till then had not raised a finger to bring it home to Germany. But now, roused by developments which made a general war seem practically inevitable, he at last decided to speak. Sending for Lichnowsky again in the early hours of the afternoon, he made an official communication to him, a summary of which he sent to Goschen at Berlin:

I told him of the communication, made by Count Benckendorff, that the Austrian declaration of war manifestly rendered vain any direct conversations between Russia and Austria. I said that the hope built upon these

[1] BD. XI, 258. [2] BD. XI, 252. [3] See pp. 419–20. [4] Oe-U. VIII, 10973.

direct conversations by the German Government yesterday had disappeared to-day. To-day the German Chancellor was working in the interest of mediation in Vienna and St. Petersburg. If he succeeded, well and good. If not, it was more important than ever that Germany should take up what I had suggested to the German Ambassador this morning and propose some method by which the four Powers should be able to work together to keep the peace of Europe. I pointed out, however, that the Russian Government, while desirous of mediation, regarded it as a condition that the military operations against Servia should be suspended, as otherwise a mediation would only drag on matters and give Austria time to crush Servia. It was, of course, too late for all military operations against Servia to be suspended. In a short time, I supposed, the Austrian forces would be in Belgrade, and in occupation of some Servian territory. But even then it might be possible to bring some mediation into existence, if Austria, while saying that she must hold the occupied territory until she had complete satisfaction from Servia, stated that she would not advance further, pending an effort of the Powers to mediate between her and Russia.[1]

Here we see Grey coming round to suggesting something resembling what Avarna had said to Bunsen and also resembling the *Halt in Belgrade* idea which had occurred to the Kaiser on the morning of the previous day (the 28th) and which, that evening, tardily and travestied, Bethmann had passed on to Vienna.[2] This letter of Grey's was followed by another also to Goschen, but both of them owing to the outbreak of war were never sent. The second letter continues the account:

After speaking to the German Ambassador this afternoon about the European situation, I said that I wished to say to him, in a quite private friendly way, something that was on my mind. The situation was very grave. While it was restricted to the issues at present actually involved we had no thought of interfering in it. But if Germany became involved in it, and then France, the issue might be so great that it would involve all European interests; and I did not wish him to be misled by the friendly tone of our conversation—which I hoped would continue—into thinking that we should stand aside.

He said that he quite understood this, but he asked whether I meant that we should under certain circumstances intervene? I replied that I did not wish to say that, or to use anything that was like a threat or an attempt to apply pressure by saying that if things became worse, we should intervene. There would be no question of our intervening if Germany was not involved, or even if France was not involved. But we knew very well that if the issue did become such that we thought British interests required us to intervene, we must intervene at once, and the decision would have to be very rapid, just as the decisions of other Powers had to be. I hoped that the friendly tone of our conversations would continue as at present and that I should be able to keep as closely in touch with the German Government in working

---

[1] BD. XI, 285.　　　[2] See pp. 469–77.

for peace. But if we failed in our efforts to keep the peace, and if the issue spread so that it involved practically every European interest, I did not wish to be open to any reproach from him that the friendly tone of all our conversations had misled him or his Government into supposing that we should not take action, and to the reproach that, if they had not been so misled, the course of things might have been different.

The German Ambassador took no exception to what I had said; indeed he told me that it accorded with what he had already given in Berlin as his view of the situation.[1]

10. *Grey's belated warning ; the grave consequences of his delay.*

So Grey was anxious not to incur the reproach of having misled the German Government into believing that England would stand aside and that, but for his misleading them thus, the course of things might have been different. But this is the very reproach which must for ever remain attached to his memory, despite the fact that he is one of the most upright, disinterested and deserving of esteem of the men in English political life. Not until the afternoon of 29 July, when the peace of Europe was already crashing headlong into the abyss, did he decide to make a statement to Germany, less explicit than, but on similar lines to, the one long since asked for by Sazonov as likely to restrain Austria and, above all, Germany. Not until the afternoon of the 29th did he take the advice given him on the 24th by the English Ambassador at St. Petersburg:

I thought you might be prepared to represent strongly at Vienna and Berlin danger to European peace of an Austrian attack on Servia. You might perhaps point out that it would in all probability force Russia to intervene, that this would bring Germany and (? France) into the field, and that if war became general, it would be difficult for England to remain neutral.[2]

If only he had done so then! In truth the study of the German documents shows beyond all shadow of doubt: (1) that in allowing Austria to attack Serbia, Germany started from the assumption that, if the attack developed into a European war, England would remain neutral; (2) that Grey's conduct until the afternoon of 29 July so strengthened the German leaders in this opinion that they went so far as to ask for the declaration of neutrality which we have mentioned above and which, by the very fact that they could ask for it, is the severest condemnation of the line taken by the Foreign Office: (3) that if Grey had spoken before 23 July, or even after the 23rd but not later than the afternoon of the 27th, as he spoke on the 29th, Germany would very likely have restrained Austria from declaring war on Serbia and the European war, at least for the time being, would have been averted.

[1] BD. XI, 286; DD. II, 357.   [2] BD. XI, 101.

This is a terrible responsibility from which Grey cannot be exonerated by the two excuses generally put forward in his defence. One is that if he had assumed a threatening attitude towards Germany, he would have encouraged Russia and France to intransigence and war. To this there is the easy reply that it would have some validity if it were true that Grey tried at all to restrain Russia. Not only did he refrain from so doing for fear of estranging her, but he went to the length of approving of her mobilizing, and this became the immediate cause of the European conflagration. He approved of it because he did not realize that mobilization made war inevitable (indeed, as we shall soon see, it seems that he did not understand this even after war had broken out) and thought of it as a necessary precaution from the Russian standpoint.

The second excuse, which seems at first sight to have more substance, is that Grey was not sure of support from his Cabinet, Parliament and public opinion and could not therefore anticipate their decision. This was the excuse put forward by Winston Churchill.

Suppose [he writes] that now after the Austrian ultimatum to Serbia, the Foreign Secretary had proposed to the Cabinet that if matters were so handled that Germany attacked France or violated Belgian territory, Great Britain would declare war on her. Would the Cabinet have assented to such a communication? . . . I am certain that if Sir Edward Grey had sent the kind of ultimatum suggested, the Cabinet would have broken up, and it is also my belief that up till Wednesday (29th) or Thursday (30th) at least, the House of Commons would have repudiated his action. Nothing less than the deeds of Germany would have converted the British nation to war. To act in advance of those deeds would have led to an exposure of division worse than the guarded attitude which we maintained, which brought our country into the war united. After Wednesday or Thursday it was too late.[1]

Later, when we turn our attention to what went on inside the Cabinet at the critical moment, we shall consider the political grounds and the practical bearing of this assertion, which seeks to establish that there could be only one means of avoiding war and it was a means which the Foreign Minister of Great Britain had no authority to employ. For the moment, the reply may be given to Churchill, and the many who share his opinion, that, in order to defend Grey, they unwittingly misrepresent the kind and scope of action which he could and should have taken. To restrain Germany he had no need to send her an ultimatum, such as Churchill mentions, which no Foreign Secretary could issue without the consent of the Cabinet, if not of Parliament. All that was needful was to talk to her privately as Grey actually did, but to talk soon, the sooner the better and certainly not later than 27 July. The reproach made against Grey to-day and which

[1] Churchill, I, p. 204.

will be made against him by posterity is not that he failed to warn Germany, but that he did not warn her until too late. If he judged it right and proper to speak to Lichnowsky on the 29th, why did he not do so earlier? By speaking as he did to Berlin, he did not commit himself to anything, he did not tie the hands of the Government or of Parliament; he simply worked for peace. He had moreover means at his disposal of guarding against misunderstanding, and preventing France and Russia from forming dangerous illusions from what he said to Germany. Before his talk with the German Ambassador Grey actually took the precaution of telling Paul Cambon in advance what he was going to say to Lichnowsky, not in order to raise the hopes of Paris, but in order that Paris might know how far he meant to go.

I told M. Cambon that I meant to tell the German Ambassador to-day that he must not be misled by the friendly tone of our conversations into any sense of false security that we should stand aside if all the efforts to preserve the peace . . . failed. But I went on to say to M. Cambon that I thought it necessary to tell him also that public opinion here approached the present difficulty from a quite different point of view from that taken during the difficulty as to Morocco a few years ago [i.e. in 1905–6 and in 1911]. In the case of Morocco the dispute was one in which France was primarily interested and in which it appeared that Germany, in an attempt to crush France, was fastening a quarrel on France on a question that was the subject of a special agreement between France and us. In the present case the dispute between Austria and Servia was not one in which we felt called to take a hand. Even if the question became one between Austria and Russia we should not feel called upon to take a hand in it. It would then be a question of the supremacy of Teuton or Slav—a struggle for supremacy in the Balkans, and our idea had always been to avoid being drawn into a war over a Balkan question. If Germany became involved and France became involved, we had not made up our minds what we should do; it was a case that we should have to con- sider. France would then have been drawn into a quarrel which was not hers, but in which, owing to her alliance, her honour and interest obliged her to engage. We were free from engagements, and we should have to decide what British interests required us to do. . . . M. Cambon said that I had explained the situation very clearly. He understood it to be that in a Balkan quarrel and in a struggle for supremacy between Teuton and Slav, we should not feel called to intervene; should other issues be raised, and Germany and France become involved, so that the question became one of the hegemony of Europe, we should then decide what it was necessary for us to do. He seemed quite prepared for this announcement and made no criticism upon it.[1]

This is easily understandable. The wise ambassador, one of the chief builders of the Anglo-French *Entente*, knew better than anyone that it had been brought into existence for reasons of European equilibrium and that at this juncture, even more than in 1905–6 and 1911, it was this

[1] BD. XI. 283.

equilibrium that was at stake. Consequently there was no need for him to use pressure. He had every reason to anticipate that in the end England would decide as she in the end did decide.

By what he said, first to Cambon and then to Lichnowsky, Grey has furnished the proof that, if he had wished, he could perfectly well have addressed his warning to Germany at the beginning of the crisis without waiting until 29 July and without in the least fettering his own freedom of action and that of the English Cabinet. The mischief he wrought by his silence shows indirectly in the long footnote which the Kaiser on 30 July appended to Lichnowsky's dispatch of the afternoon of 29 July, after sprinkling the dispatch lavishly with angry marginal notes:

England shows her hand at the moment when she thinks we are cornered ('im Lappjagen eingestellt') and, in a manner of speaking, done for. The low down shopkeeping knaves have been trying to take us in with banquets and speeches. The grossest deception is the King's message to me by Henry: 'We shall remain neutral and try to keep out of this as long as possible.'[1] Grey makes the King out a liar and these words to Lichnowsky are utterances of the bad conscience he has for having deceived us. What is more, it is a threat combined with bluff, meant to detach us from Austria, stop our mobilizing and make us take the blame for the war. He knows quite well that if he says a single serious, sharp, deterrent word at Paris or St. Petersburg and admonishes them to remain neutral, both will at once keep quiet. But he takes good care not to say the word and threatens us instead! Contemptible scoundrel! England *alone* bears the responsibility for peace or war, not we now! That must be made publicly clear. W.[2]

In the first part of this vehement note, which was certainly never intended for publication, Wilhelm unmistakably reveals that Germany pursued the policy she did because she firmly believed that England would keep out of any war that might result. At the beginning this may have been a gratuitous assumption. Berlin had, indeed, no right to build on English neutrality, which elementary political common sense would have perceived to be impossible. But Grey's behaviour from the beginning of the crisis until the 29th was such as to strengthen German illusions. Neither the appeals of Sazonov, nor the advice from Buchanan, nor the minutes of Crowe and Nicolson, who clearly perceived the complicity between Berlin and Vienna, availed to change Grey's attitude. Hence if the whole mass of the *British Documents* and the history of British policy in the previous crises had not established beyond dispute the high moral integrity which characterized Grey's

---

[1] King George V's words as reported by Prince Henry of Prussia were actually still more explicit: 'We shall try all we can to keep out of this and shall remain neutral.' (DD. II, 374. See pp. 429, 497, 687.)

[2] DD. II, 368.

whole personality and policy, one might almost be led to suspect, as did Wilhelm, that England only threw off the mask when she thought that Germany had gone too far to retreat. The opposite is the truth. The head of the Foreign Office in 1914 was a man devoid of all political perception, but he was a lover of peace and a man of honour. Nor was it true, as Wilhelm foolishly wrote, that he could dictate to St. Petersburg that Russia must let Austria attack Serbia, making himself the accomplice of Germany and thus demolishing the Triple *Entente*. Quite the contrary, where he did wrong was in taking no interest in the fate of Serbia, in failing to compose the dispute by demanding that not only Vienna and Berlin but also St. Petersburg and Paris should not resort to forceful methods and mobilization, warning them that the political and moral strength of Britain would be thrown in against the aggressor and that, if war came, his decisions would be influenced by the conduct, peaceful or aggressive, of the two sides. Grey foresaw that Russia would have to mobilize and, far from restraining her, he practically encouraged her. In his *Twenty-Five Years* he justifies his policy as follows:

I felt impatient at the suggestion that it was for me to influence or restrain Russia. I could do nothing but express pious hopes in general terms to Sazonov. If I were to address a direct request to him that Russia should not mobilize, I knew his reply: Germany was much more ready for war than Russia; it was a tremendous risk for Russia to delay her mobilization, which was anyhow a slow and cumbrous affair. If Russia took that risk, in deference to our request, would Britain support her, if war did ultimately come and she found herself at a disadvantage owing to following our advice? To such a request the only answer could be that we would give no promise. If we give a promise at all it must be to France, and my promise to Russia must be only consequential on that. The Cabinet was not prepared yet to give a promise even to France. This consideration was always present to my mind in all communications to St. Petersburg during those critical days.

But besides this I did most honestly feel that neither Russian nor French mobilization was an unreasonable or unnecessary precaution. In Germany, in the centre of Europe, was the greatest army the world had ever seen, in a greater state of preparedness than any other, and what spirit was behind?[1]

Here the first thing to note is that this plea takes no account of the lessons of the mobilizations. The Austrian partial mobilization, proclaimed for the purpose of attacking Serbia, became in its turn the cause, first of the partial, and then of the general Russian mobilization. But, as we have already seen, the iron logic of the situation would have rendered even the Russian partial mobilization a sufficient reason for Austrian general mobilization, which in its turn would have obliged Germany to mobilize, i.e. to go to war. It seems hardly possible

---

[1] Grey, I, pp. 330-1.

that even such a terrible prospect did not convince Grey, that inwardly to approve and formally to assent, as he did, to Russian mobilization was to drive Europe to war. And in saying that he could not, in good conscience, dissuade Russia from mobilizing for fear of the disadvantage at which she would be placed if war came, he loses sight of the crux of the whole matter. It is that, in those tragic days, the first concern of those in charge of the foreign policy of all the Great Powers should have been, not to consider the immediate advantage or disadvantage of their friends and allies, on the assumption that war was coming, but to see that war did not break out, and that for Russia the gain of two or three days lead in mobilizing was dearly bought at the price of dropping all efforts to save the peace. Coming now to Grey's final argument that the Cabinet was not prepared yet to give a promise even to France, a matter to which we shall return later, a sufficient answer is already given by the fact that he did in the end give Germany the warning she needed, and even gave it on 29 July, when the English Cabinet was more divided than ever before on what course to follow. If he had promised Sazonov that he would speak to Berlin, as he actually did speak, he would have had the right to enjoin prudence on him and would have found a ready hearing.

Failing this action by London, Berlin went on hugging its illusions of being able to 'localize the conflict' and persuade England not to enter the European war. The culmination of this illusion was the neutrality proposal which the Chancellor, with Wilhelm's permission, made to England on the evening of the 29th, a few hours after Grey's momentous conversation with Lichnowsky. Goschen's dispatch containing the proposal reached London on the morning of the 30th and was minuted by Crowe as follows:

The only comment that need be made on these astounding proposals is that they reflect discredit on the statesman who makes them.

Incidentally it is of interest to note that Germany practically admits the intention to violate Belgian neutrality but to endeavour to respect that of Holland (in order to safeguard German imports via the Rhine and Rotterdam).

It is clear that Germany is practically determined to go to war, and that the one restraining influence so far has been the fear of England joining in the defence of France and Belgium.[1]

No more clear-sighted comment is possible than that of Grey's able assistant. Incidentally his third paragraph is, unintentionally, an acute criticism of his Chief's policy. If he ever asked himself how Bethmann Hollweg came to form the idea of making so astounding a suggestion, he must have acknowledged at the bottom of his heart that if Grey had acted differently and had not fed German illusions by his lack of

plain speaking, the offer would never have been made. Indeed, when in
the night of 29–30 July, these illusions were destroyed, Jagow called on
Goschen on the morning of the 30th and told him that, had Lichnowsky's dispatch been received earlier, 'the Chancellor would, of
course, not have spoken to me in the way he had done'.[1]

11. The effects of Grey's warning in Berlin; Wilhelm's marginal notes.

On the evening of the 29th Goschen had only just taken leave of the
Chancellor after listening to the proposal for British neutrality when
Lichnowsky's dispatch conveying Grey's warning, which had left
London at 6.39 p.m., reaching the Wilhelmstrasse at 9.12 p.m.,
appeared, after decoding, on Bethmann's desk. It must have been a bad
blow to him who had based his whole policy on the assumption that,
in case of war, England would remain neutral and on that assumption
had put forward the demand that the Austro-Serbian conflict was to
be fought out and remain 'localized'. This was the pass to which
Germany had been brought by himself and his Imperial master in
giving Austria a free hand against Serbia and spurring her on to attack.
Late on the night of 29 July the situation presented a very black picture.
Russia was mobilizing against Austria, England was foreshadowing
her intervention. Jules Cambon had good reason to say that day, as
Szögyény telegraphed to Berchtold, at 11.40 p.m. on the 29th, 'that
England would without a doubt take her stand by us [France and
Russia] at the first shot'.[2] He had said the same thing three days earlier
to Jagow who had replied: 'You have your information, we have ours
which is absolutely the opposite. We are sure of English neutrality.'[3]
Sure of English neutrality? Churchill, who absolves Grey for not
having taken all possible precautions to avoid war, went about taking
his own precautions for winning the war, without asking the Cabinet,
acting on the principle that the Grand Fleet must be at its war station
'before Germany could know whether or not we should be in the war,
and therefore, if possible, before we had decided ourselves'.[4] On the
night of the 27th he sent to all Commanders-in-Chief the secret warning: 'This is not the Warning Telegram, but European political
situation makes war between Triple *Entente* and ·Triple Alliance

---

[1] BD. XI, 305, 677.

[2] Oe-U. VIII, 10950.—A dispatch from Sverbeev records that on reaching Berlin on
the 29th, he at once went to see his colleague J. Cambon who told him that the situation was practically irremediable, adding however that, according to a telegram from his
brother Paul, the French Ambassador in London, Vienna's refusal to regard the Serbian
reply as satisfactory had produced the effect that France and Russia could now count on
English co-operation. On reading this telegram Sverbeev did not find it as reassuring as
J. Cambon had thought and he called on Goschen to find out the truth about English intentions. But Goschen said he had no information and refused to commit himself (Schilling,
pp. 102–3; *Int. Bez.* i. V, pp. 333–4).

[3] Recouly, p. 23.   [4] Churchill, I, p. 200.

Powers by no means impossible.'[1] 'The whole of the 1st and 2nd Fleets were complete in every way for battle and were concentrated at Portland.'[2] Ships of the 3rd Fleet were fully manned, coaled and completed with ammunition and supplies. On the 28th the 1st Fleet received orders to proceed to its war station at Scapa Flow, passing the Straits of Dover during the hours of darkness on the 29th at high speed and without lights and taking the direct North Sea route. On the 29th the official 'warning telegram' was dispatched from the Admiralty authorizing the necessary preparations for immediate mobilization.

If all of this was not yet known to Berlin, the outlines of inevitable German defeat began to be perceived. This is not a hypothesis but a fact. Wilhelm's desperate footnote to Lichnowsky's dispatch, reproduced above and further borne out by the marginal notes to which we now turn our attention, fully reveal the Kaiser's state of mind. That of the Chancellor is shown by the moves he took during the night after receiving Lichnowsky's telegram. We now reproduce that telegram, not only on account of the Kaiser's annotations to it, but also because it was the cause of the Chancellor's moves. (The marginal notes are in parentheses. Italics show the passages underlined by the Kaiser.)

Sir E. Grey has just sent for me. The Minister was perfectly calm but very grave and received me with the words that the situation was growing more and more acute. ('The strongest and most unheard of piece of English pharisaicalness I have ever seen! *Never* will I make a naval agreement with such scoundrels!') Sazonov—he said—had declared that after the declaration of war he is no longer in a position to negotiate directly with Austria and *asks them here to resume mediation*. ('That means I am put out of currency, in spite of the Tsar's appeal to me.') The Russian Government regards the provisional suspension of hostilities as the preliminary condition for such mediation.

Sir E. Grey repeated his already reported suggestion that we should take part in this Four Power mediation to which we had already agreed in principle [the words 'to which we had already agreed in principle' were omitted from the copy submitted to the Kaiser]. To him personally it seemed a suitable basis for negotiation that Austria after, let us say, the occupation of Belgrade or other places should make known her terms ('Good! What we for days have in vain been trying to find out!') If, however, Your Excellency were to undertake the mediation, of which I this morning was able to hold out a prospect [the words 'of which I this morning was able to hold out a prospect' were omitted from the copy submitted to the Kaiser] that would of course be equally acceptable to him. But some *mediation* now seemed to him urgently needed, if things *were not to end in a European catastrophe*. ('Instead of mediation a serious word to St. Petersburg and Paris that England will not help them would at once calm the situation down'.)

<hr>

[1] Churchill, I, p. 206.   [2] Churchill, I, p. 195.

After that Sir E. Grey told me he had a friendly and private communica-
to make, namely that he did not want our so cordial personal relations and
our intimate exchange of views on all political questions to mislead me and
that he would like to *save himself later from the reproach of not having been quite
straightforward* ('Aha! the low down deceiver!!') The British Government
now as in the past was desirous of maintaining the friendship that had always
existed between us, and as long as the conflict *was confined to Austria and
Russia, they could stand aside* (' in other words we are to leave Austria in the
lurch utterly mean and Mephistophelian but thoroughly English'). But if
we and France were to become involved, the position would at once be different
and the British Government *might possibly find itself impelled to take rapid
decisions* ('have been taken already'). In this case *it would not do to stand aside
and wait for a long time,* 'if war breaks out it will be the *greatest catastrophe* that
the *world has ever seen*' [these words are in English]. ('That means they are
going to attack us.') Nothing was further from his thoughts than to utter
any kind of threat, all he wanted was to *spare* me illusions and *himself the
reproach of lack of straightforwardness* and that was why he had chosen the
form of a private explanation. ('All the same he has not been straightforward
all these years right up to his last speech.')

Sir E. Grey further added that the *Government* must *reckon with public
opinion* ('so must we! newly created!'); up till now, it had been on the whole
favourable to Austria in recognizing that a certain satisfaction is legitimate,
but now, as a result of Austrian stubbornness, it was beginning ('with the
help of the Jingo press') to *turn completely round* ('if they will they can change
and guide public opinion, since the press obeys them implicitly').[1]

With the grievous news of the threat of English intervention
Lichnowsky's dispatch also gave news that was good and hopeful.
Though knowing nothing of the Kaiser's proposal for a *Halt in Belgrade,* passed on more or less faithfully by Bethmann to Vienna, Grey
on his own initiative was suggesting something similar. Already before
receiving Lichnowsky's message the Chancellor was clutching at the
idea like a shipwrecked man at a lifebuoy. After all, at the end of six
days of negotiations (24–29 July), a formula of compromise had been
found acceptable to both Germany and England while leaving in the
background a very vital point to which we shall later return, namely
whether Serbia was to accept the Austrian terms in full or whether
they were to be discussed and softened.

12. *Berlin asks Vienna to agree to the* 'Halt in Belgrade' *and direct conversations
with Russia.*

At 2.55 a.m. on the 30th Bethmann sent on to Tschirschky almost
the whole of Lichnowsky's telegram, adding as his own conclusion
the following:

As things are, if Austria rejects all mediation, we are faced with a conflagration in which England will go against us, Italy and Roumania to all

---

[1] DD. II, 368. For the end of the telegram see p. 523.

appearances will not go with us and we should be two against four Great Powers. On Germany, as a result of English hostility, would fall the brunt of the fighting. Austrian political prestige, the military honour of her army and her legitimate claims on Serbia could be adequately vindicated by the occupation of Belgrade or other places. By humiliating Serbia she would make her position strong again in the Balkans and also in relation to Russia. In these circumstances we must urgently and emphatically commend to the consideration of the Vienna Cabinet the acceptance of mediation on these honourable terms. The responsibility for the consequences that might otherwise arise would be for Austria and ourselves exceedingly grave.[1]

This appeal was undoubtedly urgent and there is nothing to justify its being described as insincere. It is true that from Lichnowsky's telegram the last paragraph was omitted which we now reproduce:

To my Italian colleague, who has just left me, Sir E. Grey said that, if mediation is agreed to, he thinks he could procure every possible satisfaction for Austria; there could be no further question of a humiliating withdrawal by Austria, because in any case the Serbs would receive chastisement and with the consent of Russia would be forced to bow to Austrian wishes. Austria could obtain surety for the future without a war which would jeopardize the peace of Europe.[2]

This was news which in certain respects might have appealed to Berchtold and made him readier to accept counsels of moderation. Why, then, did Bethmann keep it from him? Certainly not for fear that it might induce Berchtold to yield, because by that evening the Chancellor was genuinely anxious that he should do so, and Berchtold himself, on the day following, received the impression that Berlin wanted to beat a retreat. Then was it for fear of the opposite, namely that Berchtold might regard Grey's proposal as intended to call the ultimatum to Serbia in question, a thing which Berchtold would never allow? This is the most likely reason. Probably Grey did not mean that, once the Austrians were in Belgrade, they should force integral acceptance of the ultimatum on Serbia, well knowing that Russia would never tolerate this.[3] Bethmann, on the contrary, had

---

[1] DD. II, 395.   [2] DD. II, 368.

[3] It is true that, as has already been said, Grey said to Mensdorff on the 29th that 'we should . . . have the support and sympathy of all the Powers, if we would be satisfied with the acceptance by Serbia of all our demands' (see p. 511). But if he did say this (his own account telegraphed to Bunsen on the 29th (BD. XI, 282) shows no sign of it), he was probably influenced by Rodd's message that the Serbian envoy had told San Giuliano 'he thought Servia might still accept the whole Austrian note if some explanations were given regarding the mode in which Austrian agents would require to intervene under Article V and Article VI' (BD. XI, 231. See p. 418). Now there was no foundation for this statement and, when Grey learnt that, he had no further reason to press for integral acceptance by Serbia of the ultimatum, his whole idea in proposing mediation being that it should be satisfactory to Russia and he, on his part, regarding the Serbian reply as fully satisfactory in itself.

based his proposal of the 28th on the full submission of Serbia to all the Austrian demands. But in his appeal to Vienna on the night of 30 July for acceptance of Four Power mediation, he no longer mentioned full submission. This would, indeed, have been in complete antithesis to mediation, since if Austria, after occupying Belgrade or other territory, had made evacuation conditional on integral acceptance of the terms of 23 July, there would have been nothing to mediate about. If this was Bethmann's reason for the omission, the conclusion must be drawn that, in his panic, he gave up this demand, the last ditch in the defence of 'localization', and put the whole dispute in the hands of the Powers.

Still on this memorable night, five minutes after the above telegram had gone off, i.e. at 3 a.m. on the 30th, Bethmann sent yet another to Vienna, pressing for the resumption of direct conversations. The opening was given by a telegram which had left St. Petersburg at 6.10 p.m. and reached Berlin at 8.29 p.m. on the 29th and in which Pourtalès reported that Sazonov had sent for him to inform him of Vienna's categoric refusal of his wish for direct conversations and that it only remained to revert to Grey's proposal for Four Power talks:

Minister spontaneously emphasized that he in no way intended this as a suggestion that Austria-Hungary should submit to a kind of European court of arbitration, he was only seeking ways of getting out of the present difficulty and clutching at every straw.[1] I again replied . . . that I could not but regard Russian mobilization, if it were really imminent, as a grave error. . . . Sazonov did not deny the imminence of mobilization, but gave it as his opinion that Russia had been driven to this step by Austria, but that mobilization was far from meaning the same thing as war.[2]

This news of Berchtold's refusal to authorize direct conversations with St. Petersburg was at variance with the account of the Berchtold-Shebeko interview telegraphed that very day (the 29th) by Tschirschky, whose message ran that Berchtold had said to the Russian Ambassador that: 'further discussion of terms with Serbia had become quite impossible for any Austro-Hungarian Government'.[3] The difference between the two accounts is important. Sazonov's was that Berchtold had refused to open conversations with Russia. Tschirschky's was that Berchtold had refused to enter into further discussion of terms with Serbia. Bethmann, therefore, sent the Pourtalès telegram on to Tschirschky with the words:

This report does not tally with your account of the tenor of Count Berchtold's conversation with M. Shebeko. Apparently there is a misunderstanding which I pray you to clear up. We cannot suggest to

---

[1] The phrase 'clutching at every straw' was omitted in retransmitting the telegram to Vienna, but this is of no importance.

[2] DD. II, 365.   [3] DD. II, 356. See p. 465.

Austria-Hungary that she should negotiate with Serbia, with whom she is in a state of war. But the refusal of all exchange of views with St. Petersburg would be a grave error, since it would provoke armed intervention by Russia which it is, more than anything, to Austria-Hungary's interest to avoid.

We are, of course, prepared to fulfil our duty as allies, but must decline to let ourselves be dragged by Vienna, wantonly and without regard to our advice, into a world conflagration. In the Italian question, too, Vienna seems to disregard our advice.[1] Pray speak to Count Berchtold at once with great emphasis and most seriously.[2]

Almost simultaneously with this (at 2.40 a.m. and 2.55 a.m. on the 30th) two short telegrams were sent off to St. Petersburg and one was sent to London. That of 2.40 a.m. forwarded to Pourtalès a telegram from the Tsar to Wilhelm in which, as will be told later, Nicholas proposed that the dispute should be submitted to the Hague Court, a proposal Germany refused to entertain, for which reason Bethmann added: 'The idea of the Hague Conference will of course be ruled out in this connexion.'[3] The telegram of 2.55 a.m. to Pourtalès ran: 'Pray tell M. Sazonov that we continue to mediate; preliminary condition, however, is suspension for the time being of all hostilities on the part of Russia against Austria.'[4] To Lichnowsky, also at 2.55 a.m., the instruction was sent:

Please thank Sir E. Grey for his frank statement and tell him that we continue to mediate at Vienna and urgently advise acceptance of his proposals.[5]

This was making the best of a bad job. But what chances were there that Vienna would comply? The whole day of the 29th had passed without Tschirschky's replying to the telegram of the evening of the 28th on the *Halt in Belgrade*. It was not until after this series of telegrams had gone to be encoded (which must have been before 2 a.m. on the 30th) that at 1.30 a.m. Tschirschky's unreassuring reply was received at the Wilhelmstrasse, reaching the Chancellor probably about half an hour later.[6] Tschirschky reported having communicated the

[1] As has already been said, the Chancellor was much concerned by the news coming in from Rome, and at 8 p.m. on the 29th had telegraphed Tschirschky to clear up the ambiguous attitude of Vienna in the matter of compensations to Italy and of the territorial *désintéressement* promised to Russia (DD. II, 361. See p. 493). At 8.15 p.m. on the 29th there had further arrived an alarming dispatch from Flotow. The question of Italy and of compensations to her will be discussed in Vol. III, Chapter VI.
[2] DD. II, 396.   [3] DD. II, 391.   [4] DD. II, 392.   [5] DD. II, 393.
[6] Some historians, one of whom is Bernadotte Schmitt (II, p. 170), think that Tschirschky's reply reached Bethmann before he sent these two imploring telegrams. It is true that they went off an hour and a half after the receipt of the reply and that at 11.15 that same morning, when Bethmann made his report to the Kaiser, his summary of the two telegrams made it seem as if they had been suggested by what Berchtold had said to Tschirschky (DD. II, 407). But it must be observed that the two telegrams make no reference to Berchtold's tardy answer to the *Halt in Belgrade* proposal, whereas usage would have certainly prescribed mention of it, had it been received in time. It did not arrive in time because it had first to be decoded; moreover the two telegrams, though dispatched an

proposal to Berchtold who thanked him and declared his readiness to renew his declaration of territorial *désintéressement* already made at St. Petersburg and to the Russian Ambassador at Vienna. But

as regards the further statement on military measures, Count Berchtold says he is not in a position to give me an immediate answer. Although I represented to him that the matter was urgent, I have this evening still not received further communication.[1]

No better success attended another *démarche* made tardily and against his will by Bethmann in obedience to his Imperial master. After Jagow's telling Szögyény on the evening of the 27th that the English proposals were being transmitted only *pro forma*, Vienna no doubt concluded that Bethmann's plea was also made only *pro forma* and would cause confusion and throw out all the Austrian plans. From 6 July to 20 July Berlin had done nothing but preach intransigence at Vienna, asking for an immediate declaration of war, a speedy opening of hostilities, the rejection of all offers of mediation, etc. Berchtold had done all he was told, even though he could not get Conrad to go into action before 12 August. Now, after war was declared, he was being asked to confine it to a trifle like the occupation of Belgrade, which would not involve the taking away of territory from Serbia for the benefit of Bulgaria and Albania, if not actually of Austria. Was this request seriously meant? Berchtold was not sure, and so he took his time. The Chancellor, on his side, thought those two last telegrams of his had made it perfectly plain that he wanted the proposal to be accepted and that his hard day's work was finished.

In this he was mistaken. Things had come to such a pass that it would have needed a very different approach to make the men at Vienna understand that they must go no further on the road along which they had advanced with the consent and at the insistence of Germany. What Bethmann would have needed to tell them was that the action of the two Central Powers had been based on a miscalculation, that they would not have Italy and Roumania with them, while they would have England siding with their enemies, that a war undertaken in such conditions was madness and would be fatal above all to

hour and a half after the Tschirschky dispatch came in, were lengthy and had first to be drafted by Jagow and Stumm respectively and then revised by Bethmann before being encoded. In making calculations of this kind considerable time must be allowed for drafting, revising and, above all, encoding and for the passing of documents from one departmental office to another before they appear on the writing table of the addressee and can be studied by him. For example the Pourtalès dispatch of the 29th announcing the Russian partial mobilization arrived at Berlin at 2.52 p.m. but only reached Jagow after he had been chatting quite a while with Sverbeev, who had called on him at 5 p.m.; hence he received it not earlier than 5.30 p.m., i.e. more than two and a half hours after its arrival. (See pp. 498–9.)

[1] DD. II, 388.

the Dual Monarchy, and that Germany was therefore obliged to retract her promise of support unless Austria agreed to the *Halt in Belgrade*, opened negotiations with Russia and, if these failed, submitted the whole question to Four Power mediation.

But the Chancellor was still a long way from taking such heroic measures. He may have believed he still had a few days before him, seeing that Austria was not to begin military operations until 12 August. It may have seemed to him that for the moment his two telegrams brought enough pressure to bear on Vienna. But he counted without the paroxysm which the Austrian declaration of war had evoked in Russia and which drove Sazonov into making an irreparable mistake.

CHAPTER XII

THE RUSSIAN GENERAL MOBILIZATION

(1) *Sazonov's optimism on 26 and 27 July* (*p. 528*). (2) *The conversation between Sazonov and Paléologue after the Austrian declaration of war on Serbia* (*p. 534*). (3) *The problem of Russian mobilization and the pressure from the Russian generals* (*p. 539*). (4) *On 29 July the Tsar signs two mobilization ukazes, one for partial, the other for general mobilization, to be used as circumstances render necessary* (*p. 545*). (5) *Sazonov's diplomatic conversations in the course of 29 July. The bombardment of Belgrade and Wilhelm's first telegram to the Tsar* (*p. 549*). (6) *General mobilization ordered and then revoked by the Tsar* (*p. 555*). (7) *An attempt to compose the conflict made during the night of 29–30 July; Sazonov finds a formula* (*p. 561*). (8) *Sazonov, Sukhomlinov, and Janushkevich press for general mobilization* (*p. 564*). (9) *The Tsar's last efforts to resist the generals; his conversation with Sazonov; the order for general mobilization issued at 5 p.m. on 30 July* (*p. 570*). (10) *Sazonov's motives, his mistakes, and their extenuating circumstances* (*p. 574*).

1. *Sazonov's optimism on 26 and 27 July.*

It has already been related that, when on 24 July Sazonov learnt of the Austrian ultimatum to Serbia, he had the feeling that there was going to be a war and went to the length of asking the Tsar for permission to mobilize thirteen army corps against Austria, should need arise. By this step Sazonov thought to put pressure on Austria and Berlin by making them understand that, this time, in contrast to 1909, Russia was determined not to knuckle under to the Central Powers. On the morning of the 25th the Tsar approved, not only the proposal for partial mobilization (not, however, to be put into operation immediately), but also the immediate adoption of measures for the 'period preparatory to war' which was a prelude to general mobilization.[1] But on the 26th Sazonov—who at the beginning had acted under the influence of the over-excited atmosphere of the Poincaré visit, which had ended on the evening of 23 July—returned to a calmer frame of mind induced by assurances from both Germany and Austria that the Monarchy had no designs on Serbian sovereignty and integrity, but only meant to safeguard itself against the anti-Austrian agitation of the Serbian nationalists. At the suggestion of Pourtalès, Sazonov had a talk on the 26th with the Austrian Ambassador Szápáry in an endeavour by direct conversations to get toned down, at least in form, the Austrian

[1] See pp. 290–308.

terms that were incompatible with Serbian sovereign rights, and he had asked Berchtold to authorize Szápáry to study and revise the ultimatum with him.[1]

In talking with the Austrian Ambassador on 26 July, Sazonov did not yet know the reply given by Pašić on the evening of the 25th to the Austrian note. When he learnt of it (most likely from Spalaiković on the morning of the 27th), he telegraphed on the 27th to all the Russian Ambassadors that it

exceeds all our expectations in its moderation and readiness to offer Austria the fullest satisfaction. We cannot understand in what Austria's demand can still consist unless she seeks a pretext for a campaign against Serbia.[2]

He remained optimistic in a way that amazed Pourtalès who, after calling on him on the 27th, told Szápáry (who shared his opinion) that 'the basis of this optimism was not discoverable'.[3] While there was no sign of yielding on the part of Austria and therefore no visible basis for an agreement, the Military Attachés of the Powers at St. Petersburg got wind of disquieting Russian military preparations. The German Military Attaché, Major Eggeling, asked Pourtalès on the 26th to tell the German General Staff: 'I regard as certain that mobilization ordered in Kiev and Odessa; Warsaw and Moscow doubtful, the rest probably not yet.'[4] In consequence of this information Pourtalès on the 26th interviewed Sazonov and was assured that no mobilization had been ordered and that it would only be ordered if Austria took up an attitude hostile to Russia. Sazonov admitted, however, that 'certain military preparations had already been taken to avoid surprises'.[5]

This was true, and in order to convince Germany and get her to use her influence with Austria, Sazonov instructed Sukhomlinov, the Minister for War, to confirm the news to Major Eggeling. Sending for Eggeling on the 27th Sukhomlinov gave him

his word of honour that no order for mobilization had been issued as yet. For the present purely preparatory measures were being taken, not a horse was being requisitioned, not a reservist called up. If Austria crosses the Serbian frontier there will be mobilization in the districts facing Austria; Kiev, Odessa, Moscow, Kazan. In no circumstances on German front: Warsaw, Vilna, or St. Petersburg. Peace with Germany was urgently desired. To my question what was the object of mobilizing against Austria, shrugging of shoulders and reference to the diplomats. I gave the Minister my opinion that . . . even mobilization against Austria alone must be regarded as very dangerous.[6]

Herein the Major was quite right, since it would lead to Austrian general mobilization, which in its turn would require Germany to

---

[1] See pp. 403–5.   [2] *Int. Bez.* i. V, 119.   [3] Oe-U. VIII, 10916.
[4] DD. I, 216.   [5] DD. I, 230.   [6] DD. I, 242.

mobilize. He little imagined that on that very day Jagow was telling Goschen and Cambon that Germany 'would only mobilize if Russia mobilized on the German frontier'.[1] Pourtalès was not at all reassured by the Russian official statements, and on the 27th reported to Berlin a talk with the Italian Ambassador Carlotti, who did not think that Russia was meditating aggression. Pourtalès, however, ended his dispatch with the words:

I should like to add that I cannot but regard the connexion between the very considerable increase in the Russian forces and the growing crisis in Austro-Russian relations as an increasing threat to European peace which is not to be underestimated.[2]

Buchanan, too, was concerned over the Russian military preparations, and in a conversation with Sazonov on the 27th, of which notice has already been taken,[3] he said he

trusted that mobilization *ukaze* would be deferred as long as possible and that, when it was issued, troops would not be allowed to cross frontier. . . . He could not tell me when *ukaze* would be issued, but spoke of day on which Austrian Army entered Servia as a likely date.[4]

According to what Paléologue writes, he, too, deplored the Russian preparations, though, if he did, it was for other motives than those of Buchanan, as will shortly be shown. However, Sazonov had no reason to take the various Ambassadors' admonitions not to mobilize very much to heart, since, for the time being, he saw no cause for partial mobilization nor, if he were to order it, reason to fear the consequences. On the 27th Bronevski, the Russian Chargé d'Affaires at Berlin, telegraphed to St. Petersburg:

Cambon saw the Foreign Minister yesterday about various current matters. The conversation came round to the Austro-Serbian conflict. Upon the Foreign Minister remarking that, if Russia began mobilizing, Germany would at once do the same, and then a clash would be inevitable, Cambon pointed out that it must make a difference where, and therefore against whom, Russia might in future mobilize. After some hesitation the Foreign Minister half agreed to this view of the matter and said that he meant our mobilizing on the German frontier. Later he said summing up: 'We shall mobilize either if Russia mobilizes on our frontier or if Russian troops invade Austrian territory.' Privately I learn that he expressed himself in similar terms to the English Ambassador who returned yesterday.[5]

If Jagow raised no objection to Russian partial mobilization, Grey went to the length of practically regarding it as necessary. This can be seen in two telegrams from Benckendorff of 25 July. The first reports Grey as having said to Lichnowsky: 'One must anticipate that an

---

[1] LJF. 67, in CDD., p. 187; DF. 3. XI, 134. See p. 482.   [2] DD. I, 253.
[3] See p. 408.   [4] BD. XI, 170.   [5] *Int. Bez.* i. V, 135.

Austrian mobilization will bring a Russian in its train',[1] the second as saying to Lichnowsky

that he could see only one way of keeping peace, namely that after Austria and Russia mobilize, Germany, France, Italy and England refrain from doing so for the time being, and first of all offer their good offices to Austria and Russia.[2]

In the face of such concessions by Jagow and Grey, what value could Sazonov attach to the admonitions of Pourtalès and Buchanan, to say nothing of Paléologue? This attitude of the Berlin and London Governments towards the possibility of Russian partial mobilization must be borne in mind if one would form a fair judgement of Sazonov's acts after he learnt of the Austrian declaration of war on Serbia. And this declaration must be seen as the main obstacle to a peaceful solution of the conflict.

But even before receiving the news, Sazonov on the 28th already began to shed his optimism and grow nervy and depressed, despite the fact that on the evening of the 27th Benckendorff had telegraphed that Grey was extremely pleased with the Serbian reply and had told Lichnowsky

that influence must be brought to bear on Vienna and that this was primarily a matter for the German Government. Grey added that the British Government was sincerely desirous of working with German Government as long as it was a question of both working for peace. In the opposite case England reserved her full freedom of action.[3]

In reality Grey had said nothing of this kind to Lichnowsky, although he was under the illusion, which he expressed to Benckendorff, that he had spoken plainly enough to show Germany that she had no grounds for reckoning on England's remaining neutral.[4] But in the first place Sazonov did not put too much reliance on these reports, and further he was greatly worried and angered at not receiving the expected reply from Berchtold authorizing Szápáry to negotiate and to examine the Austrian note to Serbia with him. In fact, as we have seen, Berchtold intentionally did not see Shebeko at all on the 27th, in order that their next interview should take place only after the declaration of war on Serbia had already been sent off.[5]

Berchtold's silence lent importance to disquieting news reaching St. Petersburg from Vienna on the 28th which caused Sazonov to take 'a pessimistic view of the situation'. Buchanan wrote:

I asked him whether he would be satisfied with assurances which I understood Austrian Ambassador had been instructed to give with regard to

---

[1] *Int. Bez.* i. V, 53. [2] *Int. Bez.* i. V, 54.
[3] *Int. Bez.* i. V, 122. [4] *Int. Bez.* i. V, 124.
[5] See pp. 463–4.

Servia's independence and integrity. . . . His Excellency replied at once that no engagement that Austria might take on those two points would satisfy Russia, and that on day that Austria crossed Servian frontier order for mobilization against Austria would be issued. . . . I asked whether it would not be possible in last resort for Emperor Nicholas to address personal appeal to Emperor of Austria to restrict Austria's action within limits which Russia could accept. [He, too, was thinking of something similar to the *Halt in Belgrade*.] His Excellency replied to my question by repeating that the only way to avert war was for His Majesty's Government to let it be clearly known that they would join France and Russia. Prince Henry of Prussia, he heard, was being sent on mission to England, and he trusted that His Royal Highness would not be left in doubt as to what England would do.[1]

Unfortunately Prince Henry sent home news to the opposite effect. The next caller after Buchanan was Pourtalès. Was this his first or second call that day? Here one is confronted with an enigma. Reconstructing the events of those days after the war, Pourtalès writes that on the afternoon of the 28th, when news reached St. Petersburg of Austria's having declared war on Serbia, Sazonov had been under the illusion that as Austria had not attacked Serbia at once on the expiry of the ultimatum, she was not venturing to take action. In extreme agitation he greeted Pourtalès—as the latter writes—

with the words that he now saw through our whole deceitful policy, he now no longer doubted that we had known the Austro-Hungarian plans and that it was all a well-laid scheme between us and the Vienna Cabinet. Angered by these reproaches, I replied that I had ,told him definitely days ago that we regarded the Austro-Serbian conflict as a concern only of those two states. . . . I rose and broke off the conversation, saying that if Sazonov took the liberty of talking like that, it was useless to continue the conversation. On returning to the Embassy I found a note from the Consulate saying the police had put the wireless installation on the German steamer *Prinz Eitel Friederich*, lying in St. Petersburg harbour, out of operation. This incident gave me the opportunity to go and see Sazonov's assistant Neratov. I told him what had just taken place between Sazonov and myself. . . . I stressed that if M. Sazonov would make the slightest advance I would at once go and see him. On returning to the Embassy I found a telephone message from him asking me to go at once to the Ministry. There he greeted me by flinging his arms round my neck and apologizing. . . . I said I regarded the incident as closed and would not report it to my Government.[2]

Thus the conversation was resumed and Pourtalès reported this to Berlin in a dispatch of 28 July which left St. Petersburg at 8.12 p.m.:

Sazonov tried to-day to persuade me that Serbia's answering note actually contained everything that Austria could want of Serbia. Hence if Austria declares the note to be unsatisfactory, that proves she wants war in any case.

---

[1] BD. XI, 247.   [2] Pourtalès, pp. 33–4.

. . . The Minister then again appealed for my co-operation in persuading my Government to take part in mediatory action. I answered that . . . I could not do more. . . . I further pointed out to the Minister that from reliable information reaching us there was no doubt that military preparations were in progress in excess of what the War Minister had told to our Military Attaché. I could only explain this by the chiefs of the military districts having exceeded their instructions.[1]

Pourtalès's language produced a most painful impression on Sazonov, which, as we shall soon see, he confided to Paléologue, and also communicated to Benckendorff in a dispatch of the 28th which ran:

From talks with the German Ambassador I have the impression that Germany rather favours the unconciliatory attitude of Austria and . . . obviously exercises no influence on her ally. German Ambassador here thinks the Serbian reply unsatisfactory. I regard this behaviour on the part of Germany as very disquieting and think that England could take steps to exercise appropriate pressure at Berlin better than the other Powers. The key to the situation lies, beyond all doubt in Berlin.[2]

These Sazonov and Pourtalès dispatches combine to show that neither of the two men, when they were talking together, knew of the Austrian declaration of war on Serbia, of which their conversation shows no trace. Nor was there any word of it in the talk between Sazonov and Szápáry which followed, because Sazonov only heard the news after Szápáry had left. It is, therefore, not possible that, in an earlier conversation than this one, Sazonov can have made a scene over news which he did not yet know. On the other hand Pourtalès can hardly have invented an incident of this kind. The only explanation that can be put forward is that the incident did take place but not over news of the declaration of war. Sazonov did not see Pourtalès again on the 28th after receiving news of the declaration of war.[3]

Hardly had Pourtalès left than Szápáry called with no cheering news, since he was still without a reply from Berchtold on the subject of direct conversations. Szápáry's report continues:

Sazonov thereupon remarked that this was none too good and that the situation was certainly serious. . . . M. Sazonov again pressed for communication of the *dossier* which had been promised to the Powers and had not been produced. . . . This was all said in a fairly calm and friendly way, despite visible disappointment, and I had the impression that he still had hopes of finding something in the *dossier* enabling him to withdraw from

[1] DD. II, 338.   [2] *Int. Bez.* i. V, 164.

[3] It must be added that among the appendices to the collection of German documents there is a 'chronological table of the last events' made by Pourtalès himself which for the 28th gives no news of the Austrian declaration of war on Serbia, but has for the 29th the entry: 'Publication of the Austrian declaration of war on Serbia' (DD. IV, Anhang V, p. 163).

Serbia. Our territorial *désintéressement*, the announcement of which he had probably expected, did not make much impression on him. That we intended to respect Serbian sovereignty he could not really believe in view of the nature of our demands. Our not wanting to pursue a Balkan policy against Russia led to a longish discussion . . . in which old grievances were aired. But this all took place in a perfectly friendly fashion. . . . My impression was that, in his disinclination for coming into conflict with us, the Minister clutches at straws, with the hope of escaping after all from the present situation. I must especially mention that, in contrast to earlier periods of tension, he says nothing this time about public opinion, Slavdom, Orthodoxy and argues with political objectivity, laying particular stress on Russia's interest that Serbia should not be reduced to a state of vassalage.[1]

Szápáry took his leave because Sazonov was due to be received in audience by the Tsar.

2. *The conversation between Sazonov and Paléologue after the Austrian declaration of war on Serbia.*

The last Ambassador to call on Sazonov on the 28th was Paléologue whose *Memoirs* give a dramatic and highly questionable version of their conversation. For the 28th they narrate:

At three o'clock this afternoon I went to the Foreign Office. Buchanan was in conference with Sazonov.

The German Ambassador was waiting his turn to be received. I addressed him quite frankly: 'So you've decided to calm down your ally at last? You're the only one of us in a position to make Austria listen to reason.'

There ensued a rather heated conversation between the two, so that when Buchanan 'came out of Sazonov's room, Pourtalès rushed in looking fierce without even shaking Buchanan's hand as he passed'. Szápáry arrived a few minutes later, pale and stiffly aloof. Realizing it was no use pressing him to talk Paléologue left with Buchanan.

As a matter of fact I did not want to see the Minister until he had received Pourtalès and Szápáry. A quarter of an hour later I sent in my name to Sazonov. He was pale and agitated: 'I think things are very bad', he said . . . 'very bad. It is quite clear now that Austria is refusing to treat with us and Germany is secretly egging her on. . . . As a matter of fact Pourtalès has lost his self-control . . . he stammered and looked scared. Why that fear?' 'Pourtalès is agitated because no doubt his personal responsibility is involved. I'm afraid he has helped to drive his Government into this terrible adventure. . . . Now he sees the abyss into which he has hurled his country. . . . Only yesterday Pourtalès assured the Dutch Minister and the Belgian

---

[1] Oe-U. VIII, 10999. That Sazonov in this talk with Szápáry did not yet know of the Austrian declaration of war is further shown by the fact that the above words of Szápáry's dispatch, which he only sent off at 10 a.m. on the 29th, were followed by the statement: 'The declaration of war on Serbia, which has since taken place, will doubtless soon make Russia's true intentions plain.'

Chargé d'Affaires that Russia would give way and that it would be a great triumph for the Triple Alliance. I have this from the best source.'

The truth is that Pourtalès had not urged his Government to take the line it did and, in saying such a thing to Sazonov, Paléologue was adding fuel to the flames. His story continues:

Sazonov heaved a despondent sigh and sat silent. I continued:
'The die is cast so far as Berlin and Vienna are concerned. It is London we must think of now. I *do* ask you to resort to no military measures on the German front and even to be very cautious on the Austrian front until Germany has definitely shown her hand. The least imprudence on your part will cost us England's help.'
'That is my opinion too, but our General Staff are getting restless and even now I am having great difficulty in holding them in.'
These last words worried me; an idea came into my head:
'However great the danger may be and however remote the chance of salvation, you and I ought to leave nothing undone to save the cause of peace. I do want you to realize that I am in a position which is unprecedented for an ambassador. The head of the State and the head of the Government are at sea. I can only communicate with them at intervals and through very uncertain channels; as their knowledge of the situation is incomplete, they cannot send me any instructions. The Ministry in Paris is without its chief, and its means of communication with the President of the Republic and the President of the Council are as irregular and defective as mine. My responsibility is thus enormous and that is why I ask you to pledge yourself forthwith to accept all the proposals France and England may make to you to save peace.'
'But it's impossible! How can you expect me to accept beforehand proposals of which I know neither the object nor the terms?'
'I have just said that we must even attempt the impossible to save the cause of peace, so I must insist on my request.'
After a brief hesitation he replied: 'All right! I accept.'
'I regard your undertaking as official and I am going to wire it to Paris.'
'You can do so.'
'Thank you. You have taken a great weight off my mind.'[1]

This dialogue is highly dramatic but has not even value as a piece of romanticized history, since it is given the lie by the documents. In vain would one search the *French Diplomatic Documents* for the telegram by which Paléologue would be supposed to have informed Paris of Sazonov's alleged undertaking. The *Yellow Book* for the 29th gives a telegram from Paléologue to Paris which runs as follows:

I am now in a position to assure Your Excellency that the Russian Government will acquiesce in any measure which France and England may propose in order to maintain peace.[2]

[1] Paléologue, I, pp. 38-41. [2] LJF. 86; in CDD., p. 201; DF. 3. XI, 192.

But this telegram has no connexion with the conversation with Sazonov which had taken place on the afternoon of 28 July. First of all, as the great collection of *French Diplomatic Documents* shows, this telegram was dispatched not on the 29th but on the 28th at 1.22 p.m., i.e. before the conversation with Sazonov took place. It was a reply to a communication from Bienvenu-Martin informing Paléologue of Sir Edward Grey's proposal for

joint action by England, Germany, France and Italy at Vienna, Belgrade and St. Petersburg for a suspension of active military operations while the Ambassadors of Germany, Italy and France in London would study with Sir E. Grey the ways of finding a solution to present complications.[1]

After the conversation with Sazonov on the evening of the 28th Paléologue sent the following telegram to Paris in which there is not the slightest hint of the undertaking which, he claims, was given him by Sazonov.

M. Sazonov this afternoon received the Ambassadors of Germany and Austria-Hungary; the impression left upon him by his two talks is bad. 'Decidedly'—he said to me—'Austria does not want to talk.' I gather the same impression from a conversation I have just had with my two colleagues.[2]

While Paléologue relates[3] that on the evening of the 28th he told Sazonov that Poincaré and Viviani were not able to send him instructions and that he would have to act on his own responsibility, Viviani on the previous day had sent him the following telegram from on board the *France*:

Kindly say to M. Sazonov that France, appreciating as does Russia, the high importance for both countries attaching to the affirmation of their perfect mutual understanding in regard to the other Powers and to the need for neglecting no effort in view of a solution of the conflict, is ready in the interests of the general peace fully to second the action of the Imperial Government.[4]

Although this telegram is not mentioned in Paléologue's book, he had undoubtedly received it when on the afternoon of the 28th he had his talk with Sazonov. What use did he make of it? Poincaré writes that the statement contained in Viviani's telegram of the 27th was 'indivisible' and was made 'in the interest of the general peace'.[5] Paléologue not only divided, but transformed it when, in the afternoon of 28 July, just before Sazonov went to his audience at Peterhof, he made a very different statement to Sazonov which caused the latter to take the fatal course of mobilization. In a diary which is very much more truthful

[1] DF. 3. XI, 123, 145.   [2] DF. 3. XI, 208.   [3] Paléologue, I, p. 41.

[4] DF. 3. XI, 138.   [5] Poincaré, IV, p. 385.

than that of Paléologue, the diary of Schilling, there is the following
entry for 28 July:

On the instructions of his Government the French Ambassador acquainted
the Foreign Minister with the complete readiness of France to fulfil her
obligations as an ally in case of necessity.[1]

What Paléologue is reported as saying here tallies exactly with what
he said in the three-cornered talks with Sazonov and Buchanan on
24 and 25 July.[2] But his assurance of French solidarity was rendered
particularly impressive and received greater value from the motive
which prompted him to give it. It is a motive on which he is silent, as
he is also silent about the statement itself. But its authenticity is proved
not only by the incontrovertible evidence of Schilling, who had no
reason for inventing it or putting a false date, but also, as we shall soon
see, by a telegram of Sazonov. Paléologue's account seems indirectly
to rule out the possibility of Sazonov's having known of the Austrian
declaration of war when the two had their talk on the 28th, there being
no mention of it either in Paléologue's diary or in his telegrams. But
the truth is that Sazonov did know of it and that it was the theme
which dominated their conversation, causing Paléologue to promise
Sazonov the full solidarity of France. Let us now look at the proofs of
this:

It is known beyond doubt that Sazonov had audience of the Tsar at
Peterhof at 6 p.m. The Tsar's diary notes: 'At 6 p.m. I received Sazonov
who informed me that to-day at noon Austria declared war on Serbia.'[3]
The journey to Peterhof, which is $17\frac{1}{2}$ miles from St. Petersburg, took
at least 40 minutes and, before starting, Sazonov had a talk about the
declaration of war with Janushkevich, the Chief of Staff. This is attested
also by Prince Trubetzkoi, a Russian Foreign Ministry official, to whom
the question was put in October 1914 by Luciano Magrini in the presence of the Italian Ambassador Carlotti. Hence it must be concluded
that the news of the Austrian declaration must have reached Sazonov
somewhere about 4 p.m. on the 28th. Paléologue, it is true, writes that
he sent in his name a quarter of an hour after Buchanan had taken his
leave. But in fact he called on Sazonov about 3 p.m. while Sazonov was
talking with Buchanan. The two Ambassadors took their leave together
and Paléologue did not return to the Foreign Ministry until after the
talks which Sazonov had with Pourtalès and Szápáry. These talks, from
the things that were said in them, must have occupied more than an
hour. Hence Paléologue cannot have paid another call on Sazonov until
after 4 p.m., when he had learnt or was about to learn of the Austrian
declaration of war. Most likely he saw Sazonov after he had not only

---

[1] Schilling, p. 43; *Int. Bez.* i: V, 172.   [2] See pp. 294–6; 306–7.
[3] *Journal intime de Nicolas II* (Paris, 1934), p. 15.

learnt the news but discussed it with Janushkevich. Sazonov had told the latter that it was intended to order partial mobilization and Janush-kevich—as we shall now see—had asked for general mobilization. Before the Austrian declaration of war on Serbia and Sazonov's inten-tion to order partial mobilization, the General Staff had no grounds for impatience. Neither had Paléologue grounds for finding Sazonov 'pale and agitated' after his bicker with Pourtalès. Indeed, after Pourtalès, he had received Szápáry, whose report to Vienna described Sazonov as very calm. Sazonov may have told Paléologue of the incident with Pourtalès, but it was over and done with, and peace had been restored with an embrace. If, therefore, Paléologue found Sazonov 'pale and agitated', it was under the immediate impact of the Austrian declaration of war, which he saw as making a European outbreak inevitable. And this must have formed the chief topic of their conversation. Sazonov's idea had been to resort to partial mobilization only when Austrian troops crossed the Serbian frontier, but now, obeying the dictates of his impulsive temperament and, as Baron Taube puts it, the 'pathological · nervosity of his nature',[1] he decided to proclaim it forthwith, possibly in the belief that the invasion of Serbia would follow immediately. Far from dissuading him from this course, Paléologue, who was always hinting at the inevitability of a European war brought on by Germany, must now have approved of Sazonov's decision and promised full French solidarity. That this was so may be gathered not only from Schilling's evidence but also from a telegram sent next day (29th) to the Russian Ambassadors in Paris, London, Vienna, Rome, and Berlin saying: 'all we can do is to speed up our armaments and reckon with the probable unavoidableness of war'. Izvolsky was instructed to communicate this to the French Government

at the same time conveying our sincere gratitude for the declaration, which the French Ambassador made to me in his Government's name, that we may count in full measure on the support of France under the alliance. In the present circumstances this declaration is of especial value to us.[2]

This is evidence which cannot be brushed aside and the French Government would have been better advised if it had shouldered the responsibility for the assurance given by its Ambassador to the Russian Government, an assurance for which it had the most excellent reasons. Instead of so doing, the Government tried to cover up the fact with versions and telegrams which do not square either with the Russian or with the English records (here are meant the words attributed by Paléologue to Buchanan) or with the situation. The result is that the French Government comes to the point of admitting that its Ambassa-dor, far from working for peace, actually fanned the flames of war.

[1] Taube, p. 363.   [2] *Int. Bez.* i. V, 221.

Paléologue realized this, and that is why he is at pains to represent the talk of the 28th as anything but what it really was, saying not a word of the declaration of war, the audience with the Tsar to which Sazonov was bidden, the partial mobilization, of which Sazonov certainly must have made no secret, since he communicated it to Berlin that very evening, above all the promise by France of full solidarity. But the effort is a vain one. Paléologue's line of conduct during the July crisis is attested by too many documents from other hands, too many acts and silences of his own, not to stand out clearly as exercising a decisive influence. On his own showing he had on the morning of the 24th begun to enjoin on Sazonov 'a policy of firmness' and had added: 'Henceforth we must recognize that war may break out at any moment. That prospect must govern all our diplomatic action.'[1]

He raised no objection when on the evening of the 24th Sazonov told him that the Council of Ministers had decided, if need arose, to mobilize thirteen army corps against Austria. On the evening of the 25th before even knowing of the rupture of Austro-Serbian relations, on greeting Izvolsky at the station, he agreed with him in concluding: 'This time it is war'. It was not from an Ambassador in this state of mind that Sazonov could receive counsels of calmness and moderation. On 26 July—writes Paléologue—

passing his hand across his eyes, as if some terrible vision flashed through his mind, he asked me in a trembling voice: 'Honestly, between ourselves, do you think we can still save peace?' 'If we had only Austria to deal with I should be hopeful. . . . But there is Germany. She has promised her ally a great personal triumph. She is convinced that we dare not resist her to the bitter end and that the Triple *Entente* will give way as it has always given way. But this time we cannot give way, on pain of ceasing to exist. We shall not avert war.'

And his entry for Monday 27 July contains the passage: 'My reflexions were utterly pessimistic. Whatever I did to fight them they always brought me back to the one conclusion—war.'[2]

3. *The problem of Russian mobilization and the pressure from the Russian generals.*

In truth not a few reservations have to be made regarding the accuracy of such memoirs, composed, in part at least, after the war was over. But that does not alter the results emerging from this lengthy exposition whose justification is that it leads to the following not unimportant conclusion: If Sazonov bears a heavy responsibility and committed a terrible mistake in resorting to mobilization before diplomacy had irreparably failed to compose the dispute, no influence was exercised either by France or England or Germany to hold him back from

---

[1] Paléologue, I, pp. 31-2. See p. 295.   [2] Paléologue, I, pp. 36-7.

the fatal step he was about to take. Paléologue urged him to be un-yielding, Grey thought it natural and Jagow permissible that Russia should mobilize against Austria. Hard on this came the Austrian declaration of war on Serbia, making him lose self-control and control of the situation, which passed into the hands of the military. Of this there is ample evidence. General Dobrorolski writes:

The 25, 26 and 27 July were days of torture for the optimists. Among them at first was also S. D. Sazonov, the Foreign Minister. . . . On 28 July, the day of the Austro-Hungarian declaration of war against Serbia, Sazonov all at once abandons his optimism. He is penetrated by the thought that a general war is unavoidable and he indicates to Janushkevich the need for not delaying the mobilization of our army any longer. Withal in Janushkevich's words, among the ideas of the Foreign Minister, astonishment was now visible that it had not been begun earlier.[1]

In the comments by Pourtalès appended to the German edition he states:

The Minister's revulsion of mood occurred only on 28 July when Russia's threatening attitude proved powerless to restrain Austria-Hungary from the declaration of war against Serbia. Undoubtedly this *démarche* of the Vienna Cabinet was above all else the cause of the revulsion in Sazonov's mood.[2]

It is not directly known what was discussed and decided at these conversations but the records written down that same evening and still more the dispatches sent by Sazonov enable some conclusions to be reached. The Russian telegrams do not bear indications of the hours of dispatch and receipt, but the following must have been sent after Sazonov's return from Peterhof. To Benckendorff he telegraphed:

In consequence of the Austrian declaration of war on Serbia, direct dis-cussions on my part with the Austrian Ambassador are obviously useless. It would be necessary for England with all speed to take action in view of mediation and for Austria at once to suspend military measures against Serbia. Otherwise mediation will only furnish a pretext for delay in bringing the matter to a decision and make it meanwhile possible for Austria to annihilate Serbia completely.[3]

To Bronevski, the Chargé d'Affaires at Berlin, the message ran:

In consequence of the Austrian declaration of war on Serbia, we shall to-morrow proclaim mobilization in the military districts of Odessa, Kiev, Moscow and Kazan. Inform the German Government of this and lay stress on the absence of any intention on the part of Russia to attack Germany. For the time being our Ambassador at Vienna is not being recalled from his post.[4]

[1] Dobrorolski, *La mobilisation de l'Armée russe en 1914* (Paris, 1923) pp. 144-5; German edition, p. 23.

[2] Dobrorolski, *Die Mobilmachung der russischen Armee, 1914* (Berlin, 1922), p. 38.

[3] *Int. Bez.* i. V, 167.　　　　　[4] *Int. Bez.* i. V, 168.

Both these telegrams were circulated to the other Ambassadors with instructions to communicate them to the respective Governments to which they were accredited.[1] The leading ideas in both are clear: determination not to yield; attempt to put pressure on Germany by the announcement of partial mobilization, but taking great care not to threaten Germany herself; renewed appeal to England. Thus war was regarded as very probable, indeed practically inevitable; but Sazonov in taking a step which in the end brought on the war, was endeavouring to avert it. His telegram to Bronevski shows that he had no realization of the consequences that would result from partial mobilization, i.e. that it would cause Austria in her turn to mobilize against Russia as a necessary measure of self-defence, that Germany, bound by alliance to go to the help of Austria, would at once follow suit and that German hopes of success lay in her speed of action; in short that to order even the partial mobilization of Russian forces necessarily led to the outbreak of war. On the other hand, while Sazonov deluded himself that his order would galvanize into action the diplomacy of the Power or Powers averse to a European war, he found his movements hampered by his own words and actions resulting from the pressure of an environment which he was no longer able to control. After advising Serbia not to yield to the Austrian demands and to let herself be invaded relying on Russian aid, after telling all the world that Russia would never allow the little Slav state to be crushed, after getting powers from the Tsar to order partial mobilization, he could no longer draw back. Nor was he advised to draw back by either France or England. On the other hand, he must have perceived that it was also difficult at this point for Austria to draw back. And so he decided to lose no time and prepare.

But was he to prepare only against Austria? This was originally his intention, until the generals persuaded him to decide on general mobilization. In the preface to his diary Schilling relates that St. Petersburg only gradually realized that no reliance was to be placed on German mediation. When this was realized Janushkevich explained to Sazonov that it was impossible to change over from partial to general mobilization and asked him for 'a categoric assurance that war with Germany would be avoided'. This, of course, Sazonov was not in a position to give and so Janushkevich asked him to explain the dangers of partial mobilization to the Tsar. According to Schilling's recollection, this discussion took place at the Ministry for Foreign Affairs on 28 July and Janushkevich returned to the subject the following day.[2] This is very probably the case. Januskevich had, in obedience to the decision of the Council of Ministers on the 24th, hastily prepared a plan for partial mobilization which received the Tsar's approval on the following day.

[1] *Int. Bez.* i. V, 169.   [2] Schilling, pp. 15-16.

But he saw that it would be disastrous to put the plan into action and brought up his objections on the 27th and 28th using the arguments of which Paléologue soon got news. Schilling testifies that his arguments 'made a great impression on S. D. Sazonov'.[1] But thinking perhaps that Russian general mobilization—which he imagined could be carried out secretly—might provoke German mobilization and that partial mobilization was agreed to by Berlin itself, Sazonov told Berlin that only partial mobilization was being put in hand, emphasizing 'that this was not a hostile measure with respect to Germany'.[2]

Not content with this he got the Tsar, whose aversion for war was very strong, to send Wilhelm the following telegram dispatched at 1 a.m. on the 30th and manifestly inspired by the desire to find a peaceful solution of the conflict.

Am glad you are back. In this most serious moment I appeal to you to help me. An ignoble war has been declared to a weak country. The indignation in Russia shared fully by me is enormous. I foresee that very soon I shall be overwhelmed by the pressure brought upon me and be forced to take extreme measures which will lead to war. To try and avoid such a calamity as a European war I beg you in the name of our old friendship to do what you can to stop your allies from going too far. Nicky.[3]

Here is another reference to the pressure from the military which Sazonov passed on that evening to the Tsar. At the back of it, states General Sukhomlinov, the Minister for War, was Grand Duke Nikolay Nikolaevich, the Russian Commander-in-Chief.[4] But the greatest influence was wielded by the Quartermaster-General, Yury Danilov. He was away on a tour of inspection in the Caucasus when he was hastily recalled to St. Petersburg, probably by the General Staff generals who thought the proposal for partial mobilization dangerous. Writing ten years later in Paris, Danilov states that he got back to St. Petersburg on 24 July. But he also says that 'during the first days following the presentation of the Austrian ultimatum to Serbia' (on the 23rd), he was absent from St. Petersburg.[5] Probably he was recalled on the 24th and returned on the 26th. Had he been in St. Petersburg on the 24th, he would have exercised his influence on Janushkevich, who, both on the 25th and 26th, favoured partial mobilization.[6] On his return Danilov found the following situation:

At the headquarters of the General Staff there still reigned an atmosphere of doubt and indecision, for it was realized that in resorting to partial mobilization, there was a big risk of upsetting plans for general mobilization. General Janushkevich, Chief of General Staff, who had been appointed only

[1] Schilling, p. 16.   [2] Schilling, p. 61.   [3] Int. Bez. i. V, 170; DD. II, 332.
[4] V. A. Suchomlinow, Erinnerungen (Berlin, 1924), pp. 363–4.
[5] Y. Danilov, La Russie dans la guerre mondiale (1914–1917) (Paris, 1927), pp. 30, 32.
[6] See pp. 292–3.

a few months earlier and had not yet had time to study the details of mobi-·lization, saw no reasons for demanding a revision of the plan for partial mobilization. His subordinates, on the contrary, opposed the plan adopted and pointed out the great technical difficulties and the dangers which might be entailed by this solution of the problem. The feeling of anxiety which never left me during all those trying days made me appeal to General Janushkevich to reconsider the question of our proposed mobilization in all its aspects and to discuss it afresh in conference with his immediate subordinates.

This conference took place. Apart from myself, the Chief of General Staff had summoned General Dobrorolski, Chief of the Mobilization Section, and General Ronzhin, Chief of Military Transport. The result was that General Janushkevich, visibly convinced by our arguments, consented to ordering the preparation of two drafts of Imperial *ukazes*, one for general mobilization, one for partial mobilization covering the four districts [Kiev, Moscow, Odessa and Kazan]. These two drafts were sent to be submitted simultane-ously to the Tsar, accompanied by a special report. All that now remained for us was to await His Majesty's final decision.[1]

Here was the crucial issue which has already been treated in a previous chapter,[2] namely the impossibility of carrying out partial mobilization. No plans existed for it and it would, in any case, have been a blunder, since, if war came, Russia realized she would have to settle accounts not only with Austria but also with Germany. As Danilov writes:

Any partial mobilization was, thus, nothing more than an improvisation. As such it could only introduce germs of hesitation and disorder in a domain in which everything ought to be based on the most accurate calculations made in advance.[3]

And he goes on:

The danger of the decision, lightly taken, to mobilize only four districts was so serious in the eyes of those who really understood the problem that they even arrived at the idea that it would perhaps be preferable to abstain for the time being from all mobilization rather than upset the calculations of general mobilization. But then Russia would be abandoning Serbia to her tragic fate, and this she could not do both for political and moral reasons. On the other hand, she equally risked losing precious time for putting her army on a war footing, especially if one remembers that the speed of her taking the field was considerably inferior to that of her western neighbours.[4]

Hence, either general mobilization or none at all. The only sensible thing to do would have been to wait and see. But this was not the view of the Russian General Staff which gave its opinion that war was inevi-table and wanted to lose no time, i.e. to mobilize forthwith. Faced with

[1] Danilov, *op. cit.,* pp. 32–3. [2] See pp. 292–3.
[3] Danilov, *op. cit.,* p. 33. [4] Danilov, *op. cit.,* pp. 37–8.

such pressure Sazonov ought to have declined to mobilize even partially. Only thus could he have taken the wind out of their sails. He did not do this and the worst happened.

On the contrary, his conversion to the views of the General Staff seems to have been so thorough that, on the evening of the 28th, it was he who ordered Janushkevich to prepare two *ukazes*, one for partial, the other for general mobilization. It has been generally thought that the decision to submit these two *ukazes* to the Tsar for signature on the morning of the 29th was taken at the above-mentioned generals' meeting which seems to have taken place on the 27th.[1] But now it seems not impossible that it was the generals who thought of the idea, hoping that Sazonov and the Tsar would come round to general mobilization. Janushkevich cannot possibly have submitted the *ukaze* for general mobilization to the Tsar without permission, especially as he had discussed the matter both with the Tsar and with Sazonov. Dobrorolski writes that Janushkevich was fully alive to the dangers of a proclamation of partial mobilization but his representations did not find a hearing with the Tsar[2] though, as Schilling tells us, they 'made a great impression on S. D. Sazonov'.[3] The truth was, as Sukhomlinov states—and as War Minister he was in a position to know—

The political department was entirely in the hands of the Foreign Minister. It was he who on orders from the Tsar instructed the Chief of the General Staff on 28 July to draft two orders: one for partial mobilization and the second for an eventual general mobilization.[4]

One cannot but suppose that Janushkevich produced very cogent reasons for his pressure which induced the Tsar and Sazonov on the evening of 28 July to take general, as well as a partial mobilization into consideration, inclining possibly more towards the former but leaving

---

[1] Historians in general regard this meeting as having taken place on 28 July. But when Janushkevich discussed matters with Sazonov on the 28th he was already convinced of the impossibility of carrying out partial mobilization. Now a letter sent by Dobrorolski to the *Kriegsschuldfrage* (May 1925, pp. 323–5), in reply to a request for information, makes it apparent that the meeting took place on the 27th: 'Janushkevich in the first days inclined to the politicians' view (i.e. partial mobilization) which is to be explained by his slight knowledge of strategic questions, he having been Chief of the General Staff for only five months, while before that he had been director of the Military Academy. But already on 27 July he had allowed himself to be convinced by the representations of his subordinates and began to regard the problem of mobilization no longer from the political but from the strategic point of view.' The letter goes on to say that the Tsar was disappointed to learn that no plan existed for partial mobilization and issued the order that one should be prepared: 'He summoned me one day, the date I have forgotten and gave me an Imperial command in the following terms: "Inform Chief of Mobilization Section . . . of my wish that, at the end of the present tense crisis, the mobilization plan shall be so revised that it affords the possibility of carrying out the mobilization of the separate military districts independently of one another." That means the Tsar wanted partial mobilization.'

[2] Dobrorolski, *Mobilmachung*, p. 22.   [3] Schilling, p. 16.

[4] Suchomlinow, *Erinnerungen* (Berlin, 1924), p. 361.

the decision open to the last minute. It thus became necessary to have the *ukazes* for both contingencies ready and signed. But it is likely that the Tsar at that early stage, though still tormented by doubts, and taking comfort from the thought that after all this was not the final decision and that he still had twenty-four hours before him in which to change it, gave his assent in principle to the importunities of Sazonov and the generals to make general mobilization operative if the experience of the next twenty-four hours should make this seem necessary, and that the probabilities were in favour of that course.

This consent in principle given by the Tsar no doubt explains why Janushkevich, on the evening of the 28th, hastened to telegraph to the commanding officers of all the military districts 'for their information' that: '30 July will be proclaimed the first day of our general mobilization. The proclamation will follow by the regulation telegram.'[1]

Immediately on his return from Peterhof Sazonov must have told Paléologue of what had passed at the audience and of the probability that general mobilization would be ordered next day. This at any rate seems to lie behind the following telegram sent by Paléologue at 7.35 p.m. on the 28th:

It has been agreed that, in case of general mobilization, two officers will be delegated to be sent to my Embassy. In that event I ask for MM. de Ridder and de Sèze. They should proceed via Christiania and Stockholm.[2]

4. *On 29 July the Tsar signs two mobilization ukazes, one for partial, the other for general mobilization, to be used as circumstances render necessary.*

On 29 July Janushkevich again discussed with Sazonov and pressed for general mobilization. If what Sazonov writes in his book is true, Janushkevich seems to have said that

at Army Headquarters news was continually arriving about the mobilization on the Russian frontier in Galicia; we heard that the mobilization there had begun a few days earlier and, as far as we knew, must have been completed.[3]

In this connexion it must be noted that the Russian *Orange Book* publishes a telegram from Shebeko in Vienna dated 28 July: 'The order for general mobilization has been signed.'[4] What Shebeko actually telegraphed on the 28th was very different: 'In all, for the time being, eight corps will be mobilized, i.e. half the Austro-Hungarian Army.' In the authoritative collection of Russian documents, below this authentic telegram, is a note that the one given in the *Orange Book* does not exist in the archives of the Russian Foreign Office.[5] It was clearly fabricated as a future justification of the Russian general mobilization

---

[1] *Int. Bez.* i. V, 210.   [2] *DF.* 3. XI, 216.   [3] Sazonov, p. 193.
[4] Russian *Orange Book* 47, in CDD., p. 283.   [5] *Int. Bez.* i. V, 190.

which Sazonov, in his talks with the Ambassadors, never claimed to have been caused by the Austrian mobilization. This makes it doubtful that on the 29th he believed the Austrian mobilization in Galicia to have taken place. Whether he did or not, it is certain that with his authorization Janushkevich was able to lay before the Tsar the *ukaze* for general mobilization. Without Sazonov's authorization, the Chief of Staff would never have done such a thing, nor, if he had, would the Tsar have ever signed the document. As it was, writes Schilling, the royal signature was given 'not at all willingly'.[1] Why, if the Tsar had ordered both *ukazes* to be prepared, did he sign unwillingly? The answer is that it was one thing to have them in readiness and another thing to take the plunge. We shall see that up till the last moment the Tsar was loth to authorize general mobilization, which was mobilization against Germany.

But did he not by his signature authorize it on the 29th? This is one of the most important points to be cleared up, if we are to understand what took place on that momentous day. And, to clear it up, we must make sure whether on the morning of the 29th the Tsar signed only the *ukaze* for general mobilization or whether he also signed the one for partial mobilization, which Janushkevich also brought with him. If he signed them both, it meant that both he and Sazonov were still undecided how to act.

The official documents do not make it clear that the Tsar signed both decrees, but Janushkevich behaved as if Nicholas had signed only the *ukaze* for general mobilization and had desired that it, and not the other, should be proclaimed. In order for the *ukaze* to be operative it had to bear the signatures of the Minister for War, the Navy Minister and the Minister of the Interior. On the afternoon of the 29th Janushkevich instructed Dobrorolski to obtain them. Dobrorolski tells that Sukhomlinov, who in the past had been bellicose, signed unwillingly, realizing that Russia was throwing herself unprepared into a venture beyond her strength. And Maklakov, the Minister of the Interior, sitting at a table laden with ikons and ritual lamps, began to talk of the revolution which only waited for war to carry all before it, adding 'we cannot escape our fate'[2] and crossing himself before putting his signature. Dobrorolski did not find the Navy Minister in his office and for this reason the order remained suspended for some hours. In any case it could not become operative without the Tsar's final consent and this had not yet been given. Feeling certain that in the end the decision for general mobilization would be taken, Janushkevich wanted to have everything ready in advance, so as to lose no time once the final consent had been obtained. If it had been, Dobrorolski would never have waited till evening before getting the Navy Minister's signature. He was, however, in no

---

[1] Schilling, p. 16.   [2] Dobrorolski, *Mobilmachung*, pp. 24-5.

hurry because, as many historians believe, the Tsar had signed both decrees and it had yet to be decided which should become operative.

If there is no direct proof of this assertion there is indirect proof. In the first place it is certain that, if general mobilization was actually ordered on the evening of the 29th, it was only because the Tsar had given his authorization by telephone just before, on receiving advice to do so from Sazonov. Thereupon Dobrorolski went first to get the still outstanding signature of the Navy Minister and then dispatched the necessary telegrams. The next thing was that, as we shall see, the Tsar rescinded the authorization he had given by telephone, suspending the proclamation of general mobilization and ordering partial mobilization instead. It is self-evident that he could not, from one moment to another, have ordered partial mobilization, as he did, if the necessary decree had not been signed beforehand, thus enabling it to be substituted for the order for general mobilization which was about to be promulgated.

Not only this, but on the morning of the 29th, as he was giving his signature, the Tsar instructed Janushkevich, as the latter said in evidence at Sukhomlinov's trial for high treason in 1917, to tell the German Ambassador at once that the mobilization 'did not constitute an act of hostility towards Germany' and to assure him 'that Russia meant to maintain friendly relations with Germany'.[1] These words do not necessarily rule out the possibility that general mobilization was in question. What does rule out the possibility of general mobilization is the message which the Tsar sent by Janushkevich to the German Military Attaché Eggeling. It happened in this way: On his return from Peterhof Janushkevich went and told Sazonov how things had gone there. Sazonov advised him to give the Tsar's message not to Pourtalès but to Eggeling. The latter's dispatch to Berlin of 7 p.m. on the 29th says:

Chief of General Staff sent for me and said he had just been with His Majesty. War Minister has instructed him to confirm once more that everything is still as the Minister told me two days ago. He gave me his solemn word of honour and offered a written undertaking that up till 3 this afternoon there was no mobilization anywhere, not the calling up of a single man or horse. He could not vouch for the future but could emphatically confirm that His Majesty, now as before, desires no mobilization on the fronts facing our confines. [2]

At the Sukhominlov trial, Janushkevich testified:

I regarded myself as justified in giving him this statement in writing because at that moment mobilization had in actual fact not taken place. The *ukaze* for mobilization I still had in my pocket.[3]

---

[1] Suchomlinow. *Die russische Mobilmachung im Lichte amtlicher Urkunden und der Enthüllungen des Prozesses* (Bern, 1927), p. 17.
[2] DD. II, 370.
[3] Charles W. C. Oman, *The Outbreak of the War, 1914-1918* (London 1919), p. 67.

Instead of being a proof to the contrary, this statement explains how, with the signed *ukaze* in his pocket, Janushkevich hoped to carry out general mobilization. The American historian Fay, who, like other historians, believes that the Tsar signed both decrees on the morning of the 29th, thinks that Janushkevich was determined to proclaim general mobilization forthwith. In agreement to some extent with our interpretation of events, Fay writes:

> From the somewhat divergent accounts of Schilling's *Diary* and Dobrorolski's narrative, and from the summary of the activities of the Russian diplomatic and military officials given above, one may conclude that the Tsar in signing the *ukazes* for general and for partial mobilization was still hesitating in his mind between the two, and expected Janushkevich to confer with Sazonov before sending out the order for the one or the other. Janushkevich, however, took the Tsar's assent to general mobilization as an authorization to proceed with it directly.[1]

There is no doubt that he made all arrangements to go forward at once with it, not showing much concern at the absence of the Navy Minister. But it is inconceivable that he can have been prepared to dispense with the consent of Sazonov, still more of the Tsar. This would have been an abuse of power which neither Russia nor any other State could have tolerated. If these conclusions have been reached by a process of deduction, let it be added that they find confirmation in the following passage in Sukhomlinov's memoirs:

> According to the development of the political situation the one *ukaze* or the other, signed by the Tsar, the War Minister and the Navy Minister, was to be put into execution only on the fresh personal order of the Tsar. Hence the provisional mobilization order was made secure against any runaway move on the part of the War Minister by this special provision. The above-mentioned two orders were submitted to the Tsar for signature by General Janushkevich. The orders bearing His Majesty's signature were submitted to the Supreme Senate for counter signature. . . . On the basis of these orders the General Staff prepared the corresponding telegrams which also received the signatures of the three Ministers.[2]

These words prove beyond doubt that the Tsar signed both *ukazes*, leaving the decision open which was to become effective. And in fact the general mobilization order was issued only after Sazonov, with the Tsar's consent, authorized Janushkevich to do so. From all this it is apparent that, contrary to what Fay and other historians maintain, Sazonov was telling not an untruth, but simply not the whole truth when he spoke of partial mobilization in his talks of 29 July.

---

[1] Fay, II, p. 463.
[2] Suchomlinow, *Erinnerungen*, p. 361.

5. Sazonov's diplomatic conversations in the course of 29 July. The bombardment of Belgrade and Wilhelm's first telegram to the Tsar.

At 11 a.m. on the 29th Sazonov received the visit of Pourtalès who had telephoned to Schilling that he was the bearer of an 'agreeable communication',[1] adding at once: 'Not too much optimism, all the same.' His warning was justified, since what he had to say was of small importance, apparent or actual. It was the message telegraphed by Bethmann at 9 p.m. on the 28th:

> We are continuing our endeavours to persuade Vienna to have a frank discussion with St. Petersburg for the purpose of clarifying the aims and extent of the Austrian procedure in Serbia in an unexceptionable manner which it is hoped will be acceptable to Russia. The declaration of war issued in the meanwhile does not change this in any way.[2]

This was an indirect allusion to the *Halt in Belgrade* proposal made to Vienna that same evening. Pourtalès at 1.58 p.m. on the 29th telegraphed to Berlin that the message

visibly made a good impression. The Minister remarked, however, that un- fortunately up till now there were no signs that Vienna was agreeing to take the road of a direct exchange of views with St. Petersburg. . . . Moreover Austria had mobilized eight army corps, and this measure must be regarded as partly directed against Russia. Therefore Russia also found herself obliged to mobilize military districts on the Austrian frontier. The relevant order is to be issued to-day.[3]

This justification of partial mobilization was hardly convincing, since the eight Austrian army corps mobilized against Serbia were in no wise a threat to Russia, whereas the mobilization of thirteen Russian army corps in addition to those of Serbia was a real threat to Austria. Sazonov would have done better to remind Pourtalès of Jagow's having agreed that Russia might mobilize against Austria. It is, indeed, incompre- hensible that he never availed himself of that argument. Instead of so doing he expatiated on the fact that

in Russia, unlike western European states, mobilization is far from being the same as war. The Russian Army could, at need, stand at ease for weeks without crossing the frontier.

Pourtalès continues:

These statements did not reassure me. I told him: the danger of all military measures lies in the counter-measures of the other side. It is to be expected that the General Staffs of eventual enemies of Russia would not want to sacrifice the trump card of their great lead over Russia in mobilization and would press for counter-measures. I urgently beg you to consider this danger.

---

[1] Schilling, p. 47.   [2] DD. II, 315. See p. 472.   [3] DD. II, 343.

M. Sazonov again solemnly assured me that no steps are being taken against us. I repeated with emphasis that it was far from my thoughts to utter any threat, but our obligations to Austria under the alliance were well known to him.[1]

This was a very appropriate reminder and should have been the determining factor in German diplomatic activity from the moment it became known that Sazonov meditated mobilizing against Austria and was drawing a distinction between Austria and Germany which it was not possible to make.

Anyway it was of partial mobilization that Sazonov spoke to Pourtalès, assuring him that no measures were being taken against Germany. Schilling tells us that after Pourtalès had left, Sazonov discussed the message he had brought with Neratov, Schilling, and Trubetzkoi, trying to make out whether Germany really meant to exercise pressure on Vienna or only to lull Russia to sleep, make her postpone mobilization and thus gain time on her.

The general impression was that even if the sincerity of the German Government could be admitted, under the circumstances the possibility of arriving at any practical results in this direction must be doubted, because if Austria had gone thus far without the co-operation, or at least the tacit approval of Germany, then it must be supposed that the influence of the latter in Vienna had greatly declined and that therefore the German Government would not succeed in effecting much there at present.[2]

This was a reason for Russia to threaten Austria, not Germany. And in fact when Buchanan called in the afternoon he was told only of partial mobilization.

Going straight to the heart of the matter, Buchanan told Sazonov what Jagow had said to Goschen on the 27th, namely that Germany would not mobilize against Russia if Russia only mobilized in the south, i.e. against Austria.[3] Sazonov told him that 'the order for partial mobilization was signed to-day', and that he had heard of Jagow's statement 'from another source'. (This source was Bronevski who learnt it from J. Cambon.[4]) Sazonov went on to say that: 'it was for this reason that it had been decided not to order the general mobilization which military authorities had strongly recommended'. Undoubtedly the whole truth was not told in this statement, since, when Sazonov made it, he knew that the Tsar had also signed the *ukaze* for general mobilization. But the fact of having suppressed this may be a sign that Sazonov still hoped not to resort to the more serious measure, which rendered much more probable the war he was striving to avoid by a fresh suggestion. He had learnt at last from Shebeko that Berchtold had declined

[1] DD. II, 343.
[2] Schilling, pp. 47–8; *Int. Bez.* i. V, 224.
[3] BD. XI, 185. See p. 482.
[4] *Int. Bez.* i. V, 135. See p. 530.

direct conversations,[1] indeed the refusal was implicit in the Austrian declaration of war. Moreover, as we have said, St. Petersburg had no illusions that Germany would succeed in getting them re-opened. So now Sazonov turned again to Grey's proposal for a conference of ambassadors. He had already put the idea to Pourtalès and now he said to Buchanan that

he proposed to urge return to your proposal for conference of four, or, at all events, for exchange of views between you [Grey], three Ambassadors less directly interested and, if you thought it advisable, Austrian Ambassador. He did not care what form such conversations took and he was ready to accept almost any arrangement that was approved by France and England. There was no time to lose, and war could only be averted if you could succeed by conversations with Ambassadors either collectively or individually in arriving at some formula which you could get Austria to accept. Russian Government had done all they could do to maintain peace and had been perfectly frank and conciliatory throughout, and he trusted British public realized it would not be their fault if their efforts to maintain peace failed.[2]

At this point Buchanan came forward with San Giuliano's suggestion of 27 July that 'Serbia may be induced to accept note in its integrity on advice of four Powers invited to conference'.[3]

His Excellency said he could not be more Servian than Servia and would agree to anything four Powers could arrange provided it was acceptable to Servia. Sharpness of ultimatum, however, would have to be toned down by some supplementary statement or explanations.[4]

After this talk with Buchanan there followed another with Pourtalès whom Sazonov had sent for to tell him, as he had said to Buchanan,

that the Vienna Cabinet had returned a categoric refusal to the wish expressed by him to enter into direct conversations. Nothing therefore remained but to revert to Sir E. Grey's proposal for a conference of four. Minister stressed that it was far from his thoughts to expect Austria-Hungary to submit to any kind of European court of arbitration, he was only seeking a means of escape from present difficulty and snatching at every straw.

Pourtalès replied:

I was not acquainted with the standpoint of my Government to Sir E. Grey's proposal, but could not regard order for Russian mobilization if it were imminent, as other than a grave mistake.

Sazonov did not deny that mobilization was imminent but repeated that 'mobilization was a long way from meaning war'.[5] This dispatch went off to Berlin at 8.29 p.m. In their talk neither Sazonov nor

[1] Int. Bez. i. V, 188. See p. 464.   [2] BD. XI, 276.   [3] BD. XI, 202. See pp. 417-8.
[4] BD. XI, 276.   [5] DD. II, 365.

Pourtalès was referring to general mobilization, which Pourtalès regarded as out of the question, but only to partial mobilization. But in the course of that afternoon two events came to persuade the excitable and impulsive Sazonov still further that general mobilization was necessary.

Szápáry, who had received instructions not to discuss the text of the Serbian note with Sazonov,[1] called on him with the idea of 'clearing up certain misunderstandings'. His account of the meeting runs:

> I confirmed that Your Excellency . . . had declined to discuss the conflict, but that I was in a position to suggest a much broader basis for an exchange of views by giving the assurance that we had no wish to injure Russian interests, take Serbian territory or infringe Serbian sovereignty. . . . M. Sazonov replied that as to territory he was persuaded, but in regard to sovereignty he remained convinced that the imposition of our terms meant vassallage. . . . He would again urge me that though there was readiness to acknowledge our legitimate interest and satisfy it to the full, this must be done in a form acceptable to Serbia. For in reality it was only a dispute about wording. I interposed that this was not a Russian but a Serbian interest, to which M. Sazonov replied that, in the present case, Russian interests are Serbian interests, so I broke the vicious circle by passing on to another subject.
>
> I mentioned having heard that Russia was disquieted because we had mobilized eight army corps against Serbia. M. Sazonov said that not he, who did not understand these things, but Tsar Nicholas had expressed concern as a result of information from the General Staff. . . . I sought to convince the Minister . . . that our southern army corps could not be a threat to Russia. . . . M. Sazonov very characteristically said he might explain this to the Chief of Staff who sees His Majesty every day. . . . The Minister further told me that a *ukaze* is being signed to-day ordering mobilization on a fairly large scale [i.e. partial mobilization, which he could not say in plain words was against Austria and so used this euphemistic expression].[2] But he could officially state that these troops were not destined to attack us; they would simply stand at ease in case Russia's Balkan interests were endangered. An explanatory note would make this clear.

While we were thus in confidential conversation, the Minister received the news over the telephone that we had bombarded Belgrade. He was completely transformed, trying to go over all his arguments again in complete defiance of common sense and saying that he now saw Tsar Nicholas was right. 'You just want to gain time by negotiations, yet you go ahead and

---

[1] Oe-U. VIII, 10915. See p. 462.

[2] In a later telegram Szápáry attributed the following tactics to Sazonov: 'The Minister, like his Imperial master, fights shy of war and, without reacting immediately to our Serbian campaign, hopes to be able to contest the fruits of it, if possible without war, and, should war come, to enter it better prepared than now. By a mobilization ostensibly directed only against Austria-Hungary, accompanied by declarations of peaceful intentions, but covering the Roumanian rear, Germany is to be kept out, Austria-Hungary is to be kept under pressure in the Serbian campaign, and as soon as our operations have led to success, the rescue of Serbia is to be taken in hand by Russia' (Oe-U. VIII, 11094).

bombard an unprotected city!' 'What more do you want to conquer now you have possession of the capital!' and other childish expressions. The argument that such a procedure against Serbia was the very opposite of a move against Russia left the Minister cold. 'What good is it for us to talk, if you go on like that!' he said. I left him in a very excited state and my German colleague, who again called on him, also had to give up hope of a calm conversation—at any rate for to-day.[1]

Nothing betrays better than this incident that Sazonov at the bottom of his heart still hoped to compose the dispute without war. The bombardment of Belgrade had not the importance he gave it, but he could not know this and saw it as the first action of a war which would oblige Russia to go to the help of Serbia and thus end all hope of peace. Hence his agitation, which this time was not without grounds. And before he had recovered Pourtalès came again with a message that drove him to take the fatal decision.

Sazonov must have still been thoroughly upset when at about 7 p.m. (not at 3 p.m. as stated in Schilling's *Diary*) Pourtalès made his third appearance as bearer of the grave communication from Bethmann Hollweg which has been already mentioned[2] and which left Berlin at 12.50 p.m. on the 29th:

Kindly impress on M. Sazonov very seriously that further progress of Russian mobilization measures would compel us to mobilize and that then European war would scarcely be to be prevented.[3]

Pourtalès reports that, in delivering this message, he emphasized 'that it was not a threat but a friendly opinion'.[4] But Sazonov received the communication 'with visible inward agitation', simply saying that he would report it to the Tsar.[5] Schilling reports him as having exclaimed: 'Now I have no doubts as to the true cause of Austrian intransigence' and adds that Pourtalès thereupon rose and replied with equal vehemence: 'I protest with all my strength, M. le Ministre, against this offensive statement', Sazonov drily replying that Germany still had time to show that he was wrong, after which the two men parted coolly.[6]

We must now return to what has been said a little way back about the discussion which took place at the Russian Foreign Ministry after Pourtalès had brought the 'agreeable communication' that Germany was pressing Vienna to open direct public talks with St. Petersburg. There was much doubt whether the German Government was in good faith and it was thought not to be impossible, though the conclusion was reached that Berlin no longer had much influence with Vienna. Now came Bethmann Hollweg's message, with its air of being an ultimatum,

---

[1] Oe-U. VIII, 11003.   [2] See p. 491.   [3] DD. II, 342.   [4] DD. II, 378.
[5] Pourtalès, p. 43.   [6] Schilling, pp. 48–9; *Int. Bez.* i. V, 224.

and settled all Sazonov's doubts: it was Berlin which stiffened Vienna, not Vienna which had taken the bit between its teeth with regard to Berlin. It was late in the day to realize this. He ought to have seen from the beginning that the Monarchy would never have acted in such a manner against the wish of its ally. Now what was beginning to happen —though Sazonov could not have guessed it—was that Germany was inclining to turn tail and that Austria, driven by Germany too far for retreat, was inclining towards action. In any case the wording of the German message was so abrupt that it was anything but suited to attaining its purpose.[1] On that same evening, as already briefly mentioned,[2] and as we shall soon see, Bethmann repaired it by a more temperate and reasoned telegram, which, however, only arrived the following morning. The result was that affairs took a turn for the worse. Schilling's *Diary* relates that after Pourtalès had left and while Schilling and Neratov were still conferring with Sazonov, the latter was called to the telephone by the Tsar. The Tsar read out to him a telegram just arrived from Wilhelm. It had crossed with the Tsar's own telegram to Wilhelm which had been sent on to the latter by the Chancellor at 1.45 p.m. on the 29th. Drafted in English by Stumm and corrected in many places by the Kaiser it ran:

It is with the greatest concern that I hear of the impression which the action of Austria against Servia is creating in your country. The unscrupulous agitation that has been going on in Servia for years has resulted in the outrageous crime, to which Archduke Franz Ferdinand fell a victim. The spirit that led Servians to murder their own king and his wife still dominates the country. You will doubtless agree with me that we both, you and me [sic], have a common interest, as well as all sovereigns, to insist that all the persons morally responsible for the dastardly murder should receive their deserved punishment. In this case politics play no part at all.

On the other hand I fully understand how difficult it is for you and your Government to face the drift of your public opinion. Therefore, with regard to the hearty and tender friendship which binds us both from long ago with firm ties, I am exerting my utmost influence to induce the Austrians to deal straightly to arrive to a satisfactory understanding with you. I confidently hope you will help me in my efforts to smooth over difficulties that may still arise.

Your very sincere and devoted friend and cousin Willy.[3]

---

[1] It had been drafted by Stumm towards whom Wolff is indulgent (Wolff, *The Eve of 1914*, pp. 354-5. London, 1935) but whom Lichnowsky in a letter to Prof. A. Mendelssohn-Bartholdy and Dr. F. Thimme, editors of the *Grosse Politik*, describes as: 'the worthy successor of Herr Fritz von Holstein. Herr von Stumm was guided by the notion that he might become my successor in London. He therefore endeavoured, with the willing support of Herr von Jagow, to paralyse and thwart my efforts with all the means at his disposal' (Lichnowsky, p. 153). Lichnowsky thinks that the conduct of German foreign policy lay almost entirely in Stumm's hands.

[2] See p. 505.   [3] DD. II, 335.

The first part of the telegram resorts to an easily discernible artifice intended to cover up the real nature of the Austro-Russian conflict. The second part lacks all semblance of truth. Up till the 28th Germany had done nothing but urge Austria to reject all compromise and attack Serbia. If, on the evening of the 28th, a change of policy took shape at Berlin, there was not the slightest sign of it in the language used by Pourtalès. His last communication contained an open threat un-tempered by any promise from the Chancellor of exercising restraint on Austria. This explains why the Kaiser's appeals made no impression on Sazonov who took occasion to inform the Tsar of the German threat, pointing out that it was out of keeping with the spirit of the Kaiser's telegram. The Tsar decided to appeal once more to Wilhelm and at 8.30 p.m. telegraphed him as follows:

Thanks for your telegram conciliatory and friendly. Whereas official message presented to-day by your Ambassador to my Minister was conveyed in a very different tone. Beg you to explain this divergency. It would be right to give over the Austro-Servian problem to the Hague conference. Trust in your wisdom and friendship.[1]

6. *General mobilization ordered and then revoked by the Tsar.*

In addition to saying that he would telegraph to the Kaiser, the Tsar gave Sazonov permission to discuss the question of mobilization with the Minister for War and the Chief of General Staff. This discussion took place in Janushkevich's office and Schilling records that Danilov, General Monkevitz, and Basili, Assistant to the Chief of the Foreign Minister's Chancery, were present in an adjoining room in readiness to carry out the decisions taken at the conference.

These decisions were awaited with some trepidation, since all concerned knew how important in respect of our military preparedness even a partial mobilization would be if it were ordered, and still more a general mobiliza-tion, as, in the first case, a partial mobilization would render difficult a general mobilization, if such should prove necessary subsequently. After examining the situation from all points, both the Ministers and the Chief of the General Staff decided that in view of the small probability of avoiding a war with Germany it was indispensable to prepare for it in every way in good time, and that therefore the risk could not be accepted of delaying a general mobilization later by effecting a partial mobilization now. The con-clusion arrived at at this conference was at once reported by telephone to the Tsar, who authorized the taking of steps accordingly. This information was received with enthusiasm by the small circle of those acquainted with what was in progress.[2]

This entry shows that up to that moment no decision had been taken as to whether to resort to partial or to general mobilization and that

[1] DD. II, 366.   [2] Schilling, pp. 49–50; *Int. Bez.* i. V, 224.

the decision was reached towards 8 p.m. at that very conference. The opinion prevailed that it was necessary to proceed to general mobilization in view of the 'small probability there was of avoiding war with Germany'. It cannot be doubted that the Austrian refusal of direct conversations, the bombardment of Belgrade, the threatening words of Pourtalès together with the technical reasons against partial mobilization brought forward by the military, and the consideration that war now seemed practically inevitable, all combined to induce Sazonov to recommend, and the Tsar to accept the more radical measure which met with the approval of both the political and the military leaders. Sazonov immediately communicated the decision to the Russian Ambassadors at London and Paris. The telegram sent to Izvolsky runs as follows:

The German Ambassador told me to-day that his Government had decided to mobilize its armed forces, if Russia did not stop her military preparations. Now we, in fact, made these preparations only on account of the already completed mobilization of eight army corps in Austria, and because she clearly shows no willingness to fall in with any arrangement for a peaceful settlement of her conflict with Serbia. As we cannot meet the German wish, all we can do is to speed up our armaments and reckon with the probable inevitability of war. Will you please communicate this to the French Government, at the same time conveying our sincere gratitude for the declaration which the French Ambassador made to me in his Government's name that we may count in full measure on the support of France under the alliance. In the present circumstances this declaration is of especial value to us. It would be extremely desirable that England too should without loss of time associate herself with France and Russia, as this is the only way in which she will succeed in averting a dangerous disturbance of the European balance of power.[1]

On 30 July Benckendorff communicated this telegram to the Foreign Office in London as far as the words 'probable inevitability of war'. Instead of the words: 'Will you please communicate this' etc., he substituted: 'Kindly inform the Government of His Britannic Majesty of the foregoing' and suppressed the rest of the message.[2]

'To speed up our armaments' was a euphemism instead of the bald statement that total mobilization was being ordered, as a consequence of German threats, to which Russia could not yield. But it is probable that these threats were the true determining factor, in the sense that they finally convinced Sazonov and his colleagues that Austrian intransigence was, if not inspired, at least approved by Germany and that Germany would make common cause with Austria. Thus war with Germany appeared practically inevitable and Russian prospects in it would have been injured by partial mobilization, which would have

---

[1] *Int. Bez.* i. V, 221.   [2] BD. XI, 300.

upset the one existing plan for general mobilization. This road, therefore, was the only possible choice.

General Dobrorolski was immediately entrusted with sending out
the mobilization order after it had received the signature of the Navy
Minister. The Navy Minister signed it with reluctance. He was loth
to believe that Russia meant to go to war with Germany, the Russian
Navy being no match for the German. It was 9 p.m. when Dobrorolski
arrived at the central telegraph office to dispatch the mobilization telegram. Everything was in readiness and—as Dobrorolski relates—

in my presence they began to type out the telegram on typewriters in order
to send out the telegram over all the lines linking St. Petersburg with the
main centre of the Empire. . . . Several dozen lines were waiting to receive
the mobilization telegram. But at that moment—about 9.30 p.m.—General
Janushkevich called me to the telephone and ordered me to hold up the
telegram until the arrival of Captain Tugan-Baranovski of the General
Staff. . . . He arrived and announced that he had chased after me through
the city to bring me the Imperial command not to dispatch the telegram
about general mobilization. General mobilization, he said, was cancelled and
His Majesty had issued the order to proceed instead to partial mobilization
on the lines previously laid down.[1]

This order was carried out at midnight.

How did the change come about? Evidently Nicholas II had, only
with extreme reluctance and under the impression of Sazonov's latest
information, agreed to mobilization, not only against Austria, but also
against Germany, to whom he had given assurances to the contrary.
His telephone conversation with Sazonov had only just ended when he
received from Wilhelm the following reply to his first telegram which
had been dispatched in the night of 28–29 July and had crossed with
Wilhelm's first one:

I received your telegram and share your wish that peace should be maintained. But as I told you in my first telegram, I cannot consider Austria's
action against Serbia an 'ignoble' war. Austria knows by experience that
Servian promises on paper are wholly unreliable. I understand its action
must be judged as tending to get full guarantee that the Servian promises
shall become real facts. This my reasoning is borne out by the statement of
the Austrian Cabinet that Austria does not want to make any territorial
conquests at the expense of Servia. I therefore suggest that it would be quite
possible for Russia to remain a spectator of the Austro-Servian conflict
without involving Europe in the most horrible war she ever witnessed. I
think a direct understanding between your Government and Vienna possible
and desirable and as I already telegraphed to you, my Government is continuing its exertions to promote it. Of course military measures on the part
of Russia which would be looked upon by Austria as threatening, would

[1] Dobrorolski, *Mobilmachung*, pp. 25–6.

precipitate a calamity we both wish to avoid and jeopardize my position as mediator which I readily accepted on your appeal to my friendship and my help. Willy.[1]

It was certainly the final words of this telegram which led the Tsar to ring up the War Minister and order the suspension of general mobilization. And at 2.30 a.m. on the 30th the Naval Chief of Staff, Vice-Admiral Russin, telegraphed to Admiral Essen, commanding the Baltic fleet, that

in consequence of negotiations between H.M. the Tsar and Wilhelm, the Tsar has revoked general mobilization, but has left the order in force for the mobilization of the Baltic and Black Sea fleets and for the four districts.[2]

In this connexion it is curious to note that on 25 July, when the Tsar looked over the minutes and resolutions of the Council of Ministers of the 24th, he not only approved them by adding 'agreed', but, where it was the question of mobilizing the districts of Kiev, Moscow, Odessa and Kazan and the Black Sea fleet he inserted in his own hand 'and Baltic', without any of his Ministers drawing his attention to the fact that the mobilization of the Baltic fleet constituted an act of hostility towards Germany.

Frederiks, the Minister of the Court, told Luciano Magrini that the Tsar was deeply perturbed by the possibility that the crisis might lead to war. But to the pressure from the army chiefs in favour of general mobilization was added that of Sazonov, who used the argument that general mobilization was not tantamount to war and that, on the contrary, by showing Russia's firm determination, it was the best means of overawing the Central Powers and saving the peace. It was in this persuasion that the Tsar gave his consent to general mobilization. But as soon as he read the Kaiser's telegram, he called Frederiks and expressed his apprehensions regarding the extreme military measures which were about to be taken. Frederiks remarked that general mobilization was an irreparable act which would precipitate war.

The Tsar said in extreme agitation: 'Everything possible must be done to save the peace. I will not become responsible for a monstrous slaughter.' And after several minutes' silence he said that he would order the suspension of general mobilization.[3]

Sukhomlinov tried to dissuade the Tsar from this step, saying that

mobilization is not a mechanical process which one can arrest at will, as one can a waggon, and then set in motion again. But with regard to the partial mobilization, if any order concerning it were issued, I considered it my duty

---

[1] DD. II, 359. The telegram was drafted by Jagow with many emendations from the Kaiser.
[2] *Int. Bez.* i. V, 331.   [3] Magrini, pp. 250–1.

to report that subsequently much time would be necessary in which to re-establish the normal conditions for any further mobilization in the four districts affected. I therefore begged the Tsar, having regard to the import-ance of the matter, to call for another report concerning it from the Chief of the General Staff.

The Tsar did so and received exactly the same opinion.[1] Did he perhaps desire to refrain from all mobilization, even on the partial scale approved by the Council of Ministers of the 25th at which he had presided? Sazonov writes that on the 30th he was told by Janushkevich and Sukhomlinov 'that it was with the utmost difficulty they had wrung from him [the Tsar] the permission to mobilize the four South-ern Districts against Austria'.[2] But at the Sukhomlinov trial Janush-kevich on 26 August 1917 deposed that the question addressed to him was: 'Is it not possible not to proclaim general mobilization, is it not possible to replace it by partial mobilization directed against Austria?'[3] Sukhomlinov's defending counsel then asked whether the ex-Tsar had not given the order to suspend the mobilization which had already begun, and Janushkevich gave an answer which deserves attention as throwing light on his reasons for asking for general mobilization:

I have the honour to inform the Senate that, unless my memory deceives me, I actually did receive such an order. But I must say that there was no word of revoking all mobilization, but only of stopping general mobilization, in other words, according to the meaning of that order, we were to proceed only to partial mobilization. . . . But we knew that Germany was the ally of Austria and that mobilization against Austria also meant mobilization against Germany. Moreover, we knew well that Germany was ready for war, that she was longing for it at that moment, because our big armaments pro-gramme was not yet completed (was to be completed only by 1917) and be-cause our war potential was not as great as it might be. . . . We knew that war was inevitable, not only against Austria, but also against Germany. For this reason partial mobilization against Austria alone, which would have left our front towards Germany open, would have been inopportune. It might have brought about a disaster, a terrible disaster.[4]

The defence pressed its point and asked whether the Tsar had not ordered the suspension not only of general mobilization but also of partial mobilization. To this Janushkevich replied:

If my memory does not deceive me, in the telephone conversation, which lasted about half an hour, I was given the positive order to stop only general mobilization.

[1] Suchomlinow, *Erinnerungen*, pp. 364–5, quoted by Schilling, p. 117.
[2] Sazonov, p. 200.
[3] Suchomlinow. *Die russische Mobilmachung im Lichte amtlicher Urkunden und der Enthül-lungen des Prozesses* (Bern, 1917), p. 21.
[4] *Ibid.*, pp. 22–3.

It would be strange if after an interval of only three years Janushkevich's memory should deceive him on such an important point and
there is something suspicious about the insistence of Sukhomlinov's
defending counsel in putting a question about which Sukhomlinov
knew as much as Janushkevich. Can the Tsar have ordered that there
should be no mobilization and can Janushkevich have pressed for
partial mobilization in the hope of getting it changed to general mobilization? This would provide some explanation of Sazonov's statement.
In this connexion it must further be added that, in the course of the
trial, Sukhomlinov stated that, half an hour after his conversation with
the Tsar, Janushkevich told him over the telephone that when he told
the Tsar that it was not possible to stop mobilization, Nicholas had
replied: 'Stop it all the same.' This being the case Janushkevich asked
Sukhomlinov what he ought to do and Sukhomlinov answered 'Just
do nothing', i.e. told him to let general mobilization take its course.
At this Janushkevich exclaimed: 'Thank God!' 'Next day [continued
Sukhomlinov] I told the Tsar a lie. I told him that only partial
mobilization was going forward in the south-western districts.'[1] This
was a falsehood to which Sukhomlinov resorted in his trial for high
treason in order to find favour with the judges. It was believed until
Dobrorolski established the truth and drew attention to the fact that
no one in 1914 would have dreamt of committing such an act of dis-
obedience. Nor does Sukhomlinov in his memoirs repeat the lie he
told at the trial.

The Tsar stood firm because he did not want to break off his conversations with Wilhelm, to whom he telegraphed at 1.20 a.m. on the 30th:

Thank you heartily for your quick answer. Am sending Tatistchev[2]
this evening with instructions. The military measures which have now come
into force were decided five days ago for reasons of defence on account of
Austria's preparations. I hope from all my heart that these measures won't
in any way interfere with your part as mediator which I greatly value. We
need your strong pressure on Austria to come to an understanding with us.[3]

This telegram was most ill-advised in speaking of military measures
ordered five days ago, justified by reasons of defence, which were non-
existent, and directed towards exercising pressure on Austria, i.e.
threatening her, not defending Russia against her. We shall see later
the effects and the sequel of this correspondence. Here we finish the
account of what took place at St. Petersburg on 29 July, noting that
the measure for partial mobilization, devised by Sazonov and ordered

---

[1] Suchomlinow. *Die russische Mobilmachung im Lichte amtlicher Urkunden und der Enthül-
lungen des Prozesses* (Bern, 1917), pp. 23–5.

[2] General Tatistchev was the Tsar's personal representative with Wilhelm as Chelius
was that of the Kaiser with the Tsar.

[3] DD. II, 390.

on the evening of that day in reply to the Austrian declaration of war on Serbia, did not meet either the demands of the General Staff, which had no such plan prepared, or the political demands of the situation, inasmuch as, if there were to be war, Russia would have to count Germany among her foes. Hence that order had either to be cancelled in order not to cause Austrian mobilization and thus bring German mobilization in its train, or transformed into general mobilization with the practically certain risk of German and Austrian mobilization.

7. *An attempt to compose the conflict made during the night of 29–30 July; Sazonov finds a formula.*

The order to suspend general mobilization and go forward with partial mobilization was not given to Sazonov, probably because the Tsar had not the courage to turn to him, preferring to deal with the Generals, whom he could order about without too much discussion. Sazonov, therefore, was kept in the dark about Wilhelm's telegram which had caused Nicholas to change his mind, and only got it to read on the afternoon of the 30th. However he learnt immediately from Janushkevich of the change from general to partial mobilization. It must have greatly disturbed him. He had by then realized the mistakenness of partial mobilization as interfering with general mobilization, which in view of the German attitude would in the long run become inevitable. But at the moment he either did not think of making a stand, or did not venture to do so and, according to the Russian documents, simply went to bed,[1] or, according to telegrams from Pourtalès, made a supreme new effort to avert the conflict.

By two dispatches, one sent off at 4.30 a.m. on the 30th, the other at 9.30 a.m., Pourtalès informed Berlin that towards midnight Sazonov sent for him and had a talk lasting an hour and a half.

The Minister's purpose was to persuade me to advise my Government to take part in Four Power conversation in order to find means in a friendly way of inducing Austria to drop the demands detrimental to Serbian sovereignty. I simply promised to pass on the conversation and took the standpoint that any exchange of views seemed to me extremely difficult, if not impossible, now that Russia had resolved on the fatal step of mobilization. . . . Once Austria by her declaration of territorial *désintéressement* . . . had promised to show consideration for Russian interests, the Austro-Hungarian Monarchy should be left alone to settle her differences with Serbia. When the time came to make peace the question of sparing Serbian sovereignty could come up again. I gravely added that the whole Austro-Serbian affair at present falls into the background compared with the danger of a European conflagration.

[1] Schilling, p. 50.

. . . I told him that the communication I had made this afternoon on instructions from Your Excellency was not a threat but a friendly warning with reference to the automatic effect which, in virtue of the Austro-German alliance, must result from Russian mobilization. Sazonov declared that the cancellation of the mobilization order is no longer possible and that Austrian mobilization was responsible for it.

During the conversation of last night Sazonov continually reverted to the theme that we were the only ones who could now hold Austria back. H.M. the Kaiser and King need only say the word and it will be heeded. . . . Russia's vital interests demanded not only respect for the territorial integrity of Serbia but also that Serbia shall not sink to the rank of a vassal state of Austria by the acceptance of Austrian demands injurious to her own sovereign rights. Serbia must not become a Bokhara.[1]

In the latter part of the morning of 30 July Pourtalès himself took steps to renew the conversation. He had to carry out the instructions contained in the Chancellor's telegram dispatched at 11.5 p.m. on the 29th and thus later than the one of 12.50 p.m. which Sazonov had regarded as an ultimatum since it threatened that Germany would mobilize if Russia went on with her mobilization.[2] The later telegram replied to one of the 29th from Pourtalès which had reached the Wilhelmstrasse at 2.52 p.m. and had reported Sazonov's statement that Russia was mobilizing only against Austria, that mobilization did not mean war, that Russian troops could remain for weeks on end standing at ease without crossing the frontier, and that no measures were being directed against Germany. Bethmann's reply struck a different note from his earlier one of intimidation. He warned that: 'Russian mobilization on the Austrian frontier will, I assume, lead to corresponding Austrian measures. How far it will still be possible to stop the avalanche then it is hard to say.' In order if possible to avert the threatening catastrophe he was trying to get a fresh formal assurance of territorial *désintéressement* from Austria, and Russia must rest satisfied with that.[3] To this, as Pourtalès reports, Sazonov answered

that an assurance of Austrian territorial *désintéressement* could not satisfy Russia. He could not now advocate another policy without endangering the life of the Tsar. Remarking that I saw no prospect of the fulfilment of his wishes by Austria, I begged Sazonov to put them once more into writing, bearing in mind that if any prospect of a peaceful solution remained, he must consent to some kind of compromise. Thereupon the Minister wrote down the following:

'If Austria, recognizing that her dispute with Serbia has assumed the character of a question of European interest, declares herself ready to eliminate from her ultimatum the clauses which are damaging to the sovereignty of Serbia, Russia undertakes to stop all military preparations.'[4]

[1] DD. II, 401, 412.   [2] See p. 491.   [3] DD. II, 380. See p. 505.
[4] French original text in DD. II, 421 and Schilling, p. 52.

Although these demands will hardly prove acceptable, it is noteworthy that Sazonov's draft contains no word of a demand for the immediate cessation of the Austrian punitive expedition. But when I proposed that Russia might perhaps declare herself satisfied if Austria were to give certain assurances in this sense for when peace was concluded, the Minister would not entertain the idea.[1]

In this dispatch which went off to Berlin at 1.1 p.m. on the 30th, Pourtalès very rightly noted that Sazonov's formula opened up the possibility of an agreement on the basis of a *Halt in Belgrade*. Sazonov writes that:

Russia consented to stop her preparations for war if Austria merely renounced her attack upon Serbia's sovereign rights [in reality he asked for something more, namely, a revision of the ultimatum], she did not require that Austria should immediately stop her military operations against Serbia.[2]

This was indeed a noteworthy concession, but if it was to be of any use, not only general, but also partial mobilization would have to be countermanded, because, as Bethmann rightly remarked, Russian partial mobilization would entail that of Austria, and it was hard to say 'how far it would be possible to stop the avalanche'. (Only this is what he ought to have said right from the beginning, and Jagow had been saying the very opposite.) Sazonov, moreover, in handing this peace formula to Pourtalès, had already made up his mind to change partial into general mobilization and thus was not acting in good faith.

The above is Pourtalès's version of what took place. But Schilling's *Diary* states: 1. That it was not Sazonov who towards midnight on the 29th sent for Pourtalès to make those proposals. It was Pourtalès who towards 1 a.m. on the 30th asked to see Sazonov who rose from bed to receive him. 2. that on being received, Pourtalès made the communication in accordance with the Chancellor's instructions, asking for and obtaining the formula for conciliation which Sazonov drafted.[3]

This would mean that the talk reported to Berlin by Pourtalès at 1.1 p.m. on the 30th was the one which took place during the night, while the one which his dispatches of 4.30 a.m. and 9.30 a.m. of the 30th give as having taken place during the night did not take place at all. Sir George Buchanan's telegram, sent off at 1.15 p.m. on the 30th, gives the following data:

Minister for Foreign Affairs received French Ambassador and me this morning. He told us he had yesterday afternoon conversation with German Ambassador in which latter had said that his Government would guarantee that Austria would not violate Serbian integrity. Minister for Foreign Affairs had replied that though territorial integrity might be respected Servia would inevitably become vassal of Austria just as Bokhara, though its territory had

[1] DD. II, 421 ; Pourtalès, p. 48.   [2] Sazonov, p. 197.
[3] Schilling, pp. 50-1; *Int. Bez.* i. V, 224.

been left intact, was a vassal of Russia. Were Russian Government to tolerate this, there would be a revolution in the country. . . . At two o'clock in the morning German Ambassador had a second interview with Minister for Foreign Affairs in which former, seeing that war was inevitable, broke down completely and appealed to latter to hold out a last straw and to make some suggestion he could telegraph to his Government. . . .[1]

There seems no reason why Sazonov should not be telling the truth to Buchanan or why he should hide the efforts made by himself during the night to arrive at a peaceful solution, knowing that this would meet with approval from Buchanan, if not from Paléologue. There also seems no reason why Pourtalès should invent the summons from Sazonov in the depth of night if it never took place. But it is useless to waste time over a discrepancy which does not alter the main facts one way or another.[2]

8. *Sazonov, Sukhomlinov, and Janushkevich press for general mobilization.*

We now return to Schilling's *Diary* from which we learn what line was taken by Sazonov on the morning of the 30th when he had to decide whether to support the Tsar's opinion that partial mobilization would be sufficient or throw his weight on the side of general mobilization. The quotation is a lengthy one but is needful in order to throw

---

[1] BD. XI, 302.

[2] Most historians accept the Pourtalès version. When he was questioned on this point on 14 February 1924 by the Commission of Inquiry into the origins of the war he reaffirmed his story, maintaining, as is also recorded in a note in Schilling's *Diary* (p. 51): i. that the Chancellor's telegram, dispatched at 11.5 p.m. on the 29th, was received by him on the morning of the 30th and could not therefore have been in his hands when he talked with Sazonov at about midnight; ii. that his talk with Sazonov, for which he asked in order to carry out the instructions contained in the Chancellor's telegram, took place about noon on the 30th. But it may be objected that Schilling's *Diary* records that Pourtalès asked for the meeting not at midnight but at 1 a.m., by which time he might well have received the short urgent telegram from Bethmann. Moreover it is not possible that the following morning Pourtalès can have been in conversation with Sazonov about noon because it is a fact that at 1.1 p.m. he telegraphed the results of the conversation to Berlin. He would not have had time to send off a rather lengthy telegram in code by 1 p.m. if he had been talking with Sazonov about noon. Still less would Buchanan have been able to send off his dispatch reporting the Pourtalès-Sazonov conversation at 1.15 p.m. Nor can it be believed that Pourtalès simply made a slip of an hour for, as we shall see in a moment, on 30 July Sazonov went away elsewhere at 11 a.m. or perhaps a little earlier and on returning received a call from Paléologue who was soon joined by Buchanan. Hence if the Pourtalès-Sazonov talk took place on the morning of the 30th and not during the night of 29–30 July, it could only have been about 10 a.m. or a bit earlier. And very likely this is what did happen, since the authenticity of the Pourtalès telegram is beyond doubt. On the other hand Sazonov, as will soon be seen, in informing Buchanan and Paléologue, spoke of two conversations with Pourtalès, one on the afternoon of the 29th and the other at 2.30 a.m. on the 30th, assigning to the earlier conversation part of what was said at the later and vice versa. Now since he cannot possibly have said certain of the things in the afternoon one is driven to the conclusion that he intentionally interchanged the conversations for motives which remain unknown to us. But in that case would it be Schilling who invented the story of Sazonov being called from his bed? How many obscure points crop up when one seeks to clear up the exact particulars of the history of those momentous days!

light on acts and words which were decisive in precipitating the crisis.

Between 9 and 10 a.m. the Minister for Foreign Affairs spoke to the Minister for Agriculture by telephone. Both of them were greatly disturbed at the stoppage of the general mobilization, as they fully realized that this threatened to place Russia in an extremely difficult position in the event of relations with Germany becoming acute. S. D. Sazonov advised A. V. Krivoshein to beg an audience of the Tsar in order to represent to His Majesty the dangers called forth by the change.

At 11 a.m. the Minister for Foreign Affairs again met the Minister for War and the Chief of the General Staff. Information received during the night still further strengthened the opinion which they all held that it was imperative to prepare for a serious war without loss of time. Accordingly the Ministers and the Chief of the Staff adhered to the view which they had expressed yesterday to the effect that it was indispensable to proceed to a general mobilization. Adjutant-General Sukhomlinov and General Janushkevich again endeavoured by telephone to persuade the Tsar to revert to his decision of yesterday to permit a general mobilization. His Majesty decidedly refused to do so, and finally shortly declared that the conversation was at an end. General Janushkevich, who at this moment was holding the telephone receiver, only succeeded in reporting that the Minister for Foreign Affairs was there with him and asked to be allowed to say a few words to His Majesty. A somewhat lengthy silence ensued, after which the Tsar expressed his willingness to hear the Minister. S. D. Sazonov requested His Majesty to receive him to-day, to enable him to present a report concerning the political situation which admitted of no delay. After a silence the Tsar asked: 'Is it all the same to you if I receive you at 3 o'clock, at the same time as Tatistchev, as otherwise I have not a free minute to-day?' The Minister thanked His Majesty and said that he would present himself at the hour named.

The Chief of the Staff warmly pleaded with S. D. Sazonov to persuade the Tsar without fail to consent to a general mobilization in view of the extreme danger that would result for us if we were not ready for war with Germany, should circumstances demand the taking of decisive measures by us after the success of a general mobilization had been compromised by recourse to a partial mobilization. . . .

On his return to the Foreign Office, S. D. Sazonov had an interview with the French Ambassador. Meanwhile Krivoshein informed S. D. Sazonov that in reply to his request that the Tsar would receive him, he was told that His Majesty was so extremely occupied to-day that he could not see him. Krivoshein then expressed a desire to see S. D. Sazonov before the latter went to Peterhof. It was decided that they should breakfast together at Donon's, and at 12.30 they and Baron Schilling met in a private room there. The general state of mind was tense and the conversation was almost exclusively concerned with the necessity for insisting upon a general mobilization at the earliest possible moment, in view of the inevitability of war with Germany, which every moment became clearer.[1]

[1] Schilling, pp. 62–4; *Int. Bez.* i. V, 284.

While this is the story given in Schilling's *Diary*, Sazonov in *Fateful Years* gives a somewhat different version. He states that the talk with Janushkevich and Sukhomlinov took place not at 11 a.m. but at 2 p.m., and that the two generals

hardly mentioned Austria, since she had no further surprises in store for us . . . and also because the menace from Germany made the Austrian danger look comparatively unimportant.

They felt certain

that the German mobilization had advanced much further than was generally supposed and that . . . Russia might find herself in an extremely dangerous situation if she mobilized partially and not as a whole.

Janushkevich added that 'war had become inevitable and that we were in danger of losing it before we had time to unsheath our sword'.

Sazonov asked him

whether he had told all this to the Tsar. The Generals answered that the Tsar knew exactly how matters stood, but that they had not so far succeeded in obtaining his consent for a general mobilization decree and that it was with the greatest difficulty they had wrung from him the permission to mobilize the four Southern Districts against Austria. . . . Our mobilization might be put off for another twenty-four hours at the utmost, but after that it would be useless, for it could not be carried out properly; in that case General Janushkevich could not hold himself responsible for the consequences. The moment was so critical that the Chief of the General Staff and the Minister for War begged me to telephone to the Tsar . . . I need not say with what feelings I regarded this request. . . .

I telephoned to the Peterhof Palace. After several minutes of agonizing expectation I heard a voice which I did not recognize at once—the voice of a man evidently not used to speaking on the telephone—asking me who was speaking. . . .[1] 'What is it you wish?' asked the Tsar. I answered that I begged him earnestly to see me in the afternoon on urgent business. This time I had to wait still longer for a reply. At last the voice was heard again and said: 'I will receive you at 3 o'clock'. The Generals heaved a sigh of relief and I hurried home to change and left for Peterhof before half past two, arriving there at the time appointed.[2]

The discrepancies between this story and Schilling's turn on the hour at which Sazonov's talk with the two generals took place, the circumstances in which he telephoned to the Tsar and the answer given him by the Tsar. There seems to be little doubt that the more trustworthy account is Schilling's, which has a flavour of authenticity and

[1] The Tsar can hardly have been so unaccustomed to the telephone, seeing that the previous evening he had talked at considerable length with Sazonov who was persuading him to assent to general mobilization, and that, during the night, he had a long telephone discussion first with Sukhomlinov and then for half an hour with Janushkevich.

[2] Sazonov, p. 201.

accuracy. Schilling cannot have invented certain of the details, including the lunch which he had with Sazonov and Krivoshein at 12.30 noon and the things that were said at it. Schilling's account, moreover, has been corroborated by Baron Frederiks, Minister of the Imperial Court.[1] Yet what motive could Sazonov have had for altering, in the first place, the chronology of events, making out that he went to the conference with the generals at 2 p.m. and hardly had time to change and go to the audience at Peterhof? Light is thrown on what he told Paléologue and Buchanan by the summary which Buchanan telegraphed to Grey at 1.15 p.m. on 30 July:

Minister for Foreign Affairs . . . told us he had yesterday afternoon conversation with German Ambassador in which latter had said that his Government would guarantee that Austria would not violate Servian integrity. Minister for Foreign Affairs had replied that though territorial integrity might be respected Servia would inevitably become vassal of Austria just as Bokhara, though its territory had been left intact, was a vassal of Russia. Were Russia to tolerate this, there would be a revolution in country. High words were exchanged on both sides, Minister for Foreign Affairs accusing Austria of pursuing a policy of blackmail and Germany of being animated by desire of gaining time to complete her military preparations. Russian Government, Minister for Foreign Affairs told us, had absolute proof of military and naval preparations being made by Germany against Russia more especially in direction of Gulf of Finland. Yesterday evening it was decided to issue this morning order for partial mobilization . . . and at the same time to commence preparations for general mobilization. At two o'clock in morning German Ambassador had second interview with Minister for Foreign Affairs in which former, seeing that war was inevitable, broke down completely and appealed to latter to hold out a last straw and to make some suggestion he could telegraph to his Government. Minister for Foreign Affairs then read out text of French formula[2] given by him to Ambassador of which following is a translation:—

If Austria, recognizing that her conflict with Serbia has assumed character of question of European interest, declares herself ready to eliminate from her ultimatum points which violate principle of sovereignty of Servia, Russia engages to stop all military preparations.

If Austria rejects this proposal, preparations for a general mobilization will be proceeded with and European war will be inevitable. For strategical reasons Russia can hardly postpone converting partial into general mobilization now that she knows that Germany is preparing and excitement in country has reached such a pitch that she cannot hold back if Austria refuses to make concession. Minister for Foreign Affairs is to see Emperor this afternoon.[3]

[1] Magrini, pp. 249-51.
[2] Here is apparent the transposition made by Sazonov of what he said at the two interviews with Pourtalès.
[3] BD. XI, 302.

These last words show that when Sazonov saw Buchanan he knew that he was due for an audience of the Tsar at 3 p.m. and that therefore his conference with Sukhomlinov and Janushkevich took place some little time before 2 p.m. Now one might have believed that it was by a sheer slip of memory that Sazonov put the conference at 2 p.m. instead of 11 a.m., were it not that he went out of his way to say that after it he had to 'hurry home to change and start off for Peterhof', saying not a word of the luncheon with Krivoshein and Schilling which cannot have dropped out of his mind on account of what was said at it. Therefore it cannot be ruled out that by transposing the times he has tried to hide the fact that on that morning he had told Buchanan an untruth (it is doubtful whether he hid the truth from Paléologue) when he said that general mobilization would only be resorted to if Austria rejected his formula, whereas in reality he was on the point of seeing the Tsar—who on his proposal the previous evening had assented to general mobilization and had then revoked it—in order to beg him to withdraw this revocation. If the conference with the generals and the telephone conversation with the Tsar had taken place after the call of the two Ambassadors, Sazonov could not be accused not only of concealing but of falsifying the truth, as he did to a serious extent, especially in relation to England (for in regard to France it is extremely difficult to ascertain the truth in view of the large lacunae in Paléologue's diplomatic correspondence, which intentionally kept Paris in the dark about what was going on at St. Petersburg). Hardly had he spoken to Buchanan and Paléologue on the lines summarized in Buchanan's telegram than he was telegraphing to the Russian Ambassadors at Berlin, Paris, London and Vienna after reproducing the formula itself[1]: 'Until the receipt of entirely satisfactory reply from Austria through the German Government we shall continue arming.'[2]

But let it be made quite clear. Sazonov's mistake was not that he sought to have partial mobilization changed to general mobilization. An improvised partial mobilization would have been fatal to Russia's military prospects, and, given the certainty that, in the event of war, Germany would rally to the cause of Austria, it would have made no sense. Called upon to decide between general and partial mobilization, any statesman with the rudiments of good sense could not do otherwise than choose general mobilization. But the dangers conjured up by either should have ruled them both out as long as there was the least hope of arriving at a peaceful solution of the dispute. Hence Sazonov's fault was, first, not to have seen at once that partial mobilization was impossible, and then, rather than give up the whole idea, to have chosen to proceed with general mobilization with all the risks it involved. If, when he perceived the slippery slope towards which the military

---

[1] *Int. Bez.* i. V, 277, 278.   [2] *Int. Bez.* i. V, 279.

authorities were pushing him, he had had the courage to turn back rather than accept general mobilization, which he knew would bring Germany on to the scene, he would undoubtedly have had the wholehearted support of the Tsar against the Generals.

The Tsar's temperament was quite unfitted to decide the destinies of his vast empire. Sukhomlinov, writing of an audience of the Tsar on 28 July, notes:

To judge by the calmness or more exactly the equanimity with which the Tsar listened to my report of current business, one might have come to the conclusion that there was nothing that might in any way threaten the peaceful life of Russia. I was amazed at His Majesty's impassiveness and the slightness of his interest in what I had to say. I could find no explanation for it.[1]

The same impression of heedlessness and childishness is given by a perusal of the Tsar's diary. The entry for 28 July (old style: 15 July) runs: 'At 6 p.m. I received Sazonov who informed me that to-day at noon Austria declared war on Serbia.' That is all! On the previous day, 27 July, he had written:

Little news of interest; but, according to a report received by Sazonov, it appears that the Austrians seem extremely amazed by the rumours circulating about our military measures and are beginning to talk of them.

On the 29th:

During the day we played tennis; the weather was magnificent. But the day was singularly unpeaceful. I was constantly being called to the telephone, now it was Sazonov, now Sukhomlinov or Janushkevich. Apart from that I was in urgent telephonic communication with Wilhelm. In the evening I read and received Tatistchev whom I am sending to-morrow to Berlin.

On the 30th, after having given assent to general mobilization:

After lunch I received Sazonov and Tatistchev. I went for a walk by myself. The weather was hot. At 6 I received Count Frederiks with Voïekov and then Nilov. Had a delightful bathe in the sea.

On the 31st: 'It has been a grey day, in keeping with my mood.'[2] But these colourless entries do not belie the fact that their author's peaceable and gentle character strongly inclined him towards keeping the peace, quite apart from the pressure exercised by the Tsarina and the many Germanophils at Court, beginning with Frederiks, however much the Grand Duke Nicholas might incline in the other direction. Sukhomlinov writes that 'in the days preceding the war the Tsar was entirely under the influence of his uncle'.[3] But Sukhomlinov was prompted to exaggerate, if not to invent, by the fact that he himself

---

[1] Suchomlinow, *Erinnerungen*, p. 361.   [2] *Journal intime de Nicolas II*, pp. 15-16.
[3] Suchomlinow, *Erinnerungen*, p. 363.

was obviously not a favourite with the Grand Duke, whom he believed to have been instrumental in bringing the Tsar into direct contact with the Chief of General Staff. One thing certain is that the Tsar on the evening of the 29th and morning of the 30th stood his ground against the Generals who were pressing for the retention of the order for general mobilization, though he did not make any effort, however unavailing, to stop partial mobilization. It is also certain that Sazonov asked Krivoshein to use his influence with the Tsar, that Sukhomlinov appealed to Rodzianko, President of the Duma, to ask for an audience on the question of mobilization (another particular forgotten by Sazonov) and that Rodzianko and Sukhomlinov saw Sazonov again before the latter's departure for Peterhof. Sazonov was asked to carry the message that Rodzianko 'as head of the representatives of the Russian people would never forgive a delay which might precipitate the country into fatal confusion'.[1]

Schilling's account, quoted above, makes it clear that neither the Generals nor Sazonov felt sure of extracting the Tsar's consent. And in fact it was not easily given.

9. The Tsar's last efforts to resist the generals; his conversation with Sazonov; the order for general mobilization issued at 5 p.m. on 30 July.

Sazonov went to Peterhof accompanied by Tatistchev. His account in *Fateful Years* states that he found the Tsar tired and anxious. Nicholas asked him whether he had anything against General Tatistchev being present at the interview and Sazonov answered that he would be very pleased, but expressed a doubt whether Tatistchev would be able to return to his position in Berlin as General in the suite of Kaiser Wilhelm.

'You think it is too late?' asked the Tsar. I had to say I did.·. . . I began my report at ten minutes past three and finished at four. I told the Tsar in detail my conversation with the Minister of War and the Chief of the General Staff, omitting nothing of what I had heard from them and mentioning the last news. . . . This news left no doubt whatever that, during the two days I had not seen the Tsar, the position had changed so much for the worse that there was no more hope of preserving peace. All our conciliatory offers . . . had been rejected. . . . I told the Tsar that I fully agreed with Janushkevich and Sukhomlinov that it was dangerous to delay the general mobilization any longer, since, according to the information they possessed, the German mobilization, though not as yet proclaimed officially, was fairly advanced. . . . On the morning of 30 July he had received a telegram from Kaiser Wilhelm saying that if Russia continued to mobilize against Austria, the Kaiser would be unable to intercede, as the Tsar had asked him. . . . I could see from his expression how wounded he was by its tone and content

[1] M. V. Rodzianko, *The Reign of Rasputin* (London, 1927), pp. 106–8.

. . . After giving me time to read the unfortunate telegram carefully, the Tsar said in an agitated voice: 'He is asking the impossible. He has forgotten, or does not wish to remember, that the Austrian mobilization had begun sooner than the Russian, and now asks us to stop ours without saying a word about the Austrians. You know I have already suppressed one mobilization decree and then consented only to a partial one. If I agreed to Germany's demands now, we should find ourselves unarmed against the Austrian Army which is mobilized already. It would be madness. . . .'

I answered that the responsibility for the precious lives carried away by the war would not fall upon him.[1]

The war had been

thrust upon Russia and Europe by the ill-will of the enemy, determined to increase their power by enslaving our natural Allies in the Balkans, destroying our influence there and reducing Russia to a pitiful dependence upon the arbitrary will of the Central Powers. . . . I had nothing further to add and sat opposite the Tsar, watching him intently. He was pale and his expression betrayed a terrible inner struggle. . . . At last the Tsar said, speaking as it were with difficulty: 'You are right. There is nothing left for us but to get ready for an attack upon us. Give then the Chief of the General Staff my order for mobilization.'[2]

This account of the historic audience, written by Sazonov many years later, is incomplete and inexact. That of Schilling written down on the very day of the 30th has much greater value and deserves full credence. It shows that the Tsar went through a long struggle before surrendering to the arguments used with him and that these are not precisely the ones given by Sazonov:

During the course of nearly an hour the Minister proceeded to show that war was becoming inevitable, as it was clear to everybody that Germany had decided to bring about a collision, as otherwise she would not have rejected all the pacificatory proposals that had been made and could easily have brought her ally to reason. . . . Therefore it was necessary to put away any fears that our warlike preparations would bring about a war and to continue these preparations carefully, rather than by reason of such fears to be taken unawares by war.[3]

The firm desire of the Tsar to avoid war at all costs, the horrors of which filled him with repulsion, led His Majesty, in his full realization of the heavy

[1] Here there is a lacuna in Sazonov's story. It is probably filled out by Paléologue's account: 'The Tsar was deadly pale and replied in a choking voice: "Just think of the responsibility you are advising me to assume! Remember it is a question of sending thousands and thousands of men to their death" ' (Paléologue, I, p. 45). It is to these words that Sazonov replies.

[2] Sazonov, pp. 201–5.

[3] Dobrorolski states that Janushkevich had also persuaded Sazonov to represent to the Tsar that partial mobilization was a violation of Russian duties under the alliance with France and that it would give Wilhelm II an opening to demand a promise of neutrality from the French Government with the further prospect of the latter's even declaring war against Russia (Dobrorolski, *Mobilmachung*, p. 28).

responsibility which he took upon himself in this fateful hour, to explore every possible means for averting the approaching danger. Consequently he refused during a long time to agree to the adoption of measures which, however indispensable from a military point of view, were calculated, as he clearly saw, to hasten a decision in an undesirable sense. The tenseness of feeling experienced by the Tsar at this time found expression, amongst other signs, in the irritability, most unusual in him, with which His Majesty interrupted General Tatistchev. The latter, who throughout had taken no part in the conversation, said in a moment of silence: 'Yes, it is hard to decide.' His Majesty replied in a rough, displeased tone: 'I will decide'—in order by this means to prevent the General from intervening any further in the conversation.[1]

Finally the Tsar agreed that in the existing circumstances it would be very dangerous not to make timely preparations for what was apparently an inevitable war, and therefore gave his decision in favour of an immediate general mobilization.

S. D. Sazonov requested the Imperial permission to inform the Chief of the General Staff of this immediately by telephone, and, this being granted, he hastened to the telephone on the ground floor of the palace. Having transmitted the Imperial order to General Janushkevich, who was waiting impatiently for it, the Minister, with reference to the conversation that morning, added: 'Now you can smash your telephone.'[2]

This was a reference to the fact that before the audience

General Janushkevich requested the Minister that in the event of his succeeding in persuading the Tsar he would telephone to him to that effect from Peterhof, in order that he might immediately take the necessary steps, as it would be requisite first of all to stop as soon as possible the partial mobilization. . . . 'After that', said Janushkevich, 'I shall go away, smash my telephone and generally adopt measures which will prevent anyone from finding me for the purpose of giving contrary orders which would again stop our general mobilization.'[3]

Janushkevich had come to an agreement with Dobrorolski that he was to act immediately on gaining the Tsar's consent. Again it was needful to get the signatures of three Ministers, but this was easy because the Council of Ministers was at that moment sitting at Mariinsky Palace. About 5 p.m. the telegram announcing general mobilization for the following day, 31 July, was handed in at the head telegraph office by Dobrorolski. But the decision had been taken at 4 p.m. Sazonov would have liked to keep it secret 'to avoid rendering more acute our

---

[1] Schilling, pp. 64–5. Of the reactions arising from the very weakness of the Tsar's character, Anna Virubova, an intimate friend of the Tsarina's and a go-between between her and Rasputin, writes that the Tsarina tried to use her influence to prevent the war. But a telegram from Rasputin predicting that the war would end with the destruction of the Russian Empire only served to irritate the Tsar (Anna Virubova, *Souvenirs de ma vie* (Paris, 1927), p. 65).

[2] Schilling, pp. 65–6; *Int. Bez.* i. V, 284.   [3] Schilling, pp. 63–4; *Int. Bez.* i. V, 284.

relations with Germany', as Schilling reports.[1] But already in the night of 30–31 July the red notices calling the classes to the colours were posted up on the walls in St. Petersburg. This particular relating to secrecy is, in the opinion of the present author, of some little importance, and, as will be shown more fully in the following chapter, explains many things. Among these things, the belief that it was possible to proceed to general mobilization without making it public may well have made Sazonov more inclined to order it.

Receiving news of the Russian general mobilization, the German Ambassador, Pourtalès, asked and obtained an audience of the Tsar in the morning of 31 July.

I drew His Majesty's attention with the utmost seriousness to the impression which this morning's order for the mobilization of the *entire* Russian army and navy could not fail to produce on us after the many assurances given us that only a partial mobilization of the districts adjoining Austria was intended. I expressed anxiety that this measure had perhaps already produced irreparable consequences. I especially dwelt on the apprehension that mobilization against Germany, in the course of the mediation carried out by Your Majesty and not yet definitely come to naught, would be regarded by the German nation as a provocative act. I entreated him, if at all possible, to stay or revoke this measure.[2]

In his diary Pourtalès further narrates:

The Tsar listened quietly to what I had to say without his countenance betraying what was passing in his mind. All he answered was: '*Vous croyez vraiment?*' I received the impression that His Majesty either possessed an unusual degree of self-control or else had not yet fully understood the gravity of the situation in spite of my very serious representations. When I remarked that the only thing that in my opinion might perhaps still prevent war would be the withdrawal of the order for mobilization, the Tsar replied that I, as an officer, must be aware that a stay of the orders already issued was no longer technically possible. The Tsar then showed me a telegram to our Kaiser, which he was about to send off, and also the beginning of a letter to His Majesty, explaining his standpoint. I ventured to remark that in my opinion it was, as things now stood, too late for such discussions by letter. The Tsar then went on to a general discussion of the situation and, unmistakably under the inspiration of Sazonov, pointed to the need for Germany to exercise strong pressure on Austria. . . . I replied that the moderating influence exercised by us on Austria-Hungary had been repeatedly apparent during the Balkan war and had been recognized by Russia. Now, too, we were not behindhand with friendly suggestions to the Vienna Cabinet, as the Tsar knew. We could not, however, be expected to use forceful pressure on Austria-Hungary. Our position in Europe precluded our imperilling our friendly relations with our ally. The Tsar listened in silence to these representations which apparently were not appreciated by him. I then made another attempt to draw the Tsar's attention to the dangers which this war represented for

[1] Schilling, p. 69; *Int. Bez.* i. V, 349.　　　　[2] DD. III, 535.

the monarchic principle. To this His Majesty agreed and finally remarked that he hoped everything would turn out right in the end. When I answered that I did not think this possible unless Russian mobilization were stopped, The Tsar pointed upwards with the words: 'Then there is only One alone who can help.'[1]

In this fateful hour the Tsar was uttering to Pourtalès practically the same thought as he had uttered some years earlier to one of his ministers at another critical moment for Russia, when he dissolved the Duma amid revolutionary turmoil while appearing perfectly calm:

If you see me so calm, it is because I have firm and absolute faith that the fate of Russia, of myself, and of my family is in the hands of God who has placed me where I am. Whatever happens, I shall bow to His will, conscious of having had no other thought than that of serving the country He has entrusted to me.[2]

The same thought was again in his mind in the days of the 1917 revolution. In July 1914 the Tsar tried to prevent war, resisting the pressure of those who clamoured for general mobilization and revoking it a first time at the last moment after he had given it his consent. But then his weak character bent under the pressure of Sazonov and the military and his fatalistic mysticism sought refuge in the aid of a Higher Power, whose grace he sought to win by the purity of his intentions. In spite of the many signs which ought to have told him that Russian general mobilization made a European war practically inevitable, the Tsar, even after his talk with Pourtalès, continued to hope 'that everything would turn out right in the end'. At 3 p.m. on 31 July he telegraphed to Wilhelm:

It is technically impossible to stop our military preparations which were obligatory owing to Austria's mobilization. We are far from wishing war. As long as the negotiations with Austria on Servia's account are taking place my troops shall not make any provocative action. I give you my solemn word for this.[3]

The Tsar was still under the illusion that the peace could yet be saved. But in reality events were moving with increasing speed. Diplomacy was being reduced to silence. The General Staffs were not concerned with averting war but with winning victory. And to come out victorious they must attempt to forestall the enemy. Every hour gained was of moment for their chance of victory.

10. *Sazonov's motives, his mistakes, and their extenuating circumstances.*

In any case, let it be clearly established that the responsibility for the fatal step of mobilizing against Austria on the evening of the 29th and

---

[1] Pourtalès, pp. 60–1.   [2] *Mémoires d'Alexandre Izwolsky* (Paris, 1923), p. 222.
[3] DD. III, 487.

against Austria and Germany at 4 p.m. on the 30th rests beyond all doubt with Russia. What happened was that about 2 p.m. on the 30th the Berlin *Lokal-Anzeiger* came out with a special issue announcing that the Kaiser had just ordered German mobilization. This false report was promptly contradicted by the Berlin Government. Its origin will be discussed in Vol. III; Ch. I of the present work. Here it may already be said that the Russian Ambassador at Berlin, Sverbeev, who telegraphed it to St. Petersburg, quickly followed it up with a *démenti*. The incident gave rise to the theory, long debated and for a time believed, that it was Sverbeev's first telegram which gave the impetus to Russian mobilization. The theory was put forward as early as the following day, 31st, by Bethmann himself in a telegram to Lichnowsky which said:

I regard it as not impossible that Russian mobilization originated in the fact that the absolutely false rumours of German mobilization circulating here yesterday, though at once officially contradicted, were reported as facts to St. Petersburg.[1]

The Bavarian Socialist, Kurt Eisner, further claimed that Sverbeev's telegram contradicting the *Lokal-Anzeiger* announcement was held back on purpose by the German authorities who wanted Russia to be tempted into mobilizing first. And, after the Sukhomlinov trial, the Kerensky Government reaffirmed the influence exercised by the news on the Government of the Tsar.[2] Montgelas, however, has conclusively shown that by some delay of transmission, Sverbeev's telegram contradicting the rumour was dispatched before the one with the announcement that mobilization had been proclaimed and that the latter cannot have reached St. Petersburg before 7 p.m.[3] Now the decision on Russian mobilization was in fact taken at 4 p.m., and in a letter of 5 March 1927 Sazonov himself states that the chronology of events shows there was no causal connexion between the *Lokal-Anzeiger* announcement and Russian mobilization.[4] Still less is it true that Russia mobilized because Austria had ordered general mobilization, as is stated in a telegram from Paléologue of 31 July published in the French *Yellow Book*,[5] since Austrian general mobilization was proclaimed at 12.23 p.m. on the 31st. This Paléologue telegram was an invention of the Quai d'Orsay to justify Russian mobilization, and shows that even the Quai d'Orsay did not regard this extreme military measure as justified.[6]

---

[1] DD. III, 488.

[2] R. Grelling, 'Le mystère du 30 juillet' in *Revue de Paris*, 3 March 1922, pp. 29–69.

[3] Max Count Montgelas. *The Case for the Central Powers* (London, 1925), pp. 216–17; *Deutsche Rundschau*, May 1922, pp. 113–24.

[4] KSF. November 1929, p. 1062.   [5] LJF. 118, in CDD., p. 223.

[6] In Vol. III, Chap. IV, it will be shown what influence this falsification of the *Yellow Book* had on statements made by Poincaré and Viviani after the war. But if Viviani in 1922 could say in good faith that Austrian mobilization preceded Russian mobilization, Poincaré

Nor, indeed, was it. Or at least there was no justification for the partial mobilization which, as being impracticable, led on to general mobilization, to which the Tsar was only induced to assent by false reasons. He was made to believe that Austria had mobilized, not only against Serbia, but also against Russia, and that Germany had completed her mobilization. The true facts are that German and Austrian military preparations (apart from Austrian preparations against Serbia) were until the 31st less extensive than those of either Russia or France. It was, however, true that war seemed practically inevitable, seeing that Austria was not prepared to make concessions and that Germany, up to the evening of the 29th, had given her no serious advice to do so. It was also true that Russia could not attach any value to the Austrian promise of territorial *désintéressement*, for it concealed a deception to which we must pay attention for a moment.

It will be remembered that at the Council of Joint Ministers of the Dual Monarchy of 19 July, at which the decision was taken to act against Serbia, Tisza had successfully insisted that territorial gains should not be aimed at, but it had been added that 'this decision does not rule out strategically necessary frontier rectifications and such temporary occupation of Serbian territory as may in the event become necessary'.[1] In other words Serbia was to be reduced to a minimum in favour of Bulgaria, Greece and Albania, if not also of Roumania.[2] Hence both the Austrian, and by reflexion the German documents, took great pains to speak of Austrian territorial *désintéressement*, something quite different from the maintenance of the territorial integrity of Serbia which Sazonov demanded without perceiving the deception contained in the other formula. But even supposing the equivocation to have been removed and Austria to have given an undertaking not to mutilate Serbia, either to her own benefit or that of other states (a pledge which would have been obtained from her with great difficulty), Serbia would none the less have fallen into vassalage. As the Austrian Prime Minister mentioned at the Council meeting on the 19th it would be possible

by the deposition of the dynasty, a military convention and other appropriate measures, to place Serbia on a relationship of dependence on the Monarchy.[3]

in 1930 can hardly have been speaking in the same good faith when he insinuated: 'According to the check undertaken by M. de Montgelas, it would seem that M. Sverbeev's first telegram did not reach St. Petersburg before the decision of Nicholas II. All the same St. Petersburg, no less than anywhere else, will doubtless have said to itself that there is no smoke without a fire' (Gerin, p. 103). And that in spite of the fact that three years earlier Pierre Renouvin, a distinguished French historian, often quoted by Poincaré and anything but indulgent to the Germans, had written: 'I believe that the news of the fictitious German mobilization reached St. Petersburg too late to have had any possible influence upon the decisions of the Russian Government' (Renouvin, p. 202).

[1] Oe-U. VIII, 10393. See pp. 256–7.   [2] See p. 257.   [3] See p. 257.

On 30 July, discussing with Berchtold and the War Minister Krobatin the question what was to be demanded of Serbia if she proved amenable, Conrad proposed that she should be compelled

to accept the demands of our ultimatum word for word and refund the entire outlay occasioned by our mobilization. I added that we ought to ask for the cession of territory such as would at least secure our military position: Belgrade and Šabac with their surrounding territory for the building of fortifications the cost of which would likewise fall on Serbia.[1]

Now if Sazonov in those days knew nothing of all this, and even showed that he believed Serbia would not be stripped of any territory, he thoroughly understood that her sovereignty would come to an end unless Austria gave an undertaking about it to Russia and the other Powers. Hence from the Russian point of view he acted rightly in standing his ground. Hermann Lutz remarks:

it was on 28 July for the first time that territorial *désintéressement* was 'proclaimed' by Austria (the earlier declarations, as we know, had come via Berlin). We further note that Sazonov greeted the assurance of sovereignty with incredulity, not without reason in view of the demands of the ultimatum.[2]

When that same day Buchanan asked Sazonov:

whether he would be satisfied with assurances which I understood Austrian Ambassador had been instructed to give with regard to Servia's independence and integrity . . . he replied at once that no engagement that Austria might take on these two points would satisfy Russia.[3]

He said the same thing to Pourtalès in the night of 29–30 July and again on the 30th on the subject of the Austrian declaration of territorial *désintéressement*.[4] 'No reproach can be levelled at the Foreign Minister for this distrust, especially after the Austrian declaration of war on Serbia.'[5] And further on, after recognizing that Sazonov did not work for war right from the beginning of the crisis, and up to the 28th, was filled with the desire to avoid the outbreak, Lutz writes that it was the declaration of war on Serbia on the afternoon of 28 July which destroyed Sazonov's hopes.

The conviction gained ground that Austria had been acting in bad faith. Moreover Sazonov already knew that the declaration of war would mean a stiffening of the Austrian demands on Serbia, as was, indeed, the intention at Vienna.[6]

It was, in fact, a great turning-point in history. If the Central Powers had this time, too, succeeded as they did in 1909 in imposing their will

[1] Conrad, IV, p. 150.   [2] Lutz, p. 174.   [3] BD. XI, 247.
[4] DD. II, 401, 412, 421.   [5] Lutz, p. 177.   [6] Lutz, p. 251.

on the rest of Europe, the results of the Balkan wars would have been annulled and the prestige of the other Powers, together with their interests in the Balkan Near East, would have suffered irreparable damage with incalculable consequences for the balance of power in the Mediterranean and the fate of European and Asiatic Turkey. But this just perception of the political position should not have caused the ruling circles in St. Petersburg to lose their heads and plunge into war preparations which would mean that control of the situation would pass from their hands into those of the military chiefs, whose idea was, not to avoid war, but to win it by forestalling the moves of the other side, getting in the first blow and thus gaining time. Sazonov was aware, and had several times got Benckendorff to say to Grey, that England was in the position of arbiter in the conflict. Benckendorff's telegrams showed him that slowly she was moving towards solidarity with France and Russia. Once Germany perceived this tendency, Berlin in all probability would urge Austria to make concessions. Therefore why not wait and refrain from setting the military machine in motion before it had been proved that diplomatic action was unavailing? Had Russia waited longer before mobilizing, probably, if not certainly, some agreement could have been found on a formula in the nature of the *Halt in Belgrade*.

There is no doubt, as will be demonstrated in the next chapter, that Sazonov did not receive any counsels of moderation from the French Government, nay more, that the French Ambassador at St. Petersburg did nothing to restrain the impulsive and impressionable Russian Minister. The French historian Isaac observes:

No doubt one cannot, one will never be able, to gauge exactly the influence which M. Paléologue (and his declarations of the 28th) may have exercised on Sazonov (and his decisions of the 29th); to deny this influence or regard it as negligible seems to me to be flying in the face of historical objectivity.[1]

Another extenuating circumstance is the consent given in advance by Grey to Sazonov on the subject of Russian mobilization measures and the consent given by Jagow to partial mobilization by Russia. If the decision was taken before the two messages of consent arrived, the carrying out of the decision did not begin until after. It was the mistaken assumption that this mobilization could be carried out against Austria alone, avoiding any threat to Germany, which set in motion the avalanche of mobilizations and the war itself. Realizing too late that partial mobilization would be a disastrous step and having announced it to the Powers, Sazonov had not the courage to turn back and took the still more disastrous step of deciding on general mobilization.

[1] Isaac, p. 198.

Never, in tracing the history of the July crisis, can too much stress be laid on the point, on which we have already dwelt,[1] that it was the political leaders' ignorance of what mobilization implied and the dangers it involved which led them light-heartedly to take the step of mobilizing and thus unleash a European war. The concatenation of Russian partial mobilization with Austrian general mobilization, of Austrian general mobilization with German mobilization, of French mobilization with German mobilization was only perceived too late by all concerned. Nor did they realize that they must in any case adapt their actions to the existing plans of mobilization and that a plan of mobilization cannot be extemporized *ad hoc*. Likewise there was a general ignorance of the fact that mobilization rendered war inevitable beyond recall.

Let us not speak of the Tsar, whose good faith is above suspicion. Having yielded unwillingly to Sazonov's pressure, he then strained every nerve to save the peace, giving Wilhelm his solemn word of honour that his troops would not commit 'any provocative action' and asking for the same guarantee in return, i.e. that the mobilization measures ordered by Austria and Germany 'do not mean war and that we shall continue negotiating for the benefit of our countries and universal peace dear to our hearts'[2]. Let us speak of Sazonov. The majority of the most reputed historians take the view that he was fully aware that to order Russian general mobilization was tantamount to giving grounds for Austrian and German mobilization. And of this there can be no doubt, particularly after what Pourtalès said to him in the name of the German Chancellor on the 29th. But is it equally certain that Sazonov was as aware of the equation: mobilization = war?

It is true that, in the negotiations which took place in 1892 for the Franco-Russian military agreement, both the Russian Chief of Staff and the head of the French military mission had made an agreed statement to that affect. General Boisdeffre had said to the Tsar: 'Mobilization is declaration of war' and the Tsar had nodded assent.[3] Further, on 12 March 1912, the Russian General Staff had sent orders to the general in command of the Warsaw military district that

the telegram relative to mobilization is to be regarded at the same time as the Imperial command for the opening of hostilities against Austria and Germany.[4]

But on 21 November of the same year this order was revoked.

Such an order may lead to serious misunderstandings in relations with those Powers with which, on the basis of political circumstances, war or the

---

[1] See pp. 479–83.   [2] DD. III, 487, 546.
[3] AF-R. 71 (pp. 95–6). See Vol. I, p. 77.
[4] Gunther Frantz, *Russlands Eintritt in den Weltkrieg* (Berlin, 1924). Appendix 80, p. 234.

opening of hostilities is at least not intended right from the beginning. On the other hand it may prove advantageous to muster forces without opening hostilities, in order that the enemy may not irrevocably be deprived of the hope that war may be avoided. In this our measures may be masked by skilful diplomatic negotiation in order as far as possible to lull the apprehensions of the enemy.[1]

Consequently on 26 November 1912 the Tsar had approved:

that the proclamation of mobilization must not be regarded as an Imperial order for the opening of hostilities. The opening of hostilities will be determined by a special telegram over the signature of the Minister for War indicating against which Power or Powers, and the moment at which, hostilities are to begin . . . or by hostile acts on the part of the enemy.[2]

Sazonov was therefore fully entitled to claim that, as far as Russia was concerned, mobilization was not equivalent to war and that the Russian Army 'could at need stand at ease for weeks without crossing the frontier'.[3]

It remains to be seen how much he realized that what was true for Russia might not be true for other Powers. When he gave that assurance to Pourtalès on 29 July he added that 'in Russia unlike Western European States mobilization is far from being the same as war'.[4] It must further be noted that both Buchanan and Pourtalès plainly and repeatedly drew his attention to the dangers of Russian mobilization, pointing out to him that Germany and Austria would not be prepared to let their enemy steal a march upon them. Nor is it in doubt that the Russian generals had no illusions as to the meaning of mobilization. Dobrorolski writes:

The choice of the moment is influenced by a complex of political factors of all kinds. But once the moment has been fixed, everything is settled, and there is no turning back. The beginning of war is automatically regulated in advance.[5]

But it is not to be thought that Janushkevich made use of this line of argument to obtain Sazonov's consent to general mobilization. In fact he quite likely said the very opposite, as he had no interest in frightening the Minister. To sum up, Sazonov realized that Russian general mobilization would be followed by that of Austria and Germany, and

---

[1] Frantz, *op. cit.*, Appendix 82, p. 236.

[2] Frantz, *op. cit.*, p. 47; Appendices 83-5, pp. 237-40.

[3] See p. 504. Sazonov writes: 'It was with the utmost difficulty that they [the generals] had wrung from the Tsar the permission to mobilize the four Southern Districts against Austria after she had declared war on Serbia and bombarded Belgrade—and this in spite of the Tsar having told the Kaiser that our mobilization did not necessarily mean war. The difference between mobilization and war was clearly recognized at every stage of our military administration' (Sazonov, p. 200).

[4] DD. II, 343.   [5] Dobrorolski, *op. cit.* (German translation), p. 10.

hence that his decision would render much more probable the war that he already saw as practically inevitable. But what he did not know was that for Germany mobilization would be practically simultaneous with crossing the Belgian and Luxemburg frontiers and thus creating a situation which was irreparable. Even in Germany this was a secret from Tirpitz and perhaps even from the Kaiser, who, as we shall see, at a certain moment tried to hold up the beginning of operations and was not able to do so. We have already noted that on 26 July Sazonov asked Pourtalès: 'Surely, mobilization is not tantamount to war with you either, is it?' and that Pourtalès replied: 'Perhaps not in theory. But . . . once the button is pressed and the machinery of mobilization set in motion, there is no stopping it.'[1] In theory, however, this was not the case and so Sazonov could hold the belief that was generally held, namely that mobilization was a matter of some days and that as long as hostilities had not broken out, it would not be impossible to turn back. He was quite sincere in saying to Paléologue on 30 July: 'Right up to the last moment I shall go on negotiating.'[2] And he went on negotiating, as we shall later see. Had he known as a mathematical certainty that to order mobilization was to decide irrevocably on war, most probably he would have hesitated yet awhile longer before advising the Tsar to take the step.

The upshot is that Sazonov bears the heavy responsibility of having at once thought of resorting to partial mobilization, of not turning back when he realized that partial mobilization was impracticable, and of advising the Tsar to order general mobilization, though well aware that this would bring Germany on the scene and render war practically inevitable. Practically, but not absolutely, because, as we shall see in a later chapter, the final, definite responsibility for the outbreak of the war lies with the German plan of mobilization, while the primary responsibility—and this must never be lost sight of—rests on the actions of the Central Powers who thought they could frighten the other Powers by their strength and thus 'localize the conflict', but made a thorough miscalculation.

[1] See p. 481.   [2] DF. 3. XI, 359.

CHAPTER XIII

FRANCE AND RUSSIAN MOBILIZATION; LAST ENGLISH EFFORTS TO SAVE PEACE

1. *Paléologue's story of the revoked Russian general mobilization of 29 July and what it did not tell.*

The Power which had the strongest right to restrain Russia from mobilizing was unquestionably France who would be involved in the consequences of this measure. The treaty of alliance was definite on that point. This does not mean that the French Government could interpret the treaty to suit itself and could be backward in lending diplomatic and military support to the Russian Government. Any such conduct would have imperilled the existence of the alliance. But the French Government had the right and the duty to intervene in the decisions of the Russian Government, to advise coolness and prudence, and to dissuade it from false steps. But, as we have already seen,[1] the French Ambassador at St. Petersburg, on whom, in the absence of the head of the Quai d'Orsay, fell a special responsibility for exercising a restraining influence, exercised an influence in the opposite direction. It has been shown above that right from the first minute on 24 July he egged Sazonov on to a 'policy of firmness', assuring him of the wholehearted support of France. This promise he repeated on the following day, 25 July, in a three-cornered conversation with Sazonov and Buchanan. Then on 28 July, at the critical hour when Sazonov was making up his mind to proceed to the fatal military measures,

[1] See pp. 295–6; 537.

Paléologue reaffirmed 'the complete readiness of France to fulfil her obligations as an ally in case of necessity'.[1] By the evening of the 28th he must certainly have learnt from Sazonov that on the following day two *ukazes* would be laid before the Tsar, one for partial and one for general mobilization. Nothing of this did he reveal to his Government, only telegraphing at 7.35 p.m. that, in case of mobilization, two army officers whom he named were to be seconded to his Embassy and that they were to proceed *via* Christiania and Stockholm.[2] This showed that he regarded general mobilization as so imminent that it would be risky for the two officers to travel by the shorter route via Germany. When on the evening of 29 July Russia ordered general mobilization, Paléologue's behaviour was devious and ambiguous, as we shall now consider in detail. The first statement contained in his diary entry for 29 July runs: 'Yesterday evening the Austro-Hungarian Government ordered the general mobilization of the army', an assertion which not only was untrue, but was not made on the 29th by any rumour or by any document. He then proceeds to relate:

At eleven o'clock to-night Nicholas Alexandrovich Basili, Deputy-Director of the Chancery of the Foreign Office, appeared at my office. He came to tell me that the imperious language used by the German Ambassador this afternoon has decided the Russian Government (1) to order this very night the mobilization of the thirteen corps earmarked for operations against Austria-Hungary; (2) secretly to commence general mobilization.

These last words made me jump:

Isn't it possible for them to confine themselves—provisionally at any rate—to a partial mobilization?

No. The question has just been gone into thoroughly by a council of our highest military officers. They have come to the conclusion that in existing circumstances the Russian Government has no choice between partial and general mobilization, as from the technical point of view a partial mobilization could be carried out only at the price of dislocating the entire machinery of general mobilization. . . .

Those are strong arguments but I still think that your General Staff should take no step without previous discussion with the French General Staff. Please tell M. Sazonov from me that I should like his most serious consideration of this matter and a reply in the course of the night.[3]

It was completely untrue that on the 29th the Russian Government had decided to order the mobilization of only thirteen corps and 'secretly to commence general mobilization'. The order was to proceed to general mobilization and hence to mobilize not only the thirteen corps detailed to operate against Austria but also the others which were to operate against Germany, in other words, the whole Russian Army.

---

[1] Schilling, p. 43; *Int. Bez.* i. V, 172.   [2] DF. 3. XI, 216. See p. 545.
[3] Paléologue, I, pp. 41-2.

When this order for general mobilization, suspended by the Tsar on the evening of the 29th, was definitively promulgated at 5 p.m. on the 30th, Paléologue, in reporting it to Paris at 9.15 p.m., repeated that the Russian Government had decided 'to proceed secretly to the first measures for general mobilization'.[1] Does it appear from this that both on the 29th and the 30th Sazonov misled Paléologue and that it was all Sazonov's fault if Paléologue sent his Government such wrong and belated information on what was happening at St. Petersburg? That Sazonov conveyed to Paléologue the message that, in order not to make relations with Germany still more acute, he was proceeding to general mobilization secretly, is entirely probable, since Sazonov was such a greenhorn in military matters as to imagine the thing could be done, and was only convinced of the contrary when on 31 July he saw the red notices, calling up reservists, posted up in the streets of St. Petersburg.[2] It was to maintain this secrecy that, in communicating the decisions taken on the evening of the 29th to Izvolsky and Benckendorff, he said: 'All we can do is to speed up our armaments',[3] instead of speaking straight out of general mobilization. We shall see later that this misled Paris, which was not kept informed by Paléologue. But there is no reason whatever to assume that towards Paléologue Sazonov was more than simply reticent or that the message he sent by Basili contained, not just vague expressions such as 'speeding up armaments', but actual falsehoods, such as that 'the mobilization of thirteen corps' had been ordered and that Russia was 'secretly to commence general mobilization'. It is easy to demonstrate this.

If the fault had lain with Sazonov, Paléologue, who was a good hand with his pen, would certainly have long since thrown the blame on Sazonov when he found himself attacked in France and elsewhere. Nowhere, however, does he claim that Sazonov kept anything hidden from him. Indeed what reason would Sazonov have had to do so, since Paléologue had unreservedly placed himself, had placed France, at his side? None can read the documents of that period, especially Buchanan's telegrams, without perceiving that Sazonov and Paléologue were hand in glove, and without to some extent getting the impression that Paléologue with his forebodings and his advice to be unyielding stiffened the backbone of Sazonov. Never would Sazonov have ventured to proceed to general mobilization without informing Paléologue, especially as Russia was bound by treaty, not only to give previous intimation of mobilization but even not to mobilize without previously concerting with the French General Staff. This is a very important point which, as Isaac pertinently observes,[4] historians have strangely overlooked.

---

[1] DF. 3. XI, 359.
[3] *Int. Bez.* i. V, 221. See p. 556.

[2] Schilling, p. 69; *Int. Bez.* i. V, 349.
[4] Isaac, p. 192.

Article II of the Franco-Russian Military Agreement in its final wording of 1913 runs:

As the French and Russian Governments recognized in 1911 and 1912, German mobilization obliges Russia and France to mobilize immediately and simultaneously all their forces at the first news of the event and without there being need of previous agreement. It shall be the same for any act of war on the part of the German Army against either one of the allied powers. But in the case of the partial, or even the general mobilization of Austria or Italy singly, previous agreement ('concert') is indispensable.[1]

If previous agreement was thus laid down by treaty, Russia, in proceeding to general mobilization without previous accord with France after Austria had only mobilized eight corps against Serbia, was violating one of the fundamental conditions of the alliance. Any such violation would give the French Republic full right not to recognize the *casus foederis*. How much greater still would be this right if Russia not only failed to concert, but actually failed to give intimation and even practised deception as to what she was about! The inference is that Paléologue was not only correctly informed by Basili on the evening of the 29th and by Sazonov on the 30th, but must have learnt some hours previously that the Tsar that same morning (29th) had signed the two *ukazes*, for partial and for general mobilization respectively, leaving it to be decided later which was to be put into application, and that Sazonov, for the strong reasons adduced by the Chief of General Staff, inclined towards general mobilization. The decision was probably taken and made known to Paléologue that very evening. So well was he informed of what had been decided on the morning of 29 July between the Tsar and Janushkevich, namely to proceed secretly to general mobilization, that in the afternoon he passed on to Buchanan the untruthful assurance, given by the Chief of the Russian General Staff to the German Military Attaché, that 'up to the present no single military preparation has been taken against Germany'.[2]

Why, then, does Paléologue conceal the truth in his *Memoirs*? He does so in order not to reveal the conflict between the facts and the telegrams he sent to Paris on the 29th and 30th. And he kept silence in these telegrams in order that the Quai d'Orsay should raise no obstacles to the Russian line of action. It is a fact that in his *Memoirs* he makes believe that he opposed this line of action, reminding Basili that the Russian General Staff could not take the proposed measures without 'conferring' with their French opposite numbers, that he drew Sazonov's attention to this matter and asked for an answer in the course of the night. This is a discreet and circumspect allusion to Article II of the Military Agreement which, it should have been Paléologue's duty to

---

[1] Isaac, p. 192.   [2] BD. XI, 271. See p. 616.

insist, must be observed. To insist on its observance at this critical moment he should at once have called on Sazonov and demanded at all costs the suspension of the mobilization order pending the consent of Paris. But the words he records that he said to Basili contain no demand for the suspension of mobilization and therefore could do nothing to change the course of events. They were superfluous, so much so that in all probability they were not what he said at all. Moreover, why should they have been said on the evening of the 29th if they were not said on the evening of the 30th when general mobilization was finally ordered? The truth is that, as the Tsar on the 29th revoked the order, Paléologue finds it easy to take credit for a protest which he never made on the 29th any more than he did on the 30th. To convince oneself of the correctness of this assumption it is sufficient to read the following page of Paléologue's *Memoirs*, in which, under the date of 30 July he narrates what he did on learning that general mobilization had been suspended by the Tsar. It throws light on the high-handed way in which Paléologue kept his Government in the dark about what was going on in St. Petersburg for fear the Quai d'Orsay should intervene with demands for restraint and negotiations for a compromise.

Basili had hardly got back to the Foreign Office before Sazonov rang up to ask me to send him my First Secretary, Chambrun, 'to receive an urgent communication'. At the same time my Military Attaché, General de Laguiche, was sent for by the General Staff. It was 11.45 p.m.

The Tsar Nicholas had received a personal telegram from the Emperor William this evening and decided to suspend general mobilization, as the Emperor William had told him 'that he is doing everything in his power to bring about a direct understanding between Austria and Russia'. The Tsar has come to his decision on his own authority and in spite of the opposition of his generals who have once more insisted upon the difficulties, or rather the dangers, of a partial mobilization. I have therefore informed Paris of the mobilization only of the thirteen Russian corps destined for eventual operations against Austria.[1]

We need not linger on the fact that in writing that the Tsar had 'decided to suspend general mobilization' Paléologue tacitly admits having known on the evening of 29 July that what had first been ordered was not partial mobilization, as he had telegraphed to Paris, but general mobilization. What we shall particularly note is the bearing of another statement of his. But it must first be mentioned that Recouly's perfectly credible account would make it appear that Paléologue's story does not quite give what really happened. As telegrams for France had to go via Germany, Basili had suggested to Paléologue, and he had agreed, that the Russian cipher code should be employed for the telegram in question, as being more difficult to decode than the French

[1] Paléologue, I, p. 43.

system. For this purpose a secretary of the French Embassy went with Basili to the Russian Foreign Office to put the telegram into Russian code. The telegram ran:

The Ambassador of Germany has come to tell M. Sazonov that, if Russia does not stop her military preparations, the German Army will receive the order to mobilize. M. Sazonov replied that Russian preparations are motivated: 1. by the obstinate intransigence of Austria; 2. by the fact that eight Austro-Hungarian corps are already mobilized. The tone in which Count Pourtalès acquitted himself of the notification has decided the Russian Government this very night to order the mobilization of thirteen corps destined to operate against Austria.[1]

As this message was being encoded, Basili came in haste to tell the secretary:

Only send the first part. The second, about general mobilization, is no longer correct. The order has just been brought. It has been decided to postpone the measure. The French Military Attaché at the same moment brought the same information. Acute embarrassment on the part of the secretary. His chief has given him the order to dispatch a telegram to Paris. Ought he to do so at all cost? Ought he to listen to the Russians who know the facts better than anyone. Sazonov in person confirmed the suspension. . . . The secretary deferred to his reasons. All that he sent to Paris towards 1 a.m. was the first part of the telegram,[2]

and he omitted the final six words of it which ran: 'and secretly to commence general mobilization'.[3] Now Paléologue not only gave approval to the change made by the secretary, but did not think it necessary to inform the Quai d'Orsay by a subsequent telegram of what had really happened at St. Petersburg on 29 July. Nothing throws more light on his behaviour than this silence which he avows with the utmost composure: 'I have therefore informed Paris of the mobilization only of thirteen Russian corps.' A decision had been taken to order the general mobilization of the Russian Army without the preliminary accord which the French General Staff had laid down as necessary in view of the fact that Russian mobilization would provoke German mobilization and consequently war. The measure had been simply 'postponed' by the Tsar 'against the opposition of the Generals' who regarded partial mobilization as disastrous and therefore renewed their insistence that it should be replaced by general mobilization. This was the danger which overhung France, and her representative at St. Petersburg did not think it necessary to inform the President of the Republic and the Prime Minister, who had just got back to Paris, and the French General Staff, of what had been going on, in order that they might give him instructions and take the measures they deemed right! No

[1] DF. 3. XI, 283.   [2] Recouly, pp. 160–1.   [3] Recouly, p. 160.

explanation of this omission can be discovered except by putting all Paléologue's words and deeds together and thus arriving at the proof that, after urging Sazonov to intransigence, promising the whole-hearted support of France and raising no objection to the mobilization proposals, he hid the true state of things from Paris for fear the Quai d'Orsay might issue instructions of a pacificatory nature. This judge-ment will be confirmed by the account of his doings on 30 July. Not only does it show Paléologue as partly, if not entirely, responsible for Sazonov's mistakes and imprudences, but it throws a shaft of light on the part played by Poincaré at St. Petersburg. One can hardly suppose that Paléologue acted as he did solely on his own initiative and after the departure of Poincaré.

To prevent this opinion from gaining acceptance it would have been needful for Poincaré to clear the question up thoroughly and give satisfactory answers to the queries that arose. If the data were not available immediately, they came to light later, not only in the British and Russian documents but also in Paléologue's own diary, published in 1921. But in *L'Union Sacrée*, published in 1927, in speeches and lec-tures, and in other writings rebutting accusations made against him, both by the Germans and by his own fellow countrymen, of bearing responsibility for the outbreak of the European war, Poincaré registers with meticulous care his own actions and those of the French Govern-ment, particularly of Viviani, who accompanied him on his journey. He uses Paléologue's diary and telegrams when they serve his purpose. But not a word does he say about the accusations levelled against Paléologue and the evidence which accompanies them. And yet it was Paléologue who represented France at St. Petersburg and what he said and did is the only thing that counts. No doubt he may also have dis-obeyed or reversed instructions received. Poincaré may have thought it impossible to draw a distinction between his own and the French Government's responsibility and that of the Ambassador, for fear of playing into the hands of the Germans. But such arbitrary behaviour on Paléologue's part hardly seems credible. It remains to be seen whether Poincaré's manner of maintaining his innocence did not do more to bolster up the German case than would have a downright condemna-tion of Paléologue's behaviour. One must also consider that, if Paléo-logue had played false to the ideas of Poincaré, with whom he was in the closest contact at St. Petersburg during the days preceding the presentation of the Austrian ultimatum, the fact would somehow have come to light. What does come to light is the very opposite.

As has already been related, Paléologue's diary tells among other things that at St. Petersburg on 21 July Poincaré warned the Austrian Ambassador: 'Serbia has some very warm friends in the Russian people. And Russia has an ally, France. There are plenty of complications to be feared.' Then, when Szápáry had taken his leave, Poincaré said to Paléologue: 'Austria has a *coup de théâtre* in store for us. Sazonov must be firm and we must back him up.'[1] This last sentence can be interpreted in several ways, but the accepted interpretation is that of the man to whom it was spoken and to whom Poincaré had certainly fully explained his views. Nor can it be objected that from the constitutional point of view the President of the Republic could not give instructions to the Ambassador. Poincaré was a personality of so much temperament and passion that he exercised an immense influence on his country's foreign policy, especially when its instrument was Paléologue who was a creature of his.

2. *The return voyage of Poincaré and Viviani. First instructions to Paléologue.*

It is time to break off the story of Paléologue's doings at St. Petersburg and turn attention to those of Poincaré and Viviani whom we last saw on the evening of 23 July ending their Russian visit. The battleship *France* was to bear them first to Stockholm, then to Copenhagen and lastly to Christiania (Oslo) on state visits to the three Sovereigns, before they returned to France. Poincaré narrates that on board the Imperial yacht which bore them to the *France*, Viviani and Sazonov together drafted a dispatch to the French Ambassador in Vienna instructing him tactfully to enjoin on Berchtold not to take any action which might infringe Serbian sovereignty or integrity:[2] We know from the *French Diplomatic Documents* that this message went off from St. Petersburg at 2.5 a.m. on the 24th,[3] twenty-two hours later than Sazonov's dispatch of similar content to the Russian Ambassador in Vienna. Poincaré's memoirs indicate a reason for this delay. To spare Berchtold's feelings every appearance was to be avoided that might suggest a joint *démarche* on the part of the two Ambassadors. Their messages were to be delivered 'en des visites séparées'.[4]

But on the 24th it was too late to make representations to Vienna, since the ultimatum had been presented the evening before. News of the ultimatum reached the *France* on 24 July and then—according to Poincaré—Viviani wirelessed to St. Petersburg and via St. Petersburg to Paris and London suggesting:

1. That Serbia should at once offer Vienna all the satisfaction compatible with her honour and independence; 2. that she should ask for an extension of the twenty-four [obviously a slip for 'forty-eight'] hour time limit; 3. that we should support this request at Vienna; 4. that the Triple *Entente* should examine whether it would not be possible to get an international inquiry substituted for the Austro-Serbian Inquiry which risks appearing humiliating for Serbia.[5]

[1] Paléologue, I, p. 19.   [2] Poincaré, IV, p. 276.   [3] See p. 195, n. 2.
[4] Poincaré, IV, p. 276.   [5] Poincaré, IV, p. 288.

No trace of this dispatch exists either in the *Yellow Book* or in the French, Russian, and British documents. Indeed the wording of the first recorded telegram from Viviani on his return voyage makes it seem doubtful whether the dispatch was ever sent. Telegraphing from Stockholm at 4.5 p.m. on 25 July acknowledging communications from Paris of 24 July Viviani says:

> In spite of the *démarche* made at Paris by the German Ambassador tending to prevent all moderating intervention between Austria-Hungary and Serbia on the part of the Powers, I am of the opinion that we should at once study with Russia and England the means to avert a conflict in which the other Powers might find themselves involved. If Austria-Hungary insists on taking part on Serbian territory in an Inquiry into the origins of the outrage on the Heir Apparent, could one not at the opportune moment, following up the precedent of the conference on anarchists held at Rome, widen the Inquiry to include the other Powers?[1]

If this telegram shows anything, it is that Viviani had—to say the least of it—not understood a thing about the whole business!

In Chapter VIII of *L'Union Sacrée* Poincaré gives an account of the return voyage, rendered disquieting no less by the wireless messages that arrived than by those that did not. Of their first day at sea, the 24th, he writes:

> Little by little we receive fragmentary wireless messages, disquieting in their confusion and obscurity. We learn that Austria has sent a threatening note to Serbia.[2]

On 25 July they reach Stockholm and find there awaiting them Bienvenu-Martin's telegram of the 24th giving news of Schoen's call with the German note asking for the 'localization of the conflict'.[3] The messages from Paléologue are at variance with those from the Quai d'Orsay. Yet, how can the two statesmen throw up their two other state visits and steam straight for home?[4]

On 26 July the *France* resumes her voyage to Copenhagen. Poincaré, Viviani and Margerie spend their time anxiously exchanging their impressions.

> From the European chancelleries only confused sounds reach us.[5] The wireless mostly brings us fragmentary and incomprehensible phrases. Our communications with the land seem to be systematically jammed and in fact they are so, as we are later to learn. During our voyage the German Government has issued the order to jam them.[6]

---

[1] DF. 3. XI, 54.   [2] Poincaré, IV, 287.   [3] Poincaré, IV, pp. 304–5.   See pp. 323–4.
[4] Poincaré, IV, p. 302.   [5] Poincaré, IV, 321.
[6] Poincaré, IV, p. 328. The evidence quoted by Poincaré in support of this assertion is an entry in the service log of the Metz wireless station dated 2 a.m. 27 July: 'Governor orders jamming of French wireless service in such a way as not to constitute a breach of the

Poincaré goes on to say, however, that messages received by the *France* during the night of the 26th were clear enough to convey the general wish of the French Cabinet and press that the remaining state visits should be cancelled and that Poincaré and Viviani should return straight to France. Viviani at once agreed and at 7 a.m. on 27 July sent back the following wireless message, duly received in Paris at 2.30 p.m. the same day.

Although the President of the Council on board the *France* has been in constant contact with the Quai d'Orsay and the representatives of France abroad; it has seemed indispensable . . . that the Head of the State and the Foreign Minister should return without delay to the midst of French public opinion.[1]

The other message wirelessed by Viviani at 7 a.m. on 27 July makes it seem likely that Poincaré and Viviani also received on board the *France* the disquieting telegram from Paléologue which had reached the Quai d'Orsay at 7.35 p.m. on the 25th. It ran:

At the Council of Ministers held this morning at Krasnoe Selo under the presidence of the Emperor, the Russian Government decided *in principle* to mobilize the thirteen army corps which are in the event destined to operate against Austria. This mobilization will only be made effective and public if the Austro-Hungarian Government means (*prétend*) to bring armed pressure to bear on Serbia. Secret preparations will, however, commence already to-day. If the mobilization is ordered, the thirteen corps will immediately be concentrated on the Galician frontier, but they will not take the offensive, in

peace.' An entry of 4 a.m., 28 July runs: 'Eiffel Tower have noticed our attempt to jam them and are clearly trying to foil us by sending to Dunkirk on a powerful wave news for the *France* which does not reply.' However in contemporary German naval records there is clear evidence that between 23 and 27 July the Germans made no attempt to jam radio communication between the *France* and France. On the contrary the battleship was in radio communication with the German radio station at Norddeich near Bremen during her return passage to France. At least two signals were made by the *France* and one by Norddeich. During this exchange of signals the battleship continually received messages from the Eiffel Tower radio station, and on being called up by the latter, interrupted her communications with Norddeich to receive the French message. The Germans intercepted two cipher telegrams transmitted by the *France*—one addressed to the French Foreign Office and signed Viviani, the other to the French Admiralty. There is, nevertheless, a possible explanation of the imperfect reception of which Poincaré complains. According to information available in 1914, both Norddeich and the Eiffel Tower had a high-pitched note, and could be clearly heard at Riga. The Eiffel Tower was also audible inside Russia, but this station's transmission power fluctuated as much as 10 per cent., so that the signal strength was variable. The selectivity of the then existing receivers was poor, and if Norddeich (or any other station within range of the Baltic) and the Eiffel Tower happened to be transmitting together on approximately the same wavelength, the *France* may well have had difficulty in tuning in to the latter station and this inadvertent interference may have given the impression of deliberate jamming.

On 28 July Poincaré notes that messages are coming through better (Poincaré, IV, 346), and in fact the *France* was by then nearer to Eiffel Tower than to Norddeich. [Translator's note.]

[1] DF. 3. XI, 128.

order to leave Germany a pretext not to invoke the *casus foederis* immediately. General de Laguiche has just been seconded to Krasnoe Selo to the Grand Duke Nicholas and the War Minister. Russian opinion affirms its determination not to let Serbia be attacked.[1]

The following day Paléologue sent the French War Minister the following telegram from the Military Attaché, General de Laguiche:

Yesterday at Krasnoe Selo the War Minister confirmed to me the mobilization of the army corps of the military districts Kiev, Odessa, Kazan and Moscow. The endeavour is to avoid any measure likely to be regarded as directed against Germany, but nevertheless the military districts of Warsaw, Vilna and St. Petersburg are secretly making preparations. The cities and governments of St. Petersburg and Moscow are declared to be under martial law. . . . The Minister for War has reiterated to us his determination to leave to Germany the eventual initiative of an attack on Russia. The information coming in from Berlin is to the effect that they are disposed there to take this initiative.[2]

In the *Yellow Book* there is no trace of either of these telegrams, although French press correspondents made no mystery of the decisions taken at St. Petersburg. On 25 July the *Figaro* correspondent telegraphed that at the Council of Ministersheld at Krasnoe Selo on the 25th the 'Minister of War had declared in a long, detailed and vigorous speech that Russia was ready for war'. The *Matin* correspondent telegraphed that at the Council of Ministers General Sukhomlinov, the Minister for War,

gave his word of honour as a soldier that Russia had never been more ready to fulfil her military obligations and Sazonov, the Foreign Minister, declared that the community of views between France and Russia was complete.

The correspondent added that the most far reaching measures were being taken and that 'the Russian Government will regard an aggression against Serbia as if it were a direct attack on Russia'. The *Temps* correspondent telegraphed that the Council of Ministers had decided that mobilization measures would be taken immediately in self-preservation 'since Russia means to follow events with the possibility of immediate action in case of need'. On the following day he telegraphed 'General Sukhomlinov personally told me yesterday: "It's done" ' and assured him that the odds in favour of war were '75 per cent.'

The *Yellow Book* only gives one telegram from Bienvenu-Martin to Viviani saying:

From St. Petersburg we learn that . . . at the Council of Ministers on the 25th . . . the mobilization of thirteen army corps intended eventually to operate against Austria was considered; this mobilization, however, would

---

[1] DF. 3. XI, 50.   [2] DF. 3. XI, 89.

only be made effective if Austria were to bring armed pressure to bear on Serbia, and not till after notice had been given by the Minister for Foreign Affairs upon whom falls the duty of fixing the day, freedom being left him to go on with negotiations even if Belgrade should be occupied.[1]

This is another of the falsifications in the *Yellow Book*. The authentic text of Bienvenu-Martin's telegram, dispatched at 4.30 p.m. on 26 July and published in the *Documents Diplomatiques Français*, runs:

This mobilization will only be put into effect and made public if Austria were to bring armed pressure to bear on Serbia; further Russia would concentrate troops on the Galician frontier, but would not take the offensive in order not to give Germany the pretext to have recourse to the *casus foederis*. Russian public opinion affirms its determination not to let Serbia be crushed.[2]

But in any case the knowledge of what Paléologue had actually communicated to Paris must have been sufficient to make Viviani, in announcing his direct return to France, instruct Paléologue at noon on the 27th:

Kindly say to M. Sazonov that France, appreciating as does Russia the high importance for both countries attaching to the affirmation of their perfect mutual understanding in regard to the other Powers and to the need for neglecting no effort in view of a solution of the conflict, is ready in the interests of the general peace whole heartedly to second the action of the Imperial Government.[3]

This telegram may have been omitted from the *Yellow Book* as being displeasing to the Russian Government. Certainly it was timely, unexceptionable in tone and indicative of a level-headed, pacific attitude on the part of Viviani, who had inserted into de Margerie's draft the words 'in the interests of the general peace'.[4] But Paléologue took no heed of these instructions on 28 July. He went so far on the evening of the 28th as to tell Sazonov, as we have seen:

The head of the State and the head of the Government are at sea. I can only communicate with them at intervals and through very uncertain channels; as their knowledge of the situation is incomplete they cannot send me any instructions.[5]

---

[1] LJF. 50, in CDD., p. 174. Obviously the compilers of the *Yellow Book* give the Russian Council of Ministers of 25 July as consenting to an Austrian occupation of Belgrade because the compilers had knowledge of what came later. They must have gathered this knowledge mainly from the *British Blue Book* which prints portions of a telegram from Buchanan of 25 July including the following phrases: 'In the event of the Austrians attacking Serbia, the Serbian Government would abandon Belgrade and withdraw their forces into the interior, while they would at the same time appeal to the Powers to help them. . . . His Excellency assured me that Russia would take no action until it was forced on her' (*British Blue Book*, 17; in CDD., pp. 21–2. BD. XI, 125 gives the full unparaphrased text). This, not Paléologue's dispatches, is probably the compilers' source of information.

[2] DF. 3. XI, 90. [3] DF. 3. XI, 138; Poincaré, IV, 385. See p. 536.
[4] DF. 3. XI, note to 138. [5] Paléologue, I, p. 41.

This fact is of extreme importance. But Poincaré glides over it, as if he did not perceive that the sensible instructions of the 27th, which he himself reproduces, were not carried out by the Ambassador to whom they were addressed and therefore had no effect on the situation.

The 27–29 July were anxious days for Poincaré and Viviani. Poincaré writes:

Not to have exact information about anything, not even to have the essential data in hand as to the problem that was to be resolved, caused M. Viviani not only mental but physical suffering. He paced the *France's* deck in his agitation, silent for long periods, then returning at intervals affectionately to pour his anguish into my ear.[1]

On 28 July Viviani telegraphed to Paris his approval of the English proposal for a conference and of Bienvenu-Martin's reply to Schoen.[2] And by another telegram he requested Paul Cambon to tell Grey that he 'fully approved the combination suggested by him' and begged Paul Cambon to support Grey's move in his conversations with the Ambassadors of Germany and Italy.[3] At last at 8 a.m. on the 29th the *France* entered the Dunkirk roads.

This story is of some significance as showing how much a guiding hand was lacking in France from the moment the crisis broke until the afternoon of the 29th when the situation was already on the verge of war. Schoen's telegrams show the acting Foreign Minister to have been ill-informed and filled with unfounded optimism, not only in the days before the 28th but still on the 28th and 29th after the Austrian declaration of war on Serbia. On the 28th he thought that Germany had raised only formal and easily superable objections to Grey's proposal for an ambassadors' conference, and that Austria should only receive advice to exercise restraint in her military operations.[4] On 29 July when Schoen confidentially told him of German

efforts to obtain from Vienna statements which could be used to tranquillize St. Petersburg, he regarded this as a gratifying proof of our good intentions to avoid the extension of the conflict.[5]

---

[1] Poincaré, IV, p. 337.

[2] LJF. 76 in CDD., pp. 194–5; DF. 3. XI, 190.—Strangely enough Poincaré does not reproduce the text of this telegram. Among other things it says: 'I entirely approve the combination suggested by Sir E. Grey, and am myself requesting M. Paul Cambon to inform him of this. . . . The action of the four less interested Powers cannot, for the reasons given above, be exerted only at Vienna and St. Petersburg. In proposing to exert it also at Belgrade, which means in fact between Vienna and Belgrade, Sir E. Grey grasps the logic of the situation; and, in not excluding St. Petersburg, he offers on the other hand to Germany a method of withdrawing with perfect dignity from the *démarche* by which the German Government have caused it to be known at Paris and London that the affair was looked upon by them as purely Austro-Serbian and without any general character.'

[3] DF. 3. XI, 193.   [4] DD. II, 310.

[5] DD. II, 345.

Such incomprehension of the situation would never have been shown by Viviani. His own telegrams and the impressions of him and of his anguish given by Poincaré justify us in asking whether, if he had remained at his post, things would have gone as they did. Those Frenchmen who attack Viviani no less than Poincaré think they would. The present writer does not share this opinion, and does not believe that Viviani played a double game or that his actions were not sincere. The present writer in 1922 attended the Washington Conference for the reduction of naval armaments as one of the representatives of Italy and had the opportunity to get to know Viviani very well. Viviani, Briand, and A. Sarraut were the representatives of France and, after Briand's departure, Viviani was head of the French delegation. The impression he made was that of a man of intense feeling and of a quick intelligence that was at the same time penetrating and simple, aiming boldly and undeviatingly for what his convictions told him was right. No doubt Poincaré influenced him considerably during their long voyage together, and certainly Viviani, no less than Poincaré, believed that in the event of war France could not forsake Russia. When he asked Nekludov, the Russian Minister at Stockholm, what he thought of the situation and Nekludov answered that war was likely, Viviani exclaimed: 'It is terrible, terrible, for if it means war for you, it most certainly also means war for us too.'[1] But the idea was 'terrible' to him. His political origins and the composition of his Ministry combined to make him feel a horror of war, even if by degrees he came to admit that it had become probable.

3. The first measures taken by the French Minister for War and by Joffre.

The atmosphere which greeted the President and Viviani on landing was one of intense excitement. A crowd acclaimed the arrival of their tender at the quayside.

It was really France waiting for us and coming to meet us. I felt I was pale with emotion and made an effort not to show my emotion. . . . What struck me was that many people here seem to think war imminent. . . . One of those speaking to me, a man of some importance . . . went so far as to say to me: 'We have had enough of this! . . . Better make an end of it once and for all.' I calmed him, answering: 'For mercy's sake, do not talk like that. We must still do everything to avoid war.'[2]

If such was the reception at Dunkirk, it may be imagined what lay before the two at Paris where ministers, prefects, municipal representatives, senators, deputies, a delegation of the League of Patriots headed by Maurice Barrès and a crowd of men 'of all ages and opinions', had been waiting for hours.

[1] A. Nekludoff, *Diplomatic Reminiscences* (London, 1920), p. 291.
[2] Poincaré, IV, pp. 361-2.

Before we emerged on to the square [Messimy, the Minister for War] said to me 'Monsieur le Président, you are going to see Paris; it is magnificent.' Indeed it was magnificent. . . . As I came out [of the station] I was greeted by an overwhelming demonstration which moved me to the depths of my being. Many people had tears in their eyes and I could hardly hold back my own. From thousands of throats arose repeated shouts of: '*Vive la France! Vive la République! Vive le Président*' . . . From the station to the Élysée the cheering never stopped. . . . Never have I felt so overwhelmed. Never have I found it more difficult, morally and physically, to maintain an impassive bearing. Greatness, simplicity, enthusiasm, seriousness, all combined to render this welcome unexpected, unbelievable and infinitely beautiful. Here was a united France. Political quarrels were forgotten. . . . It was only yesterday that the High Court after several days of lively debate acquitted Mme Caillaux. How far away the affair seems now! What different matters now claim public attention !¹

What now claimed public attention was the prospect of a possible European war which would reopen the duel between France and Germany. But the renewal of this duel, if desired by some, could not but be dreaded by others. As the procession moved forward shouts were heard of: 'To Berlin.' As Poincaré entered the Élysée the League of Patriots filed past the statue of Strasbourg in the Place de la Concorde to the strains of the 'Marseillaise'. The tone of some newspapers was anything but restrained. The *Temps* in its leading article said that all the actions of Austria seemed to have the purpose of rendering a solution by force of arms inevitable and concluded:

The Triple *Entente* is united, resolute and sincere. It places all its strength at the service of peace for which it hopes. It will place its strength at the service of war if others impose war on it.

In the *Écho de Paris* J. Herbette, after announcing that Austria had declared war on Serbia, went on to explain what could be the reasons of Austria and Germany for taking this step and continued:

To do away with Serbia means to double the strength which Austria can send against Russia; to double Austro-Hungarian resistance to the Russian Army means to enable Germany to send some more army corps against France. For every Serbian soldier killed by a bullet on the Morava one more Prussian soldier can be sent to the Moselle. This is the explanation of the huge Teuton effort. It is for us to grasp this truth and draw the consequences from it before disaster overtakes Serbia. Afterwards, as Droyn de Lhuis said in August 1866, when the fate was sealed which was to lead us to Sedan, there will remain nothing but to weep.

Nevertheless Bertie telegraphed on the 29th that though:

Many newspapers are writing about Germany in a way calculated to excite public opinion. . . . French public up to the present is disinclined to allow itself to be worked up to warlike excitement.²

¹ Poincaré, IV, pp. 368–9.   ² BD. XI, 270

Also Szécsen on the 30th reported to Berchtold that:

In spite of chauvinistic national pride and justifiable patriotic self-confidence, people here are with good reason apprehensive of war and its unpredictable consequences. But fear is a bad counsellor![1]

Meanwhile, whether from apprehension or foresight, the War Minister Messimy, who was receiving reports of German war preparations from various points of the frontier especially from Alsatians, had already before the return of Poincaré and Viviani obtained the approval of the Cabinet for effective military measures. Two hours after the rupture of diplomatic relations between Austria and Serbia, the absent generals were recalled by telegram to their garrisons. On the 26th all officers on leave were recalled immediately after the news came in of the recall of German officers to their units. In the evening, as disquieting news continued to pour in, Messimy ordered the recall of other ranks away on harvest leave and the application of the *dispositif restreint de sécurité* on the railways, but limited only to civilians. On the 27th this measure was also extended to the military, and French troops were ordered back from Morocco and Algeria. Raymond Recouly, who, after the war was ended, interviewed a series of leading figures, published in his *Les Heures Tragiques d'Avant-Guerre* the following account given him by Messimy:

In Morocco we had not far from 100,000 men, officers and other ranks, who were classed among our best troops. Were we going to leave that picked body away there when the fate of France and hence of her colonies, was about to be settled a few weeks hence on the Eastern frontier? The plan of mobilization laid down that practically all these troops were to remain in Morocco. Only a few battalions and batteries were to be sent back to France. After consultation with Abel Ferry, the Under Secretary of State for Foreign Affairs, I informed the Cabinet of this grave question. We decided at the meeting of the 27th that Morocco and Algeria were, as far as possible, to be evacuated by all combatants. At the close of the Cabinet meeting the Foreign Ministry, in agreement with me, sent the preparatory telegrams to General Lyautey. . . . He immediately sent us all that was humanly possible.[2]

Messimy goes on to speak of the decisive rôle played by these Moroccan troops in winning the battle of the Marne. But, he continues:

This was not everything. Right at that very moment my attention turned to the Russian Army. The two General Staffs had long ago formed the habit of working together. General Dubail in 1911 and General Joffre in 1912 had been in Russia working on joint plans with the Supreme Command. Through our Military Attaché, by the channel of the Foreign Ministry and our St. Petersburg Ambassador, I urged with all my might that, in spite of the

---

[1] Oe-U. VIII, 11082.   [2] Recouly, pp. 61-8.

slowness of Russian mobilization, the Tsar's armies should as soon as possible take the offensive in East Prussia.[1]

Later on Joffre in his *Memoirs* confirms this news in his entry of 27 July, taking the credit for the move to himself.

The direction which events were taking left me with no illusion—we were headed straight for war, and Russia was going to find herself drawn in at the same time as ourselves. My first thought, therefore, was to strengthen the liaison between us and our Allies, and I asked the Minister to endeavour through all possible means to make sure that, if hostilities broke out, the Government of St. Petersburg would immediately take the offensive in East Prussia, as had been agreed upon in our conventions. It will be recalled how important I considered this immediate offensive to be; we had requested our Allies to promise to undertake it, and they had agreed to do so. Our Military Attaché and, as I have been given to understand, our Ambassador, were asked to inquire of the Russian General Staff whether we could count upon them in this matter, while at the same time indicating the great importance that we attached to their offensive taking place in conjunction with ours. This question was answered by the announcement made the moment war was declared, that the Russian attack would open at once.[2]

Not without justice does Demartial, one of those Frenchmen who have the most bitterly attacked the conduct of their Government, comment:

This intervention on the part of Messimy was of capital importance. It goes without saying that to ask the Russians to take the offensive as soon as possible against Germany was to ask them to mobilize not only against Austria, but also against Germany.[3]

However it is not improbable that the steps taken by Messimy and Joffre were prompted by what Paléologue had telegraphed on 25 and 26 July, i.e. that the Russian Government had decided to mobilize only against Austria, endeavouring 'to avoid any measure likely to be regarded as directed against Germany' and determined 'to leave to Germany the eventual initiative of an attack on Russia'.[4]

This plan, as being more political than military, can hardly have appealed to Joffre and Messimy. Hence their intervention at St. Petersburg. And their intervention must have had the effect of strengthening Paléologue in the line he had taken on the 24th. Finding the French War Minister and Chief of Staff intent, not on dissuading Russia from mobilizing, but on urging her to a speedy offensive, he may well have been tempted not to pay great heed to the instructions which Viviani telegraphed him on the 27th from the high seas where after all he was out of touch with public opinion.

---

[1] Recouly, pp. 69–70.   [2] Joffre, I, pp. 117–18.
[3] Demartial, *L'Évangile du Quai d'Orsay* (Paris, 1926), pp. 24–5.   [4] See p. 592.

4. An alarming telegram of the evening of 29 July from Sazonov on Russian military measures.

On their arrival in Paris Poincaré and Viviani were certainly informed of the steps decided on by the military authorities as well as learning other significant news. At 11.15 a.m. on the 29th Izvolsky called at the Quai d'Orsay to say on behalf of Sazonov that, as Austria had declared war on Serbia, Russia was mobilizing her southern districts, i.e. against Austria, excluding all aggressive intentions towards Germany. Izvolsky further told that Sazonov had sent word to London that, in consequence of the Austrian declaration of war on Serbia, direct discussions with the Austrian Ambassador were obviously useless. 'It would be necessary for England with all speed to take action in view of mediation and for Austria at once to suspend military measures against Serbia.'[1] Viviani's first act on resuming office was to telegraph Paul Cambon in London to support the Russian demand.[2] After quickly glancing through the pile of papers accumulated during his absence, he went to the Élysée to attend a Cabinet meeting, presided over by Poincaré and lasting from 5 to 7 p.m., at which the situation was discussed and the decision taken to hold daily meetings.

The ministers had only just assembled when Schoen asked to make an urgent communication to Viviani. The Chancellor had telegraphed at 12.50 p.m. on the 29th that, if France continued to arm, Germany would be obliged to proclaim the 'danger of war' (*Kriegsgefahr*) 'which, though not meaning mobilization or recall to the colours, would undoubtedly sharpen the tension'.[3] It is evident that this telegram was much less threatening than the one which Bethmann at the same hour sent to Pourtalès and which infuriated Sazonov, to whom it seemed a kind of ultimatum.[4] Viviani did not deny to Schoen that precautionary measures had been taken, but emphasized that they were of slight proportions and inconspicuous in execution.

It was a long way from being mobilization. He

would not think it disquieting if similar measures were taken by us. Measures on our part would, however, be to be deprecated on account of their alarming effect on public opinion. The best means of avoiding this would seem to him to be to expedite mediatory action as much as possible no matter in what form. [Kaiser's marginal note of 30 July: 'If only he would get Vienna to give an answer.'] Viviani does not mean to give up hope of the preservation of peace, which is here sincerely desired.[5]

But did not Russian partial mobilization by its inevitable repercussions constitute a serious threat to peace? Paris had been informed of Jagow's statement that Germany would not object to it, i.e. would not

---

[1] *Int. Bez.* i. V, 167, 168. See p. 540.   [2] LJF. 97, in CDD., p. 208; DF. 3. XI, 260.
[3] DD. II, 341.   [4] DD. II, 342. See pp. 491, 553.   [5] DD. II, 367.

take corresponding measures on her side. But it was not wise to set too much store by this statement which took no account of the logic of the situation. Poincaré writes that he spent several hours of the night running through the dispatches which had come in during his absence and that their perusal showed him that the situation was much worse than he had realized on the voyage.[1] Recalling the events of those days he continues:

It is also to-day (29th) that General von Moltke has handed a memorandum to M. Bethmann Hollweg setting forth beforehand the fated sequence of events which are being prepared: Russian partial mobilization, Austrian general mobilization, German mobilization, French mobilization.[2]

And so indeed it was. But if it was a fatal sequence, Poincaré, Viviani, and Messimy should have been capable of foreseeing this and taking appropriate steps at St. Petersburg. If the telegram, of which we shall soon speak, sent to Paléologue by Viviani on the morning of the 30th, had been dispatched in the afternoon of the 29th, it might perhaps have produced an effect which on the 30th it was too late to achieve. Even though arriving home only on the 29th the President of the Republic and the Prime Minister should have made it their duty to formulate and communicate to St. Petersburg the French Government's objection to any degree of mobilization on account of the danger it involved Another useful, if not indispensable measure, would have been a telegram from Poincaré to the Tsar. Nothing on these lines was done. We have seen how Messimy acted. And what was said to Izvolsky before and after the Cabinet meeting led him on the 29th to send Sazonov telegrams certainly not calculated to make the latter more cautious. The first runs:

The firm attitude adopted by the French press still continues. It is very severe on the Austrian aggression and the patent complicity of Germany and unhesitatingly agrees that this touches us very closely and that we cannot remain indifferent. As to their solidarity with us, this question simply does not come under discussion as being a perfectly unequivocal fact. This is the line taken by all journalists including such prominent personalities of various parties as Pichon, Clemenceau, even Jaurès and the pioneer of anti-militarism, Hervé.[3]

The second runs:

On his arrival at Paris the President of the Republic was greeted at the station and in the streets with big demonstrations of popularity by the assembled crowds. Margerie told me that the President, from conversations with Prefects and politicians on the train journey, had convinced himself of the determined and at the same time steady tone of public opinion which is fully enlightened as to the true import of present events. The same spirit prevails

[1] Poincaré, IV, p. 376.   [2] Poincaré, IV, p. 378.   [3] Int. Bez. i. V, 232

even among a great proportion of the Radical-Socialists. The attempts at anti-militarist demonstrations by the revolutionary party are not taken seriously by the Government and it intends to take strong measures against them. The preparatory military measures are the subject of a detailed report by Count Ignatiev. The morale in military circles and the Supreme Command is very high. A further special detailed report on the press will follow.[1]

After the end of the Cabinet meeting, Izvolsky telegraphed:

Viviani has just assured me that the determination of the Government to proceed in perfect unity with us finds support in the widest circles and parties, including the Radical Socialists who, he said, had just handed him a resolution expressing their full confidence and the patriotic sentiments of their group.[2]

All these messages could not do otherwise than strengthen Sazonov in going to extremes. The desire 'to act in complete unity with Russia' did not, it is true, mean approval of Russia's unleashing war by being first with general mobilization. There was room for counsels of caution, above all for a warning against any kind of mobilization. All the more was this needful with an Ambassador like Izvolsky whose temperament inclined him to send St. Petersburg a picture of the state of opinion in France which left out all the gradations of light and shade. Did he exaggerate the statements made to him? Probably not, for when Viviani thought necessary to enjoin prudence on Sazonov, Izvolsky faithfully conveyed the Premier's warning. Sazonov must certainly have learnt more of what Viviani's ideas were from Izvolsky than from his own conversation with Paléologue. The warning was given on the morning of the 30th.

On the evening of the 29th Paléologue failed to inform Paris that general mobilization had been ordered in Russia, had then been revoked by the Tsar and replaced by partial mobilization. But before the revocation, Sazonov, as has already been shown, had sent Izvolsky a telegram saying that Pourtalès had informed him that Germany would order mobilization unless Russia suspended hers. This, however, Russia was unable to do in view of the fact that Austria had mobilized eight army corps and rejected every proposal for the composition of the conflict with Serbia. Therefore, continued the telegram,

as we cannot meet the German wish, it only remains for us to speed up our armaments and reckon with the probable inevitability of war. Will you please communicate this to the French Government, at the same time conveying our sincere gratitude for the declaration, which the French Ambassador made to me in his Government's name, that we may count in full measure on the allied support of France. In the circumstances of the present moment this declaration is particularly precious to us. It would be extremely desirable

[1] *Int. Bez.* i. V, 233.   [2] *Int. Bez.* i. V, 234.

that England too, should without loss of time associate herself with France and Russia.[1]

Izvolsky grasped the urgency and importance of this telegram and during the night of the 29/30th sent his Counsellor at the Embassy, Sevastopulo, to communicate it to Viviani, and his Military Attaché, Ignatiev, to communicate it to Messimy. Viviani must have been deeply disturbed on reading it. Here was Russia speeding up armaments, regarding war as inevitable, and taking the solidarity of France for granted! Messimy and Viviani together went to the Élysée to waken Poincaré and show him Sazonov's telegram. In reproducing it in *L'Union Sacrée* Poincaré adds a comment worthy of attention:

Sazonov is referring, and can only be referring, to a statement made by M. Paléologue, not in my name, but in that of the French Government. When was this statement made? When M. Paléologue received from M. Viviani the telegram dispatched from our battleship on 27 July 1914 and containing the phrase: 'Kindly tell M. Sazonov that France, appreciating, no less than Russia, the high importance for both countries of affirming their perfect mutual understanding in regard to the other Powers and to the need for neglecting no effort in view of a solution of the conflict, is ready in the interests of the general peace wholeheartedly to second the action of the Imperial Government.' But this statement has to be taken as a whole. It was made in the interests of the general peace, at an hour when Austria had not yet declared war on Serbia and when we did not suppose that Russia could dream of mobilizing. M. Viviani, therefore, not without reason, thought that M. Sazonov was now giving a rather wide meaning to any assurances which M. Paléologue may have given him. As he said to me, he thought it important to lose no time in making things perfectly clear (*mettre les choses au point*).[2]

Let us dwell a moment on this passage. The fact that Sazonov makes no mention of any promise given by Poincaré or Viviani during their visit is of undeniable value and cannot in fairness be called in question. But it is easy to reply that Poincaré was too skilled a master of expression and too conscious of the limits of his powers to compromise himself by outspoken statements and explicit promises. However the tone of his after-dinner toasts, the speeches he made, his blunt warning to Szápáry all created an atmosphere at St. Petersburg which was conducive to Sazonov's change of attitude. Moreover, until proof to the contrary is forthcoming, it is difficult not to believe that it was his guiding principles which determined Paléologue's handling of the situation. Not only can this be said of Paléologue's actions between the evening of 23 July and the afternoon of 30 July when Poincaré and Viviani were out of reach and he made his own decisions as to the attitude of France at St. Petersburg, but even on the 30th when he made no change in his line of policy as a result of the instructions telegraphed to him by Viviani

[1] *Int. Bez.* i. V, 221. See p. 556.   [2] Poincaré, IV, pp. 384-5.

on the morning of that day. Now the above quoted passage from *L'Union Sacrée*, far from altering this impression, only serves to strengthen it.

Poincaré cannot but reproduce Sazonov's telegram of thanks for France's unconditional support pledged by Paléologue, but he negotiates the snag by asking the question: 'When was this declaration made?' and giving the answer: 'When Paléologue received the telegram sent on 27 July' and he quotes its essential passages which say that 'in regard to the need for neglecting no effort in view of a solution of the conflict, France is ready in the interests of the general peace whole-heartedly to second the action of the Imperial Government'.[1] This declaration, maintains Poincaré, has to be taken as a whole. Very true! But Poincaré makes the gratuitous statement that this is what Sazonov referred to in his telegram, the fact being that Paléologue never communicated it to Sazonov. On the contrary Sazonov, at the tragic moment when 'it only remains for us to speed up our armaments and reckon with the probable inevitability of war', records that the French Ambassador's statement in his Government's name 'that we may count in full measure on the allied support of France . . . is particularly precious to us'.[2] No qualification of any sort, no hint of conjoint action for the saving of peace! On the contrary a promise of solidarity in the war regarded as inevitable, a promise not given now for the first time, but reiterated by Paléologue every day since 24 July. Had Paléologue received no authorization to say what in the telegrams both of Sazonov and Buchanan he is reported as saying? If so, it is not the artifices to which Poincaré resorts in the above passage that will serve to vindicate either himself or Paléologue. No doubt it is possible that he may have been genuinely mistaken and, like Viviani, have thought 'that Sazonov gave a rather wide meaning to any assurances which M. Paléologue may have given him', there being no reason for him to assume that Paléologue was not following instructions. But this mistaken view becomes inexcusable when, in later years, the English and Russian documents and the avowals contained in Paléologue's own diary threw a clear light on what had gone on.

5. *Viviani's instructions to Paléologue on the morning of 30 July.*

We now turn to the study of the decisions taken at the Élysée in the small hours of 30 July. Viviani had prepared a telegram for the Ambassador at St. Petersburg which received the assent of Poincaré, was sent off at 7 a.m., and contains the following passage:

As I have indicated to you in my telegram of the 27th inst., the Government of the Republic has decided to neglect no effort with a view to the solution of the conflict and to second the action of the Imperial Government in the

---

[1] See p. 593. [2] See p. 601.

interest of the general peace. On the other hand France is resolved to fulfil all the obligations of her alliance. But in the very interests of the general peace and in view of the fact that a conversation has been begun between the less interested Powers, I believe it would be opportune that, in the precautionary and defensive measures to which Russia believes herself obliged to resort, she should not immediately proceed to any measure which might offer Germany a pretext for a total or partial mobilization of her forces.[1]

The sincerity of this appeal to Russia not to mobilize against Austria has been called in doubt by those writers like Demartial who regard the document as having been drafted to produce a good impression on London[2] to which it was immediately communicated with the following addition:

I beg you to communicate the above to Sir Edward Grey as a matter of urgency and to remind him of the letters you exchanged with him in 1912 on the subject of the examination to which the two Governments are to proceed conjointly in the case of European tension.

The present writer does not regard this as Machiavellianism on the part of Viviani. He does not believe that Viviani was acting a part that night, that his anxiety was simulated, that he telegraphed thus to St. Petersburg to save appearances. Viviani's behaviour was consistent throughout. On 27 July when he learnt at sea that Russia was proposing to proceed to partial mobilization, he sent Paléologue the pacific instructions we have already considered. On reading Sazonov's telegram of 29 July he telegraphed a fresh appeal on the same lines as that of the 27th, making it more precise by representing to St. Petersburg the advisability of taking no measures which might give Germany a pretext to mobilize. Could his injunctions with advantage have been more emphatic? Some historians hold this view. Others, like Jules Isaac, think:

In all fairness one cannot but commend the perfect correctness of Viviani's telegram and acknowledge that the French Government at last ventured to

---

[1] DF. 3. XI, 305; BD. XI, 294. Several versions of this document exist. The first published is that of LJF. 101 (in CDD., p. 210). But as usual it has been manipulated. It omits the reference to instructions sent to Paléologue from on board the *France* on 27 July (the omission is understandable in view of the fact that the telegram sent from on board the *France* was not included in the *Yellow Book*). Further, after the words 'France is resolved to fulfil all the obligations of her alliance' there appear the following words added by the compilers of the *Yellow Book*: 'She (France) will not neglect, however, any effort towards a solution of the conflict in the interests of universal peace'. Another text, incomplete but not inaccurate, is that given by Izvolsky, to whom Viviani gave a copy of the telegram (*Int. Bez.* i. V, 289). Lastly there is the one forwarded to the Foreign Office in London by Paul Cambon, which is, of course, authentic and identical with that of the DF. 3. XI. Poincaré, however, in the first edition of *L'Union Sacrée* omitted from the last sentence the words 'which might offer Germany a pretext' and the omission substantially changes the sense of the concluding phrase. In his *Responsabilités de la Guerre* (p. 90) he explains this as a copyist's error and it was put right in later editions. These drop the final words 'total or partial (mobilization) of her forces', but this is of no importance.

[2] Demartial, *L'Évangile du Quai d'Orsay*, p. 73.

exercise the moderating action at St. Petersburg which the English Government on its side showed no willingness to do.[1]

Indeed it was not the first time that Viviani sought to exercise a moderating influence. His telegram of 27 July was in the same key, even if Paléologue took no account of it. However, to gauge the sincerity and the forcefulness of this second appeal, the first point to settle is whether he and the other members of the French Government had understood that Sazonov's words 'to speed up armaments' meant to issue the order for general mobilization. If they understood this, they were being weak and lacking in sincerity in what they said to St. Petersburg.

The opinion of the present writer is that they did not and could not understand, because Sazonov's wording was intentionally vague and certainly did not give them reason to think that what had been ordered was nothing less than general mobilization. Hence when, on the evening of 31 July, Schoen called on Viviani to present an ultimatum from Berlin on grounds of the Russian mobilization, Viviani, not having yet received Paléologue's telegram bringing news of it, replied that he had 'no information at all about an alleged total mobilization of the Russian army and navy' and wired to Paléologue 'to inform me as a matter of urgency as to the reality of an alleged general mobilization in Russia', adding: 'I do not doubt that the Imperial Government in the supreme interest of peace will, on its part, avoid anything that might open the crisis.'[2] It is true that the accusers of the French Government have tried to make out that when Viviani answered Schoen he was not telling the truth. But it is difficult to follow the reasoning of these writers who are obsessed with the idea that there was a conspiracy, concocted in all detail, between Paris and St. Petersburg to bring about war. Their obsession leads them to outstep all bounds of fairness, to the point of denying that the Central Powers had any hand in causing the war. Let us endeavour not to outstep these bounds and to make allowance for the critical and complex nature of the problem with which the French rulers were confronted by the Russian reaction to the Austrian ultimatum to Serbia. Poincaré has well summarized it as follows:

On us rested two duties, difficult to reconcile but equally sacred: to do our utmost to prevent a conflict, to do our utmost in order that, should it burst forth in spite of us, we should be prepared. And there were still two other duties which, also, at times ran the risk of being mutually contradictory: not to break up an alliance on which French policy has been based for a quarter of a century and the break up of which would leave us in isolation at the mercy of our rivals; and nevertheless to do what lay in our power to induce our

[1] Isaac, pp. 201–2.
[2] DF. 3. XI, 438. In the *Yellow Book* this document appears with alterations as No. 117 (in CDD., pp. 222–3).

ally to exercise moderation in matters in which we are much less directly concerned than herself.[1]

This is, indeed, an apt formulation of the problem which confronted France. The critics are mistaken who do not perceive it and start out from the assumption that Paris could give such advice to Russia as would lead her to accept another humiliation like that of 1909. This, however, does not rule out the comment that to set forth lucidly, as Poincaré does, the conflicting aims which it was the duty of the French Government to achieve is not, in itself, proof that the Government succeeded in reconciling these aims. What it did succeed in doing was only to save the alliance at the cost of its other aim, that of saving the peace. Nor does it establish a claim to immunity from the passion which glowed in the hearts of so many Frenchmen and in few more intensely than that of Poincaré, the man of Lorraine, a passion which might well tempt him not to let slip a favourable chance of recovering the lost provinces. But it is not within the power of man to look into the hearts and lay bare the motives of those who enacted this great tragedy, whether in leading or secondary rôles, all the more so as not one of them can have been inspired by one single motive only. Who among them can have been so clear-headed, so single-minded as never to feel hesitation, never to be assailed by conflicting impulses, and relentlessly to steer an undeviating course towards the goal of war? We must be content to judge them by their deeds, always giving the benefit of the doubt and, where no basis for forming a judgement exists, refraining from a definite expression of opinion.

With an impartial approach and an absence of preconceived ideas it often becomes possible to establish some measure of connexion between documents which, on the face of things, seem mutually contradictory. This, in the opinion of the present writer, is the case with the two different versions extant of conversations which on the morning of the 30th took place between on the one hand Izvolsky and Margerie, the Political Director at the Quai d'Orsay, and on the other the Russian Military Attaché, General Ignatiev, and the French War Minister Messimy. Poincaré writes that on the morning of the 30th Izvolsky called on Viviani and told him that Ignatiev had asked Messimy how to put into technical terms the recommendation contained in Viviani's telegram to Paléologue (a copy of which had been handed to the Russian Ambassador) adding that Messimy had advised the suspension of mobilization and particularly the avoidance of mass troop movements. Viviani said that was exactly the view of the Government and Izvolsky promised to transmit this to Sazonov.[2] It is clear that Ignatiev, who had perhaps guessed or been told that on the evening of the 29th

---

[1] Poincaré, IV, p. 412.   [2] Poincaré, IV, pp. 386–7.

St. Petersburg had decided to order general mobilization, was anxious to find out whether France, with whom previous consultations were necessary, was asking for its suspension. Viviani's telegram asked the Russian Government in general terms to refrain from measures which would furnish Germany with a pretext for mobilizing. It has not proved possible to find out how much Ignatiev was in a position to enlighten and did in fact enlighten Messimy on the Russian decisions. Poincaré certainly declares that first Messimy and then Viviani advised the suspension of mobilization. But then how could Viviani on the evening of the 31st tell Schoen, and wire to Paléologue, that he had no knowledge of Russia's having ordered general mobilization? It appears to the present writer—and this seems the only way of explaining both the attitude of Viviani and the French Government and Poincaré's statements in *L'Union Sacrée*—that Paris must have been only very vaguely aware of what was going on at St. Petersburg between 30 and 31 July. Possibly it was thought that what Russia had ordered was —in the words of Paléologue of the evening of the 30th—'to proceed secretly to the first measures of general mobilization',[1] similar to those which Joffre was advocating should be taken in France[2] but not constituting, in Viviani's words, the 'total mobilization of her forces'.[3] It was therefore thought that these early measures could be toned down and carefully regulated so as not to catch the eye of Germany. This will have been the substance of what was said to Izvolsky and Ignatiev with the intent not to offend Russia or put obstacles in the way of her taking precautions which would be timely if, as was probable, there was to be war. But there was certainly no intention of advising general mobilization, the extreme measure which would unleash war and put both France and Russia in the wrong. This impression receives confirmation from Poincaré. After quoting Paléologue's telegram of 30 July, which merely said that 'the Russian Government had decided to proceed secretly to the first measures of general mobilization' instead of announcing the fact that general mobilization had that afternoon been definitely ordered by the Tsar, Poincaré writes:

I remember how much at that moment I deplored that Russia had not more closely conformed to M. Viviani's opinion. We had at least all grounds for hoping that official and public mobilization was not near.[4]

If, in fact, Paris did not yet realize that Russia was proceeding to general mobilization and was under the illusion that only 'early measures' were being taken in view of a practically inevitable conflict, then Izvolsky's telegram, telling Sazonov of the conversations between Ignatiev and Messimy and between himself and Margerie (not with

---

[1] DF. 3. XI, 359.
[2] Recouly, p. 74; Joffre, I, p. 122.
[3] DF. 3. XI, 305. See p. 604.
[4] Poincaré, IV, p. 404.

Viviani, whom Izvolsky probably did not see until later), gives a reasonably faithful picture of the counsels and opinions at the Quai d'Orsay, torn, as it was, between the need to preserve the alliance and the need to save the peace.

Izvolsky's telegram runs:

Request urgent instructions. Margerie with whom I have just spoken, says the French Government has no intention of interfering in our military preparations but thinks it extremely desirable, in view of the further pursuance of negotiations for the preservation of peace, that these preparations should be of as little overt and provocative a character as possible. Also, dealing with the same theme, the Minister for War said to Count Ignatiev we might make a statement that in consideration of the overriding interests of peace we were prepared temporarily to slow down the measures for mobilization. This, of course, would not prevent us from determining our military measures and even speeding them up, so long as we refrain, as far as possible, from mass transport of troops. At 9.30 a.m. there is to be a Cabinet meeting at which Poincaré will preside and after which I shall immediately have a talk with Viviani.[1]

If the Russian preparations were to have 'as little overt and provocative a character as possible,' if a statement was to be issued that mobilization measures were being temporarily slowed down, even though they still went on under cover, avoiding all mass movements of troops, this indicated the taking of extensive precautions, such as would be of great use if war were to come, but were not a full-scale general mobilization which would involve such a calling up of classes, such mass movements that it could not be hidden or explained away. Hence the advice given by Margerie and Messimy may well have been motivated by the wish not to put too many obstacles in the way of Russia's plans, both in order not to offend her, and because it was a vital interest for France that the Russian Army should take the offensive in East Prussia without delay. But it does not mean, as Fabre-Luce claims, that they were giving their approval to Russian general mobilization, nor does it show 'that the French Government simply had as its aim to favour it [the Russian mobilization] while disclaiming responsibility for it'.[2] Poincaré 'vigorously rebuts' the similar accusations raised against him by the German historian Montgelas, and draws attention to the fact that Viviani's telegram was read out at the Cabinet meeting and that neither Messimy nor anyone else raised any objection to it.

The French Government [he writes] had flatly advised Russia against measures such as might, by repercussion, bring about German mobilization. We none of us, therefore, expected the *ukaze* which was issued in the afternoon, for which there had been nothing to prepare us and of which we only learnt long hours afterwards.[3]

---

[1] *Int. Bez.* i. V, 291.   [2] Fabre-Luce, pp. 211–12.   [3] Poincaré, IV, p. 408.

But if Viviani did not clearly perceive the seriousness of the situation and thought that 'appeals for general peace' would have an effect on St. Petersburg, he thought, as he told the High Court in April 1930 at the Caillaux trial: 'To tell Russia not to mobilize would have been a singular responsibility to take'.[1]

In personal notes taken at a Cabinet meeting by the Under Secretary of State, Abel Ferry, there appears the phrase: 'Not stop Russian mobilization. Mobilize but not concentrate.' It is reproduced in the *Documents Français* in an editorial footnote to Viviani's telegram to Paléologue and is followed by the Editor's comment: 'This note is dated 30 July, Friday, whereas the 30th was a Thursday.' The error of dating does not, however, alter the significance of the note. It was evidently taken at the very Cabinet meeting of 30 July. The editorial footnote goes on to reproduce part of a note drawn up on 23 January 1915 by Berthelot, the Political Director at the Quai d'Orsay, which summarized instructions issued to Paléologue on 30 July 1914 and told of Ignatiev's asking Messimy on the morning of the 30th how to translate into technical terms the recommendations contained in that telegram of Viviani to Paléologue and 'in what measure the preparatory arrangements of mobilization could be suspended in order not to give Germany the dreaded pretext'.

Berthelot's note adds that Viviani

remembers that M. Izvolsky showed him a paper in which Count Ignatiev, in the light of his conversation with M. Messimy, had indicated in what sense, from the military point of view, the formula of the Prime Minister's telegram was to be understood. Viviani has preserved not a trace of this formula. . . .[2]

In any case, however, the responsibilities of France through the actions of her Ambassador in Russia—whether or not inspired by Poincaré and the latter's attitude in St. Petersburg—even if posterior to those of the Central Powers and of Russia, are already sufficiently serious for it not to be necessary to add to them. On the other hand it cannot be overlooked that the advice given to Russia against general mobilization was timely, not only from the point of view of those whose aim was to avoid war, but also of those who saw the situation as a good chance for the *revanche*. Indeed for the *revanche* to be possible and the certain defeat of France to be prevented, two things were essential: Italian neutrality and English intervention. If the former seemed probable, the latter was extremely problematical, and if Russia did not want to render it impossible, she must refrain from hostile acts towards Germany. So true is this that the French Government itself, when pressed by Joffre to take precautionary measures which he thought necessary

---

[1] Demartial, *L'Évangile du Quai d'Orsay*, p. 40.   [2] DF. 3. XI, 305, n. 2.

and urgent, acted as we shall see with great circumspection, taking only unobtrusive measures, as it had advised St. Petersburg to do.

The same unobtrusive preparatory measures would have been taken by Russia if she had followed Margerie's and Messimy's suggestions passed on by Izolvsky. Indeed both Russia and France would have done well to be more cautious in playing with fire, remembering that, once they committed themselves to military preparations, they were on a slippery slope. But on this head the French political leaders can plead an important extenuating circumstance. They were firmly convinced that Germany's insistence on a free hand for Austria against Serbia made war a certainty,[1] and this conviction, as all know who have lived through those unforgettable days, was general all over Europe. Now if war seemed inevitable, or even only highly probable, it was natural that not only the diplomatists but also the military should turn their attentions to their defences. It was no moment to advise Russia to abstain from all preparatory measures. But then the question arises whether advice such as that tendered by Messimy and Margerie, with its equivocal implications, did not tend to neutralize the suggestion contained in Viviani's telegram that Russia should refrain from any steps which might furnish Germany with a pretext to mobilize. Various historians take the view that such was the case; but it is without justification on several grounds, one of which is decisive, namely: what emerges above all from this advice is, as has been said, that Russia was to abstain from general mobilization. In the second place the counsels they gave were not such that Sazonov could regard them as superseding Viviani's suggestion. Lastly it can conclusively be shown that Izvolsky's telegram containing them only reached St. Petersburg after the general mobilization had been decreed. Izvolsky and Ignatiev did not have their respective talks with Margerie and Messimy earlier than 9 or 10 a.m. After that Izvolsky and Ignatiev met at the Russian Embassy and exchanged impressions. The telegram had to be drafted and encoded. It can hardly have left Paris sooner than between 11 a.m. and noon at the earliest. Judging from the timing of an immense number of other telegrams, at least three hours will have been needed for transmission and decoding at St. Petersburg, where the telegram cannot have been available before 2 p.m. (Paris time). 2 p.m., Paris time, is 4 p.m. at St. Petersburg and Schilling tells us that Sazonov left the Ministry at 12.30 p.m., and at 2 p.m. left St. Petersburg with Tatistchev for Peterhof where the Tsar expected them at 3 p.m.[2] About 4 p.m. Sazonov from Peterhof telephoned the order to the Chief of Staff to issue the

---

[1] Bertie wrote to Grey on 30 July: 'The Spanish Ambassador (Urrutia) . . . says that the President of the Republic told a friend this morning that he considers war inevitable' (BD. XI, 320 b).

[2] Schilling, p. 64; *Int. Bez.* i. V, 284.

decree for general mobilization and it was handed in at the central telegraph office by Dobrorolski about 5 p.m. This time-table shows that there can be no question of any neutralizing effect exercised on Viviani's telegram of advice to Sazonov by the counsels given by Margerie and Messimy. Rather what must be settled is whether this telegram arrived in time to be read by Sazonov before he left for Peterhof.

This question is important. It is a fact that when on the following day the Tsar saw Izvolsky's telegram giving the substance of Viviani's instructions to Paléologue, he wrote at the foot of it: 'This telegram has come too late. Peterhof, 31.7.1914.'[1] This leaves one with the conviction that if Sazonov had carried Viviani's recommendation not to order general mobilization with him to Peterhof, the Tsar, already so reluctant to take the step, would have firmly refused to do so. Incidentally, it also means that if Poincaré on his return to Paris had on 29 July telegraphed to the Tsar in the same terms as Viviani telegraphed to Paléologue, Russia would not have ordered general mobilization on 30 July. Was it possible for Sazonov to learn of the French recommendations before leaving for Peterhof either from Izvolsky's telegram or from Paléologue? Viviani's telegram left at 7 a.m. It has not been possible to ascertain the hour of dispatch of Izvolsky's. But supposing Izvolsky to have telegraphed also at 7 a.m., which is anything but certain, Sazonov would have had to receive it decoded by 10.30 a.m. (French time), i.e. 12.30 (Russian time), since we know from Schilling's *Diary* that at 12.30 he went to lunch with Krivoshein and Schilling at Donon's and thence to Peterhof.[2] This would scarcely have been possible. Transmission, decoding and the passage through various departments which a decoded document undergoes before reaching the Minister's desk take a very long time, as experience proves. The historian with a thesis to defend is tempted to pay scant attention to such factors and to let the telegrams appear on the Minister's desk at the hour that suits his case. But one who seeks to be careful in drawing his conclusions must leave plenty of room for these factors of delay in the arrival of a telegram and its perusal by the minister or ambassador to whom it is addressed.[3] Hence if it is not true that Paléologue received Viviani's telegram only at 6 p.m. on the 30th, as he states in his diary, it is also quite certain that it could not have been in his hands on the morning of that day. That morning he was out calling at the Russian Foreign Ministry where he first talked alone with Sazonov before they were joined by Buchanan, Sazonov leaving at 12.30 p.m. to go to the luncheon with Krivoshein and Schilling. Buchanan's account of their conversation was dispatched to London at 1.15 p.m. This all shows that those historians are mistaken who take their stand on a sentence in a telegram

[1] *Int. Bez.* i. V, 289.　　　　[2] Schilling, p. 64; *Int. Bez.* i. V, 284. See p. 565.
[3] See p. 525, n. 6.

of Paléologue's, which, as we shall see, means nothing, and regard it as proving that Paléologue gave Viviani's message to Sazonov on the morning of the 30th.

But even assuming, for the sake of argument, that Sazonov may have learnt of Viviani's recommendations from Paléologue or Izvolsky before going to Peterhof to ask the Tsar's consent for general mobilization, it is hard to believe that he would have paid much heed to them or laid them before the Tsar at Peterhof. The previous chapter has set forth the many reasons which render it improbable. Sazonov had become convinced of the technical impossibility, indeed the disastrousness, of recourse to partial mobilization. Not wanting to cancel it after having announced it to all the Powers on 28 July he asked and received the Tsar's permission for general mobilization. The Tsar had then withdrawn this and ordered that only a partial mobilization should be carried out. But Sazonov, the generals, and his other colleagues thought it essential that the Tsar should change this decision, which, if war did break out, might well bring disaster upon the Russian armies. By agreement with the generals Sazonov had asked for and obtained an audience in order to persuade the Tsar of this necessity. Something much more than Viviani's gentle recommendations would have been needed to make him take the very opposite course. Telegraphing after the morning's talk, Buchanan's message ran: 'For strategical reasons Russia can hardly postpone converting partial into general mobilization.'[1] Hence, if she were not to proceed with partial mobilization, she must also desist from general mobilization. But with what loss of prestige and with what effects on the attitude of the Central Powers!

Had Paléologue in the name of his Government made any such suggestion, probably Sazonov would rightly have objected that this advice should have been given him earlier, instead of the advice to show the utmost firmness and the many assurances, given also in the presence of the English Ambassador, of the unlimited support of France. As has just been said, nothing less than a timely telegram from Poincaré to the Tsar, sent off from Paris on the evening of the 29th, could have changed the course of events and prevented the proclamation of general mobilization. It still remains to be seen whether war would not have broken out all the same. In Fay's opinion:

If President Poincaré had expressed himself with his usual vigour and clarity—if he had said unmistakably to Russia: 'Do not order general mobilization for the present while diplomatic negotiations are going on'—there is a possibility that war might still have been avoided.[2]

But, as will soon be shown, before knowing of the Russian general mobilization, Germany on the evening of 30 July, had decided to send

[1] BD. XI, 302.   [2] Fay, II, p. 486.

St. Petersburg an ultimatum demanding the revocation even of the partial mobilization. Now it is doubtful whether the Tsar would have bowed to such a request made in such a manner even at the desire of Poincaré and yet this was the crux of the whole matter. It does not, however, do away with the fact that the attempt should have been made and made twelve hours earlier than Viviani's telegram, with greater authority and energy than he could muster and not addressed to Sazonov but to the Tsar. The only plea which the French leaders can put forward in extenuation is that Paris was not in possession of exact information as to what was taking place at St. Petersburg and as to the activities of the French Ambassador. He, on his part, after his language and incitements from 24 July onwards, would have found it impossible on the 30th to carry out Viviani's instructions even had he received them in time. He did not, in fact, carry them out, any more than he had carried out those of the 27th, and he continued to deceive Paris about what was going on at St. Petersburg.

6. *Paléologue's telegrams of 30 July and his talk with Sazonov.*

Schilling's diary tells that on Sazonov's return to the Russian Foreign Ministry from the office of the Chief of Staff after telephoning to the Tsar, he found Paléologue waiting and had a talk with him.[1] It was their first meeting since the events of the previous evening which have already been fully dealt with above: the decision to order general mobilization, followed by the Tsar's order revoking it. Sazonov no doubt fully informed the Ambassador of all that had taken place. Did Paléologue repeat the protest which Basili was also to make on his behalf against the proposal to decree general mobilization without previous accord with the French General Staff? No doubt the fact that the Tsar had revoked this general mobilization had removed the grounds for such a protest. But it would become again necessary if the generals, whose objections were fully explained to Paléologue, were successful in overcoming the Tsar's resistance. Paléologue's diary breathes not a word of this talk which must surely have been one of the greatest importance, since Sazonov cannot but have poured all his anguish into the ear of this intimate colleague, telling him of the request he was about to make to the Tsar who was due to receive him at 3 p.m. This, however, belongs to the realm of conjecture. What is proved by the documents is that to Buchanan, who arrived during the course of the conversation, Sazonov was secretive and not quite straightforward, saying:

Yesterday evening it was decided to issue this morning order for partial mobilization . . . and at the same time to commence preparations for general mobilization.

[1] Schilling, p. 64; *Int. Bez.* i. V, 284. See p. 565.

He read out the text of the French formula for the move of conciliation, which he had given in the night to Pourtalès. He then added: 'If
Austria rejects this proposal preparations for general mobilization will
proceed and European war will be inevitable'.[1] In actual fact, without
waiting for the Austrian reply, he was about to ask the Tsar to authorize
general mobilization. But what he revealed was enough to enable
Buchanan to send home very disquieting news. Did Sazonov say exactly the same to Paléologue? And when and how did Paléologue carry
out Viviani's instructions of 28 July? When and how did he inform
Paris of the general mobilization ordered at 5 p.m. on that same
day?

To form an idea of the devious conduct of this Ambassador it is
necessary to examine in chronological order his telegrams of 30 July.
The first, dispatched at midnight on 29 July, arriving in Paris at 3.40
on the 30th, runs: 'According to information received by the Russian
General Staff, the general mobilization of the German Army will be
ordered tomorrow, 30 July.'[2]

Not a word here of what Buchanan told his Government in a telegram, sent off at 1.15 p.m. on the 30th, namely:

Russian Government, Minister for Foreign Affairs told us, had absolute
proof of military and naval preparations being made by Germany against
Russia more especially in the direction of Gulf of Finland,[3]

because this item implicitly contradicted his first telegram. Paléologue's
two next telegrams, both dispatched at 1.30 p.m., gave an account,
similar to that of Buchanan, of the Pourtalès-Sazonov interview which
the Russian documents place in the night of 29–30 July and the Pourtalès version places in the forenoon of the 30th.[4] These two telegrams
appear as No. 113 of the *Yellow Book*, altered, shortened, and dated,
not the 30th, but the 31st, Heaven knows for what obscure reason![5]
There is no point in quoting them since they do not contain anything
not given in Buchanan's telegram which has been fully discussed in the
preceding chapter.[6] There is, however, one difference. While Buchanan
reports that partial mobilization had been ordered and preparations
begun for general mobilization, which for strategic reasons could not
fail to be ordered soon if Austria did not accept Sazonov's formula,
Paléologue's telegram contains not a word of this. And whereas
Buchanan faithfully reports how Pourtalès, in dismay at the prospect
of war, implored Sazonov to draft a formula for peace, Paléologue puts
the following words into Sazonov's mouth: 'The Emperor Nicholas
has such a desire to avert war that in his name I make a last proposal'.[7]

---

[1] BD. XI, 302.
[2] DF. 3. XI, 302.
[3] BD. XI, 302; DF. 3. XI, 328.
[4] See pp. 561–4.
[5] LJF. 113 in CDD., pp. 220–1.
[6] See p. 567.
[7] DF. 3. XI, 328.

This was completely untrue! And therefore when the Quai d'Orsay learnt the true facts from Izvolsky, Berthelot drafted and Margerie signed a telegram to Paléologue which runs as follows:

I am obliged to draw your attention to the fact that M. Izvolsky, on his side, has communicated the Russian proposal to me, but indicating that it arose in consequence of an urgent request from the German Ambassador at St. Petersburg to know the conditions on which the Russian Government would stop its military preparations.

However this may be, in case, as is possible, the terms formulated by M. Sazonov were not in their present form to be regarded as acceptable by Austria, it would be your duty, while maintaining close contact with M. Sazonov and without acting counter to the English endeavour, to seek with him a formula such as might seem suitable to form a basis of conversation and conciliation.[1]

Poincaré comments that Sazonov's formula was rather belated, and in reproducing the two telegrams of Paléologue and Margerie he comments on the latter: 'Thus the French Government was determined to leave nothing undone that might save the peace and clutched desperately at every straw.'[2] Margerie's telegram deserves not only to be placed to the credit of the French Government, it also throws a favourable light on other documents which detractors of the French Government have stigmatized as insincere and double dealing. But Margerie's move came still more belatedly than Sazonov's formula, though the French leaders were not aware of this. Moreover it was addressed to an Ambassador irrevocably committed to the opposite course, so irrevocably that he could not turn back and had to go forward, whatever the consequences.

On returning home after the morning conversation, Paléologue sent off two more telegrams, one at 4.30 p.m. which runs: 'The bombardment of Belgrade arouses the most intense feeling in Russia. The moderating efforts of the Imperial Government risk being thereby paralysed.'[3] After this preamble, at 4.31 he proceeded to reply to Viviani's telegram of the morning of the 30th as follows:

This very morning I have recommended to M. Sazonov to avoid all military measures which might furnish Germany with a pretext for general mobilization. He answered that in the course of last night the Russian General Staff had actually deferred certain secret precautions, the disclosure of which might have alarmed the German General Staff. Yesterday the Russian Chief of General Staff sent for the Military Attaché at the German Embassy and gave him his word of honour that the mobilization ordered this morning is directed exclusively against Austria.[4]

[1] DF. 3. XI, 349; Poincaré, IV, pp. 402–3.   [2] Poincaré, IV, p. 403.
[3] DF. 3. XI, 340.   [4] DF. 3. XI, 342.

This telegram was published in a modified form as the first part of No. 102 of the *Yellow Book*[1] and fused with two other telegrams which were later published in the *French Diplomatic Documents* under No. 328. This manipulation and falsification was revealed in 1923 by Poincaré in circumstances which will be discussed in Vol. III.

It cannot have been a pleasant task for Poincaré to avow the manipulation of documents practised by the Quai d'Orsay in the *Yellow Book* and to publish the above telegram in which a French Ambassador so closely linked with himself is caught in the act of grossly deceiving his own Government. Paléologue knew that, the previous evening, general mobilization was on the point of being proclaimed when the Tsar intervened and suspended it against the will of the General Staff. Not content with concealing this grave news from Paris, Paléologue, for the purpose of proving the intentions of St. Petersburg to be ultra-pacific, transformed it by asserting that 'in the course of the night the Russian General Staff had actually deferred certain secret precautions the disclosure of which might have alarmed the German General Staff'. The truth was that this was anything but what was wanted by the Russian General Staff and that it was now endeavouring to get the Tsar to revoke the order for suspension. Paléologue, still with the idea of showing what a peaceful wind was blowing at St. Petersburg, added that Janushkevich on the previous day had given his word of honour to Eggeling that mobilization was directed solely against Austria. The actual incident happened at 3 p.m. on the 29th and Paléologue learnt of it at once, since he told the story to Buchanan, who informed London by a telegram dispatched at 8.30 p.m. on the 29th.[2] Eggeling with good reason telegraphed to Berlin that he regarded Janushkevich's words as 'an attempt to mislead'.[3] Paléologue, on the contrary, affected to believe them and sent the belated news on the following day without comment, though he perfectly well knew that if, on the 29th, Janushkevich's words had been worth little, by the 30th they were worth nothing. Here Morhardt is not wrong in commenting that

if Paléologue had been telegraphing to the German Government to hide the truth from it about what was happening at St. Petersburg and to mislead it, he would not have resorted to a greater number of circumlocutions, evasions and lies.[4]

And Paléologue's deception of his own Government is a far more serious thing than the deception practised on Eggeling by Janushkevich. But it is not true, as Morhardt goes on to say, that he acted as he did because he was 'in collusion with the Russian Government on one hand and the Quai d'Orsay on the other', and that he continued

[1] CDD., p. 211.   [2] BD. XI, 271.
[3] DD. II, 370.   [4] Morhardt, *Les Preuves*, p. 196.

'to send Paris misleading telegrams giving no correct or exact information on the events he witnessed but capable of serving at need as an alibi for the Government of the Republic to prove falsely that France was pacific'.[1] The Government of the Republic in this case was not the accomplice but the victim of its Ambassador. There would be no point in mentioning these exaggerations of certain accusers of the French leaders of 1914, if some in the opposite camp did not play into their hands by refraining from passing judgement on documents like these, or even bringing them forward in support of the French case as does Poincaré himself.

Even after learning the truth about the facts of the Russian mobilization from Dobrorolski's account and Schilling's *Diary*, which he frequently quotes, Poincaré uses that telegram of Paléologue's for his own purpose, which is to show that Viviani's recommendations were passed on to Sazonov in good time but that Sazonov did not pay them due heed. Poincaré writes:

On the 30th, on receiving the telegram dispatched by Viviani at 7 a.m. on the 30th, Paléologue called on Sazonov and expressed the French Government's desire to avoid all measures which might give Germany a pretext for general mobilization.

Quoting Paléologue's reply, Poincaré comments:

The formulas used by M. Sazonov and the Russian Chief of Staff give us little information on what had happened the previous day and the second in particular is not very happy.[2]

This comment is too barefaced! If the French Government was badly informed the fault lay entirely with Paléologue. Poincaré, it is true, is not alone in declaring that Paléologue on the morning of 30 July did, in fact, carry out the instructions given him. Renouvin had already written:

The advice of the French Government had therefore been interpreted as it was intended: France did not wish Russia to proceed with general mobilization. M. Paléologue's *démarche* had been made just in time, before M. Sazonov's visit to Peterhof Palace. According to Baron Schilling's *Diary*, it was about noon that the Minister had an interview with the French Ambassador.[3]

And almost all the historians hold the same opinion. It is natural that this should be the case with those who seek to maintain French innocence at all cost. But it is strange that those who challenge it fall into the same mistake. It should not have been difficult for them to perceive that a telegram leaving Paris at 7 a.m. (French time), i.e. at 9 a.m. (Russian time) could not be decoded and in Paléologue's hands by 10 to 10.30 a.m., when he presumably left the Embassy to pay his

---

[1] Morhardt, *Les Preuves*, p. 198.   [2] Poincaré, IV, pp. 399–400.
[3] Renouvin, p. 207; Schilling, p. 64.

call on Sazonov. Their talk must have taken place not about noon, as Renouvin writes,[1] but about 11 a.m., if not earlier. This can be gathered from the fact that both Paléologue's and Buchanan's fairly long telegram relating to the conversation went off in code between 1.15 and 1.30 p.m. If Viviani's telegram had reached Paléologue before his call on Sazonov, he would have replied to it at about the same time as when he actually did send Paris his account of the morning's talk in two telegrams[2] which reached Paris at 4 p.m. and 5.25 p.m. respectively and (be it repeated) were dispatched from St. Petersburg at 1.30 p.m. To Viviani's telegram he replied only at 4.31 p.m., not having received it until the early afternoon.

What then, it will be asked, was the meaning of the words 'ce matin même' in this third telegram?[3] In theory they might mean that Paléologue on his own initiative had already that morning taken the step suggested by Viviani. In practice it means nothing of the kind, since he never communicated Viviani's suggestion to Sazonov at all. Had he done so he would not have received the untruthful reply which he invents himself and attributes to Sazonov to keep Paris quiet. Moreover his words would have been reported to London by Buchanan, who makes no mention of any reaction on the part of Paléologue to the news given them by Sazonov. Paléologue's diary tells us in its entry for 30 July what he actually did say to Sazonov after receiving Viviani's telegram and it flatly contradicts the view taken by Poincaré, Renouvin and many others. The entry runs:

> At 6 p.m. I received a telegram dispatched from Paris this morning and signed by Viviani. After once more emphazing the pacific intentions of the French Government and imposing caution on the Russian Government, Viviani added: *France is determined to meet all the obligations of the alliance.*
>
> I went to tell Sazonov, who replied very simply: 'I was sure of France.'[4]

This entry makes it clear: (i) that anything said by Paléologue 'ce matin même', assuming him to have said something, was not said as a result of Viviani's telegram, since that only arrived in the afternoon

---

[1] Renouvin concludes that Paléologue's call took place at noon because Schilling's *Diary* states (*ibid.*, pp. 63–4): 'At 11 a.m. the Minister for Foreign Affairs again met the Minister for War and the Chief of the General Staff' and that these two 'again endeavoured by telephone to persuade the Tsar to . . . permit a general mobilization. . . On his return to the Foreign Office, S. D. Sazonov had an interview with the French Ambassador.' But at the Sukhomlinov trial, Janushkevich deposed that Sazonov had only a few minutes 'talk with the Chief of Staff. We were in such complete agreement that everything was settled in a few minutes' (*Revue d'Histoire de la Guerre Mondiale*, April 1924, pp. 56–7). Schilling's indication of 11 a.m. may, after all, be only approximate. The one certainty is that both Paléologue and Buchanan sent off their telegrams relating to the three cornered conversation at about 1.30 p.m. Since Buchanan's is fairly long, it must have taken at least an hour to draft and encode so that the conversation must have ended by about noon.

[2] Published together in DF. 3. XI, as No. 328.

[3] DF. 3. XI, 342.   [4] Paléologue, I, pp. 45–6.

(though not so late as 6 p.m.); (ii) that he carried out Viviani's instructions, not in the forenoon, but in the afternoon or evening, after the general mobilization had been definitely ordered; (iii) that, as Sazonov's reply shows, Paléologue only carried out that part of his instructions which consisted in reaffirming the unconditional support of France, as he had done two days previously; (iv) that 'imposing caution on the Russian Government' at that time, when the die was cast and general mobilization already ordered, would have not only been a reversal of all he had been previously saying, but quite out of place when war was imminent.

7. *Paléologue's concealments and the belated information sent by him to Paris regarding the Russian mobilization.*

Paléologue's diary entry for 30 July is not confined to the passage just quoted above. This is preceded, as is chronologically justified, by an account of the historic audience which Sazonov had of the Tsar at 3 p.m., given in the form of a dialogue worthy of Paléologue's gifts of authorship. Sazonov brings forward his reasons for asking for mobilization:

'Germany is obviously evading the mediatorial intervention for which we asked her and all she is after is to gain time to complete her military preparations in secret. . . .' The Tsar was deadly pale and replied in a choking voice: 'Just think of the responsibility you're advising me to assume! Remember it is a question of sending thousands and thousands of men to their death!' Sazonov replied: ' . . . Now I feel certain that diplomacy has finished its work. . . . If Your Majesty stops our preliminary mobilization, all you will do is to dislocate our military organization and disconcert our allies. The war will break out just the same—at Germany's appointed time— and will catch us in hopeless confusion.'

The argument that France would be disconcerted, placed in the mouth of Sazonov, betrays the part played by Paléologue in inciting Sazonov and bears the stamp of his own style and mode of thought.

The entry continues:

After a moment's reflexion the Tsar said in a firm voice: 'Sergei Dimitrievitch, ring up the Chief of Staff and tell him that I order general mobilization' [which Sazonov did]. It was exactly 4 o'clock.[1]

Just so! But besides making this entry in his diary, was it not Paléologue's duty to telegraph the substance of the interview in an accurate and truthful form to his own Government? Let us now turn to look how he acted in this supreme emergency.

It is not known at what hour he saw Sazonov and received from him (or others) the account of what took place at the audience of 3 p.m. All that is known is that at 7.40 p.m. he telegraphed Viviani asking for instructions regarding the members of the French territorial and reserve

[1] Paléologue, I, p. 45.

forces resident in Russia. 'Am I to invite them to return to France as soon as I receive news of French mobilization and advance them their travelling expenses?'[1] At 9.15 p.m. he sent off the following telegram :

In a conversation which he had this afternoon with Count Pourtalès, M. Sazonov was obliged to come to the conviction that Germany will not speak the decisive word at Vienna which would safeguard the peace.

Secret.—Tsar Nicholas has the same impression from an exchange of telegrams which he has just had personally with Kaiser Wilhelm. Moreover the Russian General Staff and Admiralty have received disquieting information concerning the preparations of the German Army and Navy. In consequence the Russian Government has decided to proceed secretly to the first measures of general mobilization. In giving me this information M. Sazonov added that the Russian Government is none the less continuing its efforts towards conciliation. He repeated to me: 'I shall continue to negotiate until the last moment.'[2]

This telegram No. 315 was inserted into the second part of No. 102 of the *Yellow Book*[3] minus the words: 'In consequence the Russian Government has decided to proceed secretly to the first measures of general mobilization'. But we are not here concerned with these manipulations of documents carried out after war had been declared. What now interests us is to ascertain and judge the acts of France's representative at St. Petersburg. Let us look closely at the document in question. First of all if we take Pourtalès's version as the accurate one, Sazonov, in the course of 30 July, saw Pourtalès not in the afternoon, but for a first time in the early hours after midnight of the 29th, for a second time in the forenoon and for a third time in the evening.[4] It was at the forenoon meeting that Sazonov gave him the well-known peace formula which, as Paléologue himself telegraphed to Paris, Pourtalès promised to support and which was not logically reconcilable with the Russian order for immediate mobilization. At the evening meeting Pourtalès communicated to Sazonov two telegrams from Bethmann, one of which runs: 'Please tell M. Sazonov that we continue to mediate; but only on the assumption that no hostilities are for the time being undertaken by Russia against Austria.'[5] The other runs: 'Vienna's refusal to open discussions must have been returned before our last *démarche* at Vienna, about the success of which information has still not come to hand.'[6] It was, therefore, a complete inversion of the sense of Pourtalès's telegram to say, as does Paléologue, that 'Sazonov was obliged to come to the conviction that Germany will not speak the decisive word at Vienna which would safeguard the peace'.

Paléologue then goes on to state—as he does more fully in his diary —that the Tsar had assented to general mobilization because of the bad

---

[1] DF. 3. XI, 355.   [2] DF. 3. XI, 359.   [3] CDD., p. 211.
[4] See p. 564, n. 2.   [5] DD. II, 392.   [6] DD. II, 397.

impression produced on him by a newly arrived telegram from Kaiser Wilhelm, which will be discussed later and which stated: 'If . . . Russia mobilizes against Austria, my rôle as mediator . . . will be compromised if not made impossible'.[1] This telegram, of which Paléologue in his diary quotes the concluding portion,[2] left Berlin at 3.30 p.m. on 30 July, arriving at Peterhof at 6.30 p.m. after general mobilization had been ordered. Wilhelm, it is true, had said something similar also in his telegram sent from Potsdam on the morning of the 29th and received by the Tsar on the evening of the same day. But, as we have seen, this telegram, far from causing the Tsar to order general mobilization, made him revoke it.[3]

But if the Russian decision was based on assumptions which were devoid of foundation, still more serious and reprehensible was the silence maintained by Paléologue in his telegrams to his Government about the nature and implication of that decision. He does not say frankly that general mobilization had been ordered but only that 'the Russian Government has decided to proceed secretly to the first measures of general mobilization', just as he had done the evening before. And the purpose was still the same, i.e. to keep the French Government in the dark, so that it should not place obstacles in the way of the Russian action (if that were possible once mobilization had been proclaimed). Of course, if what was being done remained secret and if there was no question of the general mobilization deprecated by Viviani, France would have no grounds for anxiety and could, on the contrary, feel reassured. And in fact the Quai d'Orsay, on receiving the telegram at 11.25 p.m., did not attach much importance to it. After all Margerie and Messimy had themselves advised Russia to carry out secretly something in the nature of the first measures of general mobilization. What mattered was that Germany should not know of them and use them as a pretext for mobilizing. And as long as it was a matter of 'first secret measures' and not of general mobilization, Germany might or might not hear of them without feeling undue alarm.

It may be objected that it was not Paléologue who deceived Paris,

---

[1] DD. II, 420.   [2] Paléologue, I, pp. 44–5.

[3] See p. 557. Paléologue's historical inaccuracy is incredible! In a later book (*Guillaume II et Nicolas II*, Paris, 1934) summarily reconstructing the events of the last days of July 1914 he completely omits the fact that the Tsar signed the decree for general mobilization on the 29th and makes out that he ordered partial mobilization because of the bombardment of Belgrade: 'What dominates the debate and suddenly lights up the horizon with a flash is, in the night of 28–29 July, the bombardment of Belgrade, the opening of hostilities. . . . All the passions of Orthodox Slavism burst into flames like a fork of lightning' (*ibid.* pp. 196–7). In actual fact Sazonov took the decision to order partial mobilization on the evening of the 28th and the news of the bombardment of Belgrade, which reached St. Petersburg about 4 p.m. on the 29th, made Sazonov, well before 'the passions of Orthodox Slavism burst into flames', ask and obtain the Tsar's assent to general mobilization, which would have been proclaimed on the evening of the 29th, had it not been revoked by the Tsar.

but Sazonov who deceived Paléologue. Bernadotte Schmitt writes that Sazonov 'concealed from the French Ambassador that the general mobilization had been ordered and spoke merely of "proceeding secretly to the first measures". Such conduct was not loyal.[1] But Schmitt's accusation against Sazonov is unfounded. We have already, in connexion with the events of 29 July, discussed the subject of the intimacy and complete confidence between Sazonov and the French Ambassador. In respect of the events of 30 July, it must be added that, in writing thus, Schmitt forgets that Paléologue himself, by entering in his diary under the 30th the account of Sazonov's audience of the Tsar at 3 p.m., confesses to having on the 30th received information of the general mobilization ordered on that very afternoon. And in this he may be believed, because if Sazonov had kept things from him on the 30th, it would have been to Paléologue's own interest to say so and thus clear himself of the charge of having sent Paris misleading information on that date. It is true that to a contributor to the French weekly *Vu* of 15 March 1933 Paléologue said something which seems to cast doubt on the accuracy of his own diary. He was giving an explanation of why he did not telegraph until 10.43 a.m. on the 31st, the news of the general mobilization ordered at 5 p.m. on the 30th, with the result that the news did not reach Paris until 8.30 p.m. on the 31st after Viviani had spoken with Schoen and told him that he had no knowledge of any Russian mobilization. Paléologue told the contributor to *Vu* that at 6 a.m. on Friday 31 July he got word that the mobilization order had been posted up in the streets. He at once sent his Military Attachés post haste to Staff Headquarters to find out 'if this order were operative for the whole Empire'. As soon as they returned, he telegraphed to Paris: 'An order has been issued for the general mobilization of the Russian Army.' The telegram left the Embassy at 8.30 a.m. But at 9.30 the messenger returned from the central telegraph office, situated at a distance of three and a half kilometres, saying that great agitation reigned there, as it was about to be occupied by the military. Fearing possible delays and the risks of sending the news via Berlin, Paléologue dispatched it by Scandinavian lines, a very complicated route which caused it to arrive at Paris only at 8.30 p.m. on the 31st.[2]

[1] Schmitt, II, p. 248.

[2] An editorial note to Paléologue's telegram (DF. 3. XI, 432, pp. 356-7) says that Paléologue communicated to the Editorial Committee an extract from his diary, which repeats the story given to the contributor to *Vu*. The messenger ' "found the post office premises in great agitation because the military authorities were in the act of taking over the telegraph service". It is this circumstance, thinks M. Paléologue, which explains the length of time that elapsed between the handing in of the telegram and its dispatch.' Further on the note raises the question 'whether an earlier wireless message announcing the general mobilization had not been sent direct from the Russian to the French General Staff'. But 'no such message has come to light. Only one wireless message of Russian origin figures in the "incoming messages" of the Minister for War's Cabinet for the night of 30–31 July: it indicates a German Fleet movement.'

It is a strange affair, this episode of the messenger who cannot manage to send off a telegram from the French Embassy because of the great agitation prevailing at the post office, while a short time afterwards a similar telegram from the German Ambassador was handed in and speedily dispatched. The fact that Pourtalès's telegram left at 10.20 a.m. and reached the Wilhelmstrasse at 11.40 a.m. shows that, to say the least of it, Paléologue did wrong not to send his telegram by both the German and the Scandinavian route. The news had been known for some time and, as there was no need to maintain secrecy about a matter of public knowledge, the telegram might well have been sent *en clair*.

Richard Ullrich who in 1914 was St. Petersburg correspondent of the *Kölnische Zeitung* makes the following comment on Paléologue's statements:

> Even if one is ready to believe M. Paléologue that he was still so naïf on 31 July as to ask what sort of a mobilization order was posted up at the street corners, there was really no need of a procedure lasting two hours for him to fathom the contents of the little red notices. Their heading ran: 'Imperial *ukaze* of general mobilization.'

To Paléologue's story that the distance of the French Embassy from the central telegraph office was $3\frac{1}{2}$ kilometres, Ullrich remarks that he himself had taken the shortest way along the Neva hundreds of times and that a messenger taking one of the quick cabs, which stood outside every embassy door, would have covered the distance in ten minutes at most. Ullrich denies that there was any bustle and confusion at the central telegraph office on account of its being taken over by the military.

> I was there between 9 and 10 a.m. . . . . Only three foreign correspondents were still standing chatting at the counters. The elderly, hump-backed spinster who spoke every existing language and, with her unvarying courtesy, was the friend of all correspondents, accepted my telegram as usual and asked, as I said good-bye, whether there was really going to be war. . . . Not a trace did I see of military occupation. I chatted a while with my foreign colleagues; none of them said anything about a military occupa·· tion and that would have been talked of at once as something quite out of the ordinary.[1]

This, however, is beside our point. What here concerns us is that this new story would give us to understand that Paléologue is contradicting his own diary and making out that he only learnt of the general mobilization on the morning of the 31st from the notices posted up in the St. Petersburg streets. He only warily adds that he sent his Military Attachés to find out if the order was 'operative for the whole Empire'.

[1] Richard Ullrich, *Herrn Paléologues Meldung der russischen allgemeinen Mobilmachung*, in KSF., August 1933, pp. 781-3.

What was the point of this inquiry? Does Paléologue want it to be believed that on 31 July he still thought it might be a question only of partial mobilization in the four southern districts against Austria? He does not say this, since in that case he would be confessing that his diary does not tell the truth. But if he had really been kept in the dark by Sazonov, the doubts and accusations to which his telegrams have given rise would have made him disclose that fact, even if his disclosure was belated. He made no such disclosure, nor does his one-line telegram indicate at what time the general mobilization was ordered. If the notices were already posted up in the streets that morning, the proclamation must necessarily have been made the previous evening. Why did he not say so in notifying Paris, and why, especially after Viviani's telegram deprecating such a step, does he not say that the step was taken without his knowledge?

The truth is that Paléologue was perfectly aware that general mobilization was ordered on the evening of the 30th. The only thing that surprised him was that notices were publicly posted up proclaiming it, whereas Sazonov had told him, or had arranged with him, that the order was to be kept secret. Historians have not devoted sufficient attention to this point, which provides the key to many mysteries. It to some extent explains the behaviour of Sazonov who thought Russia could mobilize without Germany's knowing of it immediately. In this connexion it is worth noting what Taube relates on the authority of Boris Nolde who was then Legal Counsellor at the Russian Foreign Ministry:

Eyewitnesses are still alive who were present at that rather tasteless (*insipide*) scene, damaging to our diplomatists, when on the morning of 31 July the German Ambassador caused real stupefaction at the Ministry for Foreign Affairs by bringing Neratov a specimen of the red notices already adorning all the streets.[1]

They evidently had not expected the measure ordered the previous evening to become so quickly public. Neither did Paléologue, who, in the opinion of the present writer, cannot have been ignorant of this bright idea of secrecy and sent his Military Attachés to G.H.Q. to find out how it was that the secret had not been kept. (This assumes that he told the contributor to *Vu* the truth and that he hastened to telegraph the news of general mobilization to Paris as soon as he learnt, perhaps by telephoning to the Russian Ministry for Foreign Affairs, that it was known to the German Ambassador.) For him it was an awkward business because, to keep Paris from raising objections, he had fobbed it off with the story that only 'the first measures of general mobilization' had been ordered secretly. The only thing he could do now was baldly to

---

[1] Taube, French Edition, p. 366.

telegraph that general mobilization had been ordered, saying nothing about when. If by sending the telegram via Scandinavia it would be likely to arrive late, so much the better.

The intimacy and identity of views between the two men and the close alliance between France and Russia make it impossible for Sazonov at such a moment to have deceived Paléologue, especially as there was a military agreement obliging the Russian General Staff not to mobilize without previously concerting with the French. Just as on the evening of the 29th Sazonov had sent Basili to the French Embassy at once with the news of the revocation of general mobilization, so on the 30th he immediately told Paléologue all about the audience with the Tsar. And just as Paléologue, on the previous evening, had telegraphed to his Government that St. Petersburg had decided secretly to begin general mobilization, so on the 30th he repeated that it had been decided 'to proceed secretly to the first measures of general mobilization', not straight out 'to general mobilization'. It is not at all inconceivable that Sazonov was aware of how Paléologue was acting. Isaac remarks that 'between the make-believe deceiver (Sazonov) and the make-believe dupe (Paléologue) the understanding would seem to have been perfect'.[1] Isaac is not mistaken. If there is not direct proof that Sazonov was aware of the manner in which Paléologue performed his duty, there is an indirect piece of evidence in the circumstance that Sazonov did not inform Izvolsky of the fact that general mobilization was ordered on the 30th.

On 31 July Izvolsky telegraphed from Paris that he did not believe the news given in a telegram from the Havas agency and told Bertie that he 'was not aware of any general mobilization of the Russian forces'.[2] Sazonov would never have kept Izvolsky in the dark, had he not known that Paléologue was keeping the Quai d'Orsay in the dark too. On the other hand he could never have kept Paléologue in ignorance, because it would have been too risky for Russia to deceive France by keeping the matter secret from France's representative at St. Petersburg.

However this may be, Paléologue, by those belated, misleading and disingenuous telegrams, created the illusion in Paris of which Poincaré speaks when, with reference to the telegram of the 30th, he writes: 'We had at least all grounds for hoping that official and public mobilization was not near'.[3] Had Paléologue done his duty, Paris would have known already on the 29th that 'official and public mobilization' in Russia was imminent. As he was told of everything that was going on at St. Petersburg, Paléologue must be presumed to have been told immediately that on the morning of the 29th the Tsar had signed the *ukaze* for

---

[1] Isaac, p. 212.   [2] *Int. Bez.* i. V, 354; BD. XI, 357.
[3] See p. 607; Poincaré, IV, p. 404.

general mobilization, just as we know he was told of the assurances given by Janushkevich to Eggeling on orders from the Tsar at the moment of signing the *ukaze*. It remains to be seen whether the French Government would have put up resistance if it had known in time of Russia's intention to mobilize. Its behaviour on the evening of the 31st to which we shall come later, justifies the doubt. But that does not mean it was not entitled to be accurately and immediately informed of all that St. Petersburg did and proposed to do. And the fact is that it was not so informed.

This long excursus on one of the most complicated, obscure and debated points in the history of those days, the attitude of France to the Russian general mobilization, leads to the conclusion that the two leaders, Poincaré and Viviani, during their return voyage, lasting from 23 to 29 July, i.e. the decisive days of the crisis, were not in a position to exercise an effective influence to restrain Russia from rash actions. Bienvenu-Martin, who acted for Viviani at the Quai d'Orsay, was in-experienced, lacking in authority and not capable of guiding French policy and so let the situation drift. This left the French Ambassador in St. Petersburg as the sole exponent of his country's views. Far from restraining Sazonov, Paléologue urged him to extremes by repeated promises of unconditional French support. Not only did he put up no opposition to Sazonov's proposals to mobilize, he also concealed them from the Quai d'Orsay, sending untrue or incomplete information to Paris, observing complete silence or sending belated telegrams about the Russian Government's decisions. It is not possible to decide with certainty whether, in so doing, he was acting on his own initiative or obeying, to good or ill effect, instructions given him by Poincaré. All that one can be sure of is that after the return of Poincaré and Viviani on the 29th, Viviani, with Poincaré's approval, acted correctly if with-out sufficient vigour. But his instructions came too late, and even if, like those of the 27th from the *France*, they had come in time, they would not have been heeded by Paléologue, whose responsibility cannot be overstressed.[1]

These conclusions stand quite apart from the question whether in such a set of circumstances France could have abandoned Russia without destroying the alliance, which she could certainly not have done. But she was in a position to have exercised friendly restraint and

[1] These conclusions coincide completely with those reached by Isaac who writes: 'The absence from France of the heads of the Government between 23 and 29 July is suffi-cient to explain the importance of the personal part played by the Ambassador, Paléologue, at St. Petersburg, but not to justify it. In what measure did the attitude taken by the Am-bassador owe its origin to the Franco-Russian agreement and conversations of 20–23 July? The relationship is obvious, its interpretation problematic. One can perceive intermittently, and particularly on the 28th, a divergence between the French Government's line and that followed by its Ambassador. This divergence reaches its maximum in the decisive days of 29 and 30 July' (Isaac, p. 213).

proffered counsels of prudence which might have averted the catastrophe. What the French representative at St. Petersburg did was, on the contrary, to fan the flames and thus expose his own country to the most serious risk, in view of the fact that, not only the neutrality of Italy, but also the intervention of England, as we shall see, appeared anything but a foregone conclusion.

8. *French covering troops take up positions; the 'ten kilometre withdrawal'.*

The news reaching Paris from Berlin on the 30th was not such as to leave much room for hope. Poincaré gives a full list of items.[1] At 2.30 p.m. Jules Cambon reported the rumour that German mobilization was to be ordered on the following day adding that the Wilhelmstrasse would neither confirm nor deny this, though telling newspaper correspondents that important decisions had been taken; feeling was deeply stirred.[2] At 3.30 p.m. came another telegram from him telling that Jagow had telephoned him to say that the news of mobilization published by the *Berliner Lokal-Anzeiger* was untrue and asking him to inform Paris of this as a matter of urgency.[3] At 4.52 p.m. Cambon reported that a colleague had been told at 2 p.m. by Zimmermann that the military were insisting on mobilization which the General Staff 'sees' to be war, but that up to then their demand had been resisted. However—he added—there must be no 'mobilization measures published in France' except after Germany had beyond doubt decided on mobilization, in order not to antagonize English public opinion. 'It is evident'—he adds—'that they are trying to get us to be the first to publish our mobilization.'[4]

Jules Cambon thus showed himself less concerned with the mobilization than with its being made known, he, too, perhaps holding the mistaken view that mobilization could go forward without publicity. To clear the matter up he called on Jagow, who inveighed against the *Lokal-Anzeiger* but failed to convince Cambon that mobilization was not imminent. Cambon asked Jagow what had been his reply to Grey's suggestion that Jagow himself should draft the formula for the intervention of the disinterested Powers.[5] Jagow answered that to save time he had asked Austria on what basis she would agree to discussions. He then went on to speak of Russian (partial) mobilization, saying that it endangered the success of any intervention. Cambon pointed out that Jagow himself had stated that Germany would not feel obliged to mobilize if Russia did not mobilize on the German frontier (i.e. undertook only partial mobilization). Jagow replied that this was true but that the army chiefs were insisting that no time must be lost. Cambon

---

[1] Poincaré, IV, pp. 418–23. [2] DF. 3. XI, 322. [3] DF. 3. XI, 330.
[4] DF. 3. XI, 339. [5] See pp. 501, 511.

ends: 'I took away from this conversation the impression that the chances of peace had again diminished.'[1]

While all this news poured in to the Quai d'Orsay, the Minister for War was receiving information of German train and troop movements towards the frontier. Could the French Government—asks Poincaré after depicting these developments—remain with eyes shut and folded arms? France must take her precautions. In actual fact she had taken her precautions on the morning of the 30th before the arrival of this last telegram from J. Cambon. If Moltke was exercising pressure in Berlin, Joffre, conscious of his responsibility, was doing the same in Paris and both of them, Joffre even more than Moltke, were overestimating the enemy's preparations. Already on the evening of the 29th Joffre asked Messimy's authorization for the French covering forces to take up position and Messimy brought up the question at the forenoon meeting of the Cabinet on the 30th. Poincaré relates that the Cabinet

is unanimous in the resolve not to shrink from the necessary precautions, but is apprehensive that our initiative may be held up against us by the German Empire in England and Italy and that, in spite of the evidence to the contrary, we should be made to appear in the rôle of the aggressors.

As a way of reconciling the exigencies of defence with the requirements of diplomacy, authorization was given for the covering troops to take up positions, but on condition that no train transport was used, no reservists called up, no horses and vehicles requisitioned, though they might be bought in the open market, and—last but not least—the covering troops were to approach not closer than ten kilometres to the frontier in order to avoid contact between German and French patrols.[2]

This famous *ten kilometre withdrawal* had Joffre's consent with the proviso, accepted by the Government, that its application should not be too rigid and that at some points cover should be posted nearer to the frontier. The order was issued at 4.55 p.m. on the 30th.[3] Both Messimy and Viviani claim the honour of having initiated the proposal for the *ten kilometre withdrawal*. Poincaré's own account states that having weighed the pros and cons with the two Ministers and with Joffre, he gave the measure his assent. Viviani writes:

To be sure the risk was terrible, yet I took it. . . . I put the proposal to the Cabinet, taking the heaviest responsibility in history upon my shoulders,

---

[1] DF. 3. XI, 380. This telegram figures with alterations as No. 109 in the *Yellow Book* (CDD., pp. 216–17). No mention is made of Jagow's denial of the news given in the *Lokal-Anzeiger*. Instead of the passage: 'He (Jagow) was astonished that, after signing, the Tsar telegraphed to Kaiser Wilhelm to ask for his mediation,' the *Yellow Book* version substitutes: 'He added that he feared that Austria would mobilize completely as a result of a partial Russian mobilization, and this might cause as a counter-measure, complete Russian mobilization and consequently that of Germany.'

[2] Joffre, I, pp. 122–3.

[3] Poincaré, IV, pp. 423–4; Recouly, pp. 74–6; Joffre, I, p. 123.

upon France. . . . I and my colleagues, whose courage has a claim to public homage from me, were haunted by the fear of seeing war spring out of a clump of trees where two patrols had an encounter, from a hasty word, a threatening gesture.[1]

This is quite true. But it is equally true that the *ten kilometre withdrawal* was prompted less by the fear that a chance clash of patrols might, unsought, bring on the calamity of war, than by the desire to make a gesture which would favourably influence English public opinion. Viviani himself confesses this in the opening paragraph of the following telegram, sent immediately after the Cabinet meeting by Abel Ferry to Paul Cambon in London:

Please inform Sir E. Grey of the following facts concerning French and German military preparations. England will see from this that, if France is resolute, it is not she who is taking aggressive steps. You will direct the attention of Sir E. Grey to the decision taken by the Council of Ministers this morning; although Germany has made her covering dispositions a few hundred metres from the frontier along the whole front from Luxemburg to the Vosges and has transported her covering troops to their war positions, we have not done so, although our plan, conceived in a spirit of the offensive, provides for the war positions of our covering troops to be as close to the frontier as are those of the German troops. We thus leave a strip of our national territory undefended against sudden aggression. In so doing we have *no other reason* than to prove to British public opinion and the British Government that France, like Russia, will not fire the first shot.[2]

These words, which are followed by details of the steps already taken by Germany, in contrast with the more limited measures taken by France, indicate the true reason for the *ten kilometre withdrawal*. The order for this, given by Messimy to the officers in command of the five covering corps at 4.55 p.m. on 30 July, ordered their commanding officers:

The troops carrying out *couverture* movement . . . will take up their appointed stations without delay in case of sudden attack. However for diplomatic reasons it is essential that no incident shall arise by our action. Consequently no element and no patrol shall on any pretext approach the frontier or pass the line.

The order was repeated by Messimy on 1 August 'in view of assuring the collaboration of our English neighbours'.[3]

---

[1] R. Viviani, *Réponse au Kaiser* (Paris, 1923), pp. 179–80.

[2] DF. 3. XI, 316; BD. XI, 319.—This document, too, has suffered manipulation at the hands of the compilers of the *Yellow Book*. Viviani's two picturesque last sentences appear as: 'By leaving a strip of territory undefended against sudden aggression of the enemy, the Government of the Republic hopes to prove that France does not bear, any more than Russia, the responsibility for the attack.' And Poincaré reproduces this revised version (LJF. 106, in CDD., pp. 214–15; Poincaré, IV, pp. 424–5).

[3] *Les Armées Françaises dans la Grande Guerre*. (Ministère de la Guerre, Paris, 1932. Annexes Nos. 15 and 25, pp. 56, 66.)

Here is visible the overriding anxiety which governed the conduct of the French leaders all through these days. It would never have let them agree lightheartedly to Russia's being the first to mobilize, had they only been informed in time. Grey, it is true, had, as has already been said, told Paul Cambon in advance of the somewhat threatening language he was to hold to Lichnowsky in the afternoon of the 29th and which so startled Berlin. As Grey himself wrote to Bertie:

I told him that I meant to tell the German Ambassador to-day that he must not be misled by the friendly tone of our conversations into any sense of false security that we should stand aside if all the efforts to preserve peace which we were now making in common with Germany failed.[1]

The purpose of this advance announcement was not to feed French hopes but to affirm the full freedom of England to decide her own action. And in fact Cambon conveyed it to Paris in a way which created an anything but favourable impression. His telegram did not give the substance of what Grey was proposing to tell Lichnowsky, nor did it say that the whole idea originated with Grey. What he reported was:

My German colleague having asked Sir E. Grey what the intentions of the British Government in case of conflict were, the Secretary of State for Foreign Affairs replied that he had nothing to state for the present.[2]

This was so far from what Grey really said that one wonders whether Paul Cambon had misunderstood or whether he did not intentionally tone down the reassuring but not decisive news to prevent the Quai d'Orsay from acting rashly.

Meanwhile his brother Jules from Berlin was pressing for a definite pronouncement from London. At 2.05 p.m. on the 30th he telegraphed that he had drawn the attention of the British Ambassador Goschen to the danger of the impression prevailing in Germany that England would remain neutral. Goschen had replied that an open declaration of British support would encourage Russia to be unyielding. Jules Cambon had answered that no public declaration was necessary. All that was needful was a private word from Grey to Lichnowsky or from Goschen to Jagow.[3] Poincaré, of course, took the same view as Jules Cambon. When, on the evening of 30 July, Bertie called on him to convey Grey's congratulations on the success of his St. Petersburg visit, Poincaré brought up the subject. Bertie's report runs:

He is convinced that preservation of peace between Powers is in hands of England, for if His Majesty's Government announce that, in the event of conflict between Germany and France, resulting from present differences

[1] BD. XI, 283. See p. 516.
[2] DF. 3. XI, 281; Poincaré IV, pp. 376–7. In the *Yellow Book* part of this telegram is given under No. 98; in CDD., p. 209.
[3] DF. 3. XI, 326; Poincaré, IV, pp. 415–16.

between Austria and Servia, England would come to aid of France, there would be no war, for Germany would at once modify her attitude.[1]

This was indeed true, but only on condition that Russian partial mobilization (the general mobilization was not known of until the 31st) did not precipitate matters at Vienna and Berlin, as it actually did on 30 July.

According to Poincaré's account Bertie replied: 'I personally agree with you'. But the *British Documents* show that, remaining faithful to his previous attitude, Bertie wrote to Grey:

The French, instead of putting pressure on the Russian Government to moderate their zeal, expect us to give the Germans to understand that we mean fighting if war break out. If we gave an assurance of armed assistance to France and Russia now, Russia would become more exacting and France would follow in her wake.[2]

This was a danger, it is true. But far greater was the danger of letting Berlin think that England would remain neutral. Then the Central Powers would refuse all compromise and war would become inevitable. Bertie has no perception of this:

I told M. Poincaré that it would be very difficult for His Majesty's Government to make such an announcement, for the majority of the House of Commons would probably not appreciate the necessity for making it. Poincaré pointed out that then 'there would be general war on the continent in which England would inevitably be involved. . . . By a declaration now of her intention to support France . . . a war would almost certainly be prevented, for Germany, though she might be ready to fight France as well as Russia, would not run the risk of having her seaborne trade destroyed, and of being starved by the British fleet. . . . Even if it did not prevent it [war], British aid to France at the outbreak of hostilities would assist in the maintenance of the balance of power in Europe. Aid given later might be too late, and if England remained neutral and Germany became omnipotent on the Continent, the position of England would be entirely altered to her detriment as a Great Power.'[3]

Poincaré writes that these unexceptionable opinions were shared by many English Conservatives. Bonar Law said to him and to the United States Ambassador to London, Walter Page, that in July 1914 he too had expressed the same views to Liberal Ministers. He added: 'If the English Government had decided to take sides earlier, the war would undoubtedly have been averted.'[4] Now Grey, on the afternoon of the 29th, had gone so far as, if not to take sides, at least to open Germany's eyes to her mistake in taking English neutrality for granted. But he had acted too late. Austria had already declared war on Serbia. This,

---

[1] BD. XI, 318.
[2] BD. XI, 320.
[3] BD. XI, 320, 373; Poincaré, IV, pp. 416–17.
[4] Poincaré, IV, pp. 418.

the bombardment of Belgrade, and Vienna's refusal of discussions with St. Petersburg had led to Russian mobilization, which in its turn brought about the failure of the peace proposals to which Grey applied his efforts on 30 and 31 July.

9. Grey's indignant rejection of the German request for neutrality; his own counter-proposal.

The request for neutrality, made on the evening of the 29th by Bethmann to Goschen, reached London at 9 a.m. on the 30th and convinced Grey that Germany was now thinking more of war than of peace.

The Imperial Government was ready to give every assurance to the British Government, provided that Great Britain remained neutral, that, in the event of a victorious war, Germany aimed at no territorial acquisitions at the expense of France. . . . His Excellency said that it would not be possible for him to give such an assurance as regards colonies. . . . As regards Belgium, his Excellency could not tell to what operations Germany might be forced by the action of France.[1]

Grey tells us:

I read it through with a feeling of despair. . . . The proposal made to us meant everlasting dishonour if we accepted it. . . . I had contemplated resignation if war came and we declined to stand by France, and I had therefore thought nothing as to making conditions for our neutrality. This bid from Bethmann Hollweg was like a searchlight lighting up an aspect of the situation which had not been looked at yet. I saw how difficult the situation would be even for those who were most resolved to keep out of war, if it came. If their policy carried the day, they would be expected to turn British neutrality to account, to ensure that the conditions for it were such that the British position was not jeopardized by the war. What stipulations could they make? If it was dishonouring and impossible to accept the price and the conditions here offered, what other price or conditions could they require in British interests that were not dishonouring to Britain? The answer was clear—there were none. If it were decided to remain neutral, we must, after this bribe offered by Bethmann Hollweg, remain neutral without conditions. There was further matter for depression in this telegram. Did Bethmann Hollweg not understand, could he not see, that he was making an offer that would dishonour us if we agreed to it? What sort of man was it who could not see that? Or did he think so badly of us that he thought we should not see it? Every thought the telegram suggested pointed to despair. But while there is still time one does not sit down under despair, only the effort to lift it must be big and the appeal must be big.[2]

Grey—like Salandra (to use a phrase of Salandra's far nobler than that of 'sacro egoismo')—was moved by the conviction that 'neutrality by negotiation would be neutrality with dishonour'. These words of

[1] BD. XI, 293. See pp. 506-7.   [2] Grey, I, pp. 326-7.

his are of a simplicity, a warmth and a moral grandeur worthy both of the man and of his office. How he felt on reading Goschen's telegram is shown in the reply which he at once sat down and penned:

You must inform German Chancellor that his proposal that we should bind ourselves to neutrality on such terms cannot for a moment be entertained. He asks us in effect to engage to stand by while French colonies are taken and France is beaten so long as Germany does not take French territory as distinct from the colonies. From the material point of view such a proposal is unacceptable, for France would be so crushed as to lose her position as a Great Power, and become subordinate to German policy without further territory in Europe being taken from her. But apart from that, for us to make this bargain with Germany at the expense of France would be a disgrace from which the good name of this country would never recover. The Chancellor also in effect asks us to bargain away whatever obligation or interest we have as regards the neutrality of Belgium. We could not entertain that bargain either. Having said so much, it is unnecessary to examine whether prospect of a future general neutrality agreement between Germany and England would offer positive advantages sufficient to compensate us for tying our hands now. My answer must be that we must preserve our full freedom to act as circumstances may seem to us to require in any development of the present crisis, so unfavourable and regrettable, as the Chancellor contemplates.

You should add most earnestly that the one way of maintaining the good relations between England and Germany is to continue to work together to preserve the peace of Europe; if we succeed in this object, the mutual relations of Germany and England will, I believe, be *ipso facto* improved and strengthened. For that object His Majesty's Government will work in that way with all sincerity and goodwill.

And if the peace of Europe can be preserved, and this crisis be safely passed, my own endeavour would be to promote some arrangement to which Germany could be a party, by which she could be assured that no hostile or aggressive policy would be pursued against her or her allies by France, Russia and ourselves, jointly or separately. I have desired this and worked for it, as far as I could, through the last Balkan crisis, and, Germany having a corresponding object, our relations sensibly improved. The idea has hitherto been too Utopian to form the subject of definite proposals, but if this present crisis, so much more acute than any that Europe has had for generations, be safely passed, I am hopeful that the reaction and relief that will follow may make some more definite *rapprochement* between the Powers possible than was possible before.[1]

The indignation roused by the German offer seems to have caused Grey to find his true voice. Bernadotte Schmitt well remarks: 'He concluded on a note which was new in European diplomacy and finally triumphed in the Treaties of Locarno eleven years later.'[2] It was the idea of collective security, put forward to take the place of the balance of power which had wrought such havoc in Europe. But to put it into

[1] BD. XI, 303.   [2] Schmitt, II, pp. 259-60.

execution, the first thing to do was to save the peace in the present emergency. How was this to be done? To Mensdorff whom Grey saw on the evening of the 30th and who asked him to calm down St. Petersburg he said that, to make any effect there, he could not come with empty hands. Mensdorff went away with the impression that if Austria engaged not to go further than occupying Belgrade and part of Serbia, provided the Serbs met the Austrian demands, with perhaps a guarantee from the Powers that there would be no defaulting, this might, in Grey's opinion, be a way out of the deadlock.[1]

But this was not at all what Grey meant. His idea of the *Halt in Belgrade* was not the prostrate submission of Serbia. It presupposed the mediation of the Powers between Austria and Russia, with Russia demanding that the Austrian demands should be softened.[2] This is how Berlin understood him, as is shown by Bethmann's telegram of 2.55 a.m. on the 30th: 'Please thank Sir E. Grey for his frank statement and tell him that we continue to mediate at Vienna and urgently advise the acceptance of his proposals.'[3] Lichnowsky at once sent the message by letter to Grey on the morning of the 30th,[4] while at the same time Jagow repeated it to Goschen, adding, however, that there had been no reply from Vienna.

He fears Russian mobilization against Austria will have increased difficulties, as Austria-Hungary, who has as yet only mobilized against Servia, will probably find it necessary also against Russia. Secretary of State for Foreign Affairs says if you can succeed in getting Russia to agree to above basis . . . and in persuading her in the meantime to take no steps which might be regarded as an act of aggression against Austria, he still sees some chance that European peace may be preserved. He begged me to impress on you difficulty of position to Germany in view of Russian [partial] mobilization and military measures which he hears are being taken in France. Beyond recall of officers on leave . . . Imperial Government had done nothing special in way of military preparations. Something (i.e. mobilization) would have soon to be done. . . . His Excellency added that telegram received from Prince Lichnowsky last night contains matter which he had heard with regret, but not exactly with surprise, and at all events he thoroughly appreciated frankness and loyalty with which you had spoken. He also told me that . . . had it been received earlier Chancellor would, of course, not have spoken to me in the way he had done.[5]

Goschen's telegram had not yet reached London when already Lichnowsky was calling on Grey with a similar message. At 11.30 a.m. on the 30th Bethmann had telegraphed him:

My hopes of mediation still being possible on the basis of Grey's proposals are seriously shaken by Russian mobilization against Austria and French war

---

[1] Oe-U. VIII, 11064. [2] BD. XI, 285; DD. II, 368. See pp. 512–3, 521–2.
[3] DD. II, 393. See p. 525. [4] DD. II, 418. [5] BD. XI, 305.

preparations. Austria will hardly be able to refrain from answering Russian mobilization with corresponding measures. Our position becomes extremely critical on this account and particularly on account of French arming. A demand from ourselves to France for a cessation of preparations could scarcely be made except in the form of an ultimatum. This could only be avoided if Grey manages to persuade France to drop her preparations at once. Grey would also have to put forth his strength to impose acceptance of terms of his proposal on Russia, and stop Russian deployment against Austrian frontier.[1]

Grey assured Lichnowsky

that the French were using their whole influence at St. Petersburg in the cause of peace. According to his information nothing more had been undertaken than the recall of men on leave on the German frontier. Real war preparations such as the calling up of reservists had not taken place. He is going to have a talk with Cambon this afternoon and has given me another appointment to let me know the result. In regard to Russian armaments he will to-day endeavour to act in the sense desired through Count Benckendorff. The Minister confidently hopes that Your Excellency's mediatory efforts will be successful in bringing about an understanding.[2]

Meanwhile the telegram from Buchanan arrived summarizing the conversation he and Paléologue had had with Sazonov on that morning of the 30th and giving the peace formula drafted by Sazonov for Pourtalès, which the Foreign Office had also received from Benckendorff.[3] Thus the news both from Berlin and from St. Petersburg seemed to give a ray of hope if France and Russia could be prevailed upon to suspend their military preparations. To ask Russia to do so after having in the preceding days regarded Russian mobilization as an obvious course was for Grey to beat a retreat. But no such consideration held him back and at 7.35 p.m. on the 30th he telegraphed to Buchanan:

German Ambassador informs me that German Government would endeavour to influence Austria, after taking Belgrade and Servian territory in region of frontier, to promise not to advance further, while Powers endeavoured to arrange that Servia should give satisfaction sufficient to pacify Austria. . . . If Austria, having occupied Belgrade and neighbouring Servian territory, declares herself ready, in the interest of European peace, to cease her advance and to discuss how a complete settlement can be arrived at, I hope that Russia would also consent to discussion and suspension of further military preparations, provided that other Powers did the same.
It is a slender chance of preserving peace, but the only one I can suggest.[4]

Thus Grey linked the *Halt in Belgrade* with the suspension of Russian military preparations. But when his telegram left London, general mobilization had already been decreed in Russia. The admonitions

[1] DD. II, 409.   [2] DD. II, 435.
[3] BD. XI, 302. See also pp. 567 and 612.   [4] BD. XI, 309.

from Paris and London came too late. Grey did not know this and sent a copy of the telegram to Bertie so that Paris might associate itself with the move. He also read it to Lichnowsky whom he saw again in the afternoon of the 30th, telling him that 'Cambon had answered him the French are doing nothing more than we are; only precautionary measures are being taken'. There are telegrams from Lichnowsky relating to this conversation with Grey. The first tells that the British fleet had proceeded northwards to Scottish bases. The 'strained relations' warning from the Foreign Office, which always preceded mobilization, had not yet been issued. 'So long as we do not mobilize the French will not do so, nor will England.'[1] The second says that Grey had given him a copy of his telegram to Buchanan which Lichnowsky communicates to Berlin adding: 'The Minister was perfectly calm and seemed not to have given up all hope.'[2]

This was also the impression Grey made on Paul Cambon, who reported it to Paris by a telegram sent off at 8.36 p.m. Only a garbled version of it figures in the *Yellow Book*,[3] and is summarized by Poincaré.[4] It was a very important talk that Paul Cambon had with Grey on the afternoon of the 29th. He had been instructed by Viviani to enlarge on the theme of the *ten kilometre withdrawal*. Poincaré tells us that Viviani had also telephoned him to find out as soon as possible what British intentions really were. So the wise and experienced Paul Cambon, who had been one of the builders of the *Entente*, decided to base the conversation on the exchange of letters between himself and Grey of 22 November 1912. In this exchange they had agreed

that if either Government had grave reason to expect an unprovoked attack by a third Power, or something that threatened the general peace, it should immediately discuss with the other whether both Governments should act together to prevent aggression and to preserve peace and if so, what measures they would be prepared to take in common.[5]

In an earlier conversation between the two men that same morning Grey had again 'repeated what he had told me yesterday of the indifference of English opinion towards Austro-Russian conflicts over the Slavs and had added that the moment had not yet come to consider the possibility of British intervention'. On receiving the telegram from Abel Ferry about the *ten kilometre withdrawal* Paul Cambon again sought out Grey and pointed out to him

that the matter was no longer confined to a struggle for influence between Austria-Hungary and Russia, that we were threatened with aggression and that from one day to another a general war might be unleashed; that it was therefore urgent to examine all the possibilities.

[1] DD. II, 438.   [2] DD. II, 439, 460.   [3] LJF. 108; CDD., p. 216.
[4] Poincaré, IV, pp. 428–9.   [5] Grey, I, pp. 97–8. See Vol. I, p. 405.

Did this French *démarche* find Grey unprepared? It is difficult to think so. He raised no objections and immediately replied that he would bring up the matter at the Cabinet meeting on the morrow (31 July) and would see Cambon again after it. He had—as has been said—not entirely lost hope of a peaceful issue, basing it, as Cambon reported to Paris, on the *Halt in Belgrade*. Cambon, however, who no doubt read Grey's letter to Buchanan, did not believe that Russia would agree.[1]

10. *Last English efforts to save peace.*

What happened at the Cabinet meeting of 31 July will be told in a later chapter.[2] Here attention will be confined to Grey's diplomatic efforts to prevent war in the last hours before the irrevocable happened, while he was endeavouring to bring about mediation after the Austrian occupation of Belgrade. It is still 30 July. Prince Henry of Prussia had telegraphed to King George V that he had conveyed to his brother Wilhelm the substance of their talk at Buckingham Palace.[3] The Kaiser had 'gratefully' received the message.

William . . . is trying his utmost to fulfil Nicky's appeal to him to work for the maintenance of peace and is in constant telegraphic communication with Nicky who to-day confirms news that military measures have been ordered by him equal to mobilization measures which have already been taken five days ago. We are further informed that France is making military preparations, whereas we have taken no measures, but may be forced to do so any moment, should our neighbours continue which then would mean a European war. If you really and earnestly wish to prevent this terrible disaster, may I suggest you [*sic*] using your influence on France and also Russia to keep neutral, which seems to me would be most useful. . . . I may add that now more than ever Germany and England should lend each other mutual help to prevent a terrible catastrophy [*sic*] which otherwise seems unavoidable. Believe me that William is most sincere in his endeavours to maintain peace, but that the military preparations of his two neighbours may at last force him to follow their example for the safety of his own country which otherwise would remain defenceless.[4]

In this appeal of Prince Henry is to be noted the renewed demand that France and Russia should remain 'neutral' in the Austro-Serbian

---

[1] DF. 3. XI, 363; BD. XI, 319; Poincaré, IV, pp. 428-9. This telegram of Cambon's figures in the *Yellow Book* as the second part of No. 108 (CDD., p. 216) in the following form : 'The information which Your Excellency has addressed to me on the subject of the military measures taken by Germany on the French frontier, gave me the opportunity of remarking to Sir E. Grey that it is no longer a question of a conflict of influence between Russia and Austria-Hungary, but that there is a risk of an act of aggression which might provoke general war. Sir E. Grey understood my feelings perfectly and he thinks, as I do, that the moment has come to consider and discuss together every hypothesis.' Grey said no such thing, and one wonders what is the idea of this pointless manipulation of documents, whose authentic text has an immediacy altogether lacking in the banalities substituted in its place.

[2] See Vol. III, Ch. VIII.   [3] See p. 497.   [4] DD. II, 417.

conflict, an impossibility for Russia and in any case outdated by the negotiations then in progress. At 8.54 p.m. King George's reply was sent off, obviously drafted or suggested by Grey:

So pleased to hear of William's efforts to concert with Nicky to maintain peace. Indeed I am earnestly desirous that such an irreparable disaster as a European war should be averted. My Government is doing its utmost suggesting to Russia and France to suspend further military preparations, if Austria will consent to be satisfied with occupation of Belgrade and neighbouring Serbian territory as a hostage for satisfactory settlement of her demands, other countries meanwhile suspending their war preparations. Trust William will use his great influence to induce Austria to accept this proposal thus proving that Germany and England are working together to prevent what would be an international catastrophe. Pray assure William I am doing and shall continue to do all that lies in my power to preserve peace of Europe.[1]

King George's reply reproduced almost textually the formula telegraphed shortly before to Buchanan by Grey, who placed all his hopes in it, refusing to regard war as inevitable and turning a deaf ear to the appeal from Poincaré contained in Bertie's telegram which he found on his table on the morning of the 31st accompanied by the following minute from Sir Eyre Crowe:

Sir E. Grey will no doubt approve Sir F. Bertie's language. What must weigh with His Majesty's Government is the consideration that they should not, by a declaration of unconditional solidarity with France and Russia, induce and determine these two Powers to choose the path of war. If and when, however, it is certain that France and Russia cannot avoid the war, and are going into it, my opinion, for what it is worth, is that British interests require us to take our place beside them as Allies, and in that case our intervention should be immediate and decided.[2]

Crowe rightly saw that war was inevitable and that the views of those who wanted no promises to be made to Paris and St Petersburg for fear of encouraging them to go to war were being overtaken by events. A point had been reached when words no longer counted and deeds were what mattered. This is what Crowe now conveys to Grey. It does not, however, do away with the fact that Grey, at an early stage, should not so much have made promises to France and Russia as threatened Germany with English intervention against her in the event of a general war.

Grey, however, remained unconvinced, and on the 31st seemed to be going into reverse even before the Cabinet met. Possibly he was annoyed and disquieted by Poincaré's statement to Bertie that 'peace between

---

[1] DD. II, 452. Neither of these two telegrams appears in the collection of *British Documents*.
[2] BD. XI, 318.

the Powers depends on England, that if she declares herself *solidaire* with France and Russia there will not be war'.[1] At any rate he telegraphed to Bertie at 7.30 p.m. on the 31st: 'I believe it to be quite untrue that our attitude has been decisive factor in situation. Germany does not expect our neutrality.'[2] He plainly resented being told that he could have saved the situation and was failing to do so. He must have been still more hurt by a telegram from Jules Cambon in Berlin which was passed to him by Paul Cambon during the Cabinet meeting and said that

it was the uncertainty with regard to whether we would intervene which was the encouraging element in Berlin, and that, if we would only declare definitely on the side of Russia and France, it would decide the German attitude in favour of peace.[3]

Grey in a telegram to Bertie tells how he rebutted this imputation when he saw Paul Cambon in the evening after the Cabinet meeting:

I said that it was quite wrong to suppose that we had left Germany under the impression that we would not intervene. I had refused overtures to promise that we should remain neutral. I had not only definitely declined to say that we would remain neutral; I had even gone so far this morning as to say to the German Ambassador that, if France and Germany became involved in war, we should be drawn into it. That, of course, was not the same thing as taking an engagement to France, and I told M. Cambon of it only to show that we had not left Germany under the impression that we would stand aside.[4]

There was truth in this but not the whole truth. It was true that on the 29th Grey had spoken plainly to Lichnowsky and that this had given Berlin a rude shock, only his warning had come four or five days too late. It was also true that he had, on the 30th, rejected the neutrality proposed by Bethmann to Goschen on the evening of the 29th. But it was not true that on the morning of the 31st he made the categoric statement to Lichnowsky which he later made to Paul Cambon. Had he done so, Lichnowsky would have passed it on to Berlin immediately, since he had always warned his Government that England would stand by France. What he did telegraph to the Wilhelmstrasse at 12.13 p.m. after his talk with Grey was the very opposite:

To-day for the first time I have the impression that the recent improvement in relations with Germany and perhaps also the friendly feelings for Germany in the Cabinet have opened up the possibility that, in a possible war, England might adopt a waiting attitude. To this end it would be of the greatest importance for us to be in the position, if war did come, to dissipate the suspicion here that we unconditionally support the Austrian standpoint

[1] BD. XI, 320.   [2] BD. XI, 352.   [3] Poincaré, IV, p. 440.   [4] BD. XI, 367.

by some tangible and not merely formal concession on the part of the Austrian Government brought about by our mediation.[1]

This makes it appear that far from declaring on the morning of the 31st that, if a Franco-German war broke out, England would intervene, Grey for the first time let Lichnowsky go away with the impression that England might assume a waiting attitude. It may be taken for granted that such was not his intention. But the fact remains that he not only led Lichnowsky to send that telegram but in the afternoon, as we shall see, spoke to Paul Cambon in a way which deeply distressed him. What can have been going on in Grey's mind to make him act in this way? As has often been emphasized already, it would be beside the mark to presuppose that the leading protagonists in this tragedy were steadfastly pursuing a single consistent line of policy throughout. They were men who may have had more or less decided aims and been governed by certain definite emotions. But they were also subject to doubts, uncertainties, changes of mind. These, again, led to a series of oscillations which, far from enabling a peaceful settlement to emerge, led to the worst solution of all.

The possibility cannot be ruled out that, besides being angered by the burden of responsibility thrust upon him by the French, Grey imagined he could evade their terrifying question by, after all, bringing about a settlement. At 9.30 p.m. on the 30th a telegram had come from Bunsen in Vienna summarizing a promising conversation which had taken place that afternoon between Berchtold and the Russian Ambassador Shebeko. Berchtold had said that, since Russia had mobilized against Austria, Austria must do the same, not as a threat, but simply as a precaution, but that he was not against the continuance of conversations between Sazonov and Szápáry.

On the whole, Russian Ambassador is not dissatisfied. He had begun to pack up his things . . . Russian Ambassador now hopes that something may yet be done to prevent war with Austria, but he hears from Berlin that German Secretary of State for Foreign Affairs was much annoyed by mobilization and threatened a German mobilization both on Russian and French frontiers.[2]

Bunsen's cheering news was confirmed, and the impression that Germany was opposing an Austro-Russian agreement dispelled, on the morning of 31 July by Lichnowsky who called with a telegram from Tschirschky which will be fully considered in the coming chapter.[3] It said that in response to the German request Berchtold had sent instructions to Szápáry to open conversations with Sazonov on the Austrian note to Servia and to reassure him on the question of Austrian mobilization. Berchtold was going to send for Shebeko and speak to him on the

[1] DD. III, 484.   [2] BD. XI, 311.   [3] See p. 680.

same lines (as Bunsen's telegram had said). Lichnowsky had instructions to add that Germany had taken the initiative in persuading Austria to open direct conversations. Tschirschky's telegram had revealed such a conciliatory spirit on the part of Vienna that it was to be hoped England was using her influence with St. Petersburg to produce a similar spirit and a suspension of military preparations.[1]

Vienna's conciliatory spirit was, as we shall see, an illusion. It was a feint put up between Tschirschky and Berchtold to evade the pressure from Berlin. But it served to produce the impression that there was immediate prospect of a real *détente* signalized by the resumption of Austro-Russian conversations. To this *détente* Grey was anxious to make his contribution and therefore launched into the statements to Lichnowsky which would produce a more kindly atmosphere in Berlin and from which, no doubt, Lichnowsky derived the impression that Britain might remain neutral. Lichnowsky's telegram, sent off from London at 12.15 p.m., summarized the conversation as follows:

The Minister said at first that Russia had become somewhat sensitive in the matter of war measures, since a suggestion from us on this point had been felt there as a threat. He will, however, endeavour to use his influence in this sense. In regard to Austro-Russian talks, he thought everything depended on Austria's making such a concession that Russia would be in the wrong if she rejected it, then he would be in a position to put pressure on Paris and St. Petersburg. . . . He would have to be in a position at need to motivate an attitude of reserve on the part of England by some tangible evidence of Russia's being in the wrong. He did not actually use this word but he let it clearly be understood that he could sponsor the idea of not immediately taking the part of France only if he were in a position to point to some tangible evidence of a conciliatory spirit. He repeatedly stressed that England was bound by no treaties. I surmise that he has in mind his original suggestion for the suspension of military operations in Serbia. . . . On my own part I should like to say that negotiations will have scant prospects if Count Berchtold were to confine himself to repeating previous statements and comments. . . . From my knowledge of Vienna I feel sure that only extremely strong pressure from Berlin will induce Vienna to make such a concession as would decisively influence the attitude of England in case war were to break out after all.[2]

Lichnowsky's perception was a true one. A point had been reached at which, had Russian partial mobilization (not the general mobilization of which Berlin and Vienna heard only on the 31st) not called the Austrian and German General Staffs on to the scene and led Bethmann on the evening of the 30th to desist from further pressure on Vienna, a way out of the crisis was almost in sight. But it happened each time during this crisis that any move which might have been effective in

<hr>

[1] DD. II, 444.   [2] DD. III, 489.

bringing about a peaceful solution either came too late or was not acted upon in good faith.

In this instance, too, Grey's statement to Lichnowsky came too late. His own account of it is contained in a telegram to Goschen, sent off at 2.45 p.m. on the 31st:

> I hope that the conversations which are now proceeding between Austria and Russia may lead to a satisfactory result. The stumbling block hitherto has been Austria's mistrust of Servian assurances, and Russian mistrust of Austrian intentions with regard to the independence and integrity of Servia. It has occurred to me that in the event of this mistrust preventing a solution being found by Vienna and St. Petersburg, Germany might sound Vienna, and I would undertake to sound St. Petersburg whether it would be possible for the four disinterested Powers to offer to Austria that they would undertake to see that she obtained full satisfaction of her demands on Servia, provided that they did not impair Serbian sovereignty and the integrity of Servian territory. . . . All Powers would of course suspend further military operations or preparations.[1]

This was a somewhat different proposal from the *Halt in Belgrade* on which Berlin and London had seemed to agree and which was now dropped. In truth, Austria had not begun military operations against Serbia and was not to do so until 12 August, so that if she now suspended preparations and operations she would find herself with empty hands and in a worse position than would be hers if she temporarily occupied Belgrade and the surrounding territory. Hence if the Berlin-London talks proposed by Grey were to be pursued, it would have to be not on the basis Grey now put forward, but ont hat of the *Halt in Belgrade*. Jagow, as will be shown in Vol. III,[2] late at night on the 31st feigned to welcome it, but only because Germany had already put the matter on a new basis by issuing an ultimatum to Russia. If, nevertheless, the talks could have gone on and if Berlin and London had reached an agreement, what would have happened next? Grey in this telegram to Goschen gives his own ideas on this point.

> I said to German Ambassador this morning that if Germany could get any reasonable proposal put forward which made it clear that Germany and Austria were still striving to preserve European peace, and that Russia and France would be unreasonable if they rejected it, I would support it at St. Petersburg and Paris and go the length of saying that if Russia and France would not accept it His Majesty's Government would have nothing more to do with the consequences; but otherwise, I told German Ambassador that if France became involved we should be drawn in.[3]

Even this text shows that Grey did not go so far as to use the words he told Paul Cambon he had used: 'I had even gone so far this morning

---

[1] BD. XI, 340.   [2] See Vol. III, Chap. I, § 11.   [3] BD. XI, 340.

as to say to the German Ambassador that, if France and Germany became involved in war, we should be drawn into it'.[1] What he did say was that if Germany put forward reasonable proposals and Russia and France rejected them, England would leave them to their fate. This was a very different thing. It must, moreover, be added that the threat in the sentence beginning 'but otherwise' did not appear in Lichnowsky's report, which thus lacks the clarity and directness of the *either—or* of Grey's account. But when all that has been said, it must be acknowledged that in placing English intervention on this basis Grey was acting in a manner which displayed both political wisdom and diplomatic skill. What is to be regretted is that he took this action only when the conflagration was on the point of breaking out and not six or seven days earlier. His telegram had probably not even been drafted when Berlin learnt the news of Russian general mobilization and the time for negotiations was gone for good. The pity is that his mind moved too slowly. In the days when these words of his would have been decisive he fumbled round, saying and advising everything but what was needed on the one hand to restrain Russia and France and on the other to make Germany and Austria see reason.

11. *The tragedy of Grey.*

Let there be no repetition, therefore, of the usual excuse that Grey was unable to act because of dissensions within the Cabinet. If he could talk to Lichnowsky on the 31st as he told Goschen he did, without consulting the Cabinet, still less Parliament, he could have done so much earlier. In his *Twenty-five Years* he tells that in the crisis of July 1914 he was convinced

that, if war came, the interest of Britain required that we should not stand aside, while France fought alone in the West, but must support her. I knew it to be very doubtful whether the Cabinet, Parliament, and the country would take this view on the outbreak of war, and through the whole of this week I had in view the probable contingency that we should not decide at the critical moment to support France. In that event I should have to resign; but the decision of the country could not be forced and the contingency might not arise and meanwhile I must go on.

His guiding principle was:

A clear view that no pledge must be given, no hope even held out to France and Russia which it was doubtful whether this country would fulfil. One danger I saw so hideous that it must be avoided and guarded against at every word. It was that France and Russia might face the ordeal of war with Germany relying upon our support; that this support might not be forthcoming, and that we might then, when it was too late, be held responsible by

[1] BD. XI, 367.

them for having let them in for a disastrous war. Of course I could resign if I gave them hopes which it turned out that the Cabinet and Parliament would not sanction. But what good would my resignation be to them in their ordeal? This was the vision of possible blood guilt that I saw, and I was resolved that I would have none of it on my head.[1]

It is the tragedy of Grey that he was to be held responsible for the rivers of blood shed in the Great War. The principles he puts forward were utterly useless. They implied abstention from all endeavour to influence the course of events. How could the country on which the eyes of both camps were anxiously fixed, the country whose weight, thrown into the scales on one side or the other, would decide the outcome of the crisis caused by the Austro-Serbian conflict, refrain from taking a definite line and leave Europe to drift on to the rocks? But the principles put forward by Grey explain why he acted as he did, why he disinterested himself in the fate of Serbia, why he said that if Russia accepted the localization of the conflict, Austria could have a free hand against Serbia, why he agreed to Russian mobilization while refusing to enter into any commitments, why he accepted the idea that both sides should mobilize and that peace negotiations could proceed after mobilization had been carried out, why he did not call Germany's bluff by plain speaking right from the beginning for fear that the Cabinet and Parliament might not approve, while Russia and France might be encouraged to go to war. This was the road that led straight to an outbreak in which, as Grey himself foresaw, England could not stand aside. And if the war, in his own words, 'would be a catastrophe for which previous wars afforded no precedent', to act as Grey did was to allow the catastrophe to happen.

Can his conduct be explained by respect for constitutional principles? Can it be conceived that the ship of state should be without the hand of the steersman in the fiercest storm, that a Foreign Minister should not act for the safety of his country as his conscience directed? Let him, so long as he remained in office, do as duty dictated. If Parliament and his colleagues failed to support him, let him then depart. He would be pledging his own word, not binding the other authorities of the State. This is so much the case that Grey himself, on 29 and 31 July, did not hesitate to speak his mind freely without waiting to consult the other authorities and this he did at a moment when the Cabinet was acutely divided. Hence if on the 31st he took the line he did, all the more easily could he have done so earlier. In acting thus on the 31st he showed how great had been his error of judgement during the preceding days. As one reads what he wrote and weighs what he said, including those words spoken to his subordinates at the Foreign Office which were not meant for French and German ears, the thought arises that his mistakes

[1] Grey, I, pp. 312–13.

may stem from the fact that the possibility—not to speak of the necessity—of English intervention had not yet really dawned on the Government or Parliament or the country.

There is a distinction to be made between holding an opinion and professing it publicly in order that by one's efforts it may triumph. Grey may well have felt, as he writes, that 'if war came, the interest of Britain required that we should not stand aside, while France fought alone in the West, but must support her' and that if the Cabinet, Parliament and the country did not 'take this view on the outbreak of war' he would have to resign. But it was his duty, when he felt convinced that England should not stand aside, to have the courage of this conviction and not, as he himself confesses, let his conduct be influenced by doubts 'whether the Cabinet, Parliament and the country would take this view on the outbreak of war'. True 'the decision of the country could not be forced'.[1] But the impression he gives is that he hesitated to shoulder the burden of the line of conduct he saw to be necessary. Let Parliament and the country take the responsibility as, indeed, they did with a stout-heartedness which seems to have taken Grey by surprise. He, meanwhile, for fear of forcing public opinion, did his best to save the peace, but made bad use of the powerful position he was in to stop war.

He made bad use of it in regard not only to Germany but also to France and Russia. After his talk with Lichnowsky he telegraphed to Buchanan:

I was asked to urge St. Petersburg to show good will in discussions and to suspend military preparations. . . . As to military preparations, I said to German Ambassador I did not see how Russia could be urged to suspend them unless Austria would put some limit to her advance into Servia.[2]

This was a very vague and perfunctory allusion to the things he had said to Lichnowsky. He had, as has been seen, engaged with Lichnowsky to leave Russia and France to their fate if Berlin, in concert with Vienna, made 'a reasonable proposal' and St. Petersburg and Paris rejected it. Why did he not say this to Sazonov and Viviani? Was it because he would have impaled himself on the other horn of the dilemma and have to promise support to France and Russia if Germany failed to make 'a reasonable proposal'? By acting as he did he made it impossible for himself to take timely steps to prevent Russia from stiffening her attitude and for France to exercise pressure on Russia in favour of moderation and prudence lest otherwise England would leave her to her fate.

One may go to the length of asserting that if on the afternoon of the 31st Grey had repeated to Paul Cambon what he said in the morning to

---

[1] Grey, I, pp. 312-13.   [2] BD. XI, 335.

Lichnowsky, he would have caused less dismay than by what he actually did say to him. In the account which he wrote to Bertie he begins, as we have seen, by the rebuttal:

> I said that it was quite wrong to suppose that we left Germany under the impression that we would not intervene. I had refused overtures to promise that we should remain neutral.

He then goes on:

> M. Cambon then asked me for my reply to what he had said yesterday. I said that we had come to the conclusion, in the Cabinet to-day, that we could not give any pledge at the present time. The commercial and financial situation was exceedingly serious; there was danger of a complete collapse that would involve us and everyone else in ruin; and it was possible that our standing aside might be the only means of preventing a complete collapse of European credit, in which we should be involved. This might be a paramount consideration in deciding our attitude.
>
> I went on to say to M. Cambon that though we should have to put our policy before Parliament, we could not pledge Parliament in advance. Up to the present moment, we did not feel, and public opinion did not feel, that any treaties or obligations of this country were involved. Further developments might alter this situation and cause the Government and Parliament to take the view that intervention was justified. The preservation of the neutrality of Belgium might be, I would not say a decisive, but an important factor, in determining our attitude. Whether we proposed to Parliament to intervene or not to intervene in a war, Parliament would wish to know how we stood with regard to the neutrality of Belgium, and it might be that I should ask both France and Germany whether each was prepared to undertake an engagement that she would not be the first to violate the neutrality of Belgium.
>
> M. Cambon expressed great disappointment at my reply. He repeated his question whether we would help France if Germany made an attack on her.
>
> I said that I could only adhere to the answer that, as far as things had gone at present, we could not take any engagement. The latest news was that Russia had ordered a complete mobilization of her fleet and army. This, it seemed to me, would precipitate a crisis, and would make it appear that German mobilization was being forced by Russia.
>
> M. Cambon urged that Germany had from the beginning rejected proposals that might have made for peace. It could not be to England's interest that France should be crushed by Germany. We should then be in a very diminished position with regard to Germany. In 1870, we had made a great mistake in allowing an enormous increase of German strength; and we should now be repeating the mistake. He asked me whether I could not submit his question to the Cabinet again.
>
> I said that the Cabinet would certainly be summoned as soon as there was some new development, but at the present moment the only answer I could give was that we could not undertake any definite engagement.[1]

[1] BD. XI, 367.

Cambon's 'great disappointment' is not surprising. Here was Grey refusing to give France any undertaking, putting the commercial and financial situation in the forefront, letting it seem doubtful whether even the violation of Belgian neutrality would bring about English intervention, making it appear that German mobilization was being forced by Russia and turning a deaf ear to every consideration and every appeal brought forward by Cambon. What would be the effect in Paris where uneasiness and anxiety were mounting from hour to hour? Not content with having telegraphed on the 30th announcing the *ten kilometre withdrawal*, Viviani sent a fresh telegram at 12.30 p.m. on the 31st telling Paul Cambon that German patrols had twice penetrated the strip of territory thus evacuated by French troops.

The populations thus left exposed to enemy attack protest; but the Government is determined to show English public opinion and the Government that the aggressor will in no case be France.

Viviani added that tens of thousands of German reservists were being called up [which was not true], while France had not called up a single one. This telegram was shown to the Foreign Office by Paul Cambon.[1] He also received a telegram from his brother, forwarded by Paris, sent off at 1.30 a.m. on the 31st and saying:

The attitude of the English Embassy at Berlin corresponds to the hesitations revealed in the language of Sir Ed. Grey. . . . This attitude is such as to entail the direst consequences, for here a hopeful view is taken of the struggle with France and Russia if they are alone. Only the eventuality of English intervention would be capable of moving the Kaiser, his Government and all interests.[2]

At 3.20 p.m. Viviani again telegraphed Paul Cambon announcing that William Martin, the *Directeur de Protocol* at the Quai d'Orsay, was arriving in London at 10.45 p.m. bringing a letter from the President

---

[1] DF. 3. XI, 390; BD. XI, 338.

[2] DF. 3. XI, 378; Poincaré, IV, pp. 434-5.—At the end of July 1914 Sir Edward Goschen wrote to Nicolson: 'My chief diplomatic difficulty has been to satisfy Cambon's curiosity as to my repeated visits to the Chancellor without giving the latter away on points which he has made me promise to keep secret. I have a stronger conviction than Cambon that both the Chancellor and Jagow would like to avoid a general war. . . . Cambon . . . considers, wrongly I think, Jagow to be a Junker of the most bellicose description. . . . As for the Chancellor, if he makes war it will be because he is forced into it. Jules Cambon is continually scolding me about England keeping her intentions so dark and says that the only way by which a general war can be prevented is by Sir E. Grey's stating *carrément* that England will fight on the side of France and Russia. But I tell him that a statement to that effect at the present stage, while it might cause Germany to hesitate, might equally urge Russia on' (BD XI, 677). These utterances make clear how little Goschen understood the situation. He was unable to see that, if Bethmann and Jagow did not want war, they were determined, even at the price of war, to win a diplomatic and political victory of the most far-reaching importance. But the level of intelligence among the British Ambassadors was not very high. Neither Goschen nor Bertie nor Bunsen were the equals in ability of the Cambon brothers, of Barrère or even of Paléologue.

of the Republic to the King. He asked that arrangements should be made to have the letter presented that same evening.[1]

Poincaré, indeed, was on thorns, shut off, as he was, at the Élysée, unable to find out at first hand what was going on or to take action himself.

I only receive brief summaries of diplomatic conversations. I have to let the responsible ministers have full freedom of action, otherwise I should be false to the spirit of the Constitution and expose the country to Government anarchy. This moral semi-paralysis has the inevitable effect of intensifying the strength of the emotions within me and I hold myself taut to hide them for fear of adding to the emotion of those with whom I am speaking.[2]

During the night Paris had received another telegram from Paul Cambon, sent off earlier than the one just quoted[3] but arriving later. Grey, it ran, had been repeating what he had said the previous day about the indifference of English public opinion towards Austro-Russian conflicts over the Slavs, and had added that the moment had not yet come to consider the possibility of British intervention.

It is noticeable that for several days powerful German influences are at work in press and Parliament emanating from the City which is peopled by financiers of German origin. Several members of the Cabinet are under these influences and it is possible that Mr. Asquith with his habit of temporizing does not dare for the moment to take a decided attitude. But personally he is in favour of intervention.

Poincaré felt so perturbed by this British 'insular serenity in the face of what was happening on the continent' that he proposed to the Council of Ministers that he should himself write a personal letter to King George V.[4]

Anxiety in Paris was intense and here was London refusing to promise support. But in his two telegrams of the 31st reporting Grey's unfavourable answer, Paul Cambon did not give way to despair. The first of them began with the statement:

The German Ambassador having this morning asked Sir E. Grey if England would observe neutrality in the conflict which seemed imminent, Sir E. Grey replied 'that England could not remain neutral in a general conflict and that if France was involved, England would also be drawn into it.

This, as we have seen, is not at all borne out by Lichnowsky's version of the conversation. The telegram then went on to summarize

---

[1] DF. 3. XI, 395; Poincaré, IV, p. 440.   [2] Poincaré, IV, pp. 432–3.
[3] DF. 3. XI, 363. See pp. 636–7.

[4] Poincaré, IV, pp. 432–7. Regarding this telegram of Paul Cambon's it must be noted that Fay is mistaken in saying that the conversation took place between Cambon and Nicolson. Not Nicolson but Grey was 'Secretary of State for Foreign Affairs' (Fay, II, p. 488).

in a few words the statements made by Grey of which we have seen his own version. The second telegram, which is a continuation of the first, tells:

I asked the Secretary of State for Foreign Affairs to give me a statement identical with the one he had just given Prince Lichnowsky. He replied that he could not give me a guarantee without the authorization of Parliament and that with the German Ambassador it was not a question of a guarantee, it was only that he had to dispel the illusions at Berlin on the attitude of England.[1]

This was not very comforting and if Cambon refrained from bitter comment, it may have been because, in a third telegram sent off much about the same time as the two others, he was able to send better news. What had happened was that on leaving Grey's office Cambon went and poured his anxieties into the ear of his friend, the Permanent Under Secretary, Arthur Nicolson, whose son, Harold Nicolson, thus describes the relations between the two men:

Nicolson had been on intimate terms with M. Paul Cambon for upwards of thirty years. This intimacy had been increased by four years of close co-operation in London, and by their common experiences during the Agadir crisis and the protracted crisis of the Balkan wars. Almost daily, during those four years, the French Ambassador had visited Nicolson at the Foreign Office. A small but distinguished figure, with startlingly white hair and beard, with prominent glaucous eyes, he would enter the room slowly, place his grey top hat upon its accustomed table, sink into his accustomed leather chair, and exclaim, as he drew off first one kid glove and then the other, 'Eh bien, mon cher, voici encore votre pain quotidien!' During those five dark days from 30 July to 3 August, Paul Cambon did not for one instant lose his imperturbability, his dignified precision or his outward calm. Nicolson felt ashamed, however, to meet the anguish in Paul Cambon's eyes.[2]

It is not impossible that in listening to Grey's statements that evening Cambon may have lost a little of his outward calm as he did the following day and that Nicolson, less than ever, ventured to meet his eye. In any case he telegraphed Paris that the Cabinet was to meet again on the morrow and that 'Grey who is a partisan of immediate intervention, will, I suppose, not fail to renew his proposals'. He added:

At this morning's meeting the question of Belgian neutrality was raised and telegrams have been sent during the day to the Ambassadors at Berlin and Paris telling them to ask the Governments to whom they are accredited for assurances in this matter.[3]

---

[1] DF. 3. XI, 445. [2] Nicolson, p. 417.

[3] DF. 3. XI, 445. These three telegrams bear the protocol numbers 167, 168, 168 *bis*. They left London respectively at 9.44 p.m., 8.42 p.m., 8.40 p.m. on 31 July, i.e. the third went off first and the first an hour after the second, thus going off last. It is not impossible that this was done on purpose to give the good news at the beginning, though it came later in point of time. In the *Yellow Book* the three with alterations are merged into one as No. 110 (CDD., pp. 217–18).

But if this was so—one asks—did Grey speak so discouragingly to Cambon merely as a measure of prudence right up to the last? Was he really 'a partisan of immediate intervention'? And did he at the Cabinet meeting on the 31st speak in favour of Cambon's request? No, not at all! At the Cabinet meeting, as we shall see, Grey is reported by Lord Morley to have

professed to stand by what he had told Cambon in his letter of 1912, that we were left perfectly free to decide whether we would assist France by armed force.[1]

Far from being a staunch supporter of immediate intervention, Grey showed himself still on 1 August a prey to such indecision that he put forward preposterous proposals which drove Cambon to despair. Hence if Nicolson gave his French friend reassuring news, it was probably to calm him down, being himself rightly convinced that England would inevitably be drawn in.

Indeed, a short time before, Schubert, Secretary of the German Embassy, had called at the Foreign Office and read out a telegram from the German Chancellor, dispatched from Berlin at 3.10 p.m., stating that Russia had proclaimed a general mobilization of her army and her fleet; that, in consequence of this, martial law (i.e. 'threatening danger of war') would be proclaimed by Germany; and that, if within the next twelve hours Russia did not withdraw her general mobilization proclamation, Germany would be obliged to mobilize in her own defence.[2] At what exact moment the communication was made to London is not known, but it may have been about 4.30 p.m., which is rendered possible by the fact that Central European time is one hour ahead of Greenwich time. In any case Asquith was able to tell the House about 5 p.m. that he had just heard from Berlin, not from St. Petersburg, that Russia had proclaimed general mobilization. War, therefore, was round the corner and would resolve the doubts and hesitations of Grey and his colleagues. This is probably what was in Nicolson's mind. And he was also in a position to tell Cambon of the telegrams which were going off to Paris and Berlin asking assurances from France and Germany that they would respect Belgian neutrality. Intervention, therefore, would come about on those grounds, not on a basis of support for France. But it would amount to the same thing in the end. And, in fact, that is how it did come about, but not before Grey had made vain and desperate attempts to find a way out for his country other than war.

---

[1] Morley, p. 10.   [2] BD. XI, 344; DD. III, 488.

CHAPTER XIV

THE AUSTRIAN GENERAL MOBILIZATION

(1) *Berlin appeals to Vienna for the* Halt in Belgrade; *Berchtold's tardy replies* (p. 651). (2) *Vienna learns on 29 July of Russian partial mobilization. Bethmann's third appeal to Vienna* (p. 655). (3) *Berchtold decides on general mobilization. Tschirschky's influence at Vienna; his evasive and misleading telegrams to his Government* (p. 658). (4) *Berchtold authorizes a feint resumption of conversations with St. Petersburg* (p. 661). (5) *Berlin's fourth solemn appeal to Vienna in the night of 30 July* (p. 664). (6) *Berchtold's doubts and uncertainties at an audience with Francis Joseph* (p. 669). (7) *Moltke overrides the Chancellor. The decree for Austrian general mobilization signed on 31 July and communicated by Francis Joseph to Wilhelm* (p. 673). (8) *Austrian mobilization announced to the Powers. Vienna's rejection of the German and English proposals* (p. 679). (9) *The resumption of direct conversations between Vienna and St. Petersburg; the quibble about Austrian territorial* désintéressement (p. 681).

1. *Berlin appeals to Vienna for the* Halt in Belgrade; *Berchtold's tardy replies.*

Having launched the declaration of war on Serbia and confronted the other Powers with the *fait accompli*, as advised by Berlin, Berchtold, as has been told above, had continued to act along lines which were the logical consequence of this premise. Serbia was being attacked with the object of 'destroying this nest of vipers'. It therefore followed that Berchtold could not but reject both the conversations with St. Petersburg, proposed by Shebeko on behalf of Sazonov on 28 July, and the Four Power mediation which Bunsen in Grey's name begged him to accept on the same day.[1] True the Chancellor on the evening of the 27th had telegraphed Tschirschky that he could not turn a deaf ear to Grey's appeal for Berlin to use its good offices in order that Vienna might regard the Serbian reply 'either as satisfactory or as a basis for negotiations'.[2] But in the first place Tschirschky, who was doing his utmost to prevent the crisis from finding a peaceful solution and enable Austria to carry out a thorough settlement of accounts with Serbia, carried out, or feigned to carry out the Chancellor's instructions of the 27th only on the afternoon of the 28th, when the declaration of war had been dispatched. In the second place Jagow, as has been described in detail, had been at pains to give the Austrian Ambassador at Berlin advance warning of this *démarche* and to tell him that it was

---

[1] See pp. 463–5.   [2] DD. I, 277. See pp. 443–4.

being made purely *pro forma*, as a means of avoiding anything 'that might disconnect the telegraph line between Germany and England which till now has been in such good working order' and that it was to be rejected by Vienna.[1] The result was that Berchtold told Tschirschky to thank Bethmann for the proposed English mediation, saying he would soon reply to it himself; for the moment he

observed that after the opening of hostilities on the part of Serbia and the declaration of war which has meanwhile taken place, he regarded the English *démarche* as coming too late.[2]

The 'opening of hostilities on the part of Serbia' was a lie and the declaration of war might have been held back if Tschirschky had lost no time in giving Bethmann's message the morning it arrived and if, instead of being a ruse, the message had been seriously meant and expressed with the necessary firmness. But, meant as it was, and communicated as it was, the message received on the 29th the reply promised on the 28th which was of course a refusal.

In regard to the utterances of the English Secretary of State to Prince Lichnowsky, the Royal and Imperial Government would in the first place point out that the Serbian reply by no means, as Sir E. Grey seems to assume, implies acceptance of all our demands with only one exception, that, on the contrary, reservations are made on most of the points, essentially diminishing the value of the concessions made. The rejection bears on the very points which contain some guarantee for the achievement of the purpose aimed at. The Royal and Imperial Government cannot conceal its surprise at the assumption that its action against Serbia could be thought to affect Russian influence in the Balkans, for this would presuppose that the propaganda directed against the Monarchy was not only of Serbian but also of Russian origin. . . . Moreover the Royal and Imperial Government regrets that it is no longer in a position to adopt an attitude towards the Serbian reply in the sense of the English suggestion, since, at the time of the German *démarche* here, the state of war had come into existence between the Monarchy and Serbia and the Serbian reply had been overtaken by events. The Royal and Imperial Government points out in this connexion that the Royal Serbian Government, before sending its reply, proceeded to the mobilization of its military forces and that it afterwards let three days pass without announcing its readiness to abandon the standpoint of its reply, whereupon the declaration of war on our part followed. If, however, the English Cabinet is prepared to use its influence with the Russian Government in the direction of preserving peace between the Great Powers and the localization of the war forced on us by long years of Serbian machinations, the Royal and Imperial Government could only welcome this.[3]

When this document was handed to Tschirschky late on the evening of the 29th (his telegram was sent off at 3 a.m. on the 30th) the fresh

---

[1] Oe-U. VIII, 10793. See pp. 445-6.   [2] DD. II, 313. See p. 465.
[3] Oe-U. VIII, 10941; DD. II, 400.

development had taken place that on the evening of the 28th, at the behest of Wilhelm, who regarded the Serbian reply as highly satisfactory and thought it removed all need for a war, Bethmann had telegraphed to Tschirschky the suggestion that Berchtold should renew the Austrian promise to St. Petersburg of territorial *désintéressement*, declaring that its military measures were 'aimed purely at a temporary occupation of Belgrade and other definite points on Serbian territory in order to compel the Serbian Government to integral fulfilment of Austrian demands'.[1] What impression can this proposal of the *Halt in Belgrade* have made on Tschirschky and Berchtold? Were they to take it seriously, or as just a new move in the diplomatic manoeuvring carried on by Berlin with regard to St. Petersburg and above all to London, the necessity for which had been explained to Szögyény, and which Vienna had been told to disregard? It will be remembered that Bethmann had carried out his Sovereign's instructions so unwillingly that, instead of sending them off in the early afternoon of the 28th, he had delayed them until 10.15 p.m., in order that his telegram should not go off until war was declared on Serbia and should be received the morning after.[2] While Vienna did not know this (unless Stumm or someone else from the Wilhelmstrasse telephoned it to Tschirschky), Bethmann's telegram enjoined on Tschirschky

carefully to avoid giving the impression that we wish to restrain Austria. It is merely a question of finding an arrangement to render possible the achievement of the aim pursued by Austria-Hungary of severing the vital nerve of Pan-Serb propaganda without at the same time bringing on a world war, and if this latter is not avoidable, to improve for us, as far as possible, the conditions in which it will be waged.[3]

Vienna could, therefore, hardly regard the *démarche* otherwise than as one more tactical move which the Ballplatz was at liberty if it chose to disregard.

Some doubts may have assailed both Tschirschky and Berchtold. The German Ambassador's immediate step should have been to hasten round to the Ballplatz the first thing in the morning with the telegram which had reached him at 4.30 a.m. When he did call, it has not been possible to ascertain. All that is known is that, late on the 29th, Bethmann had still not received a reply. And since, for reasons already discussed, Bethmann had during the day come round to the idea of the *Halt in Belgrade*, which he had not at first favoured, he telegraphed to Tschirschky twice *en clair* (at 10.18 p.m. and 10.30 p.m.) asking if his instructions had been carried out.[4] These telegrams were on the way when at 1.30 a.m. on the 30th Tschirschky's reply, which we already

---

[1] DD. II, 323. See pp. 476-7.
[2] See p. 471.
[3] DD. II, 323. See p. 478.
[4] DD. II, 377. See p. 504.

know, arrived in Berlin. Berchtold declared his readiness to renew his declaration of territorial *désintéressement* already made at St. Petersburg, but

as regards the further statement on military measures, Count Berchtold says he is not in a position to give me an immediate answer. Although I represented to him that the matter was urgent, I have this evening still not received further communication.[1]

Had Tschirschky really insisted that the matter was urgent? On 30 July Bunsen telegraphed confidentially to Grey:

Unfortunately German Ambassador is himself so identified with extreme anti-Servian and anti-Russian feeling prevalent in Vienna that he is not likely to plead the cause of peace with entire sincerity.[2]

Berchtold's memorandum, written immediately after the interview, shows that Tschirschky did not keep to himself, as he was meant to do, the instruction not to create the impression that Berlin wanted to restrain Austria, but told it to Berchtold. Berchtold notes: 'The suggestion of the . . . *démarche* with the St. Petersburg Cabinet is not, the Reichschancellor requests, to be understood as pressure from him on us, or as a wish on his part to restrain us from our action.'[3] What else was this than a hint from Tschirschky to reject it? Bethmann's instructions had stated further:

It is merely a question of finding an' arrangement to render possible the achievement of the aim pursued by Austria-Hungary of severing the vital nerve of Pan-Serb propaganda without at the same time bringing on a world war.[4]

But as they appear in Berchtold's memorandum they run: 'He was guided in this solely by the endeavour to achieve an improvement in the conditions under which we should have to wage a world war', a very different matter. Nor does Berchtold's memorandum contain a hint of insistence on the part of the German Ambassador on some kind of reply, let alone on a favourable one. All this makes it seem probable that Tschirschky on the 29th, as on the previous day, was in no hurry to carry out his instructions and was in league with Berchtold on the question of taking plenty of time and not giving an answer at once. By waiting, Berchtold would enable fresh developments to change the situation so that previous proposals would then be overtaken by events. For example: how would St. Petersburg react to the declaration of war of the previous day?

[1] DD. II, 388. See p. 526.　　　　[2] BD. XI, 307.
[3] Oe-U. VIII, 10939.　　　　[4] DD. II, 323. See p. 478.

2. Vienna learns on 29 July of Russian partial mobilization. Bethmann's third appeal to Vienna.

The Russian reaction became known to Tschirschky on the afternoon of the 29th. On the evening of the 28th Sazonov had telegraphed to the Russian Ambassadors that, in consequence of the Austrian declaration of war on Serbia, the four districts of Kiev, Moscow, Odessa and Kazan would mobilize on the following day.[1] On receiving this announcement the Russian Ambassador at Vienna thought it incumbent upon him to give the news to his colleagues, among them being Tschirschky who at 7.30 p.m. on the 29th reported it to Berlin, adding that his next caller had been Dumaine who came to talk the matter over.[2] Did Shebeko perhaps not dare personally to give the news to Berchtold? Did he give it to Tschirschky in order to test his reactions, well knowing that Tschirschky would at once pass it on to Berchtold and that Berchtold would take his cue from Tschirschky? Certainly it was from Tschirschky that the Ballplatz first heard of the Russian partial mobilization. At 1 a.m. on 30 July Berchtold telegraphed to Szögyény at Berlin:

As Herr von Tschirschky has just informed me, the Russian Ambassador tells him, he has had word from his Government that the military districts of Kiev, Odessa, Moscow and Kazan are being mobilized. . . . I beg you to bring the above at once to the notice of the German Government and emphasize that if the Russian mobilization is not suspended at once our general mobilization must ensue on military grounds. As a last attempt to avert the European war, I would regard it as desirable that our own and the German representative at St. Petersburg, perhaps also those in Paris, should receive immediate instructions to state in a friendly spirit to those Governments that the continuance of Russian mobilization would lead to counter-measures in Germany and Austria-Hungary, which would necessarily have serious consequences. Will Your Excellency add that we shall of course not allow ourselves to be deflected from our military action against Serbia. . . . We leave it to the German Government to decide whether Italy is to be informed of this step.[3]

This telegram shows that Berchtold did not decide on Austrian general mobilization on the afternoon of the 29th, though knowing that Russia was mobilizing against Austria. He only threatened it if Russia did not suspend hers. And he gave advance notice of this intention to Berlin, because he did not want to act without German approval. This point is further proved by a marginal note of Tschirschky's jotted down the following morning for his own use on a telegram from Bethmann. It runs:

Here the decision is to mobilize as soon as Berlin agrees to it, in the firm resolve not to tolerate any further Russian mobilization. It is proposed to

[1] *Int. Bez.* i. V, 168, 169. See pp. 540–1.   [2] DD. II, 386.   [3] Oe-U. VIII, 10937.

send instructions to St. Petersburg and, if need be, to Paris, saying that if mobilization continues, general mobilization will ensue here and in Germany.[1]

The proposal to send an intimation to France and Russia emanated from Conrad, whom Berchtold had consulted immediately on learning of Russian partial mobilization. It is, however, curious that in their discussion on the evening of the 29th Berchtold did not—as we gather from Conrad's diary—mention anything about the German suggestion of the *Halt in Belgrade*, so that Conrad only learnt of it the following day.[2] It can hardly be supposed that Berchtold, who had already talked with Tschirschky, was still ignorant of it. He immediately turned it down by implication in getting Szögyény to say to the Wilhelmstrasse: 'we shall, of course, not allow ourselves to be deflected from our military action against Serbia'.

The political and military reasons which led the Austrian Government to regard the occupation of Belgrade as not enough were set forth by Berchtold in a letter published in the *Kriegsschuldfrage* of July 1927:

As regards the political objections, it must be borne in mind that the question of a temporary occupation of Belgrade was linked with the English proposal for mediation *à quatre*, so that the occupation of Serbian territory was not to be for the purpose simply of securing the fulfilment of our still unsatisfied demands on Serbia, since of the four mediating Powers only one stood politically on our side. . . . Just as after our so-called 'diplomatic triumphs' of 1909 and 1913, any such manoeuvre, purely for the purpose of a demonstration, would, inasmuch as Serbia would have accommodated herself to it, have produced no other result than intensified bitterness together with renewed confidence in the ultimate success of the clearly outlined programme of destruction in regard to the Monarchy. These political repercussions would inevitably have followed if the action thus staged had proved successful. The military authorities were, however, very dubious even of their being successful and regarded the *coup de main*, as they termed it, as a risky venture for which, in view of the prevailing mood in Serbia, they could not take the responsibility. General (later Field Marshal) Baron Conrad von Hötzendorf, with whom I was in daily contact at that moment, expressed this opinion in no uncertain terms and expounded his views in an audience which he and I had of the Emperor.[3]

This reasoning was valid, but only up to a certain point. If Serbia had accepted all the demands of the ultimatum, Berchtold himself had

---

[1] *Beilagen zu den Stenographischen Berichten über die öffentlichen Verhandlungen des Untersuchungsausschusses. 1. Unterausschuss.* No. 1: '*Zur Vorgeschichte des Weltkrieges. Schriftliche Auskünfte deutscher Staatsmänner*' (Berlin, 1921), p. 98; Lutz, p. 220.

[2] Conrad, IV, p. 148.

[3] Hermann Lutz, *Das Entscheidende über den 'Halt in Belgrad'*, KSF., July 1927, pp. 683–4.

admitted that he would have been satisfied with the 'diplomatic success'.[1] But he had always laid it down as a minimum condition that this success should not be whittled down by discussions or attempts to get changes made in any of the terms of the note of 23 July. The *Halt in Belgrade* would provide an opening for Serbia to evade total submission, since, as Berchtold comments, 'the occupation of Serbian territory was not to be for the purpose simply of securing the fulfilment of our still unsatisfied demands on Serbia' but was to be ancillary to diplomatic action, i.e. Four Power mediation. Bethmann, it is true, disobeying the Kaiser's instructions, had suggested the occupation of Belgrade as a means of enforcing unconditional acceptance of the ultimatum on Serbia. But Berchtold was not mistaken in thinking that, once war operations were narrowed down, the other Powers would ask for and obtain a softening of the more extreme demands in the note. The problem remained what it was in the beginning: either the Central Powers gave way and agreed to soften the terms, or else Russia would come to the help of Serbia and there would be war. All this does not change the fact that Austria would have acted better in her own interest if she had come to an agreement with Russia and enlisted, as she could have done, the co-operation of the Powers in the suppression of Pan-Serb propaganda. But the Austrian Government with the approval, indeed under the pressure of the German Government, had embarked on a course of intransigence and now thought it fatal to its prestige abroad and damaging to its popularity at home to turn back.

Such were the motives underlying the Austrian attitude on the critical day of 30 July. Already at dawn came the first series of frantic telegrams to Tschirschky sent off overnight by the Chancellor and making clear for the first time that Berlin really wanted Vienna to show some sign of yielding. The first of the series relayed Lichnowsky's account of his talk with Grey on the morning of the 29th, when Grey suggested that Germany should herself find some formula which would 'enable Austria to receive full satisfaction without expecting Russia to look on quietly until Austria had carried her military enterprise to its extreme end'. If not, world war would be unavoidable and 'there was no knowing what houses would be spared in such a conflagration'. At the end of their talk Grey told Lichnowsky:

the Serbian Chargé d'Affaires at Rome had told Marquis San Giuliano that, under the presupposition of certain elucidations as to the manner of participation of Austrian agents, Serbia would be inclined to swallow even Articles 5 and 6 of the Austrian note, and thus her entire demands. . . . The matter might reach Serbia as advice through the channel of the Great Powers.[2]

---

[1] See pp. 376–80.   [2] DD. II, 357. See p. 501.

At the end of this relayed telegram came the message from Bethmann:

> Please communicate the enclosed to Count Berchtold at once, adding that
> we regard such compliance on the part of Serbia as suitable basis for negotia-
> tions on condition of an occupation of Serbian territory as guarantee.[1]

At the same time (12.30 a.m. on 30 July) the Chancellor sent
Tschirschky another telegram: 'Russia informs us that she mobilizes
Kazan, Kiev, Moscow, Odessa, because Austria has mobilized 8 corps
and this measure must be regarded as partly directed against Russia.'
But St. Petersburg gave the assurance that: 'Russian mobilization by
no means implies war, as in Western Europe [meaning Germany] . . .
and Russia is anxious to avoid war if at all possible' and regretted
that direct conversations with Vienna were not being continued.
Bethmann therefore added that 'in order to prevent general catastrophe,
or at any rate put Russia in the wrong, we must urgently desire that
Vienna should begin and pursue conversations as indicated in Telegram No. 174', the one proposing the *Halt in Belgrade*.[2]

*3. Berchtold decides on general mobilization. Tschirschky's influence at Vienna; his
evasive and misleading telegrams to his Government.*

This time Tschirschky was forced to take heed of the difference in tone
from that of the preceding days. He lost no time in seeing Berchtold
and informing him of the new turn of events. They had serious matters
to discuss and it is not known what advice Tschirschky proffered.
There is no proof that he counselled Berchtold to remain unyielding,
while feigning to make concessions and to reply to Russian partial
mobilization by Austrian general mobilization. But when one has examined step by step the activity of Tschirschky during the crisis, one is
forced to the conclusion that he exercised no small influence on the
weak, irresolute, hesitating Austrian Foreign Minister. On the morning
of the 30th Berchtold took the decision to ask the Emperor's assent in
principle to general mobilization without sending previous warning
to St. Petersburg or awaiting the consent of Berlin, as he had settled to
do the previous evening. Conrad's diary entry for 30 July narrates:

> On 30 July the Italian Military Attaché, Count Albricci, brought me a very
> courteous letter from General Count Cadorna, appointed Chief of the Italian
> General Staff after Pollio's death. After Count Albricci, Count Hoyos brought
> the message that I must be ready to go this very day to see the Emperor; it
> was a question of ordering general mobilization.[3]

---

[1] DD. II, 384. See p. 504.

[2] DD. II, 385. See p. 504. This is the telegram which Tschirschky annotated as is given
by Lutz, p. 220; see p. 656.

[3] Conrad, IV, pp. 146-7.

Why this decision to order general mobilization? Was it because Bethmann's telegram left no doubt about Russian mobilization? But this had been known for certain the previous evening and not even Conrad had thought it a reason for mobilizing. All he had suggested was that Berlin should be asked to make it clear to Paris and St. Petersburg 'that the continuance of Russian mobilization would lead to counter-measures in Germany and Austria-Hungary'.[1] One is therefore led to conclude that Berchtold was driven to an immediate declaration of general mobilization by the feeling that Germany had taken fright at the possible consequences of the Austrian attack on Serbia for which she had clamoured, and was now demanding a humiliating climb down on the part of the Monarchy. However this may be, there is no doubt that, if this measure did not forthwith bring about the outbreak of hostilities, it constituted another big step in the direction of war both in itself and in its effect on the attitude of the German General Staff. It is unlikely that Berchtold acted on his own initiative without getting the approval of Tschirschky. And in fact, as we shall see, after sending Hoyos with the message that Conrad was to be ready to go that very day to see the Emperor on the question of ordering general mobilization, Berchtold was assailed by doubts and hesitations, so that it remains an open question whether he would actually have put the order into execution if he had received further strong pressure from Berlin in favour of the *Halt in Belgrade* and mediation.

Let it not be objected that in Tschirschky's two telegrams to Berlin, following the morning's talk with Berchtold, there was no word of the intention to mobilize. This silence itself is damaging evidence against the German Ambassador. No one would seriously maintain that Berchtold kept him, of all people, in the dark about the intended mobilization, especially as the Russian Ambassador Shebeko was told of it that same afternoon in a talk which had been previously agreed upon by Berchtold and Tschirschky.[2] Tschirschky himself provides proof of his foreknowledge by an annotation to yet another telegram from Bethmann which reached Vienna at 10 a.m. on the 30th. The annotation runs: 'Conrad this evening with His Majesty, the general mobilization.'[3] This did not prevent him from concealing from Berlin what was decided with the Emperor, as we shall shortly see. Tschirschky's connivance with Berchtold is also apparent in the two telegrams with which he replied to those of Bethmann of the previous night. They show that, far from carrying out his instructions promptly and integrally, brushing aside Berchtold's delays and stratagems, he was playing Berchtold's game. The first of these telegrams (sent off from

---

[1] Oe-U. VIII, 10937. See p. 655.
[2] Shebeko, p. 255.
[3] Lutz, p. 235.

Vienna at 3.20 p.m. on 30 July, later than the second which went off at 2.31 p.m.) runs:

Order carried out. Count Berchtold told Bunsen that he only rejected discussion of Serbo-Austrian conflict with Russia, but, as reported elsewhere, is ready to discuss with her all questions directly affecting Austria and Russia.

That acceptance of Articles 5 and 6 of the Austrian note means integral acceptance of it is a mistake, since Serbia has made reservations also on several other points. Integral acceptance of the demands in the note would have been enough as long as it was a question of peaceful settlement of the conflict between Serbia and the Monarchy. Now that a state of war prevails, the Austrian terms would naturally be different.[1]

If Tschirschky had been honestly obeying his instructions, he would have pointed out to Berchtold that it was a mockery to reply to Berlin's advice by saying he was ready to discuss with Russia on other matters but not on the Serbo-Austrian conflict, which was the matter that threatened the peace of Europe. Still less honest, though so adroitly phrased that the Kaiser was taken in by it, was the second telegram:

Berchtold and Count Forgach ask me to communicate the following: In response to our gratefully received suggestion of yesterday, instructions have been sent to Count Szápáry to *begin* (the Kaiser underlined the word with the comment: 'Nòt till now!') conversations with M. Sazonov. Count Szápáry is empowered to elucidate the note to Serbia with the Russian Minister though it is outdated by the state of war, and to receive any suggestions that might yet emanate from Russia, as well as discussing with Sazonov all questions directly affecting Austro-Russian relations. . . .

Count Berchtold will to-day send for Shebeko and speak to him in this sense. The Minister will further say to the Russian Ambassador—Count Berchtold noted down the relevant points in my presence—that the Monarchy had no territorial aims in Serbia and that after the *conclusion of peace* (Kaiser: 'When will that be?') it planned a purely temporary occupation of Serbian territory in order to enforce on the Serbian Government the integral fulfilment of its demands and the furnishing of guarantees for future good behaviour. Step by step as Serbia fulfilled the peace terms, the evacuation of Serbian territory by the Monarchy would follow.[2]

The Kaiser marked this telegram '*good*' and minuted it: 'Practically my proposal accepted and the procedure what I had telegraphed to the Tsar as my view.' He did not perceive the trickery in Tschirschky's wording and that it meant something very different from his own. His own had implied that there was not to be war, but only the occupation of Belgrade, which was to last only until Serbia had carried out the engagements taken in the Serbian reply, with reservations on certain points of the ultimatum, there being the possibility of settling these reservations 'by negotiation' which was exactly what Russia wanted.[3]

[1] DD. II, 432.   [2] DD. II, 433; Shebeko, p. 255.   [3] DD. II, 293. See pp. 468–9.

Tschirschky's telegram, on the contrary, ruled out all negotiation on the substance of the note. Szápáry in the proposed conversations with Sazonov was only to be authorized to elucidate it. Moreover the phrase 'after the conclusion of peace', which was suppressed in the version of the telegram published by the *Norddeutsche Allgemeine Zeitung*, 11 October 1917, clearly implied that there was to be war, that it was to be fought out to a conclusion and be ended by a peace. Not therefore an occupation limited to Belgrade and the surrounding district, but the invasion and occupation of the whole land. Not until after the conclusion of a peace would the period begin during which Austria, still holding the invaded Serbia occupied, would begin to evacuate it step by step as all the points of the ultimatum successively received full satisfaction and as, in addition, guarantees were provided for future good behaviour. What these guarantees were to be, beyond those laid down in the ultimatum, was not indicated, but they would certainly have been such as to turn Serbia into a vassal of Austria. It was not even stated that she would be left territorially intact. She might quite well be reduced in size and the neighbouring Balkan States enlarged at her expense. In short Berchtold and Tschirschky were in league to throw dust in the eyes of Berlin, London and St. Petersburg, not without some success, as we shall see.

4. *Berchtold authorizes a feint resumption of conversations with St. Petersburg.*

In pursuance of his plan Berchtold at once (1.30 p.m. on the 30th) telegraphed to Szápáry that Sazonov must have misunderstood his reply on direct conversations (it certainly was a flat refusal) and continued:

I am, of course, still prepared through Your Excellency to elucidate the single points of our note to Serbia with M. Sazonov, although it has been overtaken by events.

He was ready to 'elucidate' but not, as Sazonov desired, to 'discuss'. What he expressed himself willing to discuss were 'questions directly affecting our relations with Russia'. Szápáry, therefore, was instructed 'on his own initiative' to inquire of Sazonov 'what matters the Minister would like to take as a basis of these conversations' and offer to report Sazonov's answer to Vienna.[1] This was sheer humbug on the part of Berchtold even if it was not he but Shebeko, an Ambassador of mediocre ability, who originated the idea of shifting the basis of discussions to general questions affecting Austro-Russian relations. And Berchtold carried on the humbug in the conversation he had with Shebeko on the 30th which he kept on the lines pre-arranged with Tschirschky.

[1] Oe-U. VIII, 11092.

Reporting this conversation Shebeko telegraphed to Sazonov:

Count Berchtold then adverted to his last conversation with me about empowering Count Szápáry to engage upon a private exchange of views with you for the purpose of a re-elaboration of the Austrian note of 23 July. He remarked in this connexion that he in no way intended to decline this exchange of views. It in fact seemed to him highly desirable and he had to-day telegraphed to Szápáry in this sense, proposing that he proceed with the exchange of views already begun with you.[1]

These words convey the impression that Berchtold was ready to instruct Szápáry to reopen conversations with Sazonov with a view to modifying the Austrian note, whereas in reality he ruled that out. On this point his word is to be believed because he never budged from this standpoint at any time during the crisis. If he had, there would have been no European war. In his own account of the conversation, telegraphed to Szápáry on the 30th, he writes:

I had already by telegram given Your Excellency a free hand to offer any elucidation of the note which M. Sazonov may desire, although it seems to be outdated by the outbreak of war. This, it is true, can only be by way of supplementary explanations, since it was never our intention to bargain on any point of the note.

If Shebeko had only grasped this essential and deciding element in the whole dispute, he would not have breathed optimism as he did. He declared his readiness to hold conversations on the lines of a general discussion of Austro-Serbian and Austro-Russian relations, on which it is not necessary to dwell here. He attached no great importance to Berchtold's announcement of Austrian general mobilization, in view of the fact that Russia had mobilized against the Monarchy, as Berchtold had reminded him.

What the reason of this is—said Berchtold to Shebeko—I do not know, there being no dispute between ourselves and Russia. Austria-Hungary had mobilized solely against Serbia, not at all against Russia. . . . By the fact that Russia is obviously mobilizing against us we should also have to extend our mobilization, but I wanted expressly to mention that this measure, it goes without saying, has no character of hostility against Russia and is to be regarded purely as the necessary counter-measure to Russian mobilization.[2]

Shebeko was entirely convinced by this explanation and ended his telegram with the following words:

The whole talk bore the most friendly character, and I received the impression that Berchtold would really like to arrive at an understanding with us, but is of the opinion that it is impossible for Austria to stop her operations against Serbia without having received full satisfaction and solid guarantees

---

[1] *Int. Bez.* i. V, 307.   [2] Oe-U. VIII, 11093.

for the future. At the end of the talk he once again assured me that Austria has no sort of aggressive intentions against Russia.[1]

The not very sharp-witted Shebeko communicated his favourable impression of Berchtold's statements to his French and English colleagues. Dumaine on the 30th telegraphed Paris that 'in a discussion of great importance' Shebeko and Berchtold 'reviewed the present formidable difficulties at length and with equal good will on both sides to apply mutually acceptable solutions to it'.[2] Bunsen told Grey that the interview had been 'quite friendly'. Berchtold had said:

that of course as Russia had mobilized Austria must do so also, but this was not to be considered as a threat. . . . Also there was no objection to conversations between Russian Minister for Foreign Affairs and Austrian Ambassador at St. Petersburg being continued, though Minister for Foreign Affairs did not say that they could be resumed on basis of Servian reply.[3]

Dumaine on his part reported that *pourparlers*

had only been interrupted owing to a misunderstanding, as Count Berchtold thought that the Russian Minister for Foreign Affairs claimed that the Austrian representative should be given powers which would allow him to modify the terms of the Austrian ultimatum. Count Szápáry will only be authorized to discuss what settlement would be compatible with the dignity and prestige for which both Empires had equal concern.[4]

This makes it difficult to understand how Shebeko could telegraph Sazonov in the ambiguous terms reproduced above and could think matters had taken a better turn, when they were just where they stood at the beginning, with Berchtold refusing to do what Sazonov regarded as essential, namely to modify and soften the ultimatum to Serbia.[5]

Far from taking a better turn when the Berchtold-Shebeko talk took place in the latter part of 30 July, the situation was growing worse. On learning from Hoyos what Sazonov had told Pourtalès of Russian partial mobilization, Conrad, who was ever ready to invade the province of the political leadership of the Monarchy, brought Berchtold a draft for a note to be sent to St. Petersburg saying:

Austria-Hungary has mobilized only against Serbia and will not let herself be deterred from proceeding against Serbia. Against Russia Austria-Hungary

---

[1] *Int. Bez.* 3. V, 307.   [2] DF. 3. XI, 364.   [3] BD. XI, 311.

[4] DF. 3. XI, 364. Reproduced in the *Yellow Book* as No. 104 with alterations in the first part, but not in the portion quoted above (CDD., p. 213).

[5] Shebeko's behaviour is the more incomprehensible in the light of the account he gives in his *Souvenirs:* 'He [Berchtold] had already instructed Count Szápáry to give the Foreign Minister detailed explanations concerning the Serbian reply, although after the declaration of war they seemed superfluous. These elucidations were to be solely of an explanatory character, for it was not in his intention to yield on any point' (Shebeko, p. 255). Why then did Shebeko telegraph in such a different sense to St. Petersburg, diffusing around him so favourable an impression of the statements made to him?

has not mobilized at all, as is shown by her not mobilizing the I, X and XI corps. Since Russia's mobilization is obviously directed against us, we declare ourselves therefore obliged to extend our mobilization at once—without any intention to attack or threaten Russia, but only to make provision against an attack by Russia.

Berchtold told Conrad of the pressure from Berlin

to resume diplomatic *pourparlers* with Russia in order by our conciliatory behaviour towards her to avoid the odium of starting a major war, leaving it in the event to Russia. This would, moreover, influence English public opinion in our favour.

Conrad replied

that Count Berchtold could open *pourparlers* as much as he wanted, but operations against Serbia must not be held up by them. . . . Any delay could only worsen the military position of Austria-Hungary.[1]

Conrad does not tell us what were the conclusions reached in this first conversation he had with Berchtold which must have taken place before lunch. His memoirs go on to state that he heard at 12.45 p.m. that the Russian Ambassador Sverbeev had notified Berlin of the mobilization of the four districts, Moscow, Kiev, Kazan, Odessa. At 3.30 p.m.—writes Conrad—he was again sent for by Berchtold because the Emperor was about to be asked to order general mobilization. 'Russia's move had made any delay impossible.' But only just before this he had noted down, as his first diary entry on the 30th, that, after his receiving a call from the Italian Military Attaché, 'Count Hoyos brought me the communication that I was to hold myself ready to go to see His Majesty this very day on the question of ordering general mobilization'. Evidently hesitations had arisen which were dispersed in the afternoon. Was it the step taken by Russia which dispersed them? This is what Berchtold may have led Conrad to believe, but it is not true, since no new step had been taken by Russia. Her partial mobilization had been notified to Vienna on the 29th by Shebeko, on the 30th by Sazonov's statement to Pourtalès, and Sverbeev's to Jagow, and was now a well-known fact. A new factor, however, was the strong pressure from Bethmann in favour of a peaceful solution and it was this which finally made Berchtold decide to make the situation worse by ordering the general mobilization of the Monarchy.

5. Berlin's fourth solemn appeal to Vienna in the night of 30 July.

At 10 a.m. Vienna received the telegram sent off by Bethmann at 3 a.m. which renewed the pressure brought to bear in the previous telegrams, insisting on the resumption of direct conversations and adding that Germany was prepared to fulfil the obligations of the

---

[1] Conrad, IV, pp. 147–8.

alliance but declined to be 'dragged by Vienna irresponsibly and without regard to our advice into a world conflagration'. 'In the Italian question too [ran Bethmann's dispatch] Vienna seems to disregard our advice' and Tschirschky was urged to 'speak to Count Berchtold at once with great emphasis and most seriously'.[1] Five minutes earlier, i.e. at 2.55 a.m., another telegram had left Berlin containing Grey's momentous declaration to Lichnowsky of the afternoon of 29 July that the German Government must not be 'misled into supposing that we should stand aside'.[2] To Lichnowsky's message Bethmann had appended grave words of his own:

Thus, if Austria rejects all mediation, we are on the brink of a conflagration in which England would be against us, Italy and Roumania by all appearances not with us, and we should be two against four Great Powers. Germany, as the result of England's hostility, would have to bear the brunt of the fighting. The political prestige of Austria, the military honour of her army and her just demands on Serbia could be adequately safeguarded by the occupation of Belgrade or other places. . . . In these circumstances we must urgently and emphatically recommend to the consideration of the Vienna Cabinet the acceptance of mediation on the honourable terms indicated. The responsibility for the consequences that would otherwise arise would be a very heavy one for Austria and ourselves.[3]

This telegram, though dispatched earlier than the one above, only reached Tschirschky at noon on the 30th. As soon as it was decoded, it was taken to the Austrian Foreign Ministry where Tschirschky was lunching with Berchtold. The two men were evidently keeping in unbroken contact all through that decisive day. At 5.20 p.m. Tschirschky telegraphed to his Government: 'Instructions emphatically executed. Count Berchtold will reply by return after receiving Emperor Francis Joseph's commands.'[4] This laconic telegram was followed up eight hours later by the following, which was dispatched from Vienna at 1.35 a.m. on the 31st:

Telegram 192 which arrived at noon was, immediately after decoding, handed to me at the Ministry for Foreign Affairs while I was lunching with Count Berchtold. As soon as luncheon ended I carried out my commission with Count Berchtold in the presence of Count Forgach. The Minister, who listened pale and silent while I read the message over twice—Count Forgach taking notes—said at the end that he would at once give a report of it to the Emperor.

I again particularly drew the Minister's attention to the fact that the justifiable demands of Austria-Hungary, for the chastisement of Serbia and the provision of guarantees for her further good behaviour, seemed fully safeguarded by acceptance of the mediation proposal, so that the initial purpose

[1] DD. II, 396. See p. 525.   [2] BD. XI, 286; DD. II, 368. See pp. 513, 522.
[3] DD. II, 395.   [4] DD. II, 434.

of the whole action against Serbia announced by the Monarchy would be attained without unleashing a world war. In these circumstances an outright rejection of mediation seemed to me impossible. Military honour would be satisfied by the occupation of Serbian territory by Austro-Hungarian troops. That this military occupation of Serbian territory was to take place with the express consent of Russia unquestionably meant a valuable reinforcement of Austrian influence in relation to Russia and in the Balkans. I begged the two gentlemen to bear in mind the incalculable consequences of a rejection of mediation.

When Count Berchtold had left the room to change for his audience of the Emperor, I again, when alone with Count Forgach, appealed very earnestly to his conscience. He expressed the view that an acceptance of mediation would be the right course, but thought it hardly possible to limit the military operations now in progress.

This afternoon before and after the telephone conversation with Herr von Stumm I took occasion to have a very serious discussion again with Counts Forgach and Hoyos in our sense. Both assured me that feeling in the army and among the public made them regard it as impossible to limit military operations. To-morrow morning Count Tisza is expected in Vienna and his opinion in so weighty a decision will have to be heard.

Conrad von Hötzendorf this evening was to submit the order for general mobilization to the Emperor as the answer to the measures already taken by Russia. It was not quite certain whether in the present situation mobilization was still the right course.[1]

This document would make it appear that Tschirschky this time thoroughly carried out Bethmann's instructions, backed as they were with arguments which could not be treated with levity. And yet no man knew better than he the promises given by the German Government to Austria and that he had exposed himself to a smart reprimand from Wilhelm for having at the beginning recommended prudence. The result had been that he had daily pressed for action and the rejection of all compromise. He was necessarily aware that the Monarchy could not beat a retreat without suffering humiliation and a further loss of prestige. With what authoritativeness, therefore, and with what conviction could he recommend a retreat, when he himself judged the crushing of Serbia to be essential? In other words, how much belief can be attached to his assurances on this point?

It may be noted that the first laconic and enigmatic message was only sent off at 5.20 p.m. and gave no hint that Austria was going to return a negative answer. Yet Tschirschky had been in discussion with Berchtold, Forgach and Hoyos, who had expressed opposition to the *Halt in Belgrade*. In their anxiety and impatience for further news than those few lines, the leaders at the Wilhelmstrasse got Stumm to telephone to Tschirschky and he must have replied, as we deduce from Bethmann's

[1] DD. II. 465.

telegram of 9 p.m., that 'Vienna rejected all compromise and in particular the proposal made by Grey'.[1] Why did he not telegraph that news from the first?

Presumably he was instructed over the telephone to insist once more and did in fact, return to the Ballplatz (as is to be deduced from his words 'before and after the telephone conversation with Herr von Stumm') where Forgach and Hoyos reiterated that in their opinion the limitation of military operations was impossible. This was tantamount to a rejection of the German request which was based on that very limitation. Now, at what hour did Tschirschky telegraph his report which bears the date of the 30th? Not until 1.35 a.m. on the 31st, so that it reached the Wilhelmstrasse at 4.35 a.m. and was read on the morning of the 31st. The report made the statement that the decision was to be taken the following day when Tisza was to be in Vienna.[2] The reality was, as will soon be seen, that this decision and others as well had already been taken by the Emperor. They amounted to a flat rejection of Berlin's request and the proclamation of general mobilization.

But this is not all. What creates a still worse impression is the last paragraph of the telegram, containing the statement that 'Conrad von Hötzendorf this evening was to submit the order for general mobilization to the Emperor' and ending: 'It was not quite certain whether in the present situation mobilization was still the right course.' When Tschirschky telegraphed these words, Berchtold and Conrad had already had their audience of the Emperor at which, as Conrad relates, the decision was taken that 'general mobilization will be ordered on 1 August'. It is true that Conrad adds 'however to-morrow (31 July) there will be another discussion about this',[3] but not because the matter was in any doubt. So little was it in doubt, that Conrad, that same evening of the 30th, drafted a telegram to Moltke which was dispatched on the morning of the 31st. It runs: 'By a decision of His Majesty it is resolved: to carry through war against Serbia. To mobilize remainder of army and assemble in Galicia. First mobilization day 4 August. Mobilization decree issued to-day 31st.'[4] Can it for a moment be thought that all this was kept from Tschirschky's knowledge? In the first place he enjoyed such prestige and was a man of such domineering character that he would never have allowed himself to be left out of any discussions affecting Germany. He had been told that Berchtold and Conrad were to be received by the Emperor. He had a right to know what

---

[1] DD. II, 441.

[2] While awaiting news from Tschirschky, Bethmann telegraphed Kaiser Wilhelm at 8.55 p.m. on the 30th: 'Reply from Vienna will be here to-morrow noon at the earliest, as Count Tisza does not arrive in Vienna till to-morrow morning' (DD. II, 440). This shows that Tschirschky must have given this misleading news to Stumm over the telephone.

[3] Conrad, IV, p. 151.   [4] Conrad, IV, p. 156.

decisions were taken at that audience and he was informed of them at once. Moreover, as we know, Berchtold informed not only him but also the Russian Ambassador who at once telegraphed the news to St. Petersburg[1] while Tschirschky concealed it from Berlin. Thus it came about that St. Petersburg knew long before Berlin that Austria was ordering general mobilization. Can one imagine anything more incredible?

In the face of all this, let him who will, believe in the sincerity of Tschirschky's efforts to restrain Austria at the eleventh hour. The times of dispatch and the contents of his telegrams give every reason to throw serious doubt on it and this is a fact of no small importance. It leads to the conclusion that when Bethmann Hollweg made up his mind to entreat Vienna to go into reverse, he did not find in the German representative at Vienna a faithful executor of his wishes. Very different results could have been obtained by Tschirschky, had he so willed, if he had used his great authority and applied the pressure of which he was capable in order to get the plea from Berlin accepted. The only excuse that can be put forward on his behalf is that Berlin at first, i.e. on the 27th, supported the English proposal for mediation only as a feint and on the 28th put forward the *Halt in Belgrade* with scant conviction and with injunctions to the Ambassador 'carefully to avoid giving the impression that we wish to restrain Austria'. Only in the night of 29/30 July did Berlin make up its mind to bring real pressure to bear on Vienna to accept the *Halt in Belgrade* and mediation and to resume conversations with St. Petersburg. This behaviour, lacking in coherence and common sense, was not of a nature to command particular respect or obedience from one who had been a mouthpiece and moving spirit of the warlike policy hitherto pursued. For the new line to earn credence and trust, it would have had to be·pursued with greater frankness and vigour, leaving no room for ambiguity. The Chancellor would have had to begin by admitting his mistakes and wrong doing, confessing that he had egged Austria on to the adventure in the belief that the Austro-Serbian conflict could be localized or at least that he would have England neutral and Italy a supporter of her allies in the event of a general European war. He would have had further to admit that all these calculations had proved mistaken and that therefore Germany was no longer in a position to maintain her promise to Austria to recognize the *casus foederis* and to support her in a venture which would begin under the worst auspices and might end with the defeat of both Empires and the annihilation of the Dual Monarchy. The acceptance of the *Halt in Belgrade* was thus not a suggestion but an iron necessity. If such had been Bethmann's frank statement, Tschirschky would have understood it and Berchtold could not have done otherwise than comply.

[1] *Int. Bez.* i. V, 361.

Let it never be forgotten that the Foreign Minister of the Dual Monarchy was a man entirely lacking in strength of will and power of decision, and that at moments of crisis he showed such uncertainty as to cause perplexity in those who, like Conrad, knew exactly what they wanted. Even as late as the 30th he was assailed by doubts whether Austria could venture on a war with both Serbia and Russia. He asked Conrad: 'Shall we stand it financially? Stürgkh thinks we cannot financially afford a war against Russia as well as against Serbia.' Conrad replied:

These scruples must be dropped, they come too late. Our position is such that we have no other choice. Who knows whether there will be war with Russia after all. The Russians may quite well stand still expecting to make us drop our plans against Serbia.[1]

Berchtold showed the same hesitation at the audience with the Emperor which took place in the afternoon of the 30th and was attended also by the War Minister and Conrad, the Emperor having returned at noon to Vienna from Ischl for the occasion.

6. *Berchtold's doubts and uncertainties at an audience with Francis Joseph.*

Conrad relates that all the communications made by Tschirschky were submitted to Francis Joseph. Among them was Bethmann's telegram containing Lichnowsky's summary of his talk with Grey on 29 July at the conclusion of which Grey mentioned that the Serbian Chargé d'Affaires at Rome had told San Giuliano 'that under the presupposition of certain elucidations as to the manner of participation of Austrian agents, Serbia would be inclined to swallow even Articles 5 and 6 of the Austrian note, thus of her entire demands'. Bethmann had appended the comment: 'We regard such compliance on the part of Serbia as suitable basis for negotiations on condition of an occupation of Serbian territory as a guarantee.'[2] This document seems to have played an important part in the discussions which took place at the audience. Conrad's account of them deserves to be reproduced in full:

At the audience there was a discussion on what was to be demanded of Serbia in the event of her now coming to heel. She would have to accept the terms of our ultimatum word for word and reimburse all outlay occasioned by the mobilization. I added that we should have to ask for cessions of territory which would at least secure our military position: Belgrade and Šabac with adjacent territory for the construction of extensive fortifications, the expenditure for which would also be borne by Serbia.

His Majesty: That is something they will not agree to!

Count Berchtold: Moreover Count Tisza desired that we should not demand cessions of territory.

---

[1] Conrad, IV, p. 148.   [2] DD. II, 357, 384. See pp. 501, 504.

I interposed that now everything was under way we could not suspend the hostilities against Serbia—in view of the state of feeling in the army, it was not possible. This would have to be said to Germany. If Russia mobilized, we should also have to mobilize.

Count Berchtold: That will cost millions.

Conrad: The Monarchy is at stake.

Count Berchtold: If the army is stationed in Galicia, it will mean war with Russia.

I replied that if the Russians do not touch us, we need not touch them either. The position is not a desperate one if our mobilization is ordered in good time. Then at the beginning there would be about $27\frac{1}{2}$ of our infantry divisions against about 33 Russian.

I should think it irresponsible in view of the already indubitable Russian mobilization to fold our arms and not carry out our own mobilization. The consequence of such an omission might be the invasion of the Monarchy—the road to Budapest and Vienna would lie open to the Russians.[1]

What a figure does Berchtold cut in this dialogue! It seems incredible that the very man who had raised this storm could stand aghast at the logical consequences of his own actions and raise such childish objections. Nor is it easy to understand how Conrad did not see that by insisting on war with Serbia he rendered war with Russia inevitable. And yet on the very day before, the 29th, he had written in his diary that

the hope grew ever fainter that Russia meant no more than a threat. Her vigorous, stubborn, and large-scale action left scarcely a doubt that Russia thought the moment had arrived to make war on Austria-Hungary against whom her preparations had long been aimed.[2]

Therefore

every day was of far-reaching importance—any delay might lay the forces now assembling in Galicia open to being struck by the full weight of a Russian offensive in the midst of their deployment.

But, that being the case, why did Conrad propose to the Emperor that the Austrian Supreme Command should at the beginning launch out on a war in Serbia? Conrad tells us:

The discussions in the presence of His Majesty led to the following resolution: The war against Serbia shall be carried on; a courteous reply will be returned to the English proposal, without accepting it on its merits; general mobilization will be ordered on 1 August, with 4 August as the first day of mobilization; however, to-morrow (31 July) there will be another discussion about this.

I remarked: Better to-morrow, but in the extreme case 1 August would be in time enough.

[1] Conrad, IV, pp. 150–1.   [2] Conrad, IV, p. 146.

Hereupon His Majesty approved my proposal that, in the event of general mobilization, all armies should be placed under His Royal Highness Archduke Frederick and that the Army Supreme Command should in the first instance proceed to the Serbian theatre of war. In the event of the outbreak of a subsequent war against Russia there would be still time enough for it to move to Galicia.[1]

The words 'in the event of the outbreak of a subsequent war against Russia' give the impression that Conrad did not regard it as certain even when Vienna had decided to reject the *Halt in Belgrade* and mediation. It is not inconceivable that it was Germany's attitude, which for the past forty-eight hours had seemed more cautious and conciliatory, more concerned to avoid a European war, that opened the eyes of those in charge of Austrian policy to a possible solution of the crisis which would keep Russia out of the war. It was precisely because of the fear that this solution might be based on the sacrifice of the prestige and interests of the Monarchy that the decisions taken at the audience were based on a determination to make no concessions. On 30 July at Vienna there undoubtedly reigned a deep distrust of Berlin. The sense of dissatisfaction and confusion caused by Bethmann's telegrams was heightened by one from Moltke. The following is Conrad's account of the incident:

While H.M. Emperor Francis Joseph, in this no doubt gravest hour of his life, with deep earnestness and calm resolve took the step, the serious consequences of which were no less evident to him than its inevitability, it seemed at that moment as if Kaiser Wilhelm was meditating a retreat and that the mood in Berlin had veered round in consequence of the truancy of Italy. Captain Fleischmann of the Austro-Hungarian General Staff, seconded to General Staff Military Intelligence in Berlin, telegraphed after his interview with General von Moltke:

Russian mobilization still no reason for mobilization; not until commencement of state of war between Monarchy and Russia. In contrast to customary Russian mobilizations and demobilizations, Germany's mobilization would unconditionally lead to war. Do not declare war on Russia but wait for Russia to attack.

To this I at once sent answer:

We shall not declare war on Russia and not start war.[2]

Conrad's curt reply sprang from the belief that Moltke was declaring Russian mobilization not to be a reason for mobilization by Austria, while what Moltke meant was mobilization by *Germany* and he expected Austria not to delay her mobilization. The Vienna State Archives contain no trace of this telegram from Fleischmann, who arrived at Berlin

[1] Conrad, IV, p. 151.
[2] Conrad, IV, pp. 151-2.

on the 29th as liaison officer, but they possess the letter written by him on the 30th after his interview with Moltke, which runs:

His Excellency remarked that—contrary to other press news on this subject—the definitely ordered [partial] Russian mobilization gave no occasion for a similar measure on the part of Germany, since German mobilization would only follow upon the beginning of a state of war between the Monarchy and Russia. In contrast to the already customary Russian mobilizations and demobilizations, a German mobilization would inevitably lead to war. . . . His Excellency expressed the conjecture that the mobilization of the whole Austro-Hungarian Army would now follow. His Excellency attaches extreme importance to the consideration that a declaration of war, if at all, should come from Russia, not from the Monarchy, to avoid producing any appearance of an aggressive move on our part in the eyes of Europe and because in the event of a Russian declaration of war, England would in no case co-operate within the framework of the Triple *Entente*.[1]

Fleischmann later made a statement for record in the German Imperial Archives about this interview with Moltke. When Moltke told him that Russian partial mobilization in itself did not cause the *casus foederis* to arise for Germany, Fleischmann's face registered pained surprise. Seeing this, Moltke with his own hand drafted the telegram reproduced by Conrad (Vol. IV, p. 152) and told Fleischmann to telephone it through to Conrad at once. As the text was in Moltke's own hand, Fleischmann did not venture to render it unambiguous by inserting the words '*of Germany*' after 'no reason for mobilization'.[2]

He could, however, have sent Moltke's text as it stood, adding explanations as to how it was to be interpreted, but this he did not do. Sent for again by Moltke on the morning of the 30th, he at 1.15 p.m. dispatched a second telegram as follows:

Russian Ambassador Berlin has officially communicated mobilization in districts Kiev, Odessa, Moscow, Kazan.—Chief of General Staff requests communication of decisions taken by you.[3]

Did this second telegram suffice to clear up Conrad's misunderstanding? Or was he still feeling indignant at Moltke's saying that Russian mobilization was still no reason for Germany to mobilize? At all events after the audience Conrad at 7.30 p.m. drafted the following reply to Moltke's request:

On the basis of His Majesty's decision the resolve is: to go forward with the war against Serbia. To mobilize remainder of army, assemble in Galicia. First day of mobilization 4 August. Mobilization order issued to-day 31 July. Request intimation of your first mobilization day.

This last inquiry shows that Conrad thought Germany ought to mobilize on her side without further ado. Another point to be noted

Schäfer, pp. 522–3.   [2] Schäfer, p. 524.   [3] Schäfer, p. 524.

in the telegram is the perhaps intentional indication of 31 July as the first day of mobilization instead of 1 August. Was this to prevent Berlin from knowing that there would be time to intervene and get it suspended? This supposition is supported by the very significant fact that the telegram was sent off, not on the evening of the 30th but about 8 a.m. on the 31st.[1]

7. *Moltke overrides the Chancellor. The decree for Austrian general mobilization signed on 31 July and communicated by Francis Joseph to Wilhelm.*

But, as we shall see, towards noon on the 30th a radical change took place in the attitude of Moltke. Having appeared at the beginning unwilling to urge the German Government to military action, he from noon onwards pressed for mobilization and war. The Austrian Military Attaché at Berlin, Lieutenant-Colonel Bienerth, after having been sent for by him, writes:

It may well have been about 2 p.m. His Excellency, as far as my memory serves me, came from the Foreign Office and was extremely agitated, as I had never before seen him.[2]

After the interview Bienerth, at 5.30 p.m. on the 30th, sent Conrad the following telegram which arrived in Vienna during the night:

Moltke says he would regard the situation as critical unless the Austro-Hungarian Monarchy at once mobilizes against Russia. Russian publication of the order to mobilize creates necessity for counter-measures on part of Austria-Hungary, this to be indicated in the public proclamation. This would give the *casus foederis* for Germany. Bring about honourable arrangement with Italy by assurances of compensation to keep Italy in the war on side of Triple Alliance, be sure to leave no troops on Italian frontier. Reject renewed English *démarche* for maintenance of peace. Last means of preserving Austria-Hungary is to fight out (*durchhalten*) a European war. Germany with you unconditionally.[3]

Doubtful perhaps that this categoric statement would suffice to rouse the Austrians, Moltke himself later sent Conrad the following telegram which reached Vienna at 7.45 a.m. on 31 July:

Stand firm against (*Durchhalten*) Russian mobilization. Austria-Hungary must be preserved, mobilize at once against Russia. Germany will mobilize. Compel Italy to do her duty as an ally by compensations.[4]

When Moltke made these moves, both Wilhelm and the Chancellor were still endeavouring to obtain Vienna's acceptance of the *Halt in Belgrade* in circumstances which will be dealt with fully in Vol. III,

---

[1] Oe-U. VIII, 11119.   [2] Schäfer, p. 525.
[3] Conrad, IV, p. 152.   [4] Conrad, IV, p. 152.

Chap. I. At 7.15 p.m. on the 30th the Kaiser telegraphed to Francis Joseph:

I did not think I could refuse the personal appeal of the Tsar to undertake an attempt at mediation to avert a world conflagration and preserve world peace and have yesterday and to-day had proposals laid before your Government by my Ambassador. They are, among other things, to the effect that, after occupying Belgrade or other places, Austria should make known her terms. I should be most sincerely obliged to you if you would let me know your decision as soon as possible.

In faithful friendship Wilhelm.[1]

At 9 p.m. Bethmann sent Tschirschky another urgent appeal in the same sense. It was later revoked, as we shall see, but it none the less showed a real desire for a composition of the conflict.[2] The same attitude was visible in the telegram sent at the same moment by Jagow to Tschirschky:

Count Szögyény has here proposed joint *démarche* at St. Petersburg and Paris by which our Ambassadors would in a friendly spirit draw attention to the consequences of Russian [partial] mobilization [made known on the evening of the 29th].[3] I answered Count Szögyény that as we had in the last few days already spoken in this sense at St. Petersburg and Paris, we could not repeat the *démarche*. We, therefore, would ask Austria to make the *démarche* alone. We advise your informing Rome.[4]

This was clearly a 'fin de non recevoir', inspired by the desire not to annoy Russia. How, then, did it come about that Moltke, loyal liegeman of his Kaiser as he was, ventured to impose his will not only on the Chancellor but even on his liege lord and Commander-in-Chief? Conrad relates that on the morning of the 31st he and the War Minister Krobatin went to Berchtold's office where they also found Tisza, Stürgkh and Burian. He read out Moltke's two telegrams and Berchtold exclaimed: 'How odd! Who runs the government: Moltke or Bethmann?'[5] Berchtold was thinking both of Bethmann's telegrams, made known to him by Tschirschky, and of Wilhelm's telegram to Francis Joseph, asking for anything rather than mobilization, in fact, as Conrad says, making an effort to avoid a general war. After the reading out of Wilhelm's telegram, Berchtold turned to Conrad with the words:

I have sent for you because I had the impression that Germany was beating a retreat; but now I have the most reassuring pronouncement from responsible military quarters.[6]

Thus in Berchtold's eyes the German Chief of Staff counted for more than the Chancellor and Kaiser, and Austria could now go ahead. And

---

[1] DD. II, 437.	[2] DD. II, 441.	[3] See p. 655.
[4] DD. II, 442.	[5] Conrad, IV, p. 153.	[6] Conrad, IV, p. 153.

in fact the decision was taken to submit the mobilization order for the imperial signature. Conrad's telegram to Moltke, drafted the previous evening, was now sent off. Berchtold repeated it in his own telegram to Szögyény, dispatched at 8 a.m. on the 31st for communication to the Chancellor.[1] The mobilization order, laid before Francis Joseph by General Krobatin, came back signed to the War Ministry at 12.23 p.m. and was immediately published. A few minutes later, at 1 p.m. the Emperor's answer to Wilhelm went off:

I hasten to thank you cordially and warmly for your friendly telegram. Immediately after your Ambassador yesterday handed my Government Sir Edward Grey's mediation proposal, the official announcement arrived from my Ambassador at St. Petersburg that the Tsar of Russia has ordered the mobilization of all military districts on my frontiers. Count Szögyény informs me that you had told Tsar Nicholas in unmistakable terms to arrest Russian armaments because otherwise the whole responsibility for a world war would fall on his shoulders. Conscious of my heavy responsibility for the future of my Empire, I have ordered the mobilization of all my armed forces. The action of my army against Serbia now proceeding can suffer no interruption from the threatening and challenging attitude of Russia. A fresh rescue of Serbia by Russian intervention would entail the most serious consequences for my lands and I, therefore, cannot possibly permit such intervention. I am conscious of the import of my decisions and have taken them trusting in divine justice and with confidence that your armed forces will take their stand with my Empire and the Triple Alliance in unchanging loyalty as an ally.[2]

Formal approval of the decisions was given by the Council of Joint Ministers of the Monarchy on 31 July after the morning discussion at Berchtold's office mentioned above. To the Joint Ministers Berchtold read out a report of the latest diplomatic developments: Tschirschky's communication of Grey's proposal to Lichnowsky for the suspension of hostilities against Serbia and the acceptance of Four Power mediation, Grey's threatening language to Lichnowsky,[3] and Grey's statement to Imperiali that if mediation were agreed to, he thought he could procure every possible satisfaction for Austria: Austria could obtain surety for the future without a war which would jeopardize the peace of Europe.[4] There then followed, with modifications which we shall examine in a moment, the grave words with which Bethmann had accompanied Lichnowsky's last telegram. The minutes of the Council meeting record that after the reading of the report:

Count Berchtold stated that when the German Ambassador submitted the English proposal to him, he immediately declared that a cessation of our hostilities against Serbia was impossible. In the matter of the proposal for

---

[1] Oe-U. VIII, 11119. [2] Oe-U. VIII, 11118.
[3] DD. II, 395. [4] DD. II, 368. See p. 523.

mediation he alone could not decide but must hear the commands of His Majesty and discuss it in the Council of Ministers. He then reported to His Royal and Imperial Apostolic Majesty the content of the German Ambassador's *démarche*. His Majesty at once declared that the cessation of hostilities against Serbia was impossible. His Majesty, however, approved the suggestion that we must carefully avoid accepting the substance of the English proposal, but that we should show conciliatoriness in the form of our reply and thus meet the German Chancellor's wish not to offend the [English] Government.[1]

Let us dwell for a moment on this summary of events which with its omissions and manipulations throws much light on the manoeuvres by which Berchtold with, in the present writer's opinion, the connivance of Tschirschky, eluded the pressure from Berlin. It completely hides the fact that it was Bethmann by his telegram of the evening of the 28th, and not Grey, who proposed the *Halt in Belgrade*. Berchtold twisted his account in such a way as to give the Joint Ministers, and probably in the first place Tisza, the impression that the refusal was being returned not so much to Germany as to England. In fact the seriousness of the German pressure was, if not suppressed, at least greatly played down. Tschirschky was quoted as having worded Bethmann's warning of 2.55 a.m. on 30 July to run:

If Austria-Hungary refused all mediation, Austria-Hungary and Germany would be faced with a coalition of all Europe, since even Italy and Roumania would not go with them. Austria-Hungary's political prestige etc.[2]

What Bethmann had really written was:

If Austria rejects all mediation, we are on the brink of a conflagration in which England would be against us, Italy and Roumania by all appearances not with us and we should be two against four Great Powers. Germany, as the result of English hostility, would have to bear the brunt of the fighting. The political prestige of Austria etc.[3]

Thus it is the first part of the German warning which is played down, the second part being reproduced faithfully. The alteration is of some importance. By suppressing not only the allusion to English intervention but also the observation that the brunt of the fighting would fall on Germany and the words 'we should be two against four Great Powers', implying that Italy would in the end range herself against the Central Powers, the mood of Berlin was made to appear far less serious than it really was and it was thus easier to get the consent of the Council of Ministers to the reply which Berchtold planned to send to Germany. This reply was to be based on

three basic principles: i. War operations against Serbia must be continued. ii. We cannot negotiate on the English proposal unless Russian mobilization

[1] Oe-U. VIII, 11203.   [2] Oe-U. VIII, 11025.   [3] DD. II, 395.

is suspended. iii. Our terms must be integrally accepted [by Serbia] and we could not consent to any negotiations on them.—Experience shows that in such cases the Powers always try to whittle down the demands made by the one side and this is what would probably be attempted now when, in the present grouping, France, England, and Italy too would support the Russian standpoint and we should have a very dubious supporter in the present German representative in London. From Prince Lichnowsky we can expect anything rather than warm support for our interests. If the action were now to end with a mere gain of prestige, it would in Berchtold's opinion have been undertaken entirely in vain. We should derive no benefit from a simple occupation of Belgrade, even if it were with the consent of Russia. All this would be nothing but tinsel. Russia would cut a figure as the saviour of Serbia especially of the Serbian Army. This would remain intact and we should be faced with the prospect in two or three years of another attack from Serbia in much more unfavourable conditions.

The Joint Finance Minister Bilinski observed that the terms laid down previous to the Austrian mobilization would now be inadequate. Tisza expressed agreement with Berchtold's views and thought it would be fatal to enter into the merits of the English proposal. Military operations against Serbia must continue.

He wondered whether it were necessary to acquaint the Powers at present with the new demands we were to make on Serbia and would suggest replying to the English recommendation that we were ready in principle to examine it further but only on condition that our operations against Serbia proceeded and that Russian mobilization was stopped.

This was tantamount to outright rejection. The Austrian Prime Minister Stürgkh also said that

the idea of a conference was so hateful to him that he would prefer to avoid even an appearance of agreeing to it. He therefore regarded Count Tisza's proposal as the right one. Herr von Bilinski thought Count Tisza's suggestion extremely skilful and that, by laying down the two above-mentioned conditions, we should gain time. He, too, could not feel attracted by the idea of a conference. The proceedings of the London Conference were such a hideous memory that the whole of public opinion would rise in opposition to the repetition of such a piece of play acting. But he too thought that the English proposal must not be abruptly rejected. After Baron von Burian had also expressed his agreement, Count Tisza's proposal was unanimously adopted.[1]

Berchtold then passed on to speak of Italy, and what he said will be examined in Vol. III.

The short minutes of this discussion show that the Ministers were invited to bury the English proposal for mediation, but not the German one for the *Halt in Belgrade* which was kept from their knowledge.

---

[1] Oe-U. VIII, 11203.

Thus they were not able to discuss the fundamental feature of the situation on that day, which was that Germany was extremely worried and unwilling to plunge into a European war opening under bad auspices for both the Central Powers and that Berlin no less than Britain was pressing for a conciliatory formula. But while this was a result of Berchtold's manoeuvring, it was not entirely his fault that the leading political figures of the ancient and tottering Monarchy failed to ask themselves what would be their country's prospects of victory in a European war. More blind and irresponsible it would have been impossible for them to be, and this will appear still more clearly when we look at their attitude towards Italy, even though the War Minister Krobatin in the course of the discussion reminded them that both Kaiser Wilhelm and Moltke had 'expressly pointed out how important Italy's active intervention would be in the impending conflict'. They thought they could secure Italy's co-operation in the war by holding out vague hopes of inadequate compensation (Valona) if she recognized the *casus foederis* as having arisen. In Berchtold's report to the Emperor after the Council of Ministers he wrote: 'Baron Conrad hopes to induce Italy not only to fulfil her allied obligations against France but to place troops at our disposal for Galicia.'[1] What an incredible illusion!

There was equal incomprehension of the bonds linking France to Russia. At 9.10 a.m. on 31 July the Ballplatz received a telegram of the previous evening from Szögyény with the news that

the German Government on good authority was now unfortunately certain that England would unquestionably at once attack ['losgehen'] Germany and Austria-Hungary if war against France and Russia were to break out.[2]

Perhaps it came too late for Berchtold to bring it before the Council of Ministers. But even without it, Grey's words to Lichnowsky on the evening of 29 July, only summarily reported at the Council, provided sufficient evidence that English intervention was to be expected. And even without this evidence the whole situation logically pointed to it. Well then! If Italy and Roumania were for the time being neutral, with the possibility of becoming hostile, and if the queen of the seas ranged herself against the Central Powers, what chances had they of winning the war? And if they did not win it, what would be the fate of Austria-Hungary?

But into these considerations the Ministers of the Dual Monarchy did not enter. Had they done so, they would have arrived at the conclusion that for the time being, however great the sacrifice, it would be wisest to compose the dispute, at worst waiting for Serbia to make

[1] Oe-U. VIII, 11201.   [2] Oe-U. VIII, 11127.

an attack on Austria. Indeed if a European war had developed out of a Serbo-Russian aggression, Italy could not have refused to fulfil her obligations as an ally, nor would England have intervened. But however much this was the sort of general war which Berchtold would have preferred, it was not the sort that was ever likely to happen. Russia would never have countenanced a Serbian attack on Austria, and France would have exercised restraint on Russia for fear that England would refuse to join in. All this was a matter of elementary common sense and could have provided the best of answers to Moltke's irresponsible exhortations that a European war offered 'the last possibility of salvation for Austria-Hungary', a conviction shared also by Conrad. As it was, ministers and generals worked hand in hand to lead the Dual Monarchy to its doom.

8. *Austrian mobilization announced to the Powers. Vienna's rejection of the German and English proposals.*

The best that one can say is that, even if at the moment of supreme decision in Austria there had been somebody who did reason things out, events would in any case have taken the same turn. On that very morning of the 31st Tschirschky, after receiving a telephone call from Berlin, notified Berchtold that the Chancellor intended to send an ultimatum to Russia summoning her to stop her mobilization.[1] At 1.45 p.m. Bethmann sent Tschirschky the following telegram which reached Vienna at 4.10 p.m.:

Following on the Russian general mobilization, we have proclaimed·imminent danger of war. It will presumably be followed by mobilization within 48 hours. This inevitably means war. We expect from Austria immediate active participation in the war against Russia.[2]

Thus with a lighter heart Berchtold could go ahead with the last activities of that exhausting day and, without risk, don the mask of peace to hide the lineaments of war. To the Austrian representatives abroad he circulated a telegram which runs as follows:

Since the Russian Government has ordered mobilization on our frontier, we are driven to military measures in Galicia. These measures have a purely defensive character and are taken purely under the pressure of Russian provisions which we greatly deplore, as we ourselves have no aggressive intentions towards Russia and desire the continuance of the previous good-neighbourly relations. The discussions on the situation between the Vienna and St. Petersburg Cabinets, from which we hope for an all round assuagement, are meantime being pursued in a friendly spirit.[3]

The hypocrisy of this document is consummate. It gives out that there was still the intention of carrying on negotiations between Vienna

[1] Oe-U. VIII, 11201.   [2] DD. II, 479.   [3] Oe-U. VIII, 11120.

and St. Petersburg, when the decision had already been taken to use extreme measures against Serbia, not stopping short at the occupation of Belgrade and imposing terms on Serbia more severe than those contained in the ultimatum. The same insincerity pervaded the reply sent at long last to Szögyény (and also circulated to Mensdorff and Szápáry) in answer to Bethmann's telegrams urging Austria to accept the *Halt in Belgrade* and mediation. It repeated the misleading summary of Tschirschky's *démarche* read out at the Council of Ministers, suppressing all mention of the *Halt in Belgrade*. It then proceeded to instruct Szögyény:

I request Your Excellency to thank the Secretary of State very much for the communications made by Herr von Tschirschky and say to him that, in spite of the change in the situation since caused by the Russian mobilization and in full appreciation of the English endeavours on behalf of the preservation of the peace of the world, we are willingly prepared to examine more closely Sir E. Grey's proposal to mediate between ourselves and Serbia. The premises of our acceptance, however, are of course that our military action against the Kingdom shall in the meantime take its course and that the English Cabinet shall prevail upon the Russian Government to arrest the mobilization of its troops directed against us, in which case we would naturally also at once revoke the defensive military counter-measures in Galicia necessitated by the Russian mobilization.[1]

By the time this telegram reached the capitals to which it was dispatched the situation was already beyond remedy. But even had this not been the case, it would have seemed a joke in such bad taste that Russia could hardly have regarded it otherwise than as a provocation. What else than provocation was it to lay down as a premise of acceptance that Austria should be allowed to make war on Serbia without restriction and without limits to the territory she could occupy, limits which had been recognized as necessary even by Berlin, and to demand that, while this aggression took its course, Russia should revoke the partial mobilization she had already ordered? Nevertheless between 30 and 31 July, by this feint of resuming direct conversations and by the language of his telegrams, Berchtold successfully spread the impression that he had yielded and that, if Berlin had not mobilized, matters could easily have been mended between. Vienna and St. Petersburg.

It has already been related that Jagow lost no time in sending on to Lichnowsky Tschirschky's telegram of 30 July skilfully throwing up dust, making it appear that Berchtold had authorized the resumption of conversations between Sazonov and Szápáry and expressing Austrian acceptance of the *Halt in Belgrade*.[2] Grey, to whom Lichnowsky communicated it on 31 July, was only to a certain point taken in by it. 'He said he thought everything depended on Austria's making a concession

---

[1] Oe-U. VIII, 11155.   [2] DD. II, 433, 444. See p. 640.

of such a kind as would put Russia in the wrong if she were to reject it.' Lichnowsky was still less taken in, as is shown by his comment:

If Count Berchtold confines himself to the repetition of well-known declarations, negotiations will have poor prospects. . . . Only very strong pressure from Berlin can induce Vienna to make such a concession, the granting of which might be of decisive importance for the future attitude of England in the event of war breaking out.[1]

Sazonov, however, fell right into the trap. Here is how this came about.

9. The resumption of direct conversations between Vienna and St. Petersburg; the quibble about Austrian territorial désintéressement.

We have already seen that on 30 July Berchtold had telegraphed to Szápáry that he was, as if at his own suggestion, to propose to Sazonov a resumption of direct conversations on general Austro-German relations within limits laid down for him.[2] But Szápáry answered on the 31st that he had already done this very thing on the 29th and did not see his way to beginning all over again when his first overture had been nipped in the bud by the news of the Austrian bombardment of Belgrade.[3] Moreover, as Pourtalès had also reported,[4] Sazonov had told Szápáry:

Russia would not regard it as sufficient even if there were a formal declaration that Austria-Hungary would neither diminish (!) Serbian territory, nor encroach on Serbian sovereignty, nor injure Russia's Balkan or other-interests. And as Russian general mobilization has since then been ordered, I think the démarche should be left in abeyance pending further express orders from Your Excellency.[5]

Szápáry did not judge wrongly. For conversations to be of any use, Vienna would have had to make other concessions than that. But on receiving Berchtold's telegram reporting his conversation with Shebeko of the 30th, the one which had so raised the latter's hopes,[6] Szápáry

---

[1] DD. III, 489.   [2] Oe-U. VIII, 11092. See p. 661.
[3] Oe-U. VIII, 11003. See pp. 552–3.   [4] DD. II, 412, 421. See p. 577.
[5] Oe-U. VIII, 11177. The exclamation mark after the word 'diminish' is in the Austrian text and is most revealing. It implies: 'Whoever said that Serbia was not to be diminished? Austrian territorial désintéressement does not mean that Serbia will not be diminished for the benefit of other states. And Austria reserves to herself a right to diminish her for the benefit of the neighbouring Balkan states.' In other words, this exclamation mark fully confirms what has been said on p. 576 on the deceit which Berchtold was practising towards Germany as well as towards Russia and the other Powers when he made a show of placating Sazonov by promises of Austrian territorial désintéressement. Sazonov understood it to mean respect of Serbian territorial integrity. Berchtold meant it as renunciation of territorial acquisition by the Monarchy, but not as ruling out cession of Serbian territory to Bulgaria, Greece and Albania.
[6] Int. Bez. i. V, 307. See p. 662.

thought better of it and asked for an appointment with Sazonov who saw him on the afternoon of the 31st. Szápáry opened the conversation by saying:

I had received instructions in cipher but I had first of all to remark that the present situation in Vienna, created by the Russian general mobilization, was wholly unknown to me, so that in interpreting my instructions, which had been sent me before the new situation had developed there, I should have to make allowances for the fact. The Minister interrupted me excitedly by saying that the mobilization had no significance and that Tsar Nicholas had pledged his word to Kaiser Wilhelm that the army would not budge so long as a conversation tending towards an agreement was still going on with Vienna. Moreover we had mobilized first, an assertion which I distinctly denied, so that the Minister said: 'let us leave chronology aside'. There was no fear that the guns would go off by themselves and, as regards the Russian Army, it was so well disciplined that the Tsar with one word could make it retire from the frontier. I continued by saying that Your Excellency's two instructions started from the misunderstanding that we had declined further negotiations with Russia. This was a mistake, as I had already informed him without instructions. Your Excellency was not only ready to negotiate with Russia on a broad basis, but especially inclined to discuss the text of our Note as far as interpretation was concerned. I knew, of course, that the Russian point of view was that the form of the note should be modified, whilst Your Excellency was of the opinion that its meaning could be elucidated.

This resulted in a discrepancy which could not be overlooked, though on the whole it seemed to me that it came to the same thing. M. Sazonov said this was good news, for he still hoped that in this way the matter might be directed into that channel which he had from the first imagined the best. I insisted on the fact that Your Excellency's instructions to me were a proof of good will, though I had again to remind him that the situation since created by the general mobilization was unknown to me. I could only hope that the course of events had not gone too far already. In any case I had thought it my duty again to insist on the good will of the I. and R. Government at the present most serious moment. M. Sazonov replied that he took note with satisfaction of this proof of good will; also he would like to draw my attention to the fact that negotiations in St. Petersburg would seem, for reasons easily understood, to promise less hope of success than those on the neutral ground of London. I answered . . . that I was not in a position to give any opinion concerning his suggestion about London. . . . M. Sazonov seemed greatly relieved by my information and to attribute an excessive importance to it, so that I again and again had to point to the changed situation, the discrepancy between our initial points of departure etc. Moreover, during the conversation two main points were entirely evaded: on my side, the partly retrospective and theoretical character of a conversation on the text of the Note . . ., on his side, what should happen as regards military operations during the eventual negotiations. With regard to the reservation which I made concerning the Russian general mobilization, Your Excellency is absolutely free to declare my communication devoid of basis. On the other hand, from the point of view of the allotting of rôles, it seemed to me exceedingly important to have undertaken one more *démarche* which may perhaps be described as the furthest one could go in the direction of conciliation.[1]

What a bit of play-acting! This conversation, although overtaken by events even at the moment it was happening, is of interest as showing that, in spite of the mistakes he made, Sazonov acted in good faith and, after the proclamation of mobilization, still clutched at even the faintest hope of avoiding war. Indeed he at once on the evening of the 31st telegraphed the good news to all the Russian Ambassadors (while Szápáry, who was accustomed to taking his time, did not telegraph his Government until 10.45 a.m. on 1 August) saying that Szápáry had informed him of 'his Government's consent to enter upon a discussion of the substance of the ultimatum sent to Serbia'. By his own account, Szápáry held out no such false hope. But not a few shades of expression in his telegram leave an impression that he did go to considerable lengths, or else Sazonov would hardly have misapprehended him. To the Ambassadors Sazonov wrote:

The Austrian Ambassador called on me and conveyed to me the consent of his Government to enter into a discussion on the content of the ultimatum presented to Serbia. I expressed my satisfaction over this and indicated to the Ambassador that it would be preferable that the negotiations should be carried on in London with the participation of the Great Powers. We hope that the English Government will undertake to preside over these discussions, whereby it would earn the gratitude of all Europe.

For a successful prosecution of such negotiations it would be very important that Austria should suspend her military operations on Serbian territory.[2]

Sazonov thus thought suspension of operations extremely important, but not indispensable, a sign that he would have adapted himself to the *Halt in Belgrade* provided the note were toned down. It was, however, another mistake on his part, due to his instability of temperament, that he asked for the discussion to be transferred to London now that Austria seemed to be accepting his proposal for direct conversations. The mistake was perceived by the Tsar who annotated Sazonov's telegram: 'The one thing does not rule out the other. Continue the conversations with the Austrian Ambassador.'

However, the misunderstanding did not lead to any consequences, because other events supervened and because Austria was not prepared to negotiate or yield on any point. A telegram of 26 July from Szécsen, the Austrian Ambassador to Paris, had informed Berchtold that Schoen had discussed with the Quai d'Orsay Szápáry's statement to Sazonov

[1] DA. III, 97.   [2] *Int. Bez.* i. V, 348.

of Austria's territorial *désintéressement* towards Serbia.[1] Berchtold had circulated to Szécsen in Paris his telegram to Szápáry of the 27th:

I authorize Your Excellency, without entering into a binding engagement, to converse with M. Sazonov and your Italian colleague in the sense that, as long as the war between Austria-Hungary and Serbia remains localized, the Monarchy does not plan any territorial acquisitions.

To the copy destined for Szécsen Berchtold had appended the sentence: 'Above paragraph must rest on a misunderstanding to which it does not for the moment seem to me opportune to draw attention.'[2] There seems no doubt that the misunderstanding to which Berchtold referred was the one created by himself in speaking of Austrian territorial *désintéressement*, which was generally taken to mean respect for Serbian territorial integrity, when, as has been pointed out above,[3] Austria had no intention of respecting that integrity and planned to diminish Serbia for the benefit of the neighbouring Balkan States. This was, indeed, a misunderstanding which Berchtold could not have cleared up at that moment without disturbing a hornets' nest. But Berchtold's perfidious instructions placed Szécsen in a quandary. He had not grasped the quibble contained in Berchtold's promise and telegraphed back in reply:

I can only repeat that Baron Schoen, in obedience to instructions, has stated here that we had declared to St. Petersburg we have no intention of making conquests in Serbia. . . . Any departure from this standpoint would unquestionably make the worst possible impression both here and in England.[4]

A later telegram on the same day (30th) reported that Szécsen had just had a long talk with Viviani 'whose language was pacific and conciliatory' and who expressed the view that 'a solution must be sought which would spare Russia any humiliation'. He 'reverted to the English

---

[1] Oe-U. VIII, 10741.

[2] Oe-U. VIII, 10834. To clear up the Austro-Hungarian intentions the present writer inquired by letter of Berchtold whether the following explanation of the 'misunderstanding' alluded to in his telegram to Szécsen was correct, namely that 'while Szápáry was authorized to state that, as long as the war remained localized, Austria had no territorial aspirations in Serbia, Schoen had talked of the territorial integrity of Serbia, not at all the same thing, because although Austria did not aspire to territorial annexations in Serbia, the assurance given to St. Petersburg did not rule out Serbia's being territorially reduced after the war for the benefit of the neighbouring Balkan States. In short while Austria, as long as the war remained localized, was not to make territorial annexations in Serbia (though this did not exclude strategic frontier rectifications), she considered that after the end of the war Serbia could be reduced territorially for the benefit of the neighbouring states.' The reply received from Berchtold runs as follows: 'I no longer remember the essence of this misunderstanding alluded to in my telegram of 27 July 1914 to Count Szécsen. Certainly it cannot be denied that the interpretation of the matter given by you has a concrete and objective basis.'

[3] See pp. 576–7.   [4] Oe-U. VIII, 11077.

proposal of a conference of the four Ambassadors' and took the stand-point that, before Russia was asked to suspend mobilization, she must first be given assurances that Austria did not mean to annihilate Serbia.[1] Yet another telegram from Szécsen of the same day reported:

The idea has got round here that we aim at reconquest of the Sanjak. This, it is said, would for Russia mean war. I am pressed by government quarters and other political men to give some kind of reassuring explanations about our intentions to be used against the alarmist news from Russia. Chief anxiety here: Sanjak, annexation of certain Serbian districts, encroachments on independent status, protectorate over Serbia.[2]

To these telegrams Berchtold replied on the 31st asking Szécsen to draw Viviani's attention

at once to the fact that we have already officially stated at St. Petersburg that we have no territorial aims in connexion with our action against Serbia . . . and emphatically to contradict the view that we plan a reoccupation of the Sanjak. . . . It goes without saying that all our declarations of *désintéresse-ment* only hold good for the case that the war between ourselves and Serbia remains localized.[3]

Here again, as is apparent, what was promised was Austrian *désintér-essement*, not Serbian territorial integrity, and it was promised only on condition that Austria could go ahead with her war against Serbia and impose both the old terms and others that were new and unknown—an impossible set of demands. Armed with this statement Szécsen betook himself to the Quai d'Orsay that same evening of the 31st at 11.15 p.m. Viviani was attending a Cabinet meeting, but Szécsen was received by Berthelot who

expressed the personal opinion that in view of to-day's German *démarche* [the ultimatum to France] the Serbian question falls entirely into the background. I shall endeavour as far as possible to make our conciliatory attitude known, it having been passed over in silence here by Russia.[4]

His endeavour did, in fact, have a result which will be discussed in Vol. III. Here it is enough to say that Szécsen's endeavour and the ephemeral resumption of conversations between Sazonov and Szápáry, which will also be spoken of in Vol. III, induced Viviani to telegraph on 1 August to all the French Ambassadors:

The deduction from these facts is that Austria would at last show herself ready to come to an agreement, and that the Russian Government likewise would be ready to enter into negotiations on the basis of the English proposal. Unfortunately these arrangements, which would give hope of a

[1] Oe-U. VIII, 11079.   [2] Oe-U. VIII, 11081.
[3] Oe-U. VIII, 11121.   [4] Oe-U. VIII, 11164.

peaceful solution, seem in fact about to be rendered nugatory by the attitude of Germany.[1]

Similarly in a report dated 1 September 1914, drawn up for Sir Edward Grey by Bunsen, the English Ambassador to Vienna, the statement is made that after the Berchtold-Shebeko conversation of 30 July an arrangement between Russia and Austria 'seemed almost in sight':

On 1 August I was informed by M. Shebeko that Count Szápáry had at last conceded the main point at issue by announcing to M. Sazonov that Austria would consent to submit to mediation the points in the note to Servia which seemed incompatible with the maintenance of Servian independence. M. Sazonov, M. Shebeko added, had accepted this proposal on condition that Austria would refrain from the actual invasion of Servia. Austria, in fact, had finally yielded, and that she herself had at this point good hopes of a peaceful issue is shown by the communication made to you on 1 August by Count Mensdorff to the effect that Austria had neither 'banged the door' on compromise nor cut off the conversations. . . . Unfortunately these conversations at St. Petersburg and Vienna were cut short by the transfer of the dispute to the more dangerous ground of a direct conflict between Germany and Russia. . . . A few days' delay might in all probability have saved Europe from one of the greatest calamities in history.[2]

Nothing is further from the truth! For the calamity to have been averted, Austria would have had to make concessions to which she had all along opposed a steadfast refusal. She could have been compelled to yield by the German Chancellor if on the day of 30 July he had remained in the same frame of mind as on the night of the 29th and had sternly insisted that Austria must show readiness to compromise. But in that case the credit for the peaceful issue would have been due to Berlin, not to Vienna, which had no eyes save for the Austro-Serbian conflict, never faced the possibility of a European war, and stumbled blindfold into the most hazardous and disastrous adventure that was possible.

[1] DF. 3. XI, 481; LJF. 120, CDD., p. 225. See Vol. III, Ch. II, §9.
[2] BD. XI, 676.

APPENDIX

KING GEORGE'S WORDS TO PRINCE HENRY OF PRUSSIA

(See page 429.)

No record of this conversation between King George and Prince Henry is preserved among the King's own papers or in his diary. There exists, however, an undated half sheet of notepaper on which, 'possibly some time after the event', he noted down his words to Prince Henry as follows:

I don't know what we shall do, we have no quarrel with anyone and I hope we shall remain neutral. But if Germany declared war on Russia and France joins Russia, then I am afraid we shall be dragged into it. But you can be sure that I and my Government will do all we can to prevent a European war.[1]

The warning contained in the above words appears in so indirect a form in Prince Henry's letter to the Kaiser that it fell unheeded. The quotation in English is followed by Prince Henry's guarded comment:

I am convinced that this utterance was sincerely meant, and also that England will at first stay neutral; whether she will be able to do so in the long run, I cannot judge, but have my doubts because of the relation with France.[2]

There is an earlier parallel to this backwardness on Prince Henry's part bluntly to convey a warning from King George to the Kaiser. Volume X of the *British Documents* reproduces a letter from the King to Sir Edward Grey, dated 8 December 1912:

Prince Henry of Prussia paid me a short visit here two days ago. In the course of a long conversation with regard to the present European situation he asked me point blank whether, in the event of Germany and Austria going to war with Russia and France, England would come to the assistance of the two latter Powers. I answered undoubtedly yes under certain circumstances. He professed surprise and regret but did not ask what the certain circumstances were. He said he would tell the Emperor what I had told him.[3]

The relevant passage from Prince Henry's letter of 11 December 1912 to the Kaiser runs:

Were a serious European conflict to arise which resulted in Germany's keeping faith with Austria as an ally, one would in the present state of things perhaps have to reckon with neutrality on the part of England, but not with her joining in on the German side.[4]

[1] Harold Nicolson, *King George V. Life and Reign* (London, 1952), pp. 245–6.
[2] DD. II, 374.   [3] BD. X, 452.   [4] GP. XXXIX, 15612, note, pp. 119–20.

On this earlier occasion, however, a dispatch from Lichnowsky of 3 December had conveyed a clear warning from Lord Haldane that 'England would in no circumstances tolerate the overthrow of the French'. Hence the Kaiser's comment to his brother's words runs: 'Already settled. She will side with France.'

INDEX

ABBAZIA, conversations at, 235
Adler, V., Austrian Deputy, 70 *n*
Aehrenthal, Alois, Baron Lexa (Count from 1909), Austro-Hungarian Ambassador at St. Petersburg, 1899–1906; Minister for Foreign Affairs, 1906–12, 13, 14 *n*, 122, 237, 251
Afghanistan, Russia and, 206
Africa, Anglo-German Settlement, 130
Agadir Crisis. *See* MOROCCO
Albania:
    new state, 20
    situation in, Francis Joseph on, 131 *n*
    Wied, Prince Wilhelm of, 124
    Austria-Hungary and: agreements with Italy over, 315; Austro-Italian dispute over, 218 *n*; struggle for influence, 219
    Germany and: enquiry as to position in, 146
    Italy and: expedition to, planned, 252; policy in, 218; possible move in, 238
    Serbia and, 257, 354, 454, 475–6, 493, 576
Albert I, King of the Belgians, 1909–33, 197
Albertini, Senator Luigi, Berchtold, letter to, 221, 380
    Giesl, conversation with, 152
    Hoyos, conversation with, 135
Albricci, Count, Italian General, Military Attaché at Vienna, 658, 664
Alexander III, Tsar of Russia, 1881–94, 579
Alexander, Prince, Serbian Regent, 35; King of Jugo-Slavia [1921], 95
    attempt on life of, 30, 73
    Austrian ultimatum, 348, 360
    Black Hand and, 32
    character of, 278
    Dimitriević, attitude to, 69
    Greek military attaché, conversation with, 351
    Nicholas II, appeal to, 349–50, 352, 354, 354 *n*
    Pašić's government, 70
    Russia, appeal to, 352; guidance by Russian ministers, 271
    Sarajevo plot, 100–1
    Strandtmann, conversation with, 348
    Victor Emmanuel, appeal to, intervene at Vienna, 349
    visit to St. Petersburg, 279
Alexander Obrenović, King of Serbia, 1889–1903, 30, 31 *n*, 34, 95, 108, 271
Alexandra Feodorovna, Tsarina of Russia, 569, 572 *n*
Algeria, French military measures, 597
Aliotti, Baron, Carlo, Italian Minister at Durazzo, 1914–22, 17, 131 *n*, 219

Alliances:
    Dual (Franco-Russian). *See* FRANCE, *Russia and*
    Triple:
    Art. I, 239, 249, 251; Text, 248
    Art. III, 248, 250
    Art. IV, 251
    Art. VII, 236–40, 244, 249–52, 315–16; Text, 248–9
    Balkan League and, 250
    military strength of, 221
    policy of, defensive, 121, 422
    position of Italy, 220–2, 224, 232, 242, 245, 247, 250–2, 487, 492–3, 500, 526, 678–9
    renewal of, 1887, 250; 1912, 245, 250
    Tripoli and, 250
    war, present time favourable, 383
    Austria-Hungary and. See AUSTRIA-HUNGARY
    Bulgaria and, 128, 130, 146, 167
    France and: French action in N. Africa, 250
    Germany and. See GERMANY
    Great Britain and: friendship with, 199
    Italy and. See ITALY
    Roumania and, 1914, 125
    adherence of and detachment from, 124, 142, 155, 257 *n*, 526
    King Carol and, 131 *n*
    Russia and: intervention by, a *casus foederis* for Germany, 121
    Serbia and, 121
    Sweden and, 454 *n*
    Triple Entente and: Serbian conflict, 410 *n*, 442, 451
    war possible between, 520–1
    Turkey and, 130, 167, 251
Alsace-Lorraine, autonomy of, 210
    restoration of, 194, 197
Ambassadors' Conference, 215, 392–3, 404, 677
Ambrozy, Count Ludwig, First Counsellor of Austro-Hungarian Embassy at Rome (sometimes Chargé d'Affaires), 290, 312, 313
Anastasia Nicolaievna, Grand Duchess of Russia, 194, 195
Andrassy, Count Julius, Hungarian Minister for Home Affairs, 1906–9 , 119
Andrejević, Major Z., Serbian engineer, 1914, 67
Anglo-Persian Oil Agreement, 1913, 206
Anglo-Russian agreements, Persia, 193
Anglo-Russian Convention, 1907, 188

2 Z

PRINTED IN GREAT BRITAIN AT THE UNIVERSITY PRESS, OXFORD
BY VIVIAN RIDLER, PRINTER TO THE UNIVERSITY